ENVIRONMENTAL
LAW

Text, Cases, and Materials

Elizabeth Fisher,

Bettina Lange,

and

Eloise Scotford

OXFORD
UNIVERSITY PRESS

OXFORD

UNIVERSITY PRESS

Great Clarendon Street, Oxford, OX2 6DP,
United Kingdom

Oxford University Press is a department of the University of Oxford.
It furthers the University's objective of excellence in research, scholarship,
and education by publishing worldwide. Oxford is a registered trade mark of
Oxford University Press in the UK and in certain other countries

© Elizabeth Fisher, Bettina Lange, and Eloise Scotford 2013

The moral rights of the authors have been asserted

Impression: 1

British Library Cataloguing in Publication Data

Data available

ISBN 978-0-19-927088-0

Printed in Great Britain by
Ashford Colour Press Ltd, Gosport, Hampshire

To all students of environmental law.

PREFACE

By its very nature, a volume of Text, Cases, and Materials is a collaborative enterprise. Indeed, that is the great value of such books, but it has also meant that the writing of this textbook has been a significant intellectual and practical challenge. Its existence is due to the input and patient support of many. Thus we have many people to thank. First, the editorial team at OUP, and particularly Abbey Nelms, has been wonderfully supportive at all times. Second, we would like to thank a number of research assistants who worked on this book over the years and particularly Paolo Ronchi and Stephen Dimelow – their can-do attitude was both impressive and an enormous help to all of us in finalizing the manuscript. Third, we would like to thank the reviewers and readers of draft chapters as well as all those in the wider environmental law scholarship community who have engaged with us and our writing. The very thoughtful feedback we received from reviewers was constructive and invaluable. Likewise, much in this book reflects the vibrancy of environmental law scholarship and we hope that the book will encourage students to dig deeper into the environmental law literature.

Finally, we would like to thank each other – that might seem a 'group-hug' thing to do, but this book would never have come into being in its current form without the contribution of each of us. As such, this book is a collective effort and we hope more than the sum of its parts. In light of the vast expanse of environmental law, we divided up the writing of the different chapters in the following way. Fisher was responsible for chapters 1–7, 9–10, 18–21 and the Introduction to Parts II, III, and V. Lange was responsible for Chapters 8, 12,13, 14, 17, and 22. Scotford was responsible for Chapters 11, 15 and 16. All contributed to the Introductions to Parts I and IV. This division of labour, and the different scholarly expertise we have brought to these chapters, reflects the fragmented nature of environmental law. With that said, we have each written our chapters with a view to the approaches and contents of other chapters, so there is considerable cross-referencing and cross-fertilization between them.

Liz Fisher writes: I would also like to thank the Faculty of Law and Corpus Christi College, University of Oxford for the much appreciated support they have provided over the years through funding research assistance and providing a research and teaching environment that encourages the very best. A big thank you must also go to my children, Corin and Arthur, for being their boisterous and curious selves. My most important and heartfelt thank you goes to my husband, Roderick. Writing this book has imposed much on him and I have been deeply appreciative of his loving, patient, and inspirational support (and his sense of humour).

Bettina Lange writes: I would like to thank colleagues at Oxford, including Wolfson College, for support of my academic work, Professor Bill Howarth for helpful comments on Chapter 14 (Water Pollution), Zachary Vermeer for excellent research assistance and my partner, Susan, for being lovely.

Eloise Scotford writes: I have done most of the work for this book as a Lecturer at King's College London, so my thanks go to colleagues at King's who read chapters and provided invaluable comments (in particular, Dr Rachael Walsh gave very helpful feedback on Chapter 6, Private Law), and who otherwise left me alone whilst I was in the depths of writing. My thanks are also owed to all those people – family, godparents and friends – with whom I spent not enough time whilst I was 'writing the textbook'. Finally, thank you to Michael, who took me on a first date whilst my first chapter was only half-written and put up with all the writing moments along the way with great patience, constant support and genuine interest – some of the (no doubt better) ideas about waste are the result of our discussions and emails.

Liz Fisher
Bettina Lange
Eloise Scotford
7 January 2013

OUTLINE CONTENTS

DETAILED CONTENTS

PART II CHARTING THE ENVIRONMENTAL LAW LANDSCAPE I—LEGAL CULTURES   63

3 ENVIRONMENTAL LAW IN THE LEGAL CULTURE OF THE UNITED KINGDOM   75

4   EUROPEAN UNION ENVIRONMENTAL LAW   115

5   INTERNATIONAL ENVIRONMENTAL LAW   169

PART III CHARTING THE ENVIRONMENTAL LAW LANDSCAPE II — BASIC LEGAL CONCEPTS 207

6 PRIVATE LAW 219

7 PUBLIC LAW 254

11 PRINCIPLE AND POLICY 401

12 REGULATORY STRATEGY 460

13 GOVERNANCE   501

PART IV POLLUTION CONTROL   537

CRC	Carbon Reduction Commitment (formerly), now CRC Energy Efficiency Scheme
CROW Act	Countryside and Rights of Way Act 2000
CRU	Climatic Research Unit
DCLG	Department of Communities and Local Government
DDT	Dichlorodiphenyltrichloroethane
DECC	Department of Energy and Climate Change
DEFRA	Department of Environment, Food and Rural Affairs
DES	Department for Education and Skills
DETR	Department of Environment, Transport and Regions
DG	Directorate General
DH	Department of Health
DNA	DeoxyriboNucleic Acid
DOE(NI)	Department of Environment (Northern Ireland)
DWI	Drinking Water Inspectorate
DWP	Department for Work and Pensions
EA	Environment Agency
EA	Environmental Assessment
EAC	Environmental Audit Committee
EAP	Environmental Action Programme
EC	European Community
ECHR	European Convention on Human Rights
ECJ	European Court of Justice
ECtHR	European Court of Human Rights
EDPR	Environmental Damage (Prevention and Remediation) Regulations 2009
EEA	European Environment Agency
EEC	European Economic Community
EFSA	European Food Safety Authority
EFTA	European Free Trade Association
EGA	Experimentalist Governance Architecture
EHO	Environmental Health Officer
EIA	Environmental Impact Assessment
EIR 2004	Environmental Information Regulations 2004
EIS	Environmental Impact Statement
ELD	Environmental Liability Directive
ELV	Emission Limit Value
ELV	End of Life Vehicles Directive
EM	Ecological Modernization
EMAS	Eco-Management and Audit Scheme
EMS	Environmental Management Standard
EoW	End-of-Waste
EP	European Parliament
EPA	Environmental Protection Act 1990
EPRs	Environmental Permitting Regulations 2010
EQS	Environmental Quality Standard
ERU	Emission Reduction Units
ERDF	European Regional Development Fund
ES	Environmental Statement
ESDN	European Sustainable Development Network

ETS	Emissions Trading Scheme
EU	European Union
EURATOM	European Atomic Energy Community
EWC	European Waste Catalogue
FCO	Foreign and Commonwealth Office
FESCO	Forum of European Securities Commissions
FIT	Feed-In-Tariff
FoE	Friends of the Earth
FofES	Friends of the Earth Scotland
FOI	Freedom of Information
FOIA	Freedom of Information Act
FSA	Food Standards Agency
FSC	Forest Stewardship Council
FTT	First Tier Tribunal
GATT	General Agreement on Tariffs and Trade 1947
GC	General Court
GCC	Global Climate Change
GDP	Gross Domestic Product
GHG	Greenhouse Gas
GMOs	Genetically Modified Organisms
GPP	Green Public Procurement
HC	House of Commons
HCBD	Hexachlorobutaiene
HFC	Hydroflurocarbon
HM	Her Majesty's
HMT	Her Majesty's Treasury
HRA	Human Rights Act 1998
HSE	Health and Safety Executive
IA	Impact Assessment
IBA	Inventory of Important Bird Areas
IBM	International Business Machines Corporation
ICI	Imperial Chemical Industries
ICJ	International Court of Justice
ICT	Information and Communication Technologies
IED	Industrial Emissions Directive
IEF	Information Exchange Forum
IEL	International Environmental Law
IMO	International Maritime Organization
IMPEL	EU Network on the Implementation and Enforcement of Environmental Law
IPC	Infrastructure Planning Commission
IPC	Integrated Pollution Control
IPCC	Intergovernmental Panel on Climate Change
IPPC	Integrated Pollution Prevention and Control
ISO	International Standards Organization
ITLOS	International Tribunal for the Law of the Sea
IUCN	International Union for Conservation of Nature
JNCC	Joint Nature Conservancy Committee
LAQM	Local Air Quality Management

LCP	Large Combustion Plants
LETS	Local Exchange Trading System
LGA	Local Government Act 1999
LGO	Local Government Ombudsman
LMO	Living Modified Organism
LNG	Liquefied Natural Gas
LNR	Local Nature Reserve
LPA	Local Planning Authority
MAFF	Ministry of Agriculture, Fisheries and Food
MARPOL	International Convention on the Prevention of Pollution from Ships
MCZ	Marine Conservation Zones
MEA	Multi-lateral Environmental Agreement
MHPA	Milford Haven Port Authority
MNR	Marine Nature Reserve
MOL	Metropolitan Open Land
MOX	Mixed Oxide Fuel
MP	Member of Parliament
MS	Member State
N_2O	Nitrous Oxide
NAIL	New Approaches to International Law
NAO	National Audit Office
NAP	National Allocation Plan
NAQS	National Air Quality Strategy
NDPB	Non-Departmental Government Body
NRA	National Rivers Authority
NE	Natural England
NEC	National Emissions Ceiling
NEPA	National Environmental Policy Act 1969
NERC Act	Natural Environment and Rural Communities Act 2006
NGO	Non-Governmental Organization
NH_3	Ammonia
NIEA	Northern Ireland Environment Agency
NNR	National Nature Reserve
NO	Nitrogen Oxide
NO_2	Nitrogen Dioxide
N_2O	Nitrous Oxide
NO_x	Oxides of Nitrogen
NPAC Act	National Parks and Wildlife Countryside Act 1949
NPM	New Public Management
NPPF	National Planning Policy Framework
NPS	National Policy Statement
NSDS	National Sustainable Development Strategies
NSWLEC	New South Wales Land and Environment Court
O_3	Ozone
OECD	Organization for Economic Development and Co-operation
OMC	Open Method of Co-ordination
OPRA	Operational Risk Appraisal
ORO	Offence Response Options

OSPAR	Convention on the Protection of the Marine Environment of the North Atlantic
PAT	Phosphinothricin-Nacetyltransferase
PEFC	Pan-European Forest Certification Council
Pb	Lead
PCB	Polychlorinated Biphenyls
PCO	Protective Costs Order
PIL	Public Interest Litigation
PM-10	Particular matter of a diameter less than 10 microns
PM-2.5	Particular matter of a diameter less than 2.5 microns
PMEM	Post-Market Environment Monitoring plans
PO	Parliamentary and Health Services Ombudsman
POP	Persistent Organic Pollutant
PPC	Pollution Prevention and Control
PPG	Planning Policy Guidance
PPS	Planning Policy Statement
Pt C	Part C notification under Directive 2001/18/EC.
PWD	Packaging Waste Directive
QMV	Qualified Majority Voting
RBS	Royal Bank of Scotland
RCC	Regulators' Compliance Code
RCEP	Royal Commission on Environmental Pollution
REACH	Registration, Evaluation, Authorization and Restriction of Chemical Substances
REDD	Reducing Emissions from Deforestation and Degradation
RESA	Regulatory Sanctions Act
R & D	Research and Development
RIA	Regulatory Impact Assessment
RIMAS	Research Institute for Managing Sustainability
RM	Reflexive Modernization
RNA	Ribonucleic acid
RO	Renewables Obligation
ROC	Renewables Obligation Certificate
ROMP	Review of Old Mining and Minerals Permissions
RSPB	Royal Society for the Protection of Birds
SAC	Special Area of Conservation
SCI	Sites of Community Importance
SCP/SIP	Sustainable Consumption and Production/Sustainable Industrial Production
SCR	Secondary Catalytic Reduction
SEPA	Scottish Environment Protection Agency
SET-Plan	European Strategic Energy Technology Plan
SD	Sustainable Development
SDI	Sustainable Development Indicators
SDS	EU Sustainable Development Strategy
SEA	Strategic Environmental Assessment
SEA	Single European Act Treaty
SF$_6$	Sulphur Hexafluoride
SG	Sector Guidance Note
SIGGTO	Society of International Gas Tanker and Terminal Operators
SNIF	Summary Notification Information Format database

SO_2	Sulphur Dioxide
SOx	Oxides of Sulphur
SPA	Special Protection Area
SPS	Sanitary and Phyto-sanitary
SSSI	Site of Special Scientific Interest
STW	Severn Trent Water Authority
TA	Technical Instruction Air (Technische Anleitung Luft)
TBT	Technical Barriers to Trade
TEC	Treaty establishing the European Community
TCPA	Town and Country Planning Act 1990
TEU	Treaty of the European Union
TFEU	Treaty on the Functioning of the European Union
TSAP	Thematic Strategy on Air Pollution
TWAIL	Third World Approaches to International Law
TWG	Technical Working Groups
UEA	University of East Anglia
UK	United Kingdom
UKELA	UK Environmental Law Association
UN	United Nations
UNCED	UN Convention on Environment and Development
UNCLOS	United Nations Law of the Sea Convention
UNECE	UN Economic Commission for Europe
UNEP	United Nations Environmental Programme
UNESCO	United Nations Educational, Scientific and Cultural Organization
UNFCCC	UN Framework Convention on Climate Change
US	United States
VEP	Voluntary Environmental Program
VOC	Volatile Organic Compound
WA	Water Act 2003
WCAct	Wildlife and Countryside Act 1981
WDA	Welsh Development Agency
WEEE	Waste Electrical and Electronic Equipment Directive
WFD	Water Framework Directive (in Chapter 14)
WFD	Waste Framework Directive (in Chapter 16)
WFWT	Wildfowl and Wetlands Trust
WG	Working Groups
WHO	World Health Organisation
WIA	Water Industry Act
WRA	Water Resources Act
WSR	Waste Shipments Regulation
WWF-UK	World Wildlife Fund-UK
WT	Wildlife Trust
WTO	World Trade Organization

ACKNOWLEDGEMENTS TO COPYRIGHT HOLDERS

A central purpose of this book is to introduce students to the richness of environmental law discourse and scholarship. Not only do we want our readers to see the diversity and complexity of views but we also want to encourage them to read beyond this textbook. To that end, this book contains over 550 extracts from different primary and secondary sources. Throughout the book, the full citation of all material is given. Grateful acknowledgement is made to all the authors, organizations and publishers of copyright material that appears in this book including:

Incorporated Council of Law Reporting: extracts from the *Law Reports: Queen's Bench Division* (QB), the *Law Reports: Appeal Cases* (AC) and *Weekly Law Reports* (WLR).

Publishers and organizations: Ashgate, Cambridge University Press, Edinburgh University Press, Edward Elgar, Elsevier Emerald, Europa Publishing, Green Books, Hart Publishing, Kings' Fund, Koninklijke Brill NV, Magistrates Association, Manchester University Press, MIT Press, National Academies Press, New York University Press, Oxford University Press, Penguin, Polity Press, Palgrave Macmillan, Random House, Routledge, Sage Publications, Springer, Sweet & Maxwell, Taylor and Francis Press, Thomson Reuters UK Environmental Law Association, University of California Press, Westview Press, Wiley, Wolters Kluwer, World Resources Institute, and Yale University Press.

Journals: American University Journal of International Law, Buffalo Environmental Law Journal, Cardozo Law Review, Colorado Journal of International Environmental Law and Policy, Columbia Law Review, Environmental Health Perspectives, Indiana Journal of Global Studies, Nottingham Law Journal, Pace Environmental Law Review, Southern California Law Review, Tulane Law Review, and Yale Journal of International Law.

Extracts from the Yearbook of European Environmental Law with permission from the publisher and the editor (Han Somsen), Cambridge Journal of Economics by Cambridge Political Economy Society, European Journal of International law by European University Institute, Statute Law Review by Statute Law Society, Journal of Environmental Law, Journal of Public Health, and Oxford Journal of Legal Studies, appear with kind permission of Oxford University Press.

Authors: Joel Bakan, Nick Blomley, Jane Holder, Richard Macrory, Donald McGillvray, Karen Morrow, David Vogel, and Charles Yablon.

Part I

A Dan Tarlock, 'The Future of Environmental Rule of Law Litigation' (2002) 19 Pace Environmental Law Review 575, p 576–77. Pace Environmental Law Review by Pace University Copyright © 2002 Reproduced with permission of Pace University, School of Law.

Garrett Hardin, 'The Tragedy of the Commons' (1968) 162 Science 1243, 1244, 1245. Reprinted with permission from AAAS.

Reprinted by permission of the publisher from *We Have Never Been Modern* by Bruno Latour, translated by Catherine Porter, 1. Cambridge, Mass: Harvard University Press. Copyright © 1993 by the President and Fellows of Harvard College, Reprinted by permission of the publisher.

Reprinted by permission of the publisher from *The Fifth Branch: Science Advisors as Policy Makers* by Sheila Jasanoff, 77. Cambridge, Mass: Harvard University Press, Copyright © 1990 by the President and Fellows of Harvard College.

Part II

Part III

Brian Preston, 'Leadership by the courts in achieving sustainability' (2010) 27 EPLJ 321, 329–330. Reproduced with permission of Thomson Reuters (Professional) Australia Limited, www.thomson-reuters.com.au.

Alhaji Marong, 'From Rio to Johannesburg: Reflections on the Role of International Legal Norms in Sustainable Development', (2003–4) 16 Georgetown International Environmental Law Review 21, 57–58. Reprinted with permission of the publisher, Georgetown International Environmental Law Review, Copyright © 2003.

Ida Koppen 'Environmental Mediation: An Example of Applied Autopoiesis', in: Roeland In 'T Veld, and others (eds) *Autopoiesis and Configuration Theory: New Approaches to Societal Steering* (Kluwer Academic Publishers 1991) 143, 146, 149. Copyright © Kluwer Academic Publishers 1991. With kind permission from Springer Science+Business Media.

Jonathan Borck and Cary Coglianese 'Voluntary Environmental Programs: Assessing their Effectiveness' (2009) 34 Annual Review of Environment and Resources 305, 307–9. Reproduced with permission of Annual Reviews.

Part IV

With kind permission from Springer Science+Business Media: KA Dahlberg 'Democratizing Society and Food Systems: Or How do we Transform Modern Structures of Power?' (2001) 18 Agriculture and Human Values 141, 145–6, © 2001 Kluwer Academic Publishers.

E Melanie DuPuis (ed), *The Politics of and Culture of Air Pollution: Smoke and Mirrors* (New York University Press 2004) © 2004 New York University. Reprinted with permission.

The Air Pollution and Climate Change Secretariat, Sweden for permission to reproduce Figure 15.1.

Richard Girling, *Rubbish! Dirt On Our Hands and the Crisis Ahead*, (Eden Project Books 2005) i–ii. Reprinted by permission of The Random House Group Limited.

R Nagle, 'The History and Future of Fresh Kills' in *The Filthy Reality of Everyday Life* (Profile Books London 2011) 190, 192, 198–99. With kind permission of Profile Books.

Cormac Cullinan, *Wild Law: A Manifesto for Earth Justice* (revd edn, Green Books 2011) 26–7, 29, 30–31. Extracted by permission.

Charles Yablon, 'The Indeterminacy of Law: Critical Legal Studies and the Problem of Legal Explanation' (1985) 6 Cardozo Law Review 917, 918, 919, 920, 931. Reprinted with kind permission.

Part V

Laurence H Tribe, 'Technology Assessment and the Fourth Discontinuity: The Limits of Instrumental Rationality' (1972–3) 46 Southern California Law Review 617, 627. Reprinted with kind permission of the Southern California Law Review.

David Edward, 'Direct Effect: Myth, Mess or Mystery' in J Prinssen & A Schrauwen (eds) *Direct Effect: Rethinking a Classic of EC Legal Doctrine* (Groningen, Europa Publishing 2002) 13. Printed with kind permission of the publisher.

Tim Clutton-Brock and Ben Sheldon 'The Seven Ages of Pan' (2010) 327 Science 1207, 1207–8. Reprinted with permission from AAAS.

Andrew Szsaz, *EcoPopulism: Toxic Waste and the Movement for Environmental Justice* (University of Minnesota Press 1994) 42–3. Copyright © 1994 by the Regents of the University of Minnesota. Reprinted with permission.

TABLE OF CASES

European Court of Human Rights

UNITED STATES

TABLE OF STATUTES

United States

TABLE OF STATUTORY INSTRUMENTS

TABLE OF EUROPEAN LEGISLATION

Directives

TABLE OF CONVENTIONS AND AGREEMENTS

PART I
THE BASICS

A BRIEF WORD ABOUT
OUR APPROACH

'Text, Cases, and Materials' books are scholarly misfits in the world of legal education. While they do not take the form of a fully fledged textbook that provides an authoritative version of the law, they cannot be dismissed as *ad hoc* collections of legal commentary and miscellany. Not only are there an increasing number of these books being published in the UK (and they have a long and venerable history in the US), but they are also beginning to play a role in shaping and framing how legal subjects are understood. Craig and de Burca's *EU Law: Text, Cases, and Materials* is a prime example. Any attempt to understand this breed of legal book is not made easier by the fact that the publications that describe themselves as 'Text, Cases, and Materials' come in many different forms and are the product of different ambitions. We therefore here outline our purposes in writing this particular book of 'text, cases, and materials'. For the reader wishing to 'get straight into the substance' this outline might be tempting to skip over, but we would urge you not to. By understanding what this book is (and is not) you are likely to get far more out of it.

We consider environmental law to be a legally, scientifically and socio-politically complex subject that requires lawyers, students and researchers to take law and the context in which it operates seriously.[1] Our ambition in writing this textbook is thus to highlight those complexities and the need for a rigorous intellectual approach in thinking about them as lawyers. Our strategy in each chapter of this book is to explain the complex ecological and socio-political nature of environmental problems and the interrelationships between such problems and different aspects of relevant legal systems, including different attempts to regulate these problems through law. We therefore raise many different issues that we want our readers to think critically about and to reflect on. We rarely provide solutions or a final answer to the issues that we highlight. For those readers who want neat answers, this approach may fail to satisfy or even frustrate. But our reason for taking this approach is that there are no straightforward answers to environmental law problems. As Carol Rose has noted, 'A mature environmental law is not pretty. It is past the stage of grand theory and well into the stage of acronyms and statutory sections'.[2] Among those acronyms, those statutory sections, *and* the bundles of policy documents, *and* the byzantine decision-making processes, *and* the manuals of procedure that are part of the package of 'environmental law', there lurk difficult, tricky, and very exciting legal and intellectual issues. By highlighting these, we seek to contribute to the intellectual development of the subject. The book starts from the premise that, in tackling environmental law, lawyers, students,

---

[1] Elizabeth Fisher, Bettina Lange, Eloise Scotford, and Cinnamon Carlarne, 'Maturity and Methodology: Starting a Debate about Environmental Law Scholarship" (2009) 21(2) JEL 213.

[2] Carol Rose, 'Environmental Law Grows Up (More or Less) And What Science Can Do to Help' (2005) 9 Lewis and Clark L Rev 273, 292.

and legal scholars need to be equipped with sharp skills of analysis, a reflective intellect, and an appreciation of nuance.

In this spirit, this book of 'Text, Cases, and Materials' places less emphasis on telling readers exactly *what* to think but rather provokes thinking about environmental law by exposing the themes, issues, and difficult questions in the often seemingly impenetrable detail and novel legal problems of the subject. At most, it is a guide to *what you should be thinking about*. Thus, our emphasis is upon providing good quality material that illustrates the complexity of environmental problems, and of the law that applies to them, and also provides an analytical framework for understanding that complexity. In this regard, it is also worth noting that, while we examine all the major features of the relevant legal regimes, we do not chart them in all their detail—that is the task of a practitioner's text. We do, however, inform the reader of where such detail may be found.

Moreover, in light of the large amount of teaching of environmental law to non-lawyers that occurs in England, we are aware that this book will not only be used by lawyers. In our view, this is not a reason to cut down on the coverage of legal complexities, and we have not done this. This is particularly important because any attempt at developing an interdisciplinary understanding of environmental problems requires relevant disciplines (including law) to set out their contribution to such an understanding fully and frankly. To help the non-lawyer in particular, however, we have provided some frameworks to aid those less acquainted with the law in Parts II and III of the book. These chapters will not be wasted on lawyers either—lawyers need to be dextrous and imaginative in using their basic legal skills and knowledge when thinking about environmental problems.

We are acutely aware that all of this is highly ambitious. Indeed, this book has had a long gestation period because of our ambition. We want this book of 'Text, Cases, and Materials' to provide a solid intellectual foundation for a new era of how environmental law is taught, practised, discussed, and analysed. It is an ambition that we believe can only be achieved through fostering a nuanced and sophisticated discourse about environmental law. Such a discourse requires an appreciation of the multiple contexts in which environmental law operates and the multiple perspectives that can be validly brought to bear in understanding the subject, as well as the engagement of all participants in environmental law. All of this extends beyond the more neatly bounded domains of traditional legal subjects, and the scholarly ambition in approaching the subject must accordingly reach creatively and further to capture the subject for its legal study.

WHAT IS ENVIRONMENTAL LAW?

This volume of 'Text, Cases, and Materials' is an advanced introduction to environmental law in the UK, concentrating on England. It has been written with law students, lawyers, and scholars from other disciplines in mind. It aims to be both explanatory and challenging so that while providing a clear outline of the subject it also encourages readers to think critically and independently. In particular it requires readers to appreciate the complexity of environmental problems *and* law.

As this is the case, this book requires scholars and lawyers to grapple with three interrelated matters in order to understand environmental law. First, there is a need to appreciate that environmental issues are both physically and socio-politically complex. Such an appreciation is not so much about being concerned for the environment but rather understanding the nature of environmental problems and in particular how irreconcilable and intractable environmental disputes often are. To that end, Chapter 2 discusses the nature of environmental problems and, in each chapter that examines a discrete regulatory regime, the particular environmental problems that regime is meant to address are examined.

Second, there is a need to understand that the 'law' that applies to environmental problems consists of a diverse collection of laws that draw on all parts of English and EU legal culture as well as international legal cultures. This is not to say that there is no coherence to the subject but that in many ways environmental law is an 'applied subject' in that it involves the application of basic legal concepts (albeit differently derived and influenced) to environmental problems. Practically, this means that an environmental lawyer needs a good working knowledge of all aspects of the relevant legal cultures and the laws and legal ideas that operate in them. Hence, Parts II and III of this book are overviews of the relevant legal cultures and legal concepts that inform environmental law.

The final matter for environmental law scholars and practitioners to appreciate is that the application of law to environmental problems is a complex exercise in itself. Environmental lawyers need thus not only to understand environmental problems and a diverse body of law, but the interaction between the two as well. Indeed, the process of application of existing bodies of law to environmental problems often requires the re-evaluation of existing legal concepts and doctrines. Thus, in the chapters in Parts IV and V, which analyse the substantive law in particular subject areas, we will see how specific environmental problems often force an adaptation and development of conventional legal ideas.

All of this places those who study and practise environmental law in a curious and not necessarily enviable position. An environmental lawyer needs to have not only an understanding of environmental problems and a significant amount of legal knowledge but also an ability to understand how the two interact. To put it more bluntly, to be a brilliant environmental lawyer one must be able to integrate a sophisticated interdisciplinary understanding of environmental problems with a skilful and carefully focused legal approach. We do not say this to be off-putting but rather to point out that the challenges that this book sets out for the study of environmental law are inherent in the subject itself.

This chapter provides an introductory overview of environmental law and the challenges involved in its study by examining three different ways in which the subject can be defined—descriptively, purposively, and jurisprudentially. These different approaches represent fundamentally distinct approaches to the subject and throughout the book the implications of these different approaches are considered. Each definition is also shown to be problematic but each is shown to capture an important aspect of the subject. We then consider the significance of these different definitional approaches, particularly to the practice and the critical evaluation of environmental law. In the second section, we consider some of the perceived problems with environmental law as a subject, including those relating to assumptions about its incoherence and difficulty, and the challenges for environmental lawyers that these perceptions reflect. Finally, we return to the three matters that environmental lawyers must understand to master the subject—environmental problems, the basic legal concepts underpinning environmental laws, and the interaction between those problems and those concepts. This tripartite structure provides a basic framework to help guide inquiry.

1 CHALLENGES IN DEFINING ENVIRONMENTAL LAW

Environmental law is the law relating to environmental problems. You may be thinking 'That is obvious. What I need is a more comprehensive definition that will help me understand the subject easily'. However, the difficulty is that, in attempting to develop a more comprehensive definition of the subject, scholars adopt very different perspectives. Three different approaches are identified here.

1.1 A DESCRIPTIVE DEFINITION

One approach to defining environmental law is to equate it with the laws relating to environmental protection that exist in a particular jurisdiction. This is a purely descriptive definition and requires the commentator to simply list the various laws that are concerned with environmental protection. On this definition English environmental law consists of UK statutes, delegated legislation, EU legal instruments, policies and case law concerned with regulating pollution, environmental quality, and biodiversity conservation. This approach is rather appealing in that it looks like a relatively straight-forward way to define the subject and to give it clear boundaries. It is true that the subject is dynamic and so that with new legislation and new laws the boundaries will change, but it would appear that, by this definition, the subject can be identified at any point in time. However, this approach to defining the subject is not as simple as it appears and, in particular, there are real problems in placing boundaries around the subject so as to establish its scope and nature. These problems can be broadly divided into two categories—those over the definition of 'law' and those over the definition of the 'environment'. In relation to 'defining law', there are a variety of matters that need to be considered. First, the process of identifying the relevant law is not simply a case of isolating a single statute. English environmental law is not only made up of UK domestic law but also includes EU and international law. Much of environmental law is also in the form of delegated legislation and so an environmental lawyer must have regard to a wide range of legal material. Moreover, while there are some common regimes across the UK it is also important to note that there are differences between the environmental law of England, Scotland, Wales, and Northern Ireland. A study of these differences is beyond the scope of this book.

A second problem is that it is not clear what type of 'instruments' are included under the definition of 'law' as there is an important role to be played by policy and regulatory strategy in environmental law. Likewise, as we shall see in Chapter 13, governance frameworks play a significant role in regulating environmental quality.

All this raises important questions about what is the 'law' in environmental law. That inquiry has many dimensions. Thus, for example, in some cases we shall see how environmental problems are regulated through policy, governance networks, and a range of regulatory strategies that are not traditionally legal in nature. Involved in these different frameworks are a range of public and private actors. These will be discussed in Chapters 12 and 13 but can also be seen in the substantive chapters of the book that focus on particular environmental regulatory regimes and problems.

Even if a scholar or student decides to only concentrate on what is traditionally understood as 'law', the situation is no less difficult. This is well captured by the UK Environmental Law Association's (UKELA) 2011–12 review of the state of UK environmental law, which adopted the quality of environmental legislation as its focus for inquiry:

UKELA and King's College London, The State of UK Environmental Legislation in 2011: Is There a Case for Reform? Interim Report, Revised April 2012 (funded by a King's Future Fund award) 7

[The project's research] found significant examples of UK environmental legislation that is problematic in lacking coherence, integration and/or transparency. [Coherence being understood as a reflection of clarity and comprehensibility; integration capturing how different laws and regimes overlap and interact; and transparency being a measure of legislative accessibility.] This legislative complexity is driven by:

- the idiosyncratic historical development of legislation;
- European law requirements, including the regime-specific nature of directives, and the copy-out and referential drafting techniques used to transpose EU law into UK law;
- overlapping legislative requirements;
- a reluctance to consolidate legislation sufficiently often;
- inherently complex statutory provisions and technical requirements;
- over-reliance on detailed guidance and regulatory positions to establish legal requirements; by administrative complexity; and by cross-border differences.

It should [also] be noted that EU environmental law pervades the domestic approach to environmental legislation throughout the UK administrations, and drives much of its complexity. [...]

The report went on to note various problems of the quality of legislation and the final report for the UKELA project concluded that these problems can cause real challenges for practitioners, regulators, and regulated industry (adding burdens and cost due to uncertainty and wasted time, and inhibiting investment in innovative practices). Such problems can lead to non-compliance with laws and failure to achieve regulatory goals, and they can also undermine access to justice and the rule of law.[1] They can also make life difficult for environmental law students!

[1] UKELA, King's College London and BRASS (Cardiff University) *The State of Environmental Law 2011–12: Is There a Case for Legislative Reform – Final Report*, May 2012, 5–6 and generally.

Some scholars would argue that looking at conventional sources of law—such as legislation—as a focus for studying environmental law misunderstands the nature of 'law' for this subject. Thus, for example, de Sadeleer argues much environmental law is post-modern.

Nicolas de Sadeleer, *Environmental Principles: From Political Slogans to Legal Rules*
(OUP 2002) 233

In effect, a new legal model that reflects post-modern conditions is replacing the classical law of modern societies. Under pressure from a globalizing economy, the State has lost its monopolist role as a producer of norms for multilateral and supranational institutions. The nation-state and even the system of states may be either in crisis or heading toward crisis in the face of the increasing seriousness of many environmental problems. In addition, law-makers have had to renounce general legal formulations and turn to more flexible modes of action, better adapted to dynamic social realities, in order to ensure the effectiveness of public policies. Similarly, they have had to abandon simplicity, systematization, and coherence so that legal norms might respond more rapidly to urgent and complex social needs. Finally, they have had to relinquish constraint in favour of a flexible and decentralized system of rule-making, based on regulatory flexibility.

De Sadeleer may be over-emphasizing the 'postmodernist' nature of environmental law but there is no doubt that environmental law does require students and lawyers alike to engage with many different legal forms that operate across jurisdictions. As you study the subject you should consider whether there is a different kind of legal reasoning operating in environmental law.

Furthermore, institutional behaviour and regulatory action will often have a significant role to play in environmental law, particularly in the area of enforcement. This has meant that there is a very strong socio-legal tradition in environmental law scholarship.

Bridget Hutter, 'Socio-Legal Perspectives on Environmental Law: An Overview'
in Bridget Hutter (ed), *A Reader in Environmental Law* (OUP 1999) 4–5

Environmental law represents a major, and perhaps one of the most important, regulatory regimes in Western industrialized societies. This perspective upon environmental law has been an early and enduring focus of socio-legal research into environmental law. There are many definitions of regulation. Traditionally it refers to the use of the law to constrain and organize economic activity. It therefore directs attention to state intervention through law and typically it involves regulation through public agencies charged with the implementation of the law. This is often referred to as the 'command and control' approach to regulation. It involves the 'command' of the law and the legal authority of the state. Typically it involves regulatory law backed by criminal sanctions. But this definition has been broadened to encompass both non-legal forms of regulation and supranational regulation. Indeed, the development of environmental law has led to new ways of conceptualizing regulation and new directions for socio-legal research into environmental law.

For Hutter, studying environmental law requires the analysis of regulatory forms and how they operate. It is a study in human organization. Thinking about environmental law in these terms also highlights that even where a formal legal regime exists there is often a very big difference between what the law is and how it is practised. This is particularly the case in the UK where there is a considerable role for administrative discretion. Another reason why a descriptive definition of environmental law is not as straightforward as it seems is that, just as with 'law', there is no single definition of the environment. This means that it is not obvious what areas of law the term 'environmental' law covers. This is discussed in more detail in the Introduction to Part III, and throughout this book you will see that statutes, directives, and regulatory regimes are protecting distinct aspects of the environment and in doing so they are often implicitly defining the 'environment' in divergent ways. Thus, often in the context of pollution statutes, the environment is being frequently defined in terms of different media—water, air, soil, and so on—although we will also see that in recent years a more holistic approach to the environment has also been taken in pollution control regimes. In contrast, in nature conservation law, the environment is often being defined in terms of habitats of particular species or ecosystems. Furthermore, different approaches to defining the environment can be seen in which topics different environmental law textbooks and courses choose to cover. For example, some textbooks do not cover land use planning; this particular textbook does not cover noise pollution. In fact, what might be covered by environmental law is contested and by no means obvious.

1.2 A PURPOSIVE DEFINITION

A second approach to defining environmental law is to define it in terms of the purpose the law is designed or desired to achieve. That purpose may be an environmental policy or a particular environmental outcome such as the prevention of pollution or some form of environmental degradation. Defined in this way, environmental law is primarily a social program implemented through law.

A Dan Tarlock, 'The Future of Environmental Rule of Law Litigation' (2002) 19 Pace Envtl L Rev 575, 576–77

[E]nvironmental law could be defined as the positive and common law that reflects environmentalism. Environmentalism is an unstable wedding of two policy objectives: (1) the protection of public health from the risks associated with involuntary exposures to pollutants and contaminants, and (2) the protection and preservation of natural areas. Not surprisingly, a more complete definition of environmentalism creates a more complex question with many different and contradictory answers. Following Aldo Leopold, I define environmentalism as an emerging philosophy or value system which posits that we living humans should assume science-based ethical stewardship obligations to conserve natural systems for ourselves as well as for future generations. [...] Environmental law can therefore be explained as an effort to institutionalize stewardship obligations.

To define environmental law in purposive terms is useful in that it highlights that much of environmental law is a product of ethics, policy, and/or politics. The history of environmental law can be understood in terms of a series of waves of legal initiatives that reflect different eras of environmentalism and environmental policy. Such a definition also highlights the fact that historically environmental law developed as a regulatory response to the inadequacies of the existing law.

Lord Scarman, _English Law—The New Dimension_ (Stevens & Sons 1974) 53

But the truth has to be faced. The judicial development of the law, vigorous and imaginative though it has been, has been found wanting. Tied to concepts of property, possession, and fault, the judges have been unable by their own strength to break out of the cabin of the common law and tackle the broad problems of land use in an industrial and urbanised society. The challenge appears at this moment of time, to be likely to overwhelm the law. As in the area of the social challenge, so also the guarding of our environment has been found to require an activist, intrusive role to be played by the executive arm of government.

A purposive definition also highlights that we need to understand the rationale behind laws in order to understand and to evaluate them.

Alyson C Flournoy, 'In Search of an Environmental Ethic' (2003) 28 Colum J Envtl L 63, 114–15

Environmental law is itself an important expression of social value. The adoption of laws in this field reflects concern for values previously excluded or inadequately weighed under our laws. [...] If neither the public nor the decisionmakers articulate the ethical issues involved, we cannot ultimately know whether our laws and policies are consistent with our ethics. Just as in archery one learns from seeing where the last arrow struck and adjusts one's aim, we need to know what the bulls-eye is for environmental law, or else we're simply launching arrow after arrow with only random improvement.

A functional definition thus invariably highlights the inadequacy of an approach to environmental law that simply focuses on legal rules, institutions, and processes. At the very least, an understanding of environmental policy is needed.

Yet, as with descriptive definitions, purposive definitions are not as straightforward as they seem. In particular, these definitions are under-inclusive. This can be seen from three perspectives. First, they construe the driving logic of environmental law as exterior to the law and thus the role of law is largely instrumental. As will be shown throughout this book, law is not just a bundle of rules that are akin to a computer 'app', rather it is a culture replete with a distinct body of reasoning, ideas, and processes. While Lord Scarman's comments about environmental law were valid in 1974, they are no longer. Statutory schemes and administrative action is complemented by a large body of carefully reasoned case law in which judges are not simply protecting the environment or interpreting statutes but also refashioning legal principles and developing new legal concepts. Describing environmental law in purposive terms can overlook these developments.

A second issue or problem with a purposive definition of environmental law is that it seems to suggest that the role of environmental law and environmental lawyers is to enhance environmental protection or to pursue a particular environmental ethic.

Patrick McAuslan, 'The Role of Courts and Other Judicial Type Bodies in Environmental Management' (1991) 3(2) JEL 195, 197

My view and my argument here is that this is no longer good enough and we have to raise the intellectual level of our legal discourse on environmental matters. We have to start from the proposition that given the environmental crisis that is upon us, lawyers no less than other disciplines have to contribute to the development of what I would call a new ethic of government and administration; we have to try and put flesh on the bones of the concepts of environmentalism and sustainability.

Besides the expectations that this places on lawyers it ignores the fact that while much of environmental law is concerned with environmental protection that does not mean that the operation of law is simply about preventing environmental harm. Rather, many other factors come into play in environmental law issues such as responsibilities of the state, private rights and other interests. The task of the practising environmental lawyer is not so much the promotion of a new ethic but rather being involved in decisions and disputes that are embedded in complex legal and socio-political contexts.

Finally, there is a danger that the purposive approach to defining environmental law ignores the fact that there is considerable disagreement over the nature and definition of environmental policy. Rather environmental law is described as fulfilling the purpose that the commentator wants achieved whether it is environmental justice, sustainability, or pollution prevention. Conflict over environmental protection is not just simply between those who wish to protect the environment and those who don't, but there are also many different understandings of what it means to protect the environment. Many people wish to promote sustainable development but that term can mean various things ranging from a minor adjustment to industrial activity to a radical overhaul of the whole of society (see Chapter 11). Likewise Flournoy, quoted already, identifies a number of different ethical impulses in US environmental law such as environmental justice, a land ethic, private rights ethic, a development ethic, and sustainability.[2] Environmental law thus is a battleground for different perspectives on environmental protection. A purposive account can take into account these divergences of opinion but there remains a danger that environmental law is treated as just politics in another guise.

1.3 A JURISPRUDENTIAL DEFINITION

A third approach to defining environmental law can be seen to be emerging in the literature. This definition addresses many of the concerns associated with a purposive definition and can be described as a jurisprudential approach. Under this approach, environmental law is neither a collection of laws concerned with environmental protection nor an instrument of policy, but rather a body of legal principle. The approach is jurisprudential in the sense that it is promoting the legal integrity of the subject. Consider the comments of Jewell and Steele in the introduction to a collection of essays, which explores the interface between environmental issues and other areas of law.

Tim Jewell and Jenny Steele, 'Law in Environmental Decision-Making' in Jenny Steele and Tim Jewell (eds), *Law in Environmental Decision-Making: National, European, and International Perspectives* (OUP 1998) 3

[C]urrent developments would seem to pull towards a more 'integrated' approach to the subject, and to suggest the development of environmental law as a distinctive field with distinctive subject-matter. From such a point of view, the type of analysis adopted in this collection—which emphasizes the specific qualities of particular (perhaps even traditional) legal frameworks and sources—will require some explanation. If the current emphasis is on a distinctive series of 'environmental' problems to be solved, then it would seem that 'component' categories of law would need to be amended, or even transcended, in order to achieve such goals. On the other hand, questions of environmental law are intimately associated with questions of legal technique, and even innovative techniques have both a practical and an academic history and setting. In addition, it will be suggested that it is in the nature of current environmental law to invite consideration of environmental issues as part of other concerns, and as connected with other bodies of law.

[2] Alyson Flournoy, 'In Search Of An Environmental Ethic' (2003) 28 Colum J Envtl L 63–118.

This perspective acknowledges the transformative nature of applying law to environmental problems and that this in turn raises more general issues for how legal scholars think about legal control.

Another jurisprudential approach to defining the subject can be seen in the work of Coyle and Morrow. They are writing very much from the perspective of property law.

Sean Coyle and Karen Morrow, *The Philosophical Foundations of Environmental Law: Property, Rights and Nature* (Hart Publishing 2004) 212

Environmental law, viewed as a series of arguments concerning responsibility and justice, might be thought of as the product of a sustained reflection upon the relationship between property, rights and nature: a body of philosophical speculation which has its roots in the deliberations of the natural rights theorists of the seventeenth century. For the natural lawyers, property rights are imbued with a moral (and religious) significance which shapes and refines their specific characteristics on the plane of juristic thinking. Within the natural rights tradition, property was thought of as central to the nature and political fabric of the polity itself. [...]

Coyle and Morrow's arguments are interesting. They are attempting to show that a body of environmental law thought can be recognized and that it has a long and well entrenched history. Coyle and Morrow are not attempting to argue that this means there is a coherent and well thought out set of legal principles but that the legal foundations of environmental law are well entrenched.

From the perspective of the environmental lawyer, the jurisprudential approach to defining the subject is very attractive as it puts the subject on a firm disciplinary footing and addresses the perception that environmental law is in some way a 'second rate' legal discipline, because it has little jurisprudential content. A problem, however, which can be seen from comparing these two perspectives, is that it is not obvious what that jurisprudential content is. The Jewell and Steele collection is emphasizing the interface between environmental issues and a variety of areas of law (although not directly property law) while Coyle and Morrow are specifically focused on property law. De Sadeleer's comments also offer another perspective on the jurisprudential content of the subject. Just as with the purposive approach, there needs to be awareness that what is identified as the substantive content of environmental law is more influenced by what the commentator wants it to be than what it actually is.

A second problem is that there may be a danger that a jurisprudential approach to defining environmental law overemphasizes the unique nature of the subject. Consider the comments of Cane in relation to arguments for a special liability scheme for environmental harm.

Peter Cane, 'Are Environmental Harms Special?' (2001) 13(1) JEL 3, 5–6

Unlike the law of contract or property but like product liability, environmental liability law and 'toxic tort law' are functional or practical legal categories—they do not have a conceptual unity of their own. They have grown out of attempts to use existing legal techniques and concepts to deal with new social problems. This is perfectly acceptable and, indeed helpful, so long as these new functional legal categories are used only as frameworks for organising knowledge and thinking about particular social problems. But difficulties can arise when special regimes of legal liability rules are invented to deal specifically with harms caused, for instance, by 'products' or 'environmental pollution'. [...] My basic point is in thinking about environmental liability law we should aim first and foremost to develop a fair and efficient system of compensation for harm inflicted. We should not complicate this compensation goal by trying simultaneously to punish polluters or to reduce pollution.

Cane's argument is an interesting one in that he is emphasizing the importance of established legal doctrines for how environmental issues are treated by the law. At the very least it emphasizes the danger of the jurisprudential approach to defining the subject, but if taken more seriously also undermines a purposive approach to the subject.

1.4 WHY DO DEFINITIONS MATTER?

The discussion in Sections 1.1, 1.2, and 1.3 highlights that there is no one definition of environmental law that can adequately capture the subject. Each of the definitions does have some validity but each also has serious drawbacks. As this is the case, these definitions are used as common reference points throughout this book to illustrate the different ways in which the subject can be approached. To do that, however, it is useful to consider in more detail why the definition of the subject matters so much.

It should be stressed that the problems of defining the subject are not unique to environmental law but are particularly acute in relation to it because of its wide scope and dynamic development. The variations in definitions clearly present challenges for the environmental law textbook writer or the environmental law lecturer in trying to figure out what should be included in a textbook or a course. These problems are not of direct concern to the student or the lawyer—so why do the problems in defining environmental law matter to students and scholars of environmental law?

From one perspective it could be said that how we define environmental law is of no consequence. Consider, for example, the perspective of Lord Woolf (then Sir Woolf).

Sir Harry Woolf, 'Are the Judiciary Environmentally Myopic?' (1992) 4(1) JEL 1, 2

It could be suggested that the initial difficulty is that while environmental law is now clearly a permanent feature of the legal scene, it still lacks 'clear boundaries'. It may be that, again as in the case of administrative law, it is preferable that the boundaries are left to be established by judicial decision as the law develops. After all, the great strength of English law has been its pragmatic approach. It has always been concerned more with remedies than with principles. However, environmental law does not fit conveniently into any existing legal compartment. It is easier to identify the areas of the law with which it is not concerned than those with which it is concerned. For my own purposes I regard it as being concerned with our physical surroundings rather than our political or social surroundings [...] we rely upon no single legal procedure or remedy. Instead we rely in part on the long-established common law actions for private and public nuisance; In part on the public law procedure of judicial review; in part on statutory appeals and applications and generally on the criminal law. Combined these procedures provide a formidable armoury. However at the present time, their deployment can and occasionally does result in an embarrassing succession of proceedings.

Lord Woolf's comments are very apposite. The law with which an environmental lawyer will be concerned will be driven by pragmatic concerns and the boundaries of that law will be determined by the remedies and legal procedures available. Environmental law is thus the application of those different areas of the law to environmental issues. As this is the case there is no need to draw neat boundaries around the subject and if such boundaries are drawn they are likely to be overly restrictive.

However, definitions do matter for three reasons. First, a chosen definition of environmental law will affect what is adopted as the focus for analysis. Thus, for example, defining the subject in doctrinal terms provides a very different picture than if it is defined in socio-legal terms. Any analytical framework will provide a means by which to identify particular recognized features or procedures and to draw on common approaches between them, at the expense of identifying other features, relationships, and procedures. A definition will thus affect even a pragmatic approach to the subject because it will assist in identifying what is in the 'formidable armoury' of the environmental lawyer. Thus, for example, environmental law could equally be understood as concerned with: bringing particular types of legal action, invoking particular types of laws, or ignoring formal legal processes and focusing on negotiation with administrative bodies. These different definitions will also have implications for how the subject is taught and for what is understood as acceptable to be published as 'legitimate' environmental law scholarship.

The second reason why the definition of environmental law matters is to do with the way in which the law is applied. The focus here is particularly on how the *environment* is defined, because this will affect the scope of the subject and how environmental issues are conceptualized. Consider the perspective of Holder and McGillivray in an introduction to a series of essays which explore how the environment is legally constructed.

Jane Holder and Donald McGillivray, 'Introduction' in Jane Holder and Donald McGillivray (eds), *Locality and Identity: Environmental Issues in Law and Society* (Aldershot 1999) 1

[O]ur concern is that geographic, economic and moral boundaries have been drawn around particular ways of understanding this relationship, leading to the partial defining of environmental problems and the marginalisation of particular groups in decisions about the state of the environment. Law has played an important part in drawing such boundaries, for example, by narrowly defining 'the environment' as air, water and land, and by generally dividing up matters of conservation, land use and landscape protection for separate treatment. Law's traditional preoccupation with jurisdiction compounds this state of affairs: environmental problems are conceived of, and contested, in terms of international, European Community [now Union] and national law, often with little appreciation of the operation of complex and often contradictory laws of nature, cross-media, trans-boundary and cumulative environmental effects. A further legal boundary is drawn between that which is privately owned and that which is 'common', with law having traditionally upheld private rights at the expense of common ownership. This creates some doubts about the capacity of law to protect the environment as 'commons' via individualised legal mechanisms. Much of the law relating to the environment may therefore be characterised by spatial, theoretical and disciplinary closure.

Holder and McGillivray's comments highlight the problems of a pragmatic approach. Different legal processes and remedies can be deployed to protect the environment in discrete ways and in doing so has implications for how we understand environmental problems and how to address them. Thus, for example, there is an overlap but disjunction between planning law and pollution control law that results in environmental management being distorted.

Another example of how defining the environment can shape (or confuse) the focus for environmental law can be seen in Macrory's comments concerning the role of different government departments in relation to environmental issues.

Richard Macrory, ' "Maturity and Methodology": A Personal Reflection' (2009) 21(2) JEL 251, 252–53

The difficulties that governments have in constructing coherent environmental ministries reflect the pervading nature of the environment—all the reorganisations of central government environment departments that have taken place in the UK over the last 10 years underline the sheer impossibility of fitting the environment into conventional bureaucratic structures. Universities attempting to establish environmental centres and similar initiatives face similar problems in challenging long-established departmental and faculty structures. For many of us engaged in the field, this is what makes the subject so intellectually interesting. But it makes even the use of the term 'environmental law' problematic.

Macrory also went on to consider the challenges in exploring the possibility of considering setting up an Environmental Tribunal.

One of the questions that had to be faced was what made environmental law special: if an environmental tribunal, then why not a trading standards or health and safety tribunal? We identified a number of characteristics of environmental law that did seem to place it in a distinct category, and which in themselves pose challenges for developing robust scholarship as the authors indicate. First, that in practice many of the legal disputes involved complex and often uncertain technical and scientific issues, and were thus quite different from the sorts of questions raised in planning or amenity type decisions. Next, environmental law involved a complex and fast-developing legislative and policy base. I have never seen a comparative study, but I suspect that the sheer body of new substantive law in the environmental field is higher than in many other areas. Then, there was the sheer complexity of differing and overlapping jurisdictions engaged in environmental law, from criminal and civil law to private and public law. The density of the European Community legislation in the environmental field appeared to be greater than in many others, including town and country planning and health and safety. This was coupled with the significance of a large number of international environmental treaties. In addition, fundamental principles, such as the precautionary principle and the polluters pay principle, have now entered the language of environmental law, and raised challenging questions for interpretation and application. Principles concerning third party access to justice, notably those reflected in the Aarhus Convention, had been highly developed in the environmental field. Finally, the overarching principle of sustainable development was underpinning many policy and legal developments—a concept subject to so many differing interpretations that its value was becoming suspect, but it nevertheless required understanding.

The third and perhaps most important reason why definitions definitely do matter is that how the subject is defined will directly affect how the law is evaluated. In studying a subject law students are not only concerned with knowing the law. They are also concerned with assessing the quality and integrity of that body of law. Environmental law also needs to be evaluated as part of its development and reform. How environmental law is defined will act as the benchmark for how it is judged. If environmental law is thought to be concerned with preventing environmental degradation, then any degradation that occurs will be construed as a failure of environmental law. If, however, environmental law is understood as a coherent body of principles, then a particular area of environmental law not in line with those legal principles will be understood as deficient. The definition of the subject is thus essential in assessing its validity. In analysing any critiques of environmental law, an important starting point is to understand how the commentator is defining environmental law.

2 THE CHALLENGES OF PRACTISING AND STUDYING ENVIRONMENTAL LAW

While the discussion in Section 1 has focused on definitions, as the last section also makes clear, environmental law is not a straightforward subject to either study or practice. There is much to think about in relation to how environmental problems are understood, what are understood as the relevant legal frameworks, and how those frameworks apply to particular environmental problems. It thus should come as no surprise that, among environmental lawyers, there is a great deal of soul searching about the nature of their subject. Again this might seem an annoyingly intellectual concern and enterprise, but the issues that vex environmental lawyers and environmental law scholars have significant practical implications. Before looking at those implications, it is useful to expand on those challenges. The extract from Fisher and others relates to that environmental law scholarship but there is much that is also relevant to environmental law itself, lawyers, and scholars in particular.

Elizabeth Fisher, Bettina Lange, Eloise Scotford, and Cinnamon Carlane, 'Maturity and Methodology: Starting a Debate About Environmental Law Scholarship' (2009) 21(2) JEL 213, 218–19

[T]here is a strongly held belief amongst environmental law scholars that the subject has not yet come of age as an area of legal scholarship and that the best is yet to come. To put it bluntly—environmental law scholarship is characterised as immature. Moreover, these perceptions have not shifted in over two decades. Indeed, for environmental law scholars, environmental law scholarship seems to be like the Peter Pan of legal scholarship—'the discipline that never grew up'. [...] There are many different reasons why the immature image of environmental law scholarship persists. Four are particularly significant: the intellectual incoherence of environmental law as a subject, the perceived marginality of environmental law scholarship in the legal academy, the poor quality of some environmental law scholarship and the sheer difficulty of carrying out environmental law scholarship.

We are of course included among these authors of this article, and the conclusion in this article was that much of the perceived immaturity pointed to methodological challenges in the subject, including challenges arising from: the speed and scale of change; interdisciplinarity; governance; and the multijurisdictional nature of the subject. There is no room here to go into the details of our analysis but it is worth noting interdisciplinarity in environmental law: in particular, Heinzerling makes some very pertinent comments in relation to interdisciplinarity.

Lisa Heinzerling, 'The Environment' in Peter Cane and Mark V Tushnet (eds), *The Oxford Handbook of Legal Studies* (OUP 2003) 701, 702–3

First, the nearly simultaneous passage of the major environmental laws meant that legislators often had no time to react to the experience under one law before enacting another; thus several mistakes were made in the early environmental laws, and many of these mistakes were repeated from one statute to the next. A large strand of legal scholarship on the environment has taken critical aim at these early mistakes. To this day, environmental law scholars focus much of their attention on issues of statutory design. [...]

Environmental law scholarship is pervasively interdisciplinary. Indeed, it is almost impossible to imagine a first-rate environmental law scholar who is not comfortable with, and whose work does not touch upon, scholarly disciplines beyond law. Toxicology, ecology, public health, statistics, economics, sociology, psychology, philosophy, and more—these fields have as much to do with environmental law, and environmental law scholarship, as 'law' itself (assuming that law is an autonomous discipline in any event). Outside of several constitutional issues that have special relevance to environmental problems (such as the 'takings' issue in the United States), traditional modes of legal scholarship—doctrinal analysis, case parsing, analogical reasoning—have relatively little place in cutting-edge environmental law scholarship. Most of the heavy labour is done only with the help of other scholarly disciplines. For example, to look ahead for a moment, the astonishingly popular scholarly trend in favour of market-based mechanisms for pollution control came, not from law, but from economics. In environmental law scholarship, interdisciplinarity is not a trend; it's a way of life.

Our solution to these different challenges in approaching environmental law issues was, and is, to argue for scholars to be more reflective about their methodology. In being so focused on method, scholars can be understood as developing their expertise, thus building the rigour of their analysis, arguments, and conclusions. Fisher has commented on this; although her discussion here is in relation to transnational environmental law, her analysis of expertise is relevant to environmental law more generally.

Elizabeth Fisher, 'The Rise of Transnational Environmental Law and the Expertise of Environmental Lawyers' (2012) 1 Transnational Envtl L 43, 48–50

Much has been written about expertise, but for my purposes let me use a very simple definition: namely, that the term connotes a set of skills and knowledge that other scholars are not expected to have. The focus then becomes the knowledge, skills and experience that are required for someone to be identified as a transnational environmental lawyer as opposed to another type of lawyer, including other types of environmental lawyer. Those skills and that knowledge and experience fall largely into two categories: contributory and interactional expertise. These terms are taken from the work in science and technology studies of Collins and Evans. While the questions asked within the context of their work do not relate directly to law, it provides a useful frame. This is particularly because their analysis heavily emphasizes the importance of language.

Contributory expertise refers to the sets of skills, knowledge and experience that are needed to contribute to the development of transnational environmental law as a discipline. This expertise is legal expertise [...]

Contributory expertise is not the only form of expertise that needs to be fostered in relation to transnational environmental law, however. There is also a need to develop interactional expertise. By this I refer to the need to interact with the other disciplines that relate to how environmental problems are conceptualized. In particular, there is a need to develop linguistic expertise in these other areas. The development of this type of expertise is not just about reading the right textbook or knowing what a particular scientific term means—it requires understanding the complexities, ambiguities and nuances of environmental problems and discourses. This often involves engagement with a range of different disciplines. Thus, understanding risk requires a multi-disciplinary approach, as does making sense of the activity of modelling. Fostering this type of expertise also requires the fostering of critical capacity—we should not just blindly accept concepts from other disciplines but subject them to the scrutiny we give to legal concepts. Of course, it cannot be the same scrutiny, but the point about interactional expertise is that it highlights the need to develop a distinct expertise for addressing this process of interaction.

These comments respond to many of the issues highlighted by Heinzerling, also returning to the themes highlighted in the first pages of this chapter. In other words, the practical implications of the challenges of studying and practising environmental law manifest themselves in the need for environmental lawyers to develop a range of different types of expertise.

3 HOW TO STRUCTURE ENVIRONMENTAL LAW INQUIRY

All of this is sobering reading. The study of environmental law is not just about finding simple solutions to making the world a better place. It is a difficult subject that requires scholars, practitioners, and students to think hard and carefully about what they do. In this last section we provide a very rough general framework to help students in this process. Before doing this, it is valuable to highlight two points from the discussion in Sections 1 and 2. First, defining environmental law is not easy because of (among other things): the surrounding socio-political context; the variations in legal institutions and processes concerned with environmental problems; and the subject's ambiguous legal nature. Second, how the subject is defined matters because it affects what is understood to be the relevant law, how that law is applied, and how that law is evaluated.

This state of affairs seems to leave students, lawyers, and academics in a rather difficult situation. An authoritative definition appears elusive but such a definition is necessary to both the effective practice and study of environmental law. What is thus needed is an approach that somehow captures the ambiguity of the subject but not at the cost of thwarting proper analysis. Such an approach is best achieved by starting with a very inclusive definition of the subject and returning to three matters that we highlighted as being important at the start of this chapter.

An inclusive definition of the subject is something like this: environmental law is the law concerned with environmental problems. It is a highly pluralistic subject and different areas of the law and different environmental problems have given rise to different legal frameworks. Variations in substantive legal norms, legal processes, purposes, and the involvement of different jurisdictions in environmental law reflect the wide scope of the subject. Moreover, it is also not surprising that those environmental issues and associated legal frameworks result in a range of different legal responses. Common approaches can be seen across the subject but there are also considerable differences.

At this stage, an understanding of the three issues highlighted in the introduction—environmental problems, basic legal concepts, and the interaction between the two—becomes significant. Table 1.1 sets out these three issues as a series of conceptual steps that a student or lawyer needs to reason through in thinking about a particular environmental law problem. The starting point is thus not environmental protection writ large but rather a specific issue or dispute. In a sense these steps are overly simplistic, but they also are a way of stressing the scope of knowledge and understanding that an environmental lawyer needs to understand, apply, and evaluate environmental law.

This framework should not be treated rigidly but more as a way to loosely begin or structure a legal inquiry about an environmental problem or issue. The first step is to analyse the nature of environmental issues and environmental disputes. The physical nature of environmental problems can vary considerably in scale and impact. Likewise, there may be very little knowledge about it. As the questions in the table also make clear, such an analysis is not limited to an understanding of the physical nature of an environmental problem but also requires consideration of its socio-political context. The next step is to understand the relevant environmental laws that relate to a particular issue. It should be stressed from the outset that this is not just an exercise in identifying a bundle of rules but requires a far more sophisticated analysis. These laws may come from different jurisdictions and it is important to appreciate the nature of the legal cultures they are derived from. To this end the legal cultures of England, the EU, and international environmental law are discussed in Part II. The relevant laws may take many different forms. In some cases there will be legislative regimes or legal doctrines that have been specifically developed to address a particular environmental problem but there also may be other areas of law which, for one reason or another, are indirectly relevant to environmental disputes.

Table 1.1 A Process of Inquiring into Environmental Law Problems

1. What is the Nature of the Environmental Issue or Dispute?

a) What knowledge is there about the environmental problem? What is the nature of that knowledge and how is an understanding of the environmental problem affected by scientific uncertainties, values, and decision-making context?

b) Who are the interested parties involved? Is there conflict between the parties and, if so, over what? In particular, what are the values that the different parties hold?

c) What role does the state play in decision-making? Does that role rest on a particular understanding of an environmental problem or favour a particular set of environmental values?

d) How does the existing legal framework shape understandings of the environmental problem and conflict over it?

2. What are the Relevant Legal Concepts Pertaining to the Environmental Problems?

a) Is there legislation or legal doctrine understood to regulate this particular environmental problem?

b) Is there other legislation or legal doctrine that might be relevant?

c) What legal cultures are involved and what are signficiant features of those legal cultures?

d) What are the basic legal issues and areas of law involved?

3. What is Involved in the Application of the Relevant Law to a Particular Environmental Problem?

a) How well do existing legal doctrines and frameworks address the complexity of environmental problems?

b) Does there need to be an adjustment to a particular area of law in addressing environmental problems?

c) How are understandings of environmental problems affected by the application of a particular law?

They are only 'environmental' in the loosest of senses. Most significantly, there is a need to identify the basic legal concepts that are applicable. To help in this inquiry, Part III of this book discusses these concepts independently of substantive regimes that regulate particular environmental problems.

The third and most difficult step in Table 1.1 is to think about the process of applying the relevant law to environmental problems. In the introduction we described this as a process of interaction because the process of application not only requires a reconsideration of basic legal concepts but also often involves a re-evaluation of environmental problems as well. It is at this stage that the three different definitions of the subject become particularly relevant because, as already pointed out, they will affect the focus for analysis, how the law is applied, and how the law is evaluated. Because of this, these definitions are a constant reference point throughout this book.

While each of these three steps is separate, they do require constant reference to each other. How the law is applied requires consideration of not only what the law is, but also the nature of the relevant environmental issue. Likewise, the legal framework will affect the environmental issue and the legal framework can only really properly be understood by thinking about the legal issues it raises. The important point is that an environmental lawyer must have a wider perspective than simply knowing what the applicable law is in descriptive terms. He or she must not only think about a body of environmental laws, but also think about the environmental problems that that body of law addresses and how that body of law is applied. The end result is not a neat map of the subject but a series of questions that helps to structure the lawyer's or the student's inquiry into the subject, or a particular area of it. The questions given here are not exhaustive. The important point is that a true understanding of the subject can only be gained though analysing (at least) these three aspects.

One final word of warning in understanding the nature of environmental law—nearly all legal scholarship is a normative enterprise and environmental law particularly so. This means that any reader of any text needs to consider whether what is being described or discussed is what the law *is* or what the writer would *like it to be*. Sometimes this is obvious in that the writer is calling for reform, but sometimes it is more subtle and is implicit in the analysis. This can be particularly seen when scholars will often classify the law, describe a case, or provide a particular explanation of a legal development in the hope it will lead to a 'better' application of the law or that a particular explanation of a case will lead to a 'better' interpretation. What this means is that, in such cases, the act of describing is also an act of prescribing.

This leads on to our final point. While much environmental law and environmental law scholarship is concerned with prescribing 'better' approaches to environmental disputes, there is no agreement over what is 'better'. Again, this will be discussed in Chapter 2 but here it is worth noting that even this book is an act of prescription—as an introduction to the subject, it is also one that is prescribing a particular intellectual approach, an approach that not all scholars may agree with, but which can be simply summed up as the need to take environmental problems, law, and the interaction between them seriously.

4 CONCLUSION

There often exist two perceptions among students embarking on the study of environmental law. The first is that the subject is a very worthy one about saving the world. The second is that saving the world is largely about learning and applying very dry and technical legislation. In other words, it is very dull. As this chapter demonstrates, and the rest of the book will show, both these perceptions are inaccurate. Environmental law and environmental law scholarship are important and complex. Those attempting to master the subject need to be critical and careful navigators of both law and environmental problems.

FURTHER READING AND QUESTIONS

1. For further discussions about the difficulties of defining environmental law see A Dan Tarlock, 'Is There a There There in Environmental Law?' (2004) 19 Journal of Land Use and Environmental Law 213; Todd S Aagaard, 'Environmental Law as a Legal Field' (2010) 95 Cornell L Rev 221; Andreas Philippopoulos-Mihalopoulos (ed) *Law and Ecology: New Environmental Foundations* (Routledge 2011) chs 2–3.

2. Looking at the course you are studying, can you identify a definition of the 'environment' or 'law' underpinning its design?

3. For discussions about environmental law scholarship focusing on the UK see Elizabeth Fisher and others, 'Maturity and Methodology: Reflecting on How to Do Environmental Law Scholarship' (2009) 21(2) JEL 213; Richard Macrory, '"Maturity and Methodology": A Personal Reflection' (2009) 21(2) JEL 251; and John McEldowney and Sharon McEldowney, 'Science and Environmental Law: Collaboration across the Double Helix' (2011) 13 Env L Rev 169.

UNDERSTANDING
ENVIRONMENTAL PROBLEMS

This chapter is an introduction to environmental problems. Understanding environmental problems is not just of passing academic interest, the 'fluffy' stuff you read before getting into the legal detail. Rather, as noted in Chapter 1, an understanding of environmental problems is essential for understanding environmental law. A good environmental lawyer has a sophisticated appreciation of environmental problems and understands in particular how the nature of these problems impacts on environmental law and practice. The extracts in this chapter are thus not just optional background reading. They are essential for understanding the subject.

The chapter is structured as follows. The first section analyses in more detail why an understanding of environmental problems is important for environmental lawyers. The second section gives an overview of the systemic complexity of environmental problems, paying particular attention to issues such as their collective nature and the way in which environmental problems 'cross boundaries'. The third section examines environmental knowledge and the limits of that knowledge. The fourth section is an overview of environmental values and politics, which also inform the appreciation of, and response to, environmental problems. The fifth and sixth sections examine the roles of the state and law respectively in framing and defining environmental problems. It should be noted at the outset that this chapter can only give the reader a flavour of the complexity of environmental problems. Doing this in a single chapter comes at the expense of deep analytical rigour and this chapter does not seek to provide a thorough review of the expansive literature concerning environmental problems. The extracts included in each section are wide ranging and you should constantly keep in mind how the different facets of environmental problems highlighted will impact on environmental law. At the end of each section, there is discussion of the legal implications of the material covered and a series of questions for discussion. These questions have no easy or definitive answers.

1 WHY AN UNDERSTANDING OF ENVIRONMENTAL PROBLEMS IS IMPORTANT FOR UNDERSTANDING ENVIRONMENTAL LAW

Before entering into an analysis of environmental problems, it is imperative to appreciate *why* it is important for environmental lawyers to have an understanding of environmental problems. For this purpose, it is useful to return to the definition of environmental law given in Section 3 of

Chapter 1—'environmental law is the law concerned with environmental problems'. From this defini-tion some appreciation of environmental problems is obviously needed. It is useful for a lawyer to know what issue a law is attempting to address and what legal disputes are about. But still, you may be thinking that there is not much to understand, particularly if one looks at how environmental problems are often depicted in the mainstream media. In populist discussion, environmental problems are seen as conse-quences of individuals or corporations not making environmentally responsible decisions because of apathy, lack of awareness, greed, or wickedness. An environmental problem is perceived as a product of an actor failing to adhere to easily identifiable standards of behaviour. If this is the case then what all lawyers need to understand is that people and corporations are often wayward—not a particularly new insight—and that the role of environmental law is to stop them being wayward.

However, these populist caricatures bear little relationship to the reality of environmental problems. Their main flaw is that they rest on an assumption that there are robust, universal, and uncontested understandings of environmental problems and of environmentally ethical behaviour. This is far from the case. Rather (and this is the most important feature of environmental problems), there is rarely a single and obvious answer to the question: 'is this an environmental problem, and if it is, what we should we do about it?' This is because knowledge about environmental problems is often incom-plete and views about the value of the environment vary considerably. Moreover, to make matters more complicated, knowledge and values are entangled. Values will be influenced by knowledge but values will also shape how environmental quality is perceived.

The starting point for thinking about environmental problems thus cannot involve populist caricatures. Broadly speaking, an environmental problem is a *situation where there is a collective judg-ment that environmental quality is not acceptable, or that there is a threat to acceptable environmental quality*. This definition is deliberately vague and non-restrictive. A 'collective judgment' may not be universal and it may be held by only a small group in a community. Likewise, such a judgment may be based on a mixture of values and knowledge. Moreover, what is 'acceptable' and what constitutes a 'threat' are also open to question. Whether environmental quality is 'acceptable' to an actor may depend upon that actor's values and/or the way they interpret the knowledge we have about environ-mental problems. The same is true of 'threats': what is perceived as a threat by one actor may not be seen as such by another. Further, the notion of 'environmental quality' can cover many issues, from pollution levels in the natural environment and biodiversity, to land use planning decisions that have environmental consequences.

It is now that we can begin to see why an understanding of environmental problems is so important for environmental law. If environmental law is a response to environmental problems and concerned with disputes in relation to these problems, then the fact that understandings of environ-mental problems are not settled means that the role of environmental law cannot be understood as merely enforcing a universal standard of environmental friendly behaviour. If 'collective judgment', 'acceptability', and 'threat' are all open to different interpretations, then there is no simple way of determining what the role and nature of environmental law is, and what it should be. This is the case, whether you take a descriptive, functional, or jurisprudential approach to the subject. In particular, the complexity of environmental problems has four overlapping sets of implications for environmen-tal law.

First, such complexity will impact on what is understood to *be the role of environmental law*. If environmental law is a response to environmental problems but there is no settled agreement about those problems, then this will mean that different environmental laws may be based on different 'collective judgments' and understandings of 'acceptability' and 'threat'. Second, the complexity of environmental problems will have implications for the *operation of environmental law*. The divergence in collective judgments over environmental problems will result in divergences in opinion about how environmental laws should be interpreted, applied, and enforced. Third, the nature of environmental problems will *shape the nature of environmental law disputes*. Disputes over environmental problems may take two forms and in both cases the complexity of environmental problems will cause difficulties. The first type of dispute will be over *how environmental law should be applied* and here there will be complexities created by divergent values and lack of robust knowledge of environmental problems. The second type of legal dispute will be over the *validity of environmental laws*. These disputes arise, and are also intractable, because of the variation in what is understood to be an environmental problem. Finally, the complexity of environmental problems will also mean that there will be difficulties *in evaluating the quality of environmental laws*. Not only may different actors value environmental laws differently but, because of the value-laden and uncertain nature of environmental problems, the process of evaluation may be impossible to carry out.

All this is sobering reading. It points to the fact that environmental lawyers need to engage with the complexities of environmental problems when carrying out legal analysis. The question then arises of how best to go about this process of engagement. In Chapter 1, a way of structuring an environmental law inquiry was identified. The first question was: 'what is the nature of the environmental issue or dispute?' Illustrative sub-questions were grouped into four categories:

a) What knowledge is there about the environmental problem? What is the nature of that knowledge and how is an understanding of the environmental problem affected by scientific uncertainties, values, and decision-making context?

b) Who are the interested parties involved? Is there conflict between the parties and, if so, over what? In particular, what are the values that the different parties hold? How does the decision-making context impact upon the problem?

c) What role does the state play in decision-making? Does that role rest on a particular understanding of an environmental problem or favour a particular set of environmental values?

d) How does the existing legal framework shape understandings of the environmental problem and conflict over it?

As stressed in Chapter 1, these questions are not exhaustive but they highlight the different dimensions of environmental problems. Moreover, they aid environmental lawyers in understanding which features of an environmental problem may create challenges for:

- determining the role of environmental law;
- applying environmental law;
- resolving environmental legal disputes; and
- evaluating the quality of environmental law.

The rest of this chapter explores a number of different dimensions of environmental problems. Before looking at those dimensions, Section 2 considers the sheer systemic complexity of environmental problems.

2   THE SYSTEMIC COMPLEXITY OF ENVIRONMENTAL PROBLEMS

A core feature of environmental problems is their sheer systemic complexity. This point is made beautifully by Dryzek.

John S Dryzek, *The Politics of the Earth* (2nd edn, OUP 2005) 8–9

[E]nvironmental problems tend to be interconnected and multidimensional; they are, in a word, complex. Complexity refers to the number and variety of elements and interactions in the environment of a decision system. When human decision systems (be they individuals or collective bodies such as governments) confront environmental problems, they are confronted with two orders of complexity. Ecosystems are complex, and our knowledge of them is limited, as the biological scientists who study them are the first to admit. Human social systems are complex too, which is why there is so much work for the ever-growing number of social scientists who study them. Environmental problems by definition are found at the intersection of ecosystems and human social systems, and thus are doubly complex.

The more complex a situation, the larger is the number of plausible perspectives upon it because the harder it is to prove any one of them wrong in simple terms. Thus the proliferation of perspectives on environmental problems that has accompanied the development and diversification of environmental concern since the 1960s should come as no surprise.

Dryzek's analysis highlights three closely interconnecting sources of complexity. The first is the *physical* nature of environmental problems. Physical complexity arises from the open ended and holistic nature of ecosystems, as well as from the limits of scientific knowledge. The second is the *socio-political* complexity of environmental issues—complexity created by the fact that the environment does not have a fixed value and the socio-political context of decision-making. The third form of complexity highlighted by Dryzek is due to the fact that environmental problems, in his words, 'do not present themselves in well defined boxes'.[1] These complexities are all systemic complexities and are discussed in this section. Systemic complexities arise for two reasons—the collective nature of environmental problems and the way in which environmental problems 'cross boundaries'.

2.1 COLLECTIVE NATURE OF ENVIRONMENTAL PROBLEMS

Decision-making about the environment is not an exercise that individuals can take in isolation. This is because the causes and solutions to environmental problems are not solely the product of individual autonomous actions or choices. Thus, for example, climate change is the product of many individual decisions, some due to personal preferences but most due to systemic societal influences, and values that have resulted in increasing greenhouse gas emissions. These influences include agricultural practices, transport systems, pollution control, food habits, housing design, and general lifestyle choices. Environmental problems are thus not just caused by the wayward litterbug or the evil corporate mogul—they are caused by general community practices. An individual can make decisions to use less energy in the house, use public transport, ride a bicycle, and not to use plane travel (all of which should reduce emissions). However, those actions, *by themselves*, will not result in a serious reduction in greenhouse gas emissions. Moreover, an individual's ability to take those decisions will be seriously affected by the travel required by his or her job; the distance between where that person lives and works and where his or her children attend school (which locations are in turn products of housing prices and town planning); what energy saving products are on the market; the availability and reliability of public transport; and general social customs. In other words, environmental problems are collective in nature. In part this has to do with the shared nature of the environment, and in part this has to do with the issues highlighted by Dryzek.

[1] John Dryzek, *The Politics of the Earth* (2nd edn, OUP 2005) 8.

Three features of the collective nature of environmental problems are noted here: the polycentricity of environmental problems; the way in which environmental problems arise because of disincentives in contemporary society to look after the 'commons'; and the operation of the market. An appreciation of each of these dimensions to environmental problems contributes to understanding the causes of such problems and also their potential solutions.

Polycentricity

Returning to the climate change example, there are many different causes of climate change and those causes are complex in themselves. Take, for example, the problem of fuel-inefficient cars. Such cars are undesirable both in terms of using up non-renewable energy resources and contributing greenhouse gas emissions. Yet there are many reasons for them being on the road, including: the *perception* that such cars are safer; fashion; a lack of focus on fuel efficiency in car design; traditional car manufacturing practices; and the reality that more fuel efficient cars tend to be newer and thus not as affordable to all sectors of society. In other words, the issue of fuel inefficiency is related to a wider web of actors and issues. Likewise, in thinking about solutions, there are a range of issues and parties to consider. Imagine a law that decided to ban large cars on the basis of fuel inefficiency. Such a law would arguably have serious impacts on the car industry, poorer sections of society, and car design, as well as placing more pressure on other forms of transport.

None of this is to say that action should not be taken, but in taking action there needs to be an appreciation that individuals or government are not simply weighing up a few issues or negotiating with a couple of actors in isolation. Nor are environmental problems akin to the traditional bi-polar disputes between two parties that are the subject matter of much private law—this is even when environmental problems result in court cases. Rather, they are highly polycentric. Fuller describes the concept of polycentricity.

Lon L Fuller, 'The Forms and Limits of Adjudication' (1978) 92 Harv L Rev 353, 395

We may visualize this kind of situation by thinking of a spider web. A pull on one strand will distribute tensions after a complicated pattern throughout the web as a whole. Doubling the original pull will, in all likelihood, not simply double each of the resulting tensions but will rather create a different complicated pattern of tensions. This would certainly occur, for example, if the doubled pull caused one or more of the weaker strand to snap. This is a 'polycentric' situation because it is 'many centred'—each crossing of strands is a distinct center for distributing tensions.

Fuller's analysis highlights the problems that courts have with adjudicating in relation to polycentric issues, and thus the limits of such adjudication. In that sense, the issue of polycentricity is problematic in general legal terms, but it is useful to consider it in the environmental law context because it highlights:

(a) The wide range of interests and actors that are relevant to any environmental problem.

(b) How environmental problems must be distinguished from other legal problems.

(c) That legal solutions must take into account a wide number of considerations.

Polycentricity has also been discussed in other disciplines. In particular, it has been the focus for analysis in understanding how governance systems respond to particular problems. From this perspective, polycentricity does not only define the environmental problem but is also implicated in considering appropriate responses to it.

Elinor Ostrom, 'Polycentric Systems for Coping with Collective Action and Global Environmental Change' (2010) 20 Global Environmental Change 550, 552

Polycentric systems are characterized by multiple governing authorities at differing scales rather than a monocentric unit. Each unit within a polycentric system exercises considerable independence to make norms and rules within a specific domain (such as a family, a firm, a local government, a network of local governments, a state or province, a region, a national government, or an international regime). Participants in a polycentric system have the advantage of using local knowledge and learning from others who are also engaged in trial-and-error learning processes. As larger units get involved, problems associated with non-contributors, local tyrants, and inappropriate discrimination can be addressed and major investments made in new scientific information and innovations. No governance system is perfect, but polycentric systems have considerable advantages given their mechanisms for mutual monitoring, learning, and adaptation of better strategies over time.

Polycentric systems tend to enhance innovation, learning, adaptation, trustworthiness, levels of cooperation of participants, and the achievement of more effective, equitable, and sustainable outcomes at multiple scales, even though no institutional arrangement can totally eliminate opportunism with respect to the provision and production of collective goods. Enabling citizens to form smaller-scale collective consumption units encourages face-to-face discussion and the achievement of common understanding. Creating larger collective consumption units reduces the strategic behavior of the wealthy trying to escape into tax havens where they could free ride on the contributions of others. Further, creating polycentric institutions related to climate change helps to fulfill the 'matching principal' in international law that problems involving multiple levels (eg global, national, regional, and small scales) should involve contributions at each of these levels.

The impact of polycentricity will be seen throughout the chapters of this book, and particularly in relation to governance (Chapter 13).

The commons

The second collective dimension of environmental problems relates to the part of the environment that is being affected. Generally speaking (and remembering the concept of polycentricity already discussed), environmental problems are due to the way in which individual or community behaviour impacts on others and the world around them, often in unexpected and unintended ways. However, that impact invariably falls most heavily on those parts of the environment that are not private property but which constitute the 'commons'—those parts of the natural environment that are not owned. The commons may include land, sea, and air. An extract from Hardin's famous article on the *Tragedy of the Commons* highlights how private behaviour impacts upon these areas of the 'commons'.

Garrett Hardin, 'The Tragedy of the Commons' (1968) 162 Science 1243, 1244, 1245. Reprinted with permission from AAAS.

Picture a pasture open to all. It is to be expected that each herdsman will try to keep as many cattle possible on the commons. [...]

As a rational being, each herdsman seeks to maximize his gain. Explicitly, or implicitly, more or less consciously he asks, 'What is the utility to me of adding one more animal to my herd?' This utility has one negative and a positive component.

1. The positive component is a function of the increment of one animal. Since the herdsman receives all the proceeds from the sale of the additional animal, the positive utility is nearly +1.

2. The negative component is a function of the additional overgrazing created by one more animal. Since, however, the effects of overgrazing are shared by all the herdsmen, the negative utility for any particular decision-making herdsman is only a fraction of -1.

Adding together the component partial utilities, the rational herdsman concludes that the only sensible course for him to pursue is to add another animal to his herd. And another; and another [...] But this is the conclusion reached by each and every ration herdsman sharing a commons. There is the tragedy. Each man is locked in a system that compels him to increase his herd without limit—in a world that is limited. Ruin is the destination toward which all men rush, each pursuing his own best interest in a society that believes in the freedom of the commons.

Hardin notes examples of this tragedy: overgrazing on public lands in the US, fishing, and pressure on national parks, and many other environmental problems are due to such tragedies. He then goes on to note a different problem with the commons.

In a reverse way, the tragedy of the commons reappears in problems of pollution. Here it is not a question or taking something out of the commons, but of putting something in—sewage, or chemical, radioactive, and heat wastes into water; noxious and dangerous fumes into the air; and distracting and unpleasant advertising signs into the line of sight. The calculations of utility are much the same as before. The rational man finds that his share of the cost of the wastes he discharges into the commons is less than the cost of purifying his wastes before releasing them.

Again many examples can be found and all forms of pollution are in essence 'commons' problems.

What Hardin is highlighting is that environmental problems are not just the product of individual behaviour impacting upon the environment but that they arise because social arrangements encourage environmental exploitation. The significant social arrangement here is property ownership and Hardin's analysis can be seen as promoting the virtue of private property ownership as a solution to environmental problems—if individuals have an investment in land through ownership, they are more likely to take care of it in environmental terms. Furthermore, Hardin's overall argument is that such tragedies do not have technical solutions, which he defined as 'requir[ing] a change only in the techniques of the natural sciences, demanding little or nothing in the way of change in human values or ideas of morality'.[2] Rather, the moral aspects of such decisions need to be recognized.

The market

The final collective dimension of environmental problems follows on from Hardin's analysis, which highlights not only the importance of private property ownership but also of the market. Hardin's rational man is rational because he needs to maximize his gains in a market economy. Returning to Dryzek's analysis, the socio-political complexity of environmental problems arises because of the complexity of the market economy and the incentives and disincentives it creates in relation to environmental problems. It thus comes as no surprise that the relationship between the environment and the market has been the subject of considerable inquiry. Of particular interest has been how markets promote environmentally destructive behaviour. The extract from Sagoff explains two of the major 'theories' that have influenced the understanding of the relationship between markets and environmental protection.

[2] Garrett Hardin 'The Tragedy of the Commons' (1968) 162 Science 1243, 1245.

Mark Sagoff, *Price, Principle and the Environment* (CUP 2004) 106, 112–114

Many economists, following a suggestion Arthur Pigou put forward in the 1925, have proposed to tax polluters at an amount equal to the marginal cost or damage per unit of the wastes they emit into the water or air. Such a tax would give polluters an incentive to control pollution to the point at which they would have to pay more to reduce emissions by the next unit than society would benefit from that unit of reduction. This yields an 'optimal input mix because the waste disposal services provided by the environment' will be priced along with all other resources.

Pigouvian theory chimes well with the 'tragedy of the commons' problem. The cause of environmental problems is the fact that individuals do not need to pay for their use and/or abuse of the commons and thus they ignore the adverse environmental impacts—the 'externalities'—that their activities have. The solution is thus to ensure that they do pay—that they internalize pollution costs by paying an appropriate emissions tax—and in so doing, pay the correct amount to ensure the market is operating efficiently.

However, Sagoff notes various problems with Pigouvian analysis, including the information burdens that it places on the state (particularly due to the complexity of pollution problems) and the way in which it promotes centralized planning, as it requires the state to assess the true costs of private activity and redistribute them. Sagoff then examines the 'Coasian Turn in Economics'.

In his critique of the Pigouvian approach, Coase emphasized the reciprocal nature of harm, for example, that harm arises not simply because of the emissions of a power plant but also because of the presence of the neighbours who are injured. Coase also explained that the operators of a source of pollution, such as a power plant, will negotiate with those they harm to reach an optimal outcome if they can manage the transaction costs—the costs of getting information about WTP [Willingness to Pay] and WTA [Willingness to Accept] as well as processing and implementing contracts based on that information. This resolution might require the plant install scrubbers or the people to move away. The parties will agree on the cheapest solution; the direction in which compensation is paid will differ from case to case depending on the initial distribution of property rights.

[...]

In a market with transaction costs, the status quo similarly marks a Pareto Frontier and passes the Kaldor-Hicks [efficiency] test. 'In order to carry out a market transaction', Coase wrote, 'it is necessary to discover who it is one wishes to deal with, to inform people that one wishes to deal and on what terms, to conduct negotiations leading up to a bargain, to draw up a contract, … and so on'. People have to pay transaction costs as they have to pay labour costs, materials costs, transportation costs, to name a few. If any of these costs is so great that the project results in a loss, the agents will not undertake it. Transaction costs, in other words, are ordinary costs of doing business. CJ Dahlman has written, 'It is difficult to see in what significant way [...] transaction costs differ from regular costs of production.'

Coase's original argument involved the consideration of liability rules and his core point concerned the power of bargaining. His theory had a limited role for state intervention. This also has important implications for thinking about ways to address environmental problems and for the nature and design of environmental law. Coase's theory, like all foundational theories, has been open to question and interpretation. However, while the validity of Coase's theorem might be challenged, it is important to appreciate, in relation to environmental problems, his identification of the reciprocal and multi-dimensional nature of harms involved, and the way in which actors bargain about those harms and how they might be allowed or acceptable.

2.2 CROSSING BOUNDARIES

The second feature of the complexity of environmental problems is the way in which they 'do not present themselves in well defined boxes', as Dryzek noted. In part, this is due to issues of polycentricity and the collective causes of environmental problems discussed in Section 2.1, but there are also other reasons. Consider the extract from Latour.

Bruno Latour, *We Have Never Been Modern* (Catherine Porter translator, Harvard University Press 1993) 1

On page four of my daily newspaper, I learn that the measurements taken above the Antarctic are not good this year: the hole in the ozone layer is growing ominously larger. Reading on, I turn from upper-atmosphere chemists to Chief Executive Officers of Atochem and Monsanto, companies that are modifying their assembly lines in order to replace the innocent chlorofluorocarbons, accused of crimes against the ecosphere. A few paragraphs later, I come across heads of state of major industrialized countries who are getting involved with chemistry, refrigerators, aerosols and inert gases. But at the end of the article, I discover that the meteorologists don't agree with the chemists; they're talking about cyclical fluctuations unrelated to human activity. So now the industrialists don't know what to do. The heads of state are also holding back. Should we wait? Is it already too late? Toward the bottom of the page, Third World countries and ecologists add their grain of salt and talk about international treaties, moratoriums, the rights of future generations, and the right to development.

The same article mixes together chemical reactions and political reactions. A single thread links the most esoteric sciences and the most sordid politics, the most distant sky and some factory in the Lyon suburbs, dangers on a global scale and the impending local elections or the next board meeting. The horizons, the stakes, the time frames, the actors—none of these is commensurable, yet there they are, caught up in the same story.

What Latour is really highlighting is how environmental problems require us to cross boundaries in thinking about them: two specific boundaries. First, he is highlighting that the boundary between facts and politics is so often unclear. In particular, the factual understanding of an environmental problem is not always definitive. Second, he notes the way in which understandings and perceptions of environmental problems are not confined within national boundaries. Depletion of the ozone layer is a global problem although it requires, and impacts upon, national action.

In relation to Latour's first point, the close interrelationship between facts and values is probably *the* most significant aspect of environmental problems. While this interrelationship will be explored in this chapter, it is worth noting a number of points here. In public life, we are used to the notion that facts and values are separate. The former are ascertainable through objective processes, while the latter are subjective and negotiated and debated in the realm of politics. Moreover, facts are invariably given a privileged role in public argument because of their objectivity. In environmental problems, however, this distinction is rarely clear cut. There are a range of reasons for this, including that facts are often unascertainable so there must be reliance on values in making decisions about them. Further, values and world-views direct how facts are researched, analysed, and interpreted. Recognition of boundary-crossing also means recognition of the need to take an interdisciplinary approach to understanding environmental problems, as discussed in Chapter 1.

The second form of boundary-crossing noted by Latour is useful to discuss at greater length. In the last twenty years, there has been a growing cross-jurisdictional and international discourse about environmental problems and their resolution. This is unsurprising considering that many environmental problems physically relate to transboundary causes and effects, including global effects. These new connections between international and national developments do not simply concern how national and international law and policy influence each other. Rather, the globalization of environmental issues has led to new forms of governance. The extract from Long Martello and Jasanoff describes some of these developments. This extract is taken from the introduction to an edited collection on the globalization of environmental governance, with Long Martello and Jasanoff reflecting on some of the themes that they see emerging from the works in the collection.

Marybeth Long Martello and Sheila Jasanoff, 'Introduction: Globalisation and Environmental Governance' in Sheila Jasanoff and Marybeth Long Martello (eds), *Earthly Politics: Local and Global in Environmental Governance* (The MIT Press 2004) 3–4

Over the past 30 years, some of the most interesting balancing acts between the global and the local have come from the domain of environmental governance. The willingness to seek global solutions to problems of the human environment is one of the big and as yet only partly told stories of the late twentieth century. Starting in the 1970s, nations rallied together around such issues as acid rain, ozone depletion, hazardous wastes, marine pollution, biodiversity loss, desertification, and climate change. These efforts preceded the widely discussed globalizing effects of the Internet, trade liberalization, and the marketization of socialist economies at end of the Cold War. Environmental initiatives revealed, often for the first time, emergent aspects of transnational politics that will only grow in significance in this century: the increasing interaction between scientific and political authority, highlighting fault lines in each; the salient role of non-state actors in both knowledge making and politics; the emergence of new political forms in response to novel conjunctions of actors, claims, ideas, and events that cut across national boundaries; and, of greatest interest here, the reassertion of local knowledge claims and local identities against the simplifying and universalizing forces of global science, technology, and capital.

In a time when national particularities are under pressure from many directions, it is of no small interest that the idea of the local has emerged as a salient topic in the policy discourses of environment and development. While seeking to establish common transboundary approaches to issues of sustainability, a remarkable variety of international regimes have recognized and accommodated knowledges and perspectives that are tagged as local. This juxtaposition of global and local, universal and particular, serves as the entry point for the work presented in this volume. We confront here a twofold puzzle. On the one hand, it is notable enough that environmentalism, so long associated with place-specific political phenomena such as the NIMBY ('not in my back yard') syndrome, has become global at all. On the other hand, it is equally striking that the implementation of the global environmental agenda should so quickly and on so many levels have led to a rediscovery of the local.

In other words, globalization is not just leading to the internationalization of environmental law and policy but is creating new and complex relationships between local and national levels of governance. Local communities still have a role in responding to environmental problems, but the process of globalization is adding to the systemic complexity of environmental problems. It highlights that action taken in one jurisdiction must often take into account decision-making at the international level and other national jurisdictions. This jurisdictional layering and interconnection of governance regimes is seen in many of the substantive law chapters of this book.

2.3 SYSTEMIC COMPLEXITY AND ENVIRONMENTAL LAW

The systemic complexity of environmental problems creates a number of challenges for thinking about environmental law. For present purposes, these challenges fall into two different categories of problems:

- *Framing environmental problems.* If environmental problems are polycentric and cross boundaries, then it is difficult to know how environmental lawyers should frame environmental problems. This is seen in two ways. First, we are not simply dealing with relationships between an easily identifiable set of actors. In areas such as tort law and contract law, legal issues are framed by legal relationships (e.g. agreed contracts, a duty of care) but environmental law is not defined by legally constructed relationships. Second, while most other areas of law studied at law school can focus primarily on national law (albeit with an increasingly strong element of EU and ECHR law), this is far more difficult in environmental law because of its international and transnational dimensions.

- *Difficulties in ascribing responsibility for environmental problems.* The polycentric and complex nature of environmental problems means it is not always obvious what the 'cause' of an environmental problem is. Moreover, the myriad ways in which rational actors can cause or contribute to environmental problems, including through established social practices, mean that environmentally destructive behaviour is not always the same as delinquent or wicked behaviour.

These problems are not exhaustive but they do highlight the kind of challenges created by systemic complexity in understanding and responding to environmental problems. These are, however, not the only challenges for environmental law.

FURTHER READING AND QUESTIONS

1. Pick two contemporary environmental problems (e.g. nature conservation, fly tipping, water pollution) and consider the different causes of such a problem. Then consider the nature of those causes. Are they due to long-standing practices? Are they practised by one part of the population? Now consider the possible solutions to such a problems (e.g. bans, regulation) and what the different consequences of those actions might be. Do you think the two problems differ in their polycentricity? For a good discussion of polycentricity in the environmental context, see Elinor Ostrom, 'Polycentric Systems for Coping with Collective Action and Global Environmental Law' (2010) 20 Global Environmental Change 550. For a discussion of the history of the term 'polycentricity', see Paul D Aligica and Vlad Tarko, 'Polycentricity: From Polanyi to Ostrom and Beyond' (2012) 25 Governance 237.

2. Coase's 'The Problem of Social Cost' is well worth a careful read, beyond Sagoff's analysis given in this chapter. It is a long piece, with many extended examples and Coase develops his economic argument carefully: Ronald H Coase, 'The Problem of Social Cost' (1960) 3 Journal of Law and Economics 1. Do you think those who cite Coase have engaged with all he is saying?

3. For other theoretical social science works exploring the nature of environmental problems, including the interplay between facts and values, see Ulrich Beck, *Risk Society: Towards A New Modernity* (Sage Publications 1992); Sheila Jasanoff, *Designs on Nature: Science and Democracy in Europe and the United States* (Princeton University Press 2005); Bruno Latour, *Politics of Nature: How To Bring the Sciences Into Democracy* (Harvard University Press 2004).

3 ENVIRONMENTAL KNOWLEDGE: NATURE AND LIMITS

To state the obvious in tautological terms—we only know about environmental problems because we have scientific knowledge of them. Environmental knowledge is thus crucial not only to understanding environmental problems but in actually identifying them in the first place. Many environmental problems only become apparent because of advancements in knowledge, and in particular scientific knowledge. Thus, for example, the depletion of the ozone layer was only identified in the 1970s and 1980s, while that depletion had in fact already been occurring over a number of years. Again, the tort action in *Cambridge Water Company v Eastern Counties Leather*[3] only became both necessary and possible because of advancements in scientific knowledge that allowed the amount of perchloroethene to be measured in water. Yet the problem remains that environmental knowledge is not particularly definitive. Knowledge acquisition about environmental problems is often understood as being a process of exploration and identification, the end point being complete human understanding of the natural world. However, knowledge rarely takes that form, and this section examines a number of the complexities inherent in environmental knowledge and its development.

3.1 DEFINING ENVIRONMENTAL KNOWLEDGE

Environmental knowledge is a very broad term. It can refer to many different types of knowledge ranging from anecdotal information in a local community about its environmental quality to very technical and sophisticated scientific information. The former, while not always rigorous and accurate, has played an important role in the history of environmental protection. Thus, for example, the biologist Rachael Carson in her groundbreaking work *Silent Spring* recorded anecdotal evidence of the environmental and public health impacts of pesticide use, in a way that had never been done before.[4] Further, the use of such knowledge still continues with programmes such as the Royal Society for the Protection of Birds 'Big Garden Birdwatch', asking members of the public to record their observations of populations of bird species. These examples also highlight that the collection of environmental knowledge is crucial in knowing about environmental problems. Without collection processes that have as their purpose the gauging of environmental quality, it would be very difficult to 'know' about the state of the environment. Environmental changes are often imperceptible, occurring over a long time period, across a wide area, and are due to complex ecosystem interactions.

Furthermore, law and policy are often the catalysts for the production of environmental knowledge. We often gain environmental knowledge because, as a society, we have decided to create laws and policies to protect the environment. As such, environmental knowledge is often the product of environmental regulation. This may be due to explicit monitoring programmes or, more likely, due to the fact that, if something is going to be regulated, some knowledge is needed. The role of regulation is significant for two reasons. First, it means that environmental knowledge is often produced for particular purposes and the state often takes a lead role in its production and collection. Second, it means that most environmental knowledge that environmental lawyers encounter is produced in a regulatory context and/or for regulatory purposes. Even in this context, environmental knowledge can take many different forms and range from 'state of the environment' reporting, such as measuring air pollution levels, to the collection and production of knowledge for assessing a particular activity, such as monitoring greenhouse gas emissions from industrial installations. The extract from

---

[3] [1994] 2 AC 264 (HL) 292.   [4] Rachel Carson, *Silent Spring* (Houghton Mifflin 1962).

the Royal Commission on Environmental Pollution describes, and also prescribes, environmental knowledge requirements in relation to environmental standard setting. Environmental standard setting can relate to a range of environmental problems—from acceptable water and air pollution levels to biodiversity targets/identifying endangered species and the measures that should apply to them—and these are often prescribed in the form of delegated legislation.

Royal Commission on Environmental Pollution, *Setting Environmental Standards*
(21st Report, Cm 4053 1998) paras 8.4–8.11 [bold in original text excluded]

8.4 [...] The analytical stage of the policy process [in environmental standard setting] has several complementary and closely inter-related components:

- scientific assessment;
- analysis of technological options;
- assessment of risk and uncertainty;
- economic appraisal; and
- analysis of implementation issues, including the geographical scope of standards.

Conceptually, this approach would apply to any kind of environmental policy or standard but the nature of a particular environmental problem will determine the resources which should be devoted to each type of analysis in practice.

8.5 There are well-established procedures for assessing the scientific evidence and determining, for example, dose-effect relationships to inform the decision-making process. The aim must be to indicate clearly where the boundaries of knowledge lie. To avoid the spurious accuracy often implied when only a single statement or conclusion is presented, assessments should present a range of relationships concerning the particular issue, each established under different conditions; indicate susceptibility to change (for example through increased knowledge, or changing priorities); and should acknowledge uncertainties more clearly.

8.6 Technological assessment will reveal opportunities for controlling pollution, as well as new forms of pollution resulting from technological change. Life cycle assessment will usually provide the most satisfactory basis for assessing the environmental effects of industrial products and processes, and environmental standards should not be set in ways which discourage the development of this approach, or obstruct the uptake of improved technology.

8.7 Procedures for risk assessment can help to illuminate the choice between alternative policies or standards and rationalise the choice of substances for priority control. Assessments should identify and characterise the different types and sources of risk in the situation under consideration, together with the uncertainties and their implications. Human factors strongly influence the way people conceive of risks and their tolerance of them, and they should be taken into account throughout the assessment process drawing on the evidence from consensus conferences and similar techniques used earlier in the process. Communication about risks should begin at the outset and inform the framing of the assessment.

8.8 The economic appraisal will value the costs and benefits of different courses of action so far as possible. Great care is needed to ensure that effects for which no price can be established are appropriately taken into account in making decisions. The assessment of the costs and benefits of environmental measures can be problematic when available choices raise value questions.

8.9 The way standards are implemented influences particular patterns of behaviour or courses of action by individuals, business and industry. These should be identified in advance to ensure that perverse incentives are not inadvertently created and that the strategies selected will be those most

effective in influencing behaviour. The legal status of standards should be that which will best complement those strategies.

8.10 Value questions are necessarily posed when standards are set and scientific, technological and
economic appraisals should be supplemented in ways which allow these questions to be properly
considered, in order to elucidate the consequences of setting standards. There is scope for more
trialling and experimentation in the methods by which public values may be articulated.

8.11 The presentation to decision-makers of the results of the analyses referred to above should clearly
state the assumptions and limitations of each analysis. It will usually be necessary to offer several
options and their implications, so far as these can be gauged.

This extract makes clear just how much, and how many different types of, information is required as
part of the standard setting process. Moreover, that knowledge is not presented as a series of scientific
papers, but in particular forms—technology assessments, risk assessments, economic appraisals, and
so on. The purpose of the Royal Commission's report was to identify 'a more consistent and robust
basis for setting standards in environmental protection' (para 1.2) and thus the discussion is perhaps
more prescriptive than descriptive, but the type of tools it describes are common features of most
regulatory decision-making.

While there are many different types of environmental knowledge used in environmental regulation, the two most important are derived from the disciplines of science and economics. Science is
particularly important because it is seen as the most necessary form of environmental knowledge
in identifying and knowing how to deal with environmental problems. At the same time, it is profoundly controversial within, and outside, scientific disciplines. The importance of economics in
identifying and analysing environmental problems has also been growing over recent years, with
an increasing regulatory focus on the financial impact of regulation, and with economics also being
used as a basis for appreciating the nature and importance of environmental problems in the first
place.

3.2 SCIENCE AND REGULATORY SCIENCE

Science is usually understood as the starting point for our environmental knowledge, although
as shown in Section 3.1 it is only one source of relevant information. It is understood as a starting
point for the simple reason that it is presumed to be the most authoritative source of environmental
information.

**Andrew Stirling, 'The Precautionary Principle in Science and Technology' in Tim
O'Riordan, James Cameron and Andrew Jordan (eds)** *Reinterpreting the Precautionary
Principle* (Cameron May 2001) 64.

[S]cience is conventionally held to imply a series of key properties, including a systematic methodology,
scepticism, transparency, quality control by peer review, professional independence and accountability, and an emphasis on learning. It is not that these properties are always realised in practice, but rather
that they represent central aspirations in the positive enterprise of science.

Stirling's definition highlights two important features of science. First, the term can refer to many different disciplines. In the environmental context, knowledge is drawn from nearly all the different sciences, including chemistry, physics, geology, and the wide range of biological sciences. These different scientific inquiries are often grouped together and described as 'environmental science', although it should be appreciated that that term is a very broad one, and does not refer to all scientific activities that increase scientific knowledge about the environment. Second, the definition is a prescriptive one—it refers to a set of requirements that a body of knowledge is expected to reach, and which its authority will be based on. This prescriptive dimension to the definition of science is important. Science is important not just for the information it provides about environmental problems but also for the perceived authority it brings to the decision-making process.

As already noted, environmental knowledge is invariably generated for particular purposes in specific contexts. Science is no exception and many commentators have argued for the need to distinguish the type of science used in environmental regulation from the type of science that occurs in the laboratory. Thus, for example, Sheila Jasanoff argues that the type of science developed and used in environmental and public health policy-making is quite distinct from research science.

Sheila Jasanoff, *The Fifth Branch: Science Advisors as Policy Makers* (Harvard University Press 1990) 77

Science used in the policy process differs from research science most significantly in its context, but also partly in its content. With regard to content, regulatory science can best be thought of as the aggregate of three different types of scientific activity. In the first place, regulatory science includes a component of *knowledge production*. Studies designed to fill gaps in the knowledge base relevant to regulation may either be performed or sponsored by regulatory agencies or they may be carried out under ordinary conditions of academic research. In either case [...] their status as 'science' is frequently open to question. Second, regulatory science includes a substantial component of *knowledge synthesis*. As Salter notes, secondary activities, such as evaluation, screening, and meta-analysis, play a much larger role in regulatory science than open-ended, original research.[54] The products of regulatory and research science accordingly are rather different. Whereas research science places greatest value on published papers, certified by peers as true, original, and significant, science conducted for policy is rarely innovative and may never be submitted to the discipline of peer review and publication.

The third and most contentious branch of regulatory science is *prediction*, the activity that requires the decision maker to determine how serious or significant a risk is created by a regulated technology. Because prediction involves so many elements of uncertainty and discretionary judgment, analysts seeking to understand regulatory science have paid it disproportionate attention.

54 Liora Salter, *Mandated Science* (Dordrecht, Netherlands: Kluwer, 1998), pp. 187–188.

Jasanoff's discussion is in the context of the US regulatory system in which large 'science bureaucracies' operate, equipped with the resources for research. There has been no similar institutional tradition in the UK and in the EU, but Jasanoff's analysis is equally valid for these legal cultures because regulatory science plays a similar role in UK and EU environmental policy and regulation.

This is well illustrated by briefly considering two methodological tools that have been developed in the context of environmental law and regulation—modelling and risk assessment. The extract from Fisher, Pascual, and Wagner discusses the former, which is now a ubiquitous feature of environmental law.

Elizabeth Fisher, Pasky Pascual, and Wendy Wagner, 'Understanding Environmental Models in Their Legal and Regulatory Context' (2010) 22 JEL 251, 265–67

[M]odels are 'a simplification of reality that are constructed to gain insights into select attributes of a particular … system'. Using this definition as a springboard there are five key things to note about models in environmental regulation.

First, models are simplifications of reality. Or to put the matter another way—a model is not reality. A model of a river basin will only capture some elements of that ecosystem just as a model of the solar system only captures some elements of the planets and their relationship to the sun. In relation to environmental regulations, models are particularly useful because the systems they represent are so complex and open ended that they can be difficult to conceptualise [...]

Moreover, models are frames that enable 'better questioning, exploration, handling and manipulation of the topic'. As frames, models will draw (among other things) on both scientific theories about how a system works and available data about that system. Models may draw on a single scientific discipline or many, and they may be adapted as information and disciplinary understandings change.

One of the most common types of model used in environmental regulation are computational models developed by selecting different elements of a system and formalising relationships among these elements through mathematical equations that are then codified in a computer program. That computer program is not reality however. Nor is it a 'truth telling machine' or a 'fact'.

Second, for a model to be able to provide insight it must be a *rigorous* representation of reality. It must have a level of rigour that is defensible as fit for the purpose in hand. A model of ocean currents which is based on no data and a presumption that the world is flat is clearly inferior to one incorporating ocean current data and grounded in the theory that the world is round. A good model will be a coherent representation of a system that is based on well-established scientific theories and relevant, quality data. To say this is not to say that models are facts or that a model's truth can be validated. Rather it is saying that despite this, distinctions can be made in the quality of models. Moreover, the quality of a model will determine the quality of the insight which can be gained from it. Of course that raises the difficult question of how quality is judged and who is to judge it [...]

Third, as a simplification of reality a model is constructed for a purpose or set of purposes. That purpose is defined by the NRC [National Research Council] as 'gaining insight' but this should be understood in context. In the environmental regulatory context the main role of models is not so much to gain disinterested insight into a particular system but rather models are developed to assist decision-makers in discharging their regulatory responsibilities. Those responsibilities can vary dramatically but generally speaking models are concerned with assessing the existing state of the environment, human health and the economy, and predicting impacts on these different things.

Fourth, the purpose or purposes for which a model is developed will directly influence how reality is simplified. Thus, for example, if a model is being developed to assess water quality in a river then a model may represent water flow, oxygen concentration and contaminants but is unlikely to represent how many rocks are in the river or how many bridges cross it. In other words, the regulatory purposes of a model will influence what it represents. Moreover, the purposes of a model will directly influence how simplified the representation of a model is. Thus, for example, a model may be oversimplified to increase transparency of a system or the use of a system by non-scientists. Models, then are not just products of theory and data but are also shaped by the priorities of the decision-makers who are deploying them.

Fifth, a logical consequence of all of the above is that modelling is an interdisciplinary activity. This is in two different ways—internally and externally. *Internally*, the process of modelling itself requires the integration of many different forms of information and assumptions from a variety of different disciplines. Thus, while modelling is a distinct activity, it is only semi-autonomous in nature as it is drawing on a range of different disciplines. Modelling also has an *external* interdisciplinary aspect because it is being carried out for a set of regulatory and policy-making purposes. Modelling is not just a scientific activity which is of relevance to policy-makers, but a scientific activity developed *for* policy-makers with the purposes of policy-making in mind.

Thus, while models are 'scientific', they are of profound importance to lawyers. In particular, they provide the rationale and basis for environmental decision-making.

Models are just one example of the development of specific methodological tools to aid environmental decision-making. The most high profile example of these tools, which also encompasses modelling, is risk assessment, increasingly utilized in the setting of standards and the appraisal of products, technologies, and activities. 'Risk assessment' is a term used in many different disciplinary contexts to mean many different things. Even in environmental and public health regulation, it can be defined in various ways. As such, care needs to be taken with the concept. The extract from the National Research Council gives a very general definition of the term.

National Research Council, *Understanding Risk: Informing Decisions in a Democratic Society* (National Academy Press 1996) 33

Risk assessment is usually defined as the scientific analysis and characterization of adverse effects of environmental hazards. It may include both quantitative and qualitative descriptors, but it often excludes the analysis of perceived risk, risk comparisons, and analysis of the social and economic effects of regulatory decisions (eg National Research Council 1983:18). Risk assessment is often presumed to be free of value judgments, with some important exceptions, such as choices about whether and to what extent to include worst-case assumptions in risk assessments, a choice that may be made differently depending on whether the assessment is being conducted to determine regulatory priorities or priorities for testing.

The definition given here was developed in the US context, but risk assessment also plays a significant role in UK environmental decision-making. Three points are worth noting about risk assessment. First, risk assessment plays an increasingly important role in environmental decision-making, mainly because it provides a seemingly systematic and objective way of presenting scientific information in a policy context. Second, the practice of risk assessment is contentious, with many commentators arguing that its use over-emphasizes the authority and reliability of science. Some of these issues will be explored in this chapter. Third, the use of risk assessment has led to the subject matter and purpose of environmental law being characterized in terms of 'risk'. As such, the concept of 'environmental risk' is used interchangeably with the concept of 'environmental problem', and commentators and decision-makers often discuss environmental problems in terms of risk. Care again needs to be taken as the concept of risk can mean many different things.[5]

3.3 ECONOMICS AND COST–BENEFIT ANALYSIS

The second important source of environmental knowledge is economics. As already seen in Section 1, economic understandings of environmental problems are important because of the way in which

---

[5] Elizabeth Fisher, 'Risk and Environmental Law: A Beginner's Guide' in Benjamin J Richardson and Stepan Wood (eds), *Environmental Law for Sustainability* (Hart Publishing 2006).

environmental problems are often a product of how markets works. What that discussion has also highlighted is that there are a number of different economic theories about environmental problems. As well as Pigou's and Coase's theories, within economics there are a number of different sub-disciplines, which have been developed with environmental problems in mind. They are described in the extract from Common and Stagl.

Michael S Common and Sigrid Stagl, *Ecological Economics: An Introduction* (CUP 2005) 4 (emphasis added)

Starting in the early 1970s, neoclassical economics began to show renewed interest in the natural environment and it now includes the two important specialisations, or sub-disciplines, of environmental economics and natural resource economics (sometimes just resource economics) [...] *[E]nvironmental economics* (mainly) concerns itself with the economy's insertions into the environment, and with problems of environmental pollution. *Natural resource economics* concerns itself (mainly) with the economy's extractions from the environment, and with problems associated with the use of 'natural resources'. Many university economics programmes now offer higher-level optional courses in one or both of these specialisations. The compulsory courses in most economics programmes do not pay much attention to economy-environment interactions. It is possible to qualify as an economist and to know very little about environmental and resource economics. While neoclassical economists do not ignore the natural environment, they do not think that an understanding of the connections between the economy and the environment [...] is an essential part of an economist's education.

Ecological economists do think that such an understanding is an essential of an economist's education. Ecological economics is based on the idea that the proper study of 'how humans make their living' has to include the study of the relations of the human animal to its 'organic and inorganic environment'. Whereas neoclassical economics treats the study of economy-environment interdependence as an optional extra, for ecological economics it is foundational. It *starts* with the fact that economic activity takes place within the environment.

There are a number of things to note from this extract. The first is that economics is not a monolithic discipline. Second, and following on from this, values are implicit in economic knowledge about the environment. The nature of those values will be explored in more detail.[6]

As with scientific environmental knowledge, there has been the development of specific types of economic knowledge in the context of environmental decision-making. In particular, there has been an increasing role for economic appraisal in regulatory decision-making. The extract from the Royal Commission on Environmental Pollution gives their description of economic appraisal.

Royal Commission on Environmental Pollution, *Setting Environmental Standards* (21st Report, Cm 4053 1998) para 5.13

5.13 Appraisal as characterised by the UK Treasury involves, first, defining the objectives [...] and then normally going through the following sequence:

i. consider the options;

ii. identify, quantify and where possible value the costs, benefits and risks and uncertainties associated with each option;

[6] See Sections 3.4 and 5.

iii. analyse the information;

iv. present the results.

As the extract makes clear, the Commission was drawing on UK Treasury guidance in describing this process and there is more specific government guidance on economic appraisal in environmental decision-making.[7] As with risk assessment, economic appraisal can refer to many different types of processes that have developed over time, including cost–benefit analysis and regulatory impact assessment (RIA).

The use of these tools has not just been limited to environmental regulation and these tools have been deployed right across the regulatory state. The growth of these instruments has been particularly marked in the US where cost–benefit analysis and regulatory impact assessment have been an official part of regulatory decision-making since 1981. Since the 1990s, regulatory impact assessment has also played an important role in UK and EU regulation, acting as an analytical tool accompanying new initiatives, which involves assessing the 'costs' and 'benefits' of regulatory action. Many of these developments have been due to the influence of the Organisation for Economic Development and Co-operation (OECD),[8] and are part of a broader programme of 'Better Regulation' that operates across all Western governments.[9] Radaelli discusses the nature of regulatory impact assessment in the UK and EU.

Claudio M Radaelli, 'Rationality, Power, Management and Symbols: Four Images of Regulatory Impact Assessment' (2010) 33 Scandinavian Political Studies 164, 167–68

In the United Kingdom, there are both agency-level RIAs and departmental RIAs on proposed legislation. However, the system originated in the Cabinet Office to control the regulatory production of departments—the agency dimension emerged later. Since 1996, departments have been obliged to produce benefit-cost assessments of proposed legislation (including statutory instruments) affecting business or the non-profit sector. Given the broad range of activities covered, the United Kingdom now prefers to use the notion of IA to RIA—to indicate that scrutiny is not confined to regulation. The Cabinet Office used to intervene directly in the early steps of the assessment. Now the Better Regulation Executive—which has moved from the Cabinet Office to the Department for Business, Innovation and Skills—prefers that departments prepare the RIAs more autonomously. One aim of the government throughout the last decade has been to use rigorous policy appraisals to foster joined-up governance, but empirical evidence sheds mixed light on the achievements.

In the EU, impact assessment (or IA, since the EU also dropped the 'R') covers most of the items in the legislative programme of the European Commission as well as some 'catalogue' initiatives outside the programme and some comitology decisions—the regulatory nature of the initiative is not a discriminant for impact assessment, hence the cancellation of the 'R'. IAs are prepared by the lead Directorate General. The Secretariat General supports the process by writing guidelines, and by creating inter-service groups among the lead Directorate General (DG) and other Directorates with an interest in the proposal. The European Parliament and the Council are supposed to produce their own impact assessments of substantive amendments, due to an obligation introduced in 2003 by the inter-institutional agreement on better regulation. The implementation of the 2003 agreement, however, is fraught with problems.

[7] HM Treasury, *Green Book: Appraisal and Evaluation in Central Government* (TSO 2003 with 2011 amendments).

[8] OECD, *Risk and Regulatory Governance* (GOV/PGC/REG(2006)1/ANN2 2006)

[9] Chapter 12.

In 2006, the Commission, under pressure from the Member States, created an Impact Assessment Board (reporting to the President of the Commission) to exercise oversight on the quality of RIA. The technical preparation of the opinions of this body lies de facto with the Secretariat General, whilst the opinions eventually issued are decided by the board's members (high-level officers from the lead DGs). The board is chaired by the Deputy Secretary General of the Commission.

This extract makes clear that RIAs are playing an increasingly important role in regulatory decision-making and thus in environmental law. All major new regulatory initiatives are accompanied by a RIA,[10] and these assessments influence what is understood as 'good' regulation.

3.4 THE LIMITS OF KNOWLEDGE

The discussion in Section 3.3 suggests that there are very real limits to the usefulness and reliability of environmental knowledge. The authority of environmental knowledge cannot always be taken as a given. There are three major reasons for those limits. First, environmental knowledge is always limited by uncertainty, particularly scientific uncertainty. Second, the production, organization, and acceptance of environmental knowledge is infused with values. Third, environmental knowledge is limited due to its context—it is produced for specific regulatory reasons, in short time frames, and in political context. In such situations, the knowledge produced is likely to be provisional and shaped by policy. In examining these limits in this section, the focus is mainly on scientific forms of environmental knowledge. While science has been seen as the most authoritative form of environmental knowledge, the reasons for its authority need to be questioned.

Uncertainty

Over the last twenty years, there has been an increasing appreciation that there is a much uncertainty about the causes and nature of environmental problems. This uncertainty ranges in form but the most high profile set of uncertainties have been scientific. Scientific uncertainty is a feature of all science and can never be completely eradicated; and it is also a particular feature of environmental problems. The most fundamental feature of scientific uncertainty to understand is that it is not simply a 'data gap' that can be reduced by throwing more resources at it. Rather, as Fisher explains, 'scientific uncertainty' is shorthand for a whole series of methodological, epistemological, and ontological problems in science. Fisher's discussion concerns risk assessment but it is also relevant to other areas of regulatory science.

Elizabeth Fisher, 'Drowning by Numbers: Standard Setting in Risk Regulation and the Pursuit of Accountable Public Administration' (2000) 20 OJLS 109, 115–16

There are simple experimental and sampling uncertainties in the collection of data, particularly in the ecological context. There are technological limitations placed on the process of monitoring. Risk assessment relies on modelling tools and it is difficult to assess whether a model is a constructive simplification or a misunderstanding of the reality it is attempting to represent. Likewise, there are methodological problems in assessing risks particularly in relation to long term health risks such as cancer. There are also

---

[10] HM Government, *Impact Assessment Overview* (2011).

epistemological uncertainties and these are the types of uncertainties which arise because 'we don't know what we don't know'.

Finally, and most importantly, there is the problem of indeterminacy. Risk assessment was originally developed in engineering for systems which were closed. In contrast, in ecological and health risk assessment the subject of analysis is an open ended system in which the vagaries of both the natural environment and human behaviour must be taken into account. The natural environment is a holistic system made up of numerous complex and little understood interrelationships. Likewise social phenomena are not easily subject to predictive analysis and as Rayner and Malone note we 'have inaccurate and conflicting theories about how and why people make choices, for themselves and in societies'. Thus while risk assessment can be a useful tool in the process of standard setting, it is rarely an accurate *factual* statement. Moreover, in some cases there may be no way of assessing how accurate any assessment is. The same is true for analytical tools such as cost/benefit analysis and regulatory impact assessment. Likewise, it is only one part of the standard setting process, the other and more important being the normative [aspects of standard setting].

There are various implications of these different types of uncertainty. In most cases, they mean that accurate assessment of environmental harm is not possible. For this reason, principles like the precautionary principle have increasingly played a role in environmental law and policy.[11] In other cases, scientific uncertainty may mean that, while the harm is ascertainable, the cause of the harm is not. This has been a major obstacle for bringing tort law actions in relation to environmental damage, when they rely on proof of causation.

One type of uncertainty worth expanding upon is 'indeterminacy'. This type of uncertainty is inherent in economic analysis, particularly in economic appraisal. We have already seen that, within the UK and EU, regulatory impact assessment has an important role to play, and involves cost–benefit analysis. Ackerman and Heinzerling explain some of the different techniques for calculating environmental costs in monetary terms.

Frank Ackerman and Lisa Heinzerling, 'Pricing the Priceless: Cost-Benefit Analysis of Environmental Protection' (2002) 150 U Pa L Rev 1553, 1557–59

Economists create artificial prices for health and environmental benefits by studying what people would be willing to pay for them. One popular method, called 'contingent valuation', is essentially a form of opinion poll. Researchers ask a cross section of the affected population how much they would be willing to pay to preserve or protect something that can't be bought in a store.

[...] For example, the average American household is supposedly willing to pay $257 to prevent the extinction of bald eagles, $208 to protect humpback whales, and $80 to protect gray wolves. [...]

An alternative method of attaching prices to unpriced things infers what people are willing to pay from observation of their behavior in other markets. To assign a dollar value to risks to human life, for example, economists usually calculate the extra wage—or 'wage premium'—that is paid to workers who accept riskier jobs. [...]

One final step in this quick sketch of cost-benefit analysis requires explanation. Costs and benefits of a policy frequently occur at different times. Often, costs are incurred today, or in the near future, to prevent harm in the more remote future. When the analysis spans a number of years, future costs and benefits are *discounted*, or treated as equivalent to smaller amounts of money in today's dollars.

[11] See Chapter 11.

Discounting is a procedure developed by economists in order to evaluate investments that produce future income. The case for discounting begins with the observation that $100 received today is worth more than $100 received next year, even in the absence of inflation. For one thing, you could put your money in the bank today and earn interest by next year. Suppose that your bank account earns 3% interest per year. In that case, if you received the $100 today rather than next year, you would earn $3 in interest, giving you a total of $103 next year. Likewise, in order to get $100 next year you only need to deposit $97 today. So, at a 3% *discount rate*, economists would say that $100 next year has a *present value* of $97 in today's dollars. [...] The larger the discount rate, and/or the longer the time intervals involved, the smaller the present value: at a 5% discount rate, for example, $100 twenty years from now has a present value of only $38.

Essentially these are examples of cost–benefit analysis resting on a number of different types of uncertainties relating to how costs and benefits are assessed. A consequence of this is that values will play an important role in undertaking and interpreting such analysis. In other words, uncertainty not only creates limits for knowledge production but also creates a larger role for values.

The role of values

The second limit to environmental knowledge relates to the objectivity of such knowledge. Because of the uncertain nature of much environmental knowledge, it will be infused with values. Values play a role in relation to which environmental problems are researched, what environmental information is seen as important, and how such information is interpreted. This is not to say that all environmental knowledge is subjective, but that the authority of environmental knowledge cannot be taken for granted. Its value assumptions need to be appreciated, or questioned, in accepting or challenging that authority.

The way in which economic analysis is infused with values can be seen in Ackerman and Heinzerling's extract. Decisions about economic values and discount rates must be based on particular moral values. Others argue that values are inherent in the very assumptions on which economic analysis is based.

Donald Ludwig, Marc Mangel and Brent Haddad, 'Ecology, Conservation and Public Policy' (2001) 32 Annual Review of Ecology and Systematics 481, 500

The century-old commitment of economics to mechanics and utilitarianism has imposed costs. Economists' regular use of linear dynamics, quadratic costs, and Gaussian random variables stands in contrast to ecological situations that are often unique, nonlinear, and nonGaussian. Common economic modeling assumptions such as complete reversibility of transactions and complete substitutability of goods and services are incompatible with ecologists' conceptions of evolution and uniqueness of ecosystems. The doctrinal domination of utilitarianism mutes the discussion of environmental policies that could emerge from alternative ethical bases, such as sustainability or equity. Ecologists place much greater emphasis on experiment (as opposed to theory) than do economists.

Values also have an important role to play in the scientific aspects of environmental knowledge. Again, much of this is due to the uncertainties inherent in scientific process. Shrader-Frechette highlights the uncertainties inherent in quantitative risk assessment.

Kristin Shrader-Frechette, *Burying Uncertainty: Risk and the Case Against Geological Disposal of Nuclear Waste* (University of California Press 1993) 37–38

In summary, methodological value judgments in quantitative risk assessment (QRA) as in all science typically fall into a number of categories. They are, for example, value judgments about the acceptability of

- a given definition of risk
- a given description of what factors are at risk
- a given simplification of the situation
- a given way of selecting and deleting data
- a given aggregation of the data
- a given sample size
- a given statistical test
- a given model for exposure
- a given dose-response model
- a given extrapolation from the data
- a given price/value for risk avoidance.

Each of these and other methodological value judgments enables us to respond to a situation that is uncertain or empirically underdetermined. Yet because our response involves a value judgment, it could be wrong. It could lead to error in the risk assessment. Because methodological value judgments are both unavoidable and potentially erroneous, we must learn to deal with them. We need to take account, explicitly, of all the relevant methodological value judgments on which our scientific conclusions depend.

Shrader-Frechette wrote this in the context of assessing the health risks of nuclear waste disposal. The uncertainties are arguably even more considerable when ecological impact is analysed.[12]

Value judgments do not only have a role to play because of the uncertain nature of environmental knowledge. They also ultimately lie at the heart of most regulation processes. We have environmental laws because we value the environment. The concept of values in environmental law will be discussed generally in Section 4, but it is useful here to consider how values shape what we expect of the decision-making process.

Steve Rayner and Robin Cantor, 'How Fair Is Safe Enough? The Cultural Approach to Societal Technology Choice' (1987) 7 Risk Analysis 3, 4–5

Contrary to the accepted wisdom of those who criticize the activities of intervenors and consumer advocates, our experience has been that only a tiny minority of the public expects that life ought to be entirely free of involuntary danger. So, what does the vast majority of the policymakers' constituencies care about? Our recent research indicates at least three things:

1 Is the procedure by which collective consent is obtained for a course of action acceptable to those who must bear its consequences?

---

[12] Richard Carpenter, 'Limitations in Measuring Ecological Sustainability' in Thaddeus C Trzyna (ed), *A Sustainable World: Defining and Measuring Sustainable Development* (World Conservation Union 1995).

2 Is the principle that will be used to apportion liabilities for an undesired consequence acceptable to those affected?

3 Are the institutions that make the decisions that manage and regulate the technology worthy of fiduciary trust?

We suggest that when all three of these factors are amenable to the risk-bearing population, it will hardly consider many of the low-probability, high-consequence events that currently obsess us to be worthy of the term 'risk' at all. What is needed is a polythetic definition that encompasses both societal concerns about equity at the risk-management end of the conceptual chain and engineering-type concerns about probability and magnitude at the technical end. Such a definition would truly open new approaches to large-scale technology choice for which the proper question would become not 'How safe is safe enough?' but 'How fair is safe enough?'

This is not merely a linguistic quibble, substituting *fair* for *safe*, for this would still leave us with a reified concept of risk as a thing 'out there' in nature. Risk is rather a way of classifying a whole series of complex interactions and relationships between people, as well as between man and nature. The point of changing the societal risk management question to 'How fair is safe enough?' is to encourage risk managers to debate technology options on the explicit basis of social conflicts over trust and equity, rather than on rival estimates of the probability and magnitude of unlikely events. Such a change will require a broad interdisciplinary approach to risk management.

Rayner and Cantor are highlighting how too great a focus on environmental knowledge means that there is a danger of misunderstanding what is at stake in environmental regulation and law. In particular, they highlight how the collective nature of environmental problems creates new dimensions and issues for consideration. Rayner and Cantor's concern is with equity and fairness, although these should not be seen as the only relevant values that may arise in environmental decision-making. Other values may relate to power relationships in a society, and differing assumptions about the role of the state, and in particular the administrative state. The important point is that values do not just limit the utility of environmental knowledge but play a significant role in framing it.

The contextual nature of environmental knowledge

The final set of limits on environmental knowledge relate to the context in which environmental decision-making is operating. The distinction has already been made between 'normal science' and 'regulatory science'. In particular, environmental knowledge is often produced for specific purposes and is organized and interpreted by analytical tools such as risk assessment and cost–benefit analysis. The contextual nature of environmental knowledge also means that such knowledge is limited in its authority and reliability. This takes us back to Stirling's prescriptive definition of science, and raises questions about its relevance, as seen in the extract from O'Riordan.

Tim O'Riordan, 'Environmental Science, Sustainability and Politics' (2004) 29
Transactions of the Institute of British Geographers 234, 234

[E]nvironmental science is now part of a larger environmental politics. This is even more the case as scientific analysis is shaped by the trust and support of policy providers and deliverers in the private and voluntary sectors [...]

> [...] [F]resh ways of incorporating relevant interests are now being recognized as forming the basis of scientific research and appraisal. Science has become a partnership between forms of analysis and prediction, and forms of engaging with those who have to deliver the policies and practices of such prediction. We now live in a world of co-production of scientific and policy knowledge with actual behaviour. Thus there is a science of politics, and a science for politics. It is time to merge the two perspectives.

O'Riordan is emphasizing the fact that the context in which environmental knowledge is produced will shape the nature of that knowledge. Rather than being objective and value free, environmental knowledge is being co-produced alongside policy.

3.5 ENVIRONMENTAL KNOWLEDGE AND ENVIRONMENTAL LAW

There are two main implications of this analysis for environmental lawyers:

- *Environmental knowledge is necessary for all activities in environmental law.* The development of environmental laws requires the identification of environmental problems using various forms of environmental knowledge. The application of environmental law requires environmental knowledge in understanding that to which environmental law should be applied. The attribution of responsibility and liability in legal disputes requires environmental knowledge. Environmental law can only be properly evaluated with knowledge of what differences such laws have made to environmental problems.

- *Despite the fact that environmental knowledge is a necessary feature of all aspects of environmental law, it is not always reliable and/or objective due to scientific uncertainty, the role played by values, and the fact that it is produced for particular regulatory purposes.* Uncertainty, and in particular scientific uncertainty, is a constant feature of environmental law due to limited human knowledge about the environment, the open ended nature of ecosystems, and the fact that much environmental regulation is *ex ante* and thus predictive. Environmental knowledge is not always objective—it is infused with values that fill gaps left by uncertainties, and the decision to protect the environment is itself a value choice. Environmental knowledge is generated for particular purposes and is often produced in specific forms such as risk assessment and cost–benefit analysis.

At first glance, these two implications seem in direct contradiction to each other—as environmental lawyers we need authoritative understandings of problems but such understandings are not always obtainable. This is disconcerting reading for those who have perceived environmental problems as being easily identifiable and environmental knowledge as straightforward to obtain. Yet this apparent contradiction points to the need for environmental lawyers to take a critical stance in relation to environmental knowledge and its reliability. The authority of environmental knowledge should never be taken as a given. This means that environmental lawyers must have a thorough understanding of the factual aspects of an environmental problem and appreciate the limits of environmental knowledge in any particular circumstance.

FURTHER READING AND QUESTIONS

1. Pick a very simple instance of environmental risk; for example, the risk associated with a certain activity on a particular piece of land. Then try and figure out what type of environmental

knowledge you would need to assess that 'risk'. Thinking about the discussion of scientific uncertainty described in this section, what type of scientific uncertainties may be involved in such knowledge? Now pick a more large-scale environmental controversy, such as the farming or use of genetically modified organisms or climate change, and do the same.

2. Do the uncertainties and values inherent in economic appraisal make it a waste of time? Compare Ackerman and Heinzerling and Cass R Sunstein, *Risk and Reason: Safety, Law and the Environment* (CUP 2002).

3. Examples of the importance of emerging knowledge for understanding problems such as ozone layer depletion can be found in Poul Harremoës and others (eds), *The Precautionary Principle in the Twentieth Century: Late Lessons From Early Warnings* (Earthscan 2002).

4. On risk and risk assessment, see Royal Society, *Risk, Analysis, Perception and Management* (Royal Society 1992); National Research Council, *Understanding Risk: Informing Decisions in a Democratic Society* (National Academy Press 1996); Elizabeth Fisher, 'Drowning by Numbers: Standard Setting in Risk Regulation and the Pursuit of Accountable Public Administration' (2000) 20 OJLS 109; Elizabeth Fisher, 'Risk and Environmental Law: A Beginner's Guide' in Benjamin J Richardson and Stepan Wood, *Environmental Law for Sustainability* (Hart Publishing 2006); Elizabeth Fisher, 'Risk Regulatory Concepts and the Law' in OECD (ed), *Risk and Regulatory Policy: Improving the Governance of Risk* (OECD 2010).

5. On different forms of economic analysis being used to address environmental problems, see Michael Common and Sigrid Stagl, *Ecological Economics: An Introduction* (CUP 2005); Nick Hanley, Jason F Shogern, and Ben White, *Introduction to Environmental Economics* (2nd edn, OUP 2013).

6. For more on regulatory impact assessment, see Stephen Weatherill (ed), *Better Regulation* (Hart 2007). For the OECD's latest guidance, see OECD, *Regulatory Impact Analysis: A Tool for Policy Coherence* (Paris, OECD 2009).

7. For further writings on risk and scientific uncertainty, see Brian Wynne, 'Uncertainty And Environmental Learning' (1992) 2 Global Environmental Change 111; Carlo C Jaeger and others, *Risk, Uncertainty, and Rational Action* (Earthscan 2001); Gabriele Bammer and Michael Smithson, *Uncertainty and Risk: Multidisciplinary Perspectives* (Routledge 2008).

4 ENVIRONMENTAL VALUES AND THE SOCIO-POLITICAL DIMENSION OF ENVIRONMENTAL PROBLEMS

The discussion in this chapter so far has focused on issues relating to collective knowledge about environmental problems. That discussion has established that the production and interpretation of that knowledge cannot be untangled from the values attributed to the environment. We have seen how values are often the catalysts for the production of environmental knowledge, and that such knowledge is invariably framed and infused by values. Moreover, many environmental law and policy textbooks often begin their discussion of environmental problems with a discussion of environmental values, explaining that environmental values have directly led to the development of environmental law. Here a different approach has been taken, setting out environmental knowledge as a more significant feature of environmental law. It is a study of environmental knowledge that explains why environmental values are so important.

4.1 VALUES AND ENVIRONMENTAL PHILOSOPHY

The simplest reason why environmental values are important in understanding environmental problems is that there is variation in the ethical values that actors may place on the 'environment'. Thus, even though two actors may value the environment enough to protect it, they may do so for different reasons. Environmental philosophy explores this issue and the extract from Martell explains the issues involved in this discipline.

Luke Martell, *Ecology and Society: An Introduction* (Polity Press 1994) 77

The main issues in green philosophy are on the ethical basis of environmental concern. (1) How far should obligations and moral concern be extended to entities in the environment beyond human kind and (2) for what reasons should they be extended? What should be the scope and basis for our ethical concern vis-à-vis the environment? These two points are linked because the bases on which obligations are due has implications for which entities they are due to. Because deciding why we care for things environmental determines which we care for, philosophical discussions on environmental ethics are more than just academic. They have implications for policy.

There are a number of issues and positions in green philosophy to deal with. (1) Should we care only about humans in the wider environment? Should it be because of the adverse effect of environmental problems on humans that we protect the environment? (2) If we are concerned about humans should we care about future as well as present generations of the species? (3) Should we extend rights and obligations to other 'sentient' beings (beings with the power of sensory perception), namely animals (4) Should our concern be focused not only on sentient beings but also non-sentient beings whether living (eg plants) or non-living (eg sand and stones)? (5) If we extend obligations to different groups should they be entitled to equal consideration or should obligations be weighted differently for different groups? If the latter, how and on what basis?

As Martell rightly points out, these ethical issues are not just academic; they are the basis on which policy and law are made. The literature on the questions posed by Martell is sprawling and rich, and commentators have categorized responses into different groups that are based on divergent ways of valuing the environment. The starting point is the distinction between anthropocentric and ecocentric viewpoints, as explained by Eckersley.

Robyn Eckersley, *Environmentalism and Political Theory* (UCL Press 1992) 26

Although there are many different areas of disagreement, the most fundamental division from an ecophilosophical point of view is between those who adopt an anthropocentric ecological perspective and those who adopt a non-anthropocentric ecological (or ecocentric) perspective. The first approach is characterized by its concern to articulate an ecopolitical theory that offers new opportunities for human emancipation and fulfilment in an ecologically sustainable society. The second approach pursues these same goals in the context of a broader notion of emancipation that also recognizes the moral standing of the nonhuman world and seeks to ensure that it, too, may unfold in its many diverse ways.

Others have also charted a spectrum of these different philosophical views.[13] Thus, for example, distinctions are drawn between 'light green' and 'dark green' environmental values—the former being more anthropocentric and the latter being more ecocentric. A similar distinction is drawn between 'shallow green' and 'deep green'. Three important things should be noted about this kind of spectrum. First, it is a spectrum—there is a variety of different anthropocentric values relating to the environment. We may value it because of its beauty, its economic value, its impact on our health, and so on. Likewise, there is a rich and varied strain of ecocentric thinking. Second, this spectrum is not one-dimensional. There are many other issues that interrelate with environmental thinking. As examples, issues to do with feminism, politics, and economics might also be included. Third, these different bodies of environmental thought vary in the nature of their radicalism. Anthropocentric thinking tends to be more conventional and has underpinned most environmental law and policy, while ecocentric thinking has provided the foundations for a more radical and marginalized politics. Indeed, in our current regulatory and political system, it is often difficult to imagine how a value can be placed on aspects of the environment without relating it back to a human value. Thus, wilderness is often valued because of the aesthetic pleasure it gives to humans, and biodiversity because of the potential medical and economic benefits created by a larger gene pool. To value wilderness, for its own sake, is often difficult in mainstream politics, policy, and also law.

One of the reasons for this has already been touched upon—the centrality of markets to contemporary society. That centrality has meant that a common way of valuing the environment is in economic terms, or put more crudely, in monetary terms. This is a firmly anthropocentric approach to valuing the environment (although not the only anthropocentric approach). Harvey notes that it is not only the importance of the market that has resulted in monetary values playing such an important role in environmental decision-making.

David Harvey, *Justice, Nature and the Geography of Difference* (Blackwell Publishers 1996) 150–51

There are four arguments in favour of money valuations of nature.

1. Money is the means whereby we all, in daily practice, value significant and very widespread aspects of our environment. Every time we purchase a commodity, we engage with a train of monetary and commodity transactions across space through which money values are assigned to natural resources or significant environmental features used in production, consumption, and exchange

2. Money is the only well-understood and universal yardstick of value that we currently possess. We all use it and possess both a practical and intellectual understanding (of some sort) as to what it means. It serves to communicate our wants, needs, desires as well as choices, preferences, and values, including those to be put specifically upon 'nature', to others. The comparability of different ecological projects (from the building of dams to wildlife or biodiversity conservation measures) depends on the definition of a common yardstick (implicit or acknowledged) to evaluate whether one is more justifiable than another. No satisfactory or universally agreed upon alternative to money has yet been devised for making comparative decisions on a rational basis. [...]

3. Money in our particular society is the basic (though by no means the only) form of social power. It is therefore a means to achieve, liberate, and even emancipate human desires. Its neutral and universal qualities as a mere thing can be put to use in an infinite number of ways for purposes that may be judged good or bad as the case may be. The lack of any moral judgment inherent in the money form

---

[13] This sketch draws on work by Timothy O'Riordan, *Environmentalism* (2nd edn, Pion 1983) and David Pepper, *Modern Environmentalism: An Introduction* (Routledge 1996).

itself, can liberate the individual from direct repressive social constraints (though whether with good or bad effects may be debated). This leads to the powerful argument that the market is by far the best mechanism yet devised to realize human desires with a maximum of individual freedom and the minimum of socio-political restraints.

4. To speak in money terms is always to speak in a language which the holders of social power appreciate and understand. To seek action on environmental issues often requires that we not only articulate the problem in universal (ie, money) terms that all can understand, but also that we speak in a voice that is persuasive to those in power.

Harvey goes on to record what he sees as the different problems with valuing nature in terms of money. He highlights beautifully how, for a range of reasons, monetary values placed on the environment take priority in public discourse. This will be seen time and time again in the framing of environmental problems, and in the legal responses adopted to them. Overall, prioritizing market-based or monetary values is fundamentally problematic in a society in which environmental values are pluralistic.

4.2 ENVIRONMENTALISM AND ENVIRONMENTAL DISCOURSE

In our society, we are not simply dealing with environmental ethics operating in the context of an abstract debate about values. Environmental values are not just a matter for academic debate and contemplation—they operate in the real world. Indeed philosophical debates about environmental values have generated the rise of a new politics—environmentalism. Environmentalism, as a significant political movement, appeared in the 1960s as a product of a new and high profile consciousness about the need to protect the environment. This is not to say that there were no debates about the environment before the 1960s, but that those debates were not so prominent—the 1960s marked a political turning point. The emergence of environmentalism at this time is arguably no accident. It appeared in liberal democracies alongside a range of other new political movements that were concerned with recognizing interests which had been overlooked in democracies that were socially stratified, by class in particular. These movements included feminism, ethnic equality, and gay rights—and are often labelled 'new social movements'. While this term does not apply to all forms of environmentalism, it is useful because it helps to identify some of the key features of environmental politics, as explained in more detail in the extract from Dryzek and others.

John S Dryzek and others, *Green States and Social Movements: Environmentalism in the United States, United Kingdom, Germany and Norway* (OUP 2003) 11–12

Environmentalism and feminism cover the best examples of what are often termed 'new social movements'. These new movements have a number of features that distinguish them from 'old' social movements, especially class-based ones. The first is their self-limiting radicalism. That is, the movement generally does not wish to capture, overthrow, or even share state power (though Green parties eventually compromised on this last point), even as its members may look to radical paradigms beyond industrial society. The second is that identity concerns are always close to the top of the movement's agenda: that is, there is a preoccupation with questions of 'who are we, how are we constructed, and what do we want?', rather than just 'how do we get it?' The third is an organisational style and structure that is often fluid, participatory, discursive, and impermanent; though again, more mainstream and long-established environmental groups do not always measure up. Fourth, the tactics can be unconventional, involving protests, community organizing, and media events, rather than just lobbying or negotiating through parties and pressure groups. Finally, new social movements are not explicitly class-based, though their members are drawn disproportionately from the new middle class of knowledge-workers. Clearly, not all environmental groups are 'new movements' in these terms, especially when it comes to self-limitation; but a substantial section of the movement in most countries does share these features.

As the extract makes clear, these new social movements gave rise to a new type of politics, one that although focused on the role of the state (see Section 5), also often radically alters that role, or at least challenges it.

As already seen, environmental values are not monolithic, nor are environmental politics. One might imagine that, if a group of self-described 'environmental activists' were brought together to discuss the nature of environmentalism, they would largely agree. This is rarely the case however. Rather, different actors sharply disagree about the significance of environmental protection and what collective action should be taken in relation to it. Much ink has been spilled (and trees turned into paper!) by commentators explaining these variations. One of the most useful accounts is that of Dryzek who, rather than describing different forms of environmental politics, describes different forms of environmental discourse. He describes a 'discourse' as:

[...] a shared way of apprehending the world. Embedded in language, it enables those who subscribe to it to interpret bits of information and put them together into coherent stories or accounts. Discourses construct meanings and relationships, helping to define common sense and legitimate knowledge. Each discourse rests on assumptions, judgments, and contentions that provide the basic terms for analysis, debates, agreements and disagreements.[14]

There are two important things to note from this extract. First, discourses bring together certain understandings of values and facts. This relates back to what we saw in Section 1, the way in which there is a close interrelationship between the factual and political dimensions of environmental problems. As such, environmental ideologies (which are based on different values) result in different understandings of environmental problems (as explored in more detail in *The Politics of the Earth* extract by Dryzek). Second, these different discourses are not easily reconcilable. Dryzek outlines the four different discourses that he sees as having dominated environmental policy and politics in industrialized societies.

John S Dryzek, *The Politics of the Earth: Environmental Discourses*
(2nd edn, OUP 2005) 15–16

Environmental problem solving is defined by taking the political-economic status quo as given but in need of adjustment to cope with environmental problems, especially via public policy. Such adjustment might take the form of extension of the pragmatic problem-solving capacities of liberal democratic governments by facilitating a variety of environmentalist inputs to them; or of markets, by putting

[14] John Dryzek, *The Politics of the Earth: Environmental Discourses* (2nd edn, OUP 2005) 9.

price tags on environmental harms and benefits; or of the administrative state, by institutionalizing environmental concern and expertise in its operating procedures. [...]

Survivalism is the discourse popularized in the early 1970s by the efforts of the Club of Rome [...] and others, still retaining many believers. The basic idea is that continued economic and population growth will eventually hit limits set by the Earth's stock of natural resources and the capacity of its ecosystems to support human agricultural and industrial activity. The limits discourse is radical because it seeks a wholesale redistribution of power within the industrial political economy, and a wholesale reorientation away from perpetual economic and population growth. It is prosaic because it can see solutions only in terms of the options set by industrialism, notably, greater control of existing systems by administrators, scientists, and other responsible elites.

Sustainability commences in the 1985, and is defined by imaginative attempts to dissolve the conflicts between environmental and economic values that energize the discourses of problem solving and limits. The concepts of growth and development are redefined in ways which renders obsolete the simple projections of the limits lose their force. There is still no consensus on the exact meaning of sustainability; but sustainability is the axis around which discussion occurs, and limits lose their force. [...]

Green radicalism is both radical and imaginative. Its adherents reject the basic structure of industrial society and the way the environment is conceptualized therein in favour of a variety of quite different alternative interpretations of humans, their society, and their place in the world. Given its radicalism and imagination, it is not surprising that green radicalism features deep intramural divisions [...] Everywhere, green romantics disagree with green rationalists, proponents of the rights of individual creatures disagree with more holistic thinkers, and advocates of green lifestyles disagree with those who prefer to stress green politics.

Dryzek's analysis is significant because he shows how environmental discourses cross traditional political boundaries and ideologies. Environmentalism does not necessarily belong to either the Left or the Right of politics, and there is a range of perspectives about the role of the state and the ability of contemporary society to deal with such problems. Dryzek is also highlighting the way in which these discourses have appeared over time. This is significant from an environmental point of view because it will be seen that environmental laws and regulatory approaches often reflect the mainstream ideology of the political era in which they were created. Also important to appreciate is that these discourses are often operating simultaneously and different actors within society have divergent understandings of the factual and socio-political nature of environmental problems.

These divergent discourses of environmentalism also reflect another feature of environmental problems that makes them seriously intractable. Environmental problems are difficult to identify and understand not only because environmental knowledge is incomplete and different actors hold different environmental values, but also because different values will affect those actors' perception of the environment. Differing values are embedded in different worldviews, and serve to construct fundamentally different understandings of environmental problems. The following extract from Schwarz and Thompson explains this point well. They are writing from the perspective of cultural theory, which is concerned with understanding how social institutions shape understandings of the world.

Michiel Schwarz and Michael Thompson, *Divided We Stand: Redefining Politics, Technology and Social Choice* (Harvester Wheatsheaf 1990) 4–6

Ecologists who study managed ecosystems, such as forests, fisheries, and grasslands, encounter the managing institutions as sets of interventions in those systems. Time and time again they have found that different managing institutions, faced with exactly the strategies based on one of four different interpretations of ecosystem stability. These four 'myths of nature' as they call them [...] captures *some* essence of experience and wisdom [...]

Nature benign gives us global equilibrium. Such a world is wonderfully forgiving: no matter what knocks we deliver the ball it will always return to the bottom of the basin. The managing institutions can therefore have a *laissez-faire* attitude. *Nature ephemeral* is almost the exact opposite. The world, it tells us, is a terribly unforgiving place and the least jolt may cause its catastrophic collapse. The managing institutions must treat the ecosystem with great care. [...] *Nature perverse/tolerant*, though it may look like a cross between the first two, is quite different. Its world is one that is forgiving of most events, but is vulnerable to an occasional knocking of the ball over the rim. The managing institutions must therefore regulate against unusual occurrences. [...] It accepts that the small·risk of disaster necessitates government regulation, but believes that, once minimum standards have been met, it should be free to make its own decisions. Finally, *nature capricious* is a random world; institutions with this view of nature do not really manage, nor do they learn. They just cope with erratic events.

Each of these views of nature appears irrational from the perspective of any other. [...]

This is what Schwarz and Thompson describe as plural rationality and the existence of plural rationality creates real challenges for environmental law. Disputes over environmental problems are not just ad hoc conflicts over facts and values but often disagreements between divergent rationalities, which involve fundamentally different understandings of the facts. Such plural rationalities result in actors making different collective judgments over whether an environmental problem exists, and if so what its nature is.

4.3 ENVIRONMENTAL VALUES AND ENVIRONMENTAL LAW

The discussion in this section once again makes simplistic understandings of environmental problems look highly deficient. Environmental values in society are not fixed. This means that not only will there be variation between different people over what value should be given to the environment, but that there will also be variations in 'collective judgments' in relation to whether an environmental problem exists in the first place. The implications for environmental law are as follows:

- *Environmental laws may be founded on different environmental values, which in turn may be influenced by divergent understandings of environmental problems.* Thus, some environmental laws may be a product of survivalism, while other laws may be a product of sustainability politics.

- *Values will influence the way in which environmental laws are interpreted and applied.* For example, the 'environment' will be defined differently if one takes an ecocentric as opposed to an anthropocentric approach. Likewise, the types of considerations that an administrative decision-maker should take into account in environmental protection decisions will depend upon the values and politics in operation.

- *Disputes over environmental values and environmental politics will often be at the heart of legal disputes.* This is perhaps one of the most important points to appreciate. Disputes over whether planning permission should be granted for a development, whether an environmental impact assessment should be carried out, or whether a certain species of bird should be protected, often all involve disputes over values. While these values may not figure explicitly in legal discourse, they can explain the reasons for conflicts in the first place.

- *Environmental values will mean that critical evaluation of environmental law is not an objective process.* Assessments about the success or failure of different environmental laws will rest on analytical frameworks that draw on different environmental values and politics. Thus, regulation that is understood as successful in terms of sustainability is unlikely to be so understood in terms of green radicalism.

Values and politics thus play a constant background role in environmental law. While there are few legal questions that take the form 'what values are in operation?', an understanding of values helps to makes sense of the law and its evolution.

FURTHER READING AND QUESTIONS

1. Consider how biodiversity is valued from an anthropocentric and ecocentric perspective. How reconcilable are those two perspectives? How may those perspectives result in different laws and policies? See also Roderick Nash, *The Rights of Nature: A History of Environmental Ethics* (University of Wisconsin Press 1989).

2. For further readings on environmental values and politics, see Andrew Dobson, *Green Political Thought* (4th edn, Routledge 2007); Linda Kalof and Terre Satterfield (eds), *The Earthscan Reader in Environmental Values* (Earthscan 2005); David Pepper, *Modern Environmentalism: An Introduction* (Routledge 1996).

3. Consider the four different views of nature described by Schwarz and Thompson, and consider the pros and cons of each perspective. Do you think any particular view is more convincing than another, and if so why? Can you think of other examples where 'world-views' influence understandings of environmental problems? Can you think of examples where this might have implications for law? See also Mary Douglas and Aaron Wildavsky, *Risk and Culture* (University of California Press 1982).

4. Do you think the law should favour one set of ethical values over another?

---

5 THE ROLE OF THE STATE

The discussion in this chapter so far has highlighted that the state looms large in environmental problems. Thus, we saw, in relation to environmental knowledge, that the state has a role in producing or requiring the production of information about the environment. Likewise, we saw that environmental politics tends to have the state as its focus. This section examines further the role of the state in identifying and addressing environmental problems, including why it has a role at all and why that role is controversial.

5.1 WHY DOES THE STATE HAVE A ROLE IN ADDRESSING ENVIRONMENTAL PROBLEMS?

Numerous different reasons are given in the literature for why the state has a role in addressing environmental problems. Those reasons reflect different political outlooks as well as divergent disciplinary starting points. With that said, there are generally two reasons for the state having a significant role in environmental problems. The first is that environmental problems by their very nature generate a form of politics. This has been discussed already in relation to the rise of environmentalism, and is due both to the collective nature of environmental problems and the pluralistic nature of values attributed to the environment. Environmental issues can never be characterized as matters of private autonomy and choice. Second, within the public sphere, it is the state that has the ultimate authority to take formal action in relation to the environment. That action may take many forms and may range from creating a command and control regime backed up by criminal offences, to creating frameworks that encourage private actors to take action voluntarily that will prevent environmental degradation.[15] Beyond this, however, there is little common ground among commentators writing about the role of the state and environmental law, particularly when the question is 'why should the state regulate the environment?' Environmental law literature gives at least three different answers to this question.

The first is that we need environmental regulation because of market failure, particularly the failure of the market to price environmental costs, and that the state is required to step in and regulate accordingly. This flows from the type of discussion in relation to the extracts by Sagoff and Hardin. The market failure argument has also been a common argument justifying environmental regulation. The extract from Baldwin and Cave explains this need to regulate because of the failure to price externalities.

Robert Baldwin and Martin Cave, *Understanding Regulation: Theory, Strategy and Practice* (2nd edn, OUP 2012) 11–12

The reason for regulating externalities (or 'spillovers') is that the price of a product does not reflect the true cost to society of producing that good and excessive consumption accordingly results. Thus, a manufacturer of car tyres might keep costs to consumers down by dumping pollutants arising from the manufacturing process into a river. The price of the tyres will not represent the true costs that production imposes on society if clean-up costs are left out of account. The resultant process is wasteful because too many resources are attracted into polluting activities (too many tyres are made and sold) and too few resources are devoted by the manufacturer to pollution avoidance or adopting pollution-free production methods. The rationale for regulation is to eliminate this waste and to protect society or third parties suffering from externalities by compelling the internalization of spillover costs on 'polluter pays' principles.

Environmental regulation as a solution to the problem of failing to properly price externalities is an attractive theory for those that value the environment in anthropocentric financial terms but not for those who have a more ecocentric outlook. Correctly pricing environmental harm does not necessarily prevent it, although it may incentivize its minimization.

A second related but distinct reason given for environmental regulation by the state is the failure of tort law to compensate properly for environmental damage. The starting point of this legal perspective is that there are environmental wrongs that the law should address and correct, and the question is how that is best done. If legal doctrine fails to provide adequate compensation, then the state should step in. Again this view is appealing more from an anthropocentric than an ecocentric perspective, focusing on harms done to individual 'victims' rather than natural systems. Sunstein has given one of the most interesting analyses on the issue of why and how the legal system should compensate harms.

---

[15] See Chapter 12 for a discussion of different regulatory strategies.

Cass R Sunstein, *The Partial Constitution* (Harvard University Press 1993) 319, 320–21

Principles of compensatory justice are the staple of Anglo-American legal systems. One person harms another; the purpose of the lawsuit is to ensure that the victim is compensated by the aggressor. Drawing from this basic understanding, principles of compensatory justice are organized around five basic ideas.

1. The event that produced the injury is both discrete and unitary.

2. The injury is sharply defined in time and in space.

3. The defendant's conduct has clearly caused the harm suffered by the plaintiff. The harm must be attributable to the defendant, and not to some third party or to 'society'.

4. Both plaintiff and defendant are easily identifiable.

5. Apart from the goal of compensation, narrowly defined, existing rights and the status quo are held constant.

These principles are understood to underpin contract and tort law but environmental law does not operate on these principles. As already seen, the causes of environmental problems are rarely discrete and unitary, the injuries are not always "sharply" defined, conduct and harm are not easily identifiable, and nor are the parties (particularly where environmental harm is not done to individuals). Sunstein goes on to note the limits of compensatory justice in areas such as environmental law.

In numerous areas of public and private law, however, traditional principles of compensatory justice are unattractive, or at least serve to rule out plausible alternatives. The basic problem is that in ways large or small, those principles are poorly matched to the best theories that underlie the legal claim. In these contexts, the relevant harm is not sharply defined, and it cannot be connected to a discrete event. The problem involves a shared, collective risk rather than an individual right. The defendant is not easily identifiable or has a highly ambiguous relation to the harm. Causation itself is doubtful and complex; we do not really know whether the defendant was responsible for the plaintiff's harm. The injured party cannot be specified in advance. The notion of restoration to a status quo ante seems logically incoherent, unworkable and based on fictions. Perhaps most important, the status quo should itself be questioned, or taken as unjust and non-neutral, or as a product of the legal rule or the decision at issue.

[...]

Indeed, the rise of administrative agencies and the dramatic displacement of the common law courts in the twentieth century are partly attributable to dissatisfaction with compensatory ideas and with the underlying notion of neutrality. In both the New Deal period and the "rights revolution" of the 1960s and 1970s producing protection against environmental degradation, occupational injury, poverty, and discrimination on the basis of race, gender, and disability there were self-conscious legal responses to the inadequacy of compensatory principles. The rise of new administrative institutions, foreign to the original system of checks and balances, reflects departures from compensatory thinking.

Thus, for Sunstein the rise of environmental regulation can partly be explained as a failure of private law mechanisms. Note also Sunstein's point that the failure of tort law has led to the rise of *administrative* agencies with extensive responsibility for environmental regulation—environmental decision-making is now often in the hands of non-elected public officials. That is how the 'state' is involved in addressing environmental problems.

The third, and final, justification for the role of the state in regulating environmental issues, is an ethical/democratic one, as Eckersley explains. She shows how arguments for a strong state are arguments for both a strong and ethical state, considering each of these in turn.

Robyn Eckersley, *The Green State: Rethinking Democracy and Sovereignty*
(MIT Press 2004) 12–13

That the state should be 'strong' or effective arises from the need to facilitate environmental restoration, regulate, and in some cases proscribe a wide range of environmentally and socially damaging activities. [...] The state is enlisted because it is the social institution with the greatest capacity to discipline investors, producers, and consumers. [...] The state also has the capacity to redistribute resources and otherwise influence life opportunities to ensure that the move toward a more sustainable society is not a socially regressive one—a very real prospect if environmental goals are not properly integrated with social justice goals. This state capacity arises precisely because it enjoys a (virtual) monopoly of the means of *legitimate* coercion and is therefore the final adjudicator and guarantor of positive law. In short, the appeal of the state is that it stands as the over-arching political and legal authority within modern plural societies.

This appeal to the 'strong' or effective state should not be understood as an entirely instrumental appeal; otherwise, there would be no reason, in principle, for environmentalists not to hire private mercenaries to discipline society along more ecologically sustainable lines, assuming that the necessary resources can be mustered. That the state should also be 'good' arises from the understanding that the state is (potentially) the most *legitimate*, and not just the most powerful, social institution to assume the role of 'public ecological trustee', protecting genuinely *public* goods such as life-support services, public amenity, public transport, and biodiversity. Such a normative posture toward the state harks back to the European idea of the state as the embodiment of reason, ethics, and the collective good. In this respect this view is reminiscent of the civic republican tradition insofar as the laws of the democratic state are enlisted to constitute (as distinct from merely restrict) the ecological freedom of all citizens. [...] It is precisely these democratic procedural requirements that convert the state's coercive power into *legitimate* coercive power.

Finally, there is the hope in green demands upon the state that it would not only act as a good ecological trustee over its own people and territory but also as a good international citizen in the society of states.

Eckersley is highlighting that the state has an ethical role of strong leadership. This is quite a different role than that ascribed to the state, either by the market failure theory or by Sunstein. Indeed, each of these three theories will conceivably result in different understandings of what the state should do in relation to environmental problems. Arguably Eckersley would demand that the state take a more activist role than if its intervention were justified on the grounds of market failure alone. Likewise, each of these different theories will appeal to different discourses. The market value theory makes sense for those who understand the environment in anthropocentric terms, while Eckersley's theory accommodates more radical views.

5.2 THE CONTROVERSIAL ROLE OF THE STATE

The controversial role of the state is partly a product of the fact that there is no agreement over why the state should have a role to play in environmental decision-making, as examined in Section 5.1. This section highlights two further sources of controversy. First, the state is often perceived in Janus-faced terms, as both the possible cause of, and solution to, environmental problems. Second, the state will often favour one collective judgment relating to an environmental problem over another.

In relation to the first controversy, the problem is that the state has often promoted environmentally destructive activities while at the same time attempting to address environmental problems. Take a very simple example—the granting of planning permission for the extension of a commercial port, where the extension will impact upon land already recognized as having considerable ecological value. On the one hand, both local and national government wish to support the development because of the economic growth and the jobs that the expansion will bring. A larger port means more business and that will be of great benefit to the local and national community. The port will also support interstate trade and thus (theoretically) the national economic standing of the state. As such, expansion may be formally encouraged by government through policy and government schemes (while of course observing EU laws on state aid). At the same time, local and national governments are entrusted with ensuring that such a project is compliant with environmental and planning laws. The laws may have many different justifications and come from different eras and sources: some derive from EU law on nature conservation; others may relate to the national planning scheme and be more concerned with the regulation of planning than environmental protection. Each law rests on different assumptions about the vulnerability of the environment and the value that should be accorded to it. The overall role of the state in these circumstances is a very ambivalent one—the state is simultaneously protecting the environment through the adoption of environmental laws but at the same time promoting activities that may have environmentally adverse consequences.

This, as we will see throughout this book, is a constant theme in environmental problems—they are also polycentric in terms of applicable laws and relevant government policies. Eckersley pithily describes this ambivalent role of the state in conceptual terms.

Robyn Eckersley, 'Greening the Nation-State: From Exclusive to Inclusive Sovereignty'
in John Barry and Robyn Eckersley (eds) *The State and the Global Ecological Crisis* (MIT Press 2005) 161–63

Green theorists (and many environmentalists) have been highly skeptical of the nation-state and the state system. The three most significant (and recurring) of these critiques concern:

- The anarchic character of the system of sovereign states, which is understood as structuring a dynamic that leads to the 'tragedy of the commons'.

- The parasitical dependence of states on private capital accumulation; that is, the state is inextricably bound up with, and fundamentally compromised by, the promotion of capital accumulation, which is a key driver of ecological destruction, and states are now actively promoting economic globalization in ways that further undermine their own political autonomy and steering capacity.

- The highly centralized and hierarchical character of states as institutions, with imperatives that are fundamentally at odds with the green vision of a more participatory democracy and human-scale, decentralized forms of governance.

[...]

Taken together, these three general objections would appear to provide a powerful green indictment of states per se (rather than just particular 'ecocidal' governments), with the implication that the prospects for the development of more ecologically responsive states are bleak. [...]

Yet we should not be too hasty to assume that the structures and social dynamics referred to in these three analyses are necessarily always anti ecological and always mutually reinforcing (although they often can be) or that they provide a complete green analysis and evaluation of the emancipatory potential of states as governance structures. Moreover, on their face, none of these arguments addresses the crucial question of state legitimacy or places any store on the possibilities of deepening the democratic accountability of states to the citizens of particular states, to transnational civil society, or to the society of states in general [...] Here, we might single out three, mutually informing developments that have served to moderate, and in some exceptional cases work synergistically to transform, the respective 'logics' of anarchy, capitalism, and administrative hierarchy:

- The rise of environmental multilateralism, including environmental treaties and declarations and international environmental standards;

- The emergence of sustainable development as an alternative development strategy and of ecological modernization as a new 'competitive strategy' of corporations and states;

- The emergence of domestic environmental legislation, including new democratic discursive designs within the administrative state (such as community right-to-know legislation, community environmental monitoring and reporting, third-party litigation rights, environmental and technology impact assessment, statutory policy advisory committees, citizens' juries, consensus conferences, and public inquiries).

An interesting point about Eckersley's analysis is the way in which she highlights both the external and internal nature of state sovereignty. Most of the time we are concerned with the role of the state within its relevant jurisdiction, but the state also has an important role to play in environmental protection in the international and supranational context. This can be seen in relation to both international and EU environmental law.[16]

The second source of controversy over the role of the state in environmental regulation is due to the way in which the state, through law and policy, will privilege one understanding of an environmental problem over another. We have already seen in Section 4 how different actors will perceive environmental problems differently. The problem for the state is that it is difficult to take into account all these different perceptions simultaneously. Wynne gives two examples of this problem.

Brian Wynne, 'Seasick on the Third Wave? Subverting the Hegemony of Propositionalism: Response to Collins & Evans (2002)' (2003) 33 Social Studies of Science 401, 406–07 (emphasis added)

When British Nuclear Fuels proposed THORP [thermal oxide nuclear fuels reprocessing plant] at the 1977 Windscale public inquiry, objectors argued that it was meaningless to assess the risks and implications of this one plant alone. THORP would produce plutonium to be used, it was then assumed, for nuclear bombs or for future fast-breeder reactors, and this plutonium would be regularly transported around the world along with spent fuel, nuclear wastes and other dangerous materials in a so-called global 'plutonium economy'. THORP would also hugely increase nuclear waste production, yet with no established means of disposal. Thus, objectors argued that the risk assessment of THORP must logically encompass those wider consequences of its construction; it was utterly artificial and misleadingly reductionist to confine assessment only to the immediate effects of that particular plant at that particular site. Foreshadowing current preoccupations, critical environmental analysts included questions

---

[16] See Chapters 4 and 5.

about terrorist hijacking and use of such plutonium, and about the security culture that would inevitably attend these developments. The inquiry chair dismissed this attempted issue-framing as emotive and irrational, because it was so speculative and ill-defined.

Yet it was difficult to deny that these further interconnections were indeed real possibilities, even if not precisely and deterministically specifiable. However, *the chair took the analytical and epistemological route already institutionalized and taken for granted in the prevailing policy culture, one with which his legal training also naturally resonated.* Sound science and rational policy demanded precision, and precise questions that implicitly reflected controlled empirical observation and analysis. This in turn reflects the historical domination of an implicit laboratory physical science model at the apex of the accepted hierarchy of knowledge, one in which controlled observation of relevant variables takes precedence over comprehensiveness and realistic simulation of the less controlled and more complex factors and situations outside the laboratory. There are good reasons within classical science for this epistemological commitment to precision and control before realism and comprehensiveness. But when the issue is how to assess the pros and cons of such a development as THORP, it is also reasonable to recognize responsibility for the larger consequences, and this different meaning implies a different set of criteria for defining sound knowledge, as the purposes of that knowledge have shifted. Instead of acknowledging this as a matter to be debated, however, the *chair translated all such concerns into the established reductionist and precise cultural meaning, deleting those cultural and epistemological questions from view.*

In this example, we can see the operation of plural rationalities and how the state, represented here by the chair of the public inquiry, reduced these to a single analytical and epistemological framework. The problem for the state is that law and policy work best when based on a single rationality. Moreover, in this example, the state favoured understandings of environmental problems that gave greater weight to the 'facts' rather than to (explicitly argued) values. Indeed, we can see from this example how the state itself generates environmental politics—an external political response to state decision-making that affords limited space for accommodating environmental values.

5.3 THE ROLE OF THE STATE AND ENVIRONMENTAL LAW

There are two main implications of the analysis in this section for thinking about environmental law:

- *The most significant implication of the role of the state for environmental law is that the bulk of environmental law is a form of public law.* In other words, much environmental law is concerned with reviewing how public decision-makers act in relation to the environment, and in particular administrative decision-makers. This means environmental lawyers need a solid understanding of both administrative law and EU law. The latter is relevant because, in terms of contemporary governance, the EU has supplemented the sovereignty of national states.

- *Much environmental law addresses issues arising because of the controversial role of the state.* The role of the state is controversial in that there exist different reasons for the state's role in environmental regulation, the state is seen as both the problem and the solution in relation to environmental problems, and because the state will favour one 'collective judgment' of environmental problems over another. In legal terms, these different issues translate into legal disputes over the form regulation should take and what constitutes legitimate state action.

FURTHER READING AND QUESTIONS

1. Which of the justifications for the role of the state is the most appealing to you and why? How do you think these different reasons for state regulation might translate into different bodies of environmental regulation? For further reading on the issue, see Chris Hilson, *Regulating Pollution: A UK and EC Perspective* (Hart Publishing 2000); Elizabeth Fisher, *Risk Regulation and Administrative Constitutionalism* (Hart Publishing 2007).

2. Do you think the problems that Wynne highlights are inevitable? Do you think there are ways for a decision-maker to take into account the values and assumptions of different actors in the decision-making process? See Andrew Stirling, 'Risk, Uncertainty and Precaution: Some Instrumental Implications From the Social Sciences' in Frans Berkhout, Melissa Leach, and Ian Scoones (eds), *Negotiating Environmental Change: Perspectives from Social Science* (Edward Elgar 2003); Silvio O Funtowicz and Jerome R Ravetz, 'Three Types of Risk Assessment and the Emergence of Post Normal Science' in Sheldon Krimsky and Dominic Golding (eds), *Social Theories of Risk* (Praeger 1992).

6 THE ROLE OF LAW

All of this finally brings us to the role of law in relation to environmental problems. In a sense there is no need to have a separate section to discuss the 'law', because the relationship between environmental problems and the law has been discussed in various ways in this chapter and, further, the law is the subject of the rest of this book. With that said, this chapter has been concerned with getting lawyers to take a hard look at environmental problems and that exercise also involves taking a hard look at the role of law in environmental problems.

This section does not provide an exhaustive analysis of law, but notes two important features about the role of law. First, law is a complex phenomenon and it should not be seen in monolithic terms. It involves a range of different legal actors, rules, principles, and institutions. There is no universal *legal* understanding of environmental problems and this can be seen throughout this book. Moreover, as seen in Chapter 1, the actual nature of environmental law is contested and we can see descriptive, purposive, and jurisprudential definitions of environmental law in operation. What this means is that law is a discourse with multiple voices. The overall implication for environmental law is that different environmental laws may impact on environmental problems in divergent ways.

Second, environmental law is essentially a prism through which to understand environmental problems and itself presents a discourse in which issues are understood in particular and often well-established ways. Jasanoff demonstrates this point by comparing the 'clashing cultures' of science and law. Note that in this extract Jasanoff is writing about the role of expert evidence in the courtroom and this context should be kept in mind.

Sheila Jasanoff, 'Law's Knowledge: Science For Justice in Legal Settings' (2005) 95 (S1) American Journal of Public Health S49, S51 © American Public Health Association

The formal spaces of both institutions—courts no less than labs—are claimed to be dedicated to finding the truth, though with different ends in view: the law needs facts as necessary adjuncts to doing justice; science seeks facts more as an end in itself. Legal fact-finding therefore generally remains within the framework of a specific case or controversy, whereas scientific facts must speak to wider audiences. Facts established by science are published, and so participate in further rounds of dialogue and inquiry. Facts found in litigation rarely achieve wider circulation. Nonetheless, 'speaking truth' remains an unquestioned virtue in both contexts: lying (or its legal equivalent, perjury) is among the most serious offenses one can commit in either arena, because it threatens each institution's public legitimacy. Accordingly, the processes of both institutions are geared toward producing truthful claims.

Jasanoff is thus highlighting that both law and science are concerned with establishing truth and reality, but in different ways. This extract is only one part of her analysis, but what it highlights is that the relationship between science and law is more complex than the 'clashing cultures' metaphor suggests. She also goes on to emphasize the way in which, within legal discourse itself, different ways of establishing facts have been established for particular purposes. Her work is well worth a careful read and what it makes clear is that law is a lens through which to view the world and a very different one from economics, or philosophy or politics. This point is important to keep in mind when reading every chapter of this book, and in the practice and study of environmental law more generally. In particular, it is important to remember that within the law—in the variety of legal approaches to environmental problems—the process of findings facts is always driven by a particular purpose, and you should reflect on what those purposes are in evaluating environmental laws.

7 CONCLUSION

This chapter has been a tumultuous journey through the rich literature concerning environmental problems. If it has shown anything, it has shown the danger of oversimplifying environmental problems. For some, this chapter may look a little too much like post-modern deconstruction and thus not very useful for the practising environmental lawyer. But as will be shown, time and time again in this book, a critical approach to understanding environmental problems is a key tool in mastering environmental law.

PART II

CHARTING THE ENVIRONMENTAL LAW LANDSCAPE I—LEGAL CULTURES

INTRODUCTION

In this section, three key legal cultures are examined, each of which contributes fundamentally to what is understood as 'English' and 'UK' environmental law. These are the legal cultures of: England and the UK, the EU, and international environmental law.

These jurisdictions are introduced in terms of legal culture to make clear that they are not just sources of rules but something far more substantive. This is well illustrated by noting that there is an initial challenge in thinking about UK environmental law. Ideally, a textbook of this sort should cover UK environmental law across the UK but this is not analytically or jurisprudentially possible, due to different legal cultures existing in the UK historically (consider the unique tradition of Scots law), as well as the current processes of devolution. Indeed, devolution means that there is no unitary body of UK environmental law; rather, it is becoming increasingly fragmented.[1] This creates something of a dilemma—to focus only on England is to miss the bigger picture, but to focus only on the UK is to ignore the legal significance of its different regions within the UK. Furthermore, different regimes work at different levels across the UK. In some fields of environmental protection, there is a UK-wide regime, such as under most provisions of the Climate Change Act 2008, while in others there is not, such as the integrated English permitting regime established by the Environmental Permitting Regulations 2010. In other cases again, there might be separate regimes for different devolved administrations, but they all serve to implement a single EU Directive, such as the Waste Framework Directive. An understanding of legal culture is thus important in appreciating the variety of legal and jurisdictional influences that shape English and UK environmental law. In this introductory section we briefly consider *why* overviews of different legal cultures are fundamental in studying English environmental law, as well as some of the difficulties involved in the interrelationship between these distinct cultures.

1 WHY SUCH AN OVERVIEW?

Pick up any standard environmental law textbook and it will nearly always have a section at the beginning giving an overview of English/UK, EU, and international environmental law. This textbook is no different. But why are these chapters useful? Thinking about this is important because, by their very nature, such overview sections must be brief and therefore their purpose must be limited. Moreover, a proper study of each of these legal cultures is a life-time scholarly affair. By appreciating the limited purpose of these overviews, the reader will get more out of reading them, and avoid feeling frustrated that they do not address the jurisdictions examined comprehensively.

---

[1] UKELA, *The State of UK Environmental Law in 2011–2012: Is there a Case for Legislative Reform?* (UK Environmental Law Association, King's College London, Cardiff University, May 2012) 2. This fragmentation creates particular challenges in thinking about environmental law reform.

In Chapter 2, a tension was highlighted in thinking about environmental problems. Whilst it must be appreciated that environmental problems are socio-politically embedded, at the same time they cross jurisdictional boundaries. A corollary of this tension is that legal responses to environmental problems are products of particular legal and socio-political cultures, but that such legal responses *may not be limited to one legal culture.*

The obviousness of this point also hides its complexity. It is not simply that environmental law has a range of different jurisdictional sources, or even that those different jurisdictional sources give rise to different kinds of legal statutes and instruments. Rather, environmental law is embedded in a range of profoundly different legal cultures and thus informed by a range of divergent and interrelating legal ideas, rules, principles, prescriptions, institutions, regimes, ideologies, and legal theories. It is thus not enough to know that a particular law is an EU Directive or a piece of English delegated legislation but *why* that situation came to be, and what the implications of this state of affairs are. It is for this reason that we argue in Chapter 1 that the process set out for inquiring into environmental law problems requires a scholar and/or lawyer to ask a series of questions about the nature of the legal context. Environmental law cannot be seen in isolation. To study environmental law—to understand *which* laws apply to environmental problems and *how* they do so—requires the study of a broader legal culture.

With that said, the purpose of jurisdictional overview chapters may vary considerably and range from pure descriptive accounts of legal cultures to more theoretical or prescriptive accounts. The purpose of Part II falls somewhere in between these two extremes in that it attempts to be both descriptive and thought provoking. Chapters 3, 4, and 5 thus provide a themed contextual account of each of these legal cultures as a way of highlighting the types of difficult legal issues that characterize environmental law within each legal culture. Thus, in the UK setting, we see the interface between environmental law and decentralized/devolved government as a particular theme and legal concern, while in the EU context, the interface between environmental law and the limits on Member States' discretion to take unilateral environmental action gives rise to contentious legal arguments. And of course we see interaction between the national and EU legal orders. The overview chapters in this part are thus not comprehensive descriptions of legal systems—for such accounts, readers will be far better served by looking at textbooks that focus on the nature of each legal system discretely.

2 UNDERSTANDING AND APPRECIATING LEGAL CULTURE

Our use of the concept of legal culture to describe the English, UK, EU, and international law systems may seem curious to some. Textbooks usually talk of systems, jurisdictions, or regimes rather than anything so messy sounding as legal 'culture'. The term is derived from comparative law methodology and it is useful to reflect on what comparative lawyers mean by the term. One of the most prominent scholars on the issue of legal culture, David Nelken reflects on this.

David Nelken, 'Using the Concept of Legal Culture' (2004) 29 Australian Journal of
Legal Philosophy 1, 1

Legal culture, in its most general sense, is one way of describing relatively stable patterns of legally oriented social behaviour and attitudes. The identifying elements of legal culture range from facts about institutions such as the number and role of lawyers or the ways judges are appointed and controlled, to various forms of behaviour such as litigation or prison rates, and, at the other extreme, more nebulous aspects of ideas, values, aspirations and mentalities. Like culture itself, legal culture is about who we are not just what we do.

The key point about legal culture is that law is not simply a set of rules—it is a cultural phenomenon that is not easily delineated from other cultural phenomena. In fact, it is formed by them. By thinking of environmental law in terms of legal culture, we are not just thinking about rules but also about institutions, ideas, philosophies, and motivations. Indeed, the importance of focusing beyond rules can be seen in the discussion on the definition of environmental law in Chapter 1—environmental law is a pluralistic concept in scholarly terms, which extends beyond a formalist description of the rules that comprise it.

It should be noted that some scholars have been critical of the concept of legal culture, particularly for its vagueness. Much of this debate has been about the validity of particular social science methodologies and whether the concept of legal culture can be used as an explanatory or interpretative tool. In what might be seen as a response to this debate, Webber explains key aspects of the usefulness of the concept of legal culture.

Jeremy Webber, 'Culture, Legal Culture, and Legal Reasoning: A Comment on Nelken'
(2004) 29 Australian Journal of Legal Philosophy 27, 34–35

The notion of legal culture [...] pays attention to the texts of the law and to the distinctive ordering of priority, in different legal traditions, among these texts. But it also incorporates the broader range of considerations that actors routinely rely upon, sometimes implicitly, sometimes expressly, in their interpretation and application of the law: presumptions as to the underlying principles of justice; expectations as to institutional role (the role of courts vis-à-vis legislatures, the role of provincial versus central governments, the role of state regulation in relation to private ordering); general norms of social interaction and fair dealing emergent in particular social practices; and a sense of law's historical evolution and future potential. The law is continually being fashioned and refashioned as rules are applied to new circumstances, as new enactments require that one rethink established areas of the law, as theories of law evolve, and as broader social attitudes and practices change. The concept of legal culture, if deployed well, can help reveal the broader historical and societal context that shapes the interpretation and development of law.

The last point is the most significant in adopting legal culture as an analytical framework—the historical and social context of law is critical in making sense of it, and relates to dynamic understandings of the law. As will be seen in the chapters throughout this book, such historical and social context is critical in understanding legal responses to environmental problems, and this context can be very different for different environmental issues and legal problems. Moreover, appreciation of such contextual factors is not easily transferable across legal cultures. Environmentalism in the US is thus distinct from environmentalism in the UK, as are the constitutional histories and regulatory traditions of both these jurisdictions, which set them up as fundamentally different legal contexts. Such differences of context and culture are often overlooked in environmental law scholarship. There is a tendency to argue for a shift of regulatory ideas or environmental aspirations from one legal culture to another without appreciating that such a shift is not always possible; or that contextual factors may deeply affect or reshape legal ideas in any such attempted transposition.

3 THE RELATIONSHIP BETWEEN UK, EU, AND INTERNATIONAL LEGAL CULTURES

The final point to note before examining the different legal cultures in this part is that the relationship between English, UK, EU, and international environmental law is by no means a straightforward one. This can be seen in at least four different ways.

First, these legal cultures are not discrete 'units' of analysis. Nelken makes this point well in his discussion of the concept of legal culture.

David Nelken, 'Using the Concept of Legal Culture' (2004) 29 Australian Journal of Legal Philosophy 1, 3–4

Articles, and books, very interesting ones, continue to identify legal culture within the nation state, and collections of studies of legal culture likewise use this as their organising theme. But rather than limit ourselves to the state level, patterns of legal culture can and must also be sought both at a more micro as well as at a more macro level. At the sub-national level the appropriate unit of legal culture may be the local court, the prosecutor's office, or the lawyer's consulting room. Differences between places in the same society may often be considerable. Legal culture is not necessarily uniform (organisationally and meaningfully) across different branches of law. Lawyers specialising in some subjects may have less in common with other lawyers outside their field than they have with those abroad. At the macro level, historical membership of the continental or common law world transcends the frontiers of the nation state. And, increasingly, the implications of these memberships are being challenged and reworked by globalising networks of trading and other interchanges. We also need to explore what have been described as the 'third cultures' of international trade, communication networks and other trans-national processes.

Thus, for example, in the UK setting, there is a significant role for both devolved and local government in environmental law. Likewise, in international environmental law, there are many different subsets of legal culture. There are specific regional agreements in relation to environmental problems, such as the UN Economic Commission for Europe's Convention on Long-Range Transboundary Air Pollution, as well as more overarching environmental agreements, such as those relating to sustainable development and climate change.[2]

The second notable feature of how these three legal cultures interact is that they do not necessarily exist in a hierarchical relationship with each other. Thus, environmental law is neither a top-down phenomenon derived from international law, nor is it a bottom-up development that has solely originated from English law. Nor is environmental law simply the application of EU law, albeit that the influence of EU environmental law on UK and English law is extensive. This is not to say that hierarchies do not exist. From an EU law perspective, EU law is supreme,[3] and this has implications for English environmental law. Likewise, the dualist nature of the UK legal system means that, without further national implementation, international environmental law documents have no legal force. However, these hierarchies are not always straightforward. Thus, for example, international agree-

[2] For example, Rio Declaration on Environment and Development (1992) UN Doc A/CONF 151/26 (Vol I) Annex I; UN Framework Convention on Climate Change 1992 (adopted 9 May 1992, ratified 21 March 1994) 1771 UNTS 107.
[3] Case 6/64 *Costa v ENEL* [1964] ECR 585.

ments, such as the Aarhus Convention, might be implemented indirectly in UK law through EU law measures, without direct national implementation.

This leads to the third point about the interrelationship between these three legal cultures— environmental law is a product of simultaneous and interrelated developments in all three legal cultures. Just as each legal culture is not monolithic, nor is it sealed off from other legal cultures, and there is a constant exchange of ideas and concepts between legal cultures. Thus, principles such as the precautionary principle have been subject to legal and policy development in all three legal cultures.[4] Moreover, policy and regulatory developments in one legal culture are often the product of events in other legal cultures. For instance, the Industrial Emissions Directive (2010/75/EU) can be understood as an EU translation of the English ideal of integrated pollution control.[5] This type of interface was discussed in Chapter 2, which explored how environmental problems not only encouraged more international co-ordination but also local responses.

These different interrelationships between legal cultures have been particularly well recognized in political science, more so than in legal scholarship, particularly in the EU context. This is not surprising—political scientists describe the world they see and part of that world is the close interrelationship between different levels of governance. Indeed, political scientists coined the term 'multi-level governance' in relation to this phenomenon—a concept that, in the EU, has been understood as a system 'of continuous negotiation among nested governments at several territorial tiers— supranational, national, regional, and local—as the result of a broad process of institutional creation and decisional re-allocation'.[6] In other words, there is a flexible interaction between policy and legal developments at each of these jurisdictional levels.

The final feature to note about the interrelationship between these different legal cultures is that the nature of that interrelationship is legally complex and often involves quite technical points of law. One thus needs to be wary of oversimplification. This is best illustrated by example—an example used not so much to make a point about what the law says, but rather about how the law operates. In this case example, the UK operated a plant that recycled plutonium from spent nuclear fuel by converting it into mixed oxide fuel (MOX). The Republic of Ireland, concerned about the plant's operation and the pollution it could cause, brought a number of actions under different international law conventions to challenge the building and operation of the plant. This in itself illustrates the multi-forum nature of environmental law disputes, but our focus here is on one legal dispute that arose before the ECJ. One of the actions Ireland had attempted to bring was arbitral tribunal proceedings against the UK under the UN Convention on the Law of the Sea (UNCLOS). Under this action, Ireland claimed that the UK was breaching Convention obligations in relation to marine pollution and the protection of the environment. The European Commission brought infringement proceedings in the ECJ against Ireland for bringing this UNCLOS action, claiming that it was a breach of (then) Community law and that Ireland should have dealt with the dispute before the ECJ. In particular, they claimed it constituted a breach of what was then Articles 10[7] and 292 TEC (now Article 344 TFEU). The Court of Justice concluded that such a breach had occurred. The Court's findings are in relation to the breach of what was then Article 292 TEC. That article states that:

Member States undertake not to submit a dispute concerning the interpretation or application of this Treaty to any method of settlement other than those provided for therein.

---

[4] See Chapter 11.   [5] See Chapter 17.

[6] Marks, as quoted in Jenny Fairbass and Andrew Jordan, 'Multi-level Governance and Environmental Policy' in Ian Bache and Matthew Flinders (eds), *Multi-level Governance* (OUP 2004) 149–50.

[7] Now repealed but effectively reflected in art 4(3) TEU. See Chapter 4.

Case C–459/03 *Commission v Ireland*
[2006] ECR I–4635, paras 80–86

80. It is necessary to specify at the outset that, by its first head of complaint, the Commission is criticising Ireland for failing to respect the exclusive jurisdiction of the court by bringing before the Arbitral Tribunal a dispute between it and another Member State concerning the interpretation and application of provisions of the Convention involving obligations assumed by the Community in the exercise of its external competence in regard to protection of the environment, and for thereby breaching Art.292 EC. [...]

81. Under Art.300(7) EC: '[a]greements concluded under the conditions set out in [that] Article shall be binding on the institutions of the Community and on Member States'.

82. The Convention [UNCLOS] was signed by the Community and subsequently approved by Decision 98/392. It follows that, according to settled case-law, the provisions of that convention now form an integral part of the Community legal order (see, inter alia, Case C–344/04 IATA and ELFAA [2006] ECR I–0000, para 36).

83. The Convention was concluded by the Community and all of its Member States on the basis of shared competence.

84. The court has already ruled that mixed agreements have the same status in the Community legal order as purely Community agreements, as these are provisions coming within the scope of Community competence (Case C–13/00 *Commission v Ireland*, para 14).

85. From this the court has concluded that, in ensuring respect for commitments arising from an agreement concluded by the Community institutions, the Member States fulfil, within the Community system, an obligation in relation to the Community, which has assumed responsibility for the due performance of that agreement (Case C–13/00 *Commission v Ireland*, para 15).

86. As the Convention is a mixed agreement, it is for that reason necessary to examine whether the provisions of that agreement relied on by Ireland before the Arbitral Tribunal in connection with the dispute concerning the MOX plant come within the scope of Community competence.

The nature of a mixed agreement is explained by Cardwell and French.

Paul James Cardwell and Duncan French, 'Who Decides? The ECJ's Judgment on Jurisdiction in the *MOX Plant* Dispute' (2007) 19 JEL 121, 123–24

The 'mixed' element refers to the division of obligations between the Community and the Member States. These are thus distinguished from the agreements over which the EC has exclusive competence (such as the Common Commercial Policy under [what was then] Article 133 EC), and which form an integral part of EC law. As Eeckhout states, 'the prima facie legal justification for a mixed agreement is that parts of the agreement do not come within the Community's competence, and that conclusion of the agreement therefore requires joint action by the Community and its Member states, the latter complementing, as it were, the otherwise insufficient powers of the Community'.

The nature of mixed agreements, common in many external policy areas, has been debated by the ECJ in cases stretching back many years. Despite this, the ECJ has been reluctant to set out strict demarcation lines between the respective competences of the EC and the Member States. As mixed agreements are by their nature externally focused, they are a major feature of those aspects of external relations over which the EC has competence. The EC has competence in the external environmental field by means of Article 175 EC [now Art 192], under which the EC became party to UNCLOS in the first place.

The ECJ did not need to consider the extent to which the dispute raised areas of exclusive environmental competence of the EC, but only the Commission's claim that the ECJ has the jurisdiction to interpret those provisions which are shared between the Member States and the EC. In doing so, the Commission relies on a line of case-law back to the European Road Transport Agreement (*AETR*) judgment whereby implied competence of the EC in the external field arises from the conferment of internal competence in a specific field. Clearly, competence in environmental matters is given to the EC by virtue of Article 175 EC. Yet, in this field, the Community has fixed only minimum rules (as set out in the Declaration of Community competence attached to the EC's acceptance of UNCLOS) and therefore, according to Ireland, the nature of the dispute with the UK does not cover areas in which competence has been transferred to the Community.

On this issue the Court concluded as follows.

Case C–459/03 *Commission v Ireland*
[2006] ECR I–4635, paras 104–112, 116–127

104. It is necessary to point out in this regard that the second sentence of the first paragraph of the second indent of point 2 of the Declaration of Community competence states, with regard to, inter alia, the provisions of the Convention relating to the prevention of marine pollution, that: '[w]hen Community rules exist but are not affected, in particular in cases of Community provisions establishing only minimum standards, the Member States have competence, without prejudice to the competence of the Community to act in this field'.

105. Consequently, that declaration confirms that a transfer of areas of shared competence, in particular in regard to the prevention of marine pollution, took place within the framework of the Convention, and without any of the Community rules concerned being affected, within the terms of the principle set out in the AETR judgment.

106. However, that passage of the Declaration of Community competence makes the transfer of areas of shared competence subject to the existence of Community rules, even though it is not necessary that those rules be affected.

107. In the other cases, that is to say, those in which there are no Community rules, competence rests with the Member States, in accordance with the third sentence of the first paragraph of the second indent of point 2 of the Declaration of Community competence.

108. It follows that, within the specific context of the Convention, a finding that there has been a transfer to the Community of areas of shared competence is contingent on the existence of Community rules within the areas covered by the Convention provisions in issue, irrespective of what may otherwise be the scope and nature of those rules.

109. In this regard, the appendix to the Declaration of Community competence, while not exhaustive, constitutes a useful reference base.

110. It appears that the matters covered by the provisions of the Convention relied on by Ireland before the Arbitral Tribunal are very largely regulated by Community measures, several of which are mentioned expressly in the appendix to that declaration.

111. Thus, with regard to the head of complaint alleging failure to meet the obligation to carry out a proper assessment of the environmental impact of all of the activities associated with the MOX plant on the marine environment of the Irish Sea, based on Art. 206 of the Convention, it must be stated that this matter is the subject of Directive 85/337 [the Environmental Assessment Directive], which is mentioned in the appendix to the Declaration of Community competence.

112. Ireland also cannot question the relevance of Directive 85/337 since it itself referred to that directive in its statement of claim before the Arbitral Tribunal as a measure which could serve as a reference for the interpretation of the relevant provisions of the Convention.

[...]

116. Furthermore, that complaint, in so far as it concerns international transfers of radioactive substances connected to the activity of the MOX plant, is closely linked to Directive 93/75, which is also mentioned in the appendix to the Declaration of Community competence and regulates the minimum requirements for vessels bound for or leaving Community ports and carrying dangerous or polluting goods.

117. Furthermore, with regard to the complaint derived from Arts 123 and 197 of the Convention concerning the lack of co-operation on the part of the United Kingdom and, in particular, its refusal to provide Ireland with certain information, such as the full version of the PA report, it must be held that the provision of information of this kind comes within the scope of Council Directive 90/313/EEC of 7 June 1990 on the freedom of access to information on the environment ([1990] OJ L158/56).

118. In addition, as has been stated in para 31 of the present judgment, Ireland set out that same head of complaint before the arbitral tribunal established pursuant to the Convention for the Protection of the Marine Environment of the North-East Atlantic on the basis of Art.9 of that convention, a convention which it once again invoked in its application initiating proceedings before the Arbitral Tribunal as a reference base for the interpretation of the Convention provisions in issue. The Convention for the Protection of the Marine Environment of the North-East Atlantic was concluded by the Community and, moreover, replaced the Paris conventions for the prevention of marine pollution from land-based sources, themselves mentioned in the appendix to the Declaration of Community competence.

119. It is also common ground that, in its pleadings before the Arbitral Tribunal, Ireland based its arguments in support of the head of claim in issue simultaneously on Directive 85/337, Directive 90/313 and the Convention for the Protection of the Marine Environment of the North-East Atlantic.

120. Those matters suffice to establish that the Convention provisions on the prevention of marine pollution relied on by Ireland, which clearly cover a significant part of the dispute relating to the MOX plant, come within the scope of Community competence which the Community has elected to exercise by becoming a party to the Convention.

121. It follows that the provisions of the Convention relied on by Ireland in the dispute relating to the MOX plant and submitted to the Arbitral Tribunal are rules which form part of the Community legal order. The court therefore has jurisdiction to deal with disputes relating to the interpretation and application of those provisions and to assess a Member State's compliance with them (see, in that connection, Case C–13/00 *Commission v Ireland*, para 20, and Case C–239/03 *Commission v France*, para 31).

122. It is, however, necessary to determine whether this jurisdiction of the court is exclusive, such as to preclude a dispute like that relating to the MOX plant being brought by a Member State before an arbitral tribunal established pursuant to Annex VII to the Convention.

123. The court has already pointed out that an international agreement cannot affect the allocation of responsibilities defined in the Treaties and, consequently, the autonomy of the Community legal system, compliance with which the court ensures under Art.220 EC. That exclusive jurisdiction of the court is confirmed by Art.292 EC, by which Member States undertake not to submit a dispute concerning the interpretation or application of the EC Treaty to any method of settlement other than those provided for therein (see, to that effect, Opinion 1/91 [1991] ECR I–6079, paragraph 35, and Opinion 1/00 [2002] ECR I–3493, paragraphs 11 and 12).

124. It should be stated at the outset that the Convention precisely makes it possible to avoid such a breach of the court's exclusive jurisdiction in such a way as to preserve the autonomy of the Community legal system.

125. It follows from Art.282 of the Convention that, as it provides for procedures resulting in binding decisions in respect of the resolution of disputes between Member States, the system for the resolution of disputes set out in the EC Treaty must in principle take precedence over that contained in Part XV of the Convention.

126. It has been established that the provisions of the Convention in issue in the dispute concerning the MOX plant come within the scope of Community competence which the Community exercised by acceding to the Convention, with the result that those provisions form an integral part of the Community legal order.

127. Consequently, the dispute in this case is indeed a dispute concerning the interpretation or application of the EC Treaty, within the terms of Art.292 EC.

All of this is legally complex—the issue of whether the CJEU has exclusive jurisdiction is not a straightforward one (and therefore whether there was a breach of Article 292) and this is dependent on mainstream legal principles about the nature of international agreements in EU law. It is crucial to answer the question of 'who decides' to resolve this environmental dispute. In this case, it is not driven by 'environmental law' but by European legal doctrines concerning jurisdictional matters. As such, careful *legal* attention needs to be given to the interface between these different jurisdictions, and the particular questions of law that they involve.

4 CONCLUSION

This introduction to Part II provides a framework not only for reading Chapters 3, 4, and 5 but also for thinking about environmental law more generally. Scholars and lawyers must continually question and seek to understand the context of the law they are dealing with, because that context will be integral in understanding the nature of that law. Further, it is important to acknowledge the importance of appreciating the distinction between what the framework for environmental law *is* in a particular legal culture and what scholars would *like it to be*. Evaluating environmental law, and thinking about its possible change and reform, of course makes the process of understanding environmental law an even messier business, but also a far more meaningful and constructive one.

FURTHER READING

1. For more about the nature of legal culture and comparative law methodology, see David Nelken, 'Disclosing/Invoking Legal Culture' (1995) 4 Social and Legal Studies 437; and Pierre Legrand and Roderick Munday, *Comparative Legal Studies: Traditions and Transitions* (CUP 2003); Mathias Reimann and Reinhard Zimmermann, *The Oxford Handbook of Comparative Law* (OUP 2006).

2. On the issue of multi-level governance and environmental law, see Jenny Fairbass and Andrew Jordan, 'Multi-level Governance and Environmental Policy' in Ian Bache and Matthew Flinders (eds), *Multi-level Governance* (OUP 2004); and Gerd Winter (ed), *Multi-level Governance of Global Environmental Change: Perspectives from Science, Sociology and the Law* (CUP 2006).

ENVIRONMENTAL LAW IN THE
LEGAL CULTURE OF THE
UNITED KINGDOM

This chapter is an overview of the legal cultures within the UK as they relate to environmental law. Our focus is upon England but our scope of analysis is across the UK. The purpose of this chapter is to give the reader not only a general overview of the main features of these cultures but also to highlight much of its complexity. In particular, the uniqueness of much of UK environmental law means that one must be wary of transplanting ideas and assumptions about environmental law from other jurisdictions.

This chapter is structured as follows. First, a basic overview is given of the historical and socio-political roots of UK environmental law. The second section provides an overview of the nature of UK environmental law, including the prominent role of delegated legislation; statutory rights and remedies; the marginal role of private law actions; the UK policy style; and UK approaches to enforcement. The third section gives an overview of the institutional landscape of UK environmental law including: the significance of the Westminster model of government; the role of agencies; the role for local government and devolution; and the importance of accountability mechanisms. The final section considers the impact that EU membership has had on UK environmental law.

In setting out the unique nature of UK environmental law, this chapter highlights four features of UK legal culture that are particularly influential. First, environmental thought and environmental law both have long histories and deep theoretical and socio-political foundations that reflect distinct characteristics of UK cultural life. Second, most of UK environmental law is *public law*, which entrusts considerable discretion to administrative bodies, including those enforcing environmental law. Third, there is a wide range of administrative institutions involved in UK environmental law and these operate at central, regional, and local levels. Much of environmental law is concerned with the exercise of public powers by these bodies and holding them to account. Fourth, membership of the EU has had a particularly profound effect on the law, and institutions involved in UK environmental law.

The significance of these points will be seen in all chapters of this book, which relate to the operation of environmental law in England. They are not just of passing theoretical interest but of huge practical significance. Thus, the discretionary and public law nature of much UK environmental law directly affects its operation—its framework, implementation, and evaluation all depend heavily on public institutions and structures. Likewise, EU membership means that environmental lawyers cannot treat UK environmental law as operating in a legal vacuum.

Three points should be made before starting. First, as noted in the introduction to Part II, a challenge in discussing UK environmental law is that, while the UK may have a unitary constitution, it does not operate as a unitary state in terms of legal culture. This is not simply due to devolution but is also due to the historical evolution of England, Wales, Scotland, and Northern Ireland. The focus of this book is on England but much will also be relevant to these other jurisdictions, due to overlapping and inter-connecting laws, historical connections, and common UK-wide obligations under EU and international law. This chapter does touch upon devolution but does not give an exhaustive appraisal of legal cultures across the devolved administrations, considering the book's focus on England (the inter-relationships between these historical regions, devolution, and environmental law is worthy of many books in their own right!). Second, and as already noted in the introduction to Part II, this chapter is not an exhaustive analysis of the legal cultures informing UK environmental law. Moreover, many of the features highlighted in this section will be discussed further in Parts III, IV, and V of this book.

Third, much of the discussion in this chapter is not just about the 'law' but also about the administrative and political culture of the UK. This is consistent with the idea of legal culture discussed in the introduction to Part I, and has also to do with the fact that UK environmental law, like UK public law, defies conventional understandings of 'law', as explained by Fisher.

Elizabeth Fisher, *Risk Regulation and Administrative Constitutionalism*
(Hart Publishing 2007) 52–53, 55

In the UK, administrative constitutionalism is a blurring of law, policy, political theory, ideology, and con-vention. Moreover, due to the dominance of the Westminster model, administrative and constitutional law have tended to be collapsed into each other, and thus are not distinct. All this can be disconcerting and historically has resulted in some commentators being critical of the substantive context of UK public law and suggesting it is a 'deserted territory' in which no meaningful debate has occurred. But as Harlow and Rawlings have noted:

'[t]he history of political ideas in Britain is peculiarly rich. The tradition of public law less so. It is none the less a pluralist tradition' [...]

In other words, UK administrative constitutionalism has been pluralistic but more 'political', than legal, in nature, a fact evidenced by the dominance of the concept of the 'political constitution'. Likewise, in relation to risk regulation, developments have been incremental and less marked by the creation of rule bound legal regimes.

[...]

Historically, the courts have played a marginal role in holding decision-making to account and the legal frameworks for executive action in the UK left much to the imagination in that they delegated broad powers to administration. The constituting, limiting and holding of decision-makers to account has been through organisational structures, political processes, policies, managerial technique and through the promotion of an ethos. Moreover, the lack of 'hard law' is particularly the case in the risk regulation field where regulatory strategy has historically been based on a more flexible model in which there is a significant role for negotiation between the regulated and the regulator. The setting and enforcement of standards has often been one and the same process and the legal frameworks relatively loose. There is also little in the way of judicial review litigation in this area and thus the courts have played no role in promoting particular understandings of administrative constitutionalism.

Hence, thinking about UK legal culture must encompass both political and legal ideas, as well as recognizing that there are a variety of views about the very nature of law and its role in society. This is the reason for the finding in Chapter 1 that a key challenge in seeking to define environmental law descriptively is that there is no clear understanding or definition of what constitutes 'law'.[1]

1 THE HISTORICAL AND THEORETICAL ROOTS OF UK ENVIRONMENTAL LAW

An important first step in understanding UK environmental law is to place it in its historical and social context. There is a rich history of environmental thought and environmental law in England, both of which have had a subtle and important impact on the nature of contemporary environmental law. This section gives an overview of this history. In thinking about environmental thought in particular, you should refer back to the readings in Chapter 2 concerned with environmental values.

1.1 UK ENVIRONMENTAL THOUGHT

As seen in Chapter 2, the value placed on the environment will depend on socio-political culture, which, in turn, informs UK environmental thought. By environmental thought we mean the environmental values embodied in UK culture. Environmental values are not fixed—they change over time, between cultures, and across groups in a particular legal culture. Environmentalism in the US or in Germany is distinct from environmentalism in England. Environmental values in the 1950s were different from those that prevail now. Moreover, contemporary environmentalism spans a spectrum of political and ideological views, from ecological and communitarian views to rationalist and utilitarian political approaches. Since law reflects environmental values, appreciating the nature of environmental values and thought in a particular culture is important for understanding the law and legal culture of that jurisdiction. Further, just as this value-influenced law is not static—it changes and evolves over time—the physical and natural landscape to which it relates also changes. The UK landscape of today is very different from that of 400 years ago. Changing landscapes also inspire changing values, manifesting again in different forms of environmental thought.

The history of environmental thought in the UK is a long one and the concept of landscape is an entrenched feature of the UK psyche. The starting point for discussing environmental thought is often the Industrial Revolution. This starting point makes sense in that, as explored further, the Industrial Revolution led to serious adverse environmental impacts throughout the UK. However, even before that time, there existed, within English culture at least, a body of understanding about the natural environment and about landscape. The development of this environmental thought was not just a reaction to severe environmental degradation caused by industrialization; rather, it was an established and integral part of English tradition and culture. Thomas discusses that body of environmental thought, which was forming in English culture before the Industrial Revolution.

Keith Thomas, *Man and the Natural World: Changing Attitudes in England 1500–1800* (Allen Lane 1983) 242–43

At the beginning of this book it was suggested that, at the start of the early modern period, man's ascendancy over the natural world was the unquestioned object of human endeavour. By 1800 it was

---

[1] Section 1.1 of Chapter 1.

still the aim of most people and one, moreover, which at least seemed firmly within reach. But by this time the objective was no longer unquestioned. Doubts and hesitations had arisen about man's place in nature and his relationship to other species. The detached study of natural history had discredited many of the earlier man-centred perceptions. A closer sense of affinity with the animal creation had weakened old assumptions about human uniqueness. A new concern for the sufferings of animals had arisen; and, instead of continuing to destroy the forests and uproot all plants lacking practical value, an increasing number of people had begun to plant trees and to cultivate flowers for emotional satisfaction. These developments were but aspects of a much wider reversal in the relationship of the English to the natural world. They were part of a whole complex of changes which, by the later eighteenth century, had helped to overthrow many established assumptions and to create new sensibilities of a kind which have gained in intensity ever since.

Those new sensibilities manifested themselves in many ways. In part, new understandings of nature emerged and value was placed on rural landscapes. This can be seen particularly in nineteenth-century literature and art—in the work of Romanticists such as Wordsworth, Turner, and Constable—as well as in the eighteenth-century landscape designs of Capability Brown.

However, these new sensibilities were then faced with the dramatic environmental and public health impacts of the Industrial Revolution. Implicit in the basis and success of the Revolution were very different understandings of property and land. McLaren discusses these new understandings as well as some of the associated environmental impacts of the Industrial Revolution.

John PS McLaren, 'Nuisance Law and the Industrial Revolution—Some Lessons From Social History' (1983) 3 OJLS 155, 163–65

To the new industrialist the utility of land related to its ability to accommodate his machines, buildings, workers and sources of power, and how productive it was in providing the mineral resources which he needed to fuel his manufacturing process. For him land was something to be changed and exploited to suit his industrial strategy and economic desires. The ambient air and flowing water were the convenient depositories for the waste by-products of his industrial operations. [...]

The consequences for the population of the industrial cities and the natural environment were traumatic. Those who toiled in the factories, mills and smelters bore the brunt of the social and environmental abuse. The industrial workers, many of whom, it must be admitted, saw more security and opportunity in the cities and towns than in their former rural homesteads, were rigidly regimented in large, often unsafe and unhealthy factories, and housed in the most squalid conditions close to their places of employ. [...]

The standards of construction were in the main deplorable, the consequence of rampant speculation. Long rows of cramped, overshadowed, ill-ventilated and ill-lit dwellings, built back to back without gardens and with nothing but the most limited common facilities constituted the living experience of most factory workers. The lack of sanitation and any provision for the disposal of sewage and rubbish meant that ill health was endemic. The death rate in the industrial cities was staggering. Dodds provides the following grim figures for the 1840s:

'[T]he average annual mortality rate for all of Britain was twenty-two per thousand. In Glasgow the death rate was thirty-two per thousand, in Manchester thirty-five, and in Liverpool thirty-five. A newborn child of the working classes had just about one chance in two of reaching the age of five, a child of the higher classes, four chances in five. The average age of death in London was twenty-seven years (with the working classes twenty-two); in Leeds, twenty-one, in Manchester eighteen.'

The particular misery of the workers, was matched by the more general and pervasive environmental abuse caused by the factories. The first problem was smoke. Early in the century the pervasive fact of smoke in industrial cities such as Manchester and Birmingham was noted. As Briggs records, Manchester evoked this comment: 'The town is abominably filthy,' a visitor from Rotherham (of all places) declared as early as 1808, 'the steam engine is pestiferous, the Dyehouses noisome and offensive, and the water of the river as black as ink or the Stygian Lake.'

McLaren goes on to record the serious environmental and public health impacts of noxious vapours, noise, and river pollution in similarly unrelenting terms. In light of these profoundly negative environmental impacts, it is not surprising that the state began to regulate, albeit in a piecemeal way. Indeed, the roots of contemporary UK environmental law can be found during this period and surveying the impact of the Industrial Revolution reminds us that human activity can wreak serious havoc upon environmental and public health.

At the same time, what can be seen in McLaren's account is that many of those who led the Industrial Revolution understood land as something to be exploited and the costs of externalities as something to be avoided or to be placed on others. Environmental and public health problems were thus a product of a particular understanding of capitalist endeavour—one that did not address the environmental and public health costs of that endeavour. Indeed, from that time onwards, a general cultural dichotomy existed between those who saw the environment as an exploitable resource and those who sought to protect it. That dichotomy arguably persists, in that much environmental law is understood in terms of correcting the failure of the market to price environmental degradation into its goods, services, and other productive activity. As will be examined in Chapter 11, the concepts of sustainability and sustainable development attempt to address and move beyond this dichotomous understanding of environmental law.

Despite this capitalist thinking and new wave of industrial production, environmental thought was not extinguished. Thus, the nineteenth century saw the emergence of a variety of social movements concerned with nature conservation and public health. Concern with the former took a variety of forms, ranging from protection of animals to preservation of historical landscapes. A variety of nature conservation organizations were set up, including the National Trust, the Rambler's Association, and the Society for the Protection of Birds. Likewise, the public health impacts of urbanization gave rise to a range of campaigns and organizations. Parliament at Westminster could barely meet during the 'Big Stink' of 1858, caused by sewage and pollution in the River Thames. The health problems caused by industrialization and ever-growing cities were depicted in popular novels such as Elizabeth Gaskell's *North and South* and the works of Charles Dickens, which recorded settings of putrid air and water quality, toxic work conditions, and characters suffering from cholera, typhoid, and serious respiratory illness, amongst other things. Significantly, the conservation and public health movements of this time were often mainstream and middle class, and tied to concerns about the social fabric of society. Take, for example, the extract from a sermon by Charles Kingsley, the author of the popular children's book *The Water Babies*. The topic of Kingsley's sermon was that of 'human soot'.

Charles Kingsley, 'Human Soot' in Frances Eliza Kingsley (ed), *Charles Kingsley: His Letters and Memories of His Life: Volume Two* (Henry S King & Co 1877) 323

We know well how, in some manufactures, a certain amount of waste is profitable—that it pays better to let certain substances run to refuse, than to use every product of the manufacture- as in a steam mill every atom of soot is so much wasted fuel; but it pays better not to consume the whole fuel and to let the soot escape. So it is in the present social system; it pays better. Capital is accumulated more rapidly by wasting a certain amount of human life, human health, human intellect, human morals, by producing and throwing away a regular percentage of human soot—of that thinking and acting dirt which lies about, and alas! Breeds and perpetuates itself in foul alleys and low public-houses, and all and any of the dark places of the earth. But as in the case of the manufactures, the Nemesis comes swift and sure. As the foul vapours of the mine and manufactory destroy vegetation and injure health, so does the Nemesis fall on the world of man- so does the human soot, those human poison gases, infect the whole society which allowed them to fester under its feet.

Kingsley is characterizing the problems of industrialization in both physical and social terms, and this sermon is a reminder of the socio-political dimension of environmental problems that was discussed in Chapter 2. It is also an early example of the externalities argument—that it was profitable for manufacturers to pollute the commons (air), since it involved no direct cost to them.

The social and political movements of the nineteenth century carried on into the twentieth century and were closely intertwined with other social movements, concerning class, employment, and health in particular. Specific environmental problems often galvanized public support for political and legislative action. One good example of this was the response to the London smog of 1952, which highlighted the serious problems being created by air pollution in the 1950s.

Devra L Davis, Michelle L Bell, and Tony Fletcher, 'Guest Editorial: A Look Back at the London Smog of 1952 and the Half Century Since' (2002) 110 Environmental Health Perspectives A734, A734

The modern field of environmental health owes much to the tragedy that befell Greater London, some 50 years ago this month. From 5 December through 9 December 1952 a heavy, motionless layer of smoky, dusty fumes from the region's million or more coal stoves and local factories settled in the London basin. This thick sulfurous smoky fog, the 'smog', brought traffic and people to a standstill. Not all medical and political authorities appreciated what was happening, but the undertakers and florists knew there was a problem. They ran out of caskets and flowers.

Health officials at the time did not appreciate the magnitude or severity of the problem, having previously weathered many dense 'pea-souper' fogs and smogs. This fog became known as the Big Smoke because its toll and the public reactions to it were without precedent. Hospital admissions, pneumonia reports, applications for emergency bed service, and mortality followed the peak of air pollution. Mortality remained elevated for a couple of months after the fog. A preliminary report, never to be finalized, attributed these later deaths to an influenza epidemic. New evidence shows that this could not be the case and that only a fraction of the deaths could be from influenza. Davis (2002) leaves 12,000 unexplained and additional deaths during the episode and in the two months after the peak fog ebbed.

The figure of 12,000 is debated in the academic literature, but the fog of 1952 led to a new consciousness about the problems that pollution created. It also led to the passing of one of the first pieces of modern environmental legislation—the Clean Air Act 1956.[2]

---

[2] See Chapter 15.

With that long and varied history of the cultural concern for the environment in the UK, the 1960s then saw the worldwide emergence of environmentalism—this was environmental thought on a new scale. Vogel explains the nature of these changes in relation to the UK environmental movement.

David Vogel, *National Styles of Regulation: Environmental Policy in Great Britain and the United States* (Cornell University Press 1986) 40–41

All of these developments contributed to a substantial increase in the membership of environmental organizations in Great Britain. Between 1967 and 1980, the membership of the Council for the Protection of Rural England (CPRE; formerly the Council for the Preservation of Rural England) increased from 14,000 to 31,000; that of the National Trust from 159,000 to 1 million; that of the Royal Society for the Protection m 38,000 to 300,000; that of the Ramblers' Association from 16,000 to 32,000; and that of the Society for the Promotion of Nature Conservation from 29,000 to 129,000. In 1958 local amenity societies had been established in 200 British communities; by 1975 their number had increased more than sixfold. In 1977 the total membership of the local amenity movement was estimated at 300,000, or slightly less than 1 percent of the British population. Allowing for overlapping membership, by the middle of the 1970 between 2.5 and 3 million British citizens belonged to at least one environmental organization. In addition, three new national environmental organizations were founded: Greenpeace, a British chapter of the American organization Friends of the Earth (FOE), and the Conservation Society. In its first year of existence the Conservation Society recruited 8,000 subscribers, while within four of its founding FOE had established more than a hundred local chapters.

[...]

Up through the 1960s, many British environmental organizations were extremely reluctant to encourage publicity, preferring instead to rely on private negotiations with government officials. But over the following two decades environmental groups came to rely increasingly on the shaping of public opinion as a way of influencing public policy.

Thus, from the 1960s onwards, environmental organizations not only grew in membership but also changed their practices. In particular, there was a shift from these organizations playing a relatively discreet role in public life to them playing a far more high profile one. Environmental non-governmental organizations became more media-savvy and also more significant stakeholders in policy-making.

During this period, the UK Green Party was also set up, as Dryzek and others explain.

John Dryzek and others, *Green States and Social Movements: Environmentalism in the United States, United Kingdom, Germany and Norway* (OUP 2003) 54

In the 1980s and 1990s Green Party politics on the face of it was less important in the UK than in several other European countries. This difference is a direct consequence of Britain's first-past-the-post electoral system, which makes it virtually impossible for minority parties to secure parliamentary representation (unless their strength is regionally concentrated, as for the Scottish and Welsh nationalists). The Greens have never won a seat at Westminster [but see below]; their poor electoral prospects have meant that the mainstream environmental groups found it easy to shun the Greens—and their radicalism. The British Greens actually hold the world record for percentage of votes in a nationwide election achieved by a green party; in the 1989 election to the European parliament, they secured 15 per cent of the vote. But the first-past-the-post system translated this 15 per cent into no seats. Under a new electoral system in 1999 the Greens secured two of the British seats in the European parliament with 6.3 per cent of the vote. However, their lack of parliamentary representation notwithstanding, the British Green Party and its precursor, the Ecology Party, did provide the main platform for a very visible and radical critique of established policies and practices, of a sort not engaged by the mainstream environmentalist groups.

The Green Party has played a role, in particular, at local government level. Further, in 2010, prominent Green Party member Caroline Lucas, who had been a member of the European Parliament between 1999 and 2010, was elected as MP for Brighton Pavilion.

When it emerged as a party, the Green Party was understood as being more radical in its politics than existing environmental organizations. However, the 1990s saw the emergence of an even more radical politics—that concerned with direct action and public protest, which ranged from lawful assemblies through to peaceful civil disobedience and to forms of eco-terrorism. An extract from Doherty and others explains this development.

Brian Doherty, Matthew Paterson and Benjamin Seel, 'Direct Action in British Environmentalism' in Brian Doherty, Matthew Paterson and Benjamin Seel (eds), *Direct Action in British Environmentalism* (Routledge 2000) 15–16

Before the 1990s the rise of a radical environmental movement was considered unlikely in Britain. This was because it was thought that the 'bureaucratic accommodation' of environmental organisations in Britain constrained them to moderate forms of action and the pursuit of broad political alliances. Academics thought that environmental activists would be drawn into environmental organisations with consultative or 'insider' status. It was reasoned that these organisations would constrain the ways in which affiliated activists could act because they did not want to risk their insider status either by arguing for highly radical change or by employing provocative tactics. For instance on occasion even Greenpeace was forced to stand down after being sued by BP in late summer 1997. But in contrast to these expectations, from 1991 a new wave of direct action was begun in Britain by a new wave of radical activists who were critical of organisations like Greenpeace, WWF and FoE, not to mention old guard conservation organisations such as the National Trust. Rather quickly, the UK seemed to have considerably more radical activism than many other countries in Western Europe.

These groups thus reflect a much more radical politics than early 'traditional' environmental NGOs. They have been a particularly significant force in areas such as road building and climate change. An important feature of these groups is that they are less likely to engage in formal legal and policy-making processes than more conventional green groups, and far more likely to engage in forms of civil disobedience. From a legal perspective, this has led to a variety of issues, concerned with trespass to land, obstructing the free movement of goods in EU law, and freedom of expression.[3] These groups are not just environmentally radical however—as the extract makes clear, these groups are closely interrelated with other forms of radical politics in England and their emergence can be understood as part of wider political movements, such as anti-capitalist and even anarchist movements.

[3] *Manchester Airport Plc v Dutton* [1999] 3 WLR 524 (CA); *Monsanto v Tilly* [2000] Env LR 313 (CA); Case C–265/95 *Commission v France* [1997] ECR I–6959. cf Case C–112/00 *Eugen Schmidberger Internationale Transporte Planzuge v Austria* [2003] ECR I–5659.

Hence, UK environmentalism does not just span anthropocentric and ecocentric perspectives (see Chapter 2). It also reaches from establishment politics to radical politics. The environment is an issue that features on many different public and political party agendas, and in a range of ways—it is not the preserve of any particular political party or ideology. UK environmentalism is thus a rich tapestry of political ideas and philosophies, which themselves have a long history. As a result, taking environmental protection measures can carry with it a number of different symbolic meanings, particularly because those who support ideas of environmental protection do so from very different political positions.

This point can be illustrated with a brief example—the riding of bicycles. It has become popular for those in the public eye to ride bicycles as a means of establishing that they are 'environmentally friendly'. Thus, publicly-spotted bicycle riders include conservative politicians, celebrities, and radical environmental activists. The riding of a bicycle is not just something you do to get from A to B, or that you do for fun, but it is now also an important political statement. Yet, as Horton notes, the riding of a bicycle can be interpreted in a number of different ways.

Dave Horton, 'Environmentalism and the Bicycle' (2006) 15 Environmental Politics 41, 54

So the bicycle's importance to contemporary environmentalism is as more than a mode of mobility particularly favoured by environmentalists. Bicycle riding and contemporary environmentalism are mutually constitutive: environmentalist discourse prompts activists to ride bicycles, and that bicycle riding contributes to the making of environmentalism in general and the green lifestyles of environmental activists in particular. Yet if riding a bicycle is, among environmental activists, an act of both distinction and opposition, it is also now a practice which complies with emerging state discourses, which are formed increasingly around the perceived need to shift prevailing mobility practices towards sustainability. Thus, on one hand, environmental activists use the bicycle in the formation of their distinctive and oppositional political identities; on the other hand, the state increasingly sponsors the bicycle as a legitimate and valuable mode of transport.

This bicycling example may seem a flippant one, but it illustrates that the primacy of environmental protection on the UK political agenda does not necessary translate into agreement about what such 'protection' entails, in terms of either political ideology or practical outcomes. UK environmental thought, just like 'the public interest', is a 'texture of multiple strands'.[4]

Part of that texture is the persistent notion that the environment can be justifiably exploited. While perhaps not as crudely assumed as during the Industrial Revolution, this mindset can still be seen today in a variety of ideologies and understandings of the natural environment. Wurzel explains one such variation—the assumption that England has less serious environmental problems than those that exist in other jurisdictions because it is an island.

Rüdiger K W Wurzel, *Environmental Policy-Making in Britain, Germany and the European Union* (Manchester University Press 2002) 7

One does not have to push the importance of Britain's island status as far as Samuel Finer has in arguing that it has had a profound bearing on its political institutions. However, strong winds, shortist-flowing

---

[4] To quote Justice Frankfurter in *Federal Power Commission v Hope Natural Gas Co* 320 US 591 (1944) 627.

rivers and a scouring sea have had a major impact on British environmental policy. Classic air and water pollutants are relatively quickly dispersed and diluted. They will be rendered harmless if the natural carrying capacity (that is, the self-restoring capacity) is not exceeded. However, a dilute-and-disperse policy can also be used to externalise the cost of pollution control measures by shifting the problem to other countries or international commons (such as the High Seas). Examples include a 'high chimney' policy for coal-fired power stations to disperse sulphur dioxide emissions and a 'long sea outfall' policy to dilute sewage discharges.

Wurzel highlights that this understanding of the natural environment is used to justify not taking environmental protection measures and thus for externalizing the costs of environmental degradation. This is a useful reminder that the rise of environmentalism has not necessarily resulted in everyone wishing, or feeling that it is necessary, to protect the environment.

1.2 THE RELATIONSHIP BETWEEN ENVIRONMENTAL THOUGHT AND ENVIRONMENTAL LAW

Before moving on, it is worth briefly considering the relationship between environmental law and environmental thought more carefully. Considering this interrelationship raises difficult issues about what we consider to be law, as examined in Chapter 1. Here we highlight a different issue, noting that the history of environmental thought is reflected in the way that both UK landscapes and environmental law have developed.

A good example is provided by hedgerows—those thick hedges between fields, relics of forests that once covered the countryside, which support a wide diversity of flora and fauna. Holder discusses the close relationship between law and the construction and protection of hedgerows.

Jane Holder, 'Law and Landscape: The Legal Construction and Protection of Hedgerows' (1999) 62 MLR 100, 112–13

That law has played a significant part in the construction of the landscape is seen in the case of the hedgerow. Early law legitimated a great shift in the economic structure of landowning and later provided the mechanisms by which planned and regularised enclosure could take place. The particular legal form chosen for enclosure shaped the physical landscape. The hedgerows planted to give effect to the Enclosure Acts are physical representations of the social and legal history of enclosure, particularly patterns of land ownership, and rejection of common land rights. Further examples of law bearing upon landscape are the Game Laws of the eighteenth century and the Corn Laws of the nineteenth century. Today, different legal landscapes can be seen: the Private Trust landscape, the Common Agricultural Policy landscape and the Set Aside landscape, all of which are structured and upheld by legal instruments, concepts and doctrines.

Although law has shaped the physical form of land, the legal protection of landscape is tenuous. The legislative measures remain oblique, setting out duties of taking the conservation of amenity and beauty of land into account in decision making, but imposing few specific legal obligations. The recent legislative attempts at hedgerow protection pursue a one-dimensional view of landscape as no more than the sum of its surface features, so that measurement, rather than memory or understanding, is the absolute arbiter of value. Landscape is, in this case, legally understood in scientific, objective and narrowly historical terms, less so in social, popular, or cultural terms. Law therefore fails to capture the richer, extended vision—the 'inner landscape' of perception and meaning. Doubtless one reason for this is the practical inability for law to capture the importance of such incalculable concerns using legal methods which are sufficiently objective to be workable, but what is really at stake is a legal indifference to the creation of landscape by culture. Unlike in the tradition of critical geography, law has still to appreciate that landscape, like space, is in part socially constructed and to reflect this in its representations.

Holder is not only highlighting the important interrelationship between law, culture, and landscape, but also the failure of that relationship to be fully appreciated in legal scholarship. This is an interesting point, which should be considered in thinking about different areas of environmental law—particularly those that concern or involve impacts on the natural environment. Another important example of environmental thought influencing environmental law can be seen with the concept of property, which Coyle and Morrow (see Chapter 1) argue is central to environmental law. Environmental law 'might be thought of as the product of a sustained reflection upon the relationship between property, rights and nature.'[5] The significance of this and how other private law concepts inform and fit within environmental law will be considered in more detail in Chapter 6.

Overall, while environmental thought and 'law' are distinct bodies of ideas, they are also closely interrelated. Environmental thought permeates legal culture and legal concepts permeate environmental thought. The focus of this textbook is upon the law, but this interrelationship should be kept in mind in understanding both legal developments and their wider social effects.

1.3 THE HISTORICAL ROOTS OF ENGLISH ENVIRONMENTAL LAW

The discussion so far has focused on environmental thought, which can be seen to have evolved over time. Part of that evolution has been related to the development of environmental law and changes in how we manage the environment in legal terms. This section briefly considers the history of environmental law in the UK, with a particular focus on England. This is not an easy task. A feature of nearly every chapter of this book is that the relevant area of environmental law covered will be shown to have a long history. Our purpose in this section is thus not to chart comprehensively the rise of particular laws, but rather to consider the implications of environmental law in having such deep historical roots.

Examples of 'environmental' legislation or 'environmental' litigation can be traced back to medieval times.[6] However, from the Industrial Revolution onwards, there was an increasing environmental consciousness and a pressing need for regulating the environmental and public health impacts of both industrial development and of unrestricted urbanization. For this reason, the Industrial Revolution marks a starting point for understanding contemporary environmental law. The first legal developments in this area took the form of private law actions. These actions, however, had limited impact in terms of environmental protection, and there are some rich legal historical accounts of this era, which come to a variety of conclusions as to why this was the case.

John PS McLaren, 'Nuisance Law and the Industrial Revolution: Some Lessons From Social History' (1983) 3 OJLS 155, 220–21

[...] the Common Law failed not because of doctrinal weakness, but because it was no match for the social problems spawned by industrialization. Even in less frenetic times the Common Law had

---

[5] Sean Coyle and Karen Morrow, *The Philosophical Foundations of Environmental Law* (Hart Publishing 2004) 212, discussed in Chapters 1 and 6.

[6] Indeed, we have a wonderful legal historian colleague who is always discussing environmental pollution cases from many hundreds of years ago.

exercised at best an indirect influence on patterns of social change. This was because of its basically reactive quality, the capricious nature of its operation, which depended so much on individual initiative and staying power, and its lack of general enforcement mechanisms and supervisory powers. The pristine theory of nuisance embodied in the sic utere doctrine had in its heyday not prevented earlier instances of environmental abuse. For example, as early as 1742 Daniel Defoe remarked on the dark and black facades of the houses in Sheffield caused 'by the constant smoke of the forges, which are always at work'. It is less than realistic to suppose that it could have exercised any significant influence on the relentless march of events in industrial England after 1800. Given the profound nature of the social problems generated by industrialization it was only by the boldest initiatives that the process of degradation could be stemmed and attempts made to improve the quality of life. These initiatives had to await public acceptance of a more assertive role for government as the regulator of society and of the facultative character of legislation. By the time that the 'law was on the march' in relation to pollution problems the Common Law had been relegated to an ancillary role; a role which it has retained ever since.

Raymond Cocks, 'Victorian Foundations?' in John Lowry and Rod Edmunds (eds) Environmental Protection and the Common Law (Hart Publishing 2000) 2–3

However, in large part the restriction [of the private law in protecting the environment] was intellectual. This was suggested over a quarter of a century ago by JF Brenner. More recently, in a long and sophisticated analysis of changes in water law, Getzler has reminded us that 'historians investigating the relationship between legal and economic change neglect the internal history of the law at their peril'. In his analysis he argues that:

'Principles of land and water use were developed to a high level of sophistication in centuries of legal evolution before 1800. Then, in the circumstances of industrialising England, those doctrines were adapted as judges sought legal solutions to unprecedented economic problems. The confrontation of new economic and social practices with ancient laws revealed the limits of the common law as a means of governance and this ultimately led to a shift in law-making from the courts to Parliament. Water and land-use law was one field, however, where the articulate contribution of the common lawyers always remained significant. In the court-rooms of Westminster can be found vibrant discussion of the fundamental principles of property and of civil liability, which not only had immense practical significance, but which revealed much of the common lawyers' attitudes to economic progress and its concomitant legal problems.'

In Getzler's view, the shift of attention from the courts to Parliament was of central significance, but both the shift and the remaining role of the common law could only be fully understood by reference to changes in the ideas of common lawyers. In particular, Getzler points out that, in the course of the nineteenth century, English riparian law came to have a broad discretionary character. For example, in the 1875 *Swindon* case, Lord Cairns's judgment turned upon:

'an opaque test of 'reasonableness', to be determined in the circumstances of the particular case. He did not provide indicia structuring that concept of reasonableness [...] the reasonableness standard was left to be determined on the individual facts of each case.'

Later courts took Lord Cairns's uninformative doctrine to have settled or even codified the modern law.

The marginal role of private law was in reality due to the reasons set out in both of these accounts— the overwhelming scale of the environmental problems at hand, and the shift from the courts to the

Parliament as existing common law doctrine required supplementing by stricter environmental standards more suited to the new social and economic conditions. At the same time the common law continued to develop flexibly to move with the times. What the second extract also highlights is that private law was not simply limited to tort law but also included areas of law such as riparian water law (concerning rights of landowners to make use of adjacent water bodies).

The failures of private law actions to regulate environmental problems led to legislative developments, but legislative development in this area has been by no means an organized or systematically planned experience. At the start of the nineteenth century, there was little in the way of a central executive state. Many of the first major legislative initiatives of the UK central state were piecemeal and reactive measures concerned with protecting the public from the impacts of industrialization and urbanization, particularly from the 1830s onwards. Legislation tended to focus upon factories,[7] sanitation,[8] and particular health risks such as cholera.[9] Only in the latter part of the century were problems such as generic pollution[10] and food safety subject to overarching regulation.[11] This was also a period of administrative experimentation and legislative reform. Creating environmental and public health laws did not simply involve the granting of more powers to civil servants or agencies, but often involved the very refashioning of administrative structures and laws. Significantly, while public health regimes were being set up in the early 1800s, it took until 1833 for legislation to be accompanied by any administrative structure.[12] This is because most of those early schemes involved simply creating offences—a type of regulatory strategy that still exists today for environmental control— rather than setting up administrative procedures for decision-making and applying environmental standards. This history is complicated but it is important to appreciate that many of the features of contemporary environmental law can be traced to this time. These features include reliance on central–local government interrelationships, the negotiated nature of enforcement, and the creation of offences as a means of regulation. The extract from Drewry notes one particular development—the heavy reliance on general public acts as a means of social reform.

Gavin Drewry, 'Lawyers and Statutory Reform in Victorian Government' in Roy MacLeod, *Government and Expertise: Specialists, Administrators and Professionals, 1860–1919* (CUP 1988) 34

The fact remains, however, that the main instrument of Victorian social reform was the public general Act of Parliament, and that increasingly such legislation came to be recognised as an essential part of the collectively agreed programmes of government: the Queen's Speeches at the beginning of the reign contain few, if any, specific legislative promises, but as time goes on their legislative content increases markedly. The growth of such legislation—measured not just in terms of numbers of Bills and Acts but also by their size, scope and complexity—is an important indicator of the rate at which the responsibilities of government grew during this period. Later, the picture is increasingly clouded by the expansion of delegated legislation [...]

General Acts of Parliament still play a central role in UK environmental law and we will see that these Acts are the starting point for nearly all regulatory frameworks, from pollution control to planning

---

[7] See, for example, Health and Morals Act 1802; Factories Act 1833 (both regulating children working in factories).
[8] See, for example, Public Health Act 1848; Public Health Act 1858; Sanitary Act 1866.
[9] See, for example, Cholera Act 1832; Nuisances Removal Act 1846.
[10] See, for example, Rivers Pollution Prevention Act 1876.
[11] See, for example, Food and Drugs Act 1860; Pharmacy Act 1862; Sale of Food and Drugs Act 1875.
[12] Factories Act 1833. On the development of this see SE Finer, *The Life and Times of Sir Edwin Chadwick* (Methuen & Co Ltd 1952) 50–68.

law procedures. We will also see, however, the significance of delegated legislation within these frameworks in contemporary UK environmental law. The importance of these historical roots can be seen in a number of chapters in this book. Thus, for example, an understanding of integrated pollution control is not possible without understanding its history in the nineteenth century. Likewise, UK planning law (Chapter 18) and statutory nuisance (Chapter 9) are both shaped by nineteenth-century legal debates and developments.

Legislative developments continued into the twentieth century and these developments will be charted in the relevant subject matter chapters, but here it is worth noting that this era of environmental law reform was marked by three particular features. First, many legislative developments were preceded by lengthy official debate, including Commissions of Inquiry. Second, developments in executive power for environmental protection, including its expansion and increasing organization in external agencies as well as government departments, were an integral part of the development of the UK administrative state and administrative law more generally. Thus, as an example, the Tribunals and Inquiries Act 1958 was concerned, in part, with addressing the administrative issues in planning (Chapter 18).

Third, twentieth-century legislative developments were incremental, involving amendment over time rather than wholesale reform and improvement. Thus, in terms of pollution control, besides some legislative activity in the 1950s, legislation was not significantly overhauled until the 1970s, and then amended in the decades that followed, although often in a piecemeal fashion with the main features of preceding legislation remaining. While in other jurisdictions, such as the US, Australia, and Germany, environmental law was often developed in a series of legislative packages, this has not been the case in England. This trend continued into the 1990s and beyond, even when new legislative measures were more frequently introduced and there was an attempt to consolidate the institutional frameworks for environmental protection. The UK Environmental Law Association report extract highlights how these piecemeal legislative practices continue today, despite some important legislative reforms that have integrated the administration of aspects of environmental law in ambitious ways—for example, the Environmental Permitting Regulations (EPRs), which have operated in England and Wales since 2007.[13]

UK Environmental Law Association, _The State of UK Environmental Legislation in 2011: Is There a Case for Reform?—Interim Report_ Revised April 2012 (funded by King's Future Fund Award) 32

One general drafting issue that [...] give[s] rise to problems of legislative incoherence is the use of amending legislation without consolidation. This method of updating environmental legislation can result in a patchwork of legislation that is hard to understand, giving rise to serious comprehensibility issues in practice, as well as problems of transparency. Whilst consolidation of legislation is a government priority, exercises of consolidation take time to get through policy and legislative processes due to strains on resources and competing policy priorities. A regulatory cost/benefit analysis is often undertaken, with downsides to consolidation including that prosecution under frequently consolidated legislation can lead to multiple statutes being applicable in cases and judgments covering the same legal point, causing a lack of coherence of a different kind.

---

[13] The EPRs replaced a large number of statutory instruments and provisions, underlying a number of overlapping pollution licensing regimes, with a single set of Regulations that set up a regime requiring operators to obtain only a single environmental permit. See further, Introduction to Part IV.

The report highlights the current state of the English environmental law statute book reflects this drafting practice and challenge, and also reflects all the idiosyncratic legislative history that has gone before, alongside a number of other influences that complicate the picture—from the implementation of EU environmental law to the increasing fragmentation of environmental legislation across the devolved administrations of the UK. The body of English environmental legislation today is thus very incoherent and disorganized. This gives rise to problems of legislative quality—in terms of its legal coherence as well as accessibility for all who use environmental law—as well as serious challenges for reform, as the final UKELA report concluded in 2012.[14]

FURTHER READING AND QUESTIONS

1. Have a look at a daily newspaper to see what types of environmental issues are being discussed. What type of politics do you think are involved in such issues? How do you think they relate to other political issues?

2. The following readings are useful for those interested in UK environmental history: William G Hoskins, *The Making of the English Landscape* (Penguin 1970); BW Clapp, *An Environmental History of Britain Since the Industrial Revolution* (Longman 1994).

3. The history of UK environmental law, let alone UK administrative law, is yet to be fully written. Some interesting partial accounts can be found in Roy MacLeod, 'The Alkali Acts Administration 1863–1884: The Emergence of the Civil Scientist' (1965) 9 Victorian Studies 85; Martin Loughlin, *Foundations of Public Law* (OUP 2010). Is understanding the historical roots of a law particularly relevant?

3. Do you think the reasons that private law has historically lacked a significant role in relation to environmental protection are still relevant today? For some excellent accounts of the role of private law in the nineteenth century for protecting the environment and associated issues, see JF Brenner, 'Nuisance Law and the Industrial Revolution' (1974) 3 JLS 403; AWB Simpson, 'Legal Liability for Bursting Reservoirs: The Historical Context of *Rylands v Fletcher*' (1984) 13 JLS 209; Joshua Getzler, *A History of Water Rights at Common Law* (OUP 2004).

---

2 THE NATURE OF UK ENVIRONMENTAL LAW

The discussion so far has focused on history and politics and this section considers the nature and key features of environmental law today. It identifies the characteristics of UK environmental law's legal forms and practices, which have been profoundly shaped by the history and socio-political context examined in Section 1.

The overall nature of UK environmental law today can be broadly summarized as follows: *UK environmental law consists of legislation (both primary and secondary), regulatory regimes, common law doctrine, implemented EU legislation, and policies.* Of these elements, it has been legislation, and in particular delegated legislation, which has dominated the legal landscape. A key feature of this legislation is that it often grants considerable discretion to administrative decision-makers. Moreover, UK regulatory and enforcement styles have been conventionally informal and negotiated. As such, the line between law and 'non-law' is not always easy to draw in relation to UK environmental control.

---

[14] UKELA, *The State of UK Environmental Law in 2011–2012: Is there a case for legislative reform?* (May 2012) <http://www.ukela.org/content/page/3006/Final%20report%20UK%20Environmental%20Law%20in%202011-2012.pdf> accessed 4 October 2012.

This rather bland description of the legal components, or instruments, of UK environmental law gives little feeling of their character or their relevant importance. The aim of this section is to give some depth to this description of UK environmental law.

2.1 LEGISLATION AND DELEGATED LEGISLATION

Within the environmental law field much primary legislation entrusts broad ranging powers to administration and the substantive detail of regulatory frameworks is often set out in a range of statutory instruments, or delegated legislation. The nature of this legislative structure is explained in the extract from Wilson. Wilson worked as a lawyer in what was then the Department of the Environment, Transport and the Regions, thus having the perspective of one working at the coalface of environmental law. His discussion relates to s 87(1) Environment Act 1995 that provides power for making Regulations. That section states:

> (l) Regulations may make provision
>
> > (a) for, or in connection with implementing the [National Air Quality] strategy;
> >
> > (b) for, or in connection with, implementing-
> >
> > > (i) obligations of the United Kingdom under the Community Treaties, or
> > >
> > > (ii) international obligations to which the United Kingdom is for the time being a party, so far as relating to the quality of air; or
> >
> > (c) otherwise with respect to the assessment or management of the quality of air.

William Wilson, *Making Environmental Laws Work: Law and Policy in the UK and USA*
(Hart Publishing 1998) 44

There follow three pages of particular matters which such regulations may contain. It may be worth identifying the elements for which section 87 provides statutory authority, because it is fairly typical of many hundreds of such provisions in the statute book. Section 87(1)(a) means that once the Government has formulated a National Air Quality Strategy, as it is required to do, it has the means and legislative authority to put it into effect by making binding regulations. This will be backed up as necessary by the power to create and enforce criminal offences.

The effect of section 87(1) (b) is that wherever the United Kingdom through the negotiations of its officials and the agreement of its ministers takes on or is subject to a European Community commitment, or signs an international treaty, relating to air quality, it has the means to deliver compliance by making binding regulations in national law.

Section 87(1) (c) is a catch-all, to ensure that there are no gaps in the legislative authority to make regulations "with respect to the assessment or management of the quality of air". Potentially, the management of air quality is a very wide area indeed. It is, on the whole, unlikely that a future Secretary of State would seek to close all factories in Britain, or ban all cars from its roads in regulations made under this provision. But it can be seen that in order to make effective regulations in an area of great concern to the public, large inroads are made on the freedom of individuals to do as they please. The tendency of such provisions is to shift power from Parliament to the executive, from public debate to bureaucratic discretion.

In this extract, Wilson highlights that the purpose of most primary legislation is to authorize the exercise of power on the part of the executive, leaving the substance of much of UK environmental law to delegated legislation. He also highlights the role of delegated legislation in implementing EC, now EU, Directives. This is further discussed in the final section of this chapter, since EU environmental law has its own significant implications for both UK environmental law and administration.

Hawkins considers the implications of primary legislation being used in environmental law mainly as a tool for authorizing administrative discretion.

Keith Hawkins, *Environment and Enforcement: Regulation and the Social Definition of Pollution* (Clarendon Press 1984) 22

Water pollution control shares with other forms of regulation a broad legislative mandate and an unspecified task of implementation. A characteristically legal mode of social control—the criminal sanction for misconduct—is made available to govern a social problem with technological and economic dimensions. The legislature creates a rather abstract mandate and an agency to implement it, while only defining explicitly the offences which give rise to prosecution. And even then, the content and boundaries of the offensive behaviour are matters of administrative discretion. Ironically, the power to prosecute is rarely used. Legislative mandate and legal offence are linked by an unguided and pervasive administrative discretion. It is as if the creation of a regulatory bureaucracy carries with it implicit powers to achieve agency goals. The power to negotiate, which is central to compliance systems, is one which exists by implication only but one made possible because the law is not made concrete or specific. Regulatory law is permeated with uncertainty.

As Hawkins makes clear, the discretionary nature of UK administration has implications not only for environmental standard setting but also for enforcement. This will be explored in more detail later.

All of this means that environmental law is not simply the law on the statute books, or even that found in delegated legislation. An environmental lawyer must thus have regard to delegated legislation, administrative discretion, and administrative practice in order to understand what laws apply to a given environmental problem. Moreover, as will be seen in many of the subject matter chapters, policy documents and technical guidance documents also play a significant role in this environmental law mix. The role of policy and guidance in environmental law is discussed in more detail in Chapter 11, and is a particular feature of areas such as planning, contaminated land liability, and integrated pollution prevention and control.

Another important implication of administrative discretion playing a central role in environmental legislative structures is that a significant part of UK environmental law consists of judicial review case law, which seeks to check and confine the exercise of this administrative discretion. Judicial review case law sets the legitimate boundaries of administrative action, as undertaken within a statutory framework. Judicial review sets these boundaries in many ways, as discussed in Chapter 7. In this way, in many chapters of this book, you will see that the 'law' consists of a series of judicial review decisions that define the boundaries of administrative discretion—the contexts of planning (Chapter 18) and environmental impact assessment (Chapter 19) in particular are richly populated with judicial review cases.

2.2 PRIVATE LAW, STATUTORY REMEDIES, AND OFFENCES

Readers might get the impression from the discussion so far that the development of UK environmental law has been a steady progression from private law actions to the creation of legislative regimes that establish environmental controls and standards. This is not the case, and it is useful to note in passing the role of private law, statutory remedies, and criminal offences, which are dealt with in Chapters 6, 9, and 8 respectively. The purpose of discussing them here is to make clear the legal richness of UK environmental law.

The first point to note is that, while private law still plays a marginal role in environmental law, it is an important one. There are many different forms of private law that are relevant to environmental problems, including tort law, contract law, property law, and company law. Furthermore, these different areas of law exist in a complex interrelationship with environmental problems and environmental law. Thus, for example, the discussion in Chapter 6 highlights how private law serves to establish a legal *status quo*, how it is limited in dealing with environmental problems, how conversely private law litigation can act to trigger environmental protection, how private law interrelates with public law, and finally how private law itself is shaped by environmental regimes.

Alongside private law, embedded in legislation are a range of different remedies, which are hybrids of private, public, and criminal law. These are discussed in detail in Chapter 9. As already noted, one of the first legislative initiatives in relation to environmental and public health protection was the creation of regulatory offences. Moreover, through legislation, the UK Parliament has created a number of strict liability criminal environmental offences, such as Regulation 12 of the Environmental Permitting Regulations 2010, which is one of the most heavily enforced environmental law offences.[15] These types of offences will be discussed in more detail in Chapter 8, but here it is worth noting that an important feature of these novel statutory offences and remedies is that the courts have often been quite activist in interpreting and applying them.

2.3 POLICY STYLE

Sections 2.1 and 2.2 have discussed the nature of UK environmental law in terms of legal forms but, as noted in Section 2.1, a key feature of UK environmental law (due to its particular legislative form) is administrative discretion. This means that, in thinking about the nature of UK environmental law, one must have an understanding of the nature of the administrative practice and discretion. This is a complicated topic but this section and Section 2.4 note two important aspects—policy style and enforcement. Policy style is a relevant aspect of administrative discretion in directly influencing how laws are developed, particularly when they are in the form of delegated legislation. Enforcement is relevant because the discretion applied in how laws are enforced, or administered, will directly influence what environmental standards are being achieved.

Policy style may be an issue considered more deeply by political scientists than lawyers, but the scholarship on British policy style confirms that British administration is inherently discretionary and flexible. Moreover, a brief look at the concept of policy style also highlights as a feature of British administration 'bureaucratic accommodation'.

Grant Jordan and Jeremy Richardson, 'The British Policy Style or the Logic of Negotiation?' in Jeremy John Richardson (ed), *Policy Styles in Western Europe* (George Allen & Unwin 1982) 81

[…] Britain is best characterised as emphasising consensus and a desire to avoid the imposition of solutions on sections of society. In that there is no particular priority accorded to anticipatory solutions— and the stress on negotiation itself inhibits radical change—the British style is also 'reactive'. Hayward effectively summarised the essence of the style:

---

[15] See Chapter 14.

'Firstly, there are no explicit, over-riding medium or long term objectives. Secondly, unplanned decision-making is incremental. Thirdly, hum drum or unplanned decisions are arrived at by a continuous process of mutual adjustment between a plurality of autonomous policy-makers operating in the context of a highly fragmented multiple flow of influence. Not only is plenty of scope offered to interest group spokes men to shape the outcome by participation in the advisory process. The aim is to secure through bargaining at least passive acceptance of the decision by the interests affected.'

2.4 ENFORCEMENT STYLE

The discretionary and negotiated nature of UK administration also has a direct impact upon environmental law in relation to its implementation and enforcement. An enduring feature of UK administration is reflected in the considerable discretion given to administrators in the enforcement of environmental legislation. This is because offences are often described in very broad terms or involve discretionary concepts and standards such as 'best practicable means' (See Section 1 of Chapter 17). This feature of environmental regulation is also seen in other areas of regulation, such as occupational health and safety regulation and building regulation, and has its historical roots in nineteenth-century Britain. Implementation of environmental law through discretion is thus best understood as a process of compliance and enforcement, with enforcement in the form of prosecution being a last resort. Keith Hawkins was one of the first scholars to describe systematically these practices and his work has framed thinking in this area. He explains the lack of reliance on formal regulatory processes by pollution regulators.

Keith Hawkins, *Environment and Enforcement: Regulation and the Social Definition of Pollution* (Clarendon Press 1984) 207

The formal processes of the law will be employed only where a regulatory agency can be sure they rest upon the secure foundation of a perceived moral consensus. In the vast majority of cases of regulatory deviance a confusion of interests and values exists, manifested in doubts about whether agencies are protecting the public good when sanctioning behaviour which is a consequence of economic activity beneficial to the public. *In an environment of ambivalence what is mutually recognizable assumes immense importance.* Conduct placed within a moral framework possesses just such recognisability. The formal machinery of the law is appropriate therefore only in those 'big' and 'bad' cases where the gravity or moral offensiveness of a breach renders the confusion of interest minimal. The agencies are demonstrably doing something while offending few. This is deeply-entrenched behaviour in pollution control work and perhaps a major reason for the persistence and consistency of the patterns of enforcement behaviour to be observed in a wide variety of areas of regulation. To regard a compliance strategy of enforcement at field level, or the formulation of prosecution policy at headquarters as symptomatic of the capture of the regulators misses the point. The practice of regulatory enforcement expresses an identity of moral values which transcends the regulator-regulated relationship.

This last point is particularly important. It has become popular to understand the problems of regulatory enforcement in terms of 'agency capture'—the idea that regulators for a variety of reasons promote the interests of those that they are regulating rather than the public interest—but Hawkins argues that this is not the case. Indeed, Hawkins' understanding that regulatory enforcement is about consensus—in terms of mutual moral understandings and perceptions of a problem—can be seen quite strongly in more recent enforcement policies, discussed in Chapter 8.

Implicit in this understanding of UK regulatory enforcement is the fact that environmental health officers play an important role in negotiating the conditions of compliance with laws. As Hawkins explains, that process of negotiation is a profoundly complex and subtle one. It is shaped by social norms developed 'on the ground' in interactions between enforcement officers and those who are subject to regulation. Paradoxically, what appears to be 'discretionary administration' can, in practice, be significantly patterned enforcement behaviour circumscribed, not necessarily by determinate legal rules, but by specific social practices.

Keith Hawkins, *Environment and Enforcement: Regulation and the Social Definition of Pollution* (Clarendon Press 1984)126–28

Compliance is often treated as if it were an objectively-defined unproblematic state, rather than a fluid, negotiable matter. Compliance, however, is an elaborate concept, one better seen as a process, rather than a condition. […]

Compliance is negotiable and embraces action, time, and symbol. It addresses both standard and process. It may in some cases consist of present conformity. In others, present rule-breaking will be tolerated on an understanding that there will be conformity in future: compliance represents, in other words, some ideal state towards which an enforcement agent works. Since the enforcement of regulation is a continuing process, compliance is often attained by increments. Conformity to this process itself is another facet of compliance. And when a standard is attained, it must be maintained: compliance here is an unbounded, continuing state. It is not simply a matter of the installation of treatment plant, but how well that plant is made to work, and kept working. And an ideal, once reached, may be replaced or transformed by other changes—in consent, in water resource or land use, for example—which demand the achievement of a different ideal. Central to all of this is the symbolic aspect of compliance. A recognition of the legitimacy of the demands of an enforcement agent expressed in a willingness to conform in future will be taken as a display of compliance in itself. Here it is possible for a polluter to be thought of as 'compliant' even though he may continue to break the rules about the discharge of polluting effluent.

Hawkins' analysis of pollution control was ground-breaking and represents one of the most significant socio-legal studies ever produced. It also presents a real challenge to environmental lawyers and scholars because Hawkins is also highlighting how much environmental law is not 'on the books' but is rather comprised of what goes on in practice. How that 'practice' is encompassed in the study and definition of the subject was touched upon in Chapter 1, and will be returned to again and again in the chapters that follow, particularly those concerned with pollution control.

FURTHER READING AND QUESTIONS

1. Look at any chapter of this book and consider how much of the legislative area is governed by primary legislation and how much by delegated legislation. How comprehensible is the overall legislative pattern? Compare in particular nature conservation and planning law.

2. For those wishing to acquaint themselves in more detail with the UK legal system, a good introductory text is Martin Partington, *An Introduction to the UK Legal System* (7th edn, OUP 2012).

3. Consider the interrelationship between the UK negotiated policy style and the type of direct action politics discussed in Section 1.1. Are they reconcilable? On the issue of policy style,

see AG Jordan and JJ Richardson, *British Politics and the Policy Process: An Arena Approach* (Routledge 1987).

4. There is a rich socio-legal literature concerning regulatory implementation and enforcement. An obvious starting point is the exceptional Keith Hawkins, *Law as a Last Resort: Prosecution Decision-Making in a Regulatory Agency* (OUP 2002). Also see Genevra Richardson and others, *Policing Pollution: A Study of Regulation and Enforcement* (OUP 1982); Bridget M Hutter, *The Reasonable Arm of the Law?: the Law Enforcement Procedures of Environmental Health Officers* (Clarendon Press 1988).

3 THE INSTITUTIONAL LANDSCAPE OF UK ENVIRONMENTAL LAW

The discussion so far has focused on the nature of environmental law and we now turn to the institutions that administer it. As with the different forms of environmental law, the administration of UK environmental law can also be understood to have evolved over time and to have been shaped by a long history. The end result is not particularly coherent—as suggested by the conclusion in Section 1 that UK environmental law is not systematic. This includes the administration of UK environmental law, which, like much UK public administration, amounts to an 'an untidy empire [...] continuously adapted and readapted to meet new political fashions and expediencies'.[16] There is no one single institution that governs UK environmental law—rather there is an ad hoc assemblage of different bodies, and the jurisdiction, character, and constitution of those bodies may owe more to historical accident and politics than any logical scheme. This section sketches some of the key institutions involved, although it should be stressed that a comprehensive account is very difficult due to the ad hoc nature of institutional development.

Generally speaking, the administration of statutes is carried out by large central government departments, local government, and, in some cases, specialist agencies. The role of the courts in administering environmental regimes has been historically marginal but, as will be seen, is increasingly significant, particularly as a tool of accountability. The role of agencies and local government tends to be more limited to administering particular statutes and they do not have the wide-ranging discretionary power that is entrusted to central government departments, although the power is still considerable. Moreover, central government, local government, and specialist agencies will often *all* have a role to play in administering particular schemes. A good example of this is the contaminated land regime, discussed in Chapter 21—this statutory regime (Part IIA Environmental Protection Act 1990) relies on core statutory guidance issued by the Department for Environment, Food and Rural Affairs (DEFRA), implementation responsibilities imposed on local authorities, and the Environment Agency being required to deal with the most serious cases of contaminated land. It should be noted that all these administrative bodies are public in nature, but the popularity of new public management and more 'voluntary' regulatory strategies means that there is a role for private actors. Moreover, these public bodies both increasingly contract out aspects of their work to private workers and institutions, and also adopt more 'market-based' approaches to their operations internally. The shift towards governance will be discussed in Chapter 13.

Before examining each of these public institutions, it is important to note that the institutional landscape for the administration of environmental law can change very quickly. Government

---

[16] Stuart Weir and David Beetham, *Political Power and Democratic Control in Britain* (Routledge 1999) 158.

departments can be reorganized by exercise of prerogative powers almost overnight (this most often occurs with incoming governments), and new agencies can be set up with breathtaking speed. Moreover, the institutional frameworks and strategies of such institutions are constantly subject to revision. This flexibility is a feature of the Westminster style government and means that care needs to be taken with dated accounts of administration. It may even be the case that the description given in Section 3.1 is outdated by the time you come to read it! If in doubt, always check government and agency websites.

3.1 DEFRA AND OTHER CENTRAL GOVERNMENT DEPARTMENTS

The most significant central government department from an environmental law perspective is DEFRA, which is responsible for administering many environmental issues. DEFRA was created in 2001 and was an amalgamation of the Ministry of Agriculture, Fisheries and Food with environmental responsibilities from other government departments. With that said, as we write these arrangements are being changed. Thus, in late 2012 government department websites began to move onto the gov. uk web platform. The climate team at DEFRA broke away in 2008 to join with the energy team at the then Department for Business Enterprise and Regulatory Reform (BERR) to create the Department of Energy and Climate Change (DECC). Likewise, planning and environmental impact assessment is a matter for the Department of Communities and Local Government (DCLG), and the Department for Business, Innovation and Skills (BIS, formerly BERR) plays a key role in fashioning and developing regulatory strategies, as does HM Treasury. The nature of these central government departments are described in general terms by Ross.

Andrea Ross, 'The UK Approach to Delivering Sustainable Development in Government: A Case Study in Joined-Up Working' (2005) 17 JEL 27, 31–32

In the UK, central government functions are predominantly divided up among departments. Each department is headed by a minister who is chosen by the Prime Minister from members of either House of Parliament. The doctrine of ministerial responsibility means that the Minister is ultimately responsible for all activity in his or her department and is answerable to Parliament and to the public for his or her department. The Prime Minister meets with ministers in the Cabinet where overall government policy is determined. The Prime Minister exercises a certain amount of pressure over ministers and can remove them from their posts, but ultimate responsibility remains with individual ministers. Ministerial responsibility is also essential to protect the anonymous nature of the civil service. Officials are career civil servants and are kept secure from political changes. This means expertise is not lost with a change of government, but it also means that systems within departments become firmly entrenched. Daintith and Page conclude that 'departmental primacy has been the central organising principle of the executive branch [...] The corollary of departmental primacy was an essentially decentralised system of internal control for the operation of which the ministerial head of each department was responsible to Parliament'. Ministers are accountable to Parliament directly through parliamentary questions and debates in the House as well as being subject to scrutiny by the relevant departmental select committee. As a result, control tends to rely on self-discipline. Each department works towards its own objectives in its own way and the centre has remarkably little influence on public sector behaviour. Hence, the culture of different departments may be quite distinct.

Following criticism that the UK public sector was monolithic, inward-looking and too removed from the needs of service users, the Conservative governments of the 1980s and early 1990s introduced a variety of measures designed to improve efficiency and responsiveness. To this end, several nationalised industries were privatised. Within departments, the delivery of services was hived-off and separated from policy-making by the creation of 'executive' or 'next steps agencies' and tighter financial controls and compulsory competitive tendering were imposed on local authorities. This emphasis on management reform brought improved productivity, better value for money and in many cases better quality services. However, little attention had been paid to the policy process and the way it affects government's ability to meet people's needs.

Ross's analysis highlights the generalist, permanent nature of central government departments and also the role that policy agendas have had to play in their reworking over the last two decades.

The resulting administrative character of such governmental institutions is discussed by Knill below. He discusses the British administrative state in the context of a comparison with Germany, with continental ideas of bureaucracy used as a reference point. This perspective is useful in that British public administration is often conceptualized in Prussian terms, along the lines described by Weber.[17] Lawyers often tend to think of public administration in clichéd terms as a bureaucratic hierarchy, but Knill's analysis shows that such a conceptualization is off the mark.

Christoph Knill, *The Europeanisation of National Administrations: Patterns of Institutional Change and Persistence* **(CUP 2001) 80–81**

To begin with competence allocation, there are no strongly entrenched arrangements with respect to the functional division of labour between and within different levels of central and subcentral administration. Rather the distribution of administrative competencies seems to be quite flexible, with shifting competencies and administrative reorganisation taking place frequently, at least when compared to Continental European countries.

Central government enjoys wide discretion when deciding on the allocation of administrative competencies within and between the central and local level. The constitutional position of local government is inferior to that of central government. Although there exist also elected representations at the local level, local authorities in Britain—as opposed to Germany—lack constitutionally guaranteed competencies and responsibilities, but are subject to ultra vires, empowered to undertake only those functions deliberately granted to them by Parliamentary statute. Central government has therefore not only powers to reduce administrative competencies given to the local level, but also can reorganise the entire structure of local government as well as its finances.

[...]

In contrast to the administrative development in Continental Europe, British administration has evolved over centuries by accretion with relatively little planning and without a central organisational format which would make the system more comprehensible. According to this pattern, the increase in civil service functions, which was basically a result of nineteenth-century industrialisation and the welfare state development, led to the creation of new administrative bodies on an ad hoc basis, rather than allocating new functions to already existing authorities and within existing structures.

In view of this particular evolution, a complex, but little coherent administrative structure can be observed, including different types of organisation, such as executive departments, executive agencies carrying out implementation activities separated from the sponsoring department, local government, the health services, and a large number of non-departmental bodies [...]

---

[17] Max Weber, *Economy and Society: An Outline of Interpretative Sociology* (Bedminster Press 1968).

[T]he general lack of structural coherence concerning the allocation of administrative competencies has important implications for administrative co-ordination and control. It is a basic feature of the British administrative system, that authorities responsible for a certain area enjoy a significant degree of autonomy [...] Hierarchical guidance and control by the central government departments occurs only with respect to general rather than policy-specific aspects, such as the definition of a broad legal, operational and financial framework. Within this framework, administrative authorities and agencies at both the central and local levels enjoy far-reaching discretion for specifying the generally vague regulatory provisions defined by Parliamentary statute.

Central to Knill's analysis is the importance of central–local relations, which is a particularly significant relationship in UK environmental law and is discussed in more detail in the discussion on local government in Section 3.2.

It is useful to reflect further on the nature of British public administration and its implications for environmental law in practice. An excellent analysis of British public administration in action was undertaken by the BSE Inquiry, which reported in 2000.[18] While not directly concerned with environmental administration, the Inquiry's discussion on the working of the Ministry of Agriculture, Fisheries and Food (MAFF) and the Department of Health (DH) is directly relevant to the environmental context.

Inquiry into BSE and V-CJD, *The BSE Inquiry Report, Volume Fifteen: Government and Public Administration* (2000) para 2.3–2.18

2.3 In order to assist with the collective development of policy and the handling of difficult issues, the Cabinet usually met once a week when Parliament was in session. Various Cabinet Ministers and a number of Ministers outside the Cabinet were also members of long-established Cabinet committees that focused on particular policy areas—for example, the Economic Affairs Committee—or *ad hoc* committees [...] Papers drafted within their own Departments (and sometimes brokered in advance with other Departments) would be submitted by Ministers to these committees.

2.4 Within their Departments, Cabinet Ministers were usually assisted by two or more junior ministers. These were either Parliamentary Secretaries or Ministers of State (a higher rank for particularly responsible posts), one of whom might speak for the Department in the House of Lords. Their responsibilities were decided by the departmental Minister, and they were expected to master the relevant issues and legislation, to be alert to developing problems, and to handle subordinate matters.

2.5 Mr Roger (now Lord) Freeman thought that his role as a junior Minister at the Department of Health had included:

[...] at least two aspects of keeping my eyes and ears open [...] I was certainly, throughout that period, from the receipt of the Southwood Report onwards, keeping my eyes and ears open in a Parliamentary sense, listening to what colleagues had to say, picking up comments made to me in letters. I also took [...] an even more specific interest in making sure that I was aware of Parliamentary comment and making sure that the Secretary of State was aware of it [...] I think the second way in which one was seeking to alert the Secretary of State to issues was simply in terms of what I was aware of within the Department, and indeed what one was aware of simply through reading the daily press comment.

---

[18] Inquiry into BSE and V-CJD, *The BSE Inquiry Report* (2000).

2.6 Another former junior Minister (at MAFF), Mr David Curry, put it as follows:

[...] one of the jobs which I regarded as important in assisting the Minister was trying to look a little bit round the corner ... from time to time I would pull ideas together and say 'What happens if this occurs?' [...] I thought it was part of a useful job to make sure the Department was thinking ahead, because so much was happening on a day-to-day basis that from time to time one needed to say 'What might happen if?'

2.7 Junior Ministers processed a heavy load of day-to-day business, including much parliamentary business (for example adjournment debates and the committee stages of Bills) and answering letters from MPs. Such correspondence, or the tabling of a Parliamentary Question ...., could be the initial means by which an issue came to Ministers' attention.

2.8 Mr (now Sir) Michael Forsyth (Scottish Office) emphasised the subordinate nature of the junior ministerial role—

[...] I imagine talking to the junior Minister was a bit like talking to the organ grinder—the monkey rather than the organ grinder.[6]

—and the need to avoid embarrassment to colleagues. Lord Skelmersdale (Northern Ireland Office) explained that his senior Minister had indicated that he was:

[...] only to approach him when [...] I was likely to get the Government into trouble, him into trouble and last of all myself into trouble.

2.9 The ways in which senior Ministers involved their junior colleagues in decision-making reflected their personal style of working and preferences. Junior Ministers were included in any ministerial briefing or policy discussions in their particular field of responsibility. Some senior Ministers preferred a systematic pattern of meetings, either daily or weekly (often referred to as 'Prayers') to discuss matters of topical interest, often without officials present. One Secretary of State for Health, Mr William Waldegrave, held regular 'Top of the Office' meetings which included the Permanent Secretary (the most senior civil servant in the Department), the Chief Medical Officer (CMO) and other officials.

2.10 The day-to-day running of Ministerial offices—the management of papers, meetings, diary and transport—was in the hands of the Private Secretaries or 'Private Office'. This was a small team of civil servants, led by high fliers whose spell in Private Office was a recognised stage in their career progression. The senior Private Secretary (PS) in each office determined which parts of the large volume of material passing through it should be particularly drawn to Ministers' attention, or required a meeting. One PS would attend and record all such meetings, and would also listen in to and make a written note of the Minister's important telephone conversations.

2.11 Because of pressure on time during the day, important submissions would normally be put in the Minister's 'Red Box' of papers for him or her to take home and read during the evening or the following morning before coming into the office. The 'weekend box' would be particularly substantial.

To facilitate easy contact and informal discussion between all the Private Offices within a Department (which included those of the Permanent Secretary and, within DH, of the CMO, as well as one for each Minister), these were usually located close together. Private Offices also worked closely with the Department's Chief Information Officer on how issues were presented in public, including responses to requests for media interviews. [...]

2.12 Many Ministers appointed 'special' or 'political' advisers who commented on submissions and attended policy meetings. These were personal appointments from outside the established civil service. Their role was specifically to address the political aspects of policy and its presentation, in which the role of civil servants was restricted by longstanding conventions of impartiality and propriety that were set out formally in Departments' codes of conduct for staff. Constituency business was dealt with outside the Private Office.

2.13 Officials had three roles. The first was to alert and advise: ie, to identify and consider issues on the basis of appropriate information; to identify options for addressing them; and to present the information and recommendations to Ministers. This was mainly done by a relatively small number of policy staff in each Department. The second was to assist in carrying out Ministers' decisions, a role that involved policy planning and problem-solving. The third—by far the largest in terms of the number of staff employed—was to manage and deliver services for which the Government was responsible. Policy staff, especially at senior levels, were also expected to be efficient managers in terms of keeping the administrative machine running smoothly and directing resources to where they were needed, and of ensuring that the executive outcomes of policy decisions (eg, abattoir inspection programmes, systems for licensing animal and human medicines) were implemented by:

i) the Department itself;

ii) an agency of the Department [...]; or

iii) external organisations such as non-departmental public bodies (NDPBs), local authorities and health authorities.

2.14 As with all large organisations, senior officials were responsible for advising on a wide range of issues, often simultaneously, and for facilitating the effective performance of large numbers of junior staff. Most Departments were organised in well-defined hierarchies with levels of authority and responsibility indicated by grades. Permanent Secretaries, the most senior officials, were ranked Grade 1; under them were Deputy Secretaries (Grade 2), Under Secretaries (Grade 3), Assistant Secretaries (Grade 5) and Principals (Grade 7). Some posts were graded Senior Principal (Grade 6); one relevant to BSE was held by Mr Alan Lawrence in MAFF's Animal Health Division. Specialised responsibilities, for example on the medical side in DH and the veterinary side in MAFF, were often at other grades. A number of important figures in the BSE story held such posts: at Grade 1A (the Chief Medical Officers, Sir Donald Acheson and Sir Kenneth Calman), and Grade 4 (Dr Hilary Pickles, a Principal Medical Officer in DH, and Mr Kevin Taylor, an Assistant Chief Veterinary Officer in MAFF). For reasons described in Chapter 4, the Chief Veterinary Officer was, unusually, a 'Grade 3+'.

2.15 Departmental staff at these various levels were deployed in groups, directorates, divisions and branches (the nomenclature varied between Departments), forming a hierarchical structure of units with varying spans of responsibility. The complexity or significance of an issue generally determined the level from which advice went to the Minister and the degree of involvement of the most senior officials. Annex 1 to this volume sets out the organisation of MAFF and DH, showing the hierarchical structure and responsibilities and the names of those occupying each post. [...]

[...]

2.17 Generally, officials were expected to discuss issues or raise concerns with colleagues (including professionals) at their own level. Where matters could not be resolved in this way, junior staff did not make independent approaches to senior members of other divisions or to Ministers. Instead, they would 'put things up' through their line managers to raise with colleagues 'at their level'. All those with an interest—even if not actually in the policy lead—who needed to be kept informed of progress would receive copies of the relevant submissions, minutes or letters, either inviting observations or simply 'for information'.

2.18 Officials also aimed to 'keep off other people's patch'—ie to let their colleagues exercise their responsibilities while becoming involved themselves only if invited to do so or if the actions of others impinged on their own responsibilities. Dr Jeremy Metters (DH) saw this principle encapsulated in:

Rogan's rule [...] is it for this Department? Is it for this Division? Is it for me? I found it very helpful to abide by those rules in deciding whether or not I should intervene.

This lengthy analysis really concerns the higher echelons of the Executive, but it highlights the very close interrelationship between UK policy style and UK institutions in which ministers and senior civil servants play important roles.

Finally, the challenges of interdepartmental co-operation need to be highlighted. This is a feature of nearly all governmental systems, but it has become particularly important in recent years in relation to environmental issues for two reasons. First, as already seen, DEFRA is not the only government department involved in administering environmental issues—responsibility is split across departments with the attendant risks of 'silo' working and thinking. Second, the increasing emphasis on sustainability has meant that there is a need for more integrated thinking across policy sectors.[19] Jordan discusses some of the challenges to such 'joined up' thinking.

Andrew Jordan, 'Environmental Policy' in Patrick Dunleavy and others, *Developments in British Politics 6* (rev edn, Palgrave 2002) 266–67

In simple bureaucratic terms, greening government required colonization of the key centres of power in the political system, by winning over the more powerful departments of state to its way of thinking [...] The paradox is that joined-up policy-making can be delivered only via the very institutionalized system of inter-departmental bargaining that leads to fragmented and sectorized thinking. The political difficulty of overcoming this deep-seated paradox of government should not be under-estimated. Whitehall has its own, highly effective ways of thwarting new cross-sectoral initiatives.

Of all the barriers to 'joined-up thinking', one of the most fundamental is the basic organizational structure of government. Many influential accounts stress the extent to which it is deeply fragmented into competing departments of state. Richardson and Jordan (1979) coined the phrase 'departmental pluralism' to describe the tendency for different parts to compete with one another. The segmentation of government works into independent, functionally discrete departments, insulated from external pressure by policy networks of special interests, thwarts cross-cutting initiatives such as sustainability. According to a Minister in the DTI [Department of Trade and Industry], the 'danger' of these divisions, is that Ministers find themselves 'locked into silos [...] one department does one thing, another does another, and they actually undermine each other and never talk to each other' (HC 517-11, Session 1997–8, 145). Potentially 'over-riding issues' such as the environment tend to fall between the cracks between departments, or are simply dissipated unless there is strong leadership from the centre.

3.2 LOCAL GOVERNMENT

As already noted, the administration of UK environmental law is not limited to central government. A striking feature of much UK environmental law is the prominent role of local government, in both the administering and enforcing of much environmental law. In light of the discretionary nature of many environmental law regimes, this means the power of local authorities is considerable. As seen in regimes such as air quality management (Chapter 17) and contaminated land control (Chapter 21), local authorities are involved in the regulatory processes of identification, authorization, and management. Like many features of UK environmental law, the role of local government is deeply set in the historical landscape. Beyond this historical reality, the reasons for local government existence and involvement are less clear, as Sharpe discusses in the extract from 'Theories and Values of Local Government'. The extract concerns the role of local government generally, but the issues raised are pertinent to environmental law as well. Sharpe's starting point is that the purposes of local government are poorly understood.

---

[19] See Chapter 11.

LJ Sharpe, 'Theories and Values of Local Government' (1970) 18 Political Studies 153, 154–55

One reason why local government has not attracted the political theorist's interest, and a brief glance at the literature suggests that this may apply to other countries as well, is that it exists and has existed in some form for a long time. To quote Mackenzie again, himself paraphrasing a hallowed Whitehall rubric: 'It is justified because it is an effective and convenient way to provide certain services. It is justified because we like to think that our central government needs the kind of qualities which are best trained by local self-government.' [...]

Sharpe then quotes Mill

'The very object of having local representation, is in order that those who have an interest in common which they do not share with the general body of their countrymen may manage that joint interest by themselves.'

There can be little serious objection to this claim for local government, indeed it is the least ambiguous and the most concrete of all the justifications of local government. But it embraces a very limited range of activities which it is difficult to envisage as sufficient grist for a full-dress elected and tax-raising system enjoying 'a measure of autonomy'. [...]

Linked to this functional value is the knowledge value of local government. Not only is it irrational to involve anyone else in the local problems of the local area, central government is not equipped to grasp the inimitable conditions of each locality. Local government is preferable precisely because locally elected institutions employing their own specialist staff are better placed to understand and interpret both the conditions and the needs of local communities. [...]

Arthur Maass and Paul Ylvisaker, in what remains the most exhaustive systematic discussion of the division of powers by area, have defined the values inherent in local government as being: liberty, equality and welfare. Local government promotes liberty in the sense, following Montesquieu, that it is a division of powers on an area basis which mitigates the power of the sovereign. It promotes equality in the political sense that it provides broad opportunities for citizens to participate in public policy. Finally, it promotes welfare in the sense that it provides agents that are apt for meeting the needs of society.

Sharpe's analysis highlights the fact that the role of local government is a complex one, largely because local government is playing a variety of roles—it is not just an 'agent' delivering the policy of central government. This is important to keep in mind where issues such as local expertise, local representation, and participation are valued aspects of decision-making in the operation of environmental law. The 'primordial' nature of local government is also important to remember—the power of local authorities existed before that of central government.

Following on from this, integral to thinking about the role of local government in environmental law is its relationship to central government. This relationship is again complex and numerous scholars have developed many different theories about its nature. Loughlin, in particular, has made an important contribution to this scholarship, and here we get a feel for his argument.

Martin Loughlin, *Legality and Locality: The Role of Law in Central-Local Government Relations* (Clarendon Press 1996) 416–18

[W]e cannot appreciate the modern relationship between government and law without understanding our traditions of local government and the tensions between the centre and the localities which are manifest in our constitutional arrangements. [...] It was mainly because of the work undertaken by Parliament that no formal hierarchical relationship between the central State and local authorities came to be forged, thereby enabling a tradition of local government to be maintained. And it is largely owing to this achievement that no special system of administrative law has evolved in this country. The consequent tensions between the practices of local government and the claims of the central State have largely been resolved through administrative networks whose status and importance, whilst occasionally being accommodated by the law, have not generally been entrenched in law.

[...] The central-local government relationship has been both politicized and juridified and that these related trends may be understood as reflections of an inexorable process of rationalization of social life. The emergence of ideological politics has imposed severe strains on our anti-Rationalist constitutional arrangements. The Conservative Government's agenda for local government since 1979 may be viewed as a specific illustration of this tendency. The Government's action has often failed to conform to traditional patterns of political behaviour and the administrative network, which has emerged this century as a regulatory mechanism in the conduct of central-local relations, has often been by-passed or subverted. The Government's programme for local government, being based on value-for-money criteria, has been rooted in an instrumental rationality which has occasionally been reinforced by vesting individual rights in consumers of local services. The overall impact of this programme has been to undermine the institution of local government. Further, because of the manner in which the Government has implemented the programme, the central-local relationship has been reconstructed in much more explicitly hierarchical terms.

[...]

Though local government has since the nineteenth century been placed on a statutory foundation, positive law has not been a primary determinant of this relationship. Statute law has established a facilitative framework through which conventional arrangements for regulating central-local relations could evolve and which, in effect, constituted a non-juridified structure of administrative law. One consequence of the Government's recent actions in subverting the administrative network has been to transform law into a primary instrument of regulation.

Loughlin is thus highlighting that there has been a dramatic shift in central/local relations over time, with a central feature being the shift from a less hierarchical and legal relationship to an instrumental and highly juridified one. This implies a greater role for the courts and administrative law actions. Indeed, environmental law cases are increasingly comprised of public law cases in relation to the role of local government, particularly in relation to planning disputes (Chapter 18). Another implication of Loughlin's account is that central government now plays a more directing role than it has historically, which will be seen in areas such as planning and contaminated land liability, although the relationship remains complex and evolving, as recent political and administrative changes to boost localism in England demonstrate.[20]

3.3 DEVOLUTION

While this textbook is primarily focused on England, the significance of devolution cannot, and should not, be ignored. The devolution of environmental decision-making to Scotland, Wales, and Northern Ireland has fundamentally changed the institutional dynamics of UK environmental law by

---

[20] Localism Act 2011 (Chapter 18).

devolving power to regional institutions. This has given rise to new institutional arenas and discourses, and sometimes (and it seems increasingly) different environmental legal standards and practices. Devolution is thus a foundational feature of the UK environmental law landscape.

In legislative terms, devolution has occurred through three Acts—the Scotland Act 1998, the Government of Wales Act 1998 (and subsequent legislative reforms), and the Northern Ireland Act 1998. The form devolution takes in each region is very different. Under the Scotland Act 1998, the Scottish Parliament is delegated legislative power in areas that have not been reserved to the UK Parliament under Schedule 5 of the 1998 Act. As environmental protection is not a reserved matter, it is an area in which the Scottish Parliament has competence (although energy and health and safety are reserved, causing some tensions). This environmental competence has been exercised extensively. Scottish legislation includes the Nature Conservation (Scotland) Act 2005 and the Planning etc (Scotland) Act 2006. Pieces of legislation such as the Environmental Assessment (Scotland) Act 2006 represent the Scottish implementation of that EU Directive. There is also a range of pieces of delegated legislation, and devolution has also involved executive reform—including the creation of the Scottish Environmental Protection Agency. Reflecting its progressive environmental policy, Scotland's environmental legislative agenda has been ambitious, with statutes such as Water Environment and Water Services (Scotland) Act 2005[21] and the Climate Change (Scotland) Act 2009 being innovative instruments, in their integration of environmental goals across policy spheres and in their ambitious environmental protection goals. Further, wholesale reform of environmental legislation in Scotland is now looking likely, in an effort to simplify and integrate environmental regulation and to prepare for future regulatory challenges on environmental issues.

Devolution in Wales has been a far more dynamic process. Originally, the Government of Wales Act 1998 only allowed for executive devolution, but that has now changed, in light of the Government of Wales Act 2006 and the subsequent referendum in 2011 as explained in the extract from Melding.

David Melding, 'Issue on Welsh Devolution' (2012) 33 Stat LR 97, 97–98

The latest referendum has given the National Assembly wide-ranging powers to make laws for Wales. The Assembly is now a very different creature from the single corporate body that took its first tentative steps to becoming a legislature in 1999 with few law making powers beyond the ability to make (and perhaps over scrutinize) subordinate legislation.

In the third Assembly [after the 2006 Act], the creation of a legislative Assembly legally separate from its executive in the shape of the (then) Welsh Assembly Government, together with the limited but historically important ability to make primary laws for Wales [known as Assembly Measures] laid the foundations for a genuinely parliamentary institution.

The fourth Assembly's powers are now extensive, meaningful, and relevant to the lives of people in Wales. Even with the more limited powers available to the third Assembly, new laws were passed in areas that impact directly on the citizen or affect important areas of public policy. Measures such as charging for carrier bags, seatbelts on school buses, and on healthy eating created public debate and enjoyed varying degrees of public support. Important areas of public policy were addressed with Measures on matters such as Mental Health provision, Local Government, and Education.

Some of these Measures were no doubt considered flawed by some and the ability of Government and the Assembly to pass clear unambiguous legislation was constrained by the then devolution

---

[21] Together with secondary legislation, including Water Environment (Controlled Activities) (Scotland) Regulations 2005 and the Water Environment (Oil Storage) (Scotland) Regulations 2006.

settlement. However, the referendum result must in part reflect a belief among the people of Wales that the legislation made by the Assembly was competent, relevant, and normal.

It is not an entirely appropriate metaphor, but if the first three Assemblies served, in the words of the former First Minister Rhodri Morgan AM, as an 'apprenticeship', the Assembly has now served its period of indenture and can now craft its own legislation unencumbered (mostly) by the need to work under the close direction of our colleagues in the Westminster parliament.

Whether this goes as far as the 'full law-making powers' claimed by many of the proponents of a 'Yes' vote is a moot point. The Assembly's powers are still characterized by specific competences rather than the more general competence that the Scottish parliament enjoys. Nevertheless, the Assembly, in law-making terms, can properly be considered a legislature in the full sense of the word and a parliament for Wales in all but name.

Welsh Assembly Measures can thus be introduced in areas of devolved competence, and those areas include key areas of environmental policy. Legislative competence may be devolved to Wales in one of two ways: either through clauses in UK Parliamentary Bills or through the Order in Council procedure provided for in the Government of Wales Act 2006. In relation to the latter, Transfer of Function Orders and Legislative Competence Orders (LCOs) are types of secondary legislation that transfer specific powers directly from the UK Parliament to the Welsh Assembly within general areas of competence. These general areas include environmental matters, as set out in Schedule 5 to the Government of Wales Act 2006: including waste (including disposal of waste into the sea), environmental pollution, and nuisances, as well as town and country planning. In light of the 2011 referendum, there will be greater freedom to legislate and no longer formal need for UK Parliamentary approval in legislating within the broad environmental policy areas set out in the Government of Wales Act.

While there is already a distinct body of Welsh environmental law and policy, mainly involving secondary legislation under UK primary acts, the above extract makes clear that this legal picture will undergo significant change in the next few years, particularly in light of the recent referendum that will increase the direct law-making powers of the National Assembly. As in the Scottish case, the WAG is currently consulting on plans for comprehensive reform of its environmental legislation,[22] again on the back of a progressive policy agenda. Further, the creation of independent regulatory institutions in Wales for administering environmental legislation is in development.[23]

Devolution in Northern Ireland has taken a different form again, reflecting the history of that region. The Northern Ireland Assembly, like the Scottish Parliament, has legislative power to regulate on (unreserved) environmental matters under the Northern Ireland Act 1998. The environmental legislative agenda in Northern Ireland has not been as ambitious in policy or institutional terms, although it has been prolific, particularly in implementing EU environmental law (and under the threat of EU infraction proceedings). As in the other regions, environmental issues are now being administered at the Northern Ireland level, and there is a dedicated Northern Ireland Environment Agency, although this is not independent of government.[24] Further, despite political resistance to prioritizing environmental protection and policy in Northern Ireland, considerable work is nonetheless

---

[22] Particularly through the introduction of a Sustainable Development Bill, which aims to put sustainable development at the heart of all Welsh governmental action (this was consulted on in 2012), and wider legislative reform is also contemplated. See the companian website for further details.

[23] Welsh Assembly Government, *A Living Wales—A New Framework for Our Environment, Our Countryside and Our Seas* <http://wales.gov.uk/topics/environmentcountryside/consmanagement/nef/currentwork/institutional/?lang=en.> accessed 4 October 2012.

[24] In 2012, a single official holds the operational post of CEO of the Environment Agency, as well as the administrative role of Under Secretary of Environmental Policy.

being done by both the Department of the Environment (Northern Ireland) and the Northern Ireland Law Commission concerning the simplification and reform of environmental legislation.

Turner's scholarship has been strickingly important in exploring the significance and complexities of these developments for understanding the administrative context of environmental law in Northern Ireland.

Sharon Turner, 'Transforming Environmental Governance in Northern Ireland. Part One: The Process of Policy Renewal' (2006) 18 JEL 55, 61–62

[...] [Devolution] also profoundly transformed the legal and political framework governing the enactment of legislation for Northern Ireland. For the first time in thirty years, DOE(NI) [Department of the Environment (Northern Ireland)] was required to engage with the time-intensive and technically demanding process of steering legislation through a normalised process of democratic control. Whereas experience of significant legislative projects is a valued core competence within the civil service in Great Britain, as a result of the policy vacuum of direct rule, an entire generation of civil servants in Northern Ireland had either very limited or no experience of developing policy and legislation—much less the highly technical and complex provisions required to transpose the regulatory regimes required by EU Directives on the environment. To compound matters, devolution on the basis of power sharing meant that Departments and their Ministers had neither the support of a political majority or that of a party whip to assist in steering legislative proposals through the Assembly. However, devolution also posed civil servants with scrutiny by and accountability to a political class that had been excluded from the development of policy and legislation for almost a generation. Not surprisingly, Members of the Local Assembly asserted their new parliamentary powers with considerable enthusiasm, but also with an equal measure of suspicion and in some cases, hostility towards civil servants who had effectively run Northern Ireland for thirty years and whom many believed would only reluctantly cede power.

It was in the context of this novel, tense and uncertain political landscape that relations between DOE(NI) and the Assembly scrutiny committee on the environment inevitably reached boiling point as local politicians were faced with the consequences of DOE(NI)'s long-standing neglect of its policy and legislative responsibilities concerning the environment.

Turner then conducts a very lengthy analysis of this tension, which not only highlights that devolution has given rise to some complex policy dynamics but that EU environmental law has also had a crucial role to play in the process of Northern Ireland devolution, as indicated already. This can also be seen in relation to Scottish devolution, highlighting how legal cultures interact with each other. The role of EU law will be considered in more detail in Section 4.

3.4 THE ENVIRONMENT AGENCY AND OTHER SPECIALIST INSTITUTIONS

The final institutions to consider as part of the English administrative landscape of environmental law are specialist agencies, often described as non-departmental public bodies (NDPBs). The two most significant of these are the Environment Agency and Natural England, but others, such as the Drinking Water Inspectorate and Marine Management Organisation, are also important to note. These agencies may take many legal forms, ranging from bodies set up under prerogative power to those that have statutory footings. The Environment Agency (under the Environment Act 1995) and Natural England (under the Natural Environment and Rural Communities Act 2006) fall into the latter category.

There has been a long history of the existence of ad hoc bodies charged with the administration of particular environmental statutes. The Alkali Inspectorate in the nineteenth century is a prominent historical example, as the key body involved in regulating early air pollution problems under a series of statutes starting with the Alkali Act 1863, and only ceasing to exist as an independent agency in 1975 (when it was transferred to the Health and Safety Executive). These institutions were often created in an expedient manner with very little thought given to creating a coherent scheme of administration. Moreover, their powers were amended over time to address new issues but not always in a comprehensive manner. The Royal Commission on Environmental Pollution, in their 1976 report on Air Pollution, highlighted this kind of ad hoc development in relation to the Alkali Inspectorate.[25] Even the Environment Agency, representing the most significant institutional reform in this area, was created by merging two different bodies—Her Majesty's Inspectorate of Pollution (into which the Alkali Inspectorate eventually evolved) and the National Rivers Authority. Likewise, Natural England was created by amalgamating three different organizations: English Nature, parts of the Countryside Agency, and parts of the Rural Development Service. The result of these mergers and forms of gradual evolution is that these agencies often involve complex and not always complementary mixtures of different institutional cultures and ideas. Indeed, each of these institutions will have their own peculiar cultures and practices, due to their historical component parts as well as their evolving overall structures.

The Environment Agency provides a good example for reflecting on these different environmental agencies. In existence since 1 April 1996, the Environment Agency administers a number of different environmental statutes, and also develops its own programme of research. The extract from the House of Commons Environment, Food and Rural Affairs Committee describes the function of the Agency.

Environment, Food and Rural Affairs Committee, *The Environment Agency*
(HC 2005–06, 780–I) paras 1–2

1. The Environment Agency is the leading public body protecting and improving the environment in England and Wales. It is an executive non-departmental public body (NDPB) which employs more than 11,000 staff: the second largest agency of its type in the world and the largest in Europe. It was created by the Environment Act 1995 and came into operation in April 1996, taking over the roles and responsibilities of the National Rivers Authority, Her Majesty's Inspectorate of Pollution and the waste regulation authorities in England and Wales. Its current remit includes:

   – preventing flooding and pollution incidents;

   – reducing industry's impacts on the environment;

   – ensuring waste produced is correctly disposed of;

   – advising on land use planning, including advice on regional planning development plans and planning applications;

   – cleaning up rivers, coastal waters and managing water resources;

   – improvement of contaminated land;

   – improving wildlife habitats;

   – improving and enhancing inland waterways and ensuring sustainable inland fisheries.

   The Agency consists of seven English regions and Environment Agency Wales. These are sub-divided into 26 areas.

---

[25] *Royal Commission on Environmental Pollution, Report, Air Pollution Control* (Cmd 6371, 1976).

2. The Agency currently has 14 board members, most of whom are appointed by the Secretary of State for Environment, Food and Rural Affairs. The Welsh Assembly Government appoints one member. The Board is directly responsible to Ministers for all aspects of its organisation and performance. The Board is accountable to Parliament through Ministers.

Thus, the Agency has a range of functions, and the relationship between them is not always an obvious one—a fact that reflects the historical merger of institutions. Despite this, the Agency's remit is significant in that its governing statute, the Environment Act 1995, gave the Agency a broad goal of 'achieving sustainable development' (s 4(1)). This type of broad aspiration (as opposed to having simply broad discretion) is not a conventional feature of UK administrative institutions and amounts to a new institutional norm. It has also given rise to controversy in its own right—particularly because the goal of sustainable development is such an unclear one, as discussed in Chapter 11—but here it is worth reflecting on the role played by this legislative ideal in informing the Environment Agency's work.

Derek Bell and Tim Gray, 'The Ambiguous Role of the Environment Agency in England and Wales' (2002) 11(3) Environmental Politics 76, 93

At the heart of these issues [criticisms of the Environment Agency] are serious ambiguities concerning the role of the Environment Agency: Is it primarily a 'champion' of sustainable development or a 'champion' of the environment? How is its general duty to promote sustainable development limited by the discharge of its day-to-day functions? What should be the Agency's role in the policy process? What should be its goals as a regulator? Until and unless these questions are answered, critics of the Environment Agency are unlikely to be silent.

As seen in Chapter 2, this type of tension is inherent in most environmental problems. These criticisms have resulted in a number of House of Commons Select Committee reports about the Agency.

Environment, Food and Rural Affairs Committee, *The Environment Agency*
(HC 2005–06, 780–I) Summary

The Environment Agency is the leading public body protecting and improving the environment in England and Wales. It is the second largest agency of its type in the world and the largest in Europe. Ten years after its creation, a review of the Agency's effectiveness and funding, and its relationships with Defra and other key bodies, is opportune.

The Agency's involvement in environmental protection and conservation has increased considerably over the past ten years. Stakeholders are concerned that the Agency is experiencing difficulties managing its wide range of responsibilities and, in particular, that it is struggling to combine its regulatory role with that of 'Champion of the Environment'. Defra should examine whether the Agency is adequately equipped for the cross-cutting environmental challenges facing it, not least its important role as environmental champion and how it balances this with its regulatory role. In particular, the Agency's capability to address the challenges that climate change poses for its areas of responsibility should be fully explored.

A strong case exists for placing more of the burden of enforcement costs onto fines, rather than charges. Fines for environmental offences are still relatively small and often do not reflect the severity of the offence. We also believe that consistency in sentencing of environmental crimes should be improved, and therefore support the Agency's proposal that a team of magistrates be trained specifically to deal with environmental cases. Defra should set out its proposals on the roles to be played by other branches of Government in devising ways in improving the system by which the courts administer environmental prosecutions.

We are extremely concerned that the Agency is experiencing difficulties recruiting specialist staff, such as flood risk engineers, hydrologists and geomorphologists. The Agency should issue a work plan with specific deadlines to set out how it aims to solve its recruitment problems, and publish details about its future graduate requirements. We welcome the Government's recent funding increases to the Agency in relation to its flood defence work. However, flooding risks will only increase in the future due to the effects of climate change. The Government should aim to increase the Agency's funding in this area to £1 billion per year in the long term.

We welcome the progress made by officials in the Agency and the Natural England Partnership in establishing a close and constructive working relationship. We are concerned, however, that tensions already exist relating to the potential use of the agri-environment budget. Defra should provide Natural England with clear guidance on using this agri-environmental funding to achieve both organisations' objectives.

Many of the suggestions here are specific to the range of regulatory tasks that the Environment Agency carries out. In particular, they reflect the significant resource needs of such an institution.

Overall, this section has shown that the role of agencies such as the Environment Agency and Natural England is yet fully to be worked out. In part, this is because there is always ambiguity over the role of administrative institutions. But it is also because there has been no real entrenched tradition of independent administrative agencies in England—they represent relatively unchartered administrative ground. This is in contrast to other jurisdictions, in particular the US, where the Environmental Protection Agency (EPA) has played the leading role in US environmental protection.

3.5 THE ACCOUNTABILITY OF INSTITUTIONS: A NOTE

All of the institutions examined in Section 3.4 are public in nature and an important 'rule of law' feature of public institutions is that they can, and should be, held to account. Indeed, much environmental law results from legal processes that call environmental decision-makers to account. In other words, there is a close interrelationship between the nature of UK environmental law and its institutional framework, in that much of that law is concerned with defining the boundaries of legitimate behaviour of decision-makers through public law mechanisms and actions. The issue of accountability will be considered in far more detail in Chapter 7 concerning public law and in Chapter 13 discussing governance—this section simply highlights in overview the numerous ways in which decision-makers can be held to account.

Fisher discusses how public decision-makers are nearly always acting in the context of a web of multiple accountabilities.

Elizabeth Fisher, 'Drowning by Numbers: Standard Setting in Risk Regulation and the Pursuit of Accountable Public Administration' (2000) 20 OJLS 109, 120–21

Risk regulators have been theoretically subject to multiple accountabilities. They are politically accountable to Parliament, financially accountable to the Treasury, legally accountable to the courts, as well as being subject to central policy and organizational direction from the Cabinet Office. Moreover, they are more generally and ephemerally accountable to the public for addressing risk problems. In practice however, there are few stringent accountability mechanisms in this area.

The constitutional convention of ministerial responsibility has been the traditional means of holding public administration to account, but in many risk controversies has been found to be lacking. In cases such as the BSE and *Salmonella* outbreaks, duties to put information before Parliament were ignored or problematic because of the difficulties inherent in scientific uncertainty. Likewise, judicial review of risk regulation standards occurs very rarely and the grounds of review are narrow and legalistic. The courts state that they cannot review questions of fact and also tend to defer to decision makers in matters of a complex and technical nature, particularly where delegated legislation is being passed. There has been a heavy reliance on public inquiries for national controversies such as the *E Coli 0157* and BSE outbreaks, but these are of a *post hoc* nature and tend to be more directed at 'dampening or dissembling public disquiet' rather than necessarily calling decision-makers to account. The same is true of parliamentary select committees.

In light of the spasmodic and deferential nature of these accountability mechanisms it has become difficult to know whether standards have been due to the conscientious and careful exercise of discretion or are a product of 'fudge and smudge, a quagmire of intellectual fuzziness....and administrative laxity'.

This Fisher extract may give the impression that accountability does not have an impact, but that is not necessarily the case.

Elizabeth Fisher, *Risk Regulation and Administrative Constitutionalism*
(Hart Publishing 2007) 73

A common perception about the BSE crisis was that decision-makers were operating in an accountability vacuum. From a strictly legal perspective, this is perhaps true—judicial review was not only deferential but there were few cases in which decisions had been challenged. The constraints of the Statutory Instruments Act 1946, the statute that regulated the passing of delegated legislation, were also minimal. Likewise, established mechanisms such as ministerial accountability and accountability to Parliamentary Select Committees, were perceived to be ineffectual. Indeed, in the early years of the BSE crisis there was little discussion about BSE in Parliament. Despite this, the threat of such mechanisms did influence decision-makers actions. Moreover, decision-makers were also being held to account in numerous other ways. As such, they were operating in a context in which they were subject to multiple accountabilities, albeit very few of them having a legal status. Departments were financially accountable to a number of different bodies, and operating under internal management mechanisms, individual appraisal systems, budgeting systems, and the Deregulation Initiative. [...] The Deregulation Initiative was particularly important in this regard as it required departments to justify their regulatory action by proving the factual basis for such regulation on the basis of cost/benefit analysis or risk assessment. One official involved in the crisis described the Initiative not as stopping regulation but requiring that it was 'tightly drawn' [...] decision-makers proving that they were only carrying out the regulatory tasks assigned to them.

What can be seen by comparing these two extracts is that the considerable non-legal aspects of UK administrative culture mean that it is very difficult to assess how accountable a decision-maker in fact is, or how accountability mechanisms shape decision-making. In particular, neat constitutional law accounts of accountability mechanisms do not tell the full picture of public decision-making—it is within the processes of administration that much holding to account of decision-makers actually takes place.

FURTHER READING AND QUESTIONS

1. Have a look at the different websites for the different governmental institutions discussed in Section 3. How easy is it to understand their roles and how they interact?

2 On the issue of the role of accountability mechanisms in action, a brilliant analysis is *The BSE Inquiry Report: Volume 15: Government and Public Administration* (the Inquiry into BSE and V-CJD: HMSO 2000).

3 For a more theoretical approach to webs of multiple accountabilities within and across institutions, and how they might promote accountability of a governance system overall, see Colin Scott, 'Accountability in the Regulatory State' (2000) 1 Journal of Law and Society 38.

4 THE IMPACT OF EU ENVIRONMENTAL LAW

This final section notes the key changes in UK environmental law that have come about because of the UK's membership of the EU. As noted in the introduction to Part II, a specific national legal culture is not hermeneutically sealed and separated from the cultures of other jurisdictions. This is particularly true in the EU context because of the close relationship between national (Member State) and EU law.

EU environmental law will be considered in more detail in Chapter 4 but this section highlights two different influences of EU environmental law on UK legal culture. First, much UK environmental law now involves the implementation of EU directives. Second, EU membership has resulted in a number of cultural changes in the administration of UK environmental law, in particular, the development of a new policy dynamic within administration. Both of these issues are considered here and it is important to remember that, while legal cultures are not operating in a vacuum, there is osmosis between cultures as well. Moreover, the implementation of directives is a key aspect of the cultural change seen in UK administration.

The first important influence of EU environmental law on UK environmental law is that much of, but by no means all, UK environmental law is now developed through the implementation of EU directives. This process of implementation can occur in a variety of ways, although a directive must be implemented into law and not just in policy. Most EU directives are either implemented into legislation or, more often, into delegated legislation.

One method of implementing a directive is by creating a new regulatory regime. An example is the UK's implementation of the Integrated Pollution Prevention and Control Directive (IPPC) 96/61/EC in England and Wales, which led to the passing of the Pollution Prevention and Control Act 1999 and the Pollution Prevention and Control (England and Wales) Regulations 2000. Thus, new statutory provisions were the key means for implementing the IPPC Directive although a system of integrated pollution control had existed under Part I of the Environmental Protection Act 1990. This framework is now being overhauled in light of the Industrial Emissions Directive (2010/75/EU).

Another, and perhaps more popular, approach has been to integrate a directive into an existing legislative and administrative scheme. Thus, for example, the Environmental Assessment Directive has been implemented as part of the English planning law regime through the passing of delegated legislation.[26]

---

[26] See Chapter 19.

Similar approaches can be seen in relation to EU Directives covering waste management (Chapter 16) and water and air quality (Chapter 15).

Either way, this process of EU implementation requires UK decision-makers to rethink their approach to environmental law. EU environmental law is not just a new set of laws but a new paradigm of legal culture and administration.

Derrick Wyatt, 'Litigating Community Environmental Law—Thoughts on the Direct Effect Doctrine' (1998) 10 JEL 9, 10

The current situation is one in which environmental law in the United Kingdom has become significantly Europeanized, not only because Directives have been transposed into national law [.... .], but because they have been transposed in such a way that the key provisions of the Directives in question have been incorporated into United Kingdom statutory provisions, or into statutory instruments. This technique minimizes the possibility of national judges interpreting statutory implementing measures in a way which differs from the underlying directive. It amounts in a very real sense to the *Europeanization* of United Kingdom environmental law.

An aspect of that Europeanization is an increased role for the courts and Kelemen, a political scientist, argues that we have seen the rise of adversarial legalism, or in other words greater reliance on more legal and court-bound approaches to implementing environmental law.

R Daniel Kelemen, 'Suing for Europe: Suing for Europe: Adversarial Legalism and European Governance' (2006) 39 Comparative Political Studies 101, 115–16

The EU's proclivity for formal laws and strict enforcement relying heavily on private parties is rooted in the EU's fragmented institutional structure. The agency problems and distrust discussed above have encouraged the drafting of laws designed to be strictly enforced by the ECJ and national courts. Recognizing the Commission's limited enforcement capacity, lawmakers, particularly those in the European Parliament, promote decentralized, private enforcement.

[...]

In addition to enforcement actions brought by the Commission, the EU is creating greater opportunities and incentives for private enforcement of environmental law. Many environmental directives create substantive and procedural rights for individuals. Although there are no comprehensive data on environmental litigation rates across the member states, EU environmental law has certainly increased opportunities for litigation before national courts. As for references to the ECJ, as of 2003, 71 preliminary ruling references for environmental cases had been sent to the ECJ. Although the pace of referrals from national courts accelerated in the late 1990s and has started to play an important role in areas such as nature conservation, the impact of the preliminary ruling procedure on environmental policy remains limited. One key reason for the infrequency of such cases is that many national legal systems restrict standing for environmental nongovernmental organizations. However, since the mid-1990s, the Commission and Parliament have been pressuring member states to harmonize their rules on access of private parties to national courts. In 1998, member states and the EU itself signed the UN Aarhus Convention, which includes commitments concerning access to justice in environmental policy making. The Commission and member state environmental inspectorates have interpreted them to demand that environmental NGOs have the opportunity to challenge administrative decisions.

Kelemen's point is buttressed by the fact that much of the case law in this book concerns the implementation of EU law. The Aarhus Convention will be discussed in Chapters 7 and 10.

The final point to note about the impact of EU environmental law upon UK legal culture concerns its effect on UK administration. It has generally been recognized that over the last three decades there has been a form of Europeanization of UK administration. Jordan explains this development in more nuanced terms, considering some of the impacts of EU environmental law on British environmental policy.

Andrew Jordan, *The Europeanisation of British Environmental Policy: A Departmental Perspective* (Palgrave Macmillan 2002) 202–03

European integration challenges national administrative systems because most of them were designed at a time when the political centre of gravity lay inside independent sovereign states. Some analysts claim that Whitehall has responded relatively smoothly to the challenges of EU membership. For instance, Bulmer and Burch measured Europeanization on four institutional dimensions: formal (eg the creation of new committees and coordination units); procedural (eg rules and procedures governing spending and information sharing); advisory (eg Cabinet Office negotiating guidelines); and cultural (eg the duty to inform cognate Whitehall departments). They detect substantial but gradual change along all four dimensions, which has been more or less wholly in keeping with British traditions. For example, there are new coordination networks linking departments, new European coordination offices or committees within each department, a proliferation of manuals and advisory booklets on how to negotiate in Europe, and new rules and institutional mechanisms for ironing out conflict between departments. However, these do not constitute a wholesale *transformation* of the state; rather, they reflect incremental alterations to well entrenched procedures and practices.

An alternative perspective [...] suggests that Europeanization and integration have fundamentally and irrevocably transformed the state through a series of complex and long-running policy feedbacks. These have brought national and supranational actors closer together and promoted common beliefs and identities. On this view, the co-evolving processes of integration and Europeanization have not only reshaped the administrative procedures and conventions of departmental life, but the very preferences and identities of its constituent parts (ie departments).

All of this highlights that the relationship between EU environmental law and UK environmental law entails not simply the introduction of new laws or new principles—rather, it represents a profound cultural shift. The nature of that shift will be seen in many chapters of this book.

FURTHER READING AND QUESTIONS

1. What are the advantages and disadvantages of the rise in adversarial legalism that Kelemen highlights? Further reading on the issue can be found in Robert A Kagan, *Adversarial Legalism: The American Way of Law* (Harvard University Press 2003); Alec Stone Sweet, *The Judicial Construction of Europe* (OUP 2004); Dan Kelemen, *Eurolegalism: The Transformation of Law and Regulation in the European Union* (Harvard UP 2011).

---

5 CONCLUSION

The analysis in this chapter has given an introductory overview of UK legal culture as it relates to environmental law. In particular, it has highlighted four points:

- Environmental thought and environmental law both have long histories and deep theoretical and socio-political foundations in the UK.

- Most UK environmental law is public law, which entrusts considerable discretion to administrative bodies, including those responsible for enforcing environmental law.

- There is a wide range of administrative institutions involved in UK environmental law, which operate at central, regional, and local levels. Much of environmental law is concerned with holding these institutions to account.

- Membership of the EU is having a profound effect on the law and institutions involved in UK environmental law.

These issues are not merely of passing academic interest. This chapter has shown that they are of serious practical significance for the way in which environmental law is studied and practiced. This will be seen in each chapter of this book, and the themes of this chapter should be kept in mind whenever you think that environmental law is appearing disjointed, deficient in case law, heavy on EU Directives, all about public law rather than environmental matters, or too buried in obscure sounding delegated legislation. Understanding the legal culture in which this body of UK law is operating is vital in order to appreciate what it is that constitutes UK environmental law and why it looks and operates the way it does.

4

EUROPEAN UNION
ENVIRONMENTAL LAW

The important role that the EU plays in environmental law cannot be overstated. In the last forty years, the EU institutions and Member States have formulated and built a considerable body of environmental law and policy, required its implementation, and enforced it. The Court of Justice of the European Union (CJEU) and national courts have interpreted and adjudicated upon this body of law, and national authorities have been involved in its implementation and enforcement. Much of the substance of environmental law in the UK, as well as the rights and remedies available to aggrieved individuals, are now derived from EU environmental law. Many of the key political debates over environmental policy and specific environmental issues also have important EU dimensions. Moreover, other aspects of EU law affect the ability of Member States to take action on their own in relation to environmental protection. This is seen most obviously in the internal market law relating to the free movement of goods.[1] In light of the integral role for EU law in UK and English environmental law, understanding the importance of EU law in this context does not simply involve knowing a few environmental Directives but requires understanding more deeply EU legal and decision-making processes and the different actors involved in them. At the same time, the relationship between EU law and environmental law should not be understood as only having implications for environmental law. The formulation, implementation, and enforcement of national environmental law have also had a powerful impact upon the EU and how it, and its law, is understood.

This chapter is an introduction to some of the major themes in EU environmental law. It is not a substitute for an EU law textbook (nor a good EU environmental law textbook for that matter) and it is expected that a reader has a good basic knowledge of EU law. The first section outlines aspects of EU legal culture and considers different approaches to defining EU environmental law. Sections 3, 4, 5, and 6 examine four major themes of EU environmental law. The first theme is *competence* (including the legal principle of subsidiarity), which concerns the nature of the EU's authority to act in relation to environmental matters. The second theme is *implementation and enforcement*. EU environmental law, compared with other areas of EU law, has a poor record on both of these counts. The third theme is the ability of Member States to take *unilateral environmental protection action*. Such national measures are restricted by a number of articles of the EU Treaties and by the case law of the CJEU. The final theme is the *legitimacy and accountability of EU governance*. An examination of these four themes does not provide an exhaustive account of EU environmental law, but it does highlight some of the major features of EU environmental law that will be encountered in this textbook and in the practise and study of environmental law.

---

[1] Articles 34–36 TFEU.

In navigating this chapter, and in dealing with EU environmental law issues generally, it is useful to have a copy of the Treaty of the European Union (TEU) and the Treaty on the Functioning of the European Union (TFEU) to hand as a reference. These can be found at <http://eur-lex.europa.eu/en/treaties/index.htm>. It should be remembered that these Treaties came into force in 2009 and before then was the Treaty of the European Community (the Treaty of Rome) that came into force in 1958 and the Treaty of the European Union that came into force in 1993. Each of these original Treaties has undergone revision over time. In particular, they were renumbered by the Treaty of Amsterdam 1997 (which entered into force 1999), and the structure of the Treaties (and the EU) was overhauled and they were again renumbered by the Treaty of Lisbon in 2009. A key structural change to keep in mind is the Lisbon Treaty's establishment of an integrated 'European Union'; prior to 2010, the EU had been comprised of three 'pillars' of competence and activity, one of which—the European Community—was the main source of what was then Community law relating to the environment. Note also that, while there have been some substantial changes with successive Treaty revisions, much has also stayed the same. The key point is that, in reading cases and literature on EU environmental law, you need to keep your Treaty numbering wits about you—many of these were written at times when different Treaty articles and numbering applied. Our policy throughout the book is to use the new (post-Lisbon) Treaty numbering and the label 'EU' where we can, but we have not edited extracts to include new Treaty article numbering and you will also see references to the 'EC' or European Community. However, we do highlight where there have been significant changes in the wording of relevant Treaty articles.

1 SOME COMMENTS ON EUROPEAN UNION LEGAL CULTURE

While this chapter is not a substitute for either an EU law textbook or an EU environmental law textbook, this section highlights some key features of the EU legal order. As seen in Chapter 3, having insight into the legal culture within which a body of environmental law operates helps to make sense of that body of law. In relation to the EU, this is no mean feat since its legal culture is *sui generis, dynamic and informed by the national legal cultures of a range of different Member States.*

The formal starting point of the EU is the Treaty of Rome, which entered into force in 1958 and which created the European Economic Community (EEC) amongst the six founding Member States, not at that time including the UK.[2] In general terms, the Treaty of Rome set in train two different legal processes. First, it began a process of negative harmonization by which Member States were bound by common rules that prevented them from putting in place barriers between each other, for example, Article 34 TFEU's requirement of the free movement of goods, (see Section 5). The second process was positive harmonization. Member States, acting through the Commission and Council (and later the Parliament), created common European rules in the form of Directives, Regulations, and decisions (defined in Article 288 TFEU) in order to establish a common internal market and other related EU policies. Positive and negative harmonization are not the only legal activities of the EU, particularly today, but they are processes that are significant in EU environmental law.

The original Treaty of Rome is often understood as having a singular aim of creating the 'common market' (Articles 2 and 3 of that Treaty), but a singular common market focus ignores the deeper aspirations behind the EEC. Those aspirations can be seen in Preambles 1 to 3 of the Treaty of Rome, now found in the Preamble to the TFEU:

---

[2] The UK acceded to the EEC in 1973.

> DETERMINED to lay the foundations of an ever closer union among the peoples of Europe,
>
> RESOLVED to ensure the economic and social progress of their States by common action to eliminate the barriers which divide Europe,
>
> AFFIRMING as the essential objective of their efforts the constant improvements of the living and working conditions of their peoples

Thus, even in 1958, the Treaty contained an explicit aim of the 'constant improvements of the living [...] conditions' of the peoples of Europe and thus, while there was no environmental competence in the Treaty at that time, it is also incorrect to say that the original Treaty of Rome was purely about economic integration. The desire from the outset to create 'an ever closer union among the *peoples* of Europe' also makes clear that European integration has been a dynamic process with no obvious endpoint and a process in which diversity is recognized.

The dynamic nature of the EU can be seen in the ongoing processes of Treaty amendment since 1958, which have involved five milestones of Treaty reform. First, the Single European Act (SEA) in 1987, introduced among other things, qualified majority voting in the European Council. Second, key reforms of the Maastricht Treaty in 1993 included establishing the EU with a three pillar structure and introducing the concepts of EU citizenship and attributed competence. Third, the Amsterdam Treaty in 1999 consolidated the EU on a more democratic basis and also consolidated the Treaty administratively by renumbering it. Fourth, the Nice Treaty in 2003 prepared the EU for enlargement and introduced the accompanying, non-legally binding EU Charter of Fundamental Rights (along with some more Treaty renumbering). Finally, 2005 saw the failure of the Draft Constitutional Treaty and its renegotiation as the Lisbon Treaty in 2007, which then came into force in 2009. The Lisbon Treaty again fundamentally restructured the Treaties and their numbering, and collapsed the tri-pillar structure of the EU, consolidating its policies and competences into a united structure, in formal and institutional terms. These Treaty changes were all iterative but not linear in their development of EU law. Thus, a simplistic understanding of the history of the EU legal order, particularly one which sees environmental policy simply inserted as a matter for EU concern at a certain point along its historical Treaty development and expansion into more policy areas (usually identified as the SEA with its inclusion of an explicit environmental head of EEC competence), should be avoided.

Moreover, as a result of this incremental and negotiated history, the EU has a *sui generis* legal order that defies easy categorization. Thus, the European Court of Justice (ECJ) (now CJEU) in its early case law stated that the Community amounted to a 'new legal order',[3] and a 'new legal system'.[4] MacCormick assesses the consequences of this legal development.

Neil MacCormick, *Questioning Sovereignty* (OUP 1999) 131–32

[S]ince at least 1964 it has been the doctrine of the European Court of Justice that the Community (as it now is) constitutes a new legal order, neither a subordinate part of the laws of the member states nor simply a sub-system of International law. From the point of view of a soundly pluralistic theory of law as institutional normative order, there is no difficulty about accepting this self-characterization of Community law as a distinct legal order. It owes its origin, certainly, to treaties binding under general International law. Further, from the point of view of member-state legal systems, the ground of validity of provisions of Community law is located within the state-system. Community law's validity as a

---

[3] Case 26/62 *NV Algemene Transport en Expeditie Onderneming van Gend en Loos v Netherlands Inland Revenue Administration* [1963] ECR 1, 12.

[4] Case 6/64 *Costa v ENEL* [1964] ECR 585, 593.

high level source of law is traceable to the acts of ratification or adoption of foundational or amending treaties by appropriate modes of decision-making. The appropriateness to this end of a mode of
decision-making is determined by the state constitution in question. But there has been an institutionalization of a legal order under the foundation treaties and the treaty amendments have elaborated this,
always preserving the *acquis communautaire*. There are now long-established Community organs for
law-making, for executive action, and for judicial law-application. That these have operated in a largely
efficacious way over a substantial period of time makes it both proper and necessary to recognize that
here we have a full-blown instance of an institutional normative order, and thus to confirm the Court's
representation of it as a distinct legal order.

Within that legal order and from the point of view of Community organs and persons working within
Community law, the criteria for recognition of the validity of Community legal provisions are now internal to this legal system. [...] As a system, it differentiates itself from other systems by whose distinct
criteria of validity Community legal provisions are also valid and applicable. This is the case within
the legal orders of member states, each of whose organs acknowledge Community provisions as
valid and applicable in relevant situations, in a manner coordinated with, and justifiable by, reference
to the member state's own internal criteria of validity. 'Community-validity' is a relevant fact when it
comes to assessing member-state validity. 'Member-state validity' is a relevant fact for some purposes
of Community law. The situation is one of differentiation of systems subject to mutual overlap and
interaction.

This unique and interactive legal situation has led many legal scholars to talk of the role of pluralism
in EU legal orders. EU pluralism can take many legal and constitutional forms and can be understood
in different ways, as Krisch notes.

Nico Krisch, *Beyond Constitutionalism: The Pluralist Structure of Postnational Law* (OUP 2010) 71

[P]luralism has many meanings, and it can serve as a description of the shape and diversity of society,
of substantive commitments in matters of rights or institutions, or of the structure of a polity's institutions. It is the latter meaning that interests me most, as it operates on the same (structural) level as
constitutionalism and may therefore provide a true alternative. Yet even here, the usage of pluralism
varies widely. The differences could be seen as a matter of degree—as between 'soft' and 'hard',
'weak' or 'strong', or 'moderate' and 'radical' pluralism. Analytically, though, they are better captured as
differences in kind, as between what maybe termed 'institutional' and 'systemic' pluralism.

A focus on pluralism thus highlights many types of diverse legal interaction in the EU. In relation
to EU environmental law, pluralism is a constant implicit refrain, in legal commentary and disputes
concerning subsidiarity, governance, enforcement, competence, public participation, or the ability of
Member States to take unilateral action. Consequences and tensions of legal pluralism can be seen in
Case C-459/03 *Commission v Ireland*, discussed in the introduction to Part II. In that case, we saw the
tension between Ireland wanting to resolve an environmental dispute with the UK in an international
tribunal and Ireland's duty under the TEC to use Union mechanisms for such dispute resolution.

In determining the nature of the EU legal order, and its relationship with Member State legal
orders, it is important to consider not only legal doctrines of EU supremacy and national sovereignty, but also the obligation of legal cooperation on Member States now set out in Article 4(3) TEU.
It states:

Article 4(3) TEU

Pursuant to the principle of sincere cooperation, the Union and the Member States shall, in full mutual respect, assist each other in carrying out tasks which flow from the Treaties.

The Member States shall take any appropriate measure, general or particular, to ensure fulfilment of the obligations arising out of the Treaties or resulting from the acts of the institutions of the Union.

The Member States shall facilitate the achievement of the Union's tasks and refrain from any measure which could jeopardise the attainment of the Union's objectives.

This wording was introduced in the Lisbon Treaty although a related obligation was included previously in Article 10 TEC.[5] This duty reflects a key constitutional norm of the EU legal order and has a profoundly important role to play in resolving EU environmental law disputes.

MacCormick and Krisch, in these extracts, are discussing EU legal culture at a level of considerable theoretical abstraction. However, two other legal mechanisms that operate in EU law—preliminary references (Art 267 TFEU) and direct effect—have developed as key defining aspects of the EU legal order. Both of these mechanisms have bound national legal systems and EU legal order together and have been powerful tools in the process of EU legal integration. Both concepts will be well known to those studying EU law, but it is worth reflecting on their significance as core elements of the EU legal framework, which are also important in EU environmental law. The late Judge Mancini, a former judge of the ECJ, has described the importance of the preliminary reference procedure and the doctrine of direct effect in the following way (writing at the time of the European Community).

GF Mancini, *Democracy and Constitutionalism in the European Union*
(Hart Publishing 2000) 41–43

Without direct effect, we would have a very different Community today, a more obscure, more remote Community barely distinguishable from so many other international organizations whose existence passes unnoticed by ordinary citizens. As a result of *Van Gend en Loos*, the unique feature of Community law is its ability to impinge directly on the lives of individuals, who are declared to be the 'subjects' of the new legal order, entitled as such to invoke rights 'which become part of their legal heritage'. The effect of *Van Gend en Loos* was to take Community law out of the hands of politicians and bureaucrats and to give it to the people. Of all the Court's democratizing achievements none can rank so highly in practical terms [...]

The involvement of Europe's citizens in the enforcement of Community law, as a result of the doctrine of direct effect, is, as we have said, a dramatically important democratizing factor; but it could not have borne full fruit if the reference procedure under Article 177 [now Art 267 TFEU] had not been transformed in the course of the years into the quasi-federal instrument for reviewing the compatibility of national laws with Community law [...]

The consequence is a virtuous circle. More and more Europeans are aware that a law higher than the statutes enacted by their Parliaments bestows upon them rights which are, in the last analysis, protected by the body interpreting that law. This growing awareness increases the visibility of the Court (according to a Community-wide survey of 1988, the latter was perceived as a very important policy-making institution by 18 per cent of respondents). Visibility in turn, is the first precondition of legitimacy, at least for judicial organs; and the legitimacy thus acquired by the Court reverberates on the

---

[5] TEC (Treaty establishing the European Community—the amended Treaty of Rome, post-Maastricht Treaty).

law which the Court administers and enlarges the expectations which ordinary people found on its provisions. Whether these expectations coincide with a sense of common citizenship is doubtful; but they are certainly a prelude to it and, as is evidenced by the constant growth in the number of references, they come ever closer to the real thing.

Some scholars might quibble with the use of the word (and idea of) 'federalism' but Mancini is really highlighting three important points. First, direct effect and preliminary references are the primary means of making EU law effective and thus promoting integration. Second, in doing so, they are also forms of 'democratization', in that they empower individuals to act and assert rights within the EU legal order. We will see the significance of this throughout the book as a considerable number of UK environmental law cases involve direct effect. Third, they are also mechanisms that promote the legalization of disputes. Indeed, Kelemen (Section 4 of Chapter 5) has suggested that EU integration has given rise to 'adversarial legalism' as a key feature of EU law.[6] Finally, do note that the concept of direct effect and the preliminary reference mechanism are both complex creatures of EU law. If your knowledge of them is particularly hazy then do consult a good EU law textbook before moving on.

FURTHER READING AND QUESTIONS

1. For a good EU law textbook, see Steven Weatherill, *EU Law: Cases and Materials* (10th edn, OUP 2012); Paul Craig and Gráinne de Búrca, *EU Law: Text, Cases, and Materials* (5th edn, OUP 2011); and the list at the end of this chapter.

2. Why do you think 'pluralism' as discussed above might be relevant to environmental law? Consider the issues raised in Chapter 2, particularly in relation to the role of the state in environmental law.

2 EU ENVIRONMENTAL LAW: A RANGE OF DEFINITIONS

Broadly speaking, we can define EU environmental law as the body of EU law concerned with environmental problems. However, as we saw in Chapter 1, beyond this simple definition, there are three ways in which environmental law can be defined—descriptively, purposively, or as a body of jurisprudence. This section adopts this typology to present an overview of the many dimensions of EU environmental law.

2.1 A DESCRIPTIVE DEFINITION

A simple descriptive definition of EU environmental law would begin and end with the definition in the introduction to this section. A significant bulk of EU environmental law is a product of positive harmonization and includes those Regulations, Directives, decisions, and policies that have been passed by Union institutions and which relate to, or affect, environmental problems. Yet negative harmonization—in the form of legal restrictions placed on Member States in adopting unilateral environmental protection measures—also plays an important role in EU environmental law. EU environmental law is also extensive—it touches upon nearly all environmental problems, including

---

[6] R Daniel Kelemen, 'Suing for Europe: Adversarial Legalism and European Governance' (2006) 39 Comp Pol Stud 101.

biodiversity, pollution control, waste, climate change, and land management. With that said, a considerable bulk of the subject is comprised of product and process standards, which require considerable administration and discretionary decision-making at the national level.

In the late 1960s a number of Directives were passed which although they were primarily concerned with harmonizing national product rules also regulated environmental quality.[7] It was not until the early 1970s that there was an explicit EU environmental policy in the form of the First Action Programme on the Environment.[8] Further action programmes, policies, and Directives followed.[9] Some of these Directives were still concerned with market harmonization but others had more explicit environmental protection aims even though there was nothing in the Treaty that gave the Union institutions competence. The legitimacy concerns that this raised was offset by the fact that all Union measures required unanimous voting to pass.

The SEA, signed in 1986 and in force in 1987, introduced a new environmental title (then Articles 130r–t and now Articles 191–193 TFEU), giving the EU explicit competence to legislate with respect to environmental matters. Since 1987, the Treaty has been amended to strengthen further its obligations in relation to environmental protection. These provisions will be discussed here. In terms of the EU institutional landscape, an Environment Directorate-General of the Commission (originally DG XI) was created in 1973, and it now has just over 500 staff, a considerably lower number than in any national environmental administration. The development of new environmental protection institutions at the Union level is limited by the Treaty,[10] and by CJEU case law that restricts delegation of power.[11] However, this has not stopped the creation of a new Directorate-General for Climate Action (established February 2010) and other new EU environmental bodies. The information-gathering European Environment Agency became operational in 1993, and there is a host of other committees and agencies involved in formulating and implementing EU environmental law—from the European Food Safety Authority (EFSA) to the European IPPC (Integrated Pollution Prevention and Control) Bureau in Seville. There are also various transnational governance networks, such as the European Union Network for the Implementation and Enforcement of Environmental Law (IMPEL), which is an informal network of environmental authorities of EU Member States, accession and candidate countries as well as EEA countries.

In recent years, there has been a diversification of regulatory strategies and EU environmental law can no longer simply be understood as being contained in command-and-control legislative instruments. As will be seen, there has been a greater push towards more flexible and self-regulatory schemes for governing environmental problems, as well as an interest in regulatory instruments that work with the market. Likewise, the EU has produced a considerable amount of documentation regarding environmental policy, including Action Programmes, White Papers, Strategies, and Commission Communications. None of this is strictly legally binding but it frames EU environmental law in a very powerful way, in setting out key policy ideas, and shaping its legal direction.[12]

The danger with the discussion so far is that it gives the impression that EU environmental law is just a collection of rules and that its evolution has simply been a process of adding new rules or changing the nature of those rules. Krämer, however, highlights that the evolution of the subject has also involved significant constitutional and institutional development.

---

[7] For a history see Albert Weale and others, *Environmental Governance in Europe* (OUP 1999) chs 1 and 13; John McCormick, *Environmental Policy in the European Union* (Palgrave 2001).

[8] Ibid.   [9] Ibid.   [10] Article 13 TEU.

[11] Case 9/56 *Meroni v ECSC High Authority* [1957-8] ECR 133.   [12] See Chapter 11.

Ludwig Krämer, 'Thirty Years of EC Environmental Law: Perspectives and Prospectives' (2002) 2 YEEL 155, 180

Environmental law has reached constitutional status in the EU. In numerous Member States, there now exist express constitutional provisions pertaining to the constitution which require the protection of the environment. This constitutional development has occurred over the last thirty years, reached the EU in 1987, and continues to influence constitutional developments in Central and Eastern Europe. The positioning of environmental needs at a level equal to human rights or social rights is important. It conveys the message to all stakeholders, including citizens, that the need to protect, preserve, and improve the quality of the environment is of fundamental importance, vital for the state and for society as a whole.

Environmental law in the EU has thus led to the emergence of administrative infrastructures in the Member States. Over the past thirty years, progressively, environmental bureaucracies were set up at Community, state, regional, and local level. Overall, it seems fair to say that environmental administration, policy, and law is most structured, developed, and sophisticated, where economic performance is highest.

Environmental law has now come to regulate all aspects of the environment, from the more classical areas such as water, air, products, noise, nature, and waste, to more intricate areas such as town and country planning, climate change, transport and energy law. Again, the number, substance, and intensity of regulation varies, and the evolution of environmental law, including the 'conquest' of new areas, has not yet come to a halt.

Krämer's analysis is a reminder that a descriptive definition is never a straightforward or complete one, and there are many different ways in which a subject can be described. He is not simply describing EU environmental law as a set of rules, rather he also focuses on how EU environmental law has 'permeated' public and private institutions within society such as universities, environmental organizations, and courts. The multitude of actors involved in EU environmental law is described further by Chalmers.

Damian Chalmers, 'Inhabitants in EC Environmental Law' in Paul P Craig and Gráinne de Búrca (eds), *The Evolution of EU Law* (1st edn, OUP 1999) 653, 681–82

The development of judicially enforceable norms; the establishment of formal, horizontal structures of communication between the national administrations of Member States, between national administrations and private parties, and between private parties; the administration and implementation of EC environmental policies or policies into which EC environmental considerations have been integrated have all resulted in EC environmental law being used in a multiplying number of arenas. A variety of examples come to mind. NGOs have sought to use the EC Courts to annul Community policies and acts of the EC institutions. They have also sought to use the Court and, with more success, the Ombudsman to challenge national policies. Both industry and NGOs are increasingly using national courts to pursue their own interests. Environmental norms are increasingly having to be administered by a large number of ministries or state agencies. Local authorities are having to consider questions of EC environmental law in the exercise of their duties, *inter alia* in the fields of planning, air pollution, and waste. Private parties are increasingly using EC environmental law to gain voice in these proceedings. It is claimed by one eminent practising lawyer that commercial transactions are increasingly having to be shaped around EC environmental norms. The wider diversity of venues within which there is an interest in EC environmental law is likely to be the central influence on the field in the years to come, and conclusions can only be drawn tentatively.

Chalmers was writing over a decade ago but his description is still apt. An added complexity to this, furthering the permeation of EU environmental law norms throughout multiple legal and administrative arenas, is due to the often blurred line between environmental protection and public health protection. This is seen particularly in relation to issues such as genetically modified organisms and chemicals. Likewise, EU environmental principles such as the precautionary principle, while originally only operating in relation to the environment (due to its articulation in Article 191(2) TFEU), now also operate in relation to public health as well.[13] Many 'environmental' cases are thus often public health cases, so that the definition of 'EU environmental law' covers a broad range of subjects and policy areas (see Chapter 11), in descriptive terms. This is further reinforced by the Treaty's integration principle (Article 11 TFEU), which requires environmental protection considerations to be integrated into all EU policy areas.

2.2 A PURPOSIVE DEFINITION

Defining EU environmental law in purposive terms reveals that, broadly speaking, EU environmental law might be seen to serve two different functions—market integration and the fulfilling of a political desire to have an explicit and progressive EU environmental policy. In relation to market integration, as already seen in Section 2.1, the original purpose of the EEC was the creation and maintenance of a common market among its Member States. The first 'environmental' directives were product standards passed under what was then Article 100 TEC.[14] This is not to say that such measures did not have an environmental protection aspect, but their primary rationale was enabling the common market.

Albert Weale and others, *Environmental Governance in Europe* (OUP 1999) 30–31

The creation of the single market required policy-makers to pay attention to environmental issues because measures of environmental protection, either in the form of administrative regulation or by means of economic instruments, often threatened the functioning of the market. However, since any set of markets can give rise to market failures, including pollution externalities, the creation of the single market also had implications for policies of environmental protection. Hence, just as policies of environmental protection inevitably had implications for the single market, so the creation of the single market had implications for policies of environmental protection.

Moreover, despite the inclusion of an environmental title in the Treaty in 1987, the view that environmental law should aid, or at least complement, market integration has remained and is reflected in action programmes,[15] policies,[16] and legislative measures.[17] One of the most significant

---

[13] For example, Case T-74/00 *Artegodan GmbH v Commission* [2002] ECR II-4965. See Chapter 11.

[14] For example, Council Directive 70/157/EEC of 6 February 1970 on the approximation of the laws of the Member States relating to the permissible sound level and the exhaust system of motor vehicles [1970] OJ Spec Ed 111. Note the Lisbon Treaty removed reference to the 'common market'.

[15] Decision No 1600/2002/EC of the European Parliament and of the Council of 22 July 2002 laying down the Sixth Community Environment Action Programme [2002] OJ L 242/1.

[16] Regulation (EC) No 761/2001 of the European parliament and of the council of 19 March 2001 allowing voluntary participation by organizations in a Community eco-management and audit scheme (EMAS) [2001] OJ L114/1, reflecting a policy that incentivizes private market actors to develop self-regulatory environmental management schemes.

[17] Directive 2003/87/EC of the European Parliament and of the Council of 13 October 2003 establishing a scheme for greenhouse gas emission allowance trading within the Community and amending Council Directive 96/61/EC [2003] OJ L275/32 (as amended).

examples of this is the EU chemicals regime—REACH (Registration, Evaluation, Authorisation and Restriction of Chemical Substances)[18]—adopting a policy that is as much about competitive markets as it is about environmental and public health protection.[19] In other words, within the EU, one of the major justifications for environmental law and regulation is the economic advantages it will bring. This way of thinking about environmental issues is sometimes described as 'ecological modernization'.[20]

The second reason for the growth of EU environmental law (and its second purpose) derives from the explicit decision of Member States in the early 1970s to develop an EEC environmental policy. They did so in an era of increasing international concern about environmental protection. At the 1972 Paris Summit between the Heads of Member States—a meeting of the European Council—the importance of environmental protection was declared, leading to the publication of the First Community Environmental Action Programme (EAP) the following year.

Declaration of the Council of the European Communities and of the representatives of the Governments of the Member States meeting in the Council of 22 November 1973 on the programme of action of the European Communities on the environment OJ 1973 C112/1, 5

PART I – OBJECTIVES AND PRINCIPLES OF A COMMUNITY ENVIRONMENT POLICY AND GENERAL DESCRIPTION OF THE ACTION TO BE TAKEN AT COMMUNITY LEVEL DURING THE NEXT TWO YEARS

INTRODUCTION

Among the other objectives set out in the preamble to the Treaty establishing the European Economic Community, the signatories affirmed as goals 'the constant improvement of the living and working conditions of their peoples' and 'the harmonious development of their economies'.

In Article 2 of the Treaty, the following are included in the statement of the task assigned to the Community: to promote throughout the Community a harmonious development of economic activities, a continuous and balanced expansion, an accelerated raising of the standard of living and closer relations between the States belonging to it.

When they met in Paris on 19 to 20 October 1972, the Heads of State or Government of the Member States declared that 'economic expansion is not an end in itself: its first aim should be to enable disparities in living conditions to be reduced. It must take place with the participation of all the social partners. It should result in an improvement in the quality of life as well as in standards of living. As befits the genius of Europe, particular attention will be given to intangible values and to protecting the environment so that progress may really be put at the service of mankind'.

This readiness to ensure that the Communities direct their activities towards the improvement not only of the standard of living but of living conditions and the quality of life is expressed still more precisely in point 8 of the final Declaration of the Paris Summit Conference: 'the Heads of State or

---

[18] Regulation (EC) No 1907/2006 of the European Parliament and of the Council of 18 December 2006 concerning the Registration, Evaluation, Authorisation and Restriction of Chemicals (REACH), establishing a European Chemicals Agency, amending Directive 1999/45/EC and repealing Council Regulation (EEC) No 793/93 and Commission Regulation (EC) No 1488/94 as well as Council Directive 76/769/EEC and Commission Directives 91/155/EEC, 93/67/EEC, 93/105/EC and 2000/21/EC [2006] OJ L 396/1.

[19] Elizabeth Fisher, 'The "Perfect Storm" of REACH: Charting Regulatory Controversy in the Age of Information, Sustainable Development, and Globalization' (2008) 11 J of Risk Research 54.

[20] Albert Weale, 'Ecological Modernisation and the Integration of European Environmental Policy', in Duncan Liefferink, Philip Lowe and Arthur Mol (eds), *European Integration and Environmental Policy* (Belhaven Press 1993).

of Government emphasised the importance of a Community environmental policy. To this end they invited the Community institutions to establish before 31 July 1973, a programme of action accompanied by a precise timetable'.

This programme of action has been established in response to this invitation. It also takes into account the results of the Conference of the Ministers responsible for environmental questions held in Bonn on 31 October 1972, together with the memoranda and documents forwarded by the Member States and the detailed comparison of the points of view of the Commission and the representatives of the Member States on the Commission's communication forwarded to the Council on 24 March 1972. It also takes into account the opinions expressed by the European Parliament, the Economic and Social Committee and the employers' and workers' organizations.

TITLE – OBJECTIVES OF COMMUNITY ENVIRONMENT POLICY

The aim of a Community environment policy is to improve the setting and quality of life, and the surroundings and living conditions of the peoples of the Community. It must help to bring expansion into the service of man by procuring for him an environment providing the best conditions of life, and reconcile this expansion with the increasingly imperative need to preserve the natural environment.

It should:

- prevent, reduce and as far as possible eliminate pollution and nuisances,
- maintain a satisfactory ecological balance and ensure the protection of the biosphere,
- ensure the sound management of and avoid any exploitation of resources or of nature which cause significant damage to the ecological balance,
- guide development in accordance with quality requirements, especially by improving working conditions and the settings of life,
- ensure that more account is taken of environmental aspects in town planning and land use,
- seek common solutions to environment problems with States outside the Community, particularly in international organizations.

A number of reasons can be identified as to why Member States supported the development of an EEC environmental policy, including the transboundary nature of environmental problems; the efficiency and effectiveness of Member States taking action at the Community level; its development as a by-product of international environmental politics;[21] and/or the growing concerns at all levels with environmental ethics and democracy. All these justifications for developing EU environmental law are independent of the common market. This independent rationale was confirmed by Treaty amendments enabling and embedding EU environmental action, as discussed further. Moreover, the freestanding importance of EEC environmental law was recognized by the ECJ in 1985, when the Court described environmental protection as an 'essential objective of the Community', leading to significant case law developments that allowed exceptions from internal market rules.[22] A number of further EU policy developments have entrenched the importance of environmental protection in its own right. These include the elaboration of policies such as the precautionary principle,[23] and the signing up to international environmental agreements,

---

[21] Stockholm 1972 Declaration of the United Nations Conference on the Human Environment.

[22] Case C-240/83 *Procureur de la République v Association de défense des brûleurs d'huiles usagées (ADBHU)* [1985] ECR 531; Case 302/86 *Commission v Denmark* [1988] ECR 4067.

[23] Commission, 'Communication from the Commission on the Precautionary Principle', COM (2000) 1 final. See further Chapter 11.

such as the Aarhus Convention on Access to Information, Public Participation in Decision-Making, and Access to Justice in Environmental Matters,[24] often in 'mixed agreements' with Member States also signing international environmental treaties concurrently.[25]

Observing EU environmental law through a purposive lens brings into sharp perspective a curious disconnection that lies at the heart of the subject. Both purposes—promoting the common market and building an environmental protection policy—often operate simultaneously but not always in tandem. Thus, in the 1970s, while market integration was used (instrumentally) as the legal justification for introducing some environmental protection Directives, the content of such Directives was directly concerned with environmental quality.[26] Likewise, the incidental power of the EU (then Article 235 TEC now Article 352 TFEU amended) was used as a basis for environmentally ambitious Directives such as the Wild Birds Directive.[27] In contrast, by the 1990s, the Treaty did include an environmental protection-focused head of competence, but EU regulatory strategies were far more directed at market efficiency.[28]

Sustainable development is perhaps one policy area where these two purposes combine or overlap.[29] It offers a particularly attractive policy platform in the EU setting, since sustainable development can act as a conceptual umbrella for the twin purposes of EU environmental law. Since the Treaty of Amsterdam, reference to sustainable development has been included in the Treaties.[30] It has also been an explicit and increasingly prominent aspect of EAPs, since the Fifth Environmental Action Programme in 1992. In 2001, the Presidency of the European Council reached the following conclusions in relation to sustainable development.

Presidency Conclusions, Göteborg European Council, 15–16 June 2001, SN 200/1/01 REV 1

19. Sustainable development – to meet the needs of the present generation without compromising those of future generations – is a fundamental objective under the Treaties. That requires dealing with economic, social and environmental policies in a mutually reinforcing way. Failure to reverse trends that threaten future quality of life will steeply increase the costs to society or make those trends irreversible. The European Council welcomes the submission of the Commission's communication on sustainable development which includes important proposals for curbing such trends.

20. The European Council agrees a strategy for sustainable development which completes the Union's political commitment to economic and social renewal, adds a third, environmental dimension to the Lisbon strategy and establishes a new approach to policy making. The arrangements for implementing this strategy will be developed by the Council.

21. Clear and stable objectives for sustainable development will present significant economic opportunities. This has the potential to unleash a new wave of technological innovation and investment, generating growth and employment. The European Council invites industry to take part in the development and wider use of new environmentally friendly technologies in sectors such as energy and transport. In this context the European Council stresses the importance of decoupling economic growth from resource use.

---

[24] See Chapters 7 and 10.
[25] As in the case of the 1992 UN Framework Convention on Climate Change and its 1997 Kyoto Protocol, which have been signed and ratified by both the EU and its Member States: see Chapter 15.
[26] Council Directive 76/160/EEC of 8 December 1975 concerning the quality of bathing water [1976] OJ L31/1.
[27] Council Directive 79/409/EEC of 2 April 1979 on the conservation of wild birds [1979] OJ L103/1.
[28] For example, Regulation (EC) No 1907/2006 (n 18).   [29] See Chapter 11.
[30] Now included in the Preamble and Article 3(3) TEU, and Article 11 TFEU. Also see Article 37 of the Charter of Fundamental Rights.

The Göteborg meeting launched the first EU sustainable development strategy (SDS), and the importance of sustainable development has since continued to be reaffirmed by the Union institutions and the European Council, with the EU SDS being reviewed and updated in 2006 and 2009.[31] With the introduction of the Lisbon Treaty, after some intense political negotiation to keep sustainable development as a core EU priority, the European Council stated that 'sustainable development remains a fundamental objective of the European Union under the Lisbon Treaty'.[32]

2.3 A JURISPRUDENTIAL DEFINITION

A third approach to defining EU environmental law is in jurisprudential terms—that is, defining it as a coherent body of legal principle. As with environmental law more generally, this is the least developed way of thinking about the subject and, in many ways, this is not particularly surprising. Not only does EU law cover a wide range of topics, but the legal resolution of EU environmental law issues and disputes historically primarily occurred at the Member State level. It is really only in the last twenty years that the CJEU and the General Court (formerly the Court of First Instance) have had a sufficient caseload to develop a body of doctrine with increasingly well-formed environmental jurisprudential thinking. A striking example of this is the growing body of EU doctrine in relation to environmental principles, discussed in detail in Chapter 11.

A related approach to defining EU environmental law in jurisprudential terms is to focus on the case law of the CJEU and the General Court. Such an approach recognizes that Article 263 TFEU judicial review jurisprudence and Article 267 TFEU preliminary reference jurisprudence will be important for Union institutions and Member State courts respectively in determining and applying EU law. However, to date there have been few comprehensive studies of the jurisprudence of the CJEU in environmental cases. One exception has been the Article 34 TFEU free movement of goods case law in relation to environmental matters, which has been the subject of considerable analysis.[33] The last decade has seen other areas of the CJEU's environmental law jurisprudence starting to be examined in a similarly thorough manner, albeit that such studies tend to focus on particular substantive areas.[34] However, a substantive history of the CJEU's role in the development of EU environmental law is yet to be written, albeit there have been some reflections on that role, including those offered by Sir Francis Jacobs, a former ECJ Advocate General.

Francis Jacobs, 'The Role of the ECJ in the Protection of the Environment'
(2006) 8 JEL 185, 205

[Following a lengthy analysis of some of the CJEU's environmental jurisprudence,] I have three conclusions. First, that the Court [of Justice] has performed a difficult task, if not always coherently, nevertheless imaginatively, boldly and with broadly satisfactory results. Second, that the Court's case law is exceptionally and perhaps uniquely effective in terms of enforcement. Third, that because the protection of the environment may require more, rather than less, action on the EU level, it seems that on that front the United Kingdom both faces and presents a serious problem.

---

[31] European Council, 'Review of the EU Sustainable Development Strategy (EU SDS) – Renewed Strategy', 10917/06, 26 June 2006; Commission, 'Mainstreaming sustainable development into EU policies: 2009 Review of the European Union Strategy for Sustainable Development' COM (2009) 400 final.

[32] General Secretariat of the Council, General Conclusions, European Council, 10/11 2009, EUCO 6/09, para 21.

[33] See Section 5.2.   [34] For example, waste law. See Chapter 16.

Jacobs' final point reflects the attitude of many in the UK towards the EU and its powers. The key point of this analysis is that the CJEU has often been imaginative in its doctrinal development, particularly in cases concerning environmental problems, as can be seen in many substantive chapters of this book. However, such doctrinal development is not merely a case of 'environmental exceptionalism', it also reflects the embryonic and evolving stages of much EU law doctrine generally.

2.4 MOVING FORWARD

This section has highlighted three distinct approaches to defining EU environmental law. Each approach has its advantages and disadvantages and, as with environmental law more generally, the subject has many different dimensions and a body of scholarship that has built up around its numerous agendas. None of these approaches to defining the subject is exclusive or definitively complete. Rather, appreciating their different features highlights that care should be taken not to oversimplify the subject, and that many valid lines of analytical inquiry require consideration in getting to grips with EU environmental law. Further, each of these definitions points not only to the complexity of EU environmental law but also to the challenges of European integration more generally.

The next four sections pick up on some of the legal themes outlined already in these three definitional approaches, to give a more detailed overview of the central issues of EU environmental law. In particular, four themes of EU environmental law are considered: competence, implementation, the ability of Member States to take unilateral environmental protection measures, and governance.

FURTHER READING AND QUESTIONS

1. For a thoughtful analysis of EU environmental law, see Ingmar von Homeyer, 'The Evolution of EU Environmental Governance' in Joanne Scott (ed), *Environmental Protection: European Law and Governance* (OUP 2009). Consider in particular how Homeyer's analysis intertwines with the themes in this section on defining EU environmental law.

2. A list of EU environmental law textbooks can be found at the end of this chapter. For a good overview of EU environmental law and the Lisbon Treaty, see Hans Vedder, 'The Treaty of Lisbon and European Environmental Law and Policy' (2010) 22 JEL 285.

3. Which of the different approaches to defining EU environmental law do you find the most compelling and why?

---

3 EUROPEAN UNION COMPETENCE IN RELATION TO ENVIRONMENTAL PROTECTION

The first important theme of EU environmental law concerns the competence of Union institutions to pass laws in relation to environmental protection. The majority of these laws take the form of Directives. Article 288(3) TFEU relevantly states that:

> A directive shall be binding, as to the result to be achieved, upon each Member State to which it is addressed, but shall leave to the national authorities the choice of form and methods.

Formally, this means that a Directive needs to be *implemented* in a Member State for it to become 'legally effective'. In certain circumstances, however, Directives do have legal effect independent of Member State implementation.[35] The description of Directives in Article 288(2) can give the impression that Directives are vague, but they are usually highly detailed and prescriptive in the environmental law context. Positive harmonization can also take the form of EU Regulations, which are 'directly applicable" (Article 288 TFEU), and thus do not require Member State implementation —an example is the Waste Shipments Regulation[36]—and sometimes Council decisions.

As the legal manifestation of the EU's power to act, competence is now a profoundly important issue within the EU, since the demarcation and attribution of competences between the EU and its Member States decides the constitutional balance of powers between EU and national layers of governance. Article 5(1)–(2) of the TEU states:

1. The limits of Union competences are governed by the principle of conferral. The use of Union competences is governed by the principles of subsidiarity and proportionality.

2. Under the principle of conferral, the Union shall act only within the limits of the competences conferred upon it by the Member States in the Treaties to attain the objectives set out therein. Competences not conferred upon the Union in the Treaties remain with the Member States.

A version of this Article has been in the Treaty since 1993 and its importance cannot be overstated. These provisions express a version of constitutionalism, according to which the Treaty itself sets the legal limits of the Union institutions and their powers. Those legal limits are broad and wide-ranging in relation to EU environmental law. This is because there are a number of Treaty articles that empower Union institutions, both explicitly and implicitly, to act in relation to environmental protection. Indeed, the Treaty provides an embarrassment of riches when it comes to legislating on environmental matters. Besides the environmental competence in Article 192 TFEU (discussed in Section 3.1), relevant competences include, *at least*, those concerning: the internal market,[37] agriculture,[38] the common commercial policy,[39] as well as Article 352 TFEU, which empowers Union institutions to pass laws on the basis of unanimous voting if 'action by the Union should prove necessary, within the framework of the policies defined in the Treaties, to attain one of the objectives set out in the Treaties, and the Treaties have not provided the necessary powers'. While the historical antecedents of this Article did have a role to play in allowing EU action on environmental matters, that role has been eclipsed by the subsequent introduction of other competences.

It is also noteworthy that the Treaties do not only mention the importance of environmental protection but also the need to aim for a 'high level of protection'.[40] This is an aspirational but quite ambiguous phrase, like the concept of 'an ever closer union' in the TEU and TFEU Preambles. As Joerges notes, this Treaty goal reflects and sets a standard of the 'common weal'.[41]

Since the Lisbon Treaty, the EU Treaty framework explicitly distinguishes between areas of exclusive competence (Article 3 TFEU) and shared competence (Article 4 TFEU), across which powers to act on environmental matters are divided. Article 2(1)–(2) explains the two different sets of competences:

1. When the Treaties confer on the Union exclusive competence in a specific area, only the Union may legislate and adopt legally binding acts, the Member States being able to do so themselves only if so empowered by the Union or for the implementation of Union acts.

---

[35] Under the doctrine of direct effect, see *Van Gend en Loos* (n 3).

[36] Regulation (EC) No 1013/2006 of the European Parliament and of the Council of 14 June 2006 on shipments of waste [2006] OJ L190/1.

[37] Article 114 TFEU.   [38] Article 43 TFEU.   [39] Article 207 TFEU.

[40] Article 3(3) TEU, and arts 114(3) and 191(2) TFEU.

[41] Christian Joerges, '"Good Governance" Through Comitology', in Christian Joerges and Ellen Vos (eds), *EU Committees: Social Regulation, Law and Politics* (Hart Publishing 1999) 320.

2. When the Treaties confer on the Union a competence shared with the Member States in a specific area, the Union and the Member States may legislate and adopt legally binding acts in that area. The Member States shall exercise their competence to the extent that the Union has not exercised its competence. The Member States shall again exercise their competence to the extent that the Union has decided to cease exercising its competence.

The Union's specific competences in relation to environmental policy and the internal market are both shared (Article 4), but the competences in relation to the common commercial policy (effectively international trade), the conservation of marine biological resources under the common fisheries policy, and the conclusion of certain international agreements are exclusive. In other words, different competences will give the EU, and thus Member States, varying scope for action, and this allocation of power may be influential in choosing the legal basis of legislative action relating to particular environmental policies. Thus, from a legal perspective, the issues surrounding EU environmental competence are not so much about whether the Union has competence to act in relation to an aspect of environmental policy, but raise a more difficult set of questions concerning which particular Treaty article should provide the competence basis for a specific measure. This issue has become even more complicated in an era when there are increasing moves to integrate measures across different policy sectors.

3.1 ARTICLES 191–193 AND ARTICLE 114 TFEU

Before 1987, there was no explicit competence in relation to the environment and so environmental protection measures were passed primarily under Article 100 (for the establishment and functioning of the common market) and Article 235 (now 352 TFEU) (residual powers, as set out here). Depending on which commentator you read, by 1986 there had been 100–200 Directives passed with an environmental purpose. In 1987, the SEA introduced an environmental title into the Treaty of Rome. And while there are now many possible relevant Treaty competences for EU action in relation to environmental matters, as a matter of practice the environmental title (Articles 191–192 TFEU) and the internal market (Article 114 TFEU) are the most common bases for positive harmonization in relation to environmental problems—a situation that once again expresses the dual purpose of EU environmental law.

TFEU - TITLE XX - ENVIRONMENT

Article 191

1. Union policy on the environment shall contribute to pursuit of the following objectives:
    —   preserving, protecting and improving the quality of the environment,
    —   protecting human health,
    —   prudent and rational utilisation of natural resources,
    —   promoting measures at international level to deal with regional or worldwide environmental problems, and in particular combating climate change.

2. Union policy on the environment shall aim at a high level of protection taking into account the diversity of situations in the various regions of the Union. It shall be based on the precautionary principle and on the principles that preventive action should be taken, that environmental damage should as a priority be rectified at source and that the polluter should pay.

In this context, harmonisation measures answering environmental protection requirements shall include, where appropriate, a safeguard clause allowing Member States to take provisional measures, for non-economic environmental reasons, subject to a procedure of inspection by the Union.

3. In preparing its policy on the environment, the Union shall take account of:

— available scientific and technical data,

— environmental conditions in the various regions of the Union,

— the potential benefits and costs of action or lack of action,

— the economic and social development of the Union as a whole and the balanced development of its regions.

4. Within their respective spheres of competence, the Union and the Member States shall cooperate with third countries and with the competent international organisations. The arrangements for Union cooperation may be the subject of agreements between the Union and the third parties concerned.

The previous subparagraph shall be without prejudice to Member States' competence to negotiate in international bodies and to conclude international agreements.

Article 192

1. The European Parliament and the Council, acting in accordance with the ordinary legislative procedure and after consulting the Economic and Social Committee and the Committee of the Regions, shall decide what action is to be taken by the Union in order to achieve the objectives referred to in Article 191.

2. By way of derogation from the decision-making procedure provided for in paragraph 1 and without prejudice to Article 114, the Council acting unanimously in accordance with a special legislative procedure and after consulting the European Parliament, the Economic and Social Committee and the Committee of the Regions, shall adopt:

(a) provisions primarily of a fiscal nature;

(b) measures affecting:

— town and country planning,

— quantitative management of water resources or affecting, directly or indirectly, the availability of those resources,

— land use, with the exception of waste management;

(c) measures significantly affecting a Member State's choice between different energy sources and the general structure of its energy supply.

The Council, acting unanimously on a proposal from the Commission and after consulting the European Parliament, the Economic and Social Committee and the Committee of the Regions, may make the ordinary legislative procedure applicable to the matters referred to in the first subparagraph.

3. General action programmes setting out priority objectives to be attained shall be adopted by the European Parliament and the Council, acting in accordance with the ordinary legislative procedure and after consulting the Economic and Social Committee and the Committee of the Regions.

The measures necessary for the implementation of these programmes shall be adopted under the terms of paragraph 1 or 2, as the case may be.

4. Without prejudice to certain measures adopted by the Union, the Member States shall finance and implement the environment policy.

5. Without prejudice to the principle that the polluter should pay, if a measure based on the provisions of paragraph 1 involves costs deemed disproportionate for the public authorities of a Member State, such measure shall lay down appropriate provisions in the form of:

— temporary derogations, and/or

— financial support from the Cohesion Fund set up pursuant to Article 177.

Article 193

The protective measures adopted pursuant to Article 192 shall not prevent any Member State from maintaining or introducing more stringent protective measures. Such measures must be compatible with the Treaties. They shall be notified to the Commission.

The environmental title has a number of interesting features. First, the competences in Article 192 must be interpreted in light of Article 191—a provision which contains a curious mixture of principle and policy. The significance of that Article is considered in more detail in Chapter 11. Second, there are actually two law-making competence provisions under Article 192. The majority of environmental protection legislative measures will be passed under Article 192(1) and thus in accordance with the 'ordinary legislative procedure' (the co-decision procedure pre-Lisbon), which importantly involves qualified majority voting in the Council. However, Article 192(2) includes certain specific areas in relation to which the Union can only act on the basis of unanimous voting—these include the quantitative management of water resources, town planning, and energy supply. This different type of competence is largely due to these matters being politically sensitive, so that they require all Member States to support them in the European Council before their adoption. These areas can also be understood as being particularly subject to the principle of subsidiarity (Section 3.3). Third, Article 192(3) provides a legal basis and frame for EU environmental action programmes. Fourth, legislative action pursuant to Article 192 does not necessarily preclude unilateral Member State action due to Article 193. That provision is not quite as simple as it looks however, and will be considered further in Section 5.

The second key Treaty competence for EU environmental action is Article 114(1) TFEU, which concerns measures that 'have as their object the establishment and functioning of the internal market'. Article 26(2) TFEU states that the 'internal market shall comprise an area without internal frontiers in which the free movement of goods, persons, services and capital is ensured in accordance with the provisions of the Treaties'. This is significant for two reasons. First, the concept is narrower in scope than the original concept of the common market, in that the common market was undefined but the internal market has an explicit definition. Second, the internal market is a concept that is given meaning by the Treaty and thus by the CJEU's interpretation of it.

As already noted, before 1987 many environmental measures were passed pursuant to the then significant common market competence (Article 100 TEC) and the introduction of an environmental title did not sever the relationship between the competences for EU action relating to the common/internal market and environmental protection. This can be seen from the wording of Article 114(1) and Article 114(3).

Article 114

1. Save where otherwise provided in the Treaties, the following provisions shall apply for the achievement of the objectives set out in Article 26. The European Parliament and the Council shall, acting in accordance with the ordinary legislative procedure and after consulting the Economic and Social Committee, adopt the measures for the approximation of the provisions laid down by law, regulation or

administrative action in Member States which have as their object the establishment and functioning of the internal market. [...]

3. The Commission, in its proposals envisaged in paragraph 1 concerning health, safety, environmental protection and consumer protection, will take as a base a high level of protection, taking account in particular of any new development based on scientific facts. Within their respective powers, the European Parliament and the Council will also seek to achieve this objective. [...]

Article 114(3) thus clearly envisages that Directives concerned with the establishing and functioning of the internal market may have an environmental protection aspect, although it is important to note the distinction here between the obligations of the Commission and Council and Parliament. The Commission must ensure that all their measures are based on a 'high level of protection' while the other two institutions must only 'seek to achieve' this level in considering and approving legislation. Note that Article 114(3) does not detract from the fact that measures under Article 114 must have as their essential basis—their 'centre of gravity'—the establishing and functioning of the internal market. This can be seen in *R v Secretary of State for Health, ex parte British American Tobacco (Investments) Ltd*, in which Article 114(3) was considered in determining the proper Treaty basis of an EU measure concerned with protecting public health (by banning and restricting tobacco advertising).

Case C-491/01 *R v Secretary of State for Health, ex parte British American Tobacco (Investments) Ltd*
[2002] ECR I-11453, paras 61–62

61. Also, it follows from that case-law that while recourse to Article 95 EC [now Article 114 TFEU] as a legal basis is possible if the aim is to prevent the emergence of future obstacles to trade resulting from multifarious development of national laws, the emergence of such obstacles must be likely and the measure in question must be designed to prevent them (see, to that effect, Case C-350/92 *Spain v Council* [1995] ECR I-1985, paragraph 35; the tobacco advertising judgment [C-376/98 *Germany v Parliament and Council* [2000] ECR I-2247], paragraph 86, and Case C-377/98 *Netherlands v Parliament and Council* [2001] ECR I-7079, paragraph 15).

62. Finally, provided that the conditions for recourse to Article 95 EC as a legal basis are fulfilled, the Community legislature cannot be prevented from relying on that legal basis on the ground that public health protection is a decisive factor in the choices to be made (see, to that effect, the tobacco advertising judgment, paragraph 88). Moreover, the first subparagraph of Article 152(1) EC [now 168(1) TFEU] provides that a high level of human health protection is to be ensured in the definition and implementation of all Community policies and activities, and Article 95(3) EC explicitly requires that, in achieving harmonisation, a high level of protection of human health should be guaranteed.

Thus, Article 114(3) does not broaden the competence under Article 114, but rather the type of measures that can be taken under it. It also has symbolic importance in that it is not simply concerned with integrating environmental concerns into the internal market, but it establishes that a 'high level of protection' is a baseline for Union institutions in constructing and regulating the internal market. Note that Articles 114(4)–(8) TFEU also provide a derogation procedure for Member States in relation to internal market measures, which is examined in more detail in Section 5.

3.2 THE CASE LAW ON COMPETENCE IN RELATION TO ENVIRONMENTAL PROBLEMS

Before 1987, in the era in which any EEC legislative measure required unanimous consent in the Council, there were virtually no legal challenges to the competence of Community institutions in introducing environmental protection measures. This was the case although there was often a tenuous relationship between the measure and the Treaty article under which it was passed. After the passing of the SEA, however, qualified majority voting (QMV) was introduced for measures introduced under the internal market competence (now Article 114), and new competences were added, including the environmental title of the Treaty, which retained unanimous voting. The end result was that different competences for a period of time required EU legislation to be passed pursuant to different procedures. Thus, for example, between 1987 and 1993, the 'internal market' competence—then Article 100a (now Article 114 TFEU)—required Directives to be passed by the 'co-operation procedure', which involved QMV and an increased role for Parliament in passing legislation. In contrast, during the same period the environmental competence—then Article 130s(1)—required the Parliament only to be consulted and unanimous voting in Council.

This rather untidy legislative situation led to a number of legal challenges by Union institutions involved in the law-making process, under (what is now) Article 263 TFEU. While there is no problem in principle with the EU competence for a Directive or Regulation being derived from two different Treaty articles (or having dual basis), a problem does arise in cases where those articles prescribe different procedures. In such cases, a decision needs to be made as to the legislation's centre of gravity, so as to determine the Treaty article on which it should be properly based, and thus the proper procedures for its enactment. The general thrust of the argument for those EC institutions challenging Directives (and thus the nature of their institutional involvement in the law-making process) was that the Directive had been passed pursuant to the wrong Treaty article. The most well known of these environmental competence cases is the *Titanium Dioxide* case.

Case C-300/89 *Parliament v Council*
[1991] ECR I-2867, paras 10–25

The Facts

The Council passed Council Directive 89/428/EEC of 21 June 1989 on procedures for harmonizing the programmes for the reduction and eventual elimination of pollution caused by waste from the titanium dioxide industry under Art 130s(1) TEC [now Art 192(1) TFEU although the voting procedure has also changed]. The Commission brought an annulment action arguing that it should have been passed pursuant to Art 100a(1) [now Art 114(1) TFEU].

The ECJ

10. It must first be observed that in the context of the organization of the powers of the Community the choice of the legal basis for a measure may not depend simply on an institution's conviction as to the objective pursued but must be based on objective factors which are amenable to judicial review (see the judgment in Case 45/86 *Commission v Council* [1987] ECR 1493, paragraph 11). Those factors include in particular the aim and content of the measure.

11. As regards the aim pursued, Article 1 of Directive 89/428/EEC indicates that it is intended, on the one hand, to harmonize the programmes for the reduction and ultimate elimination of pollution caused by waste from existing establishments in the titanium dioxide industry and, on the other, to improve the

conditions of competition in that industry. It thus pursues the twofold aim of environmental protection and improvement of the conditions of competition.

12. As regards its content, Directive 89/428/EEC prohibits, or, according to strict standards, requires reduction of the discharge of waste from existing establishments in the titanium dioxide industry and lays down time-limits for the implementation of the various provisions. By thus imposing obligations concerning the treatment of waste from the titanium dioxide production process, the directive conduces, at the same time, to the reduction of pollution and to the establishment of greater uniformity of production conditions and therefore of conditions of competition, since the national rules on the treatment of waste which the directive seeks to harmonize have an impact on production costs in the titanium dioxide industry.

13. It follows that, according to its aim and content, as they appear from its actual wording, the directive is concerned, indissociably, with both the protection of the environment and the elimination of disparities in conditions of competition. [...]

16. It follows that, in view of its aim and content, the directive at issue displays the features both of action relating to the environment with which Article 130s [now Art 192] of the Treaty is concerned and of a harmonizing measure which has as its object the establishment and functioning of the internal market, within the meaning of Article 100a of the Treaty.

17. As the Court held in Case 165/87 *Commission v Council* [1988] ECR 5545, paragraph 11, where an institution's power is based on two provisions of the Treaty, it is bound to adopt the relevant measures on the basis of the two relevant provisions. However, that ruling is not applicable to the present case.

18. One of the enabling provisions at issue, Article 100a, requires recourse to the cooperation procedure [...] whereas the other, Article 130s, requires the Council to [...] act unanimously after merely consulting the European Parliament. As a result, use of both provisions as a joint legal basis would divest the cooperation procedure of its very substance.

19. Under the cooperation procedure, the Council acts by a qualified majority where it intends accepting the amendments to its common position proposed by the Parliament and included by the Commission in its re-examined proposal, whereas it must secure unanimity if it intends taking a decision after its common position has been rejected by the Parliament or if it intends modifying the Commission's re-examined proposal. That essential element of the cooperation procedure would be undermined if, as a result of simultaneous reference to Articles 100a and 130s, the Council were required, in any event, to act unanimously.

20. The very purpose of the cooperation procedure, which is to increase the involvement of the European Parliament in the legislative process of the Community, would thus be jeopardized. As the Court stated in its judgments in Case 138/79 *Roquette Freres v Council* [1980] ECR 3333 and Case 139/79 *Maizena v Council* [1980] ECR 3393, paragraph 34, that participation reflects a fundamental democratic principle that the peoples should take part in the exercise of power through the intermediary of a representative assembly.

21. It follows that in the present case recourse to the dual legal basis of Articles 100a and 130s is excluded and that it is necessary to determine which of those two provisions is the appropriate legal basis.

22. It must be observed in the first place that, pursuant to the second sentence of Article 130r(2) [now in an amended form Art 191(2)] of the Treaty, 'environmental protection requirements shall be a component of the Community's other policies'. That principle implies that a Community measure cannot be covered by Article 130s merely because it also pursues objectives of environmental protection.

23. Secondly, as the Court held in its judgments in Cases 91/79 and 92/79 *Commission v Italy* [1980] ECR 1099 (paragraph 8) and 1115 (paragraph 8), provisions which are made necessary by considerations relating to the environment and health may be a burden upon the undertakings to which they apply and, if there is no harmonization of national provisions on the matter, competition may be appreciably

distorted. It follows that action intended to approximate national rules concerning production conditions in a given industrial sector with the aim of eliminating distortions of competition in that sector is conducive to the attainment of the internal market and thus falls within the scope of Article 100a, a provision which is particularly appropriate to the attainment of the internal market.

24. Finally, it must be observed that Article 100a(3) requires the Commission, in its proposals for measures for the approximation of the laws of the Member States which have as their object the establishment and functioning of the internal market, to take as a base a high level of protection in matters of environmental protection. That provision thus expressly indicates that the objectives of environmental protection referred to in Article 130r may be effectively pursued by means of harmonizing measures adopted on the basis of Article 100a.

25. In view of all the foregoing considerations, the contested measure should have been based on Article 100a of the EEC Treaty and must therefore be annulled.

The problem and reasoning in relation to *Titanium Dioxide* are in many ways unique. In other competence challenges, the CJEU has nearly always found that, while a measure may relate to two different competences, it is in fact more aligned to one than the other.[42] Moreover, the CJEU has always made clear that the choice of Treaty competence is an objective one, relating to the essential nature of the measure, and differences in law-making procedure are irrelevant.[43] However, in this case, the genuine dual basis of the contested measure led the court to take account of the democratic nature of the legislative procedures involved, thereby giving more weight to Article 100a and its use of the (former) cooperation procedure. With that said, the case highlights very well the close alignment between environmental protection measures and market integration, particularly through the use of Article 114(3) in the reasoning.

The existence of different law-making procedures between the internal market and environmental Treaty competences shifted slightly with the Maastricht Treaty—law making under Article 100a(1) was pursuant to the new 'co-decision' procedure and under Article 130s(1) required the co-operation procedure. Different procedures remained until the Treaty of Amsterdam, which brought law making under what is now Article 114(1) and Article 192(1) under the same procedure—co-decision (now the ordinary legislative procedure). However, the problems of divergences between Treaty articles have remained.[44] This is partly because other Treaty competences that overlap with environmental protection dictate different law-making procedures and partly because some give exclusive competence to the Community and others only shared.[45]

All these cases and competence disputes demonstrate that, while the EU does have competence to act in relation to environmental issues, there are many different ways to frame and understand that competence, which can raise legal questions about how it exercises its power and the institutional decision-making adopted. On the one hand, it might be said that the cases on competence are technical oddities—products of particular environmental problems and the lack of legal consistency across competences. On the other hand, however, they are perfect examples of the tensions that arise since environmental protection is both a central EU policy objective as well as one that should be integrated with other policy objectives. The legal commitment to the latter is seen in the 'integration principle'

---

[42] Case C-155/91 *Commission v Council* [1993] ECR I-939; Case C-187/93 *Parliament v Council* [1994] ECR I-2857.

[43] Case C-376/98 *Germany v Parliament and Council* [2000] ECR I-8149.

[44] eg Case C-164-5/97 *Parliament v Council* [1999] ECR I-1139 (Articles 92 and 43 TFEU); Case C-39/98 *Spain v Council* [2001] ECR I-779 (Articles 92(1)–(2) TFEU).

[45] Case Opinion 2/00 *Cartagena Protocol on Biosafety*[2001] ECR I-9713.

in Article 11 TFEU, which requires environmental protection requirements to be integrated into all EU policy areas (discussed in detail in Chapter 11).

3.3 SUBSIDIARITY

At the core of this discussion of EU competence is the concept of subsidiarity. We saw a reference to subsidiarity in Article 5(1) TEU. Article 5(3) TEU goes on to state:

> 3. Under the principle of subsidiarity, in areas which do not fall within its exclusive competence, the Union shall act only if and in so far as the objectives of the proposed action cannot be sufficiently achieved by the Member States, either at central level or at regional and local level, but can rather, by reason of the scale or effects of the proposed action, be better achieved at Union level.
>
> The institutions of the Union shall apply the principle of subsidiarity as laid down in the Protocol on the application of the principles of subsidiarity and proportionality. National Parliaments ensure compliance with the principle of subsidiarity in accordance with the procedure set out in that Protocol.

Subsidiarity, as a core constitutional principle of EU law, was first included in the TEC in 1987 in relation to environmental protection matters only.[46] That reference was taken out when subsidiarity became a general principle of the Treaty as part of the Maastricht amendments in 1993. In 1999, a Subsidiarity and Proportionality Protocol was agreed as part of the Amsterdam Treaty.[47] This was replaced by a new Protocol (Protocol No 2) as part of the Lisbon reforms.[48]

This Protocol sets out a process and framework of pre-legislative consultation between institutions in the EU in order to determine the appropriate exercise of powers at EU and Member State levels, and thus to respect the principle of subsidiarity. Indeed, as Armstrong explains, the principle can be seen as one that requires deliberation across layers of governance in the law-making process.

Kenneth A Armstrong, *Regulation, Deregulation, Re-Regulation* (Kogan Page 2000) 16

It is often difficult to separate the specific issues associated with the application of the subsidiarity principle in the EU from the broader potential of the principle and the ideas contained within it. At its most general the principle of subsidiarity asks us to think about how we relate different locations of governance to one another. What justifies decisions being taken in one location rather than another? In many ways the principle of subsidiarity does not itself contain any values that can be deployed in order to answer this question. Rather, it requires that different sorts of arguments be made for or against action in any particular location. Indeed, we might view the principle as a commitment to deliberation within a polity as to the appropriateness of governance structures.

Subsidiarity thus shapes EU competence largely in the way that it structures the law-making process. As a result, subsidiarity has not played a major role in the case law of the CJEU.[49] For many, the

---

[46] What was then Article 130r(4) TEC.

[47] Protocol (No 30) on the application of the principles of subsidiarity and proportionality (1997) [2006] OJ C321E/308.

[48] Protocol (No 2) on the Application of the Principles of Subsidiarity and Proportionality, Article 2, 4–8.

[49] cf the passing discussion of subsidiarity in Case C-491/01 *R v Secretary of State for Health, ex parte British American Tobacco* [2002] I-11453.

principle is better understood as a political principle. However, the CJEU has considered subsidiarity in some cases. One example is given here, where the principle was considered in interpreting an environmental Directive (the Waste Framework Directive).

Case C-114/01 *AvestaPolarit Chrome Oy*
[2003] ECR I-8725, paras 54–57

The Facts

Directive 91/156 amended Directive 75/442 [the old framework waste Directive] to include a European waste catalogue. The 1991 also amended the list of matters that were not covered by the directive so that wastes 'where they are already covered by other legislation' was excluded.

The ECJ

54. By part (b) of its second question, the national court asks essentially whether Article 2(1)(b) of Directive 75/442 must be interpreted as meaning that 'other legislation' within the meaning of that provision must have entered into force before 1 April 1993, the date of entry into force of Directive 91/156, or whether it may also have entered into force after that date.

55. It does not follow expressly from the wording of the provision in question that it refers only to national legislation existing on the date of entry into force of Directive 91/156. The words 'already covered by other legislation' in that provision may just as well have a material as a temporal meaning. Furthermore, the term 'already' is not used in all the language versions of Directive 75/442.

56. In accordance with Article 5 EC [now in amended form Article 5(3) TFEU], first, in areas which do not fall within its exclusive competence, which is the case at this stage as regards the environment, the Community is to take action, in accordance with the principle of subsidiarity, only if and in so far as the objectives of the proposed action cannot be sufficiently achieved by the Member States and can therefore, by reason of the scale or effects of the proposed action, be better achieved by the Community and, second, action by the Community must not go beyond what is necessary to achieve the objectives of the Treaty.

57. Consequently, since when adopting Directive 91/156 the Community legislature considered it appropriate that, until specific Community rules were adopted on the management of certain individual categories of waste, the authorities of the Member States should retain the option of ensuring that management outside the framework laid down by Directive 75/442, and since it neither expressly excluded the possibility of that option being used on the basis of national legislation subsequent to the entry into force of Directive 91/156 nor set out considerations enabling a distinction to be drawn between such national legislation and legislation prior to that entry into force, Article 2(1)(b) of Directive 75/442 must be interpreted as meaning that 'other legislation' within the meaning of that provision may have entered into force either before or after 1 April 1993, the date of entry into force of Directive 91/156.

Note that the operation of subsidiarity is entangled with the specific Directive at issue in this case. The CJEU is thus not making grand freestanding statements about the principle in legal terms, but rather analysing how it fits into a particular EU environmental regime. This is consistent with the post-Lisbon protocol. Subsidiarity is less a classic legal principle and more a lens through which to view, negotiate, and navigate legal frameworks.

FURTHER READING AND QUESTIONS

1. Consider the following hypothetical Directives. Under which Treaty article do you think they should be passed?

   (a) A Directive concerned with protecting frog habitats from being destroyed by agricultural activities. You may find it useful to refer to Case C-164–5/97 *Parliament v Council* [1999] ECR I-1139.

   (b) A Directive concerned with the allocation of water to rice farmers. You may find it useful to refer to the case above and Case C-39/98 *Spain v Council* [2001] ECR I-779, although note the case was considered before the introduction of the word 'quantitative' into article 192(2) TFEU.

   (c) A Directive concerned with the labelling of products that are environmental friendly, in the light of an international environmental law treaty requiring such a law. As well, having such a Directive will allow trading with a number of other non-EU countries. You may find it useful to have regard to the Opinion 2/00 *Cartagena Protocol on Biosafety* [2001] ECR I-9713 and Case C-281/01 *Commission v Council* [2002] ECR I-12049.

4 IMPLEMENTATION AND ENFORCEMENT

The second significant theme of EU environmental law is that of implementation and enforcement. The process of implementing EU law has been by no means straightforward or unproblematic. A common criticism of EU environmental law is that no matter how good it looks on paper, there is a problem with how it is implemented in practice. Further, it is perceived that different enforcement procedures have done little to remedy this problem. This section gives a brief overview of the nature of EU implementation, the significance of legal and administrative culture in implementing and enforcing EU environmental law, and finally surveys different modes of enforcement.

4.1 IMPLEMENTING EU ENVIRONMENTAL LAW

As already noted, the vast bulk of EU environmental law is in the form of Directives, which stipulate a period of time (usually a couple of years) for Member States to implement them into national law. The dominance of the Directive in EU environmental law is due to a number of factors but it is mainly because Directives allow Member States to control the process of implementing EU environmental law. Directives, as a legal form, also represent an expression of the principle of subsidiarity. The use of Directives means that Member States, in theory, have more flexibility to shape EU environmental laws to national conditions. However, Directives do not give unfettered discretion to Member States in implementing EU law and the CJEU has developed a rich body of doctrine concerning what are and are not legitimate forms of implementation. Two points about that case law highlight the flexible and subtle legal nature of EU environmental Directives.

First, in relation to non-implementation or partial or other forms of mis-implementation, a Member State cannot 'plead provisions, practices, or circumstances existing in its internal legal system in order to justify a failure to comply with the obligations and time limits laid down in a directive'.[50] Second, the implementation obligation will vary with the nature of the obligations included in a Directive.

---

[50] Case C-214/96 *Commission v Spain* [1998] ECR I-7661, para 18.

This is best illustrated by an enforcement action brought by the Commission against Luxembourg for an alleged incorrect transposition of the Water Framework Directive,[51] which the Commission argued needed to be implemented by specific framework legislation. The ECJ did not agree.

Case C-32/05 *Commission v Luxembourg*
[2006] ECR I-11323 paras 34–46

34. The third paragraph of Article 249 EC [now Article 288 TFEU] expressly provides that Member States may choose the form and methods for implementing directives which best ensures the result to be achieved by the directives. It follows from that provision that the implementation in domestic law of a directive does not necessarily require legislative action in each Member State. Thus, the Court has repeatedly held that it is not always necessary formally to enact the requirements of a directive in a specific express legal provision, since the general legal context may be sufficient for implementation of a directive, depending on its content. In particular, the existence of general principles of constitutional or administrative law may render superfluous transposition by specific legislative or regulatory measures provided, however, that those principles actually ensure the full application of the directive by the national authorities and that, where the relevant provision of the directive seeks to create rights for individuals, the legal situation arising from those principles is sufficiently precise and clear and that the persons concerned are put in a position to know the full extent of their rights and, where appropriate, to be able to rely on them before the national courts (see, inter alia, Case 29/84 *Commission v Germany* [1985] ECR 1661, paragraphs 22 and 23; Case C–217/97 *Commission v Germany* [1999] ECR I–5087, paragraphs 31 and 32; and Case C–233/00 *Commission v France*, paragraph 76).

35. The Court has also held that a provision which concerns only the relations between the Member States and the Commission does not, in principle, have to be transposed. However, given that the Member States are obliged to ensure that Community law is fully complied with, it is open to the Commission to demonstrate that compliance with a provision of a directive governing those relations requires the adoption of specific transposing measures in national law (see, to that effect, Case C–72/02 *Commission v Portugal* [2003] ECR I-6597, paragraphs 19 and 20, and Case C-296/01 *Commission v France* [2003] ECR I–13909, paragraph 92).

36. It is accordingly necessary in every case to determine the nature of the provisions of a directive to which infringement proceedings relate, in order to assess the extent of the obligation as to transposition which is imposed on the Member States.

37. Community legislative practice shows that there may be great differences in the types of obligations which directives impose on the Member States and therefore in the results which must be achieved (Case C–60/01 *Commission v France* [2002] ECR I–5679, paragraph 25).

38. Some directives require legislative measures to be adopted at national level and compliance with those measures to be the subject of judicial or administrative review (see, in that regard, Case C-360/88 *Commission v Belgium* [1989] ECR 3803; Case C–329/88 *Commission v Greece* [1989] ECR 4159; and Case C-60/01 *Commission v France*, paragraph 26).

39. Other directives provide that the Member States are to take the necessary measures to ensure that certain objectives formulated in general and unquantifiable terms are attained, whilst leaving the Member States some discretion as to the nature of the measures to be taken (see, in that regard, Case C–365/97 *Commission v Italy* (the '*San Rocco*' case) [1999] ECR I–7773, paragraphs 67 and 68, and Case C–60/01 *Commission v France*, paragraph 27).

---

[51] Directive 2000/60/EC of the European Parliament and of the Council of 23 October 2000 establishing a framework for Community action in the field of water policy [2000] OJ L327/1.

40. Yet other directives require the Member States to obtain very precise and specific results after a certain period (see, in that regard, Case C–56/90 *Commission v United Kingdom* [1993] ECR I-4109, paragraphs 42 to 44; Case C-268/00 *Commission v Netherlands* [2002] ECR I–2995, paragraphs 12 to 14; and Case C–60/01 *Commission v France*, paragraph 28).

41. As regards the present case, it must be noted that Directive 2000/60 is a framework directive adopted on the basis of Article 175(1) EC [now Article 192(1) TFEU]. It establishes the common principles and an overall framework for action in relation to water protection and coordinates, integrates and, in a longer perspective, develops the overall principles and structures for protection and sustainable use of water in the European Community. The common principles and overall framework for action which it lays down are to be developed subsequently by the Member States, which are to adopt a series of individual measures in accordance with the timescales laid down in the directive. However, the directive does not seek to achieve complete harmonisation of the rules of the Member States concerning water.

42. Consideration of the directive shows that it contains provisions of differing types which impose obligations on Member States (see, for example, Article 4, which requires Member States to implement the necessary measures to prevent deterioration of the status of all bodies of surface water and groundwater), on Member States as against the Commission and the Community (see, for example, Article 24(2) relating to the obligation to communicate implementing measures) and on the institutions themselves (see, for example, Articles 16 and 17 of the directive, calling on the Community institutions to adopt Community measures on pollution of water and groundwater).

43. Overall consideration of the directive shows that most of its provisions are of the type referred to in paragraph 39 of this judgment, that is to say that they require Member States to take the necessary measures to ensure that certain objectives, sometimes formulated in general terms, are attained, whilst leaving the Member States some discretion as to the nature of the measures to be taken.

44. The directive also contains provisions such as Article 1, which merely specifies the particular objectives the directive seeks to achieve and which, as the Commission itself acknowledged at the hearing, do not require transposition.

45. In reply to questions put at the hearing seeking to establish the particular provisions of the directive which formed the basis of the obligation to adopt framework legislation in order to comply with the requirements of the directive, the Commission referred to Articles 1 and 2 of the directive laying down the objectives which it seeks to achieve and the definitions on which it is based, without specifying in what way those provisions require the adoption of such legislation or why its adoption is necessary in order to permit the Member States to ensure that the objectives laid down by the directive are attained within the prescribed timescales.

46. However, neither those provisions of the directive nor any other part of it show that Member States are under a duty to adopt such framework legislation in order to implement its provisions correctly.

This case extract makes clear that implementation of Directives can take many forms and involves many different types of legal norms, as will be seen in different chapters throughout this textbook. It is also important to remember that implementation does not stop at the process of placing a Directive into national law. As most environmental Directives require continuous administration and oversight to ensure their obligations are met, there is usually a significant role for public authorities, and public administration in particular, in implementing EU environmental Directives. Demmke makes the point well.

Christoph Demmke, 'Trends in European Environmental Regulation: Issues in Implementation and Enforcement' (2003) 3 YEEL 329, 339–40

Formally, the European Commission dominates in the policy formulation phase, whereas national authorities prevail in the implementation phase. Somsen argues that:

'the perception that Member States enjoy almost total control over the implementation process has in fact in many instances softened the latter's resistance to the adoption of environmental directives, the practical impact of which they felt they could; in any event control. Losing at the policy-making stage may not be so important if there is a second round at the implementation stage when the national government. Through its bureaucracy, has an opportunity to determine what will actually happen in the policy area in that country.'

This, in turn, necessarily results in disparities amongst enforcement agencies. Moreover, inspection tasks are not always exercised by a single national authority, but are often decentralized. It has been observed that:

'national administrative traditions and their level of institutionalization influence national implementation of EU legislation. More precisely, national compliance with EU law depends on the level of adaptation pressure perceived in the Member States' [Knill].

In other words, national administrations seek to impose their national regulatory philosophies at the European level, which they do especially by lobbying the Commission, which enjoys a monopoly to propose legislation. Some Member States exercise more influence than others, however. It has been found that initiatives usually originate from Member States and/or interest groups and only a small proportion (approximately six per cent) is initiated by the Commission itself. The role of the Commission in developing proposals is, therefore, more that of a mediator than of an initiator.

Wilson, in contrast, claims that serious problems arise in the UK because directives, despite their importance, are routinely negotiated with far fewer resources and much less administrative backup than national legislation:

'[m]any opportunities to correct drafting mistakes, to clear ambiguities, to resolve problems and to avoid impossible or unreasonable obligations are thrown away at; the early stage of negotiations, when discussions take place at official level before Ministers are involved. For better law to emerge from this process, the different disciplines necessary to negotiate a directive would have to be better co-ordinated at an earlier stage, and have sufficient resources, in terms of time and manpower, to continue to co-ordinate their efforts throughout the passage of a directive's negotiation.'

Consequently, legal problems are only discovered when the directives come to be implemented into national law.

Demmke's comments highlight how a national administrative and regulatory culture will have a powerful influence on how a Directive is implemented. The same is true of legal culture. The process of implementation is not only about placing the wording of the Directive into national law but is also determined by how courts (both EU and Member State) interpret that Directive.

4.2 SOME THOUGHTS ON HARMONIZATION

The complexities of transposing EU Directives highlight that the idea of harmonizing national environmental law by means of EU measures is not a simple matter. This is because harmonization can itself mean different things, and these different meanings reflect various perspectives that may be adopted in evaluating the implementation of EU environmental law. At its simplest, harmonization means having common rules and processes across Member States. To a certain extent, this has been achieved in that the same express environmental rules are often on the statute books in each Member State (linguistic variations aside).

A second way to think of harmonization is in terms of end results. In this sense, positive harmonization by EU environmental law is designed to ensure that a similar standard of environmental quality exists in each Member State. Again, this kind of harmonization is achievable to a certain extent. If each Member State is complying with, say, the Drinking Water Directive,[52] then one can expect the quality of drinking water to be the same within each Member State. However, in reality, environmental quality between Member States varies considerably, not only because of differences in implementation of Directives, but also because the baseline environmental quality is quite distinct in each Member State. In such circumstances, it is questionable whether the same environmental standards can, or should be, achieved across the Union.

A third way of thinking about harmonization is to understand it in terms of market integration. On this basis, the issue is not so much about harmonization of laws but about ensuring that national environmental laws are not barriers to free movement within the internal market or that such laws do not distort competition. As already seen, market integration has been a powerful rationale in developing EU environmental law, albeit not the only rationale. Moreover, there is general recognition that variations in how rules of EU environmental law are implemented and enforced do affect the market.[53]

The final form of harmonization is the harmonization of policy norms. In this sense, Member States are encouraged to adopt the same regulatory strategies and similar policy frameworks and discourses. Thus, for example, the precautionary principle has become the common framework for thinking about scientific uncertainty in standard setting,[54] and the Waste Directive has set the agenda for waste policy in EU Member States.[55] This does not mean that there is always strict agreement over how a policy is understood or interpreted, but that Member States are deliberating and considering issues on the same basis and with the same policy goals in mind. This form of harmonization is best described as norm harmonization.

Each of these forms of harmonization can be seen at work in EU environmental law and each can be assessed in terms of implementation. In all aspects, it can be seen that implementing EU environmental law has not been fully achieved. There is a lack of common rules due to transposition problems, there is no uniform environmental quality across the EU, environmental laws do cause distortions in the market, and Member States do not always operate on the basis of the same policies or norms. At the same time, it is doubtful whether any form of harmonization can ultimately be perfectly attained.

4.3 THE NON-IMPLEMENTATION PROBLEM AND MODES OF ENFORCEMENT

As Wenneras puts it so beautifully, in EU environmental law, 'the most tenacious problem is not the absence of adequate laws, but the flawed and belated Member State transposition (of directives) as well as insufficient application and enforcement of those rules'.[56] In the main, these problems relate to the implementation of Directives and there are three main ways in which a Member State may fail to properly implement a Directive: (1) by not transposing it into national law at all; (2) by transposing

---

[52] Council Directive 98/83/EC of 3 November 1998 on the quality of water relating to human consumption [1998] OJ L330/32.

[53] See, for example, counsel's arguments in *Berkeley v Secretary of State for the Environment* [2001] 2 AC 603 (HL).

[54] See Chapter 11.

[55] Directive 2008/98/EC of the European Parliament and of the Council of 19 November 2008 on waste and repealing certain Directives [2008] OJ L312/3.

[56] Pál Wenneras, *The Enforcement of EC Environmental Law* (OUP 2007) 1–2.

it but not correctly; or (3) by transposing it correctly but failing to apply it properly. While transposition failures can be categorized neatly in this way, identifying such failures in the first place can be very difficult, especially in relation to the latter two types of non-implementation of Directives, which involve an understanding of the legal systems and administrative practices of particular Member States, as well as the environmental facts and enforcement practices on the ground. Providing such information about implementation failures in relation to EU environmental law is challenging for many reasons, as explained by the European Commission.

European Commission, 'Improving Delivery of Benefits from EU Environment Measures: Building Knowledge Through Better Knowledge and Responsiveness' COM(2012) 95 final, 2, 4

Knowledge is already extensive on matters such as urban air pollution levels and bathing water quality. In others, such as biodiversity and land-use, it is patchier. Moreover, the picture is difficult to fill in if we want to know precisely how implementation is undertaken in a region, city or village. While often helpful, complaints sent to the Commission and petitions submitted to the European Parliament are an incomplete source of information. [...]

[I]t is not always simple to identify quickly the provisions of national law that correspond to a given provision of a directive. Monitoring efforts are uneven across Europe and the information generated is patchy and often out-of-date. Environmental information is available through individual requests rather than systematically published.

Limited information means that studies of EU implementation problems focus on formal legal proceedings brought rather than on actual breaches. Moreover, they tend to focus on Commission infringement proceedings, since even collecting information about direct effect actions in Member States concerning EU environmental law can be very difficult. A flavour of the challenges involved can be seen in the extract from the *28th Annual Report on Monitoring the Application of EU Law*. This report focuses on Commission EU law infringement proceedings as well as petitions to the EU Parliament.

European Commission, '28th Annual Report on Monitoring the Application of EU Law (2010)' COM(2011) 588 final, 4, 6

The three most infringement-prone policy areas (environment, internal market and taxation) account for 52% of all infringement cases. More than one fifth of all active cases (444) are associated with environmental legislation, with internal market and taxation cases (326 and 324, respectively) each amounting to 15% of all infringements.

However it was not in any of the above three policy areas that the most *new* infringement proceedings were opened in 2010. It was in the sector of health and consumer protection where most of the new opened cases (273) were non-communication cases (254). Dossiers relating to environment and internal market gave rise to the second and third highest number in 2010 (229 and 191 cases, respectively). However, the Commission closed the majority of the new non-communication cases on health and consumer protection by the end of 2010, leaving only 62 active. By contrast, around two thirds of the new proceedings were still open in the fields of environment, internal market and transport (148, 131 and 116 cases, respectively), where the carry-over of new cases to 2011 was the highest. [...]

Similarly to last year, the environmental area attracted the most petitions lodged with the European Parliament (120). Problems relating to the environmental impact assessment of projects alone were the subject of 42 petitions, followed by nature conservation (32) and waste management (20). In the area of water quality and marine resources an additional 14 petitions were lodged [...]

As regards EU *environmental legislation*, deadlines are regularly missed by a large number of Member States, normally resolved after the launch of infringement proceedings, and protracted delays can be seen in a minority of Member States. An example of particularly slow transposition is Directive 2004/35/EC of the European Parliament and the Council on environmental liability with regard to the prevention and remedying of environmental damage. Just four Member States transposed it on time and the European Court of Justice had to deliver judgments against seven Member States.

This analysis identifies significant transposition and implementation problems in relation to environmental Directives through the lens of Commission proceedings, but this is only one legal avenue for enforcing EU environmental law. There are in fact three primary means of enforcing EU environmental law—enforcement action taken by the Commission, enforcement action by national authorities, and actions brought by individuals in national courts using the doctrine of direct effect. Each of these is briefly considered in turn.

Under Article 17 TEU, the Commission 'shall ensure the application of the Treaties, and of measures adopted by the institutions pursuant to them'. A key vehicle for the Commission in meeting this responsibility is the Article 258 TFEU infringement procedure. That procedure is complex in practice but essentially involves three main steps: (1) issuing a formal notice to a Member State stating that it is in breach of EU law; (2) issuing a reasoned opinion if a Member State fails to remedy the identified breach; and (3) an application to the CJEU if the Member State still fails to remedy the breach. If a Member State does not comply with a duly given CJEU judgment, then, under Article 260 TFEU, the Commission can commence proceedings for the Member State to pay a penalty payment, which can be a considerable amount and accumulates with each day of continuing infringement.[57] In spite of these powers, Somsen discusses some of the very real problems that the Commission encounters in enforcing EU environmental law.

Han Somsen, 'Current Issues of Implementation, Compliance and Enforcement of EC Environmental Law: A Critical Analysis' in Ludwig Krämer (ed), *Rech und Um-Welt: Essays in Honour of Prof. Dr. Gerd Winter* (Europa Law Publishing 2003) 421–22

Turning [...] to the Commission [...] a severe limitation is formed by the simple fact that it has no independent fact-finding powers, and in this respect is almost exclusively dependent on data provided by Member States themselves or NGOs. Unlike many other fields of policy, where a mere change in the law may sometimes bring about the desired policy-goal environmental policy seeks to bring about certain physical results. Clean water or air, or biodiversity, for example, are not realised by a change in the letter of the law. Needless to say that for the Commission to win a case involving failure to realise these physical goals without disposing of its own data is a major challenge. Instead, often the only hard data that the Commission has its disposal mostly concern the legal and/or administrative measures that Member States have adopted in response to a certain environmental directive. Not surprisingly the vast majority of cases that are dealt with by the ECJ in the context of the infringement procedure concern failure to adopt the necessary measures, in other words concern issues of 'formal' as opposed to 'practical' implementation.

---

[57] Case C-387/97 *Commission v Greece* [2000] ECR I-369.

Somsen is not only highlighting the limited resources of the Commission, but also the special nature of 'physical' environmental problems that poses challenges for implementation.

The second main way of enforcing EU environmental law is through the actions of national authorities within their jurisdictions. Such activities should, in theory, occur alongside the enforcement of national law. As an example, national criminal prosecutions can indirectly enforce EU law, if the offences are shaped by, or otherwise reinforce, standards derived from EU Directives (as can be seen in English waste law—see Chapter 16). The successes and failures of this mode of 'national' enforcement are difficult to assess because they are so decentralized and data is difficult to collect, as has been indicated. The major determinants of the form and nature of national enforcement practices (and successes) will be legal and socio-political culture. Within a particular national jurisdiction, there may be limited or no mechanisms or resources for enforcement, or there may simply be no culture of prosecution for breaches of environmental regulation.

The third, and most significant, way of enforcing EU environmental law is by individuals bringing actions in national courts via the doctrine of direct effect. Direct effect is discussed in Chapter 19 in relation to environmental impact assessment, since the doctrine has developed powerfully within, and has also shaped, that area of law. Again data about direct effect actions in national courts is difficult to gather, and the doctrinal application to EU environmental law is by no means straightforward. Whilst environmental law Directives are numerous and often very detailed, it requires close textual analysis and interpretation to determine if particular provisions meet the slowly evolving legal requirements of direct effect. Further, courts have in some cases adapted these general conditions to enable provisions in environmental Directives to become directly effective.[58]

Despite these various avenues for enforcing EU environmental law, long recognized problems remain. In 1996, the Commission produced a Communication that considered problems of EU environmental law implementation in detail.[59] This Communication made clear that problems of implementation and enforcement were multi-dimensional. They were not due to a single institution's failure or purely down to political interests but, rather, due to various factors in combination. The Communication also discussed possible solutions to the problems identified. These included getting Member States more involved in the process of drafting Directives so as to make them more implementation-friendly, as well as strengthening enforcement mechanisms. IMPEL was set up to aid monitoring and information exchange between Member States. The international Aarhus Convention was another European-driven initiative motivated by implementation concerns.[60] More broadly, there was a general shift in EU regulatory strategies adopted to make implementation more flexible, as discussed in Section 6 on governance.

In 2008, the Commission once again published a Communication on environmental law implementation.

European Commission, 'Implementing European Community Environmental Law'
COM(2008) 773/4, 3–4

The environmental *acquis* is broad and ambitious, covering such issues as climate change, air quality, waste management, protection of water resources and biodiversity, controls on chemicals, and environmental impact assessment. It deploys a wide array of techniques, such as product standards, state-of-the-environment objectives, prohibitions and restrictions, economic instruments, sensitive area

---

[58] Case C-237/07 *Janecek v Freistaat Bayern* [2008] ECR I-6221. See Chapter 15.
[59] Commission, 'Implementing Community Environmental Law' COM (1996) 500 final.
[60] See Chapters 7 and 10.

designations, plans and programmes, and public participation and information provisions. The *acquis* needs to be applied to a wide range of natural conditions, under very varied national and regional administrative arrangements, and in situations that often have a cross-border dimension. There is also a high level of public interest, reflected in the exercise of environmental rights, including complaints and petitions. [...]

2.2. Specific Challenges

Non-communication of, and defects in, national and regional implementing legislation affect all parts of the environmental *acquis*. The following specific challenges apply:

- *Waste* – the need in certain Member States to end illegal landfilling, put in place adequate networks of regulated waste facilities, prevent illegal waste shipments and intensify public awareness of the goals of preventing, reusing and recycling waste. A combination of investment and well-structured national and regional enforcement and awareness-raising activities is necessary.

- *Water* – a need in certain Member States to invest more in collecting and treating urban waste water. This requires long-term planning and financial commitments.

- *Nature* – while now substantial in coverage, a key network of European nature sites still has gaps. More effort is also necessary to manage the sites in line with nature conservation objectives.

- *Industrial installations* – significant numbers of industrial installations still have EC permit and related requirements outstanding.

- *Environmental impact assessment* – the question of compliance with EC environmental impact assessment rules is frequently invoked in objections to major projects. The challenge is to have orderly development that takes account of legitimate environmental concerns.

- *Air quality* – lack of compliance with EC air quality standards in many European cities requires concerted action to lower concentrations of pollutants.

- *Climate change* – there is an ongoing need to ensure that all Member States provide the information needed to give proper follow-up to the Kyoto Protocol to the United Nations Framework Convention on Climate Change.

Strikingly, this analysis highlights both general and specific implementation challenges that intertwine. The Commission proposed a set of responses, which included:

European Commission, 'Implementing European Community Environmental Law' COM(2008) 773/4, 2

- legislative and post-legislative work aimed at the *prevention of breaches*,
- *responding* to the specific concerns of the *European public*,
- more immediate and more intensive treatment of *the most important infringements*,
- enhanced *dialogue with the European Parliament*,
- enhanced transparency, communication and *dialogue with the public* and interested parties.

The Communication discusses all of these proposed implementation improvements in detail, which notably give a prominent role both to the public and to information.[61] These issues will be returned to in Chapter 7.

---

[61] See Chapter 7 for a further discussion of this.

FURTHER READING AND QUESTIONS

1. One matter not addressed in this section is the problems that result from poor implementation and enforcement. Two sets of problems can be identified—those relating to market integration and those relating to environmental quality. Which do you think are the more important? Are there any other problems that you can think of that result from incomplete implementation of EU environmental law?

2. Considering the four types of harmonization set out here, do you think one particular type is more important than another? Why? What kind of issues do you think this analysis of harmonization raises for the concept of European integration?

3. For a further discussion of the role of individuals in implementing EU environmental law, see Han Somsen, 'Private Enforcement of Member State Compliance with EC Environmental Law: An Unfulfilled Promise?' (2000) 1 YEEL 311; Sacha Prechal and Leigh Hancher, 'Individual Environmental Rights: Conceptual Pollution in EU Environmental Law?' (2002) 2 YEEL 89; Pál Wennaras, *The Enforcement of EC Environmental Law* (OUP 2007).

4. For more commentary on Commission enforcement, see Ludwig Kramer, *Casebook of EU Environmental Law* (Hart Publishing 2002) 55; Ludwig Krämer, 'Statistics on Environmental Judgments by the EC Court of Justice' (2006) 18 JEL 407; Koen Lenaerts and José A Gutierrez-Fons 'The General System of EU Environmental Law Enforcement' (2011) 30 YEL 3.

5. For general reflections on implementation and enforcement, see Christoph Demmke, 'Trends in European Environmental Regulation: Issues in Implementation and Enforcement' (2003) 3 YEEL 329; Richard Macrory, 'Enforcement of EU Environmental Law: Some Proposals for Reform' in Richard Macrory (ed), *Reflections on 30 Years of EC Environmental Law* (Europa Law Publishing 2006).

5 ABILITY OF MEMBER STATES TO TAKE UNILATERAL ENVIRONMENTAL PROTECTION MEASURES

The third important theme of EU environmental law is the ability of Member States to take unilateral environmental protection measures. From an EU law perspective EU law is supreme,[62] and, as seen in Section 4, Member States have agreed under Article 4(3) TEU to 'take any appropriate measure, general or particular, to ensure fulfilment of the obligations arising out of the Treaties or resulting from the acts of the institutions of the Union'. The question is how much power does that leave Member States to act independently of EU law in relation to environmental protection and environmental matters? This question is an important one not only in terms of identifying Member States' powers but also for establishing the limits of Member State regulatory autonomy.

Broadly speaking there are two different situations where the issue of unilateral Member State action and its limits may arise: (1) when the Union has already acted in relation to a particular regulatory issue, and (2) when they have not.

---

[62] *Costa* (n 4).

5.1 UNILATERAL MEMBER STATE ENVIRONMENTAL ACTION: WHERE THE EU HAS ACTED

In most cases, when the EU has acted in environmental matters, it will do so on the basis of shared competence, as has been discussed. In cases of shared competence, there remains scope for Member State action in the relevant policy field. Thus, many EU environmental measures will leave scope for complementary or related Member State action. This section sets out illustrative examples of cases in which Member States attempt to act more stringently (in terms of environmental protection) than under existing EU environmental law, through the use of national legal provisions. These examples should not be seen as exhaustive and it should be remembered that Member States can use the flexibility of Directives to interpret or implement them more (or less) strictly. Likewise, many Directives will have safeguard clauses (see Article 114(10) TFEU) that allow Member States to take unilateral Member State action in cases of emergency or pressing national health and environmental needs. CJEU case law has made clear that, while in some cases more environmentally protective interpretations of Directives will be allowed,[63] in other cases uniform interpretation is paramount, particularly in relation to Directives that set up a regulatory system for authorizing activities or products in which all Member States and the Commission participate.[64] The Court has also stressed the importance of the principle of co-operation in response to Member State attempts to derogate from EU measures on allegedly pressing environmental grounds (such as strong views on rejecting the use of GMOs).[65]

Overall, the basic point is that, once the EU has harmonized an area of environmental policy through regulation, a Member State can no longer act unilaterally in relation to the issues over which competence has been exercised. However, the Treaty provides a number of exceptions to this—in Articles 114(4), 114(5), and 193 TFEU in particular. Article 114(4)–(5) TFEU sets out two cases in which Member States can apply to derogate from EU rules where competence has been exercised in relation to the establishment and functioning of the internal market. Article 114(4) applies before a harmonized internal market rule comes into force and Article 114(5) in post-harmonization cases.

Article 114(4)–(5)

4. If, after the adoption of a harmonisation measure by the European Parliament and the Council, by the Council or by the Commission, a Member State deems it necessary to maintain national provisions on grounds of major needs referred to in Article 36, or relating to the protection of the environment or the working environment, it shall notify the Commission of these provisions as well as the grounds for maintaining them.

5. Moreover, without prejudice to paragraph 4, if, after the adoption of a harmonisation measure by the European Parliament and the Council, by the Council or by the Commission, a Member State deems it necessary to introduce national provisions based on new scientific evidence relating to the protection of the environment or the working environment on grounds of a problem specific to that Member State arising after the adoption of the harmonisation measure, it shall notify the Commission of the envisaged provisions as well as the grounds for introducing them.

---

[63] Case C-318/98 *Fornasar* [2000] ECR I-4785 [2000] ECR I-4785, although note the reliance on art 176 (now art 193 TFEU) here.

[64] Case C-236/01 *Monsanto Agricoltura Italia SpA v Presidenza del Consiglio dei Ministri* [2003] ECR I-8105.

[65] Case C-6/99 *Association Greenpeace France v Ministere de l'Agriculture et de la Peche* [2000] ECR I-1651.

Articles 114(6)–(7) TFEU then set out the process by which applications under Article 114(5) are considered. Article 114(8) states:

> 8. When a Member State raises a specific problem on public health in a field which has been the subject of prior harmonisation measures, it shall bring it to the attention of the Commission which shall immediately examine whether to propose appropriate measures to the Council.

All these procedures are essentially administrative and overseen by the Commission. Scott and Vos noted that, in what were then Article 114(4) TEC decisions up until 2002, the Commission had applied reasoning similar to that applied by the CJEU in Articles 34–36 TFEU cases.[66] Up until 2003, the CJEU had never really considered (earlier versions of) Article 114(5)–(9) directly, although Advocate General Saggio in *Kortas* had argued that the provision should be interpreted restrictively.[67] The Grand Chamber of the Court came to consider Article 114(4) in 2003, and made the following comments:

Case C-3/00 *Denmark v Commission*
[2003] ECR I-2643, paras 56–58

The Facts

In accordance with Art 95(4) [now Article 114(4) TFEU] Denmark applied to the Commission to maintain national stricter measures that a Community directive in relation to a number of additives in foodstuffs. The Commission did not approve the measures as they were 'excessive in relation to their aim' of public health. Denmark challenged the decision before the ECJ arguing among other things that the Commission's interpretation of Article 95(4) was incorrect.

The Grand Chamber of the ECJ

56. It should be recalled that the EC Treaty seeks progressively to establish the internal market, which comprises an area without internal borders, within which the free movement of goods, persons, services and capital is assured. To that end, the EC Treaty provides for the adoption of measures for the approximation of the legislation of the Member States. In the course of the evolution of primary law, the Single European Act introduced a new provision, Article 100a, into that Treaty.

57. Article 95 EC, which under the Treaty of Amsterdam replaces and amends Article 100a of the Treaty, distinguishes between notified provisions according to whether they are national provisions which existed prior to harmonisation or national provisions which the Member State concerned wishes to introduce. In the first case, provided for in Article 95(4) EC, the maintenance of existing national provisions must be justified on grounds of the major needs referred to in Article 30 EC [now Article 36 TFEU] or relating to the protection of the environment or the working environment. In the second case, provided for in Article 95(5) EC, the introduction of new national provisions must be based on new scientific evidence relating to the protection of the environment or the working environment on grounds of a problem specific to that Member State arising after the adoption of the harmonisation measure.

58. The difference between the two situations envisaged in Article 95 is that, in the first, the national provisions predate the harmonisation measure. They are thus known to the Community legislature,

---

[66] Joanne Scott and Ellen Vos, 'The Juridification of Uncertainty: Observations on the Ambivalence of the Precautionary Principle within in the EU and WTO', in Christian Joerges and Renaud Dehousse (eds), *Good Governance in Europe's Integrated Market* (OUP 2002) 267–68.

[67] Case C-319/97 *Criminal Proceedings Against Antoine Kortas* [1999] ECR I-3143.

but the legislature cannot or does not seek to be guided by them for the purpose of harmonisation. It is therefore considered acceptable for the Member State to request that its own rules remain in force. To that end, the EC Treaty requires that such national provisions must be justified on grounds of the major needs referred to in Article 30 EC or relating to the protection of the environment or the working environment. By contrast, in the second situation, the adoption of new national legislation is more likely to jeopardise harmonisation. The Community institutions could not, by definition, have taken account of the national text when drawing up the harmonisation measure. In that case, the requirements referred to in Article 30 EC are not taken into account, and only grounds relating to protection of the environment or the working environment are accepted, on condition that the Member State provides new scientific evidence and that the need to introduce new national provisions results from a problem specific to the Member State concerned arising after the adoption of the harmonisation measure.

The Court is here balancing the validity of national regulatory autonomy with market integration. In the result, the CJEU found that Denmark could retain their more restrictive standards in relation to some food additives and not others.

The CJEU has also analysed the nature of Article 114(5)—which applies after a rule based on Article 114(1) has come into force—and indicated how it understands the scope of their review in relation to Commission discretion that is exercised to assess derogating national measures. The facts are not relevant.

Case C-405/07 P *Netherlands v Commission*
[2008] ECR I-08301, paras 51–57

51. […] Under Article 95(5) EC [now Article 114(5) TFEU], after the adoption of harmonisation measures, Member States are obliged to submit to the Commission for approval all national derogating provisions which they deem necessary.

52. That provision requires that the introduction of such provisions be based on new scientific evidence relating to the protection of the environment or the working environment made necessary by reason of a problem specific to the Member State concerned arising after the adoption of the harmonisation measure, and that the proposed provisions as well as the grounds for introducing them be notified to the Commission (Case C–512/99 *Germany v Commission* [2003] ECR I–845, paragraph 80, and Joined Cases C–439/05 P and C–454/05 P *Land Oberösterreich and Austria v Commission* [2007] ECR I–7141, paragraph 57).

53. Those conditions are cumulative in nature and must therefore all be satisfied if the derogating national provisions are not to be rejected by the Commission (see *Germany v Commission*, paragraph 81, and *Land Oberösterreich and Austria v Commission*, paragraph 58).

54. To determine whether those conditions are, in fact, satisfied, which can, depending on the circumstances, necessitate complex technical evaluations, the Commission has a wide discretion.

55. The exercise of that discretion is not, however, excluded from review by the Court. According to the case-law of the Court of Justice, not only must the Community judicature establish whether the evidence relied on is factually accurate, reliable and consistent but also whether that evidence contains all the information which must be taken into account in order to assess a complex situation and whether it is capable of substantiating the conclusions drawn from it (see Case C–525/04 P *Spain v Lenzing* [2007] ECR I–9947, paragraph 57 and the case-law cited).

56. Moreover, it must be recalled that, where a Community institution has a wide discretion, the review of observance of guarantees conferred by the Community legal order in administrative procedures is

of fundamental importance. The Court of Justice has had occasion to specify that those guarantees include, in particular for the competent institution, the obligations to examine carefully and impartially all the relevant elements of the individual case and to give an adequate statement of the reasons for its decision (see Case C–269/90 *Technische Universität München* [1991] ECR I–5469, paragraph 14; Joined Cases C–258/90 and C–259/90 *Pesquerias De Bermeo and Naviera Laida v Commission* [1992] ECR I–2901, paragraph 26; and *Spain v Lenzing*, paragraph 58).

57. The review of observance of those procedural guarantees is even more important in the procedure under Article 95(5) EC since the right to be heard does not apply to it (see *Land Oberösterreich and Austria v Commission*, paragraph 44).

This case extract shows the CJEU taking its reviewing responsibilities seriously. The intensity of review in this and other Article 114(5) TFEU cases is intensive.[68]

The other key Treaty provision that concerns the ability of a Member State to take unilateral environmental protection measures is Article 193 TFEU. Despite the promising language of Article 193, it is, in reality, very limited in application. It only relates to measures passed under Article 192 and, as Krämer has suggested, a literal reading of the Article would suggest that Member States can only pass more stringent measures of the same type as the Union measure.[69] Most significantly, any action by a Member State must be in accordance with the Treaty more broadly and thus cannot breach provisions such as Article 34 TFEU.[70] Further, not every type of unilateral protective measure taken by a Member State will fall under Article 193, as the comments of Advocate General Leger suggest.

Case C-324/99 *DaimlerChrysler AG v Land Baden-Wurttemberg*
[2001] ECR I-9897, Opinion of AG Leger, paras 54–56

54. Certain parties have asked whether the decree is compatible with Article 176 EC [now Article 193 TFEU].

55. Article 176 EC authorises Member States to adopt measures which are more protective of the environment than those provided for in Community law. In *Dusseldorp* and Others the Court none the less stated that, in exercising the discretion granted by Article 176 EC, Member States must ensure that they comply with Article 28 EC [now Article 34 TFEU] et seq.

56. In the present case, the competent German authorities have only exercised a right conferred on them by Article 4(3)(a)(i) of the regulation. The decree cannot therefore be regarded as a more stringent measure provided for by Article 176 EC. It is therefore pointless to consider whether the decree is compatible with Article 176 EC.

This may give the impression that Article 193 is a very restrictive Treaty article, bound by procedure, but the *Azienda Agro-Zootecnica Franchini sarl v Regione Puglia* case explains otherwise.

---

[68] Case C-439/05 *Land Oberosterreich v Commission of the European Communities* [2007] ECR I 7141.
[69] Ludwig Krämer, *EC Environmental Law* (7th edn, Sweet & Maxwell 2012) para 3–40.
[70] Case C-203/96 *Chemische Afvalstoffen Dusseldorp BV v Minister van Volkshuisvesting, Ruimtelijke Ordening en Milieubeheer* [1998] ECR I-4075.

Case C–2/10 *Azienda Agro-Zootecnica Franchini sarl v Regione Puglia* (21 July 2011) ECJ paras 50–54

The Facts

The case was a preliminary reference from Italy concerning the refusal of permission for the building of wind turbines in a Natura 2000 site designated a SCI and SPA [see Chapter 20] under the Habitats and Wild Birds Directives. The issue was whether Italy in banning such projects through legislation was acting in a manner consistent, or more protective, than those Directives.

The CJEU

50. Nevertheless, since [the Habitats] directive was adopted on the basis of Article 192 TFEU, it should be noted that Article 193 TFEU provides that Member States may adopt more stringent protective measures. Under that provision, such measures are simply required to be compatible with the FEU Treaty and notified to the Commission. The Court has thus held that 'in connection with the Community's environmental policy, to the extent that a measure of domestic law pursues the same objectives as a directive, Article 176 EC makes provision for and authorises the minimum requirements laid down by that directive to be exceeded, in the conditions set by that article' (see *Deponiezweckverband Eiterköpfe*, paragraph 58).

51. It is apparent from both the file submitted to the Court and the parties' arguments at the hearing that the essential purpose of the national and regional legislation at issue in the main proceedings is the conservation of the areas forming part of the Natura 2000 network, and in particular the protection of the habitats of wild birds against the dangers which wind turbines may represent for them.

52. It follows that legislation such as that at issue in the main proceedings which, with a view to protecting wild bird populations inhabiting protected areas forming part of the Natura 2000 network, imposes an absolute prohibition on the construction of new wind turbines in those areas, pursues the same objectives as the Habitats Directive. To the extent that it provides for a stricter system of protection than that established by Article 6 of that directive, it therefore constitutes a more stringent protective measure within the meaning of Article 193 TFEU.

53. It is, admittedly, not apparent from the documents submitted to the Court that the Italian Government communicated those measures to the Commission in accordance with Article 193 TFEU. Nevertheless, it should be noted that, while that provision requires Member States to communicate to the Commission the more stringent protective measures which they intend to maintain or introduce in environmental matters, it does not make implementation of the planned measures conditional upon agreement by the Commission or its failure to object. In that context, as the Advocate General noted at point 38 of his Opinion, neither the wording nor the purpose of the provision under examination therefore provides any support for the view that failure by the Member States to comply with their notification obligation under Article 193 TFEU in itself renders unlawful the more stringent protective measures thus adopted (see, by analogy, Case 380/87 *Enichem Base and Others* [1989] ECR 2491, paragraphs 20 to 23; Case C–209/98 *Sydhavnens Sten & Grus* [2000] ECR I–3743, paragraph 100; and Case C–159/00 *Sapod Audic* [2002] ECR I–5031, paragraphs 60 to 63).

54. The fact none the less remains that the more stringent protective measures put in place by the national and regional legislation at issue in the main proceedings must also comply with the other provisions of the FEU Treaty.

Note the way in which the Court characterizes the nature of the right under Article 193. Unlike Articles 114(4)–(5), it involves not so much a process of considering Member State action, but more an express regulatory power of Member States. However, *DaimlerChrysler* must be kept in mind, in that the relevant Article 192 Directive or Regulation will also determine the limits of that Member State power. In very broad terms, it is simply not possible to make general statements about the nature of the EU, and its environmental law powers.

5.2 UNILATERAL MEMBER STATE ENVIRONMENTAL ACTION: WHERE THE EU HAS NOT ACTED

When the Community has not acted in relation to a specific issue of shared EU competence, such as environmental matters, a Member State is free to act. However, it is still limited by the Treaty and other rules of EU law such as those relating to state aid,[71] and public procurement.[72] The most significant EU limits on Member States' ability to act unilaterally are Articles 34–36 TFEU, as they have been interpreted through the CJEU's jurisprudence. Moreover, these free movement rules are not only relevant when the EU has *not* acted, but where it has acted as well. This is because these fundamental Treaty provisions bind Member States when they act on the basis of Article 193 TFEU, as seen in Section 5.1, and also because EU institutions are themselves bound by Articles 34–36.[73]

Article 34

Quantitative restrictions on imports and all measures having equivalent effect shall be prohibited between Member States.

Article 35

Quantitative restrictions on exports, and all measures having equivalent effect, shall be prohibited between Member States.

Article 36

The provisions of Articles 34 and 35 shall not preclude prohibitions or restrictions on imports, exports or goods in transit justified on grounds of public morality, public policy or public security; the protection of health and life of humans, animals or plants; the protection of national treasures possessing artistic, historic or archaeological value; or the protection of industrial and commercial property. Such prohibitions or restrictions shall not, however, constitute a means of arbitrary discrimination or a disguised restriction on trade between Member States.

The case law on Article 34 and Article 36 is as doctrinally complex as it is extensive, and it has been one of the greatest driving forces behind European integration. In terms of EU environmental law, it is important to appreciate that the CJEU's interpretation of 'all measures having equivalent effect' has been so broad as to catch most product and process standards relating to environmental protection, and most standards regulating conditions of product use. In *Dassonville*, the CJEU stated that 'all trading rules enacted by Member States which are capable of hindering, directly or indirectly, actually or potentially, intra-community trade, are to be considered as measures having an effect equivalent

---

[71] Case C-379/98 *PreussenElektra AG v Schleswag AG* [2001] ECR I-2099.
[72] Case C-513/99 *Concordia Bus Finland Oy Ab v Helsingin Kaupunki and Hkl-Bussiliikenne* [2002] ECR I-7213.
[73] Case C-284/95 *Safety Hi-Tech* [1998] ECR I-4301.

to quantitative restrictions'.[74] Most national environmental measures will fall into this category. This is particularly because the way the CJEU interprets Article 34, the Article catches both *distinctly applicable* measures and *indistinctly applicable* measures, that is, national measures that both distinguish in their application between national and imported goods and those that do not.[75] The CJEU has introduced restrictions on the operation of Article 34 in relation to national measures that constitute 'selling arrangements',[76] but this has had little effect on the Article's application to national environmental protection measures as few fall into this category. By contrast, the CJEU has ruled that Article 34 can cover national measures that regulate conditions of product use, which is likely to catch more national environmental measures, as seen in the *Aklagaren v Mickelsson & Roos* case.

Case C-142/05 *Aklagaren v Mickelsson & Roos*
[2009] ECR I-4273, paras 24–29

The Facts

Infringement proceedings were brought against Mickelsson and Roos in a Swedish Court for using personal watercraft (jet skis) in waters where the use of such watercraft was banned under Swedish law. The accused argued, among other things, that the Swedish law was in breach of Article 28 TEC (now Article 34 TFEU).

The ECJ

24. It must be borne in mind that measures taken by a Member State, the aim or effect of which is to treat goods coming from other Member States less favourably and, in the absence of harmonisation of national legislation, obstacles to the free movement of goods which are the consequence of applying, to goods coming from other Member States where they are lawfully manufactured and marketed, rules that lay down requirements to be met by such goods, even if those rules apply to all products alike, must be regarded as 'measures having equivalent effect to quantitative restrictions on imports' for the purposes of Article 28 EC (see to that effect, Case 120/78 *Rewe-Zentral (Cassis de Dijon)* [1979] ECR 649, paragraphs 6, 14 and 15; Case C-368/95 *Familiapress* [1997] ECR I-3689, paragraph 8; and Case C-322/01 *Deutscher Apothekerverband* [2003] ECR I-14887, paragraph 67). Any other measure which hinders access of products originating in other Member States to the market of a Member State is also covered by that concept (see Case C-110/05 *Commission v Italy* [2009] ECR I-0000519, paragraph 37).

25. It is apparent from the file sent to the Court that, at the material time, no waters had been designated as open to navigation by personal watercraft, and thus the use of personal watercraft was permitted on only general navigable waterways. However, the accused in the main proceedings and the Commission of the European Communities maintain that those waterways are intended for heavy traffic of a commercial nature making the use of personal watercraft dangerous and that, in any event, the majority of navigable Swedish waters lie outside those waterways. The actual possibilities for the use of personal watercraft in Sweden are, therefore, merely marginal.

26. Even if the national regulations at issue do not have the aim or effect of treating goods coming from other Member States less favourably, which is for the national court to ascertain, the restriction which they impose on the use of a product in the territory of a Member State may, depending on its scope, have a considerable influence on the behaviour of consumers, which may, in turn, affect the access of that product to the market of that Member State (see to that effect, *Commission v Italy*, paragraph 56).

---

[74] Case 8-74 *Procureur du Roi v Dassonville* [1974] ECR 837, para 5.
[75] Case 120/79 *Rewe-Zentral AG v Bundesmonopolverwaltung für Branntwein* [1979] ECR 649 (*Cassis de Dijon*).
[76] Case C-267-8/91 *Keck & Mithourard* [1993] ECR I-6097.

27. Consumers, knowing that the use permitted by such regulations is very limited, have only a limited interest in buying that product (see to that effect, *Commission v Italy*, paragraph 57).

28. In that regard, where the national regulations for the designation of navigable waters and waterways have the effect of preventing users of personal watercraft from using them for the specific and inherent purposes for which they were intended or of greatly restricting their use, which is for the national court to ascertain, such regulations have the effect of hindering the access to the domestic market in question for those goods and therefore constitute, save where there is a justification pursuant to Article 30 EC or there are overriding public interest requirements, measures having equivalent effect to quantitative restrictions on imports prohibited by Article 28 EC.

29. Moreover, in either case, the national provision must be appropriate for securing the attainment of the objective pursued and not go beyond what is necessary in order to attain it (see *Commission v Italy*, paragraph 59 and the case-law cited).

The broad scope of national measures that will engage Article 34 means that the contentious legal issue in EU environmental law is not so much about whether there has been a breach of Article 34 TFEU but whether that breach can be *justified*.

As the Treaty is constructed, if a national measure is found to infringe Article 34, then it needs to be justified under the provisions of Article 36, set out here, in order to be judged lawful in EU terms. Article 36 contains a limited list of exceptions, including 'the protection of health and life of humans, animals or plants', which has provided a narrow exception for justifying some national environmental measures that would otherwise infringe Article 34.[77] However, Article 36 does not include all the valid reasons why a Member State may take unilateral regulatory action. In particular, it does not include environmental protection more broadly. In the case of *Cassis de Dijon*, the CJEU held that, in relation to *indistinctly applicable measures* that breach Article 34, Member States could justify them if they were 'necessary in order to satisfy mandatory requirements', relating to certain national policy areas such as 'fiscal supervision, protection of public health and consumer protection'.[78] In the case of *Commission v Denmark* (the *Danish Bottles* case),[79] environmental protection was added to that list of mandatory requirements by the Court. This expanded case law justification for national environmental protection measures gives Member States significantly increased regulatory autonomy in regulating environmental matters unilaterally, irrespective of free movement rules. The key difference between the *Cassis* and Article 36 justifications is the requirement of the former that the relevant national measure be indistinctly applicable. However, whether a Member State seeks to justify a measure under Article 36 or as a *Cassis* mandatory requirement, it still needs to show that the measures are necessary, appropriate to their objective, and in overall terms proportionate.

The fact that distinctly applicable measures cannot be justified on the grounds of environmental protection under the *Cassis* doctrine has caused some problems for the CJEU. This is because, as we have seen, environmental protection is understood to be a fundamental objective of the EU but the doctrinal constraints limit Member State action on environmental protection to cases where it applies uniformly to national and imported goods. Reconciling these aspects of EU law has led to some curious CJEU case law, as seen most notably in the *Walloon Waste* case.[80]

---

[77] Case C-67/97 *Criminal Proceedings Against Ditlev Bluhme* [1998] ECR I-8033.
[78] *Case 120/79 Cassis de Dijon* (n 75) para 8.
[79] Case C-302/86 *Commission v Denmark* [1988] ECR 4607.
[80] Case C-2/90 *Commission v Belgium* [1992] ECR I-4431.

Case C-2/90 *Commission v Belgium*
[1992] ECR I-4431, 2nd Opinion of AG Jacobs (19 September 1991), paras 23–24

The Facts

The Commission brought an enforcement action against Belgium for a Walloon prohibition on the storage, tipping or dumping of waste in Wallonia that had originated in another Member State or another region of Belgium. The measure applied to both hazardous and non-hazardous waste. The basis of the enforcement action was that Belgium had breached Article 28 (now Article 34 TFEU) of the Treaty. The CJEU held that waste was a good and that the parts of the measure relating to hazardous waste were inconsistent with Council Directive 84/631/EEC on the supervision and control within the European Community of the transfrontier shipment of hazardous waste and thus invalid. That left those measures concerned with non-hazardous waste. As the measures were distinctly applicable then theoretically the only basis they could be justified on was on the grounds of Article 30 (now Article 36 TFEU) but as the waste was non-hazardous it did not present a risk to the health and life of humans, animals or plants. If however the measure was to be found to be indistinctly applicable then they could by justified as a mandatory requirement.

2nd Opinion of AG Jacobs

23. At the hearing, there was some discussion of what measures a Member State might be permitted to take in order to safeguard particular regions or localities from an unwanted influx of non-recyclable waste. It is clear that such measures would have to be capable of justification, in accordance with well established principles, either under Article 36 or under one or other of the mandatory requirements recognised by Community law, among which is included environmental protection: see Case 302/86, *EC Commission v. Denmark*. If justification is sought in terms of a mandatory requirement not mentioned in Article 36 itself, the measures in question must be indistinctly applicable to domestic and imported waste. Even if the transactions were to be classified as the provision of services, the justification for any restriction would in my opinion fall to be examined in accordance with similar principles. Thus, Article 56 [now Article 56 TFEU], which applies to services by virtue of Article 66 [Article 62 TFEU], provides an exception to the free movement of services on grounds of public health; and in the case of indistinctly applicable measures, restrictions on services can be justified as measures taken in accordance with imperative requirements pertaining to the general interest: Case C-288/89, *Stichting Collectieve Antennevoorziening Gouda*.

24. Applying those principles, it seems to me that at least some restrictions on the transfer of waste could be justified on environmental grounds. Since environmental protection is a mandatory requirement not mentioned in Article 36, any such measure would, however, have to be indistinctly applicable to domestic and foreign waste. As I suggested in my previous Opinion [...] that condition may not be satisfied by a measure which simply restricts the use of the waste disposal facilities of a particular region or locality to waste produced in that locality or region. A provision of that type clearly favours domestically produced waste, especially where, as is the case with the decrees of the Walloon Regional Executive, exceptions may be made in the case of waste coming from other regions of the same Member State. Hence, in the circumstances of the present case, the measures in issue cannot be justified on grounds of environmental protection. In contrast, a provision applying throughout a region of a Member State, requiring waste to be disposed of within its locality of generation, might be said to be indistinctly applicable. Such a provision would prevent the exportation of locally produced waste to another locality or another Member State in exactly the same way that it prevented the disposal of waste coming from another State or locality. Such a measure might moreover be justified in terms of the need to reduce the amount of waste in transit and to limit the areas used for waste disposal. Whether or not the measure was in fact proportionate to those objectives could be of course only be decided in the light of all the relevant circumstances.

Case C-2/90 *Commission v Belgium*
[1992] ECR I-4431, paras 34–36

34. Imperative requirements can indeed be taken into account only in the case of measures which apply without distinction to both domestic and imported products (see inter alia the judgment in Joined Cases C-1/90 and C-176/90 *Aragonesa de Publicidad Exterior and Publivoa* [1991] ECR I-4151). However, in assessing whether or not the barrier in question is discriminatory, account must be taken of the particular nature of waste. The principle that environmental damage should as a matter of priority be remedied at source, laid down by Article 130r (2) [now Article 192(2) TFEU] of the Treaty as a basis for action by the Community relating to the environment, entails that it is for each region, municipality or other local authority to take appropriate steps to ensure that its own waste is collected, treated and disposed of it must accordingly be disposed of as close as possible to the place where it is produced, in order to limit as far as possible the transport of waste.

35. Moreover, that principle is consistent with the principles of self- sufficiency and proximity set out in the Basel Convention of 22 March 1989 on the control of transboundary movements of hazardous wastes and their disposal, to which the Community is a signatory (see *International Environmental Law*, Kluwer, Deventer and Boston, 1991, p. 546).

36. It follows that having regard to the differences between waste produced in different places and to the connection of the waste with its place of production, the contested measures cannot be regarded as discriminatory.

This reasoning is considered in more detail in Chapter 11, particularly for its use of the principle of rectification at source to find the contested measure indistinctly applicable in its application to national and foreign waste, but Weatherill also provides a thoughtful explanation for the Court's reasoning in relation to the question of indistinct applicability.

Stephen Weatherill, 'Free Movement of Goods in the European Community'
(2003) 28 European L Rev 756, 758

But in some instances—in particular in connection with challenges to national measures of environmental protection—it [the CJEU] confronts the awkwardness of a discrimination-based test and it sacrifices purity of reasoning in order to achieve a result that is consistent with good environmental practice, recognised *inter alios loci* elsewhere in the EC Treaty. So Case C-2/90, *Walloon Waste*, in which, if one takes the directions of Article 174(2) EC to heart, the Court reached the correct result, is described in Oliver as involving a "manifestly discriminatory" measure (p.219). But the core problem is that choice of discrimination as a test presupposes a need to decide what constitute legitimate subjects for comparison. In *Walloon Waste* waste originating from one source was unambiguously treated differently from waste from another. But how should one define the subject matter of the regulation under challenge? Waste? Or is the place of production of waste a factor bearing on its very nature, which may be taken to mean that transported waste is simply not the same thing as local waste?

In other words, Weatherill is highlighting that one could justify this case on the grounds that an innate feature of waste is the relationship between its site of production and the location of its disposal. This is attractive reasoning in that it renders the judgment less cryptic but it does not fundamentally address the real problem at the heart of the *Walloon Waste* case—that only indistinctly applicable measures can be justified on environmental protection grounds. The CJEU and Advocate General Jacobs returned to this problem in the *Preussenelektra AG v Schleswag AG* case.

Case C-379/98 *Preussenelektra AG v Schleswag AG*
[2001] ECR I-2099, Opinion AG Jacobs, paras 225–34

The Facts

A German law required electricity suppliers to purchase electricity from renewable energy sources in the local area. As such, it was clearly distinctly applicable on its face. The law was challenged on the ground that it breached Community laws on state aid and Article 28 [now Article 30 TFEU]. The law was not found to be in breach of the state aid rules.

Opinion of AG Jacobs

225 In my view, the reasoning in *Walloon Waste* is flawed and should not be relied on in the present case. The question whether or not a measure applies without distinction to domestic and imported products is from a logical point of view a preliminary and neutral one. Its only function under the Court's case-law is to determine which grounds of justification are available. I consider therefore that in assessing whether a measure is directly discriminatory regard cannot be had to whether the measure is appropriate.

226. But the judgment in *Walloon Waste* also shows something else, namely that it is desirable that even directly discriminatory measures can sometimes be justified on grounds of environmental protection.

227. Moreover there are indications that the Court is reconsidering its earlier case-law. The Court has relied on imperative requirements in cases in which it was at least doubtful whether the measure could be considered as applying without distinction. In *Dusseldorp* the Court expressly left open whether a discriminatory restriction of exports could in principle be justified on environmental grounds'. Perhaps the most striking case is *Aher-Waggon*. That case concerned a German measure making registration of aircraft in Germany conditional upon compliance with noise limits. That measure did, it seems to me, directly discriminate between domestic aircraft and imported aircraft in that aircraft previously registered in another Member State could not be registered in Germany even though aircraft of the same construction which had already obtained German registration before the German measure was adopted could retain that registration. The Court held however without assessing whether the measure was directly discriminatory that a barrier of that type could be justified by considerations of public health and environmental protection.

228. Thus, on the one hand, it cannot be ruled out that the relevance of the distinction between Article 30 interests and rule of reason exceptions is on the decline'. On the other hand the Court has not formally abandoned the rule that imperative requirements cannot be invoked in connection with directly discriminatory measures.

229. In view of the fundamental importance for the analysis of Article 30 of the Treaty of the question whether directly discriminatory measures can be justified by imperative requirements, the Court should, in my view, clarify its position in order to provide the necessary legal certainty.

230. Two specific reasons might be invoked in favour of a more flexible approach in respect of the imperative requirement of environmental protection. In the first place the amendments to the Treaties agreed in Amsterdam show a heightened concern for the environment even though Article 36 itself was not amended.

231. Of particular importance is Article 6 [now Article 11 TFEU], which now provides that: 'Environmental protection requirements must be integrated into the definition and implementation of the Community policies referred to in Article 3' including therefore the internal market, and which adds: 'in particular with a view to promoting sustainable development'. As its wording shows, Article 6 is not merely programmatic; it imposes legal obligations.

232 Special account must therefore be taken of environmental concerns in interpreting the Treaty provisions on the free movement of goods. Moreover harm to the environment, even where it does not immediately threaten - as it often does - the health and life of humans, animals and plants protected by Article 36 of the Treaty, may pose a more substantial, if longer-term, threat to the ecosystem as a whole. It would be hard to justify, in these circumstances, giving a lesser degree of protection to the environment than to the interests recognised in trade treaties concluded many decades ago and taken over into the text of Article 36 of the EC Treaty, itself unchanged since it was adopted in 1957.

233. Secondly, to hold that environmental measures can be justified only where they are applicable without distinction risks defeating the very purpose of the measures. National measures for the protection of the environment are inherently liable to differentiate on the basis of the nature and origin of the cause of harm, and are therefore liable to be found discriminatory, precisely because they are based on such accepted principles as that .environmental damage should as a priority be rectified at source' (Article 130r(2) [now Article 192(2) TFEU] of the EC Treaty). Where such measures necessarily have a discriminatory impact of that kind, the possibility that they may be justified should not be excluded.

234. On the assumption that environmental requirements can properly be invoked (on whatever basis) in the present case, it must next be established whether the StrEG 1998 complies with the principle of proportionality. Again only the briefest comments are possible at this stage.

Case C-379/98 *Preussenelektra AG v Schleswag AG*
[2001] ECR I-2099, paras 72–81

72. However, in order to determine whether such a purchase obligation is nevertheless compatible with Article 30 of the Treaty, account must be taken, first, of the aim of the provision in question, and, second, of the particular features of the electricity market.

73. The use of renewable energy sources for producing electricity, which a statute such as the amended Stromeinspeisungsgesetz is intended to promote, is useful for protecting the environment in so far as it contributes to the reduction in emissions of greenhouse gases which are amongst the main causes of climate change which the European Community and its Member States have pledged to combat.

74. Growth in that use is amongst the priority objectives which the Community and its Member States intend to pursue in implementing the obligations which they contracted by virtue of the United Nations Framework Convention on Climate Change, approved on behalf of the Community by Council Decision 94/69/EC of 15 December 1993 (OJ 1994 L 33, p. 11), and by virtue of the Protocol of the third conference of the parties to that Convention, done in Kyoto on 11 December 1997, signed by the European Community and its Member States on 29 April 1998 (see *inter alia* Council Resolution 98/C 198/01 of 8 June 1998 on renewable sources of energy (OJ 1998 C 198, p. 1), and Decision No 646/2000/EC of the European Parliament and of the Council of 28 February 2000 adopting a multiannual programme for the promotion of renewable energy sources in the Community (Altener) (1998 to 2002) (OJ 2000 L 79, p. 1)).

75. It should be noted that that policy is also designed to protect the health and life of humans, animals and plants.

76. Moreover, as stated in the third sentence of the first subparagraph of Article 130r(2) of the EC Treaty, environmental protection requirements must be integrated into the definition and implementation of other Community policies. The Treaty of Amsterdam transferred that provision, in a slightly modified form, to Article 6 of the Treaty, which appears in Part One, headed 'Principles.

77. In addition, the 28th recital in the preamble to Directive 96/92 expressly states that it is 'for reasons of environmental protection that the latter authorises Member States in Articles 8(3) and 11(3) to give priority to the production of electricity from renewable sources.

78. It should also be noted that, as stated in the 39th recital in its preamble, the directive constitutes only a further phase in the liberalisation of the electricity market and leaves some obstacles to trade in electricity between Member States in place.

79. Moreover, the nature of electricity is such that, once it has been allowed into the transmission or distribution system, it is difficult to determine its origin and in particular the source of energy from which it was produced.

80. In that respect, the Commission took the view, in its Proposal for a Directive 2000/C 311 E/22 of the European Parliament and of the Council on the promotion of electricity from renewable energy sources in the internal electricity market (OJ 2000 C 311 E, p. 320), submitted on 10 May 2000, that the implementation in each Member State of a system of certificates of origin for electricity produced from renewable sources, capable of being the subject of mutual recognition, was essential in order to make trade in that type of electricity both reliable and possible in practice.

81. Having regard to all the above considerations, the answer to the third question must be that, in the current state of Community law concerning the electricity market, legislation such as the amended Stromeinspeisungsgesetz is not incompatible with Article 30 of the Treaty.

Advocate General Jacobs is here arguing for more transparent reasoning but the CJEU does not deliver it. They do not explain on what basis the German law is being justified, or whether the law is judged to be distinctly or indistinctly applicable (on the facts, it seems to apply in a discriminatory way in favour of local German renewable energy producers). Nor is there any deep discussion of the proportionality of the German measure. Again, the fact that Germany is applying EU environmental norms, and furthering EU renewable energy policy through national measures, is seen as desirable, at the cost of clear and consistent legal doctrine.

Thus, it can be seen that the CJEU has not applied the developed doctrine in relation to Article 34 in a strict and inflexible manner in environmental cases. Another ambiguous aspect of this body of case law is that it is not always obvious what head of justification the Court refers to—the expanded *Cassis* justification or the narrower justification through Article 36.[81] This is important since the former does not allow the justification of distinctly applicable measures (albeit that the reasoning on this point has been highly ambiguous) whereas the latter justification does. Likewise, the Court's reasoning as to whether a measure is necessary and proportionate has tended to recognize the problems of scientific uncertainty and been far more generous—in terms of justifying national measures that breach Article 34—than in other areas.[82] Having said that, the test of proportionality is the aspect of Article 34 doctrine that has really evolved in environmental cases. In cases such as the Swedish jet-ski case (the *Åklagaren* case extract), and *Nationale Radd van Dierenwerkers en Liefhebbers* (Belgian animal lovers case),[83] the Court has now developed sophisticated reasoning in assessing the proportionality of national environmental measures.

However, overall, the driving logic of this case law has been norm harmonization, as seen in the 'Danish bees' case.

---

[81] Case C-389/96 *Aher-Waggon* [1998] ECR I-4473.

[82] Compare Case C-220/98 *Estee Lauder Cosmetics GmbH & Co. OHG v Lancaster Group GmbH* [2000] ECR I-117 and Case C-473/98 *Kemikalienspektionen v Toolex Alpha AB* [2000] ECR I-5681.

[83] Case C-219/07 *Nationale Radd van Dierenwerkers en Liefhebbers* [2008] ECR I-4475. This case builds on reasoning from *Commission v Denmark* [2003] ECR I-9693; see Chapter 11.

Case C-67/97 *Criminal Proceedings Against Ditlev Bluhme*
[1998] ECR I-8033, paras 33–38

The Facts

Denmark banned 'golden' bees from the Danish island of Læsø so as to protect a group of native brown bees that lived on the island. There was some uncertainty whether these brown bees were a distinct subspecies from other brown bees and what the impact of having other bees on the island would be.

The ECJ

33. On this question, the Court considers that measures to preserve an indigenous animal population with distinct characteristics contribute to the maintenance of biodiversity by ensuring the survival of the population concerned. By so doing, they are aimed at protecting the life of those animals and are capable of being justified under Article 36 [now Article 36 TFEU] of the Treaty.

34. From the point of view of such conservation of biodiversity, it is immaterial whether the object of protection is a separate subspecies, a distinct strain within any given species or merely a local colony, so long as the populations in question have characteristics distinguishing them from others and are therefore judged worthy of protection either to shelter them from a risk of extinction that is more or less imminent, or, even in the absence of such risk, on account of a scientific or other interest in preserving the pure population at the location concerned.

35. It does, however, have to be determined whether the national legislation was necessary and pro-portionate in relation to its aim of protection, or whether it would have been possible to achieve the same result by less stringent measures (Case 124/81 *Commission v United Kingdom* [1983] ECR 203, paragraph 16).

36. Conservation of biodiversity through the establishment of areas in which a population enjoys special protection, which is a method recognised in the Rio Convention, especially Article 8a thereof, is already put into practice in Community law (in particular, by means of the special protection areas provided for in Council Directive 79/409/EEC of 2 April 1979 on the conservation of wild birds (OJ 1979 L 103, p. 1), or the special conservation areas provided for in Directive 92/43).

37. As for the threat of the disappearance of the Læsø brown bee, it is undoubtedly genuine in the event of mating with golden bees by reason of the recessive nature of the genes of the brown bee. The establishment by the national legislation of a protection area within which the keeping of bees other than Læsø brown bees is prohibited, for the purpose of ensuring the survival of the latter, therefore constitutes an appropriate measure in relation to the aim pursued.

38. The answer to be given must therefore be that a national legislative measure prohibiting the keeping on an island such as Læsø of any species of bee other than the subspecies *Apis mellifera mellifera* (Læsø brown bee) must be regarded as justified, under Article 36 [now Article 30 TFEU] of the Treaty, on the ground of the protection of the health and life of animals.

In this case, the CJEU is not requiring Denmark to prove conclusively that there is a threat to the Læsø brown bee. Rather, the Court seems to justify Denmark's actions not so much on conventional Article 36 grounds (although this very same article is applied), but more on the ground that the purpose of the Danish law is consistent with both European and international policy. As already noted, this case law needs to be read alongside the discussion of principles in Chapter 11, since environmental principles are used as important doctrinal tools in many of these cases.

FURTHER READING AND QUESTIONS

1. For further commentary on Article 34 TFEU, see Miguel Poiares Maduro, *We the Court* (Hart Publishing 1999), especially chs 2 and 3 and Catherine Barnard, *The Substantive Law of the European Union: The Four Freedoms* (3rd edn, OUP 2010).

2. For further cases on Article 114(4) and (5), see Joined Cases C-439/05P & C-454/05P *Land Oberösterreich v Commission* [2007] ECR I-7141 (see Chapter 22). Note in particular how the CJEU is interpreting Case C-3/00 *Denmark v Commission* [2003] ECR I-2643. Note also the role of the European Food Safety Authority in *Land Oberösterreich*.

3. Case C-112/00 *Schmidberger v Austria* [2003] ECR I-5659 is an interesting example of environmental protestors' fundamental rights of freedom of expression being found to constitute a justification for Austria to allow them to protest by shutting a motorway for a short period of time.

4. The problems that scientific uncertainty creates for determining whether an Article 34 TFEU infringement can be justified were seen in the Case C-67/97 *Criminal Proceedings Against Ditlev Bluhme* [1998] ECR I-8033. For another example, see Case C-473/98 *Kemikalieinspektionen v Toolex Alpha AB* [2000] ECR I-5681.

5. For a further example of the problems created by the distinctly applicable/indistinctly applicable distinction, see Case C-389/96 *Aher Waggon* [1998] ECR I-4473.

6. Consider the following circumstances. Would the Member State be allowed under EU law to maintain their relevant national law?

    (a) An EU Directive regulates the environmental impacts of ice cream manufacture. Member State A wishes to introduce a stricter set of laws because they have far more ice cream manufacturers than other Member States. Would your answer make any difference if the Member State were maintaining a national law that existed at the time that the Community passed the Directive?

    (b) Member State B has a law that prevents the importation of any roses. The reason given is that imported roses may carry disease, which will threaten Member State B's rose stock. Would your answer by any different if the law banned the import of a widely recognized weed that could affect the wilderness areas of that Member State? You may find the *Bluhme* case and Case C-131/93 *Commission v Germany* [1994] ECR I-3303 useful.

    (c) Member State C decides to set up its own battery recycling disposal scheme. Anyone can return batteries to any shop in the Member State and get a refund. The scheme requires the packaging of all batteries sold in the Member State to be labelled with details about the scheme. You may find helpful Case 302/86 *Commission v Denmark* [1988] ECR 4607.

    (d) Member State D passes the following laws: (i) a law requiring that school children must ride a bicycle, take public transport, or go on foot to school; (ii) a law requiring that no cars with engines larger than 1.6 litres can be sold in Member State X; and (iii) a law requiring that no car parking places will be provided in any new development granted planning permission. No cars are manufactured in Member State E and it has a very large and significant bicycle industry that is world famous for its production of bicycles for children and families. Advise Member State E whether these laws would be in breach of its free movement of goods obligations under EU law.

6 LEGITIMACY AND THE DEVELOPMENT OF EU ADMINISTRATIVE LAW

In the discussion so far we have touched upon matters of EU competence, implementation and enforcement, and the ability of Member States to take unilateral action. However, we have not considered the role of EU institutions in detail. The discussion above hints at the existence of a rich hinterland of principles and policy, regulatory strategy, and governance structures. These different issues are discussed in detail in Chapters 11, 12, and 13 respectively. In short, these chapters show that the various legal frameworks and regulatory ideas and institutions of EU environmental *law* are not operating in isolation—they interconnect and interrelate with regulatory strategy and governance structures.

The discussion here is also stalked by an elephant in the room—the issue of the EU's legitimacy. The EU is commonly recognized as suffering from a legitimacy problem, but 'legitimacy' is a complex and multi-dimensional beast. Indeed, there are at least three different sets of legitimacy problems that concern and affect EU environmental law. First, problems of legitimacy arise because the EU suffers from a 'democratic deficit', since EU legislative processes are not dominated by democratic representatives but by the representatives of Member States. Given the largely 'administrative' (that is, involving discretion exercised by non-elected civil servants) nature of *national* environmental law,[84] EU environmental lawyers have not been particularly pre-occupied with the problems of legislation having little direct democratic input. By contrast, they have been very concerned about the wider public having few opportunities to contribute to the processes of formulating EU environmental law and making environmental decisions, and ensuring accountability of public actors. These issues are discussed in Chapters 7, 10, and 13.

Second, legitimacy can be understood in 'output' terms. That is, the legitimacy of governing institutions is considered to derive mainly from the results they achieve, rather than the procedure chosen to achieve that result.[85] On this front, it could be argued that the EU has been quite successful in relation to market integration. In relation to environmental protection, however, desired and required standards of environmental quality have not been achieved throughout the EU, largely because of problems with implementation and enforcement as already seen.

The final category of legitimacy problems may be described as those associated with the 'rule of law' and 'accountability'. There is a general belief that EU institutions, particularly in relation to environmental law, are unaccountable and have few constraints on their power. This has resulted in the growth of EU administrative law, a focus on transparency and public participation in relation to EU decision-making, and greater attention being paid to the role of the CJEU in holding both Member States and EU decision-makers to account (as seen in Case C-405/07 P *Netherlands v Commission*).

Chapter 7 considers the role of UK public law in environmental law, but it is also important to appreciate that a body of administrative law is also beginning to emerge at the EU level. By 'EU administrative law', we mean a body of law concerned with constituting EU institutions, limiting the power of decision-makers and holding them to account. Some of this law manifests in the form of annulment actions under Article 263 TFEU but much of it comprises rules and frameworks that govern action in the Commission, in agencies, and between Member States and EU institutions. This is an area that has undergone rapid change and is highly complex. This change has been partly driven by a number of important Treaty articles introduced by the Lisbon Treaty. The first is Article 290 TFEU.

---

[84] See Chapter 3.   [85] Fritz Scharpf, *Governing in Europe: Effective and Democratic?* (OUP 1999).

Article 290

1. A legislative act may delegate to the Commission the power to adopt non-legislative acts of general application to supplement or amend certain non-essential elements of the legislative act.

   The objectives, content, scope and duration of the delegation of power shall be explicitly defined in the legislative acts. The essential elements of an area shall be reserved for the legislative act and accordingly shall not be the subject of a delegation of power.

2. Legislative acts shall explicitly lay down the conditions to which the delegation is subject; these conditions may be as follows:

   (a) the European Parliament or the Council may decide to revoke the delegation;

   (b) the delegated act may enter into force only if no objection has been expressed by the European Parliament or the Council within a period set by the legislative act.

   For the purposes of (a) and (b), the European Parliament shall act by a majority of its component members, and the Council by a qualified majority.

3. The adjective 'delegated' shall be inserted in the title of delegated acts.

Article 290 TFEU is an affirmation of the principles that have constrained delegation of EU legislative power since the time of the European Coal and Steel Community.[86] However, it creates a formal distinction between legislative and delegated acts in EU law that did not previously exist. The Lisbon Treaty also reformed the labyrinthine process of comitology (Article 291 TFEU), by which committees decide important issues that supplement and inform EU secondary legislation. In short, these Lisbon reforms both formalize and constrain the power of EU institutions, including the range of administrative institutions that support the EU's primary legislative organs.

The Treaty also sets out (and has since the Treaty of Amsterdam) a duty to provide access to documents in Article 15 TFEU. This is reinforced by Regulation 1049/2001 regarding public access to European Parliament, Council, and Commission documents,[87] which is currently under review. The application of that Regulation to environmental problems is exemplified in the *WWF European Policy Programme v Council* case.

Case T-264/04 *WWF European Policy Programme v Council*
[2007] ECR II-911, paras 39–45

Facts

WWF applied under 1049/2001 for access to documents in relation to a meeting concerning trade and sustainability. They were refused access to one document on the ground that release would harm the sensitive negotiations.

The General Court (then CFI)

39. According to the case-law relating to that legislation, the rule is that the public is to have access to the documents of the institutions and refusal of access is the exception to that rule. Consequently, the provisions sanctioning a refusal must be construed and applied strictly so as not to defeat the application of the rule. Moreover, an institution is obliged to consider in respect of each document to which

---

[86] Case 9/56 *Meroni* [1957–58] ECR 133.   [87] [2001] OJ L145/43.

access is sought whether, in the light of the information available to that institution, disclosure of the document is in fact likely to undermine one of the public interests protected by the exceptions which permit refusal of access. In order for those exceptions to be applicable, the risk of the public interest being undermined must therefore be reasonably foreseeable and not purely hypothetical (see Case T-211/00 *Kuijer v Council* [2002] ECR II-485, paragraphs 55 and 56 and the case-law cited).

40. It is also apparent from the case-law that the institutions enjoy a wide discretion when considering whether access to a document may undermine the public interest and, consequently, that the Court's review of the legality of the institutions' decisions refusing access to documents on the basis of the mandatory exceptions relating to the public interest must be limited to verifying whether the procedural rules and the duty to state reasons have been complied with, the facts have been accurately stated, and whether there has been a manifest error of assessment of the facts or a misuse of powers (see, to that effect, Case T-14/98 *Hautala v Council* [1999] ECR II-2489, paragraphs 71 and 72, and *Kuijer v Council*, cited in paragraph 39 above, paragraph 53).

41. As to whether there was a manifest error of assessment of the facts, as the applicant essentially submits is the case, it must be noted that the Council refused to grant access to the note so as not to risk upsetting the negotiations that were taking place at that time in a sensitive context, which was characterised by resistance on the part of both the developing and the developed countries and the difficulty in reaching an agreement, as illustrated by the breakdown of negotiations at the WTO Ministerial Conference in Cancun in September 2003. Thus, in considering that disclosure of that note could have undermined relations with the third countries which are referred to in the note and the room for negotiation needed by the Community and its Member States to bring those negotiations to a conclusion, the Council did not commit a manifest error of assessment and was right to consider that disclosure of the note would have entailed the risk of undermining the public interest as regards international relations and the Community's financial, monetary and economic policy, which was reasonably foreseeable and not purely hypothetical.

42. It follows from the above that the Council has, first, given sufficient reasons for its refusal to grant access to the note and, secondly, not misinterpreted the conditions for applying the exceptions to public access to documents laid down in the third and fourth indents of Article 4(1)(a) of Regulation No 1049/2001.

43. Those conclusions cannot be altered by the applicant's arguments concerning the need to balance its interest in having access to the note against the Council's interest in not disclosing it.

44. The exceptions set out in Article 4(1) of Regulation No 1049/2001 are framed in mandatory terms and it follows that the institutions are obliged to refuse access to documents falling under any one of those mandatory exceptions once the relevant circumstances are shown to exist (see, by analogy, Case T-105/95 *WWF UK v Commission* [1997] ECR II-313, paragraph 58). Those exceptions are therefore different from the exceptions relating to the interest of the institutions in maintaining the confidentiality of their deliberations laid down in Article 4(3) of Regulation No 1049/2001, in the application of which the institutions enjoy a discretion which allows them to balance, on the one hand, their interest in maintaining the confidentiality of their deliberations against, on the other hand, the interest of the citizen in gaining access to documents (see, by analogy, *Carvel and Guardian Newspapers v Council*, cited in paragraph 26 above, paragraphs 64 and 65).

45. Since the exceptions at issue in the dispute fall under Article 4(1) of Regulation No 1049/2001, the Council was not required in the present case to balance the protection of the public interest against the applicant's interest in gaining access to the note.

The issue of access to information is also governed by the Aarhus Convention on the Access to Information, Public Participation in Decision-making and Access to Justice in Environmental

Matters, which will be discussed in Chapters 7 and 10. Many of the Union's obligations under that Convention were implemented into Regulation 1367/06/EC.[88] Article 3 of that Regulation makes clear that Regulation 1049/2001 applies to any request for environmental information. Aarhus applies to both EU and Member State, and it is also a prime example of the development of EU environmental administrative law.

The final and most obvious thing to note about the nature of EU administrative law is the role of the General Court and the Court of Justice in hearing judicial review/annulment actions under Article 263 TFEU.

Article 263 TFEU

The Court of Justice of the European Union shall review the legality of legislative acts, of acts of the Council, of the Commission and of the European Central Bank, other than recommendations and opinions, and of acts of the European Parliament and of the European Council intended to produce legal effects *vis-à-vis* third parties. It shall also review the legality of acts of bodies, offices or agencies of the Union intended to produce legal effects *vis-à-vis* third parties.

It shall for this purpose have jurisdiction in actions brought by a Member State, the European Parliament, the Council or the Commission on grounds of lack of competence, infringement of an essential procedural requirement, infringement of the Treaties or of any rule of law relating to their application, or misuse of powers.

The Court shall have jurisdiction under the same conditions in actions brought by the Court of Auditors, by the European Central Bank and by the Committee of the Regions for the purpose of protecting their prerogatives.

Any natural or legal person may, under the conditions laid down in the first and second paragraphs, institute proceedings against an act addressed to that person or which is of direct and individual concern to them, and against a regulatory act which is of direct concern to them and does not entail implementing measures.

Acts setting up bodies, offices and agencies of the Union may lay down specific conditions and arrangements concerning actions brought by natural or legal persons against acts of these bodies, offices or agencies intended to produce legal effects in relation to them.

The issue of standing under paragraph 4 is dealt with in Chapter 10 but here it is worth noting that, over the last two decades, the General Court and CJEU have developed a rich body of doctrine concerning the grounds of legality review in EU law. In particular, it should be noted that 'of any rule of law relating to their application' is an open-ended category and includes grounds of review such as legitimate expectations, fundamental rights, and manifest error of assessment. Likewise, as discussed in Chapter 11, environmental principles inform these grounds of review.

There are a couple of things to note about the procedure of this legality review framework. First, as a matter of general practice, the General Court hears Article 263 cases from non-privileged applicants (that is, those under Article 263(4)) while the CJEU hears appeals from the General Court and cases brought by privileged applicants (that is, those listed in Article 263(2)). Second, questions of validity can also be raised as part of a preliminary reference action (Article 267(2)), meaning that locating relevant legality doctrine in EU cases is a complicated exercise.

---

[88] Regulation (EC) No 1367/2006 of the European Parliament and of the Council of 6 September 2006 on the application of the provisions of the Aarhus Convention on Access to Information, Public Participation in Decision-making and Access to Justice Environmental Matters to Community Institutions and bodies [2006] OJ L264/13.

All of this only gives a very rough outline for the structures of legal accountability in the EU. You will see how those structures operate in almost all chapters in this textbook. In short, the important point to appreciate is that understanding EU law is vital for understanding more specific areas of UK and English environmental law.

7 CONCLUSION

This chapter has provided an overview of some of the major themes in EU environmental law. It has not attempted to be an exhaustive examination of the subject, but to show its many different dimensions. For nearly every English environmental problem, an environmental lawyer will need to think about its EU law aspects, including the way in which relevant EU law has been created, implemented, and enforced. Likewise, they will also need to think about the limits of the UK's ability to take unilateral action on environmental matters. Questions of accountability and legitimacy at the EU level will also be important in appraising the quality of English environmental law.

The discussion in this chapter may be frustrating for those readers hoping for something more linear and definitive. That lack of linearity reflects the nature of EU law, which is a subject that needs to be understood 'in the round'. This will become ever more obvious in the different substantive chapters of this book, since EU environmental law is omnipresent but in many different ways, as specific aspects of EU law are triggered or engaged by different environmental problems. Without an understanding of the bigger picture of EU law, an understanding of the detail of a particular area of English environmental law can be hard to grasp. To put the matter another way, the EU is not just a source of rules but a site for legal practice.

FURTHER READING AND TEXTBOOKS ON EU LAW

Catherine Barnard, *The Substantive Law of the EU: The Four Freedoms* (3rd edn, OUP 2010).

Paul Craig and Gráinne de Búrca, *EU Law: Text, Cases and Materials* (5th edn, OUP 2011).

Paul Craig, *EU Administrative Law* (2nd edn, OUP 2012).

Ludwig Kramer, *EU Environmental Law* (7th edn, Sweet & Maxwell 2012).

Stephen Weatherill, *EU Law: Cases and Materials* (10th edn, OUP 2012).

5

INTERNATIONAL
ENVIRONMENTAL LAW

When many students think of environmental law, they think of (public) international law—of treaties, of conventions, of high profile international meetings at which heads of state fly in and sign agreements in front of the cameras. These agreements, if successful, can save the world, and if they are not successful (or even signed) … well … back to the drawing board. In either case, the perception is that the triumphs and tragedies of environmental law are determined by what occurs in the international legal order.

Much is wrong with this perception. As already made clear, most environmental law with which lawyers must engage is national and EU in character and, as we will see in Parts III and IV, its operation is deeply embedded in those legal cultures. Likewise, while international law may be international, the relationship between national and international legal orders is not a top-down hierarchical one. This is because the concept of state sovereignty is fundamental. Furthermore, the history of the pursuit of environmental protection at the international level has shown that saving the world—or even just responding to environmental problems in legal terms—is a fiendishly complex and incremental business.

Thus, while international law may not be a top-down authoritarian regime that delivers solutions to environmental problems, a study of its role is fundamentally important in understanding the complexity of environmental law. A glimpse of this was seen in the Introduction to Part II with the *Commission v Ireland*[1] case, which concerned whether an EU or international dispute resolution forum was the proper legal arena for hearing the Ireland–UK dispute over alleged pollution of the sea from nuclear waste processing. Further, there are many different legal cultures relevant to environmental protection in international law, which are all part of the fabric and thread of the tapestry of environmental law. A true understanding of environmental law thus cannot be gained without regard to the many relevant arenas, discourses, norms, and regimes of the international legal order.

In light of all this, and the fact that international environmental law is a topic in itself,[2] the aim of this chapter is to give an overview of the landscapes and dynamics of international environmental law and public international law, and to get you thinking about key issues. The chapter is structured as follows. First, it briefly examines the concept of international environmental law and the different ways it can be defined. Second, the nature and complexity of public international law are considered more broadly. Particular emphasis is placed on the sources of public international law, the role of state sovereignty, the increasing phenomenon of fragmentation in international law, and the different ways

---

[1] Case C–459/03 *Commission v Ireland* [2006] ECR I–4635.

[2] See, for example, Patricia Birnie, Alan Boyle, and Catherine Redgwell, *International Law and the Environment* (3rd edn, OUP 2009), and the textbooks listed at the end of this chapter.

in which public international law can be understood theoretically. The purpose of this analysis is to highlight the deeply embedded complexity of international legal orders.

Section 3 considers the history and scope of international environmental law. In terms of subject matter, international environmental law can be understood to consist of environmental protection regimes, sustainable development regimes, and regimes that indirectly regulate environmental problems—thus the scope of international environmental law is extensive and overlapping, and its history multifaceted. The fourth section surveys the nature of international environmental law, considering the respective and overlapping roles of treaties, customary law, and soft law. The fifth section then examines the institutional arrangements of international environmental law, including dispute settlement mechanisms. In these three sections (Sections 3, 4, and 5), the highly fragmented nature of international environmental law is evidenced. Finally, the sixth section discusses the enforcement and national implementation of international environmental law.

One point should be made before starting. This chapter does not attempt to cover the substance of international environmental law comprehensively. Such a task requires a (lengthy) book rather than a chapter. And the purpose of this chapter is different—it focuses on the complex underlying nature of international environmental law. Attention is thus paid to its structure and its legal composition, rather than the precise obligations included within it. In this regard, this chapter provides a launch pad for engaging with international environmental law more closely.

1 DEFINING INTERNATIONAL ENVIRONMENTAL LAW

From the outset, the study of environmental problems in the context of international law encounters a problem of definition and scope. The problem is similar to that outlined in Chapter 1 for environmental law generally, in that there is no definitive and tightly bounded subject labelled 'international environmental law'. This is particularly because, as we will see, the international legal order is fragmented.

Broadly speaking, international environmental law can be understood to consist of a series of disputes, ad hoc treaties, Conventions, Protocols, regimes, and governance networks that are constantly evolving and exist in varying interrelationships with other. What they have in common is their relationship to environmental problems, albeit more or less directly. Moreover, as in Chapter 1, descriptive, purposive, and jurisprudential definitions of international environmental law can be identified. Birnie, Boyle, and Redgwell's descriptive approach to defining the subject is extracted here.

Patricia Birnie, Alan Boyle, and Catherine Redgwell, *International Law and the Environment* (3rd edn, OUP 2009) 2–3

A number of preliminary problems arise in any attempt to identify 'international environmental law'. Although international courts make use of the term, some scholars have avoided doing so, arguing that there is no distinct body of 'international environmental law' with its own sources and methods of law-making deriving from principles peculiar or exclusive to environmental concerns. Rather, they stress that such relevant law as does exist originates from the application of general rules and principles of classical or general international law and its sources.

It is unquestionably correct that international environmental law is part of international law as a whole, not some separate, self-contained discipline, and no serious lawyer would suggest otherwise. The problem with over-emphasizing the role of general international law, however, is that 'the traditional legal order of the environment is essentially a *laissez-faire* system oriented toward the unfettered freedom of states. Such limitations on freedom of action as do exist have emerged in an *ad hoc* fashion and have been formulated from perspectives other than the specifically environmental'. As environmental problems have risen in importance it has been necessary to develop a body of law more specifically aimed at protection of the environment. A study of contemporary international environmental law thus requires us to consider this evolving body of specifically environmental law, as well as the application of general international law to environmental problems.

In this work the expression 'international environmental law' is thus used simply as a convenient way to encompass the entire corpus of international law, public and private, relevant to environmental issues or problems, in the same way that use of the terms 'Law of the Sea', 'International Criminal Law', and 'International Economic Law' are widely accepted. It is not intended thereby to indicate the existence of some new discipline based exclusively on environmental perspectives and principles, though these have played an important role in stimulating legal developments in this field, as we shall observe.

Birnie, Boyle, and Redgwell's definition highlights the difficulties of describing the area of international environmental law—a distinctive but not a new legal discipline—and also makes clear its nuanced relationship to public international law, which is considered further in Section 2, and to international law more broadly.

Other definitions of international environmental law are purposive in nature. Thus, Bodansky describes a 'policy' approach to international environmental law and argues that such an approach is typical of newly emerging fields.[3] Within the international context, this kind of approach quickly leads to a great deal of questioning, both about how to achieve policy outcomes and the extent to which this process raises distinctly legal questions. Implicit in this analysis are questions about what constitutes law and what its purpose is. This issue is highlighted in the extract from the philosopher Crisp.

Roger Crisp, 'Ethics and International Environmental Law' in Samantha Besson and John Tasioulas (eds), *The Philosophy of International Law* (OUP 2010) 473

International environmental law (IEL) is primarily an instrument for human purposes, and these purposes may be moral ones. As an instrument, it could not plausibly be described as blunt. It is difficult to make, to interpret, and to apply or enforce. Nor are its conceptual boundaries sharp. Not only is it hard to say what constitutes 'the environment' (should cultural heritage be included along with the mountains and oceans, for example?), but exactly what counts as law here is unclear. The term often used—'soft'—is more appropriate. But soft, hard-to-define, hard-to-use things can be valuable, and the ends or goals of IEL include some among the most significant yet adopted by humanity.

Environmentalists, lawyers, politicians, citizens, and others who participate in the processes of establishing and applying IEL are pursuing many different goals.

As suggested in the introduction, purposive approaches to international environmental law have populist appeal. However, these two extracts make clear that a simplistic purposive understanding of international environmental law is not credible, due to the complexity of international legal orders.

---

[3] Daniel Bodansky, *The Art and Craft of International Environmental Law* (Harvard UP, 2010) 6.

As for a jurisprudential approach to international environmental law, Bodansky quickly moves on to consider a quite different, and more normatively-focused, approach to understanding international environmental law, which he describes as an 'explanatory approach'.

Daniel Bodansky, *The Art and Craft of International Environmental Law* (Harvard UP 2010) 8–9

The explanatory approach to international environmental law focuses on two topics: first, the emergence (or non-emergence) of international environmental norms, and second, their effectiveness (or ineffectiveness). To what extent, for example, can the development and effects of international environmental law be explained in terms of the rational self-interest of states? What are the roles of scientific knowledge, intergovernmental organizations, and non-governmental groups? These are the kinds of questions that political scientists ask.

Political scientists have traditionally separated into different 'schools' each with a different causal model to explain how international norms emerge and affect behaviour, or fail to do so. *Realists* emphasize the role of power;[21] *institutionalists* the role of interests more generally;[22] *liberals* the role of domestic politics;[23] and *constructivists* the role of values and knowledge.[24] Interestingly, students of international environmental politics have tended to eschew the methodological preference of most political scientists for a single explanatory model, and have instead acknowledged the multiplicity of causal factors and pathways that help explain the emergence and effectiveness of international environmental norms.[25] My approach, too, will be eclectic: I will consider the role of power and interests and knowledge and ideology and domestic politics, as appropriate to the occasion. To my mind, the traditional schools of international relations are like the blind men and the elephant: each has something to contribute but presents only part to the picture. State interests are important, but how a state conceives of its interests depends on its values and knowledge, as well as on its domestic political processes. Actors apply a 'logic of consequences' calculating the costs and benefits of their actions. But what counts as a cost and benefit depends on many other factors. In any event, individuals (and states) not only calculate consequences; they also consider the appropriateness of different courses of action, based on their values and their self-identity—their conception of 'who they are.' Attempts to reduce this complex reality to a simple causal model hold the promise of scientific rigor but at too steep a price for the international environmental lawyer, who must operate in the real world—in all its messiness.

[21] For a general survey of realism, see Robert O. Keohane, ed., *Neorealism and Its Critics* (New York: Columbia University Press, 1986); *see also* John J. Mearsheimer, "The False Promise of International Institutions," *International Security* 19 (1994/1995), pp 5–49.

[22] See e.g., Robert O Keohane, *After Hegemony: Cooperation and Discord in the World Political Economy* (Princeton, NJ: Princeton University Press, 1984); Stephen D. Krasner, ed. *International Regimes* (Ithaca, NY: Cornell University Press, 1983). A game theoretic vision of instrumentalism is found in Scott Barrett, *Environment and Statecraft: The Strategy of Environmental Treaty Making* (Oxford: Oxford University Press, 2003).

[23] See, e.g., Andrew Moravcsik, "Taking Preferences Seriously: A Liberal Theory of International Politics," *International Organization* 51 (1997), pp. 513–533.

[24] *See, e.g.,* Peter M. Haas, *Saving the Mediterranean: The Politics of International Environmental Cooperation* (New York: Columbia University Press, 1990); Martha Finnemore and Kathryn Sikkink, "International Norm Dynamics and Political Change," *International Organization* 52 (1998), pp. 887–917. For an international law approach, see Jutta Brunnée and Stephen S. Toope, "International Law and Constructivism: Elements of an Interactional Theory of International Law," *Columbia Journal of Transnational Law* 39 (2000), pp. 19–74.

[25] *See, e.g.*, Oran R. Young, *International Governance: Protecting the Environment in a Stateless Society* (Ithaca, NY: Cornell University Press, 1994); Peter M. Haas, Robert O. Keohane, and Marc A. Levy, eds, *Institutions for the Earth: Sources of Effective International Environmental Protection* (Cambridge, MA: MIT Press, 1993).

At first glance, Bodansky's 'explanatory' approach seems to bear very little resemblance to the jurisprudential approach to environmental law seen in Chapter 1. But there is much in common with it. In particular, Bodansky is focused on identifying the norms of international environmental law just as the jurisprudential approach to environmental law more broadly is focused on a normative understanding of the subject. The approaches differ because discourses about international law are different from those concerning domestic law. In particular, the creation of environmental international law is highly dependent on the political actions of state actors, whereas domestic legal orders have less contingent and more settled forms of norm (and law) creation. Bodansky thus highlights the relationship of international environmental law with other disciplines—political science and international relations in particular—which shape the different ways in which the subject can be understood in normative terms. The issues he is highlighting are also features of public international law more generally. Just as the descriptive approach defines international environmental law in terms of public international law, so too does a jurisprudential or explanatory approach.[4] The fundamental character of international environmental law thus involves, in whole or in large part, public international law, which is examined further in Section 2.

FURTHER READING AND QUESTIONS

1. Which of the definitional approaches discussed in Section 1 do you find the most attractive? And which do you consider as the most useful? Why? Consider how these definitional approaches vary from those seen in Chapter 1.

2. What does Bodansky's 'explanatory' approach extracted here tell you about how international treaties relating to environmental problems might be agreed? Does this suggest that international environmental law will end up as 'fragmented'?

---

2 PUBLIC INTERNATIONAL LAW

The need for environmental lawyers to understand public international law flows from the fact that international legal regimes, instruments, and norms concerned with environmental problems are, for the most part, regimes, instruments, and norms of public international law. Since public international law is a discipline in its own right, we, as textbook writers, face the Hamlet-like prospect of writing a textbook within a textbook within a textbook (public international law in international environmental law in environmental law, as it applies to UK and English environmental problems). However, our approach is to give an overview of key aspects of public international law, highlighting four features that are of particular relevance to international environmental law: the definition and sources of public international law, the role of state sovereignty, the fragmented nature of the international legal order, and the different theoretical perspectives that can be applied to the subject.

---

[4] For another example of this approach, see Philippe Sands and Jacqueline Peel, *Principles of International Environmental Law* (3rd edn, CUP 2012).

2.1 PUBLIC INTERNATIONAL LAW AND ITS SOURCES

Shaw's definition of public international law is a useful starting point for understanding the subject.

Malcolm Shaw, *International Law* (6th edn, CUP 2009) 2

Public international law covers relations between states in all their myriad forms, from war to satellites, and regulates the operations of the many international institutions. It may be universal or general, in which case the stipulated rules bind all the states (or practically all depending upon the nature of the rule), or regional, whereby a group of states linked geographically or ideologically may recognise special rules applying only to them, for example, the practice of diplomatic asylum that has developed to its greatest extent in Latin America. The rules of international law must be distinguished from what is called international comity, or practices such as saluting the flags of foreign warships at sea, which are implemented solely through courtesy and are not regarded as legally binding. Similarly, the mistake of confusing international law with international morality must be avoided.

This is a relatively straightforward definition, although as Lowe notes:

Archetypal international law is concerned with the rights and duties of States towards one another; but the principles, materials and techniques of international law are applied more widely.[5]

This point is particularly significant in relation to environmental problems because, as seen throughout this book, the 'principles, materials and techniques' of international law indeed operate in other legal orders, in ways that both incorporate and depend on norms of those implementing, interacting legal orders. This can be seen particularly in relation to the UK and EU legal systems, as explored further in Section 6.

The final part of Shaw's definition—concerning the distinction between law, comity, and morals—also reveals a real difficulty in the subject because the distinction between these concepts is not always clear. Accordingly, it is important to appreciate carefully the *sources* of public international law, and their legal nature, as a major aspect of defining the subject. Thirlway gives one view of the sources of international law.

Hugh Thirlway, 'The Sources of International Law' in Malcolm Evans (ed), *International Law* (3rd edn, OUP 2010) 96–97

It is traditional to distinguish between what are called the *material* sources of international law, and the *formal sources*. In relation to a particular rule which is alleged to be a rule of international law, the material source is simply the place—normally a document of some kind—in which the terms of the rule are set out. This may be a treaty, a resolution of the UN General Assembly, a proposal of the UN International Law Commission, a judicial decision, a 'restatement' by a learned body, or even a statement in a textbook. In identifying a material source, no account need be taken of the legal authority of the textual instrument: for example, a treaty which has never come into force at all, and is thus not binding on anyone as a treaty, may still be the material source for a rule which has acquired the force of binding law by another route.

---

[5] Vaughan Lowe, *International Law* (Oxford, Clarendon Press 2007) 5.

The question of the authority for the rule as a rule of law, binding on States, is determined by the *formal* source of the rule. The generally recognized formal sources are identified in Article 38 of the Statute of the International Court of Justice [...] the two most important sources in practice are treaties and international custom.

Article 38(1) of the Statute of the International Court of Justice is as follows:

The Court, whose function is to decide in accordance with international law such disputes as are submitted to it, shall apply:

(a) international conventions, whether general or particular, establishing rules expressly recognized by the contesting states;

(b) international custom, as evidence of a general practice accepted as law;

(c) the general principles of law recognized by civilized nations;

(d) subject to the provisions of Article 59, judicial decisions and the teachings of the most highly qualified publicists of the various nations, as subsidiary means for the determination of rules of law.

The role of these different sources of public international law is considered further in Section 4, but note that *this* understanding of legal sources is positivistic in outlook—representing international law largely as a set of posited rules that can be explicitly identified rather than perceptions of obligations embedded within legal systems. Lowe explains, and questions, the real world application of, this idea.

Vaughan Lowe, *International Law* (Clarendon Press 2007) 26–27

In essence, positivists say that a State is bound by rules of international law because it has signed up to them, either literally in the case of treaty rules or metaphorically by the State's participation in the making of customary law. That has been the dominant ideology of international law throughout the last century. The practical significance of this ideology upon the day-to-day operation of international law is not entirely negligible [...] but it is small. The most important characteristic of twentieth century international law was its bureaucratization and the pervasive colouring of inter-governmental dealings by the concepts and vocabulary international law; the nature of international governmental dealings is, as they say, subdued to what it works in, like the dyer's hand. Those who actually engage in international lawyering are troubled seldom and little by the question of the theoretical basis of obligation. James Brierly who devoted one of his more substantial articles to the question of the basis and obligation in international law, wisely observed that 'we are all of us obliged to act as if we were convinced of the reality of an objective order, both physical and moral, if we are to go on living and acting at all'. Quite what the theoretical basis of that objective order might be is a matter that can in practice usually remain a mystery.

Despite its limitations, the positivist theoretical approach to public international law has historically dominated public international law scholarship. However, Section 2.4 shows that it is not the only theoretical approach to the subject, and goes some way in unpacking the theoretical 'mystery' of international law's objective order.

From the perspective of an environmental lawyer, understanding the nature of the norms and legal instruments that emerge from the international legal order is important. This is because international environmental law regimes can take a range of different forms and their authority as formal, or otherwise authoritative, sources of international law is often ambiguous or at least contested by scholars and commentators. This kind of scholarly debate is seen in Sections 4 and 5.

2.2 STATE SOVEREIGNTY

The next important aspect of public international law to note, which is also important to international environmental law, is state sovereignty. The concept is explained by French.

Duncan French, 'A Reappraisal of Sovereignty in the Light of Global Environmental Concerns' (2001) 21 LS 376, 377

The sovereignty of each nation state is the most fundamental principle of international law. It is the idea that all states, whatever their size or political influence, are deemed to be independent of all other states and that they exercise control over their own subjects, their own affairs and their own territory. As Judge Huber noted in the *Island of Palmas Arbitration*:

'[s]overeignty in the relations between States signifies independence. Independence in regard to a portion of the globe is the right to exercise therein, to the exclusion of any other State, the functions of a State ... Territorial sovereignty involves the exclusive right to display the activities of a State.'

Such sovereignty manifests legally in many different ways in public international law, but most fundamentally in the concept that a state must *consent* to being bound by international obligations. At the same time, as French notes, the concept of sovereignty is also limited by public international law. As Okowa explains, an important corresponding duty comes with the rights of state sovereignty—state responsibility.

Phoebe N Okowa, *State Responsibility for Transboundary Air Pollution in International Law* (OUP 2000) 65–66

The sovereignty that a state enjoys in respect of its territory embodies a catalogue of rights and duties the character of which as *lex lata* is not in doubt. Thus, it is generally accepted that territorial sovereignty confers a licence on a state to exploit and enjoy the resources within its territorial confines. But the freedom is double-edged, in so far as it also requires source states to respect equally the sovereignty of others and refrain from conduct that may be injurious to other states in a manner that is contrary to the rules of international law. In particular, it is generally accepted that where a state harbours a source of harm on its territory, it is in principle responsible to other states that may suffer injury as a result. The obligations of the source state to prevent harm is grounded on the actual or presumed control that international law vests in it. It follows from this principle that the state is responsible for polluting activities directly operated by it as well as those under private control.

A number of judicial decisions, multilateral and bilateral treaties, diplomatic exchanges, as well as resolutions of international organizations, discussed below, may be cited in support of the basic proposition that a state 'is not permitted to use its territory for purposes injurious to the interests of other states'. This principle has been reaffirmed repeatedly and its legal quality is not in doubt. However, much uncertainty has centred on its practical application, and in particular the standard of conduct required of states in specific situations. Nevertheless, it is increasingly accepted that it involves a duty to exercise control over sources of transboundary harm and to pay reparation for any resultant damage.

The relationship between state sovereignty and state responsibility is a major theme in international law and environmental protection, particularly in relation to state activities that have a transboundary impact. This relationship has its roots firmly in the foundations of public international law.

2.3 FRAGMENTATION

A third important feature to note about public international law is that it has become increasingly fragmented as a legal order over time. This legal fragmentation, of which scholars have become progressively aware, has been the subject of scrutiny by the International Law Commission, which explains the phenomenon.

International Law Commission, *Fragmentation of International Law: Difficulties Arising From the Diversification and Expansion of International Law* UN Doc A/CN.4/L.682 (13 April 2006) paras 7–8

One of the features of late international modernity has been what sociologists have called 'functional differentiation', the increasing specialization of parts of society and the related autonomization of those parts. This takes place nationally as well as internationally. It is a well-known paradox of globalization that while it has led to increasing uniformization of social life around the world, it has also lead to its increasing fragmentation—that is, to the emergence of specialized and relatively autonomous spheres of social action and structure.

The fragmentation of the international social world has attained legal significance especially as it has been accompanied by the emergence of specialized and (relatively) autonomous rules or rule-complexes, legal institutions and spheres of legal practice. What once appeared to be governed by 'general international law' has become the field of operation for such specialist systems as 'trade law', 'human rights law', 'environmental law', 'law of the sea', "European law' and even such exotic and highly specialized knowledges as 'investment law' or 'international refugee law' etc.—each possessing their own principles and institutions. The problem, as lawyers have seen it, is that such specialized law-making and institution-building tends to take place with relative ignorance of legislative and institutional activities in the adjoining fields and of the general principles and practices of international law. The result is conflicts between rules or rule-systems, deviating institutional practices and, possibly, the loss of an overall perspective on the law.

Thus, fragmentation not only raises issues about legal and institutional coherence at the international level, but also issues about how environmental problems are framed within this legal order, and what is understood as the relevant (legal) expertise required to address them. Koskenniemi, who chaired the committee that produced the ILC report above, explains this legal framing problem and its consequences.

Martti Koskenniemi, *The Politics of International Law* (Hart Publishing 2011) 67

Think about an everyday international occurrence such as the transport of hazardous chemicals at sea. This can be conceptualised at least through half a dozen vocabularies accompanied by the same number of forms of expertise and types of preference: law of trade, law of transport, law of the environment, law of the sea, 'chemical law', and the law of human rights. Each would have something to say about the matter. Each would narrate it as part of a different set of human pursuits, values, and priorities. Trade law might focus on trade agreements between the countries and their relations with third parties. Transport law might highlight the legal-technical relationships between the different parties to a single contract of carriage and allocate jurisdiction differently between the legal systems to which they adhere. Environmental law might examine the nature of the cargo and the properties of the environment through which it is passing. Law of the sea might fix on the jurisdiction of the coastal state and the port state, or perhaps on the relevant International Maritime Organisation (IMO) standards, while 'chemical law' would examine it from the perspective of the best practices, standard operation forms, and the economic position of the industry. Finally, the law of human rights might concentrate on the dangers of the voyage to the persons involved in it, the conditions on board the ship and during the off-loading of the cargo to the local populations, and so on. Each such vocabulary is likely to highlight some solutions, some actors, some interests. None of them is any 'truer' than the others.

An example of this framing problem is seen in the *Commission v Ireland* case, extracted in the introduction to Part II. That case involved a dispute over which tribunal should consider the case, and also which legal regime should govern it, as Koskenniemi explains.

Martti Koskenniemi, *The Politics of International Law* (Hart Publishing 2011) 337

The question of the possible environmental effects of the operation of the 'MOX Plant' nuclear facility at Sellafield, United Kingdom, has been raised at three different institutions: an Arbitral Tribunal set up under the United Nations Convention on the Law of the Sea (UNCLOS), another Tribunal under the Convention on the Protection of the Marine Environment of the North-East Atlantic (OSPAR Convention) and within the European Court of Justice (ECJ) under the European Community and Euratom Treaties. Three rule-complexes—the UNCLOS, the OSPAR Convention, and EC law—each address the same facts. Which should be determinative? Is the problem principally about the law of the sea, about (possible) pollution of the North Sea, or about inter-EC relationships? To pose such questions already points to the difficulty of providing an answer. Surely the case is about all of these matters?

Moreover, even if these different, potentially applicable regimes include similar obligations, they will interpret them differently. That is the practical result and significance of different legal cultures in operation. This reinforces why, in light of fragmentation in international law, the international legal order cannot be understood in monolithic terms. The types of challenges thus highlighted by Birnie, Boyle, and Regdwell in defining international environmental law (in Section 1) are not just problems of the subject's scope, but also problems of bringing together and integrating different legal cultures.

This is not the only consequence of fragmentation in public international law. Koskenniemi argues that another consequence is a 'deformalization' of international law, which Carlarne explains.

Cinnamon Carlarne, 'Good Climate Governance: Only a Fragmented System of International Law Away?' (2008) 30 Law & Policy 450, 457

As a result of deformalization, standard-making takes places within the framework of multilateral treaty law-making processes and, thus, creates issue-specific substantive and procedural rules rather than developing general behavioral standards—as was common in the early days of international law.

Deformalization is evidenced by the compartmentalization of law as well as by the delegation of law-making authority from traditional international law actors—that is, states—to new international organizations—that is, multilateral environmental agreement (MEA) secretariats and conferences of the parties (COPs). This creates a cycle whereby international law becomes increasingly detailed and clustered by topic.

Deformalization encourages the proliferation of 'soft' law and, at times, erodes treaty legitimacy, but it also facilitates informed, issue-specific negotiations. For international environmental law, this is a critical development. Environmental law is intrinsically tied to complex scientific and social processes and divides countries down cultural and economic lines. In the absence of deformalized law-making procedures that facilitate extensive negotiations and compromise, it is doubtful that much international environmental law would exist. Deformalization, thus, offers essential opportunities for advancement in specialized, but no less important, areas of international law.

Deformalization, however, also creates substantive and administrative divisions and challenges the overarching unity and role of international law in interstate relations. The creation of specialized branches of international law creates new opportunities for interstate negotiations, but it also raises concerns about the coherence and legitimacy of international law as a whole.

The concept of soft law is discussed in more detail in Section 4.3, but it is also closely bound up with the fragmentation of public international law. These themes of fragmentation and de-formalization of law can also be seen in national and EU law,[6] but they are particularly significant in public international law. This is partly due to the fact that the international legal order is more nascent that these other legal orders, but also because international legal scholars are aware that the conceptual foundations of the subject are not as well established as they might be. We saw this in Section 1, in considering a jurisprudential or normative approach to international environmental law, where this involved drawing on political science concepts and knowledge to account for the arrangements between, and behaviours of, state actors. Compared to the English legal system, public international law thus lacks firm intellectual as well as legal foundations, which has meant that scholars have been particularly interested in international law theory, as Section 2.4 explains.

2.4 INTERNATIONAL LAW THEORY

To appreciate different theoretical approaches to the subject, it is useful to consider the nature of public international law scholarship. This might appear an obscure line of inquiry, but the Boyle and Chinkin extract makes clear that there is a considerable divergence in scholarly opinion over how public international law should be understood, conceptualized, and studied. These differences reflect different theoretical approaches, or different scholarly approaches for building a theoretical framework for public international law. These differences are also particularly relevant for environmental lawyers because they influence how environmental law, to the extent that it comprises or incorporates norms of international environmental law, is also understood and how emerging legal forms and processes of international environmental law are, or should be, studied.

Alan Boyle and Christine Chinkin, *The Making of International Law* (OUP 2007) 11–15

The origins of contemporary international law are rooted in natural law thinking categorised by Van Hoof under the umbrella of 'legal idealism'. While many versions of natural law have been influential,

---

[6] See further Chapters 3 and 4.

especially (but by no means exclusively) in Western thought over many centuries, its 'constant factor has been the appeal to something superior to positive law, whether this superior factor was seen as a directive [rooted in religious doctrine, or secular appeal to reason] or as a guide to positive law'. [...]

The legal positivist, seeking rules deriving from state consent will tend to adhere to recognisable sources of authority, treaties and custom, and will give weight to those other sources identified in the Statute of the ICJ, Article 38(1). The positivist is less willing to accept the normative effect of non-legal instruments such as GA [General Assembly] resolutions or the final documents of global summit meetings, seeing any concept of so-called soft law as seeking 'unprecedented expansion of the concept of law into areas of normative regulation which have never been considered as belonging to the law proper'. While 'enlightened' positivism retains the centrality of formal sources as the core of international legal discourse, it is more flexible, recognises change in patterns of state behaviour and wider methods of determining state consent and evidence of that consent. [...]

The adherent to the New Haven (Yale) policy science approach to international law focuses not on rules but explicitly on the processes by which legal decisions and policies are made. The method of analysis involves first identification of the observer's standpoint to allow disengagement and objectivity, second consciousness of the conceptual categories used by the observer to analyse particular situations, and third an understanding of the processes used to influence particular outcomes. The constitutive process therefore requires identification of trends in decision-making with reliance on past decisions in the light of their contexts (conditioning factors) and the desired outcome, thereby incorporating policy objectives and values. Unlike the positivist view, under the New Haven approach the decision-making process that generates international law is not limited to states or the actions of state officials. [...]

Critical legal scholars have used the form of legal argument to expose the indeterminacy of and contradictions in international (and national) legal rules and processes and thereby to challenge the view that law is rational, neutral, objective and principled. They emphasise that law is premised on substantive political or other values. [...] The self designated task of the critical legal scholar is to reveal the concealed biases and hierarchies of international law and hence to expand its discourse. Accordingly the decision-maker should not rely solely on either rules or process but must use 'socio logical enquiries into causal relationships and political enquiry into acceptable forms of containing power'. Critical scholars in what has become known as the 'New Approaches to International Law' (NAIL) have exposed a range of different biases that are obscured and marginalised by accounts of law-making that ignore the interests of disempowered groups. Studies include the gendered nature of international law, Third World Approaches to International Law (TWAIL) that show the failure to take account of third world analyses and resistance movements, and historical accounts that have demonstrated the 'dark' side of international law in upholding the interests of the colonial powers, for example by masking their violent acquisition and exploitation of overseas territories through the civilising doctrines of legality. Critical analysis has also charged that international law-making is in fact 'part of the problem' and that lawyers mistake law-making for problem solving and substitute process for substantive solutions.

The critiques just addressed might be perceived as coming from the 'left' of the political spectrum. Other challenges to the place of international law in the contemporary world come from its other end. Commitment to an international rule of law has long been challenged by the realists who dispute the applicability of law to the powerful when it restrains their choices. Another challenge to the position of law in international affairs has gained prominence in the post-cold war era, especially from within the US. Writers such as Goldsmith and Posner have argued that international law empirically results from state interests: 'international law emerges from states acting rationally to maximise their interests, given their perceptions of the interests of other states and the distribution of state power.' On this reasoning law is no more than a factor to be taken into account in decision-making and the concept of *opinio juris* is rendered meaningless. Treaty-making is also reduced in importance for the text has little bearing on state behaviour.

This long extract shows that there is a real diversity of opinion over how one should go about studying public international law, and thus its relationship to environmental protection and its application to environmental problems. Thus, for some, the focus for understanding and studying international environmental law should be Treaties, with perhaps some attention paid to soft law. For others, attention should be directed to the processes and mechanisms by which legal decisions and policies are made; for others again, the institutions and governance regimes created and involved are central. Thus, returning to Shaw's definition quoted at the start of this section, we can see that it conceals a number of complexities. Moreover, Boyle and Chinkin's analysis relates to that of Bodansky, in that his questions about the proper focus of international environmental law raise questions about how to understand the subject in theoretical terms.

FURTHER READING AND QUESTIONS

1. What role do you think state sovereignty plays in contributing to environmental problems and their solutions? In particular, do you think it helps or hinders the search for effective solutions? In thinking about these questions, you might wish to return to the discussion about the role of the state in Chapter 2. For further reading, see Robin Eckersley, *The Green State: Rethinking Democracy and Sovereignty* (MIT Press 2004).

2. Think more carefully about the theoretical discussions of Bodansky, and Boyle and Chinkin. How might these different theoretical approaches affect understandings of the following problems: (a) climate change negotiations; (b) biodiversity; and (c) water pollution.

---

3 THE HISTORY AND SUBJECT MATTER OF INTERNATIONAL ENVIRONMENTAL LAW

It may appear to the reader that the analysis in Section 2 was heavily bogged down in public international law, without much focus on environmental issues. But engagement with the different features of public international law identified—from state sovereignty to fragmentation to varying scholarly approaches and traditions—is vital in understanding the nature and complexity of international environmental law. These features should be kept in mind when reading any piece of international environmental law scholarship. In short, the subject of international environmental law cannot be treated instrumentally, and international law cannot be understood as a crude tool for achieving particular (environmental) ends. It is a deeply rich and complex realm of legal ordering with its own principles, processes, and legal forms. It is also open to differing interpretations.

With that legal picture in mind, this section focuses on how we got there, setting out a brief overview of the history of international environmental law, and also considers in more detail the scope of the subject. Since this chapter does not cover comprehensively the subject matter of international environmental law, the discussion primarily sets the scene, although there is some closer focus on the substance of international trade law, since this background informs issues considered in a number of other chapters.

3.1 THE HISTORY OF INTERNATIONAL ENVIRONMENTAL LAW

International environmental law, like environmental law, is often understood as being a 'new' subject. However, as Redgwell explains, it actually has a relatively long history.

Catherine Redgwell, 'International Environmental Law' in Malcolm Evans (ed), *International Law* (3rd edn, OUP 2010) 690–91

It is common to divide the development of international environmental law into three or four stages. The first pre-dates the 1972 Stockholm Conference and is characterized by piecemeal and reactive responses to particular problems of resource use and exploitation [...] Some writers sub-divide this first stage into two, commencing the second stage with the creation of international institutions from 1945 and seeing its culmination in the 1972 Stockholm Conference on the Human Environment inaugurating on this analysis the third phase of development. It produced a Declaration and an Action Programme, a template followed by the 1992 Rio Conference on Environment and Development 20 years later. In addition, the run-up to and conclusion of the Stockholm Conference stimulated a great deal of regional and global treaty making activity, much of it directed towards protection of the marine environment. [...] The terrestrial environment was also the focus of attention, with the conclusion of major treaties regarding the natural and cultural heritage (the 1972 UNESCO Convention Concerning the Protection of the World Cultural and Natural Heritage), species and habitat protection (eg, the 1971 Ramsar Convention on Wetlands of International Importance Especially as Waterfowl Habitat, the 1973 Convention on International Trade in Endangered Species and, in direct response to a recommendation at Stockholm, the 1979 Bonn Convention on the Conservation of Migratory Species of Wild Animals). [...]The third (or fourth) period adopts a holistic approach to environmental protection and seeks to marry such protection with economic development, embraced in the principle of sustainable development. This was the theme of the 1992 Rio Conference on Environment and Development which, in addition to producing a Declaration of Principles and a programme of action for the twenty-first century (Agenda 21) saw the conclusion of two major treaties under UN auspices—the 1992 Framework Convention on Climate Change and the 1992 Convention on the Conservation of Biological Diversity. [...] the general outcome of the Rio Conference and the conclusion of the Biodiversity and Climate Change Convention in particular marked a new phase in international environmental regulation with the acknowledgement in each that the conservation of biological diversity or preventing further adverse changes in the earth's climate are the common concern of humankind. Proposals further to develop the institutional framework of international environmental law to reflect these common and intergenerational concerns have not yet made any significant headway.

Since the time of Redgwell's writing, the twenty year follow up to the Rio Conference, the 2012 Rio+20 Conference, has been held, with similarly limited legal and institutional developments. This pithy analysis highlights not only the way in which the subject matter has evolved over time but also how its scope has changed. In particular, a shift can be seen from quite limited sectoral approaches to the more integrated and wide ranging programmes that are part of the sustainable development programme. Implicit in this shift to a broader regulatory framework is the growing relevance of areas of international law that relate to environmental problems but were not created to regulate them—reflecting both the expansive possibilities of what constitute environmental problems and the interconnection of international laws that relate to them (as well to other problems). The international trade regime of the World Trade Organisation (WTO) is a very good example of this widening body of international 'environmental' law. Likewise, one can see a shift from more conventional public international law regimes (based largely on treaty formation) to ones that are more legally novel and *sui generis* in nature (involving soft law agreements, and focusing on institutional frameworks). This shift is not simply one of subject matter but in the very nature of legal obligations at the international level. Yet, with that said, one should not understand these changes in wholesale terms as one legal approach completely yielding to another. Rather, there is a panoply of existing legal regimes and instruments that are products of different times, different politics, and different levels of awareness of environmental problems.

So, as a result of this history, what types of environmental issues does this panoply of regimes address today? The short answer is: many. Further, a lot of these issues are not dealt with in an isolated way at the international level—there are also significant and interacting regulatory efforts at the national and supranational levels. For example, in Chapter 22 on Genetically Modified Organisms (GMOs) and Chapter 20 on nature conservation law, we will see that national and supranational regimes are closely interrelated with international regimes, albeit not in hierarchical ways.

The resulting scope of international environmental law can be understood as falling into three distinct categories—those regimes that have an environmental protection focus, those concerned with sustainable development, and those that are relevant to international environmental law because they indirectly govern environmental problems. Each of these classifications is considered in this section. As will become obvious, these labels do not reflect the adoption of identical legal forms or strategies but refer to an array of different regulatory arrangements, united only by general themes of legal approach.

3.2 ENVIRONMENTAL PROTECTION REGIMES

As is clear from Redgwell's historical analysis in Section 3.1, there is a range of different regimes promoting environmental protection at the global level. Young explains how we can understand these regimes as being concerned with three (albeit overlapping) categories of environmental issues: international commons, shared natural resources, and transboundary externalities.

Oran Young, 'Rights, Rules and Resources in World Affairs' in Oran Young (ed), *Global Governance: Drawing Insights From the Environmental Experience* (MIT Press 1997) 7–9

International commons are physical or biological systems that lie wholly or largely outside the jurisdiction of any individual member of international society but that are of interest to two or more of them— or their nationals—as valued resources. Examples of such systems of current interest include high seas fisheries, deep seabed minerals, the electromagnetic spectrum, the stratospheric ozone layer, the global climate system, the global hydrological system, and outer space. Three broad options are available to those concerned with the governance of international commons: (1) enclosure through the extension of national jurisdictions, (2) the creation of a supranational or world government, and (3) the introduction of codes of conduct analogous to common property arrangements in small-scale stateless societies. Although students of international relations have long focused their attention on the first two options, the idea of 'governance without government' has stimulated a marked growth of interest in the third option.

Shared natural resources, by contrast, are physical or biological systems that extend into or across the jurisdictions of two or more members of international society. They may involve renewable resources (eg, migratory stocks of wild animals or straddling stocks of fish), non-renewable resources (eg, pools of oil that underlie areas subject to the jurisdiction of two or more states), or complex ecosystems that transcend the boundaries of national jurisdictions (eg, shared river basins). As these examples suggest, there may be significant asymmetries among the states concerned with shared natural resources. [...]

Transboundary externalities arise when activities occurring wholly within the jurisdiction of one state nevertheless produce (normally unintended) consequences that affect the welfare of those located in other jurisdictions. Classic cases involve tangible impacts, such as the acidification of Swedish lakes from transboundary fluxes of airborne pollutants, or the loss of biological diversity (which is of actual or Potential value to people located everywhere) associated with the destruction of moist tropical forests in the Amazon basin. [...] As these examples suggest, transboundary externalities can and often do give rise to asymmetries between the victims and the perpetrators of environmental harms, which accounts for the widespread interest both in devising liability regimes that will cover the transboundary impacts of actions occurring within individual jurisdictions and in promulgating general rules or principles pertaining to such situations (for example, the 'polluter pays' principle).

This taxonomy of environmental problems reflects many of the themes we saw in Chapter 2—from the collective and transboundary nature of environmental problems to their polycentricity. However, this taxonomy also reflects the global context in which international environmental law operates. Thus, the concept of a 'commons' takes on a whole new meaning at the global level,[7] and encompasses areas over which there is no asserted jurisdiction. Likewise, the sharing of natural resources is not just between legal actors operating within the same legal culture but also between those across legal cultures. In these circumstances, for example, ideas of property may vary. Further, the concept of an 'externality' is not simply what is externalized by the activities and pricing of a particular market, but also by the operation of jurisdiction and sovereignty. So, we can see that in the international sphere some regulatory concepts and environmental problems become understood in new ways, differently from the way those concepts and problems are understood at the national or EU level. Here are some examples, in relation to each of these categories:

- International environmental law that addresses the management of global commons includes: Part XII of the International Law of the Sea 1982; the Madrid Protocol to the Antarctic Treaty on Environmental Protection 1991; the Montreal Protocol on Substances that Deplete the Ozone Layer 1987; and the United Nations Framework Convention on Climate Change 1992.

- Examples of international environmental law that address the problem of shared natural resources include the Convention on the Protection of the World Cultural Heritage and Natural Heritage 1972; the Convention on Biological Diversity 1992; the Convention on International Trade in Endangered Species of Wild Flora and Fauna 1973; and the International Convention for the Regulation of Whaling 1946.

- Examples of international environmental law addressing transboundary environmental problems, besides the principles of state responsibility discussed here, include: the Convention on the Protection and Use of Transboundary Watercourses and Lakes 1992; Convention on the Control of Transboundary Movements of Hazardous Waste and their Disposal 1992; and the Convention on Environmental Impact Assessment in a Transboundary Context 1991.

While these categories overlap in some senses and do not provide a rigid classification, they highlight the scope and distinct nature of these various international environmental protection regimes.

3.3 SUSTAINABLE DEVELOPMENT

The second set of international law regimes that govern environmental problems are those concerned with sustainable development. Sustainable development regimes are distinct from those concerned with environmental protection alone because their ambitions are more wide ranging, as French explains.

---

[7] Cf the discussion of Hardin in Section 2.1 of Chapter 2.

Duncan French, *International Law and Policy of Sustainable Development*
(Manchester UP 2005) 10–11

Sustainable development is therefore an attempt to reconcile environmental protection and human development; it is a term that is intended to go beyond the 'either/or style of debate over environment and development'. This is the idea that one can either have environmental protection or one can have development—usually in the form of economic growth—but one cannot have both. Fragments of such an idea can be found in the history of both environmental and economic theory. In terms of environmental theory, its most obvious emanation was the limits to growth literature, which suggested that economic growth could not continue indefinitely, but that the level and extent of human activity would ultimately be restricted by environmental restraints, such as the permanent loss of non-renewable natural resources. This essentially negative approach to the relationship between economic growth and environmental protection was rejected by the World Commission in favour of a more positive— some have argued idealistic—correlation between development and the environment.

In one sense, sustainable development is an amalgamation of Young's categories of environmental issues. But it goes further than covering the different dimensions of environmental problems, addressing the interrelationship not only between environmental protection and economic development but also social issues. Sustainable development, including its history, is discussed in more detail in Chapter 11, which analyses sustainable development as a principle of environmental law.

3.4 INTERNATIONAL LAW REGIMES THAT GOVERN ENVIRONMENTAL PROBLEMS INDIRECTLY

The third category of international environmental regimes is made up of those that govern environmental problems indirectly. These are regimes that apply to environmental problems, but which have been set up to regulate other issues and/or for other purposes. Such indirect forms of environmental regulation can have a profound impact upon our understanding and handling of an environmental problem.[8]

The most dominant and high profile regime that falls into the 'indirect regulation' category is the multilateral trade regime of the WTO. As we saw in Chapter 4, in relation to free movement of goods, trade regulation indirectly regulates the power of national regulators to act unilaterally in relation to environmental matters.[9] The same is true of international trade law and, as we see in Chapter 22 on the regulation of GMOs, international trade law has had a significant impact on aspects of national and EU environmental law regimes. The WTO trade regime is therefore briefly sketched here.

The WTO trading system has evolved from the public international law framework of the General Agreement on Tariffs and Trade 1947 (GATT). That system was introduced with a limited formal institutional structure, and dispute settlement under GATT originally took a diplomatic rather than legal form, working on the basis of consensus. The WTO system itself only came into being in 1995, after several years of negotiation. At its core remained the trade obligations of the GATT but it added a series of new institutional structures (including a dispute settlement system) and further agreements, which both strengthened the obligations under GATT and broadened the scope of WTO jurisdiction.

---

[8] For example, see the discussion of transgenic agriculture in Chapter 22.   [9] See Chapter 4.

An important point to note about the WTO is that it reflects, and is characterized by, a legal culture in itself. Thus Weiler has noted that:

> Law – legal cultures, legal rules, and legal discourse – does not simply act as a neutral medium or transmission belt for policies determined by economic, political, and even moral considerations. Law is, additionally, both reflective and constitutive of political culture, indeed of culture in its broadest sense.[10]

In other words, the institutions, concepts, and legal reasoning in the WTO must be taken seriously on their own terms. This creates an extra analytical burden for students, scholars, and lawyers, since understanding how environmental issues are indirectly regulated by the WTO regime requires understanding the WTO regime writ large. The description given here does not provide a full analysis of the WTO legal system and its legal culture, but it is a starting point.

From an environmental law perspective, there are three WTO agreements of relevance: the General Agreement on Tariffs and Trade (GATT); the Agreement on Technical Barriers to Trade (the TBT Agreement); and the Sanitary and Phytosanitary (SPS) Agreement.

The General Agreement on Tariffs and Trade (GATT)

The GATT is the foundation for the substantive obligations of WTO law. Article I of the GATT imposes a non-discrimination obligation according to which imports from WTO members must be treated no less favourably than imports from other states (the 'most favoured national principle'). Article III of the GATT requires that imported products should not be treated less favourably than domestic products (the 'principle of national treatment'). Article XI also prohibits national quantitative restrictions on imports or exports—other than duties, taxes, and charges—that are made effective through 'quotas, import or export licences or *other measures*'. Despite the similarity of Article XI to Articles 34 and 35 TFEU, these three GATT principles amount to a relatively 'light touch' approach to trade liberalization when compared with the EU (see Chapter 4). This is also partly due to the way in which the exceptions to these GATT rules are applied, as examined further. However, these GATT principles can be complex to apply to particular sets of facts and require subtle analysis.[11]

Article XX provides a framework for derogation from the main GATT obligations, on the grounds of a closed list of fairly narrowly defined social objectives. Articles XX (a), (b), and (g) are the most relevant in relation to derogating national environmental measures, but note also the 'chapeau' at the start of Article XX, which acts as an extra qualification on any derogation from the Agreement.

Article XX GATT

General Exceptions

Subject to the requirement that such measures are not applied in a manner which would constitute a means of arbitrary or unjustifiable discrimination between countries where the same conditions prevail, or a disguised restriction on international trade, nothing in this Agreement shall be construed to prevent the adoption or enforcement by any contracting party of measures:

   (a) necessary to protect public morals;

---

[10] Joseph Weiler, 'Law, Culture and Values in the WTO—Gazing into the Crystal Ball', in Daniel Bethlehem, and others (eds) *The Oxford Handbook of International Trade Law* (OUP 2009) 752–53.

[11] Rob Howse and Petros Mavroidis, 'Europe's Evolving Regulatory Strategy for GMOs: The Issue of Consistency with WTO Law: of Kine and Brine' (2000) 24 Fordham Int'l LJ 324.

> (b) necessary to protect human, animal or plant life or health; [...]
>
> (g) relating to the conservation of exhaustible natural resources if such measures are made effective in conjunction with restrictions on domestic production or consumption.

As with all Treaty obligations various interpretation issues arise in relation to these exceptions and a series of decisions of the WTO dispute resolution fora—the Dispute Settlement Panels and Appellate Body—have elucidated some of these matters. Thus, the Appellate Body has confirmed that Article XX(g) can be relied upon in order to justify restrictions on international trade for the purposes of environmental protection in quite broad terms (in adjudications relating to the protection of turtles,[12] dolphins,[13] and clean air[14]). This now includes measures that prescribe environmental process standards as a condition of import and which have extra-territorial application. More broadly, states can define and choose their own level of protection in order to achieve the social objectives specified in Article XX (including public morals, health, and the environment). However, restrictions under grounds (a) and (b) must also be 'necessary' and hence it must not be possible to take less trade-restrictive measures that meet the same objective, which are 'reasonably available' in terms of costs and technical availability. Finally, the chapeau of Article XX makes clear that any derogating measures must not be applied 'in a manner which would constitute a means of arbitrary or unjustifiable discrimination between countries where the same conditions prevail, or a disguised restriction on international trade'.[15]

The Agreement on Technical Barriers to Trade ('TBT Agreement')

The TBT Agreement aims to ensure that technical standards, as well as testing and certification procedures, do not create unnecessary international trade barriers. While the TBT Agreement is *lex specialis* to the GATT, it can be applied cumulatively with that main agreement, so that a single provision in a national regulatory regime for, say, GMOs (see Chapter 22) might engage both the GATT and TBT Agreements. According to Article 1.5 of the TBT Agreement, it does not apply to any sanitary or phytosanitary measures (that is, food safety and animal and plant health measures), as defined in Annex A of the SPS agreement, considered further here. However, these two associated WTO agreements might still overlap in their operation. Thus, if a measure restricting trade in transgenic agricultural products pursues various objectives, a measure that is a sanitary or phytosanitary measure, and thus evaluated for its lawfulness under the SPS Agreement below, may also be considered to constitute *independently* a TBT measure in relation to its non-SPS purposes and thus might be justified in any case on the grounds of the TBT Agreement.[16]

> ### Article 2: Preparation, Adoption and Application of Technical Regulations by Central Government Bodies
>
> With respect to their central government bodies:
>
> [...] 2.2 Members shall ensure that technical regulations are not prepared, adopted or applied with a view to or with the effect of creating unnecessary obstacles to international trade. For this purpose, technical regulations shall not be more trade-restrictive than necessary to fulfil a legitimate objective,

---

[12] United States—Import Prohibition of Certain Shrimp and Shrimp Products (WT/DS58/AB/R, 12 October 1998), para 153.

[13] United States Restrictions on Imports of Tuna (1992) 30 ILM 1598 (Tuna/Dolphin I); United States Restrictions on Imports of Tuna (1994) 33 ILM 839 (Tuna/Dolphin II).

[14] United States—Standards for Reformulated and Conventional Gasoline (WT/DS2/AB/R, 29 April 1996).

[15] For example, *US Shrimp Turtle* case n 12; *US Gasoline* case n 14.

[16] Maria Lee, *EU Regulation of GMOs* (Edward Elgar 2008) 202.

taking account of the risks non-fulfilment would create. Such legitimate objectives are, *inter alia:* national security requirements; the prevention of deceptive practices; protection of human health or safety, animal or plant life or health, or the environment. In assessing such risks, relevant elements of consideration are, *inter alia:* available scientific and technical information, related processing technology or intended end-uses of products.

Examples of TBT 'technical regulations' include product specifications and labelling requirements. In the context of GMO regulation, an example of such 'technical regulations' is the EU GMO Traceability and Labelling Regulation,[17] which imposes a labelling requirement for GM food and feed products circulating within the EU.

The Agreement on Sanitary and Phytosanitary Measures ('SPS Agreement')

Of all the WTO Agreements, the SPS Agreement is the most controversial.[18] The Agreement, like the TBT Agreement, was developed as part of the Uruguay Round and came into force in 1994. The Agreement applies to 'measures' that are applied to protect animal, plant, and human life and health from a variety of different risks, ranging from the spread of pests to additives in food.[19] The Agreement entrenches the right of Members to act so as to protect human, animal, and/or plant health,[20] but regulates the process by which such standards can be set and the basis on which they are set. The Agreement thus includes provisions relating to the basis for decisions,[21] what can be taken into account,[22] decision-making transparency,[23] who should be consulted,[24] and how trade-restrictive standards can be.[25]

Article 2.2 states that:

2. Members shall ensure that any sanitary or phytosanitary measure is applied only to the extent necessary to protect human, animal or plant life or health, is based on scientific principles and is not maintained without sufficient scientific evidence, except as provided for in paragraph 7 of Article 5.

The process for setting SPS measures is set out in Article 5 of the Agreement. Article 5.1 thus provides:

'Members shall ensure that their sanitary or phytosanitary measures are based on an assessment, as appropriate to the circumstances, of the risks to human, animal or plant life or health, taking into account risk assessment techniques developed by the relevant international organizations.'

As Scott has pithily noted, the Agreement is generally understood as positing:

'scientific principle, scientific evidence, and risk assessment, as benchmarks according to which the lawfulness of Member State regulatory intervention will be assessed.'[26]

---

[17] Regulation (EC) No 1830/2003 of the European Parliament and of the Council of 22 September 2003 concerning the traceability and labelling of genetically modified organisms and the traceability of food and feed products produced from genetically modified organisms and amending Directive 2001/18/EC [2003] OJ L268/24.

[18] David Victor, 'The Sanitary and Phytosanitary Agreement of the World Trade Organisation: An Assessment After Five Years' (2000) 32 NYU J Int'l Law & Pol 865.

[19] Annex A.1.   [20] A right also evidenced in Article XX(b) of the GATT.

[21] Articles 2.2, 3.2, and 5.1   [22] Articles 5.2 and 5.3.   [23] Article 7 and Annex B.

[24] Articles 3.4, 9, and 12.   [25] Articles 5.4, 5.5, and 5.6.

[26] Joanne Scott, *The WTO Agreement on Sanitary and Phytosantiary Measures* (OUP 2007) 3.

The impact of these SPS Agreement provisions will be considered further in Chapter 22 in relation to transgenic agriculture, but it is worth highlighting the complexity of the different approaches of the Appellate Body and the Dispute Settlement Panels in interpreting the SPS Agreement. Fisher takes up the point. Her concept of administrative constitutionalism essentially concerns the ways in which administrative decision-makers are constituted, limited, and held to account.

Elizabeth Fisher, *Risk Regulation and Administrative Constitutionalism*
(Hart Publishing 2007) 204

There needs to be recognition of the fact that the SPS Agreement is not a neutral document and dispute settlement is not just about an objective assessment of the facts. The Agreement's interpretation and the resolution of disputes both require normative choices to be made. Likewise there is a mutually constitutive interrelationship between paradigms of administrative constitutionalism, risk regulation regimes, WTO trade law, and WTO dispute settlement proceedings in which each are co-produced alongside each other. Thus as seen above, understandings about the trade law purposes of the SPS Agreement are co-produced with paradigms of administrative constitutionalism.

Implicit in this recognition of co-production must be a recognition of the thickness of WTO legal culture [...] Dispute settlement is creating a substantive body of normative rules and Panels and the AB are not neutral arbiters but are regulating understandings of good administration.

Fisher's point returns to those of Koskenniemi and Weiler—the WTO is a thick legal culture. The SPS Agreement has been interpreted as requiring scientific analysis and certain levels of scientific knowledge in order to justify trade restrictive measures on food, animal, and plant safety grounds. According to Fisher, this interpretation of the Agreement is certainly not a given on its terms, and has been adopted for reasons that relate to, and essentially reflect, the legal culture of the WTO.

FURTHER READING AND QUESTIONS

1. Return to Hardin's discussion of the 'tragedy of the commons' in Chapter 2. How applicable are his ideas to environmental issues at the global level?

2. On issues of global environmental problems and their politics, the following works are good starting points: Oran Young, *International Governance: Protecting the Environment in a Stateless Society* (Cornell UP 1994) and Peter Dauvergne (ed), *Handbook of Global Environmental Politics* (Edward Elgar 2005).

3. On issues relating to WTO law and the SPS Agreement in particular, see Joanne Scott, *The WTO Agreement on Sanitary and Phytosanitary Measures* (OUP 2007) and Simon Baughen, *International Trade and the Protection of the Environment*, (Routledge-Cavendish 2007).

4 THE NATURE OF INTERNATIONAL ENVIRONMENTAL LAW

Beyond outlining the broad reaching scope of international environmental law, it is also important to consider the legal nature of this body of law. Section 2 demonstrated that the nature of the international legal order is complex, which can be viewed and analysed in a range of ways. The same is true of international environmental law. In broad terms, while much international environmental law is in Treaty form, there is considerable discussion over whether other aspects of international environmental law constitute general principles of customary international law. To further complicate matters, many of the obligations in international environmental law—no matter what their source—are recognized as 'soft' in nature.

4.1 TREATIES

Treaty law is the main recognized source of international environmental law. In *Principles of International Environmental Law*, Sands and Peel explain the nature and role of treaties in international environmental law.

Philippe Sands and Jacqueline Peel *Principles of International Environmental Law* (3rd edn, CUP 2012) 96–97

Treaties (also referred to as conventions, accords, agreements and protocols) are the primary source of international legal rights and obligations in relation to environmental protection. A treaty can be adopted bilaterally, regionally or globally, and is defined by the 1969 Vienna Convention on the Law of Treaties (1969 Vienna Convention) as 'an international agreement concluded between states in written form and governed by international law, whether embodied in a single instrument or in two or more related instruments and whatever its particular designation'. At the heart of this definition is the idea that the instrument is intended to create international legal rights and obligations between the parties. Whether an instrument is intended to create such binding obligations will usually be clear from its characteristics and the circumstances in which it was adopted. [...]

Numerous attempts have been made to classify treaties in one form or another, such as whether they are bilateral or multilateral, or of general or universal in effect. These efforts frequently have not shed a great deal of light on the practical consequences of a particular treaty. Certain treaties nevertheless have greater authority than others, and may assume the quality of 'law-making treaties' in the sense that they have been concluded for the purpose of laying down general rules of conduct among a large number of states. Factors which are relevant in assessing the authority of a treaty include: the subject-matter it addresses; the number and representativity of states participating in its negotiation, and signing it or becoming parties; the commitments it establishes and practice prior to and following its entry into force. In relation to environmental obligations, certain treaties of potentially global application might be considered to have 'law-making' characteristics, particularly where they have attracted a large number of ratifications and are established to 'manage' a problem area over time.

Sands and Peel note many treaties and state that over 2000 are relevant to environmental problems. That is a huge number of treaties, and clearly illustrates the fragmented nature of international environmental law. It is important to remember that each of these treaties sets up detailed regimes, which differ considerably in their obligations and institutional mechanisms. Thus, the 1946 International Convention for the Regulation of Whaling restricts the rights of states to hunt whales, in order to guarantee the conservation of whale stocks over time, with its obligations monitored by the International Whaling Commissions. This covers very different ground from, say, the UN Framework Convention on Climate Change, which deals with a fundamentally different environmental problem and contains flexibility mechanisms as well as varying obligations applying to different states to set up an international framework for mitigating climate change, which also relies on further treaties and protocols being signed to achieve its goal. The difficulty in studying these treaties, in isolation and in comparison, should not be underestimated.

4.2 CUSTOMARY INTERNATIONAL LAW AND GENERAL PRINCIPLES

Many commentators have argued that international environmental law does not only take the form of treaties. Other sources of international environmental law include international custom or state practice, and recognized general principles (see Section 2.1). In fact, very little international environmental law is in these forms but some scholars are often keen to expand the corpus of international environmental law by arguing that aspects of the subject amount either to customary practice or to general principles of international law, as Bodansky considers.

Daniel Bodansky, 'Customary (and Not So Customary) International Environmental Law' (1995–96) 3(1) Ind J Global Legal Studies 108–09, 111–112, 119

According to the standard account of customary international law, claims about customary law are empirical claims about the ways that states (and other international actors) regularly behave. [...]

In saying that customary rules represent regularities of behavior, several points should be noted. First, the approach is empirical rather than normative. [...]

Second, customary rules are not equivalent to simple behavioral regularities. Behavioral regularities are like physical laws; they can be identified by an external observer, whose 'view will be like the view of one who, having observed the working of a traffic signal in a busy street for some time, limits himself to saying that when the light turns red there is a high probability that the traffic will stop.' [...]

Finally, customary rules represent regularities, but not necessarily uniformities, of behavior. The behavioral approach requires a general congruence between rules and behavior. If a purported rule says one thing and states generally do something else, one can no longer say that the rule 'governs' behavior. Nevertheless, mistakes and violations of rules are possible. [...]

As a growing number of international legal scholars are recognizing, there is a divergence between the traditional theory of customary law, which emphasizes consistent and uniform state practice, and the norms generally espoused as 'customary.' Robert Jennings has observed, 'Most of what we perversely persist in calling customary international law is not only *not* customary law; it does not even faintly resemble a customary law.' [...] scholars characterize the duty to prevent transboundary pollution and the precautionary principle as customary obligations when there is little support for them in the actual behavior of states. As Jennings concludes, 'Perhaps it is time to face squarely the fact that the orthodox tests of custom—practice and *opinio juris*—are often not only inadequate but even irrelevant for the identification of much new law today.'

Bodansky goes on to argue that, in actual fact, what is described or argued for as 'customary' international law by environmental lawyers is often more concerned with what states declare than what they do. He argues that this form of declarative law is not binding but that also this is largely irrelevant because:

[the] functions of international environmental norms do not depend on a norm's legal status. Whether the duty to prevent transboundary pollution or the precautionary principle are part of customary international law, they will set the terms of international discussions and serve as the framework for negotiations. If so, the current debates over the legal versus non-legal status of these norms are of little consequence. They would matter if dispute resolution were more prevalent.

Bodansky is highlighting three issues. First, many arguments about customary international law or general principles of international environmental law are wishful thinking in light of traditional public international law understandings of those legal sources. Second, the experience and arguments in international environmental law around these issues are forcing a process of reflection about what is international custom or what are 'general principles', and perhaps that considering 'general norms of international environmental relations' might be of more consequence for international environmental law. This leads to Bodansky's final point, which is essentially that much of this debate about putting international environmental law ideas into ill-fitting public international law boxes may in fact be a red herring.

4.3 SOFT LAW

Beyond formal sources of public international law, much international environmental law is understood to take the form of 'soft law'. Soft law is the manifestation of deformalization, as discussed by Carlarne in Section 2.3. The idea of 'soft law' originated in the international economic law sphere but it has been a central feature of international environmental law since at least the 1990s. Chinkin explains some of its main features.

Christine Chinkin, 'Normative Development in the International Legal System' in Dinah Shelton (ed), *Commitment and Compliance: The Role of Non-Binding Norms in the International Legal System* (OUP 2000) 30, 42

There are various ways of categorizing international soft law. Instruments may be included within this generic term for a number of reasons:

   (i) they have been articulated in non-binding form according to traditional modes of law-making;

   (ii) they contain vague and imprecise terms;

   (iii) they emanate from bodies lacking international law-making authority;

   (iv) they are directed at non-state actors whose practice cannot constitute customary international law;

   (v) they lack any corresponding theory of responsibility;

   (vi) they are based solely upon voluntary adherence, or rely upon non-juridical means of enforcement.

Chinkin is highlighting that an instrument may be identified as 'soft law' for many different reasons and take a variety of different forms. In particular, it is difficult to draw a clear distinction between hard (or 'formal') law and soft law in public international law, especially because an obligation included in a Treaty may still amount to soft law if 'articulated in non-binding form' or 'vague and imprecise terms'. Chinkin goes on to consider why there has been a prevalence of soft law in international environmental law, discussing both the positive and negative aspects of this development.

The complexity of international legal affairs has outpaced traditional methods of law-making, necessitating management through international organizations, specialized agencies, programmes, and private bodies that do not fit the paradigm of Article 38(1) of the Statute of the ICJ. Consequently the concept of soft law facilitates international co-operation by acting as a bridge between the formalities of law-making and the needs of international life by legitimating behaviour and creating stability.

Behaviour in conformity with soft law principles is unlikely to be denounced, even by those who have remained outside their enunciation, while the appropriateness of rigid adherence to hard obligations may be undermined by emerging soft law. Even the expectation that soft law instruments will be ignored is an important factor in anticipating future behaviour. Their negotiation requires response, even negative response, that clarifies the stance of others.

These developments also have a negative aspect. The contradictions both within the concept of soft law and, more specifically, between provisions articulated within different fora and by different protagonists lack coherence. Claimants can pick and choose between these instruments to support their position while decision-makers can either assert their validity or resort to formalism. Soft law may maintain the fiction of a universal international law, while in reality leading to its destruction through the formulation of relative standards.

Chinkin sums up wonderfully both the benefits and problems of soft law, particularly as they relate to international environmental law. On the one hand, the use of soft law reflects the inadequacies of traditional forms of public international law to address environmental problems, whether due to problems in reaching agreement or due to lack of flexibility in regulatory strategy. On the other hand, she also highlights that soft law can give the impression that there is agreement or some form of legal framework when in actual fact there is none (at least in formal terms). This last point is particularly important for national environmental lawyers—not every Treaty or international declaration is meant to give rise to legal consequences in the context of public international law, let alone national law. However, soft law agreements can still have significant impacts, particularly on policy discourses, in framing international negotiations on environmental issues, and in paving the way for next normative steps, as Bodansky highlights.

FURTHER READING AND QUESTIONS

1. What do you think are the challenges involved in developing a coherent understanding of international environmental law in light of the range and number of environmental treaties? Is this a different type of challenge from that seen in national systems in relation to environmental legislation?

2. The precautionary principle provides a good example of an environmental concept that scholars have argued over as to its status as a general principle or custom of international law. See Owen McIntyre and Thomas Mosedale 'The Precautionary Principles as a Norm of Customary International Law' (1997) 9 JEL 222; Ari Trouwborst, *Evolution and Status of the Precautionary Principle in International Law* (Kluwer 2002); cf Vaughan Lowe, 'Sustainable Development and Unsustainable Arguments', in Alan Boyle and David Freestone, (eds), *International Law and Sustainable Development* (OUP 1999).

3. For further analysis of soft law in public international law, see Part IV of Daniel Bodansky, Jutta Brunnée, and Ellen Hey (eds), *Oxford Handbook of International Environmental Law* (OUP 2007); Gregory Shaffer and Mark Pollack, 'Hard vs Soft Law: Alternatives, Complements and Antagonists in International Governance' (2010) 94 Minn L Rev 706; Alan Boyle and Christine Chinkin, *The Making of International Law* (OUP 2007) 211–29.

4. One important topic not addressed in detail in this chapter is how international environmental law is made. There have been a number of good works on this issue including Scott Barrett, *Environment and Statecraft: The Strategy of Environmental Treaty Making* (OUP 2003) and Alan Boyle and Christine Chinkin, *The Making of International Law* (OUP 2007).

5 INSTITUTIONS AND INTERNATIONAL ENVIRONMENTAL LAW

To understand fully the nature of international environmental law, it is important to look beyond the sources of international environmental law to consider their institutional arrangements. This section first considers the types and nature of institutional arrangements for making and administering international environmental law. It then briefly analyses the role of dispute settlement at the international level. Throughout this discussion, the significance of governance arrangements (see Chapter 13) should be kept in mind, both in building up a broader picture of environmental law and in spotting contentious issues, particularly relating to the legitimacy and accountability of those empowered to act and make decisions.

5.1 THE INSTITUTIONAL ARRANGEMENTS OF INTERNATIONAL ENVIRONMENTAL LAW

As already noted , the most significant institution in public international law is the sovereign state, which has the ability to negotiate and enter into international agreements. Alongside sovereign states, there are many other institutions involved in international environmental law. The United Nations (UN) is the most important of these—besides its General Assembly, which has direct law-making powers, there are also a range of organizations that are run by it or affiliated to it. These include the UN Environment Programme (UNEP), UN Development Programme (UNDP), UN Commission on Sustainable Development (UNCSD), World Health Organisation (WHO), International Atomic Energy Agency (IAEA), and the Food and Agricultural Organisation (FAO). Beyond these institutions, other international bodies, particularly those involved in trade and economic development, also act as fora for the discussion and negotiation of environmental issues, and the implementation of norms relating to environmental problems. These include the World Trade Organisation (WTO) and Organisation for European Economic Co-operation (OECD). There are also a wide range of non-governmental organizations, both private and public interest focused, which are also involved in international environmental governance.

Not surprisingly, this institutional landscape has resulted in the development of co-operative networked approaches to addressing environmental problems, such as private actor self-ordering. Thus, for example, 'Agenda 21'—a product of the Rio Conference on Environment and Development—amounted to an ambitious and detailed programme of activities across almost all sectors and aspects of social and economic activity, rather than constituting a body of law, either soft or hard. However, this programme has had a widespread influence on international (including national) action relating to sustainable development.

These different sets of institutional arrangements are often described as forms of *international environmental governance*. In the last decade, some scholars have begun to describe specific institutional arrangements as 'autonomous' in nature because of the way in which they operate separately from states.[27] French highlights that the situation is somewhat more complicated.

[27] Robin Churchill and Geir Ulfstein, 'Autonomous Institutional Arrangements in Multilateral Environmental Agreements: A Little Noticed Phenomenon in International Law' (2000) 94 AJIL 623.

Duncan French, 'Finding Autonomy in International Environmental Law and Governance'
(2009) 21 JEL 255, 260–61

Though difficult to present in summary form, it is possible to highlight some of the bodies that comprise what one might loosely characterise as 'global environmental governance'. These include the UN Environment Programme (UNEP), UN specialised agencies and other institutions such as the Food and Agriculture Organisation, the World Meteorological Organisation, UNESCO, the World Bank, UN-HABITAT, and the World Food Programme. Moreover, whereas some environmental treaties have created bespoke inter-governmental organisations and/or commissions, such as the International Whaling Commission and commissions established to govern certain international rivers and international fisheries, other treaties rely on pre-existing international organisations, such as the International Maritime Organisation (IMO). [...]

More significant is the creation of institutional bodies within the framework of environmental treaties themselves, often referred to as 'Conference of the Parties' (CoPs), together with any subsidiary bodies and attached secretariats. Though, as the name suggests, such bodies are comprised of the parties to the treaty, thus appearing to lack any semblance of autonomy with which this article is concerned, the elaboration of such institutions has been heralded as a key feature of the institutional development of international environmental law [...]

The challenges posed by the existence of different institutional bodies have not gone unnoticed at the global level. UNEP, as the principal institution within the UN family on the global environment, has sought to bring a measure of coherence to the situation, though it must be doubted whether the necessary structural measures have yet truly been taken. Thus, work has been undertaken on what has been called 'international environmental governance', including the establishment (through the auspices of the UN) of the Global Ministerial Environmental Forum and the Environmental Management Group to promote coordination at both the political and inter-agency level, respectively. However, ultimately such processes seek to manage better the international community's organisational response to environmental problems within the current global paradigm rather than provide the means to forge ahead with proactive, consensus-based action, unfettered by the traditional constraints of State consent.

French's analysis highlights two important points. First, there are many different institutional arrangements that might fall under the heading 'international environmental law', reinforcing the complexity of the institutional picture. Second, the concept of autonomy does not mean that there is no role for the state in these arrangements—characterizing them does not involve a sharp delineation between state and non-state actors or processes. This is another aspect of fragmentation in international environmental law. There is not only a range of different institutional creations operating in international environmental governance but they are also highly fragmented, in form, processes, and structure.

5.2 DISPUTE SETTLEMENT

The second important feature of the institutional landscape of international environmental law is the range of fora for dispute settlement. Dispute settlement is a substantive topic in itself and only a few central points are outlined here.

As Bodansky has noted, there is often an assumption that dispute settlement is the means by which non-compliance (discussed further) might be addressed by the relevantly 'injured' party bringing an action.[28] It is important to remember that the injured party in this context is a state—dispute settlement at the international level is between states and does not involve individual legal actors. Furthermore, international dispute settlement often consists of a series of disputes in which different international tribunals rule on different points of international law. Cases are frequently quite technical and are embedded in particular international law regimes, which can often be quite esoteric and subject-specific. This means that international law cases need to be read with care and with a broader awareness of the legal issues and culture involved (as seen in the discussion in relation to WTO law and the decisions of WTO dispute resolution bodies).

Despite all of this, dispute settlement is also an institutional mechanism by which international environmental law principles have been developed and established. The most well-known and classic (albeit rather dated) example of this is the *Trail Smelter* case. Stephens describes the implications of that case.

Tim Stephens, *International Courts and Environmental Protection* (CUP 2009) 133

The *Trail Smelter* case is best remembered for the statement that states must not permit their territory to be used in such a way as to cause damage to the territory of other states by atmospheric pollution. The influence of the case was ensured because even though it considered only airborne pollutants as required by the Trail Smelter Arbitral Agreement it had adapted a general principle regarding sovereignty and territorial integrity that could extend to other forms of transboundary damage. For this reason the tribunal's statement ultimately found expression in principle 21 of the Stockholm Declaration which was substantially repeated in principle 2 of the Rio Declaration.

The longevity of the dictum is a consequence of the flexible and negotiable standard articulated by the tribunal. It is implicit in the tribunal's reasoning that the duty to prevent transboundary harm is not a strict or absolute one, but rather applies only to harm that is foreseeable and preventable. Moreover, the tribunal found that states required to prevent transboundary harm of 'serious consequence' and that any injury be 'established by clear and convincing evidence'. The imposition of a more demanding threshold of damage would clearly have been desirable from an environmental viewpoint.

Stephens states two important points. First, the principle established in *Trail Smelter* did become a general principle of international law. Second, it did so because of the nature of the legal reasoning deployed. In other words, to understand the legal implications of the case, there is a need to understand the wider body of international law in relation to which it was being decided.

However, a significant complication in making general points about international dispute resolution fora is one that we have repeatedly seen in international law—fragmentation—as Romano describes.

Cesare PR Romano, 'International Dispute Settlement' in Daniel Bodansky, Jutta Brunnée and Ellen Hey (eds), Oxford Handbook of International Environmental Law (OUP 2007) 1054–55

There are no international judicial or quasi-judicial bodies solely dedicated to environmental disputes, the partial exception being the Chamber for Environmental Matters of the ICJ. However, the polymorphic nature of environmental disputes makes a wide variety of fora potentially usable, which are almost impossible to list. Cases involving environmental issues have been brought before the ICJ, ITLOS, the WTO dispute settlement system, the European Court of Human Rights, the InterAmerican Court of Human Rights, judicial bodies of regional economic integration organizations (such as the ECJ),

[28] Bodansky (n 2) 245.

inspection panels, international and transnational arbitral tribunals, and compensation and reparations bodies. This also explains why. Besides dispute management and settlement procedures endogenous to international environmental regimes, there are no international judicial or quasi-judicial bodies solely dedicated to deal with environmental disputes.

The fragmentation of law in specialized and self-contained regimes; the institutionalization of international decision-making and enforcement processes; the proliferation of international judicial bodies; the erosion of the divide between the domestic and international legal spheres; and the multiplication of subjects of international law beyond the state-centric classical models, are all characteristics of contemporary international law. Many of these changes to the international law fabric originally took place in the environmental field.

Despite this fragmentation, there are those, like Stephens, who argue that an environmental jurisprudence is beginning to emerge in international dispute resolution fora around issues such as transboundary environmental harm, international water law, and the protection and preservation of the marine environment.[29] This may be the case, but this jurisprudence still requires very careful analysis, particularly in appreciating the precise legal contexts and cultures in which it develops. Moreover, even if a common jurisprudence might be identified across international dispute resolution bodies, it needs to be remembered that the *enforcement* of international environmental judgments and decisions are limited by the very foundations of public international law, in particular by the concepts of state sovereignty and state responsibility.

FURTHER READING AND QUESTIONS

1. For further discussion of the institutional landscape of international environmental law, see Oran Young, *Institutional Dynamics: Emergent Patterns in International Environmental Governance* (MIT Press 2010). For a similar discussion in relation to a specific issue, see Lavanya Rajamani, 'From Berlin to Bali and Beyond: *Killing Kyoto Softly?*' (2008) 57 ICLQ 909; Lavanya Rajamani, 'The Making and UnMaking of the Copenhagen Accord' (2010) 59 ICLQ 824.

2. For a good overview of international dispute settlement in relation to environmental problems, see Tim Stephens, *International Courts and Environmental Protection* (CUP 2009).

3. The impact of the WTO dispute settlement process in developing and shaping principles can be seen in relation to the precautionary principle in particular. See Elizabeth Fisher, *Risk Regulation and Administrative Constitutionalism* (Hart Publishing 2007) ch 6.

4. There have been arguments made for an international environmental court. What advantages do you think would such a bespoke international forum bring? Is it enough in itself? See Tim Stephens, *International Courts and Environmental Protection* (CUP 2009) 56–61.

6 IMPLEMENTATION OF INTERNATIONAL ENVIRONMENTAL LAW

The discussion in this chapter so far has focused on international environmental law *at the international level*. This final section considers the relationship between international environmental law and

[29] Tim Stephens, *International Courts and Environmental Protection* (CUP 2009) 13.

national and supranational regimes. This issue is often understood simply as one of implementation of international norms into national and regional legal systems but, as we have written elsewhere, the relationship between these regimes is far more complicated than the word 'implementation' suggests.

Elizabeth Fisher, Bettina Lange, Eloise Scotford, and Cinnamon Carlane, 'Maturity and Methodology: Starting a Debate about Environmental Law Scholarship'
(2009) 21 JEL 213, 241–42

The second methodological challenge [for studying and researching environmental law] is the need to develop rigorous techniques for analysing the interrelationship between local, national, regional and international environmental laws. This interrelationship remains underexplored and scholarly debate on the proper methodology for undertaking such analyses remains virtually non-existent. This is despite the practical importance of this interrelationship becoming more obvious in case law and legislation. Scholars tend to work in one jurisdiction with only occasional and rather crude inroads into another, often with a single-minded purpose in mind. Where there are attempts to provide a more overarching approach, they tend to suffer from being overly simplistic and from a lack of appreciation of the significance of legal culture.

There are many instances of the need to study the importance of jurisdictional interrelationships and to understand the complexity of both national and international legal cultures. There is, for example, an urgent need to recognise that national climate change and nature conservation policies are closely related to international and other national regulatory initiatives. Beyond describing this state of affairs, however, it is not clear how to develop a deeper legal understanding of these relationships, particularly when much of what going on is 'not law' and/or is at the very boundaries of international law and national law. While more scholars are beginning to look at cross-issue linkages, the disciplines of domestic and international environmental law continue to inhabit relatively distinct scholarly domains. Add to this parallel existence the growing field of regional environmental law (such as European Community environmental law) and the situation grows even more complicated. The end result is that there is no obvious way to negotiate the national/international legal relationship, but it must be negotiated to make sense of these regimes.

This extract highlights two important and related issues. First, there are numerous interrelationships between national, supranational, and international regimes. Second, in thinking about these interrelationships, it is important to think about legal culture. With this in mind, this final section briefly considers examples of implementation of international environmental law in the UK and EU legal orders.

6.1 IMPLEMENTATION—GENERAL PERSPECTIVES

National implementation of international environmental law may involve administrative, judicial, or legislative implementation but, as Redgwell explains, the process of implementation is not well researched or recorded.

Catherine Redgwell, 'National Implementation' in Daniel Bodansky, Jutta Brunnée and Ellen Hey (eds), *Oxford Handbook of International Environmental Law* (OUP 2007) 945–46

Notwithstanding very significant evolution in international environmental law during the past 30 years, in particular, we still do not have a complete picture of the extent to which it is implemented by legislative/

executive action at the domestic level. A recent trend in international environmental law doctrine is to emphasize the need for effective implementation and enforcement of the existing rules rather than the promulgation of further substantive norms. This emphasis upon national implementation is evident in the influence of the Rio Conference—'Think Globally, Act Locally.' Yet the techniques available for assessing the extent—not to mention the effectiveness—of such implementation are still rudimentary and incomplete. In consequence, it is difficult to examine, say, the relative paucity of international environmental case law and to draw from it conclusions regarding the effectiveness of national implementation. Is national legislation so well designed and implemented that few cases arise in practice? Or is this relative paucity a result of judicial restraint/ aversion to international environmental law? Or is there a record of poor implementation that is coupled with very restrictive standing requirements, cost rules, or the like, deterring potential litigants? Or is it that there are cases we simply do not know about—a general problem of the dissemination of state practice in the environmental context? What is clear is that, as a relatively new area of international law, international environmental law will be increasingly invoked in horizontal and vertical proceedings before national courts, and legislative implementation and enforcement will continue to be scrutinized by supranational bodies via national reporting and monitoring obligations as well as (in some cases) via non-compliance procedures. It is unlikely that international environmental law will achieve as high a profile as international human rights law before national courts. Yet there is some cause for optimism in the extent to which international environmental law is permeating national policy discourse, legal instruments, and, slowly but inexorably, judicial decision-making.

The situation as described by Redgwell is further complicated by at least three other issues.

First, only a small number of national environmental laws can be understood as implementing international environmental law directly (and explicit implementation might not even be required where states already comply with international norms through existing legal provisions). However, international environmental law can impact national legal systems in a number of *indirect* ways. These include the promotion of particular policies by national governments or regulators, encouraging international co-operation, and forcing states to focus on particular issues within their systems of law and governance. How these indirect impacts are identified and analysed is a legal challenge but throughout this book we will see the pervasive influence of international law.

Second, studying implementation of international environmental law is also difficult in that international concepts are often the *starting point* for national legal reform but the nature of that reform as it is formulated and introduced is a product of that particular legal culture, and is thus unique. International environmental law is akin to the grain of sand in the (national law) oyster but the resulting pearl is more to do with the oyster than the sand. Thus, for example, the precautionary principle was introduced into—'implemented' in—many national laws in the 1990s, largely because of its inclusion as Principle 15 of the Rio Declaration on Environment and Development 1992,[30] but was defined and utilized differently in each legal culture.[31] These national efforts thus represent the implementation of international environmental law in only the most general sense.

The final complicating factor in thinking about implementation of international environmental law is that implementation may not always involve implementation into the national law of a sovereign state. Rather, it may involve implementation through inter-state legal interaction (including through supranational legal arrangements such as the EU legal order), or through the management by states of the global commons.

---

[30] See Chapter 11.
[31] Timothy O'Riordan, James Cameron and Andrew Jordan (eds), *Reinterpreting the Precautionary Principle* (Cameron May 2001).

6.2 LEGAL AUTHORITY OF INTERNATIONAL ENVIRONMENTAL LAW IN UK AND EU LAW

Beyond general reflections on the implementation of international environmental law, this final section considers the legal authority of international environmental law in UK and EU Law. The basic starting point in determining that legal authority, whether considering the position in national or EU law, is to recognize that the relationship with public international law is not simply a hierarchical one but is determined primarily by national or EU law. Thus, analysis begins by determining the national or EU legal position on the status of international environmental law, rather than presupposing the supremacy of international law.

However, beyond this basic starting point, it must be noted that the relationship between *UK and international law* is different from that between *EU and international law*. The UK legal system is dualist in nature, which means that national law and international law are understood to operate independently of one other. Thus, for treaties signed by the UK at the international level to become 'national law', they must be implemented into UK law, usually by legislation. As a result, there is little UK case law considering the legal authority of international environmental law, but there is legislation that has its origins in international law. Moreover, much of this legislation implements international law at one remove, by implementing an EU Directive (that itself implements international law). An example is the introduction of the Environmental Information Regulations 2004 (see Chapter 7),[32] which implement the EU Directive on public access to environmental information,[33] that in turn implements (in part) the international Aarhus Convention on Access to Information, Public Participation in Decision Making and Access to Justice in Environmental Matters.[34] In other words, EU law provides an important conduit for international law into UK law. The EU Emissions Trading Scheme, which seeks to facilitate Member States meeting their greenhouse gas emissions reduction obligations under the Kyoto Protocol, is another example of this.[35]

By contrast, the EU legal system is monist in nature. This means that there is an embedded or 'automatic' relationship between the EU and international legal orders, so that in some cases international law will have 'direct effect' in EU law. However, the finer doctrinal details of this monism are deeply complicated, as the *Intertanko* case makes clear. At issue in this case was the legal validity of Directive 2005/35/EC on ship-source pollution and whether, in passing it, the EU needed to be consistent with international obligations under the UN Convention on the Law of the Sea (UNCLOS) and the International Convention for the Prevention of Pollution from Ships (MARPOL).

**Case C-308/06 *R (on the application of International Association of Independent Tanker Owners (Intertanko) v Secretary of State for Transport*
[2008] ECR I–4057 paras 42–65**

42. It is clear from Article 300(7) EC [reworded version now Article 216(2) TFEU] that the Community institutions are bound by agreements concluded by the Community and, consequently, that those agreements have primacy over secondary Community legislation (see, to this effect, Case C-61/94 *Commission* v *Germany* [1996] ECR I-3989, paragraph 52, and Case C-311/04 *Algemene Scheeps Agentuur Dordrecht* [2006] ECR I-609, paragraph 25).

---

[32] The Environmental Information Regulations 2004 SI 2004/3391.

[33] Directive 2003/4/EC of the European Parliament and of the Council of 28 January 2003 on public access to environmental information and repealing Council Directive 90/313/EEC [2003] OJ L41/26.

[34] UNECE, *Aarhus Convention on Access to Information, Public Participation in Decision Making and Access to Justice in Environmental Matters*, 25 June 1998.

[35] See Chapter 15.

43. It follows that the validity of a measure of secondary Community legislation may be affected by the fact that it is incompatible with such rules of international law. Where that invalidity is pleaded before a national court, the Court of Justice thus reviews, pursuant to Article 234 EC [now Art 267 TFEU], the validity of the Community measure concerned in the light of all the rules of international law, subject to two conditions.

44. First, the Community must be bound by those rules (see Joined Cases 21/72 to 24/72 *International Fruit Company and Others* [1972] ECR 1219, paragraph 7).

45. Second, the Court can examine the validity of Community legislation in the light of an international treaty only where the nature and the broad logic of the latter do not preclude this and, in addition, the treaty's provisions appear, as regards their content, to be unconditional and sufficiently precise (see to this effect, in particular, Case C-344/04 *IATA and ELFAA* [2006] ECR I-403, paragraph 39).

46. It must therefore be examined whether Marpol 73/78 and UNCLOS meet those conditions.

47. First, with regard to Marpol 73/78, it is to be observed at the outset that the Community is not a party to this Convention.

48. Furthermore, as the Court has already held, it does not appear that the Community has assumed, under the EC Treaty, the powers previously exercised by the Member States in the field to which Marpol 73/78 applies, nor that, consequently, its provisions have the effect of binding the Community (Case C-379/92 *Peralta* [1994] ECR I-3453, paragraph 16). In this regard, Marpol 73/78 can therefore be distinguished from GATT 1947 within the framework of which the Community progressively assumed powers previously exercised by the Member States, with the consequence that it became bound by the obligations flowing from that agreement (see to this effect, in particular, *International Fruit Company and Others*, paragraphs 10 to 18). Accordingly, this case-law relating to GATT 1947 cannot be applied to MARPOL 73/78.

49. It is true that all the Member States of the Community are parties to Marpol 73/78. Nevertheless, in the absence of a full transfer of the powers previously exercised by the Member States to the Community, the latter cannot, simply because all those States are parties to Marpol 73/78, be bound by the rules set out therein, which it has not itself approved.

50. Since the Community is not bound by Marpol 73/78, the mere fact that Directive 2005/35 has the objective of incorporating certain rules set out in that Convention into Community law is likewise not sufficient for it to be incumbent upon the Court to review the directive's legality in the light of the Convention.

51. Admittedly, as is clear from settled case-law, the powers of the Community must be exercised in observance of international law, including provisions of international agreements in so far as they codify customary rules of general international law (see, to this effect, Case C-286/90 *Poulsen and Diva Navigation* [1992] ECR I-6019, paragraphs 9 and 10; Case C-405/92 *Mondiet* [1993] ECR I-6133, paragraphs 13 to 15; and Case C-162/96 *Racke* [1998] ECR I-3655, paragraph 45). None the less, it does not appear that Regulations 9 and 11(b) of Annex I to Marpol 73/78 and Regulations 5 and 6(b) of Annex II to that Convention are the expression of customary rules of general international law.

52. In those circumstances, it is clear that the validity of Directive 2005/35 cannot be assessed in the light of Marpol 73/78, even though it binds the Member States. The latter fact is, however, liable to have consequences for the interpretation of, first, UNCLOS and, second, the provisions of secondary law which fall within the field of application of Marpol 73/78. In view of the customary principle of good faith, which forms part of general international law, and of Article 10 EC [Art 4(3) TEU], it is incumbent upon the Court to interpret those provisions taking account of Marpol 73/78.

53. Second, UNCLOS was signed by the Community and approved by Decision 98/392, thereby binding the Community, and the provisions of that Convention accordingly form an integral part of the Community legal order (see Case C–459/03 *Commission* v *Ireland* [2006] ECR I–4635, paragraph 82).

54. It must therefore be determined whether the nature and the broad logic of UNCLOS, as disclosed in particular by its aim, preamble and terms, preclude examination of the validity of Community measures in the light of its provisions.

55. UNCLOS's main objective is to codify, clarify and develop the rules of general international law relating to the peaceful cooperation of the international community when exploring, using and exploiting marine areas.

56. According to the preamble to UNCLOS, the Contracting Parties agreed to that end to establish through UNCLOS a legal order for the seas and oceans which would facilitate international navigation, which would take into account the interests and needs of mankind as a whole and, in particular, the special interests and needs of developing countries, and which would strengthen peace, security, cooperation and friendly relations among all nations.

57. From this viewpoint, UNCLOS lays down legal regimes governing the territorial sea (Articles 2 to 33), waters forming straits used for international navigation (Articles 34 to 45), archipelagic waters (Articles 46 to 54), the exclusive economic zone (Articles 55 to 75), the continental shelf (Articles 76 to 85) and the high seas (Articles 86 to 120).

58. For all those marine areas, UNCLOS seeks to strike a fair balance between the interests of States as coastal States and the interests of States as flag States, which may conflict. In this connection, as is apparent from numerous provisions of the Convention, such as Articles 2, 33, 34(2), 56 and 89, the Contracting Parties provide for the establishment of the substantive and territorial limits to their respective sovereign rights.

59. On the other hand, individuals are in principle not granted independent rights and freedoms by virtue of UNCLOS. In particular, they can enjoy the freedom of navigation only if they establish a close connection between their ship and a State which grants its nationality to the ship and becomes the ship's flag State. This connection must be formed under that State's domestic law. Article 91 of UNCLOS states in this regard that every State is to fix the conditions for the grant of its nationality to ships, for the registration of ships in its territory and for the right to fly its flag, and that there must exist a genuine link between the State and the ship. Under Article 92(1) of UNCLOS, ships are to sail under the flag of one State only and may not change their flag during a voyage or while in a port of call, save in the case of a real transfer of ownership or change of registry.

60. If a ship is not attached to a State, neither the ship nor the persons on board enjoy the freedom of navigation. In this connection, UNCLOS provides inter alia, in Article 110(1), that a warship which encounters a foreign ship on the high seas is justified in boarding it if there is reasonable ground for suspecting that the ship is without nationality.

61. It is true that the wording of certain provisions of UNCLOS, such as Articles 17, 110(3) and 111(8), appears to attach rights to ships. It does not, however, follow that those rights are thereby conferred on the individuals linked to those ships, such as their owners, because a ship's international legal status is dependent on the flag State and not on the fact that it belongs to certain natural or legal persons.

62. Likewise, it is the flag State which, under the Convention, must take such measures as are necessary to ensure safety at sea and, therefore, to protect the interests of other States. The flag State may thus also be held liable, vis-à-vis other States, for harm caused by a ship flying its flag to marine areas placed under those States' sovereignty, where that harm results from a failure of the flag State to fulfil its obligations.

63. Doubt is not cast on the foregoing analysis by the fact that Part XI of UNCLOS involves natural and legal persons in the exploration, use and exploitation of the sea-bed and ocean floor, and subsoil thereof, beyond the limits of national jurisdiction, since the present case does not in any way concern the provisions of Part XI.

64. In those circumstances, it must be found that UNCLOS does not establish rules intended to apply directly and immediately to individuals and to confer upon them rights or freedoms capable of being relied upon against States, irrespective of the attitude of the ship's flag State.

65. It follows that the nature and the broad logic of UNCLOS prevent the Court from being able to assess the validity of a Community measure in the light of that Convention.

In this case, the ECJ is not simply asking whether international law has direct effect in EU law as a crude instrument, but rather is asking a series of more subtle questions. Thus, by subjecting UNCLOS and MARPOL to careful legal analysis, the Court is seeking to establish and/or apply the following points:

- whether the EU is in fact bound by these Treaties (Member States individually being bound is not enough to bind the EU as a whole), in which case they prevail over EU legislation;
- whether the nature and the broad logic of any binding Treaty in fact allow the EU courts to review EU legislation for compatibility with the Treaty and thus their validity (in EU law terms);
- if so, whether the Treaty's provisions, in terms of their content, are unconditional and sufficiently precise to as to overlap with and potentially invalidate EU law provisions; and
- further, whether or not a Treaty is directly binding on the EU, the customary principle of good faith (general international law, and Article 4(3) TEU) requires that secondary EU legislation falling within its scope is interpreted to take account of its provisions.

A wider implementation point was also clarified in the recent *Air Transport of America* case, which concerned the validity of including aviation within the scope of the EU emissions trading scheme, in light of various potentially overlapping and arguably conflicting international conventions and laws relating to aviation. In ultimately finding the relevant EU Directive valid, the Court of Justice found that:

[I]n conformity with the principles of international law, European Union institutions which have power to negotiate and conclude an international agreement are free to agree with the third States concerned what effect the provisions of the agreement are to have in the internal legal order of the contracting parties. Only if that question has not been settled by the agreement does it fall to be decided by the courts having jurisdiction in the matter, and in particular by the Court of Justice, in the same manner as any question of interpretation relating to the application of the agreement in the European Union.[36]

This reinforces the general point that the implementation of international law can involve implementation through inter-state legal interaction. In short, the relationship between EU and international law is one that requires careful legal navigation of both EU and international law.

FURTHER READING AND QUESTIONS

1. Bodansky highlights three ways of thinking about the effectiveness of international law: legal effectiveness, behavioural effectiveness, and problem solving effectiveness; Daniel Bodansky, *The Art and Craft of International Environmental Law* (Harvard UP 2010) 253. Much of the

---

[36] Case C-366/10 *Air Transport Association of America and Others v Secretary of State for Energy and Climate Change* (ECJ, 21 December 2011), para 49.

discussion here has concerned legal effectiveness but how relevant and important do you think the other types are in relation to international environmental law?

2. What factors do you think influenced the Court of Justice's conclusion in the *Intertanko* case? To what extent do you consider the issues highlighted in this chapter—state sovereignty, fragmentation, multiple sources of international law—are relevant to that reasoning?

3. For more detail on the *Air Transport of America* case, in which the relationship between international and EU legal orders was reasoned at length and in detail, see Case C-366/10 *Air Transport Association of America and Others v Secretary of State for Energy and Climate Change* (ECJ, 21 December 2011). After examining the reasoning in this case closely, and in light of *Intertanko*, do you think the Court of Justice has a predilection (doctrinal or otherwise) for finding EU law, which interconnects with international law, to be generally valid?

4. For a discussion of direct effect of Article 9(3) of the Aarhus Convention, see C-240/09 *Lesoochranárske zoskupenie* [2011] ECR I-1255; Case T-338/08 *Stichting Natuur en Milieu v Commission* (General Court, 14 June 2012); *Vereniging Milieudefensie v Commission* (General Court, 14 June 2012). Consider how EU law is read down and invalidated in light of international law obligations in these cases.

7 CONCLUSION

The purpose of this chapter has been to give UK environmental law students and lawyers a feeling for the scope and complexities of international environmental law and to dispel common but incorrect characterizations of the subject. In doing so, it has reinforced the importance of appreciating legal culture, legal technique, legal landscapes, and legal relationships. In short, international environmental law is not a subject consisting of a set of binding rules that exist in a hierarchical relationship with national law. Rather, it is embedded and fragmented within public international law, covering a diverse range of topics, varying in its legal nature, and involving a variety of different institutional arrangements. Its relationship with national and supranational law is also far from straightforward. From all of this, there is only one conclusion—environmental lawyers must approach international environmental law with care and considerable legal skill.

FURTHER READING AND QUESTIONS

1. There are numerous very good international environmental law textbooks, including Patricia Birnie, Alan Boyle, and Catherine Redgwell *International Law and the Environment* (3rd edn, OUP 2009) and Philippe Sands and Jacqueline Peel, *Principles of International Environmental Law* (3rd edn, CUP 2012). Daniel Bodansky, *The Art and Craft of International Environmental Law* (Harvard UP 2010) is a wonderful overview for a more generalist audience. See also Daniel Bodansky, Jutta Brunnée, and Ellen Hey (eds), *Oxford Handbook of International Environmental Law* (OUP 2007).

2. For good accounts of public international law, see Vaughan Lowe, *International Law* (Clarendon Press 2007); Malcolm Shaw, *International Law* (6th edn, CUP 2009); and Malcolm Evans (ed), *International Law* (3rd edn, OUP 2010). Martti Koskenniemi, *The Politics of International Law* (Hart Publishing 2011) is also an excellent read.

3. Bodansky has commented that '[a]s international environmental law continues to grow more like domestic environmental law, it will be held to the same standards of legitimacy, and its lack of transparency and accountability will become increasingly problematic': Daniel Bodansky, 'The Legitimacy of International Governance: A Coming Challenge for International Environmental Law?' (1999) 93 AJIL 596, 606. Do you agree? On the topic of legitimacy in international environmental law, see Steven Bernstein 'Legitimacy in Global Environmental Governance' (2005) 1 JILIR 139 and Daniel Bodansky, 'Legitimacy' in Daniel Bodansky, Jutta Brunnée, and Ellen Hey (eds) *Oxford Handbook of International Environmental Law* (OUP 2007).

PART III

CHARTING THE ENVIRONMENTAL LAW LANDSCAPE II—BASIC LEGAL CONCEPTS

INTRODUCTION

The discussion so far has focused upon giving an overview of environmental law, environmental problems, and the relevant legal cultures that contribute to the body of law understood as environmental law. We have seen that environmental law is not a discrete subject in its own right with clear and rigid boundaries and that there are different definitional approaches to the subject. It was also shown very clearly at the end of Chapter 1 that environmental law is in many cases *applied* law, involving the application of public or private law to a particular environmental problem. Being an environmental lawyer thus requires understanding both what is unique about environmental law and environmental problems, as well as understanding basic principles and concepts of other legal subjects. Indeed, we would go so far as to argue that, to be a good environmental lawyer, one needs to be an excellent private lawyer, an excellent public lawyer, an excellent EU lawyer, and so on. To put the matter another way—there is no getting around the fact that the study of environmental law involves the study of law, legal principles, legal concepts, and legal ideas in all their glorious complexity.

The purpose of Part III of the textbook is thus to give an overview of basic legal concepts that arise in environmental law. This part includes eight chapters covering private law, public law, criminal liability, statutory liability, the role of the courts, principle and policy, regulatory strategy, and governance. These chapters do not provide an exhaustive survey of these topics; rather they aim to provide intellectual road maps that are both guides to the basics and also assist the reader in thinking creatively and critically about environmental law.

For lawyers, reading these chapters should be akin to a trip down memory lane, though with a twist. Many of the issues discussed in these chapters will be familiar to those studying, or who have studied, compulsory legal subjects. The twist is that the legal issues discussed here are examined in a new light because they arise in the context of environmental problems. Thus, thinking about property rights, for instance, takes on a new dimension in the context of environmental problems, which often transcend traditional ideas of property. Likewise, the public law concept of participation has a new frame and urgency in the environmental context. What is 'fair' in terms of general criminal justice also needs reconsidering in the environmental field. The overall aim is for lawyers and law students to think critically about these basic legal concepts and appreciate how their meaning might be subtly different in the context of environmental law.

For non-lawyers these chapters will provide an introduction, albeit a rather advanced one, to many of the basic legal concepts that underpin environmental law. These chapters offer a platform for examining the wider field of law and show that the legal concepts operating in environmental law have long pedigrees and also operate in other contexts. In particular, these chapters highlight the fact that law is not just an instrument that can be relied on to achieve certain (environmental) ends. Rather, as already discussed in the Introduction to Part II, it is a culture replete with its own ideas, concepts, and institutions—all of which have long and significant histories.

Before looking in detail at different legal concepts that operate in environmental law, it is important to understand that, despite the diverse nature of the chapters in Part III, they have a common theme. The underpinning idea is that the development of environmental law has largely concerned *giving legal expression to the issues that arise in dealing with environmental problems*. The need to frame environmental issues in legal terms is due to the fact that, historically, the environment did not figure as a concept in either law or public discourse. This may sound like an ideological issue, but we understand it as a pragmatic problem. As seen in Chapter 2, concern about the environment and its protection is a recent socio-political phenomenon, which stems partly from the problems we have faced since industrialization. As Dryzek notes:

> The environment did not exist as a concept anywhere until the 1960s (though concerns with particular aspects of what we now call the environment, such as open spaces, resource shortages, and pollution do of course pre-date the 1960s).[1]

It is thus unsurprising that, within law, there was no explicit legal discourse about the protection of the environment and much environmental law evolution over the last forty years has been concerned with developing that discourse. Moreover, as is also clear from Chapter 2, environmental problems cross boundaries and involve difficult questions about the role and nature of knowledge, values, and the state. In those circumstances, giving legal expression to environmental problems was never going to be easy. The challenges involved in giving legal expression to environmental concerns can be seen by examining three interrelated issues: developing legal definitions of the 'environment' and related concepts; developing environmental rights and remedies; and developing ways of factoring environmental concerns into public and private decision-making.

1 DEVELOPING LEGAL DEFINITIONS OF THE 'ENVIRONMENT'

Developing legal definitions of the 'environment' has been a preoccupation of many environmental lawyers. As such, there is considerable commentary in relation to how the 'environment' and associated terms can be defined and whether such definitions are legitimate ones. The reason for this obsession is that a legal definition of the environment is needed because it defines the role and nature of environmental law, as Wilkinson explains.

David Wilkinson, *Environment and Law* (Routledge 2002) 40

Whether law is successful in protection of the environment will depend significantly upon the range of entities that it is able to protect. Law can only succeed in protecting an object if that object is clearly defined in law. This is exemplified in the well-known law, present in all legal systems, against murder. Murder, it is generally accepted, is the unlawful killing of *a person* accompanied by a certain mental state (roughly speaking 'intention'). In order for this to be effective there has to be clarity about the meaning of 'person'. Is, for instance, an unborn child covered by this term? If so, how can abortion be legally justified? Are persons in permanent comas or other forms of severe brain function depletion to be regarded as legal persons? By analogy it is apparent that any body of law which seeks to protect the environment needs to have a workable and sufficiently broad conception of the subject of its concern.

Generally, it may be best to adopt a concept of environment that is broad in scope. If one defines 'environment' too narrowly then it may not be possible for law to make a meaningful contribution to the resolution of ecological degradation.

---

[1] John S Dryzek, *The Politics of the Earth: Environmental Discourses* (2nd edn, OUP 2005) 5.

The point is that, with the introduction of environmental legislation and legal definitions of the environment, legislation both triggers and defines the scope of environmental protection. Likewise, there is a preoccupation with the related concepts of 'pollution' and 'harm'. Such definitions are important for scoping a new area of legal activity and thus specifying what is to be protected by that activity. However, a problem arises when different pieces of legislation define legislative provisions relating to the environment differently. See, for example, the two different UK legislative provisions in the extracts from the Environmental Protection Act 1990 and the Pollution Prevention and Control Act 1999.

Environmental Protection Act 1990, Part II Waste on Land[2]

s 29(2) The 'environment' consists of all, or any, of the following media, namely land, water and the air.

s 29(3) 'pollution of the environment' as:

pollution of the environment due to the release or escape (into any environmental medium) from—

(a)   the land on which controlled waste or extractive waste is treated,

(b)   the land on which controlled waste or extractive waste is kept,

(c)   the land in or on which controlled waste or extractive waste is deposited,

(d)   fixed plant by means of which controlled waste or extractive waste is treated, kept or disposed of,

of substances or articles constituting or resulting from the waste and capable (by reason of the quantity or concentrations involved) of causing harm to man or any other living organisms supported by the environment.

Pollution Prevention and Control Act 1999[3]

s. (1)2 [. . .] 'environmental pollution' means pollution of the air, water or land which may give rise to any harm; and for the purposes of this definition (but without prejudice to its generality)—

(a)   'pollution' includes pollution caused by noise, heat or vibrations or any other kind of release of energy, and

(b)   'air' includes air within buildings and air within other natural or man-made structures above or below ground.

(3)   In the definition of 'environmental pollution' in subsection (2), 'harm' means—

(a)   harm to the health of human beings or other living organisms;

(b)   harm to the quality of the environment, including—

(i)   harm to the quality of the environment taken as a whole,

(ii)   harm to the quality of the air, water or land, and

(iii)   other impairment of, or interference with, the ecological systems of which any living organisms form part;

(c)   offence to the senses of human beings;

(d)   damage to property; or

(e)   impairment of, or interference with, amenities or other legitimate uses of the environment (expressions used in this paragraph having the same meaning as in Council Directive 96/61/EC).

---

[2] See Chapter 16.   [3] See Chapter 17.

The first of these definitions is relatively straightforward but the second is complicated enough to make you want to throw this textbook out the window. It is not an isolated example. Throughout this textbook, there are many examples of such definitions—such as that of 'statutory nuisance' under s 79 of the Environmental Protection Act 1990 (see Section 3 of Chapter 9) and 'environmental damage' under Article 2 of Directive 2004/35/EC on environmental liability (see Chapter 9).

Interacting with these definitions is a part of environmental law practice and study and it is important to appreciate that the 'environment', and related concepts such as pollution and harm, can be understood and constructed in many different ways. The same is true with environmental protection policies such as sustainable development.[4] The (potential) variation in definitions is not simply of academic interest—these definitions will play an important role in shaping the scope of the law to which they relate.

Different definitions of the 'environment' will relate to different ways of valuing it and of understanding what is an 'environmental problem'. Thus, for example, the definition of the environment from Part II of the Environmental Protection Act 1990 refers only to land, water, and air and does not refer to animals or buildings, and thus they would not theoretically receive protection under that Part of the Act—they are not considered to be relevant environmental problems. By contrast, the definition of 'environmental damage' under the Environmental Liability Directive (see Chapter 9), while including damage to plant and animal species, does not include protection of man-made objects. Legal definitions also depend on different facts being proved to demonstrate relevant environmental problems. Thus, for example, under the Environmental Liability Directive again, damage or impairment must be 'measurable'. This in turn raises the problems associated with the formulation and proof of environment knowledge examined in Chapter 2.

The importance of legal definitions of the environment for determining the scope of environmental protection—and thus environmental problems themselves—does not stop there. Some scholars have highlighted how such definitions promote particular environmental values in environmental law. The challenge for environmental law is thus not simply the introduction of environmental legislation but also being able to understand what that legislation embodies and how it embodies it. As we saw in Chapter 2, there is a range of environmental values and these will result in a number of different ways of defining environment and environmental protection in legislation.

Overall, legal definitions of the environment are by no means straightforward. They did not exist historically; there is no one single definition of the environment; and how we define the environment will be influenced by different sets of environmental values. Defining aspects of the environment also depends on proof of different facts—such facts are required for defining the environmental problems at issue. But they are also susceptible to the complexities associated with constructing and legitimizing environmental knowledge.

2 RIGHTS AND REMEDIES

The need to develop a legal definition of the environment has not been the only challenge for lawyers. More significantly, there has also been the need to develop rights and remedies that aid in protecting the environment, or at least in addressing environmental problems and solving disputes. The development of such rights and remedies is largely the focus of Chapters 6, 7, 8, 9, and 10. It is also one of the most vexed issues in environmental law because it has been commonly recognized that law has not historically catered well for providing rights and remedies in relation to environmental problems. Establishing such rights and remedies has been the main concern of the development of much environmental law.

---

[4] See Chapters 11 and 12.

Defining what is a legal right and a legal remedy is a notoriously difficult business. Such definitions risk not only being under or over inclusive but also promoting a particular theory of law. What constitutes a 'right' or a 'remedy' are major themes in legal theory but here it is useful to have a simple working definition. Van Gerven offers a particularly useful approach.

Walter van Gerven, 'Of Rights Remedies and Procedures' (2000) 37 CML Rev 501, 502–03

The concept of *right* refers, in my view, to a legal position which a person recognized as such by the law—thus a legal 'subject' (hence the name 'subjective' right)—may have and which in its normal state can be enforced by that person against (some or all) others before a court of law by means of one or more *remedies*, those are classes of action, intended to make good infringements of the rights concerned, in accordance with *procedures* governing the exercise of such classes of action and intended to make the remedy concerned operational. I would like to add two comments only. The first is that the legal position which the right confers upon a legal 'subject' and which is based on, ie can be derived from, a legal rule, can be general—such as the basic right to life, body and health or the fundamental freedom of expression or the equally fundamental freedom to make contracts, or assign property, but also such as the economic freedoms, as embodied in the EC Treaty—in that they pertain to very large classes of persons, even, for some, to all human beings. However, such a legal position can also be very specific, such as a right *in rem* or *in personam*, in that it gives a full or limited dominance over a specific object or over some form of behaviour by another person who is bound to behave in that way. The second comment is that, as seen hereinafter, it is often difficult to distinguish between remedies and procedures (or remedial and procedural rules).

In this piece, van Gerven is concerned with the effect of EU law in national courts and his definition is limited by the fact that he is defining rights as legal concepts that are recognized by courts. In one sense, such a definition is too narrow (particularly in environmental law) in that there are some legal rights that are not within the province of the judiciary, particularly in the context of innovative regulatory strategies.[5] On the other hand, his definition highlights that judicial recognition is vitally important in giving authority to a legal right and that rights are closely associated with remedies as well as obligations.

Legal rights and remedies can take many different forms—including private rights, public rights, rights before courts, and the creation of criminal offences—all generating remedies for environmental harm and disputes. As we will see in Chapter 6, considerable academic focus has been on rights and remedies in the private law context. However, the most significant development of rights and remedies in pursuit of environmental protection and resolving environmental problems has been in the public law sphere, particularly through public law litigation.

Indeed, one of the most famous attempts to create 'environmental' rights was in the United States, where there was an ambitious scholarly attempt to argue that trees should have legal standing in court cases.[6] The legal scholar who formulated this argument describes how he chanced upon it.

Christopher D Stone, *Should Trees Have Standing? Law, Morals and the Environment* (3rd edn, OUP 2010)) xi–xii (emphasis added)

I was teaching an introductory class in Property Law, and simply observing that societies, like human beings, progress through different stages of growth and sensitivity. In our progress through these

---

[5] See Chapter 12.
[6] See Chapter 10 and the arguments in Christopher D Stone, 'Should Trees Have Standing?—Towards Legal Rights for Natural Objects' (1972) S Cal L Rev 450; *Sierra Club v Morton* 405 US 727 (1972).

stages the law, in its way, like art and literature, in theirs, participates. Our subject matter, the evolution of property law, was illustration. Throughout history, there have been shifts in a cluster of related property variables, such as *what things*, at various times, were recognized as ownable (land, movables, ideas, other persons (slaves)); *who* was deemed capable of ownership (individuals, married women); the powers and privileges ownership conveyed (the right to destroy, the immunity from a warrantless search); and so on. It was easy to see how each change shifted the locus and quality of power. But there also had to be an internal dimension, each advance in the law-legitimated concept of 'ownership' fuelling a change in consciousness, in the range and depth of feelings. For example, how did the innovation of the will—of the power to control our property after death—affect our sense of mortality, of out selves? Engrossing stuff (I thought). But we were approaching the end of the hour. I sensed that the students had already started to pack away their enthusiasms for the next venue. (I like to believe that every lecturer knows this feeling.) They needed to be lassoed back.

'So', I wondered aloud, reading their glazing scepticisms, 'what would a radically different law-driven consciousness look like? ... One in which Nature had rights,' I supplied my own answer. 'Yes, rivers, lakes, ...' (warming to the idea) 'trees , . . animals. . .' (I may have ventured 'rocks'; I am not certain.) 'How would such a posture *in law* affect a community's view *of itself*?'

This little thought experiment was greeted, quite sincerely, with uproar. At the end of the hour, none too soon, I stepped out into the hall and asked myself, 'What did you just say in there? How could a tree have '*rights*'?' I had no idea.

The important point highlighted by Stone is that it is not so much that there were no legal rights and remedies in law that could be used to protect the environment. As we will see in Chapter 6, tort law has historically been used for environmental protection in innovative and indirect ways. Rather, Stone is stressing that there were no legal rights that gave *explicit* expression to environmental concerns. Moreover, the process of reasoning in relation to such rights is not straightforward within conventional legal thought and doctrine. Students thus often laugh at the idea of trees having standing and dismiss it as a legally preposterous idea, and in many ways it is ridiculous, but it is the ridiculousness and preposterousness of the idea that highlight the disjunction between what the law historically protected and what in fact needs protecting in the environment. This raises questions about why this state of affairs exists.

Daniel H Cole, *Pollution and Property: Comparing Ownership Institutions for Environmental Protection* (CUP 2002) 2–3

It is frequently said that pollution and other environmental problems stem, in the first instance, from the absence of property rights in natural resources (or 'environmental goods') [. . .] This reductionist assertion is repeated so often that it has become a truism. But it begs a further reductionist question: what accounts for the absence of property rights in many environmental goods? If some other factor is responsible for the lack of completely specified property rights, then the lack of property rights itself cannot be the ultimate 'cause' of pollution and other environmental problems. This reflects a standard problem with reductionist arguments: at what point does the process of reduction end?

As economists know (at least since Coase 1960), property rights are not completely specified for all—really any—environmental goods because they are costly to define, sometimes too costly. We might legitimately claim, therefore, that the cost of establishing property rights, rather than the absence of such rights, is the ultimate cause of environmental problems. But that only leads us to the next reductionist question: why are the costs of imposing property rights sometimes, but not always, too high? With this question we finally arrive at the twisted root of the matter: the economic, institutional, technological, and ecological *circumstances* that in large measure determine the costs of defining property rights in, and transacting over, environmental goods. Relations between pollution and property are ultimately determined by the economic, institutional, technological, and ecological circumstances that prevail at a given time and place.

Cole's statement is a reminder of the fact that our understanding of environmental problems is embedded in particular contexts.

Moreover, it should be noted that in thinking about rights and remedies, we also need to think about how law is implemented and enforced. These matters will affect how important traditional ideas of rights and remedies still are for the implementation of environmental law in particular. Thus, Chapter 12 shows that, over the last decade a range of regulatory strategies have been promoted, which focus on negotiation rather than on the assertion of rights.[7] Likewise, the traditional UK regulatory enforcement strategy has tended to be informal—a factor again which tends to deemphasize the importance of legal rights and remedies.[8]

3 FACTORING ENVIRONMENTAL CONCERNS INTO DECISION-MAKING

The third and final legal challenge arising from giving legal expression to environmental concerns consists of factoring environmental concerns into private and public decision-making. As seen in Chapter 2, environmental problems involve numerous parties, cross jurisdictional borders, and require the consideration of both facts and values. This state of affairs means that making decisions about environmental problems requires the careful consideration of a wide range of factors and issues, which are often spread widely both in a spatial and temporal sense. Accordingly, environmental problems are classic polycentric problems.[9] In terms of the law, this challenge has seen the rise of many different legal institutions, concepts, and frameworks, the basic aim of which is to get decision-makers to think broadly about environmental issues. That is, of course, easier said than done. There are at least four different ways in which the law has developed to promote a consideration of environmental issues.

The first and most traditional legal technique consists of requiring decision-makers to take environmental issues into account *within the context of a regime set up to promote environmental protection*. This has been mainly in the context of public law,[10] and requires a decision-maker to take environmental protection or some other related environmental goal into account. We will see many different obligations throughout the chapters in this book requiring (public) decision-makers to take environmental goals into account. Likewise, in some cases, special legal processes and procedures, such as environmental impact assessment and strategic environmental assessment, have been created.[11]

A second legal technique has been *the creation of environmental regimes that involve many different jurisdictions*. For example, the Kyoto Protocol (relating to climate change) involves the interaction of national and international jurisdictions in establishing legal obligations and procedures.[12], A key

---

[7] See Chapter 12.   [8] See Section 2.4 and Chapter 8.   [9] See Section 2.1 of Chapter 2.
[10] See Chapter 7.   [11] See Chapter 19.   [12] See Chapters 14 and 15.

aspect of multilevel regimes is that they involve the creation of new institutions and new governance regimes, which often challenge existing understandings of what amounts to law and regulation.[13]

A third legal technique involves *the development of principles and policies that emphasize the importance of particular issues in environmental decision-making.*[14] Thus, the precautionary principle requires scientific uncertainty to be acknowledged and the principle of intergenerational equity requires decision-makers to think about future generations. Both of these principles raise issues to which decision-makers traditionally did not have regard to in legal decision-making. Indeed, the promotion of principles in environmental law is often part of the promotion of a new agenda for decision-making.[15]

Finally, there has been increasingly emphasis *on integrating environmental concerns into mainstream decision-making.* This technique is at the heart of the idea of sustainable development, and is included in Article 11 of the TFEU.

> Environmental protection requirements must be integrated into the definition and implementation of the Union's policies and activities, in particular with a view to promoting sustainable development.

Article 11 and the ideas it encompasses were briefly discussed in Chapter 4 and are further elaborated in Chapter 11,[16] but here it is worth noting that, when we talk about integrating environmental concerns into decision-making, this can mean a variety of things. Jewell explains this, making an important distinction between the assimilation and integration of environmental concerns legally.

Tim Jewell, 'Public Law and the Environment' in Tim Jewell & Jenny Steele (eds),
*Law in Environmental Decision-Making: National, European and Environmental
Perspectives* (OUP 1998) 79

> This use of the words 'assimilation' and 'integration' suggests that they are synonymous, or at least similar. A more precise usage is preferred here [. . .] 'assimilation' is taken, for these purposes, to refer to the incorporation of environmental considerations within wider, often existing, decision-making systems; 'integration', by contrast, is used to refer to the bringing together of disparate controls into less fragmented controls over environmental harm. To this extent it represents significant legal change, but this is still change within a relatively narrow body of recognized 'environmental' law.

Jewell is highlighting here a useful distinction and you will find examples of both assimilation and integration across the textbook.

4 CONCLUSION

This has been an introduction to the discussion of basic legal concepts in environmental law. The label 'basic' should not make one think that the issues addressed in Part III of the textbook are simple or straightforward. Rather, the term 'basic' highlights the foundational nature of the legal concepts that underpin environmental law. However, as seen in this Introduction, those foundations are by

---

[13] See Chapter 13.   [14] See Chapter 11.
[15] Nicolas de Sadeleer, *Environmental Principles: From Political Slogans to Legal Rules* (OUP 2002).
[16] See Chapter 11.

no means solid and the development of environmental law has been essentially concerned with developing those firm footings.

In conclusion, the most significant point to appreciate is that law, as it relates to environmental problems, is profoundly complex. It is not just a 'plug and play' tool. And while law is closely inter-twined with society, it is not merely an instrument; rather, it is a thick cultural phenomenon.[17] Galligan makes the point in the introduction to his study of law and society.

DJ Galligan, *Law in Modern Society* (OUP 2007) 4

Anyone entering into the study of law in society faces the dilemma of either not taking law seriously enough or taking it too seriously. If the view prevails that there is nothing distinctive about it and that its place and importance are marginal to society, law is not taken seriously enough. If, on the other hand, it is thought that law is simply a system of rules that exerts authority over society while being insulated from it, then its character is miss-described and its importance exaggerated. The direction of this study is to do justice to the ideas implicit in the two approaches: that law is both a fairly distinctive social phenomenon and yet closely intertwined with other aspects of society; that law exerts authority over society, and yet in doing so is restrained and influenced by society; that law is in some sense an inde-pendent social formation while at the same time being interdependent with other social formations. A study of law in society must draw out these apparently competing qualities. On the one hand it must reveal the qualities particular to law, and on the other hand unravel its entanglement with society.

While we need to recognize that law is closely related to socio-political culture, it is also a separate entity, which requires distinct appreciation and close study, as Part III guides you to undertake.

---

[17] Clifford Geertz, *Local Knowledge* (Fontana Press 1993) 214.

PRIVATE LAW

Andreas Philippopoulos-Mihalopoulos has noted that:

> On the one hand environmental law encompasses, actually or potentially, everything that may ever be encompassed by law in general. On the other hand, and simultaneously to the above, what we commonly refer to as the legal discipline of environmental law does not really exist.[1]

There is much truth in that statement, particularly in relation to private law. Private law areas such as tort law, property law, and contract law have a profound impact on how societies understand and deal with environmental problems through the ways in which they define rights, responsibilities, and liabilities. At the same time, these subjects are not directly concerned with environmental problems and contemporary environmental law is understood as primarily deriving from legislation and regulatory schemes—as a 'public law' rather than 'private law' discipline.

Philippopoulos-Mihalopoulos notes the 'everything and nothing' nature of environmental law as its 'foundational paradox'.[2] That may be true, but it leaves textbook writers with a conundrum in explaining the interface between environmental law, environmental problems, and private law. In this chapter, we could give a comprehensive overview of private law or we could just focus on examples of when it directly affects environmental law. The former would be impossible, as it would require providing an account of huge swathes of the law. The latter, however, would be misleading as it would suggest that the small handful of 'environmental' private law cases are the sum total of the interrelationship between environmental problems, environmental law, and private law. That is not the case—they are simply examples of where that relationship has been litigated. The approach in this chapter is thus to find an uneasy middle way, attempting to capture both the general significance of the relationship between private law, environmental problems, and environmental law, and the direct relevance of private law to particular environmental problems.

The chapter is structured as follows. First, the concept of private law is defined and its general relationship with environmental law considered. Sections 2, 3, 4, and 5 give an overview of property law, tort law, contract law, and company law and their relationship to environmental law. This analysis shows that private law has a role in framing our understanding of environmental law and environmental problems, while environmental law and environmental problems also shape understandings of private law, and of property law in particular. Section 6 discusses the multi-dimensional nature of

[1] Andreas Philippopoulos-Mihalopoulos, 'Towards a Critical Environmental Law' in Andreas Philippopoulos-Mihalopoulos (ed), *Law and Ecology: New Environmental Foundations* (Routledge 2011) 18.

[2] Ibid.

the interrelationship between private law, environmental problems, and environmental law in more detail.

Two points should be made before moving on. First, this chapter is not a replacement for reading good textbooks on the relevant private law area under consideration—a further reading list can be found at the end of this chapter. Indeed, an expert in these different private law areas will likely baulk at the simplicity of the analysis of the different legal doctrines covered and want to supplement them with much more detail and analysis. Second, this chapter should not be taken as a definitive statement of all the possibilities of the relationship between private law, environmental law, and environmental problems. Rather, it offers a framework and raises the kinds of questions you need to think about as an environmental lawyer.

1 PRIVATE LAW AND ENVIRONMENTAL LAW: SOME GENERAL POINTS

Private law is often understood to be concerned with self-ordering amongst private actors; however, there is no singular way to define private law. Various approaches to defining private law can be taken,[3] and there is a lively debate between private lawyers about the nature and scope of their subject.[4] To keep the sanity of both the authors and readers of this textbook in this chapter, we avoid the jurisprudential complexities of private law and use the term 'private law' to refer to the areas of law that are conventionally understood to fall under that category—property law, tort law, and contract law. We also include company law, as one of the main means of self-ordering amongst private actors. This is not an exhaustive list. This convenient list of private law areas still offers the environmental lawyer, and environmental law student, plenty of scope to see the nuanced legal interactions at play between private law and environmental problems as an aspect of environmental law. In this section we briefly discuss each of these private law areas but, before doing that, it is important to highlight a number of features of private law.

First, private law subjects have a significant common law element but they are not solely a product of the common law—statutes have a role to play in private law subjects, particularly in company law. Likewise, there are also common law elements in public law. Second, private law is often understood not only in terms of its legal and doctrinal content but also how it structures the litigation relationship between different parties (see Chapter 10).[5] Third, definitions of private law are both descriptive and normative, thus defining both what private law *is* and what it *ought* to be. This latter point means that it is important for environmental lawyers to see that there are different scholarly and doctrinal issues (and agendas) at play when private law relates to environmental problems.

In short, the relationship between private law, environmental law, and environmental problems is complex and we can begin to see that complexity by returning to the three different ways of defining environmental law in Chapter 1. Those who take a descriptive approach to environmental law consider that certain aspects of private law are part of environmental law. Thus, Woolf (later Lord Woolf) defined environmental law to include 'the long-established common law actions for private and public nuisance'.[6]

By contrast, those who take a more purposive approach to defining environmental law find private law difficult to categorize. On the one hand, private law is at best irrelevant to environmental law, and

---

[3] William Lucy, *Philosophy of Private Law* (Clarendon Press 2007) 22–25.
[4] Andrew Robertson and Tang Hang Wu (eds), *The Goals of Private Law* (Hart Publishing 2009).
[5] Lucy (n 3).
[6] Sir Harry Woolf, 'Are the Judiciary Environmentally Myopic?' (1992) 4 JEL 1, 2.

at worst obstructive to it, because the values private law promotes—individualism and freedom of choice in particular—are understood to be at odds with environmental protection. On the other hand, litigants will often seek to use private law as a tool for environmental protection (see Section 6.3).

Finally, in terms of a jurisprudential definition of environmental law, the reasoning in private law cases becomes relevant if it can be seen to contribute to a more rigorous legal account of environmental law. Thus, we saw in Chapter 1 how Coyle and Morrow used an account of private law, focusing in property law, to show that the jurisprudential foundations of environmental law run deep.[7]

These three different definitional approaches should be kept in mind throughout the chapter. They highlight not only the ambiguity in the nature of the relationship between private law, environmental problems, and environmental law but that that relationship has many different dimensions. Sections 2, 3, 4, and 5 outline property law, tort law, contract law, and company law as they relate to environmental problems.

2 PROPERTY LAW

Property law is the law concerning relationships over things—in most cases this involves ownership of things and the rights that flow from that ownership, but as a social institution, property encompasses relationships about things that come in many shapes and sizes (essentially in as many shapes and sizes as the law might create and recognize). Particularly important for environmental lawyers is that property law regulates the right of access to a resource. Most of the time when thinking about property law the focus is on land law (including landlord and tenant law), but other areas of law also involve proprietary interests, such as the law in relation to personal property, intellectual property, and aspects of financial law. Likewise, property rights and interests, in both land and chattels, can come in many different forms—both legal and equitable. All this means is that the boundaries of property law are not sharply drawn and just as there are debates about the nature of environmental law there is also extensive debate about the nature of property law.[8]

One fundamental aspect of property law, as Lawson and Rudden point out, is that it is an area of law which underlines day-to-day transactions that are 'entirely, normal, peaceful and useful'.[9] It does not, like other areas of the law, only operate in times of conflict and 'all of us all the time take peacefully for granted the business of getting things and then keeping them and utilising them'.[10] In terms of environmental law and environmental problems, property law can be understood to frame our understanding of environmental problems and environmental law, and vice versa, through specific legal interrelationships. This is best seen by first considering concepts of property in general terms, and then turning to consider private property rights and alternative ideas of property in the commons against this backdrop.

2.1 CONCEPTS OF PROPERTY

There is no single idea of private property. It can be conceptualized in multiple ways —as an individual right that is inherently valuable (and even deserved), as a negotiated social agreement over use

---

[7] See Section 2.2.

[8] See, for example, James Penner, *The Idea of Property in Law* (OUP 1997) (presenting an essentialist idea of property). Cf Joseph W Singer, *Entitlement: The Paradoxes of Property* (Yale UP 2000) (property as a bundle of rights).

[9] FH Lawson and Bernard Rudden, *The Law of Property* (Clarendon Press 2002) 4.

[10] Ibid, 3.

of a resource, as an expression of a communal decision and interest in how land and other resources should be treated, and so on. Such different conceptualizations exist because property law deals in legally constructed ideas of property that are derived from legal and socio-political culture. Thus, the idea of property has a number of different dimensions, as Barnes explains.

Richard Barnes, *Property Rights and Natural Resources* (Hart Publishing 2009) 22

Property, in its broadest sense, is an institution governing the use of things. It is an economic institution in the sense that it is concerned with the allocation and use of goods and it is a social institution in that property provides a means to achieve social order. It is also a legal institution: law is the vehicle for the definition and regulation of any regime of property is thus a shared paradigm, our understanding of which is legitimately informed by a variety of intellectual disciplines. In providing an account of the legal institution of property, the point here is not to dispute the validity of non-legal perspectives on property. Rather it is to point to the fact that property rights must be legally constructed. Property rights are the product of property rules and property rules are located within legal systems. This means that property rights are invariably exposed to the values and limitations which inhere within a legal system and any analysis of property that disregard such values and limitations is incomplete.

Thus, there is a complex interrelationship between legal culture and the socio-political culture to which it relates, and there is a rich and exciting literature on property theory that explores different understandings of property rights. Hence, for example, US scholar Purdy argues that there are three ways in which property rights are 'celebrated'—the libertarian, welfarist, and personhood conceptions.[11] Purdy argues that these are not 'high theory intrusions from outside' but inherent in legal culture.[12] Purdy also notes that there are three different critiques of property rights—'the realist, romantic and republican veins' of legal thought.[13] Likewise, Barnes highlights in his work a range of different public and private roles of property law.[14] While there is no room here to go into detail about these debates, the swathe of categories for conceptualizing property show that real care should be taken in presuming that property law and property rights mean only one thing. Moreover, what the different critiques of property law theory also highlight is that thinking about the concept of property raises tricky jurisprudential questions about the relationship between law and society, and the extent to which property rights are shaped by, as much as they shape, social relations.

Debates over concepts of property and how they legally operate also interact with environmental law and environmental problems, thus, demonstrating the different ways in which property rights are promoted and critiqued in operation. For example, in some environmental law and property law scholarship, private property is understood as antithetical to environmental protection because it is seen as a tool of exploitation (the realist vein of legal thought). Lucy and Mitchell have noted that 'the institution of private property was denounced as theft and attacked as the product of exploitation and class antagonism'[15] in much early scholarship. An obvious legal consequence of this is to create environmental regulation regimes that limit the ways in which property rights can be exploited or to create 'commons' ownership, which is distinct from private property ownership and focused on group access to environmental resources.

---

[11] Jedediah Purdy, *The Meaning of Property: Freedom, Community, and the Legal Imagination* (Yale UP 2010) 19–20.
[12] Ibid, 19.   [13] Ibid, 21–25.
[14] Richard Barnes, *Property Rights and Nature Resources* (Hart Publishing 2009).
[15] William NR Lucy and Catherine Mitchell, 'Replacing Private Property: The Case for Stewardship' (1996) 55 CLJ 566, 566.

But this is not the only way to view the interrelationship between property rights and environmental regulation and examples here show private property rights being recast so as to incorporate ideas of stewardship as well as new property rights being created in the interests of environmental protection and managing resource scarcity. In thinking about each of these examples, the fact that concepts of property are themselves multiple and contested needs to be kept in mind.

2.2 PRIVATE PROPERTY RIGHTS

In terms of private property, the conventional starting point is the idea of 'liberal property rights'. Purdy has described 'liberal property theory' as a 'social imaginary', a concept akin to Dryzek's discourses examined in Section 4.2 of Chapter 2.[16] A very famous statement of 'liberal property rights' is given by Demsetz.

Harold Demsetz, 'Toward A Theory of Property Rights' (1967) 57 American Economic Review 347, 347

In the world of Robinson Crusoe property rights play no role. Property rights are an instrument of society and derive their significance from the fact that they help a man form those expectations which he can reasonably hold in his dealings with others. These expectations find expression in the laws, customs, and mores of a society. An owner of property rights possesses the consent of fellowmen to allow him to act in particular ways. An owner expects the community to prevent others from interfering with his actions, provided that these actions are not prohibited in the specifications of his rights.

In reaction to this, a common view has been that concepts of liberal private property are antithetical to environmental concerns, as Coyle and Morrow explain.

Sean Coyle and Karen Morrow, *The Philosophical Foundations of Environmental Law: Property Rights and Nature* (Hart Publishing 2004) 157

The modern legal order thus reflects a view of property rights as competing with environmental values and concerns, rather than emerging from moral reflection upon mankind's place in the world. Such a view is not inevitable: the natural rights theories of the seventeenth and eighteenth centuries rooted property rights in a teleological view of nature, and hence as determined and shaped by concerns which we could now aptly characterise as 'environmental'. Yet this conception of property is one no longer open to us. Our more complex way of life presents impossible challenges to the underlying assumption that human interests and environmental protection coincide. The natural rights theorists regarded human beings as possessing a duty to transform the environment from a barren, hostile wasteland into fruitful Eden; hence, we can see in those accounts an attempt to provide a philosophical basis for the systems of agrarian capitalism and agrarian communism which constituted the most important economic structures of the time. [...]

The perception of any intrinsic relationship between property and the environment came to be replaced by a view of property understood overwhelmingly in terms of subjective, rather than objective, right, and a view of environmental protection as instrumentally and prudentially desirable rather than morally necessary.

---

[16] Purdy (n 11) 11.

In this way, planning law and some aspects of nature conservation law limit what a property owner can do with his or her land. These regimes can thus be understood to stand in opposition to property rights, with legal disputes arising concerning how private property rights are reconciled with environmental protection goals.

There are many different legal ways that this conflict might manifest. It can be seen as a background theme in planning law, since planning law is constantly balancing the need to regulate development with the rights of property owners.[17] But the conflict can also arise in more complicated and oblique ways. Thus, for example, in private nuisance actions the rights of a property owner are limited if they cause an unreasonable interference with the right of enjoyment of land of another who has an interest in land. Questions of enjoyment of land in this context inevitably relate to issues of environmental quality but a private nuisance action only arises legally when such quality concerns interfere with someone else's property right.[18] In other words, this situation presents not so much a conflict between private property and environmental protection, but a conflict between property interests where environmental protection issues are relevant. Likewise, in recent years there have been examples of trespass actions against environmental protestors, which are less to do with property rights being in conflict with environmental protection and more concerned with property rights in conflict with the rights of protest, as seen in the *Monsanto v Tilly* case.

Monsanto v Tilly
[1999] EWCA Civ 3044 (Mummery LJ)

The Facts

Monsanto, among other things, argued that a group of protestors that were part of a protest movement called GenetiX Snowball had committed a trespass to land and goods by entering property that Monsanto had an interest in and destroying crops. The action was found to be made out and Mummery LJ made the following comments in relation to the possibility of the defendants running a defence of public interest to the trespass action.

Judgment

On the one hand, there is a public interest in the enforcement of law for the protection of private property in particular and in the maintenance of public order in general. Public confidence in the legal system and in the rule of law would be undermined if the courts refused to enforce the law on the ground that defendants, who wished to establish the validity of beliefs sincerely and genuinely held, were entitled to rely on the public interest to justify wrongs to the property of others who did not share their point of view. It is extremely improbable that a reasonable man would regard the defence proposed as an acceptable reason for the unauthorised presence of anyone, public official or fellow citizen, on his property or on the property of anyone else.

On the other hand, the unavailability of public interest as a justification for trespass does not in any way curtail or prejudice the exercise by the defendants of their undoubted right in a democratic society to use to the full all lawful means at their disposal to achieve the aims and objects of GenetiX Snowball. Supporters can peacefully and effectively pursue those aims and gain publicity and public support for them in many different ways without the need to commit unlawful acts of trespass against Monsanto or anyone else.

The Court of Appeal found that the 'public interest' defence failed. Note that the conflict between private property and the right to protest is not happening in a legal vacuum. In his reasoning, Mummery LJ also took into account public confidence in the legal system, the rule of law, and the

---

[17] See Chapter 18.   [18] *Hunter v Canary Wharf Ltd* [1997] AC 655.

values that exist in a democratic society—legal values that showed the public interest, in legal terms, to be far from straightforward.

More obvious examples of conflicts between environmental protection and private property rights can been seen in legal disputes where Article 1 of the 1st Protocol (Article 1P1) of the European Convention of Human Rights is invoked against a public authority under s 6 of the Human Rights Act 1998.[19] Article 1P1 states:

(1) Every natural or legal person is entitled to the peaceful enjoyment of his possessions. No one shall be deprived of his possessions except in the public interest and subject to the conditions provided for by law and by the general principles of international law.

(2) The preceding provisions shall not, however, in any way impair the right of a State to enforce such laws as it deems necessary to control the use of property in accordance with the general interest or to secure the payment of taxes or other contributions or penalties.

The issue that has been raised in a growing number of cases is whether environmental regulation by the state can result in a restriction of property rights, so as to oblige the state to compensate a property owner. One example can be seen in the *R (Trailer & Marina (Leven) Ltd) v Secretary of State for the Environment, Food & Rural Affairs* case. The facts are not important, other than to know that the case concerned nature conservation legislation that operated in a way that restricted property owners' rights.

R (Trailer & Marina (Leven) Ltd) v Secretary of State for the Environment, Food & Rural Affairs
[2004] EWCA Civ 1580, [2005] 1 WLR 1267 paras 42–47, 50–53, 58 (Neuberger LJ)

42. There is no doubt that [...] deprivation of property without compensation will normally infringe Article 1P1, is correct. Thus, in *James v United Kingdom* (1986) 8 EHRR 123, [54], the ECtHR said:

'the taking of property in the public interest without payment of compensation is treated as justifiable only in exceptional circumstances not relevant for present purposes. As far as article 1 is concerned, the protection of the right to property it affords would be largely illusory and ineffective in the absence of any equivalent principle.'

43. The court immediately went to say:

'Clearly, compensation terms are material to the assessment whether the contested legislation respects a fair balance between the various interests at stake and, notably, whether it does not impose a disproportionate burden on the [persons deprived of their property].'

44. Furthermore, as the ECtHR held in that case, and indeed has held in other cases:

'Article 1 does not, however, guarantee a right to full compensation in all cases, since legitimate objectives of 'public interest', such as pursued in measures of economic reform or measures designed to achieve greater social justice, may call for less than reimbursement of the full market value.': see *Lithgow v United Kingdom* (1986) 8 EHRR 329, [121].

45. Those observations were concerned with deprivation of ownership of property, whereas the present case is concerned with control of use of property. [...]

46. If article 1P1 required the provision of compensation in legislation which restricted the use of property, the results would be very far-reaching indeed. The financial consequences of introducing laws concerned with town and country planning, listed and historic buildings, health and safety at work, and hygiene, to take some obvious examples, would be such as severely to cripple the legislature's freedom to introduce such socially beneficial legislation.

[19] See Chapter 7.

47. However, the jurisprudence of the ECtHR demonstrates that what is not an actual expropriation may amount to what one might call a de facto expropriation for the purposes of article 1P1. [...]

50. Where there is no actual or de facto expropriation, the proper approach of the court to a complaint that there has been an infringement of article 1P1 was spelled out in *Jacobsson v Sweden* (1989) 12 EHRR 56. The ECtHR, after explaining why *Sporrong* was distinguishable, said at [55]:

'Under the second paragraph of article 1 of Protocol No 1, the Contracting States are entitled, among other things, to control the use of property in accordance with the general interest by enforcing such laws as they deem necessary for the purpose. However, as this provision is to be construed in the light of the general principle enunciated in the first sentence of the first paragraph, there must be a reasonable relationship of proportionality between the means employed and the aim sought to be realised. In striking the fair balance thereby required between the general interests of the community and the requirements of the protection of the individual's fundamental rights, the authorities enjoy a wide margin of appreciation.'

51. In this connection, it is worth mentioning what, in the context of the Convention, is the exceptional nature of the second paragraph of Article 1P1. It expressly excludes from the ambit of the right granted by the first paragraph any interference which is 'deem[ed] necessary' by the state 'in accordance with the general interest' (or to secure payment of taxes). This subjective approach to necessity is in marked contrast to the objective requirement of necessity in the second paragraph of articles 8, 9, 10 and 11.

52. The reasoning of the ECtHR [...] appears to us to establish that, when considering whether legislation, which controls the use of property in the public interest, infringes article 1P1, a fair balance has to be struck between the general public interest and individual rights, which is tantamount to a requirement of proportionality (as the ECtHR recognised in *Jacobsson*). In appraising this, the court must accord to the legislature the measure of judgment discussed by Lord Hoffmann in *Alconbury* at [72]–[73], and by Lord Nicholls of Birkenhead in *Wilson v First County Trust (No 2)* [2004] 1 AC 816 [68]–[70].

53. At [70] in *Wilson*, Lord Nicholls said:

'...[C]ourts should have in mind that theirs is a reviewing role. Parliament is charged with the primary responsibility for deciding whether the means chosen to deal with a social problem are both necessary and appropriate. Assessment of the advantages and disadvantages of the various legislative alternatives is primarily a matter for Parliament.'

As Mr Rabie says, it is debatable whether the legislation with which this case is concerned can be characterised as aimed at 'a social problem'. In our view, however, the legislation in the present case was plainly enacted for 'the general interests of the community' (to quote from *Jacobsson* at [55]) and the observations of Lord Nicholls are equally applicable to it.

[...]

58. The right analysis seems to us to be that provided the state could properly take the view that the benefit to the community outweighs the detriment to the individual, a fair balance will be struck, without any requirement to compensate the individual. Should this not be the case, compensation in some appropriate form may serve to redress the balance, so that no breach of article 1P1 occurs.

This case is merely one example of how property rights and the public interest can be balanced in the ECHR context and it shows that the nature of that balance is very much dictated by the framework of the ECHR and the body of legal doctrine that has built up around it. Thus, to the extent that environmental regulation can be understood to promote the public interest, the legal relationship between private property rights and environmental protection should not be understood as having only one form.

Indeed there are scholars who have argued that liberal property rights can be deployed *for* environmental protection purposes.[20] Likewise, there have been scholars, such as Rodgers, who have understood property rights from a different conceptual starting point altogether, understanding the relationship between such rights and environmental protection in a fundamentally different way.

Christopher Rodgers, 'Nature's Place? Property Rights, Property Rules and Environmental Stewardship' (2009) 68 CLJ 550, 557–58

An altogether different approach would categorise property rights as elements (or strands) of utility that together combine to make up the constituent elements of a land interest. According to this analysis 'property' consists not of a bundle of abstract rights protected by legal rules, but rather a bundle of individual elements of land based utility. As Gray has observed, it follows that where there is any addition to, or subtraction from, the bundle of utility rights enjoyed by a person, it is possible to argue that a transaction or movement in 'property' has occurred—a proposition of great relevance to modern environmental regulation. Viewed in this sense, a property right gives a legally protected right of access to a resource. Moreover, the advent of modern land use planning, and of legislation protecting living natural resources, has arguably produced a situation where the 'property' of the owner, viewed in this sense, represents merely a residuum of socially permitted power over land resources. [...]

The primary impact of much environmental legislation is concerned with the limitation or redistribution of property rights in this sense—as elements of utility—in order to pursue public policy objectives. Property rights are therefore fundamentally important to an understanding of the *impact* of the legal and economic instruments used to implement environmental policy. Gray's analysis of property rights as elements of land-based utility provides a more promising framework of analysis for the interaction of environmental regulation with property rights. In particular, it can be used to examine the resource allocation function of property rules and to identify the inherent tensions between the use of public resources for environmental protection on the one hand and the restriction of private property rights of land use and utility on the other. Modern environmental regulation plays an important role in determining and shaping future resource allocation, and in shaping future land management to enhance biodiversity. It is not concerned solely with determining the nature and allocation of existing land use resources and entitlements. A theory of 'environmental property' must also, therefore, capture the forward looking role of modern environmental instruments, many of which are designed to change *future* land use practices in order to *improve and enhance* biodiversity and the environment.

Rodgers' analysis also highlights that property is not merely a limitation on environmental protection but can also be part of the legal framework for pursuing it. In this way, the right to property might be used in human rights cases as a tool for demanding a certain level of environmental quality.[21] More recently, property rights have been deployed as legal devices in regulatory strategies, such as emission trading schemes, which have fundamental environmental protection aims (see Chapter 15).

2.3 COMMONS

The complexity of property rights thickens again when one turns to another concept of property: 'the commons'. As we saw in Section 2.1 of Chapter 2, the idea of the 'commons' has been an important

---

[20] Elizabeth Brubaker, *Property Rights in the Defence of Nature* (Earthscan 1995).
[21] *Hatton v UK* (2002) 34 EHRR 1 (based on Article 8 ECHR).

theme in understanding environmental problems and Hardin's article on 'The Tragedy of the Commons' has been a touchstone for understanding and conceptualizing environmental problems. Hardin was not a lawyer and his idea of a commons is not a legally precise one, and was, using Barnes' terminology, more concerned with understanding a *social* institution. Indeed, as Ostrom notes, the idea of the 'tragedy of the commons' has come to 'symbolise the degradation of the environment to be expected whenever many individuals use a scarce resource in common'.[22] Thus, the problem is one of collective action.

But the idea of the commons can also be understood as a *legal* institution. At its most simple, a 'commons' is conceptually distinct from private property rights, as seen in the approach of Holder and Flessas.

Jane B Holder and Tatiana Flessas, 'Emerging Commons' (2008) 17 Social and Legal Studies 299, 300

A generic definition of commons is almost impossible to formulate, because the shared interests and values that produce (legally determined) commons are themselves in constant flux, producing fluid and often unpredictable groupings and initiatives across industries, historical public spaces and cultural identities. Nonetheless, a tentative description that spans the different forms of commons discussed in this collection is 'the collective and local ownership of land, resources, or ideas, held in an often communal manner, sometimes in opposition to private property'.

A striking aspect of this legal definition is that a commons is not defined as an absence of ownership, but rather as collective ownership. Indeed, a number of scholars argue that 'the conceptual binary of private/commons property creates too paltry a framework',[23] because it fails to provide a schema for understanding that many different types of public and private ownership might exist. Thus, for example, there is a very big difference between a 'commons' being understood as an open access free-for-all and an identifiable group owning something collectively, as explained by Rose.

Carol M Rose, 'Common Property, Regulatory Property, and Environmental Protection: Comparing Community Based Management to Tradable Environmental Allowances' in *Committee on the Human Dimensions of Global Change, The Drama of the Commons* (National Academy Press 2002) 233–34

In the Hardin/Ophuls view, environmental degradation—overfishing, deforestation, overgrazing, pollution, whatever—is only a bleak set of repetitions of the 'tragedy', and only two solutions are possible to stave off the tragic decimation: individual property on the one hand, which internalizes the externalities of common pool exploitation, or 'Leviathan' on the other, where governmental directives force individuals to perform in ways that promote the common good (Hardin, 1968; Ophuls, 1977).

The great service of Ostrom and her colleagues has been to contest this unattractive view, and to offer a powerful set of counterexamples of conservationist social institutions. Ostrom and others have

---

[22] Elinor Ostrom, *Governing the Commons: The Evolution of Institutions for Collective Action* (CUP 1990) 2.
[23] Hanoch Dagan and Michael A Heller, 'The Liberal Commons' (2001) 110 YLJ 549, 552.

pointed out that the problem that Hardin called 'the commons' was really a problem of 'open access', whereas a common resource that is limited to a particular group of users may suffer no such decimation. Indeed, Hardin's dominating example of the medieval common fields was not tragic at all, but was rather an example of a set of community-based sustainable agricultural practices that lasted for centuries, if not millennia [...]

Thus, once we begin to understand the 'commons' as a legal institution, we begin to see that it can refer to a range of different specific legal rights and obligations. In English land law, for example, a 'commons' has a specific legal meaning.

Christopher Rodgers, 'Reversing the "Tragedy" of the Commons? Sustainable Management and the Commons Act 2006' (2010) 73 MLR 461, 463–64

Far from suffering a 'tragedy of the commons' in Hardin's sense, common land in England and Wales was, prior to the Commons Registration Act 1965, subject to common law principles of customary origin that promoted 'sustainable' management. These were expressed through property rights, in the form of qualifications on the resource use conferred by property entitlements, and administered by local manor courts [...] the administration of customary rules by the courts represented a wholly different means for organising the management of common resources than the model posited by Hardin, which stresses the need for exclusive ownership by either individuals or government in order to promote the effective management of the resource.

The management principles applied by manorial institutions were not expressed in terms of the 'sustainable' management of the common land resource. This reflects the fact that the focus of common law discourse is on rights and remedies, with which the notions of intergenerational equity and futurity implicit in sustainable development sit uneasily. There is ample evidence, however, that until their demise in the eighteenth and nineteenth centuries, the manor courts administered a sophisticated system of land use regulation that fulfilled many, but not all, of the objectives that modern environmental policy now seeks for the 'sustainable' management of common land.

The idea of the commons is not simply a historical artefact. The Commons Registration Act 1965 required that common land and the rights over it be registered, and more recently the Commons Act 2006 has provided a framework for management of areas registered under it. This has led to litigants bringing actions to have land registered as a village green under the Commons Registration Act 1965 as a means of protecting it. Section 22(1) of that Act (as amended) states:

'town or village green ' means land [a] which has been allotted by or under any Act for the exercise or recreation of the inhabitants of any locality or [b] on which the inhabitants of any locality have a customary right to indulge in lawful sports and pastimes or [c] on which the inhabitants of any locality have indulged in such sports and pastimes as of right for not less than 20 years [...]

(1A) Land falls within this subsection if it is land on which for not less than 20 years a significant number of the inhabitants of any locality, or of any neighbourhood within a locality, have indulged in lawful sports and pastimes as of right, and either—(a) continue to do so, or

(b) have ceased to do so for not more than such period as may be prescribed, or determined in accordance with prescribed provisions.

A rich body of case law concerning what constitutes a village green and how it should be established has developed around this statute.[24] In the extract from McGillivray and Holder, they consider the nature of the 'village green', in property law terms and as a feature of environmental law more generally.

Donald McGillivray and Jane Holder, 'Locality, Environment and the Law: The Case of Town and Village Greens' (2007) 3 International Journal of Law in Context 1, 3–4

Greens do not fall easily into existing (public and private) categories of property law. Greens are neither un-owned nor 'public' land—as with commons more generally, they belonging to someone (although a significant amount have no registered owner). Greens are primarily created by the activities of those within the locality, or neighbourhood within the locality, over time. Their registration carries with it features of an easement—the enjoyment of rights over another's land. But, as with public rights of way, this is an unconventional type of property right since its main method of creation is by the actions of communities rather than individuals, and the mechanism for registration is by application to a county council under statutory provisions. The registration of land as a green does not transfer property to the community or give it exclusive possession—the land remains in private ownership, whether by a private individual or public body—but the effect is to curtail severely the rights of the landowner so that, in effect, existing activities may continue but little more than this. In a sense, possession of land is shared between the owner and the community, with neither being able to oust the other over their respective pre-existing interests (*Oxfordshire County Council v Oxford City Council* [2006] UKHL 15): the law relating to greens produces a public right to land, but in a private form.

The hybrid nature of greens also arises from the way in which they come into being. In line with the idea that designation as a green involves a measure of clashing private rights rather than public law control, the instigation of the right to register land is by individual citizens, campaigning groups, or representative bodies such as parish councils. There is invariably a public inquiry, and challenges to the registration of land as a green is [sic] made by way of judicial review, both of which suggest a strong public law element in the acquisition of the public right to use greens without the threat of their future development. But the legal test for the registration of greens, requiring a connection between the land and its use by a significant number of the local community, also demonstrates features of property law.

Village greens may not fall into a narrow or liberal understanding of property but their meaning only makes sense within the context of property law. Thus, overall, it is important to take a broad view of property rights and their relationship to environmental law. As one final example and food for thought, the regulation of parking on public roads is a form of creating and regulating different types of property rights,[25] which is probably not found in a property law textbook (but perhaps should be!) and which is an important type of regime for controlling the use of scarce resources (space and arguably clean air).

3 TORT LAW

Following on from discussing the interaction of property law, environmental law, and environmental protection, this section turns to tort law, a considerable amount of which is in fact dependent on the

---

[24] *Oxfordshire County Council v Oxford City Council* [2006] UKHL 25, [2006] 2 AC 674; *R (on the application of Lewis) v Redcar and Clevland Borough Council* [2010] UKSC 11 [2010] 2 AC 70.

[25] Richard A Epstein, 'The Allocation of the Commons: Parking on Public Roads' (2002) 31 JLS S515.

operation of property law. That is, property rights are triggers for tort law actions and remedies. In other words, different areas of private law (and public law also for that matter) should not be seen as hermetically sealed. This section briefly outlines what tort law is and how various torts play a role in environmental law and environmental protection.

Tort law is the law of civil wrongs. As McBride and Bagshaw note:

> the function of tort law is to determine what legal rights we have against other people, free of charge and without our having to make special arrangements for them, and what remedies will be available when those rights are violated.[26]

Tort law is understood to include (but is not limited to) the laws of trespass, negligence, nuisance, breach of statutory duty, defamation, and a range of economic torts. Much tort law is common law but it has also been significantly supplemented by statute.[27] The main remedies for tort law wrongs are compensation and/or an injunction.

Generally speaking, tort law has been understood as the area of private law most relevant to environmental problems and there is a significant literature on the interface between tort and environmental law.[28] This is for three reasons. First, tort actions provide possible remedies for environmental harm without the need for a 'special arrangement', such as a contract or a legislative duty, being in place. Second, tort law has historically served as a basis or legal inspiration for the development of statutory liabilities like statutory nuisance (addressed in Chapter 9). Third, the language of tort law has been appealing to non-lawyers as concepts such as 'nuisance' and 'duty of care' seem to chime with how they think about environmental problems. However, there is a very wide gap between everyday language and precise legal terms—something may be a 'nuisance' in common speech but that is very different from it constituting a private or public nuisance actionable in law. In reality, tort cases concerning environmental protection are relatively few when considering the full spectrum of tort law cases. The analysis in Sections 3.1 to 3.4 touches on these relatively rare cases.

3.1 PRIVATE NUISANCE

A tort of private nuisance is established if it is found that someone 'created, authorised, adopted or continued a state of affairs that has unreasonably interfered, or is unreasonably interfering with either the use and enjoyment of land' that another has a sufficient interest in or 'some right associated with that land'.[29] There are three particular things to note about the action from an environmental law perspective.

First, the action only provides remedies for those who have an interest in land, thereby limiting those who can bring an action.[30] Second, the remedies available in nuisance cases are usually an injunction to stop any future unreasonable interference and damages to compensate for past unreasonable interference. Third, and most importantly, the action does not provide remedies for any interference but only 'unreasonable' interference, which often involves the balancing of respective uses of land of the claimant and defendant, as the reasoning in the *Halsey v Esso Petroleum Co Ltd* case illustrates.

---

[26] Nicholas J McBride and Roderick Bagshaw, *Tort Law* (4th edn, Pearson 2012) 1.

[27] See, for example, Occupiers' Liability Acts 1957 and 1958; Consumer Protection Act 1989.

[28] Jenny Steele, 'Assessing the Past: Tort Law and Environmental Risk' in Tim Jewell and Jenny Steele (eds), *Law in Environmental Decision-Making* (OUP 1998).

[29] McBride and Bagshaw (n 26) 434.   [30] *Hunter v Canary Wharf Ltd* [1997] AC 655.

Halsey v Esso Petroleum Co Ltd
[1961] 1 WLR 683 (QB) 691–92 (Veale J)

The Facts

The plaintiff brought a private nuisance action arguing that emissions from an oil depot (described as 'noxious acid smuts') amounted to an unreasonable interference in land.

Judgment

So far as the present case is concerned, liability for nuisance by harmful deposits could be established by proving damage by the deposits to the property in question, provided of course that the injury was not merely trivial. Negligence is not an ingredient of the cause of action, and the character of the neighbourhood is not a matter to be taken into consideration. On the other hand, nuisance by smell or noise is something to which no absolute standard can be applied. It is always a question of degree whether the interference with comfort or convenience is sufficiently serious to constitute a nuisance. The character of the neighbourhood is very relevant and all the relevant circumstances have to be taken into account. What might be a nuisance in one area is by no means necessarily so in another. In an urban area, everyone must put up with a certain amount of discomfort and annoyance from the activities of neighbours, and the law must strike a fair and reasonable balance between the right of the plaintiff on the one hand to the undisturbed enjoyment of his property, and the right of the defendant on the other hand to use his property for his own lawful enjoyment. That is how I approach this case.

It may be possible in some cases to prove that noise or smell have in fact diminished the value of the plaintiff's property in the market. That consideration does not arise in this case, and no evidence has been called in regard to it. The standard in respect of discomfort and inconvenience from noise and smell which I have to apply is that of the ordinary reasonable and responsible person who lives in this particular area of Fulham. This is not necessarily the same as the standard which the plaintiff chooses to set up for himself. It is the standard of the ordinary man, and the ordinary man, who may well like peace and quiet, will not complain, for instance, of the noise of traffic if he chooses to live on a main street in an urban centre, nor of the reasonable noises of industry, if he chooses to live alongside a factory.

As the extract indicates, the unreasonableness of the interference is partly determined by the nature of the locality in which the alleged nuisance is taking place. This locality factor in determining what is a 'reasonable user' of land is relevant only in nuisance cases that concern acts that produce 'sensible personal discomfort' (reduced amenity through smells, noise, and vibration etc) rather than material damage to land.[31] Determining what is a reasonable use of land in private nuisance terms is a well litigated topic,[32] particularly as issues of unreasonable interference with land use rights and the nature of the locality overlap with planning law (see Chapter 18). These overlapping concerns and legal issues can be seen in the *Watson v Croft Promo Sport Ltd* case.

Watson v Croft Promo Sport Ltd
[2009] EWCA Civ 15 paras 24, 29–34 (The Chancellor of the High Court)

The Facts

The claimants brought an action in nuisance in relation to noise from a race circuit. The defendants argued that there the noise was not unreasonable interference due to the grant of planning permissions

---

[31] *St Helen's Smelting Co v Tipping* [1865] 11 HLC 642.
[32] *Gillingham Borough Council v Medway (Chatham Docks) Co Ltd* [1993] QB 343 (QB); *Wheeler v JJ Saunders Ltd* [1996] Ch 19 (CA); *Watson v CP Ltd* [2009] EWCA Civ 15, [2009] All ER 249.

in 1963 and 1998 in relation to the circuit. The Divisional Court found that the defendant's actions did constitute an actionable nuisance. The defendants appealed.

The Court

24. The [trial] judge started by setting out two principles of law which he described as 'reasonably well settled'. They were that (1) a planning authority (including a minister and an inspector) have no jurisdiction to authorise a nuisance, though they may have the power to permit a change in the character of a neighbourhood and (2) the question whether a permissive planning permission has changed the character of a neighbourhood so as to defeat what would otherwise constitute a claim in nuisance is one of fact and degree

[...]

29. The submissions for the defendants on this appeal may be summarised as follows: (1) the judge was wrong in law in not concluding that the nature and character of the locality had been changed by the planning permissions of 1963 and 1998 and by the s 106 Agreement; (2) the correct test for resolving that question is whether (a) there is some new and distinctive feature about the locality which has been effected by the planning consent under consideration and, if so, (b) whether that feature was the product of a planning process which involved a fair and conclusive adjudication on matters of public interest in such a way as to restrict private right or is otherwise 'strategic' in nature [...]

30. Logically the second submission should be considered first, notwithstanding that in his oral argument counsel for the defendants made it plain that it was very much a secondary argument. Counsel for the defendant emphasised the inconvenience which may result if the outcome of a statutory process such as that which governs whether any particular development should be permitted from a public perspective is to be revisited in a private law tort claim. He stressed that in this case both the permission of 1963 and that of 1998 was granted after an exhaustive consideration of the consequences of the noise which would be generated by the developments for which permission was then being sought. He suggested that the consequence of those permissions was to introduce an element of noise which, necessarily, qualified the essentially rural character of the locality to the extent of the noise element so introduced. Given that that noise element was restricted by the terms of the s 106 Agreement that should be the benchmark for a consideration of both the nature and character of the locality and/or the standard of reasonable user.

31. In support of that submission counsel for the defendants relied on certain dicta in *Wheeler v JJ Saunders Ltd* [1996] Ch 19, 30E and *Hunter v Canary Wharf Ltd* [1997] AC 655, 722E in relation to the effect of those planning decisions which may properly be regarded as 'strategic planning decisions affected by considerations of public interest'. It is suggested that in such cases the grant of planning permission of itself affects the private rights of the citizen to complain of a common law nuisance.

32. I would reject this submission for a number of reasons. First, it is well established that the grant of planning permission as such does not affect the private law rights of third parties. This was clearly stated by Cumming-Bruce LJ in *Allen v Gulf Oil Refinery* [1980] QB 156, 174G–H and has been consistently applied in all the subsequent cases [...] Second, the implementation of that planning permission may so alter the nature and character of the locality as to shift the standard of reasonable user which governs the question of nuisance or not. This too is clearly recognised in the judgments of Staughton and Peter Gibson LJJ in *Wheeler v JJ Saunders Ltd* [1996] Ch 19, 30D–E and 35G and the speech of Lord Cooke of Thorndon in *Hunter v Canary Wharf Ltd* [1997] AC 655, 722G.

33. In the light of these two well established principles I find it hard to understand how there can be some middle category of planning permission which, without implementation, is capable of affecting private rights unless such effect is specifically authorised by Parliament. It has not been suggested to us that there is any section in the statutory code governing the application for and grant of planning permission which could have that result. For that reason alone I would reject the second ground of appeal put forward by the defendants.

34. In any event, even if there be some middle category such as that for which the defendants contend neither of the grants of planning permission on which the defendants rely can be properly described as 'strategic'. The 1963 grant was specific to the part of the airfield to which it applied. It dealt with the issue of noise, but in a more confined context than what might reasonably be described as 'strategic'. In the case of the 1998 grant it is plain from the passages in the inspector's report to which I have drawn attention that the purpose and effect of that grant was to introduce some restriction and control over the otherwise unrestricted activities authorised by the 1963 grant. In effect it dealt with the unimplemented parts of the 1963 grant. It follows that, on the facts of this case, neither grant of permission can come within any such third category.

The judge then went on to consider the first question and concluded that the trial judge had been correct in his findings. This analysis shows that the interaction between nuisance claims and planning permission is by no means simple. Section 6.4 shows that it becomes even more complicated in light of other forms of statutory authorization, such as pollution permits, which are commonly used in environmental regulation.

3.2 PUBLIC NUISANCE

Public nuisance is not strictly a tort.[33] Rather, it is a crime prosecutable by a public authority, but it is also actionable in tort by certain individuals, if they suffer 'special damage' as a result (over and above damage to the public).[34] Lee highlights both the complexity of this doctrine[35] and also the way in which it frames this area of environmental law.

Maria Lee, 'Personal Injury, Public Nuisance, and Environmental Regulation'
(2009) 20 King's Law Journal 129, 136

The proper place of public nuisance in either criminal or tort law is not easy to pin down, and remains open in many respects. Neither private nor public nuisance has ever been 'about' environmental protection, notwithstanding an occasional overlap. Much maligned, undoubtedly clumsy and still incoherent, public nuisance is however potentially a highly revealing tort in the environmental arena. In particular, public nuisance conceptualises harm as a public event that has an impact on communities, avoiding the misrepresentation of environmental harm as a series of individual harms, but recognises that individuals may also suffer, as individuals. And whilst allowing recovery brings the law closer to addressing the human impact of pollution, the true environmental impact (to biodiversity, for example) may be picked up (albeit in a highly anthropocentric manner) by the criminal element.

The complexity of public nuisance concerns not only its legal status but also what kinds of activity and harm amount to a public nuisance. There has been much judicial consideration of the latter point, with the case of *Corby Group v Corby Borough Council* providing an example. In *Corby Group*, the nature of public nuisance needed to be elucidated in order to determine whether damages might be available for personal injury under the tort.

---

[33] JR Spencer, 'Public Nuisance—A Critical Examination' (1989) 48 CLJ 55.
[34] *Tate & Lyle Industries v GLC* [1983] 1 All ER 1159 (HL).
[35] See also Neil Papworth, 'Public Nuisance in the Environmental Context' [2008] JPEL 1526.

Corby Group v Corby Borough Council
[2008] EWCA Civ 463, [2009] QB 335 paras 27, 29–30 (Dyson LJ)

The Facts

The claimants argued that the defendants by allowing the escape of toxic material during the reclamation of a steelworks endangered the health of the public and caused personal injury to the claimants and their mothers. This they argued gave rise to an action in public nuisance recoverable in damages. The defendants argued that a remedy for damages was not available in public nuisance. Dyson LJ, after a lengthy analysis of both the judicial and scholarly (Newark being a leading one) authorities came to the following conclusions.

Judgment

27. It seems to me that it is at least arguable that Professor Newark was wrong to describe a public nuisance as a 'tort to the enjoyment of rights in land'. The definition of the crime of public nuisance says nothing about enjoyment of land and some public nuisances undoubtedly have nothing to do with the interference with enjoyment of land. As Lord Bingham said, the ingredients of the crime and the tort are the same. A public nuisance is simply an unlawful act or omission which endangers the life, safety, health, property or comfort of the public. As was said in *Salmond and Heuston on the Law of Torts* (21st edition 1996) 54–55: 'Public and private nuisances are not in reality two species of the same genus at all. There is no generic conception which includes the crime of making a bomb-hoax and the tort of allowing one's trees to overhang the land of a neighbour'.

29. [...] The essence of the right that is protected by the tort of private nuisance is the right to enjoy one's property. It does not extend to a licensee: see *Hunter's case* [1997] AC 655 . The essence of the right that is protected by the crime and tort of public nuisance is the right not to be adversely affected by an unlawful act or omission whose effect is to endanger the life, safety, health etc of the public. This view is reflected in the *American Law Institute, Restatement of the Law, Second, Torts 2d* (1979) chapter 40 para 821B (h) which states: 'Unlike a private nuisance, a public nuisance does not necessarily involve interference with use and enjoyment of land'.

30. In these circumstances, it is difficult to see why a person whose life, safety or health has been endangered and adversely affected by an unlawful act or omission and who suffers personal injuries as a result should not be able to recover damages. The purpose of the law which makes it a crime and a tort to do an unlawful act which endangers the life, safety or health of the public is surely to protect the public against the consequences of acts or omissions which do endanger their lives, safety or health. One obvious consequence of such an act or omission is personal injury. The purpose of this law is not to protect the property interests of the public. It is true that the same conduct can amount to a private nuisance and a public nuisance. But the two torts are distinct and the rights protected by them are different.

As could also be seen in relation to private nuisance, this reasoning shows that analysis of public nuisance in an environmental context requires an understanding of the tort writ large and its relationship to other torts. The wider tort law context has also driven the development of the rule in *Rylands v Fletcher*, considered in Section 3.3 and often claimed by environmental lawyers as a significant common law development in relation to environmental protection. The tort law context of these cases raises a question about how much these cases concern environmental problems and how much they are driven by more general theories of the role of tort.[36] This is particularly the case when, like public nuisance, torts do not only relate to environmental problems.

[36] Peter Cane, 'Are Environmental Harms Special?' (2001) 13 JEL 3.

3.3   THE RULE IN *RYLANDS V FLETCHER*

The rule in *Rylands v Fletcher* derives from litigation in the mid 1860s. At the Court of Exchequer level in *Rylands*, Blackburn J stated that:

> We think the rule of law is, that the person who, for his own purposes, brings on his land and collects and keeps there anything likely to do mischief if it escapes, must keep it in at his peril; and if he does not do so, is *prima facie* answerable for all the damage which is the natural consequence of its escape. He can excuse himself by showing that the escape was owing to the claimant's default; or perhaps that the escape was the consequence of *vis major*, or the act of God.[37]

In the House of Lords, Lord Cairns LC ruled that Blackburn's formulation would only apply where land was being put to a non-natural use.[38]

The rule in *Rylands v Fletcher* looks deeply appealing from an environmental protection perspective—it appears to be a rule of strict liability that provides a remedy for 'non-natural' uses of land, and what could be more non-natural than industrial pollution? But the rule has rarely given rise to a successful action. There are a number of reasons for this. There has clearly been judicial restraint in its application, particularly in determining what a 'non-natural use' is.[39] The development of the rule has also been driven by a policy presumption on the part of judges that 'as a general rule, it is more appropriate for strict liability in respect of operations of high risk to be imposed by Parliament, than by the courts'.[40] However, the limits of the rule can partly be found in its first incarnation, as Lord Hoffmann explains.

Transco Plc v Stockport Metropolitan Borough Council
[2003] UKHL 61, [2004] 2 AC 1 paras 28–29, 39, 45–46 (Lord Hoffmann)

> 28. Although the judgment of Blackburn J is constructed in the traditional common law style of deducing principle from precedent, without reference to questions of social policy, Professor Brian Simpson has demonstrated in his article 'Legal Liability for Bursting Reservoirs: The Historical Context of *Rylands v Fletcher*' (1984) 13 J Leg Stud 209 that the background to the case was public anxiety about the safety of reservoirs, caused in particular by the bursting of the Bradfield Reservoir near Sheffield on 12 March 1864, with the loss of about 250 lives. The judicial response was to impose strict liability upon the proprietors of reservoirs. But, since the common law deals in principles rather than ad hoc solutions, the rule had to be more widely formulated.

> 29. It is tempting to see, beneath the surface of the rule, a policy of requiring the costs of a commercial enterprise to be internalised; to require the entrepreneur to provide, by insurance or otherwise, for the risks to others which his enterprise creates. That was certainly the opinion of Bramwell B, who was in favour of liability when the case was before the Court of Exchequer: (1865) 3 H & C 774. He had a clear and consistent view on the matter: see *Bamford v Turnley* (1862) 3 B & S 62, 84–85 and *Hammersmith and City Railway Co v Brand* (1867) LR 2 QB 223, 230–231. But others thought differently. They considered that the public interest in promoting economic development made it unreasonable to hold an entrepreneur liable when he had not been negligent: see *Wildtree Hotels Ltd v Harrow London Borough Council* [2001] 2 AC 1, 8–9 for a discussion of this debate in the context of compensation for

---

[37] (1866) LR 1 Ex 265.   [38] *Rylands v Fletcher* [1868] LR 23 HL 330, 340.
[39] *Read v J Lyons & Co Ltd* [1947] AC 156 (HL).
[40] *Cambridge Water Company v Eastern Counties Leather plc* [1994] 2 AC 264 (HL), 305 (Lord Goff).

disturbance caused by the construction and operation of works authorised by statutory powers. On the whole, it was the latter view—no liability without fault—which gained the ascendancy. With hindsight, *Rylands v Fletcher* can be seen as an isolated victory for the internalisers. The following century saw a steady refusal to treat it as laying down any broad principle of liability.

After surveying those conclusions, Lord Hoffmann considered the contemporary state of the rule.

39. I pause at this point to summarise the very limited circumstances to which the rule has been confined. First, it is a remedy for damage to land or interests in land. As there can be few properties in the country, commercial or domestic, which are not insured against damage by flood and the like, this means that disputes over the application of the rule will tend to be between property insurers and liability insurers. Secondly, it does not apply to works or enterprises authorised by statute. That means that it will usually have no application to really high risk activities. As Professor Simpson points out ([1984] 13 J Leg Stud 225) the Bradfield Reservoir was built under statutory powers. In the absence of negligence, the occupiers whose lands had been inundated would have had no remedy. Thirdly, it is not particularly strict because it excludes liability when the escape is for the most common reasons, namely vandalism or unusual natural events. Fourthly, the cases in which there is an escape which is not attributable to an unusual natural event or the act of a third party will, by the same token, usually give rise to an inference of negligence. Fifthly, there is a broad and ill-defined exception for 'natural' uses of land. It is perhaps not surprising that counsel could not find a reported case since the Second World War in which anyone had succeeded in a claim under the rule. It is hard to escape the conclusion that the intellectual effort devoted to the rule by judges and writers over many years has brought forth a mouse.

Lord Hoffmann chose not to abolish the rule but did consider how the concept of non-natural use should be considered today.

45. Two features of contemporary society seem to me to be relevant. First, the extension of statutory regulation to a number of activities, such as discharge of water (section 209 of the Water Industry Act 1991) pollution by the escape of waste (section 73(6) of the Environmental Protection Act 1990) and radio-active matter (section 7 of the Nuclear Installations Act 1965). It may have to be considered whether these and similar provisions create an exhaustive code of liability for a particular form of escape which excludes the rule in *Rylands v Fletcher*.

46. Secondly, so far as the rule does have a residuary role to play, it must be borne in mind that it is concerned only with damage to property and that insurance against various forms of damage to property is extremely common. A useful guide in deciding whether the risk has been created by a 'non-natural' user of land is therefore to ask whether the damage which eventuated was something against which the occupier could reasonably be expected to have insured himself. Property insurance is relatively cheap and accessible; in my opinion people should be encouraged to insure their own property rather than seek to transfer the risk to others by means of litigation, with the heavy transactional costs which that involves. The present substantial litigation over £100,000 should be a warning to anyone seeking to rely on an esoteric cause of action to shift a commonplace insured risk.

There are a number of interesting points to note here. Again, there is an important relationship between social and legal culture. Further, the rule in *Rylands v Fletcher* is also dependent on property law and only makes sense in relation to other torts. Likewise, it is shaped by statutory obligations. In other words, the rule is not a simple tool for environmental protection but part of a complex area of legal doctrine. For a pithy statement of what non-natural use now requires under the rule in *Rylands*, Lord Bingham in *Transco* stated that the relevant use must involve an 'exceptionally high risk of danger or mischief' and be 'extraordinary and unusual', with the value of the activity to the community not being relevant. Combining this with Lord Hoffmann's guidance, there remains a high bar to proving liability under this common law rule.[41]

3.4 NEGLIGENCE

The final area of tort law of some relevance to environmental problems is negligence law. An action for negligence will be successful if: a) a duty of care can be found owing by the tortfeasor to the claimant; b) that duty was breached through the fault of the tortfeasor; c) the breach of that duty caused loss actionable in negligence.[42] As every tort student knows, the application of these different requirements is terribly complex, with negligence being potentially relevant to a vast array of different situations. However, the relevance of negligence to environmental problems is more limited than expected, for a range of reasons including: environmental law being a field in which statutory liability schemes have a significant role to play (see Chapter 9); the types of scientific uncertainties discussed in Chapter 2 makes causation difficult to establish; and the practicalities of bringing tort litigation act as a major limitation on such actions.

However, negligence actions may be arguable and appropriate in some environmental cases, as can be seen in the *Corby Group* litigation already discussed in Section 3.2. Besides public nuisance, negligence was also alleged and a later Group Litigation Order sought to address general issues. The discussion of negligence by the judge in that later case gives a good feeling for how a negligence action operates in the environmental context.

Corby Group Litigation v Corby DC
[2009] EWHC 1944 (TCC) paras 680–84, 689 (Akenhead J)

680. There is no real issue between the parties as to the duty of care owed in tort by CBC (Corby Borough Council). CBC admits in Paragraph 115 of the Defence that a duty was owed by it to the Claimants and their mothers to take reasonable care in the execution of the works to avoid injury to the Claimants and their mothers. [...]

681. The standard of care to be exercised by CBC is that of an ordinarily careful local authority embarked on reclamation works of the type involved in Corby. The duty is to be judged by reference to the standards known or reasonably ascertainable and knowledge available at the time. Thus, if standards had materially changed over the period within which this claim is concerned, any breach of the duty would be determinable by reference to the standards applicable at the time of the breach, and not by the later standards.

682. This case is necessarily and obviously concerned with the dispersal of toxic substances from the CBC site. Primarily, the Court must be concerned therefore with any breaches of the duty that caused the dispersal of such substances into areas in which the Claimants' mothers might have ingested or inhaled such substances.

683. So far as foreseeability is concerned, it is not necessary that CBC would or could reasonably have foreseen the precise type of birth defect suffered by the Claimants. It is enough that it was reasonably foreseeable that harm or damage might be caused to embryos or foetuses being carried out by mothers at the material time. It was argued by CBC initially that it had to be established that it was reasonably foreseeable to the defendant that its wrongful act would be likely to cause injury of the types sustained by the Claimant concerned. However, it was accepted in argument, properly, that the formulation referred to above was sufficient.

---

[41] *Transco* [10]–[11].   [42] McBride and Bagshaw (n 26) 96.

684. It is generally the case, in negligence, that, provided that the defendant in question has selected independent contractors with reasonable care and skill, that defendant will not be liable for the negligence of those independent contractors save to the extent that it had been negligent itself in supervising and monitoring the work of those contractors. [...]

689. There was much discussion during the trial as to legal issues relating to causation in the context particularly of Issue 3: 'whether any such breach [of duty] had the ability to cause upper hand or lower limb defects to the Claimants of the type complained of'. It is uncontroversial that, at least generally, a claimant has the burden of proving on the balance of probabilities that the injuries (or in this case the birth defects) were caused by any breaches of duty or public nuisance which are established.

This case is only provided as an example. It shows the judge having to reason very carefully to clear the different hurdles of a negligence action, and it is easy to imagine environmental cases where one or more of those hurdles are not easily met (and where there might be no actionable personal injury or individual property damage on which to base a claim).

4 CONTRACT LAW

Contract law is the law relating to agreements between two parties and the obligations that flow from such agreements. Like property law, contract law plays a foundational role in that it regulates the status quo of relationships, and in particular commercial relationships. In this regard, contract law plays an important role in managing the expectations of legal actors in relation to any agreement that they make.

In relation to environmental law, the role of contact is significant. As Waite notes:

Contract law [...] allocates environmental liabilities between parties to an agreement for the acquisition of property, business assets or company shares, or requires one party to carry out work to remediate or protect the environment.[43]

Contract law is thus a major vehicle by which other areas of private law and regulatory environmental obligations in particular are put into operation. Indeed, the role of environmental lawyers in practice is often grounded in contract law in that their task is to make sure that a) a legal actor is complying with the law and b) that a legal actor by engaging in a commercial transaction is not exposing themselves to an unwanted environmental obligation. This is discussed further in Section 6.5.

This is not the only role for contract law however. In light of its role in managing relationships, contract has also been used as a regulatory technique.[44] Thus, regulators might negotiate individual contracts with those whom they are regulating, often described as 'environmental agreements'. As Affolder notes:

Environmental agreements occupy an amorphous and ill-defined space between command and control regulation and voluntary initiatives. Broadly defined, environmental contracts are negotiated and enforceable agreements addressing environmental issues. Agreements may be between companies and regulators, companies and community groups, or companies and indigenous peoples. They may transcend the individual company unit and involve entire industries. An environmental

---

[43] Andrew Waite, 'The Quest for Environmental Law Equilibrium' (2005) 7 Env L Rev 34, 58.
[44] David A Dana, 'The New "Contractarian" Paradigm in Environmental Regulation' (2000) U Ill L Rev 35.

contract can supplement existing regulation or it can offer an alternative to an otherwise applicable regulatory regime.[45]

In other words, a contract can act as a regulatory strategy (see Chapter 12). It can also act as a regulatory strategy in concert with property law, as seen in the emerging technique of nature conservation covenants. Such covenants are voluntary, individually negotiated contracts that restrict landowner activities that might threaten the land's conservation values, but can also constitute easements that attach to land title.

The analysis here makes clear that contract law has a central role to play in the practice of environmental law. Whilst it is little discussed in most chapters of the textbook, its background role should be kept in mind.

5 COMPANY LAW

The final area of private law that is particularly relevant to environmental problems is the law of business associations, in particular company law. There are legal institutional frameworks (both through statute and common law doctrines) for carrying on businesses such as partnerships and limited liability companies. These frameworks are important for environmental law because they not only define the obligations and powers of commercial actors but they also influence the way in which commercial actors define and prioritize their responsibilities.[46]

The most well-known of these frameworks is the limited liability company, the most popular corporate form, with its division between management and ownership. Blankenburg and others explain the nature and significance of the concept.

Stephanie Blankenburg, Dan Plesch, and Frank Wilkinson, 'Limited Liability and the Modern Corporation in Theory and in Practice' (2010) 34 Cambridge Journal of Economics 821, 823–24

Corporate limited liability refers to a widespread legal principle that limits the accountability of shareholders-owners for the debts of their companies to the current value of their shareholding. Therefore, for any amount beyond their investment, shareholder-owners are exempt from any claims by creditors whatever the cause of their company's indebtedness. What might, at first sight, appear to be a fairly straightforward financial arrangement becomes on closer inspection a rather more complex matter: as well as constituting a 'veil' obscuring corporate structuring and restructuring, limited liability is at the heart of the formation of the modern corporation as a separate legal and 'real' entity, and many of its most problematic features, including excessive risk-taking and 'shareholder primacy'. The nature of shareholding, and the lack of transparency surrounding it, largely accounts for a dangerous deterioration of what can be described as an economically and politically viable balancing of privatised gains and socialised risk, and of private and public interests, brought sharply into focus by the evolution of the global financial crisis.

---

[45] Natasha A Affolder, 'Rethinking Environmental Contracting' (2010) 21 Journal of Environmental Law and Practice 155, 156.

[46] Mark Stallworthy, 'Sustainability, the Environment and the Role of UK Corporations' (2006) 17 International Company and Commercial L Rev 155.

Corporate limited liability has two important implications for environmental law. First, the primary duty of the management of a company is to increase shareholder value rather than address other social and public interests, including environmental issues. The movement to recognize 'corporate social responsibility' (CSR) reflects one attempt to deal with this problem.

Associated with CSR have been attempts to recognize a more nuanced understanding of the duties owed to shareholders. Thus, s 172(1) of the Companies Act 2006 provides that:

(1) A director of a company must act in the way he considers, in good faith, would be most likely to promote the success of the company for the benefit of its members as a whole, and in doing so have regard (amongst other matters) to—

(a) the likely consequences of any decision in the long term,

(b) the interests of the company's employees,

(c) the need to foster the company's business relationships with suppliers, customers and others,

(d) the impact of the company's operations on the community and the environment,

(e) the desirability of the company maintaining a reputation for high standards of business conduct, and

(f) the need to act fairly as between members of the company.

Section 417 of the Act also requires Directors' reports to include information about 'environmental matters (including the impact of the company's business on the environment)'. This can be understood to reflect an idea of 'enlightened shareholder value'.

The second significant implication of limited corporate liability for environmental law is that shareholders are limited as to their liability.[47] Thus, if a company causes serious environmental harm, 'the corporate veil' cannot necessarily be lifted to pursue compensation from owners. Many debates about the appropriateness of this legal situation and exceptional cases for lifting the corporate veil are carried on at the international level due to the transnational aspects of much corporate behaviour that results in serious environmental harm.[48]

6 PRIVATE LAW AND ITS COMPLEX RELATIONSHIP WITH ENVIRONMENTAL PROBLEMS AND ENVIRONMENTAL LAW

The discussion so far is not an exhaustive survey of private law but it shows that different areas of private law have both a general and also more specific relationships to environmental problems and environmental law, and that the different areas of law are often interrelated. In this last section, we consider in a more conceptual and detailed way the different dimensions of the relationship between private law, environmental law, and environmental problems. Five particular aspects of that relationship are explored. First, we analyse how private law as a body of common law establishes the legal status quo—a background state of legal normality against which activities take place (and environmental problems occur). Second, we consider how regulatory regimes have been created in response

---

[47] Paddy Ireland, 'Limited Liability, Shareholder Rights and the Problem of Corporate Irresponsibility' (2010) 34 Cambridge Journal of Economics 837.

[48] David M Ong, 'The Impact of Environmental Law on Corporate Governance: International and Comparative Perspectives' (2001) 12 EJIL 685.

to the perceived limits of private law. Third, we analyse how private law actions can provide a remedy for individuals to protect the environment and thus to agitate for legal change. Fourth, we analyse how private law fundamentally interacts with legislation relating to environmental issues in a variety of ways. Finally, we consider how public environmental law shapes private ordering and has given rise to transactional environmental law.

6.1 PRIVATE LAW AS THE STATUS QUO

Purdy described property law as a 'social imaginary'.[49] The same is true of other areas of private law. Thus, tort law and contract law establish pre-existing rights and responsibilities that frame our understanding of what we can expect of others. This means that private law is often understood to represent the foundational status quo that exists before statute-based environmental law intervenes in an area of social and/or legal activity.

In creating this legal status quo, private law is often a mixture of legal norms and social norms. A good example can be seen with the introduction of the Carbon Reduction Commitment (CRC) Energy Efficiency Scheme in the UK.[50] The scheme essentially requires various large organizations to purchase annual carbon allowances to cover their emissions for each year, encouraging them to be more energy efficient. As Bright notes, many of those organizations will be large commercial landlords—this creates a problem in terms of their responding to the CRC scheme's incentives, considering the nature of commercial leases.

Susan Bright, 'Carbon Reduction and Commercial Leases in the UK' (2010) International Journal of Law and the Built Environment 218, 220, 222

This idea of the institutional lease is important [...] for two reasons. First, the fact that for many landlords the lease is primarily an investment requires the lease to be readily marketable as an asset, and this is a driver towards investment leases taking a common format and not containing unusual provisions. As Williams and Eddington explain, standard lease terms carry the advantages of acceptability in the marketplace, easier negotiation and familiarity [...] Leases that reflect a standard pattern are much easier to attach a capital value to [...] This leads to the second aspect of the institutional lease that is important. For an investor landlord the ideal is a lease that delivers a long-term secure income. One outworking of this principle, important in the CRC context, is that all unknown servicing costs (such as repair and insurance) are borne by the tenant. This means that the landlord receives a net rent, one that is not vulnerable to deduction of variable costs. In most cases, therefore, it is the tenant that pays for energy costs for the premises.

Although it is the tenant who will usually pay for energy, it does not follow that the tenant is in charge either of energy supply, or of how much energy is used.

[...]

The fact that tenants pay for the energy costs is one dimension of the widely discussed 'split-incentive' problem. The other dimension relates to responsibility for the provision of energy supply equipment under the lease, providing for core services such as heating, air conditioning, and electricity. [...] it is usually the landlord that supplies energy to a multilet property, at least in part. [...] To the extent that the tenant is able to invest in energy efficient works, it will only be motivated to do so if there is sufficient pay back. Given that relatively short leases have become the norm in the UK, there may not be a strong

---

[49] Purdy n 11.   [50] See Chapter 15.

enough return. This means that the energy management opportunity lies with the landlord, but the financial incentive is with the tenant who pays for the energy [...]

This 'split-incentive' is not simply the outcome of 'lawyer's drafting' but is core to the way that the UK commercial property market has developed. Attempts to move away from the net lease model to accommodate occupier preferences have generally not taken off because investors find it difficult to attach value to buildings let in this way.

The private law status quo is thus important to take into account in thinking about environmental law and the development of any regulatory strategy (including those that depend on voluntary action). No such activity should ever be understood to be taking place in a legal vacuum—there are always existing legal structures in which are embedded particular practices. This means that environmental lawyers need to spend time understanding what the legal status quo actually is—for an environmental law student, this means building on the foundations of what you have learned in the rest of your legal studies. Appreciating the finer points of this status quo is not always an easy task, as highlighted in the discussion on property law in Section 2.

6.2 THE LIMITS OF PRIVATE LAW

Thinking about private law is also relevant to environmental problems and environmental law in that many studies of private law highlight that private law is at best limited, and at worse obstructive, in dealing with environmental problems. This has been a significant reason why regulatory regimes aimed at environmental protection were developed.[51] An understanding of the limits of private law is thus needed to understand why environmental law has developed as it has.

There is a rich body of literature that highlights a range of different limitations of private law—three are noted here. First, as already seen, private law is understood as limited to the protection of private rights, and in particular private property rights, while environmental problems raise issues to do with the commons and the public interest.[52] For some this presents a purely conceptual misalignment that could be remedied with a creative application of the law. For others, this means that private law is ideologically at odds with environmental protection because it promotes a narrow vision of property rights and responsibilities. As Richard Epstein puts it, 'one characteristic of the modern environmental movement is its manifest distrust of private law approaches to environmental protection'.[53]

The second recognized limitation of private law is that it operates in a post hoc way in response to individual problems that have already occurred.[54] We saw discussions concerning this in Chapters 2 and 3. A related point is that judges have also seen the development of private law for environmental protection as less appropriate than legislative law reform. Or, to put the matter another way, they have not seen a significant role for the common law in protecting the environment. This point of view is summed up by Lord Goff in considering the nature of the foreseeability tests in the rule in *Rylands v Fletcher*. For present purposes, the facts are irrelevant.

---

[51] See the discussion in Chapter 2.
[52] See Chapter 2 and Introduction to Part III.
[53] Richard A Epstein, *Simple Rules for a Complex World* (Harvard University Press 1995) 275.
[54] Cass R Sunstein, *The Partial Constitution* (Harvard University Press 1993) ch 11. See Section 5.1 of Chapter 2.

Cambridge Water Co v Eastern Counties Plc
[1994] 2 AC 264 (HL), 305 (Lord Goff)

Like the judge in the present case, I incline to the opinion that, as a general rule, it is more appropriate for strict liability in respect of operations of high risk to be imposed by Parliament, than by the courts. If such liability is imposed by statute, the relevant activities can be identified, and those concerned can know where they stand. Furthermore, statute can where appropriate lay down precise criteria establishing the incidence and scope of such liability.

It is of particular relevance that the present case is concerned with environmental pollution. The protection and preservation of the environment is now perceived as being of crucial importance to the future of mankind; and public bodies, both national and international, are taking significant steps towards the establishment of legislation which will promote the protection of the environment, and make the polluter pay for damage to the environment for which he is responsible—as can be seen from the WHO, EEC and national regulations to which I have previously referred. But it does not follow from these developments that a common law principle, such as the rule in *Rylands v Fletcher*, should be developed or rendered more strict to provide for liability in respect of such pollution. On the contrary, given that so much well-informed and carefully structured legislation is now being put in place for this purpose, there is less need for the courts to develop a common law principle to achieve the same end, and indeed it may well be undesirable that they should do so.

The third reason why private law is understood to play a limited role in environmental protection relates to the procedural aspects of a private law action. Disputes in private law are constructed as bi-polar while environmental problems tend to be polycentric (see Section 2.1 of Chapter 2). Moreover, many private law actions require proof of past harm. As private law actions are civil law actions, such proof only needs to be established on the balance of probabilities but this can often act as a serious barrier to compensation or to an environmental problem being taken seriously.[55]

In sum, the limits of private law relate to both the substantive and structural aspects of private law. This inevitably has implications for the type of legal and regulatory interventions that then develop in relation to environmental problems.

6.3 PRIVATE LAW LITIGATION AND ENVIRONMENTAL PROTECTION

While it has been understood that the limits of private law have led to the rise of statutory-based environmental law, in some instances private law litigation can be seen to operate as a tool of environmental protection—as demonstrated by the various tort cases and cases concerning 'village greens' already discussed. Indeed, as highlighted by the Environmental Justice Project extract, such actions are significant in terms of their success.

Environmental Justice Project, *A Report by the Environmental Justice Project*
(2004) 26–27

26. At first sight it seems private law claims are more likely to be successful than public law claims [...] Some practitioners report a success rate of just over 70%. [...] However, the average success rate for

---

[55] Carl F Cranor, *Toxic Torts: Science, Law and the Possibility of Justice* (CUP 2006).

solicitors responding to the EJP [Environmental Justice Project] was 51% in relation to 'other environmental claims'.

27. However, there is a distinction to be made between the different types of private law claims. Overall, practitioners involved in nuisance and land damage report a higher level of success and a reasonable degree of satisfaction with the manner in which the Courts deal with their claims. For injury related claims the picture is very different.

There are three different reasons why private law actions are understood as an important tool for environmental protection. First, as McGillivray and Whightman explain, private rights can be used to protect a broader range of concerns.

Donald McGillivray and John Whightman, 'Private Rights and Environmental Protection' in Paddy Ireland and Per Laleng (eds), *The Critical Lawyer's Handbook 2* (Pluto Press 1997) 177

[T]he 'reach' of an injunction against some polluting activity is not limited to the more obviously private interests of neighbours. There may be other classes of 'collateral beneficiaries' of a nuisance action. Thus, anglers may benefit from a riparian owner's success in obtaining an injunction to prevent pollution of a river by a sewage outfall because of the improvement in habitat for fish, while environmentalists may approve of the outcome simply because it conserves a part of the natural world, rather than on account of any amenity use they make of the river.

A second reason why environmental lawyers are preoccupied with private law efforts to pursue environmental protection is due to the symbolism of private law actions. If environmental protection is achieved through a private law action, then mainstream law is recognizing the importance of protecting the environment, whether directly or indirectly. These cases are thus significant in the recognition of rights and remedies in relation to environmental protection, discussed in the Introduction to Part III.

The final reason why private law actions are important tools for environmental protections is that they provide a way to agitate for legal change on behalf of individual litigants. Private law actions do not depend on a legislature or administrative body deciding to protect something. Rather, there is a possibility of legal action based on an individual's own initiative. A limit on this is that an individual needs to fit their legal action into existing legal categories and existing legal practices, but the point remains that they do not need the permission or the acquiescence of the state to do so, as Stanton and Willmore explain.

Keith Stanton and Christine Willmore, 'Tort and Environmental Pluralism' in John Lowry and Rod Edmunds (eds), *Environmental Protection and the Common Law* (Hart Publishing 2000) 93–94

What has been called the 'unofficial' nature of private law makes it a tool which can be a voice for views and priorities which may otherwise not be heard. We see two significant roles for tort actions in a pluralist society. First, they provide the primary mechanism for individuals to seek compensation for losses they have suffered. Secondly, tort can be used to assert perspectives which are unorthodox or in some way question mainstream priorities, for example challenges to established scientific wisdom or to our attitudes to risk and the allocation of loss. Law is not the only mechanism through which such diverse or dissenting views can be aired, but the particular power associated with legal discourse can lend weight to views.

In short, for environmental lawyers, both private law doctrine and private law litigation practices are important. The latter is touched on further in Chapter 10.

6.4 THE INTERRELATIONSHIP BETWEEN PRIVATE LAW AND (PUBLIC LAW) REGULATION

Private law does not exist in its own legal universe, separate from regulation and public law; rather, there are simultaneous interactions between these two areas of law in relation to environmental problems. As Lord Bingham noted in *Transco* 'it must be remembered that common law rules do not exist in a vacuum, least of all rules which have stood for over a century during which there has been detailed statutory regulation of matters to which they might potentially relate'.[56] Whether one chooses to focus analysis on private law or environmental regulatory regimes, the other cannot be ignored. There are three reasons for this.

First, private law techniques have become elements of innovative regulatory strategies.[57] As indicated already, contract has been used to impose environmental obligations on particular landowners and even industries.[58] Likewise, property rights have been used as the basis for emission trading schemes.[59] Second, as already discussed, private law is the starting point, or reason, for developing many regulatory regimes. Third, private law does not disappear with the creation of a regulatory regime. It operates alongside it and will continue to interact with those regimes. This chapter has already seen a number of examples of this interaction, particularly in relation to private nuisance and property law. The extract from Lee gives some feeling for the complexity of that interrelationship in considering regulation and tort law.

Maria Lee, 'Safety, Regulation and Tort: Fault in Context' (2011) 74 MLR 555, 555

[T]he real contours of the relationship between tort and regulation are nevertheless surprisingly under-explored, especially given the increased scope and complexity of regulatory activity in recent decades. The dimensions along which tort and regulation interact are endless. Some view tort as a form of regulation; or regulation might so completely occupy the field that there is no space at all for tort. Regulatory norms of quality can influence the point at which pollution becomes damage, or the nature and scope of common law duties; regulation may affect the reasonableness of an activity in private nuisance, the nature of a defect in products liability, and even causation. The scope of the debate is vast, and the different interactions difficult and potentially dense.

Indeed, much tort law that applies to environmental problems involves determining the interrelationship between actions in tort and a range of different statutory schemes. Thus, questions arise about whether an otherwise tortious activity has been authorized under legislation (examined in the *Allen*

---

[56] *Transco plc v Stockport Metropolitan Borough Council* [2003] UKHL 61, [2004] 2 AC 1 [6].

[57] Chapter 12.

[58] See, for example, voluntary agreement with the catering and hospitality industries to reduce food waste and associated packaging (WRAP Hospitality and Food Service Agreement 2012).

[59] Sanja Bogojevic, 'Ending the Honeymoon: Deconstructing Emissions Trading Discourses' (2009) 21 JEL 443. See Chapter 15.

v Gulf Oil case), the status of private law norms in light of more recent regulatory developments,[60] and whether a legislative or a judicial response to an environmental problem is more appropriate.[61] Moreover, remedies under statute and in private law may also be pursued in relation to the same environmental problem, and procedural choices may need to be made. Overall, there is no general rule— the nature of the interrelationship between private law and any applicable regulation will depend very much on the particular legal circumstances.

As a consequence, it is important not to oversimplify any aspect of the laws that apply to a single environmental problem. This is highlighted by Lee in discussing the interaction between private nuisance and planning law.

Maria Lee, 'Tort Law and Regulation: Planning and Nuisance' [2011] JPEL 986, 988

The idealised propositions about regulation and tort in the introduction to this article provide a crude argument in each of two diametrically opposed directions: that planning permission should be decisive, or that it should be irrelevant. But both tort and regulation are too diverse and too complicated to be captured by any simple allocation of authority. The courts are unlikely to simply defer across the board to standards set in another forum, but equally they cannot simply ignore the existence and legitimacy of those other fora. The cases tell us that whilst planning permission does not in principle diminish the rights and interests of third parties, planning law and private law are not entirely separate. There is no easy hierarchy; some planning permissions will have greater normative impact in the determination of a private nuisance than others. The difficulty is in working out the criteria according to which that impact varies.

Those difficulties in determining how private law doctrine and regulation work in relation to each other are not just limited to the planning and nuisance interface. Other such legal interactions are best illustrated by providing two different examples of private nuisance actions interacting with legislative and regulatory schemes.

The first example involves the question of whether a statute under which an oil refinery was authorized to be built and to operate provided an immunity from any private nuisance action in relation to the refinery's activities.

Allen v Gulf Oil Refining Ltd
[1981] AC 1001 (HL), 1011–14 (Lord Wilberforce)

It is now well settled that where Parliament by express direction or by necessary implication has authorised the construction and use of an undertaking or works, that carries with it an authority to do what is authorised with immunity from any action based on nuisance. The right of action is taken away: *Hammersmith and City Railway Co v Brand* (1869) LR 4 HL 171, 215 *per* Lord Cairns. To this there is made the qualification, or condition, that the statutory powers are exercised without 'negligence'—that word here being used in a special sense so as to require the undertaker, as a condition of obtaining immunity from action, to carry out the work and conduct the operation with all reasonable regard and care for the interests of other persons: *Geddis v Proprietors of Bann Reservoi* (1878) 3 App Cas 430, 455 *per* Lord Blackburn. It is within the same principle that immunity from action is withheld where the terms of the statute are permissive only, in which case the powers conferred must be exercised in strict conformity with private rights: *Metropolitan Asylum District v Hill* (1881) 6 App Cas 193.

---

[60] *Transco plc* (n 56).
[61] *Cambridge Water Company* (n 40).

What then is the scope of the statutory authority conferred in this case? The Act was a private Act, promoted by the appellants, no doubt mainly in their own commercial interests. In order to establish their projected refinery with its ancillary facilities (jetties, railway lines, etc), and to acquire the necessary land, they had to seek the assistance of Parliament and so they necessarily had to satisfy Parliament that the powers they were seeking were in the interest of the public to whom Parliament is responsible. The case they undertook to make, which they had to prove, and which, as the passing of the Act shows, they did prove, is shown by the preamble. This recites 'increasing public demand for [the company's] products in the United Kingdom' and that 'it is *essential* that further facilities for the importation of crude oil and petroleum products and for their refinement should be made available' (emphasis supplied). It proceeds to recite the intention of the company to establish a refinery at Llanstadwell, that it was expedient that in connection therewith the company should be empowered to construct works including jetties for the accommodation of vessels (including large tankers) and for the reception from such vessels of crude oil and petroleum products for the proposed refinery and for conveying oil and petroleum products therefrom: that it was expedient for the company to be empowered to acquire lands: and that 'plans… showing… the lands which may be taken or used compulsorily under the powers of the Act for the purposes thereof… have been deposited.'

My Lords, all of this shows most clearly that Parliament considered it in the public interest that a *refiner*, not merely the works (jetties etc), should be constructed, and constructed upon lands at Llanstadwell to be compulsorily acquired.

To show how this intention was to be carried out I need only quote section 5:

'(1) Subject to the provisions of this Act, the company may enter upon, take and use such of the lands delineated on the deposited plans and described in the deposited book of reference as it may require for the purposes of the authorised works or for the construction of a refinery in the parish of Llanstadwell in the rural district of Haverfordwest in the county of Pembroke or for purposes ancillary thereto or connected therewith. (2) The powers of compulsory acquisition of land under this section shall cease after the expiration of three years from October 1, 1965.'

The lands in question were the specific lands—about 450 acres in extent—shown with precise detail in the deposited plans.

I cannot but regard this as an authority—whether it should be called express or by necessary implication may be a matter of preference—but an authority to construct and operate *a refinery* upon the lands to be a acquired—a refinery moreover which should be commensurate with the facilities for unloading offered by the jetties (for large tankers), with the size of the lands to be acquired, and with the discharging facilities to be provided by the railway lines. I emphasize the words *a refinery* by way of distinction from *the refinery* because no authority was given or sought except in the indefinite form. But that there was authority to construct and operate a refinery seems to me indisputable.

[…]

The respondent alleges a nuisance, by smell, noise, vibration, etc. The facts regarding these matters are for her to prove. It is then for the appellants to show, if they can, that it was impossible to construct and operate a refinery upon the site, conforming with Parliament's intention, without creating the nuisance alleged, or at least a nuisance. Involved in this issue would be the point discussed by Cumming-Bruce LJ in the Court of Appeal, that the establishment of an oil refinery, etc was bound to involve some alteration of the environment and so of the standard of amenity and comfort which neighbouring occupiers might expect. To the extent that the environment has been changed from that of a peaceful unpolluted countryside to an industrial complex (as to which different standards apply—*Sturges v Bridgman* (1879) 11 Ch D 852) Parliament must be taken to have authorised it. So far, I venture to think, the matter is not open to doubt. But in my opinion the statutory authority extends beyond merely authorising a change in the environment and an alteration of standard. It confers immunity against proceedings for any nuisance which can be shown (the burden of so showing being upon the appellants) to be the inevitable result of erecting a refinery upon the site—not, I repeat, the existing refinery, but any refinery—however carefully and with however great a regard for the interest of adjoining occupiers it is sited, constructed and operated. To the extent and only to the extent that the actual nuisance (if any) caused by the actual refinery and its operation exceeds that for which immunity is conferred, the plaintiff has a remedy.

In other words, the operators of the refinery were immune from having a nuisance action brought against them.

The second case is a more recent private nuisance action brought by a group of residents in relation to odours from a waste tip, which was operating pursuant to a regulatory permit. The facts and regulatory history are both complex and Coulson J gave a very lengthy judgment at trial finding for the defendants, before the case went on appeal. Note in particular how the case is distinct from *Allen v Gulf Oil Refining*.

Barr v Biffa Waste Services
[2012] EWCA Civ 312, paras 41–46, 146 (Carnwath LJ)

41. Judged by these principles and in the light of these authorities, the case against Biffa seems reasonably clear-cut. The introduction of 'pre-treated' tipping had resulted in a series of episodes of unpleasant smells, affecting the ordinary enjoyment of residents' houses and gardens. They were not just isolated or trivial occurrences, but continued to attract substantial and credible complaints, intermittently and particularly in warm weather, over five years. Until Biffa's attitude changed in October 2007, there was no real dispute about the significance of the problem, or Biffa 's responsibility for it. The likely area of controversy would be about the extent of the problem within the Estate, as between those most directly affected, and the rest of the 150 households who had joined in the group action. It was also clear, judged by conventional principles (notably *Allen v Gulf Oil Refining Ltd* [1981] AC 1001) that Biffa did not have statutory immunity, express or implied.

42. However, Biffa argued, and succeeded in persuading the judge, that this conventional view of the case was too simplistic a view. Their case was that the correct understanding of more recent case law, taken in the context of the elaborate modern statutory framework, European and domestic, justified and required the reshaping of conventional principles to fit the modern world. In the judge's words:

'The common law must be flexible in order to survive. What was appropriate in Victorian England may need to be modified in the rather more complex world of the twenty-first century.' ([359])

43. To develop a modified set of principles appropriate for the modern age, the judge embarked on an arduous journey through 200 paragraphs of legal analysis. Similar industry has been shown in the arguments in this court, the combined skeletons running to more than 120 pages. Biffa's arguments are directed principally to upholding the reasoning of the judgment. In addition, by the cross-appeal, they seek to establish, contrary to the judge's view, that similar flexibility should apply to the principles of statutory immunity.

44. Without disrespect to those efforts, I continue to believe that the applicable law of nuisance is relatively straightforward, and that the 19th century principles for the most part remain valid. Although I will examine the judge's reasoning in more detail in Part II, the essential points can in my view be shortly stated and shortly answered.

45. The following are the main building blocks of the judge's reasoning:

   i) The 'controlling principle' of the modern law of nuisance is that of 'reasonable user'. If the user is reasonable, then absent proof of negligence, the claim must fail ([203]).

ii) In the context of the modern system of regulatory controls under EU and domestic environmental legislation, and the specific waste permit granted in 2003, the common law must be adapted to 'march in step with' the legislation ([304]). Biffa's user must be deemed to be have been reasonable, if it complied with the terms of the permit ([350]).

iii) Furthermore, the permit was relevant in two other ways:

a) The grant of a permit for what was the first site for tipping of pre-treated waste was 'strategic' in nature, and therefore altered the character of the neighbourhood in which reasonableness was to be judged ([371]).

b) The permit (in particular condition 2.6.12) by implication gave statutory licence for 'inevitable teething troubles'; and for escape of 'a certain amount of odour emission', which was 'inevitable', and 'inherent' in the granting of the permit and the underlying statutory scheme ([371], [388], [567]).

iv) It followed that in the absence of any specific allegation of negligence or breach of the permit, Biffa's user must be deemed reasonable, and the claims must fail ([376]).

v) In any event, in the light of recent authorities, and since some level of odour was inherent in the permitted activity and accepted by residents, it was necessary to set a precise 'threshold', to distinguish between the acceptable and the unacceptable ([385]).

vi) In the absence of any alternative suggestion by the claimants, the judge set the threshold at 'one odour complaint day each week (ie 52 each year) regardless of intensity, duration, and locality' ([446]). Judged by that test all but two of the claims would have failed ([538]).

46. In my view there are short answers to all these points:

i) 'Reasonable user' is at most a different way of describing old principles, not an excuse for reinventing them;

ii) The common law of nuisance has co-existed with statutory controls, albeit less sophisticated, since the 19th century. There is no principle that the common law should 'march with' a statutory scheme covering similar subject-matter. Short of express or implied statutory authority to commit a nuisance (rule (v) above), there is no basis, in principle or authority, for using such a statutory scheme to cut down private law rights.

iii) Further:

a) The 2003 permit was not 'strategic' in nature, nor did it change the essential 'character' of the neighbourhood, which had long included tipping. The only change was the introduction of a more offensive form of waste, producing a new type of smell emission.

b) The permit did not, and did not purport to, authorise the emission of such smells. Far from being anticipated and impliedly authorised, the problem was not covered by the original Waste Management Plan, and the effects of the change seem to have come as a surprise to both Biffa and the Environment Agency. Nor can they be dismissed as mere 'teething troubles', since they continued intermittently without a permanent solution for five years.

iv) There was no requirement for the claimants to allege or prove negligence or breach of condition. Even if compliance with a statutory permit is capable of being a relevant factor, it would be for the defendant to prove compliance, not the other way round;

v) There is no general rule requiring or justifying the setting of a threshold in nuisance cases. The two cases mentioned do not support such a general rule, and in any event concerned noisy activities which could readily be limited to specific days (unlike smelly tipping at Westmill).

vi) By adopting such a threshold, the judge deprived at least some of the claimants of their right to have their individual cases assessed on their merits.

As this was the case, and the findings were complex, in the Court of Appeal Carnwath LJ, in delivering judgment, refers paragraphs of Coulson J's judgment:

146. This case is a sad illustration of what can happen when apparently unlimited resources, financial and intellectual, are thrown at an apparently simple dispute such as one about nuisance by escaping smells. The fundamental principles of law were settled by the end of the 19th century and have remained resilient and effective since then. Isolated statements in individual cases, at whatever level, are of limited value unless they have been absorbed into the stream of accepted authority. Parliament may alter by statute, or the higher courts by reinterpretation of the old cases. But there is a salutary presumption that neither does so without making their intention clear. Parliament may also enact parallel systems of regulatory control; but, unless it is says otherwise, the common law rights and duties remain unaffected. The judge was faced with a very difficult task, given the way the case was developed and presented on both sides. But he should not have allowed himself to be deflected from his ordinary task of assessing the evidence against the established legal principles and exercising his judgement on the facts of the case.

These are wise words but the case also illustrates just how complex the interaction between regulation and tort law is, which can result in complicated, deeply contested, and expensive litigation.

6.5 THE IMPACT OF ENVIRONMENTAL LAW ON PRIVATE LAW AND PRIVATE ORDERING

The final aspect of the interrelationship between private law and environmental law to note is that environmental law and environmental problems will inevitably affect private law and private ordering. We have already seen a number of examples of this in this chapter. Thus, the CRC scheme will have implications for commercial leases, and groundwater contamination and poorly done remediation work will provide specific problems for tort law. Contract law will need to accommodate the new liabilities and responsibilities created by statutory regimes.

The ways in which private ordering and private law are affected by environmental law has increasingly become a topic of interest for legal scholars.[62] Thus, we shall see a very important study by Lee and Vaughan in Chapter 21 concerning transactional environmental law and the contaminated land liability regime. An American academic, Vandenbergh, has described most commercial and everyday activity carried on by private actors as being involved, in legal terms, with second-order agreements, defined as 'agreements entered into between regulated firms and other private actors in the shadow of public regulations'. These agreements are essentially contracts and Vandenbergh explains the reasons for them (in the US context, but his analysis equally applies to the UK).

Michael P Vandenbergh, 'The Private Life of Public Law' (2005) 105 Colum L Rev 2029, 2044, 2062, 2045

The environmental regulatory regime has two principal characteristics that induce second-order bargaining and that are shared by many other regulatory schemes. First, the costs imposed by environmental regulations pose a substantial risk for private parties. Not only are ongoing compliance costs often substantial, but an unwitting buyer or other party may face liabilities arising from past releases of

---

[62] Eric W Orts, 'Reflexive Environmental Law' (1995) 89 Northwestern University L Rev 1227.

hazardous substances and the current condition of the property, regardless of whether caused by their regulatory violations.

Second, most environmental costs can be allocated between the parties, whether implicitly through adjustments in the purchase price, interest rate or rent, or through explicit terms allocating known or contingent liabilities. Environmental statutes typically have been interpreted to allow private parties to transfer the costs of environmental compliance among themselves but not to allow an indemnity to serve as a defense to liability in the first instance. As a result, although the primary compliance duty often remains with the business or facility owner or operator, in many cases there is no bar to trading the business or facility itself or reallocating the costs of compliance through indemnification. Thus, firms often have both the incentive and the ability to reduce compliance costs through private bargaining.

As Vandenbergh goes on to note, companies may enter into both stand-alone agreements and agreements about environmental obligations that are part of bigger agreements. In the former category he includes:

environmental insurance agreements and a catchall category that this Article calls 'environmental performance agreements'. The performance agreement category includes agreements between private firms and agreements between private firms and nonprofit groups.

The latter category he identifies as including the following:

Corporate acquisition agreements (whether structured as mergers, asset purchases, or in other ways), credit agreements, commercial real estate agreements (including sales agreements and leases), and agreements for the sale of goods or services are reviewed here.

In other words, environmental protection and regulatory responsibilities can be identified in a whole series of large commercial transactions as well as being the subject of individual contracts and agreements. In light of this, Vandenbergh argues that the vast majority of environmental law practice is transactional work rather than either litigation or regulatory work. Many examples support this position. For example, the Equator principles (which operate in a transnational context) require banks to take into account social rights (and thus environmental issues) as part of their operational practices.[63] There is also an emerging body of transactional environmental litigation.[64] With that said, little substantive research has been done on these issues in the UK beyond some good texts on environmental law in commercial transactions[65].

7 CONCLUSION

The path taken in this chapter has reflected Philippopoulos-Mihalopoulos' paradox—environmental law is everything and nothing. Thus, on the one hand, the chapter has shown how the relationships between environmental law, environmental problems, and private law are multifarious and multi-dimensional. Thinking about the interrelationship requires thinking about private law in all its forms, conceptual as well as doctrinal. On the other hand, as soon as one begins to do this, it quickly

---

[63] Nigel Clayton, 'Equator Principles and Social Rights: Incomplete Protection in a Self Regulatory World' (2009) 11 Env L Rev 173.

[64] *Colour Quest Ltd v Total Downstream UK Plc* [2009] EWHC 540 (Comm), [2009] 2 Lloyd's Rep 1.

[65] Andrew Waite, Tim Jewell, Goronwy Jones and Michael Woods, *Environmental Law in Property Transactions* (3rd revised edn, Tottel 2009).

becomes clear that to understand the environmental aspects of these different private law subjects requires us to understand the nuances and subtleties of each of these private law areas. This chapter could not even begin to undertake that task but it has hopefully reinforced the point that the private law aspects of environmental law are not simply a handful of tort cases. It has also made clear that, while the role of private law might not always be directly significant to environmental problems, environmental lawyers need to think carefully about its relevance—as establishing the background legal status quo, as a reason for environmental regulation, as an indirect potential means of litigating for environmental protection, or as a transactional space in which to deal with the commercial reality of environmental regulation.

FURTHER READING

There are many excellent textbooks in the areas of private law that are covered in this chapter. A few examples of further reading are suggested here:

Paul Davies, *Introduction to Company Law* (2nd edn, Clarendon Press 2010).

FH Lawson and Bernard Rudden, *Law of Property* (3rd edn, Clarendon Press 2002).

Nicholas M McBride and Roderick Bagshaw, *Tort Law* (4th edn, Pearson 2012).

Ewan McKendrick, *Contract Law: Text, Cases and Materials* (5th edn, OUP 2012).

Jenny Steele, *Tort Law: Text, Cases and Materials* (2nd edn, OUP 2010).

PUBLIC LAW

Whichever way you look at it, much environmental law is public law, or more precisely, administrative law. That is not to say environmental law is only administrative law—otherwise the other chapters in this part would be redundant (and the title of this chapter would be administrative law rather than public law)—but it is certainly very hard to practice or study environmental law without a good grasp of administrative law. To make matters more complicated, the relationship between administrative law and environmental law is not a one-way street. Developments in administrative law have influenced environmental law and vice versa. Moreover, the nature of environmental problems creates serious conceptual and practical challenges for public law. Environmental lawyers do not just need to know about administrative law but they also need to appreciate that administrative law doctrine does not always apply easily in environmental law settings.

As a result, environmental lawyers must not only know and understand basic concepts of administrative law, but they must also understand its finer details. Therein lies a dilemma. Not only is administrative law a notoriously difficult subject—Justice Scalia of the US Supreme Court once describing it as 'not for sissies'[1]—but in most law schools, while basic administrative law is compulsory, more detailed study of the subject is often optional. For some lawyers, administrative law is even 'something of an acquired taste'.[2] This is perhaps not surprising when basic advice to approaching the subject is: '(1) read the statute; (2) read the statute; (3) read the statute!'[3] Let's face it—that doesn't exactly sound like the most exciting thing to do.

This chapter attempts to address this challenge in studying administrative law (for environmental law purposes) by providing an overview of the subject as it relates to environmental law in England and Wales, and setting out a framework for making sense of its interrelationship with environmental law. While that might sound comforting to the novice, we recommend proceeding with some caution. As most readers will know, learning public law is like, well, learning to ride a bicycle. Until you understand all the different aspects involved and how they interact, the subject can remain a mystery. Moreover, just like bicycle riding, even after you have mastered the basics, the learning experience does not stop. For cyclists, it is about how to ride in traffic. For public lawyers, it is about appreciating the nuanced and complex application of public law, which reduces the chance that a chapter like this can provide a simple framework.

The structure of this chapter is as follows. First, it gives an overview of administrative and constitutional law and the relevance of these legal subjects for environmental law. In this section,

---

[1] Antonin Scalia, 'Judicial Deference to Administrative Interpretations of Law' (1989) 38 Duke LJ 511, 511. It should be noted that Scalia's point was that administrative law was a painfully dull subject, not that it required a particularly macho approach.

[2] David S Tatel, 'The Administrative Process and the Rule of Environmental Law' (2010) 34 Harv Envtl L Rev 1, 1.

[3] Felix Frankfurter, as quoted in ibid, 3.

the role of EU and international law is also considered. Section 2 addresses the challenges that environmental problems create for public law. Three particular challenges are considered—the novel nature of environmental interests, the need for information and expertise in environmental decision-making, and the importance of public participation. Unsurprisingly, these challenges have resulted in legal responses—the most high profile being the United Nations Economic Commission for Europe (UNECE) Convention on Access to Information, Public Participation in Decision-Making and Access to Justice in Environmental Matters (the Aarhus Convention), which is discussed. Section 3 provides examples of different, non-judicial ways in which the administrative process is regulated and held to account, including through access to environmental information, public participation, and other non-judicial accountability mechanisms. Section 4 gives an overview of the most high profile accountability mechanism in administrative law—judicial review—while Section 5 examines the role of the Human Rights Act 1998 (HRA) in environmental law. Finally, Section 6 briefly considers the significance of EU administrative law for environmental law.

Three important points on using this chapter should be made at the outset. First, the chapter cannot attempt to be an exhaustive survey of public law and environmental law. Its purpose is to illustrate the complexity of the interface between these two areas of law; it is not a substitute for reading a good administrative or public law textbook. Indeed, this chapter should inspire you to turn to such books—the Further Reading section at the end of the chapter recommends other texts that students might find useful. Second, this chapter needs to be read alongside other chapters in this textbook. In particular, it is presumed that the reader has read Chapter 3 concerning the English and UK environmental law landscape. There is also clear overlap between this chapter and the chapters on regulatory strategy and governance (Chapters 12 and 13). Indeed, there is a strong argument that some of the issues discussed in this chapter are eclipsed by the developments discussed in those chapters. Finally, the access to justice aspects of the Aarhus Convention will be dealt with in Chapter 10, which focuses on the role of the courts.

1 PUBLIC LAW: A BRIEF OVERVIEW

Public law in the UK can be defined as the law relating to the UK state, and it can be understood as consisting of two parts—constitutional law and administrative law. As we shall see, the latter subject is of more direct concern to environmental lawyers. In this section, these two areas of law are briefly sketched and their relevance to environmental law is considered. The relationship of these areas of law to international and EU law is also examined, before reflecting on the fundamentally complex aspects of public law, which are relevant also for thinking about UK environmental law.

1.1 CONSTITUTIONAL LAW

Constitutional law is broadly understood as the law concerning the overarching relationships between the different constituent elements of the state as well as the relationship between citizen and state. It involves the study of general constitutional doctrines (such as parliamentary sovereignty, the rule of law, and the separation of powers), conventions (such as individual and collective ministerial responsibility), the wider issue of UK devolution, the relationship of the UK with the EU, civil liberties, and the HRA. The key starting point for studying UK constitutional law is that there is no formal written constitution in the UK. The UK constitution is understood historically as a 'political' constitution, in that limitations on the exercise of state powers have been established through political processes rather than by legal means.[4] However, over the last decade, there has been a shift to a more 'legal' constitution, with the introduction of constitutionally significant legislation (HRA, Scotland Act 1998, Northern Ireland Act 1998, Government of Wales Act 2006) and also through case law.[5]

UK constitutional law is relevant to environmental law in three ways. First, it provides the framework that regulates the ability of the UK Parliament, the Scottish Parliament, and the Welsh and Northern Irish Assemblies to legislate in relation to environmental issues. These issues of devolved competence were discussed in Section 3.3 of Chapter 3. In relation to the UK Parliament, the limits on legislative competence are few in light of the principle of parliamentary sovereignty, although membership of the EU and the HRA place limits on legislative action in practice. This UK situation is very distinct from federal jurisdictions, such as Australia, where there are very real constitutional limits on the ability of the federal (Commonwealth) government to legislate in relation to the environment.[6]

Second, by regulating the relationship between citizen and state, through legal mechanisms such as the HRA, constitutional law affects the ability of individuals to act in relation to environmental problems and to demand action from the state in relation to such problems. These issues will be considered in Section 5.

Third, general constitutional doctrines, such as the rule of law and separation of powers, are an ever present influence on how legislation is drafted and how administrative as well as judicial decisions are made. Most of the time this will be implicit in legal discourses—these doctrines are deeply ingrained in legal thinking and reasoning. These constitutional doctrines also infuse administrative law. Jewell describes the general implication of this for environmental law.

Tim Jewell, 'Public Law and the Environment' in Tim Jewell and Jenny Steele (eds), *Law in Environmental Decision-Making* (Clarendon Press 1998) 75

In general terms, environmental decision-making of the sort being considered here operates within a theoretical context concerned with constitutional principles of fairness and legitimacy. The most direct impact of this is in the extent to which such principles transcend individual decisions or decision-making processes: in other words, the extent to which normative principles of law precede legislation, rather than 'just' emanate from it. An important implication of this is the potential it creates for tension between views of what 'fair process' should be, and goals of contemporary environmental policy. This tension lies at the heart of the relationship between process and substance in environmental decision-making. Legislation might be seen in very instrumental terms as the mechanism for implementing the priorities of government: in this sense, descriptions of law as a tool or technique take on a very real significance. The tension emerges however in considering the extent to which high-profile environmental priorities should be influenced by or accommodate principles of public law which go beyond individual statutory contexts.

Principles of constitutional concern or importance most obviously relate to the powers of Parliament, the Courts, and the Crown, and to the relationship between them. As such they would seem to be most relevant to types of decisions which are not directly relevant to this chapter. However, the impact of principles of this sort extends throughout the whole of public law. In particular, discussions of the unwritten principles of the UK constitution demonstrate the central importance of 'procedural fairness'

---

[4] Adam Tomkins, *Public Law* (Clarendon Press 2003) 18.

[5] For an exploration of the complexity of this issue, see Graham Gee and Gregoire Webber, 'What Is A Political Constitution?' (2010) 30 OJLS 273.

[6] Most significantly seen in the Australia: *Commonwealth v Tasmania* (1983) 158 CLR 1 (Tasmanian Dam Case).

to UK public law. Descriptions of the Rule of Law, for example, and its 'disabling function' in respect of the theoretically unlimited sovereignty of Parliament, emphasize notions of legal certainty, limitation of administrative discretion, and procedural fairness.

Two important points should be taken from Jewell's analysis. First, a focus on constitutional law makes clear that legislation is not simply a tool to achieve desired policy ends. Rather, legislation is a legal practice that is embedded in other rules and principles. Second, and following on from this, environmental legislation, and decision-making under it, must conform to these other doctrines and principles. It does not matter how urgent or serious an environmental problem might be. The state cannot take action that breaches its constitutional (and administrative law) framework. Thus, like private law, constitutional law often plays a foundational role in environmental regulation—it establishes the legal status quo in a different sense. Hence, while there may not be a great deal of explicit 'environmental constitutional law' in UK law, the fundamental significance of the subject should not be forgotten.

1.2 ADMINISTRATIVE LAW

Administrative law is the law relating to the executive and administrative arms of the state. It has three main aspects.[7] The first is that administrative law constitutes administrative bodies. That constituting can be done in a variety of ways. Most obviously, it is done by statute. Thus, for example, the Environment Agency was set up under the Environment Act 1995. More often, however, government departments and organizational structures for the exercise of public powers are created through the Royal Prerogative. Thus, for example, the structure and nature of central government departments such the Department of Environment, Food and Rural Affairs (DEFRA) is determined by Royal Prerogative. It must also be remembered that administrative law constitutes local authorities, which are significant actors in environmental law and its implementation.[8] Furthermore, a range of independent, non-governmental bodies, such as Natural England (the nature conservation regulator), have also been constituted to aid the delivery of environmental law. This is the 'untidy empire'[9] referred to in Chapter 3. Hence, the constituting of different administrative institutions in environmental law is legally complex in and of itself.

Second, administrative law both empowers and limits public administration. This occurs for the most part through legislation and delegated legislation. Thus, in nearly every chapter of this book that analyses a regulatory regime (Parts IV and V), the focus is on powers granted to administrative bodies. A particular feature of English environmental law is that such granting of powers mainly occurs through delegated, not primary, legislation. Moreover, both primary and secondary legislation can often grant power in quite a piecemeal fashion, creating fragmented statutory landscapes for particular areas of environmental regulation. To make matters more complicated, these legislative powers are often further fleshed out through extensive official policy documents.[10] In some cases, such as contaminated land and planning law, such policy documents are referred to in the relevant legislation (albeit in different ways), but in other cases government or regulatory bodies create them

---

[7] Adapted from Frank Goodnow, *Comparative Administrative Law: An Analysis of the Administrative Systems National and Local of the US, England, France and Germany* (GP Putnam & Sons 1893) 8.

[8] See Chapter 3.

[9] David Weir and David Beetham, *Political Power and Democratic Control in Britain* (Routledge 1999) 158.

[10] See Chapter 11.

independently. As will be seen in the chapters in this book, such official policy guidance may not be strictly legally binding, but it can define the powers of decision-makers, and also limit them.

Furthermore, limiting public administration occurs not only by defining the powers of administrative decision-makers in legislation and accompanying policy instruments. It also occurs through legal provisions and principles that dictate *how* such powers should be exercised. Indeed, this is the primary focus of administrative law, rather than the outcomes of decision-making, particularly in light of the extent to which administrative decision-makers are given discretion to act under environmental legislation. Thus, legislation and administrative law doctrine will often regulate the procedures by which decisions under statute should be made. In recent years, there has also been a concern that decision-making should be transparent.[11] These different limits are often described as 'principles of good administration' and they highlight the fact that the legitimacy of administrative decision-making is not only determined by whether decision-makers stay within the limits of the powers granted to them, but also by how they exercise that power.

The final role of administrative law is to hold public decision-makers to account. The concept of accountability is dealt with in a wide-ranging way in the context of discussing governance in Chapter 13. For our purposes here, let us focus on the role of accountability in UK public law. At its most basic, being held to account means needing to give reasons or explanations for what one has done. More usefully, accountability is best understood as a process, the key steps of which Davies outlines.

ACL Davies, *Accountability: a Public Law Analysis of Government by Contract* (OUP 2001) 81

Oliver describes the components of an accountability mechanism in the following way: '[Accountability] is about requiring a person to explain and justify—against criteria of some kind—their decisions or acts, and then to make amends for any fault or error, whether by reversing the decision, or paying compensation or in some other way—even resigning from office' (Oliver 1994: 246, based on Marshall 1986). On the basis of this description, it can be seen that an accountability mechanism consists of four key features: setting standards against which to judge the account; obtaining the account; judging the account; and deciding what consequences, if any, should follow from it. These are common to all mechanisms of accountability, although they can be manifested in a variety of ways.

Davies' analysis is particularly useful because it provides a framework for thinking about the vast diversity of different accountability mechanisms in English administrative law. These include: ministerial responsibility, audit committees, internal management oversight, Treasury oversight, regulatory impact assessments, commissions of inquiry, internal appeals, review by a Tribunal, the Parliamentary Commissioner of Administration, Local Government Ombudsmen, the use of performance indicators and league tables, and judicial review. An important feature of these different mechanisms is that they are all arenas where conflict often occurs. This is because accountability inevitably involves the challenging of decisions. More fundamentally, as will be seen in the sections below, issues of accountability in administrative law often involve questioning the legitimacy of standards on which an accountability mechanism is based.[12]

---

[11] Elizabeth Fisher, 'Transparency and Administrative Law: A Critical Evaluation' (2010) 63 CLP 272.
[12] Elizabeth Fisher, 'The European Union in the Age of Accountability' (2004) 24 OJLS 495.

1.3 EU AND INTERNATIONAL DIMENSIONS

The discussion so far may seem to suggest that the UK legal system is hermetically sealed off from other jurisdictions. Chapters 4 and 5, however, make clear that this is not the case—there is a constant overlap between UK, EU, and international law, which, amongst other things, shapes the nature of public law and its relevance to UK environmental law. This is particularly because much substantive UK environmental law is derived from EU law. The EU and international law dimensions of public law relevant to the UK have two different aspects.

The first is largely UK constitutional in nature, concerning the relationship between these three legal systems—the UK, the EU and international law. As discussed in Section 6.2 of Chapter 5, the UK legal system is a dualist legal system in relation to international law, which means that international law and national law do not have an automatic interconnection in formal terms. For an international treaty to have any legal force, it must first be transposed into national law by the UK government.

The constitutional situation in relation to EU law is very different. The European Court of Justice declared very early on that EU law is supreme,[13] and, while the acceptance of that supremacy by UK courts has been neither straight-forward or absolute, it is grudgingly accepted in practice (albeit less so in theory).[14] As a result, EU environmental law has significant legal authority in UK law and failure to comply with it can have a range of public law implications. The most obvious legal implication is through enforcement actions brought against the UK government (explored in Chapter 4), which challenges the (in)action of the UK government and in some cases UK parliamentary sovereignty. The implications for judicial review of not complying with EU law will be considered in Section 4.

The second public law implication of EU and international law relevant for UK environmental law is the body of EU and international administrative and constitutional law that exists,[15] quite separately from national public law. Thus, in EU law, there are legal avenues for challenging the actions of EU institutions, and the creation of frameworks to limit and hold EU and international decision-makers to account. All of this raises both a distinct body of EU administrative law (see Section 6) and questions of governance (see Chapter 13).

1.4 THE COMPLEXITIES OF UK PUBLIC LAW

The analysis so far has been largely descriptive and, while some of it might sound straightforward, there are obvious examples of complexity, which are useful to reflect on before proceeding further. Four examples are examined here: complexities concerning the dynamic nature of the subject; complexities created by normative disagreement over the role of the state; complexities created by legal pluralism; and complexities created by a lack of administrative coherence. In each case, the relevance of these issues for environmental lawyers is considered.

The first complicating aspect of public law is the constant evolution of both the constitutional and administrative structures of the state—the latter evolving more than the former. As the state itself has evolved, so too have administrative legal frameworks and subjects. Thus, during the Victorian era, the lack of a centralized executive meant that there was very little in the way of a coherent framework for administrative (or environmental) law. Yet this changed with the growth of the administrative state

---

[13] Case 6/64 *Costa v ENEL* [1964] ECR 585.

[14] *R v Secretary of State for Transport, ex p Factortame Ltd (No 2)* [1991] 1 AC 603 (HL); *Thoburn v Sunderland CC* [2003] QB 151. For a more wide-ranging discussion of parliamentary sovereignty, see *Jackson v AG* [2005] UKHL 56, [2006] 1 AC 262.

[15] In EU law, see Paul Craig, *EU Administrative Law* (2nd edn, OUP 2012)

throughout the twentieth century and, by the 1970s, there was a growing recognition of administrative law as a separate subject. Environmental law was part of that development.[16]

That change has continued and, in the last thirty years, both subjects have undergone radical transformations. Thus, in the late 1990s, constitutional law underwent significant change with devolution and the passing of the HRA in 1998. The structure and scope of public administration has also changed over this time, most obviously with large-scale privatization of public services in the late 1980s and early 1990s.[17] More specifically, environmental law regimes have undergone dramatic evolution in the last thirty years. Some of these reforms have been through primary legislation, but others are often introduced through secondary legislation.[18] This creates real challenges for both practitioners and scholars, who must keep up with dramatic and sometimes obscurely drafted changes.[19]

The second deeply complex aspect of public law is its normative status. Paul Craig put this well when noting that:

> the nature and content of constitutional and administrative law can only be properly understood against the background political theory which a society actually espouses, or against a such a background which a particular commentator believes that a society ought to espouse.[20]

Likewise, Harlow and Rawlings have noted that '[b]ehind every theory of administrative law there lies a theory of the state'.[21] The normative nature of public law thus raises some rather tricky questions about what constitutes the legal content of public law[22]—does it include norms for direct public participation in government? To what extent does public law, or how should it, further human rights protection? How do courts (properly) reflect their constitutional role in applying judicial review doctrines? But such questions themselves concern two different issues—they address both what public law *is* and what it *should* be. Thus, for example, there are scholars who argue that there should be a constitutional right to a clean environment—but this position is a prescription, rather than a description, of current law (see Section 5). The distinction between these two categories is not always clear, particularly in administrative law where arguments about what the law is, and what it should be, are often intertwined. None of this is made any easier by the fact that there is no settled normative agreement about the nature and purpose of public law itself.

The third complex aspect of public law is that much of it is non-legal in nature. Thus, as already noted, the UK constitution is often described as being political. Furthermore, public administration is also in some respects constituted, limited, and held to account on non-legal grounds. This raises some rather tough questions about where public lawyers should focus their study and analysis.[23] As will become apparent in this book, these are also questions for environmental lawyers—for one thing, they cannot simply focus on environmental legislation but must also consider a range of policy and other documents in appraising the full legal depths of the subject.

---

[16] David Roberts, *Victorian Origins of the British Welfare State* (Yale UP 1960).   [17] See Chapter 13.

[18] For example, Conservation of Habitats and Species Regulations 2010 SI 2010/490 (as amended). See Chapter 20.

[19] Elizabeth Fisher and others, 'Maturity and Methodology: Starting a Debate about Environmental Law Scholarship' (2009) 21 JEL 213, 228–30.

[20] Paul Craig, *Public Law and Democracy in the United Kingdom and the United States of America* (Clarendon Press 1990) 1.

[21] Carol Harlow and Richard Rawlings, *Law and Administration* (3rd edn, CUP 2009) 1.

[22] Peter Cane, 'Theory and Values in Public Law', in Paul Craig and Richard Rawlings (eds), *Law and Administration in Europe: Essays in Honour of Carol Harlow* (OUP 2003).

[23] Richard Thomas, 'Deprofessionalisation and the Postmodern State of Administrative Law Pedagogy' (1992) 42 J Leg Ed 75.

The final complexity to note about public law, particularly in relation to environmental law, is that it is not particularly coherent. Part of the incoherence is due to the interrelationship between EU and UK law, but much of it relates to the fact that the administrative state in the UK has rarely been rationalized and is not codified. Thus, we do not have a single administrative body that oversees environmental law in the UK. Rather, we have a web of different interrelated institutions that have different powers. Likewise, the powers of institutions in relation to environmental problems are derived from a range of different pieces of primary and secondary legislation. As a result, it requires a steady analytical eye to see the full public law picture, and its potential implications, in UK environmental law.

FURTHER READING

1. There is a list of constitutional and administrative law textbooks at the end of this chapter. Note that each will have a different normative agenda. See Martin Loughlin, *Public Law and Political Theory* (Clarendon Press 1992) for a historical discussion of this.

2. For an interesting reflective piece on environmental law and constitutional change, see Richard Macrory, 'Environmental Regulation as an Instrument of Constitutional Change' in Jeffrey Jowell and Dawn Oliver (eds), *The Changing Constitution* (7th edn, OUP 2011).

3. For further discussion of the normative complexity of public law, see Elizabeth Fisher, *Risk Regulation and Administrative Constitutionalism* (Hart Publishing 2007) ch 1; Carol Harlow and Richard Rawlings, *Law and Administration* (3rd edn, CUP 2009) ch 1.

---

2 THE CHALLENGES OF ENVIRONMENTAL LAW FOR ADMINISTRATIVE LAW

Section 1 explained how any environmental law regime must be consistent and act in tandem with existing constitutional and administrative law. In particular, administrative law will be an ever-present feature of environmental law regimes in providing the framework by which those regimes are constituted, limited, and held to account. While less prominent, the same is true of constitutional law.

However, environmental law regimes have themselves contributed to the development of administrative and constitutional law and created real challenges for these two areas of law. This section considers the three most significant challenges: the 'novel' nature of interests in environmental law, the need for considerable amounts of information and expertise in environmental decision-making, and the need for participatory input into environmental decision-making. These different challenges have not gone ignored, however, and the Aarhus Convention can be understood as a significant legal response to meet them.

2.1 THE NATURE OF INTERESTS IN ENVIRONMENTAL PROBLEMS

The Introduction to Part III showed that the type of interests raised by environmental problems do not naturally map onto traditional legal categories of rights. The most significant manifestation of this can be seen in relation to the laws of standing in judicial review actions, which will be considered in Chapter 10. However, this is not the only implication for public law. Two other aspects of legal interests in environmental problems are worth noting.

First, such legal interests often do not have any basis in common law but are derived from legislation that relates to environmental problems. This may seem obvious but it is important to appreciate that the existence of the legal interest involved depends very much on how the legislation at issue is interpreted. Thus, many environmental law cases will focus on questions of interpretation, since a particular legislative interpretation will result in particular interests (and not others) being protected.[24] Moreover, in contrast to other areas of public law, the interest being protected is legally novel—being constructed by statutory duties and considerations and rights of participation and appeal—rather than being a conventionally recognized legal right (such as a right to sue in private law). This is not to say that common law rights are legally straightforward or that the law will not protect novel rights, but it does mean that courts will be less experienced with them and, along with lawyers, may take time to make sense of a new legislative regime that recognizes new interests specific to a particular regime. A good example of this is in environmental assessment where it took over ten years for English lawyers and courts really to understand the legal significance of that regulatory regime.[25] That regime requires decision-makers to engage in a certain procedure, which at the time of its introduction was quite legally novel. Moreover, the nature of what legislation protects, and thus the relevant legal interests involved, can vary. For instance, in nature conservation law, there is a range of different regimes that protect various interests, from listed protected species, to 'enclaves' that are marked out for protection from damaging development and activity, to agreements between landowners and regulators.

The second challenging aspect of legal interests in relation to environmental problems concerns how public law accommodates their consideration in decision-making. As Jewell put it so aptly over a decade ago:

> [T]he mere fact that environmental considerations are increasingly considered in statutorily constituted processes of decision-making is less significant than the details of the process for assessing them, and especially for assessing the relative importance, against other substantive goals.[26]

Thus, many chapters of the book cover legislative and judicial struggles to reconcile environmental interests with economic, social, and other interests. This struggle can be particularly difficult because, not only are environmental protection interests often incommensurable with other considerations, particularly in terms of the values at stake, but they are often perceived as 'softer' and more complex in nature. Laurence Tribe, writing in the US context, described this concern vividly nearly four decades ago.

Laurence H Tribe, 'Ways Not to Think about Plastic Trees: New Foundations for Environmental Law' (1974) 83 Yale LJ 1315, 1317

> Statutes and judicial decisions typically mandate 'systematic' and 'interdisciplinary' attempts to 'insure that presently un-quantified environmental amenities and values may be given appropriate consideration in decision-making along with economic and technical considerations.' Public interest challenges to decisions alleged to be environmentally unsound are diverted by the pressures of doctrine and tradition from claims about the value of nature as such into claims about interference with human use, even when the real point may be that a particular wilderness area, for example, should be 'used' by no-one.

---

[24] *Berkeley v Secretary of State for the Environment* [2001] 2 AC 603 (HL) being the most high profile example of this.
[25] See Chapter 19 and *Berkeley* (n 24).
[26] Tim Jewell, 'Public Law and the Environment' in Tim Jewell and Jenny Steele (eds), *Law in Environmental Decision-Making* (Clarendon Press 1998).

Such tension between environmental concerns and the conventional constraints of common law actions (in public as well as private law) can also be evidenced in English law and, as will be seen, these interests can be very difficult to reconcile.

2.2 INFORMATION AND EXPERTISE

As seen in Chapter 2, environmental decision-making is intensive in its need for, and use of, information. Knowledge is needed to understand environmental problems and decision-making requires the collection, collation, and assessment of information. That information might relate to many different things, including the current state of environmental quality, the nature of the impacts of a particular activity, the causes of those impacts, and the potential consequences of administrative action. Expertise is also often required for such processes of assessment. Legal decisions must also be made about what is 'relevant' and 'necessary' information, where that information might include scientific information, economic data, lay observations, and judgments based on experience. Such information must also be organized and interpreted. As we saw in Chapter 2, there are many ways of doing this, including a variety of risk assessment, modelling, and cost–benefit analysis methodologies, as well as regulatory impact analysis. The nature of expertise required in environmental decision-making thus refers to a wide range of disciplines, including the sciences, social sciences, professional vocations, and those who have experience of environmental issues.

The large amount of information and expertise needed in environmental decision-making presents a number of challenges for public law, and particularly administrative law. First, there is the practical problem of how such knowledge and expertise can be integrated into administrative decision-making. This issue arises because administrative law doctrine developed in areas with more limited information requirements, for example, in relation to administrative decisions over whether to award social security benefits. Furthermore, in the UK, the historical approach was to keep research and expertise at arm's length from government and administration, whether through the use of committees, independent bodies, or contracting out.[27] In contemporary UK environmental law, the collection and assessment of information is carried out by a variety of public and private actors, and the role of these different actors varies from regime to regime. It often requires some digging to see all the actors who were involved in making an environmental decision.

Second, there is the problem of how to limit discretion in relation to decision-making, which requires expertise and is information intensive. This is a major theme in judicial review, as Moules explains.

Richard Moules, *Environmental Judicial Review* (Hart Publishing 2011) 15–16

Environmental judicial review claims are amongst the most factually complex judicial review proceedings. Frequently they involve voluminous factual, policy and technical material, often requiring a court to understand complicated scientific processes or modelling. Not only does this threaten to compromise the speed and efficiency of the judicial review jurisdiction, but it also has the potential to draw the courts beyond their constitutional function and lead them to consider the merits of decisions made by scientific experts and democratically accountable decision-makers.

This is not only a problem for judicial review but for any process of accountability applied in relation to environmental decision-making. It presents a real challenge for developing regulatory regimes that control and limit discretion, as discussed further in Section 2.3.

[27] Elizabeth Fisher, *Risk Regulation and Administrative Constitutionalism* (Hart 2007) ch 2.

Finally, the need for information and expertise in administrative decision-making creates a normative legitimacy problem. The simple reason for this is that the information and expertise requirements of environmental decision-making make the role of public administration necessary. However, due to administrative discretion being difficult to limit and to hold to account, there are ongoing attempts to explain, justify, and legitimize the exercise of administrative power in this area. In other words, there are debates over what *should* be the role and nature of public administration in this area.[28]

2.3 PUBLIC PARTICIPATION AND CONSULTATION

The final significant challenge that environmental law poses for public law is that, axiomatically, environmental law is quintessentially 'public'. The public nature of environmental law is due to the fact that the subject is dealing with collective interests. This has led to an expectation that environmental decision-making should involve some form of participation by the public. As the US National Research Council has noted:

> Some arguments for participation rest on normative theories of democracy and collective action, some are based on ideas of what constitutes a high-quality decision, and some are grounded mainly in considerations of improving agency practice and the policy process.[29]

Thus a study of public participation is often a study of the role and nature of the *state*, and the types of discourses discussed in Section 5 of Chapter 2. Debates about public participation also require consideration of the appropriate relationship between values and science in environmental decision-making. Hence, it is not surprising that public participation in environmental decision-making has become the subject of dense theoretical debates, which have many implications for political theory and science, as well as for lawyers. For environmental lawyers, the most significant implication is appreciating that public participation can take many different forms, as explained in the extract from Richardson and Razzaque.

Benjamin J Richardson and Jona Razzaque, 'Public Participation in Environmental Decision-Making' in Benjamin J Richardson and Stepan Wood (eds), *Environmental Law for Sustainability: A Reader* (Hart Publishing 2006) 167

Different models have been proffered to analyse the range of forms of public participation. One model, known as Arnstein's 'ladder', shows the spectrum of participation opportunities, beginning with mere notification, and extending to consultation and even joint decision-making power. The lowest levels of participation may effectively amount to non-participation. The highest level of participation, says Arnstein, is where the public has the power to negotiate with decision-makers and to veto proposed decisions. Another model of participation distinguishes between 'top-down' and 'bottom-up' approaches. The former is where the government initiates participation, the latter where communities do so. Thirdly, some commentators distinguish between substantive and procedural dimensions of participation. Participatory rights may derive from substantive human rights, such as a right to live in a healthy, unpolluted environment, and may be enshrined in a constitution or statutory bill of rights.

---

[28] Ibid.
[29] National Research Council, *Public Participation in Environmental Assessment and Decision Making* (NAS 2008) 33.

By contrast, procedural rights concern the methods of decision-making, and typically encompass public consultation, information provision and access to the courts. Substantive and procedural rights are often intertwined: for instance, a substantive right to a healthy environment usually requires procedural rights to be heard in decisions that might affect those substantive rights.

From an administrative law perspective, this means that, just as with information, the constituting, limiting, and holding to account of public administration will inherently involve constituting participation processes, governing the limits of them, and ensuring that such processes are subject to accountability mechanisms. There was very little emphasis on this in UK administrative law historically but, as will be seen, that has changed dramatically over the last ten years. In part, this is due to specific EU Directives, such as the Environmental Assessment Directive (see Chapter 19), which mandate public involvement in decision-making; in part, this is due to a change in basic assumptions about the nature of administrative law, and, in part, to the introduction of the Aarhus Convention.

2.4 THE AARHUS CONVENTION

The Aarhus Convention can be understood as a response to the types of challenges that environmental problems create for public law. Concerns with recognizing different interests and the roles of information and participation in environmental decision-making all figured in the United Nations Convention on Environment and Development (UNCED) in 1992 and in its accompanying plan for action, *Agenda 21*. They also featured in the preceding 1991 Espoo Convention, which established a regime for environmental assessment and consultation between states for major projects likely to have significant adverse transboundary environmental impacts, and included advanced public participation provisions.[30] Following on from these developments, the UNECE negotiated and drafted the Aarhus Convention on Access to Information, Public Participation in Decision-making and Access to Justice in Environmental Matters. It was signed in 1998 and now has forty-six parties, including the EU and the UK. The Convention entered into force in October 2001. The objective of the Convention is described in Article 1:

In order to contribute to the protection of the right of every person of present and future generations to live in an environment adequate to his or her health and well-being, each Party shall guarantee the rights of access to information, public participation in decision-making, and access to justice in environmental matters in accordance with the provisions of this Convention.

As Article 1 suggests, the Convention has three pillars—the rights of access to information, public participation in decision-making, and access to justice. The last of these will be considered in Chapter 10 in considering access to the courts, but it can be seen that the first two pillars flow from the types of challenges environmental law poses for public law. Moreover, as Lee and Abbot note, the Convention reflects the various ambiguities and complexities of these challenges considered in this section.

---

[30] UNECE Convention on Environmental Impact Assessment in Transboundary Matters (Espoo 1991, in force since 1997). See Section 2.2 of Chapter 19.

Maria Lee and Carolyn Abbot, 'The Usual Suspects? Public Participation Under the Aarhus Convention' (2003) 66 MLR 80, 86

The Aarhus Convention is certainly ambiguous in its objectives, with the recitals recognising diverse, yet interrelated motivations. The recitals refer to rights and duties to an 'environment adequate to ... health and well-being', and posit that rights advocated in the Convention enhance 'the quality and the implementation of decisions' and 'public awareness of environmental issues'. In addition, they state the need for 'public authorities to be in possession of accurate, comprehensive and up-to-date environmental information'. The Convention also aims 'to strengthen public support for decisions on the environment'. In process terms, 'accountability of and transparency in decision-making' is mentioned and more radically, the Convention 'will contribute to strengthening democracy'.

Although the Aarhus Convention has very mixed motives, perhaps the clearest and strongest link is with improving environmental protection. So far, we have mentioned that procedure might improve problem solving, but the level of environmental protection is still potentially open-ended. In the Aarhus Convention, the understanding seems to be that public participation actually improves environmental protection, implying *more* environmental protection. Given the fundamental controversy over claims as to the state of the environment, or what constitutes environmental protection, that is not a straightforward objective. And it is by no means clear that general public involvement will prioritise long term environmental protection over, say, short term economic benefits. The involvement of environmental interest groups is probably crucial, and indeed the distinct role for NGOs is perhaps the most significant innovation of the Convention. The Aarhus Convention defines the 'public concerned' as 'the public affected or likely to be affected by or having an interest in, the environmental decision-making ... non-governmental organisations promoting environmental protection and meeting any requirements under national law shall be deemed to have an interest.'

Note how Lee and Abbot conclude by focusing on the Convention's definition of the public. Through this definition, the Convention plays an important and powerful role in framing how public participation is understood as a concept, particularly considering the international application of the Convention. This means that Aarhus, and the legal instruments that implement it in EU and UK law, need to be carefully scrutinized. Aarhus is not a panacea for environmental problems but a complex legal regime that has a significant role to play in relation to them.

In relation to the first pillar of the Convention—access to environmental information—Article 4 imposes a duty on public authorities to make certain environmental information available on request, subject to certain limitations. Article 5 places a duty on public authorities to collect and publish information. The details of the English regime implementing these duties, particularly in relation to Article 4, are covered in Section 3, but here it is worth noting the very broad definition of 'environmental information' set out in Article 2(3) of the Convention.

3. 'Environmental information' means any information in written, visual, aural, electronic or any other material form on:

(a) The state of elements of the environment, such as air and atmosphere, water, soil, land, landscape and natural sites, biological diversity and its components, including genetically modified organisms, and the interaction among these elements;

(b) Factors, such as substances, energy, noise and radiation, and activities or measures, including administrative measures, environmental agreements, policies, legislation, plans and programmes, affecting or likely to affect the elements of the environment within the scope of subparagraph (a) above, and cost-benefit and other economic analyses and assumptions used in environmental decision-making;

(c) The state of human health and safety, conditions of human life, cultural sites and built structures, inasmuch as they are or may be affected by the state of the elements of the environment or, through these elements, by the factors, activities or measures referred to in subparagraph (b) above;

Information is thus not only what is published or written but can take many different forms. This makes this pillar of the Aarhus Convention potentially a very powerful tool that applies to a wide range of environmental decision-making situations, as well as information creation, collection, and collation more broadly.

The second pillar of the Convention relates to public participation, which notably does not create a general right of participation in relation to *all* environmental decision-making. Article 6(1)(a) requires public participation in relation to the listed permitting decisions set out in Annex 1, which essentially includes the activities governed by the EU environmental impact assessment regime (see Chapter 19), the EU integrated pollution prevention and control regime (see Chapter 17), and the international Espoo Convention. Annex 1.20 also explicitly recognizes that Article 6 applies 'where public participation is provided for under an environmental impact assessment procedure in accordance with national legislation'. The purpose of these provisions is to require public involvement in all administrative decisions relating to the permission of activities that might have a significant effect on the environment. Article 6(1)(b) goes a step further, requiring public involvement in relation to decisions on proposed activities not listed in Annex 1 but which 'may have a significant effect on the environment', as determined by the relevant Party to the Convention, in accordance with its national law. Articles 7 and 8 set out the requirements of public participation for these various situations:

Article 7: PUBLIC PARTICIPATION CONCERNING PLANS, PROGRAMMES AND POLICIES RELATING TO THE ENVIRONMENT

Each Party shall make appropriate practical and/or other provisions for the public to participate during the preparation of plans and programmes relating to the environment, within a transparent and fair framework, having provided the necessary information to the public. Within this framework, article 6, paragraphs 3, 4 and 8, shall be applied. The public which may participate shall be identified by the relevant public authority, taking into account the objectives of this Convention. To the extent appropriate, each Party shall endeavour to provide opportunities for public participation in the preparation of policies relating to the environment.

Article 8: PUBLIC PARTICIPATION DURING THE PREPARATION OF EXECUTIVE REGULATIONS AND/OR GENERALLY APPLICABLE LEGALLY BINDING NORMATIVE INSTRUMENTS

Each Party shall strive to promote effective public participation at an appropriate stage, and while options are still open, during the preparation by public authorities of executive regulations and other generally applicable legally binding rules that may have a significant effect on the environment.

> To this end, the following steps should be taken:
>
> (a) Time-frames sufficient for effective participation should be fixed;
>
> (b) Draft rules should be published or otherwise made publicly available; and
>
> (c) The public should be given the opportunity to comment, directly or through representative consultative bodies.
>
> The result of the public participation shall be taken into account as far as possible.

These Articles are fairly uninspiring, reading more like administrative guidance than a declaration of some deeply entrenched right. However, this reflects the reality of public participation—it nearly always concerns the minutiae of administrative processes. Thus, while the discourses about public participation are often phrased in very general and conceptual terms, the operation of participatory processes in practice is quite the opposite—they are detailed and dependent on the precise construction (and implementation) of the regimes involved.

In relation to EU institution decision-making and legal processes, the three pillars of the Convention have been implemented through Regulation 1367/2006/EC on the application of the provisions of the Aarhus Convention on Access to Information, Public Participation in Decision-making and Access to Justice in Environmental Matters to Community Institutions and Bodies.[31] Article 3 makes clear that Regulation 1049/2001/EC regarding public access to EU institution documents extends to cover 'environmental information', defined in Article 2(d) to pick up the Aarhus concept of environmental information. Articles 4 and 5 of Regulation 1367/2006 promote the 'active and systemic dissemination' of environmental information to the public and ensure such information is 'up to date, accurate, and comparable'. Article 9 requires 'early and effective opportunities for the public to participate' during the preparation, modification, or review of plans or programmes that concern the environment, at a stage 'when all options are still open'. Articles 10, 11, and 12 relate to the access to justice pillar of the Convention and provide, in the first instance, for a right to internal review. These latter aspects have been subject to recent significant litigation and are considered further in Section 2.5 of Chapter 10.

In relation to environmental decision-making in England and Wales, the situation is more complicated, as we shall see in Section 3 and in Chapter 10. Some implementation of the Convention into UK law has been accomplished through EU Directives. Thus, Directive 2003/4/EC on public access to environmental information[32] aimed to implement Article 4 of the Directive within EU Member States and has resulted in the passing of the Environmental Information Regulations 2004 in England and Wales (see Section 3.1).[32a] Likewise, Directive 2003/35/EC providing for public participation in respect of the drawing up of certain plans and programmes relating to the environment,[32b] amended the Environmental Assessment Directive (then Directive 85/337/EEC) so as to include Aarhus-compliant public participation and access to justice provisions (see Section 2.3 of Chapter 10).

Overall, the Aarhus Convention is playing two different roles in UK environmental law. First, distinct from other international treaties, it has legal authority in UK law through the EU's implementation of it. As we shall see, this has actually led to legal reform in English law. Second, the Convention has significant symbolic importance as it relates to the challenges discussed in this section. Thus, while the Convention may not be legally relevant in all cases, it neatly and powerfully reflects the problems inherent at the interface between administrative law and environmental law.

---

[31] [2006] OJ L264/13.   [32] [2003] OJ L41/26.

[32a] European Parliament and Council Directive 2003/4/EC of 28 January 2003 on public access to environmental information and repealing Council Directive 90/313/EEC [2003] OJ L41/26.

[32b] [2003] OJ L156/17.

> **FURTHER READING**
>
> 1. For further discussion of the specific challenges that environmental decision-making creates for public law, see Elizabeth Fisher, *Risk Regulation and Administrative Constitutionalism* (Hart Publishing 2007) ch 1.
>
> 2. See Jenny Steele, 'Participation and Deliberation in Environmental Law: A Problem Solving Approach' (2001) 21 OJLS 415 and Amy Cohen, 'Negotiation Meet New Governance: Interests, Skills and Selves' (2008) 33 Law and Social Inquiry 503, for excellent discussions of the role of public participation in environmental law.

3 REGULATING THE ADMINISTRATIVE PROCESS

As is already clear from the analysis in this chapter, administrative law is not just what happens in the courtroom in judicial review cases. The subject is also concerned with how administrative processes are constituted and limited in general. There are two particular features to note in relation to the regulation of administrative processes.

First, in most cases, how administration is regulated will be specific to the regime involved. This is one of the reasons that environmental law can look dull—its various regimes are essentially detailed frameworks for making decisions in relation to environmental issues. The specificity of these regimes, as well as the fact that they are constantly undergoing change, means that their analysis is not easily covered in a textbook.[33] The best advice one can give to a budding environmental lawyer hoping to see how environmental regimes are regulated is to paraphrase Frankfurter's direction in the Introduction—'read the statute', and the 'delegated legislation, and the associated policy guidance'. With that said, some overarching regimes also operate in UK law to regulate decision-making and acts of public officials in relation to environmental issues—the Environmental Information Regulations 2004 (EIR 2004),[34] which implement the Aarhus Convention's first pillar, are a case in point.

Second, legislation and guidance are not the only means by which administrative decision-making is regulated. There is a range of different mechanisms or techniques by which decision-makers are held to account. Thus, judicial review doctrine plays an important role in regulating administrative processes since each judicial review case sets down a precedent that will guide future decision-makers. Accordingly, the Treasury Solicitor has produced a publication entitled *The Judge Over Your Shoulder*, extracted here, which provides guidance to civil servants on judicial review doctrine and explains its significance.

Treasury Solicitor, *The Judge Over Your Shoulder* (4th edn, HMSO 2006) paras 2.3–2.4

When a Minister or a Department decides to act, or to act in a particular way, or not to act, they are 'exercising a discretion'. The discretion may appear to be unlimited ('unfettered')—for example, the statutory provision conferring the discretion may say 'the Secretary of State shall grant or refuse the application', without any qualification. But however unlimited the decision-maker's discretion may appear to be, there are legal limits on the exercise of that discretion.

---

[33] For another aspect of this challenge, see Chapter 9.

[34] SI 2004/3391. The EIR 2004 apply throughout the UK, but do not apply to Scottish authorities, which are bound by a separate but similar set of Scottish Regulations.

Some limitations on the exercise of the discretion may be *express*: the purposes for which a particular power was given, or the criteria to be applied in exercising it, may actually be set out in the legislation. Other limits will be *implied* by the statutory scheme. But others may be derived from the principles of administrative law [judicial review doctrine], or from rights recognised under the European Convention on Human Rights. It is an axiom that public law powers must be exercised for the purpose for which they were conferred, not for any extraneous or ulterior purpose. At the same time, those purposes do continue to evolve or be re-interpreted in the light of constitutional and democratic developments— such as the Human Rights Act.

Judicial review is not the only mechanism that will regulate administrative processes. There are also ombudsmen and other forms of oversight. As a result, administrative processes are regulated in many different ways and the framework for what is acceptable administrative action can come from a range of sources. This section examines four different ways in which administrative environmental processes are regulated in UK law, beyond judicial review—the EIR 2004, the regulation of the use of information and its analysis in decision-making, public participation, and other forms of non-judicial oversight. The analysis is brief but gives some feeling for the various, often complicated, issues in this area.

3.1 ACCESSING INFORMATION: ENVIRONMENTAL INFORMATION REGULATIONS 2004

The EIR 2004 are atypical of legislation that regulates administrative processes because, rather than limiting discretion, they provide an overarching framework for access to environmental information. The general nature of the Regulations is due to the fact that they implement (and largely directly transpose) Directive 2003/4/EC and thus implement the first pillar of the Aarhus Convention, as discussed already. Note that this Directive superseded an earlier EU regime so this is not the first legal framework on accessing environmental information in either the UK or the EU.[35] There is also a more general right to access to information in the UK under the Freedom of Information Act 2000 (FOI Act 2000), although the EIR 2004 is a distinctive regime.[36]

The EIR 2004 relates to 'environmental information', as defined in the Aarhus Convention and set out in Section 2.4. Regulation 5 sets out a duty of disclosure on public authorities:

Regulation 5

5.—(1) Subject to paragraph (3) and in accordance with paragraphs (2), (4), (5) and (6) and the remaining provisions of this Part and Part 3 of these Regulations, a public authority that holds environmental information shall make it available on request.

(2) Information shall be made available under paragraph (1) as soon as possible and no later than 20 working days after the date of receipt of the request.

(3) To the extent that the information requested includes personal data of which the applicant is the data subject, paragraph (1) shall not apply to those personal data.

---

[35] Directive 2003/4/EC repealed Council Directive 90/313/EEC [1990] OJ L158/56, as implemented by the Environmental Information Regulations 1992 SI 1992/3240.

[36] Note that 'environmental information' is exempt from the Freedom of Information Act 2000 regime (s 39 FOI Act 2000).

(4) For the purposes of paragraph (1), where the information made available is compiled by or on behalf of the public authority it shall be up to date, accurate and comparable, so far as the public authority reasonably believes.

(5) Where a public authority makes available information in paragraph (b) of the definition of environmental information, and the applicant so requests, the public authority shall, insofar as it is able to do so, either inform the applicant of the place where information, if available, can be found on the measurement procedures, including methods of analysis, sampling and pre-treatment of samples, used in compiling the information, or refer the applicant to a standardised procedure used.

(6) Any enactment or rule of law that would prevent the disclosure of information in accordance with these Regulations shall not apply.

The relevant request for information can basically come in any form. Under the Regulations, a public authority is defined in the following way:

Regulation 2(2)

(2) Subject to paragraph (3), 'public authority' means—

(a) government departments;

(b) any other public authority as defined in section 3(1) of the Act, disregarding for this purpose the exceptions in paragraph 6 of Schedule 1 to the Act, but excluding—

   (i) any body or office-holder listed in Schedule 1 to the Act only in relation to information of a specified description; or

   (ii) any person designated by Order under section 5 of the Act;

(c) any other body or other person, that carries out functions of public administration; or

(d) any other body or other person, that is under the control of a person falling within sub-paragraphs (a), (b) or (c) and—

   (i) has public responsibilities relating to the environment;

   (ii) exercises functions of a public nature relating to the environment; or

   (iii) provides public services relating to the environment.

Regulation 12 then sets out the exceptions to disclosure:

Regulation 12

12.—(1) Subject to paragraphs (2), (3) and (9), a public authority may refuse to disclose environmental information requested if—

   (a) an exception to disclosure applies under paragraphs (4) or (5); and

   (b) in all the circumstances of the case, the public interest in maintaining the exception outweighs the public interest in disclosing the information.

(2) A public authority shall apply a presumption in favour of disclosure.

(3) To the extent that the information requested includes personal data of which the applicant is not the data subject, the personal data shall not be disclosed otherwise than in accordance with regulation 13.

(4) For the purposes of paragraph (1)(a), a public authority may refuse to disclose information to the extent that—

(a) it does not hold that information when an applicant's request is received;

(b) the request for information is manifestly unreasonable;

(c) the request for information is formulated in too general a manner and the public authority has complied with regulation 9;

(d) the request relates to material which is still in the course of completion, to unfinished documents or to incomplete data; or

(e) the request involves the disclosure of internal communications.

(5) For the purposes of paragraph (1)(a), a public authority may refuse to disclose information to the extent that its disclosure would adversely affect—

(a) international relations, defence, national security or public safety;

(b) the course of justice, the ability of a person to receive a fair trial or the ability of a public authority to conduct an inquiry of a criminal or disciplinary nature;

(c) intellectual property rights;

(d) the confidentiality of the proceedings of that or any other public authority where such confidentiality is provided by law;

(e) the confidentiality of commercial or industrial information where such confidentiality is provided by law to protect a legitimate economic interest;

(f) the interests of the person who provided the information where that person—

(i) was not under, and could not have been put under, any legal obligation to supply it to that or any other public authority;

(ii) did not supply it in circumstances such that that or any other public authority is entitled apart from these Regulations to disclose it; and

(iii) has not consented to its disclosure; or

(g) the protection of the environment to which the information relates. [...]

[...]

(8) For the purposes of paragraph (4)(e), internal communications includes communications between government departments.

(9) To the extent that the environmental information to be disclosed relates to information on emissions, a public authority shall not be entitled to refuse to disclose that information under an exception referred to in paragraphs (5)(d) to (g). [...]

The EIR 2004 also sets out requirements in relation to the charges that public authorities can impose on those requesting information (regulation 8), and other matters relating to the provision of advice and assistance for those making a request (regulation 9), and empowers public authorities to issue a code of practice (regulation 16).

There are two important things to note about these provisions. First, this regime is free-standing—it provides independent rights of access and an autonomous definition of public authority, notably different from those under the Freedom of Information (FOI) regime. In particular, it is striking that there is an overriding assumption that disclosure should occur (regulation 12(1)(b)). Second, these provisions are detailed but require interpretation and the exercise of discretion. Not surprisingly, considering the sensitive and often valuable interests at stake in releasing information covered by the Regulations, there have already been disagreements over their scope and operation. The regime allows for an appeal process, largely paralleling the appeals mechanisms under the FOI regime. First, there is an internal appeal process, so that an unsatisfied applicant can make representations to the public authority if it appears that the authority has failed to comply with a requirement of the Regulations in dealing with a request for information.[37] Appeals can then be made to the Information Commissioner,[38] then to the First Tier (Information Rights) Tribunal (previously the Information Tribunal),[39] and ultimately to a court.[40] There has also been a preliminary reference to the Court of Justice from the UK Supreme Court after a series of such appeals.

This structure has led to an 'administrative law of transparency',[41] in that there are a range of decisions that now exist, from different bodies, concerning how the Regulations should operate in relation to the disclosure of environmental information. Two examples are considered here. The first case addresses which public bodies owe a duty under the Regulations, and the second is a preliminary reference before the Court of Justice that considers how the exceptions to disclosure under the Regulations operate.

Smartsource v Information Commissioner
[2010] UKUT 415 (AAC) paras 63–68 (Judge Wikeley)

The Facts

Smartsource requested information from sixteen water companies under the EIR 2004 arguing they were 'public authorities' for the purposes of regulation 2(2)(c). They claimed they were not.

The UT (Administrative Appeals Chamber)

63. We agree with the submission on behalf of the Information Commissioner that the ambit of regulation 2(2)(c) is narrower than the scope of section 6(3)(b) of the Human Rights Act 1998, which in dealing with public authorities refers to 'persons certain of whose functions are functions of a public nature'. We also accept that regulation 2(2)(c) is narrower than CPR 54.1 which, in the context of proceedings for judicial review, refers to bodies 'performing a public function'. It follows that a body may be a public authority for the purpose of the Human Rights Act 1998, and/or amenable to judicial review under CPR 54.1, and yet still fall outside regulation 2(2)(c). In our view the human rights and judicial review case law needs to be read with that important qualification in mind.

64. We agree with, and approve of, the multi-factor approach taken by the Information Tribunal in both the *Network Rail* and the *Port of London Authority* cases, namely that the decision on whether a body is a "public authority" within regulation 2(2)(c) of the EIR 2004 depends on a range of factors. [...]

65. We also agree [...] that the question of whether a water company is a public authority for the purpose of regulation 2(2)(c) (and indeed (d)) is a mixed question of fact and law, and that the onus lies on the Appellant to demonstrate that the companies fall within the statutory definition. [...]

66. Applying the multi-factor approach means that we have to identify the relevant factors which point one way or the other and weigh them in the balance in the process of determining whether the body in question is performing functions of public administration and so a public authority within regulation 2(2)(c). There are, firstly, a number of similarities between the position of the water companies and Network Rail. In particular, the water companies:

- own and manage a major utility industry which serves paying customers;

---

[37] EIR 2004, reg 11. [38] EIR 2004, reg 18; FOI Act 2000, s 50.
[39] FOI Act 2000, s 57. [40] Tribunals, Courts and Enforcement Act 2007, s 13.
[41] Fisher, 'Transparency and Administrative Law' (n 11).

- operate under a licence supervised by a regulator;
- have considerable commercial freedom, e.g. in setting staff salaries, pension arrangements and other terms and conditions of employment;
- are subject to a degree of price regulation;
- neither set nor enforce health and safety standards, but are rather subject to a regulator.

67. There are also a number of differences between the position of the water companies and Network Rail. Unlike Network Rail, the water companies:

- have institutional and private shareholders to whom the companies are accountable through their AGMs (and indeed in several instances the majority shareholdings are owned by foreign companies);
- receive no public funding by way of income or capital, other than that public sector bodies buy water and sewerage services in the same way as other customers, e.g. there is no public funding in England and Wales for major capital projects in the water industry, such as replacing the Victorian water mains in major cities (in contrast 70 per cent of Network Rail's funding came from the government or government-backed borrowing);
- do not have government nominees on their boards of directors.

68. [...] [T]he cumulative effect of these factors amounts to a compelling argument that water companies have fewer of the characteristics of a public authority than Network Rail and so fall outside the reach of regulation 2(2)(c) . In this context we also note that several of the water companies are foreign-owned and that they can buy each other, or buy parts of each other, subject only to competition legislation. On this basis the preponderance of factors points to the water companies not being public authorities.

Case C-71/10 *Office of Communications v Information Commissioner* (28 July 2011 CJEU) paras 21–32

The Facts

The UK Office of Communications operated a website that provided information about the location of mobile phone masts although the website did not give the precise location of a mast. An Information Manager for Health Protection Scotland asked for the grid references of masts and was denied by the Office of Communications who argued that disclosure would not be in the interests of public safety and also adversely affect the intellectual property rights of the mobile phone operators. This decision was appealed to the Information Commissioner who ordered disclosure of the information and that decision was ultimately appealed to the Supreme Court who referred the following question to the Court of Justice.

The CJEU

21. By its question, the national court asks in essence whether a public authority, where it holds environmental information or such information is held on its behalf, may, when weighing the public interests served by disclosure against the interests served by refusal to disclose, in order to assess a request for that information to be made available to a natural or legal person, take into account cumulatively a number of the grounds for refusal listed in Article 4(2) of Directive 2003/4, or whether it must weigh the interests served by refusal to disclose, one at a time, against the public interests served by disclosure.

22. It should be noted that, as is apparent from the scheme of Directive 2003/4 and, in particular, from the second subparagraph of Article 4(2) thereof, and from recital 16 in the preamble thereto, the right to information means that the disclosure of information should be the general rule and that public authorities should be permitted to refuse a request for environmental information only in a few specific and clearly defined cases. The grounds for refusal should therefore be interpreted restrictively, in such a way that the public interest served by disclosure is weighed against the interest served by the refusal.

23. It should be observed that, according to the introductory wording in Article 4(2) of Directive 2003/4, 'Member States may provide for' exceptions to the general rule that information must be disclosed to the public. That provision does not specify any particular procedure for examining the grounds for refusal in cases where a Member State has provided for such exceptions on that basis.

24. In that regard, it should be noted, first, that the second sentence of the second subparagraph of Article 4(2) provides that '[i]n every particular case, the public interest served by disclosure shall be weighed against the interest served by the refusal'. As the Advocate General stated in her Opinion, that sentence has an independent function, separate from that of the first sentence of the same subparagraph. The first sentence of the second subparagraph sets out the duty to weigh each of the grounds for refusal against the public interest served by disclosure of the information. If the sole purpose of the second sentence of the second subparagraph of Article 4(2) of Directive 2003/4 were to establish that duty, that sentence would be no more than a redundant and unnecessary repetition of the meaning conveyed by the first sentence of the same subparagraph.

25. Secondly, it should be observed that, when the interests involved are weighed, a number of separate interests may, cumulatively, militate in favour of disclosure.

26. Recital 1 to Directive 2003/4 sets out the various reasons for disclosure; they include, in particular, 'a greater awareness of environmental matters, a free exchange of views, more effective participation by the public in environmental decision-making and … a better environment'.

27. It follows that the concept of 'public interest served by disclosure', referred to in the second sentence of the second subparagraph of Article 4(2) of that directive, must be regarded as an overarching concept covering more than one ground for the disclosure of environmental information.

28. It must accordingly be held that the second sentence of the second subparagraph of Article 4(2) is concerned with the weighing against each other of two overarching concepts, which means that the competent public authority may, when undertaking that exercise, evaluate cumulatively the grounds for refusal to disclose.

29. That view is not undermined by the emphasis placed in the second sentence of the second subparagraph of Article 4(2) on the duty to weigh the interests involved '[i]n every particular case'. Such emphasis is intended to stress that interests must be weighed, not on the basis of a general measure, adopted by the national legislature for example, but on the basis of an actual and specific examination of each situation brought before the competent authorities in connection with a request for access to environmental information made on the basis of Directive 2003/4 (see, to that effect, Case C-266/09 *Stichting Natuur en Milieu and Others* [2010] ECR I 0000, paragraphs 55 to 58).

30. Moreover, the fact that those interests are referred to separately in Article 4(2) of Directive 2003/4 does not preclude the cumulation of those exceptions to the general rule of disclosure, given that the interests served by refusal to disclose may sometimes overlap in the same situation or the same circumstances.

31. It should also be pointed out that, since the various interests served by refusal to disclose relate, as in the case in the main proceedings, to the grounds for refusal set out in Article 4(2) of Directive 2003/4, taking those interests into consideration cumulatively when weighing them against the public interests served by disclosure is not likely to introduce another exception in addition to those listed in

that provision. If weighing such interests against the public interests served by disclosure were to result in a refusal to disclose, it would need to be acknowledged that that restriction on access to the information requested is proportionate and accordingly justified in the light of the overall interest represented jointly by the interests served by refusal to disclose.

32. In those circumstances, the answer to the question referred is that Article 4(2) of Directive 2003/4 must be interpreted as meaning that, where a public authority holds environmental information or such information is held on its behalf, it may, when weighing the public interests served by disclosure against the interests served by refusal to disclose, in order to assess a request for that information to be made available to a natural or legal person, take into account cumulatively a number of the grounds for refusal set out in that provision.

These cases are just two of many tribunal and court cases concerning the operation of the EIR 2004. Three important aspects of these cases are important to highlight. First, the EIR 2004 regime requires decisions to be made about *how* it will operate in practice. These Regulations are not self-executing and there is legitimate scope for disagreement over how they should work. Second, the wording of the Regulations and the Directive is still critical in determining how the regime should work and both cases show careful and close reasoning in interpreting the provisions of the Regulations and the Directive. However, with limited precedent for construing the Regulations, other more familiar regimes are drawn on as frames of reference in this reasoning—not as determinative but as useful guides for interpreting the Regulations within their broader legal context. Thus, in *Smartsource*, Wikeley J also considered the definitions of a public authority under the HRA and for the purposes of judicial review actions at common law. Third, each of these cases is highly dependent on its facts. That is again reflected in *Smartsource* with the explicit recognition that the question of what constituted a public authority was a question of mixed fact and law, so that a multi-factor approach was needed to resolve the interpretive point.

3.2 REGULATING THE USE AND ANALYSIS OF INFORMATION IN ENVIRONMENTAL DECISION-MAKING

The EIR 2004 regulate access to environmental information by the public but they do not directly regulate how information is taken into account in environmental decision-making.[42] Section 3 of Chapter 2 explained how knowledge and expertise are needed for environmental decision-making and we have already seen that this creates significant challenges for public law. Historically, the discretion of decision-makers was very broad under UK legislation,[43] meaning that the use of environmental information by officials was quite unregulated. By the 1960s, the House of Lords was making it clear that such discretion was not completely unfettered.[44]

In the last twenty years, the way in which decision-makers exercise their expert discretion and take information into account has become far more regulated by public law. This is the result of three different, but overlapping, developments. First, legislation and statutory guidance have become much more specific about how factual analysis should be carried out within environmental regimes. An obvious example of this is the statutory guidance that contains detailed provisions on the operation of the contaminated land regime, as discussed in Chapter 21. There are many other such examples in most areas of environmental regulation; where guidance on information assessment was once

---

[42] Although it could be argued that regs 4 and 6 play a minor role in this regard.
[43] *Liversidge v Anderson* [1942] AC 206 (HL).
[44] *Padfield v Minister of Agriculture Fisheries & Food* [1968] AC 997 (HL).

non-existent, it is now normal practice (see Chapters 14 and 17). Moreover, more overarching reforms to executive government have placed increasing emphasis on carrying out different forms of regulatory impact assessment and risk assessment, which, among other things, require rigorous scrutiny of the information used in administrative decision-making.[45] Connected to these frameworks is the increasing focus on making decision-making transparent, as reflected by the EIR 2004.[46]

Second, while national legislation has tended to grant relatively broad discretion to decision-makers, EU Directives often have not when it comes to the collection, use, and analysis of environmental information. In particular, the annexes of many environmental EU Directives often set out in considerable detail frameworks for how information gathering and scientific analysis should be carried out by national decision-makers. The Annexes to the Water Framework Directive are a good example of this.[47] As a result, questions about the implementation of the Directive become questions about whether national administrators have met the technical requirements of the Directive.[48]

Finally, public law has taken on a greater role in regulating the use of environmental information through the courts in judicial review cases increasingly intervening in relation to questions of factual analysis. This is discussed in more detail in Section 4 but here it is important to note that court decisions concerning how information is assessed will play an important role in regulating decision-making with decision-makers using these precedents as guiding examples, in line with the discussion of *The Judge Over Your Shoulder*.

The overall implication of these developments is that administrative law is playing an increasingly important role in regulating how administrative decision-makers carry out factual analysis and many disputes in environmental law now concern this kind of issue. This creates a number of challenges for environmental lawyers. First, as we saw in Section 3.4 of Chapter 2, our knowledge in relation to environmental problems is riddled with uncertainty. Thus, issues to do with scientific uncertainty have been of particular interest to environmental lawyers who work in public law, with the precautionary principle in particular coming to have a high profile for lawyers (see further Chapter 11). Second, there are fundamental problems of competence. Environmental lawyers are not environmental scientists and yet environmental law is partly concerned with regulating scientific analysis. We will see the problems that this creates for judicial review, in relation to its doctrinal nature and proper constitutional role, in Section 4.

3.3 PUBLIC PARTICIPATION

As we saw in Section 2.3, public participation has been a major theme in environmental law and the expectation of such participation in relation to environmental decisions poses a real challenge for administrative decision-making. However, it is a challenge that cannot be avoided, with public participation now inherent in environmental decision-making, as Justice Sullivan noted in *Greenpeace v Department of Trade and Industry*[49]:

> Whatever the position may be in other policy areas, in the development of policy in the environmental field consultation is no longer a privilege to be granted or withheld at will by the executive.

---

[45] Elizabeth Fisher, 'The Rise of the Risk Commonwealth and the Challenge for Administrative Law' [2003] PL 455; Robert Baldwin, 'Is Better Regulation Smarter Regulation?' [2005] PL 485.

[46] Fisher, 'Transparency and Administrative Law' (n 11).

[47] Maria Lee, 'Law and Governance in Water Protection Policy', in Joanne Scott (ed), *Environmental Protection: European Law and Governance* (OUP 2009). See also the Annexes to the Air Quality Framework Directive, discussed in Chapter 15.

[48] *Downs v Secretary of State for Environment, Food and Rural Affairs* [2008] EWHC 2666 (Admin).

[49] [2007] EWHC 311, [2007] Env LR 29, para 49.

Sullivan J went on in this case to cite the Aarhus Convention (an example of its symbolic use), but even before the Aarhus Convention most environmental regimes allowed for some form of public participation or consultation. Thus, as seen in Chapter 18, there is a duty under the Town and Country Planning Act 1990 to publicize planning applications and to consider submissions, along with various mechanisms for consulting a range of interests in relation to planning applications, from citizens to other public bodies (such as Natural England when nature conservation issues are relevant). Likewise, as seen in Chapter 19, public participation and consultation with interested bodies are an integral part of environmental assessment. Public participation is thus another significant aspect of environmental decision-making and its constitution and control by public law demonstrates a further avenue of accountability in the regulation of environmental decision-making.

Three points are worth making in relation to the public law regulation of public participation processes. First, rights in relation to public participation and consultation are often understood as *procedural* rights. They are therefore distinguished from rights concerned with the exercise of discretion and rights to particular outcomes. In the context of judicial review, failure to observe such rights are thus linked to arguments about procedural fairness[50] and other related review grounds, such as the duty to give reasons[51] and procedural legitimate expectations.[52]

Second, the nature of rights of consultation and participation set out in legislation varies significantly, which affects their precise constitution and thus control through public law. We have already seen the particularity of the rights of participation under the Aarhus Convention, and in general there is no overarching participation right in relation to environmental matters in the way that there is for accessing environmental information. The environmental regime that grants the most significant participation rights to the public is the environmental assessment regime,[53] but these rights are not universal and other regimes provide fewer public participation rights. The rights set out explicitly in primary and delegated legislation are also often supplemented by both policy and case law. Examples of the latter can be seen in judicial review cases in Section 4. An example of policy supplementing participation rights is the UK Government's Consultation Principles,[54] which applies to formal public consultation exercises of central government. Hence, determining what rights of consultation actually exist is often not straightforward and usually requires painstaking analysis of statutory provisions and the related policy context.

Third, in relation to most environmental regimes, there is considerable disagreement over whether certain participation rights are adequate, either in theory or in practice. In part this relates to the themes highlighted in Section 2.3—there are many different types of public participation. However, disagreements over the adequacy of participation exercises also reflect substantive conflicts in relation to the particular environmental issue at stake. Thus, for example, a lack of adequate participation will often be framed as a failure of a decision-maker to take into account particular points of view (that is, relevant considerations in a substantive sense) in exercising their discretion.[55] Thus, while public participation is often understood as a matter of procedure, it also relates to more substantive matters, as will be seen in many environmental judicial review cases, in Section 4 and throughout the textbook.

[50] *Bushell v Secretary of State for the Environment* [1981] AC 75 (HL).

[51] *Resource Recovery Solutions (Derbyshire) Ltd v Secretary of State for Communities and Local Government* [2011] EWHC 1726 (Admin) (QB) and *R(Wye Valley Action Association Ltd) v Herefordshire Council* [2011] EWCA Civ 20, [2011] Env LR 20.

[52] *Greenpeace* (n 49) and *The Bard Campaign & Anor v Secretary of State for Communities and Local Government (Rev 1)* [2009] EWHC 308 (Admin) (QB).

[53] Directive 85/337/EC, art 6. See Chapter 19.

[54] HM Government, Consultation Principles, Cabinet Office 2012. Available from <http://www.cabinetoffice.gov.uk/resource-library/consultation-principles-guidance> accessed 28 January 2013.

[55] *Greenpeace* (n 49).

3.4 OTHER (NON-JUDICIAL) ACCOUNTABILITY MECHANISMS

We have already seen in this section how environmental decision-making is regulated in various ways, through statutory rights of the public to information and to participate in decisions, and through legal controls on the use and analysis of environmental information. Public law plays a role in guaranteeing these rights and enforcing these limits on decision-making, through the backstop of judicial review and appeals, but also in the very construction and application of these regulatory controls. They are examples of how public administration in the UK is subject to multiple accountabilities. This section concludes by considering some other, non-judicial accountability mechanisms relevant to environmental decision-making, before Section 4 considers the role of the courts in holding administrators to account, through judicial review and HRA actions in particular. Non-judicial forms of accountability include various forms of both internal and external oversight.[56] In this sub-section, three examples are briefly noted—forms of parliamentary oversight, the ombudsmen, and tribunals.

It should be noted that there are not just multiple forms of accountability but that they operate as a network of oversight. Hence, in many cases, different forms of oversight and accountability will be operating simultaneously.[57] For example, in the case of *Downs*, extracted in Section 4.2, the pesticides standards of the UK government were the subject of consideration by the (now defunct) Royal Commission on Environmental Pollution,[58] and were also subject to a judicial review action.[59] The many different accountability mechanisms that exist not only represent different routes for redress, but they can also produce documentation that is a valuable resource for understanding what is going on in UK public administration. Seeing administrative activity clearly, beyond its description and analysis in administrative law cases, can be difficult without conducting wide empirical studies.

Considering, first, parliamentary oversight as a mechanism for holding administration to account—this mechanism reflects the political nature of the UK constitution. Tomkins has described a political constitution.

Adam Tomkins, *Public Law* (Clarendon Press 2003) 18–19

A political constitution is one in which those who exercise political power (let us say the government) are held to constitutional account through political means, and through political institutions (for example, Parliament). Thus, government ministers and senior civil servants might be subjected to regular scrutiny in Parliament. The scrutiny may consist of taking part in debates, answering questions, participating in and responding to the investigations of committees of inquiry, and so forth.

As discussed in Section 1.1, it has been recognized that there has been a shift towards the UK constitution being more legal in nature, but that does not mean that these political accountability mechanisms are now irrelevant. In particular, parliamentary select committees conduct important oversight of all policy areas, including how environmental issues are dealt with by government. Many of these committees oversee the work of a particular government department. Thus, there exist House

---

[56] There is no room in a chapter like this to highlight all these different mechanisms, even an administrative law textbook struggles with this task.

[57] A very good overview of this can be found in Inquiry into BSE and vCJD in the UK, *The BSE Inquiry Report, Volume Fifteen: Government and Administration* (HMSO 2000). See Section 3.1 of Chapter 3.

[58] Royal Commission on Environmental Pollution, *Crop Spraying and the Health of Residents and Bystanders* (Royal Commission on Environmental Pollution 2005).

[59] *Downs* (n 48) and *Secretary of State for Environment, Food and Rural Affairs v Downs* [2009] EWCA Civ 664.

of Commons Committees in relation to Energy and Climate Change (overseeing the work of the Department of Energy and Climate Change) as well as the Environment, Food and Rural Affairs Committee (overseeing the work of DEFRA). There are also cross-cutting select committees. For example, in 1997 the Environmental Audit Committee (EAC) was set up to assess whether UK public administration across the board was contributing to environmental protection and sustainable development. Likewise, the Science and Technology Committee of the House of Commons plays an important role in reviewing the scientific aspects of administrative decision-making. These committees also produce reports that can be a useful resource for understanding the practices of public administration.

The second set of non-judicial accountability mechanisms to note is that of ombudsmen. Ombudsmen are independent bodies that have powers of investigation. Originally ombudsmen acted in relation to the public sector, but in the 1990s a number of private sector ombudsmen were set up, particularly to oversee newly privatized industries. Our focus here is on public sector ombudsmen. The most high profile is the Parliamentary and Health Services Ombudsman (PO), which was set up in 1967 and was originally known as the Parliamentary Commissioner.[60] There is also a Local Government Ombudsman (LGO) as well as ombudsmen for specific areas including privatized industries. The focus here is on the PO and LGO.

Historically, the idea was that ombudsmen would investigate 'maladministration'.[61] However, this concept has never been defined and the investigatory powers of both these bodies are broad-ranging. As s 5 of the Parliamentary Commissioner Act 1967 makes clear, the powers of the PO are very wide, although they do have limits.

Parliamentary Commissioner Act 1967, ss 5(1)–(2)

(1) Subject to the provisions of this section, the Commissioner may investigate any action taken by or on behalf of a government department or other authority to which this Act applies, being action taken in the exercise of administrative functions of that department or authority, in any case where—

(a) a written complaint is duly made to a member of the House of Commons by a member of the public who claims to have sustained injustice in consequence of maladministration in connection with the action so taken; and

(b) the complaint is referred to the Commissioner, with the consent of the person who made it, by a member of that House with a request to conduct an investigation thereon. [...]

(2) Except as hereinafter provided, the Commissioner shall not conduct an investigation under this Act in respect of any of the following matters, that is to say—

(a) any action in respect of which the person aggrieved has or had a right of appeal, reference or review to or before a tribunal constituted by or under any enactment or by virtue of Her Majesty's prerogative;

(b) any action in respect of which the person aggrieved has or had a remedy by way of proceedings in any court of law:

Provided that the Commissioner may conduct an investigation notwithstanding that the person aggrieved has or had such a right or remedy if satisfied that in the particular circumstances it is not reasonable to expect him to resort or have resorted to it. [...]

---

[60] Parliamentary Commissioner Act 1967.
[61] JUSTICE, *The Citizen and Administration: The Redress of Grievances* (Steven & Sons Ltd 1961).

There are two important points to note here. First, complaints must be referred to the PO by an MP. This is known as the 'MP filter'. Second, the Ombudsman cannot conduct an inquiry where other accountability mechanisms exist though rights of review or appeal to tribunal or courts (unless there are reasonable grounds for not pursuing these). The main outcome of an inquiry is a report, which can recommend compensation (albeit not in significant amounts). Ombudsman reports can be very influential, as the Parliamentary and Health Service Ombudsman example shows.

Parliamentary and Health Service Ombudsman, *Environmentally Unfriendly: a Report of a Joint Investigation by the Parliamentary Ombudsman and the Local Government Ombudsman* (Stationery Office 2010) 7

I am laying this report before Parliament under section 10(4) of the *Parliamentary Commissioner Act 1967*.

The report relates to an investigation which I have conducted as Parliamentary Ombudsman jointly with the Local Government Ombudsman, Anne Seex, in accordance with the powers conferred on us by amendments to our legislation due to the Regulatory Reform (*Collaboration etc. between Ombudsmen*) Order 2007.

The complaint, made by a woman and her son, was that the relevant authorities, namely the Environment Agency, Lancashire County Council and Rossendale Borough Council, had failed both individually and jointly over a seven-year period to take appropriate action to prevent their neighbour from using his land as an illegal landfill site. As a result, the woman and her son had found it impossible to live peacefully in their family home, yet had been unable to sell it. The neighbour's illegal activities had also made the landscape, which had been a local beauty spot, unrecognisable.

Our investigation found that the relevant authorities failed to take urgent or robust enforcement action, despite the very evident and unacceptable activities taking place on the neighbouring farm. They also failed to work together, despite the existence of a national protocol between the Environment Agency and the Local Government Association which clearly required a co-ordinated joint approach on waste enforcement. The consequence of that failing was a significant failure of all the safeguards introduced by Parliament to protect citizens and the environment from uncontrolled waste operations. Being able to undertake a joint investigation and issue a joint report with the Local Government Ombudsman has allowed us to consider maladministration and injustice in the round. We have been able to make joint recommendations which address individual remedy for the complainants. Moreover, we have made joint recommendations for the central and local government bodies to implement individually and jointly to prevent recurrence of their maladministration.

The extract shows that reporting the actions of public decision-makers enables an assessment of their behaviour, and thus public scrutiny of the acceptability of their action. This kind of report also highlights issues that are not the subject of other accountability mechanisms, such as interactions between different public bodies, which are not the subject of direct scrutiny by judicial review and tribunals.

The final non-judicial accountability mechanism to note is the network of UK tribunals and planning inspectors. Planning inspectors are dealt with in Section 6.2 of Chapter 18 but they are not the only form of tribunal-type body that can be appealed to in relation to environmental decision-making (or public decision-making more generally). Indeed, many different pieces of environmental legislation contain rights of appeal to a tribunal.[62] One example has already been seen under the EIR

---

[62] Richard Macrory and Michael Woods, *Modernising Environmental Justice: Regulation and the Role of an Environmental Tribunal* (UCL Centre for Law and the Environment 2003).

2004. Historically, the tribunal structure in the UK lacked unity but this changed with the Tribunals, Courts and Enforcement Act 2007,[63] which created a more unified two-tier system of tribunals. In 2010, a first-tier 'environmental tribunal' was created, which Macrory describes.

Richard Macrory, *Consistency and Effectiveness: Strengthening the New Environmental Tribunal* (UCL Centre for Law and the Environment 2011) paras 11–13

11. At present there are six appointed judges, all with at least seven years professional experience, together with ten non-legal members with a wide range of expertise. Members sit part-time, and the tribunal has a great deal of flexibility in how it handles cases. A judge and two non-legal members can be appointed to handle more serious or complex cases, but it is perfectly possible for a case to be heard by a single judge or a single non-legal member. The Tribunal is not based in a single location but can sit wherever it is needed, taking advantage of the common approach to administrative support provided by the new tribunal system. Procedures are governed by the Tribunal Procedure (First-tier Tribunal) (General Regulatory Chamber) Rules 2009 as amended. and there is a fast track procedure for handling appeals against Stop Notices.

12. As is common practice in tribunal appeals, each party normally bears their own costs, although the 2009 Rules allows for a Tribunal, acting either on its own initiative or in response to an application, to make an Order for Costs where, for example, it considers a party has acted unreasonably in bringing, defending, or conducting proceedings. The Rules also require that, where appropriate, the Tribunal must bring to the attention of the parties any appropriate alternative dispute resolution procedure and facilitate this as the parties wish.

13. The jurisdiction of the Environment Tribunal was originally limited to hearing appeals against civil sanctions, imposed by environmental regulators, pursuant to regulations made under the Regulatory Enforcement and Sanctions Act 2008. But other environmental appeals have now been added to this jurisdiction, notably appeals against decisions of the National Measurement Office concerning civil sanctions under eco-design regulations, and appeals under the new Welsh plastic bag regulations.

The Environment Tribunal represents some consolidation of appeal routes from environmental decisions but not complete consolidation, and Macrory goes on to argue that its role could be broadened and strengthened. Some of those arguments will be dealt with in Chapter 10, but here it is important to note that tribunals play an important role in holding decision-makers to account and in creating precedents.[64] Thus, the vast majority of disputes concerning the EIR 2004 have been considered by tribunals, generating in the process a body of doctrine around the Regulations.[65] Likewise, as will be seen in Chapter 18, the planning inspectorate plays an important role in shaping the planning regime. Much of this oversight activity has been ignored by legal scholars,[66] which is unfortunate as tribunals are fundamental features of the public law landscape that play a key role in regulating the environmental decision-making of public officials.

---

[63] See Robert Carnwath, 'Tribunals Justice: A New Start?' [2009] PL 48 for a discussion.
[64] Trevor Buck, 'Precedent in Tribunals and the Development of Principles' (2006) 25 CJQ 458.
[65] *Archer v Information Commissioner* [2007] UKIT EA 37; *Port of London Authority v Hibbert* [2007] UKIT EA 83.
[66] Cf Genevra Richardson and Hazel Genn, 'Tribunals in Transition: Resolution or Adjudication' [2007] PL 116.

FURTHER READING

1. There are a number of very good works on access to information, which cover the Environmental Information Regulations 2004. See Patrick Birkinshaw, *Freedom of Information: The Law, The Practice and the Ideal* (4th edn, CUP 2010) and Philip Coppel, *Information Rights* (3rd edn, Hart Publishing 2011).

2. For a very good discussion of the role of different accountability mechanisms in holding decision-makers to account in the environmental context, see Andrea Ross, *Sustainable Development Law in the UK: From Rhetoric to Reality?* (Routledge 2011) ch 10.

3. The Law Commission has recently published a report that provides an excellent overview of ombudsmen. See Law Commission, *Public Service Ombudsmen* (Law Comm No 329, 2011).

4 JUDICIAL REVIEW

Out of all the different accountability mechanisms in administrative law, judicial review has been given the most attention by lawyers. Some have criticized this, arguing that it reflects a preoccupation with courts. But another way of understanding is to see this area as one that needs considerable legal expertise to understand. Other mechanisms, while practically important, are not characterized by legal complexity of the same order. Moreover, most of the cases that you will read in this book about the operation of UK environmental regulatory regimes are judicial review cases, which cannot be fully appreciated without a firm grasp of judicial review doctrine and processes.

The purpose of this section is twofold—to provide an overview of judicial review and some of its generic and conceptual features, and to offer some examples of grounds of judicial review operating in the environmental law context. Again, it must be remembered that the reasoning in these latter cases is heavily dependent on the specific environmental regulatory regime at issue. They are also just an illustrative selection—judicial review in the environmental law context has grown exponentially over the last decade (this case law is easy to access through electronic databases),[67] and so the case examples given should not be understood as definitive examples of the law of environmental judicial review.

4.1 JUDICIAL REVIEW: A GENERAL OVERVIEW

Judicial review can be understood as review by a court of a decision by a public official to ensure that the decision-maker has not committed an *error of law*. A court thus cannot interfere with a decision simply because they happen not to like it, or because an error of fact has been committed. With that said, in some cases, errors of fact can amount to errors of law. Likewise, the distinction between fact and law is notoriously blurry. Administrative, including environmental, decisions are understood to consist of a mixture of facts, law, policy, and discretion, although decisions do not come with labels identifying which bits are which. Thus, a significant role for a reviewing court is to identify which elements of a decision are law, fact, and discretion.[68] The process of arguing judicial review cases

---

[67] <http://www.bailii.org> accessed 15 September 2012.

[68] Compare *R (on the application of Jones) v Mansfield District Council* [2003] EWCA Civ 1408, [2004] Env LR 21; and *R (on the application of Goodman) v Lewisham* [2003] EWCA Civ 140, [2003] Env LR 28.

is thus a fine-grained one in scrutinizing precise aspects of administrative decisions, and litigants cannot walk into court and simply argue that a decision was not to their liking.

From a practical perspective, judicial review actions may be brought either pursuant to a statutory section allowing appeal to the High Court for an error of law or via the common law. These two routes are now understood as allowing identical grounds of review.[69] The procedural nature of judicial review proceedings will be considered in Chapter 10 and here the focus is on the *grounds* of review. The classic starting point for understanding grounds of judicial review is Lord Diplock's obiter dicta in *Council of Civil Service Unions v Minister for the Civil Service*. That judgment came a few years after the introduction of Order 53 of the Rules of the Supreme Court in 1977, which for the first time spelled out the procedure for bringing a judicial review claim. It has now been replaced by Part 54 of the Civil Procedure Rules 1998. Lord Diplock's reasoning can be understood as an act of judicial codification of the grounds of review. The facts of the case are not relevant.

Council of Civil Service Unions v Minister for the Civil Service
[1984] AC 374 (HL) 410–11 (Lord Diplock)

Judicial review has I think developed to a stage today when without reiterating any analysis of the steps by which the development has come about, one can conveniently classify under three heads the grounds upon which administrative action is subject to control by judicial review. The first ground I would call 'illegality,' the second 'irrationality' and the third 'procedural impropriety.' That is not to say that further development on a case by case basis may not in course of time add further grounds. I have in mind particularly the possible adoption in the future of the principle of 'proportionality' which is recognised in the administrative law of several of our fellow members of the European Economic Community; but to dispose of the instant case the three already well-established heads that I have mentioned will suffice.

By 'illegality' as a ground for judicial review I mean that the decision-maker must understand correctly the law that regulates his decision-making power and must give effect to it. Whether he has or not is par excellence a justiciable question to be decided, in the event of dispute, by those persons, the judges, by whom the judicial power of the state is exercisable.

By 'irrationality' I mean what can by now be succinctly referred to as 'Wednesbury unreasonableness' (*Associated Provincial Picture Houses Ltd. v. Wednesbury Corporation* [1948] 1 KB 223). It applies to a decision which is so outrageous in its defiance of logic or of accepted moral standards that no sensible person who had applied his mind to the question to be decided could have arrived at it. Whether a decision falls within this category is a question that judges by their training and experience should be well equipped to answer, or else there would be something badly wrong with our judicial system. To justify the court's exercise of this role, resort I think is today no longer needed to Viscount Radcliffe's ingenious explanation in *Edwards v. Bairstow* [1956] A.C. 14 of irrationality as a ground for a court's reversal of a decision by ascribing it to an inferred though unidentifiable mistake of law by the decision-maker. 'Irrationality' by now can stand upon its own feet as an accepted ground on which a decision may be attacked by judicial review.

I have described the third head as 'procedural impropriety' rather than failure to observe basic rules of natural justice or failure to act with procedural fairness towards the person who will be affected by the decision. This is because susceptibility to judicial review under this head covers also failure by an administrative tribunal to observe procedural rules that are expressly laid down in the legislative instrument by which its jurisdiction is conferred, even where such failure does not involve any denial of natural justice. But the instant case is not concerned with the proceedings of an administrative tribunal at all.

---

[69] *E v Secretary of State for the Home Department* [2004] EWCA 49, [2004] QB 1044, paras 41–43.

It needs to be stressed, and stressed again, that as Beloff has put it so beautifully, Lord Diplock's judgment 'was never intended to be exhaustive, and is manifestly inadequate as a classification of all the flowers in the judicial review garden'.[70] Not only have there been many other formulations, both judicial and academic, of the grounds of review,[71] but Diplock's statement is overly general. Thus, for example, under 'illegality' may be found a whole series of grounds of review, such as improper purpose,[72] taking into account irrelevant considerations, and failing to take into account relevant considerations.[73] Further, other grounds of review, such as 'no fettering of discretion',[74] do not easily fit into Diplock's scheme and nor do other aspects of judicial review, such as discretion over whether remedies should be granted.[75] Perhaps most importantly, since Diplock's judgment, the English courts have developed new grounds of review,[76] and re-invigorated old ones. It is fair to say that there has been a process of increasing, if modest, activism on the part of the judiciary in reviewing administrative decisions.

Furthermore, Diplock's categorization ignores the role of EU law. As is clear from many chapters in this book, much UK environmental law has its source in EU environmental law and much UK legislation involves the implementation of an EU Directive. As a consequence, many environmental judicial review claims will relate to EU law matters. Thus, for example, arguments about the correct interpretation of a statutory term will often concern how such a term is interpreted in EU law.[77] Likewise, legal arguments can be raised in judicial review proceedings concerning whether a particular action is consistent with a Directive in light of the Directive having vertical direct effect.[78] Hence, English courts carrying out judicial review will often refer to Directives and the CJEU judgments interpreting those Directives. There are also some examples where the EU Treaties themselves may be a basis for a judicial review action.[79] Judges and lawyers thus cannot ignore EU law in thinking about judicial review and UK administrative law.

4.2 JUDICIAL REVIEW: CONCEPTUAL AND THEORETICAL ASPECTS

The discussion so far has focused on judicial review as a legal process, but its conceptual and theoretical aspects are also important in appreciating and critiquing how judicial review operates in practice. The last twenty years have seen an ongoing debate about the constitutional justifications for judicial review. Some scholars argue that the justification for such review lies in ensuring decision-makers adhere to their statutory mandate. Others argue that judicial review is about preventing abuse of power.[80] These, and associated debates, highlight that the theoretical underpinnings of judicial review are in no way settled. The grounds of judicial review should therefore not be understood as

---

[70] Michael Beloff, 'Judicial Review—2001: A Prophetic Odyssey' (1995) 58 MLR 143, 150.

[71] For example, *R v Hull University Visitor, ex p Page* [1993] AC 682 (HL) 701–02.

[72] *R v Somerset CC ex p Fewings* [1995] 3 All ER 20 (CA).

[73] *Barbone v Secretary of State for Transport* [2009] EWHC 463 (Admin).

[74] *In re Findlay* [1985] AC 318 (HL).

[75] It is important to remember that public law remedies are discretionary: *R (Edwards) v Environment Agency (No 2)* [2008] UKHL 22, [2008] 1 WLR 1587 and *Walton v Scottish Ministers* [2012] UKSC 44.

[76] *E* (n 69) and *R v North and East Devon Health Authority, ex p Coughlan* [2001] QB 213 (CA).

[77] There are many examples but see Chapters 19 and 20 in relation to environmental assessment and nature conservation.

[78] Case C-201/02 *Wells* [2004] ECR I-723.

[79] *R v Chief Constable of Sussex, ex p International Trader's Ferry Limited* [1998] 2 AC 418 (HL), which involved a breach of Article 34 TFEU of the then Treaty of the European Communities (TEC).

[80] Christopher Forsyth (ed), *Judicial Review and the Constitution* (Hart Publishing 2000).

neat formulas, and their application in individual cases is based on evolving and contested premises. Furthermore, as Jowell explains, the grounds of review relate to conceptual questions of institutional and constitutional competence.

Jeffrey Jowell, 'Of Vires and Vacuums: The Constitutional Context of Judicial Review'
[1999] PL 448, 451

In seeking to justify judicial review on any ground, we must surely begin with a notion of competence. In order to second-guess the primary decision-maker the courts must first establish that the decision is within their appropriate realm of decision. There are two senses of competence, *constitutional competence* and *institutional competence,* both of which are necessary to ground the court's jurisdiction. The question of constitutional competence involves a normative assessment of the proper role of institutions in a democracy. It starts with the assertion that it is not the province of courts, when judging the administration, to make their own evaluation of the public good, or to substitute their personal assessment of the social and economic advantage of a decision. We should not expect judges therefore to decide whether the country should join a common currency, or to set the level of taxation. These are matters of policy and the preserve of other branches of government and courts are not constitutionally competent to engage in them.

The question of institutional competence involves a practical evaluation of the capacity of decision making bodies to make certain decisions. It starts with the recognition that some matters are not ideally justiciable. It thus focuses not upon the appropriate role of the judge, but upon the inherent limitations of the process of adjudication. This is because courts are limited in their capacity to decide matters which admit of no generalised or objective determination. Such matters (such as whether a local authority's expenditure was 'excessive', or the question of a university department's rating for research), are not amenable to decision by a non-specialist. In addition, the adjudicative process is not ideally suited to deciding polycentric questions—those which cannot be settled in isolation from others which are not before the court—such as whether scarce resources should be allocated to one project or proposal in preference to others whose claims are not in issue.

The discussion of constitutional competence is a useful reminder that constitutional law plays a constant background role in judicial review actions. The discussion of institutional competence is highly relevant in relation to environmental decision-making, which is characteristically polycentric (see Section 2.1 of Chapter 2). These two types of competence will have an important influence on the nature of judicial review, as explained by Fisher (in the context of a broader discussion on the legal role of precautionary principle).

Elizabeth Fisher, 'Is the Precautionary Principle Justiciable?' (2001) 13 JEL 315, 321–22

What are understood to be the constitutional and institutional competences of a court are closely interrelated. Moreover, such understandings have a powerful influence on judicial review and their impact can be seen in three main facets of judicial review doctrine. First, some issues are ruled as being inappropriate subjects for review. High level policy issues are an excellent example of this. Second, the grounds of judicial review are shaped by the courts understanding of their competence. Until recently the court saw themselves limited to a discrete number of questions of law. Even now with the 'jettisoning [of] many of the conceptual barriers' which had held back the development of more intensive judicial review doctrines this has not changed. While the courts and commentators may describe judicial review as being concerned with 'principles of good administration' the doctrines of judicial review are still limited. As noted by Jowell, matters of *procedure* are far more likely to be understood as matters within the courts' competence than matters of substance. Likewise in regards to matters of substance, the courts are far happier dealing with the *process* by which the decision was made (improper purpose, relevant and irrelevant considerations etc) rather than ruling on the whether the final *impact* of the decision was the correct one.

The final way in which issues of competence manifest themselves is in regards to the *intensity* of review. Whether courts are reviewing the procedures or process by which a decision was made or even its impact they will exhibit varying degrees of self-restraint. While courts may be happy to review on a certain ground, for reasons of competence, that review may be minimal because they feel the decision is beyond their expertise, is finely balanced or polycentric. Thus, the courts in scrutinising a decision will defer to the decision-maker.

All this means that raising a ground of judicial review is not like throwing a basketball slam dunk into a hoop—under each ground of review there are a number of issues for courts to consider. More specifically, and as already noted, in relation to environmental law, issues of institutional competence loom large due to the polycentric and often highly politicized nature of decisions, as well as the role of expertise in environmental decision-making. Consider Collins J's statement in the Divisional Court in *Downs*, a judicial review case challenging the lawfulness of UK measures implementing the EU Plant Products Directive (91/414/EEC) concerning the control of pesticides. A range of arguments were put before Collins J relating to the adequacy of a scientific model used by DEFRA in assessing the risks of pesticides to bystanders. Some of the arguments concerned the scientific adequacy of the model, and others concerned legal adequacy, in light of the operation of the EU Directive.

Downs v Secretary of State for Environment, Food and Rural Affairs
[2008] EWHC 2666 (Admin), para 38 (Collins J)

I am not qualified to decide between those views nor is it an appropriate exercise for a judge to undertake on judicial review. No doubt if it were clear that one view was tainted by irrationality in the *Wednesbury* sense, the court could so declare. But that is most unlikely to be established and, as it seems to me, we are here at the very fringe of what should properly be the subject of judicial review. As May LJ said in a different context in *R(Campaign to End All Animal Experiments) v Secretary of State for the Home Department* [2008] EWCA Civ 417 in paragraph 1:-

'The scientific judgment is not immune from lawyers' analysis. But the court must be careful not to substitute its own inexpert view of the science for a tenable expert opinion.'

Collins J is rightly highlighting the fact that he should not review questions of fact in a judicial review action. The problem is that, in practice, it is often the *assessment* of the facts that provides the rationale and basis for a decision and thus gives rise to legal grounds of review. Hence, in *Downs*, the legal issue was whether DEFRA had complied with the relevant EU Directive.[81] In other cases, the assessment

---

[81] He found that it had not so complied but this was reversed on appeal. See *Downs* (n 48) and *Secretary of State for Environment, Food and Rural Affairs v Downs* (n 59).

of facts can give rise to arguments concerning statutory interpretation,[82] procedural fairness,[83] irrationality,[84] and the taking into account of relevant and irrelevant considerations.[85] In other words, while the fact/law distinction is fundamental to the operation of judicial review, it is constantly being blurred or crossed in the context of environmental law since factual assessment is closely interwoven with questions about the legality of decisions. The fact that judges are required to engage with environmental facts on some level in judicial review cases is one of the reasons why there have been arguments for a specialist environmental court (see Section 3 of Chapter 10).

4.3 EXAMPLES OF GROUNDS OF REVIEW IN ENVIRONMENTAL LAW CASES

This section gives a handful of examples of different grounds of judicial review operating in the environmental law context. Each of them makes clear the complexity and craft involved in judicially reviewing an environmental administrative decision. In analysing these cases, four things are important to remember. First, isolated examples are extracted from the different cases. In practice, a range of different grounds of review will be argued simultaneously in a case. Second, the reasoning of the cases is heavily dependent on the specific facts and legislative framework at issue. Third, these grounds are legal devices by which to raise the range of legal issues discussed throughout this textbook—from the meaning of 'waste' (Chapter 16) and the protection of nature conservation areas (Chapter 20), to the application of planning rules (Chapter 18) and pollution control regimes (Chapters 14, 15, and 17). The proper and lawful application of these regimes is most often challenged through judicial review actions, which involve answering all manner of legal questions in these different areas of environmental law. Fourth, the application of these different grounds of judicial review to a decision in a particular circumstance reflects the skill of a lawyer to relate existing grounds of review to an administrative decision that they wish to challenge. To put the matter another way, when making a decision, a decision-maker is not explicitly recognizing that there are legal flaws in the process he applies or leaving obvious markers to identify such flaws. Rather, it is the role of a lawyer to identify them by carefully construing the decision-making process.

The grounds of judicial review are not static and the history of their development in the twentieth century was long and torturous. As we have already made clear, Diplock's three grounds of review are just one step in this process of development. Since the early 1990s, English courts have also made it apparent that they will intervene in relation to errors of law.[86] How this principle operates, and what it means, is by no means straightforward, as we have already seen. It is not helped by terminological overlap. Thus, each of Diplock's three grounds may be understood broadly as errors of law, but the first head of review is also referred to discretely as 'illegality'. In broad terms, if there is an error in interpreting a statute or an EU Directive, then this can amount to an error of law.[87] Many examples of such (alleged) legal errors are seen throughout this book. Good examples can be seen in relation to environmental assessment (Chapter 19), concerning how the categories in Schedules 1 and 2 of the Environmental Impact Assessment Regulations,[88] which are central to the environmental assessment scheme, should be interpreted.[89]

---

[82] *Morge v Hampshire County Council* [2011] UKSC 2, [2011] 1 WLR 268.

[83] *R (Eisai Ltd) v NICE* [2008] EWCA Civ 438, (2008) 11 CCL Rep 385.

[84] *R (Friends of Basildon Golf Course) v Basildon District Council* [2010] EWCA Civ 1432, [2011] Env LR 16.

[85] *Badger Trust v The Welsh Ministers* [2010] EWCA Civ 807, [2010] 6 Costs LR 896.

[86] *Page* (n 71).   [87] *Morge* (n 82) although the argument failed in that case.

[88] Town and Country Planning (Environmental Impact Assessment) Regulations 2011, SI 2011/1824.

[89] Note most of these cases were considered under the 1999 Regulations (SI 1999/293), now replaced with the 2011 Regulations, but the Schedules remain basically the same.

R (on the application of Goodman) v Lewisham LBC
[2003] EWCA Civ 140 paras 7–8, 13–14 (Buxton LJ)

The Facts

The applicants challenged the respondent's grant of planning permission to the interested party on the basis that development fell into Sch.2 para.10(b) of the Town and Country Planning (Environmental Impact Assessment) (England and Wales) Regulations 1999 as it amounted to 'a infrastructure projects that are urban development projects'.

The CA

7. The first question for a planning authority is, therefore, to determine whether the application before it is a 'Schedule 2 application': that is [...] whether the development falls within the descriptions and limits set out in Schedule 2. Although the application becomes a Schedule 2 application by decision of the authority; and does not thereafter become an application for EIA development unless the authority further so decides; the authority cannot avoid the implications of the application being for EIA development simply by not taking the preliminary decisions at all. That is clear from the observations of Lord Hoffmann (albeit in relation to the obligations of the Secretary of State under an earlier version of the Regulations, the Town and Country Planning (Assessment of Environmental Effects) Regulations 1988) in *Berkeley v Secretary of State for the Environment* [2001] 2 AC 603 at pp 614G–615A. The authority is bound to enter upon consideration of whether the application is for Schedule 2 development unless it can be said that no reasonable authority could think that to be the case: *Berkeley*, loc.cit. If the development is found to be a Schedule 2 development, responsibilities of the same order attach to the authority's consideration of whether it is an EIA development.

8. In the present case, the only serious contender for a category of Schedule 2 development under which the application might fall is paragraph 10(b) of the Schedule: infrastructure projects that are urban development projects. These are very wide and to some extent obscure expressions, and a good deal of legitimate disagreement will be involved in applying them to the facts of any given case. That emboldened Lewisham to argue, and the judge to agree, that such a determination on the part of the local authority could only be challenged if it were *Wednesbury* unreasonable. I do not agree. However fact-sensitive such a determination may be, it is not simply a finding of fact, nor of discretionary judgement. Rather, it involves the application of the authority's understanding of the meaning in law of the expression used in the Regulation. If the authority reaches an understanding of those expressions that is wrong as a matter of law, then the court must correct that error: and in determining the meaning of the statutory expressions the concept of reasonable judgement as embodied in *Wednesbury* simply has no part to play. That, however, is not the end of the matter. The meaning in law may itself be sufficiently imprecise that in applying it to the facts, as opposed to determining what the meaning was in the first place, a range of different conclusions may be legitimately available. That approach to decision-making was emphasised by Lord Mustill, speaking for the House of Lords, in *R v Monopolies Commission ex p South Yorkshire Transport Ltd* [1993] 1 WLR 23 at p 32G, when he said that there may be cases where the criterion, upon which in law the decision has to be made,

'may itself be so imprecise that different decision-makers, each acting rationally, might reach differing conclusions when applying it to the facts of a given case. In such a case the court is entitled to substitute its own opinion for that of the person to whom the decision has been entrusted only if the decision is so aberrant that it cannot be classed as rational.'

Buxton LJ then went on to apply this approach to the facts of this case.

> 13. [...] 'Infrastructure project' and 'urban development project' are terms of wide ambit, perhaps more easily understood by those versed in planning policy than by mere lawyers, and attracting the observations of Lord Mustill quoted in §8 above. But the examples of urban development projects set out in paragraph 10(b) of the Regulation demonstrate that in this instance 'infrastructure" goes wider, indeed far wider, than the normal understanding, as quoted to us from the *Shorter Oxford Dictionary*, of 'the installations and services (power stations, sewers, roads, housing, etc) regarded as the economic foundations of a country'. I am unable to accept that a storage and distribution facility (particularly when, as in the present case, it provides services to business and the community at large, and is not simply a private operation), however large and extensive, can never be reasonably regarded as part of the infrastructure as understood in the Regulations. Nor can I accept the contention of Mr Lindblom QC, in his helpfully succinct submissions on behalf of the interested party, that some assistance can be gained from the fact that storage is specifically referred to in other paragraphs of Schedule 2 , but not in paragraph 10 with which we are concerned. The storage there referred to is ancillary to the major operations controlled, of the energy industry. The storage with which we are concerned is a general and free-standing operation that must be assessed on the basis of its own function in the general economy. Indeed, it may well have been the absence of any specific reference to storage in the examples of urban development projects given in paragraph 10(b) that misled Miss Sterry into thinking that any storage function was necessarily excluded from that definition.
>
> 14. I accordingly consider that the view taken by Lewisham of the reach of paragraph 10(b) was outside the range of reasonable responses that was open to that authority.

As will be seen in Chapter 19, this case has played a foundational role in how courts review decisions concerning assessment of whether a project is 'likely to have a significant effect on the environment'. Issues concerning statutory interpretation can be seen in relation to a number of other regimes as well.[90] An often litigated example is the question of what constitutes a 'material consideration' in the context of planning law.[91] While courts decide legal points in these cases, they will also often defer to the interpretation of an expert decision-maker or to their application of the contested statutory term to the facts.[92]

Other 'illegality' grounds of judicial review, which also engage questions of statutory interpretation, involve the failure to take into account relevant considerations and taking into account irrelevant considerations. These grounds relate to the errors of law because what amounts to a relevant or irrelevant consideration is not a subjective choice but is dependent on the wording and structure of the regulatory regime at issue. While the question of relevancy turns on the legislative framework in many cases, it can also turn on policy guidance and other documents—the full statutory and regulatory context is significant.[93] It is also important to remember that, while a court will be willing to determine what is relevant and irrelevant, it will not rule what weight should be given to any particular factor.[94] The *R (People and Planet) v HM Treasury* case example gives some feeling for how this ground of judicial review operates in practice.

---

[90] For example, *R (Boggis) v Natural England* [2009] EWCA Civ 1061, [2010] 1 All ER 159 in the nature conservation context.

[91] See Section 5.1 of Chapter 18.

[92] For example, *Tesco Stores Ltd v Secretary of State for the Environment* [1995] 1 WLR 759 (HL) and *R (Fisher) v English Nature* [2004] EWCA Civ 663, [2005] 1 WLR 147. See Section 3.1 of Chapter 20.

[93] *T-Mobile UK Ltd v The First Secretary of State* [2004] EWCA Civ 1763, [2005] Env LR 18.

[94] *Barbone* (n 73).

R (People and Planet) v HM Treasury
[2009] EWHC 3020 (Admin) paras 21–30 (Sales J)

The Facts

The applicant brought an action of judicial review in regards to the HM Treasury's 70% ownership of the Royal Bank of Scotland (which is owned by a Treasury owned company—UK Financial Investment Ltd ('UKFI')). The applicant's argument was that through their shareholding, the Treasury should persuade RBS to adopt lending practices that were more protective of the environment and human rights than their current lending practices. In relation to this argument they stated that HM Treasury should be bound by the *Green Book—Appraisal and Valuation in Central Government*. HM Treasury were not operating under legislation but under their common law powers and Sales J made it clear that in doing so they were subject to 'public law principle'.

The HC

21 In my judgment, the legal framework is important here. HM Treasury was exercising the common law powers of the Crown in deciding what to do in relation to the management of its investment in UKFI and, through UKFI, in RBS. HM Treasury had a very wide discretion as to the matters which should be taken into account or left out of account in formulating its policy.

22. Next, it is relevant to refer to the nature of the Green Book. The Green Book contains guidance as to the general approach to formation of policy in relation to the whole of central government. It does not lay down a prescriptive regime setting out clear indications of what are to be treated as mandatory relevant considerations or as irrelevant considerations in any particular evaluation exercise. This much is clear both from its general context and its purpose. It is a document which is addressed to the formulation of all forms of government policy and, clearly, having regard to the very wide area of activity which it covers and provides guidance for, it is not intended to be highly prescriptive.

23. In that regard, I refer in particular to paragraph 1.1 of the Green Book, which provides:

'All new policies, programmes and projects, whether revenue, capital or regulatory, should be subject to comprehensive but proportionate assessment, wherever it is practicable, so as best to promote the public interest. The Green Book presents the techniques and issues that should be considered when carrying out assessments.

The purpose of the Green Book is to ensure that no policy or project is adopted without first having the answer to these questions:

- Are there better ways to achieve this objective?
- Are there better uses for these resources?'

24 Paragraph 2.25 of the Green Book states (with emphasis added):

'There is a wide range of generic issues that may need to be considered as part of any assessment. The following listed should be checked for relevance to options under appraisal, and used for later evaluations:

- Strategic impact- new proposals can be said to have strategic impacts on organisations if they significantly affect the whole or major part of an organisation over the medium to long term. Proposals should therefore be considered in terms of their potential scale of impact, and how they fit in with the strategy of the organisation(s) they affect.
- Economic rationale - proposals need to be underpinned by sound economic analysis, which should be provided by a cost benefit analysis in an option appraisal. See Chapter 5 in particular.

- Financial arrangements and affordability - proposals need to be affordable, and an affordable financial plan needs to be developed. See Chapter 6.

- Achievability - all proposals should be assessed for their achievability, and recognised programme and project management arrangements set up as necessary. See Chapter 6.

- Commercial and partnering arrangements - proposals need to take account of commercial, partnering and procurement arrangements; what can be delivered in the market; how costs and benefits can guaranteed through commercial arrangements; how contracts will be managed through to completion. See Chapter 6.

- Regulatory impact - as discussed previously, the impacts of new proposals on businesses, voluntary sector and charities should be assessed. See Chapter 2.

- Legislation - consideration should be given to legislation specific to the case in hand, as well as statutes that affect many proposals, such as the Human Right Act, or the Data Protection and Freedom of Information Acts.

- Information management and control - The information requirements of proposals, including the data needed for later evaluation, and the supporting IT that may be required. Further guidance is available from the OGC.

- Environmental impacts - The effects on the environment should be considered, including air and water quality, land use, noise pollution, and waste production, recycling and disposal. Further guidance is available from ODPM, Defra and DFT.

- Rural issues - The government is committed to ensuring that all its policies take account of specific rural circumstances. Appraisers should assess whether proposals are likely to have a different impact in rural areas from elsewhere. Further guidance is available from Defra.

- Equality - Impacts on various groups in society should be considered as part of an appraisal. Chapter 5 describes how distributional impacts should be brought into the appraisal process... [etc] ...'

25. In my judgment, these passages underline the point that policy-makers retain a large measure of discretion as to what considerations they may take into account or leave out of account when conducting an assessment in accordance with the Green Book in formulating policies and taking decisions. The Green Book left HM Treasury with a very wide discretion to decide what factors to treat as relevant or weighty or not for the purposes of formulating its policy in respect of UKFI, in accordance with ordinary principles of public law (as illustrated by *CREEDNZ v Governor General* [1981] 1 NZLR 172 , 183; *Re Findlay* [1985] AC 318 , 333-334; and *Tesco Stores Ltd v Secretary of State for the Environment* [1995] 1 WLR 759). The Green Book also left HM Treasury a wide discretion to decide what investigations it thought were required to inform itself about relevant factors applying the guidance in *Secretary of State for Education and Science v Tameside MBC* [1977] AC 1014 .

26. In the present case, paragraphs 3 and 10 to 13 of the Green Book assessment, in particular, show that regard was had by HM Treasury to environmental and human rights considerations in the formulation of the policy. As with all reasons for administrative decisions, the approach of the court is strongly against trawling with a fine tooth comb through reasons which are given looking for errors. Even after looking carefully for errors, I can detect no arguable error here.

27. The primary objective for the policy is properly identified in paragraph 6 of the Green Book assessment, which identified a consideration of very great weight. HM Treasury was perfectly entitled to give the factor identified there that weight. That paragraph inevitably then affects the reasoning in the rest of the document and the extent to which consideration of other matters was required in order to arrive at a conclusion in accordance with the Green Book procedure.

28. Paragraphs 3 and 10 of the Green Book assessment show that environmental and human rights considerations were taken into account. Paragraphs 12 and 13 show that a sensible reconciliation of

those factors with the main consideration set out at paragraph 6 was identified as being available. In the context of that reasoning, it was not necessary under the Green Book approach for HM Treasury to analyse the matter further.

29. It is also relevant that any analysis of what could in practice be done in relation to RBS, which might be capable of affecting its dealings in respect of particular projects, would be likely to be very onerous and difficult. That underlines, in my view, the rationality of the approach adopted here by HM Treasury.

30. Accordingly, in my judgment there is no arguable case identified by the claimant based on that particular ground of challenge.

This case shows how the ground of relevant considerations is closely constrained by the legal and policy framework. Even in this context, without any relevant legislation, this ground of review does not operate independently from the legal regime involved. The case also shows how a judge will not rule on what weight should be given to a particular relevant consideration.

Questions concerning relevancy can quickly slip into questions concerning irrationality—Diplock's second ground of review, also often described as *Wednesbury* unreasonableness.[95] This ground of review has a certain appeal in environmental law where challenges to the rationality of decision-making are a constant theme (see Section 4 and Chapter 2). However, while there are many examples of *Wednesbury* unreasonableness being pleaded, in both planning and other environmental cases, these arguments rarely succeed.[96] This is because this ground of review raises the issues of institutional and constitutional competence highlighted by Jowell. An argument about irrationality can look too close to an argument about the merits of a particular decision, which is beyond the institutional, and arguably the constitutional, competence of the courts.[97]

This area has become further complicated by the new action of 'illegality' introduced by s 6 of the *Human Rights Act 1998*. Under ECHR review, where an ECHR right allows for interference by the state on certain grounds (as under Articles 8, 9, 10, and 11), that interference can only be justified and valid if it is proportionate. The relationship between proportionality review and *Wednesbury* unreasonableness is often understood as a close one,[98] although the courts have made it clear that review under the HRA and under the grounds of judicial review are distinct.[99]

The situation is different in relation to Diplock's third ground of review—procedural impropriety—in relation to which there are more successful claims in environmental cases. This is a ground that includes procedural flaws under specific statutes and the common law ground of procedural fairness. The relationship between statutory and common law procedural impropriety is very close due to the fact that what is procedurally fair will depend on the statutory context, although it is important to distinguish between regimes that explicitly and implicitly grant procedural rights. Where a statute sets out a procedure explicitly, the role of the court is simply to enforce that procedure. This is very different from when a statute sets out no or minimal procedure and the courts apply common law principles of procedural fairness.

The environmental assessment regime (Chapter 19) is an example of one that grants procedural rights explicitly. As a ground of review, procedural impropriety also covers the requirement that a decision-maker should not be biased.[100] While it is very difficult to say anything very general about procedural fairness, the discussion by the Court of Appeal in *Edwards v Environment Agency* is instructive.

---

[95] *Associated Provincial Picture Houses Ltd v Wednesbury Corporation* [1948] 1 KB 223 (CA).

[96] For example, *R (Newport City Council) v The Welsh Minsters* [2009] EWHC 3149 (Admin); *R (Cheshire East BC) v Secretary of State for Environment Food and Rural Affairs* [2011] EWHC 1975, [2011] NPC 92.

[97] See the discussion on this point in *Secretary of State for Environment, Food and Rural Affairs v Downs* (n 59) in the CA.

[98] *R v Secretary of State for the Home Department, ex p Daly* [2001] UKHL 26, [2001] 2 AC 532.

[99] *Belfast City Council v Misbehavin' Ltd* [2007] UKHL 19, [2007] 1 WLR 1420.

[100] *R (Island Farm Development Ltd) v Bridgend CBC* [2006] EWHC 2189.

R (Edwards) v Environment Agency (No 2)
[2006] EWCA Civ 877 paras 90–94, 105–6 (Auld LJ)

The Facts

Edwards challenged the granting of an IPPC permit by the Environment Agency to a company for the operation of a cement plant, including the burning of waste tyres as a substitute for conventional fuel. Among the arguments put before the court was the argument that the Environment Agency had breached a common law duty of fairness for failing to disclose certain scientific (AQMAU) reports as part of the consultation process. The relevant regulations set out some requirements for consultation.

The CA

90. It is an accepted general principle of administrative law that a public body undertaking consultation must do so fairly as required by the circumstances of the case. Lord Woolf MR, as he then was, giving the judgment of this Court in *R v North Devon HA, ex p Coughlan* [2001] QB 213, at paragraph 112, articulated and stated the limitations of this principle in the following terms:

'… consultation is not litigation: the consulting authority is not required to publicise every submission it receives or (absent some statutory obligation) to disclose all its advice. Its obligation is to let those who have a potential interest in the subject matter know in clear terms what the proposal is and exactly why it is under positive consideration, telling them enough (which may be a good deal) to enable them to make an intelligent response. The obligation, although it may be quite onerous, goes no further than this.'

91. Focusing more closely on the issue thrown up by this case, namely whether fairness in decision-making subject to public consultation requires internal workings of a decision-maker also to be disclosed as part of the consultation, the answer given by the House of Lords in *Bushell & Anor v Secretary of State for the Environment* [1981] AC 75 and in a number of other authorities since, is generally not. In Bushell, Lord Diplock, with the agreement of the majority, expressed the principle in the context of a minister's decision-making role on his department's motorway proposal, in which the minister took into account governmental policy as to the method of assessing future traffic growth, unavailable or unpublicised at the material time. He said, at 95E–96A and 102E/F:

'[…] What is fair procedure is to be judged […] in the light of the practical realities as to the way in which administrative decisions involving forming judgments based on technical considerations are reached. […] Discretion in making administrative decisions is conferred upon a minister not as an individual but as the holder of an office in which he will have available to him in arriving at his decision the collective knowledge, experience and expertise of all those who served the Crown in the department of which, for the time being, he is the political head. The collective knowledge, technical as well as factual, of the civil servants in the department and their collective expertise is to be treated as the minister's own knowledge, his own expertise. … This is an integral part of the decision-making process itself; it is not to be equiperated with the minister receiving evidence, expert opinion or advice from sources outside the department after the local inquiry has been closed. […]

Once he has reached his decision he must be prepared to disclose his reasons for it, […] but he is, in my view, under no obligation to disclose to objectors and give them an opportunity of commenting on advice, expert or otherwise, which he receives from his department in the course of making up his mind. If he thinks that to do so will be helpful to him in reaching the right decision in the public interest he may, of course, do so; but if he does not think it will be helpful — and this is for him to decide — failure to do so cannot in my view be treated as a denial of natural justice to the objectors.'

92. The House of Lords approved and applied those observations in *R (Alconbury Developments Ltd) v Secretary of State for the Environment, Transport and the Regions* [2003] 2 AC 295—again in the context of a ministerial decision involving considerations of policy as well as judgment on the instant facts in a planning context. However, Lord Clyde, at paragraph 141, expressed an important qualification that parties should be allowed to comment if 'some significant factual material of which the parties might not be aware comes to his notice through departmental inquiry'.

93. Lord Diplock's rationale in Bushell for internal decision-making not being an apt candidate for disclosure does not, in my view, indicate an intention by him to establish a rule so absolute that it would override in particular circumstances the requirement of fairness, the conceptual setting in which he was considering the disclosability or non-disclosability of internal decision-making. The need expressed by Lord Clyde in Alconbury for a more pragmatic approach when circumstances demand it, were presaged by Lord Diplock himself in his speech in *Bushell*, at 96D:

'Fairness ... also requires that the objectors should be given sufficient information about the reasons relied on by the department as justifying the draft scheme to enable them to challenge the accuracy of any facts and the validity of any arguments on which the departmental reasons are based.'

94. Thus, if in the course of decision-making a decision-maker becomes aware of a new factor, as in *Interbrew SA v Competition Commission* [2001] EWHC Admin 367, or some internal material of potential significance to the decision to be made, as in *R v Secretary of State for Health, ex p United States Tobacco International Inc* [1992] QB, 353, CA , at 370–371 (per Taylor LJ) and 376 (per Morland J), fairness may demand that the party or parties concerned should be given an opportunity to deal with it.

Auld LJ found that the case was not covered by Bushell. He noted, in particular, two important points.

105. First, AQMAU, in conducting its modelling, did so only in relation to the predicted emissions from the burning of waste tyres and, for the purpose, obtained additional information from Rugby Ltd going to the predicted environmental impact of the proposals, which was not put in the public domain until the Agency issued its Decision Document. Secondly, for the reasons given by the Judge in that paragraph, the highly technical nature of AQMAU's predictions and the possible significance of their conclusions were such that their non-disclosure in the consultation process cannot be dismissed as unimportant. For one thing, as Mr Wolfe emphasized, the Agency, in its Decision Document, distanced itself from AQMAU's predictions. Moreover, those predictions were, as the Judge described them, highly specialized, breaking new ground and going beyond merely testing or verifying material in the application and in the public domain. They clearly raised subjects potentially—I stress the word 'potentially'—important to an adequate assessment of the proposal of which interested members of the public were unaware and might well fail to examine for themselves. The fact that no environmental damage has, as yet, resulted from the proposal is, it seems to me, no more of an answer to a finding of a breach of a common law obligation in such a context than it is to a breach of a legislative obligation; cf. *Thornby Farms v Daventry DC* [2003] QB 503, CA, per Pill LJ at para 60.

106. In short, the non-disclosure of the AQMAU Reports left the public in ignorance, until the Agency's grant of the permit, of the only full information as to the extent of the low level emissions of dust and the only information at all on their possible impact on the environment. I agree with the Judge that such information was potentially material to the Agency's decision and to the members of the public who were seeking to influence it, and that failure by the Agency to disclose it at the time was a breach of its common law duty of fairness to disclose it. It does not follow, however, that they were thereby 'clearly and materially disadvantaged' as Mr Wolfe maintained.

Despite this being the case, the Court of Appeal agreed with the Divisional Court's refusal to grant relief. The case was then appealed on other grounds to the House of Lords. While the issue of breach of procedural fairness at common law was not the subject of the appeal, Lord Hoffmann commented on the matter.

R (Edwards) v Environment Agency (No 2)
[2008] UKHL 22, [2008] 1 WLR 1587 para 44 (Lord Hoffmann)

44. The third basis for the duty of consultation is that the Agency owed a duty of fairness at common law to disclose one or both of the AQMAU documents: see *Regina v. North and East Devon Health Authority, Ex p Coughlan* [2001] QB 213. It was, it was said, a procedural irregularity not to do so. This argument was accepted by Lindsay J (at paras 42–64) and the Court of Appeal (paras 86–106). There is no challenge to this finding in the Agency's printed case and I shall therefore not spend much time upon it, except to say briefly that I would not have come to the same conclusion. The IPPC directive specifies with some precision what information should be made available to the public. The regulations both give effect to these requirements and extend them. When the whole question of public involvement has been considered and dealt with in detail by the legislature, I do not think it is for the courts to impose a broader duty. Secondly, the AQMAU documents were part of the Agency's decision-making process, prepared after a lengthy period of public consultation. If the Agency has to disclose its internal working documents for further public consultation, there is no reason why the process should ever come to an end.

Many points can be taken from this line of cases. First, as made clear by *Bushell*, the concept of procedural fairness does not amount to full disclosure. Second, as already stressed, determining what the duty of fairness means in any particular situation will depend upon the legal framework at issue. A complexity in this case, as in many environmental law cases, is that the source of the framework is in EU law. Third, the difference of opinion between the Court of Appeal and Lord Hoffmann in the House of Lords highlights the fact that what is procedurally fair is open to interpretation. Fourth, questions of procedural fairness relate to a number of other grounds of review, including legitimate expectations (a significant ground of review in its own right)[101] and Article 6 of the ECHR. The final point to note in this case is that the issue of procedural fairness is intertwined with both issues of participation and methods of scientific analysis. It provides yet another example of the blurring of the fact/law divide. This is also one of a number of recent cases in which procedural fairness issues have been raised in relation to consultation exercises.[102]

FURTHER READING

1. The discussion in Section 4 provides but a few examples of environmental judicial review. A brilliant overview of judicial review in the environmental law context is Richard Moules, *Environmental Judicial Review* (Hart Publishing 2011).

2. It is interesting to note how judicial review challenges often cluster around particular issues. Airport expansion is a case in point. See *Wandsworth LBC v Secretary of State for Transport* [2005] EWHC 20 (Admin); *Barbone v Secretary of State for Transport* [2009] EWHC 463 (Admin); *R (Hillingdon LBC) v Secretary of State for Transport* [2010] EWHC 626 (Admin).

---

[101] Legitimate expectations can be both procedural or substantive, the former ground overlapping significantly with the procedural impropriety ground—see, for example, *Greenpeace* (n 49).

[102] For example, *Greenpeace* (n 49) and *Bard* (n 52).

5 THE HUMAN RIGHTS ACT 1998

Much of the discussion so far in this chapter involves individuals exercising legal rights in relation to environmental problems—particularly through participation in decision-making or bringing judicial review actions or other appeals. We have already noted that these rights are often novel in nature and come in many different forms, depending often on the statutory context of the environmental regimes involved. Distinct from these rights, albeit overlapping in their potential application, are rights that relate to environmental protection, which are understood to have a more constitutional status.[103] There is a vast scholarly literature concerned with constitutional environmental rights and human rights. These rights are distinct from those already discussed in that they are understood to be meta-principles that override other considerations, and focus on achieving substantive environmental protection outcomes. They thus address directly the types of problems that arise due to the novel nature of environmental interests. While arguments for such rights can be powerful, the reality is that, in the UK, their role has been minimal. The reason for this is very simple. There is no constitutional right to environmental protection, and the related human rights that exist do not easily relate to environmental issues. This section briefly considers the role of the European Convention on Human Rights (ECHR) and the Human Rights Act 1998 (HRA) in relation to environmental law. Note that the issue of environmental rights is not only relevant to public law but has implications also for private law and for the role of the courts (see Chapters 6 and 10).

The primary source of human rights in UK public law is the HRA, which implements the ECHR.[104] The HRA places a number of duties on public authorities. Section 2 requires a court or tribunal to 'take into account' any judgment, decision, or advisory opinion of the European Court of Human Rights. Section 3 requires that primary and subordinate legislation 'must be read and given effect in a way which is compatible with the Convention Rights' and, if this cannot be done, courts can make a declaration of incompatibility (section 4).[105] Section 6 makes it 'unlawful for a public authority to act in a way which is incompatible with a Convention right'. Section 8 allows courts to grant a range of remedies for breaches of Convention rights, including damages in certain circumstances. There have been a number of cases that address the implications of the HRA for private law which are dealt with in Chapter 6. The focus here is on the public law implications of the HRA.

The HRA has had a significant impact on UK public law, but its effect on environmental law has not been significant. This is mainly due to the nature of the rights protected by the ECHR, as explained by Morrow.

K Morrow, 'Worth the Paper they are Written On? Human Rights and the Environment in the Law of England and Wales' (2010) 1 JHRE 66, 67–68

Established instruments such as the 1950 European Convention on Human Rights (ECHR) provide for both procedural rights and substantive rights. While the ECHR contains no rights pertaining

---

[103] Roderick Nash, *The Rights of Nature* (University of Wisconsin Press 1989); Tim Hayward, *Constitutional Environmental Rights* (OUP 2004).

[104] Also note that the ECHR has some legal effect through EU law. In the context of EU law, there is also the Charter of Fundamental Rights. The legal effect of this document is so far marginal in relation to UK environmental law and so is not discussed in this chapter.

[105] Such a declaration does not quash an offending statute, but Parliament must take it into account and decide how to proceed in light of it (considering also the fact that the UK government will be accountable under the ECHR for any Convention violation).

directly to the environment (as indeed is to be expected of a document of its vintage), the European Court of Human Rights has adopted an innovative approach to its jurisprudence in general which has had important ramifications for its application to environmental matters. Chief among the procedural rights that have provided fruitful ground in this regard is Article 6 (the right to a fair hearing), and in the substantive rights category, Articles 8 (the right to respect for family and private life) and 1 to the First Protocol (the right to peaceful enjoyment of possessions) are of most significance for the purposes of this paper. Under these heads, environmental claims, have, on occasion been recognized as an adjunct to, or perhaps more accurately, contingent upon recognized substantive Convention rights, notably in landmark cases such as *Lopez Ostra v Spain, Guerra v Italy* and *Fadeyeva v Russia*. That said, there are some significant limitations on the viability of the ECHR in environmental cases, not least being that the regime applies only to actual harm, risk is not covered and thus the protection offered on the ground is decidedly limited. Another significant factor curtailing the impact of the ECHR in environmental cases lies in the fact that the Convention offers only limited access to the courts for nongovernmental organizations (NGOs) raising public interest cases. While such groups can bring cases, and indeed in the environmental sphere they are frequent litigants on all legal stages, under the Convention they are subject to the general requirement imposed by Article 34 that substantive rights must have been violated in order to proceed. This can prove particularly problematic as such groups are often better positioned to invoke generally applicable procedural rights than substantive claims.

A further problem is that, in deciding whether a breach of a Convention right is proportional, the ECHR applies a 'margin of appreciation'.[106] This effectively means that a court conducting human rights review will not immediately intervene in a case where a Convention right is breached. In the UK context, this has translated sometimes uneasily into courts showing deference to public authorities in relation to Convention rights questions.[107]

Chapter 6 included some analysis of the role of the HRA and ECHR in considering conflicts between environmental protection and private property rights and discussed *R (Trailer & Marina (Leven) Ltd) v Secretary of State for the Environment, Food & Rural Affairs*,[108] which was a challenge to nature conservation legislation under Article 1 of the ECHR Protocol 1. There are other examples of HRA claims being argued in environmental cases[109] including, for example, those that involve different rights such as freedom of assembly.[110] Overall, these cases show that the relationship between environmental protection and human rights is not a natural one. Indeed, as we saw in *Trailer*, environmental law actions based on the HRA are challenges to action taken by public officials to *promote* environmental protection but which is considered to interfere with another human right.[111]

Some UK environmental law cases raising Convention issues have gone to the European Court of Human Rights (ECtHR).[112] An extract from a recent case brought against the UK in the ECtHR is included here. The analysis in the case was lengthy and here we only extract some of the arguments raised.

---

[106] *Handyside v UK* App no 5493/72 (ECHR 7 December 1976).

[107] For example, *R (ProLife Alliance) v BBC* [2003] UKHL 23, [2004] 1 AC 185;

[108] [2004] EWCA Civ 1580, [2005] 1 WLR 1267. See Chapter 6.

[109] For example, *Secretary of State for Environment, Food and Rural Affairs v Downs* (n 59), paras 106–114.

[110] *Kay v Commissioner of The Police of The Metropolis* [2008] UKHL 69, [2008] 1 WLR 2723.

[111] *R (Alconbury Developments Ltd) v Secretary of State for the Environment Transport and the Regions* [2001] UKHL 23, [2001] 2 WLR 1389.

[112] *Hatton v UK* (2003) 37 EHRR 28 (aircraft noise).

Hardy v UK App no 1965/07
(ECHR, 14 February 2012) paras 187–92, 217–21, 245–50

The Facts

The applicants alleged breaches of Article 2 and 8 of the ECHR in relation to the building of a LNG terminal at Milford. The Court found that the 'complaints are most appropriate examined from the standpoint of Article 8 alone' (para 184). There issues were relevant—the applicability of Article 8, whether Article 8 had been breached in relation to the assessment of risks from the terminal and whether Article 8 had been breached in relation of a failure to disclose risks.

The ECtHR (Fourth Section)

187. As the Court noted in *Fadeyeva v. Russia*, no. 55723/00, § 68, ECHR 2005 IV, Article 8 has been relied on in various cases in which environmental concerns are raised. However, in order to raise an issue under Article 8 the interference about which the applicant complains must directly affect his home, family or private life.

188. In cases concerning environmental pollution, the pollution must attain a certain minimum level if the complaints are to fall within the scope of Article 8 (see *López Ostra*, cited above, § 51; and *Fadeyeva*, cited above, §§ 69-70). The assessment of that minimum is relative and depends on all the circumstances of the case, such as the intensity and duration of the nuisance and its physical or mental effects. The general context of the environment should also be taken into account. There would be no arguable claim under Article 8 if the detriment complained of was negligible in comparison to the environmental hazards inherent to life in every modern city.

189. The Court has also found Article 8 to apply where the dangerous effects of an activity to which the individuals concerned are likely to be exposed have been determined as part of an environmental impact assessment procedure in such a way as to establish a sufficiently close link with private and family life for the purposes of Article 8 of the Convention (see *Taşkın and Others*, cited above, § 113). In the subsequent case of *Tătar v. Romania*, no. 67021/01, 27 January 2009, the Court found Article 8 to be applicable in a case concerning a risk posed by a mineral extraction plant. In that case the absence of any internal decision or other official document indicating, in a sufficiently clear manner, the degree of risk which the hazardous activities posed to human health and the environment was held not to be fatal to the claim, given that the applicant had attempted to pursue domestic remedies, and that a previous incident involving an accidental spillage had resulted in a higher than usual reading of certain toxic products in the vicinity (at §§ 93–97 of the Court's judgment).

190. In the present case, there is no suggestion that the normal operation of the LNG terminals poses any risk to the applicants or to the environment. In particular, there is no allegation of any continuing pollution caused by the transport of LNG in Milford Haven. The risk, according to the applicants, arises from the possibility of a collision in the haven, leading to the escape of a large quantity of LNG and the potential for an explosion or a fire as a result of such an accident. The applicants allege that the possibility of collision and the risks and consequences associated with such an event have not been properly assessed.

191. The Court notes that in order to establish and operate the LNG terminals, the operators were required to obtain planning permission and hazardous substances consent (see paragraphs 9–11, 129 and 138 above). The projects were of such a nature as to require, pursuant to the EIA Directive, that environmental impact assessments be prepared (see paragraphs 130–131 above). The installations were classified as "top tier" for the purposes of the COMAH Regulations, entailing more onerous conditions on the operators (see paragraph 46 above). The SIGTTO guidance to which the applicants referred makes recommendations regarding the manner of selection of a site for an LNG terminal in order to minimise marine risks. It also makes reference to the risk of fire and explosion in the event of

an escape of LNG into the atmosphere (see paragraphs 161–170 above). A report by the HSE, following an initial examination of the consequences of a major release from a delivery ship moored at the jetty, concluded that released LNG plumes would be capable of engulfing Milford Haven (see paragraph 33 above), the town where both applicants reside.

192. In the circumstances, the Court is satisfied that the potential risks posed by the LNG terminals were such as to establish a sufficiently close link with the applicants' private lives and homes for the purposes of Article 8. Article 8 is accordingly applicable.

Note how the Court approaches the question of the scope of Article 8 ECHR and, in particular, the role of regulatory frameworks in forcing an identification of possible risks to human health and the environment so as to establish a sufficiently close link to individuals' private lives and homes. The Court went on to consider the question of assessment of risk and stated the general principles that would apply in cases such as this:

217. The Court reiterates that in a case involving decisions affecting environmental issues there are two aspects to the inquiry which it may carry out. First, the Court may assess the substantive merits of the national authorities' decision to ensure that it is compatible with Article 8. Second, it may scrutinise the decision-making process to ensure that due weight has been accorded to the interests of the individual (see, *mutatis mutandis, Hatton and* Others, cited above, § 99; *Giacomelli,* cited above, § 79; and *Taşkın and Others,* cited above, § 115).

218. It is for the national authorities to make the initial assessment of the 'necessity' for an interference. They are in principle better placed than an international court to assess the requirements relating to the transport and processing of LNG in a particular local context and to determine the most appropriate environmental policies and individual measures while taking into account the needs of the local community. The Court has therefore repeatedly stated that in cases raising environmental issues the State must be allowed a wide margin of appreciation (see *Hatton and Others,* cited above, § 100; *Giacomelli,* cited above, § 80; *Taşkın and Others,* cited above, § 116).

219. As the Court has previously indicated, although Article 8 contains no explicit procedural requirements, the decision-making process leading to measures of interference must be fair and must afford due respect to the interests safeguarded to the individual by Article 8 (see *Giacomelli,* cited above, § 82; and *Taşkın and Others,* cited above, § 118). It is therefore necessary to consider all the procedural aspects, including the type of policy or decision involved, the extent to which the views of individuals were taken into account throughout the decision-making process and the procedural safeguards available (see *Hatton and Others,* cited above, § 104; *Giacomelli,* cited above, § 82; and *Taşkın and Others,* cited above, § 118). However, this does not mean that the authorities can take decisions only if comprehensive and measurable data are available in relation to each and every aspect of the matter to be decided (see *Giacomelli,* cited above, § 82; and *Taşkın and Others,* cited above, § 118).

220. A governmental decision-making process concerning complex issues of environmental and economic policy must in the first place involve appropriate investigations and studies so that the effects of activities that might damage the environment and infringe individuals' rights may be predicted and evaluated in advance and a fair balance may accordingly be struck between the various conflicting interests at stake (see *Hatton and Others,* cited above, § 128; *Giacomelli,* cited above, § 83; *Taşkın and Others,* cited above, § 119; *Dubetska and Others v. Ukraine,* no. 30499/03, § 143, 10 February 2011; and *Grimkovskaya v. Ukraine,* no. 38182/03, § 67, 21 July 2011).

221. Finally, the individuals concerned must also be able to appeal to the courts against any decision, act or omission where they consider that their interests or their comments have not been given sufficient weight in the decision-making process (see, *mutatis mutandis, Hatton and Others,* cited above, § 128; *Taşkın and Others,* cited above, §§ 118-119; and *Giacomelli,* cited above, § 83).

After a careful consideration of the facts and framework in this case, the ECtHR found that there was no violation of Article 8 ECHR on the facts. The Court then finally considered the issue of disclosure of information:

245. In cases concerning hazardous activities, the importance of public access to the conclusions of studies undertaken to identify and evaluate risks and to essential information enabling members of the public to assess the danger to which they are exposed is beyond question (see, *mutatis mutandis*, *Guerra and Others*, cited above, § 60; *McGinley and Egan*, cited above, § 97; *Giacomelli*, cited above, § 83; and *Taşkın and Others*, cited above, § 119).

246. The Court has previously indicated that respect for private and family life under Article 8 further requires that where a Government engages in hazardous activities which might have hidden adverse consequences on the health of those involved in such activities, and where no considerations of national security arise, an effective and accessible procedure must be established which enables such persons to seek all relevant and appropriate information (see *McGinley and Egan*, cited above, § 101; and *Roche v. the United Kingdom* [GC], no. 32555/96, § 162, ECHR 2005 X).

(ii) Application of the general principles to the facts of the case

247. The Court observes at the outset that the planning and hazardous substances applications were public documents and formed the subject of extensive public consultation (see paragraphs 17, 29, 37, 43 and 53 above). The Environmental Statements accompanying the applications were also made available to the public and the applicants do not dispute that they had access to them. The MHPA responded to the consultations and in its response provided details of its conclusions regarding the safety of the proposals (see paragraphs 26-27, 49 and 55 above). MHPA also responded to a number of queries by letter and in response to journalists' queries reiterating its conclusions on the risks posed by the terminals, and providing details of the simulation exercises conducted, involving MHPA pilots, under different weather and wind conditions (see paragraphs 40, 56, 64-66 and 68 70 above).

248. The Court further notes that the provisions of the Environmental Information Regulations and the FOI Act establish an extensive regime to promote and facilitate public access to environmental information (see paragraphs 171–178 above). The definition of 'environmental information' is relatively wide and can include information pertaining to public safety (see paragraph 177 above). In the event that information requested is not provided by the relevant authority, a challenge to the Information Commissioner is possible, followed by an appeal to the Information Rights Tribunal, the Upper Tribunal and, ultimately, the Court of Appeal (see paragraph 178 above). Further requirements to provide specific information to the public are contained in the EIA Directive and the COMAH Regulations (see paragraphs 133 and 149-151 above). The applicants availed themselves of the possibilities afforded to them by this legislation, and obtained a favourable decision from the Information Commissioner ordering the release of two reports requested by them (see paragraphs 119 120 above). In so far as they now seek to complain that the reports were heavily redacted, the Court observes that they have not suggested, nor have they provided any evidence to support the suggestion, that they made a complaint to the relevant domestic authorities regarding the information provided. It appears that section 50 of the FOI Act would have allowed the applicants to apply to the Information Commissioner for a ruling as to whether the information provided satisfied the obligations incumbent on MHPA pursuant to the Environmental Information Regulations (see paragraph 178 above).

249. The Court reiterates the importance of informing the public of the conclusions of studies undertaken and to other essential information to identify and evaluate risks. As the Information Commissioner explained in his decision notice (see paragraph 119 above), disclosure of environmental information of the type requested by the applicants can add significantly to public knowledge of the risks posed by the development and better inform public debate. However, the Court considers that in the present case, a great deal of information was voluntarily provided to the public by MHPA and the developers of the projects. The applicants have failed to demonstrate that any substantive documents were not

disclosed to them. In any event, in respect of any information which they allege was not provided, they had access to a mechanism established by law to allow them specifically to seek particular information, a mechanism which they employed successfully. In the circumstances, the Court is satisfied that the authorities provided information as required by Article 8 and that there was an effective and accessible procedure by which the applicants could seek any further relevant and appropriate information should they so wish.

250. In conclusion, having regard to the information provided during the planning stage of the projects, to the provisions of the Environmental Information Regulations allowing access to environmental information and to the routes of appeal available in the FOI Act, the Court finds that the respondent State has fulfilled its positive obligation under Article 8 in relation to these applicants. There has accordingly been no violation of this provision. In view of this conclusion, it is not necessary for the Court to rule on the Government's preliminary objection (see paragraph 236 above).

Overall, these are small extracts from a long case but two important points can be taken from them. First, human rights arguments are not made in a legal vacuum. The Court considered them by referring to the wider regulatory matrix, which includes various environmental regimes. Second, as can be seen in relation to the issue of disclosure of information, many rights are protected by other regimes and not solely under the HRA.

FURTHER READING

1. This section's discussion of the HRA and ECHR was brief. Further information can be found in the public law textbooks at the end of this chapter. There are also more specific texts relating to the HRA, including David Harris and others, *Law of the European Convention on Human Rights* (2nd edn, OUP 2009) and Richard Clayton and Hugh Tomlinson, *The Law of Human Rights* (2nd edn, OUP 2009).

2. There is a large literature concerning the relationship between environmental law and human rights. A good starting point is Donald Anton and Dina Shelton, *Environmental Protection and Human Rights* (CUP 2011). For a good discussion of the concept of constitutional environmental rights in the UK, see Ole Pedersen, 'A Bill of Rights, Environmental Rights, and the UK Constitution' [2011] Public Law 577.

---

6 A NOTE ABOUT EU ADMINISTRATIVE LAW

The discussion in this chapter has focused on public law in England and the UK. However, EU administrative law (as discussed in Chapter 4) must also be kept in mind. Issues relating to accountability, public participation, and the judicial review of environmental decision-making can also be seen within the EU legal realm. Thus, in Chapter 11, we will see how the CJEU has reasoned about environmental principles in applying EU grounds of review and Chapter 15 covers challenges under Article 263 TFEU to decisions made under the EU emissions trading regime.

Here it is worth emphasizing two general points about EU administrative law. First, EU administrative law is not identical to English administrative law, as both bodies of law are derived from different legal cultures. Thus, in both systems, there are grounds of judicial review, but they differ. As an example, 'manifest error of assessment' is a ground of review in EU law, but no such ground is recognized in UK law.[113] Understanding administrative law in one system does not mean understanding it in the other.

Second, an understanding of the EU administrative realm requires a broader understanding of governance issues, which are discussed in Chapter 13. In many ways, it is difficult to talk of public administration in the EU because the structure of the EU does not fit a traditional separation of powers framework of government. Thus, there are significant overlaps between executive and legislative functions, as seen particularly in the role of the Commission. With that said, many EU institutional structures might seem to resemble public administration in that they are not directly elected, although they clearly have a *sui generis* nature (see further Chapter 4). In light of this ambiguous familiarity, extra care must be taken in translating pre-existing assumptions about accountability, as shaped by national legal systems and based on particular political theories of government and democracy, into the EU context. Moreover, when discussing the accountability of EU institutions, one needs to consider carefully how an institution or process should be characterized, as Fisher points out.

Elizabeth Fisher, 'The European Union in the Age of Accountability' (2004) 24 OJLS 495, 511–12

A discussion of accountability in the EU cannot be disentangled from discussion about what is and should be the role and nature of European institutions. As such, debates about accountability resemble those over constitutionalism. Weiler has described the importance of constitutional choices as 'not only in the structure and process of government they put in place' but also about moral commitment and identity'. The same can be said of accountability.

This is also true of discussions about accountability in national settings but in the EU it has the added dimension that so many of the decision-making structures are innovative and the processes of integration many. Thus for example while many have argued the need to make comitology procedures more accountable there are actually profound disagreements over the nature and significance of the comitology phenomenon. Committees and agencies have been simultaneously described as 'corridors linking the EU architecture', 'intergovernmental Trojan horses', forms of 'deliberative supranationalism', sites for multi-level governance, technocratic, and a means of creating a 'European' administration. Proposals for agencies have been heralded as a new step in European integration but those steps may simultaneously lead to the creation of a regulatory state, a governance network, or a system of centralised administration. Indeed Slaughter notes that is unclear whether comitology is either the 'source' or the 'solution' to the EU's democratic deficit. If inter-institutional relationships (or the purpose of certain institutional arrangements) are not agreed then proposals for different forms of accountability become proposals for different European futures. This ambiguity is also reflected in the fact that while the term 'governance' may have become the 'private patois' of political scientists and EU lawyers it is a highly malleable term. By some it is used in a generic sense as a synonym for governing or the exercise of authority and by others it is a technical term of art, albeit having a multitude of different meanings. Governance can thus simultaneously refer to new public administration, policy networks, market regulation, private modes of ordering, and international regimes.

Thus, discussions about EU administrative law become quickly entangled in debates about EU governance and how it should be characterized. It is not simply that the EU is a different legal culture with a different, distinct body of administrative law, but that a consideration of EU administrative law involves different intellectual challenges, including the kinds of governance issues raised in Chapter 13.

---

[113] Case T-13 *Pfizer v Council* [2002] ECR II 3305.

7 CONCLUSION

This chapter has provided only a brief sketch of the public law aspects of environmental law. That brevity may irritate some readers, yet the chapter did not aim to provide a comprehensive overview of the public law aspects of environmental law. Rather, it provided an insight into the complexities of the interface between public and environmental law in the UK, and a feeling for how a student or lawyer might approach those complexities. Three overall points can be drawn in conclusion.

The first is that environmental problems pose particular challenges for the application and operation of public law, in light of the interests to be taken into account, and the roles of public participation and environmental information. The existence of the Aarhus Convention is thus no accident—it reflects a response to these challenges. Likewise, the judicial review cases extracted in Section 4 are not simply examples of judicial review doctrine being applied to environmental matters. In each case, judges, lawyers, and decision-makers are struggling with the interrelationship between public law and environmental law. Second, Judge Frankfurter was right: in applying public law principles to environmental problems, you need to read the statute—and the delegated legislation—and the Directive— and the policy guidance—and be aware of the bigger institutional picture. To put the matter another way, there is a real danger of talking too generally about issues of public law in environmental law. There is very little that is general about the relationship between public and environmental law, which explains the brevity of this chapter but does little to make the life of an environmental lawyer easy. Finally, this is an area in which there is considerable conflict and disagreement and thus where the complexity of environmental problems is constantly under the spotlight. Likewise, there is a constant shifting between what *is* and what *ought* to be, in legal and regulatory terms. All in all, understanding the interrelationship between environmental law and public law requires constant vigilance. Or to put it another way, this is a tough bicycle to ride! (See the Introduction…)

FURTHER READING

There are many good public law textbooks on the market. Here are a number of suggestions for further reading.

Anthony Bradley and Keith Ewing, *Constitutional and Administrative Law* (15th edn, Longman 2010).

Peter Cane, *Administrative Law* (5th edn, Clarendon Press 2011).

Paul Craig, *Administrative Law* (7th edn, Sweet & Maxwell 2012).

Paul Craig, *EU Administrative Law* (2nd edn, OUP 2011).

Timothy Endicott, *Administrative Law* (2nd edn, OUP 2011).

Carol Harlow and Richard Rawlings, *Law and Administration* (3rd edn, CUP 2009).

Adam Tomkins, *Public Law* (Clarendon Press 2003).

Colin Turpin and Adam Tomkins, *British Government and the Constitution: Text and Materials* (7th edn, CUP 2011).

William Wade and Christopher Forsyth, *Administrative Law* (10th edn, OUP 2009).

8

CRIMINAL LIABILITY

This chapter introduces criminal liability for non-compliance with English environmental law. Environmental crime can be defined as behaviour that contravenes statutory provisions for the protection of the ecological and physical environment,[1] where there is some kind of punitive sanction imposed for the contravention, with such provisions sometimes also pursuing the protection of public health. Environmental crime can also include criminal offences created through the common law, such as public nuisance.[2]

The purpose of the chapter is to discuss overarching themes, such as key elements of strict liability offences, in criminalizing behaviour that damages the environment, rather than details of specific offences spelt out in particular statutes, such as the general water pollution offence under Regulations 12 and 38 of the Environmental Permitting Regulations 2010, discussed in Chapter 14, waste offences under s 33 of the Environmental Protection Act 1990, discussed in Chapter 16, or the offence of killing, injuring, or taking any wild bird under s 1(1)(a) of the Wildlife and Countryside Act 1981.

The chapter argues that environmental crime sits uneasily within the environmental law regulatory landscape, which has been shaped in the UK in recent years by co-operative, 'better regulation' agendas that seek to reduce burdens on business. From this perspective, state intervention in economic activity in order to protect the environment should be limited. But defining, prosecuting, and sanctioning environmental crime constitutes one of the most severe forms of state intervention into citizens' and businesses' behaviour in order to achieve protection of the environment and public health. The chapter suggests that this tension within the environmental law regulatory landscape reflects a fundamental moral ambiguity in the nature of environmental crime.[3] This moral ambiguity is further reinforced by the fact that there is no agreement on what types of environmentally damaging behaviour actually deserve the moral condemnation associated with a criminal offence. Can we really single out specific behaviours of individuals and corporations and label them as criminal, given the fact that widespread high-consumption, carbon-intensive lifestyles are adopted by large sections of the population in the developed world that cause significant environmental damage? The chapter suggests that this moral ambiguity of environmental crime can be traced at several levels. First, it informs the scope of legal doctrine. Arguments about whether we should have strict liability or fault-based environmental offences, or whether environmental law should hold to account company directors through environmental criminal offences, or whether we should deploy criminal or administrative law to create offences for harm done to the environment, are arguments that are informed by specific assumptions

---

[1] Neal Shover and Aaron S. Routhe, 'Environmental Crime' (2005) 32 Crime and Justice 321.
[2] For a further discussion of public nuisance, see Chapter 9 on Statutory Liability.
[3] See also Stuart Bell and Donald McGillivray, *Environmental Law* 8th edn, OUP 2013, 277.

about how morally reprehensible crimes against the environment are. Second, the chapter traces how the moral ambiguity of environmental crime contributes to enforcement behaviour that considers criminal prosecutions, and also civil sanctions, only as a last resort.

In developing these points, the chapter links to themes developed in other chapters. It complements the focus in Chapter 12 on regulatory strategies that seek to promote compliance with environmental law through educative, 'reflexive', co-operative, and 'flexible' enforcement strategies, manifested, for instance, in the rise of various hybrid forms of state and self-regulation.[4] This chapter shows that there is still a role for traditional state punitive 'command and control' regulation. Moreover, the chapter illustrates the increasing transnationalization of environmental law discussed in Chapters 4 and 5. Section 4 of this chapter introduces the recent EU initiative to provide a basic framework for the harmonization of criminal liability for environmental harms in the different EU Member States. The chapter further illustrates that, despite what appears to be significant fragmentation in English environmental law, we can identify various legal threads that integrate and render coherent this area of the law. For instance, environmental criminal offences can contribute to the legal implementation of the preventive and polluter pays principles, discussed further in Chapter 11.

The chapter develops these points through four main sections. Section 1 starts to tackle the question of why we may want to criminalize behaviour that damages the environment. Section 2 analyses how legal mechanisms are employed to criminalize environmental wrongdoing, focusing on the role of strict liability offences in English environmental law. Section 3 points to structural reasons that relegate criminal prosecutions to the background of actual enforcement practices of English environmental regulators. This section also provides an introduction to the new civil sanctions regime, which sets up a range of sanctions for English regulators in the 'enforcement pyramid'. These sanctions are to be used for a limited number of environmental offences to date, with the prosecution of offences also acting as a last resort enforcement option in this regulatory scheme. Finally, Section 4 illustrates attempts by the EU to achieve at least some minimum consensus across Member States on the use of the criminal law in order to protect the environment, within the context of scholarly discourse on the transnationalization of legal efforts to protect the environment. In reading this chapter it should be remembered that criminal law and criminology are vast disciplinary fields. The chapter is thus an introduction to thinking about the interface between environmental law and these fields.

1 WHY CRIMINALIZE BEHAVIOUR THAT HARMS THE ENVIRONMENT?

There is nothing self-evident about criminalizing behaviour that harms the environment, even though we may assume that criminal law is one of the most powerful weapons in the toolkit of environmental regulators. Various specific reasons have therefore been marshalled to justify the criminalization of environmentally damaging behaviour. First, it can impose significant intangible losses, such as adverse effects on public health and the biosphere, for instance through the extinction of species and the depletion of water resources. It can also impose significant economic losses on current and future generations of humans. Second, environmental justice considerations may justify the criminalization of environmentally damaging behaviour, given the fact that environmental harms often fall disproportionately on lower socio-economic groups or racial groups who experience discrimination. For instance, in the US industrial installations and hazardous waste disposal facilities are often situated in

---

[4] See also Neal Shover and Aaron S Routhe, 'Environmental Crime' (2005) 32 Crime and Justice 321, 357.

close proximity to African-American and Native American neighbourhoods.[5] Third, criminologists have suggested that, like other offenders, those breaching environmental standards often deploy 'techniques of neutralization'.[6] These are 'rhetorical constructions' that excuse or justify and thereby facilitate the environmentally damaging behaviour. They can be powerful because they tap into culturally accepted ways of downplaying the seriousness of the environmental damage caused. They turn illicit into permissible conduct.[7] They can draw, for instance, on rhetorical tropes, such as the importance of preserving jobs and/or the competitiveness of the national economy, the right for companies to trade, the notion that the pollution was 'just an accident', an 'unfortunate series of coincidences', or involved merely 'two-and-a-half-bucketfuls' of pollutants.[8] The reason for criminalizing environmental behaviour is then to communicate strongly a message of moral opprobrium in relation to environmentally damaging behaviour and thus to lessen the salience of 'techniques of neutralization'.

While these are all important reasons for criminalizing environmentally damaging behaviour, two issues need to be addressed for further building a case for criminalizing environmental law-breaking. First, while for some environmentally damaging behaviour is another type of white-collar crime (particularly when carried out by corporations), for others, it does not carry sufficient moral blame to amount to 'crime'. Justifying the criminalization of environmentally damaging behaviour therefore has to grapple with the moral ambiguity of environmentally crime. It might be easy to overlook this ambiguity considering that, particularly within the Environment Agency of England and Wales (EA), environmental crime has an institutional identity in English environmental law, with a dedicated EA team that deals with environmental crime.[9] Second, criminalizing environmentally damaging behaviour can be justified on the grounds that environmental crimes promote individual and general deterrence. But this claim rests on an assumption that offenders calculate rationally the risk of being detected and sanctioned when considering whether to engage in environmental crime or not, as well as on the nature and size of the relevant sanction imposed. This assumption needs to be questioned and critically examined.

1.1 THE MORAL AMBIGUITY OF ENVIRONMENTAL CRIME

Criminalizing behaviour that harms the environment can be understood as a strong expression of a polity's moral understanding that harming the environment and the health or property values of fellow citizens is ethically objectionable. But this implies that we can draw a clear dividing line between what is morally acceptable and what is objectionable environmental behaviour. It also implies that, empirically, we can distinguish between businesses that have environmental impacts, but are operated in an acceptable and legitimate way, and those that are not.

Recent contributions to 'green criminology' question this assumption and point to unholy alliances between criminal and legal business activity causing environmental damage. In the particular context of the regulation of waste disposal in Naples, southern Italy, Ruggiero and South argue that environmental crimes (that is, the illegal dumping of waste) were committed due to the failure of

---

[5] Nigel South, 'A Green Field for Criminology?: A Proposal for a Perspective' (1998) 2 Theoretical Criminology 217, referring to Williams, 1996.

[6] Gresham Sykes and David Matza, 'Techniques of Neutralization: A Theory of Delinquency' (1957) 22 American Sociological Review 664–670.

[7] Neal Shover and Aaron S Routhe, 'Environmental Crime' (2005) 32 Crime and Justice 321, 335.

[8] Paula De Prez, 'Excuses, Excuses: The Ritual Trivialization of Environment Prosecutions' (2000) 12 JEL 65–77, 74.

[9] There are also extensive policies on how the EA should use its prosecutorial powers: see, for example, Better Regulation Executive and National Audit Office, *Effective Inspection and Enforcement: Implementing the Hampton Vision in the Environment Agency*, 1 March 2008.

local politicians and public administration officials to properly oversee and control the tendering of contracts by local authorities for waste disposal. Private companies that had no technical ability or even willingness to fulfil these contracts won on the basis of low bids, and then failed to deliver waste disposal services. This, in turn, created an opportunity for organized crime, linked to the Camorra, to enter the market and become involved in the illegal disposal of waste. Ruggiero and South argue that some features of their Italian case study are by no means unusual.

Vincenzo Ruggiero and Nigel South, 'Green Criminology and Dirty Collar Crime' (2010) 18 Critical Criminology 251, 257

Dirty Collar Crime

Some aspects of the case just described are far from unique. Much previous research conducted has shown that processing industrial waste without a licence and sidestepping environmental regulations 'is cheaper and faster' (Szasz 1986, 1994). Cases uncovered in the Netherlands proved that illegal enterprises may offer service packages which comprise false invoices, transport facilities, mendacious chemical reports as to the nature of the substances dumped and forged permits to dump. In most European countries some legally registered companies also operate illegally. They either establish part-nerships with legitimate firms or run their own in house parallel illicit business. The choice between the two services is the result of how much the customer is prepared to pay. It is otiose in this respect, to question whether customers are aware of the illegal nature of the cheaper option, as its very cheapness speaks for itself (van Duyne 1993; Brants 1994; Moore 1994; South 1998). In the USA research has indicated that the involvement of organised crime reaches all aspects of the business, including control of companies officially licensed to dispose of waste and those earning contracts with public or private organisations, or the payment of bribes to dump site owners or outright ownership of such sites (Block and Scarpitti 1985; Szasz 1986; Salzano 1994).

Recent cases which occurred in Germany show that even in countries where the legislation is progres-sive and clear, illegal disposal of waste is widespread. Such cases emerged when a mismatch was noted between the quantity of waste expected and that actually received by incinerators operating in the eastern regions of the country. The missing portion of waste was found to have been dumped in illegal disposal sites.

Entrepreneurs utilising such dumps opted for the cheapest way of waste management, thus circum-venting the rules which impose a fee of around 200 euros per tonne of waste treated (Natale 2009). Cases also emerged in which the composition of the waste treated was falsely certified so that sub-stances which should have been disposed of in special sites were instead dumped in inappropriate ones. That cases such as these occur in highly ecologically aware Germany may be surprising but the paradox is that the development of illegal dumping services has run parallel with the steep increase in environmental awareness, the latter forcing governments to raise costs for industrial dumping which indirectly encourages industrialists to opt for cheaper, if illicit, solutions.

Hence, Ruggiero and South paint a picture here in which the boundaries between illegal and legal busi-ness become blurred. They also suggest that a mutual learning process takes place through which legiti-mate entrepreneurs learn from illegitimate ones how to bend the rules. Illegitimate entrepreneurs learn how to access public resources, for instance through public procurement contracts for environmental services, while legitimate entrepreneurs learn how fraud can become a way of doing business.[10]

---

[10] Vincenzo Ruggiero and Nigel South, 'Green Criminology and Dirty Collar Crime' (2010) 18 Critical Criminology 251.

Thus, the development of reasons for criminalizing behaviour that harms the environment has to grapple with the problem that such behaviour can be linked to legitimate business activity. Ruggiero and South go so far as to suggest that there are 'crime facilitative industries', which attract persons with criminal records and are characterized by 'rule-bending' and 'criminal opportunism'.[11] More fundamentally, Ruggiero and South argue that obstacles to entrenching a conception of 'environmental crime' also arise from the fact that environmental law itself is ambiguous in relation to environmentally destructive behaviour. As a 'new' legal subject, environmental law draws on doctrine and legal concepts developed in pre-existing fields of law, such as property law, administrative law, and torts. In Ruggiero's and South's view these fields of law have transplanted into environmental law a style of legal reasoning that is geared towards 'the protection of socio-economic systems heavily orientated towards unfettered industrial growth, production, and consumption',[12] and thereby potentially promoting environmental damage.

But there are also other factors that contribute to the moral ambiguity of environmental crime. Brickey has argued in the US context that the 'aspirational, evolutionary and complex nature' of environmental law raises the question whether violations of environmental standards should be criminalized.[13] She considers US environmental law to be 'aspirational' in the sense that a number of key US environmental statutes, such as the US Clean Water Act and the US Clean Air Act are 'technology forcing' statutes. Environmental standards were set at deliberately high levels in these statutes, so that they would force the development of more advanced pollution reduction technologies, which would enable operators to meet these standards. In the UK, however, standards are set also with reference to 'regulatory impact assessments' that consider the costs and benefits of environmental standards and thus take into account what operators can achieve through existing, at times 'state of the art', technology. Brickey considers US environmental law also as 'evolutionary' and 'complex', because environmental standards are often in flux, also due to scientific uncertainty surrounding the environmental harms caused by various economic activities. She considers environmental law to be 'complex' due to the legal intricacies involved in legislating for environmental harms, as well as the various types of technical and scientific expertise required in order to be able to apply environmental law to specific environmental problems. She suggests that in criminalizing environmental violations three key distinctive concerns of the criminal law are imported into environmental law: harm, culpability, and deterrence. She argues that in developing environmental offences legislatures have often given insufficient thought to how three specific characteristics of environmental law may make it difficult to address the key concerns of criminal law.

Kathleen Brickey, 'Environmental Crime at the Crossroads: The Intersection of Environmental and Criminal Law Theory' (1996–1997) 71 Tulane LR 500, 501, 503

B. Evolutionary Nature

Environmental law is in a constant state of flux. Continual change in environmental regulation is all but inevitable. Setting environmental standards requires making 'scientifically informed value judgments' based on evolving and often tentative scientific principles.

Environmental policymaking also reflects the volatile forces of public opinion and political conflict over a hierarchy of competing values and interests. Stated simply, environmental policymaking occurs in a

---

11 Ibid, 253.   12 Ibid.
13 Kathleen Brickey, 'Environmental Crime at the Crossroads: The Intersection of Environmental and Criminal Law Theory' (1996–1997) 71 Tulane LR 500.

rough-and-tumble world. In contrast with the stability normally associated with traditional criminal law, environmental law must perpetually respond to prevailing scientific, political, and social norms.

The evolutionary nature of environmental law creates uncertainty about what the law is or is likely to be, including what conduct will be considered criminal. The unpredictability of the governing legal standards thus may implicate questions of fairness in the context of criminal enforcement and reinforce the belief that the distinctive features of environmental law should not only inform criminal enforcement policymaking, but should also prescribe its bounds.

C. High Degree of Complexity

No one would argue with the premise that environmental law is highly complex. It is fraught with highly technical scientific, engineering, and economic jargon that, even to one schooled in the intricacies of environmental science and economics, can be truly mind-boggling.

Apart from the special expertise needed to penetrate the technical facets of environmental law, the draftsmanship in the statutes and regulations is notoriously flawed. The Clean Water Act has been variously described as a 'poorly drafted and astonishingly imprecise statute, that is "difficult to understand, construe and apply" and (needless to say) "devoid" of plain meaning.' Hazardous waste regulations are so complex that they 'defy the comprehension of any one person.' The Oil Pollution Act of 1990 contains only '[p]ockets of certainty' amidst its 'broad mixtures of complex and ambiguous provisions.'' And so it goes down the line.

In addition to these barriers to understanding environmental law, much of the law itself is obscure. The Oil Pollution Act of 1990, for example, 'buries laws within laws and jumbles concepts within a huge legal stew.' And as environmental regulations consume literally thousands of pages in the Code of Federal Regulations, 'the quantity of minutely detailed language [...] beggars description'. To complicate this overlay of complexity, much of environmental law is hidden in detailed preambles that are not published in the Code of Federal Regulations with the regulations they explain, and in private informal guidance memoranda and letters -hence, the problem of 'underground' environmental law.

Brickey concludes that, given the aspirational, evolutionary, and complex nature of environmental law, it is difficult to clearly ascertain what behaviour constitutes compliance with environmental standards. In the light of such uncertainty, is it really fair to use the criminal law to punish environmental wrongdoing? Brickey further pushes the fairness point by invoking contract imagery. She suggests that—in return for a conditional licence to pollute being granted by the public administration to operators—the operators agree to observe the terms of the permit when applying for it and accepting it from the public administration.[14] To conclude, Brickey therefore locates the moral ambiguity of environmental crime in the structure and nature of environmental and criminal law, as traditionally conceptualized. In contrast to this, Ruggiero and South locate the moral ambiguity of environmental crime mainly in the fluid boundaries between legal and illegal business practices that harm the environment.

FURTHER READING AND QUESTIONS

1. The environmental policy goal of sustainable development and 'Green Deal' economic programmes[15] aspire to a wholesale restructuring of societies in order to achieve greater synergy

---

[14] Ibid, 525.
[15] Such as government supported schemes for home insulation—on the UK 'Green Deal' policy, see further Chapter 15.

between economic development, environmental protection, and social cohesion. Is the criminalization of environmentally damaging behaviour in conflict with this structural and potentially voluntary approach towards achieving environmental protection?

2. For further reading on criminality in the environmental law context, see Rob White, *Crimes Against Nature: Environmental Criminology and Ecological Justice* (2008 Willan Publishing) 88; Colin Scott 'Regulatory Crime: History, Functions, Problems Solutions', in Shane Kilcommins and Ursula Kilkelly (eds) *Regulatory Crime in Ireland* (2010 First Law/Lonsdale Law Publishing, Dublin); Andy Szasz, 'Corporations, Organized Crime, and the Disposal of Hazardous Waste: An Examination of the Making of a Criminogenic Regulatory Structure' (1986) 24 Criminology 1–27.

3. For a philosophical discussion of when to use criminal law, see HM Hart, 'The Aims of the Criminal Law' (1958) Law and Contemporary Problems, 401.

4. For further discussion on the ambiguous nature of criminal law in a modern regulatory context, see John Coffee, 'Paradigms Lost: The Blurring of the Criminal and Civil Law Models—And What Can be Done about It' (1992) 101 Yale LJ 1875.

2 HOW TO CRIMINALIZE ENVIRONMENTALLY DAMAGING BEHAVIOUR?

2.1 REGULATORY VS CRIMINAL OFFENCES

The debate about the moral ambiguity of environmental crime in Section 1 is not merely of criminological theoretical interest. It is reflected in debates among lawyers about the appropriate legal classification of 'environmental crime'. Should behaviour that harms the environment be subject to the full force of the criminal law, or are lesser 'regulatory' or 'administrative' offences sufficient to ensure compliance with environmental law?

This debate is complicated by the fact that there are no clear-cut or agreed definitions of these different types of offences. In fact, practitioners tend to talk about 'regulatory crime', and scholars certainly see the rise of regulatory offences as influencing and impacting upon the traditional scope of criminal law.[16] The Law Commission has defined an 'administrative offence' as an offence where not necessarily a public body, but even a private sector employee, may determine whether such an offence has been committed and impose a penalty or preventative measure on the offender, or may report the offender to a higher authority.[17] Also, in order to satisfy due process requirements required under the criminal law, even administrative offences still allow for rights of appeal, for instance to a tribunal or court. Lord Diplock has characterized 'regulatory' offences in general terms as being those offences that regulate a particular activity involving *potential* danger.[18] However, this characterization is increasingly losing significance in light of the fact that a number of criminal environmental offences, such as the waste offences created under s 33(1)(c) EPA 1990, have been extended to behaviour that involves merely the likelihood of environmental pollution or harm to human health. 'Criminal' offences can be identified through the procedure that is being used for imposing sanctions. For instance, proceedings in the Magistrates or Crown Court are indicators of a criminal offence,

[16] See the Ashworth extract.
[17] The Law Commission, Consultation Paper No 195, 'Criminal Liability in Regulatory Contexts: A Consultation Paper', para 3.23, 31.
[18] *Sweet v Parsley* [1970] AC 132, 163.

as is the requirement that the offence must be proven in a court beyond reasonable doubt.[19] Serious sanctions that go beyond merely preventative, compensatory or rehabilitative measures are a further indicator of a criminal offence.[20]

Such attempts to distinguish between administrative, regulatory and criminal environmental offences hinge also on intuitive appeals to differentiations between different degrees of harm to be prevented or sanctioned through the offence. The criminal law affirms such distinctions through its categories of 'mala prohibita' (that is, regulatory offences) and 'mala in se', acts which are wrong in themselves. In the words of the Law Commission:

> The criminal law should be employed only when engagement in the prohibited conduct in question warrants official censure, because it involves a harm-related moral failing, not just a breach of a rule or simple departure from a standard.[21]

Hence, administrative or regulatory offences are to be reserved for less serious environmental wrong-doing, such as mere breaches of an administrative requirement of environmental law, including non-compliance with an obligation to provide information, failing to monitor emissions, or providing false information about emissions. In contrast to this, criminal offences should tackle serious and direct endangerment of either public health of natural resources, such as watercourses, air, or land. Examples of such environmental crimes are pollution of the air in breach of discharge permits or accidental oil spills polluting a river. But how much analytical substance is there to such bright-line distinctions? In order to answer this question, the following points should be borne in mind.

First, mere technical infractions of procedural administrative requirements, such as a failure to comply with monitoring and reporting requirements, can enable engagement in and often conceal from regulatory agencies more serious environmental crimes. Also, in terms of preventing environmental harm, there may not be a significant distinction between administrative and criminal offences. For instance, failure to comply with reporting requirements can also make it more difficult for the regulator to engage in clean-up or even preventative measures in the case of environmental accidents. Second, the criterion of whether there is a 'harm-related moral failing', in contrast to a 'mere breach of a rule or simple departure from a standard' may be too general in order to distinguish administrative from criminal environmental offences. In the case of environmental offences, in contrast to, for example, offences against the person, such harm may be more difficult to identify because it may be removed in time and space from the cause of the harm, but that does not make it less serious. In the case of environmental offences, it may therefore have to be decided *within the specific context* whether a 'mere breach of a rule or simple departure from a standard' does not involve a 'harm-related moral failing'. For instance, a failure to report the amount of greenhouse gas emissions emitted in a year by an operator under an emissions trading regime may simply be an administrative oversight. It may also be an expression of a complete disregard of the operator for the need to gain knowledge of its environmental impacts, in terms of the level of its greenhouse gas emissions, and to control such emissions. The environmental harm may be significant, even though distant in terms of future generations being affected by climate change, or populations at a distance from the installation being affected. Third, there is no easy consensus as to where the dividing line falls between 'mere breaches of a rule or standard' and 'harm-related moral failings'. While fly-tipping of contaminated construction waste may be considered as a mere departure from a standard; it may equally represent a harm-related moral failing, particularly when carried out on a large-scale by organized criminal syndicates.

---

[19] Law Commission (n 17), para 3.39, 36.
[20] Ibid.   [21] Law Commission (n 17) 68.

The answer to these difficulties of anchoring the distinction between 'administrative/regulatory' and 'criminal' environmental offences into clear analytical distinctions, is not to abandon such classifications. They do matter for lawyers, because serious offences trigger due process protections for defendants. Those environmental offences that are considered as essentially 'criminal' in nature by the European Court of Human Rights, regardless of how they are classified according to national law, will have to conform to Article 6(3) ECHR. In determining whether an offence can be labelled as 'criminal', the ECHR will consider the nature of the offence and the severity of the penalty for it.[22]

In practice, the normative question of whether administrative, regulatory, or criminal sanctions should be employed in order to achieve compliance with environmental law is resolved in the UK in a piecemeal and *ad hoc* fashion. There is no general administrative or criminal offence regime in England and Wales, but it depends on the specific statutory provision at issue whether an offence can be classified as administrative or criminal. By contrast, since the late 1970s, Germany has had distinct fields of, on the one hand, environmental criminal law, which forms part of the general, comprehensive German Criminal Code ('Strafgesetzbuch'), and administrative regulatory offences on the other hand, for mere breaches of regulations ('Ordnungswidrigkeiten').[23] A similar distinction between regulatory and criminal environmental offences exists in France.[24]

To summarize, criminalizing environmentally damaging behaviour is just one option for sanctioning such behaviour. In practice, administrative/regulatory offences also play an important role in punitive strategies for achieving compliance with environmental law, albeit that it might not always be obvious on the face of a statutory provision whether it provides for a regulatory or a truly criminal offence. This again reflects the moral ambiguity of environmental crime, with administrative/regulatory offences signalling that some infractions of environmental law are not really 'crime'. Ashworth, by contrast, argues that the wide range of administrative offences (in environmental law and more broadly in the modern regulatory state) undermines the nature of the criminal law, and in particular dilutes its censuring function.

Andrew Ashworth, 'Is the Criminal Law a Lost Cause?' (2000) LQR 225, 249–50

For [some regulation scholars], the prevention of harm is a primary goal of social policy, and the criminal law is regarded as one among a number of mechanisms for bringing this about. It should therefore be used as and when it is efficient, and replaced by other mechanisms when it is not efficient and/or cost-effective. This view underlies the idea of responsive regulation, as a means of dealing with the varying contexts in which regulatory agencies have to operate. My conception of the criminal law gives primary place to its censuring function, a public function with possibly severe consequences for citizens, which should be exercised in as fair and non-discriminatory a manner as possible [...] In principle, the prevention of harm should be pursued through a range of initiatives in social, criminal and environmental policy. In practice, there is no shortage of examples of governments either repeatedly over-estimating the preventive efficacy of the criminal law or deliberately ignoring the poor prospects of prevention in favour of the politically symbolic effect of creating a new crime. The aim should be to produce a set of criminal laws that penalise substantial wrongdoing and only substantial wrongdoing, enforcing those fairly and dealing with them proportionately [...]

[22] *Engel v Netherlands* (1979–1980) 1 EHRR 647, 679–80.

[23] To complicate matters further Austria does not clearly distinguish between 'administrative' and 'criminal' environmental offences. It has what it considers to be 'administrative criminal law' (Annex to the Council Framework Decision on the 2003/80/JHA of 27 January 2003 on the protection of the environment through criminal law).

[24] Law Commission (n 17), para 3.22, 31.

A further question that needs to be addressed, in order to understand how environmentally damaging behaviour can be criminalized, is whether to employ strict liability or fault-based offences. The threshold for justifying strict liability for fully-fledged criminal offences is higher, given the default presumption of the criminal law that criminal wrong-doing usually involves the requirement to prove *mens rea*, that is, some form of fault.

2.2 STRICT LIABILITY OFFENCES AND CORPORATE LIABILITY

Mens rea is usually required for the commission of a criminal offence, that is, there has to be a guilty mind, as evidenced in the intent to commit the offence and cause harm. Strict liability offences, however, are at the heart of key English statutory regimes for the protection of watercourses and land.[25] These include the offences of polluting watercourses, under Regulations 12 and 38 of the Environmental Permitting Regulations 2010 (discussed in Chapter 14), and the waste offences under s 33 EPA 1990 (discussed in Chapter 16). Judicial rationalizations of strict liability have emphasized their contribution to efficient enforcement.[26] In doctrinal terms, strict liability offences raise a number of difficult questions. What exactly must the defendant have known in order to be found guilty of a strict liability offence? How can a body corporate be held liable for a strict liability offence if it—or its senior managers—may not have known of any environmentally damaging behaviour having occurred at a particular site?

Strict liability in the context of corporate liability

The leading case on the issue of when a company can be held liable for the acts or omissions of its employees is *Tesco Supermarkets Ltd v Nattrass*.[27] Tesco was charged with an offence under s 11 (2) of the Trade Descriptions Act 1968. That offence did not require fault and provided that:

> If any person offering to supply any goods gives, by whatever means, any indication likely to be taken as an indication that the goods are being offered at a price less than that at which they are in fact being offered he shall, subject to the provisions of this Act, be guilty of an offence.

On the particular facts, there was no question that Tesco had in fact committed such an offence. In one of its stores, the shop manager, Mr Clement, had failed to properly supervise a shop assistant, Ms Rodgers, in her duties to display goods in the shop. Washing powder which had been advertised to be available at a lower price, was sold at a higher price, contrary to s 11 (2) of the Trade Descriptions Act 1968. The main question in the case was whether Tesco could avail itself of the defence under s 24 (1) of the Trade Descriptions Act 1968:

> In any proceedings for an offence under this Act it shall, subject to subsection (2) of this section, be a defence for the person charged to prove - (a) that the commission of the offence was due to a mistake or to reliance on information supplied to him or to the act or default of another person, an accident or some other cause beyond his control; and (b) that he took all reasonable precautions and

---

[25] The Law Commission is in favour of reserving strict liability offences for 'regulatory' and not fully fledged criminal offences (Law Commission Consultation Paper (n 17) para 4.5, 67).

[26] *R v Woodrow* (1846) 14 M & W 404, 153, Eng Rep 907, discussed by Paula De Prez 'Excuses, Excuses: The Ritual Trivialization of Environmental Prosecutions', (2000) 12 JEL 65–77, 70.

[27] [1971] UKHL 1; [1972] AC 153.

exercised all due diligence to avoid the commission of such an offence by himself or any person under his control.

In order to avoid conviction Tesco had to show that both parts (a) and (b) of the defence were made out. Key legal issues were, firstly, whether Mr Clement was sufficiently distant from Tesco, as a corporation, to count as 'another person'. Tesco argued that this was the case, because, although he was clearly an employee of the company, Mr Clement was distinct from Tesco by virtue of the fact that he was not part of the 'controlling brain' of the company, since he was not a director, manager, secretary, or other similar type of employee.[28] The second key legal issue was whether, only the acts of Tesco or also those of Mr Clement could be taken into account, when considering whether the due diligence defence had been proven.

The House of Lords allowed Tesco's appeal and acquitted the company. It held that a person in the employment of a company could be 'another person' for the purposes of the s 24 (1) defence. Thus, Viscount Dilhorne reasoned that a shop manager could be 'another person' because he was distinct from company directors, secretaries, or similar persons who would be considered as the controlling mind of the company. The House of Lords also ruled that Tesco had adequately discharged its due diligence obligation and had not delegated it to Mr Clement, the store manager. Both limbs of the s 24(1) defence were therefore proven. Discussions about the appropriate interpretation of the s 24(1) defence raised complex questions about the meaning of, and relationship between, the legal doctrines of delegation and vicarious liability in the context of strict liability offences. For Viscount Dilhorne, the question in the case here was not whether the company was criminally liable and responsible for the act of a particular servant, such as Mr Clement, but whether it could avoid liability by proving that it exercised all due diligence and took all reasonable precautions and that the commission of the offence was due to the act or omission of another person.[29] The key legal issues of this case are further discussed in the extract from Lord Pearson's speech.

Tesco Supermarkets Ltd v Nattrass
[1972] AC 153, 190, 192–93 (Lord Pearson)

In order to complete its defence the company must also prove that the company took all reasonable precautions and exercised all due diligence to avoid the commission of such an offence by itself or any person under its control. The question in this appeal is whether the company has proved those two points.

[…]The magistrates' opinion that Mr. Clement was not 'another person'—a person other than the company—seems to me to be clearly unsustainable. It would be immediately obvious in the case of an individual proprietor of a business and the manager of one of his shops. It is less obvious in the case of a company which can only act through servants or agents and has generally in the law of tort and sometimes in criminal law vicarious responsibility for what they do on its behalf. But vicarious responsibility is very different from identification. There are some officers of a company who may for some purposes be identified with it, as being or having its directing mind and will, its centre and ego, and its brains. Lennard's Carrying Co. Ltd. v. Asiatic Petroleum Co. Ltd. [1915] A.C. 705

Clearly the Divisional Court's decision was based on the theory of 'delegation.' One has to examine the meaning of the word 'delegation' in relation to the facts of this case and the provisions of the Trade Descriptions Act 1968, ss. 11 (2) and 24 . In one sense the meaning is as wide as the principle of the master's vicarious liability for the acts and omissions of his servants acting within the scope of their

---

[28] *Tesco v Nattrass*, 153.   [29] *Tesco v Nattrass*, 185 (Viscount Dilhorne).

employment. In this sense the master can be said to 'delegate' to every servant acting on his behalf all the duties which the servant has to perform. But that cannot be the proper meaning here. If the company 'delegated' to Miss Rogers the duty of filling the fixture with appropriate packets of washing powder, and ''delegated' to Mr. Clement the duty of supervising the proper filling of fixtures and the proper exhibition or withdrawal of posters proclaiming reduced prices, then any master, whether a company or an individual, must be vicariously liable for all the acts and omissions of all its or his servants acting on its or his behalf. That conclusion would defeat the manifest object of section 24 which is to enable defendants to avoid vicarious liability where they were not personally at fault (emphasis added).

[...]Section 24 requires a dividing line to be drawn between the master and any other person. The defendant cannot disclaim liability for an act or omission of his ego or his alter ego. In the case of an individual defendant, his ego is simply himself, but he may have an alter ego. For instance, if he has only one shop and he appoints a manager of that shop with full discretion to manage it as he thinks fit, the manager is doing what the employer would normally do and may be held to be the employer's alter ego. But if the defendant has hundreds of shops, he could not be expected personally to manage each one of them and the manager of one of his shops cannot in the absence of exceptional circumstances be considered his alter ego. In the case of a company, the ego is located in several persons, for example, those mentioned in section 20 of the Act or other persons in a similar position of direction or general management. A company may have an alter ego, if those persons who are or have its ego delegate to some other person the control and management, with full discretionary powers, of some section of the company's business. In the case of a company, it may be difficult, and in most cases for practical purposes unnecessary, to draw the distinction between its ego and its alter ego, but theoretically there is that distinction.

Mr. Clement, being the manager of one of the company's several hundreds of shops, could not be identified with the company's ego nor was he an alter ego of the company. He was an employee in a relatively subordinate post. In the company's hierarchy there were a branch inspector and an area controller and a regional director interposed between him and the board of directors.

The case thus establishes that, depending on the specific wording of the strict liability offence and its defence, a due diligence offence may provide significant scope for a body corporate to avoid liability.

The question of whether the actions of a site manager could be attributed to the company that employed him arose again in the recent environmental case of *R v St Regis Paper Co Ltd*.[30] The case concerned the fabrication of false records about emissions to water from a paper mill by the site manager, contrary to Regulation 32(1)(g) of the then Pollution Prevention and Control (England and Wales) Regulations 2000. The Court held that the intention to make a false entry could only be attributed to the company on the basis of the rule in *Tesco v Nattrass*. The Court also ruled that, on the facts of the case, the intentions of the site manager could not be attributed to the company, St. Regis Paper Co Ltd, because the site manager was not the directing mind and will of the company. Hence, the Court of Appeal followed *Tesco v Nattrass*.

R v St Regis Paper Co Ltd
[2011] EWCA Crim 2527 (Court of Appeal (Criminal Division)) Official Transcript
paras 14–18 (Lord Justice Moses)

There is, in those circumstances, no basis for suggesting that the Regulations, designed as they are to protect the environment and prevent pollution, cannot function without imposing liability on

---

[30] Court of Appeal (Criminal Division), 4 November 2011, [2011] EWCA Crim 252 [2012] Env LR 16.

the company in respect of one who is not the directing will and mind of the company. We do not, accordingly, agree with the judge that it is necessary to relax the rule in Tesco v Nattrass to avoid emasculating the legislation, as he put it. Parliament has chosen to protect the environment against pollution in circumstances to which the Regulations apply by imposing strict liability in some cases but requiring *mens rea* in others.

15. Thus the only question, in relation to attribution, is whether it was open to the jury to conclude that the technical manager Mr Steer was, within the meaning of Tesco v Nattrass , the controlling mind and will of St. Regis for the purposes of the submission of records of emissions. As the Recorder put it, was Mr Steer in actual control of the operations of the company in relation to the submission of records and not responsible to another person for the manner in which he discharged his duties in the sense of being under that other person's orders?

16. In our view, it was not open to the jury to conclude that Mr Steer fell within the category of one whose state of mind can be attributed to the company. We do not agree with HH Judge Wassall that the facts which, of course, he had to assume on the basis of the prosecution case, admitted such a conclusion.

17. As we have mentioned, the Higher Kings Mill plant was but one of five mills and the smallest. As Technical and Environmental Manager, Mr Steer reported to the Mill Operations Manager, Mr Stoddart, who reported to the mill's Managing Director. The mill's Managing Director reported to divisional technical managers and a Divisional Environmental Director, who formed part of the senior management team of some 8–10 divisional directors.

18. The directors set an express company environmental policy which formed part of the prosecution exhibits: this did not grant any discretion to falsify records. On the contrary, the company's key objectives required achievement of environmental targets set by the relevant standards and reporting daily the previous day's performance of effluent plant operation. The 'key accountability' statement of Mr Steer required him to ensure environmental standards and promote and develop 'best practice in health and safety and environmental performance at Higher Kings Mill'. On those facts, it was not open to any jury to conclude that Mr Steer fell within the category described by Viscount Dilhorne as someone who was in actual control of the operations of a company or part of them and not responsible to another person in the company for the manner in which they were discharged.

In other environmental cases, however, the courts have sidestepped the application of the rule in *Tesco v Nattrass*, and instead relied on the precedent of *Alphacell v Woodward*.[31] Moreover, in some cases, the courts have adopted a purposive interpretation in order to ensure that the environmental protection objectives of the relevant strict liability offence are achieved.

In this way, the reasoning in *National Rivers Authority (Southern Region) v Alfred McAlpine Homes East Ltd* suggests that the courts will look at the question whether criminal liability can be attributed to a company differently if significant environmental pollution is at stake.[32] In this case, the Court adopted a purposive interpretation of the strict liability offence under the now repealed s 85 of the WRA 1991. The court sought to give expression to the objective of this offence, which was to prevent and sanction water pollution. The historical and current water pollution offences are discussed further in Chapter 14. Here, the construction of the former water pollution offence in s 85(1) WRA 1991 is relevant:

a person contravenes this section if he causes or knowingly permits any poisonous, noxious or polluting matter [...] to enter any controlled waters.

[31] *Alphacell Ltd v Woodward* [1972] AC 824. See further analysis of this case in Chapter 14.
[32] Queen's Bench Division , 26 January 1994, [1994] Env LR 198.

The company McAlpine Homes East Ltd was involved in a house-building project in East Malling. A nearby stream, which was controlled water for the purposes of s 104 of the Water Resources Act 1991, ran in a man-made culvert through the building site. The stream entered first a lake and then the river Medway. A water quality engineer of the Southern Region branch of the then National Rivers Authority (NRA) inspected the stream on 21 May 1992, and found it to be cloudy and containing dead fish downstream of the building site. The building company's site agent and site manager admitted to the NRA that the stream had become polluted due to cement being washed from the building site into the stream.

McAlpine argued that they had no case to answer for two reasons. First, they argued that the company could not be held liable, because the statute here did not expressly provide for vicarious liability of the body corporate for the acts of its servants and employees. They suggested that if Parliament had intended to create vicarious liability in the case of a s 85 WRA 1991 offence, it would have also provided a due diligence defence for companies that would allow companies to exonerate themselves if they have taken all reasonable steps, for instance through their management procedures, to avoid the commission of a strict liability offence. Second, the company argued that, on the basis of the rule in *Tesco v Nattrass*, they could only be held liable if the individuals who committed the actual offence could be considered as the controlling mind and will of the company.

On appeal, the question for the Divisional Court was, whether the Magistrates were correct in law to hold that a strict liability offence under s 85 WRA 1991 could only be committed if the offence was committed by a sufficiently senior employee.[33] The Divisional Court found that this was not the case. It therefore allowed the NRA's appeal and remitted the case for a rehearing. The Divisional Court distinguished *Tesco v Nattrass* and relied instead on *Alphacell v Woodward*.[34]

National Rivers Authority (Southern Region) v Alfred McAlpine Homes East Ltd
[1994] EWHC J0126–9, 12, 14 (Lord Justice Simon Brown)

Perhaps rather oddly, that decision [i.e. Alphacell v Woodward] appears not to have been placed before the justices in the present case. Their approach seems rather to have been dictated by the earlier decision of the House of Lords in Tesco Supermarkets Ltd v. Nattrass [1972] A.C. 153 (not cited in Alphacell, although two members of the Appellate Committee were party to both). To Tesco v. Nattrass I shall return. First, however, it is important to see how the company seek to explain and distinguish Alphacell.

[...]

I for my part see Alphacell as an illustration of vicarious liability rather than a case where the House of Lords concluded that those representing the directing mind and will of the company had themselves personally caused the polluting matter to escape. The failure in the pumps which was the immediate cause of the pollution was unexplained; but there was certainly nothing to link it to any senior officer in the company. True, none of their Lordships' speeches specifically referred to the company's servants or agents as such; nor did they expressly use the language of vicarious liability. But to my mind the whole tenor of the judgments is consistent only with that approach.

[...]The implication from these various dicta is surely unmistakable: an employer is liable for pollution resulting from its own operations carried out under its essential control save only where some third party acts in such a way as to interrupt the chain of causation.

[33] *National Rivers Authority (Southern Region) v Alfred McAlpine Homes East Ltd*, [1994] EWHC JO126, para 23.
[34] *Alphacell Ltd v Woodward* [1972] AC 824.

Is the present case then properly distinguishable from Alphacell in point of fact? I believe not, at least not on the evidence as it stood before the justices at the close of the authority's case. I see no difference in principle between the design and maintenance of a storage tank for pollutants (Alphacell), and the carrying on of building operations involving the use of pollutants (here cement to construct a water feature), each occurring on land adjacent to controlled waters. Either system, if ineffectively devised or operated, can result equally in the escape of polluting material into the adjacent stream

Similarly, in other environmental cases, the courts have also side-stepped the application of the rule in *Tesco v Nattrass* when deciding whether the acts of a site manager could be attributed to the company itself. In *Shanks & McEwan (Teesside) Ltd v Environment Agency*, the court took a narrower view and held the company liable for a strict liability waste offence.[35] The Court again followed *Alphacell v Woodward*,[36] holding that the company simply had to knowingly cause the operation of the underlying business.

In *Shanks*, the defendant waste management company, Shanks & McEwan, operated a licenced waste disposal site. On 31 July 1995, the site supervisor, Mr Hanlon, allowed a consignment of controlled waste to be offloaded into a specified tank. He completed an advice note accordingly. But the waste was in fact discharged by operatives on the site into a bund, and no further advice note was completed that would have stated the actual location into which the discharge was made. The company was prosecuted for having knowingly caused controlled waste to be deposited on land, with the deposit being in breach of condition 27 of the site waste management licence,[37] contrary to s 33(1)(a) of the Environmental Protection Act 1990 ('EPA'). Note that the waste offences under s 33 are discussed in further detail in Chapter 16. In the first instance, the justices convicted the company of the offence.

One key legal issue in the company's appeal before the High Court was the question of what had to be shown in order to find a company guilty of an offence under s 33(1)(a), which made it an offence to 'knowingly cause the deposit of controlled waste in contravention of a licence condition'.[38] Was it necessary for the prosecution to prove that a person who comprises or is part of the directing mind and will of the defendant company had knowledge that the deposit had occurred and that the deposit was in contravention of condition 27 of the site licence? If so, could the site supervisor, Mr Hanlon, be considered as the directing mind and will of the defendant company?

The High Court dismissed the appeal by Shanks & McEwan and found that s 33(1)(a) required only knowledge in relation to causing or permitting controlled waste to be deposited in or on any land. The knowledge requirement did not extend to knowing whether a waste management licence was in force for a *specific* deposit and whether that deposit was in accordance with particular site licence conditions, here condition 27. It was sufficient for the prosecution to show that Shanks & McEwan had, on

[35] *Shanks & McEwan (Teesside) Ltd v Environment Agency* [1998] 2 WLR 452.

[36] *Alphacell Ltd v Woodward* [1972] AC 824.

[37] Condition 27 of the site licence established what is in effect a standard procedure at waste disposal sites, including waste treatment plants. Condition 27 set out a procedure for off-loading liquid wastes from tankers, which required a site chemist to assess whether the load conformed to its description on its accompanying delivery note and whether it was compatible with existing liquid wastes in the storage tanks. The site chemist also had to issue an advice note that recorded where the liquid waste was deposited, and in case it was incompatible with existing wastes in the storage containers, the note had to record that the waste load was to be rejected.

[38] Note that the wording of s 33(1)(a) has now changed in minor respects, but the substance of the offence remains the same. See further, Chapter 16.

the relevant day, knowingly operated the site for the reception and deposit of controlled waste, and that the deposit in fact had been in breach of condition 27 of the site licence. Hence, criminal liability for the company did not arise here on the grounds that Mr Hanlon could be considered to be acting as the directing mind and will of the company.[39]

Shanks & McEwan (Teesside) Ltd v Environment Agency
[1999] QB 333, 342–43 (Mance J)

The second question assumes that under section 33(1) whatever knowledge is referred to by the word 'knowingly' must be by a person comprising or part of the directing mind and will of the company. As the case was argued before us, without objection, that was in issue. In the prosecutor's submission, section 33(1) imports vicarious responsibility for the conduct and knowledge of any servant of the defendant company acting in the course of his authority. As to what must be known, the prosecutor submits that section 33(1)(a) only requires knowledge of the fact of deposit and not of the breach of condition. The defendant submits that there must not only be knowledge of both, but that in the present case not even knowledge of the relevant deposit is established, since, in the defendant's sub-mission, that would have involved knowledge of the deposit into the bund on the part of the defend-ant's senior management.

I take first the issue whether the knowledge required by section 33(1)(a) goes to the breach of condition as well as the deposit (however that may be identified). On this issue, the prosecutor is in my judgment clearly correct. The structure of the section is that the word 'knowingly' qualifies on its face two (out of three) of the cases identified in its first part; and the exception beginning 'unless a waste management licence ...' appears as a separate factual qualification on all three cases, not involving any requirement of knowledge. The mitigation of the strictness of section 33(1)(a)—and indeed of section 33(1) and (6) generally—is on this basis to be found in the exceptions provided by section 33(7) . Section 33(7) not only mitigates section 33(1) and (6), it indicates why it is appropriate to read those subsections strictly; the defendant's submissions would in fact introduce a considerable element of overlap into the provisions of section 33(1) and (7).

The case clarifies that, for the strict liability waste offence under s 33(1)(a), the senior management of a company need not have knowledge of the specific waste deposit being in contravention of the site licence. The company's knowledge simply has to extend to the operation of the underlying business, that is, the acceptance of waste for storage and processing at the site.

The question of what knowledge the defendant must have in the case of the strict liability offence of unlawful deposit of waste under s 33 EPA is further complicated by the fact that the definition of waste is complex and not entirely clear, as further discussed in Section 1 of Chapter 16. The strict liability offence under s 33 is made out if waste is unlawfully deposited on land. But what if the defendant claims he or she did not know that it was waste that was deposited on their land, and that he or she considered the material to be of value? The issue arose in the case of *R v Evan Jones, John Jones & Sons Ltd*,[40] which shows how uncertain definitions of key statutory terms in criminal environmen-tal offences can in fact *increase* the threshold of meeting the knowledge requirement, even in the case of strict liability offences. Thus, in the case of complex environmental offences, such as s 33(1)

---

[39] The Court found that Mr Hanlon could not be considered as the directing mind and will of the company.
[40] [2011] EWCA Crim 3294 (Court of Appeal, Criminal Division).

EPA, the question about what knowledge the defendant must have had at the time of the commission of the offence can be difficult to answer.

FURTHER READING AND QUESTIONS

1. In this section, we have outlined key generic features of criminal environmental offences. Most of these offences are spelt out in specific environmental regulatory regimes, which provide an important context to these offences, such as Regulations 12 and 38 of the Environmental Permitting Regulations 2010 for the water pollution offence and s 33 EPA 1990 for the waste offence. There are, however, also a number of other criminal offences that are significant for regulatory agencies efforts to combat environmental crime. Given limitations of space, only a few will be mentioned here. There is, for instance, the Fraud Act 2006, which provides for the criminal offences of fraud by false representation and fraud by failing to disclose information. This is particularly valuable in case the particular environmental statute does not provide for offences in relation to the provision of information. Where environmental wrongdoing by corporations leads to citizens' deaths the criminal offence under s 1 of the Corporate Manslaughter and Corporate Homicide Act 2007 may be applicable. Moreover, environmental regulators may bring prosecutions for conspiracy and fraud, as well as apply for orders under the Proceeds of Crime Act 2002 that seek to deprive environmental offenders of financial gains obtained from their offences.

2. Read the case of *O'Grady Plant and Haulage Limited, Paul O'Grady, Sarah O'Grady v London Borough of Tower Hamlets*[41] for a further clarification of the scope of the strict liability offence under s 33 EPA 1990 in case exemptions from the waste management licensing regime apply, such as those set out in Regulations 17 (1) and (4) of the then Waste Management Licensing Regulations 1994.

3. For further analysis of criminal activity in the context of corporate conduct, see Brent Fisse and John Braithwaite, *Corporations, Crime and Accountability* (1993).

---

3 ENVIRONMENTAL CRIMINAL 'LAW IN ACTION'

3.1 WHY IS CRIMINAL PROSECUTION A LAST RESORT OPTION?

While the criminal law is a potentially powerful tool for environmental regulators, it plays only a limited role in actual enforcement practice.[42] For instance, only 25% of local authorities prosecute offenders under s 33 of the Environmental Protection Act (EPA) 1990 for fly-tipping. Even for strict liability offences, prosecution is only a last resort.[43] When deciding whether to bring a prosecution the EA will consider whether a number of criteria are met, beyond the simple requirement that there is sufficient evidence for supporting an allegation that the criminal offence has been committed.

---

[41] [2011] EWCA Crim 1339; [2011] Env LR 30.

[42] This chimes with a limited use of criminal prosecutions for regulatory purposes in general. Only about 1.5–2.0% of defendants in the Crown Court are tried for regulatory offences (excluding motoring offences). In the Magistrates' Courts this figure is ca. 10%. Law Commission Consultation Paper (n 17) para 1.26.

[43] Paula De Prez, 'Excuses, Excuses: The Ritual Trivialisation of Environmental Prosecutions' (2000) 12 JEL 67; Neal Shover and Aaron S Routhe, 'Environmental Crime' (2005) 32 Crime and Justice 321, 322.

In the past, the EA had a relatively straightforward and standalone Prosecutions Policy setting out these criteria. However, this has been replaced by a more holistic and strategic approach to regulatory enforcement, which requires regulators to consider their full range of regulatory options before bringing a prosecution. Thus, the criteria to guide decisions to bring a prosecution are now found in the EA's 'Enforcement and Sanctions—Guidance' document, which is one of a suite of three documents that set out the EA's enforcement policy.[44] The most detailed of these documents—'Offence Response Options'—goes through the available enforcement options for each environmental offence, one by one (and there are a lot of offences).[45] This is because the range of enforcement options varies for different offences, for reasons that are explained further in the Guidance and internal EA procedures for structuring the exercise of civil sanction powers section. The relevant criteria for bringing a prosecution are thus now those set out here.

Environment Agency, 'Enforcement and Sanctions—Guidance' (4 January 2011) 13–16

When we are considering our response to an offence there will normally be a range of possible sanctioning responses available for us to use [...] A list of all available sanctions for each offence is contained within our Offence Response Options (ORO) document.

First we will consider the outcome that we are seeking to achieve in accordance with our commitment to outcome-focused regulation. [...] These outcomes may include lasting compliance with the law, redress for environmental harm and obtaining a good and lasting benefit for the environment, affected local communities, and ensuring a level playing field for businesses and others. [...]

Where we consider that advice and guidance has not or will not achieve the necessary outcome, and that some form of sanction (either criminal or civil) is required to secure that outcome, then we will consider the facts against public interest factors (set out below) in order to decide what type of sanction to impose. [...]

The Public Interest Factors

General

The importance of each public interest factor may vary on a case by case basis. Deciding on the public interest is not simply a matter of adding up the number of factors in favour of and against applying a sanction. We will decide how important each factor is in the circumstances of each case and make an overall judgement.

[...]

Intent

Offences that are committed deliberately, recklessly or with gross negligence are more likely to result in prosecution. Where an offence was committed as a result of an accident or a genuine mistake this is more likely to result in the use of advice and guidance, warning or an available civil sanction.

---

[44] Environment Agency, 'Enforcement and Sanctions—Guidance', at: <http://www.environment-agency.gov.uk/static/documents/Business/Enforcement_and_Sanctions_Guidance.pdf>.

[45] Environment Agency, 'Offence Response Options' at: <http://www.environment-agency.gov.uk/business/regulation/31851.aspx>. See also Environment Agency, 'Enforcement and Sanctions—Statement', at: <http://www.environment-agency.gov.uk/business/regulation/31851.aspx>.

Foreseeability

Where the circumstances leading to the offence could reasonably have been foreseen, and no avoiding and/or preventative measures were taken, the response will normally be to impose a sanction beyond advice and guidance or the issuing of a warning.

Environmental Effect

The response will address the potential and actual harm to people and the environment.
[...]

Nature of the Offence

Where the offending impacts on our ability to be an efficient and effective regulator, for instance where our staff are obstructed in the conduct of their duties, where we are targeting a particular type of offending or where we are provided with false or misleading information, we will normally prosecute.

Financial Implications

Where legitimate business is undercut, or where profits are made or costs are avoided, such as costs saved by not obtaining a permit, this will normally lead to the imposition of a Variable Monetary Penalty or a prosecution. This will include offences motivated by financial gain.

Deterrent Effect

When choosing a sanction we will consider the deterrent effect, both on the offender and others. Prosecutions, because of their greater stigma if a conviction is secured, may be appropriate even for minor non-compliances where they might contribute to a greater level of overall deterrence.

Where the use of a sanction is likely to reduce future self-reporting of offences or non-compliance, a different sanction may be appropriate.

Previous History

The degree of offending and/or non-compliance (including site-specific offending or generic failures by the offender) will be taken into account. We will normally escalate our enforcement response where previous sanctions have failed to achieve the desired outcome [...]

Attitude of the Offender

Where the offender has a poor attitude towards the offence and/or is uncooperative with the investigation or remediation, this will normally mean that we consider a prosecution or a Variable Monetary Penalty. Conversely, where the offender provides us with the details of an offence voluntarily or through a self-reporting mechanism, we will take this into account when deciding on a sanction or whether advice and guidance will suffice.

Personal Circumstances

We will consider the personal circumstances of the offender (for example if the offender is suffering from a serious illness). A first offence by a juvenile will not normally result in prosecution.

When we are considering a sanction that incorporates a financial penalty or a requirement to perform costly remediation we will carefully consider the offender's ability to pay.

A range of 'other public interest consideration' are then set out, including those for serious offences, minor breaches, repeat offending, offences by bodies corporate, offences over multiple sites, and combining sanctions.

In light of this policy, it is perhaps not surprising that, once cases have passed through this significant filtering process, conviction rates are high, at just over 90% for the EA for England and Wales and the Forestry Commission.[46] But the use of criminal prosecutions is patterned in specific ways, raising questions about whether criminal sanctions are used in the most effective way. For instance, in 2006 the vast majority of companies fined £5,000 or more were small and medium-sized businesses,[47] leaving potential regulatory breaches of larger companies unsanctioned. So why are criminal prosecutions not more widely used? Three key reasons can be identified.

Insufficiently severe sentences

The first reason are insufficiently severe sentences, including a low level of fines, which undermines the effectiveness of using criminal prosecutions for general or individual deterrence. Empirical studies suggest that increasing the severity of threatened penalties for violating, for instance hazardous waste regulations, improves compliance by facilities with legal obligations.[48]

Low fines also further reinforce the moral ambiguity of environmental crime, discussed in Section 1, thereby undermining the symbolic power of criminal law to promote compliance with environmental obligations.[49] Evidence submitted to the Hampton Review further illustrates the point that, on average, fines currently imposed by UK courts are too low to exert a function of individual or general deterrence:

For example, a person who was paid £60,000 to dump toxic waste and which cost the local authority £167,000 to clean up, was fined only £30,000. A waste disposal company which had illegally dumped waste for two years, saving £250,000, was fined only £25,000. A company which illegally dumped several thousand tonnes of waste over a ten year period was fined only £830.[50]

Water and waste offences attract the highest fines.[51]

However, in specific instances high fines are imposed by the courts in order to reflect the seriousness of the crime. For example, Cardiff Crown Court imposed in 1999 a record £4 million fine on the Milford Haven Port Authority for the Sea Empress oil disaster, in addition to an order to pay £825,000 towards the costs of the prosecution.[52] The Court of Appeal, however, reduced the fine to £750,000, reflecting still the cultural reluctance of the courts to treat environmental crime as deserving of severe punishment.

---

46 Julia Black, 'Appendix A, A Review of Enforcement Techniques' in Law Commission Consultation Paper No 195, Criminal Liability in Regulatory Contexts (August 2010) para A.14. Moreover, a high percentage of prosecutions for environmental offences are settled by guilty pleas (Shover and Routhe (n 1) 351).

47 Effective inspection and enforcement: Implementing the Hampton Vision in the Environment Agency, at: <http://www.nao.org.uk/publications/0708/hampton_environment_agency.aspx>, 36–37.

48 Neal Shover and Aaron S Routhe, 'Environmental Crime' (2005) 32 Crime and Justice 321, 337.

49 DEFRA, Fly-Tipping Strategy: A Consultation Document (London, February 2004), at: <http://archive.defra.gov.uk/environment/quality/local/flytipping/measures.htm>; Neal Shover and Aaron S Routhe, 'Environmental Crime', (2005) Crime and Justice 321, 322–3.

50 Black Evidence to Law Commission, (n 46), para A.16. The average fine imposed by Magistrates' Courts for environmental offences in 2003–4 was £ 6.680; In the Crown Court the figure was ca. £34,000.

51 Effective inspection and enforcement: Implementing the Hampton Vision in the Environment Agency, at: <http://www.nao.org.uk/publications/0708/hampton_environment_agency.aspx>, 36–37.

52 Regina v Milford Haven Port Authority, Official Transcript, para 7.

Regina v Milford Haven Port Authority **Court of Appeal Criminal Division**
[16 March 2000] 2000 WL 331173 Official Transcript paras 49–50 (Lord Bingham of Cornhill)

49. We fully appreciate the judge's reasons for regarding this as a very serious case calling for a substantial penalty. He was rightly anxious to make clear that offences of this kind on this scale come high in the scale of seriousness. But we conclude that he did fall into error in failing to give effect to the agreed basis of the Port Authority's plea of guilty, in failing to give full credit for its plea of guilty, and in failing to consider the possible impact of a £4m fine on the Port Authority's ability to perform its public functions. We also conclude (although largely on the basis of material which was not before the judge) that he took much too rosy a view of the Port Authority's financial position and prospects.

50. We are satisfied that in the result the fine imposed was in all the circumstances manifestly excessive. That leaves us with the difficult task of substituting what we consider an appropriate fine. It must be at a level which recognises the seriousness of such disasters and the need to ensure the highest levels of vigilance. But it should not be such as to cripple the Port Authority's business and blight the economy of Pembrokeshire. We conclude that, in the light of all the circumstances now known to us, an appropriate fine is one of £750,000. We will grant a reasonable period of time for payment to be made

Various reasons informed the Court of Appeal's justification of the lower fine.[53] A significant consideration was the impact of the fine on the economic viability of the Port Authority. The Port Authority could not simply recoup the cost of the fine from raising charges to its customers. Cuts to its capital expenditure due to the fine could jeopardize safety and operational requirements. The Port Authority's financial position had already been affected by the order to pay the prosecution costs, its own legal costs, the costs of the clean-up of the oil spill, and the costs of conducting an extensive review of safety procedures in the operation of the port.[54] The case thus illustrates the limits of using fines to achieve general and specific deterrence of environmental crimes.

The case also illustrates the moral ambiguity of environmental crime. Counsel for the *Milford Haven Port Authority* argued that since a strict liability offence was at stake here—that is, a conviction for breach of the then s 85(1) WRA 1991—the Port Authority did not have a blameworthy mind. This lack of culpability of the Port Authority should be considered as a mitigating factor in the sentencing decision. But Parliament has imposed strict liability offences especially for those risks and harms that are considered as serious, a point that the Court of Appeal recognized.[55] Hence, conviction for a strict liability offence indicates that a very serious offence has been committed, even though a blameworthy mind is absent.

At times (and it seems increasingly), the courts will also impose custodial sentences for serious environmental crime. In *R v Hinchcliffe*,[56] the Court of Appeal imposed a sentence of two years imprisonment on the defendant Roy Hinchcliffe, who was seventy-one years of age, for four offences

---

[53] The Court also reviewed a range of previous environmental pollution and safety accident cases in which substantial fines had been imposed both on private companies and public operators, which it considered to turn on its own facts. For instance, the Court referred to the imposition of a £1 million fine on Shell in 1990 for oil pollution of the Mersey due to a spill from their pipeline and the imposition of a £250,000 fine in the case of the Clapham rail crash in 1988, as well as the imposition in 1997 of a fine of £1.7 million for the collapse of a walkway at Port Ramsgate. The Court of Appeal also referred to the fine of £1.5 million imposed on Great Western Trains Company Ltd for the Southall train crash, as well as a fine of £1.2 million imposed on Balfour Beatty for the collapse of a tunnel at Heathrow airport (*Regina v Milford Haven Port Authority*, Official Transcript, paras 26–33).

[54] *Regina v Milford Haven Port Authority*, Official Transcript, paras 23, 43.

[55] Magistrates Association, 'Costing the Earth: Guidance for Sentencers', (2009) 2; *Regina v Milford Haven Port Authority*, Official Transcript, para 38.

[56] [2012] EWCA Crim 169.

in breach of Regulations 12 and 38 of the then Environmental Permitting (England and Wales) Regulations 2007. A sixteen-month sentence was imposed on the son, Neil Roy Hinchcliffe. The Court found that there had been 'flagrant, deliberate and sustained disregard of the regulations'.[57]

The circumstances of the case were stark. The defendants, Roy and Neil Roy Hinchcliffe had stored waste at a licenced waste disposal site in complete excess of the amount the waste licence allowed to be stored there. They were also accepting waste onto two other sites that had no environmental permit. Over a period of two years waste enforcement officers had sought unsuccessfully to get the defendants to reduce the amount of waste stored. The waste piles had finally fallen onto the riverbank.

R v Hinchcliffe
[2012] EWCA Crim 1691 para 18 (Mr Justice Edwards-Stuart)

18 The judge said that the appellant's purpose was financial gain. There was clear evidence of the amount saved by not observing the regulations. As he observed, it was of course the community that had to pay for the consequences of these infringements. The judge said he could find no mitigation apart from the appellant's plea of guilty for which he was given full credit. He also had regard to the appellant's age and medical condition but he said that the prison authorities would cope with both of those factors. The judge took as his starting point 3 years' imprisonment and then reduced it to 2 years to reflect the early plea of guilty. In the case of the appellant's son, Neil, the sentence was 16 months' imprisonment.

The problem is that magistrates have tended to impose low fines in the case of environmental offences, often leading to a situation where it is financially more rewarding for the defendant to continue committing environmental offences and pay fines than to comply with environmental regulations. There is now guidance available, which structures Justices' discretion in sentencing, and seeks to reverse this sentencing trend for environmental crimes.

Magistrates Association, *Costing the Earth: Guidance for Sentencers* (London 2009) 3

Justices hearing environmental cases, and their legal advisers, may wish to ask a range of questions. Hopefully much of the guidance provided in the following sections will provide a helpful basis for further points of clarification. For instance, for any given case the following questions, principally of the prosecution, could be asked:

- What is the cost of any damage arising from the illegality—both financial and qualitative (damage to the environment etc)?
- What is the cost of any clear-up of the damage; and who will bear/has borne it?

Can a compensation order be made to cover some or all of that cost?

- Are the company's accounts available? What do they show about the impact of the illegality on the firm's finances?
- What is the cost of conducting the business legally—obtaining licences, permits, remedial/preparatory/compliance works to enable a licence to be granted etc?
- What are the court's powers—fine, custody etc? Compensation? Prosecution costs? Confiscation order or any other ancillary orders?
- What sentences have been imposed in other similar cases?

---

[57] *R v Hinchcliffe* [2012] EWCA Crim 169 para 29.

The Magistrates' Guidance points to further key criteria that Justices should consider when imposing sentences for environmental offences. These criteria flesh out ss 142, 143, and 144 of the Criminal Justice Act 2003. The guidance, overall, seeks to direct Magistrates' attention to two issues. First, a greater understanding of the integrated nature of the environment should be embraced. The guidance encourages Magistrates to go beyond a narrow focus on the localized offence, in order not to overlook its potentially wider environmental consequences. The guidance thus encourages Justices to consider 'the bigger picture, diffuse impact, cumulative effects and long-term effects' of the environmental crime.[58] For instance, is a specific fish kill linked to the wider extinction of fishing stocks? Secondly, the guidance addresses traditional criminal law sentencing points that focus on the individual offender and the specific offence. Under this rubric, Magistrates are advised to ensure that the level of a fine is higher than the profits made by the defendant from breaching environmental law. Companies will be presumed to be able to pay unlimited fines unless they have presented evidence to the contrary.[59] Moreover, the guidance asks Magistrates to consider the state of mind, such as intention and recklessness, of the defendant in their sentencing decision, even in the case of strict liability offences.[60] In sentencing, Magistrates should also consider whether offenders have co-operated with enforcement authorities, their previous offence patterns, and whether there has been abatement of harm and mitigation by the defendant.[61] Note that, during 2013, the Sentencing Council plans to issue updated guidelines for environmental offences, with a view to improving further the robust and fair sentencing of environmental crimes.

Overall, the key consideration that should inform sentencing is the seriousness of the offence, which is determined by reference, firstly, to the culpability of the offender and, secondly, to the harm caused or risked by the offence.[62] In case Magistrates consider their own sentencing powers as insufficient, they can commit a case for sentencing to the Crown Court. Sentencing powers in the Crown Court usually involve an unlimited fine or a custodial sentence. Some statutory environmental regimes provide for specific sanctions. For instance, under Regulation 29 of The Conservation of Habitats and Species Regulations 2010, the court can impose an order requiring the offender to restore harm caused to protected habitats. Section 33B EPA enables the court to order the defendant to pay for clean-up costs in the case of waste offences.

Perceived lack of effectiveness of criminal prosecutions

A second reason for the limited use of criminal prosecutions for environmental crime is that they may not be the most effective use of the regulator's limited staff and financial resources. It can take a year from discovery of the offence to a hearing in court, thus involving significant delay not only for the regulator but also the defendant businesses or individuals.[63] Moreover, regulators who pursue a risk-based regulatory strategy will focus their resources, including inspections and enforcement action, on the most hazardous operations. But this leaves potentially a large range of installations with moderate environmental impacts below the radar of the regulator's attention.[64] This effect is further reinforced by the fact that there are not always specific victims of environmental crime that raise complaints with law enforcement agencies.

---

[58] Magistrates Association, 'Costing the Earth: Guidance for Sentencers' (2009), 10.
[59] *R v Howe & Son (Engineers) Ltd* [1999] 2 All ER 249. The case concerned Health and Safety offences.
[60] Magistrates Association, 'Costing the Earth: Guidance for Sentencers' (2009) 11.
[61] Ibid, 14.   [62] Ibid, 17.   [63] Law Commission (n 17) 2.
[64] Helena Du Rées, 'Can Criminal Law Protect the Environment?' (2001) 2 Journal of Scandinavian Studies in Criminology and Crime Prevention 114.

Prosecution versus co-operative regulatory approaches

The third reason that criminal prosecutions are only used as a last resort is because they conflict with another key role that regulators have to fulfil, which is to advise, educate, and co-operate with installations that have impacts on the environment.[65] In this capacity, the EA seeks to reconcile its aim to protect the environment with the objective to facilitate rather than shut down economic operations:

[t]he EA has taken a national enforcement position not to take action against businesses who store certain waste materials, without causing harm, above the legal limit in the light of the severe economic downturn, prevailing market conditions and the relatively low level of risk to people and the environment arising from this activity. [66]

Operators are likely to withdraw co-operation, including voluntary reporting of potentially unlawful emissions, if they will be prosecuted.

Given the fact that there are structural reasons for the low use of criminal prosecutions, such as limited resources, role conflicts for the regulator, and an entrenched moral ambiguity of environmental crime, reform of the enforcement of environmental law has led to the creation of a new civil sanctions regime. English environmental law now provides for a hybrid system of sanctioning. Under the new civil sanctions regime, regulators can chose whether to prosecute certain offences or otherwise to impose themselves one of a range of civil sanctions. This regime is examined in Section 3.2.

3.2 CIVIL RATHER THAN CRIMINAL SANCTIONS

The current trend in English law is to decriminalize some regulatory offences and to reserve the criminal sanction for only the most serious of regulatory non-compliance.[67] The proposals of the Law Commission Consultation on 'Criminal Liability in Regulatory Contexts', which have been implemented through guidance to government departments,[68] further reinforce this point.

The Law Commission, Consultation Paper No 195, 'Criminal Liability in Regulatory Contexts: A Consultation Paper', at: <http://lawcommission.justice.gov.uk/areas/criminal-liability-in-regulatory-contexts.htm> paras 1.28; 1.29; 1.30; 1.38; 1.46; 1.48; 1.50, 1.55

1.28. The criminal law should only be employed to deal with wrongdoers who deserve the stigma associated with criminal conviction because they have engaged in seriously reprehensible conduct. It should not be used as the primary means of promoting regulatory objectives.

---

[65] Ibid, 117. See also the debate between Hawkins and Tombs about the relative merits of a compliance or deterrence approach to enforcement, Frank Pearce and Steve Tombs 'Ideology, Hegemony and Empiricism' (1990) 30 British Jnl of Criminology 423 and Keith Hawkins 'Compliance Strategy, Prosecution Policy and Aunt Sally' (1990) 30 British Jnl of Criminology 444.

[66] Department for Business, Innovation and Skills and the Better Regulation Executive, The Environment Agency: A Review of Progress since its Hampton Implementation Review, February 2010, 18, at: <http://www.bis.gov.uk/assets/biscore/better-regulation/docs/10-564-environment-agency-progress-since-hampton-implementation-review>.

[67] Richard Macrory *Regulatory Justice: Making Sanctions Effective* Final Report (Better Regulation Executive, November).

[68] Ministry of Justice, Criminal Offences Gateway Guidance, at: <http://www.justice.gov.uk/legislation/criminal-offences-gateway>.

1.29. Proposal 2: Harm done or risked should be regarded as serious enough to warrant criminalisation only if,

    (a) in some circumstances (not just extreme circumstances), an individual could justifiably be sent to prison for a first offence, or

    (b) an unlimited fine is necessary to address the seriousness of the wrongdoing in issue, and its consequences.

1.30. Proposal 3: Low-level criminal offences should be repealed in any instance where the introduction of a civil penalty (or equivalent measure) is likely to do as much to secure appropriate levels of punishment and deterrence.

General principles: avoiding pointless overlaps between offences

1.38. Proposal 4: The criminal law should not be used to deal with inchoate offending when it is covered by the existing law governing conspiracy attempt, and assisting or encouraging crime.

1.46. Proposal 7: More use should be made of process fairness to increase confidence in the criminal justice system. Duties on regulators formally to warn potential offenders that they are subject to liability should be supplemented by granting the courts power to stay proceedings until noncriminal regulatory steps have been taken first, in appropriate cases.

1.48. Proposal 8: Criminal offences should be created and (other than in relation to minor details) amended only through primary legislation.[69]

1.50. Proposal 9: A regulatory scheme that makes provision for the imposition of any civil penalty, or equivalent measure, must also provide for unfettered recourse to the courts to challenge the imposition of that measure, by way of re-hearing or appeal on a point of law.

1.55. Proposal 11: In relation to wrongdoing bearing on the simple provision of (or failure to provide) information, individuals should not be subject to criminal proceedings—even if they may still face civil penalties—unless their wrongdoing was knowing or reckless.

The Law Commission's preference for civil sanctions, such as fixed penalties, warning, 'stop' or remediation notices, as well as powers of search and seizure, rather than criminal sanctions, chimes with the language of new public management,[70] which has also shaped regulatory strategies in the UK.[71] According to the Law Commission, using criminal law for regulatory purposes is 'uncertain, expensive and ineffective'.[72] Its proposals seek to ensure that the 'three Es' at the core of new public management—economy, efficiency, and effectiveness—are also applied to prosecution behaviour.[73] It should be noted that this preference for civil sanctions is already pervasive in environmental law. This is because various civil sanctions have been introduced within environmental regimes—for example, a range of notices, powers, and orders exist for regulators to issue or exercise under the contaminated land regime (Part IIA Environmental Protection Act 1990),[74] and the Environmental Damage (Prevention and Remediation) Regulations 2009.[75] The new civil sanctions regime thus overlays such existing civil sanctioning powers within particular regimes.[76] Since the civil sanctions regime does

---

[69] This is interesting also in light of the fact that the new water pollution offence was created through secondary legislation, through Regulations 38 and 12 of the Environmental Permitting Regulations (England and Wales) 2010. See further, Chapter 14.

[70] Discussed in further detail in Chapter 12.   [71] See further, Chapters 12 and 13.

[72] Law Commission (n 17) para 1.8.   [73] Ibid, 9.   [74] See further, Chapter 21.

[75] See further, Chapter 9.

[76] Civil sanctions apply in English law, for example, in relation to hazardous waste regulation and under the mandatory Carbon Reduction Commitment Energy Efficiency Scheme.

not apply in a blanket fashion to all environmental offences (as examined in Section 3.3), these different statutory sources of civil sanctions do not necessarily overlap, but there is a fragmentation in the kinds of civil sanctions now available in relation to environmental offences. Section 3.3 focuses on the new civil sanctions regime in detail, but do keep in mind that, while it is the most ambitious programme in this area of enforcement, it is not the full story.

3.3 THE ENVIRONMENTAL CIVIL SANCTIONS REGIME

Part III of the Regulatory Enforcement and Sanctions Act (RESA) 2008 introduces a new framework for civil regulatory sanctions by enabling ministers through secondary legislation to grant new civil sanctioning powers to regulators in relation to specific offences.

Thus, in relation to environmental offences, the Environmental Civil Sanctions (England) Order 2010 ('Civil Sanctions Order') and the Environmental Civil Sanctions (Miscellaneous Amendments) (England) Regulations 2010[77] confer RESA civil sanction powers upon the Environment Agency for England and Wales and Natural England. This new environmental civil sanctions regime became law in England in April 2010. In Wales similar statutory instruments were passed in July 2010.[78]

The key point of the new environmental civil sanctions regime is that regulators themselves—that is, the Environment Agency and Natural England—now have the power to impose sanctions without having to bring legal actions before the courts. More specifically, the Civil Sanctions Order and the Environmental Civil Sanctions (Miscellaneous Amendments) (England) Regulations 2010 confer upon the EA and Natural England powers to impose a range of specific civil sanctions for criminal offences that already exist in English environmental law.[79] Thus, civil sanctions exist for offences under the following key legislative provisions:

- Control of Pollution (Oil Storage) (England) Regulations 2001.
- Environment Act 1995.
- Environmental Protection Act 1990, s 33(1).
- Environmental Protection (Disposal of Polychlorinated Biphenyls and other Dangerous Substances) (England and Wales) Regulations 2000.
- Hazardous Waste (England and Wales) Regulations 2005.
- Hazardous Waste (Wales) Regulations 2005.
- Land Drainage Act 1991.
- Nitrate Pollution Prevention Regulations 2008 (England only).
- Producer Responsibility Obligations (Packaging Waste) Regulations 2007.
- Salmon Act 1986.
- Salmon and Freshwater Fisheries Act 1975.
- Sludge (use in agriculture) Regulations 1989.

---

[77] Environmental Civil Sanctions (England) Order 2010 SI 2010/1157 ('Civil Sanctions Order'). Environmental Civil Sanctions (Miscellaneous Amendments) (England) Regulations 2010 SI 2010/1159.

[78] The Environmental Civil Sanctions (Wales) Order 2010, SI 2010/1821 (W. 178) and the Environmental Civil Sanctions (Miscellaneous Amendments) (Wales) Regulations 2010, SI 2010/1820 (W. 177).

[79] Schedule 5 of the Environmental Civil Sanctions (England) Order 2010 lists which criminal offences in existing environmental legislation the new civil sanctions can be applied to.

- Transfrontier Shipment of Waste Regulations 2007.
- Water Industry Act 1991.
- Water Resources (Environmental Impact Assessment) (England and Wales) Regulations 2003.
- Water Resources Act 1991.

Note that this is a relatively embryonic and likely to be an evolving list of offences for which RESA civil sanctions are available. Civil sanctions are currently not available for many environmental offences, including the environmental permitting and water pollution offence under Regulations 12 and 38 of the Environmental Permitting (England and Wales) Regulations 2010, as well as most nature conservation offences.

The new civil sanctions regime is complex because not all of the six civil sanctions are available for each of the specific offences to which a civil sanction can be applied. Schedule 5 of the Civil Sanctions Order therefore specifies which of the six civil sanctions:

- *fixed* monetary penalty for minor offences (£ 300 for a body corporate, £ 100 for individuals);[80]
- *variable* monetary penalty for more serious offences (must not exceed £ 250,000);[81]
- compliance notice;
- restoration notice;
- stop notice (this is the only civil sanction that can be combined with prosecution); or
- enforcement undertaking

can be imposed for particular offences.

For instance, in relation to the waste criminal offence under s 33(6) EPA, schedule 5 to the Civil Sanctions Order lists in a table only the stop notice being available as a new civil sanction (see Table 8.1).

Note also that, in November 2012, the Government issued guidelines on the use of civil sanctioning powers. As a general rule, RESA powers to impose fixed monetary penalties, variable monetary penalties, and restoration notices will only be granted where their use is restricted to undertakings with more than 250 employees, while powers to impose enforcement undertakings, stop notices and compliance

Table 8.1 Civil sanctions available for the criminal offence under s 33(6) EPA 1990

Provision creating an offence	FMP	VMP	CN	RN	SN	EU
section 33(6)	No	No	No	No	Yes	No

[80] Schedule 1 para 1(3) of the Environmental Civil Sanctions (England) Order 2010.

[81] Schedule 2 para 1(5) of the Environmental Civil Sanctions (England) Order 2010. Most importantly, in calculating the amount of the variable penalty that can be imposed the regulator can take into account the financial benefit that the offender obtained from the offence. Schedule 2 para 1(6) of the Environmental Civil Sanctions (England) Order 2010 provides a power for the regulator to obtain information from the defendant about the size of the financial gain he or she obtained when committing the offence.

notices may be granted without restriction.[82] The rationale behind this development is that smaller businesses with fewer resources need protecting from potentially over-zealous regulators - they may face unfair difficulties in challenging the imposition of financial sanctions in particular. Larger regulated businesses, however, should be able to look after themselves. This development also fits with the coalition Government's agenda to cut regulatory burdens in relation to small businesses.

The six new civil sanctions provide important sanctioning powers for the Environment Agency and Natural England. Prior to RESA 2008, fixed or variable financial penalties were the main regulatory sanction available to regulators.[83] Now there are a whole range of civil sanctions available to the regulator, including stop notices. A stop notice prohibits a person from carrying on an activity that is specified in the notice until the person has taken the steps specified in that notice.[84] The notice can be imposed if the regulator reasonably believes that an activity is causing, or presents a significant risk of causing, serious harm to human health or the environment, including animal and plant health. A stop notice can also be imposed if the regulator reasonably believes that an offence, under a provision specified in Schedule 5, is likely to be committed by the person upon whom the notice is to be served.[85] It is thus an interim precautionary step.[86]

The imposition of civil sanctions as a staged process

The new civil sanctions regime seeks to achieve compliance with environmental law through a staged, gradual process. Before the regulator can impose any of the civil sanctions (apart from enforcement undertakings) it has to serve a Notice of Intent upon the defendant. This can initiate a process of advice and voluntary compliance by the regulated. Third party undertakings, for instance, can be a more formal step in the gradual process of achieving compliance with environmental law and remedying any harm that may have arisen from breach of environmental law obligations. They are struck between a defendant upon whom a notice for a civil sanction has been served by the regulator and a third party, who has been affected by the defendant's offence. The defendant will undertake to confer benefits, which may be financial benefits, upon the third party who has been affected by the offence. Third party undertakings have to be approved by the regulator, and it is up to the regulator's discretion whether to accept or to reject them.[87] This is an anthropocentric provision, which stops short of requiring the defendant to remedy any *environmental* harm caused by the offence. It focuses on harms as they affect a third party. Further, it gives the regulator considerable power to decide on questions relating to the distribution of resources in society, which arguably become even more problematic when the regulator agrees to financial payments being made to charities or local authorities under an enforcement undertaking (examined further in this section).

Moreover, those upon whom a notice has been served that indicates the intent of the regulator to impose a variable monetary penalty, a restoration, or a compliance notice, can submit written representations and objections to the regulator in relation to the notice.[88] In response to these objections and representations the regulator will then finally decide whether to proceed with the imposition of the civil sanction or whether it will modify the original notice of intent served.[89]

---

[82] Department for Business Innovation and Skills, Written Ministerial Statement: Use of Civil Sanctions Powers Contained in the Regulatory Enforcement and Sanctions Act 2008, 8 November 2012.

[83] Black, (n 46) para A.38.   [84] Schedule 3, para 1(2).   [85] Schedule 3, para 1(4) and (6).

[86] Anne Brosnan, 'The Environment Agency and Civil Sanctions: Steps Towards Implementation' (2010) Environmental Law Management 230.

[87] Schedule 2, para 4(2).   [88] Schedule 2, para 3.   [89] Schedule 2, para 5.

In the case of non-compliance with a compliance or restoration notice, or a third party undertaking, the regulator can serve a non-compliance penalty notice on the defendant, even if a variable monetary penalty notice has been already imposed for the same offence.[90] The EA or Natural England can themselves determine the amount of the penalty, with the penalty having to be 'a percentage of the costs of fulfilling the remaining requirements of the notice or third party undertaking'.[91]

The new civil sanctions regime provides new powers for regulators. Hence, safeguards for defendants to challenge the exercise of these powers are important, also in order to meet human rights requirements under Article 6(3) of the ECHR, as implemented through the Human Rights Act 1998. Those upon whom a civil sanction has been imposed can appeal against it to the General Regulatory Chamber of the First-tier Tribunal (Environment) (FTT), established under the Tribunals, Courts and Enforcement Act 2007.[92] An appeal suspends all notices with the exception of stop notices.[93] The regulator must prove in an appeal that the offence (except in relation to stop notices) has been committed 'to the same standard and burden of proof as in a criminal prosecution'.[94] In reviewing the imposition of a civil sanction, the FTT can consider the merits of the regulator's decision.[95] The FTT can confirm, withdraw or vary the requirement or notice, or 'take such steps as the regulator could take in relation to the act or omission giving rise to the requirement or notice'.[96]

Guidance and internal EA procedures for structuring the exercise of civil sanction powers

The staged process of imposing a civil sanction involves significant discretion for the regulator at each step of the decision-making process, though the exercise of these discretionary powers is further guided by the principles set out in s 5(2) RESA 2008. Regulatory activities should be carried out in a transparent, accountable, proportionate, and consistent manner. Moreover, regulatory activities should be targeted only at those cases in which action is needed. This fits well with the British flexible and discretionary approach to regulatory enforcement, but also raises questions about compliance with Article 6(3) ECHR as implemented through the HRA 1998 and compliance with Article 47 of the Charter of Fundamental Rights of the European Union. Hence, Article 11(1) of the Civil Sanctions Order requires the regulator to structure the exercise of its discretion through the publication of guidance in relation to the use of civil sanctions. As set out in Section 3.2, there is a three-tiered system of guidance. At the top level there is the EA's Enforcement and Sanctions Statement, then there is the Enforcement and Sanctions Guidance (extracted already), and finally the most detailed guidance is provided by the Offence Response Options (ORO) document. The ORO document is particularly important in light of the highly fragmented enforcement picture that now exists for the full range of environmental offences—a guide is required in order to know which sanctions are in fact available for each offence. Finally, the EA's discretion is guided by the generic Regulators' Compliance Code (RCC), which reflects the 'better regulation', co-operative approach to regulation. This requires regulators to carry out enforcement

---

[90] Article 7(1) Of the Environmental Civil Sanctions (England) Order 2010.   [91] Ibid, art 7(2).

[92] Article 10(1) of the Environmental Civil Sanctions (England) Order 2010. On the First-tier Tribunal, see further Chapter 10.

[93] Article 10(4) of the Environmental Civil Sanctions (England) Order 2010.

[94] Article 10(2) of the Environmental Civil Sanctions (England) Order 2010.

[95] Richard Macrory (2011) Consistency and Effectiveness; Strengthening the New Environmental Tribunal, 5. At: <http://www.ucl.ac.uk/laws/en/content/Consistency&Effectiveness_webfinal.pdf>

[96] Article 10(5)(6)(d) Environmental Civil Sanctions (England) Order 2010.

with minimum disruption to business activity and requires the regulated to be involved in the development of regulatory guidance.[97]

In addition to this formal guidance, the EA has established internal organizational procedures that seek to ensure the fair and consistent exercise of the new civil sanctions enforcement powers. Initial recommendations from EA field officers to impose a civil sanction will be reviewed by legally qualified EA staff and senior managers. Representations made by those upon whom a Notice of Intent has been served will be considered, not by the officer who originally served the notice, but by a more senior EA officer.[98] Moreover, all recommendations for the imposition of civil sanctions will be considered by a new National Panel, led by EA directors, which is sought to achieve consistency across different EA regions in the exercise of the new powers.

The new civil sanctions regime raises a range of interesting questions about the nature of the enforcement regime created by the civil sanctions, in particular its relationship to more co-operative approaches to enforcement, the criminal law process, and economic incentives for achieving compliance with environmental law.

Enforcement undertakings: a co-operative approach

Enforcement undertakings (EUs) have been the most popular RESA civil sanctions used to date. In the early phase of the civil sanctions regime, this was indeed the only civil sanction issued in relation to environmental offences, although a handful of fixed monetary penalties were also issued in the first eighteen months of the regime's operation (to June 2012). EUs demonstrate that the new civil sanctions regime is an integral part of the 'better regulation' agenda, which seeks to promote compliance with regulatory requirements without imposing excessive burdens upon business, as further discussed in Chapter 12. In particular, the new civil sanction of the EU reflects a co-operative, contractual approach to enforcing environmental law. The EU entails an offer by a person whom the regulator has reasonable grounds to suspect has committed an offence under the provisions specified in Schedule 5 of the Civil Sanctions Order, and an acceptance of that offer by the regulator. EUs can only be concluded if Schedule 5 indicates that an enforcement undertaking may be accepted in relation to the specific offence. An EU must specify the action that is necessary to secure that the offence does not continue or recur.[99] A key issue for the Environment Agency in deciding whether or not to accept an EU will be whether they make adequate provisions for 'fair and proportionate reparation of harm caused'.[100] An EU can spell out the actions that are necessary to ensure that the position is restored to the state it would have been in if the offence would not have occurred. This can include the payment of money to a person who has been affected by the offence. The person, who is suspected to have committed an offence, has to accept liability in relation to a specific set of facts set out in the EU, but does not have to admit guilt. Non-compliance with an enforcement undertaking is likely to lead to prosecution.

A co-operative approach is also reflected in other provisions of the Civil Sanctions Order 2010. Article 9, for instance, provides powers for the regulator to withdraw at any time in writing a fixed monetary penalty notice, variable monetary penalty notice, a non-compliance penalty notice, or an enforcement cost recovery notice. It is also possible for the regulator to reduce the level of penalty specified in a notice or to reduce the work specified as necessary. This provides significant flexibility and seems to suggest that the civil sanctions legal framework may induce 'bargaining in

---

[97] Brosnan (n 86) 229.   [98] Brosnan (n 86) 231.
[99] Para 2(1)(a) of Schedule 4 of the Environmental Civil (England) Sanctions 2010.   [100] Brosnan (n 86) 231.

the shadow of the law'.[101] So what is the nature of the new civil sanctions regime? Is it co-operative and negotiated, or punitive? Can the two approaches be successfully combined? Does a combination of these two approaches further affirm the moral ambiguity of environmental crime? What legal questions does the potential blurring of the boundary between criminal and civil sanctions raise?

A blurring of boundaries between civil and criminal sanctions?

The case of the enforcement undertakings already discussed reveals a wider phenomenon at play in relation to the role of civil sanctions in environmental law enforcement—the blurring of the boundaries between civil and criminal sanctions. Thus, it can be seen that, during an informal, co-operative phase of negotiating EUs, persons whom the EA has reasonable grounds to believe have committed a criminal offence will need to provide information in order to negotiate an EU. However, appropriate safeguards need to be in place here for defendants given the fact that a formal criminal investigation can be launched later by the regulator in case of non-compliance of the regulated with the terms of the enforcement undertaking. The prosecution unit of the EA has explicitly stated that it will not use information provided during the negotiation of EUs for criminal prosecutions, but information from a finalized EU may be used in subsequent criminal proceedings.[102]

In principle, the new civil sanctions are intended to be *alternative* courses of enforcement action, distinct from criminal prosecutions. Paragraph 9 of Schedule 2 of the Civil Sanctions Order clarifies that in case a variable monetary penalty, a compliance notice, or restoration notice is imposed on any person, that person cannot be criminally prosecuted for any act or omission. But if the person fails to comply with the variable monetary penalty, compliance notice, or restoration notice, it is possible to bring a criminal prosecution against that person for that act or omission. The provisions in relation to fixed monetary penalties are slightly tighter. Here there is only a prohibition to start criminal proceedings for twenty-eight days running from the day the notice of the regulator's intention to impose a fixed monetary penalty was received by a person.[103]

Moreover, if the person upon whom the Notice of Intent has been served discharges their liability under the fixed monetary penalty, then he or she can no longer be convicted of a criminal offence relating to their actions.[104] But this structure of criminal and civil sanctions as alternative sanctions is modified by the fact that failure of compliance with some of the civil sanctions can give rise to criminal liability. For instance, non-compliance with a stop notice by the time limit specified in that notice constitutes a criminal offence.[105]

Considering criminal prosecutions and sanctions as an *alternative* to the new civil sanctions regime, however, begs the question whether the new 'civil' sanctions are really very different in nature from 'criminal' sanctions. Various provisions in the new civil sanctions regime seem to suggest that the civil sanctions may not be entirely different in nature from criminal sanctions. First, Article 5 of the Civil Sanctions Order limits the cumulative use of civil sanctions, which seems to implement the criminal law principle of avoiding double jeopardy, that is, that a person should not be sanctioned twice for the same act or omission. Article 5(1) establishes that once the regulator has started with civil sanctions, such as the variable monetary penalty, or a compliance,

---

[101] R Harris Mnookin and Lewis Kornhauser 'Bargaining in the Shadow of the Law: The Case of Divorce', (1978–1979) 88 Yale LJ 950.

[102] Brosnan (n 86) 231.   [103] Schedule 1, para 10(1).   [104] Schedule 1, para 10(2).

[105] Schedule 3, para 6(1).

restoration, or stop notice, the civil sanction, of the fixed monetary penalty, cannot be imposed as well. Mirroring Article 5(1), Article 5(2)(a) adds to Article 5(1) that, if the regulator started enforcement proceedings with the serving of a fixed monetary penalty, other civil sanctions cannot be 'added on'.[106]

Second, some of the civil sanctions do not appear to be very different from criminal sanctions because they also require a criminal standard of burden of proof to be applied. For instance, in relation to fixed monetary penalties 'the regulator must be satisfied *beyond reasonable doubt* that the person has committed the offence', before the regulator can impose a fixed monetary penalty.[107] The same applies to variable monetary penalties, compliance and restoration notices.[108] Hence, when deciding whether to impose a civil sanction the EA will apply a threshold that is even higher than the one applied when deciding whether a criminal prosecution should be mounted. The EA currently applies for criminal prosecutions the test of whether there is 'a realistic prospect of securing a conviction'.[109]

But, in contrast, the standard of proof for EUs is that the regulator must have *reasonable grounds to suspect* that a criminal offence has been committed, while in the case of a stop notice, the regulator has to have merely *reasonable belief* that the activity to be stopped is causing harm to the environment or human health, or involves or is likely to involve the commission of an offence as specified under Schedule 5 of the Civil Sanctions Order.

To conclude, the new environmental civil sanctions regime further entrenches in law what has been long established enforcement practice—that criminal prosecutions are only to be used as a last resort.[110] In practice, the new regime is envisaged to also deploy civil sanctions merely as a last resort. The prosecution unit of the EA has clearly stated that it intends to make use of the new civil sanctions only in serious cases. It anticipates, for example, that in practice only very few fixed monetary penalties will be issued.[111] Whether the new regime will be able to implement the new public management aspiration of 'efficiency, effectiveness, and economy' in enforcement practice remains to be seen. Significant in this context is also a substantial power under Article 8(1) of the Civil Sanctions Order. Under this provision, the regulator can impose cost recovery notices upon the regulated. Costs recovered include the costs of expert advice, including legal advice. But 'effectiveness' in enforcement practices is difficult to achieve. It is not unusual for defendants to be unable to pay for restoration orders. This shifts the financial burden back to the taxpayer, potentially contrary to the polluter pays principle. The Environment Agency, for instance, estimates that there are about 50,000 cases of illegal dumping of waste each year, which cost local authorities between £50 million and £150 million to clean up.[112] In achieving the 'three Es' through the new civil sanctions regime it may therefore be necessary to consider extending provisions that seek to provide for financial guarantees for clean-up of pollution to a wider range of statutory regimes than the waste management regime. For instance, under s 39 EPA operators of waste disposal sites can be required to meet the continuing costs of managing waste disposal sites. For landfill sites specifically, the EA requires

---

[106] Article 5(2)(b) further clarifies that the regular no longer has powers to serve a notice of intent in relation to a variable monetary penalty, compliance notice or restoration notice, or a stop notice, if the defendant has already discharged his or her liability under a fixed monetary penalty.

[107] Schedule 1, para 1(2) of the Environmental Civil Sanctions (England) Order 2010.

[108] Schedule 2, para 1(2).   [109] Brosnan (n 86) 231.

[110] The regulatory impact assessment for the civil sanctions regime suggested that the Environment Agency may take potentially up to 20% fewer criminal prosecutions, now that alternative civil sanctions are available (Peter Kellett, 'Will civil penalties trump criminal sanctions'?, at: <http://www.ukela.org/content/page/1613/UP-ENVI-MI10038_BK_Civil%20Liberties.pdf>, 2).

[111] Brosnan (n 86) 230.

[112] Black (n 46) para A.74.

operators to enter into formal financial arrangements underwritten by financial institutions in order to cover potential future environmental clean-up liabilities, also in response to the EU Directive on Environmental Liability.[113]

FURTHER READING AND QUESTIONS

1. 'Environmental civil sanctions defy clear classification as either administrative or criminal legal provisions. This raises difficult questions about what, if any, administrative and criminal law principles should govern their application, also in order to protect defendants.' Do you agree? Specify which administrative and criminal law principles inform, in your view, the civil sanctions regime, and whether they provide sufficient safeguards for defendants.

2. In his report 'Regulatory Justice: Making Sanctions Effective' (Better Regulation Executive) (Final Report, November 2006, 10), Richard Macrory set out 'six penalties principles'. A sanction should:

   '1. Aim to change the behaviour of the offender;

   2. Aim to eliminate any financial gain or benefit from non-compliance;

   3. Be responsive and consider what is appropriate for the particular offender and regulatory issue, which can include punishment and the public stigma that should be associated with a criminal conviction;

   4. Be proportionate to the nature of the offence and the harm caused;

   5. Aim to restore the harm caused by regulatory non-compliance, where appropriate; and

   6. Aim to deter future non-compliance.'

   What do you consider as the respective strengths and weaknesses of civil and criminal sanctions in implementing these six penalties principles?

3. Pick one of the case studies from Part II of the 'Magistrates Association, 2009, Costing the Earth: Guidance for Sentencers'. Specify which sentence you would consider as appropriate to be imposed in the particular case you have chosen and justify your proposed sentence with reference to the criteria for sentencing discussed here.

---

4 TRANSNATIONALIZING ENVIRONMENTAL PROTECTION THROUGH CRIMINAL LAW

The criminalization of behaviour is usually perceived as a prerogative of nation states. The imposition of criminal sanctions upon citizens, one of the most coercive ways in which states can interact with their citizens, is at times justified on the grounds that a state's criminal code reflects the moral judgments of a national polity. Despite this strong link between nation states and criminal law there is, however, a developing body of international environmental criminal law. This body of international environmental law also seeks to respond to the fact that in an age of globalized economic relationships the control of environmentally damaging behaviour of corporations needs to be transnationalized.

---

[113] European Parliament and Council Directive 2004/35/EC on environmental liability with regard to the prevention and remedying of environmental damage [2004] L143/56. See further, Chapter 9.

Moreover, international responses to environmental pollution matter, given the fact that pollution often travels across state boundaries.

Initiatives for the protection of the environment through criminal law have also been developed in Europe. The Council of Europe adopted on 4 November 1998 a Convention on the protection of the environment through criminal law. While the Convention is important as a precursor to the adoption of the EU Directive on the protection of the environment through criminal law, note that the Convention itself has not yet entered into force. It has been signed only by fourteen states and ratified by one state to date, leaving 46 states to still ratify.[114] The UK has neither signed nor ratified the Convention.

4.1 LIMITED EU HARMONIZATION OF ENVIRONMENTAL CRIME

Legally most significant for shaping English environmental criminal law is, however, the recent EU Directive on the protection of the environment through criminal law (Environmental Crime Directive),[115] which takes into account the main provisions of the Council of Europe Convention. The Directive was passed because of the then European Community's concern about an increase in environmental offences in the EU and the transborder effects of a number of environmental harms (Preamble 2 to Environmental Crime Directive). The Directive is based on the idea that it is important to harness the capacity of environmental criminal law to provide general deterrence, a capacity that is considered to be greater for criminal law than administrative offences or civil liability (Preamble 3 to the Directive). The Directive provides only for a basic level of harmonization of environmental criminal law throughout the EU, because it does not spell out in detail specific environmental criminal offences that must be prosecuted consistently. It only requires Member States to ensure that criminal sanctions are available for the breach of specific obligations in EU environmental legislation (reading Articles 2(a), 3, and 5 together). Through this basic harmonization the Directive also seeks to facilitate co-operation between Member States in combating environmental crime. By requiring all Member States to criminalize the breach of key provisions of EU environmental law, opportunities for offenders to escape sanctions by 'forum shopping' for the location of environmentally damaging behaviour should be minimized. But the EU Directive on the protection of the environment through criminal law, in contrast to Article 8(1)(a) of the annulled Framework Decision on the same topic based on Articles 29, 31(e), and 34(2)(b) of Title VI of the EU Treaty, does not explicitly address the question of whether a Member State has power to criminalize environmental damaging behaviour where the effects of this behaviour occur entirely in another Member State.

The chequered legislative history of the Directive reflects concerns about the jurisdiction of the supranational EU institutions in relation to criminal environmental law. The Framework Decision was annulled in 2005 by the European Court of Justice (ECJ), which held that Article 34 TEU was the wrong legal basis for harmonized provisions on environmental crime.[116] The ECJ held that ex-Article 175(1) EC should have been the correct basis, and that the EU institutions did have powers under the then EC Treaty to pass legislation in relation to basic, harmonizing provisions on environmental crime.

The Directive strikes a delicate, if not entirely clear, balance between the jurisdiction of the EU supranational institutions and EU Member States in relation to environmental criminal law, by leaving the

---

[114] <http://www.conventions.coe.int/Treaty/en/Treaties/Html/172.htm>
[115] Directive 2008/99/EC [2008] OJ L 328/28.
[116] Case C-176/03 *Commission v Council (Environmental Crime)* [2005] 3 CMLR 20.

application of criminal sanctions or *other enforcement mechanisms in individual cases* within the ambit of Member Sates' national legal powers (Articles 5 and 7). All the Directive therefore does is to require Member States to create criminal offences (or maintain already existing national criminal offences) for the breach of EU environmental obligations already laid down in a range of existing EU environmental legislation, listed in Annexes A and B to the Environmental Crime Directive. Hence, the Directive requires that 'unlawful' conduct is sanctioned through criminal law in the Member States:

Article 2

Definitions

For the purpose of this Directive:

(a) 'unlawful' means infringing:

   (i) the legislation adopted pursuant to the EC Treaty and listed in Annex A; or

   (ii) with regard to activities covered by the Euratom Treaty, the legislation adopted pursuant to the Euratom Treaty and listed in Annex B; or

   (iii) a law, an administrative regulation of a Member State or a decision taken by a competent authority of a Member State that gives effect to the Community legislation referred to in (i) or (ii);

Note that Article 2(a)(iii) considerably widens the definition of 'unlawful' conduct by requiring that criminal offences are not just committed if a natural or legal person breaches primary statutory provisions that implement EU environmental law, as further defined in Annexes A and B to the Directive, but breach of administrative regulations or decisions taken in furtherance of the implementation of EU environmental law is sufficient. Article 3 of the Directive, then goes on to outline in general terms which types of environmentally harmful conduct should be subject to criminalization through national law in the Member States.

Article 3

Offences

Member States shall ensure that the following conduct constitutes a criminal offence, when unlawful and committed intentionally or with at least serious negligence:

(a) the discharge, emission or introduction of a quantity of materials or ionising radiation into air, soil or water, which causes or is likely to cause death or serious injury to any person or substantial damage to the quality of air, the quality of soil or the quality of water, or to animals or plants;

(b) the collection, transport, recovery or disposal of waste, including the supervision of such operations and the aftercare of disposal sites, and including action taken as a dealer or a broker (waste management), which causes or is likely to cause death or serious injury to any person or substantial damage to the quality of air, the quality of soil or the quality of water, or to animals or plants;

(c) the shipment of waste, where this activity falls within the scope of Article 2(35) of Regulation (EC) No 1013/2006 of the European Parliament and of the Council of 14 June 2006 on shipments of waste and is undertaken in a non-negligible quantity, whether executed in a single shipment or in several shipments which appear to be linked;

(d) the operation of a plant in which a dangerous activity is carried out or in which dangerous substances or preparations are stored or used and which, outside the plant, causes or is likely to cause death or serious injury to any person or substantial damage to the quality of air, the quality of soil or the quality of water, or to animals or plants;

(e) the production, processing, handling, use, holding, storage, transport, import, export or disposal of nuclear materials or other hazardous radioactive substances which causes or is likely to cause death or serious injury to any person or substantial damage to the quality of air, the quality of soil or the quality of water, or to animals or plants;

(f) the killing, destruction, possession or taking of specimens of protected wild fauna or flora species, except for cases where the conduct concerns a negligible quantity of such specimens and has a negligible impact on the conservation status of the species;

(g) trading in specimens of protected wild fauna or flora species or parts or derivatives thereof, except for cases where the conduct concerns a negligible quantity of such specimens and has a negligible impact on the conservation status of the species;

(h) any conduct which causes the significant deterioration of a habitat within a protected site;

(i) the production, importation, exportation, placing on the market or use of ozone-depleting substances.

Hence, the Directive requires EU Member States to classify as criminal offences environmentally damaging behaviour referred to as 'unlawful' behaviour in general terms in Article 2, with this conduct being further specified through two lists of existing EU Directives and Regulations. The first list is contained in Annex A to the Directive, which refers to a number of EU environmental legislation; the second list is in Annex B and contains three environmentally relevant Directives adopted under the EURATOM Treaty. Breach of the EU environmental legislation listed in Annex A or B (in one of the ways further specified in Article 3, many of which require that 'substantial damage' be caused) must also have occurred intentionally or be the result of serious negligence for the Directive's requirement of criminality to be engaged. This core legal obligation of the Directive, the duty imposed upon Member States to penalize certain types of EU environmental law infringements through national criminal offences, is dynamic, because new EU environmental legislation, adopted after the coming into force of the Environmental Crime Directive, can specify whether the provisions of the new EU environmental legislation should be subject to this duty under the Directive.

Article 4 of the Directive requires Member States to also criminalize 'inciting, aiding and abetting' the intentional breach of EU environmental law, as defined in Articles 2 and 3 of the Directive. Article 5 explicitly requires Member States that perform environmentally damaging behaviour as defined through Articles 2 and 3 in connection with Annexes A and B be subject to criminal sanctions. Article 5 thus codifies and augments a long existing legal duty established through ECJ judgments [117] that required Member States to ensure that national law provides for 'effective, proportionate and dissuasive' penalties in order to ensure compliance also with EU law. This legal duty fleshed out further the fundamental duty of Member States to give expression to the supremacy of EU law. It may be argued that Article 5 does not require environmental offences under the Directive to be *in fact* punished by effective, proportionate, and dissuasive criminal penalties—Member States retain discretion in applying criminal sanctions but the requirement of 'effectiveness' at least should guide the enforcement strategies of Member States. Thus, in considering whether Member State

[117] See, for example, Case 68/88 *Commission v Greece* [1989] ECR 2965.

practices in relation to the Directive's offences are effective, proportionate and dissuasive, all aspects of Member State enforcement should be considered. In England and Wales, this includes civil sanctions, which close the gap between enforcement tools and criminal penalties. In contrast to Article 5 of the annulled Framework Decision on the protection of the environment through criminal law, however, the Directive does not further specify possible criminal penalties, such as custodial sentences, or the combination of criminal sanctions with sanctions, such as disqualification from, for example, operating installations that can cause harm to the environment, or from managing a company the activities of which can harm the environment, where the facts of the criminal case suggest that the person may engage again in environmental criminal activity. Under the Directive it is up to the discretion of the Member States to determine what specific types and mix of sanctions to deploy.

Most importantly, in light of the fact that environmental crime is often committed not just by individual 'criminal outlaws' or organized crime, such as some waste crime, but by more routine business behaviour that, in principle, is often considered as legitimate, it is important to note that Article 6 of the Directive requires Member States to ensure that not just individual citizens, but also legal persons can be held criminally liable.

This duty to criminalize breach of EU environmental law as listed in Annexes A and B to the Directive by 'legal persons' applies where 'such offences have been committed for the benefit [of the legal person] by any person who has a *leading position* within the legal person, acting either individually or as part of an organ of the legal person'. This position must be based on 'a power of representation of the legal person' or an 'authority to take decisions on behalf of the legal person' or 'an authority to exercise control within the legal person'. This suggests that the person to be held liable must be in a sufficiently leading position in order to be considered to represent the legal person. What this really means varies according to national law. [118]

Article 6 (3) of the Directive clarifies that its provisions on corporate liability (in the terminology of the Directive, liability of 'legal persons') shall not exclude the liability of individual citizens (liability of 'natural persons' in the terminology of the Directive) who commit, incite, or are accessories to the offences set out in Articles 3 and 4 of the Directive.

But Article 7 of the Directive reflects the moral ambiguity of environmental 'crime', discussed in Section 1. Article 7 reduces the stringency with which environmentally damaging behaviour of corporations is sanctioned, at least symbolically. In the case of legal persons, EU Member States do not have to impose *criminal* liability, but are free to impose administrative or civil liability, so long as the penalties available are 'effective, proportionate, and dissuasive'.

Finally, the Directive explicitly states that Member States can adopt more stringent measures when using the criminal law to protect the environment as long as such national measures are compatible with the provisions of the EU Treaties.

While the EU Directive on the protection of the environment through criminal law represents an important step in the direction of developing a body of EU environmental criminal law, it also has serious shortcomings. The Directive has been criticized for neglecting to incorporate victims of environmental crime into the environmental criminal justice process. While it is often difficult to identify individual human victims of environmental crime and while the focus on such victims reflects a narrow anthropocentric perspective, involving victims of environmental crime in the criminal justice process strengthens public participation in environmental law. While there have been recent attempts to strengthen public participation in environmental governance, for instance

---

[118] See, for instance, the discussion in *Tesco v Nattrass*, House of Lords, [1972] AC 153.

through the Environmental Information Regulations 2004, further discussed in Chapter 7, the EU Directive on the protection of the environment through criminal law constructs environmental crime mainly as a matter of a legal relationship between the state and the offender. The extract from Cardwell, French, and Hall considers what form victim involvement in environmental justice processes could actually take.

Paul Cardwell, Duncan French, and Matthew Hall, 'Tackling Environmental Crime in the European Union: the case of the missing victim?' (2011) 23(3) Environmental Law and Management 118, 119–120

In his discussion, Edwards describes four possible forms of victim participation in criminal justice. The most significant casts victims in the role of *decision-makers*, such that their preferences are sought and applied by the criminal justice system. Less far-reaching would be *consultative* participation, where the system seeks out victims' preferences and takes them into account when making decisions. Edwards sees the traditional role of victims in terms of *information provision*, where victims are obliged to provide information required by the system. Finally, under *expressive* participation, victims express whatever information they wish, but with no instrumental impact; here Edwards highlights the danger of victims wrongly believing their participation will actually affect decision-making.

A common distinction drawn in these debates is that between 'service rights' and 'procedural rights'. For Ashworth, victim participation should not be allowed to stray beyond service rights into areas of public interest. Ashworth is particularly concerned by victims being afforded the right to influence sentencing (and other decision-making within the process) citing the difficulties of testing victims' claims and taking account of unforeseen effects on victims. The more limited service rights Ashworth has in mind include respectful and sympathetic treatment, support, information, court facilities and compensation from the offender or state, but exclude consultative participation.

[...] [T]he US Crime Victims' Rights Act has been applied to victims of environmental harm; in this case in practice as well as in theory. Of particular note is the case of *W.R Grace & Co.*, in which the named company was prosecuted under environmental legislation for 'knowingly endangering' the residents of Libby, Montana., by exposing them to asbestos through mining activities. The federal judge in the case ruled that 34 prospective victims of these activities (local residents) did not fall under the definition of victim within the Crime Victims' Rights Act and as such excluded them form the trial proceedings. In *re Parker; U.S. v. U.S. District Court and W.R. Grace & Co.*, Nos. 09-70529, 09-70533 (9th Cir.), the United States Ninth Circuit Court of Appeals reversed this decision, thus confirming that prospective victims of environmental harm are indeed included within the ambit of rights provided under the 2004 Act.

Cardwell and his colleagues go on to consider the 2001 EU Council Framework Decision on the Standing of Victims in Criminal Proceedings as a relevant legal provision in the EU that can strengthen the rights of victims of environmental crime in the criminal justice process.[119] It requires all EU Member States to provide basic levels of services and support to victims. Moreover, the 2001 Framework Decision seeks to afford victims respect and recognition by criminal justice actors, to

---

[119] Council Framework Decision of 15 March 2001 on the standing of victims in criminal proceedings, 2001/220/ JHA (2001) OJ L 82/1.

protect victims from intimidation, and provides also for mediation. In general terms the Framework Decision aims for victims to have a significant role in the criminal justice system.

> **FURTHER READING**
>
> 1. See also the Report for the EU Commission by Huglo Lepage & Partners, 'Study on Environmental Crime in the 27 Member States, 2007', which provides for an interesting comparative perspective (accessible at: <http://ec.europa.eu/environment/legal/crime/pdf/report_environmental_crime.pdf>).

5 CONCLUSION

This chapter has introduced key features of environmental criminal law in England. It has in particular highlighted the moral ambiguity of environmental crime. The chapter traced this moral ambiguity of environmental crime in the doctrinal construction of strict liability offences, where the absence of a *mens rea* requirement is sometimes read as an indicator of less reprehensible behaviour. The moral ambiguity of environmental crime can also be traced in the application of strict liability offences to corporate bodies. Does environmental crime have to be traced to individual offenders, such as a site manager causing pollution, or should the criminal law train the spotlight on the systems of management that senior officers of the company have put in place? The finer points of legal doctrine framing environmental offences may, however, have only limited bearing on day-to-day routine enforcement by environmental regulators who consider criminal prosecution merely as a last resort. It is therefore questionable to what extent environmental criminal law provides for individual and general deterrence.

Hence, environmental criminal law sits uneasily in a regulatory landscape that is shaped by co-operative, negotiated 'better regulation' approaches that seek to limit interference with commercial freedoms, a theme that has gained further significance in the context of the post-2007 economic crisis. We see here again how the vision of sustainable development, that is, the aspiration to reconcile economic, social, and environmental protection aims, is fraught with tension.

> **FURTHER READING AND QUESTIONS**
>
> 1. The criminal law is not just used as a weapon in the fight against environmental harms, but is also deployed by the state against environmental protesters, for instance through prosecutions for public order offences during climate change protests. A notorious case here is *R v Barkshire (David Robert)* [2011] EWCA Crim 1885. The criminal convictions of climate change protesters for conspiracy to commit aggravated trespass were declared as unsafe by the Court of Appeal, because evidence obtained from an undercover police agent was not sufficiently disclosed to the defence of the climate change protesters. The climate change protesters had planned to occupy a power station. They justified their actions on the grounds of necessity and justification. The undercover police agent had recorded some of the climate change protesters group's briefings and had signed a police statement. Moreover, the undercover police agent had acted as an *agent provocateur*, also by going in his actions beyond what he was authorized to do by his police handlers. The defence was not provided with either of these documents though they contained information which could have assisted the defence.

What, in your view, does this case and the prosecution of pollution incident discussed here tell us about how criminal law allocates power in struggles over protection of the environment? What balance does the criminal law strike in these cases between the state, companies, the environment, and politically active citizens? Whose interests does the criminal law serve in the various cases?

2. For further discussions of enforcement see Keith Hawkins, *Environment and Enforcement: Regulation and the Social Definition of Pollution* (OUP 1984) and Carolyn Abbot, *Enforcing Pollution Control Regulation: Strengthening Sanctions and Improving Deterrence* (Hart 2009). Hawkins is discussed in Chapter 3.

STATUTORY LIABILITIES
AND REMEDIES

A striking feature of English environmental law is the existence of a series of different statutory regimes that create liabilities, obligations, or provide remedies to address a range of environmentally-related problems. The two most prominent of these are statutory nuisance and, more recently, the Environmental Damage (Prevention and Remediation) Regulations 2009, which implement the EU Environmental Liability Directive.[1] These regimes do not have the profile or contain the legislative detail of other environmental regimes but they are both important and interesting, for at least three reasons. First, these regimes are practically important. Statutory nuisance, in particular, is one of the most common tools for dealing with local environmental problems. Second, despite the apparently simple nature of these legal tools, they are in actual fact legally complex hybrids of public law, private law, and sometimes criminal law. Third, these legal regimes highlight how pragmatic responses on the part of local authorities have been a significant feature of the English legal approach to environmental protection.

This chapter is structured as follows. First, it provides a brief conceptual overview of different types of statutory liability techniques. The second and third sections analyse two of the most prominent regimes—statutory nuisance and the Environmental Liability Directive. The final section briefly considers more specific regimes. The overall purpose the chapter is to give some feeling for both the conceptual complexity and the practical significance of these areas of law.

As always, we have caveats. First, it should again be stressed that this chapter is not a replacement for a comprehensive textbook on the topics covered and a further reading list can be found at the end of the chapter. This is particularly for areas, such as statutory nuisance, where their practice generates considerable legally complexity. Second, this area overlaps with the discussion of criminal law in Section 3 of Chapter 8 and the Regulatory Enforcement and Sanctions Act 2008, also discussed in that chapter. Third, the types of liabilities discussed in this chapter also operate in more specific areas covered by other chapters in this textbook—the contaminated land regime and waste regulation being notable examples.[2]

1 LEGISLATING FOR LIABILITY AND OTHER REMEDIES

A curious feature of environmental law is that it is often discussed in compartmentalized boxes. Thus, as seen in this part, we have separate chapters on private law, public law, criminal law, the role of courts, regulatory strategy, and governance. Yet, as those chapters show, there are overlaps

---

[1] European Parliament and Council Directive 2004/35/EC of 21 April 2004 on environmental liability with regard to the prevention and remedying of environmental damage [2004] OJ L14/30.

[2] See Chapters 21 and 16 respectively.

between these different areas of legal activity. In some cases, there is more than simply overlapping legal areas—there is the creation of legally hybrid tools and institutions to deal with environmental problems. The types of regimes covered in this chapter provide a perfect example of this latter phenomenon. Their hybrid nature means that, to make sense of them, we need to take a step back from our normal presumptions about what is public, private, or criminal law.

The focus in this chapter is on the creation of different types of legal tools through legislation that imposes duties on individual actors that require them to deliver certain remedies, or to make good certain obligations, in relation to environmental problems. These are often described as liabilities but in actual fact, as we shall see here, that term is misleading. Winter and others explain the problem in discussing the Environmental Liability Directive.

Gerd Winter and others, 'Weighing Up the EC Environmental Liability Directive' (2008) 20 JEL 163, 167

It may well be that old divisions between private and public law have to be reconsidered in the light of contemporary environmental and other social challenges. Certainly the reference to 'Environmental Liability' in the title to the Directive in itself gives little clue as to the final focus of the Directive on administrative liabilities or responsibilities, and indeed may add to the confusion for a national lawyer or non-legal expert. One of the lessons to be learnt from the lengthy period of development of the Directive is the continual need to be absolutely clear as to the concepts being used, and to be alive to the possibility of confusion that can arise from the loose use of linguistic terms that may resonate differently in different jurisdictions. In the context of the subject matter of the Directive, a more robust basis for discussion would be to acknowledge that the concept of 'environmental liability' can encompass at least three distinct categories of liability: civil liability under private law; criminal liability; and administrative responsibility, and to be explicit in any discussion as to which concept is being referred to.

This robust basis and subtle analytical appreciation of environmental 'liabilities' imposed through legislation provides the starting point for this chapter. Thus, in thinking about these different regimes, an open-minded approach needs to be taken. In particular, there is no point in attempting to pigeon hole these regimes into a particular private or public law framework. They are hybrids—and profoundly complex ones at that!

The regimes covered by this chapter can take many different forms but they tend to have three features. First, as already noted, 'liability' can take a range of different forms and does not usually reflect a conventional private law model where liability stems from a relationship between two parties (that is, a duty of care owed by one legal actor to another, or a pre-existing legal agreement between the parties). Rather, the term 'liability' simply refers to a situation where a legal actor becomes responsible for remedying a state of affairs. That remedy may take many forms. It may involve some form of compensation for loss, remediation, stopping an activity, or compensating those who have engaged in remediation of environmental damage. In many ways, liability is another word for responsibility.

A second feature of these regimes is that they have an important administrative dimension. In particular, such liability or responsibility is only triggered if an administrative body takes action, such as serving a notice on the person deemed to be carrying out an activity, which results in liability under a particular regime. Even if such notice is not required, the operation of such regimes often has a significant administrative aspect. As a result, legal disputes over the operation of these regimes often take the form of judicial review actions. Disputes over the scope and operation of individual liability are thus not private law issues but administrative law disputes.

Third, like much public environmental law, the emergence of these regulatory tools reflects the ways in which traditional common law concepts did not deal adequately with environmental problems. However, they also build on those common law concepts. As a consequence, while these different legal tools can be thought of as regulatory strategies, they have not been considered as such by most scholars and textbook writers. Indeed, the focus areas of this chapter—statutory nuisance and the Environmental Liability Directive—have received relatively little attention in the regulatory strategy context.

Thus, while as Maria Lee has noted 'liability, in broad terms, is a frequently used regulatory tool in environmental law',[3] the focus in this chapter does not fit an obvious legal compartment. It is not private law, public law, criminal law, or even regulatory strategy. This perhaps explains why, although legal tools such as statutory nuisance represent some of the first examples of UK environmental law, they have never yielded easily to scholarly study, with their analysis being more the domain of practice than academia. This is not a criticism—more food for thought about how the scholarly pre-occupations of academic environmental lawyers have often been shaped by understandings of the pre-existing boundaries of different areas of law.

Section 2 considers two of the most high profile examples of these forms of liability—statutory nuisance and the regime under the Environmental Liability Directive. The purpose here is to give some feeling for the nature of these different areas rather than the doctrinal detail of these complicated and quite technical areas of law.

2 STATUTORY NUISANCE

From a practical and pragmatic perspective, statutory nuisance provides one of the most important tools for addressing *ad hoc* environmental and public health problems. It is used on a daily basis by local authorities and is very much a workhorse of environmental law. Statutory nuisance works in the following way. If a local authority is satisfied a statutory nuisance exists (as defined in s 79 of the Environmental Protection Act 1990 or 'EPA'), then it may serve an abatement notice requiring specific steps to be taken to abate the nuisance (s 80). Such a notice may be appealed to a Magistrates' Court (s 80(3)) and failure to comply with an abatement notice is a criminal offence (s 80(4)).

The apparent simplicity of this process hides a number of complexities. First, statutory nuisance has a long history in English law—a history that reflects the nature of English environmental law, as discussed in Chapter 3. Second, as is obvious from the description, statutory nuisance is a mixture of public, private, and criminal law elements. It thus has the potential to be legally challenging in practice—requiring as it does the interrelating of different legal world-views, as well as attracting a variety of potential legal consequences. Third, the administrative and procedural nature of statutory nuisance means that few statutory nuisance actions end up as reported cases. This area of the law is an important reminder that court cases (and judicial reasoning) are only one aspect of environmental law. In this section, the concept of statutory nuisance and its history are discussed and some of its key legal features highlighted.

2.1 STATUTORY NUISANCE: THE CONCEPT AND ITS HISTORY

The starting point for understanding what constitutes a statutory nuisance is the rather ungainly s 79 of the Environmental Protection Act 1990.

---

[3] Maria Lee, 'Tort, Regulation, and Environmental Liability' (2002) LS 33, 33.

Environmental Protection Act 1990, section 79

(1) Subject to subsections (1A) to (6A) below, the following matters constitute "statutory nuisances" for the purposes of this Part, that is to say—

(a) any premises in such a state as to be prejudicial to health or a nuisance;

(b) smoke emitted from premises so as to be prejudicial to health or a nuisance;

(c) fumes or gases emitted from premises so as to be prejudicial to health or a nuisance;

(d) any dust, steam, smell or other effluvia arising on industrial, trade or business premises and being prejudicial to health or a nuisance;

(e) any accumulation or deposit which is prejudicial to health or a nuisance;

(f) any animal kept in such a place or manner as to be prejudicial to health or a nuisance;

(fa) any insects emanating from relevant industrial, trade or business premises and being prejudicial to health or a nuisance;

(fb) artificial light emitted from premises so as to be prejudicial to health or a nuisance;

(g) noise emitted from premises so as to be prejudicial to health or a nuisance;

(ga) noise that is prejudicial to health or a nuisance and is emitted from or caused by a vehicle, machinery or equipment in a street or in Scotland, road]

(h) any other matter declared by any enactment to be a statutory nuisance; and it shall be the duty of every local authority to cause its area to be inspected from time to time to detect any statutory nuisances which ought to be dealt with under section 80 below [or sections 80 and 80A] and, where a complaint of a statutory nuisance is made to it by a person living within its area, to take such steps as are reasonably practicable to investigate the complaint.

Section 79(1A)–(1B) exempts contaminated land and the rest of the section lists a number of other activities that are excluded as well as definitions. Looking at the list in s 79, one can see that it has become a somewhat *ad hoc* tool for dealing with a range of local problems. Smoke, insects, artificial light, or noise do not form a coherent group of activities but they do reflect the fact that 'we are not all simply independent spheres knocking around, occasionally intruding into another person's orb'.[4] They are thus all examples of where the activity of one individual impinges upon, another so as to cause problems, and the nature of those problems can be generally agreed upon and legally classified as requiring a remedy.[5] In some cases, such as public health, they may cause problems also for the individual creating the nuisance, but in other cases, such as smoke, the problems created are largely an externality.

The *ad hoc* nature of what is included in s 79 thus reflects the diverse range of local activities that can impinge on others. As Malcolm and Ponting note, this eclectic expediency also reflects its history.

Rosalind Malcolm and John Ponting 'Statutory Nuisance: The Sanitary Paradigm and Judicial Conservatism' (2006) 18 JEL 37, 38–39

Today statutory nuisance is concerned with a whole range of matters, including industrial atmospheric pollution and its effect on public health, as well as domestic problems, such as the noise and light pollution. But the earliest legislation passed in the late-1840s was intended as a short-term response to

---

[4] Christopher H Schroeder, 'Rights Against Risk' (1986) 86 Colum LR 495, 534.

[5] AI Ogus and GM Richardson, 'Economics and the Environment: A Study in Private Nuisance' (1977) 36 CLJ 284, 288.

combat serious outbreaks of cholera then occurring in the major towns and cities. In a wider sense, enacting statutory nuisance legislation was a response to the huge changes and adverse environmental conditions brought about during the latter phases of the Industrial Revolution in Great Britain. The concept of nuisance was central to the sanitary legislation first enacted on a national scale, in England, with the Nuisances Removal Act of 1855 and subsequently consolidated in the 1875 Public Health Act [... Statutory nuisance legislation continued in essentially the same form through to the next century with the 1936 Public Health Act [...], being re-enacted and consolidated in legislation still in force [Part III of the Environmental Protection Act 1990 (EPA)].

Section 79(1) EPA 1990 brings together nuisances that were first enacted in their current form in the 1850s with newer forms, such as noise which first became a statutory nuisance with the Noise Abatement Act 1960, and now light and insects, further to the Clean Neighbourhoods and Environment Act 2005. It can be appreciated that these statutory provisions, which are central to local pollution control in the modern world, have a long and an interesting history over a lengthy period of extensive socio-economic change.

Indeed, that history is closely intertwined with the history of industrialization and urbanization. Implicit in that history is also a tension between local and central government in addressing public health and environmental issues. The Nuisances Removal Act 1855 was understood to place power in local government and was interpreted by many as far more effective a legal regime than grand regulatory regimes.[6] Thus, the simplicity of the regime should not be taken for it being legally or institutionally meaningless—rather the concept of statutory nuisance is a symbol of the historical importance of developing local solutions to local problems in the UK,[7] as well as faith being placed in pragmatism (that faith also being seen in criminal enforcement—see Chapter 8).

The question then arises: what is the nature of statutory nuisance? Particularly, how does it relate to public and private law nuisance? The latter point is examined by Parpworth.

Neil Parpworth, 'Public Nuisance in the Environmental Context' [2008] JPL 1526, 1537

It will be noted that the formula 'prejudicial to health or a nuisance' appears in each of these examples of a statutory nuisance. These words make it clear by the use of the disjunctive 'or' that a statutory nuisance may arise where, for example, smoke emitted from premises is either prejudicial to health *or* it amounts to a nuisance. The phrase 'prejudicial to health' is thus very important to the operation of the statutory nuisance regime and, not surprisingly, its statutory definition has received considerable judicial consideration. For present purposes, however, the more important term is 'nuisance'. This is not defined in the 1990 Act. Accordingly, in the absence of a statutory definition it would seem that the word ought to be given the meaning which it has at common law. Thus in the case of *National Coal Board v Thorne*, where the Board was served an abatement notice pursuant to s 93 of the Public Health Act 1936 in respect of its premises which, by reason of having fallen into disrepair, were alleged to constitute a statutory nuisance, the Divisional Court held that:

'... a nuisance cannot arise if what has taken place affects only the person or persons occupying the premises where the nuisance is said to have taken place. A nuisance coming within the meaning of the Public Health Act 1936 must be either a private *or a public nuisance* as understood by common law.'

[6] Christopher Hamlin, *Public Health and Social Justice in the Age of Chadwick, Britain 1800–1854* (CUP 1998) 263.
[7] See Section 3.2 of Chapter 3; Martin Loughlin, *Legality and Locality: The Role of Law in Central-Local Government Relations* (Clarendon Press 1996).

These remarks have received judicial endorsement since the enactment of Pt III of the EPA. Thus it is clear that the word 'nuisance' in s 79(1) signifies a common law nuisance, ie a private *or* a public nuisance. It follows from this, therefore, that an activity or state of affairs which amounts to a statutory nuisance may also, as Lord Bingham opined in *R v Rimmington* and *R v Goldstein*, amount to a public nuisance.

It needs to be remembered that, while there is this relationship to common law nuisance, s 79 also refers to a number of other categories of statutory nuisance. Thus, if one turns to the case law, there are some cases where particular statutory terms are being interpreted and others where the connection between common law nuisance and statutory nuisance is being drawn. Two examples are given here.

The first example comes from a case not directly concerned with environmental issues but considers whether a steep staircase can be 'prejudicial to health' under s 79. It is the judicial approach rather than the actual facts of the case that are relevant.

R v Bristol City Council, ex p Everett
[1999] 1 WLR 1170 (CA), 1180–81 (Buxton LJ)

However, whatever may be thought of the verbal infelicities forced on the Act of 1990 by the applicant's case, as the judge said everything falls into place once one looks at the history of the legislation, as expounded by Mummery LJ in his judgment. It is quite clear, as the judge indeed concluded, that the provisions of s 79(1) come without significant amendment from nineteenth century statutory provisions directed at premises that create a risk of disease or illness. The provisions with which we are concerned are first found in general public health legislation of a recognisably modern type, in almost identical terms to the Act of 1990 formulation, in s 91 of the Public Health Act 1875. Reading through that Act, and referring to its predecessors, it cries out from the page that the target of the legislators was disease and not physical injury. And that was clearly understood or assumed at the time the legislation was passed. One of the predecessor statutes, consolidated in the 1875 Act, was the Nuisances Removal Act 1855, section 8 of which addressed 'Premises in such a state as to be a nuisance or injurious to health'. In *Great Western Railway Co v Bishop* (1872) LR 7 QB 550, where the issue was whether water running from a railway bridge on to highway users below constituted such a nuisance, Mr Lopes QC, at p551, pointed to the origins of the legislation and concluded that the Act was a sanitary Act, and so a 'nuisance' under it must affect health. Cockburn CJ, at p552, agreed with him. True it is that the actual issue in the case was whether the inconvenience, as opposed to physical injury, suffered by the passers by could be a nuisance; but that point was seen as concluded by the status of the legislation as, in nineteenth century terms, a sanitary provision. That perception was expressed in the 1875 Act by the nuisance provisions in section 91 being included in Part III, 'Sanitary Matters'; and by the implementation of that Act being in the hands of the sanitary authorities that had been created by the Public Health Act 1872. Changing the language, but not the concept, into twentieth century form, the successor provisions of 1990 are about disease or ill-health, and not about physical danger.

In other words, the concept of being 'prejudicial to health' is not understood as a wide-ranging concept but one that must be seen in the context of its legislative history.[8]

The second case example returns to Parpworth's discussion concerning the relationship between statutory nuisance and common law nuisance. The comments from Scott Baker LJ are instructive.

---

[8] Although that is not always straightforward to see.

R (Hackney LBC) v Rottenberg
[2007] EWHC 166 (Admin) paras 26–27 (Scott Baker LJ)

26. The short point is that what amounts to a nuisance for the purposes of the Environmental Protection Act 1990 is no different from what amounts to a nuisance at common law. Whether the threshold was crossed in this case so as to amount to an offence under the statute was a matter for the court, not the environmental health officers, however great their experience might be. The judge and the justices considered the whole of the evidence and concluded it was not proved that the threshold had been crossed. In my view, they were entitled to come to that conclusion.

27. In *R v Stockwell* [1993] 97 Cr App R 60, this court made clear that a court is not bound to accept uncritically the evidence given by a witness, even an expert. The fact that the environmental health officers called by the Council thought there was nuisance noise in this case was not determinative of the issue.

In other words, the question of what constitutes a statutory nuisance is a legal term for a court to construe not for an environmental health officer to finally determine. This effectively means that, in a difficult case, the court will have a role to play.

2.2 ABATEMENT NOTICES

The statutory nuisance regime places two duties on local authorities. The first was seen in s 79(1) in placing a duty of inspection on local authorities. As Murphy notes, that duty is a 'rather vague direction',[9] which means that it will be difficult to establish whether a local authority has complied with that duty.

The more significant duty is that of serving abatement notices. The serving of an abatement notice is a summary proceeding and failure to comply with an abatement notice is a criminal offence (s 80(4) EPA). As this is the case (and as this is the main form of breach in relation to this statutory duty), the nature of the abatement notice and the processes involved in its framing and issuance are the key aspects of the statutory nuisance process.

Section 80(1) EPA 1990 states:

Environmental Protection Act 1990, section 80(1)

[...] where a local authority is satisfied that a statutory nuisance exists, or is likely to occur or recur, in the area of the authority, the local authority shall serve a notice ("an abatement notice") imposing all or any of the following requirements—

(a) requiring the abatement of the nuisance or prohibiting or restricting its occurrence or recurrence;

(b) requiring the execution of such works, and the taking of such other steps, as may be necessary

for any of those purposes, and the notice shall specify the time or times within which the requirements of the notice are to be complied with.

The case law that has developed concerning this process is significant, particularly as those served with an abatement notice have a right to appeal against it (s 80(3) EPA). It is also important that, since

---

[9] John Murphy, *The Law of Nuisance* (OUP 2010) para 8.46.

breach of an abatement notice can result in criminal liability, local authorities must ensure that they serve an abatement notice properly. However, as Thornton has pithily put it, this is 'a thorny area where local authorities still get it wrong'.[10] The case law in this area is voluminous and detailed. Here an illustrative selection of those cases provides three examples of the types of legal questions that emerge out of the statutory nuisance process.

The first case example concerns the question of whether the person causing the statutory nuisance should be consulted before an abatement notice is served. The facts are not relevant. Simon Brown LJ began his judgment by explaining what the judge had decided on the point.

Falmouth & Truro Port Authority v South West Water Ltd
[2001] QB 445 (CA), 454-5, 458 (Simon Brown LJ)

Under this heading I shall consider also the various related arguments advanced with regard to legitimate expectation, failure to take account of relevant considerations, and irrationality. First, however, it is convenient to quote the conclusions of the judge below on these issues. [...]

First, under the heading "duty to consult":

"Having considered those competing submissions, I have come to the conclusion, after some hesitation, that there is no duty on the enforcing authority to consult the alleged perpetrator before serving the abatement notice, either as part of the statutory scheme or by implication in order to achieve fairness. I do not accept that the statutory duty under section 79 of the 1990 Act to investigate complaints of a statutory nuisance necessarily includes a duty to consult the alleged perpetrator. In the vast majority of cases, consultation with the alleged perpetrator by the enforcing authority would form both a sensible and appropriate part of the investigative process, but that arises at the enforcing authority's discretion, not as part of a statutory duty. The investigation of complaints of statutory nuisances arises in a myriad of different circumstances and there will be situations where the enforcing authority could quite properly conclude that it would not be appropriate to consult the alleged perpetrator, whether for reasons relating to the nature of the alleged perpetrator, the need for urgent action or for any other reason. If a lack of consultation thereby leads to service of an abatement notice when it should not have been issued, the alleged perpetrator can appeal to the magistrates' court under section 80(3) of the 1990 Act on any of the grounds set out in regulation 2(2) of the 1995 Regulations.

There will be many situations where fairness may suggest that the enforcing authority should consult with the alleged perpetrator, particularly in cases like the present one, where the notice is not suspended pending appeal because the nuisance is injurious to health, but the very fact that statute has provided for non-suspension of the notice in those circumstances indicates the more draconian nature of the power given to the enforcing authority where injury to health in involved. The more serious the alleged injury to health, the more urgent is the need for action by the enforcing authority. The more urgent the need for action, the greater the likelihood that it may not be possible or appropriate to consult the alleged perpetrator.

In view of the fact that there will be cases where consultation with the alleged perpetrator is not possible or is inappropriate, it would be wrong to hold that such a duty of consultation exists before an abatement notice is served. That being so, the difficulty then arises in determining when there should be consultation. As I have said, there may be many cases where fairness may suggest that there should be consultation, but, if there is to be a duty to consult in those circumstances, the enforcing authority needs to know when that duty arises, but it is not something that is capable of precise definition. The resulting uncertainty about whether the circumstances are such as to give rise to a duty to consult would militate against effective action being taken

---

[10] Justine Thornton, 'Siginficant UK Environmental Cases 2009/2010' (2010) JEL 315, 321.

by the enforcing authority, thereby frustrating the statutory purpose of protecting the public against statutory nuisances, particularly those injurious to health…"

[…]Suffice it to say that I, like the judge below, would reject this contention for the reasons he gave (although in my case without 'some hesitation'). I would furthermore respectfully question the judge's view that 'in the vast majority of cases, consultation with the alleged perpetrator by the enforcing authority would form both a sensible and appropriate part of the investigative process' in the exercise of the enforcing authority's discretion. That seems to me to go altogether too far. Often, certainly, it will be appropriate to consult the alleged perpetrator, at least on some aspect of the matter, before serving an abatement notice, but the enforcing authority should be wary of being drawn too deeply and lengthily into scientific or technical debate, and warier still of unintentionally finding itself fixed with all the obligations of a formal consultation process.

Note how the issues in this case are cast in a public law light. The question of consultation is seen as raising administrative law issues.

The second case example concerns the wording of a noise abatement notice and its legal significance. Again the facts need not concern us.

Elvington Park Limited v City of York Council
[2009] EWHC 1805 (Admin), para 36 (Silber J)

36. The authorities show clearly that if an abatement notice requires not merely abatement of noise but also steps to be taken, they should be specified but if as in the present case, the notices did not do so, they are invalid. Unless this was so, the recipients of these notices would not know what they had to do to avoid criminal proceedings being brought against them. In this case, this is a particularly potent point because, […] at the Crown Court neither the expert called by the appellant nor the expert of the council could state what work had to be done to abate the nuisance.

Here we see the implications of the criminal law aspects of statutory nuisance—if the consequence of not meeting the requirements of an abatement notice is criminal action, then it legally must follow that such a notice must be clear on its face.

The final case to note in relation to abatement notices concerns how the courts have used their role within the statutory nuisance 'machinery' to interpret the concept of nuisance. Consider the comments of Keene LJ in an action that involved considering whether a lack of adequate sound-proofing was a statutory nuisance.

Vella v London Borough of Lambeth
[2005] EWHC 2473 (Admin) paras 79–82 (Keene LJ) (emphasis added)

79. It would in my judgment be a considerable extension of the long-established meaning of this provision to regard it as encompassing a situation where the state of the premises does not itself cause a risk to health but merely fails to prevent external activities from causing such a risk. In the present case, the inadequate sound insulation did not itself threaten the claimant's health in the way in which, for example, an accumulation of debris would have done. It was the activities of other tenants which gave rise to the prejudice to the claimant's health, and those do not constitute 'the state' of the premises. If

the claimant were right in his interpretation of s 79(1)(a), it would produce a situation where statutory nuisances would exist on an enormous scale throughout the towns and cities of this country, not only because of noise from neighbouring occupiers but also because of noise from other sources. I note that, whereas noise caused by aircraft (other than those of the model variety) is excluded from s 79(1)(g) by virtue of section 79(6), no such exclusion applies to s 79(1)(a). Mr Watkinson conceded that it would be consistent with his argument for a *statutory nuisance* to arise under para (a) where inadequate sound insulation gave rise to prejudice to health because of aircraft noise. That seems to me to have been a proper concession.

80. I find it impossible to accept that this was Parliament's intention when it re-enacted this well-worn phraseology. Moreover, the comment by Lord Hoffmann in *Oakley* at page 632 D–F applies as much to the present case as it did to the situation with which he was there dealing:

'For the courts to give section 79(1)(a) an extended "modern" meaning which required suitable alterations to be made to existing houses would impose a substantial financial burden upon public and private owners and occupiers. I am entirely in favour of giving the 1990 Act a sensible modem interpretation. But I do not think that it is either sensible or in accordance with modem notions of democracy to hold that when Parliament re-enacted language going back to the 19th century, it authorised the courts to impose upon local authorities and others a huge burden of capital expenditure to which the statutory language had never been held to apply. In my opinion the decision as to whether or not to take such a step should be made by the elected representatives of the people and not by the courts.'

81. There is a further consideration which supports this narrower construction: s 80, which imposes the duty on local authorities to serve an abatement notice in respect of a statutory nuisance, is providing for a summary remedy. That can readily be illustrated. Under s 81(3), where an abatement notice has not been complied with, the local authority may itself step in and abate the nuisance, and then it can recover the reasonable expenses of so doing from the person who caused the nuisance: see s 81(4). Moreover, it is a criminal offence under s 80(4) to contravene or to fail to comply with an abatement notice without reasonable excuse. These provisions indicate that the statutory nuisance machinery is intended to deal with situations requiring a quick remedy because of the threat to health or the nuisance. As Lord Hoffmann said in *Oakley*, the provisions are dealing with a threat to health 'which requires summary removal': page 631A. In such a context, the courts should be slow to adopt an enlarged interpretation of the statutory wording.

In other words, the statutory nuisance procedure needs to be understood as a whole in two ways. First, it needs to be recognized that it not only applies to environmental problems. Second, the procedure needs to be understood writ large.

2.3 SECTION 82—PRIVATE PROSECUTION

Part of the bigger legal picture in relation to statutory nuisance is the fact that Part III of the EPA (on Statutory Nuisances) also provides for private prosecution. Section 82 thus allows for the following summary proceeding:

Environmental Protection Act 1990, section 82

(1) A magistrates' court may act under this section on a complaint made by any person on the ground that he is aggrieved by the existence of a statutory nuisance.

(2) If the magistrates' court is satisfied that the alleged nuisance exists, or that although abated it is likely to recur on the same premises, the court shall make an order for either or both of the following purposes—

(a) requiring the defendant to abate the nuisance, within a time specified in the order, and to execute any works necessary for that purpose;

(b) prohibiting a recurrence of the nuisance, and requiring the defendant, within a time specified in the order, to execute any works necessary to prevent the recurrence; and may also impose on the defendant a fine not exceeding level 5 on the standard scale.

This amounts to a form of private prosecution (and thus a criminal proceeding), which can be an important legal route where the potential defendant is the local authority (that is, the body who is meant to detect nuisances and serve an abatement notice under s 80). This may also give the appearance of providing a tool for litigants to act independently of local authorities, but in practice this is not the case. Consider the comments here in *Vella*, extracted already in Section 2.2. A preliminary argument put to the Court was that the claimant should not be able to bring a judicial review action in relation to the local authority's failure to act under s 80 because an alternative remedy was open to the claimant under s 82.

Vella v London Borough of Lambeth
[2005] EWHC 2473 (Admin) para 23 (Poole J)

23. Faced with the argument that an alternative remedy is open to the Claimant ie by himself prosecuting the Interested Party under s 82 of the EPA, as at one stage he proposed to do, the Claimant submits that for a number of reasons this would not be as 'equally effective and convenient a remedy' as Judicial Review (see *R v Birmingham City Council ex p Ferrero Ltd* [1993] 1 All ER 530, 536f). Firstly, this is a case requiring expert evidence from those holding noise nuisance or Environmental Health qualifications. It would be strenuously defended because of the financial implications of an order should other tenants decide to take the same course at the Claimant. The Interested Party is obviously better placed in terms of access to expert and legal advice and representation than he is. Moreover the Claimant does not have the financial resources to fund a private prosecution himself. These are, he argues, severe limitations to such a prosecution.

Thus, the prosecution process under s 82 should not be understood as a simple route by which to bring a statutory nuisance action. This is particularly so because another complex body of practice and procedure must be followed. However, s 82 is used regularly in the context of housing law, particularly by tenants bringing actions against landlords.

2.4 APPEALS AND DEFENCES

As already noted, s 80(3) allows for a person to appeal an abatement notice with which they have been served. The various grounds of appeal are set out in Regulation 2 of the Statutory Nuisance (Appeals Regulations) 1995 and they include: that the 'abatement notice is not justified' (Regulation 2(2)(a)); that the notice should have seen served on another person (Regulation 2(2)(h)–(j)); and that there has been some 'informality, defect, or error' in the abatement notice (Regulation 2(2)(b)). The Act also provides a range of defences for specific nuisances (s 80(9)). The structure of s 82 also provides a number of implicit and explicit defences. The way in which the appeal process and the defences inter-relate is once again another example of the legally hybrid nature of statutory nuisance, with issues arising in both an administrative and criminal law context.

The most interesting defence is that of 'best practicable means', which the Act and the Regulations allows as a defence to certain nuisances (s 80(7)–(8), s 82(9)–(10), Regulation (2)(2)(e)). We will see the concept of best practicable means (and related concepts) discussed in Chapter 17 in relation to integrated pollution control, and it is a concept with a long history in the UK.[11] The concept is defined in s 79(9).

Environmental Protection Act 1990, section 79(9)

In this Part "best practicable means" is to be interpreted by reference to the following provisions—

(a) "practicable" means reasonably practicable having regard among other things to local conditions and circumstances, to the current state of technical knowledge and to the financial implications;

(b) the means to be employed include the design, installation, maintenance and manner and periods of operation of plant and machinery, and the design, construction and maintenance of buildings and structures;

(c) the test is to apply only so far as compatible with any duty imposed by law;

(d) the test is to apply only so far as compatible with safety and safe working conditions, and with the exigencies of any emergency or unforeseeable circumstances

---

The *R (South Kesteven District Council) v Grantham Magistrates Court* case shows how this best practicable means concept operates in practice. Note the way in which the criminal and administrative law aspects of statutory nuisance proceedings become entangled on the facts of the case.

R (South Kesteven District Council) v Grantham Magistrates Court, [2010] EWHC 1419 (Admin) paras 21–26 (Wyn Williams J)

The Facts

South Kesteven DC served an abatement notice on the interested parties in this case due to amplified music and other noise that came from their pub and its garden. There were discussions between the DC and pub owners but after these discussions there were further complaints about noise and the DC concluded that there had been a breach of the abatement notice and prosecuted. The Magistrates found the interested parties not guilty and an important basis for their decision was that they concluded the defence of 'best practicable means' had been made out. This decision was subject to a judicial review action by the DC. The question for the court was whether it was open to them to conclude that the statutory defence had been made out.

Wyn Williams J

21. In the present case, the interested parties' evidence, as summarised by Mrs Gulson in her statement, suggested that they had advised their neighbours of the event, and asked them to telephone if the noise

---

[11] Royal Commission on Environmental Pollution, *Best Practicable Environmental Option, Twelfth Report* (Cmnd 310, HMSO 1988).

had become too loud; given an instruction to the disc jockey to keep the noise down; double-lined the marquee; and had walked around the outside of the marquee checking that the noise was kept down. In my judgment, on the basis of such information as is contained in Mrs Gulson's statement, it is very difficult to understand how the Magistrates could have concluded that the interested parties had taken the best practicable means to prevent or counteract the effects of the nuisance. As was pointed out in evidence by Ms Coulthard, at least one alternative, which simply was not addressed at all, was having the music played inside the public house. That simply does not feature in the reasoning process which is set out in Mrs Gulson's statement.

22. In *St Albans District Council v Patel* [2008] EWHC 2767 (Admin), Forbes J had this to say about s 80(7) and s (79)(9) of the 1990 Act:

'14. Mr Reed submitted, uncontroversially, that the expression "best practical means" must be construed having regard to the factors set out in section 79(9) of the 1990 Act but requires, ultimately, that a decision be reached that the person relying on that defence has established that he used the best practicable means on the balance of probabilities. Mr Reed contended that if the means undertaken are not established to be the best then the defence has not been made out. I agree with those submissions which, as I have indicated, are essentially uncontroversial and not in dispute.

15. It was Mr Reed's submission that, in order to be satisfied that the statutory defence under section 80(7) has been established, the court must reach the conclusion that the means employed were the best practicable to prevent or counteract the effects of the nuisance in question when compared with any other means or methods which are before the court for its consideration and which, on their face, are practicable and have the ability to prevent or counteract the effects of the nuisance more effectively than has been achieved by the defendant. Mr Reed submitted that, in short, the defendant must establish why all other obvious or, on the face of it, practicable means are not practicable, otherwise it has not been established that the best practicable means have been used. Again, I agree with those submissions which were, in effect, uncontroversial.'

I would take a great deal of persuading that I should depart in any way from the views expressed by Forbes J in the *St Albans* case, he being such an experienced and knowledgeable judge of this court. I intend to adopt precisely the approach adopted by Forbes J in the *St Albans* case.

23. That being so, it does not seem to me to be permissible for the Magistrates in this case to have reached the conclusion on s 80(7) that they did, when they simply had no regard, so far as I can see, to the possibilities raised by Ms Coulthard in her evidence, the primary one being that the music could have been played indoors and not in the marquee. It may very well be that the interested parties could have explained to the Magistrates why Ms Coulthard's suggestion was not reasonably practicable; however, that does not appear to have occurred. Indeed, they appear to have said nothing upon that topic.

24. In those circumstances, and following the guidance given by Forbes J, I simply do not see how it was open to the Magistrates to conclude that the statutory defence had been made out, since there was another obvious, or on the face of it practicable means unexplored by the interested parties which might have had a far greater chance of reducing or ameliorating the noise nuisance which was emanating from their premises.

25. Accordingly, I take the view that the Magistrates, when considering the statutory defence, reached a conclusion which was not open to them on the whole of the evidence put before them. In summary, they should not have concluded that the interested parties, on the balance of probability, had proved that they had used the best practicable means to prevent or counteract the effects of the proved breach of the enforcement notice, namely the proved noise nuisance.

Note here the role of the evidence before the Magistrates' Court.

3 THE ENVIRONMENTAL LIABILITY DIRECTIVE

In 2004, the EU (then Community) institutions passed the Environmental Liability Directive after a long and protracted discussion about what form such a Directive should take. That debate reflected the fact, as discussed in Section 2, that 'liability' is an inherent ambiguous and malleable idea. The final version was based less on a private law model of liability than a public law one. The UK implemented the Directive in 2009 with the Environmental Damage (Prevention and Remediation) Regulations 2009 (EDPR Regs). At this stage, there have been few cases concerning those Regulations. This is not surprising considering both their administrative nature and their limited scope. With that said, there have been a number of significant CJEU judgments concerning the interpretation of the Directive. In this section we give a brief overview of the history and nature of the Directive, one CJEU case as an example, and a brief word about the EDPR Regs.

3.1 THE HISTORY AND NATURE OF THE DIRECTIVE

The Environmental Liability Directive is often described as being an example of the polluter pays principle in action, but it is a far more complex legal framework than simply imposing compensation obligations on polluters. It is less about direct liability and more about requiring polluters to *prevent* imminent environmental damage (of certain kinds), to *remedy* certain environmental damage they cause, whilst also providing a means for public authorities to obtain compensation for preventing or remedying such environmental damage themselves. Winter and others explain the shift in focus of the Directive.

Gerd Winter and others, 'Weighing Up the EC Environmental Liability Directive'
(2008) 20 JEL 163, 163–64

Directive 2004/35 essentially provides for a system that requires public authorities to ensure that the polluter restores the damaged environment. All damage which is suffered by private persons, and in particular physical injury and economic loss—the so-called 'traditional damage'—is not covered. This administrative approach is significantly different from the line of discussion which had prevailed at Community level during the years of preparation of the Directive and which was largely based on a system of private law compensation.

This shift is perhaps not surprising in light of the discussion here on conceptualizing statutory liability. In creating these regimes, law-makers are often looking for pragmatic solutions to address a range of problems rather than to create a liability regime *per se*. In other words, liability is simply one means for providing a desired remedy. One of the desired remedies in introducing the Environmental Liability Directive—beyond setting up an administrative scheme for the prevention and remediation of environmental damage—was to provide an effective enforcement tool for various EU environmental regimes, including EU waste management regulation, EU integrated pollution control, and EU protected species and natural habitats. As a result, the nature of debate in the abstract about this kind of liability regime and how it ended up being legally constructed was quite different. Lee describes the result well.

Maria Lee, '"New" Environmental Liabilities: the Purpose and Scope of the Contaminated Land Regime and the Environmental Liability Directive' (2009) 11 Env LR 264, 266–67

The Environmental Liability Directive (the 'ELD') is the relatively modest outcome of a more ambitious debate about environmental liability at EU level. By the time of the Directive, environmental liability had become a purely public or administrative law issue, consisting of an administrative scheme for the remediation or prevention of 'environmental damage'. Environmental damage falls into three categories: damage to protected species and natural habitats; water damage; and land damage. The notion of land damage most obviously overlaps with the contaminated land regime, but in fact there is some overlap with all three categories. The operators of certain categories of 'occupational activity', listed by reference to EC environmental legislation, are subject to strict liability for the prevention or remediation of environmental damage. Fault-based liability is imposed on unlisted occupational activities in respect of damage to protected species and habitats only. The ELD is a minimum scheme, so that more stringent provisions can be maintained or adopted by the Member States; the text of the Directive also leaves considerable discretion to the Member States over, for example, defences.

[...][T]he role of liability as an economic instrument of regulation is limited by other purposes of the Directive. So, for example, one of the roles of economic instruments is to move towards efficient production by internalising environmental externalities. The detail of the Directive [...] restricts the internalisation of environmental externalities in its narrow identification of both 'damage' and 'defendant', together with the availability of certain defences. The point is not that the ELD is 'inefficient', but simply that the internalisation of environmental externalities is not the overwhelming purpose of the Directive. Another common objective of economic instruments is to provide for dynamic regulation, incentivising operators to go 'beyond compliance'. But again, the Directive has other concerns, as witnessed by the availability of a defence of compliance with a regulatory permit. In short, the Directive relies heavily on more substantive environmental regulation to set the boundaries of liability. This limits its role as a free-standing economic instrument, whilst emphasising that enforcement and implementation are a key objective of the legislation. In fact, the Directive is explicitly called upon by the Commission as a tool to 'support' implementation and enforcement, and this rationale is clearly followed through in the detail of the ELD

Lee is highlighting that the Directive does not create an overarching liability regime that can operate in any circumstances where there is environmental damage. This is partly because 'environmental damage' is given a very specific definition under the Directive.

Directive 2004/35/EC of the European Parliament and of the Council of 21 April 2004 on Environmental Liability with Regard to the Prevention and Remedying of Environmental Damage OJ L143, Article 2(1)–(2)

1. 'environmental damage' means:

(a) damage to protected species and natural habitats, which is any damage that has significant adverse effects on reaching or maintaining the favourable conservation status of such habitats or species. The significance of such effects is to be assessed with reference to the baseline condition, taking account of the criteria set out in Annex I;

Damage to protected species and natural habitats does not include previously identified adverse effects which result from an act by an operator which was expressly authorised by the relevant authorities in accordance with provisions implementing Article 6(3) and (4) or Article 16 of Directive 92/43/EEC or

Article 9 of Directive 79/409/EEC or, in the case of habitats and species not covered by Community law, in accordance with equivalent provisions of national law on nature conservation.

(b) water damage, which is any damage that significantly adversely affects the ecological, chemical and/or quantitative status and/or ecological potential, as defined in Directive 2000/60/EC, of the waters concerned, with the exception of adverse effects where Article 4(7) of that Directive applies;

(c) land damage, which is any land contamination that creates a significant risk of human health being adversely affected as a result of the direct or indirect introduction, in, on or under land, of substances, preparations, organisms or micro-organisms;

2. 'damage' means a measurable adverse change in a natural resource or measurable impairment of a natural resource service which may occur directly or indirectly;

Furthermore, the Directive only applies to such damage, or to an imminent threat of it, where it is 'caused by any of the occupational activities listed in Annex III', which include activities regulated under various EU environmental regimes (integrated pollution control, waste management, water discharges, and so on).[12] Exceptionally, it applies more widely to the damage of natural species or habitats, as already defined, caused by any operator who was negligent or otherwise at fault.[13] Thus, the ELD regime can only really be understood through a close analysis of the text of the Directive, as can be seen in Advocate General Kokott's opinion. The facts of the case are not relevant.

Case C–378/08 *Raffinerie Mediterranee SpA (ERG) v Ministero dello Sviluppo Economico* [2010] ECR I–1919, Opinion of AG Kokott, paras 87–95

87. The Environmental Liability Directive gives concrete expression to the 'polluter pays' principle in particular by requiring the operators responsible to take remedial action under art.6 and by providing, in art.8(1), that the operator must bear the costs for the preventive and remedial actions taken pursuant to the directive. Under art.2(6), the operator is the person who is responsible for the activity which has caused the damage. He is in principle best placed to prevent the environmental damage deriving from his activity.

88. In practice, there could be a need for further regulation in relation to damage on third party land. The directive refers to the owners of such land only insofar as it provides in art.7(4) that they are to be consulted. However, it cannot be inferred from this that the person required to take remedial action is automatically able to take measures on third party land.

89. Furthermore, under art.3(1), the Environmental Liability Directive does not establish liability for all environmental damage and also distinguishes between different types of damage in connection with such liability.

90. First, the directive covers environmental damage caused by any of the occupational activities listed in Annex III (art.3(1)(a) of the Environmental Liability Directive). Annex III lists various activities which are associated with particular environmental risks under other provisions of Community environmental law. [...]

91. Secondly, art.3(1)(b) of the Environmental Liability Directive provides for liability for action where the operator has been at fault or negligent in the case of other activities where protected species

---

[12] ELD, Article 3(1). Thus, you need to keep the Directive in mind as a remedy when studying these different areas of regulation, in Chapters 14, 16, 17, and 22 in particular, and also in relation to EU nature conservation law in Chapter 20.
[13] Note also the temporal limits to the operation of the Directive in Article 17.

and natural habitats are damaged which are protected under art.6(3) and (4) or art.16 of the Habitats Directive or Article 9 of the Birds Directive. [...]

92. Because liability for damage to protected species and natural habitats is expressly linked to fault, in principle liability for damage as a result of activities in Annex III may be invoked, *a contrario*, irrespective of fault. This is confirmed by the options available to the Member States under art.8(4) to provide for exemption from remediation costs where the operator was not at fault *and* the causal activity was authorised or was carried out according to the current state of technology. The more stringent liability mechanism of strict liability is associated with the particular risks to the environment which are accepted in connection with the activities in question, which by their nature involve risks.

93. In both cases, liability under art.3(1) of the Environmental Liability Directive requires in any event that the damage is caused by the activities covered. Under art.11(2), the duty to establish which operator has caused the damage rests with the competent national authority. Irrespective of any such finding, under arts.5 to 7, the operator is required to take preventive and, if necessary, remedial action and to inform the competent authorities. That liability is limited under art.8(3) if the operator proves that the damage was caused by a third party or resulted from orders emanating from a public authority.

94. The Environmental Liability Directive therefore seeks to implement the 'polluter pays' principle in a certain form. In essence, operators are to bear the costs of environmental damage which they cause. This allocation of costs creates an incentive for operators to prevent environmental damage. This is fair insofar as the operators carry on an activity involving risk, particularly in the case of strict liability, and generally also benefit from an economic return on that activity.

95. Where the person who caused damage is not known, on the other hand, there is no duty to take remedial action under the directive. [...]

The key statement here is that 'the Environmental Liability Directive therefore seeks to implement the "polluter pays" principle in a certain form'. As is obvious from the discussion here, that form is more complicated than simply requiring polluters to pay compensation for harm that they cause. This also reflects the fact that environmental principles like the polluter pays principle, as legal concepts, can only be understood within the legal contexts in which they operate.[14]

3.2 THE ENVIRONMENTAL LIABILITY DIRECTIVE AND CJEU

There have been numerous Article 258 TFEU enforcement actions brought by the Commission in relation to the Environmental Liability Directive.[15] These cases contain little substantive legal discussion, but there have also been a handful of cases in which the CJEU has considered and interpreted the Environmental Liability Directive. This case law is not only interesting in providing insight into the Directive but, because the Directive is understood as an example of the polluter pays principle, it is also included in the body of doctrine concerned with environmental principles.[16] In terms of elucidating the Directive itself, the Court in the *Raffinerie Mediterranae (ERG) SpA v Ministero dello Sviluppo economico* case considered the question of ascertainment of liability under the Directive, focusing on the notion of 'causation' of damage that must be established.

---

[14] See Chapter 11.

[15] See, for example, Case C-330/08 *Commission v France* [2008] I–191; Case C-417/08 *Commission v UK* [2009] ECR I–106; Case C-422/08 *Commission v Austria* [2009] I–107.

[16] See, for example, the extract from Case C–188/07 *Commune de Mesquer v Total France SA* [2008] ECR I–4501 in Section 1.2 of Chapter 16.

Case C–378/08 *Raffinerie Mediterranae (ERG) SpA v Ministero dello Sviluppo economico* [2010] ECR I–1919, paras 34, 52–62

The Facts

Administrative authorities in Sicily had for many years attempted to address environmental pollution problems in a particular region. This involved requiring certain companies to either carry our remediation themselves or reimburse the administrative authority for carrying our remediation. A number of questions were sent for preliminary reference.

The Grand Chamber

34. By its first three questions, which it is appropriate to examine together, the *Tribunale amministrativo regionale della Sicilia* asks, in essence, whether the 'polluter pays' principle, as laid down in the first subparagraph of art.174(2) EC, and the provisions of Directive 2004/35, which seeks to give that principle concrete expression in the field of environmental liability, preclude national legislation which allows the competent authority to impose measures for remedying environmental damage on commercial operators on account of the fact that their installations are located close to a contaminated area, without carrying out any preliminary investigation into the occurrence of the contamination or establishing a causal link between the environmental damage and those operators or indeed intent or negligence on the part of those operators [...]

52. As stated in recital 13 in the preamble to Directive 2004/35, not all forms of environmental damage can be remedied by means of the liability mechanism and, for the mechanism to be effective, there needs to be, inter alia, a causal link established between one or more identifiable polluters and concrete and quantifiable environmental damage.

53. As is apparent from art.4(5) and art.11(2) of Directive 2004/35, if it is necessary for the competent authority to establish such a causal link in order to impose remedial measures on operators irrespective of the kind of pollution involved, then that requirement is also a condition for the application of the directive in the case of pollution of a diffuse, widespread character.

54. Such a causal link could easily be established where the competent authority is confronted with pollution which is confined to a particular area and period of time and is attributable to a limited number of operators. On the other hand, that is not the case with diffuse pollution phenomena and, therefore, the legislature of the European Union considered that, in the case of such pollution, a liability mechanism is not an appropriate instrument where such a causal link cannot be established. Consequently, art.4(5) of Directive 2004/35 provides that the directive is to apply to that kind of pollution only where it is possible to establish a causal link between the damage and the activities of individual operators.

55. In that regard, it must be noted that Directive 2004/35 does not specify how such a causal link is to be established. Under the shared competence enjoyed by the European Union and the Member States in environmental matters, where a criterion necessary for the implementation of a directive adopted on the basis of Article 175 EC has not been defined in the directive, such a definition falls within the competence of the Member States and they have a broad discretion, in compliance with the Treaty rules, when laying down national rules developing or giving concrete expression to the 'polluter pays' principle (see, to that effect, Case C–254/08 *Futura Immobiliare v Comune di Casoria* [2009] ECR I–6995, paras 48, 52 and 55).

56. Accordingly, the legislation of a Member State may provide that the competent authority has the power to impose measures for remedying environmental damage on the basis of the presumption that there is a causal link between the pollution found and the activities of the operator or operators concerned due to the fact that their installations are located close to that pollution.

57. However, since, in accordance with the 'polluter pays' principle, the obligation to take remedial measures is imposed on operators only because of their contribution to the creation of pollution or the risk of pollution (see, by analogy, Case C–188/07 *Commune de Mesquer v Total France SA* [2008]

ECR I–4501, para 77), in order for such a causal link to thus be presumed, the competent authority must have plausible evidence capable of justifying its presumption, such as the fact that the operator's installation is located close to the pollution found and that there is a correlation between the pollutants identified and the substances used by the operator in connection with his activities.

58. Where the competent authority has such evidence, it is thus in a position to establish a causal link between the operators' activities and the diffuse pollution found. In accordance with art.4(5) of Directive 2004/35, such a situation therefore falls within the scope of the directive, unless those operators are able to rebut that presumption.

59. It follows that, if the *Tribunale amministrativo regionale della Sicilia* considers that the pollution in question in the main proceedings is diffuse and no causal link can be established, such a situation does not fall within the scope ratione materiæ of Directive 2004/35 but within that of national law, in accordance with the conditions set out at para 44 above.

60. On the other hand, if the referring court reaches the conclusion that Directive 2004/35 is applicable to the case before it, the following considerations are to be borne in mind.

61. It is apparent from art. 3(1)(b) of Directive 2004/35 that, where there is damage to protected species and habitats caused by any occupational activities other than those listed in Annex III to the directive, the directive applies, provided that it is established that the operator has been at fault or negligent. On the other hand, there is no such requirement where one of the occupational activities listed in Annex III has caused environmental damage, namely—as defined in art. 2(1)(a) to (c) of the directive—damage to protected species and habitats, and water and land damage.

62. Subject to the findings of fact, which are a matter for the referring court, where environmental damage is caused by operators active in the energy and chemical industry sectors as referred to in ss2.1 and 2.4 of Annex I to Directive 96/61, which are, for that purpose, activities falling within Annex III to Directive 2004/35, precautionary measures or remedial measures may be imposed on such operators without there being any need for the competent authority to establish that they are at fault or negligent.

There are two interesting things to note about this reasoning. First, as with AG Kokott's opinion in the same case, much of the analysis cleaves closely to the Directive. Second, the Directive imposes a considerable analytical burden on Member States.

3.3 THE ENVIRONMENTAL DAMAGE (PREVENTION AND REMEDIATION) REGULATIONS 2009

As we saw in Chapter 4, EU Directives must be implemented into the law of Member States, with the 'choice of form and methods' left up to the Member States (Article 288 TFEU). The question of implementation in the case of the Environment Liability Directive is particularly challenging when one considers that the Directive not only creates its own regime, which may not sit easily with existing legal structures in Member States, but its operation relies on legal terminology that is dependent upon a wider EU legal context for its meaning. This was clearly an issue in the development of the Directive but is also relevant in its implementation into Member State legal systems.

Gerd Winter and others, 'Weighing Up the EC Environmental Liability Directive'
(2008) 20 JEL 163, 166

European Community law has to be created against a background of different legal traditions, and this has proved particularly complex in dealing with issues concerning liability where all national systems already have well developed approaches. Terms such as 'civil liability', 'public liability', 'administrative liability' and 'environmental liability' peppered the debates and discussion papers, but often in an ill-defined way, even though they may well resonate rather differently from jurisdiction to jurisdiction. This lack of clarity as to precisely what was being considered at any particular time certainly did not always assist a clear development of the Directive.

In terms of implementation of the Directive into England, the EDPR Regulations 2009 read nothing like a liability regime but more as an administrative process for dealing with a small category of circumstances where environmental damage has occurred, or could occur. There have been relatively few applications of it so far but it is still early days.[17] There are two further notable features of the Regulations:

1. They do not apply in relation to relevant environmental damage occurring due to an emission or incident before 1 March 2009, or otherwise caused by activities before that date, or to any damage where more than thirty years have passed since the incident that caused it.

2. The UK has opted *not* to excuse operators from responsibility under the Regulations in cases where they have not been at fault or negligent and damage was caused by regulated and permitted activities or activities that were unlikely to cause damage according to the state of scientific or technical knowledge at the time (cf Article 8(4) ELD).

It is also worth considering how these Regulations, in their remedial function in respect of land contamination, overlap with the UK contaminated land regime in Part IIA of the Environmental Protection Act 1990, which is covered in Chapter 21. Despite covering overlapping legal terrain, there are some notable differences between the regimes, including: when the relevant land damage must have occurred (the EDPR Regulations do not largely deal with historical land contamination); the standard of remediation that is required; and which polluters are covered.

4 OTHER STATUTORY LIABILITY SCHEMES

Besides statutory nuisance under the EPA and the Environmental Liability Directive, it is also important to note that the UK and EU legislatures have created a series of *ad hoc* environmental liability schemes over the years. Each of these has their own complexities and gives rise to their own bodies of practice, and sometimes doctrine. An obvious example is s 73(6) of the Environmental Protection Act 1990, which creates liability for damage caused by waste crime.[18] Other examples can be seen in other chapters of this textbook, such as the contaminated land regime of Part IIA of the Environmental Protection Act 1990 in Chapter 21. Another example is the Nuclear Installations Act 1965, which creates a liability regime that implements the UK's international obligations under the Paris Convention on Nuclear Third Party Liability.[19] That regime makes the licensee of a nuclear installation liable for injuries to persons and damage to property of others, which is caused by nuclear matter or the escape of ionizing radiation.[20] These schemes, of course, raise questions about the interaction between statutory liability regimes and the common law. Thus, all these schemes raise again the questions

---

[17] DEFRA provide yearly reports to the Commission. See <http://www.defra.gov.uk/environment/quality/environmental-liability/> accessed 9 August 2012.

[18] See Chapter 16.   [19] 956 UNTS 251.

[20] Nuclear Installation Act 1965, ss 7 and 12. See the judicial consideration of this scheme in *Blue Circle Industries Plc v Ministry of Defence* [1999] Ch 289 (CA).

considered in Chapter 6 concerning the legal interrelationship between legislation and the common law.

5 CONCLUSION

This chapter has been an overview of some of the most misunderstood regimes in environmental law. Statutory nuisance may give the appearance of being a straightforward concept and process but, as the case law considered in this chapter illustrates, it is anything but. Likewise, the Environmental Liability Directive establishes more of an administrative regime than a private law compensation scheme. These are just two of many different examples of liability regimes that exist in environmental law and in each case their operation raises difficult legal questions. In short, they are fascinating areas of legal practice that require legal agility and nimbleness.

FURTHER READING

As stressed throughout this chapter, the discussion in this chapter provides only a very cursory overview of profoundly complex areas of law. For further reading the following texts are useful.

On Statutory Nuisance:

- Robert McCracken, Gregory Jones and James Pereira, *Statutory Nuisance* (3rd edn, Bloomsbury Professional 2012)
- Rosalind Malcolm and John Ponting, *Statutory Nuisance: Law and Practice* (2nd edn, OUP 2011).
- John Murphy, *The Law of Nuisance* (OUP 2010), ch 8.

On Noise Pollution more generally:

- Melville Adams and Francis McManus, *Noise and Noise Law: A Practical Approach* (John Wiley & Sons 1994) (this focuses on industry and the commercial experience with noise controls).

On the Environmental Liability Directive:

- European Commission, 'Report Under Article 14(2) of Directive 2004/35/CE on the Environmental Liability with Regard to the Prevention and Remedying of Environmental Damage' COM(2010) 581 final.

10

THE ROLE OF THE COURTS

In many ways, all the chapters in this book concern the role of the courts in environmental law and there are few chapters without an extract from a case or consideration of judical doctrine. It thus may seem odd to have a separate chapter to consider the role of the courts, particularly when few students would doubt the importance of focusing on courts in the study of law. Yet there are two important issues that are not covered in other chapters and which are important for environmental lawyers to understand and keep in mind in reading other chapters in this book.

The first issue, and the primary focus of this chapter, concerns access to the courts and the role that procedure (including costs) plays in limiting the ability of litigants to take cases to court. The second issue is the ongoing discourse about the need for some form of specialist environmental court. Both of these topics are constant background themes in environmental law and raise issues about how environmental problems interact with adjudicative procedure. They are also important because, without access to courts or competent dispute resolution forums, there would be no adequate resolution of disputes, nor any environmental law for that matter.

This chapter is structured as follows. First, there is a general discussion about the nature of a court and the type of courts and associated adjudicative bodies that are relevant in thinking about UK environmental law. It will be seen that environmental law involves a broad spectrum of adjudicative institutions including Planning Inspectors, tribunals, English courts, EU courts, and the European Court of Human Rights (ECtHR). Second, access to justice in environmental matters is considered in both England and the UK. Over the last decade, the third pillar of the Aarhus Convention on Access to Information, Public Participation in Decision-making and Access to Justice in Environmental Matters has become the touchstone for this issue. The third section surveys the debates for a specialist environmental court. While the analysis focuses on debates in England, environmental courts exist in many other jurisdictions. (See Section 2.1 of Chapter 7.)

Three points should be made at the outset. First, this chapter does not look at the substance of judicial doctrine but, rather, focuses on the procedural and institutional nature of courts. At times that distinction can be a very artificial one,[1] and you should consider the relationship between issues of procedure and the doctrinal matters discussed in other chapters. Second, we are well aware of the dangers of placing too much emphasis on the role of courts and ignoring the wider, more complex legal and regulatory landscape of environmental law. In particular, this chapter should be read alongside Chapters 12 and 13 in relation to regulatory strategy and governance, as well as the other chapters in this part. Third, this chapter does not consider the role of courts in criminal law. This issue is discussed in Chapter 8 and also requires consideration of the material in Chapter 12 concerning regulatory strategy.

---

[1] Particularly when, as in England and Wales, questions of merits and *locus standi* are considered together. See *R v Secretary of State for Foreign & Commonwealth Affairs, ex p World Development Movement* [1995] 1 WLR 386 (HC).

1 WHAT ARE COURTS AND TRIBUNALS? AND WHY ARE THEY IMPORTANT IN ENVIRONMENTAL LAW?

In order to discuss the role of courts, it is useful to consider briefly what a court actually is. This is easier said than done, but the description from Martin Shapiro is a useful starting point.

Martin Shapiro, *Courts: A Comparative and Political Analysis* (University of Chicago Press 1981) 1

Students of courts have generally employed an ideal type, or really a prototype, of courts involving (1) an independent judge applying (2) pre-existing legal norms after (3) adversary proceedings in order to achieve (4) a dichotomous decision in which one of the parties was assigned the legal right and the other found wrong.

Shapiro goes on to note the many problems with this prototype but then comments:

The root concept employed here is a simple one of conflict structured in triads. Cutting across cultural lines, it appears that whenever two persons come into conflict that they cannot themselves solve, one solution appealing to common sense is to call upon a third for assistance in achieving resolution. So universal across time and space is this simple social invention of triads that we can discover no society that fails to employ it. And from its overwhelming appeal to common sense stems the basis political legitimacy of courts everywhere. In sort, the triad for the purposes of conflict resolution is the basic social logic of courts, a logic so compelling that courts have become a universal social phenomenon.

There are two important things to note from this analysis. First, there is no single model of a court. While this basic triadic relationship exists in many different legal cultures, it is also subject to many variations in terms of both institutional structure and procedure. The most obvious variation is seen in the differences between civil law systems (where judges are more inquisitorial) and common law systems (where litigation is more adversarial), but courts will also play different roles depending on the constitutional structure of a polity, particularly in light of how the separation of powers is understood. Likewise, in some jurisdictions such as Australia and England, there is a long tradition of specialist tribunals as well as courts. Indeed, much of the discussion in Section 3 concerns the role of tribunals. While tribunals have very different powers and procedures, they too adhere to the triadic structure outlined by Shapiro.

The second notable aspect of Shapiro's analysis is that he is not only talking of courts in legal terms but also in terms of politics and society. As he is a political scientist, this is not surprising and it is an important reminder to keep in mind the role that courts play in a wider context. Litigation and court cases will resonate differently in different legal and socio-political cultures. For example, the US is often described as having a legal culture of 'adversarial legalism' where litigation is an everyday occurrence; whereas, in the UK, up until recently litigation was a relatively rare occurrence.[2]

With all that said, within common law legal cultures, courts can be identified as carrying out three sets of overlapping functions. The most obvious set of functions relates to the finding, interpreting and applying of the law, and in some cases its creation. The nature of these different enterprises and how they should be carried out are core themes in legal theory and in most areas of law.[3] The second set of functions of common law courts involves fact-finding and, as Birks, has noted adjudication

[2] Robert Kagan, *Adversarial Legalism: The American Way of Law* (Harvard UP 2003).
[3] Ronald Dworkin, *Law's Empire* (Fontana 1986).

plays an important role in 'stabilizing' the facts.[4] Thus, in deciding upon the legal aspects of a case, courts must also decide upon an authoritative understanding of the facts. This function is especially important in relation to environmental problems since the facts are particularly disputed and often require expert analysis—one of the main arguments for a specialist environmental court or tribunal is that they would be a competent specialist finder of facts. Thirdly, courts will perform a variety of roles depending on the body of law with which they are dealing. Thus, in private law disputes, courts resolve disputes within a bi-polar structure (that is, a dispute between two sets of parties), while in judicial reviewing administrative action, they seek to ensure that a decision-maker has made a legally valid decision. In other words, courts do not fulfil the same legal function all the time and care must be taken in generalizing about the role of courts between different areas of the law.

This discussion may give the impression that the role of a court is blandly functional. Yet courts are more than the sum of their parts and the judgment of a court has a symbolism and authority that few other legal documents have. A judgment is an 'icon of the rule of law' and a particular case is a 'carefully orchestrated process through which indeterminate aggregations of persons, words, stories, and materials are transformed into facts of intention, causality, responsibility and property'.[5] Law, in the form of a judgment, has a 'homeostatic' quality in which any argument must be integrated into the 'the integrity of the legal edifice'.[6] The processes of courts are thus fundamental both to the construction of legal discourse and to the authority of law itself.

In light of these features of courts, it should come as no surprise that the role of courts has been a matter of considerable scholarly interest in environmental law. This interest is best analysed by classification in terms of descriptive, purposive, and jurisprudential understandings of environmental law.[7] From a descriptive perspective, the role of the courts arises because environmental problems lead to a range of legal disputes that require adjudication. These may include property disputes, tort law claims, and judicial review actions. In a descriptive sense, a focus on the role of the courts is important since their involvement in environmental law is inevitable.

From a purposive perspective, the role of the courts is emphasized because judicial decisions are viewed as a (potential) means of furthering environmental protection.

Christopher Riti, 'Issue Editor's Note: The Role of the Environmental Judiciary'
(2010) 3 Journal of Court Innovation iii, iii–iv

> Visionary world leaders at the 1992 Rio Earth Summit agreed that sustainable development is the only way forward given the constraints and limitations inherent in the Earth's natural systems, and formally recognized the fundamental relationship between such development and public participation in no uncertain terms. Environmental adjudicative bodies are a necessary component of this vision as institutions that check the undue influence of political and economic interests while enforcing effective accountability measures.

Thus, the role of courts has been promoted in the pursuit of environmental protection, and Principle 10 of the Rio Declaration on Environment and Development accordingly requires 'effective access to judicial and administrative proceedings' in relation to environmental issues. The United Nations Economic Commission for Europe fleshed out this requirement in the third pillar of the Aarhus

---

[4] Peter Birks, 'Adjudication and Interpretation in the Common Law: A Century of Change' (1994) 14 LS 156, 158.
[5] Susan Sibley and Ayn Cavicchi, 'The Common Place of Law' in Bruno Latour and Peter Weibel (eds) *Making Things Public: Atmospheres of Democracy* (MIT Press 2005) 556.
[6] Bruno Latour, *The Making of Law* (Polity Press 2009) 243.   [7] See Section 5 of Chapter 1.

Convention (discussed in Section 2). Further, there are purposive understandings of litigation that understand a court case as a form of political mobilization. From this perspective, courts are important forums for political discourse, more than being legal forums. From a jurisprudential perspective, courts are of interest to environmental lawyers for the doctrines that they develop. Thus, for example, much of the literature on environmental principles focuses upon how courts have developed these principles, rather than upon how legislators or administrators have defined them.[8]

Despite this intense interest of environmental lawyers in courts and other adjudicative bodies, environmental problems and environmental law have not easily interrelated with traditional adjudicative structures historically. In terms of the role of courts in finding, developing, and applying law, a number of problems have been recognized. To begin with, the right of access to a court (or standing to sue) was traditionally based on having a private right infringed. However, as we have already seen in many chapters, environmental problems do not always involve the infringement or engagement of private rights. Moreover, traditional adjudicative structures were developed to accommodate bi-polar disputes while, as we have seen (Section 2.1 of Chapter 2), environmental problems tend to be polycentric.[9] Further, generalist courts have struggled to apply novel legal concepts embedded in bespoke environmental law regimes, such as environmental impact assessment.[10] Courts have also confronted a number of problems in 'stabilizing the facts' in legal disputes in environmental cases. Due to the range of issues concerning scientific knowledge and scientific uncertainty, establishing the facts on traditional rules of evidence, developed for more straightforward factual settings, has been difficult.[11]

As a result, discourses about the role of courts in environmental law exhibit an almost paradoxical quality in that there is simultaneous emphasis on both the *importance* and *limits* of courts in environmental law. This paradox can be seen in the two themes to which we now turn—access to justice and the need to develop specialist environmental tribunals. As we shall see, this paradox is illusory—by considering together the importance and limits of courts in environmental law, environmental law forces us to look at the need to reflect on types of adjudication.

2 ACCESS TO JUSTICE AND ENVIRONMENTAL LAW

Over the last decade, the most prominent and fashionable theme in environmental law has been the issue of access to justice. This is partly due to Article 10 of the Rio Declaration and the third pillar of the Aarhus Convention, but to focus on these instruments alone is to ignore the problems that those wishing to protect the environment, or otherwise to engage in environmental disputes, have encountered in attempting to litigate. This section briefly considers the procedural aspects of litigating judicial review actions in both English and EU law, before providing an overview of the third pillar of the Aarhus Convention and how it is transforming law and practice in this area.

2.1 SOME BACKGROUND ON PROCEDURE

The issue of access to justice in environmental matters has been primarily understood as a public law issue, not a private law one. This is because of the way in which the substance of a legal action relates to the right of litigation—for public law actions, standing rules require more legal construction and are more contentious as a result. Sunstein provides some background to this.

---

[8] See Chapter 11.
[9] Abram Chayes, 'The Role of the Judge in Public Law Litigation' (1976) 89 Harv LR 1281.
[10] Harold Leventhal, 'Environmental Decision Making and the Role of the Courts' (1974) 122 U Pa L Rev 509.
[11] Carl Cranor, *Toxic Torts: Science, Law and the Possibility of Justice* (CUP 2006).

Cass Sunstein, 'Standing and the Privatization of Public Law' (1988) 88 Colum LR 1432, 1434–35

In the modern period [...] judicial review of administrative action has been an outgrowth of a simple framework. If administrators intruded on interests protected at common law, judicial review was available to test the question whether there was statutory authorization for what would otherwise be a common-law wrong. If no common-law right were at stake, judicial protection was unavailable. The most distinctive feature of this framework was the use of common-law understandings to define the judicial role in public-law cases.

The basic framework was built on an analogy and an identifiable underlying theory. The analogy was to private law, in which the issues of standing, cause of action, and the merits are closely intertwined. In an action in which A causes an injury to B, the question whether B has a cause of action overlaps a great deal with the question whether B has standing and whether B is correct on the merits. For all three issues, the question is whether A has violated a duty it owes to B. C, an affected third party, generally may not bring suit when A injures B-even if C is materially affected. At private law, there is no need for a distinctive set of principles to govern standing.

In public law, there is no inherent right to sue that matches an identifiable individual legal interest, thus a private rights model of standing does not work. Administrative law involves questions about legal validity and not individual rights (see Chapter 7). While, in some regulatory areas, there will be overlap between questions of validity and individual rights, in many areas (and particularly environmental law) that involve public decision-makers making decisions in the public interest, there will not be.

As most public law systems historically used private law as a basis for defining public law standing, in the way that Sunstein explains here, the need to develop standing on a different foundation has been part of their environmental law and administrative law histories.[12]

England and Wales

In England and Wales the history of standing in public law actions has been relatively straightforward. Before 1977, the test was fleshed out in common law doctrine and grounded on a private rights framework.[13] In 1977 the application to a court for judicial review was reformed and in 1981 put on a statutory footing. What is now the Senior Courts Act 1981 states:

s 31(3) No application for judicial review shall be made unless the leave of the High Court has been obtained in accordance with rules of court; and the court shall not grant leave to make such an application unless it considers that the applicant has a sufficient interest in the matter to which the application relates.

Judicial review thus requires permission to be granted by the High Court and permission will be only granted if an applicant is found to have a 'sufficient interest'. Over the next two decades, there were a variety of judicial interpretations of what constituted a 'sufficient interest', with a growing emphasis on the importance of ensuring that abuses of power did not go unchecked because of strict standing

---

[12] See the famous Christopher Stone, 'Should Trees Have Standing?: Towards Legal Rights for Natural Objects' (1972) 45 S Cal L Rev 450, a discussion of which can be found in the Introduction to Part III. The US Supreme Court did not accept this argument but ultimately took a different approach: see *Sierra Club v Morton* 450 US 727 (1972).

[13] *Boyce v Paddington BC* [1903] 1 Ch 109.

rules.[14] Thus, even though some approaches to the question of standing followed the private rights model,[15] by the late 1990s it had become common for public interest groups in environmental and related matters to be granted standing.[16] The basis for granting standing in these cases varies significantly.[17] Recently the Supreme Court has asserted the importance of standing for concerned citizens in environmental law. The facts need not concern us beyond the fact that the Court was considering standing both in the context of common law standing ('the sufficient interest' test) and under the relevant legislation in this case (the test being 'person aggrieved').

Walton v Scottish Ministers
[2012] UKSC 44 paras 90, 94, 152, 153

Lord Reed JSC

90. In *AXA General Insurance Ltd and others v HM Advocate and others* [2011] UKSC 46; [2012] 1 AC 868; 2011 SLT 1061, this court clarified the approach which should be adopted to the question of standing to bring an application to the supervisory jurisdiction. In doing so, it intended to put an end to an unduly restrictive approach which had too often obstructed the proper administration of justice: an approach which presupposed that the only function of the court's supervisory jurisdiction was to redress individual grievances, and ignored its constitutional function of maintaining the rule of law.

Lord Reed thus when on to note that, while it was important to distinguish between someone who is a 'mere busybody' and someone who has a 'sufficient interest':

94. In many contexts it will be necessary for a person to demonstrate some particular interest in order to demonstrate that he is not a mere busybody. Not every member of the public can complain of every potential breach of duty by a public body. But there may also be cases in which any individual, simply as a citizen, will have sufficient interest to bring a public authority's violation of the law to the attention of the court, without having to demonstrate any greater impact upon himself than upon other members of the public. The rule of law would not be maintained if, because everyone was equally affected by an unlawful act, no-one was able to bring proceedings to challenge it.

Lord Hope also commented on the question of standing.

Lord Hope

152. [...] An individual may be personally affected in his private interests by the environmental issues to which an application for planning permission may give rise. Noise and disturbance to the visual amenity of his property are some obvious examples. But some environmental issues that can properly be raised by an individual are not of that character. Take, for example, the risk that a route used by an osprey as it moves to and from a favourite fishing loch will be impeded by the proposed erection across it of a cluster of wind turbines. Does the fact that this proposal cannot reasonably be said to affect any individual's property rights or interests mean that it is not open to an individual to challenge the proposed

---

[14] For example, *R v IRC, ex p National Federation of the Self Employed* [1982] AC 617 (HL) per Lord Diplock 644 and *R v Somerset CC, ex p Dixon* [1997] COD 322 (QB).

[15] For example, *R v Secretary of State, ex parte Rose Theatre* [1990] 1 QB 504 (QB); Konrad Schiemann 'Locus Standi' [1990] PL 342.

[16] For example, *R v Inspectorate of Pollution, ex p Greenpeace (No 2)* [1994] 4 All ER 329 (QB); *World Development Movement Ltd* (n 1).

[17] Chris Hilson and Ian Cram, 'Judicial Review and Environmental Law—Is There a Coherent View of Standing?' (1996) 16 LS 1 and Peter Cane 'Standing Up For the Public' [1995] PL 276.

development on this ground? That would seem to be contrary to the purpose of environmental law, which proceeds on the basis that the quality of the natural environment is of legitimate concern to everyone. The osprey has no means of taking that step on its own behalf, any more than any other wild creature. If its interests are to be protected someone has to be allowed to speak up on its behalf.

153. Of course, this must not be seen as an invitation to the busybody to question the validity of a scheme or order under the statute just because he objects to the scheme of the development. Individuals who wish to do this on environmental grounds will have to demonstrate that they have a genuine interest in the aspects of the environment that they seek to protect, and that they have sufficient knowledge of the subject to qualify them to act in the public interest in what is, in essence, a representative capacity. There is, after all, no shortage of well-informed bodies that are equipped to raise issues of this kind, such as the Scottish Wildlife Trust and Scottish Natural Heritage in their capacity as the Scottish Ministers' statutory advisers on nature conservation. It would normally be to bodies of that kind that one would look if there were good grounds for objection. But it is well-known they do not have the resources to object to every development that might have adverse consequences for the environment. So there has to be some room for individuals who are sufficiently concerned, and sufficiently well-informed, to do this too. It will be for the court to judge in each case whether these requirements are satisfied.

These two judicial comments encapsulate much of the reasoning of the courts over the last decade. The test they create is not one of open standing but one in which the importance of environmental protection is recognized. As is also noted in the judgment, the right to open standing will also be balanced against the discretion of the court to grant a remedy.[18]

The EU

The procedure for bringing judicial review actions is very different in the EU. Article 263 TFEU was discussed in Section 6 of Chapter 4 and paragraph (4) regulates standing for non-privileged applicants (that is, applicants other than EU institutions and other Member States). It should also be remembered that cases brought by non-privileged applicants are heard, as a general rule, by the General Court not by the Court of Justice. Article 263(4) states:

Any natural or legal person may, under the conditions laid down in the first and second paragraphs, institute proceedings against an act addressed to that person or which is of direct and individual concern to them, and against a regulatory act which is of direct concern to them and does not entail implementing measures.

Article 263(4) was introduced with the Treaty of Lisbon in 2009. The wording of the previous version of this paragraph (Article 230 TEC) was:

Any natural or legal person may, under the same conditions, institute proceedings against a decision addressed to that person or against a decision which, although in the form of a regulation or a decision addressed to another person, is of direct and individual concern to the former.

This provision was included in the original Treaty of Rome in 1958, and considering that the Treaty was then an international agreement, its giving of a right to individuals to bring annulment actions was remarkable.[19] However, it was an awkwardly worded provision and it resulted in a difficult body of

---

[18] *Walton v Scottish Ministers* [2012] UKSC 44 per Lord Carnwath.
[19] Eric Stein and Joseph Vining, 'Citizen Access to Judicial Review of Administrative Action in a Transnational and Federal Context (1976) 70 AJIL 219.

case law developing around the concept of 'individual' concern' that required the litigant to belong to a 'closed class'.[20] Difficulties in applying this test were encountered in many cases.[21]

Four particular issues emerged as problematic in relation to standing under the pre-Lisbon test. First, the CJEU was developing exceptions to a fundamentally restrictive standing test in the case law but there was little in the way of overarching logic to these developments.[22] Second, it was utterly clear that public interest groups could never be found to have 'individual concern'.[23] Third, one of the reasons often cited for the restrictive 'individual concern' test was problematic. This was the notion that individuals could bring actions challenging the validity of Union action via national courts and the preliminary reference procedure, but as AG Jacobs showed in his analysis in *UPA*, this alternative route to the EU courts was not always a realistic prospect for individuals.[24] Fourth, with the emergence of the EU as a constitutional order, the restricted ability to challenge acts of the EU institutions directly was seen as increasingly problematic.[25] This concern was a general one in relation to standing to challenge EU institutions, not a concern in the environmental law context alone.

It is not obvious that the new Article 263(4) addresses all of these concerns. It retains the concept of 'individual concern' but in a different textual setting, and introduces a new concept of 'regulatory act' that does not entail implementing measures, in relation to which standing can be established without showing individual concern. There have been a number of cases considering these phrases.[26] The *Europäischer Wirtschaftsverband der Eisen- und Stahlindustrie (Eurofer) ASBL v Commission* case provides an excellent example of the current approach of the General Court to standing. It is a lengthy extract and there are four important things to note in reading it. First, while this case concerns environmental regulation (the EU emissions trading scheme), it is being brought by an industry litigant. This is an important reminder that the issue of standing in environmental law is not only an issue concerning public interest groups. Second, the significance of the historical case law can also be seen, particularly in relation to the test of 'individual concern'. Third, the question of what constitute 'implementing measures' is more complicated than it may first seem. Finally, note how the Court rests much of its analysis on the specific legal framework at issue in this case.

Case T-381/11 *Europäischer Wirtschaftsverband der Eisen- und Stahlindustrie (Eurofer) ASBL v Commission*
[Order of the GC, 4 June 2012] paras 26, 29–32, 34–38, 42–47, 56–58

The Facts

Eurofer, a trade association representing the interests of the European steel industry wished to challenge the Commission adopted Decision 2011/278/EU that determined transitional Union-wide rules for harmonised free allocation of emission allowances pursuant to Article 10a of Directive 2003/87 establishing a scheme for greenhouse gas emission allowance trading. To establish standing Eurofer needed to argue that some of its members had standing under Article 263(4) TFEU either because that

---

[20] Case 25/62 *Plaumann* [1963] ECR 95.

[21] Cases C-358/89 *Extramet* [1991] ECR I-2501; C-309/89 *Codorniu* [1994] ECR I-1853.

[22] Paul Craig, 'Legality, Standing, and Substantive Review in Community Law' (1994) 14 OJLS 507.

[23] Case T-585/93 *Greenpeace* [1995] ECR II-2205 and on appeal [1998] ECR I-2305.

[24] Case C-50/00P *UPA* [2002] ECR 1-6677, although note the Court did not accept his suggestion of reinterpreting the concept of 'individual concern'.

[25] Anthony Arnull, 'Private Actions for Annulment Under Art 173 of the EC Treaty' (1995) 32 CML Rev 7.

[26] Case T-18/10 *Inuit Tapiriit Kanatami v Parliament* (GC, 6 September 2011) and Case T-262/10 *Microban International Ltd v Commission* (GC, 25 October 2011).

had individual concern or because the measure they were challenging was a regulatory act without implementing measures.

The GC

26. In the present case, it is common ground that the contested decision was [...] addressed to the Member States. Neither Eurofer nor its members are addressees of that act. Therefore, under the fourth paragraph of Article 263 TFEU, Eurofer can bring an action against that act only if it is of direct and individual concern to its members, or if the contested decision constitutes a regulatory act which is of direct concern to them and does not entail implementing measures. [...]

29. With regard to whether the applicants are individually concerned by the contested decision, it should be pointed out that the decision is a measure of general application in that it applies to situations which have been determined objectively, and has legal effects as regards a category of persons viewed in a general and abstract manner. Under Article 2 of the contested decision, that decision applies to the free allocation of emission allowances in relation to the stationary installations referred to in Chapter III of Directive 2003/87 in trading periods from 2013, with the exception of transitional free allocation of emission allowances for the modernisation of electricity generation pursuant to Article 10c of that directive. The contested decision therefore concerns all operators of those installations which, like Eurofer's members, are required to participate in the emission allowance trading scheme in accordance with Article 2(1) and Annexes I and II to Directive 2003/87, in general and abstract terms, under the rules established by the contested decision and that directive.

30. However, it is not excluded that, in certain circumstances, the provisions of a measure of general application can be of individual concern to certain natural or legal persons and the measure can be therefore in the nature of a decision in their regard. In accordance with settled case-law, natural or legal persons other than the person to whom a measure is addressed can claim to be individually concerned, for the purposes of the fourth paragraph of Article 263 TFEU, only if they are affected by the measure in question by reason of certain attributes peculiar to them, or by reason of a factual situation which differentiates them from all other persons and distinguishes them individually in the same way as the addressee (Case 25/62 *Plaumann* v *Commission* [1963] ECR 95, 107; Case C-50/00 P *Unión de Pequeños Agricultores* v *Council* [2002] ECR I–6677, paragraph 36; and Case C-263/02 P *Commission* v *Jégo-Quéré* [2004] ECR I–3425, paragraph 45).

31. The fact that Eurofer's members are operators of stationary installations referred to in Chapter III of Directive 2003/87 cannot distinguish them since, as regards the provisions of the contested decision referred to in paragraph 29 above, they are only concerned by that decision by reason of their objective capacity as operators of those installations, in the same way as any other trader which is currently or potentially in the same situation.

32. Eurofer claims that its members are individually concerned by the contested decision because of the procedural guarantees referred to in the fifth subparagraph of Article 10a(1) and the first subparagraph of Article 10a(2) of Directive 2003/87. According to those provisions, the Commission is to consult the relevant stakeholders in defining the principles for setting ex ante benchmarks in individual sectors and subsectors [...]

34. According to the case-law, the fact that a person participates in the process by which a European Union measure is adopted does not distinguish him individually with regard to the measure in question unless provision has been made under the European Union rules for procedural guarantees in his favour. Where a provision of European Union law requires that, for the purposes of adopting a decision,

a procedure must be followed in respect of which a natural or legal person may assert rights, such as the right to be heard, the special legal position which that person enjoys has the effect of distinguishing him individually within the meaning of the fourth paragraph of Article 263 TFEU (see order of 16 September 2005 in Case C–342/04 P *Schmoldt and Others* v *Commission*, not published in the ECR, paragraphs 39 and 40 and the case-law cited).

35. However, it must be pointed out that a person or entity enjoying such a procedural right will not, as a rule, where there is any type of procedural guarantee, have standing to bring proceedings contesting the legality of a Community act in terms of its substantive content. The precise scope of an individual's right of action against a Community measure depends on his legal position as defined by EU law with a view to protecting the legitimate interests thus afforded him (see order in *WWF-UK* v *Council*, cited in paragraph 22 above, paragraph 44 and the case-law cited).

36. As noted in paragraph 20 above, it is clear from the fifth sub-paragraph of Article 10a(1) and the first sub-paragraph of Article 10a(2) of Directive 2003/87 that Eurofer's members, as relevant stakeholders within the meaning of those provisions, had a right to be heard by the Commission and that the Commission was therefore required to consult them on the principles referred to in those provisions prior to the adoption of the contested decision.

37. However, that right to be heard does not create an obligation for the Commission to implement the proposals contained in the observations submitted by Eurofer on behalf of its members. An obligation to consult Eurofer's members cannot be considered the same as an obligation to follow the observations that they submit. Moreover, it is not apparent from the relevant legislative provisions that Eurofer's members may be recognised as having the right to challenge the validity of the contested regulation in terms of its substantive content (see, to that effect, order in *WWF-UK* v *Council*, cited in paragraph 22 above, paragraphs 45 and 46).

38. Thus, merely invoking the existence of a procedural guarantee before the courts of the European Union does not mean that an action will be admissible where it is based on pleas alleging the infringement of substantive rules of law (see, to that effect, order in *WWF-UK* v *Council*, cited in paragraph 22 above, paragraph 47; see, by analogy, order of 11 January 2012 in Case T–58/10 *Phoenix-Reisen and DRV* v *Commission*, not published in the ECR, paragraph 33). [...]

42. [...] as regards the question of whether the contested decision constitutes a regulatory act within the meaning of the fourth paragraph of Article 263 TFEU, it must be recalled that the meaning of 'regulatory act' for the purposes of that provision must be understood as covering all acts of general application apart from legislative acts.

43. In the present case, the contested decision is of general application, in that it applies to objectively determined situations and produces legal effects with respect to categories of persons envisaged in general and in the abstract (see paragraph 29 above).

44. Moreover, the contested decision does not constitute a legislative act since it was not adopted in accordance with either the ordinary legislative procedure or the special legislative procedure within the meaning of paragraphs 1 to 3 of Article 289 TFEU. The contested decision is an act adopted by the Commission on the basis of Article 10a(1) of Directive 2003/87.

45. Consequently, the contested decision constitutes a regulatory act within the meaning of the fourth paragraph of Article 263 TFEU.

46. Secondly, as regards the question of whether the contested decision entails implementing measures, within the meaning of the fourth paragraph of Article 263 TFEU, it must be recalled that under Article 1 of that decision, it lays down transitional Union-wide rules for the harmonised free allocation of emission allowances under Directive 2003/87 from 2013 onwards.

47. In order to examine that question, it necessary to point out, as a preliminary, the respective roles and powers allocated to the Commission and the Member States under the scheme established by Directive 2003/87 and the contested decision concerning the free allocation of emission allowances in trading periods from 2013 onwards.

The Court then engaged in a lengthy analysis of the emissions trading regime and concluded the following:

56. In the light of the respective roles and powers of the Commission and the Member States and the different steps of the decision-making process under the scheme established by Directive 2003/87 and the contested decision, as set out in paragraphs 47 to 55 above, it must be held that the contested decision entails implementing measures within the meaning of the fourth paragraph of Article 263 TFEU.

57. Article 15 of the contested decision entails implementing measures that the Member States and the Commission must adopt on the basis of that decision. Hence, first, the Member States must, in accordance with Article 11(1) of Directive 2003/87 and Article 15(1) of the contested decision, submit to the Commission a list of installations covered by Directive 2003/87 in their territory which must contain, under Article 15(2)(e) of the contested decision, the preliminary annual number of emission allowances allocated free of charge over the period from 2013 to 2020 as determined in accordance with Article 10(2) of that decision. Secondly under the second subparagraph of Article 15(3) of the contested decision, the Commission is to determine the uniform cross-sectoral correction factor. Thirdly, pursuant to Article 15(4) of the contested decision, the Commission may reject an installation's inscription on that list, including the corresponding preliminary total annual amounts of emission allowances allocated free of charge for that installation. Fourthly, the Member States are to determine the final total annual amount of emission allowances allocated free of charge for each year in the period 2013 to 2020, in accordance with Article 10(9) of the contested decision.

58. It follows that the contested decision provides that the Member States and the Commission are to adopt several implementing measures, which culminate in the determination, by the Member States, of the final total annual amount of emission allowances allocated free of charge for each of the installations concerned whose inscription on the abovementioned list has not been rejected by the Commission. Consequently, the contested decision does not constitute a regulatory act which does not entail implementing measures, within the meaning of the fourth paragraph of Article 263 TFEU.

Eurofer thus did not have standing.

2.2 THE AARHUS CONVENTION—ARTICLE 9

The discussion so far on the general frameworks for judicial review procedure in England and Wales and in the EU has highlighted two access to justice issues in different regimes. In the EU, the main concern has been about standing before the Court of Justice; in England and Wales, by contrast, standing rules have been liberalized and the primary access to justice issue has been the cost of litigation. These issues are not confined to environmental law but, since the early 2000s, the third pillar of the Aarhus Convention has been the focal point for access to justice debates in the environmental law arena.

Aarhus Convention on Access to Information, Public Participation in Decision Making and Access to Justice in Environmental Matters, 25 June 1998, Article 9

1. Each Party shall, within the framework of its national legislation, ensure that any person who considers that his or her request for information under article 4 has been ignored, wrongfully refused, whether in part or in full, inadequately answered, or otherwise not dealt with in accordance with the provisions of that article, has access to a review procedure before a court of law or another independent and impartial body established by law. In the circumstances where a Party provides for such a review by a court of law, it shall ensure that such a person also has access to an expeditious procedure established by law that is free of charge or inexpensive for reconsideration by a public authority or review by an independent and impartial body other than a court of law. Final decisions under this paragraph 1 shall be binding on the public authority holding the information. Reasons shall be stated in writing, at least where access to information is refused under this paragraph.

2. Each Party shall, within the framework of its national legislation, ensure that members of the public concerned

    (a) Having a sufficient interest or, alternatively,

    (b) Maintaining impairment of a right, where the administrative procedural law of a Party requires this as a precondition, have access to a review procedure before a court of law and/or another independent and impartial body established by law, to challenge the substantive and procedural legality of any decision, act or omission subject to the provisions of article 6 and, where so provided for under national law and without prejudice to paragraph 3 below, of other relevant provisions of this Convention.

    What constitutes a sufficient interest and impairment of a right shall be determined in accordance with the requirements of national law and consistently with the objective of giving the public concerned wide access to justice within the scope of this Convention. To this end, the interest of any non-governmental organization meeting the requirements referred to in article 2, paragraph 5, shall be deemed sufficient for the purpose of subparagraph (a) above. Such organizations shall also be deemed to have rights capable of being impaired for the purpose of subparagraph (b) above.

    The provisions of this paragraph 2 shall not exclude the possibility of a preliminary review procedure before an administrative authority and shall not affect the requirement of exhaustion of administrative review procedures prior to recourse to judicial review procedures, where such a requirement exists under national law.

3. In addition and without prejudice to the review procedures referred to in paragraphs 1 and 2 above, each Party shall ensure that, where they meet the criteria, if any, laid down in its national law, members of the public have access to administrative or judicial procedures to challenge acts and omissions by private persons and public authorities which contravene provisions of its national law relating to the environment.

4. In addition and without prejudice to paragraph 1 above, the procedures referred to in paragraphs 1, 2 and 3 above shall provide adequate and effective remedies, including injunctive relief as appropriate, and be fair, equitable, timely and not prohibitively expensive. Decisions under this article shall be given or recorded in writing. Decisions of courts, and whenever possible of other bodies, shall be publicly accessible. 5. In order to further the effectiveness of the provisions of this article, each Party shall ensure that information is provided to the public on access to administrative and judicial review procedures and shall consider the establishment of appropriate assistance mechanisms to remove or reduce financial and other barriers to access to justice.

5. In order to further the effectiveness of the provisions of this article, each Party shall ensure that information is provided to the public on access to administrative and judicial review procedures and shall consider the establishment of appropriate assistance mechanisms to remove or reduce financial and other barriers to access to justice.

Article 9 shows that the access to justice pillar of Aarhus is closely interrelated with the other two pillars of the Convention (see Section 2.4 of Chapter 7). Moreover, Article 9 imposes a number of different requirements.

As outlined in Section 2.1, even before the Aarhus Convention, there were concerns about access to justice in the EU and in England and Wales, in relation to environmental law specifically and public law more generally. There were similar concerns in other Member States. Aarhus was transformational—it resulted in a flurry of debate and reform in the EU and its Member States. This section considers three sets of developments that have flowed from Article 9: the ways in which Article 9 has required an evolution in specific areas of EU environmental law and thus Member State law (most obviously in environmental assessment); how Article 9 has been a catalyst for a debate over litigation costs in England and Wales; and how the Convention has been implemented in terms of accessing justice at the EU level.

Before discussing these three developments, it is useful to note one failed reform. In 2003, the Commission published a proposal for a directive that would seek to implement Article 9 into Member State legal systems.[27] The proposal never progressed, which is not surprising when questions of access to justice raise issues about the nature and role of the judiciary within each Member State legal culture. Eleftheriadis also explains how the proposal was in tension with the principle of procedural autonomy.

Pavlos Eleftheriadis, 'Environmental Rights in the EC Legal Order' (2007) 26 YEL 297, 307

In principle, Member States' legal systems remain autonomous. National courts are to implement EU law directly, but they are to do so on their own terms. They need not change the judicial or other procedural methods with which they apply the law. Their procedures and remedies remain autonomous. There are, however, two conditions for such autonomy. The first is the principle of equivalence: the procedural rules enforcing Community law must be no less favourable than those applied in domestic law actions. The second is the principle of 'effectiveness': the application of national procedural rules should not make the protection of Community rights excessively difficult. The two conditions were summarised in the Peterbroeck judgment:

'[T]he Court has consistently held that, under the principle of cooperation laid down in Article 5 of the Treaty, it is for the Member States to ensure the legal protection which individuals derive from the direct effect of Community law. In the absence of Community rules governing a matter, it is for the domestic legal system of each Member State to designate the courts and tribunals having jurisdiction and to lay down the detailed procedural rules governing actions for safeguarding rights which individuals derive from the direct effect of Community law. However, such rules must not be less favourable than those governing similar domestic actions nor render virtually impossible or excessively difficult the exercise of rights conferred by Community law' [...]

The proposed Directive on Access to Justice in environmental matters seems to be going beyond this general principle. The Commission's view on such issues is expressed in the explanatory memorandum accompanying the proposal. For the Commission the protection of the environment under the Aarhus Convention constitutes a significantly different area of policy, within which uniformity is more important than autonomy.

This is a reminder that the Aarhus Convention cannot be seen in isolation, particularly in relation to the role of the courts. Access to justice obligations raise issues of procedural autonomy and, as

---

[27] Commission, 'Proposal for a Directive of the European Parliament of Council on Access to Justice in Environmental Matters' COM (2003) 624 final.

Eleftheriadis goes on to analyse, questions about the interrelationships between the EU and national constitutional orders. As we now turn to consider where Article 9-related reforms have occurred, it should be stressed that this is a fast moving and dynamic area of legal development (reference should be had to our companion website).

2.3 THE AARHUS CONVENTION AND SUBSTANTIVE EU ENVIRONMENTAL LAW

In light of Article 9 of the Aarhus Convention, reforms were made to several substantive areas of EU law. In 2003, the EU passed Directive 2003/35/EC providing for public participation in respect of the drawing up of certain plans and programmes relating to the environment and amending with regard to public participation and access to justice Council Directives 85/337/EEC and 96/61/EC.[28] As is clear from its title, the Directive was not only concerned with the third pillar. In relation to Article 9 in particular, it inserted Article 10a into the Environmental Assessment Directive (Directive 85/337). Article 10a is now Article 11, since the Directive has since been codified in 2011. This is extracted in Section 3.6 of Chapter 19. This is effectively a reiteration of the obligations in Article 9, although there is a variation in wording. Note that there have also been similar amendments to the Integrated Pollution Prevention and Control Directive (now Industrial Emissions Directive) and the Environmental Liability Directive, with access to justice provisions being included within the framework of these EU environmental regimes.[29]

Article 11 of the Environmental Assessment Directive, in particular, has been considered in a number of cases. A striking feature of the analysis in these cases is the CJEU's purposive approach to interpreting the obligations of the Aarhus Convention. These examples of how the Court has approached these EU access to justice provisions are illustrations of the Court's approach rather than an exhaustive analysis of the case law.

Case C-263/08 *Djurgården-Lilla Värtans Miljöskyddsförening v Stockholms kommun genom dess marknämnd*
[2009] ECR I-9967, Opinion of AG Sharpston, paras 61–64, and decision of the Court, paras 43–49

The Facts

A preliminary reference from Sweden raised a number of questions about the interpretation of what was then Article 10a of Directive 85/337/EC. The third of these of these questions concerned whether national law could allow small NGOs a right to participate in proceedings but no right to challenge the decision. In her opinion AG Sharpston made some interesting comments about the role of NGOs in considering these questions.

Opinion of AG Sharpston

61. First, non-governmental organisations promoting environmental protection give expression to the collective interest. Because they represent a number of different parties and interests, they protect

---

[28] Respectively, [1985] OJ L175/40 and [1996] OJ L257/26.
[29] Directive 2004/35/EC of the European Parliament and of the Council of 21 April 2004 on environmental liability with regard to the prevention and remedying of environmental damage [2004] OJ L143/56, art 13 (note the different wording of this access to justice provision); Directive 2010/75/EU of the European Parliament and of the Council of 24 November 2010 on industrial emissions (integrated pollution prevention and control) [2010] L334/17, art 25 (note art 24 also provides for access to information and public participation in the permit procedure).

general objectives. This gives them the requisite 'collective dimension'. They also contribute special-ised knowledge which helps to distinguish important cases from cases of lesser significance. They speak with one voice on behalf of many, with a level of technical specialisation which is often not available to the individual. By so doing, they can rationalise the way in which the various conflicting interests are voiced and placed before the authorities.

62.   Second, this approach to environmental policy is also intended to strengthen the functioning of the courts. By encouraging people to channel environmental disputes through non-governmental organisa-tions promoting environmental protection, the Aarhus Convention and Directive 85/337, as amended, recognise that these organisations do not overload or paralyse the courts. Rather, they bring together the claims of many individuals in a single action. Although it is true that nothing prevents members of a non-governmental organisation also taking part in proceedings on an individual basis, the overall result of this policy is to create a filter which, in the long run, assists the work of the courts. In addition, as I have just indicated, these associations often have technical knowledge that individuals generally lack. Bringing this technical information into the process is advantageous, because it puts the court in a bet-ter position to decide the case.

63.   Thirdly, it is important to emphasise that the Aarhus Convention and Directive 85/337, as amended, rejected introducing an *actio popularis* for environmental matters. Although Member States can opt to make such a procedure available in their domestic legal orders, neither international nor Community law has chosen in this instance to do so. However, it seems to me that, precisely because that course was rejected, the authors of the Aarhus Convention decided to strengthen the role of non-governmental organisations promoting environmental protection. That formula was adopted in an attempt to steer a middle course between the maximalist approach of the *actio popularis* and the minimalist idea of a right of individual action available only to parties having a direct interest at stake. Giving special standing to non-governmental organisations reconciles these two positions. It seems to me to be a very sensible compromise.

64.   For these reasons I take the view that the Aarhus Convention and Directive 85/337, as amended by Directive 2003/35, have deliberately chosen to reinforce the role of non-governmental organisations promoting environmental protection. They have done so in the belief that such organisations' involve-ment in both the administrative and the judicial stages not only strengthens the decisions taken by the authorities but also makes procedures designed to prevent environmental damage work better.

The Court

43.   The directive leaves it to national law to determine the conditions for the admissibility of the action. Those conditions may be having 'sufficient interest' or 'impairment of a right', and national laws gener-ally use one or other of those two concepts.

44.   As regards non-governmental organisations which promote environmental protection, Article 1(2) of Directive 85/337, read in conjunction with Article 10a thereof, requires that those organisations 'meeting any requirements under national law' are to be regarded either as having 'sufficient interest' or as having a right which is capable of being impaired by projects falling within the scope of that directive.

45.   While it is true that Article 10a of Directive 85/337, by its reference to Article 1(2) thereof, leaves to national legislatures the task of determining the conditions which may be required in order for a non-governmental organisation which promotes environmental protection to have a right of appeal under the conditions set out above, the national rules thus established must, first, ensure 'wide access to jus-tice' and, second, render effective the provisions of Directive 85/337 on judicial remedies. Accordingly, those national rules must not be liable to nullify Community provisions which provide that parties who have a sufficient interest to challenge a project and those whose rights it impairs, which include environ-mental protection associations, are to be entitled to bring actions before the competent courts.

46. From that point of view, a national law may require that such an association, which intends to challenge a project covered by Directive 85/337 through legal proceedings, has as its object the protection of nature and the environment.

47. Furthermore, it is conceivable that the condition that an environmental protection association must have a minimum number of members may be relevant in order to ensure that it does in fact exist and that it is active. However, the number of members required cannot be fixed by national law at such a level that it runs counter to the objectives of Directive 85/337 and in particular the objective of facilitating judicial review of projects which fall within its scope.

48. In that connection, it must be stated that, although Directive 85/337 provides that members of the public concerned who have a sufficient interest in challenging projects or have rights which may be impaired by projects are to have the right to challenge the decision which authorises it, that directive in no way permits access to review procedures to be limited on the ground that the persons concerned have already been able to express their views in the participatory phase of the decision-making procedure established by Article 6(4) thereof.

49. Thus, the fact relied on by the Kingdom of Sweden, that the national rules offer extensive opportunities to participate at an early stage in the procedure in drawing up the decision relating to a project is no justification for the fact that judicial remedies against the decision adopted at the end of that procedure are available only under very restrictive conditions.

This purposive approach can also be seen in the *Solvay v Région Wallonne* case, which considered whether the right of review in Article 10a (now Article 11) applied to a legislative act.

Case C-182/10 *Solvay v Région Wallonne*
(CJEU, 16 February 2012) paras 48–50

48. Article 9 of the Aarhus Convention and Article 10a of Directive 85/337 would lose all effectiveness, however, if the mere fact that a project is adopted by a legislative act which does not satisfy the conditions set out in paragraph 31 above were to make it immune to any review procedure for challenging its substantive or procedural lawfulness within the meaning of those provisions (see *Boxus and Others*, paragraph 53).

49. The requirements flowing from Article 9 of the Aarhus Convention and Article 10a of Directive 85/337 presuppose in this regard that, when a project falling within the scope of Article 6 of the Aarhus Convention or of Directive 85/337 is adopted by a legislative act, the question whether that legislative act satisfies the conditions laid down in Article 1(5) of that directive and set out in paragraph 31 above must be amenable to review, under the national procedural rules, by a court of law or an independent and impartial body established by law (see *Boxus and Others*, paragraph 54).

50. If no review procedure of the nature and scope set out above were available in respect of such an act, any national court before which an action falling within its jurisdiction is brought would have the task of carrying out the review described in the previous paragraph and, as the case may be, drawing the necessary conclusions by disapplying that legislative act (see *Boxus and Others*, paragraph 55).

This opinion is an application of the Grand Chamber's reasoning in C-128/09 *Boxus*.[30]

A final issue to consider concerning the impact of the Convention in EU environmental law is the question of whether Article 9(3) of the Convention has direct effect in EU law, and through this its

[30] (ECJ, 18 October 2011).

implementation in Member State law. This issue arose in relation to the Habitats Directive, which has not been explicitly amended to implement the Aarhus Convention. Direct effect of international obligations in EU law is governed by its own body of doctrine,[31] and, applying those EU law principles, Article 9(3) was not found to have direct effect in EU law. However, the Grand Chamber went on to comment. Note the Court's focus on issues of procedural autonomy, as discussed by Eleftheriadis.

C- 240/09 *Lesoochranárske zoskupenie VLK v Ministerstvo životného prostredia Slovenskej republiky*
[2011] ECR I 1255, paras 45–52

45. It must be held that the provisions of Article 9(3) of the Aarhus Convention do not contain any clear and precise obligation capable of directly regulating the legal position of individuals. Since only members of the public who meet the criteria, if any, laid down by national law are entitled to exercise the rights provided for in Article 9(3), that provision is subject, in its implementation or effects, to the adoption of a subsequent measure.

46. However, it must be observed that those provisions, although drafted in broad terms, are intended to ensure effective environmental protection.

47. In the absence of EU rules governing the matter, it is for the domestic legal system of each Member State to lay down the detailed procedural rules governing actions for safeguarding rights which individuals derive from EU law, in this case the Habitats Directive, since the Member States are responsible for ensuring that those rights are effectively protected in each case (see, in particular, Case C-268/06 *Impact* [2008] ECR I-2483, paragraphs 44 and 45).

48. On that basis, as is apparent from well-established case-law, the detailed procedural rules governing actions for safeguarding an individual's rights under EU law must be no less favourable than those governing similar domestic actions (principle of equivalence) and must not make it in practice impossible or excessively difficult to exercise rights conferred by EU law (principle of effectiveness) (*Impact*, paragraph 46 and the case-law cited).

49. Therefore, if the effective protection of EU environmental law is not to be undermined, it is inconceivable that Article 9(3) of the Aarhus Convention be interpreted in such a way as to make it in practice impossible or excessively difficult to exercise rights conferred by EU law.

50. It follows that, in so far as concerns a species protected by EU law, and in particular the Habitats Directive, it is for the national court, in order to ensure effective judicial protection in the fields covered by EU environmental law, to interpret its national law in a way which, to the fullest extent possible, is consistent with the objectives laid down in Article 9(3) of the Aarhus Convention.

51. Therefore, it is for the referring court to interpret, to the fullest extent possible, the procedural rules relating to the conditions to be met in order to bring administrative or judicial proceedings in accordance with the objectives of Article 9(3) of the Aarhus Convention and the objective of effective judicial protection of the rights conferred by EU law, so as to enable an environmental protection organisation, such as the zoskupenie, to challenge before a court a decision taken following administrative proceedings liable to be contrary to EU environmental law (see, to that effect, Case C-432/05 *Unibet* [2007] ECR I-2271, paragraph 44, and *Impact*, paragraph 54).

52. In those circumstances, the answer to the first and second questions referred is that Article 9(3) of the Aarhus Convention does not have direct effect in EU law. It is, however, for the referring court to interpret, to the fullest extent possible, the procedural rules relating to the conditions to be met in order to bring administrative or judicial proceedings in accordance with the objectives of Article 9(3) of

[31] See Chapter 5.

that convention and the objective of effective judicial protection of the rights conferred by EU law, in order to enable an environmental protection organisation, such as the zoskupenie, to challenge before a court a decision taken following administrative proceedings liable to be contrary to EU environmental law.

These are only a few examples of a growing body of EU case law and they show a purposive approach in EU law to the wording of both Article 9 of the Convention and to what is now Article 11 of the Environmental Assessment Directive. They also show the limits of the Convention's implementation in EU law—its access to justice provisions do not apply across the board in EU environmental law.

2.4 ENGLAND AND WALES

The Aarhus case law considered so far has mainly concerned situations where Member States have limited the ability of NGOs to bring actions. However, unlike in EU law, this has not been a significant issue in England and Wales, due to the generous interpretation by the courts of 'sufficient interest' in s 31 of the Senior Courts Act 1981, as explained already. Standing can nonetheless be an issue in some cases, which has implications for the UK's implementation of its access to justice obligations under Aarhus. For example, consider the case of *Ashton*,[32] which concerns review under s 288 of the Town and Country Planning Act (TCPA) 1990 (an alternative avenue of judicial review for planning decisions, rather than the more general action under s 31 of the Senior Courts Act). Section 288 requires a 'person' to be 'aggrieved' by any relevant action or order by a planning decision-maker in order to have standing to challenge that action for errors of law. Note that Pill CJ interprets s 288 in line with Article 11 (ex-Article 10a) of the Environmental Assessment Directive, since the Directive is implemented in the law of England and Wales through the planning regime. This case thus involves implementation of the access to justice provisions of the Aarhus Convention in English law via EU law implementation of the Convention (in the manner discussed in Section 2.3).

Ashton v Secretary of State for Communities and Local Government, Coin Street Community Builders Ltd
[2010] EWCA Civ 600 paras 53–56 (Pill LJ)

The Facts

Ashton was a local resident and a member of a local group—the Waterloo Community Development Group (WCDG) who wished to challenge a grant of planning permission under section 288 of the TCPA 1990. As an environmental impact assessment had been carried out then what was then section10a (now section 11) of the Environmental Assessment Directive needed to be complied with.

The CA

53. The following principles may be extracted from the authorities and applied when considering whether a person is aggrieved within the meaning of section 288 of the 1990 Act:

　1. Wide access to the courts is required under section 288 (article 10a, *N'Jie*).

---

[32] See (n 26).

2. Normally, participation in the planning process which led to the decision sought to be challenged is required. What is sufficient participation will depend on the opportunities available and the steps taken (*Eco-Energy, Lardner*).

3. There may be situations in which failure to participate is not a bar (*Cumming*, cited in *Lardner*).

4. A further factor to be considered is the nature and weight of the person's substantive interest and the extent to which it is prejudiced (*N'Jie* and *Lardner*). The sufficiency of the interest must be considered (article 10a).

5. This factor is to be assessed objectively. There is a difference between feeling aggrieved and being aggrieved (*Lardner*).

6. What might otherwise be a sufficient interest may not be sufficient if acquired for the purpose of establishing a status under section 288 (*Morbaine*).

7. The participation factor and the interest factor may be interrelated in that it may not be possible to assess the extent of the person's interest if he has not participated in the planning procedures (*Lardner*).

8. While recognising the need for wide access to the courts, weight may be given, when assessing the prior participation required, and the interests relied on, to the public interest in the implementation of projects and the delay involved in judicial proceedings (Advocate General Kokott in *Ireland*).

54. I do not consider that the appellant had standing under section 288 to bring the present claim. His participation in the planning process was insufficient in the circumstances to acquire standing. He was not an objector to the proposal in any formal sense and did not make representations, either oral or written, at the properly constituted Public Inquiry. Mere attendance at parts of the hearing and membership of WCDG, which has not brought proceedings in this court, were insufficient. I agree with the judge's conclusion set out at paragraph 32 above.

55. Moreover, the absence of representations before or at the Inquiry about the loss of amenity at his property, either personally or by WCDG, deprived CSCB [Coin Street Community Builders] and the local planning authority of the opportunity to test the extent of the alleged loss and to call evidence in response. That being so, the Inspector, the fact finding tribunal, was not in a position to assess the extent of the loss and whether it amounts to a sufficient interest. This Court cannot make good that deficiency.

56. I make no finding as to whether the appellant would also fail under the interest limb of the test, though it appears to me likely that he would do so. A major project, approved following proper public consultation and a Public Inquiry, should not readily be challengeable on this or other grounds on the basis of a grievance about amenity such as the appellant's appears to be. What is a sufficient interest will always be a question of fact and degree. That reinforces the need to place the facts relied on before the decision maker during the planning process.

On the one hand, this case must be understood in the context of s 288 and thus is a decision primarily focusing on the planning regime and the role of s 288 within it. On the other hand, since the planning regime implements the Environmental Assessment Directive in England and Wales, the case is an important reminder that standing will still be a barrier to access to justice, even where (or arguably because) it implements EU law access to justice requirements.[33]

---

[33] See also *Coedbach Action Team Ltd v Secretary of State for Climate Change and Energy* [2010] EWHC 2312 (Admin) [2011] Env LR 11 (campaigning action group had no relevant sufficient interest, despite the EA Directive applying).

However, standing is not the most significant barrier to access to justice in environmental matters in England and Wales. Article 9(4) of the Aarhus Convention requires that procedures should not be 'prohibitively expensive'—historically, litigation in England and Wales has been exactly that. First, the cost of legal services themselves (solicitor and barrister fees) is very high. Second, there has been a long-standing principle of civil procedure (in common law systems generally) that, if a litigant is unsuccessful, then they should pay a proportion of the other side's costs. Justice Michael Kirby, a retired judge of the High Court of Australia, explains the significance of the law of costs in public interest litigation.

Michael Kirby, 'Deconstructing the Law's Hostility to Public Interest Litigation' (2011) 127 LQR 537, 549–50

In the common law tradition, orders for costs for parties and other participants in litigation are governed by statute. They are generally reserved to a broad discretion in the court concerned. However, this general principle is subject, [...] to a normal practice, of awarding basic (party and party) costs at the conclusion of the litigation in favour of the party which has succeeded in the proceedings.

The fact that this is the ordinary principle and that it is known to everyone entering into litigation presents particular risks for those who embark on public interest litigation not for their own private profit but in support of their view of the public interest and requirements of the rule of law. If they lose, will they generally suffer not only the disappointment in the case but also the burden of a substantial costs order? Is this consequence justifiable where the private individual, or perhaps a small civil society organisation, takes on a minister or a governmental department or agency or a large corporation? If that is the risk that must be run by private litigants, who would be so bold as to put themselves in peril of the obligation to pay very large costs that are now incurred in taking a matter to court, especially if that matter proceeds to the appellate hierarchy with an ever-growing accumulation of potential costs burdens?

It was considerations such as these that led the Hon John Toohey, then a Justice of the High Court of Australia, writing extra-curially, to draw to attention the inescapable connection between cost rules and the initiation and maintenance of public interest proceedings:

Relaxing the traditional requirements for standing may be of little significance unless other procedural reforms are made. Particularly is this so in the area of funding of environmental litigation and the awarding of costs. There is little point in opening the doors to the courts if litigants cannot afford to come in. The general rule in litigation that 'costs follow the event' is in point. The fear, if unsuccessful, of having to pay the costs of the other side (often a government instrumentality or wealthy private corporation), with devastating consequences to the individual or environmental group bringing the action, must inhibit the taking of cases to court. In any event, it will be a factor that looms large in any consideration to initiate litigation.

It should thus come as no surprise that the issue of costs has been a flashpoint for debate concerning the implementation of the Aarhus Convention in England and Wales. That debate has interrelated with a more general debate about the awarding of costs in judicial review actions, as explained by Carnwath LJ in *Morgan v Hinton Organics (Wessex) Ltd*. The facts of this case need not concern us, but note that there already existed a set of distinct principles for awarding costs in public interest cases, as had been formulated by Lord Phillips MR in *R (Corner House) v Secretary of State for Trade & Industry*.[34]

---

[34] [2005] EWCA Civ 192; [2005] 1 WLR 2600, para 74.

Morgan v Hinton Organics (Wessex) Ltd [2009] EWCA Civ 107 paras 28–33, 47
(Carnwath LJ)

The Court

28.   In England and Wales the principles governing the award of costs are found in CPR Part 44. The court has a general discretion, but this is subject to certain well established rules, including the ordinary rule that the unsuccessful party pays the costs of the successful party (CPR44.3). Recent years have seen a greater willingness of the courts to depart from ordinary costs principles in cases raising issues of general public interest, in environmental cases as in other areas of the law. A recent example an environmental case (albeit in the Privy Council) was the Bacongo case of (*Belize Alliance of Conservation Non-Governmental Organisations v. Department of the Environment* [2004] UKPC 6) where, as we were told, no order for costs was made against the Association, in spite of losing the appeal, because of the public interest of the case.

29.   The same trend has been reflected also in greater willingness to make 'Protective Costs Orders', by which the risk of an adverse costs order can be limited in advance. The principles governing such orders in relation to public interest cases were restated by this court in *R (Corner House) v. Secretary of State for Trade and Industry* [2005] EWCA Civ 192. Certain aspects of those principles have proved controversial, particularly the requirement that the claimant should have no private interest in the outcome of the case (on which we shall comment further below).

30.   There have been some specific references in judgments to the Aarhus principles. For example, in *R (Burkett) v Hammersmith and Fulham LBC* [2004] EWCA Civ 1342 paras 74-80, Brooke LJ referred to the Aarhus convention, and to concerns expressed in a recent study as to whether the current costs regime is compatible with the Convention. In the light of the costs figures revealed by that case, he thought that there were serious questions 'of ever living up to the Aarhus ideals within our present legal system'. He called for a broader study of the issues.

31.   In 2006 there was published a report of an informal working group of representatives of different interests, (including private practitioners, NGO lawyers and private sector lawyers in a personal capacity) sponsored by Liberty and the Civil Liberties Trust, and chaired by Lord Justice Maurice Kay (Litigating the Public Interest—Report of the Working Group on Facilitating Public Interest Litigation July 2006). Its recommendations were directed principally to the principles for the granting of protective costs orders in public interest cases generally.

32.   The 2008 Sullivan report, to which Carnwath LJ referred in granting permission in the present case, was a report of another informal working group representing a range of interested groups, this time under Sullivan J (Ensuring Access to Environmental Justice in England and Wales—Report of the Working Group on Access to Environmental Justice May 2008). The report expressed views on the application of the Aarhus principles, in the context of domestic procedures relevant to environmental proceedings, including protective costs orders. The present case was mentioned, without further discussion, as apparently the first which has reached this court raising issues under the Convention in relation to a costs order in private law proceedings. The following points from the report are possibly relevant in the present context:

  i)   That the 'not prohibitively expensive' obligation arising under the Convention extends to the full costs of the proceedings, not merely the court fees involved (in this respect differing from the Irish High Court in *Sweetman v An Bord Pleanala and the Attorney General* [2007] IEHC 153);

  ii)   That the requirement for procedures not to be prohibitively expensive applies to all proceedings, including applications for injunctive relief, and not merely the overall application for final relief in the proceedings;

  iii)   That costs, actual or risked, should be regarded as 'prohibitively expensive' if they would reasonably prevent an 'ordinary' member of the public (that is, "one who is neither very rich nor very poor, and would not be entitled to legal aid") from embarking on the challenge falling within the terms of Aarhus (para 20). iv) That there should be no general departure from the present 'loser pays' principle, provided that the loser's potential liability does not make litigation prohibitively expensive in the way described above (para 38).

33.   Since the grant of permission in this case, there have been two further judgments of this court dealing with the issue of protective costs orders in public interest cases: *Val Compton v Wiltshire Primary Care Trust* [2008] EWCA Civ 749; *R (Buglife) v Thurrock Gateway Development Corp and another* [2008] EWCA Civ 1209. In both, reference was made to the Kay and Sullivan reports, and to their comments on the Aarhus Convention. The latter, as an environmental case, is more directly relevant to the scope of the Convention. However, the Master of the Rolls (in the judgment of the court) agreed with Waller LJ in *Compton* that there should be –'…no difference in principle between the approach to PCOs in cases which raise environmental issues and the approach in cases which raise other serious issues and vice versa.' (para 17) He also indicated that the principles stated in Corner House were to be regarded as binding on the court, and were to be applied 'as explained by Waller LJ and Smith LJ' (para 19). We take the last words to be a reference to the comments of Waller and Smith LJJ respectively that the Corner House guidelines were 'not… to be read as statutory provisions, nor to be read in an over-restrictive way' (Compton para 23); and were 'not part of the statute and… should not be read as if they were' (para 74). These comments reflect the familiar principle that: 'As in all questions to do with costs, the fundamental rule is that there are no rules. Costs are always in the discretion of the court, and a practice, however widespread and longstanding, must never be allowed to harden into a rule.' (per Lord Lloyd of Berwick, *Bolton MDC v Secretary of State for the Environment* [1995] 1 WLR 1176, 1178; cited in *Corner House* at para 27). [...]

47.   It may be helpful at this point to draw together some of the threads of the discussion, without attempting definitive conclusions:

  i)   The requirement of the Convention that costs should not be 'prohibitively expensive' should be taken as applying to the total potential liability of claimants, including the threat of adverse costs orders.

  ii) Certain EU Directives (not applicable in this case) have incorporated Aarhus principles, and thus given them direct effect in domestic law. In those cases, in the light of the Advocate-General's opinion in the Irish cases, the court's discretion may not be regarded as adequate implementation of the rule against prohibitive costs. Some more specific modification of the rules may need to be considered.

  iii) With that possible exception, the rules of the CPR relating to the award of costs remain effective, including the ordinary 'loser pays' rule and the principles governing the court's discretion to depart from it. The principles of the Convention are at most a matter to which the court may have regard in exercising its discretion.

  iv) This court has not encouraged the development of separate principles for 'environmental' cases (whether defined by reference to the Convention or otherwise). In particular the principles governing the grant of Protective Costs Orders apply alike to environmental and other public interest cases. The Corner House statement of those principles must now be regarded as settled as far as this court is concerned, but to be applied 'flexibly'. Further development or refinement is a matter for legislation or the Rules Committee.

  v)   The Jackson review provides an opportunity for considering the Aarhus principles in the context of the system for costs as a whole. Modifications of the present rules in the light of that report are likely to be matters for Parliament or the Civil Procedure Rules Committee. Even if we were otherwise attracted by Mr Wolfe's invitation (on behalf of CAJE) to provide guidelines on the operation of the Aarhus convention, this would not be the right time to do so.

vi) Apart from the issues of costs, the Convention requires remedies to be 'adequate and effective' and 'fair, equitable, timely'. The variety and lack of coherence of jurisdictional routes currently available to potential litigants may arguably be seen as additional obstacles in the way of achieving these objectives.

There have been a number of subsequent cases concerning the issue of costs in environmental cases.[35] Currently, this case law has not gone further than deciding that more relaxed costs rules should apply in judicial review cases that involve an application of an EU Directive that implements explicitly the access to justice provisions of Aarhus. In 2010, the Supreme Court referred to the CJEU a question concerning the nature of the 'prohibitively expensive' test, which has been unresolved in the English case law. At the time of writing, [35a] that case was yet to be decided but, in referring the case, Lord Hope made numerous comments. A discussion of the procedural background is also included here to give some feeling for how the awarding of costs works in practice. Note that Edwards originally initiated the case but Mrs Pallikaropoulos later stepped in as the primary litigant.

R (Edwards) v Environment Agency
[2010] UKSC 57, [2011] 1 WLR 79 paras 1–5, 29–33 (Lord Hope DP)

1. This is an appeal against a decision by two costs officers appointed by the President of the Supreme Court under rule 49(1) of the Supreme Court Rules 2009, Mrs Registrar di Mambro and Master O'Hare, a copy of which is annexed to this judgment. From the issues they were asked to decide they selected two preliminary issues which arose in the detailed assessment of bills of costs lodged by the respondents in an appeal to the House of Lords in which they were successful. The appellant, Mrs Pallikaropoulos, had been ordered to pay the costs of the appeal. The first respondent, the Environment Agency, had lodged a bill totalling £55,810. The second respondent, the Secretary of State for the Environment, Food and Rural Affairs, had lodged a bill totalling £32,290.

2. The preliminary issues were about the proper application of article 10a of Council Directive 85/337/EEC of 27 June 1985 on the assessment of the effects of certain public and private projects on the environment ('the EIA Directive') and article 15a of Council Directive 96/61/EC of 24 September 1996 concerning integrated pollution prevention and control ('the IPPC Directive'). Those articles had been inserted by articles 3(7) and 4(4) of Council Directive 2003/35/EC of 26 May 2003 to implement provisions which first appeared in the Convention on Access to Information, Public Participation in Decision-Making and Access to Justice in Environmental Matters of 25 June 1998 ('the Aarhus Convention'). Among the provisions as to access to justice in article 9 of the Aarhus Convention is a requirement that the procedures to which it refers should be fair, equitable and timely and not prohibitively expensive: article 9(4).

3. In proceedings to which the EIA Directive applies, article 10a requires Member States to ensure that members of the public have access to a review procedure before a court of law or another independent and impartial body established by law to challenge the substantive or procedural legality of decisions, acts or omissions subject to the public participation provisions of the directive. It also provides that

'Any such procedure shall be fair, equitable, timely and not prohibitively expensive.' Article 15a of the IPPC Directive makes identical provision with respect to proceedings to which that directive applies.

4. The costs officers were asked to consider the proper application of those articles to this case. The issues which were identified from the skeleton arguments provided by the parties were as follows:

---

[35] For example, *Coedbach* (n 33) and *R (Garner) v Elmbridge Borough Council* [2010] EWCA Civ 1006.
[35a] Although AG Kokott delivered her opinion in C-260/11 *Edwards* on 18 October 2012.

(i) where an order for costs has been made, whether as a general rule the court assessing those costs has any jurisdiction to implement the directives;(ii) if so, whether in the particular circumstances of this case the costs officers should seek to do so; and (iii) if so, whether on the evidence presented the amount of costs payable by the appellant should be moderated or even excluded altogether. The costs officers decided the first two issues in favour of the appellant. They reserved their opinion on the third issue until they had given written reasons for their decision on the first two issues and the parties had had an opportunity to consider whether to appeal against it.

5. The respondents appealed against the costs officers' decision under rule 53 of the Supreme Court Rules. They asked the single Justice to refer the following questions to a panel of Justices under rule 53(2):

(1) whether it was open to the costs officers, in the circumstances of this case in which applications to the court to reduce or cap a party's liability had been made to and considered by and rejected by the Court, to achieve that result through the detailed assessment process; and

(2) if it was, whether the test indicated by the phrase 'prohibitively expensive' should be focused exclusively on the actual circumstances of the parties to the litigation and not on the question what would be prohibitively expensive for the ordinary member of the public. The single Justice referred the application to a panel of five Justices and directed that these questions should be decided after an oral hearing. The panel, having now heard counsel, is grateful for their assistance on these issues of principle. [...]

29. The question however is whether, when it made these decisions, the House [in this case costs officers] the was proceeding upon a correct understanding of the test that is to be applied in order to determine whether the proceedings in question are prohibitively expensive. There are various possible approaches to this issue. In *R (Garner) v Elmbridge Borough Council* [2010] EWCA Civ 1006 the judge had refused to grant a protective costs order because he was of the view that it was impossible to tell whether the proceedings would be prohibitively expensive unless there was detailed information about the appellant's resources to fund the proceedings. In the Court of Appeal Sullivan LJ said of his decision in para 42:

'This raises an important issue of principle. Should the question whether the procedure is or is not prohibitively expensive be decided on an "objective" basis by reference to the ability of an "ordinary" member of the public to meet the potential liability for costs, or should it be decided on a "subjective" basis by reference to the means of the particular claimant, or upon some combination of the two bases?'

30. Sullivan LJ observed that in an ideal world he would have preferred to defer taking a decision on such an important issue of principle until after the findings of the Aarhus Convention Compliance Committee as to whether our domestic costs rules are Aarhus compliant, and until after it was known whether the European Commission will accept or reject the United Kingdom's response to the Commission's reasoned opinion, announced in a press release dated 18 March 2010, in which the Commission was contending that the United Kingdom is failing to comply with the EIA Directive because challenges to the legality of environmental decisions are prohibitively expensive: para 43. But as the court had to reach a decision as to whether the judge was wrong to refuse to grant a protective costs order, he went on to say this in para 46:

'Whether or not the proper approach to the "not prohibitively expensive" requirement under article 10a should be a wholly objective one, I am satisfied that a purely *subjective* approach, as was applied by Nicol J, is not consistent with the objectives underlying the directive. Even if it is either permissible or necessary to have some regard to the financial circumstances of the individual claimant, the underlying purpose of the directive to ensure that members of the public concerned having a sufficient interest should have access to a review procedure which is not prohibitively expensive would be frustrated if the court was entitled to consider the matter solely by reference to the means of the claimant who happened to come forward, without having to consider whether the potential costs would be prohibitively expensive for an ordinary member of "the public concerned".'

There was evidence that without a protective costs order the liability and costs of an unsuccessful appellant was likely to be prohibitively expensive to anyone of ordinary means. So the judge's decision was set aside.

31. The importance that is to be attached to Sullivan LJ's observations in *R (Garner) v Elmbridge Borough Council* gathers strength when they are viewed in the light of the proposal in para 4.5 of Chapter 30 of the Jackson Review of Civil Litigation Costs (December 2009) as to environmental judicial review cases that the costs ordered against the claimant should not exceed the amount (if any) which is a reasonable one for him to pay having regard to all the circumstances, and the entirely different proposal in para 30 of the Update Report of the Sullivan Working Group (August 2010) that an unsuccessful claimant in a claim for judicial review should not be ordered to pay the costs of any other party other than where the claimant has acted unreasonably in bringing or conducting the proceedings. They have to be viewed too in the light of the conclusion of the Aarhus Convention Compliance Committee which was communicated by letter dated 18 October 2010 that, in legal proceedings in the UK within the scope of article 9 of the Convention, the public interest nature of the environmental claims under consideration does not seem to have been given sufficient consideration in the apportioning of costs by the courts and that despite the various measures available to address prohibitive costs, taken together they do not ensure that the costs remain at a level which meets the requirements of the Convention: see paras 134–135. It is clear that the test which the court must apply to ensure that the proceedings are not prohibitively expensive remains in a state of uncertainty. The balance seems to lie in favour of the objective approach, but this has yet to be finally determined.

32. It is unclear too whether a different approach is permissible at the stage of a second appeal from that which requires to be taken at first instance. The question in *R (Garner) v Elmbridge Borough Council* was about the approach that was required to be taken at first instance. In this case Mrs Pallikaropoulos did not appear at first instance. She was given a protective costs order in the Court of Appeal, where her appeal was unsuccessful, because her liability in costs was capped at £2,000. By the stage when her appeal reached the House of Lords the question which she wished to raise had already been considered twice in the courts below without the claimant having been deterred from seeking judicial review on grounds of expense. It is questionable whether the public interest is best served if a limit must be set on the amount of the costs payable to the successful party in the event of a second appeal as this will inevitably mean that, if the public authority wins, some of the costs reasonably incurred by it will not be recoverable.

33. It is plain from the reasons that were given by the House of Lords for its decision to refuse a protective costs order on 22 March 2007 that these difficult issues were not addressed at that stage. It took a purely subjective approach to the question whether a case for such an order had been made. No reasons were given for the costs order of 18 July 2008. But it is to be inferred from its terms that the House was not satisfied that a case had been made out for any modification of its approach. It must be concluded that here too the House took an approach to this issue which was a purely subjective one. It is to say the least questionable whether in taking this approach, which has now been disapproved by the Court of Appeal in *Garner v Elmbridge Borough Council*, it fulfilled its obligations under the directives.

These different extracts show the issue of costs being debated in many different forums, all questioning and incrementally shifting costs rules in public interest litigation in England and Wales. Alongside the various cases and legal forums mentioned in these extracts, the Aarhus Compliance Committee has upheld a complaint against the UK in relation to Article 9(3) of the Convention.

Findings and Recommendations of the Aarhus Convention Compliance Committee with Regard to Communication ACCC/C/2008/33 Concerning Compliance by the United Kingdom and Northern Ireland Addendum to the Report of the Compliance Meeting on its 29th meeting, Meeting of the Parties to the Convention on Access to Information, Public Participation in Decision-making and Access to Justice in Environmental Matters, 21–24 September 2010, ECE/MP.PP/C.1/2010/6/Add 3, paras 128–36

128. When assessing the costs related to procedures for access to justice in the light of the standard set by article 9, paragraph 4, of the Convention, the Committee considers the cost system as a whole and in a systemic manner.

129. The Committee considers that the 'costs follow the event rule', contained in rule 44.3(2) of the Civil Procedure Rules, is not inherently objectionable under the Convention, although the compatibility of this rule with the Convention depends on the outcome in each specific case and the existence of a clear rule that prevents prohibitively expensive procedures. In this context, the Committee considers whether the effects of 'costs follow the event rule' can be softened by legal aid, CFAs and PCOs as well as by the considerable discretionary powers that the courts have in interpreting and applying the relevant law. At this stage, however, at least four potential problems emerge with regard to the legal system of England and Wales. First, the 'general public importance', 'no private interest' and 'in exceptional circumstances' criteria applied when considering the granting of PCOs. Second, the limiting effects of (i) the costs for a claimant if a PCO is applied for and not granted and (ii) PCOs that cap the costs of both parties. Third, the potential effect of cross-undertakings in damages on the costs incurred by a claimant. Fourth, the fact that in determining the allocation of costs in a given case, the public interest nature of the environmental claims under consideration is not in and of itself given sufficient consideration.

130. While the courts in England and Wales have applied a flexible approach to *Corner House* criteria when considering the granting of PCOs, including the 'general public importance', 'no private inter-est' and 'exceptional circumstances' criteria, they have also indicated that, given the ruling in Corner House, there are limits to this flexible approach. The Committee notes the numerous calls by judges suggesting that the Civil Procedure Rules Committee take legislative action in respect of PCOs, also in view of the Convention (see para. 102 above). These calls have to date not resulted in amendment of the Civil Procedure Rules so as to ensure that all cases within the scope of article 9 of the Aarhus Convention are accorded the standards set by the Convention. The Convention, amongst other things, requires its Parties to 'provide adequate and effective remedies' which shall be 'fair, equitable [...] and not prohibitively expensive'. The Committee endorses the calls by the judiciary and suggests that the Party concerned amend the Civil Procedure Rules in the light of the standards set by the Convention.

131. Within such considerations the Committee finds that the Party concerned should also consider the cost that may be incurred by a claimant in those cases where a PCO is applied for but not granted, as suggested in Appendix 3 to the Sullivan Report. The Committee endorses this recommendation.

132. The Committee also notes the limiting effect of reciprocal cost caps which, as noted in *Corner House*, in practice entail that 'when their lawyers are not willing to act pro bono' successful claim-ants are entitled to recover only solicitor fees and fees for one junior counsel 'that are no more than modest'. The Committee in this respect finds that it is essential that, where costs are concerned, the equality of arms between parties to a case should be secured, entailing that claimants should in practice not have to rely on pro bono or junior legal counsel.

133. A particular issue before the Committee are the costs associated with requests for injunctive relief. Under the law of England and Wales, courts may, and usually do, require claimants to give cross-undertakings in damages. As shown, for example, by the Sullivan Report, this may entail poten-tial liabilities of several thousands, if not several hundreds of thousands of pounds. This leads to the

situation where injunctive relief is not pursued, because of the high costs at risk, where the claimant is legitimately pursuing environmental concerns that involve the public interest. Such effects would amount to prohibitively expensive procedures that are not in compliance with article 9, paragraph 4.

134. Moreover, in accordance with its findings in ACCC/C/2008/23 (United Kingdom) and ACCC/C/2008/27 (United Kingdom), the Committee considers that in legal proceedings within the scope of article 9 of the Convention, the public interest nature of the environmental claims under consideration does not seem to be given sufficient consideration in the apportioning of costs by the courts.

135. The Committee concludes that despite the various measures available to address prohibitive costs, taken together they do not ensure that the costs remain at a level which meets the requirements under the Convention. At this stage, the Committee considers that the considerable discretion of the courts of England and Wales in deciding the costs, without any clear legally binding direction from the legislature or judiciary to ensure costs are not prohibitively expensive, leads to considerable uncertainty regarding the costs to be faced where claimants are legitimately pursuing environmental concerns that involve the public interest. The Committee also notes the Court of Appeal's judgment in *Morgan v. Hinton Organics*, which held that the principles of the Convention are 'at most' a factor which it 'may' (not must) 'have regard to in exercising its discretion' , 'along with a number of other factors, such as fairness to the defendant'. The Committee in this respect notes that 'fairness' in article 9, paragraph 4, refers to what is fair for the claimant, not the defendant.

136. In the light of the above, the Committee concludes that the Party concerned has not adequately implemented its obligation in article 9, paragraph 4, to ensure that the procedures subject to article 9 are not prohibitively expensive. In addition, the Committee finds that the system as a whole is not such as 'to remove or reduce financial [...] barriers to access to justice', as article 9, paragraph 5, of the Convention requires a Party to the Convention to consider.

Being an international committee, the finding of the Committee is not directly legally enforceable in the UK. However, this finding is not an isolated conclusion and the EU Commission also began infringement proceedings against the UK in relation to this issue in 2011.[36] The Ministry of Justice circulated a consultation paper in 2011 proposing a cost-capping scheme for cases that fall within the scope of Article 9.[37] In late August 2012 the Ministry published an 'outline proposal' in light of the consultation process. Further details can be found on the companion website.

2.5 ARTICLE 9 AND EU INSTITUTIONS

The final issue in considering the legal developments that have flowed from Article 9 of the Aarhus Convention is in relation to challenging the actions of the EU institutions. As seen in Section 2.1.2, standing for non-privileged applicants under Article 263(4) TFEU is very limited and clearly not consistent with Article 9. The EU Parliament and the Council thus passed Regulation 1367/2006/EC on the application of the provisions of the Aarhus Convention on Access to Information, Public Participation in Decision-making and Access to Justice in Environmental Matters to Community Institutions and bodies,[38] establishing a framework that allowed a certain group of NGOs (as defined in Article 11 of the Regulation) to request internal review of an 'administrative act' by any 'Community institution or body'[39] (Article 10). Article 12 allows review before the CJEU in limited circumstances.

[36] C-530/11 *Commission v UK* (action brought on 18 October 2011).

[37] Ministry of Justice, Cost Protection for litigants in Environmental Judicial Review Claims (MOJ Consultation Paper CP16/11, 2011).

[38] [2006] OJ L264/13.

[39] Defined as 'any public institution, body, office or agency established by, or on the basis of, the Treaty except when acting in a judicial or legislative capacity' (art 2(1)(c)).

The framework created by Regulation 1367/2006 can be understood as attempting to find a balance between the requirements of Aarhus and the spirit of the structure created by Article 263(4). In doing so, it represents a very restrictive interpretation of Article 9, particularly in relation to which NGOs are entitled to review, and what can be reviewed. The former limitation can be understood as concerned with stopping non-genuine environmental interests from using Aarhus as a loophole. Thus, the requirements of Article 11 set out a series of criteria to determine a 'genuine' environmental group for the purpose of the Regulation. The latter limitation rests on the concept of 'administrative acts' and their limited review under the Regulation, the validity of which was recently challenged in two cases before the General Court. The court found that the Aarhus Convention did bind the Union institutions in these circumstances and thus turned to consider the validity of this limitation.[40]

Case T-338/08 *Stichting Natuur en Milieu v Commission* (GC, 14 June 2012) paras 71–84

71. It is appropriate, therefore, to examine the validity of Article 10(1) of Regulation No 1367/2006—which limits the concept of 'acts' to 'administrative act[s]', defined in Article 2(1)(g) of that regulation as 'measure[s] of individual scope'—in the light of the Aarhus Convention.

72. The term 'acts', as used in Article 9(3) of the Aarhus Convention, is not defined in that convention. According to well-established case-law, an international treaty must be construed by reference to the terms in which it is framed and in the light of its objectives. Article 31 of the Vienna Convention of 23 May 1969 on the Law of Treaties and Article 31 of the Vienna Convention of 21 March 1986 on the Law of Treaties between States and International Organisations or between International Organisations, which express to this effect general customary international law, state that a treaty is to be interpreted in good faith, in accordance with the ordinary meaning to be given to its terms in their context and in the light of its object and purpose (see Case C-344/04 *IATA and ELFAA* [2006] ECR I-403, paragraph 40 and the case-law cited.

73. It is appropriate first of all to recall the objectives of the Aarhus Convention.

74. Thus, it emerges from the sixth and eighth recitals in the preamble to the Aarhus Convention that the authors of that convention, '[r]ecognising that adequate protection of the environment is essential to human well-being and the enjoyment of basic human rights, including the right to life itself', consider that, 'to be able to assert this right and observe this duty, citizens must have access to information, be entitled to participate in decision-making and have access to justice in environmental matters, … acknowledging in this regard that citizens may need assistance in order to exercise their rights'. Moreover, the ninth recital to the Aarhus Convention states that 'in the field of the environment, improved access to information and public participation in decision-making enhance the quality and the implementation of decisions, contribute to public awareness of environmental issues, give the public the opportunity to express its concerns and enable public authorities to take due account of such concerns'.

75. In addition, Article 1 of the Aarhus Convention, which is entitled 'Objective', provides that '[i]n order to contribute to the protection of the right of every person of present and future generations to live in an environment adequate to his or her health and well-being, each Party shall guarantee the rights of access to information, public participation in decision-making, and access to justice in environmental matters in accordance with the provisions of this Convention'.

76. It must be held that an internal review procedure which covered only measures of individual scope would be very limited, since acts adopted in the field of the environment are mostly acts of general application. In the light of the objectives and purpose of the Aarhus Convention, such limitation is not justified.

77. Also, as regards the terms in which Article 9(3) of the Aarhus Convention is framed, it should be noted that, under those terms, the Parties to that Convention retain a certain measure of discretion

[40] See also Case T-396/09 *Vereniging Milieudefensie and Stichting Stop Luchtverontreiniging Utrecht v Commission* (GC, 14 June 2012) paras 42–77, which was delivered the same day.

with regard to the definition of the persons who have a right of recourse to administrative or judicial procedures and as to the nature of the procedures (whether administrative or judicial). Under Article 9(3) of the Aarhus Convention, only 'where they meet the criteria, if any, laid down in [the] national law, [may] members of the public have access to administrative or judicial procedures'. However, the terms of Article 9(3) of the Aarhus Convention do not offer the same discretion as regards the definition of the 'acts' which are open to challenge. Accordingly, there is no reason to construe the concept of 'acts' in Article 9(3) of the Aarhus Convention as covering only acts of individual scope.

78. Lastly, so far as the wording of the other provisions of the Aarhus Convention is concerned, it should be noted that, under Article 2(2) of that convention, the concept of 'public authority' does not cover 'bodies or institutions acting in a judicial or legislative capacity'. Accordingly, the possibility that measures adopted by an institution or body of the European Union acting in a judicial or legislative capacity may be covered by the term 'acts', as used in Article 9(3) of the Aarhus Convention, can be ruled out. That does not mean, however, that the term 'acts' as used in Article 9(3) of the Aarhus Convention can be limited to measures of individual scope. There is no correlation between measures of general application and measures taken by a public authority acting in a judicial or legislative capacity. Measures of general application are not necessarily measures taken by a public authority acting in a judicial or legislative capacity.

79. It follows that Article 9(3) of the Aarhus Convention cannot be construed as referring only to measures of individual scope.

80. That finding is not undermined by the argument, raised by the Council at the hearing, that limiting 'administrative acts' to measures of individual scope is justified in the light of the conditions laid down in Article 230 EC. In that regard, it should be noted that, under Article 12(1) of Regulation No 1367/2006, a non-governmental organisation which has made a request for internal review pursuant to Article 10 of Regulation No 1367/2006 may institute proceedings before the Court of Justice in accordance with the relevant provisions of the Treaty, hence in accordance with Article 230 EC. However, whatever the scope of the measure covered by an internal review as provided for in Article 10 of Regulation No 1367/2006, the conditions for admissibility laid down in Article 230 EC must always be satisfied if an action is brought before the Courts of the European Union.

81. Moreover, the conditions laid down in Article 230 EC—and, in particular, the condition that the contested act must be of direct and individual concern to the applicant – apply also to measures of individual scope which are not addressed to the applicant. A measure of individual scope will not necessarily be of direct and individual concern to a non-governmental organisation which meets the conditions laid down in Article 11 of Regulation No 1367/2006. Contrary to the assertions made by the Council, limiting the concept of 'acts' exclusively to measures of individual scope does not ensure that the condition laid down in Article 230 EC—that the contested act must be of direct and individual concern to the applicant—will be satisfied.

82. Accordingly, the Council's argument that limiting 'administrative acts' to measures of individual scope is justified in the light of the conditions laid down in Article 230 EC must be rejected.

83. It follows from the above that Article 9(3) of the Aarhus Convention cannot be construed as referring exclusively to measures of individual scope. Consequently, in so far as Article 10(1) of Regulation No 1367/2006 limits the concept of 'acts', as used in Article 9(3) of the Aarhus Convention, to 'administrative act[s]' defined in Article 2(1)(g) of Regulation No 1367/2006 as 'measure[s] of individual scope', it is not compatible with Article 9(3) of the Aarhus Convention.

84. It follows that the plea of illegality raised in respect of Article 10(1) of Regulation No 1367/2006, read in conjunction with Article 2(1)(g) of that regulation, must be upheld—as must, in consequence, the second plea in law. The contested decisions must therefore be annulled.

This is a significant judgment, which found the EU to be in breach of the Aarhus Convention, and clearly Regulation 1376/2006 is in need of revision. The judgment also highlights how the institutions of the EU do not easily fit into a separation of powers framework. The case has been appealed to the CJEU.[40a] The EU is a complex governance regime—a theme further explored in Chapter 13.

3 ARGUMENTS FOR A SPECIALIST ENVIRONMENTAL COURT

This section considers the second important theme of the role of courts in environmental law—arguments for specialist environmental courts. There are now over 350 adjudicative bodies in forty-one countries understood to be 'specialist environmental courts',[41] and for many years there have been arguments in the UK for an environmental court as well. This is a very different debate than that relating to access to justice because, in England and Wales at least, until recently, it has been largely academic. However, an analysis of debates over specialist environmental courts is useful for three reasons. First, it is an issue also closely related to the question of access to justice. As Carnwath LJ noted in *Hinton*, 'the variety and lack of coherence of jurisdictional routes currently available to potential litigants may arguably be seen as additional obstacles in the way of achieving these objectives'.[42] Second, debating the need for an environmental court helps lawyers to understand both the strengths and limitations of the judiciary in environmental law. Third, with the recent creation of the First Tier Tribunal (Environment), there are now the possible foundations for a specialist environmental court in England and Wales. This section highlights these matters by considering general debates about environmental courts, examples from other jurisdictions, and finally how the idea of an environmental court has been considered (and arguably now implemented) in the UK.

3.1 THE GENERAL DEBATE OVER THE ROLE OF ENVIRONMENTAL COURTS AND TRIBUNALS

An environmental court or tribunal can be understood as a body created to adjudicate environmental disputes. There is no single institutional structure for such a body and, as we shall see here, environmental courts and tribunals can take many different forms. There are many arguments that have been put forward *in support of* having environmental courts. Pring and Pring identify seventeen arguments used in support of such courts, which they list under the following headings: expertise, efficiency, visibility, cost, uniformity, standing, commitment, government accountability, prioritization, creativity, alternative dispute resolution, issue integration, remedy integration, public participation, public confidence, problem solving, and judicial activism.[43] They also list fourteen arguments made *against* the creation of environmental courts under the titles of: competing areas also needing expertise, marginalization of environmental cases, fragmentation, reform from within, insufficient caseload, cost, public confusion, problems with determining what is 'environmental', capture, judicial bias, talent gap, problems with judicial activism, judicial careers, and the creating of an 'inferior' court.[44] These are two very long lists that highlight the scope and complexity of debates over environmental courts and tribunals. The nature of those debates will also vary from jurisdiction to jurisdiction.

We saw in Section 1 how courts have been a focus for environmental lawyers in descriptive, purposive, and jurisprudential terms. Debates over the need for specialist environmental courts can be categorized similarly. In terms of a descriptive understanding of environmental law, environmental

---

[40a] C-404/12 P *Council v Stichting Natuur en Milieu and Pesticide Action Network Europe*.

[41] George Pring and Catherine Pring, *Greening Justice: Creating and Improving Environmental Courts and Tribunals* (The Access Initiative 2009).

[42] *Morgan v Hinton Organics (Wessex) Ltd* [2009] EWCA Civ 107; [2009] Env LR 30, para 47.

[43] Pring and Pring (n 41) 14–16.   [44] Ibid, 17–18.

courts emerge as a viable adjudicative institution for the simple reason that they offer a pragmatic solution to the problem that environmental law gives rise to a diverse range of legal disputes in relation to complex environmental issues. Woolf's descriptive approach to environmental law, set out in Chapter 1,[45] offered this kind of descriptive perspective. Consider here some of the reasons he gives for the creation of a new environmental tribunal.

Sir Harry Woolf, 'Are the Judiciary Environmentally Myopic?' (1992) 3 JEL 1, 12

A High Court, overburdened already and without the specialist input to deal with an influx of complex environmental issues. Problems of multiplicity of proceedings. The Criminal Courts which have more than enough work already having to deal with quasi-criminal offences often giving rise to technical crimes which do not fit easily into the structure of a criminal trial. [...] In other areas of the law, even where the issues are more readily susceptible of judicial decision, for sensible practical reasons the issues are now determined by tribunals and I suggest that consideration at least should be given to adopting the same approach to the complex issues to which environmental law gives rise.

Woolf is proposing a specialist environmental tribunal as a logical response to the need for both legal and technical expertise in this area of law.

For other scholars, Article 10 of the Rio Declaration on Environment and Development has promoted a more purposive understanding of the role of environmental courts—as a means of achieving sustainable development. With that said, analysing environmental courts from this perspective does not treat them as mere instruments. This is because, as the discussion of the work by Pring and Pring highlights, any debate about the role of environmental courts requires an analysis of many different dimensions of adjudication. Thus, Pring and Pring highlight that there are twelve 'building blocks' that must be taken into consideration in developing a specialist environmental court: type of forum; legal jurisdiction; level of decisional review; geographical coverage; case volume; standing; costs; scientific and technical expertise; alternative dispute resolution; competence of judges and decision-makers; case management; and enforcement of tools and remedies.[46] In light of these considerations, it is impossible to contemplate a court as a simple tool in aid of environmental protection.

Finally, there are jurisprudential understandings of the role of environmental courts. From this perspective, the role of an environmental court is to produce a body of environmental law doctrine. A prime example of thinking about specialist environmental courts in this way can be seen in relation to their development of a body of jurisprudence around environmental principles (Chapter 11). Brian Preston, the Chief Justice of the Land and Environment Court, explains the role of an environmental court in these terms.

Brian Preston, 'Leadership by the Courts in Achieving Sustainability' (2010) 27 EPLJ 321, 329–30

Each branch of government, including the judicature, has a role to play in achieving sustainable development. The nature and extent of the role necessarily varies depending on the functions exercised by the branch.

Traditional thinking sees the legislature and executive as playing the lead role, with the judicature acting merely as an agent in the implementation of the will and action of the legislature and the executive. But such thinking is too cramped. The judicature legitimately can make a meaningful contribution in the exercise of its central function of judging.

---

[45] See Section 1.4 of Chapter 1.   [46] Pring and Pring (n 41) 20–21.

The process of judging inherently involves judicial law-making. Judicial interpretation of legislation, both primary and subordinate, involves law-making, although this is interstitial and incremental. By fulfilling this interpretive role, courts have been described as 'the judicial partner in the legislative project'.

This process is especially significant for environmental legislation, which characteristically is drawn as a framework of rules expressed at a high level of generality. The principles of ESD [ecologically sustainable development] are a case in point. A court can, by interpretation, flesh out the skeletal framework, both in meaning and application, to the facts of the dispute before the court.

The judicial branch also acts as a partner to the legislative and executive branches by upholding and enforcing the lawful exercise of legislative and executive functions by the other branches. The upholding and enforcing of laws encouraging sustainable development ensures good governance.

In addition to its central function of judging, the judicature exercises some executive and legislative functions. In doing so, the judicature also acts as a partner with the other branches of government. The most significant exercise of executive functions is where a court is vested with authority to undertake merits review of administrative decisions and conduct. Merits review of environmental decisions provides opportunity for courts to achieve sustainability in the case at hand and add value to decision-making by the executive branch in future matters.

The judicature can also facilitate access to justice, including environmental justice, in the exercise of its executive functions, including court administration, and its legislative functions by making delegated legislation in the form of court rules.

Note how Preston's analysis flows from understanding an environmental court as a certain kind of legal institution—one that is involved in 'law-making'.

It is important to note that an increased role for a general or specialized judiciary in environmental cases is not necessarily a progressive way forward for environmental law. Much of the debate about environmental courts focuses on what they *could* achieve rather than what they actually deliver. The distinguished scholar Rajamani has analysed the Indian Supreme Court's public interest litigation (PIL) practices in relation to environmental law issues. In this area, the Indian Supreme Court is seen as a progressive world leader, promoting environmental protection outcomes judicially in a very activist way, but Rajamani's analysis sounds a note of caution in promoting the role of courts in environmental cases unhesitatingly.

Lavanya Rajamani, 'Public Interest Environmental Litigation in India: Exploring Issues of Access, Participation, Equity, Effectiveness and Sustainability' (2007) 19 JEL 293, 320

Yet, the improved governance triggered by these litigations has not yet led to governance-related reform, the improved delivery of public services has not yet been institutionalised, and the enhanced accountability of public servants has been imposed in a situation of limited technical, financial and infrastructural capacity. Further, despite the best intentions, the Court set in motion processes that were less than participatory, which therefore arguably led to solutions that were less than fair, just and impartial to all the stake-holders. The solutions have also been criticised in some quarters as ineffective and unsustainable.

More broadly, the growth of judicial activism and PIL has led to concerns that: the judges and their predilections play far too significant a role in the shape the litigations take; the leverage particular litigants have with the Court results in converting one strain of opinion into policy while annihilating others; the Court merely substitutes executive governance with judicial governance in sectors highlighted by public interest litigants; and the Court has over time developed into a 'policy evolution fora', a role it is ill-equipped to play. These concerns, real or perceived, reveal certain disaffection with the judicial process which needs to be addressed for PILs to be both effective and equitable.

The Indian Supreme Court, and how it operates, is of course a product of Indian legal culture. The point remains that the arguments for and against environmental courts, and over the role of courts in environmental law generally, have many different dimensions.

3.2 ENVIRONMENTAL COURTS IN OTHER JURISDICTIONS

These multiple aspects of environmental courts can be seen starkly in any study of environmental courts in other jurisdictions. As noted already, there are said to be over 350 examples of such adjudicative bodies in different jurisdictions. In 2010, a National Green Tribunal was created in India,[47] and there have been many arguments for an international environmental court as well.[48]

The most notable examples of environmental courts are those in Australia, where there exists a state-based network of environmental courts and tribunals. The New South Wales Land and Environment Court (NSWLEC) was created in 1979 as one of the first environmental law courts in the common law world. In the 1990s, other Australian states also set up such courts.[49] Even within the same country, these specialist environmental courts and tribunals do not conform to a common template. They occupy different places in the judicial hierarchy, vary in how they are staffed with those with legal training, and have different jurisdictions and powers. Most of the legislative frameworks for these courts and tribunals encourage mediation, although this ranges from promoting traditional forms of settlement, to creating more innovative forms of community dispute resolution. Each court and tribunal also operates within distinct environmental and planning law regimes.

The diversity in these different adjudicative bodies is not only interesting in itself but it also raises the question of whether it is possible talk about environmental courts generically at all.[50] With that said, three common features of these different institutions can be identified. First, nearly all of them evolved out of the planning system and many of them resolve disputes that, in England and Wales, would be resolved by the Planning Inspectorate (see Section 6.2 of Chapter 18). Second, all of these environmental court and tribunals review decisions on the merits (although some have other powers, including powers to conduct judicial review, as well). The NSWLEC was described by the Minister introducing the legislation into Parliament as:

[a] somewhat innovative experiment in dispute resolution mechanisms. It attempts to combine judicial and administrative dispute resolving techniques.[51]

This is not surprising and, as we saw in Section 1, a strict and conventional adjudicative procedure is problematic for the resolving of polycentric environmental disputes.

[47] Gitanjali Nain Gill, 'A Green Tribunal for India' (2010) 22 JEL 461.

[48] Ole Pedersen, 'An International Environmental Court and International Legalism' (2012) 24 JEL 547.

[49] See generally Malcolm Grant, *Environmental Court Project: Final Report* (Department of Transport, Environment and the Regions 2000) chs 5–8.

[50] A more comprehensive analysis can be found in Elizabeth Fisher, 'Administrative Law, Pluralism and the Legal Construction of Merits Review in Australian Environmental Courts and Tribunals' in Linda Pearson, Carol Harlow and Michael Taggart (eds), *Administrative Law in a Changing State: Essays in Honour of Mark Aronson* (Hart Publishing 2008).

[51] Minister Paul Landa as quoted in Stewart Smith, *A Review of the Land and Environment Court, Briefing Paper 13/2001* (Parliament of New South Wales 2001).

Finally, all these tribunals have been given considerable scope in how they regulate their own procedure and rules of evidence.[52] This has led them to introduce novel forms of adjudicative practice. Thus, for example, the NSWLEC has developed a framework for the delivery of concurrent forms of expert evidence (known as 'hot-tubbing'!).[53]

3.3 THE DEBATE OVER A SPECIALIST ENVIRONMENTAL COURT IN THE UK

The Australian experience of environmental courts and tribunals has been a source of inspiration in the UK,[54] and, since the late 1980s, there have been on-going calls for the creation of a specialist environmental court[55] in England and Wales as well as in Scotland.[56] An interesting feature of these debates is that the development of an environmental court in the UK has been seen as an enterprise distinct from the planning regime, and the role of the Planning Inspectorate in that regime. Moreover, there is nothing inherently radical in these arguments in the UK setting, which has a long history of specialist tribunals.[57]

In the 2000s, two more general reforms took place, which changed the court landscape for environmental cases. First, the Macrory Report[58] and the subsequent passing of the Regulatory Enforcement and Sanctions Act 2008 (see Section 3 of Chapter 8),[59] provided a new framework for sanctioning environmental offences. Second, the increasingly byzantine tribunal system in England and Wales was re-organized under the Tribunals, Courts and Enforcement Act 2007. The Act created a two-tier structure that allowed for some consolidation of the many tribunals that existed in England and Wales, while still recognizing the importance of retaining different tribunals with different specializations.

In 2010, on the basis of the Regulatory Enforcement and Sanctions Act 2008, the First Tier Tribunal (Environment) was introduced into the new tribunal structure. An overview of Tribunal was given in Section 3.4 of Chapter 7,[60] and some argue that it serves as the foundation for a specialist environmental court in England and Wales.

Richard Macrory, 'Environmental Courts and Tribunals in England and Wales—A Tentative New Dawn' (2010) 3 Journal of Court Innovation 61, 76–77.

After over twenty years of debate and political inaction, an environmental tribunal was established in England and Wales in 2010 with little fuss or fanfare. Admittedly its jurisdiction remains modest, being confined to hearing appeals concerning new civil sanctioning powers given to the core national environmental regulators. Nevertheless, this new tribunal may form the nucleus of a more substantial institution which will hear many types of environmental appeals. In many ways, the approach is

---

[52] Patrick Ky, 'Qualifications, Weight of Opinion, Peer Review and Methodology: A Framework for Understanding the Evaluation of Science in Merits Review' (2012) 24 JEL 207.

[53] Garry Edmond, 'Secrets of the "Hot Tub": Expert Witnesses, Concurrent Evidence and Judge-led Law Reform in Australia' (2008) 27 CJQ 51.

[54] For example, see the careful study of the Australian experience in Grant (n 49).

[55] Harry Woolf, 'Are the Judiciary Environmentally Myopic?' (1992) 3 JEL 1 and Robert Carnwath, 'Judicial Protection of the Environment: At Home and Abroad' (2004) 16 JEL 315.

[56] Scottish Government, *Strengthening And Streamlining: The Way Forward For The Enforcement Of Environmental Law In Scotland* (2006).

[57] Chantal Stebbings, *Legal Foundations of Tribunals in Nineteenth Century England* (CUP 2007).

[58] Richard Macrory, *Regulatory Justice: Making Sanctions Effective* (Cabinet Office 2006).

[59] See Chapter 8.   [60] See Chapter 7.

typically British—cautious, pragmatic, learning from experience, yet containing elements of a radical vision. The key is that the principle of an environmental tribunal has now been accepted, and, indeed, implemented. How can one explain this dramatic change in approach?

Paradoxically, the two main drivers for change providing the opportunity for establishing the environmental tribunal were not environmental factors. Rather, the new tribunal system was established as a result of a general recognition that the existing tribunal system could be run more efficiently and with greater flexibility. The new civil sanctions and rights of appeal to a tribunal are derived from a review of regulatory sanctions cutting across all areas of business regulation.

How this new tribunal will develop is anyone's guess but, as is clear from the analysis here, the tribunal is not a mere tool for achieving environmental protection outcomes—it is, and will keep on being, a complex adjudicative body in legal terms, as well as one that continues to evolve as a bespoke 'environmental court' in the UK. The debate over the UK's implementation of Article 9 of the Aarhus Convention is sure to be influential in this process of institutional evolution.

4 CONCLUSION

This chapter has been an overview of two major themes in relation to the role of the courts in environmental law. The first, and most significant, is the issue of access to justice, in relation to which Article 9 of the Aarhus Convention has acted as a powerful catalyst for reform in England and Wales, and in the EU. The second theme is the debate over specialist environmental courts. That debate has occurred in many different jurisdictions and gives some insight into the challenges and limitations of the role of the judiciary in environmental law. The new First Tier (Environment) Tribunal can be understood as a form of environmental court—although its jurisdiction is currently quite limited, this looks set to change in coming years. How issues develop in relation to the Tribunal, and more generally within the UK judiciary in deciding environmental cases, will be interesting to see. In conclusion, it is hoped that this chapter will have fostered a critical perspective on the role of courts in environmental law and you should keep in mind the issues raised in this chapter as you read about environmental law litigation throughout this book.

FURTHER READING

1. For those who wish to read more about the laws of standing in England and Wales, and in the EU, a good starting point is a comprehensive administrative law textbook. See the list at the end of Chapter 7.

2. For a discussion about the nature of environmental courts and tribunals, see George Pring and Catherine Pring, *Greening Justice: Creating and Improving Environmental Courts and Tribunals* (The Access Initiative 2009). There is also a very good collection of articles on environmental courts around the world in: 'Special Issue: The Role of the Environmental Judiciary' (2010) 3 Journal of Court Innovation 1.

3. An excellent history of the UK debate over environmental courts in England and Wales can be found in Richard Macrory, 'The Role of the First Tier Environment Tribunal' [2010] JR 54.

11

PRINCIPLE AND POLICY

This chapter concerns two key concepts for environmental law—environmental principles and environmental policy. Both concepts—principle and policy—are well-known to those who study and practise UK and EU law, but that familiarity can be deceiving when it comes to understanding their role in environmental law. This is because both principles and policy perform important but also distinctive and evolving functions in environmental law. Exploring these distinctive roles helps to elucidate different aspects of environmental law as a subject, both interrogating the jurisprudential nature of environmental law and revealing key characteristics of its developing doctrine. Further, the chapter demonstrates how environmental law, as a subject with distinct challenges, shapes our understanding of 'principle' and 'policy' as legal ideas more broadly.

To appraise the legal functions and relevance of principles and policy in English environmental law, it is thus important to keep in mind Mashaw's scholarly warning that 'we are often captives of our pictures of the world, and [...] if the world does not look just like them, their influence on our perception is nevertheless profound'.[1] When it comes to legal pictures of principle and policy in environmental law, the jurisprudential ideas of Ronald Dworkin profoundly influence the instinctive perceptions of legal scholars and law students alike.[2] In broad Dworkinian terms, principles are legal concepts that guide judicial decision-making, describe and promote individual rights, and inform the interpretation of more precise legal rules. Policies, by contrast, are conceptually and functionally separate from legal principles and rules; they concern the collective goals of a community that have no proper role in legal reasoning, and for good constitutional reasons should be within the province of governmental and political decision-making alone.[3] This stark theoretical distinction between ideas of principle (legal) and policy (non-legal) is not without its critics outside environmental law,[4] but it has a strong influence on basic doctrinal concepts and their mapping across English law. For example, there is the foundational view in administrative law doctrine that questions relating to the formulation and merits of government policy are non-justiciable and must be immune from judicial review by courts (which involves applying legal doctrines and principles) or accorded significant deference in that legal process.[5]

This chapter challenges these conventional legal ideas, by demonstrating that principles and policies are prolific in environmental law, but that they also have unique legal roles and influences. The first part of the chapter considers the nature and roles of *environmental principles* in environmental law. Environmental principles include such concepts as the 'principle' of sustainable development, the precautionary principle, and the polluter pays principle. This part starts by attempting to identify

---

[1] Jerry Mashaw, *Greed, Chaos and Governance: Using Public Choice to Improve Public Law* (Yale UP 1997) 1.
[2] Ronald Dworkin, *Taking Rights Seriously* (2nd edn, Duckworth 1978).   [3] Ibid, 22–28, 84–85.
[4] See, for example, Neil MacCormick, *Legal Reasoning and Legal Theory* (Clarendon Press 1994).
[5] *R v Secretary of State for the Environment (ex parte Nottinghamshire County Council)* [1986] AC 240, 250–51.

and characterize such principles, and concludes that they have no clear legal identity in universal terms. It then considers why they are increasingly popular concepts in environmental law in the UK and beyond—examining how such general statements (of environmental *policy* it should be noted—'principles' are not quarantined from concepts of policy, even in this general sense) are assumed to be central features of environmental law. This part of the chapter goes on to examine what legal roles environmental principles are in fact taking on, in both EU law and UK law, and what roles they might take on. Here we are in uncharted legal territory—this is a pioneering journey for the environmental lawyer. Accordingly, this snapshot of environmental law is very much part of a moving picture, and there will no doubt be developments that continue to shape and define this aspect of environmental law.

The second part of this chapter considers the role of *policy* in environmental law. This is where environmental law gets particularly idiosyncratic. It relies on policy to do all sorts of things that a UK constitutional lawyer or theorist might baulk at. Policy thus comes under review by the courts, even when made at a high strategic level; policy also acts as an effective source of legal obligation in some cases, alongside and instead of statutory regimes and measures. Significantly, however, environmental law shows that the concept of 'policy' is not monolithic when viewed from a legal perspective. It comes in all shapes and sizes—from Ministerial statements, to local development plans required under planning statutes, to guidance issued by the Environment Agency (EA) and other regulatory bodies—and these different forms need to be appreciated independently in order to see and appraise their legal roles and effects. In this sense, the Dworkinian distinction between principle and policy is not so much wrong, but not addressed to the full variety of policies that exist in environmental law and give rise to litigation. The focus of this chapter begins with environmental principles, rather than policy, but the point is equally important—environmental law is a complex and often doctrinally novel subject, which challenges us to find our focus for legal analysis carefully. This is the key lesson of the chapter in appraising environmental principles and policy from a legal perspective. In reading this chapter, it is also important to keep other chapters of this textbook in mind, particularly Chapter 7 concerning public law.

1 ENVIRONMENTAL PRINCIPLES

Environmental principles are an amorphous group of policy ideas concerning how environmental protection and sustainable development ought to be pursued. They are pithy catchphrases—including the polluter pays principle, the precautionary principle, the preventive principle, the principle of intergenerational equity, and the 'principle' of sustainable development—that are increasingly used in policy, political, and philosophical jargon internationally, whether in relation to debates on biodiversity conservation, climate change, waste pollution, or the use of genetically modified organisms. They are also increasingly taking on legal roles, featuring across jurisdictions in legal academic debates and in a variety of instruments, including legislation and various forms of soft law.

The most commonly cited catalogue of environmental principles internationally is found in the Rio Declaration on Environment and Development, which was agreed and proclaimed at the 1992 United Nations Conference on Environment and Development in Rio de Janeiro (UNCED), at which the UN Framework Convention on Climate Change and Convention on Biodiversity were also agreed.[6] This 'Declaration' falls short of being an international treaty, constituting only a document of 'soft law' in international law terms, which characterization also contributes to the legal ambiguity of these principles. Another reason for their legal ambiguity is the generality, and thus definitional uncertainty

---

[6] Note these follow on from principles in earlier UN-sponsored soft law agreements: United Nations Environment Programme, 'Declaration of the United Nations Conference on the Human Environment' (Stockholm, 16 June 1972) UN Doc A/CONF.48/14, 11 ILM 1461 (1972); World Commission on Environment and Development, 'Report of the World Commission on Environment and Development: Our Common Future' (20 March 1987) UN Doc A/42/427 ('Brundtland Report') Annex I.

of their terms. Keep this in mind as you read some of the key principles extracted here—can you identify any principles that might give rise to legal obligations in light of their express terms?

United Nations General Assembly, *Rio Declaration on Environment and Development* (1992) UN Doc A/CONF 151/26 (Vol I) Annex I

[The UNCED] proclaims that:

Principle 1

Human beings are at the centre of concerns for sustainable development. They are entitled to a healthy
and productive life in harmony with nature.

Principle 2

States have… the sovereign right to exploit their own resources pursuant to their own environmental
and developmental policies, and the responsibility to ensure that activities within their jurisdiction or
control do not cause damage to the environment of other States or of areas beyond the limits of national
jurisdiction.

Principle 3

The right to development must be fulfilled so as to equitably meet developmental and environmental
needs of present and future generations. [*a version of the 'principle of intergenerational equity'*]

Principle 4

In order to achieve sustainable development, environmental protection shall constitute an integral part
of the development process and cannot be considered in isolation from it. [*a version of the 'integration
principle' and on one view the 'principle of sustainable development'*]

[…]

Principle 6

The special situation and needs of developing countries, particularly the least developed and those
most environmentally vulnerable, shall be given special priority. International actions in the field of environment and development should also address the interests and needs of all countries.

Principle 7

States shall cooperate in a spirit of global partnership to conserve, protect and restore the health and
integrity of the Earth's ecosystem. In view of the different contributions to global environmental degradation, States have *common but differentiated responsibilities*. The developed countries acknowledge
the responsibility that they bear in the international pursuit to sustainable development in view of
the pressures their societies place on the global environment and of the technologies and financial
resources they command.

[…]

Principle 10

Environmental issues are best handled with *participation* of all concerned citizens, at the relevant level.
At the national level, each individual shall have appropriate *access to information* concerning the environment that is held by public authorities, including information on hazardous materials and activities in their
communities, and the opportunity to participate in decision-making processes. States shall facilitate and
encourage public awareness and participation by making information widely available. Effective *access
to judicial and administrative proceedings*, including redress and remedy, shall be provided.

[…]

Principle 13

States shall develop national law regarding *liability and compensation* for the victims of pollution and other
environmental damage. States shall also cooperate in an expeditious and more determined manner to

develop further international law regarding liability and compensation for adverse effects of environmental damage caused by activities within their jurisdiction or control to areas beyond their jurisdiction.

[...]

Principle 15

In order to protect the environment, the precautionary approach shall be widely applied by States according to their capabilities. Where there are threats of serious or irreversible damage, lack of full scientific certainty shall not be used as a reason for postponing cost-effective measures to prevent environmental degradation. [*a version of the 'precautionary principle'*]

Principle 16

National authorities should endeavour to promote the internalization of environmental costs and the use of economic instruments, taking into account the approach that the polluter should, in principle, bear the cost of pollution, with due regard to the public interest and without distorting international trade and investment. [*a version of the 'polluter pays principle'*]

Principle 17

Environmental impact assessment, as a national instrument, shall be undertaken for proposed activities that are likely to have a significant adverse impact on the environment and are subject to a decision of a competent national authority.

[...]

Principle 21

The creativity, ideals and courage of the youth of the world should be mobilized to forge a global partnership in order to achieve sustainable development and ensure a better future for all.

[...]

Principle 27

States and people shall cooperate in good faith and in a spirit of partnership in the fulfilment of the principles embodied in this Declaration and in the further development of international law in the field of sustainable development.

Within this extracted list of 'Rio principles', there is a diverse set of ideas about environmental protection, sustainable development, and international co-operation on these issues. Note that there is no consistent concept of a 'principle' here. The various 'Rio principles' represent economic ideas, procedural ideas (public participation and environmental impact assessment), social justice goals, and access to justice provisions; some involve scientific issues (the precautionary approach of Principle 15), and others are more overarching, such as the thread of sustainable development that weaves throughout. From a legal perspective, some of these principles represent established norms of public international law—state sovereignty, common but differentiated responsibilities—whereas others, such as rallying the youth of the world in Principle 21, represent more aspiration ideals. The entire document itself, being an instrument of soft law, is of uncertain legal status. Lang tries to get to grips with all this legal uncertainty to determine what it means for the Declaration's principles.

Winfried Lang, 'UN Principles and International Environmental Law' (1999) 3 Max Planck Yrbk UN L 157, 159, 162–65

Principles, even if they are part of the law, are norms of a general nature which give guidance to state behaviour, but are not directly applicable; the violation of such principles cannot be pursued in international courts unless they are made operational by means of more concrete norms. But whatever definition is chosen, whatever distinction one applies, nobody can deny that principles are important tools, but that their normativity in many cases remains a grey-zone phenomenon [in international environmental law] that policy-makers and lawyers have to live with.

[...]

[...] One could very well share the view that the soft obligations of the Rio Declaration, initially only formulated as programmatic statements *de lege ferenda*, will increasingly take on legal status, will inspire the creation of new customary law and will become a standard text providing interpretative aid for a large number of actual conventions. As a matter of fact many general lessons could be learned from this process of crystallizing political statements into legal duties.

[...]

Using the term 'principles and/or concepts' means that one avoids drawing a line between them as regards their normative value and entering into the futile exercise of debating their legally-binding or compulsory nature versus their legally non-binding or simply recommendatory value. But this broad approach does not mean that we will not reflect on the legal situation of one or the other text. The value is reflected either in the contents of the principle itself or in the context in which it is enumerated [...]

[The Rio Declaration carries] more political weight [than some other UN-originating documents]; but [it has] been subject to diplomatic scrutiny, [it dilutes] important ideas and [tries] to balance competing political-economic interests especially in the North-South dimension. [It is] certainly important but [it does] not necessarily reflect the state of international law, or the direction into which international law is moving.

Lang goes on to compare the principles enumerated in the Rio Declaration with those in other (then) key UN environmental documents, including the 1972 Stockholm Declaration and other expert legal reports identifying principles of sustainable development, in order to ascertain which Rio principles were developing international profiles as identifiable 'environmental principles'. This process is at the heart of the emerging prominence of environmental principles in environmental law—rather than any firm kind of legal doctrine supporting their legal evolution in a systematic way, various environmental principles have become popular concepts in environmental law scholarship with developing, if idiosyncratic, legal profiles in different jurisdictions due to their inclusion in a range of legal instruments and court judgments. Thus, legal scholars have identified some of the Rio principles as a cluster of important principles for environmental law, due to their increasing legal profile in various international, regional, and national jurisdictions. These include: the *principle of sustainable development*, the *integration principle*, the *preventive principle*, the *polluter pays principle*, the *precautionary principle*, and the *principle of intergenerational equity*. This selective grouping is not an exhaustive one nor is it consistent. In particular, the shorthand names of these principles can cause confusion, since their general terms are susceptible to different interpretations, and similarly-named principles in different jurisdictions can perform different legal roles depending on the particular legal contexts in which they are used. Thus, the sections that follow first illustrate varying meanings for these principles, and then identify some different legal roles taken on by these principles in EU and UK law to date. This is an area of environmental law about which it is easy to make broad and overarching generalizations—and the reasons for wanting to do this are set out in Section 1.2—but the legal reality is both less grand and more interesting in the detail, as well as being in a state of evolution.

Three other general points arise from Lang's extracted piece. The first is terminological—Lang refers to 'principles and/or concepts' to avoid deciding on their precise legal status, and this looseness of language can be seen in the inconsistent identification of some environmental 'principles' in cases, legal and policy instruments, and environmental law scholarship. This is most often seen in relation to sustainable development, which is identified variously as a principle, a concept, or simply as a stand-alone phrase. Equally, the precautionary principle is sometimes referred to as a 'precautionary approach', as in Principle 15 of the Rio Declaration. The legal importance of this varying nomenclature, without more legal context, is of little significance, but it reinforces that the legal context will dictate the particular legal meanings of these principles. This connects to the second point to highlight, which is that many of these pithy statements of environmental principles, particularly in international instruments, are the result of political negotiation and compromise, so that their final form can vary and represents what different parties and interests were all happy to sign up to at the relevant time.

Third, Lang's interest in seeing how political statements might 'crystallize' into legal duties demonstrates a common scholarly concern and aspiration of environmental lawyers—that the policy ideas represented by environmental principles might become legally binding through their evolving roles as 'principles' of environmental law. Whilst the group of principles highlighted here implicitly underlies many policies that we see reflected in modern environmental law—from laws focusing on the prevention of environmental damage, to regulatory strategies that foster sustainable use of natural resources, to liability regimes that impose obligations on polluters—the legal 'cystallization' of these principles is shorthand for more complicated and contextual legal developments that relate explicitly to environmental principles. Before we focus on these legal developments in EU and UK law, an overview of the various environmental principles that have high profiles in environmental law is set out in Section 1.1, followed by further consideration of why and how they are such popular concepts in environmental law.

1.1 WHAT ARE ENVIRONMENTAL PRINCIPLES?

As indicated already, there is no definitive or comprehensive catalogue of environmental principles in environmental law, despite their reflection in key international instruments such as the Rio Declaration. Rather, there are certain principles that are commonly invoked as the policies on which environmental regulation is based, and which have other legal roles, without forming a closed or definitive group. This section focuses on those principles that have developed the highest profiles in environmental law, internationally and also within the EU, and gives a sense of their contested meanings.

Sustainable Development

The most contested of environmental principles is the principle or concept of sustainable development. This principle gained significant international prominence with the 1987 Brundtland Report, a key document that launched an ongoing international discussion about building a strategic framework for sustainable development across nations. This discussion has continued with further UN conferences on sustainable development, in Rio de Janeiro in 1992, in Johannesburg in 2002, and again in Rio in 2012. These conferences have further refined a programme for sustainable development and produced more soft law instruments, including the Rio Declaration's 'sustainable development' principles.[7] Even though not the last word on sustainable development, the Brundtland Report includes the oft-cited 'definition' of sustainable development—'development that meets the needs of

---

[7] See also UNCED, *Agenda 21* (1992) UN Doc A/CONF151/PC/100/Add.1 (a programme for action that accompanied the Rio Declaration); World Summit on Sustainable Development, *Johannesburg Declaration on Sustainable Development* (2002) UN Doc A/CONF199/20; UN, *Report of the United Nations Conference on Sustainable Development* (Rio 2012) UN Doc A/CONF216/16.

the present without compromising the ability of future generations to meet their own needs'—as well as many ideas beyond this pithy statement. As you read the extract from the Report, consider how you would define its articulated concept of sustainable development, and whether such definition is possible.

World Commission on Environment and Development, *Our Common Future* (1987) UN Doc A42/427 (Brundtland Report) Annex, ch 2

1. Sustainable development is development that meets the needs of the present without compromising the ability of future generations to meet their own needs. It contains within it two key concepts:

- the concept of 'needs', in particular the essential needs of the world's poor, to which overriding priority should be given; and
- the idea of limitations imposed by the state of technology and social organization on the environment's ability to meet present and future needs.

2. Thus the goals of economic and social development must be defined in terms of sustainability in all countries—developed or developing, market-oriented or centrally planned. Interpretations will vary, but must share certain general features and must flow from a consensus on the basic concept of sustainable development and on a broad strategic framework for achieving it.

3. Development involves a progressive transformation of economy and society. A development path that is sustainable in a physical sense could theoretically be pursued even in a rigid social and political setting. But physical sustainability cannot be secured unless development policies pay attention to such considerations as changes in access to resources and in the distribution of costs and benefits. Even the narrow notion of physical sustainability implies a concern for social equity between generations, a concern that must logically be extended to equity within each generation.

4. The satisfaction of human needs and aspirations in the major objective of development. The essential needs of vast numbers of people in developing countries—for food, clothing, shelter, jobs—are not being met, and beyond their basic needs these people have legitimate aspirations for an improved quality of life. A world in which poverty and inequity are endemic will always be prone to ecological and other crises. Sustainable development requires meeting the basic needs of all and extending to all the opportunity to satisfy their aspirations for a better life.

[...]

10. Growth has no set limits in terms of population or resource use beyond which lies ecological disaster. Different limits hold for the use of energy, materials, water, and land. Many of these will manifest themselves in the form of rising costs and diminishing returns, rather than in the form of any sudden loss of a resource base. The accumulation of knowledge and the development of technology can enhance the carrying capacity of the resource base. But ultimate limits there are, and sustainability requires that long before these are reached, the world must ensure equitable access to the constrained resource and reorient technological efforts to relieve the presume [sic].

11. Economic growth and development obviously involve changes in the physical ecosystem. Every ecosystem everywhere cannot be preserved intact. A forest may be depleted in one part of a watershed and extended elsewhere, which is not a bad thing if the exploitation has been planned and the effects on soil erosion rates, water regimes, and genetic losses have been taken into account. In general, renewable resources like forests and fish stocks need not be depleted provided the rate of use is within the limits of regeneration and natural growth. But most renewable resources are part of a complex and interlinked ecosystem, and maximum sustainable yield must be defined after taking into account system-wide effects of exploitation.

[...]

15. In essence, sustainable development is a process of change in which the exploitation of resources, the direction of investments, the orientation of technological development; and institutional change are all in harmony and enhance both current and future potential to meet human needs and aspirations.

From these paragraphs and others in chapter 2 of the Report, a range of issues are driving the concept of sustainable development in policy terms—from equity between nations in sharing the world's resources, to ecological protection, to the concerns of developing nations in promoting their own economic wellbeing to prosperity, to demographic (population) developments, to the 'satisfaction of human needs and aspirations', to boosting productivity generally. These are big and complicated policy issues, which countries confront under a range of political, environmental, and social conditions; and all are drawn together here under a governing rubric of 'sustainable development', aiming to guide these many aspects of human development along a sustainable path. The scale of the ambition, breadth, and aspiration of these ideas is why the definition of sustainable development is so contested and difficult to pin down. As Tarlock points out, sustainable development is a 'paradox', which can mean many things to many people depending on their viewpoints and agendas, and is an idea that lacks operational clarity, and is arguably impossible to convert into practical reality.

A Dan Tarlock, 'Ideas Without Institutions: The Paradox of Sustainable Development' (2001) 9 India Journal of Global Legal Studies 35, 36–39

The beauty of principles that attempt to reconcile inconsistent ideas is that each side can interpret those ideas to its advantage. The principal message of the Commission's report—that environmental protection and development are not incompatible—was welcomed by developing countries. Linking development and environmental protection vindicated their long-standing position that the North's argument that environmental protection is a universal imperative was simply a new form of colonialism imposed by the more powerful developed countries to preserve their access to raw commodities and to prevent industrial and political development.

While developing countries naturally embrace the development component of [sustainable development, 'SD'], developed countries, especially in Europe, were enthusiastic in their reception of SD for a different reason: because it offered a vision of a more humane, less materialistic society [...] [vindicating] the argument that environmental protection is a permanent part of the global political agenda [...]

[This acceptance] achieved the Commission's immediate, primary purpose: it allowed the debate about environmental protection to proceed with the participation of most developing nations. Each side had to accept a key principle of the other. It also achieved the Commission's secondary purpose: environmental protection was enshrined as an integral part of the development debate [...]

The ultimate test of a concept intended to have legal force and profound social and economic consequences is whether it changes behavior at both the individual and institutional levels. The jury is still out on SD [...] More radical environmentalists argue that environmental protection and development are not in fact compatible, and thus the concept will not further environmental protection and may indeed undermine it [...] Other critics suggest that because SD attempted to marry two incompatible ideas, environmental protection and development, the resulting formulation has no consequences [...] There is considerable merit in this argument, as SD's concepts are so vague and open that any action can be justified as the practice of SD.

[...] However, the post-Rio de Janeiro story of SD [...] has two contradictory narratives. First, the principles of SD [and environmentally sustainable development, 'ESD'...] have in fact been quickly adopted throughout much of the world as *the* standard against which public policy should be judged [...] This said, the second narrative is that this implementation will never take place, because there is a virtual disconnect between the adoption of SD [...] as a policy standard and the institutional structures necessary to implement [it]. This disconnect exists in almost all countries regardless of their political system.

Another prominent aspect of the debate concerning the meaning of sustainable development is how anthropogenic its focus should be. The more anthropogenic the concept, the more likely that any balancing of environmental, social, and economic considerations—generally identified as the three pillars of sustainable development—will squeeze out environmental priorities in light of pressing human development concerns. In *The Principle of Sustainability*, Bosselmann reacts against this possibility and makes a powerful case for the promotion of an ecologically-focussed 'legal' principle of *sustainability*, which is separate from the politically (and legally) messy concept of sustainable development.

Klaus Bosselmann, *The Principle of Sustainability* (Ashgate 2008) 52–53 (emphasis added)

To identify the normative core [of sustainable development] is not difficult, at least from a logical point of view. If 'sustainable' qualifies 'development' as distinguished from unsustainable development, its meaning must be clear. [...] [T]he necessary clarity cannot be gained by merely referring to social, economic and environmental goals as all being relevant to sustainable development. Nor does it help to consider these goals as equally important. To identify, and act upon, potential conflicts between them, it is necessary to know how they should be resolved [...]

Clarity can only come from defining the essence of 'sustainable' with respect to its object. The essence is neither 'economic sustainability', nor 'social sustainability', nor 'everything sustainable', but 'ecological sustainability'. This is not the same as saying economic and social goals are less important. [...] [but rolling] the three forms of sustainability into one principle would be impossible without giving up its core meaning [...]

[...] The conceptual argument is that the principle of sustainability has been in existence for centuries with never any other object than the natural resource base. While this object may have been broadened—from local resources in ancient times to ecosystems in recent times to planetary ecosystems today— the principle of ecological sustainability never changed... [Only because of this ecological] core is it possible to relate the social and economic components of sustainable development to a central point of reference. As a consequence, the entire concept becomes operable: development is sustainable if it tends to preserve the integrity and continued existence of ecological systems; it is unsustainable if it tends to do otherwise.

This holistic, yet structured, concept of sustainable development equals 'ecologically sustainable development' and [...] [a]s a norm this can be formulated as the obligation to promote long-term economic prosperity and social justice *within the limits of ecological sustainability*.

The principle of sustainability itself is best defined as the duty to protect and restore the integrity of the Earth's ecological systems. [...] [I]t should become clear that the principle has a normative quality. It is reflective of a fundamental morality (respect for ecological integrity), requires action ('protect and restore') and is, therefore, capable of causing legal effect. The standards of a legal principle are all met.

With respect to the concept of sustainable development, the principle provides important guidance to make the concept operable. Whether this amounts to determinable legal content, making sustainable development a legal principle, is a matter of debate.

Both Tarlock and Bosselmann outline contested ideas of sustainable development, which give rise to definitional ambiguity and also give different views over the 'operability' or 'legal normativity' of sustainable development. In light of such contrasting views, how can it be said that sustainable development is a legal principle of any kind? In one sense, sustainable development is often described as a concept or principle simply to connote that it involves general ideas that nations have been prepared to sign up to at the level of abstract 'principle'. Its articulation as a principle in a legal sense, as suggested by Bosselmann, has been encouraged by theoretical reliance on Dworkin and other jurisprudential ideas of legal principles.[8] It has also been encouraged in international law terms by the soft law nature of sustainable development instruments, and by passing judicial comments in the International Court of Justice.[9] However, sustainable development is yet to find a strong base of state practice or scholarly support for its identification as a principle of public international law in doctrinal terms. This is unsurprising considering its multiple aspects, contested meanings, and overarching nature.

The overarching nature of sustainable development also means that it can be understood as a different kind of 'environmental principle', in being an umbrella concept that is constituted by other ideas and principles, including other environmental principles. Thus, the Rio Declaration sets out its programme of sustainable development through a suite of more particular principles, and the Brundtland Report itself sets out in Annexe 1 a list of 'Proposed Legal Principles for Environmental Protection and Sustainable Development'. Again, while these different catalogues of principles are not purely environmentally focused, nor consistent in their names and groupings, the idea of there being a set of environmental principles with some kind of legal status has been a persistent trend throughout these international programmes of sustainable development.[10]

The following sub-sections outline briefly the ideas underlying other environmental principles that have high profiles internationally, most of which are considered further in this chapter in relation to legal developments in EU and UK law. This is not a comprehensive catalogue of environmental principles—as indicated already such a list is not possible—but reflects the different environmental principles that emerge as particularly popular or legally resonant in different policy and legal settings. Other principles that are relevant in EU or UK law in particular are raised in Sections 1.3 and 1.4.

Principle of intergenerational equity

The principle of intergenerational equity has been developed and championed by Edith Brown Weiss.

---

[8] See, for example, Alhagi BM Marong, 'From Rio to Johannesburg: Reflections on the Role of International Legal Norms in Sustainable Development' (2004) 16 Geo Intl Envtl L Rev 21, as extracted in Section 1.2.

[9] See, for example, *Gabčikovo-Nagymaros Project (Hungary v Slovakia)* [1997] ICJ Rep 7, 90 (separate opinion of Weeramantry J, finding that sustainable development constitutes a principle of customary international law): cf *Gabčikovo-Nagymaros Project*, 78 (majority opinion), and *Case concerning Pulp Mills in the River Uruguay (Argentina v Uruguay)*, Judgment of 20 April 2010, General List No 135, 75–77, 177 (sustainable development as a guiding 'concept' or 'objective').

[10] It is also a persistent idea amongst scholars: see A Dan Tarlock, 'Ideas Without Institutions: The Paradox of Sustainable Development' (2001) 9 Ind J Global Legal Stud 35, 38; Marong (n 8) 58–64.

Edith Brown Weiss, 'In Fairness to Future Generations and Sustainable Development'
(1992) 8 Am U Intl LR 19, 20–23

All generations are linked by the ongoing relationship with the earth. The theory of intergenerational equity states that all generations have an equal place in relation to the natural system, and that there is no basis for preferring past, present or future generations in relation to the system

[...]

Every generation should use the natural system to improve the human condition. But when one generation severely degrades the environment, it violates its intergenerational obligations to care for the natural system. In such cases, other generations may in fact have an obligation to restore the robustness of the system, though not to bear all the costs. Those costs should be distributed across generations.

[...]

There are three normative principles of intergenerational equity. First, each generation must conserve options. This means conserving the diversity of the natural and cultural resource base, so that each generation does not unduly restrict the options available to future generations in solving their problems and satisfying their own values. It does not necessarily mean maximizing diversity, for this might be inconsistent with maintaining robustness. Future generations are entitled to diversity comparable to that which has been enjoyed by previous generations. This is an intergenerational principle of options, or conservation of options.

Second, each generation should be required to maintain the quality of the planet so that it is passed on in a condition no worse than that in which it was received. Each generation should be entitled to quality comparable to that enjoyed by previous generations. One can think of this as the intergenerational principle of quality or conservation of quality.

[...]

Third, each generation should provide its members with equitable rights of access to the legacy of past generations and conserve this access for future generations. This is an intergenerational principle of access, or conservation of access. This applies, for example, to access to potable water supplies

[...]

The principles proposed here recognize the right of each generation to use the Earth's resources for its own benefit. They also constrain the present generation's use of the Earth's resources. These principles provide guidance, but do not dictate how each generation should manage its resources [...] One could refer to them as planetary rights and obligations held by each generation.

The principle of intergenerational equity is reflected in the international sustainable development instruments discussed in this section so far, and there is increasing interest in the principle in policy and legal terms in various jurisdictions.[11] However, it has no identifiable role in EU or UK law to date.

Principle of prevention

Quite simply, this principle expresses the idea that pollution or other environmental damage should be prevented, as opposed to remedied once generated. De Sadeleer describes how this principle represented an evolution in environmental law from an originally 'curative approach', which only dealt

---

[11] See, for example, UN, *Report of the United Nations Conference on Sustainable Development* (Rio 2012) UN Doc A/CONF216/16; Protection of the Environment Administration Act 1991 (NSW) s 6(2).

with environmental problems once they had arisen. However, whilst the preventive principle reflects an overall change of policy and regulatory approach in environmental law, in the UK and EU in particular, its definition and outlines remain ambiguous.

Nicolas de Sadeleer, *Environmental Principles: From Political Slogans to Legal Rules* (OUP 2002) 61

[The preventive principle] gives rise to so many questions that any attempt at interpretation calls for constant clarification. We may, for example, ask whether a preventive measure presupposes complete knowledge of the risk to be reduced, if all forms of inquiry must be foreseen, if intervention should take place at the level of the sources of damage or of their effects, and whether it is preferable to monitor the progress of damage or to prohibit damage the moment it becomes evident.

This extract reinforces the definitional ambiguity that accompanies all of these generally stated environmental principles, even when they are stated in apparently simple terms.

Precautionary principle

When it comes to definitional problems, the precautionary principle is in a league of its own amongst environmental principles. It has been described as 'deeply ambivalent and apparently infinitely malleable',[12] accommodating, for example, extreme views mandating cautionary regulation in cases of controversial and uncertain environmental risks, as well as more procedural ideas requiring the conduct of adequate assessment of risks before introducing regulation in relation to scientifically complex environmental and public health problems. Fisher paraphrases what she finds to be the most common version of the precautionary principle:[13]

[W]here there is a threat to human health or environmental protection a lack of full scientific certainty should not be used as a reason to postpone measures that would prevent or minimise such a threat.

In de Sadeleer's view, a clear distinction can also be drawn between this principle and the preventive principle—the former is concerned with regulating and preventing harm from *uncertain* environmental risks, whereas the latter concerns minimizing harm associated with *known* environmental problems.[14]

As with the other principles discussed here, the definitional uncertainty of the precautionary principle highlights that any 'legal' definition of the principle depends on the particular legal contexts in which it plays a role—this is seen in relation to EU law developments, examined in Section 1.3, where the precautionary principle has been implicated in a significant and complicated body of case law.

---

[12] Joanne Scott and Ellen Vos, 'The Juridification of Uncertainty: Observations on the Ambivalence of the Precautionary Principle within the EU and the WTO' in Christian Joerges and Renaud Dehousse (eds), *Good Governance in Europe's Integrated Market* (OUP 2002).

[13] Elizabeth Fisher, *Risk Regulation and Administrative Constitutionalism* (Hart 2007) 40.

[14] Nicolas de Sadeleer, *Environmental Principles: From Political Slogans to Legal Rules* (OUP 2002) 91.

Polluter pays principle

This principle has origins in the work of the Organisation for Economic Co-operation and Development,[15] and has an economic dimension and justification that differentiates it from other environmental principles. It can be understood as a principle that seeks to correct market failures by internalizing the costs of environmental pollution—in broad terms, it requires that polluters should pay for the environmental harm they cause. Again, there are a number of uncertainties associated with the principle: who constitutes a polluter? What does it mean to cause pollution? Should polluters pay for damage caused or also for restoring the environment to its unpolluted state? How long does such liability last? These are the types of questions that are examined and answered in more precise legal and regulatory settings that engage the polluter pays principle.

FURTHER READING AND QUESTIONS

1. International environmental law is often looked to as the source of environmental principles and to confirm or examine their 'legal' status. To what extent can it be said that environmental principles are legal principles in international law terms? Further reading to help with this: see Chapter 5 and Vaughan Lowe, 'Sustainable Development and Unsustainable Arguments' in Alan Boyle and David Freestone (eds), *International Law and Sustainable Development: Past Achievements and Future Challenges* (OUP 1999).

2. Are there areas of overlap between the different environmental principles set out here? How important is it to try and define these principles?

1.2 WHY ARE ENVIRONMENTAL PRINCIPLES SO POPULAR IN ENVIRONMENTAL LAW?

As seen from the international law and policy developments in Section 1.1, environmental principles are popular in policy terms because they are pragmatic points of agreement in international negotiations—they represent suitably ambitious goals of environmental protection and sustainable development, without binding states to particular commitments, and also allowing states to mean different things through their agreement to principles. Whatever may be the evolving status of these principles in international environmental law, there are a number of reasons why their policy popularity has been matched by a legal appetite for environmental principles. This is partly driven by a desire to make the policy commitments embodied in environmental principles binding in some way—to force policy change to bring about good environmental outcomes.

However, there are other reasons why environmental principles have a high profile in environmental law and scholarship. Two different reasons dominate the literature. First, there is a drive to connect environmental law to foundational ideas concerning 'legal principles' in other legal subjects so as to legitimize environmental law as a subject and guide its development in doing so. This is where the ideas of Dworkin—distinguishing principles from policies and rules, and identifying roles for legal principles that involve guiding but not determining legal outcomes—and other respected jurisprudential scholars have particular appeal. Second, there is a countervailing concern to make sense of the doctrinally disparate, factually complex, and often policy-driven

---

[15] 1974 Council Recommendation on the Implementation of the Polluter Pays Principle, OECD C(74) 223 final.

nature of environmental law, which is unlike other legal subjects, and thus needs a new conceptual framework to represent the subject. The Marong and de Sadeleer extracts here highlight these differing views of environmental law, and of the roles of principles within the subject, whilst having in common a focus on environmental principles as central jurisprudential ideas of the subject.

Alhaji BM Marong, 'From Rio to Johannesburg: Reflections on the Role of International Legal Norms in Sustainable Development' (2004) 16 Geo Intl Envtl L Rev 21, 57–58 (emphasis removed)

Legal systems can contribute towards the transition to sustainability through incorporating certain principles which appear as 'good conduct norms' necessary for the realization of sustainable development. An understanding of lawmaking as a continuous social enterprise, rather than the sole prerogative of a hierarchical authority, is fundamental to the analysis of how law can contribute to the attainment of sustainable development. This is because the concept of sustainable development is not a static notion [...]

Principles do not operate as guidance norms in the area of actor conduct; rather, they provide frameworks for decision that could be invoked in deliberation geared towards the construction of legal rules, as well as in the application of legal rules in a judicial or administrative context [...]

How does one identify these principles? How do they differ from rules of law? In my mind, rules and principles differ at both a substantive and functional level. At a substantive level, it has been argued that [...] principles are couched in general terms and that they lack specificity. Ronald Dworkin makes a similar point, arguing that rules require specific courses of action, whereas a principle 'states a reason that argues in one direction, but does not necessitate a particular decision'. In discussing his 'concept of right' Rawls argued that the principles of such a concept must possess certain features including generality, universality and publicity.

With respect to rules, Thomas Franck has identified 'determinacy' as one of the elements that is relevant to the question of rule legitimacy. [Fuller argued that legal legitimacy depends on] tests of internal morality including generality of rules (in the sense of non-discrimination), rule clarity and the avoidance of contradiction. At a substantive level therefore, rules differ from principles with respect to the degree of their specificity [...]

[...] [A]t a functional level, it is arguable that while rules prescribe courses of action, and as such operate to regulate conduct, principles guide discourse, deliberation, discussion and argument, including deliberation geared towards the construction and interpretation of legal rules. In this manner, while principles of law may not bind actor conduct, they could serve as instruments of legal development and change when taken into account in rule making and interpretation. I would argue that this is the normative role of principles of law. Through the exercise of this role the [environmental principles] could contribute to the evolution of legal regimes towards sustainable development.

Other scholars take a more radical view of environmental law as a subject, going so far as to suggest that it represents a new form of legal order. For de Sadeleer, this is 'post-modern law', which is characterized by an increase in discretion, competing norms, multiple jurisdictions, and openness to 'extra-legal spheres', including economic, ethical, and policy spheres.[16] Within this new form of law, of which environmental law is representative, environmental principles have core roles as legal principles.

---

[16] de Sadeleer (n 14) (OUP 2002) 248–50.

Nicolas de Sadeleer, *Environmental Principles: From Political Slogans to Legal Rules* (OUP 2002) 250–51

'[P]rinciples' no longer serve merely to rationalize law or to fill gaps in a given legal system [...] Rather, they are intended to spur public policies, to allow courts to weigh and reconcile highly divergent interests. These principles mark a policy path to be followed, outline the context within which the law-maker must act, and guide the course of his passage. [Environmental principles are] 'directing principles' [...] As legal systems multiply and intersect, this new generation of principles plays an important role in maintaining the links among weakly structured networks, ensuring the practical effectiveness of the legal system as a whole [...]

They are needed to introduce a degree of rationality in a world that has become Kafkaesque though the production of an excessive number of rules and a high degree of instability [...] They provide order to this new view of the legal system.

Whatever the merits of framing environmental principles as jurisprudential foundations in environmental law, and however best to do this, there is certainly a developing body of doctrine involving principles in environmental law, which paints a picture of the legal roles of environmental principles beyond their being mere policy prescriptions. Relevantly for UK law, these developments are mostly occurring in EU law, and to that extent affect UK law as a matter of implementation of EU law. Independent legal developments relating to environmental principles in UK and English law are fewer. These developments are examined in Sections 1.3 and 1.4 and they show that environmental principles are not, or are yet to be, central concepts in UK environmental law. Environmental law is messier and more disparate than a single set of codifying principles can bring into some form of legal order.

FURTHER READING AND QUESTIONS

1. Do you think it helps to view environmental law as a new form of law? What analytical advantages or disadvantages does this viewpoint bring?

2. For further scholarship on environmental principles that connects to broader jurisprudential ideas, including those of Dworkin and other leading theoretical scholars, see Richard Macrory, 'Principles into Practice' in Richard Macrory (ed), *Principles of European Environmental Law* (Europa Law Publishing 2004) (especially the Introduction); G Winter, 'The Legal Nature of Environmental Principles in International, EC and German Law' in Richard Macrory (ed), *Principles of European Environmental Law* (Europa Law Publishing 2004); Philippe Sands and Jacqueline Peel, *Principles of International Environmental Law* (3rd edn, CUP 2012) 188–90. Do these scholars all agree that Dworkin's ideas about principles and policies work in conceptualizing environmental principles in environmental law? If not, why do you think engagement with these theoretical ideas is important in framing and analysing environmental principles in environmental law scholarship?

1.3 LEGAL ROLES OF ENVIRONMENTAL PRINCIPLES IN EU LAW

The legal roles of environmental principles in EU law begin with their articulation in the Treaty on the Functioning of the European Union, which largely restates former incarnations of environmental principles in the preceding Treaty on the European Community.[17] In particular, Article 11 TFEU provides that:

> Environmental protection requirements must be integrated into the definition and implementation of the Union's policies and activities, in particular with a view to promoting sustainable development.

This contains the EU versions of the 'integration principle' and the principle of 'sustainable development'.[18] Further, there is a key set of environmental principles included in the primary Treaty provision outlining EU environment policy—Article 191 TFEU. A full extract of Article 191 can be found in Chapter 4 but here it is worth noting Article 191(2) again.

> 2. Union policy on the environment shall aim at a high level of protection taking into account the diversity of situations in the various regions of the Union. *It shall be based on the precautionary principle and on the principles that preventive action should be taken, that environmental damage should as a priority be rectified at source and that the polluter should pay.* (emphasis added)

On one view, the principles in Article 191(2), as suggest by the Treaty provision itself, are no more than principles of policy, giving rise to no direct legal consequences. The provisions surrounding Article 191(2) might support this view, including prescribed 'objectives' and 'relevant considerations' for EU environmental policy, which carry ever less legal connotation in their generalized formulations. This view is reflected in the case of *Re Peralta*, which involved a preliminary reference to the ECJ from an Italian court asking whether an Italian law that prohibited national vessels from discharging certain harmful substances into the sea, in contravention of internationally accepted practice, was precluded by the EU preventive principle (or the principle that preventive action should be taken).[19] The ECJ held that the preventive principle did not preclude the Italian legislation because Article 191 TFEU (ex-Article 174 TEC) is 'confined to defining the general [environmental] objectives of the Community'.[20] It is the responsibility of the EU Council to determine what action is to be taken in this policy field and, while the EU could take action in this unharmonized area of environmental policy, whether it does so is not a legal issue for the EU courts to decide. The preventive principle did not have legal force in compelling EU action beyond its general policy prescription role in the Treaty.[21] Further, these principles are undefined in the TFEU. As examined already, generally stated environmental principles are susceptible to various definitions, which militates against their having a direct legal impact.

On another view, however, the presence of this collection of 'policy principles' within the TFEU is legally significant, particularly since the Treaty is a legally binding document. Indeed, we can now see that these environmental principles do have roles in EU law, in at least the following ways: (1) they are articulated increasingly in secondary EU legislation; (2) they are used to interpret other uncertain legislative terms; and (3) they inform and generate legal tests in the development of EU law doctrine

---

[17] Other environmental principles, not mentioned in the Treaty, also have evolving legal roles in EU law. For example, the principles of proximity and self-sufficiency have a role in waste regulation—see Council Directive 2008/98/EC of 19 November 2008 on waste [2008] OJ L312/3, art 16.

[18] See also Treaty on European Union, recital 9, arts 3 and 21.

[19] The argument put to the Italian court was that the level of environmental protection required by the preventive principle in the Treaty should match that set out in the MARPOL Convention, the relevant provisions of which were not as stringent as those in Italian national law.

[20] Case C-379/92 *Re Peralta* [1994] ECR I-3453, para 57.

[21] See also Case C-378/08 *Raffinerie Mediterranee (ERG) v Ministero dello Sviluppo Economico* [2010] 3 CMLR 9, Opinion of AG Kokott, para 45.

by the courts. The following sub-sections here give illustrative examples of these legal developments.[22] Note that most examples concern the precautionary principle or polluter pays principle.

As you read the cases and legal analysis here, keep in mind that this is an evolving picture, and a legally novel one. Despite the jurisprudential associations between environmental principles and Dworkinian (or other types of) legal principles in environmental law scholarship discussed already, there is no pre-existing model of how these principles work in EU law, and their increasing incorporation into legal doctrine does not fit an established or comprehensive pattern. Rather, there are lines of legal reasoning that are starting to form patterns in relation to some principles, and these are closely connected to questions of EU law concerning exercises of environmental competence, which is unsurprising considering that the principles establish the basis of EU environmental competence in Article 191(2). The basic premise underlying many EU cases involving environmental principles is that they relate to a relevant *exercise* of EU environmental competence, usually by way of secondary EU legislation based on the Treaty's environmental title (Title XX). Legal questions then arise in relation to the interpretation of that legislation or whether the competence was properly exercised.

In other cases, however, the connection to the environmental competence in Article 191(2) is more tenuous, and this is where the case law continues to evolve. Thus, *Member State* action within the scope of EU law is sometimes reviewed in accordance with Article 191(2) environmental principles, being understood broadly as exercises of '*EU* environmental competence' that must fit the overall policy prescription of Article 191(2) and so comply with its principles. Further, the integration principle in Article 11 *expands* the legal roles of Article 191(2) principles in some cases to resolve EU legal issues that concern other EU policy areas (such as transport and state aid).

However, the case law also shows that there are no free-standing roles for environmental principles as binding legal norms or grounds of review against which *all* actions of EU, or of Member State institutions within the scope of EU law, might be tested. A case demonstrating this point is *Monsanto Agricoltura Italia*,[23] in which the ECJ found that there was no general basis for reviewing the GMO-authorization procedure in Regulation 258/97 (for authorizing novel GM-derived foods)[24] against the precautionary principle, and no basis on which Member States could deviate from the Regulation's procedures for allowing GMO foods onto the market on the basis of the precautionary principle alone. The Regulation was a measure properly based on the internal market title of the Treaty (Article 114 TFEU), and environmental risks had been adequately taken into consideration in its formulation, including through the inclusion of a safeguard clause. To this extent, environmental principles remain policy ideas that inform legislative measures but do not have overarching legal roles in EU law.

One final overall aspect of the legal roles played by environmental principles in the cases that follow is that they give meanings or definitions to the generally stated but undefined environmental principles in the TFEU. These are not consistent definitions, but marginal ones that depend upon and elucidate the legal and regulatory contexts in which they are formulated.

Environmental principles in EU legislation

Increasingly, environmental principles are being included explicitly in EU secondary legislation—in substantive legislative provisions as well as preambles that connect the relevant measure back to the environmental title (Article 191 TFEU) on which it is based. There are many other provisions of environmental Directives that might be said to reflect or embody environmental principles—such

---

[22] These legal developments concerning EU environmental principles are mapped and analysed comprehensively in Eloise Scotford, *Environmental Principles and the Evolution of Environmental Law* (Hart Publishing 2013). The categorizations and arguments adopted in this section largely draw on this research.

[23] Case C-236/01 *Monsanto Agricoltura Italia* [2003] ECR I-8105.

[24] Council Regulation (EC) 258/97 of 27 January 1997 concerning novel foods and novel food ingredients [1997] OJ L43/1.

as the requirements for conducting environmental assessments under the Environmental Impact Assessment Directive 85/337/EEC or for operating industrial facilities according to standards that minimize pollution under the Directive 2010/75/EU on Industrial Emissions (both reflecting the preventive principle).[25] However, the *explicit* articulation of environmental principles in legislative measures bolsters their profile in EU law and also indicates that they have legal relevance beyond their role in delineating EU environmental policy competence in Article 191 TFEU. Here are some examples from key EU environmental Directives.

Council Directive 2000/60/EC of 23 October 2000 Establishing a Framework for Community Action in the Field of Water Policy [2000] OJ L327/1 (Water Framework Directive), Article 9(1) (emphasis added)

Member States shall take account of the principle of recovery of the costs of water services, including environmental and resource costs, having regard to the economic analysis conducted according to Annex III, and in accordance in particular with the *polluter pays principle*.

Council Directive 2001/42/EC of 27 June 2001 on the Assessment of the Effects of Certain Plans and Programmes on the Environment [2001] OJ L197/30 (SEA Directive), Article 1 (emphasis added)

The objective of this Directive is to provide for a high level of protection of the environment and to *contribute to the integration of environmental considerations* into the preparation and adoption of plans and programmes *with a view to promoting sustainable development*, by ensuring that, in accordance with this Directive, an environmental assessment is carried out of certain plans and programmes which are likely to have significant effects on the environment.

Council Directive 2008/98/EC of 19 November 1998 on Waste [2008] OJ L312/3 (Waste Framework Directive), Recital 30 and Articles 4(2) and 14(1)

(30) *In order to implement the precautionary principle and the principle of preventive action* enshrined in Article 174(2) [now Article 191(2)] of the Treaty, it is necessary to set general environmental objectives for the management of waste within the Community. By virtue of those principles, it is for the Community and the Member States to establish a framework to prevent, reduce and, in so far as is possible, eliminate from the outset the sources of pollution or nuisance by adopting measures whereby recognised risks are eliminated [...]

[Article 4(2)] When applying the waste hierarchy referred to in paragraph 1, Member States shall take measures to encourage the options that deliver the best overall environmental outcome [...] Member States shall take into account the general environmental protection *principles of precaution and sustainability* [...]

[Article 14(1)] In accordance with the *polluter pays principle*, the costs of waste management shall be borne by the original waste producer or by the current or previous waste holders.

---

[25] See Chapters 19 and 17 respectively.

Whilst not a legislative measure of EU law in strict legal terms, the Commission's Communication on the Precautionary Principle should also be mentioned here. It represents the main EU exposition of the principle and shows how difficult this principle is to articulate in terms of its precise application and definition. Whilst it is a policy document, it has had a significant effect on the judicial treatment of the precautionary principle, as discussed further in the sub-sections that follow environmental on principles acting as interpretive tools, as informing tests of legal reviews, and as generating legal review tests.

Commission, 'Communication on the Precautionary Principle' COM (2000) 1, 3–4 (emphasis added)

4. The precautionary principle should be considered within a structured approach to the analysis of risk which comprises three elements: risk assessment, risk management, risk communication. The precautionary principle is particularly relevant to the management of risk. The precautionary principle, which is essentially used by decision-makers in the management of risk, should not be confused with the element of caution that scientists apply in their assessment of scientific data.

Recourse to the precautionary principle presupposes that potentially dangerous effects deriving from a phenomenon, product or process have been identified, and that scientific evaluation does not allow the risk to be determined with sufficient certainty.

The implementation of an approach based on the precautionary principle should start with a scientific evaluation [a risk assessment], *as complete as possible*, and where possible, identifying at each stage the degree of scientific uncertainty.

5. Decision-makers need to be aware of the degree of uncertainty attached to the results of the evaluation of the available scientific information. Judging what is an 'acceptable' level of risk for society [a decision of risk management] is an eminently political responsibility. Decision-makers faced with an unacceptable risk, scientific uncertainty and public concerns have a duty to find answers. Therefore, all these factors have to be taken into consideration. In some cases, the right answer may be not to act or at least not to introduce a binding legal measure. A wide range of initiatives is available in the case of action, going from a legally binding measure to a research project or a recommendation. The decision-making procedure should be transparent and should involve as early as possible and to the extent reasonably possible all interested parties.

6. Where action is deemed necessary, measures based on the precautionary principle should be, inter alia:

- proportional to the chosen level of protection,
- non-discriminatory in their application,
- consistent with similar measures already taken,
- based on an examination of the potential benefits and costs of action or lack of action (including, where appropriate and feasible, an economic cost/benefit analysis),
- subject to review, in the light of new scientific data, and
- capable of assigning responsibility for producing the scientific evidence necessary for a more comprehensive risk assessment.

The Communication goes on to explain in some detail the elements of the tripartite decision-making process outlined here—risk management, assessment, and communication—with a close focus on the level of scientific information and logical reasoning required to amount to an 'adequate' risk assessment in this process. Despite the assertion that the precautionary principle is primarily engaged at the stage of risk management, the process outlined in the Communication emphasizes the importance of risk assessment procedures that are scientifically rigorous, as Fisher indicates.

Elizabeth Fisher, *Risk Regulation and Administrative Constitutionalism* (Hart Publishing 2007) 228

The Communication is thus creating a rigid ['rational-instrumental'] framework for decision-makers to follow if they wish to apply the precautionary principle. Decision-makers are being consigned two specific tasks of assessing and managing risks, and in regard to each are constrained by methodologies such as risk assessment and regulatory impact assessment. Not only must a decision-maker use those methodologies in making those decisions but a decision made pursuant to those methodologies is held to be valid because, so long as a decision-maker has followed these preordained processes, a decision is held to be within the power of the decision-maker. Decision-making pursuant to the principle should start with a 'scientific evaluation', must be based on 'a scientific evaluation, as complete as possible', and will probably involve commissioning scientists to perform 'as objective and complete as possible scientific evaluation'. In other words, scientific evaluation, according to this document, is the central activity in the application of the precautionary principle.

The overall result of the Communication is that it creates a 'highly cryptic set of guidelines',[26] particularly since the principle is applied in cases of scientific uncertainty, meaning that the Communication's call for scientific rigour in its application inevitably generates a tension. This tension, and the general focus of the document on processes of risk assessment and robust scientific knowledge, has now filtered through to judicial developments concerning the principle in EU law. This is despite the Communication's aim being to 'inform all interested parties [...] of the manner in which the Commission applies or intends to apply the precautionary principle when faced with taking decisions relating to the containment of risk', and its provisions being 'only intended to serve as general guidance and in no way to modify or affect the provisions of the Treaty or secondary Community legislation.'[27] As disputes concerning the regulation of controversial and scientifically uncertain environmental and health issues—relating to pharmaceutical drugs, food additives, and genetically modified organisms in particular—have unsurprisingly led to legal cases and arguments, this has created a forum for making sense of this complicated principle *legally*, and the Communication has presented itself as an authoritative starting point for courts in this endeavour.

Environmental principles as interpretive tools

Where European courts find that ambiguous EU legislative provisions reflect an environmental principle, or come within the scope of the EU environmental policy discretion that is informed by the Article 191(2) principles, they will in some cases turn to those principles to interpret relevant ambiguous legislative measures. The style of legal reasoning involved—relying on legislative purposes to construe the meanings of contested provisions—is teleological reasoning. When environmental principles are drawn on as purposes to guide interpretive reasoning, they take on legal roles and their meanings are further elucidated. The following seminal nature conservation case of *Waddenzee*—identifying the circumstances under which an 'appropriate assessment' is required to

---

[26] Elizabeth Fisher, *Risk Regulation and Administrative Constitutionalism* (Hart Publishing 2007) 228.
[27] Commission, 'Communication on the Precautionary Principle' COM (2000) 1, 9.

examine the impact of plans and projects on protected habitats—shows how influential the *precautionary principle* can be, in an interpretive role, in leading to a decisive and environmentally protective legal outcome.

Case C-127/02 *Landelijke Vereniging tot Behoud van de Waddenzee v Staatssecretaris van Landbouw*
[2004] ECR I–7405 paras 39–40, 43–44 (emphasis added)

39. According to the first sentence of Article 6(3) of the Habitats Directive, any plan or project not directly connected with or necessary to the management of the site but likely to have a significant effect thereon, either individually or in combination with other plans or projects, is to be subject to appropriate assessment of its implications for the site in view of the site's conservation objectives.

40. The requirement for an appropriate assessment of the implications of a plan or project is thus conditional on its being likely to have a significant effect on the site.

[...]

43. [This] subordinates the requirement for an appropriate assessment of the implications of a plan or project to the condition that there be a probability or a risk that the latter will have significant effects on the site concerned.

44. In the light [...] of the *precautionary principle*, which is one of the foundations of the high level of protection pursued by Community policy on the environment [under Article 191(2) TFEU], and by reference to which the Habitats Directive must be interpreted, such a risk exists *if it cannot be excluded on the basis of objective information* that the plan or project will have significant effects on the site concerned.

Here, the precautionary principle meant that the protective measures of the Habitats Directive should apply where uncertain environmental risks could not be excluded. In relation to this particular regulatory scheme, the precautionary principle thus required erring on the side of caution, representing a strong interpretation and application of the principle.

Different interpretive roles for the precautionary principle can be seen in relation to other EU legislative provisions. Thus, in relation to the definition of waste—the central regulatory concept in UK and EU waste law—the CJEU relies on the principle to find that the concept of waste should not be construed restrictively (see Section 1.2 of Chapter 16), but is not focused on the quality or existence of scientific information, as in *Waddenzee*. In cases relating to public health measures, the principle has also been understood as giving institutions discretion to take cautionary action in the face of uncertain health risks, which is more akin to the general definition of the principle set out in Section 1.1. This more permissive version of the principle has been used to interpret some EU provisions—see, for example, the interpretation of the GMO safeguard clause in Case C-236/01 *Monsanto Agricoltura Italia*[28]—but has also been implicated in further legal roles for the precautionary principle, in cases where the lawfulness of discretion exercised on the basis of the principle is challenged, as examined in the sub-sections that follow. All of this shows that there is no single definition or role for the precautionary principle in EU law, and that its legal evolution is contingent on both the legal question being asked and the regulatory context under consideration. Overall, it is the general and open nature of these environmental principles allows for flexibility, and contestation, in their legal meaning and roles.

A series of cases has also involved the *polluter pays principle* as an interpretive aid in relation to ambiguous provisions in various EU Directives all considered to involve different manifestations

[28] [2003] ECR I-8105.

of the principle—including the Waste Directive, Landfill Directive, and Environmental Liability Directive. Not only does the interpretive reasoning in these cases again give rise to different marginal definitions of the principle across different environmental regulatory contexts, but the ECJ also makes some generally consistent statements about the nature and meaning of the polluter pays principle. Thus, the ECJ clarifies that the polluter pays principle applies only to impose on polluters the burden of remedying pollution to which they have *contributed*.[29] This can be seen in *Commune de Mesquer*,[30] discussed and extracted in Chapter 16, in which the polluter pays principle is used to interpret the provisions of the Waste Framework Directive that allocate liability for the costs of waste management. Consider, by contrast, how the ECJ uses the polluter pays principle to interpret relevant provisions of the principle in the Environmental Liability Directive 2004/35/EC in *Raffinerie Mediteranee (ERG) v Ministero dello Sviluppo*,[31] which shows a different aspect of how a polluter might 'contribute' to pollution within the interpretive scope of the polluter pays principle.

Environmental principles as informing tests of legal review

Beyond the interpretive roles performed by environmental principles in EU case law, other cases have shown that the principles in Article 191(2), and the precautionary principle in particular, have legal roles in *informing legal tests* in EU law. Following these developments requires recollecting EU law principles and doctrine, which are often central in understanding UK environmental law, as explored in Chapter 4. Outlines of relevant EU legal tests, particularly of EU administrative law, are also given here—it is this level of legal detail in which roles for environmental principles in environmental law can be seen.

There are a number of ways in which the European courts have used environmental principles, particularly the precautionary principle, to inform legal tests in deciding cases. These cases involve various questions of EU law, but all essentially concern review by the courts of acts by EU or Member State institutions, when they are acting on the basis of environmental principles or otherwise within the scope of EU environmental competence, so that the principles set out in Article 191(2) both guide and constrain their actions. The roles of environmental principles in these cases show a number of things—how environmental principles are shaping EU law by filling in gaps when existing EU doctrine is insufficient to resolve legal questions; how environmental principles are extending beyond the environmental title of the Treaty to shape legal developments in other EU policy fields (thus being legally 'integrated' into other policy areas); and how further marginal definitions develop for environmental principles when they are applied and relied on in different legal settings. As a result, environmental principles have a significant role in the review of EU law-making and institutional decision-making. Note that the examples in this section are only a survey of cases in which environmental principles inform EU legal tests, and this is an evolving area of EU law as well as environmental law.

First, environmental principles are used in some cases to inform *legal basis tests* applied by the courts. That is, they are used to determine the proper extent and scope of EU competence when EU legislative measures are subject to constitutional challenge over their legal basis in the Treaty.[32] Thus, in *Commission v Council (Waste Directive)*,[33] the ECJ considered whether the (former) Waste Framework Directive was properly adopted on the basis of Article 192 TFEU (ex-Article 130s TEC) as an environmental measure, rather than being a measure primarily concerned with the internal market due

---

[29] See, for example, Case C-254/08 *Futura Immobiliare srl Hotel Futura v Comune di Casoria* [2009] 3 CMLR 45, para 45; Case C-378/08 *Raffinerie Mediteranee (ERG) v Ministero dello Sviluppo* [2010] 3 CMLR 9, paras 57, 67.

[30] [2008] ECR I-4501.   [31] *ERG* (n 29).   [32] See Section 3 of Chapter 4.

[33] Case C-155/91 *Commission v Council (Waste Directive)* [1993] ECR I-939. See also Case C-187/93 *Parliament v Council (Waste Regulation)* [1994] ECR I-2857, para 20.

to its effects in harmonizing conditions for the treatment and regulation of waste. In finding that the Directive was properly adopted as an environmental measure, the ECJ looked to its aim and content— the relevant legal test for legal basis challenges in EU law. The ECJ used environmental principles to inform this test, finding that the Directive's aim was to implement the principle of rectification at source, and that its content included, amongst other things, a 'confirmation' of the polluter pays principle in Article 15.[34]

That may seem straightforward enough, since the ECJ was looking to determine whether the measure was properly based on Title XX TFEU and thus used the principles in that Title to test the purposes of the Directive. A second kind of case shows some more doctrinal creativity on the part of the EU courts in using environmental principles to resolve legal tests and inform EU law doctrine. These are cases that involve the much litigated Article 34 TFEU, which prevents barriers to the free movement of goods within the EU internal market, except in certain circumstances, including on grounds of public health, and only when such interferences with free movement comply with the test of proportionality. Those exceptional circumstances also include those that come within the doctrine of 'mandatory require-ments' set out *Cassis de Dijon*—the so-called 'rule of reason'.[35] The rule of reason provides that Member States can justifiably infringe Article 34 if this is in pursuit of a legitimate national mandatory require-ment, which can include environmental protection, so long as the measure is non-discriminatory (in its application to Member State and non-Member State goods) and proportionate.

In applying the 'non-discriminatory' element of this test, the ECJ has drawn on the principle of rec-tification at source in a case concerning the free movement of waste, *Wallon Waste*. The case involved proceedings against Belgium in relation to a measure that banned any waste from being brought into the Belgian region of Wallonia for disposal. The measure aimed to keep waste processing in the region both self-sufficient and manageable, and effectively prevented the import of waste from other Member States, thus giving rise to an infringement of Article 34. As you read the extract, consider how the Court is using the principle to answer a legal test to which it did not otherwise have a (satisfactory) answer.

Case C-2/90 *Commission v Belgium (Walloon Waste)*
[1992] ECR I–4431 paras 34, 36 (emphasis added)

34. In assessing whether or not the barrier in question is discriminatory, account must be taken of the particular nature of waste. The *principle that environmental damage should as a matter of priority be remedied at source*, laid down by [Article 191(2)] of the Treaty as a basis for action by the Community relating to the environment, entails that it is for each region… to take appropriate steps to ensure that its own waste is collected, treated and disposed of; it must accordingly be disposed of as close as possible to the place where it is produced, in order to limit as far as possible the transport of waste […]

[…]

36. It follows that having regard to the differences between waste produced in different places and to the connection of the waste with its place of production, the contested measures cannot be regarded as discriminatory.

The ECJ thus found that the rule of reason applied and the infringement of Article 34 was justified. The decision has been criticized by EU lawyers as doctrinally unsatisfactory—it is hard to say that the Belgian measure treated Wallonian and non-Wallonian waste alike—but the reasoning shows how environmental principles are used in some cases to shape EU law doctrine in relation to environmental problems, and thereby pursue the policy aims represented by the principles in Article 191(2).

---

[34] Ibid, paras 9, 13–14.   [35] See Section 5.2 of Chapter 4.

Note also that the legislation under review in this case is a Member State measure, to which the environmental principles in Article 191(2) were found to be relevant. This shows that when Article 191(2) requires that 'Union policy on the environment' be based on its environmental principles, this also includes the policy pursued by *Member State* measures where these are found to be within the scope of EU law, such as when they infringe one of the Treaty's fundamental freedoms. In the result, the legal roles played by environmental principles again tell a wider story about EU law—in permitting Member State measures that infringe Article 34, they also constrain Member State environmental action, setting legal boundaries for national environmental policies pursued unilaterally by Member States.

A different, third type of case in which environmental principles are used by the EU courts to inform legal tests again concerns measures challenged for being unlawful or beyond power in EU law terms, in particular for failing to meet the requirement of proportionality. The test of proportionality, which is a general principle of EU law constraining all actions by EU institutions, involves three limbs: the relevant measures should be necessary or 'appropriate' to pursue a legitimate objective; they should be the least restrictive means of doing so; and the disadvantages caused by the measures must not be disproportionate in relation to the aims pursued.[36] Particularly in cases of scientific uncertainty, the appropriate way to pursue an objective can be difficult to determine—thus the limbs of the proportionality test need something more to answer the legal questions they pose. In a number of cases, the precautionary principle has been used to fill this gap,[37] often in a complicated way that involves also generating a further test of legal review. This development is examined further in the following sub-section.

Environmental principles as generating legal review tests

The final, and doctrinally most complicated, way in which the EU courts use environmental principles in their reasoning is in using the precautionary principle (only) to generate new legal tests for reviewing EU and Member State measures that are purportedly based on the principle. Again, these cases concern review under EU law of acts of EU or Member State institutions done on the basis of the precautionary principle—both within the scope of the environmental title and in relation to other EU policy fields, such as public health and agriculture, to which the precautionary principle is found to be relevant. In these various areas of EU competence, the precautionary principle is legally prescribed as a policy goal by the Treaty, and, in order to determine whether that goal is properly pursued, the Court of First Instance (CFI, now General Court) and European Court of Justice (ECJ, now CJEU) have spent some time getting to grips with the meaning and application of this controversial principle. Long and complicated decisions have resulted, from the CFI in particular, showing that the European courts are taking seriously their constitutional role in policing the Treaty and scrutinizing the acts of EU institutions and Member State governments within the scope of EU law. The complexity of the reasoning involved is also not surprising considering that the precautionary principle is so illusive to define, it concerns situations of scientific uncertainty, and at its widest it could give considerable (unreviewable) scope to institutions to act with little accountability in controversial policy areas.

The decision in *Pfizer*, extracted here, is the leading case in which the CFI spent considerable time determining how to scrutinize a Commission measure purportedly made on the basis of the precautionary principle. In doing so, the Court elucidated many aspects of the precautionary principle in EU law, including that it does not involve any bright line rules either requiring preventive action in the face

[36] Case C-331/88 *Fedesa* [1990] ECR I-4023, para 13.
[37] For example, Case C-219/07 *Nationale Radd van Dierenwerkers en Liefhebbers* [2008] OJ C209/11. See also Case C-180/96 *UK v Commission* [1998] ECR I–2265 (applying what was later recognized as a version of the precautionary principle).

of scientific uncertainty or sanctioning all cautionary measures by public actors, and generating in the process a further test of legality review that focuses on adequate scientific evidence. The particular decision under review in *Pfizer* was a Regulation that withdrew Community authorization for an antibiotic, virginiamycin, used as a growth promoter in animals reared for human consumption.[38] The Regulation had been explicitly adopted on the basis of the precautionary principle, in light of the risk that use of virginiamycin as an animal growth promoter might promote antibiotic resistance in humans through animal consumption.

Case T-13/99 *Pfizer Animal Health SA v Council*
[2002] ECR II-3305 paras 135, 139, 142–4, 146, 148–52, 154–5, 157, 159, 162–3 (emphasis added)

135. [I]t is necessary, first, to define the 'risk' which must be assessed when the precautionary principle is applied. It is then appropriate to identify the two components of the task which falls to the competent public authority when a risk assessment is performed.

[...]

139. It is appropriate to bear in mind that, as the Court of Justice and the Court of First Instance have held [including in the *BSE case*], where there is scientific uncertainty as to the existence or extent of risks to human health, the Community institutions may, by reason of the precautionary principle, take protective measures without having to wait until the reality and seriousness of those risks become fully apparent.

[...]

142. Thus, in a situation in which the precautionary principle is applied, which by definition coincides with a situation in which there is scientific uncertainty, a risk assessment cannot be required to provide the Community institutions with conclusive scientific evidence of the reality of the risk and the seriousness of the potential adverse effects were that risk to become a reality.

143. However, it is also clear from the case-law [...] that a preventive measure cannot properly be based on a purely hypothetical approach to the risk, founded on mere conjecture which has not been scientifically verified.

144. Rather, it follows from the Community Courts' interpretation of the precautionary principle that a preventive measure may be taken only if the risk, although the reality and extent thereof have not been 'fully' demonstrated by conclusive scientific evidence, appears nevertheless to be adequately backed up by the scientific data available at the time when the measure was taken.

[...]

146. The precautionary principle can therefore apply only in situations in which there is a risk, notably to human health, which, although it is not founded on mere hypotheses that have not been scientifically confirmed, has not yet been fully demonstrated.

[...]

148. Consequently, in a case such as this, the purpose of a risk assessment is to assess the degree of probability of a certain product or procedure having adverse effects on human health and the seriousness of any such adverse effects.

[...]

149. As the Commission stated in its Communication on the Precautionary Principle, which may be taken as a codification of the law as it stood at the time when the contested regulation was adopted (see

---

[38] Council Regulation (EC) 2821/98 amending, as regards withdrawal of the authorisation of certain antibiotics, Directive 70/224/EEC concerning additives in feeding stuffs [1998] OJ L351/4.

paragraph 123 above), risk assessment includes for the competent public authority, in this instance the Community institutions, a two-fold task, whose components are complementary and may overlap but, by reason of their different roles, must not be confused. Risk assessment involves, first, determining what level of risk is deemed unacceptable and, second, conducting a scientific assessment of the risks.

150. As regards the first component, it is appropriate to observe that it is for the Community institutions to define, observing the applicable rules of the international and Community legal orders, the political objectives which they intend to pursue within the parameters of the powers conferred on them by the Treaty [...]

151. In that regard, it is for the Community institutions to determine the level of protection which they deem appropriate for society [...]

152. Although they may not take a purely hypothetical approach to risk and may not base their decisions on a 'zero-risk', the Community institutions must nevertheless take account of their obligation under the first subparagraph of [ex-]Article 129(1) of the Treaty to ensure a high level of human health protection, which, to be compatible with that provision, does not necessarily have to be the highest that is technically possible...

154. As regards the second component of risk assessment, [...]

155. a scientific risk assessment must be carried out before any preventive measures are taken.

[...]

157. [...] [W]hen a scientific process is at issue, the competent public authority must, in compliance with the relevant provisions, entrust a scientific risk assessment to experts who, once the scientific process is completed, will provide it with scientific advice.

[...]

159. ...[I]n order to fulfil its function, scientific advice on matters relating to consumer health must, in the interests of consumers and industry, be based on the principles of excellence, independence and transparency.

[...]

162. [...] [Where such] experts carry out a scientific risk assessment, the competent public authority must be given sufficiently reliable and cogent information to allow it to understand the ramifications of the scientific question raised and decide upon a policy in full knowledge of the facts. Consequently, if it is not to adopt arbitrary measures, which cannot in any circumstances be rendered legitimate by the precautionary principle, the *competent public authority must ensure that any measures that it takes*, even preventive measures, *are based on as thorough a scientific risk assessment as possible*, account being taken of the particular circumstances of the case at issue. Notwithstanding the existing scientific uncertainty, the scientific risk assessment must enable the competent public authority to ascertain, on the basis of the best available scientific data and the most recent results of international research, whether matters have gone beyond the level of risk that it deems acceptable for society. That is the basis on which the authority must decide whether preventive measures are called for.

163. Furthermore, a scientific risk assessment must also enable the competent authority to decide, in relation to risk management, which measures appear to it to be appropriate and necessary to prevent the risk from materialising.

Note the similarity of the CFI's explanation of the precautionary principle to that in the Commission's Communication on the precautionary principle, examined already,[39] on which the Court effectively

---

[39] See n 27 above and accompanying text.

relies to generate its review test, placing a premium on risk assessment and scientific evaluation and also perpetuating the conceptual problems and challenges of that approach to the principle. This doctrinal reaction and development is a good example of a guidance or policy document—here the Communication—informing and provoking legal developments. This is a common phenomenon in environmental law, as explored in Section 2. It also demonstrates a broader point about the nature of the review being undertaken here and the role of the courts in reviewing and limiting administrative decision-making, as Fisher points out.

Elizabeth Fisher, *Risk Regulation and Administrative Constitutionalism*
(Hart Publishing 2007) 239

[With cases concerning the precautionary principle after the Commission's Communication, including *Pfizer*,] there has been a shift from understanding the principle and risk evaluation in [Deliberative-Constitutive] terms to understanding them in [Rational-Instrumental] terms. The focus is less upon deliberative problem-solving than upon accurate analysis and the application of methodology. This shift is consistent with more general regulatory developments at the Community level and has meant that the courts have gone from understanding precautionary reasoning as broad ranging and deliberative to understanding it as an exception that operates in specific circumstances. Likewise, risk evaluation has [broadly] gone from being understood as being an analytical-deliberative process to being divided neatly into risk assessment and risk management.

Whilst the approach of the CFI to the precautionary principle marks a significant legal shift in *Pfizer*, it is noteworthy that the Court ultimately held that the Regulation at issue was validly based on the precautionary principle. This was despite scrutinizing the relevant scientific evidence and risk assessment closely and finding it wanting in some respects. The Court was looking for a 'manifest error of assessment' on the part of the Commission's decision-making process, as well as inadequate scientific assessment, thereby according a margin of discretion to the EU institutions in their assessment and decision-making, and softening the intensity of the Court's oversight.

The reasoning in *Pfizer*, or similar reasoning, has been applied in a number of other cases challenging EU measures, mostly also ultimately deferential to the EU institutions in the discretion that they can exercise on the basis of the precautionary principle,[40] despite the rigour of the test of adequate scientific evidence and risk assessment requirements set out in *Pfizer*. A notable exception is *Artegodan*,[41] in which the CFI found that there was no new scientific evidence on the basis of which the Commission could withdraw marketing authorization for medicinal anti-obesity products—the precautionary principle could not be relied on to justify such an action; the legal conditions for doing so had not been met.

The review test generated in *Pfizer* has also been applied to scrutinize Member State action based on the precautionary principle, when this relevantly falls within the scope of EU law. There have been a series of cases in which Member States have sought to justify infringements of Article 34 TFEU on public health grounds, claiming reliance on the precautionary principle. As indicated in the previous sub-section, the ECJ has used the precautionary principle to inform the legal tests used

---

[40] See, for example, Case T-475/07 *Dow AgroSciences Ltd v Commission* (ECJ 9 September 2011); Case T-71/10 *Xeda* (General Court, 19 January 2012); cf Case T-392/02 *Solvay Pharmaceuticals BV v Council* [2004] ECR II-4555.

[41] Joined Cases T-74/00, T-76/00, T-83/00 to T-85/00, T-132/00, T-137/00, T-141/00 *Artegodan v Commission* [2002] ECR II-4945.

to determine whether Member States are properly derogating from EU free movement rules, including by informing the test of proportionality. But, as *Pfizer* showed, the precautionary principle does not just grant an area of unrestrained policy discretion, it also requires certain conditions to be met for its application, generating its own test of review. This doctrinal development, explicitly based on the precautionary principle can be seen in *Commission v Denmark* and a series of challenges to Member State measures following it.[42] At issue was the Danish administrative practice of banning nutrient-enriched foods lawfully marketed or produced in other Member States unless they met a need in the Danish population. This infringed Article 34 TFEU, and the Danish government sought to justify this on public health grounds (under Article 36 TFEU) in light of the precautionary principle, since the risks of overexposure to vitamins and minerals were uncertain and so danger to human health could not be excluded.

Case C-192/01 *Commission v Denmark*
[2003] ECR I-9693 para 48

48. A decision to prohibit marketing, which indeed constitutes the most restrictive obstacle to trade in products lawfully manufactured and marketed in other Member States, can only be adopted if the real risk alleged for public health appears sufficiently established on the basis of the latest scientific data available at the date of the adoption of such decision. In such a context, the object of the risk assessment to be carried out by the Member State is to appraise the degree of probability of harmful effects on human health from the addition of certain nutrients to foodstuffs and the seriousness of those potential effects.

The Court concluded that the contested Danish practice, which systematically prohibited the marketing of all enriched foods without distinguishing between them according to the particular vitamins and minerals added or according to the level of public risk that their addition might pose, failed the test of adequate scientific evidence generated by the precautionary principle, since no adequate risk assessment was carried out. This failure informed the proportionality inquiry, thereby vitiating reliance on Article 36—it could not be said that the practice was 'necessary' for the purpose of protecting public health. The layers of reasoning here are again a bit complicated to follow, demonstrating the doctrinal difficulty associated with giving a legally identifiable role to a policy principle focused on scientific uncertainty, whilst also highlighting the detailed EU law context within which this legal role for the precautionary principle sits.

It is also noteworthy that there is limited deference given to Denmark—a Member State—in relation to its failure to conduct adequate scientific risk assessments in this case. This contrasts with *Pfizer* where an EU measure was under review. Do you think there is a justifiable reason for this perceived distinction in judicial treatment of precautionary measures?

The special case of the integration principle and sustainable development: Article 11 TFEU

The integration principle in Article 11 TFEU—requiring that 'environmental protection requirements' be integrated into all areas of EU policy, particularly with a view to promoting sustainable development—has been instrumental in extending the legal roles of Article 191(2) environmental principles to other policy areas in the Treaty. It has thus legally integrated (at least) the areas of public

---

[42] For example, Case C-24/00 *Commission v France* [2004] ECR I-1277; Case C-41/02 *Commission v Netherlands* [2005] ECR I-11375.

health and agriculture with that of the environment,[43] by extending its binding policy principles to have legal functions in constraining and interpreting measures in those other policy areas. There has also been a suggestion in one case—*Commission v Sweden*—that a stand-alone argument based on the integration principle might be possible to challenge EU measures in non-environmental policy fields for their compliance with environmental protection requirements, including the environmental principles in Article 191(2).[44] But note that, while such a broad concept of justiciability for the integration principle could introduce wide-scale review and interpretation of EU measures on environmental grounds, this has not yet occurred.

The integration principle has also had a different kind of legal effect in EU law, expanding the areas of policy over which the EU institutions have competence to legislate. This was seen in the *Environmental Crime* case,[45] in which the ECJ found that the (then) Community institutions should have introduced a measure concerning the enforcement of environmental law through criminal measures under the environmental title of the (then) EC Treaty. This was despite criminal law being a matter traditionally reserved for Member State action, and was because environmental protection was a 'fundamental' objective of the Community, as emphasized by the integration principle.[46] The integration principle was effectively relied on to accrue more policy power to the EU institutions.[47]

These are again very EU law-specific legal roles for the integration principle, and they contrast with other versions of an environmental 'integration principle', particularly at the international level. In international instruments, such as the Rio Declaration, the integration principle refers to a broader idea that 'environmental protection shall constitute an integral part of the development process and cannot be considered in isolation from it'.[48] On other similarly broad interpretations, which identify the integration principle as a core idea of sustainable development, the principle requires that economic and environmental (and sometimes social) considerations be integrated in decision-making, which implies more balance between these different components of sustainable development. Similarly, the integration principle might refer to the necessity to integrate the principle of inter-generational equity and the acceptance of limits on exploitation and consumption into individual as well as public choices.[49] These different versions of the principle all say something about 'integrating' environmental considerations into other policies and decision-making, but they also show that there are various integration principles and any legal formulation or role for the principle is thus contingent on the particular legal setting in which it is implicated. This is seen particularly in EU law, where the Article 11 integration principle is very much concerned with issues of EU competence and how it is shaped, legally constrained and even expanded.

At the same time, like various international versions of the principle suggested here, the EU version of the integration principle ties into the concept of sustainable development, since Article 11 prescribes integrating environmental protection requirements into other EU policies particularly 'to promote sustainable development'. The EU has a core commitment to sustainable development, as seen in Article 3(3) TEU, which establishes sustainable development as a (if not the) central goal of the EU and its internal market, where EU sustainable development is 'balanced economic growth and price stability, a highly competitive social market economy, aiming at full employment and social progress, and a high level of protection and improvement of the quality of the environment.' This concept of sustainable development puts environmental considerations as equivalent priorities to economic success and social progress. In support of this Treaty imperative, the EU has an extensive sustainable development policy agenda—as explained in Chapter 12—which is reflected

---

[43] See *Artegodan* (n 41) and Question 3 in the Further Reading and Questions section.
[44] Case T-229/04 *Sweden v Commission* [2007] ECR II-2437.
[45] Case C-176/03 *Commission v Council (Environmental Crime)* [2005] 3 CMLR 20.   [46] Ibid, para 42.
[47] Cf Case C-440/05 *Commission v Council (Ship–Source Pollution)* [2008] 1 CMLR 22.
[48] Rio Declaration, Principle 4.   [49] See, for example, Tarlock (n 10).

in its 2006 EU Sustainable Development Strategy,[50] subsequently reviewed and reaffirmed by the European Council in 2009.[51] The Strategy manifests in all manner of new legislative initiatives, from the EU 2008 Climate and Energy Package,[52] to the promotion of clean and energy-efficient road transport vehicles as part of a 'Green Transport Package',[53] amongst many examples. Further, key EU environmental legislative measures either reflect or have been updated to further sustainable development goals—the revised Waste Framework Directive 2008, with its focus on promoting the life-cycles of resources and products,[54] and the new Industrial Emissions Directive, consolidating a range of key EU pollution control measures with a greater emphasis on promoting clean industry,[55] are both examples of this.

However, in doctrinal terms, Article 11's reference to promoting sustainable development has not had any notable legal effects in terms of judicial reasoning or legal actions brought to confirm or interpret its meaning. At most, it might be said that it has an evolving albeit ill-defined legal role. Strong statements have been made that it is a 'fundamental concept of environmental law', deriving from the international sustainable development agenda, which finds specific expression in Article 11.[56] And that it is an EU objective of such importance (including sustainable development of 'Europe, and even of the Earth') that the other EU principles 'framing environmental law' are suggested to take on ever-increasing importance in the future of EU law.[57] In the *Environmental Crime* case, Advocate-General Ruiz-Jarabo Colomer describes sustainable development differently again, as a '*legal interest* the protection of which inspires other [EU] policies, a protective activity which may be clarified, furthermore, as an essential objective of the [EU] system'.[58] What these various statements indicate about the doctrinal influence of sustainable development in EU law terms is (as yet) uncertain, but they do indicate that the overarching nature of sustainable development, and its connection to the international sustainable development agenda, gives this 'principle' a different complexion in EU law. Other cases also highlight the definitional ambiguity of the principle, which is not surprising considering the range of definitions and interpretations to which it gives rise.[59]

Concluding remarks

In *Artegodan*, considered in this section, the CFI boldly stated that the precautionary principle is a 'general principle of EU law' (as other principles of EU law such as equal treatment, legitimate expectations and proportionality are described), which requires 'competent authorities to take appropriate measures to prevent specific potential risks to public health, safety and the environment, by giving precedence to the requirements related to the protection of those interests over economic

---

[50] European Council, 'Review of the EU Sustainable Development Strategy (EU SDS)—Renewed Strategy', 10917/06; see Maria Lee, 'Sustainable Development in the EU: The Renewed Sustainable Development Strategy 2006' (2007) 9 Env LR 41.

[51] Commission, 'Mainstreaming sustainable development into EU policies: 2009 Review of the European Union Strategy for Sustainable Development' COM (2009) 400 final.

[52] <http://ec.europa.eu/environment/climat/climate_action.htm> accessed 7 February 2013. See further, Chapter 15.

[53] <http://ec.europa.eu/transport/strategies/2008_greening_transport_en.htm> accessed 7 February 2013.

[54] See Chapter 16.   [55] See Chapter 17.

[56] Case C-371/98 *R v Secretary of State for the Environment, Transport and the Regions ex parte First Corporate Shipping* [2000] ECR I-9235, Opinion of AG Leger, para 56.

[57] Case C-277/02 *EU-Wood-Trading v Sonderabfall-Management-Gesellschaft Rheinland-Pfalz* [2004] ECR I-11957, Opinion of AG Leger, para 9.

[58] Case C-176/03 *Commission v Council (Environmental Crime)* [2005] 3 CMLR 20, Opinion of AG Colomer, para 59.

[59] See, for example, Case C-91/05 *Commission v Council (Small Weapons)* [2008] 3 CMLR 5; cf Case C-371/98 *R v Secretary of State for the Environment, Transport and the Regions ex parte First Corporate Shipping* [2000] ECR I-9235, Opinion of AG Leger.

interests [...] in *all their spheres of activity*'.[60] However, this isolated reference does not reflect the more piecemeal, incremental, and multi-faceted developments of environmental principles in EU law, as demonstrated by the finding in *Artegodan* itself. Environmental principles have a range of legal roles and manifestations in EU law, often highly contingent on the specific EU law questions at issue and varying between different environmental principles. This demonstrates that the policy ideas reflected in environmental principles do not translate directly into legally binding or programmatic obligations in EU law, despite their presence in the EU Treaties. The legal accommodation of these binding policy ideas in this context is more nuanced and doctrinally specific. As ever, the devil is in the detail. With this introduction to environmental principles and their manifestation in EU environmental law in mind, keep an eye out for the kinds of legal roles that principles are playing in various cases and EU law developments as you study other aspects of environmental law, and consider how different environmental principles are shaping, and being defined by, legal issues and disputes.

FURTHER READING AND QUESTIONS

1. To what extent do environmental principles unify EU environmental law?

2. Another case in which a free-standing argument based on the precautionary principle was unsuccessful, similar to *Monsanto Agricoltura Italia*, is Joined Cases C-439/05 P and C-454/05 P *Land Oberösterreich v Commission* [2007] 3 CMLR 52 (see also the decision of the CFI: Joined Cases T-366/03 and T-235/04 *Land Oberösterreich and Austria v Commission* [2005] ECR II-4005). Consider in particular Advocate-General Sharpston's opinion, especially at paragraph 145. What was it about the legal questions involved in this case that made the precautionary principle irrelevant?

3. For examples of how environmental principles—the integration principle and precautionary principle in particular—have been used to interpret EU legislation based on areas of competence beyond the environmental title of the Treaty (Title XX), see Case C-513/99 *Concordia Bus Finland Oy Ab v Helsingin Kaupunki and HKL-Bussiliikenne* [2002] ECR I-7213; Case C-236/01 *Monsanto Agricoltura Italia* [2003] ECR I-8105; Case T-229/04 *Sweden v Commission* (ECJ 11 July 2007). In the latter two cases, how is the precautionary principle being used in different ways to interpret provisions of these regulatory schemes involving the approval of genetically modified organisms and pesticides for release and use? What does the use of environmental principles in relation to the different policy areas in these cases (transport, the internal market, and agriculture respectively), which extend beyond Title XX on environmental policy, tell you about the demarcation of 'environmental' issues in EU law?

4. Does the CFI's treatment of the precautionary principle in *Pfizer* elucidate the meaning of the principle helpfully? How tied up with EU law doctrine—in particular, in relation to questions of proportionality and the review test of manifest error of assessment—is the Court's reasoning involving the precautionary principle in this case? What does this tell you about the legal roles taken on by environmental principles?

5. Consider other Article 34 TFEU cases in which environmental principles have been used to test and sanction Member State action, which pursues environmental or public health aims but otherwise unlawfully interferes with the free movement of goods—for example, Case C-473/98 *Kemikalienspektionen v Toolex Alpha* [2000] ECR I-5681; Case C-379/98 *PreussenElektra v Schhleswag* [2001] ECR I-2099 (including the opinion of Advocate-General

---

[60] *Artegodan* (n 41) para 184.

Jacobs); Case C-219/07 *Nationale Radd van Dierenwerkers en Liefhebbers* [2008] OJ C209/11. How have environmental principles shaped the EU rule of reason or other Article 34 TFEU exceptions in these cases? Are the cases doctrinally convincing or are they more pragmatic? How have the doctrinal roles of environmental principles in these cases evolved over time?

6. For further reading on environmental principles in EU law, see Eloise Scotford, 'Mapping the Article 174(2) Case Law: A First Step to Analysing Community Environmental Law Principles' (2008) 8 Yearbook of European Environmental Law 1; Chris Hilson, 'Rights and Principles in EU Law: A Distinction without Foundation?' (2008) 15 Maastricht Journal of European and Comparative Law 193.

1.4 LEGAL ROLES OF ENVIRONMENTAL PRINCIPLES IN UK LAW

In light of the EU developments in Section 1.3, there are legal roles for environmental principles in UK law to the extent that EU doctrine concerning principles binds or implicates Member State action. Thus, Directives interpreted by the ECJ in light of the precautionary principle or polluter pays principle would need to be understood similarly in their implementation in UK law. A good example of this is seen in the case of *Downs v Secretary of State for Environment, Food and Rural Affairs*, where UK action governed by the EU Plant Products Directive was found to be inadequate for failing to take all necessary steps to avoid the risk of harm of a pesticide before approving it, as required by the precautionary principle, in light of 'solid evidence' raising doubt as to its safety.[61] Similarly, unilateral action by the UK to derogate from or infringe internal market rules on environmental or public health grounds will be sanctioned and constrained by compliance with environmental principles in some cases, as in *Walloon Waste* and *Commission v Denmark*.[62] More broadly, any implementation or manifestation of environmental principles in EU legislative measures will filter down into UK law as those measures are transposed—this is the very point of environmental principles guiding EU environmental policy in Article 191 TFEU—and this may happen across more policy areas than narrowly-defined environmental issues as the integration principle in Article 11 takes effect.

However, beyond these EU law effects in UK law, there are to date minimal legal roles for environmental principles in UK law, and English law in particular. Article 191(2)'s prescription to base EU environmental policy on its set of principles is not directly effective in EU law terms, imposing no directly enforceable legal obligations on state actors within Member States, short of legislative action first being taken by EU institutions.[63] Even where environmental principles are explicitly included in EU secondary legislation, their legal impact in UK law would ultimately depend on UK legal doctrine and the legal question at issue. Since environmental principles are by nature general and policy-directing, their manifestations in EU legislation (as seen in Section 1.3) tend to be as legislative objectives or matters to be taken into account, or acted in accordance with, in fulfilling certain more specific obligations. Implemented in UK law, the legal impacts of such EU requirements would most likely manifest in public law disputes relating to failure to take the principles into account as relevant material considerations in environmental decision-making,[64] or in arguments relying on the principles to construe other more specific and contested provisions. Examples of the latter type of case are seen in this section in relation to the precautionary principle and polluter pays principle.

---

[61] *Downs v Secretary of State for Environment, Food and Rural Affairs* [2008] EWHC 2666 (Admin), [2009] Env LR 19 [23], applying the CFI's reasoning in Case T-229/04 *Sweden v Commission* [2007] ECR II-2437. Note that the finding of 'solid evidence' was overturned on appeal: *Secretary of State for Environment, Food and Rural Affairs v Downs* [2009] EWCA Civ 664; [2009] Env LR 19.

[62] Cf *R (Sinclair Collins) v Secretary of State for Health* [2011] EWCA Civ 437, [2012] QB 394.

[63] *R v Secretary of State for Trade and Industry, ex p Duddridge* [1996] 2 CMLR 361 (CA) paras 17–21.

[64] See Section 4.3 of Chapter 7.

In relation to the former type of case, any judicial review undertaken by UK courts to enforce a public law obligation to take into account an environmental principle would likely be quite light-touch, considering the lack of technical expertise of judges in environmental and scientific matters. In addition, any close, substantive consideration of whether environmental principles have been properly considered by decision-makers would involve something very like merits review, with which judges and UK public law doctrine alike are uncomfortable. Thus, how a general principle might work as a material consideration is not straightforward. This was seen in a related context concerning the central 'objectives' of the EU Waste Framework Directive. Whilst not environmental principles, these waste objectives are similarly general concepts that express desired policy outcomes. They can be seen as an expression of the preventive principle, and were made binding on Member States under Article 4 of the former Waste Directive 75/442/EEC[65] (as amended, and relevantly transposed into UK law by secondary legislation):[66]

> Member States shall take the necessary measures to ensure that waste is recovered or disposed of without endangering human health and without using processes or methods which could harm the environment, and in particular:
>
> - without risk to water, air, soil and plants and animals,
> - without causing a nuisance through noise or odours,
> - without adversely affecting the countryside or places of special interest.

In attempting to determine the legal relevance of these obligatory EU waste objectives in relation to decisions by relevant English authorities, Maurice Kay J in *R (Murray) v Derbyshire County Council* held that 'it does seem a little odd that obligations arising from supra national negotiations and expressed in apparently strong language are reduced in national implementation to material considerations of unquantifiable weight'.[67] He thought that they should have some greater overriding legal weight in public law terms. On appeal, however, the approach of the Court of Appeal was more nuanced.

R (Thornby Farms Ltd) v Daventry DC
[2002] EWCA Civ 31 para 53 (Pill LJ)

> 53. An objective in my judgment is something different from a material consideration. I agree [...] that it is an end at which to aim, a goal. The general use of the word appears to be a modern one. In the 1950 edition of the Concise Oxford Dictionary the meaning now adopted is given only a military use: 'towards which the advance of troops is directed'. A material consideration is a factor to be taken into account when making a decision, and the objective to be attained will be such a consideration, but it is more than that. An objective which is obligatory must always be kept in mind when making a decision even while the decision maker has regard to other material considerations. Some decisions involve more progress towards achieving the objective than others. On occasions, the giving of weight to other considerations will mean that little or no progress is made. I accept that there could be decisions affecting waste disposal in which the weight given to other considerations may produce a result which involves so plain and flagrant a disregard for the objective that there is a breach of obligation. However, provided the objective is kept in mind, decisions in which the decisive consideration has not been the contribution they make to the achievement of the objective may still be lawful. I do not in any

---

[65] See now art 13 of the Directive 2008/98/EC on waste, discussed further in Chapter 16.
[66] Former Waste Management Licensing Regulations 1994, SI 1994/1056, sch 4(4).
[67] [2001] Env LR 26 (QB) para 14.

event favour an attempt to create a hierarchy of material considerations whereby the law would require decision makers to give different weight to different considerations.

In the result, the Court saw no reason to overturn the decisions under review, including planning permission by a local authority to extend a landfill site:[68]

A council with the [Article 4] objectives well in mind may still grant a permission for the reasons given in the Director [of Environmental Services'] report. This modest extension of landfill is not so contrary to the achievement of the objective that Derbyshire [County Council] were obliged to refuse permission. The discretion available to them permitted them to take a broader view than merely to ask which of two possible outcomes contributes more to the objective. The obligation is not overriding in that sense.

This case shows that, even with greater weight given to general environmental protection objectives in applicable EU legislation, English public law doctrine is unlikely to lead to the overturning of administrative decision-making for failure to comply with those objectives, at least in the absence of their 'plain and flagrant disregard'. Despite this limitation, there are some indications in decided cases that English courts are willing to engage with legal arguments based on environmental principles, although overall the tendency is one of judicial reluctance to engage with matters perceived to be policy issues as well as deference to the judgment of public decision-makers.

Precautionary principle

Despite largely dismissive responses by English courts to arguments based on the precautionary principle—*R v Leicester City Council and others, ex parte Blackfordby and Boothorpe Action Group Ltd* is an example[69]—some cases have acknowledged that the principle might have a doctrinal role in reviewing UK administrative decision-making, but not in general terms. Thus, in *R(Amvac Chemical) v Secretary of State for Environment, Food and Rural Affairs*, Crane J was willing to review a decision suspending regulatory approval of a particular pesticide on the basis of its compliance with the precautionary principle, but only if the governmental decision-maker had purported to apply the precautionary principle 'as a term of art or any settled, specific or identifiable mechanism or methodology'.[70] Since the Secretary of State had not sought to rely on the principle, there was no reason to examine the appropriateness of the risk assessment undertaken, although Crane J also found that there was 'at least so far—no settled, specific or identifiable mechanism of risk assessment in the field of pesticide approval' that the claimant could rely on to challenge the regulatory suspension on this ground.[71] This case mirrors the approach under EU law—there is no free-standing ground to test the legality of public action on the basis of the precautionary principle, but there is scope for introducing legal tests on that basis if discretion is purportedly exercised on the basis of the principle (albeit that this will be less common in UK law due to the lack of any national binding policy prescription to do so).

Another example of how the precautionary principle has been used in English judicial reasoning is in an interpretive sense in the context of a planning policy document that incorporated the principle explicitly. In *R (Thomas Bates) v Secretary of State for Transport, Local Government and the Regions*, Harrison J considered an appeal against a refusal to grant planning permission for a property

---

[68] [2002] EWCA Civ 31, para 64.

[69] [2001] Env LR 2 (an argument based on the precautionary principle was 'briefly advanced and again plucked out of the air in the course of oral argument, that the decision was *Wednesbury* unreasonable in its application of the principle'). See also *Duddridge* (n 63).

[70] [2002] ACD 34, para 86.   [71] Ibid, para 84.

development on the grounds that it posed too high a flood risk. As part of his reasoning, Harrison J considered Planning Policy Guidance 25 (as it then was), which constituted a relevant material consideration in this planning decision and set out a 'sequential test' for analysing the suitability of sites vulnerable to flooding, and also relied on the precautionary principle. In determining how the policy's sequential test for flood-risk development sites should apply, Harrison J held that:[72]

> The guidance in PPG 25 relating to the issue of flood risk is that planning authorities should apply the precautionary principle which requires a risk-based search sequence to avoid such risk where possible and to manage it where that is not possible. It follows that the lowest risk option should be adopted when it is possible to do so.

Whilst the decision in this case—overturning a planning consent refusal—ultimately rested on broader judicial review grounds, this interpretive role for the precautionary principle shows a different, marginal definition for precautionary principle in this planning context, and also indicates that the principle might have more of a legal role in English law, independent of EU law developments, if it were included in more domestic statutory and policy measures.

Polluter pays principle

Again there are no express references to the polluter pays principle in UK legislation, but there are notable statutory regimes and obligations that implement the polluter pays principle in different ways—including the contaminated land regime in Part IIA of the Environmental Protection Act 1990, and pollution control obligations in relation to waste management sites, including after they cease operation.[73] In relation to the interpretation and application such regimes, legal arguments based on the polluter pays principle have been less than successful to date in English courts. The *National Grid* case concerns the Part IIA regime for allocating liability for restoring contaminated land—covered in detail in Chapter 21. The Environment Agency had argued that the statutory regime, which imposes liability for cleaning up contaminated land on past polluters, should be interpreted on the basis of the polluter pays principle to extend to the successors-in-title of past polluters. The House of Lords rejected that argument.

R (National Grid Gas plc (formerly Transco plc)) v Environment Agency
[2007] UKHL 30, paras 32–33 (Lord Neuberger) (emphasis added)

> 32. The increasing awareness, during the last quarter of the previous century, of the seriousness and extent to which land had been contaminated by industrial processes, must inevitably have previously unanticipated consequences which are not only physical but also economic. The legislature has decided that the force of grievances such as those described in the previous paragraph is outweighed by the public and private interests in decontaminating land at the expense of the polluter, ie the person who contaminated it. Where the polluter has ceased to exist and the whole of its business, or at least the whole of its relevant business, has been acquired by another company, it might well appear to many people to be similarly justifiable, at least in some circumstances, if liability for decontamination was extended to apply to that other company. After all, by acquiring all the assets (or relevant assets) of the polluter, such a company could be said to be, at least in commercial terms, the successor of

---

[72] *R (Thomas Bates & Son Ltd) v Secretary of State for Transport, Local Government and the Regions* [2004] EWHC 1818 (Admin), [2005] 2 P & CR 11, para 23.

[73] See Chapter 16. Aftercare obligations also exist in relation to large industrial installations under the Industrial Emission Directive (see Chapter 17), carbon capture and storage sites, and to nuclear plants.

the polluter, or to stand in some respects in the shoes of the polluter. However, to other people, the imposition of such a liability might appear to be an unjustifiable and unfair extension of the principle that the polluter pays.

33. Whether, and, if so, in what circumstances and on what basis, it would be right to extend the concept of a polluter paying in such a way is a *matter of policy for the legislature, not for the courts*. The role of the courts is to interpret the relevant statutory provisions which the legislature has enacted, in order to determine whether they have that effect.

On the facts, it was found that the statutory successor-in-title company (National Grid) to the original polluter (Transco) was not relevantly implicated by the liability provisions of the Part IIA regime. To interpret the legislation in that way would involve 'redefining, rather than interpreting, the relevant statutory words', and the polluter pays principle was a matter of policy that was inappropriate for the courts to take into consideration in developing its reasoning. This case reflects Dworkinian ideas about legal principles and policy in its treatment of the polluter pays principle, but also shows why the polluter pays principle is not a 'legal principle' in the Dworkinian sense. Whereas Dworkin finds that legal principles legitimately guide judicial reasoning but matters of policy do not, this case acknowledges that the polluter pays principle reflects policy goals, which are properly left for the political branches of government to consider.

Using similar reasoning, the Court of Appeal has also rejected an argument based on the polluter pays principle that a waste operator should be prevented from disclaiming its pollution control obligations (including obligations to pay for remedial work necessitated by licence breaches) on becoming insolvent. This case is connected more closely to EU law interpretive roles for environmental principles, in that the waste management obligations being disclaimed by the insolvent company fulfilled permitting and environmental protection obligations under the Waste Framework Directive. However, Morritt LJ found that the polluter pays principle could not assist in interpreting the relevant English statutory provisions on the surrender of waste management licences, which were silent on cases of insolvency.

Re Celtic Extraction Ltd and Bluestone Chemical Ltd
[2001] Ch 475 490–91 (Morritt LJ)

There is nothing in the Directive to suggest that the 'polluter pays' principle is to be applied to cases where the polluter cannot pay so as to require that the unsecured creditors of the polluter should pay to the extent of the assets available for distribution among them. Yet this is the consequence of the argument for the Agency that the costs of compliance have priority over provable debts and that the assets of the company must be set aside to pay for future compliance with the terms of the licence before the company is dissolved.

Thus, overall, English judges to date to have not embraced 'environmental principles' as transformational ideas in judicial reasoning and environmental law doctrine, beyond their binding influence through EU law.

Sustainable development in UK law—legislative developments

Sustainable development is the most high profile environmental principle in UK law, which is increasingly incorporated in legislative form, usually as a consideration for regulators or decision-makers to take into account, either as a general aim or in relation to the exercise of particular powers. Thus, s 4 of the Environment Act 1995 provides that the principal aim and objective of the Environment Agency is to protect the environment and to contribute to sustainable development. Similarly, s 39(2) of the Planning and Compulsory Purchase Act 2004 provides that a 'person or body [with certain planning powers under the Act] must exercise the [relevant] function with the objective of contributing to the achievement of sustainable development'.[74] Section 4(1) of the Local Government Act 2000 puts an obligation on every local authority in England to 'prepare a strategy for promoting or improving the economic, social and environmental well-being of their area and contributing to the achievement of sustainable development in the United Kingdom.'

The first thing to note about such statutory references to sustainable development is that they operate at a level of broad generality. They also provide considerable leeway to the relevant public body in requiring it only to 'contribute' towards the achievement of sustainable development. This is not a very onerous obligation, and seems more aspirational than giving rise to identifiable legal obligations. However, it remains a legal duty. Second, combining such general duties with the definitional ambiguity of sustainable development as a concept,[75] which remains undefined in these statutory settings, again minimizes the extent to which these duties give rise to precise legal obligations that might be reviewable by a court.

However, wider statutory or policy context may help to refine and clarify the meaning of these general sustainable development duties. Thus, for example, s 39(1) of the Environment Act 1995 imposes a general duty upon the Environment Agency to have regard to likely costs and benefits of exercising its powers under the Act in considering whether or not, and how, to exercise such powers. Whilst this does not affect the Agency's overall obligation to contribute to the achievement of sustainable development,[76] it might suggest that the 'sustainable' aspect of its s 4 obligation is to be understood (at least? primarily?) in terms of economic costs.

An example of where the policy context of a sustainable development duty can shape its meaning is seen in relation to a far-reaching and ambitious Northern Irish statutory reference to sustainable development. This is found in the Northern Ireland (Miscellaneous Provisions) Act 2006, which imposes a general statutory duty on all Northern Ireland central and local government bodies to have regard to sustainable development. Section 25(1) provides that:[77]

> A public authority *must*, in exercising its functions, *act* in the way it considers best calculated *to contribute to the achievement of sustainable development* in Northern Ireland, except to the extent that it considers that any such action is not reasonably practicable in all the circumstances of the case.

However, despite this statutory duty, the Northern Irish government has since consulted on a draft Planning Policy Statement that seeks to prioritize economic considerations in planning applications, in some cases so that they outweigh environmental and social considerations.[78] This presents a definition of sustainable development, at least in the Northern Ireland planning context, which is at odds with most interpretations of sustainable development, which either promote environmental considerations or at least require a balance between economic, environmental, and social considerations (even though such a balance may be elusive in practical terms). On one view, similar economically-focused

---

[74] See also Water Industry Act 1991, ss 2(3)(e) and 27A(12); Greater London Authority Act 1999, ss 30(4) and (5); Transport Act 2000, s 207(2).
[75] See Section 1.   [76] Environment Act 1995, s 39(2).
[77] See also The Planning (Northern Ireland) Order 1991, art 10A.
[78] Department for Environment (Northern Ireland), *Draft PPS 24: Economic Considerations*, January 2011 (consultation period for this PPS ended on 6 May 2011).

planning policy developments were adopted in England in 2012, with a differently stated statutory sustainable development duty, or 'golden thread', framing the new English planning policy framework. This is discussed further in Section 2.3. By way of contrast, the planned Welsh Sustainable Development Bill aims to incorporate a legislative concept of sustainable development that will sit at the heart of all Welsh public decision-making, giving priority to living within the limits of the earth's resources, within an approach to sustain and improve people's quality of life, now and in the long term.[79] Another example of a statutory context that seems geared towards an environmentally-driven conception of sustainable development can be found in the Climate Change Act 1998, which sets binding carbon reduction commitments for the UK government up until 2050 and requires the government to adopt policies to meet those commitments.[80] In doing so, the relevant 'proposals and policies, taken as a whole, must be such as to contribute to sustainable development.'[81]

Other legislative incorporation of sustainable development may use a different form of words than a simple reference to 'sustainable development'. Such references can give further indications of the principle's meaning, and also show that sustainable development is not just a principle that exists in a general and overarching formulation, but it can also be implemented in different ways through the detail of environmental and other regulatory regimes.[82] An example is found in the following waste management regulation, which implements EU law obligations found in the Waste Framework Directive.[83]

Waste (England and Wales) Regulations 2011, Regulation 12(3)

(3) When considering the overall impacts mentioned in paragraph (2) [that is, overall impacts of the generation and management of the waste, to be considered in determining whether the waste hierarchy set out in (1) can be departed from], the following considerations must be taken into account—

   (a) the general environmental protection principles of precaution and sustainability;

   (b) technical feasibility and economic viability;

   (c) protection of resources;

   (d) the overall environmental, human health, economic and social impacts.

Even here, the requirement to take into account 'overall environmental, human health, economic and social impacts' does not give an indication of the priority to be given to these different considerations, often identified as elements of sustainable development, which also sit amongst a number of other relevant considerations. Establishing that this requirement (to consider aspects of sustainable development) has been breached would be a difficult task, particularly in light of the reasoning as to the legal effects of binding EU policy objectives on English administrative decision-making discussed in *Thornby*. The sustainable development considerations set out in the Waste Regulations are thus an obligatory guide to decision-making by waste authorities and operators, whilst also granting a degree of discretion due to the generality of their formulation and their breadth of meaning. Accordingly, this kind of statutory manifestation of sustainable development would likely be subject to only limited review and enforcement in English public law.

---

[79] <http://wales.gov.uk/docs/desh/publications/111201susdevdiscussionen.pdf>, accessed 7 February 2013. At the time of writing, a consultation on a White Paper relating to the Bill was underway, closing in March 2013.

[80] See Section 3.4 of Chapter 15.   [81] Climate Change Act 1998, s 13(3). See also s 58(2).

[82] For example, Sustainable Communities Act 2007.

[83] Directive 2008/98/EC, art 4(2). See further, Chapter 16.

In addition to the statutory manifestations of sustainable development considered here, there are important policy documents containing expressions of sustainable development and strategies to pursue sustainable development, which guide administrative decision-makers in England, particularly in the planning context. These policy instruments, and their legal effects, are considered in Section 2.3.

FURTHER READING AND QUESTIONS

1. For a case in which another environment principle—the 'principle of producer responsibility'—informs the interpretive reasoning of the English courts, see *R(Repic) v SS for Business, Enterprise and Regulatory Reform* [2009] EWHC 2015 (Admin), [2010] Env LR 24. Where does this principle come from, and how is it used to inform the reasoning of the High Court in this case? Why do you think the court is willing to consider this principle in its reasoning here, whereas it rejects the interpretive argument based on the polluter pays principle in *Transco*?

2. Might some environmental principles be able to take on further legal roles in English law? If so, which ones and how?

3. Is sustainable development a 'principle' that has legal consequences in English law? For further reading on sustainable development in UK legislation and its legal effects, see Andrea Ross, 'Why Legislate for Sustainable Development? An Examination of Sustainable Development Provisions in UK and Scottish Statutes' (2008) 20 JEL 35.

4. Can it be said that environmental principles are the jurisprudential foundation of English environmental law?

5. From your reading of EU and UK legal developments relating to environmental principles in this chapter, do you think that they are principles that translate directly from international law, or are they more independent phenomena within legal systems?

---

2 ENVIRONMENTAL POLICY

At its broadest, 'environmental policy' refers to a course of action adopted to secure, or that tends to secure, a state of affairs in relation to environmental matters that is conceived to be desirable.[84] In legal theory, and particularly in the work of Ronald Dworkin discussed so far, robust conceptual attempts have been made to separate such courses of action from law and legal decision-making—policy is preserved as the proper domain of politicians and governments, not judges and laws. Whatever the jurisprudential merits or disputes concerning this theoretical separation of matters of policy from matters of law, environmental law—in its typically messy and challenging way—reveals a picture of policy that is not so clear-cut. Policy is most definitely an important part of environmental law. This is so for two main reasons. First, there is a range of documents, strategies, and instruments that might fall under the general banner of environmental policy, which have a varying range of legal effects. These range from overarching policy papers and documents issued by central government that set the direction of environmental and planning regulation, to regulator-generated guidance for industry concerning their compliance with environmental regulation, to technical reference documents on

---

[84] Neil MacCormick, *Legal Reasoning and Legal Theory* (Clarendon Press 1994) 261.

best industrial practice generated at the EU level, to statutory guidance required by particular regimes (such as the land contamination regime) to fill in the detail of their operation. This range of 'policy' types shows that policy is not a monolithic and discrete concept when it comes to environmental law,[85] and that understanding its role in environmental law requires unravelling the concept of policy and examining more closely what role it is in fact playing in environmental law.

Second, while the role of many of these policy documents is to fill in the detail of how environmental regimes work in practice, this is often to the point that policy documents contain primary obligations that are to be enforced. This kind of operational role for policy shows that, in socio-legal terms and also in doctrinal terms, policy documents are doing the work of 'law', creating and containing legal obligations and regimes themselves. Legislation alone cannot always manage to do this, due to the high technical demands of some areas and the pace of change in technological processes and industrial practice. The nature and evolution of BAT Reference documents under the EU integrated pollution prevention and control regime provide a good example of this—under EU law, these guidance documents, which apply sector by sector, provide key references for determining whether industrial operators are meeting required technical standards of 'best available techniques' (BATs).[86]

That policy instruments contain regulatory obligations is also reflected in the reality that industrial operators, subject to environmental regulation, rely on guidance documents as their main source of information about the legal obligations with which they have to comply. Their compliance officers (who tend not to be lawyers) find statutory regimes complicated and often impenetrable, and so rely on government and regulator guidance to indicate how various regulatory regimes work, including on points of considerable legal complexity and contestation.[87] This kind of industrial practice enhances the legal relevance of guidance documents even further.

The important jurisprudential point to take away here is that environmental law, due to its challenging job of regulating complex environmental problems, itself has a complex legal nature. One way to understand this legal picture is to look at different kinds of policy that exist in UK environmental law and to examine the legal constraints that affect their formulation and the legal effects that they in turn have. Sections 2.1, 2.2, and 2.3 undertake such an analysis, with a focus on English law. Note that they do not present a perfect mapping of this area of environmental law, but they draw out some key differences and aspects of environmental policy, and their associated legal constraints and doctrinal effects. The overall point that policy is 'protean',[88] and a failure to define or characterize relevant policies in environmental law will lead to legal issues being overlooked or misunderstood.

It is important to note that theoretical accounts of the 'proper' role of policy within legal systems remain useful in critically evaluating the place of policy in environmental law, once the character of a relevant policy issue or instrument has been determined. In fact, it is in seeing how policy documents and instruments operate to supplement, implement, and otherwise shape environmental regimes in different ways that we can then ask questions about the constitutional consequences of those roles, and whether they are appropriate or problematic in any way. Thus *who* generates policy documents, how that process is *scrutinized* by democratically elected officials (or not), and the *legal effects* of such policies, including the extent to which they are *reviewable by courts*, are all relevant in considering the constitutional issues raised by different forms of policy in environmental law.

---

[85] Environmental law is not necessarily special in this respect. See, for example, the complex role of policy in immigration law: *R (Pankina) v Secretary of State for the Home Department* [2010] EWCA Civ 719, [2011] QB 376.

[86] See <http://eippcb.jrc.es/reference/> accessed 7 February 2013; see further, Chapter 17.

[87] UK Environmental Law Association, *The State Of UK Environmental Law in 2011–12: Is There A Case For Legislative Reform?* (Final Report, May 2012) 5, 9.

[88] *Bushell v Secretary of State for the Environment* [1981] AC 75 (HL) 98 (Lord Diplock).

2.1 HIGH-LEVEL GOVERNMENTAL ENVIRONMENTAL POLICY: LEGAL EFFECTS

Conventionally, high-level governmental and ministerial environmental policy originates within and at the discretion of government, and its content is thus politically devised. Such high-level policy refers to overarching strategic policy, which contains detailed plans for governmental action and its priorities and vision in different areas, setting the agenda for government and how it will deploy resources, change and reform existing systems, and also legislate. For example, the UK Government (in 2012) has policies that related to 'mainstreaming sustainable development',[89] securing the value of the natural environment,[90] energy and electricity market reform,[91] and planning nationally significant waste water infrastructure.[92] Often these policies are devised through the Green Paper/White Paper process, or they might be required under particular pieces of legislation.[93] Once established, such strategic policies can have legal effects, despite being politically derived (and motivated) in their agenda-setting function for government. This section considers such legal *effects*. Section 2.2 goes on to consider the legal *constraints* on the development of high-level governmental policy on environmental issues.

At a basic level, overarching governmental policy has legal effects in that it often leads to legal obligations being established. This is because environmental regimes, including legal obligations with which relevant people, bodies, and operators must comply, are introduced to pursue a relevant policy. Such regimes are usually in the form of legislation—primary and often secondary legislation—but can also be contained or elaborated in supporting policy and guidance documents. On the latter point, see further Section 2.3.

Further, the setting of policy might also have legal effects in and of itself. Such high-level policy does not generally bind the Government, in that it can resile from it. Further, the merits of its substance are beyond direct challenge in the courts,[94] and some areas of policy are found to be non-justiciable, such as military and defence matters and international relations.[95] Accordingly, high-level policy has no strictly binding effects in administrative law terms, and as a general rule is subject to only limited judicial review as to its lawful creation (although see Section 2.2)—this is for reasons of fundamental constitutional principle concerning the appropriate separation of powers between the executive and the courts.[96] However, high-level governmental policy can have some administrative law implications once published and even at preliminary stages of environmental policy development.

Two recent cases show these kinds of effects. In the first case, *Cala Homes (South) Limited v Secretary of State for Communities & Local Government*,[97] a Ministerial announcement concerning a prospective change in planning law was held to be a material consideration that was legally relevant to planning decision-making. The Secretary of State for Communities and Local Government had issued a statement confirming the Government's commitment to abolish Regional Spatial Strategies

---

[89] DEFRA, *Mainstreaming Sustainable Development: The Government's Vision and What this Means in Practice* (February 2011).

[90] HM Government, *The Natural Choice: Securing the Value of Nature* (The Stationery Office, London, June 2011).

[91] HM Government (DTI), *Meeting the Energy Challenge: A White Paper on Energy* (May 2007); HM Government (DECC), *Planning for Our Electric Future: A White Paper for Secure, Affordable and Low Carbon Electricity* (July 2011).

[92] HM Government (DEFRA), *National Policy Statement for Waste Water: A Framework Document for Planning Decisions on Nationally Significant Waste Water Infrastructure* (The Stationery Office, London, March 2012). Note that there are also EU policies on environmental issues, and these can overlap with and inform UK government policy development—see, for example, Commission, *Green Paper: Reform of Common Fisheries Policy*, COM (2009) 163 final.

[93] Thus, the *National Policy Statement for Waste Water* (n 92) was created and presented to Parliament pursuant to Planning Act 2008, s 5(9).

[94] *Bushell* (n 88).   [95] *R (Marchiori) v Environment Agency* [2002] EWCA Civ 3.

[96] See further, Richard Moules, *Environmental Judicial Review* (Hart Publishing 2011) 45–46.

[97] [2011] EWCA Civ 639, [2011] 2 EGLR 75. Extracted in Section 3.1 of Chapter 18.

(until then a key plank of the planning system, and the Government's first attempt to remove them had been overturned on judicial review), and setting out that it planned to do this by legislating in the form of the Localism Bill (now the Localism Act 2011). The Government's chief planning officer also wrote to all local planning authorities to the same effect, indicating that this planned change should be taken into consideration by planning decision-makers as relevant. Note that planning law is itself constituted by key policy documents as well as a complex legislative scheme—see further Section 2.3 and Chapter 18—but the case here concerns a *Ministerial* policy announcement about how this regime would change. The Court of Appeal held that the 'prospect of a change in planning policy is capable of being a material consideration', and so the Ministerial statement at issue had a legal impact in shaping the planning regime.[98]

The second case—*R (London Borough of Hillingdon) v Secretary of State for Transport*—is more cautious in its conclusions about the legal impacts of high-level policy, and also pragmatic about the processes of governmental policy development, but it indicates that in some cases high-level policy developments might restrain future government policy and action, if they would be unjustifiably inconsistent. Note there was also a legislative framework involved in this case—the Planning Act 2008, which applies to nationally significant infrastructure and requires the government to produce National Policy Statements (NPSs) in key infrastructure areas (here airports). However, it is Carnwath J's acknowledgement that an evolving policy environment might be significant enough, in some cases, to influence subsequent high-level policy choices and governmental action that is striking.

Hillingdon concerned the ongoing controversy on whether there should be a third runway at Heathrow Airport. It was a judicial review challenge to the then Labour Government's announcement to commit to a third runway, following a limited consultation exercise that expressly excluded climate change concerns from its remit. However, since a 2003 White Paper that had in principle backed a third runway, there had been considerable developments in the Government's climate change policy (as well as legislative commitments to meet ambitious climate change targets),[99] and the applicants in the case argued that such policy developments were relevant material considerations that had wrongfully not been taken into account. A key reason why the judicial review challenge was unsuccessful was its timing—the Government's decision still had to go through the legislatively prescribed airports NPS formulation process, which could allow climate concerns to be taken into account (and Carnwath J found that they should be). However, Carnwath J's reasoning also suggested that the kind of judicial review challenge brought in this case could succeed on different facts, even with its premature timing.

R (London Borough of Hillingdon) v Secretary of State for Transport
[2010] EWHC 626 (Admin), [2010] ACD 64 paras 69, 77 (Carnwath LJ) (emphasis added)

69. It is not simply the 'high-level' character of some of the policy judgments which limits the scope for review. I would also emphasise the preliminary nature of the decision. As I have said, any grounds of challenge at this stage need to seen in the context, not of an individual decision or act, but of a continuing process towards the eventual goal of statutory authorisation. A flaw in the consultation process should not be fatal if it can be put right at a later stage. There must be something not just 'clearly and radically wrong', but also such as to require the intervention of the court at this stage. Similarly,

---

[98] Ibid, para 25. It would however have been unlawful if the Ministerial direction had been to tell decision-makers to ignore the policies in the regional strategies altogether, or what weight they should give to the Government's proposed change. See further, Section 3.1 of Chapter 18.

[99] See Section 3.4 of Chapter 15.

failure to take account of material considerations is unlikely to justify intervention by the court if it can be remedied at a later stage. It *would be different if the failure related to what I described in argument as a 'show-stopper': that is a policy or factual consideration which makes the proposal so obviously unacceptable that the only rational course would be to abort it altogether without further ado* [...]

77. *However*, the claimants' submissions add up, in my view, to a powerful demonstration of the *potential significance of developments in climate change policy* since the 2003 White Paper [on the future of air transport]. They are clearly matters which will need to be taken into account under the new Airports [National Policy Statement (NPS)]. As has been seen, the Act specifically requires an explanation as to how the NPS takes account of the government's climate change policy. Whether or not these matters should have been treated as 'fundamentally' affecting the scope of the 2007 consultation [on local environmental impacts of a third runway at Heathrow] seems to me of little moment, given that they will be subject to further statutory consultation and consideration under the NPS procedure.

This case is also an example of how high-level policy can be legally constrained. Thus, any final decision on proceeding with a third runway (as an element of the Aviation NPS) would be limited by other previous developments in high-level policy, by the requirements of a statutory framework (the Planning Act 2008), and by consultation processes. These and other legal constraints on high-level environmental policy are examined in Section 2.2.

2.2 LEGAL CONSTRAINTS ON HIGH-LEVEL ENVIRONMENTAL POLICY

Section 2.1 considered how high-level governmental policy can legally constrain decision-making, but a more difficult issue is whether high-level governmental policy can also be shaped and constrained by law and legal doctrine. As indicated already, a basic constitutional principle, central to administrative law, is that evaluating the merits of high-level policy is beyond the proper scope of judicial review, and that its review on grounds of legality should be very limited. Lord Bridge explains this principle, and the reasons for it, in relation to national economic policy, but the reasoning applies equally to all high-level Government policy.

R v Secretary of State for the Environment, ex p Hammersmith and Fulham LBC
[1991] 1 AC 521 (HL) 597 (Lord Bridge)

The restriction which the [...] [common law] imposes on the scope of judicial review operates only when the court has first determined that the ministerial action in question does not contravene the requirements of the statute, whether express or implied, and only then declares that, since the statute has conferred a power on the Secretary of State which involves the formulation and the implementation of national economic policy and which can only take effect with the approval of the House of Commons, it is not open to challenge on the grounds of irrationality short of the extremes of bad faith, improper motive or manifest absurdity. Both the constitutional propriety and the good sense of this restriction seem to me to be clear enough. The formulation and the implementation of national economic policy are matters depending essentially on political judgment. The decisions which shape them are for politicians to take and it is in the political forum of the House of Commons that they are properly to be debated and approved or disapproved on their merits. If the decisions have been taken in good faith within the four corners of the Act, the merits of the policy underlying the decisions are not susceptible to review by the courts and the courts would be exceeding their proper function if they presumed to condemn the policy as unreasonable.

However, this seemingly bright line limit that prevents courts from reviewing the merits of high-level Government policy has been blurred by other cases and legal developments, which show that there are a number of ways in which high-level Government policy on environmental matters can be legally constrained. These include: (1) intensive judicial review, (2) statutory constraints, (3) EU law constraints, and (4) requirements of public consultation and participation. In some respects, environmental law is unique in the number and type of legal constraints that affect high-level policy, but these constraints have consequential effects for the English legal system more broadly by challenging doctrinal and constitutional understandings in public law. It should be noted that the kinds of constraints considered in this section in relation to high-level governmental policy show that the label 'high-level governmental policy' is itself somewhat misleading—there is no monolithic set of high-level policy instruments, but a range of ways in which such Government policy manifests and has legal roles in environmental law. Section 3 of Chapter 18 also maps the different roles that central government policy has in planning law, reinforcing the point that 'high-level policy' is too simple a label to reflect all the different types of policy that are part of the planning framework. Thus, it can be seen that broad constitutional distinctions about what responsibility courts or the elected government should have over high-level policy is insufficiently nuanced in the context of environmental law.

Intensive judicial review

In some cases, courts have undertaken intensive judicial review, applying judicial review principles broadly and purposively to extend 'legality' review to cover the substance of high-level policy decisions made by Government. Policy decisions made under a statutory power are particularly susceptible to this type of reasoning. As a matter of law, such policy must conform to the statutory frameworks under which it is made, but the requirements of that statutory framework are matters of interpretation for a court. If courts interpret such statutes purposively, or otherwise imaginatively, review of the 'legality' of policy decisions can extend to cover matters of substance (or the merits), which courts might discern as being statutorily required. Such interpretative reasoning, and consequently intensive judicial review, thus elides the public law distinction between legality and merits review.

One example of this kind of intensive review is the judicial review of the decision of the Secretary of State for Foreign and Commonwealth Affairs in the *Pergau Dam* case to support the building of a hydroelectric dam in Malaysia.[100] The case is commented on here by the then Treasury Solicitor, as an example of the courts' increasingly substantive review of government policy. This extract also starts by making the important point that all judicial review actions have a constraining effect on policy, since public acts subject to judicial review are policy decisions, or otherwise legal acts or administrative decisions that implement a relevant governmental policy.

AH Hammond, 'Judicial Review: the Continuing Interplay between Law and Policy'
(1998) PL 34, 34–35

Every application for judicial review, however routine, has some implication for policy, and for the extent to which policy can be created and exercised without restraint [...]

[100] *R v Secretary of State for Foreign Affairs, ex p The World Development Movement* [1995] 1 All ER 611 (QB).

There has been a general increase in the reach of judicial review [...]

Perhaps the most interesting of [the] cases [demonstrating this] was the challenge by the World Development Movement to the FCO in the *Pergau Dam* case, in which the power to be exercised by the Secretary of State was contained in section 1 of the Overseas Development and Co-operation Act 1980.

The challenge was on the footing that the project for which the financial assistance was granted (the Pergau Dam Hydroelectric Scheme) was 'uneconomic'; that it would not therefore genuinely promote development; that after it became clear that it was uneconomic, the true reason for continuing with the project was political. On behalf of the Crown, it was argued that the Secretary of State was entitled to take into account political considerations, but that he had concluded reasonably that the project was for a development purpose.

Counsel for the Crown had presented the case in terms of rationality: that the Secretary of State's decision that it was a developmental purpose was a reasonable one. The Court however decided that the question was rather one of legality: was the purpose in fact within the purposes permitted by the statute? Parliament could have intended that assistance should be given only to *sound* development projects. The evidence was that this was not such a project and the decision would be quashed.

The case was in some respects a 'hard' one on the facts. Even so it is interesting that in a case of this sort, where the power had been exercised on the face of it within the powers conferred by the statute—and where considerations of policy were present both in the interpretation of the statutory power and in dealing with the recipient country—the Court was prepared to construe the section purposively, so as in effect to add a criterion to those laid down on the face of the statute.

Hammond then goes on to point out the constitutional law consequences of intensive judicial review of high-level policy in environmental cases like *Pergau Dam*. Not only does it shift the balance of power between the courts and the executive, but it also exposes the reality that the constitutional balance between the arms of government is not a contest or fight for power but a symbiotic and (largely) constructive relationship.

Statutory constraints on high-level policy

As indicated in the previous section, governmental policy, including high-level policy, is often made under powers granted by statutes. Those statutes might not only empower the making of policy, but also require it, and set requirements or constraints as to how it should be formulated and what it should contain. An example is the formulation of a NPS (National Policy Statement) under the Planning Act 2008. NPSs are policy statements issued by the government to set out its objectives for developing nationally significant infrastructure in key sectors within transport, energy, water, and waste. The policies must contain certain elements—how the policy reflects government climate change and will contribute to sustainable development, how actual and projected capacity and demand have been taken into account, amongst other things. NPSs must also be formulated by a prescribed process, involving both public consultation and parliamentary scrutiny. This kind of formalized, democratic process is a long way from the pre-election policies of political parties, in relation to which politicians have complete discretion. In government, ministers and their departments are thus constrained in various respects as to the high-level policies they can produce. One consequence of having more 'legalized' policies is that they also have significant legal effects themselves, in public law terms, in shaping the decision-making to which they relate (for the example of NPSs, these in turn constrain individual decisions approving, amending, or rejecting plans for national infrastructure development).

Another prominent example of high-level policies being constrained by statute can be seen under the Climate Change Act 2008, which puts high-level policy relating to decarbonizing the UK economy (and all aspects of UK-based greenhouse gas (GHG) emitting activity) on a legislative footing. The overall legal impact of this Act has been questioned, since there are no explicit sanctions for a Government's failure to reach the (long-term) GHG emission reduction target set in the legislation—to reduce GHG emissions by 80%, against a 1990 baseline, by 2050—despite this being a legally binding obligation.[101] However, the Act has significant legal influence in shaping and constraining government climate change policy, since it gives a key role to the independent Climate Change Committee in advising the Government on matters under the Act, including on setting five year carbon budgets (which are enshrined in secondary legislation). Thus, even Cabinet decisions concerning the setting of these carbon budgets are made against a backdrop of statutory advice from the Climate Change Committee, and are arguably vulnerable to judicial review if they fail to depart from the advice of the Committee, expertly and properly prepared, including taking into account the broad range of matters listed in section 10(2).[102] This suggests a remarkable legal and constitutional situation, considering the political controversy around setting carbon plans, which have wide-ranging impacts on the UK economy and its industrial life, as well as its environment.

EU law constraints on high-level policy

There are also EU law constraints on high-level UK Government policy relating to the environment. EU law requirements: (1) shape the *substance* of particular strategic environmental policies; and (2) require general *environmental assessments* in relation to policies, when they are likely to have 'significant environmental effects'.

In relation to the first kind of EU law constraint, the UK is increasingly under obligations from EU law to establish certain types of national environment policy, and is legally directed to some extent as to their content. Thus, for example, the UK is required to devise river basin management plans under the Water Framework Directive,[103] and waste management and prevention programmes under the Waste Framework Directive.[104] These plans and programmes are key mechanisms by which the obligations of these EU Directives are implemented, and their substance must contain prescribed elements and also fulfil the objectives and obligations of these Directives more broadly. Beyond *requiring* particular policies to be created, EU law can also *constrain* the content of UK environmental policies in other ways. A good example can be seen in the Waste Framework Directive, in the form of the policy-directing 'waste hierarchy', set out here. The strongly prescriptive nature of this hierarchy implies that it imposes significant legal constraints—although the precise nature of these are somewhat unclear[105]—and that it applies to Member State governments and the EU institutions alike.

Council Directive 2008/98/EC of 19 November 2008 on Waste [2008] OJ L312/3 (Waste Framework Directive), Article 4 (emphasis added)

1. The following waste hierarchy *shall apply as a priority order in waste prevention and management legislation and policy*:

---

[101] Climate Change Act 2008, s 1. See further, Section 3.4 of Chapter 15.

[102] Climate Change Act 2008, ss 9 and 10.

[103] Council Directive 2000/66/EC of 23 October 2000 establishing a framework for the Community action in the field of water policy [2000] OJ L327/1, art 13. See further, Section 2 of Chapter 14.

[104] Council Directive 2008/98/EC of 19 November 2008 on waste (Waste Framework Directive) [2008] OJ L312/3, arts 28 and 29. See further, Section 2 of Chapter 16.

[105] See further, Chapter 16.

(a) prevention;

(b) preparing for re-use;

(c) recycling;

(d) other recovery (for example energy recovery);

(e) disposal.

2. When applying the waste hierarchy referred to in paragraph 1, Member States shall take measures to encourage the options that deliver the best overall environmental outcome [...]

Member States shall ensure that the development of waste legislation and policy is a fully transparent process, observing existing national rules about the consultation and involvement of citizens and stakeholders.

In relation to the second kind of EU law constraint, UK government policy may be subject to environmental assessment requirements under Directive 2001/42/EC on the assessment of the effects of certain plans and programmes on the environment (Strategic Environmental Assessment or 'SEA' Directive).[106] The SEA Directive requires an environmental assessment to be undertaken for any governmental plan or programme likely to have significant environmental effects. For this purpose, a 'plan or programme' is one that is 'subject to preparation and/or adoption by an authority at national, regional or local level or which [is] prepared by an authority for adoption, through a legislative procedure by Parliament or Government', and 'required by legislative, regulatory or administrative provisions'.[107] Thus, not all governmental policies will be captured by this environmental assessment requirement, but some high-level policies certainly will, including the NPSs for sectoral infrastructure development discussed already.

The full reach of this assessment obligation will depend particularly on the interpretation of the condition that a plan or programme is 'required by legislative [etc] provisions'.[108] It is yet to be seen how widely the key terms of the SEA Directive might be interpreted to impose legal limitations on strategic governmental policy in Member States, which could then be reviewable by a national or European court. However, early indications are that the Directive could have a wide-ranging influence on governmental policy. Thus, in *St Albans Council v Secretary of State for Communities and Local Government*, policies in the East of England Plan regional spatial strategy were quashed for failure to comply with the UK implementing legislation of the SEA Directive.[109]

Consultation and public participation requirements for high-level policy formulation

This category of legal constraints on high-level governmental policy overlaps with the previous two—a statutory framework that governs the formulation of a policy can require consultation or public participation, and such requirements are also included in the SEA Directive and other EU legislation[110]—but

[106] See further, Section 7 of Chapter 19, particularly in relation to the nature of the environmental assessment required under the SEA Directive.

[107] SEA Directive, art 2(a).

[108] For a narrow interpretation of this condition, see *Central Craigavon Limited v Department of the Environment for Northern Ireland* [2011] NICA 17, [2012] NI 60.

[109] *St Albans City and District Council v Secretary of State for Communities and Local Government* [2009] EWHC 1280 (Admin), [2010] JPL 70.

[110] SEA Directive, arts 6 and 8. See also European Parliament and Council Directive 2000/60/EC of 23 October 2000 establishing a framework for Community action in the field of water policy [2000] OJ L327/1, art 14.

there are other legal reasons for consultation and participation requirements in the process of formulating environmental policy. In fact, it is arguable that all high-level environmental policy should involve the public in its formulation, so that their views are taken into account to shape the final policy.[111]

First, full public consultation in relation to high-level environmental policy decisions is legally required when the government has promised this. Full consultation is not satisfied by consulting on narrow issues, nor can it be a box-ticking exercise that has no impact on the final policy. This was explained by Sullivan J in a controversial 2007 judicial review decision concerning the Government's plans announced in 2006 to support the building of new nuclear power plants. This Government policy statement came after a 2003 White Paper on energy policy, which had promised that there would be the 'fullest public consultation' before any decision was taken to support nuclear new build. A consultation had preceded the 2006 policy announcement, asking for views on 'particular questions the Government should consider when it re-examines the issues relating to possible nuclear new build', but critically *not* asking for views on whether nuclear new build should be supported at all.

R (Greenpeace) v Secretary of State for Trade and Industry
[2007] EWHC 311 (Admin) paras 48, 51, 116–17 (Sullivan J)

48. While the decision which is said to have broken the promise of 'the fullest public consultation' is fairly described as one which was dealing with a 'high-level, strategic issue', the promise itself was given at the highest level: in a Government White Paper. It would be curious, to say the least, if the law was not able to require the Government to honour such a promise, absent any good reason to resile from it.

[...]

51. [...] [Counsel for the defendant's] submission that the decision in the Energy Review 'that nuclear has a role to play in the future UK generating mix' was not a statutory decision, did not itself permit any new nuclear power station to be built and was but a step in the process of the formulation of Government policy, which was continuing, is true as far as it goes, but it ignores the fact that the decision is the critical stage in the formulation of Government policy in respect of new nuclear build. To use the defendant's own words: it opens the door, which had been left ajar in 2003 [and the 'policy' process will proceed to set up a conclusion on new nuclear build that will operate legally as a material consideration in planning inquiries into the construction of new nuclear power plants].

[...]

116. [In conclusion], the consultation exercise was very seriously flawed. ['Something] has gone clearly and radically wrong.' The purpose of the 2006 Consultation Document as part of the process of 'the fullest public consultation' was unclear. It gave every appearance of being an issues paper, which was to be followed by a consultation paper containing proposals on which the public would be able to make informed comment. As an issues paper it was perfectly adequate. As the consultation paper on an issue of such importance and complexity it was manifestly inadequate. It contained no proposals as such, and even if it had, the information given to consultees was wholly insufficient to enable them to make 'an intelligent response'. The 2006 Consultation Document contained no information of any substance on the two issues which had been identified in the 2003 White Paper as being of critical importance: the economics of new nuclear build and the disposal of nuclear waste.

117. [...] Elementary fairness required that consultees, who had been given so little information hitherto, should be given a proper opportunity to respond to the substantial amount of new material before

---

[111] See Chapter 7, Sections 2.3 and 3.3 on the significant role of public participation in environmental law.

any 'in principle' decision as to the role of new nuclear build was taken. There could be no proper consultation, let alone 'the fullest public consultation' as promised in the 2003 White Paper, if the substance of these two issues was not consulted upon before a decision was made. There was therefore procedural unfairness, and a breach of the claimant's legitimate expectation that there would be 'the fullest public consultation' before a decision was taken to support new nuclear build.

Note that Sullivan J first justifies why such high-level policy is reviewable by a court at all. His Honour acknowledges that:

in the absence of any statutory or other well-established procedural rules for taking such strategic decisions it may well be very difficult for a claimant to establish procedural impropriety. Similarly, given the judgmental nature of 'high-level, strategic' decisions it will be well-nigh impossible to mount a 'Wednesbury irrationality' challenge absent bad faith or manifest absurdity.

However, he also finds that such 'practical considerations do not mean that decisions such as those contained in the Energy Review are unreviewable by the courts simply because they are matters of "high policy"'.[112]

A more ambitious argument as to why the public should be fully consulted in relation to the formulation of any strategic UK environmental policy is that the Aarhus Convention, to which the UK is a signatory, requires this.[113] The Convention relevantly provides, in Article 7, that each Party to the Convention 'shall endeavour to provide opportunities for public participation in the preparation of policies relating to the environment'. The Aarhus Convention does not have directly binding force in UK law, but it is partially implemented through several EU Directives (including the SEA Directive), and it also constitutes persuasive authority in the application and development of English public law doctrine. In the latter sense, Sullivan J in *Greenpeace* indicated that a Government statement about the future of UK energy policy would infringe the Convention if it were not based on adequate public consultation.[114] As Sullivan J put it, '[w]hatever the position may be in other policy areas, in the development of policy in the environmental field consultation is no longer a privilege to be granted or withheld at will by the executive.'[115] This was particularly the case in relation to a decision as important as whether new nuclear build should be supported. Whilst this line of reasoning based on Aarhus was strictly obiter dicta, Sullivan J still drew on it to support his conclusion that the relevant policy statement approving new nuclear plants was unlawful.

Concluding remarks

This section has shown a number of ways in which high-level environmental policy relating to the environment is subject to legal constraints. In particular, it is conceivable that the obligations of the SEA Directive, as well as those arising under the Aarhus Convention, might render a significant body of government policy subject to legal obligation and scrutiny. In light of this, the Dworkinian position that governments alone should be charged with decision-making on matters of policy loses its force, at least in relation to *environmental* policy. One possible qualification is that the SEA Directive does not allow general review of environmental plans or programmes on the merits, rather it imposes environmental *assessment* obligations, which, if met, still allow the government to develop its own environmental policy direction. However, assessment obligations are not simply procedural and can

---

[112] *R (Greenpeace) v Secretary of State for Trade and Industry* [2007] EWHC 311, [2007] JPL 1314, para 54.
[113] For analysis of the Aarhus Convention in UK environmental law, see Section 2.4 of Chapter 7.
[114] [2007] EWHC 311, paras 49–51.   [115] Ibid, para 49.

have substantive impacts on decision-making. In any case, while the legal constraints outlined in this section are enforceable in court, much will depend on the intensity of any judicial review undertaken in determining whether government decision-makers have met these legal obligations.

2.3 POLICY RELEVANT TO ENVIRONMENTAL REGIMES: LEGAL CONSTRUCTION AND EFFECTS

This section focuses not on high-level government policy, but on the broader range of policy instruments that are required and relied on to elaborate, implement, and influence the operation of environmental regimes. It shows the significant role of policy instruments—variously described as 'guidance', 'policies', 'circulars', 'reference documents', 'statements', 'frameworks'—in constructing environmental regimes. Such documents are issued by a variety of sources, from the UK government (often DEFRA), to English environmental regulators (the Environment Agency and Natural England primarily), to the EU Commission and other EU institutions and agencies. Key reasons for the extensive role of such policy in environmental regimes include: the difficulty of including all relevant detail in primary and secondary legislation (particularly in relation to the technical detail of complex environmental issues and industrial operations); the need to update elements of regulatory regimes relatively frequently; governments changing the strategic directions of regimes from time to time (this is particularly the case with planning law); and the need for clarifying advice on the implementation of regimes once lessons have been learned.

This section firstly considers two main aspects of such diverse types of policy: (1) how they are legally empowered or constructed in many cases, and (2) the legal effects of such policies. It does not give a comprehensive account of these legal aspects of environmental policy instruments, but gives representative examples to demonstrate the issues. The section concludes by considering the special case of sustainable development—sustainable development is reflected in key planning policy documents in England, and the legal implications of these are examined.

Note that while a variety of policy documents are considered in this section, it does not cover guidance documents that simply elaborate legal obligations to users of environmental law in plain language, or industry-specific, terms. Such documents are explanatory rather than legally constitutive of a regime or otherwise legally influential in relation to its operation.[116]

Legal construction of policy

Policy documents that are important elements of environmental regimes are often required by or allowed under statute, although this is not always the case. In the planning regime, for example, local development plans are required under the Planning and Compulsory Purchase Act 2004, and these plans are central to the planning regime.[117] By contrast, *national* planning policy statements (other than those relating to national infrastructure, required under the Planning Act 2008, discussed in Section 2.1), which are also key documents in the planning regime, are not legislatively prescribed. Section 2.2 gave some examples of other policy or guidance documents required by statutory frameworks, but a more mundane and typical example can be found in the Waste Regulations.

---

[116] Albeit that industrial operators rely on such guidance as their primary source of information on environmental law and regulation relevant to their businesses, as mentioned already: n 87. See also Section 2.4.

[117] Planning and Compulsory Purchase Act 2004, s 15. See further, Chapter 18.

Waste (England and Wales) Regulations 2011 SI 2011/988, Regulation 15 (emphasis added)

Guidance

(1) The appropriate authority *may give guidance* on the discharge of the duties in regulations 12 to 14.

(2) An establishment or undertaking discharging any of the duties in regulations 12 to 14 *must*, in doing so, *have regard to any such guidance.*

When guidance is so empowered by statute, it is referred to as 'statutory guidance'—its legislative imprimatur giving it a heightened relevance in terms of its legal effect.

A slightly notorious piece of statutory guidance in English environmental law is that issued by the Secretary of State in relation to contaminated land, under s 78YA of the Environmental Protection Act 1990. This guidance was reissued in April 2012 after lengthy consultation, in light of ten years of operation of the contaminated land regime in Part IIA of the Act, as well as the latest scientific evidence. The notoriety of this guidance is due to the fact that it contains the key obligations relating to contaminated land, effectively performing a quasi-legislative role. Section 78YA, and other relevant provisions of the Act, not only indicates what should be included in the guidance in terms of content (detailed provisions on defining and identifying contaminated land, and identifying the appropriate persons responsible for remediation), but also the procedure for formulating the guidance, including consultation requirements and parliamentary approval. Note also that the legal construction of policy instruments does not stop with the terms of any legislation that directly empowers the creation of a policy document. Other legal influences may inform their construction, including other legislative instruments. Thus, for example, the Conservation of Habitats and Species Regulations 2010 contain a number of provisions that control the formulation of key planning policy documents.[118]

Other examples of environmental policy instruments prescribed by legislation can be seen at the EU level. As set out in Section 2.2, some EU legislation requires Member States to adopt particular environmental policies, such as waste prevention programmes. In addition, many environmental Directives also require or allow for further, usually more technical, regulatory details to be decided through the negotiation of supplementary measures in EU committee processes. These range from end-of-waste criteria for particular waste streams under Article 6 of the Waste Framework Directive 2008/98/EC, to BAT reference documents under Article 13 of the Industrial Emissions Directive 2010/75/EU. The Directives themselves contain criteria with which these supplementary measures must comply and matters that they must include, constraining their content to that extent, as well as prescribing the committee procedure for their formulation (in the case of BAT reference documents, also requiring Commission approval for some elements). Whether such technical documents, devised through EU comitology processes, constitute 'law' or 'policy' is unclear jurisprudentially, but the point is that they constitute key elements of these environmental regimes, which need to be worked out with the input of experts, and also updated over time. This hybrid and evolving kind of regulatory instrument is the result of the complex nature of environmental problems.[119]

Where policy documents are empowered or otherwise shaped by statutory regimes, they will be susceptible to challenge by way of judicial review if they do not conform to relevantly applicable statutory frameworks, on grounds of illegality or the failure to take into account relevant considerations. A controversial example of how a court can draw on a statutory context to find guidance unlawful is seen in *Dimmock v Secretary of State for Education*.[120] In that case, a guidance note issued by the

---

[118] Conservation of Habitats and Species Regulations, 2010 SI 2010/490, regs 39, 102, 103, 106.

[119] See Chapter 2.

[120] *Dimmock v Secretary of State for Children, Schools and Families* [2007] EWHC 2288 (Admin), [2008] 1 All ER 367.

Secretary of State for Education to state schools, to accompany a film to be shown to school children on climate change, was found to promote unlawfully 'partisan political views', in contravention of the Education Act 1996.

Legal effects of policy

There are two related aspects to the legal effects of policy documents. They can act as a primary source of legal obligations for those who are subject to a relevant regime, and they can also control acts of administrative decision-making to which they relate, as a matter of public law. These legal effects might be prescribed by the statutory framework that empowers the formulation of policy, as seen in Regulation 15(2) of the Waste Regulations, which requires regulated undertakings to 'have regard to' any guidance issued by the regulator in carrying out various duties under the regulations. They might arise as a matter of administrative law doctrine; and they might arise simply because, in practice, policy instruments contain important regulatory and technical details that dictate how an environmental regime in fact works.

In terms of policy documents that act as a primary source of obligations within particular regimes, two examples have already been identified here, in relation to the Part IIA contamination land regime and the EU integrated pollution prevention and control regime (IPPC) under the Industrial Emissions Directive. In the former case, DEFRA's statutory guidance contains key provisions for the determination of contaminated land liability. In the latter case, BAT reference documents constitute the BAT process standard, which sits at the heart of the IPPC regime as the regulatory standard that installations covered by the Directive must meet.[121] These documents set out the technical detail of the best techniques available in a given industrial sector.

As for legal effects of policy instruments that arise as a matter of public law doctrine, such effects arise when policy instruments are either statutorily required to be taken into account or are otherwise 'material' and 'relevant' to an act of public decision-making. In such cases, they must be properly considered and taken into account in that decision-making process. Chapter 7 considers these public law doctrines in more detail,[122] but the discussion in this section highlights the extent to which policy documents are embraced by judicial review doctrine in environmental law.

The most prominent examples of policy documents constituting relevant material considerations in environmental decision-making can be seen in the planning regime. Section 70(2) of the Town and Country Planning Act 1990—the central provision on how planning applications are to be determined by local authorities—provides that, in making a determination, the relevant authority must have regard to the applicable local development plan 'and other material considerations'. Whether or not policy documents are legally relevant to a particular planning decision is judged in the following way.

R v Derbyshire County Council, ex p Woods
[1997] EWCA Civ 971 (Brooke LJ)

In his well-known judgment in *Bolton MBC v Secretary of State for the Environment* [1991] 6 P&CR 343 Glidewell LJ at pp 352–3 gave useful guidance about the expression 'a material consideration' when it is found in a planning context. First, the decision maker ought to take into account a matter which might cause him to reach a different conclusion to that which he would reach if he did not take it into account ('might' in the sense of a real possibility); and secondly, there is a distinction between material matters which statute obliges the decision maker to take into account, and those which arise from the nature

---

[121] See further, Chapter 17.   [122] See Section 4 of Chapter 7.

of the decision and its subject matter: in the latter case, in the event of a challenge, it is for the court to decide if they should have been taken into account.

In practice, non-statutory plans, government planning guidance, and other relevant policy documents are routinely taken into account in planning decisions. Even evolving planning policy can be found to have legal effects on decision-making, as seen in *Cala Homes (South) Limited v Secretary of State for Communities and Local Government*.[123]

It is important to keep in mind the nature of the legal effects that such environmental policy instruments can have. When a policy is legally relevant to an instance of decision-making, its legal effects are those that follow from public law doctrine. Thus, policies do not prescribe the outcome of planning decisions—the outcome is ultimately a matter of expert planning judgment, but relevant policies must be fairly considered and applied as appropriate in the decision-making process. In particular, different policies will carry different weight, depending on their relevance to the decision at issue, and their overall relevance will be determined by also taking into account the weight of other relevant considerations, which may point in different directions. Further, the legal relevance of a policy can itself be a matter of legal interpretation, as the extract from *Woods* shows, again within the bounds of public law doctrine. It is only if a perverse interpretation of a policy is adopted by a decision-maker that a court will intervene. Thus, policies are different from statutes when it comes to their legal interpretation.

R v Derbyshire County Council, ex p Woods
[1997] EWCA Civ 971 (Brooke J)

[Counsel for the applicant's] final point was that the Council failed to take into account national policy as set out in paragraphs 60–61 of [National Minerals Planning Guidance 3 (MPG 3)], when properly interpreted. Paragraphs 60 and 61 of MPG 3 are two paragraphs which appear under the heading 'Consideration of planning objections and benefits' and are in these terms:

'60. Where there are material planning objections to a proposal, [mineral planning authorities] should take into account any material arguments which might outweigh these. These could include the clearance of dereliction or other improvements to the land and economic benefits such as the contribution to, or maintenance of, local, regional or national employment. There may also be other positive aspects of the proposal such as the provision of a certain grade of coal for blending or other specialised requirements.

61. However, there will be cases where the particular impacts, either singly or together, would have such an adverse effect on the environment and on the quality of life for a locality that planning permission should not be given unless the development would produce overriding benefits.'

[...]

If there is a dispute about the meaning of the words included in a policy document which a planning authority is bound to take into account, it is of course for the court to determine as a matter of law what the words are capable of meaning. If the decision maker attaches a meaning to the words they are not properly capable of bearing, then it will have made an error of law, and it will have failed properly to understand the policy [...] If there is room for dispute about the breadth of the meaning the words may properly bear, then there may in particular cases be material considerations of law which will deprive a word of one of its possible shades of meaning in that case as a matter of law.

[...]

---

[123] See n 97, and accompanying text in Section 2.1.

If in all the circumstances the wording of the relevant policy document is properly capable of more than one meaning, and the planning authority adopts and applies a meaning which it is capable as a matter of law of bearing, then it will not have gone wrong in law.

For a recent example of the way these well-known principles are applied in a planning context, see *Cooper v Secretary of State for the Environment* [1996] JPL 945, where Mr Lockhart-Mummery QC [said] that the need for consistency in the construction of policies as between two policy sources might be a relevant consideration when determining the meaning which the words in a policy document were capable of bearing. But the decision whether a dangerous inconsistency might in fact exist on one interpretation of the words (so as to suggest that a particular meaning should be afforded to them in the circumstances) would be a matter in the first instance for expert planning judgment, and not a matter of law. A court would only intervene if that judgment was demonstrated to be perverse, or otherwise bad in law.

In the present case, it is necessary to remember that MPG 3 is not a set of rules written by lawyers for lawyers. It is a Guidance Note on Coal Mining and Colliery Spoil Disposal provided by the government for mineral planning authorities and for the coal industry, and it should not be interpreted as if it contained the words of a statute.

Chapter 18 examines the planning regime in detail, but the ways in which policy documents are legally relevant to the operation of that regime obtain in relation to other environmental regimes as well—from pollution control, to nature conservation laws, to contaminated land regulation.

Sustainable development policy and planning law

Now that you are more aware of the extensive role that policy plays in environmental law, it should not be surprising that sustainable development features more prominently in UK policy documents than in legislation. Thus, the statutory implications of sustainable development identified in Section 1.4 reflect a wider and increasingly entrenched strategic priority of the UK government to put sustainable development at the heart of its policy-making. Chapter 12 sets out the government's high-level sustainable development strategy in some detail,[124] but this section reflects on how sustainable development is implicated in other forms of policy as well, and considers the legal construction and effects of these policy instruments.

First, some legislative provisions require the creation of guidance that will further sustainable development in some way. For example, section 4(3) of the Environment Act 1995 requires Ministers to issue guidance for the Environment Agency, which covers the contribution that the Ministers consider it appropriate for the Agency to make, by the discharge of its functions and having regard to the Agency's responsibilities and resources, towards attaining the objective of achieving sustainable development. This requirement is not only heavily qualified but it also raises the issue of the legal status of such guidance, once issued. Section 4(4) requires the Environment Agency to have regard to the guidance, and this legislative imperative has legal consequences, although the prospect of a judicial review challenge to Agency actions on the basis of failing to meet Ministerial guidance on sustainable development seems far-fetched (but that might just be a sign of the political times).

Second, sustainable development has also informed many of the relevant planning policies in England, both past and present. Until April 2012, Planning Policy Statement 1 sat at the heart of the English planning system, giving some detail as to the meaning of sustainable development in the planning context and making it a 'core principle' in all planning decisions.[125] Sustainable development, or

---

[124] See Section 2.2 of Chapter 12.
[125] DCLG, *Planning Policy Statement 1: Delivering Sustainable Development* (2005). See Chapter 18.

sustainability, also featured strongly in other more specific planning policies—in particular Planning Policy Statement 3 on Housing (PPS 3), and Planning Policy Guidance 13 on Transport.[126] Thus, to return to the question posed in Section 1.4 as to the legal role of sustainable development in English law, determining this role partly depends on determining the legal impact of these planning policies, in light of their explicit promotion of sustainable development and considering that these policy documents were, until recently, key elements of the planning law regime.

However, rather than imposing a strong and overarching idea of sustainable development in the planning context, it can be seen that these planning policies have had modest legal impacts in planning cases in terms of promoting sustainable development. This is for two reasons: they represented material considerations to be balanced against other relevant considerations in relation to planning decisions—they do not have priority;[127] and the ideas of sustainability that they promoted were narrowly drawn and interpreted, focusing on the capacity of local infrastructure to sustain local communities more than on longer-term and wider environmental considerations. This can be seen in a case like *Horsham*, extracted here. In this case, a planning inspector had allowed a planning application for a residential development in a remote village, despite the local council having earlier rejected the development on the grounds that the site was unsustainable for new development. The planning inspector's decision was successfully appealed in the High Court on the ground that the inspector had failed to take into account the sustainability requirements of Planning Policy Guidance 3 (PPG 3), a precursor to PPS 3.

Horsham DC v First Secretary of State
[2004] EWHC 769 (Admin) paras 25, 28 (Sullivan J)

25. Although it is true that paragraph 70 of PPG3 was not raised by the claimant, I accept [...] that it should have been considered by the inspector if he proposed to accept the second defendant's submission that:

' ... sustainability does not only concern the matter of transportation. It also embraces matters such as maintaining or increasing population in order to support local services and facilities, including the local school.'

The policy underpinning the approach advocated by the second defendant was contained in paragraph 70 of PPG3.

[70. Villages will only be suitable locations for accommodating significant additional housing where:

- it can be demonstrated that additional housing will support local services, such as schools or shops, which could become unviable without some modest growth. This may particularly be the case where the village has been identified as a local service centre in the development plan;

- additional houses are needed to meet local needs, such as affordable housing...]

Although paragraph 70 was merely referred to in parenthesis in the second defendant's statement, [...] it formed the basis of the claimant's sustainability analysis on which the claimant [Council] relied for the proposition that there was no need to grant planning permission for the proposed development on this site because more sustainable sites in terms of PPG3 were available. Paragraph 70 thus became potentially relevant precisely because of the basis on which the inspector decided to reject the claimant's and the County Council's case on sustainability. He accepted the argument that was being advanced by the second defendant. Having done so, it was incumbent upon him to deal properly with the paragraph 70 issue. It is unnecessary to consider whether the appeal proposal would amount to 'significant additional

---

[126] DCLG, *Planning Policy Statement 3: Housing* (4th edn, June 2011); DCLG, *Planning Policy Guidance 13: Transport* (May 2006).

[127] See, for example, *R (Ludlam) v First Secretary of State* [2004] EWHC 99 (Admin).

housing' for the purposes of paragraph 70. There is clearly an issue as to whether significant additional housing means significant in terms of the overall housing provision, or significant in terms of the amount of housing in the particular village in question. Equally, it is unnecessary to consider the implications of the requirement to demonstrate that additional housing will support local services and/or whether it is necessary to produce specific evidence that particular services could become unviable without modest growth. It is unnecessary to do so because those would have been matters for the inspector to consider had he properly approached the policy on which the second defendant's sustainability argument was based. The inspector was undoubtedly correct in accepting the argument that sustainability is not simply concerned with transportation. It is also concerned with local services and facilities [...]

28. I do not accept [...] that the inspector dealt compendiously with all the issues raised under the head of sustainability.... At the most the inspector addressed the issue of local services, although what services he had in mind apart from the school is not clear. He failed to address the implications of the lack of public transport at a relatively remote location [...] Indeed, there is nothing to indicate that the inspector dissented in any way from the County Council's analysis of the transportation position. Rather, the contrary: [the inspector also shared the concerns of the highway authority]. Those concerns, if valid, could not on any rational basis be met by simply reducing the number of car parking spaces from two per dwelling to 1.5 per dwelling. One would then be left with a residential development in an unsustainable location, with inadequate off-street parking for the cars the occupiers would have to use, since they would have 'very little modal choice other than by private car'.

This case might seem very focused on local detail and not to reflect big ideas of sustainable development, but that is the point—this is how ideas of sustainable development, framed in policy instruments, have been filtering through into legal outcomes. Moreover, it demonstrates that applicable planning policies are critical in determining the content or definition of sustainable development in the planning context. While *Horsham* reflects a relatively narrow concept of sustainability, a differently formulated concept of sustainable development in the underlying planning policies would change how the idea of sustainable development is legally relevant in planning decisions. And such change has come.

The coalition Government introduced a radical overhaul of the planning policy framework in April 2012, scrapping all existing planning policy statements and guidance documents and replacing them with a single overarching National Planning Policy Framework (NPPF), which is relevant for all planning decision-making. The details of this Framework are set out in Chapter 18, but for now it is relevant that sustainable development is a central concept in the NPPF.

Department of Communities and Local Government, *National Planning Policy Framework* (March 2012) para 14

14. At the heart of the National Planning Policy Framework is a *presumption in favour of sustainable development*, which should be seen as a golden thread running through both plan-making and decision-taking.

For plan-making this means that:

- local planning authorities should positively seek opportunities to meet the development needs of their area;

- Local Plans should meet objectively assessed needs, with sufficient flexibility to adapt to rapid change, unless:

  - any adverse impacts of doing so would significantly and demonstrably outweigh the benefits, when assessed against the policies in this Framework taken as a whole; or

> – specific policies in this Framework indicate development should be restricted.
>
> For decision-taking this means:
>
> - approving development proposals that accord with the development plan without delay; and
> - where the development plan is absent, silent or relevant policies are out-of-date, granting permission unless:
>   - any adverse impacts of doing so would significantly and demonstrably outweigh the benefits, when assessed against the policies in this Framework taken as a whole; or
>   - specific policies in this Framework indicate development should be restricted.

Whilst 'sustainable development', as a presumption, remains ambiguously defined in the NPPF, having a precise definition is not what matters, nor is it possible.[128] Rather, the overall context and content of the document indicate what sustainable development means for the purposes of the Framework—'policies in [the Framework], taken as a whole, constitute the Government's view of what sustainable development in England means in practice for the planning system'.[129] The main legal consequence of this is to require all English planning authorities and decision-makers to act in accordance with *this* version of sustainable development. And the context of the document suggests that its golden thread of 'sustainable development' is designed to ensure sustainable levels of *development*, particularly house building, more than balancing economic growth based on development with environmental concerns.[130] However, the Government, in introducing the Framework, maintained that its sustainability focus caters for a green agenda. Ultimately, interpreting the Framework's version of 'sustainable development' will be a question of law that courts will face in judicially reviewing any planning decisions that are argued to depart from the planning policy framework. In any such case, arguments based on ideas of sustainable development beyond the NPPF will not be relevant—it is the Framework itself that is central.

Overall, even if it can be said that the principle of sustainable development or 'sustainability' has a legal role in English law due to the legal influence of the planning policies in which it is included, this does not resolve the definitional problems caused by the general and open-textured nature of principle outlined in Section 1.1. Thus, to say that the concept of sustainable development is legally binding due to its policy prominence does not dictate the legal obligations to which it gives rise, without a closer examination of the policy context in which it is articulated and ultimately without its consequences being tested in court by way of judicial review. This is why there was such heated political debate around the 'presumption of sustainable development' in the consultation period leading up to the adoption of the NPPF. Whilst the definitional looseness of sustainable development allowed a polarized political debate to play out, the fact that legal consequences *will* follow from the NPPF (thereby defining sustainable development in more detail, one way or another, case by local case) no doubt intensified the debate about how exactly to articulate and use the concept of 'sustainable development' in this key government policy document.

2.4 CONCLUSION

Legislation, even detailed secondary legislation, does not tell the full story about how environmental regimes are constituted or how they apply in practice. That story in UK environmental law is often completed by large amount of governmental policy and guidance, the latter often issued by a

---

[128] See Section 1.1.

[129] Department of Communities and Local Government, *National Planning Policy Framework* (March 2012) ('NPPF') para 6.

[130] Consider, for example, the wording in paras 19, 82, 84, 88, 110 of the NPPF.

regulator. There are many examples of such policies, since environmental law regimes are often highly complex to construct and implement. This chapter has discussed a range of examples of such policies, but you will encounter many more as you examine discrete environmental regimes throughout this textbook and in your practice of environmental law.

Note that there are increasingly new and different forms of guidance being issued, which are important for environmental lawyers. A key example can be seen in the Environment Agency's guidance on the enforcement of environmental offences. What used to be a relatively succinct single-document prosecution policy is now a set of three documents (two of considerable length), which set out the increasingly complex enforcement powers and strategy of the Agency: the Agency's 'Enforcement and Sanctions—Statement', its 'Enforcement and Sanctions—Guidance and Enforcement', and 'Sanctions—Offence Response Options'.[131] This proliferation of guidance documents shows how complicated the effective enforcement of environmental regulation can be, and also how seriously enforcement goals are taken in England. It also generates a lot of policy.

When it comes to guidance that is directed primarily at industrial operators to assist them in making sense of regulatory obligations to which they are subject, again there is an increasing proliferation of guidance types. A good example can be seen in relation to the Environmental Permitting Regulations (England and Wales) 2010,[132] which unite the permitting processes for a range of pollution control regimes and industries. DEFRA has issued 'core guidance' for the Regulations, which aims to provide 'comprehensive help for those operating, regulating or interested in facilities' covered by the Regulations, and which begins by presenting a map of all the interacting guidance documents associated with the Regulations, as issued by a range of public bodies (from European institutions, to the English Environment Agency and local authorities, to the Government department itself).

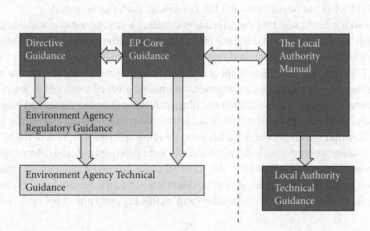

Figure 11.1 Illustration of guidance relationships

Source: DEFRA, *Environmental Permitting Guidance: Core Guidance, for the Environmental Permitting Regulations (England and Wales) 2010*, revised March 2012, 9

As a result of the proliferation of guidance and policy documents, which are subject to various legal constraints and issued by a variety of bodies in many different forms, such policy documents have a

---

[131] <http://www.environment-agency.gov.uk/business/regulation/31851.aspx> accessed 7 February 2013. See further, Section 3.1 of Chapter 8.

[132] SI 2010/675. See further, Introduction to Part IV.

range of legal effects. The precise legal impact of a relevant policy document depends on the type of regulatory situation or legal dispute involved, and the relevant legal question being asked, as well as the content and context of the policy itself. Thus, as seen in this section's discussion, policies can act as relevant material considerations in administrative decision-making, or they can set out key obligations of a regulatory regime. They can also shape the evolution of legal doctrine. As an example of the latter influence, EU Commission policy documents (from its own Communication on the precautionary principle to technical reference documents relating to food, animal, and chemical safety) have influenced the application of the precautionary principle by EU courts.[133] In some cases, unsurprisingly, guidance documents can have ambiguous, even confusing, legal status in English law.[134]

It is not only legal confusion that can arise from the proliferation of policy, but users of environmental law—particularly those in industry, but also practitioners—find the proliferation of guidance documents in environmental law to be frustrating. Whilst a heavy reliance on, and volume of, guidance documents is understandable in light of the wide-ranging and complicated problems to which environmental regulation applies, its variability—of form and source—comes at a cost of transparency, which can give rise to compliance problems.[135] Similar problems can also arise where regulators or agencies issue conflicting guidance, particularly across the different devolved UK administrations, which can have implications for those who operate across the English border.[136]

In conclusion, policy constitutes a central component of environmental law, albeit not a monolithic one. Environmental law is a subject that is not only framed and influenced by its public policy background, but policy instruments also constitute key aspects of environmental law regimes. The legal analysis of environmental law and its evolution thus requires paying close attention to policy documents, in a way that is not required in other legal subjects, and being open-minded about seeing their legal roles and implications.

FURTHER READING AND QUESTIONS

1. Are high-level environmental policy decisions and statements issued by the UK Government reviewable in court? For further cases on this issue, see *R (Medway Council) v Secretary of State for Transport, Local Government and the Regions* [2002] EWHC 2516 (Admin), [2003] JPL 583 and *R (Wandsworth LBC) v Secretary of State for Transport* [2005] EWHC 20 (Admin), [2006] 1 EGLR 91.

2. Considering both Sections 1.4 and 2.3, is there a definition of sustainable development in English environmental law? And does the concept of sustainable development have any identifiable legal consequences in English law?

3. Is it sensible to talk about 'policy' as a generalized concept in environmental law, or are there too many different types of policy for this to be meaningful? Why is there such a proliferation of policy types (and sources) in UK and EU environmental law?

4. Coming back to the theoretical issue identified at the beginning of the chapter, does the Dworkinian idea of maintaining a bright line distinction between 'law' and 'policy' work in environmental law?

---

[133] See *Pfizer*, as discussed in Section 1.3.

[134] See, for example, *R (Hart District Council) v Secretary of State for Communities and Local Government et al* [2008] EWHC 1204 (Admin), [2008] 2 P & CR 16.

[135] UKELA Final Report (n 87).

[136] See, for example, variation between SEPA and EA guidance on the definition of waste (in light of different views on *Environment Agency v Thorn International UK Ltd* [2008] EWHC 2595 (Admin), [2009] Env LR 10): ibid.

12

REGULATORY STRATEGY

This chapter discusses the meaning and role of regulatory strategy in English and EU environmental law. Regulatory strategies are often thought of as instruments to achieve certain environmental protection ends but, despite the availability of a plethora of regulatory tools to implement them, this chapter argues that regulators face often very significant challenges to act in a strategic manner and to turn environmental regulatory strategies into effective instruments of behavioural change. Hence, the chapter questions the idea that environmental regulatory strategies are purposefully driven by key objectives specified in government and regulatory agencies' environmental policies. Instead environmental regulatory strategy is often characterized by multiple, sometimes conflicting, objectives. Its ability to steer from 'the top down' is also impaired by corporate actors, citizens, and NGOs resisting government's and regulatory agencies' implementation efforts and seeking to influence the content of environmental regulatory strategy through lobbying. In fact, environmental regulation has moved towards co-regulation, which explicitly recognizes the contribution of non-state actors to the development and enforcement of environmental regulatory strategy.

By questioning regulators' capacity to deploy environmental regulatory strategy in an instrumental and targeted manner, this chapter links to key themes introduced in Chapter 1. Chapter 1 suggested that we need to consider the social foundations of environmental law, such as the political ideologies and economic reasoning that shape environmental regulatory strategies. This chapter shows that environmental regulatory strategy is often informed by political ideologies and economic reasoning that not only can be in conflict with each other, but are also contested on their own terms. They therefore pull environmental law in different directions, rather than giving it one clear strategic, focused purpose. Chapter 1 further suggested that we need to consider legal concepts and legal culture in order to understand how environmental law becomes applied to environmental problems. This chapter suggests that environmental regulatory strategy also needs to be factored into this equation in order to understand how environmental law becomes applied to environmental problems. Moreover, understanding regulatory strategy also matters in order to assess what counts as 'effective' environmental law.

This chapter is organized into four sections. In Section 1 we explain what is meant by regulatory strategy and provide an overview of different types of regulatory strategies. The crowded landscape of regulatory technique may give the impression that regulators can just pick and choose their regulatory strategies. This is incorrect. How regulatory strategies are developed and operate depends on the existing legal and socio-political culture. Thus, in Section 2 we discuss the economic and political rationales for regulating environmental problems. In particular, we focus on how the concepts of sustainable development and better regulation have been touchstones for debates over regulatory strategy in the UK and EU. While this might give the impression that regulatory strategy is targeted towards a specific set of ends we will see that this is not the case. In Section 3 we examine three theoretical perspectives on legal regulation in order to further understand the opportunities for and limits to deploy environmental regulatory strategy in an instrumental manner. Three key theoretical perspectives are introduced: systems-theory, the 'emotions and regulation' perspective, and the regulatory space approach. Systems-theory and the 'emotions and regulation' approach highlight the importance of communication for facilitating and constraining the potential of environmental regulatory strategy to shape the behaviour of human actors. The regulatory space approach introduces space—imagined as the scope of the environmental policy field and the boundaries of networks consisting of both public and private regulators and regulatees—as a further variable that influences the implementation of environmental regulatory strategy. Section 4 further critiques an instrumentalist conception of regulatory strategy by pointing to the limits of key regulatory tools, such as state 'command and control' regulation, economic incentive regulation, responsive regulation, and self-regulation, for translating environmental regulatory strategies into behavioural change.

One point should be made before continuing. Much of the discussion in this chapter overlaps with and/or frames the discussion in many other chapters of this book. This reflects the fact that discussions about regulatory strategy are fundamental to nearly all aspects of environmental law. Regulatory strategy is thus not just an element of the environmental law toolbox that can be produced or put away when needed or not needed. It is part of the fabric of environmental law. The literature discussed here and other socio-legal literature are thus relevant right across the length and breadth of environmental law.

1 REGULATORY STRATEGY: AN OVERVIEW

This chapter defines regulatory strategy widely to include the ideas, policies, programmes, and enforcement practices[1] that inform environmental regulation. Regulation, in turn, is understood as:

[t]he sustained and focused attempt to alter the behaviour of others according to standards or goals with the intention of producing a broadly identified outcome or outcomes, which may involve mechanisms of standard-setting, information-gathering and behaviour-modification.[2]

This definition indicates the broad range of regulatory activities that are captured when discussing regulatory strategy, with formal state law (legislation) not necessarily being central. In this section, we provide an overview of different regulatory strategies, examine the classic reasons given for regulation, and the problems with the tendency to see regulatory strategy in highly instrumental terms.

1.1 TYPES OF REGULATORY STRATEGIES

Environmental regulation takes many forms. A typical narrative is that in the 1970s command and control regulation was the dominant regulatory strategy. Hilson explains what is meant by command and control in relation to pollution control.

---

[1] Criminal enforcement is discussed in Chapter 8.

[2] Julia Black 'What is Regulatory Innovation?' in J Black, M Lodge, and M Thatcher (eds), *Regulatory Innovation* (Edward Elgar 2005) 11.

Chris Hilson, *Regulating Pollution: A UK and EC Perspective* (Hart Publishing 2000) 101–02

But what do we mean by command and control regulation? For present purposes, the regulatory process can be divided up into three stages: first, the setting of general policy; secondly, the setting of ambient targets and national waste or energy reduction targets; and finally, the setting of mandatory individual plant pollutions standards, company waste, or energy reduction targets, and product standards. [...] Strictly speaking, the term command and control should be used only in relation to these individual plant pollution standards, reduction targets and product standards, for it is individual companies or product specifications and framework and uses that are being commanded and controlled.

By the late 1980s, however, there was a shift to the use of other regulatory strategies and regulation can now be understood to cover a whole range of different techniques.

Neil Gunningham, 'Enforcement and Compliance Strategies' in Robert Baldwin, Martin Cave and Martin Lodge (eds), *The Oxford Handbook of Regulation* (OUP 2010) 131.

Gunningham and Grabosky (1999) advocate the concept of 'Smart Regulation', a term they use to refer to an emerging form of regulatory pluralism that embraces flexible, imaginative, and innovative forms of social control which seek to harness not just governments but also business and third parties. For example, it is concerned with self regulation and co-regulation, with using both commercial interests and NGOs (non-governmental organisations) and with finding surrogates for direct government regulation, as well as with improving the effectiveness and efficiency of many conventional forms of direct government regulation.

Thus, regulatory strategy is not just a set of legal rules. It encompasses social norms, the market, and design, as a means for shaping social actors' behaviour.[3] For instance, individual[4] carbon budget calculators seek to develop social norms for the reduction of citizens' carbon footprints. The market has been at the heart of environmental regulatory strategies that involve trading in water or greenhouse gas emission allowances.[5]

Regulatory strategies are thus less like instruments and more akin to architectures. Architecture in its metaphorical sense captures that environmental policies and programmes can influence social actors' behaviour by shaping their decision contexts.[6] In a more literal sense, architecture highlights the contribution of urban design to implement environmental regulatory strategies, through green transport options and low energy eco-housing built from recycled building materials. Before looking at that architecture in more detail, we consider the common arguments given for why environmental regulation is needed. This question is separate but related to the discussions about environmental values developed in Chapter 2.

1.2 WHY REGULATE?

Clearly there are a different range of values that operate in relation to environmental problems, but asking why environmental problems should be regulated may sound odd from an

---

[3] Lawrence Lessig, 'The New Chicago School' (1989) 27 JLS 661–63.
[4] <http://www.berkeley.edu/news/media/releases/2008/02/28_carboncalc.shtml> accessed 4 October 2012.
[5] See Chapter 15 and Section 4. [6] A point further discussed in Section 1.2.

environmental protection perspective. However, it is important to appreciate that, also in the context of de-regulation debates, there is by no means consensus about state intervention into economic activity in order to halt environmental degradation. Most importantly, asking 'why regulate?' matters because how we justify regulation of environmental problems often has a bearing on the particular regulatory strategy chosen. For instance, economic justifications for environmental regulation are sensitive to the economic consequences of environmental law, and thus may include the application of cost–benefit analysis in order to identify legislation that causes the least cost overall to society. Here we consider two of the most dominant justifications for regulation—economic and political.

Economic justifications for environmental regulation[7]

Neo-classical economic analysis has not been deployed merely in order to draw attention to the costs imposed by environmental regulation, and thus to promote de-regulation, but actually also provides important justifications for state regulation. Economic arguments for environmental law are based on the idea that the main purpose of economic transactions is the maximization of welfare for a society as a whole. This is achieved if individuals maximize their own individual welfare. Normally markets—a device for co-ordinating individual economic transactions—enable this wealth maximization. But in the case of *market failure* legal regulation is necessary in order to achieve allocative efficiency; that is, the maximization of economic welfare for a society as a whole. From an economic perspective, the aim of environmental regulation is therefore to promote what otherwise markets achieve, the efficient allocation of resources for production.

Neo-classical economists distinguish between three key market failures. The first occurs when there is insufficient competition in markets, for instance in the case of natural monopolies. These arise, for example, in the utilities sector, concerning railways, energy generation, and the provision of drinking water and sewerage services. Natural monopolies develop because the capital costs for setting up, for example, the infrastructure for networked utility services are high, thereby creating barriers to entry into these markets for potential competitors. Monopolies can handle these capital costs also by taking advantages of economies of scale. They can also keep their costs down through 'cream skimming'. Where utility services are supplied across a diverse area the fixed costs, such as of providing drinking water and sewerage services, will be particularly high in sparsely populated rural areas with limited demand in comparison to cities. Natural monopolists, supplying both rural areas and cities, can even out such differences in return on fixed capital costs. Moreover, for a society as a whole it can be cheaper for one firm to supply the utility service, rather than for the service to be supplied on the basis of competition between a number of firms.

For neo-classical economists market failure in the case of monopolies is a sufficient reason for state intervention through environmental law. From an environmental protection perspective there are arguments both for maintaining monopolies, for example, in environmentally sensitive utility sectors and for breaking up utilities in order to enable consumer choice. On the one hand, limited competition should increase revenues for monopoly utility operators, which can be ploughed back into the business to finance costly infrastructure upgrades, for instance of water treatment plants, which will enhance environmental protection. On the other hand, introducing choice in the supply of utility services may also contribute to enhanced environmental protection, for instance when customers can choose on the basis of environmental criteria which utility service supplier to contract with. For instance, in New South Wales, Australia, the 2006 Water Industry Competition Act has opened up

---

[7] The discussion in this section draws in particular on Anthony Ogus, *Regulation: Legal Form and Economic Theory* (Clarendon Press 1994) ch 3.

supply of drinking water and sewerage services to competition.[8] The Act enables private water companies to enter the market, as competitors to the former monopolist operator, Sydney Water. New entrants may be able to supply new services such as a water recycling service.

Neo-classical economists have also identified a second type of market failure—externalities—which are considered to justify legal regulation. In particular negative externalities are often a reason for environmental regulation. A negative externality occurs if a producer's activity imposes costs on third parties that are not reflected (or 'internalized') in the prices which he or she charges for his or her products or services. This leads to a misallocation of resources because purchasers of the product or service do not pay for its true cost of production. Consequently more units of the product or service are supplied than is allocatively efficient. Pollution is a key negative externality. Here, for example, an industrial manufacturer imposes costs, such as a reduced value in land for a neighbouring landowner or increased health care costs for the wider public. This market failure thus also provides a reason for environmental law to intervene and ideally to prevent the pollution externality from arising in the first place, or if pollution is created to allocate the costs of mitigating it. Often environmental law simply mitigates the impacts of pollution externalities and this should be achieved from an economic perspective at the least cost to a society as a whole. But it can be difficult to determine who is the 'least cost abater'. Is it the factory by installing scrubbers or are residents the least cost abaters by moving away from the source of pollution. Calculating who incurs the least cost in abating the pollution will also be rendered complex by the fact that air, water, and land pollution often also impose costs on future generations.

Information deficits are a third type of market failure that justify—from an economic perspective— legal regulation. When information deficits occur consumer preferences are not accurately revealed and demand is no longer a reliable measure of actual consumer preferences. Examples are insufficient information about the energy efficiency of white goods or the nutritional value of genetically modified foods. Information deficits occur because information itself is a public good and therefore may be undersupplied. Sellers may also have an economic incentive to supply misleading information, such as to assert that organic crunchy peanut butter is healthier than conventional crunchy peanut butter. Most importantly, information about the environmental quality of a good or service is usually complex and thus more difficult and potentially more costly for consumers to process than simple price information. For instance, claims about the greater health properties of organic compared to non-organic food were contested in the controversial 2009 report of the UK Food Standards Agency.[9]

The neo-classical economic concept of market failure has been an influential justification in public policy discourse for intervention into economic activity through environmental law. But it also suffers from various shortcomings. First, market failures are addressed in order to achieve allocative efficiency, but this does not consider the distribution of incomes between different individuals and thus neglects a fairness dimension in its conception of the economic welfare of a society as a whole. This matters, in particular, in light of the suggestion that 'environmental bads' are disproportionately imposed onto lower socio-economic groups, for instance through the siting of waste incinerators, that emit harmful air pollutants such as dioxins and furans, in poor neighbourhoods; the provision of workers' housing in the close vicinity of factories; and the greater susceptibility of lower socio-economic groups to pollution related illness due to poverty related poor health.[10] Second, neo-classical economics works with an abstract, and thus a potentially impoverished, understanding of how 'real life' economic actors and markets actually work. Markets are steered by an 'invisible hand', governed by the laws of supply and demand, and populated by rational utility maximizers. But a rich body of economic sociology scholarship has questioned these conceptions of economic

---

[8] Schedule 7(1)(b) of the New South Wales Water Industry Competition Act 2006.
[9] <http://www.food.gov.uk/multimedia/pdfs/organicreviewreport.pdf> accessed 28 September 2012.
[10] Kristin Shrader-Frechette, *Environmental Justice* (OUP 2002) 7.

behaviour[11] and has emphasized the importance of political and legal institutions for constituting and regulating markets, a point further discussed in the next sections. Given these criticisms of economic justifications for environmental regulatory strategy and law, we will briefly examine political justifications.

Political justifications for environmental regulation

Alongside economic justifications for regulation there are also a range of political justifications for regulation that may derive from both eco-centric and anthropocentric environmental values.[12] Thus, for example, the environmental justice (EJ) movement provides political justifications for environmental law that are based on a vision of social justice that seeks to limit the distribution of 'environmental bads' to lower socio-economic groups.

Andy Gouldson, 'Do Firms Adopt Lower Standards in Poorer Areas? Corporate Social Responsibility and Environmental Justice in the EU and the US' (2006) 38 Area 402, 403

EJ has been defined as the fair treatment and meaningful involvement of all people – regardless of race, colour, national origin or income – in the development, implementation and enforcement of environmental policies (Bass 1998; Bullard and Johnson 2000). EJ therefore recasts many environmental issues so that they are not only to do with resource use or pollution but also to do with equity, justice and human rights (Boyle and Anderson 1998; Agyeman 2002; Zarsky 2002). Like CSR, EJ has both procedural and substantive dimensions. By calling for the meaningful involvement of different social groups, EJ raises important procedural questions about the ability of different social groups to engage in and exert influence over environmental decision making in different contexts. Similarly, by promoting the fair treatment of different social groups, substantive issues about the level and distribution of different environmental impacts are brought to the fore. The debate on EJ has become more significant because of observations that poorer and more deprived communities are often excluded from exerting influence in the decision making processes that affect them and that they are disproportionately affected by negative social and environmental outcomes (Adeola 1994 2000; Dobson 1998; Foreman 1998; Schlosberg 1999; Shrader-Frechette 2002; Walker *et al.* 2003; Mitchell and Dorling 2003). [...]

Similarly, the Environment Agency for England and Wales has recently promoted the inclusion of environmental and social justice as a key theme in the UK's Sustainable Development Strategy (Environment Agency 2004; UK Government 2005).

It is worth bearing in mind, though, that distributional justice and economic efficiency do not have to be considered as two conflicting goals for legal regulation. Regulatory measures designed to correct allocative inefficiency can also be subject to constraints on the grounds of distributional justice. Similarly, re-distributional measures that form part of an environmental regulatory strategy can be fine-tuned by ensuring that they contribute to allocative efficiency. Hence, in practice policy-makers will often seek trade-offs between economic and political justifications, such as efficiency and distributional justice, for a regulatory strategy. But there is no scientific method or magic formula for resolving such trade-offs, also because non-economic values are difficult to measure, a point that is not always explicitly acknowledged in regulatory impact assessments for proposed new environmental laws. Environmental rights, however, can provide a framework through which politically

---

[11] For example, Neil Fligstein, *The Architecture of Markets: An Economic Sociology of 21st Century Capitalists Societies* (Princeton UP 2002).

[12] Chris Hilson, *Regulating Pollution: A UK and EC Perspective* (Hart Publishing 2000) 3–5.

determined trade-offs between economic and political justifications for environmental regulatory strategies become fixed. For instance, a human right to water will, in theory, trump and qualify economic justifications for the efficient operation of water markets that would deprive customers unable to pay for drinking water of high quality from access to water.

Liberal paternalism provides another example of a set of political justifications for environmental regulatory strategy and law, but again, in a way that can be reconciled with a neo-classical economics preference for choice in economic transactions. Thaler's and Sunstein's version of liberal paternalism justifies limited intervention by states or private corporations into the way citizens exercise consumption choices. They advocate such regulation on the grounds that it will enable citizens to realize their interests more fully. They make a case for 'choice architecture'. Choice architecture seeks to steer subtly economic actors' behaviour without providing direct price signals for changed behaviour, in the way economic incentive regulation does. A 'choice architect' 'has responsibility for *organizing the context* in which people make decisions'[13] but people should be free to do what they like and be able to opt out of undesirable arrangements if they want to do so. An example of their approach is the placing of environmentally friendly cleaning products at eye-level locations on supermarket shelves where they are likely to attract customers' attention in order to promote more sustainable consumption behaviour.

1.3 THE DANGERS OF THINKING INSTRUMENTALLY ABOUT REGULATION

To summarize, what can be seen here is that both neo-classical economics and political justifications provide important reasons for developing environmental regulatory strategy. While basic elements of neo-classical economics, such as a belief in the superior ability of markets to co-ordinate economic transactions, have been influential in steering the content of environmental regulatory strategy, this section has suggested that economic analysis may play a more limited role, as a technical tool, for instance in the case of cost–benefit analysis, in order to determine which environmental regulatory strategy—justified on political, not economic, grounds—imposes least cost. Furthermore, key economic concepts have significant rhetorical influence. Thus, concepts such as free choice in markets shape the development of regulatory strategy, for instance in the case of liberal paternalism. This influence can also be seen in the development of sustainable development strategies and the 'better regulation' agenda, the topics of Section 2.

In light of the pluralism of both regulatory strategies and the range of answers to 'why regulate?' there is a temptation to see regulatory strategy in instrumental terms. Fisher considers this development in relation to EU environmental law.

Elizabeth Fisher, 'Unpacking the Toolbox: Or Why the Public/Private Divide Is Important in EC Environmental Law' Mark Freedland and Jean-Bernard Auby (eds), *The Public Law/Private Law Divide: une entente assez cordiale* (Hart 2006) 222–245

In the last decade that reckoning has occurred in relation to EC environmental law. The end result has been what has been commonly described as the 'new' approach to EC environmental law and policy. In 1992 the Community published the Fifth Action Programme on the Environment – *Towards Sustainability*. The main thrust of that programme was that a 'broader mix' of regulatory 'instruments' should be developed and applied. [...]

[13] Richard Thaler and Cass Sunstein, *Nudge: Improving Decisions about Health, Wealth and Happiness* (Yale UP 2008) 3.

The Fifth Action programme was not the only statement of the new approach but it captured and stated the new philosophy like no other document did in the EC context. It contained numerous recommendations for action based on this 'new approach'. It identified, however, market based mechanisms, financial support mechanisms and 'horizontal supporting instruments' as areas for specific development. [...]

Yet regulatory innovation did not stop there. In the last decade, there have been a number of different regulatory schemes created. These include a co-operative system of integrated pollution prevention and control, a voluntary environmental management and audit scheme (EMAS), an eco-labelling scheme, and a framework for environmental agreements. There have also been a number of experiments in negotiated policymaking such as the Auto Oil programme [...]

As Demmke and Unfried note the new approach is a 'conscious effort by regulators to enlarge their toolbox'. The expansion of the 'toolbox' is viewed as part of the growing sophistication of EC environmental law and the diversification of regulatory strategies as resulting in more innovative, imaginative and flexible approaches to regulation. Indeed the imagery of instrumentality and choice has come to pervade the new policy and academic literature. Environmental regulation is concerned with choosing from an 'arsenal' so as to design of the most optimal regulatory instrument. Moreover, such regulation is 'smart' because it recognises and takes seriously the role of private actors and is not hemmed in by entrenched and 'outdated' conceptions of the administrative state. [...]

Following on from this, the purpose of EC environmental law is primarily a functional one concerned with achieving this non-controversial goal. EC environmental law exists as a mechanism for addressing market failure or, because of the trans-boundary nature of environmental problems, the Community is the most efficient site for governance.

This image is appealing but is in stark contradiction to the complexity of environmental problems and environmental law. The best way to understand this is by showing how regulatory strategies are embedded in social and legal contexts. Thus, in Section 2 we highlight the limited instrumental capacity of environmental regulatory strategy by pointing to the unresolved conflicts between political, economic, and social dimensions of sustainable development strategies as well as the diluting of distinct and discrete environmental regulatory strategies by 'mainstreaming' environmental regulatory strategy into other policy fields.

FURTHER READING AND QUESTIONS

1. For overviews of different regulatory strategies see Chris Hilson, *Regulating Pollution: A UK and EC Perspective* (Hart Publishing 2000) and Carolyn Abbot, 'Environmental Command Regulation' in Benjamin Richardson and Stepan Wood (eds), *Environmental Law For Sustainability: A Reader* (Hart Publishing 2006). For a thoughtful study of the evolution of the US regulatory state see Cass Sunstein, *After the Rights Revolution: Reconceiving the Regulatory State* (Harvard UP 1990).

2. Bronwen Morgan 'The Economization of Politics: Meta-Regulation as a Form of Nonjudicial Legality' (2003) 12 Social & Legal Studies 489. This article critiques the increasing dominance of economic rationality in regulatory public policy-making. It suggests that the requirement imposed in some jurisdictions on public policy-makers to consider the impact of regulation on the competitiveness of economic actors amounts to 'meta-regulation' of public policy-making.

3. Anthony Ogus, *Costs and Cautionary Tales: Economic Insights for the Law* (Hart Publishing 2006).

2 SHAPING REGULATORY STRATEGIES: SUSTAINABLE DEVELOPMENT AND 'BETTER REGULATION'

To understand the importance of social and political contexts we need to turn from the general and abstract discussion in Section 1 and examine in more detail the contents of actual environmental regulatory strategy. Our starting point for doing this is sustainable development.

Sustainable development was discussed in detail in Chapter 11 in relation to principle and policy. It has been a key policy idea also driving regulatory strategies in the UK and EU. Principles, policies, and regulatory strategies do overlap but they are also distinct. By focusing on regulatory strategy we can see how principles and policies are transformed into methods for changing behaviour. If you have not already done so you may find it useful to read the discussion in Chapter 11 concerning sustainable development.

Discussions about sustainable development have always been infused with discussions about regulatory strategy. Thus, the Brundtland report considered technological innovation as a key catalyst for achieving economic growth that does not cause environmental destruction. How exactly economic growth and environmental protection can be reconciled was, however, left open in the report and is also an unresolved and contested issue in sustainable development strategies that have since been developed. The general mantra of SD strategies is that economy, environment, and society are inter-related in the development of environmental regulatory strategy. The focus on integration can be seen in Agenda 21 where changes in behaviour were recommended across all sectors in society and a range of activities including education, business, and farming.

Not surprisingly sustainable development has given rise to a lot of discussion about the use of regulatory strategies. Indeed, sustainable development was one of the major catalysts for the 'new approach' to environmental policy discussed by Fisher. What can be seen in this section, however, is that the way in which sustainable development has transformed into regulatory strategies in the EU and the UK has been shaped by the socio-political and legal cultures in those regimes.

2.1 THE EU

We discussed the development of the concept of sustainable development in the EU, and the EU's Sustainable Development (SD) Strategy, in Chapter 11. The EU SD strategy forecasts a number of new EU legislative initiatives. In June 2006 the European Council adopted a renewed SD strategy. It is an 'umbrella' strategy that seeks to link to all of the EU's policy fields. It has identified seven key challenges:

- Climate change and clean energy.
- Sustainable transport.
- Sustainable consumption and production.
- Conservation and management of natural resources.
- Public health.
- Social inclusion, demography and migration.
- Global poverty and sustainable development challenges.

The following extract from the 2009 review of the EU SD strategy highlights two examples that illustrate how ambitious the EU SD strategy is in seeking to 'green' production and consumption in the EU and how detailed—in comparison to the UK strategy—EU policy-makers' assessment is of progress towards a green economy.

Communication from the Commission to the European Parliament, the Council, the European Economic and Social Committee and the Committee of the Regions, 'Mainstreaming Sustainable Development into EU Policies: 2009 Review of the European Union Strategy for Sustainable Development' COM (2009) 400 final, 3–7

Climate change and clean energy

Although EU greenhouse gas emissions grew over the period from 2000 to 2004, the trend over the last three years has been favourable and the EU is on track to meet its Kyoto Protocol target. However, if global climate change policies are not applied quickly, global greenhouse gas emissions will be in 2020 at least 60% higher than in 1990. Even though the share of renewables in gross inland energy consumption has been growing faster since 2002, it is still far from the 2010 target of 12%. In recent years, the EU has been at the forefront of the fight against climate change. In December 2008, the EU legislator agreed on a Climate and Energy Package that sets ambitious targets for the EU. The EU committed itself unilaterally to reducing its overall emissions by 20% below 1990 levels by 2020, and to upgrading this effort to a 30% emissions reduction in the event of a comprehensive international climate agreement in Copenhagen in December 2009. It also set itself the target of increasing the share of renewables in energy use to 20% by 2020. As part of the package, the directive on the EU Emission Trading System (ETS) was amended and directives on carbon capture and storage (CCS) and on renewable energy sources were adopted. The Energy Efficiency Package reinforces the key energy efficiency legislation on buildings and energy-using products. Additional energy savings will be provided by the extension of the Ecodesign Directive to energy-related products, in accordance with the sustainable consumption and production/sustainable industrial production (SCP/SIP) Action Plan. The rules governing the European Regional Development Fund (ERDF) have been amended to support sustainable energy in the housing sector, providing a further boost to investment in this sector. The European Strategic Energy Technology Plan (SET-Plan) accelerates the development and deployment of cost-effective low-carbon technologies. Similarly, a Communication on mobilising information and communication technologies (ICT) to improve energy efficiency was adopted in 2009. Agreement on the climate and energy package was a major achievement in the light of the economic crisis and provides a significant contribution by the EU to the efforts for achieving a comprehensive climate change agreement in Copenhagen. However, EU greenhouse gas emissions make up only a limited share of global emissions. While the EU is on track to achieve its greenhouse gas emission reduction targets resulting from the Kyoto protocol, global CO_2 emissions are today some 40% higher than they were in 1990, the Kyoto base year. It is estimated that in order to limit the average global temperature increase to less than 2°C compared to pre-industrial levels, global greenhouse gas emissions must be reduced to less than 50% of 1990 levels by 2050. [...]

Sustainable consumption and production

Changes in sustainable consumption and production show a rather mixed picture, with some progress being achieved in terms of decoupling environmental degradation and the use of natural resources from economic growth. Consumption patterns, mainly regarding energy consumption, however, show clear unfavorable developments, whereas production patterns show positive signs. The Sustainable Consumption and Production and Sustainable Industrial Policy (SCP/SIP) Action Plan will help to improve the environmental performance of products, boost demand for more sustainable goods and production technologies and foster innovation. The Action Plan was accompanied by proposals for a recast of the Ecodesign and Energy Labelling Directives and the revision of the Ecolabel and EMAS Regulations. Retailers play a key role in influencing consumer choices, and a Forum has been established with the aim of reducing the environmental footprint of the retail sector and better informing consumers. On

Green Public Procurement (GPP), important policy initiatives include the Energy Star Regulation and a Communication on public procurement for a better environment, which proposes a voluntary 50% GPP target for Member States to be reached as from 2010.

The European Commission's attempt to turn sustainable development into an environmental regulatory strategy that will really shape public authorities', corporate actors', and citizens' behaviour is further buttressed through the development of Sustainable Development Indicators (SDIs) by Eurostat. These indicators and an 'SD scoreboard' should help to monitor progress in implementing the EU SD strategy in the Member States.[14]

But even these sustained attempts to implement SD strategies cannot gloss over the continuing conflict between traditional conceptions of economic growth and environmental protection. In the original Lisbon Strategy the European Council proclaimed in 2000 that the EU should 'become the most dynamic and competitive knowledge-based economy in the world by 2010 capable of sustainable economic growth with more and better jobs and greater social cohesion and respect for the environment'.[15] This was understood to require an increase in productivity and competitiveness of the EU given the challenges of increasing global competition and an ageing population in the EU.

European Commission, 'Commission Staff Working Document, Lisbon Strategy evaluation document' SEC (2010) 114 final, 5

Links between the Lisbon Strategy and other EU instruments and/or strategies, such as the Stability and Growth Pact, the Sustainable Development Strategy or the Social Agenda, have not been sufficiently strong, so that rather than being mutually reinforcing some of the strategies have been operating in isolation.

The Lisbon Strategy seeks to unleash the competitiveness of EU economic actors in a global economy by keeping regulation 'light touch'. This is at odds with the vision of some sections of the environmentalist movement that favour the development of strong local communities whose economic practices are not governed by international markets controlled by global capital but by fair-trade relationships that stay within the carrying capacity of the ecosystems that enable economic activity in the first place.

The Lisbon Strategy was replaced on 3 March 2010 with the new Europe 2020 Strategy. Europe 2020 is part of the EU's response to the 2008 financial crisis. It seeks to develop the EU economy over the next decade by stimulating 'smart, sustainable and inclusive growth'. In more conventional and specific terms this means that the EU is aiming for high levels of employment, productivity, and social cohesion in the face of the threat of sovereign debt default by Member States such as Greece, Italy, Spain, and Portugal in 2011. The Strategy is further specified through five targets, which should be achieved by 2020 and will be translated into more specific targets applicable in the EU Member States: in relation to employment, 75% of the 20–64 year-olds are to be in employment; in relation to Research & Development (R&D) and innovation 3% of the EU's GDP (public and private combined) is to be invested in R&D and innovation. For climate change and energy the goal is a reduction of

---

[14] <http://epp.eurostat.ec.europa.eu/portal/page/portal/sdi/indicators> accessed 17 November 2012.
[15] European Commission, 'Commission Staff Working Document, Lisbon Strategy evaluation document' SEC (2010) 114 final, 2

greenhouse gas emissions by 20% (or even 30%, if the conditions are right) compared to 1990, with 20% of energy to come from renewable sources and a 20% increase in energy efficiency. In relation to education, the school drop-out rate is to be reduced below 10% and at least 40% of 30–34 year olds should complete third level education. Finally, Europe 2020 seeks to ensure that 'at least 20 million fewer people [are] in or at risk of poverty and social exclusion'.[16]

Thus, under the label of sustainable development environmental regulatory strategies have been developed in the EU that seek to reconcile economic growth and environmental protection. This has meant that concern about the costs of implementing environmental policies has always been an issue in the development of environmental regulatory strategy: a concern, however, that in the light of the 2008 financial crisis has become more pressing.

It is also important to appreciate that regulatory strategies based on sustainable development can give rise to considerable political and legal conflict. The EU chemicals law REACH is a good example of this.[17] REACH developed out of the interface between the Lisbon Strategy and discussions about sustainable development. Article 1(1) states:

> The purpose of this Regulation is to ensure a high level of protection of human health and the environment, including the promotion of alternative methods for assessment of hazards of substances, as well as the free circulation of substances on the internal market while enhancing competitiveness and innovation.

The way in which REACH pursues this purpose is through the 'no data, no market' rule set out in Article 5 which requires that 'substances on their own, in preparations or in articles shall not be manufactured in the Community or placed on the market unless they have been registered'. The registration process requires that safety data about a chemical be produced. Thus, rather than a system of command and control regulation, REACH makes the provision of safety data a precondition for sale on the EU market. This has proved controversial.

Elizabeth Fisher, 'The "Perfect Storm" of REACH: Charting Regulatory Controversy in the Age of Information, Sustainable Development, and Globalization' (2008) 11 J. of Risk Research 541, 552–53

> [T]here are many reasons why the explicit pursuit of sustainable development is controversial. The first set of reasons for it being so have concerned whether the costs of REACH to private actors exceed the public benefits. A number of impact assessments were conducted by both Community institutions and others as part of the process of debate and the results of these assessments were themselves queried [...] This has resulted in a sub-politics concerned with the legitimacy of impact assessment as a regulatory technique and also highlights the difficulties of making these types of assessment [...]
>
> The second set of reasons why the sustainable development aspect of REACH has proved controversial has concerned whether environmental and economic concerns can be properly integrated. In particular, there are those that have been concerned about the balance between the environmental and economic imperatives. [...], some have argued that the economic costs are too great [...], while there are those

---

[16] Target No 5 for the EU in 2020 available at <http://ec.europa.eu/europe2020/europe-2020-in-a-nutshell/targets/index_en.htm> accessed 3 March 2013.

[17] Regulation 1907/2006/EC concerning the Registration, Evaluation, Authorisation, and Restriction of Chemicals (REACH), establishing a European Chemicals Agency, amending Directive 1999/45/EC and repealing Council Regulation (EEC) No 793/93 and Commission Regulation (EC) No 1488/94 as well as Council Directive 76/769/EEC and Commission Directives 91/155/EEC, 93/67/EEC, 93/105/EC and 2000/21/EC [2006] OJ L396/1.

who have argued that REACH places too much emphasis on economic concerns at the cost of environmental protection [...] Moreover, there are some who have argued that increased costs of registration will impact on research and development [...]

The final set of reasons for the controversial nature of REACH is to do with how the requirements of registration regulate the market. Historically, most environmental regulation operates as a limit on market activity, 'you can do what you like but not *x*'. [...] In contrast, registration is operating as a precondition to market activity: without registration, a manufacturer cannot even begin to operate in the Community market. Moreover, the information requirements of registration are resulting in the production of information which is making the market work more effectively. In other words, REACH is playing a constitutive role in that it regulates who can participate in the market and on what basis they do so. [...]

The significance of this is twofold.

First, REACH is a distinct departure from other techniques of environmental regulation not just because it is 'innovative' or 'market based' but because its role is far more to do with creating the market than just regulating it. While reconstituting markets is at the heart of the sustainable development agenda, there have been relatively few examples of it actually occurring in practice. Second, REACH as a law concerned with the constituting of the market is a reminder that markets are social constructions whose existence owes much to state action [...] The significance of this reminder is not particularly great in the EU where it has always been appreciated that the internal market is a creation of legal and political forces [...] It is more radical, however, in those jurisdictions where markets have tended to be understood as domains of action that exist before the state.

All of this shows the way in which sustainable development does promote a range of different regulatory strategies, but which regulatory strategies are developed within a legal culture will depend considerably on social and political context. Moreover, that process of development may be controversial.

2.2 THE UK

Discussions about sustainable development have not been limited to the EU, and we discussed examples of it in law and policy in the UK and its regions in Chapter 11.[18] The first UK SD strategy was published in 1994, the second in 1999 and the third in 2005. On 28 February 2011 the Conservative-Liberal Party UK coalition Government[19] published its particular vision for sustainable development.

---

[18] It is worth noting that s 79(1) of the Government of Wales Act 2006 imposes a legal duty upon the Welsh Ministers to make a 'sustainable development scheme', which sets out how they propose, in the exercise of their functions, to promote sustainable development. This scheme was published on 22 May 2009 under the name of 'One Wales: One Planet' <http://wales.gov.uk/topics/sustainabledevelopment/publications/onewalesoneplanet/?lang=en> accessed 5 March 2013. See also the progress report on this: 'One Wales: One Planet', Sustainable Development Annual Report 2010–2011, September 2011, at: <http://wales.gov.uk/about/cabinet/cabinetstatements/2011/22septembersusdevlopm ent/?lang=en>. The Scottish Government published in December 2005 a Scottish Sustainable Development Strategy, entitled 'Choosing our future: Scotland's sustainable development strategy' <http://www.scotland.gov.uk/Publicati ons/2005/12/1493902/39032> accessed 5 March 2013. Northern Ireland also has its distinct sustainable development strategy, entitled 'Everyone's Involved', which was launched on 27 May 2010. Its implementation is overseen by the Office of the First Minister and the Deputy First Minister for Northern Ireland at: <http://www.ofmdfmni.gov.uk/ index/economic-policy/economic-policy-sustainable-development.htm>.

[19] <http://sd.defra.gov.uk/>

DEFRA, *Mainstreaming Sustainable Development—The Government's Vision and What This Means in Practice* (February 2011) para 2.2

2.2 Green Economy

The Government is committed to sustainable growth, economically and environmentally, and there are many opportunities for UK businesses in moving to a green economy. We will publish a Roadmap to a Green Economy in April 2011 that will outline how Government will seek to maximise economic growth, whilst decoupling it from impacts on the environment. Natural capital is an essential part of a productive economy and we need to value appropriately the goods and services it provides. This will be a key theme of the Natural Environment White Paper, the first such for 20 years. Building on the National Ecosystem Assessment, the White Paper will set out the state of our natural asset base and will strengthen Government commitments to ensure we properly measure and recognise the value of natural capital in policy decisions. This Government has made a number of announcements and policy decisions which will support delivery of the transition to a green economy – including the Green Deal, a carbon price floor, greater support for export of clean technologies and the review of waste policies. In the Spending Review the Government committed £1bn for the Green Investment Bank with a commitment for additional significant proceeds from asset sales to help unlock the finance necessary to help move to a green economy. We are also committed to introducing a presumption in favour of SD in the planning system, which will be at the core of the new simplified National Planning Policy Framework.HM Treasury (HMT) will support green growth and build a fairer, more balanced, economy. Specifically, its business plan sets out commitments to increase the proportion of revenue accounted for by environmental taxes. For example, plans to introduce a carbon price floor by 2013 and to replace air passenger duty with a per flight duty. And through Accounting for Sustainability, HMT will introduce connected sustainability reporting in 2011/12—bringing together reporting on expenditure and carbon reduction, waste management and use of finite resources.

The UK government's SD strategy also addresses the key relationship between environment, economy, and society, by discussing 'fairness and improving wellbeing'. This picks up on a wider debate[20] about the importance of capturing a society's development not just by measuring its economic development through increases in gross domestic product, but by recognizing a wider notion of citizens' 'quality of life'. The SD strategy therefore also refers to the Department for Work and Pensions' (DWP) commitment to develop a child poverty strategy, focused on eradicating child poverty by 2020, as well as measures to encourage the unemployed to become self-employed and to promote community focused work schemes, such as work clubs and work experience placements.

As indicated in the title of the current UK sustainable development strategy a key aspect of sustainable development is to integrate environmental protection into a range of related public policies, such as employment, industrial, taxation, transport, energy, and public health policies. It is questionable, however, whether this move towards abandoning a discrete and distinct environmental regulatory strategy will enhance its effectiveness or simply contribute to its dilution in policy agendas dominated by other powerful government departments, such as the Treasury. In the UK, mainstreaming environmental regulatory strategy, by including it into other policies, is merely a voluntary commitment of central government policy-makers, though the UK government has put in place an institutional framework for achieving it.

---

[20] See, for example, Joseph Stiglitz, Amartya Sen, and Jean-Paul Fitoussi, 'Report by the Commission on the Measurement of Economic Performance and Social Progress', <http://www.stiglitz-sen-fitoussi.fr/documents/rapport_anglais.pdf> accessed 5 March 2013.

DEFRA, Mainstreaming Sustainable Development—*The Government's Vision and What This Means in Practice* (February 2011) para 2.1

Ministerial leadership and oversight:

The Environment Secretary will sit on the key domestic policy Cabinet committees, including the Economic Affairs Committee, to enforce the government's commitment to sustainability across domestic policy making.

A Ministerial Steering Group will oversee delivery of new Commitments for Greening Government's Operations and Procurement

Leading by example

Reducing Government's waste generation, water use and greenhouse gas emissions. Waste will be cut by 25 per cent (approximately 74,000 tonnes) by the end of this Parliament. Best practice water efficiency methods will be put in place across government, as well as a new stretching commitment on greenhouse gas reduction which builds on the current 10 per cent announced by the Prime Minister in May 2012.

Ensuring the government buys more sustainable and efficient products and engages with its suppliers to understand and reduce the impacts of supply chains.

Embedding sustainable development in government policy

Defra will take the lead responsibility for reviewing departmental business plans in relation to SD principles. The Minister for Government Policy will then hold departments to account through the quarterly business plan review process.

The government also seeks to promote 'mainstreaming' through the development of sustainability indicators for government activity. Publication of progress in relation to these indicators shall enhance transparency and accountability for 'mainstreaming'. But more could have been done to 'mainstream' environmental regulatory strategy, for instance by making sustainable development a responsibility of the Cabinet Office, as recommended by the House of Commons Environmental Audit Committee.[21]

As this discussion makes clear the UK government's SD policy is not operating in a vacuum but interacting with the wider socio-political and legal context. Thus, when evaluating the UK government's SD policy it is worth bearing in mind the government's response to the 2008 financial crisis. The UK government imposed severe cuts in public expenditure, which also lead to the demise of a number of regulatory agencies. Thus, for example, the Sustainable Development Commission which provided independent advice to the government has been abolished. Its functions will be taken over by the House of Commons Environmental Audit Committee, which may, however, be less effective given that it is composed of MPs with limited specialist environmental expertise. Also the Royal Commission on Environmental Pollution (RCEP), the Health Protection Agency, and the Sustainable Schools programme have been axed. Budgets for the Environment Agency for England and Wales and Natural England—the main nature conservation body—have also been cut.

Moreover, the SD strategy must integrate with other government policies. Thus, in Chapter 3 we discussed the 'Better Regulation' agenda and the role of regulatory impact assessment. Hence, s 4(1) of the Environment Act 1995 states that the principal aim and objective of the Environment Agency is to protect or enhance the environment and to contribute to sustainable development, while s 39(1) of the Act imposes a general duty upon the EA to have regard to costs and benefits in exercising its powers. Section 39(2) clarifies that the EA does not have to consider costs and benefits when carrying out its duties.

---

[21] Jonathan Porritt, 'First they killed the SDC. Now they are trying to kill off Sustainable Development itself' (3 March 2011) <http://www.jonathonporritt.com/blog?page=8>, accessed 9 November 2012.

The UK Better Regulation Task Force Report 'Regulation: Less is More', published in 2005, set out various recommendations for streamlined regulatory strategy in the UK.[22] The Better Regulation Task Force was set up by the then Labour UK government in 1997 as an independent body whose task was to advise the government on the development of proportionate, accountable, consistent, transparent, and targeted regulation. In 2006 the Better Regulation Task Force became the Better Regulation Commission. It has now been replaced by the Better Regulation Executive, which was formerly based in the Cabinet Office but has been transferred to the UK central government department for Business, Innovation and Skills.[23] The previous UK Labour government had started to implement the Taskforce's recommendations through its Administrative Burdens Reduction Programme. Its focus on promoting economic development is clear.

National Audit Office, *Reducing the Cost of Complying with Regulations: The Delivery of the Administrative Burdens Reduction Programme, 2007, Report by the Comptroller and Auditor General* (2006–07, HC 615) 5

The Government's aim is to improve the UK business environment by: ensuring that regulation is used only when necessary; simplifying and removing unnecessary regulations; and making sure that EU law is not gold-plated when transposed into UK law. The ultimate objective is to achieve a faster rate of productivity growth in the UK.

In 2010 the new Conservative–Liberal UK government further developed this 'better regulation' agenda by setting out four key specific commitments for regulatory reform. Firstly, regulatory burdens shall be alleviated through a 'one-in, one-out rule' according to which no new primary statutory or secondary regulation will be adopted without an existing one being abolished. Second, regulation shall be less bureaucratic by avoiding a 'tick-box' approach to enforcement. Instead, inspections shall be more meaningful by being in-depth for high-risk organizations. For less high-risk installations professional standard-setting organizations and the regulated themselves are enlisted as self-regulators. Third, the government intends to time-limit regulation, so that the need for a particular regulation is regularly reviewed. All new environmental regulation will be subject to a seven-year 'sun-set' clause. Fourth, there is a rather wide and unspecified commitment 'to give the public the opportunity to challenge the worst regulations'.[24] The UK government claims that its 'better and risk regulation' agenda is driven by concerns about the cost burdens of regulation on business,[25] but DEFRA's response to the 'better regulation' agenda illustrates some of the complexities associated with assessing costs of environmental regulation to businesses.

---

[22] Better Regulation Task Force, *Regulation—Less is More: Reducing Burdens, Improving Outcomes* (2005) at: <http://www.bis.gov.uk/files/file22967.pdf>.

[23] See <http://www.bis.gov.uk/policies/better-regulation> accessed 29 September 2012.

[24] <http://www.defra.gov.uk/corporate/about/how/regulation/> accessed 29 September 2012.

[25] The government has collected information from businesses about the time they spend on meeting obligations to supply information to regulatory authorities in response to regulation (NAO Report, *Reducing the Cost of Complying with Regulations*, 6). It seems somehow ironic that the NAO also notes in its report *Reducing the Cost of Complying with Regulations* (6) that £17 million was spent on consultancy fees for gauging regulatory burdens imposed on businesses, a figure which does not include 'other departmental costs' spent on the reducing administrative burdens initiative, given the fact that this central government expenditure is financed by tax payers, including businesses.

DEFRA, *Defra's Approach to Regulatory Reform*, May 2011 para 2.1 <http://archive.defra. gov.uk/corporate/about/how/documents/defra-regulat-reform-1105.pdf> accessed 9 November 2012

2.1 Defra's policy landscape is characterised by the breadth and diversity of its responsibilities. Scope of Defra's Regulation.

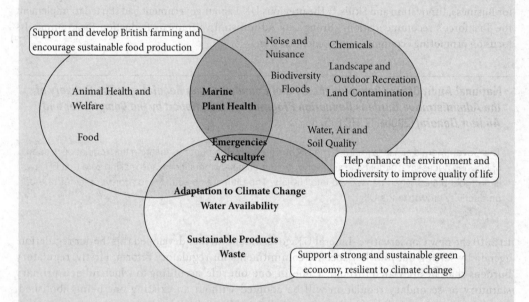

2.2 Work is underway to produce a complete picture of Defra's regulatory stock and its associated costs and benefits. Defra probably has the biggest stock of regulations in Whitehall by number, but with lower costs overall to business and civil society compared with many other parts of Government whilst providing generally strong benefits (particularly societal).

2.3 Early findings suggest that Defra is responsible for some 400-500 sets of regulations with direct or indirect costs to business and that the direct annual costs to business are likely to fall in the range £4bn-£8bn. Defra's regulation therefore represents between 0.43% and 0.86% of GDP - compared with the estimated total burden of regulation on business in this country equivalent to 10% of GDP. However, this does not take account of the direct or indirect benefits to business and civil society.

2.4 The costs of regulation include both the costs of compliance with regulations (eg installing pollution abatement equipment) and the administrative burden arising from compliance with regulations (eg providing information to regulators and filling in forms). Defra's administrative burden was estimated in May 2010 as £287m (about 3% of the total administrative burden imposed by all Government Departments) or around 3.5%-7% of the total costs of all Defra's regulations.

Hence, DEFRA needs to incorporate both sustainable development and regulatory reform into how they develop policy. Another aspect of the socio-political and legal context that shapes how sustainable development transforms into regulatory strategy is the process of passing primary and secondary legislation. It is important to bear in mind that before draft legislation is introduced into Parliament, the government department responsible for the bill will have discussed its contents with interested parties, such as professional bodies, for example, the Chartered Institution of Wastes Management, voluntary organizations, corporate actors, and environmental pressure groups. In the case of a major environmental policy initiative the government will usually publish a White Paper, which is sometimes preceded by so-called Green Papers that invite interested parties to express their views. Where environmental regulatory strategy has already solidified into a draft bill it can be considered by a departmental select committee in the Commons or by a joint committee of the Lords and Commons. This pre-legislative scrutiny has become more widespread in recent years and presents an important opportunity for MPs and Lords to influence early on the shape of a bill.

Once a bill is formerly introduced, usually in the House of Commons, though bills can also start in the House of Lords, the bill is scrutinized through Parliamentary debate (including committee debate) and thus environmental regulatory strategy is further developed. The composition of the general committees,[26] which scrutinize a bill through debate, reflects the allocation of seats in the Commons to the various political parties, and the government thus has a majority in them. General committees include what were formerly called 'standing committees'. From the beginning of the 2006–7 Parliamentary Session Standing Committees on Bills were renamed Public Bill Committees. A number of Commons Committees are 'General Committees' such as the Scottish Grand Committee, the Welsh Grand Committee, and the Northern Ireland Grand Committee, as well as Committees on Delegated Legislation and European documents. A specific type of general committee, a Public Committee is appointed for each bill that goes through Parliament. The capacity of Public Bill Committees[27] to scrutinize each piece of newly proposed environmental legislation is also enhanced by their powers to obtain written and oral evidence from civil servants and experts outside the Westminster Parliament.[28]

The House of Commons Select Committee on the Environment, Food and Rural Affairs monitors and holds DEFRA accountable and thereby can also contribute to the development of environmental regulatory strategy. There is also a separate House of Commons Energy and Climate Change Select Committee, which scrutinizes environmental policy development, as well as expenditure and administration carried out by the Department of Energy and Climate Change (DECC) and its related public bodies. The House of Commons Environmental Audit Committee has a cross-cutting scrutiny function. It examines the work of a range of government departments and non-departmental public bodies by auditing their performance in relation to any sustainable development and environmental protection targets the government may have set for these bodies. Moreover, both the House of Commons and House of Lords Science and Technology Committees contribute to the development of environmental regulatory strategy in the UK. The Committees' high quality reports have been influential in debates about environmental regulatory strategy.

Parliamentary debates will clearly shape the final outcome of legislation. Regulatory strategy is thus not a crude instrument but a set of ideas shaped by a whole range of different legal and socio-political contexts and practices. We therefore need to take into account those contexts and practices in any study of regulatory strategy.

[26] 'General Committees (including Public Bill Committees)' <http://www.parliament.uk/about/how/committees/general/> accessed 17 November 2012.
[27] Which are named after the specific piece of draft legislation they scrutinize, for example, the Public Bill Committee considering a UK government bill on waste recycling would be called the 'Waste Recycling Bill Committee'.
[28] Membership of General Committees ranges from ca. sixteen to fifty, see: <http://www.parliament.uk/about/how/committees/general/> accessed 29 September 2012.

FURTHER READING AND QUESTIONS

1. Christopher Rootes and Neil Carter 'Take Blue, Add Yellow; Get Green? The Environment in the UK General Election of 6 May 2010' (2010) 19 Environmental Politics, 992 discusses the UK Liberal-Conservative coalition Government's environmental politics.

2. The UK Government has established a new Green Economy Council, which seeks to support the transition to a green, low carbon economy in co-operation with business (at: <http://www.decc.gov.uk/en/content/cms/news/bis_pn11_064.aspx>). Executives of major corporations, such as Ford, Centrica, and IBM, are members of the Council as well as Ministers from the Department for Business, Innovation and Skills, the Department of Energy and Climate Change, and the Department for Environment, Food and Rural Affairs. This Council has published a 'Roadmap to a Green Economy': HM Government, *Enabling the Transition to a Green Economy: Government and Business Working Together* (2011) <https://online.businesslink.gov.uk/Horizontal_Services_files/Enabling_the_transition_to_a_Green_Economy__Main_D.pdf> accessed 9 November 2012.

3. Kyla Tienhaara, 'A Tale of Two Crises: What the Global Financial Crisis Means for the Global Environmental Crisis' (2009) Global Governance Working Paper No 37. <www.glogov.org> accessed 9 November 2012.

4. Michael E Porter and Claas van der Linde 'Toward a New Conception of the Environment-Competitiveness Relationship' (1995) 9(4) Journal of Economic Perspectives 97. A classic study which argues that environmental regulation can enhance a business' competitiveness by forcing innovation in production technologies.

5. The Department of Business, Innovation and Skill's report 'Better Regulation,Better Benefits: Getting the Balance Right—Case Studies' (2009) refers to the Environmental Permitting Programme as a successful Better Regulation project delivering a reduction of the regulatory burden on low risk business, redirecting 'resources from unnecessary inspection to providing advice on how to improve compliance', <http://www.berr.gov.uk/files/file53251.pdf> accessed 9 November 2012.

6. 'Better Regulation' in Scotland: SEPA 2010 Better Environmental Regulation: SEPA's Change Proposals, <http://www.sepa.org.uk/about_us/news/2010/better_env_regulation.aspx> accessed 9 November 2012. Scottish Executive 2006 Strengthening and Streamlining, The Way Forward for the Enforcement of Environmental Law in Scotland, <www.sepa.org.uk/about_us/consultations/idoc.ashx?docid=1effdde6-6b9d-4792-9f2a-aac3dc3adf41&version=-1> accessed 5 March 2013.

7. In practice the effect of environmental mainstreaming on public policy-making has been limited, see, for example, Mark A Pollack & Emilie M Hafner-Burton, 'Mainstreaming international governance: The environment, gender, and IO performance in the European Union' (2010) 5(3) The Review of International Organizations 285. What legal, if any, remedies can be pursued if EU public policy-makers fail to implement Article 11 TFEU?

8. For a fascinating account of the development of sustainable development strategies across the EU that allows for comparisons between different Member States see, in particular, chapter 4 of the report commissioned by the Committee of the Regions: 'Contributions of the Regional and Local Authorities to Sustainable Development Strategies, Committee of the Regions, 2009, a study conducted by the Research Institute for Managing Sustainability (RIMAS), Vienna University of Economics and Business Administration, at: <http://cor.europa.eu/en/Archived/Documents/7834329b-22d2-4066-a592-030f1de40d19.pdf>

accessed 17 November 2012. The report contains some interview data and case studies from eleven northern and southern, old and new EU Member States that examine the development of national SD strategies in Austria, the Czech Republic, Denmark, Finland, France, Germany, Italy, Malta, Slovenia, Spain, and the UK. When reading the report, bear in mind that since its publication the details of central, regional, and local government relationships in some Member States may have changed due to new central governments coming into power.

3 THE COMMUNICATIVE AND SPATIAL DIMENSIONS OF ENVIRONMENTAL REGULATORY STRATEGY

In light of the discussion in Section 2, we provide in this section examples of some richer theories of regulatory strategy. In order for environmental regulatory strategy to change behaviour it needs to be communicated to private companies, citizens, and public authorities. It also needs to be made to work within a specific regulatory space, that is, the bounded field occupied by networks of both public and private regulators and regulated organizations. In practice, and as already seen, communicating environmental regulatory strategy and implementing it in a specific regulatory space are replete with a range of challenges that can jeopardize the successful realization of environmental objectives. For instance, communicating environmental regulatory strategy faces the challenge of messages about environmental objectives being distorted due to the particular perceptions and 'rationalities' through which the regulated 'hear', interpret, and apply environmental regulatory objectives. Moreover, emotional factors, such as fear of environmental risks and trust in scientific and regulatory procedures for managing them, can impede but also facilitate the communication, and ultimately implementation, of environmental regulatory strategy.

Such communicative challenges to deploying environmental regulatory strategy have been addressed by social-theoretical analysis of legal regulation, in particular the systems-theoretical and 'emotions and regulation' approaches discussed here.

3.1 SYSTEMS THEORY'S TAKE ON LIMITS TO COMMUNICATING ENVIRONMENTAL REGULATORY OBJECTIVES

Systems-theory, a sociological theory of communication,[29] provides strong reasons for the limited capacity of regulatory law to be deployed strategically. It suggests that society is organized into different autopoietic sub-systems, such as a legal, political, and economic system. Each system re-constitutes itself self-reflexively (autopoietically) by observing the differences between itself and its environment. Moreover, each of these social sub-systems operates according to its own binary 'code'. In the case of the legal system, the code mobilizes the distinction between legal and illegal. Given that each social sub-system works with a different code, there are limits to communication between the different sub-systems and therefore limits to how each sub-system can influence another sub-system and change behaviour of social actors within another sub-system. This means that law's capacity to steer the behaviour of political and economic actors—an issue particularly salient in the field of communicating and implementing environmental regulatory strategies—is doubtful. As that is the case, other

[29] Niklas Luhmann, *Ecological Communication* (Chicago UP 1989).

understandings of law must be developed. Teubner, one of the main writers in the field, has set out different perspectives for improving law's 'effectiveness'. He is particularly interested in 'procedural law' which attributes a modest role to law, to control only the self-regulatory processes of social systems:

Gunther Teubner 'After Legal Instrumentalism? Strategic Models of Post-Regulatory Law' in Gunther Teubner (ed), *Dilemmas of Law in the Welfare State* **(Walter de Gruyter 1986) 307, 312**

3. Control of Self-Regulation

As alternative solutions transcending the distinction between formal and substantive law, strategies are discussed that amount to a more abstract, more indirect control through the law. The law is relieved of the burden of direct regulation of social areas, and instead given the task of the active control of self-regulatory processes (eg Bohnert and Klitzsch, 1980). Empirically, the crisis of regulatory law is identified as an incompatibility of the internal logics of different social systems. It has been demonstrated that regulatory law programs obey a functional logic and follow criteria of rationality and patterns of organization which are poorly suited to the internal social structure of the regulated spheres of life (Reidegeld, 1980: 281; Pitschas, 1980: 150). In consequence, law as medium of the welfare state either turns out to be ineffective or it works effectively but at the price of destroying traditional patterns of social life (Habermas, 1981 II: 531 and supra). [...]

In the operative dimension 'proceduralization' is offered as a formula for the role of the law in promoting and controlling the setting up of 'social systems with a learning capacity' (Wiethölter, 1982 and supra; Mayntz, 1983b; cf. as well Brüggemeier, 1982: 60 and Willke supra). The empirical basis is a whole variety of new forms of non-directive legal interventions (Winter, 1982: 9). This approach emphasizes the design of self-regulation mechanisms, combining competition, bargaining, organization and countervailing power (Hart, 1983: 22).

Teubner concludes that:

The simple model of 'political goal—legal norms—social effects' would have to be enriched with social knowledge of how self-referential systems receive regulatory information and how they process it according to their autonomous rules of internal interaction.

A further explanation of the modest regulatory capacity of 'procedural' or 'reflexive' law is provided by Teubner.

Gunther Teubner 'Substantive and Reflexive Elements in Modern Law' (1983) 17 Law and Society Review 239, 271, 275

The 'crisis' of autonomous law exists because law, particularly in its conceptual structures, has not yet adapted to the exigencies of a highly differentiated society. Legal doctrine is still bound to the classical model of law as a body of rules enforceable through adjudication. The legal order lacks a conceptual apparatus adequate for the planning and social policy requirements that arise in the interrelations among specialized social subsystems (Luhmann, 1972b: 325). [...]

Reflexive law, in other words, will neither authoritatively determine the social functions of other sub-systems nor regulate their input and output performances, but will foster mechanisms that systematically *further the development of reflexion structures within other social subsystems*.

This account, however, does not tell us much about how conflicting interests should be dealt with in the development and implementation of regulatory strategies. Social actors—and their *interests*—are curiously absent from this analysis. This can be seen in the Koppen extract, which discusses Teubner's work in the context of environmental mediation.

Ida J Koppen 'Chapter 12: Environmental Mediation: An Example of Applied Autopoiesis' in Roel J in T Veld and others (eds), *Autopoiesis and Configuration Theory: New Approaches to Societal Steering* (Kluwer Academic Publishers 1991), 143, 146, 149

Environmental mediation is the general term for different intervention mechanisms that rely on the role of a neutral intermediary to resolve conflict situations through a process of assisted negotiations. Representatives of all the groups that have an interest in the outcome of a particular conflict, generally referred to as *stakeholder groups*, are asked to participate in the negotiations. The principal features of mediation that make an autopoietic analysis interesting are the specific function performed by the *mediator* and the process of *interactive bargaining* in which the parties engage.

[...]

From an autopoietic point of view it is the operative closure between the different functional social subsystems involved in environmental regulation that renders the steering of environmental parameters problematic. Four subsystems are involved: politics, economy, science and law. Each system is autopoietically closed and self-referential. It can receive information from the outside, but it can only react to that information by reproducing it in its own internal code. The information that scientists pass on to lawyers, economists and politicians about the state of the environment, enters into their respective subsystems. It causes 'noise': initiatives are developed, activities of various kinds take place. Typically, lawyers develop legal doctrine, start a court case or propose new rules; economists want to find out how much protective measures cost; politicians appoint expert committees and put an issue on the political agenda. But the information then stays there, trapped as it were in the subsystem.

[...]

From an autopoietic point of view the interest analysis becomes secondary to a systems analysis of the conflict situation. Instead of looking at the parties in the negotiation as representatives of different interests in the conflict, the negotiation is seen as so-called interference between the different social subsystems involved. Teubner calls it a reformulation of the 'balancing of interests', which must no longer be interpreted with reference to individual or collective actors, but instead 'cast in terms of a conflict between communicative networks' (Teubner, 1989b, p. 418). It is not the interests of the stakeholders that determines the interaction in the negotiation, but the interest of the social subsystem that they belong to. The interest of a social subsystem is expressed in its internal coding: if I talk law and you talk politics we have a different interest even if we are both green.

3.2 EMOTIONAL ASPECTS OF COMMUNICATING ENVIRONMENTAL REGULATORY STRATEGY

In public policy debates, emotional and cognitive aspects of risk perception and communication are often distinguished, with emotive elements in particular of lay views perceived as hindering the implementation of 'rational' environmental regulatory strategies. For instance, a recent report by the European Parliament (EP) on genetically modified organisms (GMOs) suggests that:

> GMOs are often perceived by society in a very emotional way not necessarily based on scientific grounds. Member States should address this issue in a practical and rational [...] rather than political way.[30]

This perception of a disjuncture between 'emotional, scientific, practical, rational' and 'political ways' of perceiving environmental risks needs to be questioned. Each of these terms is broad, vague, and its meaning contested. Whether they really refer to distinct social phenomena needs to be carefully examined. For instance, as argued in Chapter 2 the science/politics divide is not as clear-cut as made out in this quote from the EP's report. Moreover, a number of sociologists of emotion[31] understand cognitive and affective elements in social action as closely linked:

> [emotion is] a relatively short-term *evaluative* response essentially positive or negative in nature involving distinct somatic (and often *cognitive*) components [...] Cognitive components consist of verbal judgments or labels that identify the emotion (emphasis added). [32]

How then do interlinking affect and cognition influence how environmental risks are perceived and how environmental regulatory strategy can be communicated?

Susan A Bandes, 'Emotions, Values, and the Construction of Risk' (2008) 156 University of Pennsylvania Law Review 421–25, 427, 430

> Emotions help us to interpret, organize, and prioritize the information that bombards us. We categorize this information based on assumptions about what is to be feared, who is to be trusted, and who is within our circle of care and compassion. We organize it into a coherent account of human behavior and causality. We cannot function without creating markers of saliency and value, and our emotions aid us in identifying which information is especially salient, valuable, or urgent—or indeed, worthy of notice or action at all. [...]
>
> Emotion is an integral part of normative judgment, but emotions are not entitled to *a priori* normative weight in determining the shape of policy. Kahan's work sheds much light on the social dynamics of belief formation, but it tends to treat values as inherently good rather than interrogating their content or their susceptibility to change. Kahan views emotion 'as a perceptive faculty uniquely suited to discerning what stance toward risk best coheres with a person's values.' The values (or cultural worldviews) themselves, in this account, are stable and reflective, rather than context sensitive. They are trait-like attributes like an 'egalitarian' ethic or 'individualistic' values. I suggest that value and fact have a more fluid and mutually constitutive relationship. We construct the world in light of assumptions about how it ought to work, but what we perceive helps shape what we feel and what we value. Neither emotion nor value is inert; both shape and are shaped by social milieu. [...]

---

[30] European Parliament Committee on the Environment, Public Health and Food Safety, 'Draft Report on the implementation of EU legislation on GMOs, in particular Directive 2001/18/EC and Regulations (EC) No 1829/2003 and 1830/2003', (2008/2306) 4, at <http://www.europarl.europa.eu/RegistreWeb/search/simple.htm?relNanme=NUPE&reference=418.031&language=EN>

[31] See also Arlie Hochschild 'Ideology and Emotion Management: A Perspective and Path for Future Research' in Theodore Kemper (ed), *Research Agendas in the Sociology of Emotions* (SUNY Press 1990) 118–19.

[32] Theodore Kemper, *A Social Interactional Theory of Emotions* (John Wiley & Sons 1978) 47.

[Sunstein] suggests that one solution to the prevalent problem of factual error is to delegate certain risk regulation issues to experts. But as Kahan persuasively argues, values and facts are not easily disentangled—by either ordinary citizens or experts. Therefore it is not easy—and not necessarily desirable—to give weight to judgments about the former and not the latter. This debate about the value/fact distinction is critical to the question of risk regulation. [...]

Determining what constitutes a risk is not a mechanical calculus. It is a task of identification and definition that requires deciding what questions to ask, what temporal and causal links to draw, what assumptions about 'social' or 'natural' forces to make, and how to fit the answers into a coherent narrative amenable to policy recommendations. In short, identifying and delineating risks implicates a cognitive process that is both normative and affect-laden.

Bandes highlights that successful communication of an environmental regulatory strategy requires some meeting of minds between policy-makers and the regulated about what constitutes an environmental risk that is serious enough to be tackled through regulation, including law. She argues that emotions play an important and valuable part in our perceptions of risk because they facilitate the processing of information and ultimately express social actors' values. Bandes also recognizes that emotive perceptions can sometimes distort comprehension of risk, and she therefore makes a case for rendering explicit the impact of affect on risk perception, for instance during public participation procedures. This perspective moves far beyond the EP report's simple distinctions between 'emotional', 'rational', 'scientific', 'practical', and 'political' elements of risk perception and communication. That an understanding of both interlinked cognitive and affective aspects of risk perception matters is also illustrated by Lofstedt, who highlights the importance of trust for deploying successfully environmental regulatory strategy.

Ragnar Lofstedt, 'Risk Communication: Pitfalls and Promises' (2003) 11 European Review 417, 417–19

Whilst risk communication cannot be defined as an independent discipline, it is perhaps best described as 'the flow of information and risk evaluations back and forth between academic experts, regulatory practitioners, interest groups, and the general public'. Thus at its best, risk communication is not a top-down communication from expert to the lay public, but rather a constructive dialogue between all those involved in a particular debate about risk.

To date, the outcomes of the various risk communication programmes relating to environmental hazards in Europe and the United States have largely been ineffective. The public tends to remain hostile to the local siting of waste incinerators and nuclear waste dumps, a reaction that has not been significantly influenced by the risk communication programmes. Whilst, in part, such responses might be attributable to the lack of funding of risk communication programmes and hence failure to conduct proper evaluations to learn why programs failed, it is more a failure to understand that it is necessary to work together with the public rather than simply 'educate' them. More attention must be paid to the social amplification of risk and the role of trust.

[...]

One of the most likely explanations for the failures of risk communication initiatives is that reactions to risk communication are not only influenced by the message content and the hazards, but also by trust in those responsible for providing the information.

[...]

What exactly is trust? Trust can be an expression of confidence between the parties in an exchange transaction and can be both process/system - or outcome-based. For example, in some cases, the public will trust regulators even if they do not agree with a regulatory decision, as long as they see the process as credible, ie fair, competent and efficient. However, in most cases, the public judges regulators on their past decisions. If the public perceives the regulator as competent, fair and efficient, based on previous decisions, the public is likely to trust these regulatory bodies in the future. I use the term trust in the sense of a complexity reduction thesis, in which the public delegates to authority. That is to say trust means acceptance of decisions by the constituents without questioning the rationale behind it. In such a case, constituents are in effect agreeing to accept a 'risk judgement' made by the regulators. The three most important components of trust are fairness, competence, and efficiency.

Two points in Lofstedt's analysis are particularly striking. First, an account of the role of scientific and legal professionals in generating and destroying trust, as well as an analysis of their own judgments to trust other actors and institutions involved in risk regulation does not feature in this article. For example, scientific experts need to 'trust', but also need to critically question risk information. The need to critically question information arises in particular when applicants—who have an interest in the positive outcome of the authorization—submit risk assessments of the genetically modified agricultural product to be authorized by the regulatory authority under Directive 2001/18/EC.[33]

Second, trust is not perceived as a distinct psychological phenomenon but seems to be equated with accepting authority, in particular when this authority is exercised in accordance with principles of good administration. Trust therefore can consist of a judgment that somebody in a position of power will not act in violation of one's interests. Lofstedt refers to 'fairness, competence and efficiency' as *'components'* not just facilitators of trust. That trust, however defined, is crucial to risk regulation and is further illustrated in the Lofstedt extract, which indicates that demand for risk regulation may also be driven by declining levels of trust in risk regulators. This questions whether 'efficient use of public money'—a justification that looms large in the 'better and risk regulation' public policy agenda—is sufficient for convincing citizens of the necessity of de-regulatory and 'better' regulation measures.

Ragnar Lofstedt, 'Risk Communication and Management in the Twenty-First Century' (2004) 7 International Public Management Journal 335, 337

In the countries where I have conducted most of my research, namely the UK and Sweden, the public's trust toward policy makers has fallen. In the UK, polls indicate that the public's trust decreased from 39 to 22 percent in the period 1974-1996 (House of Lords 2000), while trust in Swedish policymakers has declined from 65 percent in 1968 to 30 percent in 1999 (Holmberg and Weibull 1999).

The issue of falling trust levels is important. First, past research indicates that it is much easier to destroy trust than to build it (Slovic 1993). It is therefore highly unlikely that regulators in the UK, for example, will be able to rebuild public trust levels to the same height as they were prior to the BSE scandal, although one should note that the falling trust levels have tapered off. Second, research that Paul Slovic, myself, and others have done over recent years shows that public trust is one of the most important explanatory variables of the public's perceptions of risk (Lofstedt 1996). That is,

---

[33] See Chapter 22.

if the public trusts regulators they will perceive risks to be less than when they do not trust regulators. In fact, there is a correlation between low public-perceived risk and a high level of public trust and vice versa. In sum, as the public becomes increasingly distrustful, the public is increasingly risk averse.

Given this decline of citizens' trust in regulators, environmental regulators have become interested in reviving 'trust based environmental regulation'.

Bettina Lange and Andy Gouldson, 'Trust-Based Environmental Regulation' (2010) 408 Science of the Total Environment 5235, 5236–38

In broad terms, we define trust-based environmental regulation as a specific regulatory style that involves openness and cooperation in interaction between regulated, regulators and third-party stakeholders in order to achieve environmental protection objectives. [...]

But what we understand as trust in environmental regulation also depends on the perspective we adopt. Psychological definitions need to be complemented with a sociological perspective. Some social psychologists define trust as an internal state [...] Whether or not to display trust is considered as a matter of individual choice. But in a regulatory context, trust may be simply required. For instance, regulators do not always know the regulated process as well as the regulated do. Hence, they may not have a choice about whether to trust the regulated, but have to trust the information that they provide, for instance in the context of licensing and enforcement. Extensive collection and scrutiny of information may involve a disproportionate investment of both business' and regulators' resources. Sociological perspectives further highlight that trust is an interactional concept and this fits with the fact that environmental regulation seeks to steer relationships between regulator, regulated and third parties. Trust can facilitate interactions by reducing complexity and perceptions of uncertainty [...] Trust is shaped by culture and social norms which create expectations of specific behaviour that–if fulfilled–generate trust

[...]

there is no simple association between cooperative and trust-based environmental regulation, because cooperation often involves less trust than trust relationships. Cooperation means to recognise the distinct interests of each actor in a regulatory regime and to seek to merely align these. Trust relationships involve a surrender of control over the pursuit of one's own interests. Trust exists where we consider others to act in our own best interests. [...]

If there is a regulatory style with which trust-based environmental regulation–of the type where regulators still retain some oversight over the activities of the regulated–can be associated, it is a contractual regulatory style. Regulator and regulated consider each other as partners. In fact, it has been suggested that a psychological contract is in place which is informed by 'motivational postures' which in turn are shaped by 'coping sensibilities', such as 'thinking morally' or 'feeling oppressed'. Motivational postures are 'the social signals that individuals send to authority, to others, and to themselves to communicate preferred social distance from that authority' (Braithwaite et al., 2007, p. 138). They are also influenced by how trustworthy the regulated perceive the regulator to be.

While trust based environmental regulation explicitly acknowledges the role of emotions in communicating environmental regulatory strategy, it is worth bearing in mind that at its heart is a dilemma, which results from the fact that the building of trust between regulators and regulated through contractual styles of regulation can engender distrust between citizens and regulators.

3.3 REGULATORY SPACE ANALYSIS AND ENVIRONMENTAL REGULATORY STRATEGY

'Regulatory space' analysis is a third important perspective for understanding how environmental regulatory strategy works. By highlighting that regulation is communicated and implemented within the boundaries of organizational, legal, and political imagined 'spaces' this perspective further contributes to questioning instrumental understandings of regulatory strategy, which assume that regulatory strategy can be implemented according to a linear-causal model. Instead, what regulatory strategy can achieve also depends on how it travels through 'regulatory spaces' and how it is refracted and changed through the specific configurations of these spaces. This spatial metaphor includes the idea that space configures power relationships between regulated and regulatory organizations. Hence, 'regulatory space' analysis questions the simple notion of 'regulatory capture'.[34] This suggests that, in particular, economic regulation of corporate actors often fails because independent regulatory agencies—that frequently work day-to-day very closely with regulated organizations—gradually perceive the world increasingly through the eyes of those they are meant to regulate, and thus become captured by their interests and perceptions. Hancher's and Moran's regulatory space analysis paints a more subtle picture of power relationships between regulatory and regulated organizations.

Leigh Hancher and Michael Moran 'Organizing Regulatory Space' in L Hancher and M Moran (eds), *Capitalism, Culture and Economic Regulation* (Clarendon Press 1989) 276–79, 283, 286, 291–92

The critical question for the analyst of the European regulatory scene is not to assume 'capture', but rather to understand the nature of this shared space: the rules of admissions, the relations between occupants, and the variations introduced by differences in markets and issue arenas.

Public Space and Regulatory Space

Framing the problem in this way mirrors the approach recently adopted by Crouch in his attempt to make sense of different national configurations in the place given to organized interests in the policy process. Crouch begins with the notion that it is possible in any particular community at any particular time to identify a 'public space', which he describes as the 'range of issues over which general universal decisions are made within a given political unit'. He then explores the historical experiences which have, in different European countries, allowed different groups of participants into this public space. We can likewise speak of a 'regulatory space' whose dimensions and occupants can be understood by examining regulation in any particular national setting, and by analysing that setting in terms of its specific political, legal, and cultural attributes.

The concept of 'regulatory space' is an analytical construct. It is defined, to adapt Crouch's language, by the range of regulatory issues subject to public decision. A number of obvious consequences follow from this. First, precisely because it is a space, it is available for occupation. Secondly, because it is a space it can be unevenly divided between actors: there will, in other words, be major and minor participants in the regulatory process. Thirdly, just as we can identify a general concept of regulatory space in operation in a particular community we can also speak of specific concepts of regulatory space at work in individual sectors: in pharmaceuticals, for instance, issues of safety and price control are subjects, or potential subjects, of regulatory activity, whereas in the automobile sector only the former set of issues are included. Fourthly, because 'regulatory space' is an image being used to convey a concept, it can

---

[34] Marver Bernstein, *Regulating Business by Independent Commission* (Princeton UP 1955).

be augmented by similar images: thus because an arena is delineated space we sometimes speak of a 'regulatory arena'. The boundaries which demarcate regulatory space may be furiously contested. Its occupants are involved in an often ferocious struggle for advantage. Any investigation of the concept involves examining the outcomes of competitive struggles, the resources used in those struggles, and the distribution of those resources between the different involved institutions. In other words, the play of power is at the centre of this process.

Discovering who has power in regulation involves paying close attention to the relations between the organizations which at any time occupy regulatory space. But the idea of a space also directs us to a far more important aspect of power. It encourages us not only to examine relations between those who enjoy inclusion, but also to examine the characteristics of the excluded. [...]

Understanding why some issues are prioritized, included, or excluded, at different times and in different places, thus demands an exploration of how organizations become committed to, and maintain a commitment to, particular definitions of the scope of regulatory space. [...]

Understanding economic regulation therefore involves understanding the terms under which organizations enter regulatory space and defend their position within it. This is in turn heavily influenced by the prevailing general political attitudes and legal traditions existing in any community to the place of organized interests in the policy process. In other words, *place* matters in determining the nature of regulation, an insight also central to Crouch's exploration of national peculiarities and public space. We therefore next sketch the importance of place. [...]

Regulation occurs, it is a truism to observe, in particular places, and therefore place matters. The most important delineation of place is provided by the boundaries of the nation-state. Nations arrange their regulatory spaces in distinctive ways. Yet it is also plain that national peculiarities are by no means the whole story. Within particular countries the characters of different regulatory communities show great variety. [...]

Organizational space and regulatory space [...]

Common issues and common arenas bind actors together in relations of interdependence. Analysis of the process of regulation from the perspective of interdependence is by no means new, but the concept of regulatory space offers additional insights into the character of interdependence. [...]

One advantage of approaching the subject of interdependence through the concept of 'regulatory space' is that it alerts us to the problem of defining the character of the social relations between the occupants of that space. The notion of a 'regulatory space' focuses attention not only on who the actors involved in regulation are, but on the structural factors which facilitate the emergence and development of networks and which contribute to the institutionalization of linkages. In taking the nature of the links between actors as the staring-point of analysis, it offers the chance of developing a systematic comparison of their character in different industrial sectors and within different national settings.

Scott's analysis, which builds upon Hancher's and Moran's work, provides further insight into the role of law in 'regulatory space'.

Colin Scott, 'Analysing Regulatory Space: Fragmented Resources and Institutional Design' [2001] PL 329, 330–31, 334, 352

The chief idea of the regulatory space metaphor is that resources relevant to holding of regulatory power and exercising of capacities are dispersed or fragmented. These resources are not restricted to formal, state authority derived from legislation or contracts, but also include information, wealth and organisational capacities. Put another way, capacities derived from possession of key resources are not necessarily exercised hierarchically within the regulatory space, regulator over regulatee. We recognise the presence within the space not just of regulators and regulates, but of other interested organizations, state and non-state, possessing resources to a variable degree. Relations can be characterized as complex, dynamic and horizontal, involving negotiated interdependence. [...]

The dispersed nature of resources between organisations in the same regulatory space means regulators lack a monopoly both over formal and informal authority. This observation draws our attention to the need to conceive of strategies of regulation as consisting of a wide range of negotiated processes, of which rule formation and enforcement are but two. [...]

Regulatory reform, 'renegotiation of regulatory space', might then focus not exclusively, or even mainly, on a single organisation, but rather on the whole configuration of resources and relations within the regulatory space. Some capacities might be enhanced and some constrained. [...]

Fragmented Resources

Governmental resources are not restricted to legal authority, but include also wealth (or "treasure"), information (or 'nodality') and organisational capacities. The objectives of regulatory regimes can, of course, be sought through the deployment of governmental resources other than authority. [...]

Normatively the regulatory space analysis does not offer any clear prescription as to what structures and processes will have the desired behaviour modification effects in any particular policy domain, but rather leaves the identification of appropriate institutions and processes for detailed analysis in each case. Nevertheless the regulatory space metaphor is useful in challenging overstated claims for what is possible through regulatory activity.

Regulatory space analysis also prompts us to rethink accountability of regulators, a theme further discussed in Chapter 13. It suggests that not just traditional public bodies such as courts and Parliament can hold regulators to account, but also a variety of private organizations, such as powerful regulated organizations and environmental NGOs. Hence, regulatory space analysis paints a picture of regulatory strategy as constituted by complex relationships of interdependence between both public and private institutions. This complexity is further increased if we consider that regulatory space—also in environmental regulation—is usually no longer a national regulatory space, but an EU-wide one. In the context of economic regulation of utilities, such as electricity, telecommunications, and financial services, Thatcher and Coen further develop the idea of European regulatory space, defined as 'the structures for taking decisions about implementing EU legislation concerning regulation of markets'.[35] They describe European regulatory space as 'fragmented, cluttered and complex'.

---

[35] Mark Thatcher and David Coen, 'Reshaping European Regulatory Space: An Evolutionary Analysis' (2008) 31 West European Politics 806, 810.

Mark Thatcher and David Coen, 'Reshaping European Regulatory Space: An Evolutionary Analysis' (2008) 31 West European Politics 806, 809, 829

But, there has been no movement towards a neat and tidy regulatory space. Instead, that space is filled with multiple organisations and is strongly marked by past steps. Indeed, evolution has been far from painless or consensual: rather it has involved strong debates about the extent of centralisation of powers at the European level and the respective roles of the European Commission and national and EU regulatory agencies, showing that implementing institutions link to wider political battles about integration and the form of the EU.

The institutions for implementing EU regulation have been reformed in an evolutionary manner since the late 1980s. Analysis of three key sectors—financial services, telecommunications and energy—has revealed how each stage has influenced later ones. New organisational forms have arisen from old ones, offering examples of institutional 'conversion'. In securities regulation, the new European Regulatory Network CESR grew out of the network of national independent regulatory authorities FESCO, while in energy and telecommunications, current proposals are to strengthen and convert existing European Regulatory Networks.

Thatcher and Coen then outline reasons for the *evolutionary*, rather than revolutionary, development of EU regulation. They include power struggles in which existing bodies resist loss of powers or the entry into regulatory space of new institutions which may detract from their powers. Existing, in particular national, regulatory institutions therefore often act as buffers to radical change and may block the development of EU federal regulatory agencies. For instance, the European Environment Agency in Copenhagen[36] has powers to gather information about the state of the environment in the EU, but lacks stronger executive powers to monitor the implementation of environmental law in the Member States or to directly enforce EU environmental regulation.

While regulatory space analysis provides important insights into the dynamics of power relationships that shape the development and implementation of regulatory strategy, it also has some shortcomings. First, regulatory space is a metaphor—and it may be just that, thus not amounting to a fully fledged concept or inductive theory of 'regulation in action'. In order to count as a concept it requires further specification, in particular criteria that determine how to draw the boundaries of regulatory space, rather than just inferring this case by case inductively from the context of specific regulatory regimes. Second, for 'regulatory space' analysis to amount to a distinct theory, it needs to say something beyond what we already know from other accounts of de-centred regulation. For instance, institutional economics also recognize that, in practice, often multiple 'principals', such as politicians and legislators, who develop regulatory strategy, can pursue conflicting objectives or form coalitions with subsets of principals. Institutional economics further recognize that their agents, such as senior bureaucrats who are entrusted with the implementation of regulatory strategy, can build implementation coalitions that interpret legislative strategy differently from the way it was interpreted by the original legislative coalition. But—further in line with the ideas of regulatory space analysis—it also suggests that, nevertheless, a degree of control over regulators is possible. However, this does not involve hierarchical control by politicians over bureaucratic agents. Instead it takes the form of carefully calibrated checks and balances in a particular regulatory arena:

The new institutional theories of regulation show precisely that regulators can be monitored and kept politically accountable only by means of a *combination of control instruments*: oversight by specialized

---

[36] More info at <http://www.eea.europa.eu/> accessed 5 October 2012.

congressional committees, presidential power of appointment, strict procedural requirements, professional standards, public participation and judicial review. When this system works properly nobody controls the independent agency but the agency is 'under control'.[37]

FURTHER READING AND QUESTIONS

The discussion in this section has highlighted the need to engage with a wide array of literature in thinking about regulatory strategy. We thus provide quite a substantive list of further reading here. We should stress that this reading will be relevant to thinking about regulatory strategy across all areas of environmental law. The questions thus encourage broad thinking.

1. Do you agree with the systems-theoretical idea that law and politics are two distinct social sub-systems? Are environmental law and politics not intertwined?

2. For a further discussion of systems theory and reflexive law see Andreas Philippopoulos-Mihalopoulos, *Niklas Luhmann: Law, Justice, Society* (Routledge 2010) ch 4; Gunther Teubner, L Farmer, and D Murphy (eds), *Environmental Law and Ecological Responsibility, The Concept and Practice of Ecological Self- Organization* (Wiley 1994); Bettina Lange, 'Understanding Regulatory Law: Empirical versus Systems-Theoretical Approaches?' (1998) 18 OJLS 449 (discusses what conception of agency informs systems-theoretical analysis); Marleen Brans and Stefan Rossbach, 'The autopoiesis of administrative systems: Niklas Luhmann on public administration and public policy' (1997) 75 Public Administration 417; Eric Orts (1995) 'Reflexive environmental law' (1995) 89 Northwestern University Law Review 1227; and Niklas Luhmann, *Ecological Communication* (Chicago UP 1989).

3. On the important role of risk perception and trust see A Spence, NF Pidgeon, and D Uzzell, 'Climate change—psychology's contribution' (2008) 21 The Psychologist 108; D Metlay, 'Institutional trust and confidence: a journey into a conceptual quagmire' in G Cvetkovich and R Loefstedt (eds), *Social Trust and the Management of Risk* (Earthscan 1999) 100; and W Poortinga and NF Pidgeon, 'Trust in risk regulation: cause or consequence of the acceptability of GM food?' (2005) 25 Risk Analysis 199.

4. Do you think that trust based environmental regulation chimes with the government's 'better regulation' agenda, also because co-operative styles of regulation can reduce the cost of regulation?

---

4 THE LIMITS OF AN INSTRUMENTAL PERSPECTIVE OF REGULATORY STRATEGY: THE DIFFICULT SEARCH FOR 'EFFECTIVE' REGULATORY TOOLS

The discussion so far has highlighted the need to have a richer understanding of regulatory strategy. This is not to say, however, that a discussion about regulatory strategy must be wholly theoretical, but that it is important to use theoretical insights for understanding regulatory strategy. In this final section, we build on this analysis by mapping four key regulatory tools that are deployed in order to make

---

[37] Giandomenico Majone, *Regulating Europe* (Routledge 1996) 39–40.

environmental regulatory strategy happen. The extracts illustrate challenges to using these tools in a 'strategic' and 'effective' manner, and thus to realize an instrumental vision of environmental law.

4.1 STATE 'COMMAND AND CONTROL' REGULATION

As we saw in Section 1, state 'command and control' regulation is a core element of environmental regulatory strategy—though, as this section illustrates, one that is increasingly becoming supplanted by or has to interact with a whole range of other strategies, such as economic incentive and self-regulation. State 'command and control' regulation involves the establishment of usually statutory environmental standards, which are enforced by independent regulatory agencies, such as the Environment Agency for England and Wales. Such standards are often backed up by sanctions, frequently enshrined in criminal law.

While state 'command and control' environmental regulatory strategy aspires to provide 'strict' and uniform state regulation, empirical research has shown that its implementation is mediated by the way in which enforcement officers and regulated organizations interpret statutory provisions. Hence, while there may be formally 'strict' environmental law on the statute book, a process of interpreting and communicating environmental law obligations to and by those subject to regulation can change the content of the environmental regulatory strategy. What environmental law actually means and what constitutes compliance with it is, in practice, determined also with references to the social practices of regulated organizations. These consist of organizational cultures, 'customary law' at a regulated facility, and operating practices. In other words, environmental law and what constitutes compliance with it are socially constructed.

Bettina Lange, 'Compliance Construction in the Context of Environmental Regulation' (1999) 8(4) Social and Legal Studies 549

The social construction approach—in contrast—has different implications for addressing the compliance problem. According to this perspective, we would not be concerned with achieving 'more compliance' because compliance simply reflects a subjective process of the construction of the relationship between rules and social practices. Indeed some research has stated that compliance might be the problem, not the solution to enforcement deficits, particularly if it is achieved by creative means [...] Hence, official compliance assessments might not tell us much about the question of whether the regulated have achieved the substantive aims of regulation

[...]

If precise and detailed legal rules might not assist in compliance evaluations there might be alternative indicators for making meaningful statements about the activities of the regulated. [...] In the area of environmental regulation, alternative indicators of compliance could be based on technical information, for example, about the release of emissions into the environment. Evaluations of facilities would be based on what emissions they cause rather than if they 'comply' with legal rules. If facilities report about their operations without reference to formal standards in relation to which compliance has to be demonstrated, and hence if the normative element is taken out of the provision of information, greater authenticity and openness in the accounts presented may result. More openness might be a valuable goal in regulation but this might be difficult to embody in legal standards. One particular form of strong integration between rules and social practices that occurred in waste management regulation was the 'double institutionalization' of customary rules [...] Customary rules can become part of the formal law. Once customary rules have been formally restated they can be referred to by formal legal

> institutions as norms of decisions [...] The term 'customary rules' covers norms which are generated out and then abstracted from actual social practices rather than being imposed by an external agency of social control [...] Customary norms at the waste treatment plant concerned, for example, procedures set up for testing incoming waste loads. The 'double institutionalization' of customary rules occurred in connection with the licensing process. The operator of the waste management site would draw up a working plan which described the way in which the regulated carried out their operations. The working plan which in effect contained a statement of customary rules at the plant—including, for example, the testing routines—became part of the formal law through incorporation into the site licence.

This extract points out that waste management plans, a detailed statement of operating procedures at a waste management facility, are key to evaluations of what constitutes compliance at regulated plants. This descriptive account of what the regulated actually do thus merges with a normative perspective on the environmental standards they should comply with. The fact that the environmental standards they should comply with are often informed by the wider theoretical approaches to regulatory strategy discussed already, thus shows the value of being aware of theoretical ideas that inform regulatory strategies.

4.2 ECONOMIC INCENTIVE REGULATION

As noted, various criticisms of state 'command and control' regulation have led to increasing interest in economic incentive type regulation. State 'command and control' regulation has been considered as potentially inefficient by imposing excessive bureaucratic regulatory burdens upon businesses, in particular small and medium-sized companies. In contrast to this, economic incentive regulation claims that it can provide particularly powerful tools for the implementation of environmental regulatory strategy because it harnesses the entrenched aim of economic actors to maximize their economic gain.

Key examples of economic incentive regulation are, firstly, charges, taxes, and subsidies. Sections 41, 42, and 43 of the Environment Act 1995 grant powers to the EA to develop financial charges.[38] Where the amount of the charge for the licensing activity is proportionate to the magnitude and hazardousness of the pollution being regulated the charge for the licence will act as an economic incentive for the operator to reduce pollution. Where a charging system is simply recovering costs for the administration of the regulator for the licensing activity and the enforcement to be recovered it will act less as an economic incentive for the reduction of pollution. Environmental taxation poses the challenge for state actors to set the tax at the appropriate level so that it sets a sufficient price signal for environmentally damaging behaviour to be altered. In the UK the landfill tax, which is payable for every tonne of waste disposed off in a landfill site, for instance, was set initially at too low a level for sufficiently preventing the generation of waste.[39]

Further examples of charges, taxes, and subsidies are charges for licensing polluting companies, the taxation of energy use, or the promotion of environmentally beneficial activities, such as subsidies for green energy generation. Secondly, there are deposit and refund schemes, such as deposits

---

[38] See also the EA's Environmental Permitting Scheme 2011/12. The Environment Agency is developing its Operational Risk Appraisal (Opra) tool, extending its risk-based approach where appropriate to the candidate EPP2 (and other) regimes. These developments are linked to the Environment Agency's Unified Charging Framework. The full Opra methodology only applies to activities with bespoke permits, with a simplified approach being taken for the rest.

[39] Anthony Seely, 'Landfill Tax: Recent Developments', 15 December 2009, House of Commons Library, Standard Note: SN/BT/1963 at <http://www.parliament.uk/briefing-papers/SN01963.pdf>.

and refunds for reusable drinks containers.[40] Thirdly, there are markets in emission allowances in which, for example, allowances for polluting air are traded.[41] Fourthly, civil liability provisions,[42] which require polluters to pay, such as the tort of negligence, can act as an economic incentive for environmental protection.

The most innovative type of economic incentive regulation is emissions trading. We discuss the EU emissions trading scheme in detail in Chapter 15, but here it is useful to say something about such schemes in general. In theory, an emissions trading scheme is a regulatory mechanism that involves constructing a market in the right to emit certain pollutants, and setting the rules of the market. There are two basic kinds of emissions trading schemes: 'cap and trade' and 'baseline and credit' schemes.[43] Under a cap and trade scheme, an overall pollution cap for the market is set, with allowances to pollute then auctioned or allocated to players in the market (initially those who emit the relevant pollutants, but the market can also include brokers). These allowances or permits are the market's unit of trade and the total number of allowances adds up to the binding cap set for the market—no more can be issued. Market players are required to hold the number of allowances equivalent to their emissions, which may involve them reducing their emissions if they operate heavily polluting installations, or otherwise they may have to purchase additional allowances on the market. In theory, the cost of doing so should create incentives to abate pollution and invest in cleaner technology. Over time, the cap can be reduced to make allowances scarcer and more expensive, whilst ensuring that the overall level of pollution is decreasing. In a baseline and credit scheme, in contrast, polluting market players are given a baseline or performance target for their relevant polluting emissions, and they acquire credits if they come in under their emissions targets, or alternatively have to purchase them from other market players if their baseline target is exceeded.

Emissions trading is not entirely distinct from state regulation because state regulation is key to constituting and regulating a market in emission allowances. Trading schemes can also be used in other contexts such as in relation to rights to access and use water resources.

Vicky Waye and Christina Son 'Regulating the Australian Water Market' (2010) 22 JEL 431–34, 436, 457

Australia has become increasingly subject to a lack of water security. Markets have emerged as a means of responding to increased water scarcity by facilitating improvements in the efficiency of water allocation and management. However, to attain efficiency, markets have to operate competitively. Competitive markets require: low barriers to entry; low transaction costs; perfect or near-perfect information; the absence of collusion among suppliers; clear rules of exchange; enforceable property rights; and effective governance structures. [...]

However, analogous to problems encountered in the USA and Europe realisation of reform has been complicated by federalism. Under the Australian constitution, the power to regulate water use is largely devolved to Australia's seven State governments. The exercise of national Commonwealth regulatory power is further constrained by §100 Constitution which provides that the Commonwealth's power to regulate trade and commerce does not authorise the enactment of laws abridging 'the right of a State or of the residents therein to the reasonable use of the waters of rivers for conservation or irrigation.' [...]

Water reform has, therefore, not just comprised the introduction of water trading and restructuring of the water supply industry, but has also strived to achieve more coherent and sustainable management

---

[40] See the Danish scheme that was the focus of Case C–302/86 *Commission* v *Denmark* [1988] ECR I–4607, further discussed in Chapter 4.

[41] Discussed further here and see Chapter 15.   [42] See Chapter 9.

[43] See Robert Baldwin, 'Regulation Lite: The Rise of Emissions Trading' (2008) 2 Regulation and Governance 193, 194–95.

of scarce water resources. Public health externalities associated with water consumption have also been a factor which has taken water reform well beyond the promotion of competition, and into the realm of 'market environmentalism. […]

2. Water Trading

The philosophy underlying the promotion of water trading is to assure that water is allocated to its most efficient use. By imposing a market price and an opportunity cost upon water, users are encouraged to use what water they have more conservatively, or to transfer their water to others if the market price for water exceeds the cost of using it themselves. Water trading is also seen as an efficient vehicle for clawing back over-allocations of water so as to improve environmental flows. The abolition of riparian rights and the creation of water entitlements independent of land are necessary precursors to water trading.

[…]

8. Conclusion

The enactment of laws that enable the creation of tradable entitlements, prohibit barriers to trade such as exorbitant termination fees, minimise regulatory restrictions on transfer and impose fair dealing obligations on water-industry participants, have been identified as necessary pre-requisites for the development of a 'mature' water market.

In Australia, the Australian Consumer and Competition Commission, in particular, has played an important role in regulating water trading. Moreover, both the Commonwealth and state governments have been active participants in Australia's water market, also by buying water for 'environmental use', in order to support environmental resources, such as habitats.[44] In the UK, water scarcity is not yet as much of an issue as in Australia, the driest continent on earth, but availability of sufficient water is becoming a concern in the South East. The recent UK government White Paper 'Water for Life' is exploring the use of economic incentive mechanisms, including water trading, in order to address increasing water scarcity in some parts of the UK.[45] We can thus see the need to develop rich and nuanced accounts of regulatory strategy in order to capture these various developments in environmental policy.

4.3 RESPONSIVE REGULATION

Economic incentive regulation seeks to turn the regulated into willing collaborators by establishing state regulatory frameworks that provide financial reasons for reducing polluting activities. In systems-theoretical terms this is an attempt by the political sub-system of society to become 'cognitively open' to the economic sub-system. 'Responsive regulation' takes this approach further in that it seeks to 'open up' state regulation to the attitude of the regulated towards compliance with law. Enforcement activity thus becomes calibrated to how the regulated approach implementation of legal rules, a point further illustrated through 'enforcement pyramids'.

---

[44] See, for example, the activities of the Commonwealth Environmental Water Office, at <http://www.environment.gov.au/ewater/index.html>.

[45] DEFRA, *Water for Life* (Cm 8230, 2011).

Ian Ayres and John Braithwaite, *Responsive Regulation: Transcending the Deregulation Debate* (OUP 1992) 35–36

Most regulatory action occurs at the base of the pyramid where attempts are initially made to coax compliance by persuasion. The next phase of enforcement escalation is a warning letter; if this fails to secure compliance, imposition of civil monetary penalties; if this fails, criminal prosecution; if this fails, plant shutdown or temporary suspension of a licence to operate; if this fails permanent revocation of licence. This particular enforcement pyramid might be applicable to occupational health and safety, environment or nursing home regulation, but inapplicable to banking or affirmative action regulation. It is not the content of the enforcement pyramid on which we wish to focus during this discussion, but its form. Different kinds of sanctioning are appropriate to different regulatory arenas.

Defection from cooperation is likely to be a less attractive proposition for business when it faces a regulator with an enforcement pyramid than when confronted with a regulator having only one deterrence option. This is true even where the deterrence option available to the regulator is maximally potent.

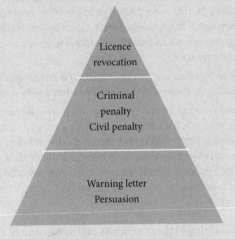

Figure 12.1 Example of an enforcement pyramid. The proportion of space at each layer represents the proportion of enforcement activity at that level

Figure 12.2 Example of a pyramid of enforcement strategies

Ayres' and Braithwaite's 'responsive regulation' approach thus makes the point that the implementation of environmental regulatory strategy benefits from a clever and careful co-ordination of different regulatory tools available to the regulator, such as state 'command and control' regulation, economic incentive, and self-regulation. But from a 'regulatory space' perspective, the regulated may have significant informal resources of power and regulators' formal authority may be dispersed among different state institutions, for instance when a regulatory agency is dependent on courts to impose sanctions. If regulatory space is configured like this, regulators may not be able to issue strong and credible threats to escalate up the enforcement pyramid.[46] In addition, the 'responsive regulation' approach has been further developed into a more ambitious 'really responsive' regulation approach.

Julia Black and Robert Baldwin 'Really Responsive Regulation' (2008) 71 MLR 59, 61, 71, 76

We argue that to be *really* responsive, regulators have to be responsive not only to the compliance performance of the regulatee, but in five further ways: to the firms' own operating and cognitive frameworks (their 'attitudinal settings'); to the broader institutional environment of the regulatory regime; to the different logics of regulatory tools and strategies; to the regime's own performance; and finally to changes in each of these elements. [...]

Really responsive regulation emphasises the relevance of the institutional context not only of the regulatee, but also of the regulator, in shaping the regulators' enforcement activities. [...]

In introducing our argument we stated that a 'really responsive' regulation approach needs to be applied across all of the different tasks that are involved in regulatory activity. In the case of enforcement, this requires that the enforcement function is broken down into its different elements. We propose that there are five such elements or tasks. These involve detecting undesirable or non-compliant behaviour, developing tools and strategies for responding to that behaviour, enforcing those tools and strategies on the ground, assessing their success or failure and modifying approaches accordingly.

Black and Bladwin, while pointing to the complexity and dynamism of a really responsive regulation approach, seek to enhance opportunities for regulators to act in a strategic and effective manner. They make this clear in a later article considering risk-based approaches to regulation.

Robert Baldwin and Julia Black, 'Really Responsive Risk-Based Regulation' (2010) 32 Law and Policy 181, 194

A really responsive approach to risk-based regulation emphasizes the degree to which regulatory interactions, processes, or outcomes are shaped by the institutional environments of both regulatee and regulator. These environments are constituted by the organizational/regulatory, normative, cognitive, and resource-distribution structures in which these actors are situated [...] The actions and decisions of organizations and individuals (both regulators and regulatees) are thus structured by the norms regulating their conduct, by the senses of appropriateness of actions, by understandings of how the environment operates, and by the distribution of resources between themselves and others with whom they interact. For regulatees, this includes the market and, in particular, its value chain. For both regulatee and regulator, it includes other regulators within a decentered or polycentric regulatory regime. A really responsive

---

[46] Colin Scott, 'Analyzing regulatory space: fragmented resources and institutional design' [2001] PL 329, 346.

approach, accordingly, demands that when regulators apply risk-based approaches, they take into account the challenges and limitations imposed by institutional environments that are both internal and external to regulatory organizations and regulatees and that involve these actors in active as well as passive roles.

Again we can see that this is an approach where regulation is not treated as a mere instrument. A more wide-ranging analysis is needed to understand how a regulatory strategy is constructed, how it can work in specific organizational contexts, and how different elements of an organizational strategy may interact.

4.4 SELF-REGULATION

Regulatory strategies based on self-regulation are a fourth set of strategies that a regulatory agency can deploy. They involve the control over polluting activities by the regulated themselves, rather than the imposition of standards by an external government regulator. In practice, however, self-regulation often involves complex hybrid state–private co-regulatory arrangements, in which the state seeks to incentivize and monitor self-regulation. UK DEFRA's core guidance on environmental permitting explicitly states that:

environmental management systems have relevance to other aspects of regulation, such as determining risk-based inspection frequencies. Recognised quality assurance schemes may also be relevant, and regulators may also take account of non-certified systems where these can be demonstrated to provide an equivalent role in safeguarding compliance and continual improvement of environmental performance.[47]

Borck and Coglianese discuss experiences with voluntary environmental programs in the US.

Jonathan C Borck and Cary Coglianese 'Voluntary Environmental Programs: Assessing their Effectiveness' (2009) 34 Annual Review of Environment and Resources 305, 307–9

By contrast, VEPs—sometimes referred to as voluntary environmental agreements—neither impose mandatory limits nor require specific forms of behaviour. As such, they offer yet another alternative to traditional forms of regulation. VEPs establish positive incentives to encourage businesses and other organizations to address environmental issues that are not subject to regulation or to reduce their regulated environmental impacts to well below the levels permitted by law. Unlike regulations—whether traditional or market based—they do not rely on built-in sanctions as a force for motivating environmental improvements. [...]

A common typology distinguishes three types of programs on the basis of the number of participating businesses and on the degree of governmental involvement: (a) unilateral initiatives, (b) bilateral agreements, and (c) public voluntary programs. Unilateral initiatives are actions that individual businesses or trade associations pursue without any specific involvement or prompting by government. Sometimes individual firms take voluntary steps without any specific programmatic encouragement by outside entities—voluntary behaviour that is typically referred to as corporate social responsibility. Businesses can also voluntarily impose environmental requirements on their business partners, such as when General Motors Corporation and Ford Motor Company unilaterally required their suppliers to implement

---

[47] DEFRA, *Environmental Permitting Guidance: Core Guidance, For the Environmental Permitting (England and Wales) Regulations 2010* (version 4.0, revised March 2012, edn 2010) paras 9.7 and 53.

EMSs [Environmental Management Standards] that met ISO [International Standards Organisation] standards. In addition, trade associations can unilaterally take action by imposing environment-related standards on their members. These trade association standards can be mandatory on those companies that choose to remain members of the industry group, such as the American Chemistry Council's Responsible Care Program, which requires members to implement EMSs. [...]

Bilateral agreements are negotiated between specific businesses and the government to pursue environmental objectives. Typically these agreements aim to establish a target for pollution reduction (or any other environmentally responsible behaviour) and a timetable for an individual business or a group of businesses to meet this target, with government offering tax or regulatory incentives in exchange. [...]

Public voluntary programs—the third type of voluntary initiative—are designed and sponsored by governments to recognize companies that go beyond compliance with existing regulations. Public voluntary programs in the United States appeared in the late 1980s and have since multiplied in number. One of the earliest national programs was called 33/50 because it sought to reduce overall emissions of designated toxic chemicals by 33% over a four-year period and 50% over a seven-year period, simply by publicly recognizing firms that voluntarily committed to reducing toxic pollutants. [...]

As Prakash & Potoski suggest, the effectiveness of any type of VEP will be a function of both the level of participation in these programs and the environmental and other improvements that result from the inducements for participation.

Borck and Coglianese are cautious about what voluntary environmental programmes can achieve, even though they also consider 'spill-over' effects of VEPs, that is, their impact on corporate actors that are not participating in the programme, but reduce nevertheless their environmental impact due to pressure from economic competitors, workers, or other stakeholders, such as shareholders, consumers, and neighbours in the communities in which they operate. The potential for stakeholders to prise a corporation 'open' to demands for improvements in its social, including environmental, impact has been considered in the literature on corporate social responsibility.

Christine Parker, _The Open Corporation_ (CUP 2002) 292–93, 295, 300–1

Corporate self-regulation is necessary to democracy. It is neither naive optimism nor a concession to market power to advocate reliance on corporate self-regulation as a matter of policy. We have no choice but to inquire into the conditions in which corporate self-regulation will occur effectively, because there will be no legal or socially responsible action by corporations if there is no self-management of responsibility. It is corporate management that will ultimately determine corporate compliance or non-compliance with social and legal responsibilities. [...]

But mine is an ideal of self-regulation that is not purely self-regulation at all. Rather, it is a marriage between law, corporate self-management and external stakeholders.

Corporate management should be open to a broad range of stake-holder deliberation about values; and legal regulation should facilitate (and enforce) their permeation. In the open corporation, management self-critically reflects on past and future actions in the light of legal responsibilities and impacts on stakeholders. They go on to institutionalize operating procedures, habits and cultures that constantly seek to do better at ensuring that the whole company complies with legal responsibilities, accomplishes the underlying goals and values of regulation, and does justice in its impacts on stakeholders (even where no law has yet defined what that involves). [...]

As we have seen, the integrity of individual self-regulation professionals, in particular, is a critical point of leverage for corporate responsibility and therefore the broader democracy. [...]

If corporate self-regulation systems have a tendency to privatize, individualize and deflect conflict in remedying injustice, *then* the role of regulation ought to be to connect individual corporate self-regulation initiatives back up to the question for social justice by gathering intelligence on patterns of injustice in corporate self-regulation, and using its problem-solving and enforcement capacities to restore justice.

[…]

If corporate self-regulation management systems frequently lack the capacity or commitment to improve on past performance, to learn from individual mistakes and consumer complaints, and to engage in the discipline of self-evaluation, *then* the role of regulation is to meta-evaluate corporate self-evaluation and organizational learning and to hold companies responsible for how they react to and resolve injustices that they cause.

Parker's analysis of self-regulation emphasizes again the theme of the interconnectedness of various regulatory tools for implementing environmental regulatory strategy, here self-regulation and state regulation.

FURTHER READING AND QUESTIONS

1. For a further discussion of a social interactionist approach to the enforcement of environmental law based on extensive qualitative empirical research involving participant observation and interviews with water pollution control inspectors of the former Regional Water Authorities in England in the late 1970s and 1980s, see the classic study by Keith Hawkins, *Environment and Enforcement: Regulation and the Social Definition of Pollution* (Clarendon Press 1984).

2. Bettina Lange, 'What does Law Know?—Prescribing and Describing the Social World in the Enforcement of Legal Rules' (2002) 30 International Journal of the Sociology of Law 131.

3. Do you think that state regulation has to draw on the actual operating practices of regulated facilities? If so, where does this leave the distinction between self-regulation and state 'command and control' regulation?

4. Further discussion of responsive regulation can be found in John Braithwaite, 'Enforced Self-Regulation: A New Strategy for Corporate Crime Control' (1982) 80 Mich L Rev 1466; and Christine Parker (ed), '20 Years of Responsive Regulation: A Critical Appraisal', special issue of Regulation and Governance (2013), forthcoming.

3. How do you think 'responsive regulation' differs from Cass Sunstein's idea of 'choice architecture', discussed in Section 1?

4. Neil Gunningham, Peler Grabosky and Darren Sinclair *Smart Regulation* (Clarendon Press 1998). This is a critique of the 'responsive regulation' approach and suggests that *preventative* regulation is also important, as is consideration of non-state actors, in enforcing regulation, such as trade associations, corporations themselves, and the professions.

5. 'Risk based' regulation (discussed by Black and Baldwin) is yet another regulatory tool for implementing environmental regulatory strategies. In the UK, the Hampton Review (Philip Hampton, *Reducing Administrative Burdens* (HM Treasury 2005)) recommended the uptake and development of this approach for a range of regulators, including the EA. It focuses upon enforcement and aims to target enforcement and inspection resources upon those organizations that pose the most severe risks, both in terms of breaching legal regulation and in terms of environmental hazards.

6. Which regulatory tools do you consider as the most important for implementing environmental regulatory strategy? Why? What role do political and legal institutions play in your
preferred regulatory tool?

5 CONCLUSION

This chapter has developed a critical perspective of the very idea of 'strategy' in the context of continuing beliefs of policy-makers in the development of environmental regulatory strategies. The chapter has
analysed the operation of regulatory strategy at three levels, theory and ideology, policy programmes,
and enforcement practices. The chapter has suggested that the development and implementation of
environmental regulatory strategy is often not 'strategic' and 'effective' for three key reasons. First,
the economic and political background assumptions that inform the development of environmental
regulatory strategy are contested. Do we regulate the environment for the purpose of economic efficiency, social justice, or the preservation of ecosystems? Second, social-theory reminds us that implementation of environmental regulatory strategy involves a range of complex social processes, such as
the communication of environmental objectives against the backdrop of powerful emotive responses
to environmental risk and regulation. It also involves the reception of environmental policy messages
in specific regulatory spaces that are configured by distinct power relationships between regulators
and regulated. Third, when examining the various regulatory tools available for implementing environmental regulatory strategy, it transpires that complex interactions between them make it difficult
for regulators to use them in a 'strategic' manner. Moreover, this chapter has decentred law. It has
implied that regulatory strategy drives environmental law, rather than environmental law driving
strategy. Some of the material discussed in this chapter shows that non-legal regulatory strategy can
displace formal state law, a trend particularly observable in EU regulation. Other material has shown
that regulatory strategy often provides policy ideas that shape environmental law. The purpose of the
chapter is thus to provide a framework for a critical examination of the specific environmental strategies that underpin UK regulation of polluting activities discussed in Parts IV and V of this book.

FURTHER READING

Robert Baldwin, Martin Cave, and Martin Lodge *Understanding Regulation: Theory, Strategy,
and Practice* (2nd edn, OUP 2011).

Robert Baldwin, Martin Cave, and Martin Lodge (eds), *The Oxford Handbook of Regulation* (OUP
2010).

Bronwen Morgan and Karen Yeung, *An Introduction to Law and Regulation: Text and Materials*
(CUP 2007).

Anthony Ogus, *Regulation: Legal Form and Economic Theory* (Hart Publishing 2004).

13

GOVERNANCE

In order to understand environmental law it is essential to be aware of the wider political structures and programmes that shape its development. Public environmental law and public regulatory agencies are a core aspect of environmental regulation in the UK. But we are also witnessing a subtle, though significant, shift that involves private actors, often operating in a transnational sphere, increasingly being mobilized in environmental regulation. This reflects a wider change in how power is exercised in contemporary societies: a shift from state government to governance. Networks, often transcending the boundaries of a nation-state and composed of both public and private actors, are a central aspect of governance.

This chapter traces the implications of this shift from government to governance for the development and implementation of environmental law in the UK. It maps, in the first section, the increasing role of private actors in environmental regulation and the imprint of new public management techniques on environmental law in the UK. The second section discusses recent, innovative EU governance initiatives that have been described as 'experimentalist' and which have the potential to also transform the development and implementation of national, including environmental, law in the UK. In the third section, this chapter analyses how traditional procedures for ensuring the legitimacy and accountability of environmental law actors are challenged by the shift from government to governance. In its fourth and final section the chapter comes back to the question of what the shift from government to governance actually means by asking whether it can be explained with reference to a wider change from industrial to reflexive modernity. The discussion in these four key sections of the chapter links to core themes examined in other chapters of this book. This chapter paints a wider picture of how environmental law and regulation are changing, and thus provides a context for Chapter 12 on Regulatory Strategy. It also links to key themes discussed in Chapter 4, such as the increasing importance of the EU for environmental law in the UK, as well as debates about the role of scientific knowledge addressed in Chapter 2.

1 ENVIRONMENTAL GOVERNANCE

Governance is a popular word in both the practice and scholarship of environmental law and the term has become a 'catch-all' for 'any strategy, tactic, process, procedure, or programme for controlling, regulating, shaping, mastering or exercising authority over others in a nation, organization or locality'.[1] Governance, then, clearly requires us to understand that environmental problems can be governed by arrangements that are very different from the traditional, hierarchical modes of regulation that we tend to think of when we imagine environmental law. In this section we examine what is understood by the concept of governance and provide some examples of environmental governance 'in action' in the UK.

1.1 THE SHIFT FROM GOVERNMENT TO GOVERNANCE

What does the shift from government to governance actually entail? While government refers to the exercise of public powers by traditional executive state actors, such as central and local government and its agencies, governance is a potentially vague concept. It blurs the distinction between state and civil society, by enrolling private actors into regulation. A hallmark of new governance techniques is the use of networks composed of both public and private actors, and sometimes voluntary sector organizations, in order to govern. These networks are considered as a specific form of exercise of public powers, distinct from 'hierarchies', that is, traditional public bureaucracies and 'markets'. They have a degree of autonomy from the state and are often self-organizing. A hallmark of these networks is that they rely not on hierarchical managerial rules in order to function, nor the discipline of the market, but on trust.[2] Networks are also characterized by interdependence between different actors and organizations within these networks. Resources exchanged include money, information, and expertise. Networks are a way for governmental actors to get things done through other organizations.[3] Privatization of public services, contracting out the delivery of public services, and the introduction of competitive quasi-markets in the delivery of public services are further examples of introducing 'markets' into the business of governing. Guy Peters further elaborates on the significance of 'governance' in the context of environmental regulation:

B Guy Peters, 'Governance as Political Theory' in David Levi-Faur (ed), *Oxford Handbook of Governance* (OUP 2012) 20

The root of the word governance, and indeed government, relates to steering a boat. A steering metaphor is indeed a useful way in which to approach the idea of governance in contemporary societies. Societies require collective choices about a range of issues that cannot be addressed adequately by individual action, and some means must be found to make and implement those decisions. The need for these collective decisions has become all the more obvious when the world as a whole, as well as individual societies, are faced with challenges such as climate change, resource depletion and arms control. Governance also implies some conception of accountability, so that the actors involved in setting goals and then in attempting to reach them, whether through public or private action, must be held accountable for their actions to society.

Here, Peters is showing that the term governance resonates particularly strongly in relation to environmental problems. Levi-Faur gives us more insight into what the term actually means.

---

[1] Nicholas Rose, *Powers of Freedom: Reframing Political Thought* (CUP 1999) 15.
[2] Rod Rhodes, 'The New Governance: Governing Without Government' [1996] Political Studies 652, 653.
[3] Ibid, 658.

David Levi-Faur, 'From "Big Government" to "Big Governance"' in David Levi-Faur (ed), *Oxford Handbook of Governance* (OUP 2012) 8

Governance, much like government, has at least four meanings in the literature: a structure, a process, a mechanism, and a strategy. While the distinction between these four meanings is often not clearly elaborated, it might be useful to clarify them for analytical and theoretical purposes. As a structure, governance signifies the architecture of formal and informal institutions; as a process it signifies the dynamics and steering functions involved in lengthy never-ending processes of policy-making; as a mechanism it signifies institutional procedures of decision-making, of compliance and of control (or instruments); finally as a strategy it signifies the actors' efforts to govern and manipulate the design of institutions and mechanisms in order to shape choice and preferences.

Levi-Faur is thus highlighting that governance has a number of different dimensions. In all cases, governance is referring to governing arrangements that can incorporate a range of very different types of public and private actors. Those arrangements can mean many different things.

Rod AW Rhodes, 'The New Governance: Governing without Government?' (1996) 44 Political Studies 652–53, 655, 660

There are at least six separate uses of governance:

- as the minimal state,
- as corporate governance,
- as the new public management.
- as 'good governance',
- as a socio-cybernetic system,
- as self-organizing networks,

[...]

The last of these is especially significant in the UK. A distinct move from government to governance occurred in the 1980s, under the conservative central government of Margaret Thatcher. This is often described as the entrenchment of new public management. Rhodes explains what he means by this.

Initially the 'new public management' (NPM) had two meanings: managerialism and the new institutional economics. Managerialism refers to introducing private sector management methods to the public sector. It stresses: hands-on professional management, explicit standards and measures of performance; managing by results; value for money; and, more recently, closeness to the customer. The new institutional economics refers to introducing incentive structures (such as market competition) into public service provision. It stresses disaggregating bureaucracies; greater competition through contracting-out and quasi-markets; and consumer choice. Before 1988, managerialism was the dominant strand in Britain. After 1988, the ideas of the new institutional economics became more prominent. NPM is relevant to this discussion of governance

We will discuss NPM below but here it is also useful to remember that NPM is only a subset of governance. Rhodes thus goes on to provide what he describes as a 'stipulative definition':

Any stipulative definition is arbitrary but my definition incorporates significant elements of the other uses, most notably governance as the minimal state, as a socio-cybernetic system and as self-organizing networks. I list below the shared characteristics of 'governance'.

(1) Interdependence between organizations. Governance is broader than government, covering non-state actors. Changing the boundaries of the state meant the boundaries between public, private and voluntary sectors became shifting and opaque.

(2) Continuing interactions between network members, caused by the need to exchange resources and negotiate shared purposes.

(3) Game-like interactions, rooted in trust and regulated by rules of the game negotiated and agreed by network participants.

(4) A significant degree of autonomy from the state. Networks are not accountable to the state; they are self-organising. Although the state does not occupy a privileged, sovereign position, it can indirectly and imperfectly steer networks.

Environmental regulation in the UK has mobilized what appear, at first glance, to be startling combinations of public and private actors in governance networks. For instance, in order to be able to issue a large number of new permits by a specific deadline for installations covered by the then new EU Directive on Integrated Pollution Prevention and Control (96/61/EC) the Environment Agency for England and Wales asked private environmental consultants to write draft IPPC permits.[4] While the final permits were signed off by an employee of the EA under statutory licensing powers, private actors were involved here in the standard setting process by drafting permit conditions. A less controversial and more widespread example of contracting out regulatory services is the use of private laboratories for testing and analysing water and waste samples relied upon in the EA's enforcement work.

Some commentators, such as Rosenau, perceive globalization as a key driver for the shift from government to governance. For Rosenau, government involves 'activities that are backed by formal authority', whereas governance is much more loosely defined as simply the activities backed by shared goals. Governance therefore captures the exercise of powers in an era of transnationalism where formal state legal and political authority are not necessarily available to establish regulatory regimes.

James N Rosenau, 'Governance, Order, And Change in World Politics' in James N Rosenau and Ernst-Otto Czempiel, *Governance without Government* (CUP 1992) 4–5

As indicated by the title of this book, governance is not synonymous with government. Both refer to purposive behaviour, to goal-oriented activities, to systems of rule; but government suggests activities that are backed by formal authority, by police powers to insure the implementation of duly constituted policies, whereas governance refers to activities backed by shared goals that may or may not derive from legal and formally prescribed responsibilities and that do not necessarily rely on police powers to overcome defiance and attain compliance. Governance, in other words, is a more encompassing phenomenon than government. It embraces governmental institutions, but it also subsumes informal, non-governmental mechanisms whereby those persons and organizations within its purview move ahead, satisfy their needs, and fulfil their wants.

Governance is thus a system of rule that is as dependent on intersubjective meanings as on formally sanctioned constitutions and charters. Put more emphatically, governance is a system of rule that works only if it is accepted by the majority (or, at least, by the most powerful of those it affects),

---

[4] Bettina Lange, *Implementing EU Pollution Control: Law and Integration* (CUP 2008) 198–99.

whereas governments can function even in the face of widespread opposition to their policies. In this sense governance is always effective in performing the functions necessary to systemic persistence, else it is not conceived to exist (since instead of referring to ineffective governance, one speaks of anarchy or chaos). Governments, on the other hand, can be quite ineffective without being regarded as non-existent (they are viewed simply as 'weak'). Thus it is possible to conceive of governance without government – of regulatory mechanisms in a sphere of activity which function effectively even though they are not endowed with formal authority.

Some environmentalists are sceptical about the shift from government to governance for two reasons. First, 'hollowing out the state' can simply mean reducing the scope of *public powers* available to environmental regulators. Privatization, for instance of local council waste collection and disposal services, may achieve greater economic efficiency in the delivery of these services, but also weakens direct environmental regulation by the council over these services, often replacing these with more indirect controls, such as terms in public procurement contracts.

Second, new public management regimes steer public sector employees through performance standards which may detract from achieving the actual purposes of environmental regulation. For instance, licensing work by employees of the Environment Agency for England and Wales under various EU Directives, including the Directive on Industrial Emissions (2010/75/EU),[5] is subject to financial accountability, which means that permits have to be delivered 'on budget' with a limited amount of EA employee time available for the writing of each permit.[6] Similarly, performance standards guide inspection work by EA enforcement officers. The emphasis of the financial performance culture on targets, often defined so that their achievement can be measured quantitatively, runs the risk of generating superficial targets that impede the solution of complex environmental problems on the basis of professional knowledge. For instance, a numerical target for inspections of polluting installations may be meaningless unless it is coupled with indicators for the quality, in particular the depth of scrutiny of a particular unannounced inspection visit, and indicators of operator responses to inspections.

But the shift from environmental government to governance also increases the range of regulatory tools available to public regulators, for instance through the development of *new powers of oversight* over privatized and contracted-out environmental regulatory services, as well as new powers for controlling self-regulation by corporations. In addition, involving a range of private actors in environmental governance can also help to develop more flexible, innovative, and creative forms of legal regulation that would not flourish in the context of bureaucratic, state environmental regulation that relies mainly on statutory powers. In order to further understand what the shift from government to governance entails, Section 1.2 traces the enrolment of private actors into environmental regulation in the UK.

1.2 ENROLLING PRIVATE ACTORS INTO ENVIRONMENTAL REGULATION IN THE UK

Chapter 3 introduces key environmental actors in the UK, in particular the central government Department for Environment, Food and Rural Affairs (DEFRA), as well as public bodies acting at arms' length from the government, such as the Environment Agency for England and Wales[7] as well

---

[5] OJ L 334/17.   [6] Lange (n 4) 198–99.

[7] From 1 April 2013 there will be a separate Environment Agency for England and a regulatory agency called 'Natural Resources Wales', which will be responsible for both environmental protection and the conservation of nature in Wales, thus including the former Countryside Council for Wales and the Forestry Commission Wales <http://www.environment-agency.gov.uk/aboutus/145716.aspx>.

as the Scottish and Northern Ireland Environment Protection Agency. Chapter 3 also highlights the role of non-governmental campaigning organizations in environmental regulation. They contribute to the development of environmental law, for instance through strategic litigation, for example, against large infrastructure projects that contribute to climate change. Much more pro-actively, non-governmental organizations have also set up new governance regimes, such as certification initiatives that mimic elements of public law state licensing powers and are increasingly developing in a transnational sphere, also because international agreements seeking to protect free trade may limit the legal competencies of nation-states to impose trade-restrictive environmental regulation.

Tim Bartley, 'Certifying Forests and Factories: States, Social Movements, and the Rise of Private Regulation in the Apparel and Forest Products Fields' (2003) 31 Politics & Society 435, 440–41

While quality and technical certification have existed for a long time—through Underwriters Laboratory, the 'Good Housekeeping Seal of Approval,' and a variety of industry standards bodies—the use of certification to address the larger societal and ecological impacts of production processes is rather new. This form has emerged alongside a discourse of corporate social responsibility, a rise of partnerships between companies and nongovernmental organizations (NGOs), and a range of experiments with corporate codes of conduct, sustainability reporting, eco-labeling, social auditing, independent monitoring, and Fair Trade products. At first, these trends may seem to be little more than responses to consumer demand or public relations ploys. But with closer attention, both of these images are lacking as explanations for certification programs. First, in contrast to the notion that certification and labeling initiatives are merely responses to the rise of socially and environmentally responsible consumerism, research on these programs suggests that stable markets for certified products rarely exist before the programs are begun—at least not at a scale that would warrant the amount of effort being put into these programs. Instead, making markets for certified products is part of a larger institution-building project that occurs along with the construction of certification associations. [...]

No single set of actors is responsible for creating certification initiatives. Instead, a number of actors—including states, social movements, NGOs, companies, and in the labor standards case, trade unions—have played roles at various moments.

Forest certification emerged as a response to campaigns about tropical deforestation and has so far focused primarily on wood products. The first overarching forest certification body was the Forest Stewardship Council (FSC), founded in 1993.

[...]

it is important to keep in mind some limits and potentials of these sorts of systems for fundamentally altering the conditions of workers and the natural environment. First, certification systems deal in reputation, which means they have the potential effect of 'greenwashing' reality, or cleaning up corporate images without changing practices on the ground. In addition, these are privatized forms of regulation, so they potentially conflict with democratic ideals of openness and accountability. Since corporations typically play some role, whatever impacts these programs may have will likely be limited—although not necessarily unsubstantial. Furthermore, their impacts depend on the enforcement activity of external actors, like consumers, investors, suppliers, and so forth—without which they have little power.

Bartley explains that not just private actors matter in new environmental governance regimes but governments still play a role, for instance by recognizing and supporting through public procurement regimes 'private' certification initiatives. His analysis suggests—as does the *Dimmock* case extract—that not merely political cultures but also existing legal frameworks shape whether we see a shift from government to governance and what form that shift takes. Bartley states that private certification initiatives were developed by non-governmental organizations in conjunction with corporations because national public bodies have only limited regulatory powers left if states have signed international free-trade agreements agreed under the auspices of the World Trade Organization (WTO). But new environmental governance can also involve public–private partnerships, a point made in Section 3, in the extract by Meidinger on forest business certification schemes. It is important to note though, that significant involvement of public bodies in national labelling and certification schemes may be in breach of Article 34 TFEU, which seeks to ensure the free movement of goods in the EU. The European Court of Justice (ECJ) has found that national certification schemes set up to promote national agricultural produce, established, for instance, under the direction of a government minister[8] and involving an obligation of producers to make payments to a fund supporting such marketing campaigns, may be in breach of Article 34 TFEU.[9] In the *Commission v France* case,[10] the ECJ further found that in some circumstances trade limiting activities of private actors can be attributed to the state, for instance, if the state had taken insufficient measures to prevent breach of Article 34 TFEU by private actors.

In the *Dimmock* case, an English statute, the Education Act 1996, and not just the government of the day determined what powers public actors—here a central government department—had in a campaign to raise awareness about climate change. This campaign bore many of the hallmarks of an environmental governance regime linking both public and private actors, in particular involving school teachers and school children. The then Environment Secretary David Miliband and the then Education Secretary Alan Johnson had enthusiastically endorsed an initiative by the then Department for Education and Skills[11] to send out the Al Gore video about climate change, 'An Inconvenient Truth', to all secondary schools in England.

Stuart Dimmock v Secretary of State for Education and Skills
[2007] EWHC 2288 (Admin) 1 (Burton J)

Stuart Dimmock is a father of two sons at state school and a school governor. He has brought an application to declare unlawful a decision by the then Secretary of State for Education and Skills to distribute to every state secondary school in the United Kingdom a copy of former US Vice-President Al Gore's film, An Inconvenient Truth ('AIT'), as part of a pack containing four other short films and a cross-reference to an educational website ('Teachernet') containing a dedicated Guidance Note. [...]

The [...] nub of the dispute are the statutory provisions described in their side headings as respectively relating to '*political indoctrination*' and to the '*duty to secure balanced treatment of political issues*' in schools, now contained in ss 406 and 407 of the Education Act 1996, which derive from the identical provisions in ss 44 and 45 of the Education (No 2) Act 1986. The provisions read as follows:

'406. The local education authority, governing body and head teachers shall forbid ...

the promotion of partisan political views in the teaching of any subject in the school.

407. The local education authority, governing body and head teacher shall take such steps as are reasonably practicable to secure that where political issues are brought to the attention of pupils while they are

(a) in attendance at a maintained school, or

[8] Case C-325/00 *Commission v Germany* [2002] ECR I-9977.
[9] Case 222/82 *Apple and Pear Development Council v KJ Lewis Ltd* [1983] ECR 4083.
[10] Case C-265/95 [1997] ECR I-6959.   [11] Now the Department for Education.

(b) taking part in extra-curricular activities which are provided or organised for registered pupils at the school by or on behalf of the school

they are offered a balanced presentation of opposing views.'

The plaintiff, Mr Dimmock, claimed that the views presented by Al Gore about climate change were political and thus contrary to sections 406 and 407 of the Education Act 1996. He alleged that, while they were not party political, the views presented in the video and the actions urged by it were political in the sense that they were intended to influence a range of government policies:

'(i) Fiscal policy and the way that a whole variety of activities are taxed, including fuel consumption, travel and manufacturing ...

(ii) Investment policy and the way that governments encourage directly and indirectly various forms of activity.

(iii) Energy policy and the fuels (in particular nuclear) employed for the future.

(iv) Foreign policy and the relationship held with nations that consume and/or produce carbon-based fuels.'

It was undisputed that Al Gore's documentary contained political views. The key legal issues therefore were whether the views presented were partisan and whether schools would be offering a balanced presentation of opposing views when showing the documentary:

I turn to deal with the outstanding issues of law relating to the construction of the two relevant statutory provisions. These are, in s. 406, the meaning of *partisan*, as in *partisan political views*: and the meaning and ambit of the duty of the local education authority etc to '*forbid the promotion of partisan political views in the teaching of any subject in the school*'. In s. 407 the dispute has been as to the meaning of the duty to '*offer a balanced presentation of opposing views*' when '*political issues are brought to the attention of pupils*'.

The judge adopted a narrow interpretation of section 406 of the Education Act 1996. He decided that the mere showing of a film that promotes a partisan political view by itself is not in breach of the Education Act 1996, as long as it is shown in the context of appropriate tuition and critical debate. In order to determine whether the distribution of the film to schools and its showing to pupils would amount to the promotion of partisan political views, the Guidance issued to schools by the then Department for Education and Skills (DES) had to be considered as well as the context. The Guidance was available for teachers to download from the internet. The plaintiff, Mr Dimmock, alleged that in order to comply with s 407 of the Education Act 1996 'equal air time' had to be given to the opposing view. Mr Justice Burton, however, stated that the term 'balanced' in s 407 of the Education Act 1996 meant simply a 'fair and dispassionate' presentation of opposing views. The next question, then, for the judge to consider was whether Al Gore's documentary did present such a 'fair and dispassionate' view. Mr Justice Barton identified nine erroneous statements in the documentary. But the modification of the Guidance issued by DES in response to the arguments heard in court, which now included a consideration of the nine errors, meant that teachers could now put forward a more considered view in relation to the climate change issues raised by Al Gore's documentary. The changed Guidance also clarified that teachers should not advocate any specific political response to climate change. Mr Justice Barton therefore ruled that—accompanied by the amended Guidance note—the documentary was now set in a context that would enable it to be shown without a breach of sections 406 and 407 of the Education Act 1996. The judge further found that sections 406 and 407 of the Education Act 1996 did not require the then Department for Education and Skills to stop distributing the video to schools.

Mr Justice Burton referred to the case as an example of 'constructive litigation', suggesting that without the changes he asked to be made to the Guidance also in response to the nine errors the screening of Al Gore's movie would probably have been in breach of sections 406 and 407 of the Education Act 1996. The case illustrates that statutory frameworks, here the Education Act 1996, regulate what role public and private actors can assume in environmental governance regimes. One issue in the critical assessment of the policy implications of the High Court's decision is the matter of a balance of views to which children were exposed. The High Court's decision limited the power of a public actor, the then Department for Education and Skills, to make a particular argument in the climate change debate. But private actors, such as transnational energy companies, which rely mainly on fossil fuels, had access for some time to class rooms in the UK, in some cases influencing teaching materials.[12]

1.3 NEW AND OLD PUBLIC MANAGEMENT FOR ENVIRONMENTAL LAW IN THE UK

As noted in Section 1.1, governance has been strongly associated with the NPM agenda. In this subsection we provide some examples of how that has operated in practice.

Reshaping the implementation of environmental law through new public management in the UK

As pointed out in the extract by Rhodes, new public management is a political programme that has also promoted a shift from government to governance. New public management (NPM) seeks to instil private sector discipline into the running of the public administration and the delivery of public services. NPM reforms were implemented in the late 1970s and 1980s in a number of European countries in order to transform public administration that was perceived to be costly, inefficient, inflexible, and overly bureaucratic.[13] Also, in the UK private sector, management techniques were introduced in the running of the civil service and local government. These techniques involve the setting of targets for public sector work and monitoring compliance with them, payment by results and auditing, as well as hiving off public administration work to the private sector through 'contracting out' or privatization. These reforms sought to implement the three Es, efficiency, effectiveness, and economy, in public sector activity.[14] Some of the rhetoric of new public management is undoubtedly vague. There is no agreement on how 'efficiency, economy, and effectiveness' can be differentiated, though the terms have been enshrined in local government legislation.[15] But the political ideology of 'rolling back the frontiers of the state' has nevertheless shaped in significant ways the development and implementation of environmental regulation in the UK.

---

[12] The Impact of the Commercial World on Children's Wellbeing: Report of an Independent Assessment for the Department for Children, Schools and Families and the Department for Culture, Media and Sport, 141 at <https://www.education.gov.uk/publications/eOrderingDownload/00669-2009DOM-EN.pdf> accessed 5 March 2013. The potential influence of private commercial sponsors, also on curriculum content, is likely to increase under the UK Conservative-Liberal coalition Government's academies program. Private corporations, such as Shell, have been able to influence teaching resources, since the 1980s and 1990s by entering into public-private partnerships with failing schools in so-called Education Action Zones, such as in the London Borough of Lambeth, see eg <http://www.shell.co.uk/gbr/environment-society/shell-in-the-society/social-investment/science-education/shell-education-service/about.html> accessed 5 March 2013.

[13] Carol Harlow, 'Global Administrative Law: The Quest for Principles and Values' (2006) 17 EJIL 200.

[14] Carol Harlow and Richard Rawlings, Law and Administration (3rd edn, CUP 2009) 60–61.

[15] Despite their lack of terminological clarity, the three Es have been invoked in the definition of statutory duties. For instance, s 3(1) of the Local Government Act (LGA) 1999 imposes a duty upon 'best value authorities' to continuously improve the exercise of their functions 'having regard to a combination of economy, efficiency and effectiveness'. Section 1(1) LGA 1999 includes in its definition of 'best value authorities' three authorities whose activities have significant environmental consequences, Transport for London, the National Park Authority, and waste disposal authorities.

The UK Government's 'better regulation' agenda encapsulates the new public management vision for UK regulators. Key elements of this vision are set out in the Hampton Report[16] 'Reducing administrative burdens: effective inspection and enforcement'.[17] The report had many detailed recommendations, some of which will be discussed here. The extract from Hampton's front letter to the Chancellor outlines the general approach of the report and its main conclusions.

Philip Hampton, Reducing Administrative Burdens: Effective Inspection and Enforcement (HM Treasury 2005) 1–2

As a society, we have increased expectations that regulations can and will protect consumers, businesses, workers and the environment, coupled with an increasing need to keep our businesses efficient and flexible to face new competitive challenges. Our regulatory system has the pivotal role in resolving the regular conflict between prosperity and protection.

The enforcement of regulations affects businesses at least as much as the policy of the regulation itself. Efficient enforcement can support compliance across the whole range of businesses, delivering targeted, effective interventions without unreasonable administrative cost to business. Inflexible or inefficient enforcement increases administrative burdens needlessly, and thereby reduces the benefits that regulations can bring.

Administrative burdens are the costs that come from enforcement activities. If regulators operate effectively, and use the best evidence to programme their work, administrative burdens on compliant businesses can be reduced while maintaining or even improving regulatory outcomes.

In investigating the regulatory system over the last twelve months, I have found much that is good, and some excellent, innovative practice. However, the system as a whole is uncoordinated and good practice is not uniform. There are overlaps in regulators' responsibilities and enforcement activities. There are too many forms, and too many duplicated information requests.

Risk assessment—though widely recognised as fundamental to effectiveness—is not implemented as thoroughly and comprehensively as it should be. Risk assessment should be comprehensive, and should be the basis for all regulators' enforcement programmes. Proper analysis of risk directs regulators' efforts at areas where it is most needed, and should enable them to reduce the administrative burden of regulation, while maintaining or even improving regulatory outcomes.

I am therefore recommending that:

- comprehensive risk assessment should be the foundation of all regulators' enforcement programmes;
- there should be no inspections without a reason, and data requirements for less risky businesses should be lower than for riskier businesses;
- resources released from unnecessary inspections should be redirected towards advice to improve compliance;
- there should be fewer, simpler forms;
- data requirements, including the design of forms, should be coordinated across regulators;
- when new regulations are being devised, Departments should plan to ensure enforcement can be as efficient as possible, and follows the principles of this report; and
- thirty-one national regulators should be reduced to seven more thematic bodies.

[16] The report was compiled for the Treasury by Philip Hampton, a business leader.

[17] Available at <https://whitehall-frontend-production.s3.amazonaws.com/system/uploads/attachment/file/695/file22988_Hampton.pdf> accessed 5 March 2013.

Risk assessment means something different here from the way it was discussed in Chapter 2.[18] Hampton is using it in relation to enforcement, not directly in relation to setting standards.

The Hampton Report provided the benchmarks according to which the EA, and other UK regulators, have been reviewed by the National Audit Office and the central government Better Regulation Executive.[19] Our focus here is upon the EA. A review report issued by the Department for Business, Innovation and Skills and the Better Regulation Executive, entitled 'The Environment Agency: A Review of Progress since its Hampton Implementation Review',[20] the Hampton Review Report, suggests that the EA should become more responsive to its 'customers',[21] that is, regulated businesses. The EA's role is perceived as one of 'encouraging economic progress' and intervening only 'when there is a clear case for protection'.[22] This appears to tilt the balance between economic development, environmental protection, and social cohesion, the three elements of sustainable development, towards economic development. More specifically, the emphasis on greater responsiveness to regulated businesses means that advice and guidance are being prioritized over inspections.

Prioritizing advice and guidance over inspections

The Hampton Review Report recommends that the EA (and other UK regulators) should spend less time and financial resources on inspections and instead rely more on advice and guidance in order to promote compliance of businesses with legal regulation.[23] 'Protection' and 'prosperity' (of businesses) should be balanced.[24] Inspection regimes should also be more effective and cost-efficient by being targeted at the most risky operations and operators. This is to be achieved through the EA's pollution hazards and operational risk appraisal tool (OPRA), which scores operators according to the likely risk that they pose.[25] The frequency of inspections and the level of fees charged to an operator increase with its OPRA calculated hazardousness score.

The Hampton Review team's recommendation to reduce the overall number, and thus frequency, of inspections is controversial. For some EA staff inspection frequencies and securing environmental outcomes are linked,[26] though the first Report 'Implementing the Hampton vision in the EA' criticized that the EA did not provide any evidence of such a link.[27] Moreover, local enforcement staff members do not necessarily see offering advice to businesses as part of their role.[28] The Hampton Review team's *recommendations* for reduced inspection frequencies should also be considered in the light of the legal duty imposed upon the EA by Regulation 34(2) of the Environmental Permitting Regulations 2010, which requires the EA 'to undertake appropriate periodic inspections of regulated facilities'. It is also questionable whether extensive advice and guidance by the EA for regulated businesses complies with the 'polluter pays' principle[29], if the principle is interpreted as shifting the costs of pollution to

---

[18] On the different meanings of risk and risk assessment see Elizabeth Fisher, 'Risk Regulatory Concepts and the Law' in OECD (ed), *Risk and Regulatory Policy: Improving the Governance of Risk* (OECD 2010).

[19] For more info see <https://www.gov.uk/government/policies/reducing-the-impact-of-regulation-on-business> accessed 5 March 2013.

[20] Hereafter referred to as the 'Hampton Review Report'.

[21] Department for Business, Innovation and Skills and the Better Regulation Executive, 'The Environment Agency: A Review of Progress since its Hampton Implementation Review' (February 2010) 4 <http://www.bis.gov.uk/assets/biscore/better-regulation/docs/10-564-environment-agency-progress-since-hampton-implementation-review> accessed 6 October 2012.

[22] 'Effective inspection and enforcement: Implementing the Hampton Vision in the Environment Agency' 15, 44 <http://www.nao.org.uk/publications/0708/hampton_environment_agency.aspx> accessed 6 October 2012.

[23] Hampton Review Report (n 21) 3, 4, 5, 8.   [24] 'Effective inspection and enforcement' (n 22) 3.

[25] <http://www.environment-agency.gov.uk/business/regulation/31827.aspx> accessed 6 October 2012.

[26] 'Effective inspection and enforcement' (n 22) 3.   [27] Ibid.

[28] 'Effective inspection and enforcement' (n 22) 11.

[29] For a discussion of the legal force of this principle in English law, see Chapter 11.

producers rather than consumers of goods and services. EA advice saves expenditure for businesses that would otherwise have to pay for private consultancy services or in-house expertise. In addition, the Hampton Review team's enthusiasm for advice as a 'regulatory tool'[30] ignores important issues, such as the potential liability of the EA for detailed guidance provided to businesses and the risk of the EA fettering its discretion or creating legitimate expectations in pre- and post-permit discussions that may be enforceable by regulated companies through judicial review. DEFRA's core guidance on environmental permitting clearly states that 'the regulator should not be expected to provide advice that might prejudice its determination of an application'.[31] Finally, it is questionable whether the recommendation of the first report 'Implementing the Hampton vision in the EA' that the EA should 'provide authoritative, accessible advice easily and *cheaply*' (emphasis added) is really in the interests of businesses. Can cheap advice be authoritative and thus valuable for regulated businesses?[32] But new public management, as fleshed out in 'Implementing the Hampton vision in the EA' and the subsequent Hampton Review Report, does not just seek to reform enforcement practices of the EA, but also advocates a changed approach to the development of environmental legislation.

A new public management take on setting environmental standards

The Hampton Review Report also counsels against the development of excessive legislation and recommends wide consultation with sectors affected by environmental legislation.[33] A recent example of this is the extensive consultation of farmers over the implementation of the agricultural waste regulations.[34] Moreover, the EA has now also set up an internal 'legislative scrutiny panel', which is meant 'to challenge new legislative and policy development'.[35] The Report: 'Effective inspection and enforcement: implementing the Hampton vision in the Environment Agency' also echoes another key theme of new public management, collaboration between public regulators and private regulated businesses. The report advocates the setting up of joint lobby groups, composed of DEFRA, the EA, and the relevant industry sector in order to influence the European Commission in relation to new proposals for EU environmental legislation.[36] Such a hybrid public–private group already exists for the water industry.[37]

In relation to the development of detailed environmental standards through permitting, the Report 'Effective inspection and enforcement: implementing the Hampton vision in the Environment Agency' advocates standard rather than bespoke permits for regulated companies within an industry sector.[38] It does so with reference to a surprising, new interpretation of transparency. Transparency is understood to impose a duty upon regulators to treat all operators within one industry sector equally.[39] This is to be achieved by issuing standard rather than bespoke permits, because standard permits allow for easier comparability of permit conditions between plants within one sector.[40] Traditionally transparency is understood as openness in the conduct of public administration, with information about the activities of the regulator being available to citizens, including regulated businesses, in order to hold the regulator accountable. The Hampton Review Report thus derives a substantive equal treatment obligation from the good government standard of transparency, rather than considering

---

[30] 'Effective inspection and enforcement' (n 22) 25.

[31] DEFRA, 'Environmental Permitting Guidance, Core Guidance, For the Environmental Permitting (England and Wales) Regulations 2010, Revised March 2013, <http://www.defra.gov.uk/publications/2013/03/07/pb13897-ep-core-guidance/> accessed 9 November 2012, para 5.4.

[32] 'Effective inspection and enforcement' (n 22) 44.

[33] Hampton Review Report (n 21) 14.   [34] 'Effective inspection and enforcement' (n 22).

[35] 'Effective inspection and enforcement' (n 22) 41.   [36] 'Effective inspection and enforcement' (n 22) 20.

[37] Ibid.   [38] 'Effective inspection and enforcement' (n 22) 38.

[39] 'Effective inspection and enforcement' (n 22) 16.   [40] Ibid.

availability of information about different operators' permit conditions as sufficient to meet this standard. Moreover, the Hampton Review Report's preference for standard permit conditions sits uneasily with NPM's aim to eradicate inflexibility and a bureaucratic approach among public regulators, a goal that in parts of the Report 'Effective inspection and enforcement: implementing the Hampton vision in the Environment Agency' is affirmed by valuing the exercise of discretion in the application of environmental law by EA staff.[41]

1.4 CONCLUDING REMARKS

To conclude, environmental government has been 'hollowed out' in the UK, also through greater involvement of private actors in environmental governance regimes. But the exercise of public powers—and thus environmental government—by the public administration, through permitting and enforcement of permits with the help of a range of administrative, criminal, and civil sanctions, is still at the heart of environmental regulation in the UK. This is further illustrated through the discussions in Chapter 7 on Public Law and in Chapter 8 on Criminal Liability.

FURTHER READING AND QUESTIONS

1. Read the complete transcript of *Stuart Dimmock v Secretary of State for Education and Skills* [2007] EWHC 2288 (Admin), [2008] 1 All ER 367. The case raises important, wider issues about the quality of debates about climate change. What is the legitimacy of the court as a judicial actor to identify the 'errors' in Al Gore's video? Why did it valorize a notion of 'expert' knowledge when stating that 'As Mr Downes has pointed out, if (sic) it has taken this hearing to identify and correct the flaws, it is impossible to think that teachers could have done so untutored' ([45])? Some of the recipients of the video would have been secondary school science teachers who may well have been able to subject the claims in the Al Gore documentary to critical scrutiny. The question of whether the High Court's intervention in the *Dimmock* case was legitimate is even more sharply raised in relation to its amendment of the DES Guidance note. The High Court limited the range of political actions that teachers could discuss with pupils in order to combat climate change, in response to the information provided by Al Gore's video. The original Guidance note had encouraged teachers to discuss with pupils why politicians may ignore climate change. Teachers were specifically invited to ask 'what pressures can be put on politicians to respond to climate change?' The High Court removed this sentence from the Guidance. It also rewrote a section of the Guidance, which provided information to teachers about organizations that could be invited as guest speakers. The revision included climate sceptic organizations in order to provide a more balanced view. Most controversially, though, the rewritten Guidance asked teachers not to promote any particular political response to climate change. Do you think that this infringes teachers' fundamental human right to freedom of speech? Why do you think the High Court itself rewrote the Guidance note, rather than issue an order requiring the DES to rewrite it? Would such an order have been more in accordance with the constitutional doctrine of separation of powers and the assumption that the administrative court should not engage in merits review than the actual judgment delivered?

2. Is certification regulation a type of information regulation that seeks to address the externality of information deficits, as identified by economic perspectives, discussed in Chapter 12 Regulatory Strategy?

---

[41] 'Effective inspection and enforcement' (n 22) 31.

3. Brian Doherty, *Ideas and Actions in the Green Movement* (Routledge 2002).

4. The report 'Review of Progress of Effective Enforcement and Inspection: A Progress Review of the Environment Agency' recommends a 'trading places' scheme in which EA enforcement officers are to be seconded to spend some time in regulated businesses and vice versa, in order to provide EA 'officers with an understanding of business'.[42] Do you think that this will enhance effective implementation of environmental law or will this simply lead to the 'capture' of regulators' perception by business interests?

5. *R (People and Planet) v HM Treasury* [2009] EWHC 3020 (Admin) was extracted in Chapter 7. The case illustrates the significance of private actors in contemporary environmental governance in the UK. Consider the following issue in light of that case. Section 13(1) of the Climate Change Act 2008 imposes a duty upon the Secretary of State to 'prepare proposals and policies' 'which will enable the carbon budgets that have been set under the Act to be met'. Section 13(4) of the Climate Change Act 2008 provides a power for the Secretary of State to take into account the policies and proposals made by other national authorities when developing his or her own plans. Develop a legal argument in relation to the question of whether the Climate Change Act 2008 imposes a duty upon UK government ministers to consider whether and how the exercise of their public powers may affect the level of greenhouse gases emitted in the UK.

3. Cary Coglianese, John Braithwaite, and David Levi Faur, 'Can Regulation and Governance Make a Difference?' (2007) 1 Regulation & Governance 1.

2 THE FRONTIERS OF NEW ENVIRONMENTAL GOVERNANCE: EXPERIMENTS AND TRANSNATIONALISM

The shift from government to governance and its implications for the development and enforcement of environmental law has also been further analysed in debates about 'experimentalist governance'. These debates have developed in response to the proliferation of risk regulatory regimes that operate at multiple levels of governance, such as environmental regulation in the EU and the US. Given that environmental problems often affect the global commons, should regulatory powers be best exercised at an international level? 'Experimentalist governance' suggests that we should also leave significant discretion to the lowest level of regulatory decision-making, even though we see a rise in transnational environmental governance. Experimentalist governance thus recognizes that solving environmental problems often has to be iterative. This involves the need to take into account experience gained in implementing environmental law in order to learn and further optimize the development and implementation of environmental law standards. In fact, regulatory standards may not be necessarily stipulated 'ex ante', but may be discovered and specified during the actual process of implementing regulation.

Charles Sabel and Jonathan Zeitlin, 'Experimentalist Governance' in D Levi-Faur (ed), *Oxford Handbook of Governance* (OUP 2012) 169–70, 175

Far-reaching transformations in the nature of contemporary governance are underway, within and beyond the nation-state. They can be observed across multiple levels and locations, from the reform

---

[42] Department for Business, Innovation and Skills and the Better Regulation Executive, 'The Environment Agency' (n 21) 10.

of local public services such as education and child welfare to the regulation of global trade in food and forest products. At the heart of these transformations is the emergence of what may be called 'experimentalist governance', based on framework rule-making and revision through recursive review of implementation experience in different local contexts. [...]

Experimentalist governance in its most developed form involves a multi-level architecture, whose four elements are linked in an iterative cycle. First, broad framework goals and metrics for gauging their achievement are provisionally established by some combination of 'central' and 'local' units, in consultation with relevant civil society stakeholders. Examples of such framework goals, to which we will refer in this chapter, include 'good water quality', 'safe food', an 'adequate education', and 'sustainable forests'. Second, local units are given broad discretion to pursue these goals in their own way. In regulatory systems, the 'local' units will typically be private actors such as firms or the territorial authorities (state regulators in the US; or member state authorities in the EU) to whom they immediately respond. In service-providing organizations, the 'local' units will typically be frontline workers, such as teachers, police, or social welfare workers, or the district or regional entities supervising them.

But, third, as a condition of this autonomy, these units must report regularly on their performance and participate in a peer review in which their results are compared with those of others employing different means to the same ends. Where they are not making good progress against the agreed indicators, the local units are expected to show that they are taking appropriate corrective measures, informed by the experience of their peers. Fourth and finally, the goals, metrics, and decision-making procedures themselves are periodically revised by a widening circle of actors in response to the problems and possibilities revealed by the review process, and the cycle repeats.

Experimentalism correspondingly diverges not only from conventional hierarchical governance, but also from other contemporary reform movements focused on reinforcing principal-agent relations, whether from the top-down, as in the New Public Management (NPM), or from the bottom-up, as in devolved or 'interactive' governance. Experimentalism is based neither on a sharp separation between policy conception and administrative execution as in conventional hierarchical governance and NPM, nor on their fusion in the hands of local communities or citizens' councils as in interactive governance. Instead, it is based on the reciprocal redefinition of ends and means through an iterated, multi-level cycle of provisional goal-setting and revision, thereby giving structure to apparently fluid practices of 'network governance'.

Sabel and Zeitlin seek to distinguish experimentalist governance from NPM, but we should also remember shared features of these two approaches. Both emphasize the role of comparison and competition between public or private regulators for driving performance. In EU wide experimentalist governance this happens through comparing outcomes in the delivery of public services between different members states. This is facilitated, for example, through reporting obligations. For instance, member states have to report by 2015 to the Commission on progress with achieving 'good water status', an objective imposed by the Water Framework Directive (WFD, 2000/60/EC).[43] Within a nation-state comparisons can be enabled through the publication of league tables 'measuring' and 'ranking' performance of service providers. Moreover, experimentalist governance shares with some approaches towards NPM a preference for flexible regulatory decision-making, and thus values discretion. Law is decentred in experimentalist governance because it features only in framework rule-making and provisional goal-setting. The exercise of discretion is not considered a dubious activity—potentially in conflict with a strict interpretation of the rule of law—but as part

---

[43] The WFD has been considered as a key example of experimentalist governance and is further discussed in Chapter 14.

of the flexible, open, transparent search for context sensitive regulatory solutions to specific regulatory problems. Von Hohmeyer discusses under what conditions we are likely to see the emergence of experimentalist environmental governance in the EU.

Ingmar von Hohmeyer, 'Emerging Experimentalism in EU Environmental Governance' in Charles F Sabel and Jonathan Zeitlin (eds), *Experimentalist Governance in the European Union: Towards a New Architecture* (OUP 2010) 121, 127–28, 135, 139

A major development which has characterized EU environmental policy in recent years is the rise of experimentalist governance. Existing mechanisms of top-down environmental regulation have been underpinned and complemented by mechanisms relying on broad framework goals, locally devised implementation measures, information provision, and recursive procedures to encourage policy learning from experience. In contrast to more traditional mechanisms, these structures frequently operate on the basis of long time horizons of ten, twenty, or more years for implementation. Drawing on two main examples—the EU Sustainable Development Strategy and the Water Framework Directive – this chapter discusses the factors which led to the emergence of experimentalism in EU environmental governance, together with its characteristics and functioning. [...]

Hohmeyer then further explains that experimentalist governance in the field of the environment is likely to emerge in relation to specific types of environmental problems. These problems are characterized by:

a relatively close causal link between the problem and the operating logic of the economic sectors causing the problem. Consequently, the effectiveness of technical fixes is limited and problem solutions require changes in the behaviour of sectoral actors.

High complexity: frequently, the sources of persistent problems are diffuse and involve a large number of actors, including important indirect contributors. In addition, cause and effect tend to be significantly delayed.

Low 'visibility': due to the 'creeping' character of many persistent problems, measures must be taken well in advance of the manifestation of serious effects. However, this means that such measures must deal with uncertainty and react to models of the future and scenarios rather than direct threats. The resulting low problem visibility and uncertainty reduces political pressure for action.

Global dimension: persistent environmental problems often have an important global dimension in the sense that, ultimately, they can only be addressed effectively by internationally coordinated measures. This tends to create political barriers to change as issues relating to social justice (eg differentiated contributions by developed and developing countries), national sovereignty, and weak international enforcement mechanisms need to be taken into account (cf. Jänicke and Jörgens 2006: 167–71). [...]

The EGA [Experimentalist Governance Architecture] benefited from the rise of SD because SD is associated with governance functions – recursiveness and learning—which are similar to those underlying the EGA. This becomes clear, for example, if one looks at the guidelines for designing SD strategies. According to the OECD Resource Book for SD strategies, being 'strategic is about developing an underlying vision through a consensual, effective, and iterative process; and going on to set objectives, identify the means of achieving them, and then monitor that achievement as a guide to the next round of this learning process' (Dalal-Clayton and Bass 2002: 29). SD strategies therefore 'move [...] towards operating an adaptive system that can continuously improve'. Similarly, the European Sustainable Development Network (ESDN) concludes that 'overall, the guidelines for SD strategies put a strong emphasis on procedural and institutional aspects of an iterative governance process. [...]

By contrast, the institutional characteristics of the 2006 revised EU-SDS correspond more closely to the EGA and, on the whole, can be expected to be more effective than those of the original Strategy. While framework goals and metrics remain somewhat vague and lack originality, they tend to be more concrete than those of the original EU-SDS. Provisions on planning by lower level units were strengthened and links with the EU level were established. Reporting and monitoring are institutionally anchored in various specialized bodies, such as the national focal points and the working group on SDIs. Peer review has also been incorporated into the EU-SDS. [...]

While it is too early for a reliable assessment of the actual implementation of the renewed EU-SDS, several implementing measures which point to improved conditions for learning have been taken. For example, the activities of the national SDS coordinators group have been extended beyond reporting on NSDSs to include exchange of experience and best practice, discussion of progress made on peer reviews, and provision of input and suggestions on new SD policy initiatives. The Commission has also made co-financing available to support peer reviews of NSDSs and selected themes.

Von Hohmeyer expects experimentalist EU environmental governance to deliver a lot, including fundamental behavioural change in relation to consumption and production patterns.[44] Further empirical research will be necessary in order to assess whether experimentalist governance can provide this. More fundamentally, enthusiasm for open-textured experimentalist governance should not overlook its potentially hidden politics. As Radaelli[45] has pointed out in the context of learning through the EU governance tool of the open method of co-ordination, who learns what from whom is ultimately a political issue. 'Learning' in experimentalist governance regimes may therefore simply be a cloak for political dynamics that affirm entrenched interests and power structures rather than transform existing patterns of consumption and production.

Experimentalist governance grants significant discretion to local standard setters, but seeks to control this through 'dynamic peer accountability'. Karkkainen discusses 'destabilisation of regulators' as another strategy for ensuring that locally set environmental standards are ambitious.

Bradley C Karkkainen, 'Information-forcing Regulation and Environmental Governance' in G de Búrca and J Scott (eds), *Law and New Governance in the EU and the US* (Hart Publishing 2006) 314–15, 317

Chuck Sabel and Bill Simon recently advanced a provocative theory of 'destabilisation rights', defined as 'claims to unsettle and open up public institutions that have chronically failed to meet their obligations and that are substantially insulated from the normal processes of political accountability'. On their view, much recent 'public law litigation'—typically, litigation to vindicate constitutional or statutory rights allegedly violated by important public institutions, like schools, prisons, police forces or various arms of the welfare state – seeks as a remedy the destabilization and disentrenchment of the failing institutions. The aim and effect of these suits, they argue, is to 'widen the possibilities of experimentalist collaboration' in crafting far-reaching institutional restructuring, while avoiding the pitfalls of a detailed, prescriptive, judicially imposed remedy. This reorientation in public law litigation, they argue,

[44] Ingmar von Hohmeyer, 'Emerging Experimentalism in EU Environmental Governance' in Charles F Sabel and Jonathan Zeitlin (eds), *Experimentalist Governance in the European Union: Towards a New Architecture* (OUP 2010) 148.

[45] Claudio Radaelli, 'Who learns what? Policy Learning and the Open Method of Co-ordination' (Economic and Social Research Council seminar series on Implementing the Lisbon Strategy: Policy Learning inside and outside the open method, Birmingham, November 2004) 3, <http://www.eu-newgov.org/database/DOCS/P22_D02_Radaelli_OMC_Learning_Birmingham_Nov2004.pdf> accessed 6 October 2012.

is part of a broader trend away from 'command-and-control' solutions and toward experimentalist 'new governance'. Analyzing the cases, they conclude that a prima facie case for destabilisation consists of two elements: first, a clear and persistent violation of standards, and second, 'political blockage', that is, a structural defect in the conventional mechanisms of political accountability that systematically blocks movement toward a solution to the underlying problem. [...]

In particular, a form of *administrative* destabilisation right may prove useful as a disciplining mechanism in the context of centrally coordinated networks of locally devolved, collaborative new governance institutions – the sort of two-tiered structure of accountability contemplated by advocates of the brand of new governance styled 'democratic experimentalism'. [...]

My modest ambition here is to reintroduce the Sabel-Simon notion of 'destabilization rights' and adapt it to elaborate on the redefined role of the 'new center' in experimentalist regulation. The idea is that while refraining from prescribing *ex cathedra* and in excruciating detail the procedures, standards, goals, objectives, performance targets, operating principles, institutional forms and mandatory rules by which local units must operate, the 'new center' might retain the whip hand through an administrative destabilisation right over local arrangements. That is, the centre would retain the right to intervene, destabilise and disentrench local efforts that are deemed to be failing, either because they evidence regulatory capture, distortions arising from strategic bargaining on the part of one or more participants, or any of the other assorted procedural defects from which devolved, collaborative deliberation is said by its critics to suffer. These two elements-chronic underperformance relative to established norms, coupled with 'political blockage'—correspond to Sabel and Simon's prima facie case for a destabilisation remedy in the public law litigation context.

The crucial difference, of course, is that the sort of destabilisation right proposed here is an administrative control mechanism, not a judicial remedy for a constitutional or statutory violation. The two are not incompatible. In principle at least, we might authorise both external checks on the entire system through the judicial process and internal checks on the performance of local units through central administrative oversight and a right of destabilising administrative intervention.

Karkkainen considers citizen suits, that is, judicial review actions brought by citizens against public regulators, as well as actions brought by private citizens against other private citizens, as an important plank of 'destabilization' in experimentalist governance. But it should be borne in mind that, given standing rules and limits to funding, citizens' judicial review actions play a limited role in environmental regulation in the UK, a point further discussed in Chapter 7 on Public Law. Private environmental actions brought by citizens against citizens, as well as private prosecutions, are even less significant in the UK, a theme further discussed in Chapter 6 on Private Law.

Karkkainen's extract also points to what seems to be a lack of internal coherence in experimentalist governance. Experimentalist governance values discretion for regulators at the local level. But where statutory powers and duties for local regulators are phrased in discretionary terms, it will be more difficult to invoke administrative destabilization rights, that is, challenges to the exercise of such powers or failure to exercise duties through legal actions. Thus, the potentially more important avenue for realizing experimentalist environmental governance in the UK is Karkkainen's notion of the 'new centre'. This refers to a central environmental regulatory body that oversees the performance of local environmental regulators who are invested with significant discretion in developing and enforcing environmental standards. Oversight by a central body, one step removed from local standard setting and enforcement, may provide extra safeguards against 'regulatory capture', that is, the gradual co-optation of regulators by the perspectives and ultimately interests of regulated companies.[46] The 'new

---

[46] Marver Bernstein, *Regulating Business by Independent Commission* (Princeton UP 1955).

centre' could be further strengthened by enrolling a range of stakeholders, including statutory consultees, environmental NGOs, and local citizens, as well as environmental scientists.

FURTHER READING AND QUESTIONS

1. Is experimentalist governance democratic? What conception of democracy informs your answer?

2. 'Localism' has been of particular interest to environmental regulation scholars and public policy-makers. Various conceptions of localism have been advanced. First, 'localism' means that in regimes of multi-level governance local, not just national or federal, government has an important role to play, for instance in combating diffuse pollution in the US.[47] For Farber, localism captures the idea that a close geographic nexus should exist between the environmental harm that has been caused and the citizens who seek to judicially review the exercise of public powers that are alleged to have caused harm. Hence, citizens of a state that is different from the one in which the environmental harm has occurred should not have standing to bring judicial review actions. A version of this understanding of localism informed the decision of the ECJ in the red grouse case.[48] The court held that the Netherlands could not ban local sales of birds if they had been killed lawfully in other EU Member States. It was irrelevant that the red grouse was a protected species in the Netherlands under Dutch law. Stricter local environmental measures could only be taken for birds inhabiting Dutch territory for those migratory or endangered birds not listed in what was then the harmonizing EC Directive 79/409 on the conservation of wild birds (see Chapter 20). Critically assess what type of 'localism' is implied in experimentalist environmental governance. Do you agree with Karkkainen that experimentalist governance provides a clear vision for balancing the exercise of regulatory powers at different levels of government? Do you think that Article 34 TFEU unduly limits the scope for 'localism' in EU experimentalist environmental governance? Also see the discussion concerning localism and planning law in Chapter 18.

3. Further reading in this area can be found in Charles Sabel, Archon Fung, and Brad Karkkainen, *Beyond Backyard Environmentalism* (Beacon Press 2000) and Katharina Holzinger, Christoph Knill, and Ansgar Schäfer 'Rhetoric or Reality? New Governance in EU Environmental Policy' (2006) 12 ELJ 403.

4. Read the discussion of the EU Water Framework Directive (WFD) 2000/60/EC) in Chapter 14 and list the features of this Directive that reflect experimentalist environmental governance.

---

3 RETHINKING ACCOUNTABILITY AND LEGITIMACY IN ENVIRONMENTAL GOVERNANCE

3.1 WHAT IS ACCOUNTABILITY?

As indicated in Karkkainen's extract in Section 2 the shift from government to new forms, including experimentalist governance, is associated with a changing conception of key building blocks of regulatory systems, such as accountability procedures and legitimacy for the development and enforcement of environmental standards. Traditional mechanisms for holding public regulators

[47] John R. Nolon, 'In Praise of Parochialism: The Advent of Local Environmental Law' (2002) 26 Harvard Env LR 365.
[48] Case C-169/89 *Gourmetterie van den Burg* [1990] ECR I-02143.

to account, for instance, through judicial review, individual ministerial responsibility, or parliamentary questions, may be sidelined where private actors play an important role in governance.[49] Mashaw further explains how we can define 'accountability'.

Jerry L Mashaw, 'Structuring a "Dense Complexity": Accountability and the Project of Administrative Law' (2005) 5 Issues in Legal Scholarship 1, 16–17

The millions of words spilled on the subject of accountability are often confusing for a quite simple reason: authors are talking about different methods and questions of accountability without specifying with any precision either the particular accountability problem that engages their attention or the choices that they are making implicitly among differing accountability regimes. The challenge is to devise a general approach to analysing instances of accountability that will allow us to see and discuss common problems across multiple domains.

Start with a dictionary definition: 'Liable to be called to account; answerable.' So far so good, but this definition is pretty vague. Accountability seems to be a relational concept, but the parties to the relationship remain unspecified. Some sort of account is to be given by someone to someone else, but what is the subject matter of this accounting? And, how is an account to be given? How are its facts and reasons developed, conveyed and tested? What are the criteria or standards by which the acceptability of conduct is to be judged? Finally, someone is supposed to be 'liable' or answerable for consequences, but liable for what and to what extent? Unless we know the answers to these questions we do not know much about what accountability means in any particular domain or instance.

On the other hand, by simply unpacking this vagueness we can begin to make some progress. For what our concerns tell us is something like this—in any accountability relationship we should be able to specify the answers to six important questions: *Who* is liable or accountable *to whom*; *what* they are liable to be called to account for; *through what processes* accountability is to be assured; *by what standards* the putatively accountable behaviour is to be judged; and *with what effects*, describe what I will call an 'accountability regime'. These six inquiries allow us to give an account of accountability. With the answers to these questions in hand, we can not only evaluate the potential capacity of any particular regime to satisfy our demands or aspirations, but also compare it to other regimes, evaluate their differential capacities, and perhaps articulate hybrid regimes that approximate optimal institutional designs.

Mashaw's analysis points to the importance of context for understanding an accountability regime.[50] This means that accountability processes often vary according to the particular regulatory regime in which they are enacted, but in particular what Marshaw calls 'governance accountability' measures seek to ensure the overarching aims of affirming democracy and the rule of law.[51] Reinforcing democracy matters in particular in the context of EU governance which has been criticized for suffering from a severe democratic deficit.[52] Ensuring compliance with the rule of law, such as the standards of framework legislation, acquires particular salience in the context of experimentalist EU governance, which relies to a great extent on soft law. Mashaw further explains that different, though sometimes connected, types of accountability, such as political, managerial, and legal, can be distinguished.

---

[49] Carol Harlow, 'Global Administrative Law: The Quest for Principles and Values' (2006) 17 EJIL (n 13) 194.

[50] Jerry Mashaw, 'Structuring a "Dense Complexity": Accountability and the Project of Administrative Law' (2005) 5 Issues in Legal Scholarship 1, 10.

[51] Ibid, 32.

[52] Kevin Featherstone, 'Jean Monnet and the "Democratic Deficit" in the European Union' (1994) 32(2) JCMS 149.

Jerry L Mashaw 'Administrative Law and Agency Accountability' in David S Clark (ed), *Encyclopedia of Law and Society: American and Global Perspectives* (Sage Publications 2007) 31–32

The emergence of managerial and legal accountability is, in part, a response to the inefficacy of electoral control in the modern administrative state. [...]

Managerial Control

One solution to the deficiencies of political accountability is an attempt to assert managerial control. People in developed democracies live in what scholars have called an *audit* society. The audit, broadly understood, is the managerial accountability mechanism of choice in both public and private organisations for ensuring that those who "have the doing in charge" act both competently and honestly.

Managerialism as a mode of accountability is, of course, not unique to democracies. The monarchical model of accountability involved a simple hierarchical relationship. Officials were accountable to the monarch and the monarch to God [...] Modern governments are rife with inspectorates of one or another type. In some cases, the inspectorate is designed to reinforce political control by providing the expertise and continuous observation that politicians lack. In other cases, the inspectorate is inside the bureaucracy itself as a device to promote the hierarchical control of top-level administrators. Indeed, modern managerial techniques emphasize the role of *external* audits in the creation of *internal* accountability systems that will produce appropriate controls over official (or private) behaviour.

Legal Control

Although today we mostly think of judicial review as a means of protecting individual rights against administrative tyranny, judicial review has historically played another role as well. Hauling the king's officers before the king's courts to answer for their conduct promotes central administrative control by the sovereign at the same time that it protects private rights. Judicial review consolidates state power, and with the shift of power to the people in constitutional democracies, judicial review becomes a device for reinforcing the democratic accountability of administrative officials.

Viewed from this perspective, judicial review of administrative action—the demand for 'legal' accountability of officials-carries out a democratic political project: the reinforcement of democratic control of official behaviour. However, like managerial accountability regimes, the techniques of accountability available through judicial review are hardly a perfect fit with the project of democratic political control. Accountability through judicial review is accountability to law. And so it must be. For, to premise accountability in politically unaccountable courts on anything other than the law would be to undermine the democratic political accountability that judicial review is struggling to reinforce. Judicial review, therefore, can only obliquely reinforce political accountability.

3.2 NEW FORMS OF ACCOUNTABILITY AND LEGITIMACY

While legal and political accountability are traditional forms of accountability key to rendering *government* accountable, managerial accountability is closely associated with new *governance* regimes. Audit is a key accountability technique of NPM reforms discussed in Section 1.3. Traditional conceptions of legal and political accountability rely on assumptions of a hierarchical relationship between a legal or political principal and his or her agents. For instance, the European Commission can hold member states accountable for the implementation of EU environmental law, ultimately with the aid of Article 258 TFEU. But the traditional principal–agent imagery does not chime with experimentalist governance, because such governance does not specify precise, specific regulatory standards at the outset, but instead encourages the development of regulatory standards during the process of implementing environmental law.

Charles F Sabel and William H Simon, 'Epilogue: Accountability Without Sovereignty' in G de Burca and J Scott (eds), *Law and New Governance in the EU and the US* (Hart Publishing 2006) 398, 400, 402

[...] new governance seems radically unsettling because of its flagrant disrespect for the distinction between enactment (or law making) and enforcement (or law application) on which principal-agent accountability depends. In new governance, agents are expected to revise their mandates in the course of implementing them. Sovereigns set frameworks that describe vague goals and invite elaboration. They do not purport to confine discretion within narrow channels.

Peer review is the answer of new governance to the inadequacies of principal-agent accountability. Peer review imposes on implementing 'agents' the obligation to justify the exercise of discretion they have been granted by framework-making 'principals' in the light of pooled comparable experience. In peer review, the actors at all levels learn from and correct each other, thus undermining the hierarchical distinction between principals and agents and creating a form of dynamic accountability-accountability that anticipates the transformation of rules in use. Dynamic accountability becomes the means of controlling discretion when that control cannot be hard-wired into the rules of hierarchy.

Sabel and Simon then further flesh out the EU variant of peer review as an accountability mechanism for experimentalist governance:

The democratic legitimacy of these peer review processes cannot depend on the conformity of their results to prior legislative decision. Rather, democracy will have to be established within the review processes themselves. Legitimacy will depend on their transparency and more ambitiously, on their openness to directly deliberative participation by affected stakeholders. Deliberative because preferences, even ideas of the possible, change in the course of decision making (otherwise we could count on principals to define solutions in advance); directly so because new preferences and possibilities arise through hands-on problem solving by those in urgent need of an answer, not dispassionate reflection of first principles by a magisterial elite secure against life's pressures.

Sabel's and Simon's advocacy of peer review as an accountability mechanism has further interesting implications for how we think about the relationship between accountability and legitimacy. They no longer clearly distinguish accountability from legitimacy. Moreover, accountability no longer occurs *subsequently* to the enactment of legitimate legal rules, in order to determine whether agents have complied with the principals' rule. Instead, accountability and legitimacy become intertwined. Legitimacy emerges as accountability for the exercise of public powers and is achieved through peer review. But this is a potentially weak form of legitimacy. It relies on the consent of a narrow range of stakeholders—rather than a whole EU demos—to the regulatory measure in question. Moreover, it is often the regulator that determine who counts as a 'stakeholder' in a particular regulatory space. For instance, the Environment Agency for England and Wales wields significant powers of inclusion and exclusion by 'mapping stakeholders'; that is, identifying local interested parties that should be involved in the drafting of river basin management plans as part of the implementation of the EU

Water Framework Directive (2000/60/EC).[53] In contrast to Sabel's and Simon's conception of legitimacy flowing from accountability processes in new governance regimes, Mashaw's understanding of government considers legitimacy also as a necessary *prior* requisite for the successful operation of accountability procedures.[54] He suggests that regulators will only answer those claims asking them to explain and justify their actions that regulators consider to be legitimate claims.

In order to further flesh out Sabel's and Simon's account of 'dynamic accountability', the extract from Meidinger discusses the operation of new accountability procedures in the specific context of new governance regimes regulating logging.

Errol Meidinger, 'The Administrative Law of Global Private-Public Regulation: the Case of Forestry' (2006) 17 EJIL 47, 55, 59, 81 83, 85–86

For the past decade a major institutional focus of this emergent system has been 'forest certification', wherein experts certify to a broader public that specific forestry operations meet applicable standards for proper forest management. [...]

After initially resisting certification, European forest owners gradually came to accept it as inevitable and then decided to establish their own programme. The resultant Pan-European Forest Certification Council (PEFC) was formed during 1998 and 1999. It drew upon the by then substantial lore of forest certification and sustainable forest management to form a system with many similarities to, but also important differences from, the FSC.[55] The first difference was that the PEFC portrayed itself not as promulgating a single overall standard to be adapted to variable local conditions, but rather as providing a common framework for the mutual recognition of nationally based certification programmes that had adopted their own legitimate rules of sustainable forestry, as well as an appropriate set of certification institutions to implement them. Second, although formed as a multi-stakeholder structure nominally independent of governments, the PEFC is controlled largely by traditional forestry interests, primarily landowners and European forest products corporations. These interests also have longstanding relationships with and influence on European government forestry ministries, and the PEFC has brought government agencies into more direct interactions with forest certification. The PEFC grew quickly and now includes approximately 18 endorsed national programmes with another dozen in process. In late 2003 the PEFC rechristened itself the Programme for the Endorsement of Forest Certification, thereby opening membership to non-European programmes and laying claim to global reach. [...]

Meidinger's analysis also highlights that the shift from government to governance can still involve a role for governmental actors:

Recently, governments have become more directly involved in certification. Most strikingly, a number of government agencies have chosen to obtain certification of state owned and managed forests. While these actions sometimes reflect a desire to retain or obtain market access, agencies sometimes also seem to think that their broader political credibility or legitimacy may be enhanced by certification. Second, a growing number of governments, particularly in Europe, have adopted certified forest products procurement programmes, thus helping to create markets for certified products and lending further legitimacy to certification requirements. Third, several governments either make certification a requirement for producing commercial timber in their jurisdictions or treat certification as de facto compliance with applicable laws. Certification standard-setting processes also appear to have had

---

[53] OJ L 327/73. Jeremy Carter and Joe Howe, 'Stakeholder Participation and the Water Framework Directive: the Case of the Ribble Pilot' (2006) 11(2) Local Environment: The International Journal of Justice and Sustainability 217.

[54] Jerry Mashaw, 'Structuring a "Dense Complexity": Accountability and the Project of Administrative Law' (n 50) 17.

[55] Forest Stewardship Council.

considerable influence on the legal requirements of some governments. Finally, many governments have become actively involved in an alliance with certification organizations, environmental NGOs, and some transnational corporations in efforts to combat 'illegal logging'.

Meidinger suggests that in order to answer Mashaw's question 'accountable to whom?' in the particular context of forest certification programmes, we should not focus on single actors and groups, but recognize that accountability mechanisms are often 'cumulative' and 'interactive':

Indeed, the underlying principal-agent connotations of the term may cause further problems by allowing the analyst too easily to focus on and critique one or another source of accountability in isolation—NGOs by themselves, for example, or industry associations by themselves—when in fact accountability mechanisms are cumulative and interactive. This problem can be put off to some extent by focusing on institutional proxies for accountability, two of which on the *ex ante* side are transparency and participation mechanisms. These can be considered before returning to the larger question of accountability in forest certification.

Hence, Meidinger tackles an analysis of accountability in new modes of governance by examining two indicators of accountability procedures, transparency and public participation. By definition certification programmes seek to promote greater availability of information about the environmental credentials of a production process or product. But information actually available under such schemes is often also limited due to commercial confidentiality considerations, in particular in the case of forest industry sponsored certification schemes in comparison to those promoted by the Forest Stewardship Council. Moreover, certification 'information' is shaped by a company's aim to present its production in a positive light and to successfully market its products, in particular when certification becomes a decisive factor in the award of government contracts. Certification 'information' is provided by certifiers hired by forestry businesses. Meidinger therefore suggests that certification information does not just enhance transparency in relation to logging and its regulation but may also obscure business activity and thus impede attempts by members of the public to hold the forestry industry to account, because they will need reliable, valid, and extensive 'information' to do so.

The second indicator of accountability discussed by Meidinger is public participation in a governance regime. Meidinger notes that all forest certification programmes have now adopted at least basic US-style administrative law 'notice-and-comment' procedures, which inform affected citizens of the existence of a draft rule and invite their comments on the proposed regulatory measures. But crucial to the effectiveness of such 'notice and comment' procedures as accountability tools is that citizens are involved early enough in the process of drafting standards for sustainable logging and that their comments will actually be taken into account when the regulator writes the final version of the standards. Meidinger then discusses in more detail how new modes of governance for forests require us to rethink how we understand accountability:

To whom or to what is the global forest regulatory system, as manifested by forest certification, accountable? There is no single accountability structure in this system. Rather, multiple, mutually reinforcing accountability structures are operating at three conceptual levels. First, organizationally, there are the competing certification programmes, each seeking to demonstrate the capacity to certify proper forest management. These are in turn accountable to constituents of various kinds, including members, forestry operations, consumers, governments and public observers. Second, there is the overarching discourse of sustainable forest management to which they all profess allegiance. This discourse has several fixed elements, such as the requirement of sustained yield, but it also encompasses considerable debate about other values. Third, the various concepts of sustainability are embodied in the institutional structures [...] These include documented rule-making processes which increasingly require reasoned responses to criticisms, structured adjudication by experts, increasing visibility through public information and consultation requirements, and competition in the market for forest certification, which is itself driven by a desire for public legitimacy. [...]

A third approach to accountability is to view the package of actors, norms and institutions as a larger system whose attributes are not reducible to the individual elements of the system. This is the approach that Charles Sabel and his colleagues are developing. They describe multi-centred, mutually adjusting, yet also institutionalized structures as learning systems capable of evolving both new values and new solutions, new goals and new strategies. This learning accountability perspective seems to match up fairly well with the emerging global forestry regulatory system described in this paper. The system seeks to clarify and sometimes modify policy goals in the course of implementation. It relies heavily on applied normative arguments backed up with reasons that are often based on practical experience. Certification programmes compete with each other by offering institutions that claim to efficiently assess and ultimately to legitimate forest management, and to do so in a way that is responsive to changing and sometimes only latent public values. To implement these claims the certification programmes rely on institutionalized procedures that provide public explanations for decisions as well as multiple (and multiplying) forums for public criticism. The programmes and their allies also criticize each other in larger public arenas, sometimes vehemently, while simultaneously recognizing a degree of mutual dependence and participation in a common project. Thus, forest certification seems to be instituting a continuing process of broad, cross-disciplinary, multi-interest internal and external surveillance and review.

Meidinger thus suggests that in the context of new, experimentalist governance prior abstract conceptions of what accountability looks like are of limited value. Instead the shape and nature of accountability systems emerges from the actual empirical operation of regulatory regimes in which various accountability systems are embedded, that sometimes compete or complement each other.

3.3 CONCLUDING REMARKS

This section has suggested that accountability and legitimacy, key concepts that inform both systems of government and governance, have to be rethought in the context of new, experimentalist environmental governance. While their meaning—based on hierarchical principal–agent relationships—is well established in the context of national legal and political government, accountability systems that are based on peer review, learning, and iterative revision of standards are only beginning to be developed as new, experimentalist governance regimes, for example, for logging, are emerging. The idea that learning is not necessarily a neutral activity, but also informed by power dynamics, that is, who determines who learns what from whom, has been already discussed in Section 2. Hence, new forms of accountability, such as peer accountability, may be a sub-species of Mashaw's conception of political accountability, though they operate at a small-scale level of political interactions between participants in an environmental regulatory regime. Furthermore, we see in governance regimes, particularly those influenced by new public management, economic values shaping accountability procedures, such as reliance on *competition* between different standard setting bodies and accountability mechanisms as enhancing accountability of public and private regulators. NPM philosophies also underpin the idea that financial and market discipline, imposed through audit and accountability to market actors, can enhance accountability of regulators. Market discipline seeks to ensure that regulatory powers do not impede but facilitate the operation of markets, such as those in forestry products.

The rise of new regimes of market accountability raises the question of to whom those who wield regulatory powers should be accountable, a question that becomes particularly difficult to answer in transnational governance regimes.[56] This question also matters in light of the fact that regulatory institutions in the transnational sphere are not necessarily subject to no accountability procedures but may be held to account by the 'wrong' accountability community.[57] Of course this raises a question about who is, and is not, the 'wrong 'accountability community'. For instance, is it the case that the European Food Safety Authority[58] should not just be accountable to the Member States that have granted it legal regulatory powers, but also to the EU citizens who are affected by its decisions and who fund it through their contributions to national Member States' tax income? The designation of 'right' or 'wrong' accountability communities has clear implications for the distribution of power in a political system.

Finally, to rethink accountability and legitimacy in the context of transnational environmental governance requires ultimately to be more explicit about what *values* of 'good' and 'democratic' governance *new* governance seeks to promote. How can such values be 'constitutionalized' in transnational legal orders that may draw on both public and private law?[59] A constitutionalization of fundamental values that provides scope for pluralism seems to be called for in the light of a 'disorderly and highly unstructured rugged landscape' of different accountability mechanisms in the transnational sphere, which may undermine, complement, or substitute for each other.[60] The pluralist vision of a global administrative law grants the various constituencies that have an interest in the exercise of regulatory measures the power to contest, but not veto, the measures in question.[61]

To conclude, the shift from environmental government to governance requires us to rethink the meaning of accountability for and legitimacy in the exercise of regulatory powers. While it is necessary to liberate our thinking from the blue prints of established national legal and political accountability and legitimacy procedures, it is clear that concepts such as constitutional values of good government originally developed in a nation-state context, still hold sway as the exercise of regulatory powers changes in a transnational sphere.

FURTHER READING AND QUESTIONS

1. Useful readings on governance and accountability include; John Braithwaite 'Accountability and Governance Under the New Regulatory State (1999) 58 Australian Journal of Public Administration 90; and Colin Scott, 'Accountability in the Regulatory State' (2000) 27 Journal of Law and Society 38; Julia Black, 'Constructing and Contesting Legitimacy and Accountability in Polycentric Regulatory Regimes' (2008) 2 Regulation & Governance 137.

2. For an analysis of accountability and EU governance see Carol Harlow, *Accountability in the European Union* (OUP 2002) and Elizabeth Fisher, 'The European Union in the Age of Accountability' (2004) 24 OJLS 495.

3. Read one of the chapters that discuss a specific environmental regulatory regime, such as Chapter 22 on GMOs, Chapter 21 on contaminated land, Chapter 14 on water pollution, or Chapter 15 on air pollution and climate change. To what extent is the exercise of government powers central to the operation of these regimes? Do you detect a shift from government to governance in their operation?

---

[56] Nico Krisch, 'The Pluralism of Global Administrative Law' (2006) 17 EJIL 247.
[57] Ibid, 250. [58] See Chapter 23.
[59] Carol Harlow, 'Global Administrative Law: The Quest for Principles and Values' (2006) 17 EJIL (n 13) 197.
[60] Krisch (n 55) 248. [61] Krisch (n 55) 249.

4 THE GOVERNANCE TURN IN ENVIRONMENTAL LAW: QUESTIONING INDUSTRIAL MODERNITY?

In this final section we examine the work of a group of scholars who suggest that the shift from environmental government to governance can be located in wider changes in power dynamics in contemporary societies. We first consider the work of reflexive modernity and then the literature on ecological modernization. What is particularly striking about each of these theoretical approaches is the way in which environmental problems have been the starting point for reconfiguring an understanding of governance and government.

4.1 FROM INDUSTRIAL TO REFLEXIVE MODERNITY

Some social theorists argue that we no longer live in an age of industrial modernity but instead have moved on to a reflexive modernity. One of the most significant of these is Ulrich Beck who published *Risk Society* in German in 1986, translated into English in 1992. The book opens with a significant argument.

Ulrich Beck, *Risk Society: Towards and New Ecology* (Sage 1992) 19–20

In advanced modernity the social production of wealth is systematically accompanied by the social production of risks. Accordingly, the problems and conflicts relating to distribution in a society of scarcity overlap with the problems and conflicts that arise from the production, definition and distribution of techno-scientifically produced risks.

The production and distribution of techno-scientifically produced risks is part of a wider significant phenomenon, called by Beck the 'new paradigm of the risk society':

which is based on the solution of a similar and yet quite different problem. How can the risks and hazards systematically produced as part of modernization be prevented, minimised, dramatized, or channelled? Where they do finally see the light of day in the shape of 'latent side effects', how can they be limited and distributed away so that they neither hamper the modernization process nor exceed the limits of that which is 'tolerable'—ecologically, medically, psychologically and socially? We are therefore concerned no longer exclusively with making nature useful, or with releasing mankind from traditional constraints, but also and essentially with problems resulting from techno-economic development itself. Modernization is becoming reflexive; it is becoming its own theme. Questions of the development and employment of technologies (in the realms of nature, society and the personality) are being eclipsed by questions of the political and economic 'management' of the risks of actually or potentially utilized technologies—discovering, administering, acknowledging, avoiding or concealing such hazards with respect to specially defined horizons of relevance. The promise of security grows with the risks and destruction and must be reaffirmed over and over again to an alert and critical public through cosmetic or real interventions in the techno-economic development.

Thus, Beck is showing how environmental problems are giving rise to a new understanding of society and modernity.

Inherent in Beck's theory is the idea that because risks have become difficult to calculate, it is more difficult to insure for them. Hence, he suggests that risk society is characterized by the decline of the provident and providing state that delivers regulatory measures for dealing with calculable risks.

Ulrich Beck, 'Risk Society and the Provident State' in S Lash, B Szerszynski and B Wynne (eds), *Risk, Environment & Modernity* (Sage Publications 1996) 31, 34, 42

In contrast to early industrial risks, nuclear, chemical, ecological and genetic engineering risks (a) can be limited in terms of neither time nor place (b) are not accountable according to the established rules and causality, blame and liability, and (c) cannot be compensated or insured against. Or, to express it by reference to a single example: the injured of Chernobyl are today, years after the catastrophe, not even *born* yet. [...]

Reflexive modernisation contains both elements: the reflex-like threat to industrial society's own foundations through a successful further modernisation which is blind to dangers, *and* the growth of awareness, the reflection on this situation. [...]

No one knows, however, how, whether and by what means it might be possible to really throttle back the self-endangering momentum of the global risk society. Talk of the nature state-by analogy with the social state-remains just as empty in this context as attempts to cure industrial society of its suicidal tendencies with more of the same: morality, technology and ecological markets. The necessary learning step still lies ahead of the global risk society on the threshold of the twenty-first century.

Hence, governance rather than government, in particular the experimentalist governance regimes already discussed by Sabel and Simon, are an attempt to institutionalize the type of reflexive learning that Beck considers as characteristic of the risk society and as simply necessary in order to deal with its embedded pollution side-effects. What shape governance regimes take is also a reflection of how environmental problems are debated within a 'public sphere'. A public sphere consists of actual political institutions as well as the discursive spaces that are created through debates among citizens about environmental problems. McCright and Dunlap suggest that debates about environmental problems are becoming increasingly pluralized, including not just environmentalist perspectives, but also those who challenge the idea that reflexive modernity is characterized by risks that are difficult to calculate and understand, such as climate change.

Aaron M McCright and Riley E Dunlap, 'Anti-reflexivity The American Conservative Movement's Success in Undermining Climate Science and Policy' (2010) 27(2–3) Theory, Culture & Society 100, 103–4, 106, 111

Forces of Reflexivity and Anti-reflexivity

Especially after the Second World War, the dominant mode of science was oriented toward providing knowledge that generated innovative technologies that increased industrial capitalist production. This science in the service of production, or 'production science', has expanded the hegemony of economic producers by giving them more control over resources (environment) and people (workers and consumers). However, the decades after the Second World War saw the gradual rise of other areas of science more oriented toward identifying the negative impacts of science and technology (as discussed in Rachel Carson's *Silent Spring*). This 'impact science' challenged the assumption that production science inevitably led to advancement and progress for society. [...]

Social movements comprise a second major force of reflexivity within the era of RM. Social movements—especially environmental movements—help raise public consciousness of unintended and unanticipated effects of the industrial capitalist social order, while providing a vision of the social transformations needed to address them. [...]

Crucial for scholars of the second dimension of power is the idea that political systems develop a 'mobilization of bias', in that some issues are included within the system and others are excluded. Bachrach and Baratz define the mobilization of bias as 'a set of predominant values, beliefs, rituals, and institutional procedures ("rules of the game") that operate systematically and consistently to the benefit of certain persons and groups at the expense of others' (1970: 43–4). The primary method for sustaining a given mobilization of bias is 'non-decision-making', whereby a 'nondecision' is 'a decision that results in suppression or thwarting of a latent or manifest challenge to the values or interests of the decision-maker' (1970: 44). Thus, the essence of the second dimension of power is that actors prevent a decision that may directly challenge their interests by agenda setting or creating a non-decision.

McCright and Dunlap then turn to consider the US conservative movement's attack on climate change science and note the different techniques deployed.

The American conservative movement has employed four non decision-making techniques associated with the second dimension of power to make climate change a non-issue and prevent significant progress on climate policy-making. This countermovement has (1) obfuscated, misrepresented, manipulated and suppressed the results of scientific research; (2) intimidated or threatened to sanction individual scientists; (3) invoked existing rules or created new procedures in the political system; and (4) invoked an existing bias of the media.

McCright's and Dunlap's analysis continues to be relevant also in light of the failure of the US administration to facilitate the achievement of an ambitious agreement at the COP 17 /CMP 7 Climate Conference in Durban in December 2011 that sought to develop a successor agreement to the Kyoto Protocol. McCright's and Dunlap's points matter also in the context of environmental debates in the UK. For instance, Nigel Lawson, the Conservative Party politician and former chancellor of the exchequer, has expressed scepticism about the significance of climate change, questioned the scientific statements in the reports of the Intergovernmental Panel on Climate Change, and rejected the idea that international law should regulate greenhouse gas emissions.[62]

Antonio and Brulle, building on the work of McCright and Dunlap, show the development of climate change denial in the US overlaps with neoliberal politics.

Robert Antonio and Robert Brulle, 'The Unbearable Lightness of Politics: Climate Change Denial and Political Polarization' (2011) 52 The Sociological Quarterly 195, 197, 199–200.

Thus, anti-environmentalism has been, from the start, a keystone of neoliberal antiregulatory politics. But the perceived threats posed by climate change discourse intensified this opposition, mobilizing energy companies and other related industries and broader free-market forces. Discrediting global climate change claims began in earnest in 1989 when the Marshall Institute issued their first report disputing climate science. Although climate change denial is a latecomer to neoliberal anti-environmentalism, it has now become the countermovement's pivotal issue in battles against environmental regulations. Neoliberals hold that the issue provides license for wholesale intervention everywhere. Conservative columnist and climate change denier George Will (2008) has argued that the fanatical 'green left's' charges that CO_2 emissions and fossil fuel industries pose a 'planetary menace' provide a rationale for the government to 'intrude' everywhere, curtail consumer choice and property rights, and increase the state's size and surveillance. Reeling from conservative attacks over liberal

---

[62] Nigel Lawson, *An Appeal to Reason: A Cool Look at Global Warming* (Duckworth Overlook 2008). He also participated in the climate change sceptic documentary 'The Great Global Warming Swindle'.

bias, 'mainstream media,' seeking 'editorial balance,' often grant parity to 'climate skeptic' news releases and policy papers, from right-wing think tanks and their bought experts and pundits, with peer-reviewed science. Having increased leverage in recessions and periods of economic insecurity, many Americans are receptive to conservative views—eg, that regulating fuel efficiency, and thereby vehicle size and weight, increases energy prices and taxes, 'kills jobs,' violates freedom of choice, and threatens overall liberty.

The current situation parallels the1920s when the market liberal discourse ruled in a climate dominated by nationally consolidated markets, major technical innovations (eg, radio, electrification), unchecked corporate power, and plutocratic inequality. John Dewey argued that the 'rugged individualist' cultural vocabulary left the American public 'lost' and 'bemused' (Dewey [1929–1930] 1999). So it is today. [...] Although many Americans believe in anthropogenic warming and fear its consequences, it is uncertain if even they are ready to expend significant resources or alter their way of life to meet the challenge. Belief in the need for continuous economic growth, at almost any cost, is transparent in a time of high unemployment, insecurity, and jobless growth.

The anti-reflexive tendencies, discussed by McCright and Dunlap play out in the context of a larger one-dimensional political culture and a citizenry resistant to the idea of public goods and the need to share their costs. Margaret Thatcher famously asserted about neoliberalism—'There is no alternative!' Arguably, this is the taken-for-granted reality today (Judt 2010).

Lively debate about the reliability of climate science, in McCright's and Dunlap's terminology 'environmental impact science'—was also sparked in 2009 in the UK in response to controversies about data generated by scientists at the Climatic Research Unit (CRU) at East Anglia University.[63]

The CRU is a significant institution in contributing to scientific research in relation to climate change. It is linked to the Hadley Centre for climate research at the UK meteorological office.[64] The CRU dealt with two key data sets in relation to global temperature developments, which fed into the reports of the Intergovernmental Panel on Climate Change. Climate sceptic computer hackers gained access to emails from staff at the CRU and published them on the internet. The language and conversation of the emails were asserted as proof that the science behind climate change had been manipulated. The fact that one of the main scientists at CRU, Professor Phil Jones, had not wanted to disclose data and that Freedom of Information requests were denied was also criticized.

The House of Commons Science and Technology Select Committee set up an inquiry into the matter and their conclusion is given in their discourse of climate data from the CRU.

Science and Technology Select Committee, The Disclosure of Climate Data from the Climatic Research Unit at the University of East Anglia (2009–10, HC 387) 3

The disclosure of climate data from the Climatic Research Unit (CRU) at the University of East Anglia (UEA) in November 2009 had the potential to damage the reputation of the climate science and the scientists involved.

---

[63] Science and Technology Select Committee, *The Disclosure of Climate Data from the Climatic Research Unit at the University of East Anglia* (2009–10, HC 387) 43–5.

[64] See, for example, links between the work of the CRU and the Hadley Centre: <http://www.metoffice.gov.uk/news/releases/archive/2012/hadcrut-updates> accessed 5 March 2013.

We believe that the focus on CRU and Professor Phil Jones, Director of CRU, in particular, has largely been misplaced. Whilst we are concerned that the disclosed e-mails suggest a blunt refusal to share scientific data and methodologies with others, we can sympathise with Professor Jones, who must have found it frustrating to handle requests for data that he knew—or perceived—were motivated by a desire simply to undermine his work.

In the context of the sharing of data and methodologies, we consider that Professor Jones's actions were in line with common practice in the climate science community. It is not standard practice in climate science to publish the raw data and the computer code in academic papers. However, climate science is a matter of great importance and the quality of the science should be irreproachable. We therefore consider that climate scientists should take steps to make available all the data that support their work (including raw data) and full methodological workings (including the computer codes). Had both been available, many of the problems at UEA could have been avoided.

We are content that the phrases such as "trick" or "hiding the decline" were colloquial terms used in private e-mails and the balance of evidence is that they were not part of a systematic attempt to mislead. Likewise the evidence that we have seen does not suggest that Professor Jones was trying to subvert the peer review process. Academics should not be criticised for making informal comments on academic papers.

In the context of Freedom of Information (FOIA), much of the responsibility should lie with UEA. The disclosed e-mails appear to show a culture of non-disclosure at CRU and instances where information may have been deleted, to avoid disclosure. We found prima facie evidence to suggest that the UEA found ways to support the culture at CRU of resisting disclosure of information to climate change sceptics. The failure of UEA to grasp fully the potential damage to CRU and UEA by the non-disclosure of FOIA requests was regrettable. UEA needs to review its policy towards FOIA and re-assess how it can support academics whose expertise in this area is limited.

There is much of interest in this statement. Note the web of institutions, the role of freedom of information, and how there are assumptions about scientific practice operating. Overall the Inquiry further highlights the emergence of a new very particular environmental politics in relation to climate science. One interesting question is whether critical scrutiny of environmental impact science should be interpreted as a force of 'anti-reflexivity' as McCright and Dunlap suggest. They may in fact be part and parcel of a reflexive modernity as defined by Beck, a modernity that increasingly questions the power of scientific knowledge to solve the risks it generates. In any case, McCright and Dunlap, as well as Beck, question the possibility of scientific knowledge and technological innovation providing lasting solutions to contemporary environmental problems.

4.2 ENTRENCHING INDUSTRIAL MODERNITY THROUGH ENVIRONMENTAL GOVERNANCE?

The final perspective to consider, in order to understand whether and how a wider shift from government to governance may be associated with a questioning of industrial modernity, is ecological modernization. This is an approach to environmental regulation that relies significantly on technological development and scientific knowledge in order to find solutions to environmental problems. Ecological modernization does not perceive a rupture between industrial and reflexive modernity. It sees environmental problems simply as an opportunity for industrial modernity to reform itself. Ecological modernization has been influential among public policy makers and chimes with the policy idea of sustainable development, as Mol and Sonnenfeld explain.

Arthur PJ Mol and David Sonnenfeld 'Ecological Modernisation Around the World: An Introduction' (2000) 9 Environmental Politics 1, 4–5

The first contributions, especially those by Joseph Huber were characterised by a heavy emphasis on the role of technological innovations in environmental reform, especially in the sphere of industrial production; a critical attitude towards the (bureaucratic) state; a favourable attitude towards the role of market actors and dynamics in environmental reforms; a systems-theoretical and rather evolutionary perspective with a limited notion of human agency and social struggles; and an orientation towards analyses at the level of the nation-state.

The second period, from the late 1980s to the mid-1990s, showed less emphasis on technological innovation as the key motor of ecological modernisation; a more balanced view on the respective roles of states and 'the market' in ecological transformation; and more attention to institutional and cultural dynamics of ecological modernisation. During this period, scholarship on ecological modernisation continued to emphasise national and comparative studies of industrial production in the Organisation for Economic Co-operation and Development (OECD) countries.

Since the mid-1990s, the frontier of Ecological Modernisation Theory has broadened theoretically and geographically to include studies on the ecological transformation of consumption; ecological modernisation in non- European countries (newly industrialising countries, less developed countries, the transitional economies in Central and Eastern Europe, but also OECD countries such as the USA and Canada); and global processes.

The relationship between markets, states, and governance are at the heart of ecological modernization. The extract from Bailey, Gouldson, and Newell also explains how it is an approach that leads us back to the discussions about governance seen at the start of the chapter.

Ian Bailey, Andy Gouldson, and Peter Newell, 'Ecological Modernisation and the Governance of Carbon: A Critical Analysis' (2011) 43 Antipode 682, 684–85

As with many forms of modernism, EM is essentially optimistic about the future. [...]

However, climate change, as a classically 'wicked' environmental problem, has challenged the optimism of EM. [...]

For a period, then, the optimism of the modernists seemed to falter. However, in recent years a substantial degree of technological and economic optimism has emerged. Technologically, authors [...] have claimed that "humanity can solve the carbon and climate problem in the first half of this century simply by scaling up what we already know how to do". Economically, Stern's (2006) claim that the costs of tackling climate change are both relatively affordable and much lower than the costs of not acting have changed the political landscape by making it economically possible and economically necessary to act on climate change. This combination of technological and economic optimism—coupled with claims that tackling climate change could have social, economic, environmental and geo-political co-benefits—has in turn made it politically viable for many governments to set ambitious targets for decarbonisation.

However, this has happened in a context where state capacities to intervene in the economy have become more limited. Globalisation and liberalisation have meant that the political capital needed to intervene escalates significantly if interventions have any negative impacts on economic competitiveness—and such interventions may lead not to the management but merely to the displacement of economic activities through phenomena such as carbon leakage. EM theory would suggest that these limits have led to innovation and policy learning—particularly through a transition away from traditional state-centred forms of intervention and towards more neoliberal and de-centred forms of governance that include a greater emphasis on markets as key delivery mechanisms for environmental governance.

This 'governance turn' has thus been associated with a shift away from the 'controller' state with its reliance on the hierarchical application of rules and regulations towards the 'facilitator' or 'enabler' state. [...] These changes have been reflected in the range of environmental policy instruments that are used in many settings, with experiments with economic and information-based instruments and an increased emphasis on voluntary approaches and different forms of self-regulation. Within these decentred approaches, authority and responsibility are dispersed within broader networks—and so governance becomes a multi-level, multi-actor phenomenon which is complex and fragmented, with new patterns of interaction emerging as a variety of economic and social actors are enlisted to 'do the governing'.

Thus, here we can see a connection between ecological modernization and neoliberalism, and how it shapes regulatory strategies and our understanding of the climate change issue.

4.3 MODERNITY AND GOVERNANCE: SOME CONCLUDING THOUGHTS

This section has suggested that the shift from environmental government to governance needs to be explained also with reference to wider changes in the dynamics of power in contemporary societies. Some social theorists, such as Beck, argue that we have moved into a new and distinct phase of modernity, called reflexive modernity. Reflexive modernity is characterized by a decline of regulatory powers in relation to contemporary environmental crises. That includes the decline of state regulatory powers, and the shift to governance can be interpreted as an attempt to address this. Beck's account of the risk society also changes how we think about key building blocks of environmental regulatory regimes, such as accountability relationships. Given the decline in regulatory powers—because risks become difficult to know about—accountability is no longer focused on whether the exercise of public or private or hybrid regulatory powers can be actually justified to particular constituencies. Instead, Beck focuses on political accountability, that is, the need to provide justifications for the distribution of 'bads', such as impacts of environmental risks on human health and ecosystem functioning. But Beck's perspective is challenged by ecological modernization, which relies on the refinement of scientific knowledge and technological innovation to retain environmental government and governance regulatory capacity.

FURTHER READING AND QUESTIONS

1. The idea of reflexive modernity suggests that scientific knowledge and technological innovation are limited in addressing complex, and often not fully known contemporary environmental challenges. But environmental policy development in the UK, in particular in the context of new public management, also increasingly relies on neo-classical economics as a social science discipline for shaping how both public and private actors should respond to environmental problems. Do you think that the significant role of economics in environmental

policy-making signals a continuity between industrial and reflexive modernity? If so, how would you critique Beck's idea of the risk society as a distinct form of modernity?

3. 'Beck's aim to chart a distinct shift from industrial to reflexive modernity can help to understand the changing form of environmental law in the UK, in particular a shift from a modernist approach to environmental law that pursues rational, coherent legal orders to a postmodern approach, that accommodates a patchwork of fragmented hybrid public–private regulatory controls'. Critically discuss this statement.

4. Sacci Lloyd's two books, *Carbon Diaries 2015* and *Carbon Diaries 2017* (Hodder Children's Books 2008 and 2009) provide a dystopian fictional account of environmental regulation in the UK in an age of personal carbon accounts. Critically assess the image of environmental government and governance, the roles for both state and private actors, that her fictional account presents.

5. To read further on ecological modernization, see Arthur PJ Mol, David A Sonnenfeld, and Gert Spaargaren (eds), *The Ecological Modernisation Reader: Environmental Reform in Theory and Practice* (Routledge 2009).

5 CONCLUSION

This chapter has sought to chart and contextualize a shift from environmental government to governance, a shift from reliance on public state bodies as key actors in environmental regulation, to greater reliance on private actors, including the development of hybrid public–private regulatory networks. The chapter identified two main drivers for this shift, first, the reform of public sector bureaucracies under the banner of 'new public management' and, second, the increasing transnationalization of environmental regulation. Transnationalization has prompted a search for innovative, experimentalist governance models, which enrol also at the local level various private actors in the definition and enforcement of environmental standards. The chapter then explained that the shift from government to governance also requires us to rethink fundamental building blocks of environmental regulation, such as accountability procedures and tools for rendering the exercise of regulatory powers legitimate. The chapter has contextualized the fundamental shift from environmental government to governance by relating it to wider debates about a move from industrial to reflexive modernity. On the one hand, the idea that society has changed from industrial to reflexive modernity can account for the decline in state environmental regulatory powers and the associated search for innovative environmental governance mechanisms that emphasize 'learning' and 'iteration' in environmental policy-making, because central state regulators no longer know the best solutions to environmental problems. On the other hand, the chapter suggested that we also need to question this perception of a shift from a distinct phase of industrial to a reflexive modernity. The increasing pluralization of voices in environmental debates, illustrated through the debate between climate change sceptics and those who suggest that scientific knowledge supports the idea of serious, irreversible damage caused by global warming, shows that within public debate images of industrial society are also being re-affirmed. Moreover, the perspective of ecological modernization, which has also been influential in UK public policy-making, perceives environmental problems as an opportunity for industrial modernity to simply reform itself according to its existing growth trajectory and on the basis of its established social orders. The chapter therefore sought to remind the reader that an analysis of the form that environmental law takes, that is, its association with environmental government or governance, benefits from an understanding of the fundamental changes in social order that social theory seeks to capture through the concepts of 'industrial' and 'reflexive' modernity.

FURTHER READING

David Levi-Faur, *Oxford Handbook of Governance* (OUP 2012).

PART IV

POLLUTION CONTROL

INTRODUCTION

So far, this textbook has charted the complexity, vastness, and variety of the legal landscape of UK environmental law. We now turn to examining legal regimes in detail. Part IV considers pollution control, while Part V covers various aspects of land management. This twofold division, as well as the organization chapters within each part, gives the impression that the landscape of environmental regimes is easily susceptible to a neat schema, but do not be fooled—it can't be. In the Introductions to both parts, we set out some of the overarching intellectually challenges in thinking about these areas of law and regulation.

In relation to pollution control, this Introduction notes five important things before embarking on a survey of different pollution control regimes. First, it briefly considers the nature of 'pollution'. Second, it considers how pollution control has emerged as a set of legal regimes. Third, it focuses on one particular development in the evolution of pollution control regimes in England and Wales—the environmental permitting system. This system integrates the administration of pollution control regulation (beyond the substantive integration of pollution control considered in Chapter 17), highlighting the scale of administration involved in regulating pollution and also providing a common point of reference for most of the separate regimes covered in Part IV. Fourth, this Introduction considers different aspects of the *legal* content of these pollution regimes to highlight that they are not as straightforward as they may seem—they incorporate laws from across jurisdictions, have significant socio-legal and theoretical dimensions, and interact with other areas of environmental law and legal doctrine more broadly. In conclusion, we reflect upon the interrelationship between the material in this part and the descriptive, purposive, and jurisprudential definitions of environmental law.

1 WHAT IS POLLUTION?

Before considering the nature of pollution control law, it is useful briefly to consider what pollution is. The *Oxford English Dictionary* contains a number of definitions but the most significant for an environmental lawyer is pollution defined as:

> Physical impurity or contamination; (now) esp. the presence in or introduction into the environment (esp. as a result of human activity) of harmful or poisonous substances, or excessive levels of light, noise, organic waste, etc.

Pollution is thus something that is 'impure' or that 'contaminates', but this raises a further question of what we mean by these terms. The work of the late anthropologist Mary Douglas is particularly significant in this regard. Along with the political scientist Aaron Wildavsky, she discusses some of the ideas that emerged from that work.

Mary Douglas and Aaron Wildavsky, *Risk and Culture: An Essay on the Selection of Technological and Environmental Dangers* (University of California Press 1983) 35–36

Pollution, defilement, contagion, or impurity implies some harmful interference with natural processes. It assumes something about normality because it implies an abnormal intrusion of foreign elements, mixing, or destruction. It is used in two senses. There is a strict technical sense, as when we speak of river or air pollution, when the physical adulteration of an earlier state can be precisely measured. The technical sense rests upon a clear notion of the prepolluted condition. A river that flows over muddy ground may be always thick; but if that is taken as its natural state, it is not necessarily said to be polluted. The technical sense of pollution is not morally loaded but depends upon measures of change. The other sense of pollution is a contagious state, harmful, caused by outside intervention, but mysterious in its origins. This nontechnical idea of pollution is particularly useful in political argument because it carries the idea of moral defect. Usually the dangerous impurity is attributed to moral transgression of one kind or another: it is presented as a penalty, plagues or famines descending to punish perjury, incest, adultery, or breach of ritual. Sometimes the evil effect is held to fall on the original perpetrator, or it may punish him the more by falling on his wife and children, or he may be seen as causing a community wide threat. [...] [T]he words *pollution beliefs* or *pollution ideas* refer to mysterious, nontechnical pollution.

[...] [P]ollution ideas are the product of an ongoing political debate about the ideal society.

Much of the explicit discussion about pollution in environmental law uses the term in the technical sense—accordingly, the chapters in this part involve considerable discussion about pollution standards. But the non-technical understanding of pollution is always important to keep in mind. Douglas' work on ideas of pollution began with anthropological studies of understandings of taboo in tribal communities and her work draws important comparisons between these ideas of taboo and ideas of pollution. In both cases, the focus is on identifying and preventing what is viewed as socially undesirable.[1] In the same way, inherent in debates about pollution are debates about what is normal and acceptable. Having read Chapter 2, this is unsurprising—we highlighted there how environmental values shape our understanding of environmental problems.

In short, pollution cannot only be understood as a technical question—it is also a question about what in a society we understand to be an acceptable level of environmental quality. Furthermore, and related to this, it is important to note that pollution does not need to lead directly to *physical* harm. An 'abnormal intrusion' might simply amount to harm because it is 'abnormal'. With that said, the fact that pollution has physical consequences is usually one of the reasons why it comes to be regulated, but the relationship between pollution and harm should not be understood too strictly.

2 THE DEVELOPMENT OF POLLUTION CONTROL LAW

Pollution control is often understood as the core of environmental law. This is not surprising as many of the first 'environmental' laws were concerned with controlling polluting discharges into air and water and onto land. In the nineteenth century, the focus was upon both discharges from certain industrial facilities (initially alkali works) and dealing with the hygiene problems created by the

---

[1] Mary Douglas, *Risk And Blame: Essays in Cultural Theory* (Routledge 1992); Mary Douglas, *Purity and Danger* (Routledge Classics 2002).

dramatic growth of cities.[2] In the mid-twentieth century, the regulatory focus on pollution turned to emissions from a broader range of industrial and other activities. As we saw in Chapter 3, the Clean Air Act 1956 was a response to the smog (and the subsequent health problems) created by industrial and coal emissions in cities. As Egan notes below, this history of regulation was largely one of states responding reactively to the problems of pollution.

Michael Egan, 'Forum: Toxic Knowledge: a Mecurial Fugue in Three Parts' (2008) 13 Environmental History 636, 636

In a provocative discussion on the nature and historicity of scientific knowledge, Bruno Latour asks: 'Where were microbes before Pasteur?' He concludes: 'after 1864 airborne germs were there all along,' which presents the historian with an interesting portal into the history of scientific knowledge and its relationship with environmental politics. The history of toxic environments is largely reactionary in nature: the framing of new environmental standards comes in response to the discovery of hazards and those standards are frequently revised as new information becomes available. Reactionary history and the changing contexts of awareness of toxic hazards are suggestive of what Latour called the 'historicity' of scientific knowledge: 'History not only passes but transforms.' Scientific discoveries alter our reading of the past.

Egan's point is that the reactionary process of regulation depends on hazards being discovered, and such discovery is both a scientific and a socio-political process. The introduction of new regimes to control pollution was thus often accompanied by wide ranging public debates about the hazards created by pollution. For example, there was a rich political discourse around public health regulation in the nineteenth century.[3] Further, the emergence of pollution control regimes in most countries in the 1960s and 1970s was directly related to the rise of the environmental movement in those different jurisdictions, which responded to developing scientific knowledge about environmental effects but also involved the social response to, and partly the construction of, that knowledge.[4] These examples highlight the significance of non-technical beliefs about pollution, as discussed by Douglas and Wildavsky.

Early pollution control regimes tended to be sector-specific and thus water pollution, air pollution, and so on, tended to be regulated separately, with a focus on regulating polluting discharges into those media. However, over the last several decades, there has been a shift towards more holistic approaches. This is most obviously seen in integrated pollution control (Chapter 17)[5] and water pollution regulation (Chapter 14). Howarth explains this shift in the context of environmentally quality standards, which regulate the overall quality of aspects of the environment.

William Howarth, 'The Progression Towards Ecological Quality Standards' (2006) 18(1) JEL 3, 6

Until fairly recently at least, the focus has been upon what things laws can be used to prevent, rather that what positive environmental goals laws can facilitate. Legislatures and environmental activists

---

[2] Ben Pontin, 'Integrated Pollution Control in Victorian Britain: Rethinking Progress within the History of Environmental Law' (2007) 19 JEL 173; Richard Lewis, *Edwin Chadwick and the Public Health Movement 1832–1854* (Longmans, Green & Co 1952).

[3] Christopher Hamlin, *Public Health and Social Justice in the Age of Chadwick, Britain 1800–1854* (CUP 1998).

[4] Philip Shabecoff, *A Fierce Green Fire: The American Environmental Movement* (Hill & Wang 1993).

[5] Although note there are strong arguments that this is not a new development. See Chapter 17 and Pontin (n 2).

seem to have had firm convictions about what activities needed to be banned, but have tended to reflect less fully upon what state of the environment should count as 'satisfactory' or 'acceptable', nor how that state might be realised by legal means.

The major turning point in environmental quality law was the recognition that it could be redirected towards the realisation of positively stated environmental quality objectives specified through precisely formulated environmental quality standards. [...] Typically, these consist of a scientifically informed numerical specification of what concentration of a particular contaminant is permissibly present in some part of an environmental media, with corresponding obligations upon the Member States to take necessary legal and administrative measures to ensure that each parameter is realised.

It should be noted, however, that these ostensible environmental quality standards are actually strongly anthropocentric in character, insofar as they are primarily guided by scientific knowledge of levels of exposure to different substances that are likely to cause adverse health effects in human beings.

Howarth's final comment is a further reminder of the importance of pollution ideals, and thus environmental values, in the development of pollution control. From a legal perspective, the shift to more holistic approaches has resulted in the growing legal and regulatory complexity of pollution control regimes. While many of these regimes were seen as traditional command-and-control regimes, which prevented or controlled certain polluting activities, there has been increased use of novel legal and regulatory techniques in controlling pollution. Thus, we see the role of emission trading schemes in air pollution control (Chapter 15) and the creation of transboundary governance regimes in water pollution control (Chapter 14). In short, while different pollution control laws were some of the first examples of environmental law, pollution control remains a dynamic and evolving area of environmental law today.

3 ENVIRONMENTAL PERMITTING IN ENGLAND AND WALES: ADMINISTRATIVE INTEGRATION OF POLLUTION CONTROL REGIMES

One particular example of the evolution of pollution control law is the environmental permitting system in England and Wales. Permits are the regulatory devices by which the command-and-control regulation of pollution control has traditionally operated. So if you plan to discharge a polluting substance into a waterway, you must first get an environmental permit (previously a discharge consent).[6] Similarly, if you plan to operate a highly polluting industrial plant, you will need an environmental permit to do so.[7] Failure to obtain a permit in these cases, or to breach a permit once obtained, is an offence. However, the system of environmental permitting has evolved over time, in light of successive waves of EU environmental regulation on pollution control and in response to the ever-increasing complexity of administering permitting systems, as highlighted further in Section 4. The most recent and most innovative reform of environmental permitting in England and Wales was introduced in 2007, in an effort to integrate the permitting processes.[8] The basic features of the new system, now set out in the Environmental Permitting Regulations 2010 (EPRs),[9] are outlined here. This outline serves firstly as a common reference point for the various pollution control regimes examined in the

[6] See Chapter 14.   [7] See Chapter 17.
[8] Environmental Permitting (England and Wales) Regulations 2007 (SI 2007/3538). Section 2.2 of Chapter 17 sets out a fuller explanation of how this integration of permitting came about in England and Wales.
[9] SI 2010/676 (EPRs).

different chapters of this part, to the extent that they involve the EPR framework for implementing permitting obligations (water pollution control, waste regulation, and integrated pollution control in particular).[10] Second, this outline highlights both the continual evolution of pollution control law and the depth of its administrative processes.

The EPRs are structured by setting out a core set of permitting obligations and then providing the substantive details for different regulated polluting activities in the voluminous schedules to the Regulations, which deal with large industrial installations, waste operations, landfill, water discharge activities, plant and operations involving asbestos, and so on. It is worth having a skim read over these schedules to get a sense of the structure and substance of the EPRs. Further details of the schedules relating to particular activities and operations are covered where relevant in the chapters of this part. Here the core obligations and mechanisms of the EPRs are explained.

The central obligation of the EPRs is the requirement for an environmental permit in regulation 12:

Requirement for environmental permit

12. (1) A person must not, except under and to the extent authorised by an environmental permit—

    (a) operate a regulated facility; or

    (b) cause or knowingly permit a water discharge activity or groundwater activity.

What constitutes a 'regulated facility' is then defined in Regulation 8:

8. (1) In these Regulations, 'regulated facility' means any of the following—

    (a) an installation,

    (b) mobile plant,

    (c) a waste operation,

    (d) a mining waste operation,

    (e) a radioactive substances activity,

    (f) a water discharge activity,

    (g) a groundwater activity.

(2) But the following are not regulated facilities—

    (a) an exempt facility [...]

All these terms are then further explained and defined in the EPRs, and are explored as relevant in the chapters of this part. Note in particular that an 'installation' is defined to include facilities subject to the integrated pollution prevention and control regime covered in Chapter 17. If a facility can be classified as more than one of the operations or activities stated here, then regulation 8(4) provides some relief from duplicate permitting obligations under the EPRs:

(4) A regulated facility of any of the following classes may be carried on as part of the operation of a regulated facility of another class—

    (a) waste operation;

---

[10] Note that climate change regulation, which also employs a permitting system to implement the emissions trading scheme (see Section 3.3 of Chapter 15), has not been included in the environmental permitting regime to date. Other activities and operations may also yet be included within the system, including water abstraction activities.

(b) mining waste operation;

(c) water discharge activity;

(d) groundwater activity.

Further, some of these facilities will be exempted from permitting requirements altogether—when they pose minimal environmental risks as characterized in various ways for the different types of facilities and processes involved. These exemptions are subject to the conditions, and administered through the processes, set out in Schedules 2 and 3.

Schedule 5 to the EPRs sets out the procedure for issuing environmental permits. To obtain a new permit, or to vary an existing one, an applicant operator must make an application (and pay a fee) under paragraph 2, submitting this to the relevant regulator. The 'regulator' under the EPRs is either the Environment Agency (EA) or relevant local authority—local authorities act as regulators under the EPRs only for smaller scale facilities and activities (paragraphs 32 and 33). Once an application has been made, the regulator has a duty to determine it, and may issue a permit subject to 'such conditions as it sees fit'. The considerations that a regulator will take into account in this decision-making process are those dictated by public law doctrine (taking into account relevant material considerations, legitimate expectations and so on),[11] and include the more specific considerations dictated by the Schedules for particular kinds of permits. Further, the regulator must consider certain representations, including those of the operator and the interested public (persons whom the regulator considers are affected by, are likely to be affected by, or have an interest in, an application).[12] These public participation provisions are significant, and partly fulfill requirements under EU law.[13] Note however the narrow interpretation of these public participation provisions in the English courts to date.[14] Finally, under paragraph 13(1), a regulator must refuse to issue (or transfer) a permit where it considers that the requirements of paragraph 13(2) will not be satisfied:

(2) The requirements are that the applicant for the grant of an environmental permit, or the proposed transferee, on the transfer of an environmental permit (in whole or in part), must—

(a) be the operator of the regulated facility; and

(b) operate the regulated facility in accordance with the environmental permit.

Note also that pollution control standards set under environmental permits are intended to be dynamic rather than static, hence they can be varied as indicated above, and the practical mechanism for this process is in regulation 34:

34. (1) The regulator must periodically review environmental permits.

(2) The regulator must make appropriate periodic inspections of regulated facilities.

---

[11] See Section 4 of Chapter 7.

[12] See EPRs, sch 5, paras 5, 6, 8 for precise details of when and how public consultees are involved.

[13] See, for example, Council Directive 2010/75/EU of 24 November 2010 on industrial emissions (integrated pollution prevention and control) [2010] OJ L334/17, art 24.

[14] *Yates-Taylor v Environment Agency* [2010] EWHC 3038 (Admin), [2011] Env LR 14.

Once a permit has been issued, there are provisions relating to breach of a permit or its conditions, which are criminal offences, as set out in regulations 38 and 39:

Offences

38. (1) It is an offence for a person to—

    (a) contravene regulation 12(1); or

    (b) knowingly cause or knowingly permit the contravention of regulation 12(1)(a).

(2) It is an offence for a person to fail to comply with or to contravene an environmental permit condition.

(3) It is an offence for a person to fail to comply with the requirements of an enforcement notice or of a prohibition notice, suspension notice, landfill closure notice or mining waste facility closure notice.

[...]

(6) If an offence committed by a person under this regulation is due to the act or default of some other person, that other person is also guilty of the offence and liable to be proceeded against and punished accordingly, whether or not proceedings for the offence are taken against the first mentioned person.

Penalties

39. (1) A person guilty of an offence under regulation 38(1), (2) or (3) is liable—

    (a) on summary conviction to a fine not exceeding £50,000 or imprisonment for a term not exceeding 12 months, or to both; or

    (b) on conviction on indictment to a fine or imprisonment for a term not exceeding 5 years, or to both.

A couple of defences are also provided in Regulation 40, with the most general defence set out here:

Defences

40. (1) It is a defence for a person charged with an offence under regulation 38(1), (2) or (3) to prove that the acts alleged to constitute the contravention were done in an emergency in order to avoid danger to human health in a case where—

    (a) the person took all such steps as were reasonably practicable in the circumstances for minimising pollution; and

    (b) particulars of the acts were furnished to the regulator as soon as reasonably practicable after they were done.

[...]

There are cases, particularly in relation to water pollution, that consider the nature of this defence.[15]

However, the process of enforcing permits is more complicated than simply bringing criminal prosecutions for permit breaches. First, breaches need to be identified, which requires a considerable effort of personnel and process on the part of the regulator. Second, regulators are focused on outcomes rather than prosecutions under the EPRs. Thus, the EPRs provide a range of tools for regulators to enforce the requirements of permits and to prioritize the minimization of pollution risks.

---

[15] See, for example, *Express Ltd v Environment Agency* [2003] EWHC 448 (Admin), [2004] 1 WLR 579.

There are powers for the regulator to vary, revoke, or suspend environmental permits,[16] and to issue enforcement notices.[17] These powers are significant. In relation to enforcement notices issued under regulation 36, the regulator can issue these as a preventative measure when it has reasonable grounds to suspect that a breach of the conditions of an environmental permit is *likely* to occur, rather than having to establish that such a breach has already occurred. Regulation 36 further requires the regulator to be specific in issuing an enforcement notice, requiring it to spell out the steps that the operator must take in order to ensure compliance with the environmental permit and the date by which such steps must be taken. These powers are also far-reaching because the regulator can require operators to carry out clean-up operations (regulation 36(3)(b)). In relation to the power to suspend an environmental permit, this exists regardless of whether a permit condition has been breached (regulation 37(3)). The regulator must show reasonable grounds that the operation is giving rise to a 'risk of serious pollution'.

Thus, it can be seen that the EPRs allow regulators to pursue a *risk-based* approach to enforcement. Beyond regulation 37(2), regulation 57(1) grants a wide discretionary power to regulators to take 'steps' for the 'removal of the risk' if the operation of a regulated facility under an environmental permit involves a risk of serious pollution. Regulation 57(4) enables the regulator to recover the costs of taking any such steps from the operator. Overall, the streamlining of the permitting system for a wide range of plants and operations—including IPPC and waste installations and those involved in water discharge activities—under one system of 'environmental permitting' is considered to allow proportionate permitting and enforcement in relation to the risks that installations pose. Environmental permitting thus promotes the UK government's 'better regulation' agenda.[18]

Finally, operators also have some rights in relation to the EPR process, beyond the right to make representations in relation to the setting and varying of environmental permits, discussed above. First, regulation 31 grants a right of appeal to an operator in relation to decisions on the granting, refusing or varying of environmental permits, and in relation to enforcement measures. Further, operators may wish to surrender environmental permits in certain circumstances, in which case they must follow the procedure in regulations 24 and 25. However, Schedule 5, paragraph 14 puts conditions on any surrender of a permit, requiring the operator to minimize pollution risks in the future and to remediate the site of the regulated facility by returning it to a 'satisfactory state' (in light of its state before the permitted operation began).[19] However, it should be noted that the insolvency of an operator might bring to an end its obligations under a permit in the way that a formal surrender of a permit does not.[20]

In short, the EPRs are an ambitious reform of environmental law regulation—they structure and legalize aspects of the discretion of administrators under pollution control regimes, but also equip regulators with tools to be flexible in their enforcement of 'command-and-control' pollution regimes. Above all, the EPRs represent one of the most recent stages in a continuum of evolving pollution control law, which should not be seen simply as the standard and static core of UK environmental law.

---

[16] EPRs, regs 20, 22, and 37. Note that, in accordance with the 'polluter pays' principle there is no provision for compensation for economic losses that arise for the operator from the variation of a permit by the regulator.

[17] EPRs, reg 36.

[18] See Section 2 of Chapter 12.

[19] Note this might constitute a higher remediation requirement than under Part IIA of the Environmental Protection Act 1990 relating to the clean up of contaminated land (see Chapter 21).

[20] See, for example, *Re Celtic Extraction Ltd (In Liquidation)* [2001] Ch 475.

4 POLLUTION CONTROL LAW AND ENVIRONMENTAL LAW

Highlighting the legal and regulatory evolution of pollution control regimes leads us onto the next important question to consider - what in fact constitutes the *legal* content of pollution control law. While much will depend on the specific regime involved, it is useful to make a number of general comments.

The first is that there are pollution control regimes in national, EU and international law. This is not an area, like planning law (which is English/UK based) that is primarily the focus of only one jurisdiction. Concern over pollution has thus led to debate and the creation of new regulatory regimes at all levels of governance. Discourses about pollution (in both its technical and non-technical sense) are multi-level phenomena. The primary focus in this part is upon the UK and EU regimes and in this regard it is significant to note that, over the last thirty years, EU environmental law has framed most of the discussion about pollution control law, albeit that there have also been innovative UK legal developments, including the environmental permitting regime outlined in Section 3. The influence of EU developments pervades all four chapters in this part.

The second point to note returns us to the point about legal and regulatory evolution. Historically, in England and Wales, at least, pollution control law was largely understood as a classic example of command and control regulation. In theory, standards or rules were set and if they were breached this resulted in criminal prosecution. This meant that the legal content of pollution control law had a significant criminal law element. However, the story is not a simple one of criminal prosecutions constituting pollution control regulation. Pioneering studies of the 1970s and 1980s by socio-legal scholars highlighted the important role of administrative and prosecutorial discretion in the implementation of these laws. We saw one example of those studies, in the work of Keith Hawkins, in Section 2.4 of Chapter 3.[21] Those studies have continued and grown as an area of scholarship—for example, the recent work of Carolyn Abbot in this area is significant.[22] Even if pollution control regimes take a 'simple' command and control' form, they still raise difficult and complex questions. Furthermore, as seen in Chapter 8, this is an area in which there has been considerable policy and legal development, particularly in light of the Macrory Review relating to civil sanctions and the enforcement of regulation.[23]

By the late 1980s, and as already noted, this was an area in which regimes were being reshaped on the basis of different theories of regulation. Thus, theories of responsive regulation,[24] autopoiesis/ reflexive modernization,[25] and market-based theories of regulation[26] have had considerable influence on both scholarship and practice in the areas of pollution control law. Many of these theories have been touched upon in Chapters 12 and 13 in discussing regulatory strategy and governance, so the chapters in this Part should be read alongside those earlier chapters. This shift in regulatory focus

---

[21] Keith Hawkins, *Environment and Enforcement* (OUP 1984); Keith Hawkins, *Law as Last Resort: Prosecution Decision-Making in a Regulatory Agency* (OUP 2002). See also Genevra Richardson, Anthony Ogus and Paul Burrows, *Policing Pollution: A Study of Regulation and Enforcement* (Clarendon Press 1982); Bridget Hutter, *Compliance: Regulation and Environment* (Clarendon Press 1997).

[22] Carolyn Abbot, *Enforcing Pollution Control Regulation: Strengthening Sanctions and Improving Deterrence* (Hart 2009).

[23] Richard Macrory, *Regulatory Justice: Making Sanctions Effective: Final Report* (Department of Business Innovation and Skills, November 2006).

[24] Neil Gunningham and Duncan Sinclair, 'Policy Instrument Choice and Diffuse Source Pollution' (2005) 17(1) JEL 51. See Section 4.3 of Chapter 12.

[25] Gunther Teubner, Lindsay Farmer and Declan Murphy (eds), *Environmental Law and Ecological Responsibility: The Concept and Practice of Ecological Self Organisation* (John Wiley & Sons 1994); Eric W Orts, 'Reflexive Environmental Law' (1995) 89 NWULR 1227. See Section 3.1 of Chapter 12.

[26] Sanja Bogojevic, 'Ending the Honeymoon: Deconstructing Emissions Trading Discourses' (2009) 21(3) JEL 443. See Section 3.3 of Chapter 15.

has also led to a greater role for administrative discretion. This can be particularly seen in the context of water quality and air quality regulation (Chapters 14 and 15). Moreover, this shift in regulatory approach raises questions about whether one can really talk in terms of pollution *control* to describe these regimes when they are largely concerned with matters of management and governance.

The final important point to note in regard to pollution control writ large is that the pollution control regimes discussed in this part do not exist in splendid isolation. The most obvious reason for this is that much environmental law is applied law and pollution control law is no exception to this. More specifically, pollution control regimes will overlap with one another and with other areas of environmental law. Thus, we will see in Section 5.3 of Chapter 18 (in Part V) that there is a significant question over how planning law and pollution control regimes interrelate.

5 CONCLUSION

This discussion makes it clear that pollution control law is complex and evolving. Care should be taken not simply to understand the different legal regimes in this part through a single analytical lens, despite the integration of some aspects of pollution control law, as seen with the introduction of the EPRs. This plurality of aspects of pollution control law can best be seen by relating the discussion in this Introduction to the descriptive, purposive, and jurisprudential definitions of environmental law discussed in Chapter 1.

On the one hand, the different chapters in this part easily fit into a *descriptive* definition of environmental law. All these chapters concern control and/or management of pollution and the law in each area is so described. On the other hand, the limitation seen in relation to a descriptive definition of environmental law in Chapter 1 can be seen more specifically here. Thus, we do not consider all forms of pollution in this part—for example, light and noise pollution are excluded. Likewise, some material in these chapters is not what would be conventionally understood as 'law'. As already noted, we will see a significant role for regulatory strategy and governance and thus also for other disciplines such as economics and science.

The situation is no more straightforward in relation to a *purposive* definition of environmental law. As we have seen, the purposes of pollution control law have been changing and evolving away from a reactive approach to a more holistic and quality-based conception of regulation. Indeed, as already noted, the label 'pollution control' is inappropriate for some areas. Yet, this change of approach is not wholesale and you will see a range of different regimes with different purposes in the chapters of this part.

Finally, what is striking when one considers pollution control law in relation to *jurisprudential* definitions of environmental law is that the development of legal doctrine relating to pollution control has occurred in isolated pockets. Thus, there is a large body of case law concerning the definition of waste (Chapter 16); emission trading schemes have given rise to a number of Article 263 TFEU challenges (Chapter 15); and water pollution offences have raised a number of interesting questions about responsibility in criminal law (Chapter 14). In these specific areas, the legal reasoning is often nuanced and sophisticated. However, there is little in the way of an overarching jurisprudential approach to pollution control law, seen either in these cases or more broadly. Much of this has to do with the diversity of the regimes involved, and the ways in which they operate legally. Thus, some regimes give rise to few doctrinal developments because they primarily operate outside conventional legal fora and/or give rise to few legal challenges. Integrated pollution control (Chapter 17) is a good case in point—there is a large amount of legal and regulatory activity relating to the implementation and enforcement of the EU IPPC regime but few court cases.

Overall, there are two important points to remember in reading the chapters of this part. First, these areas of law are complex and required a sophisticated legal approach to understand. Second, it is vital always to remind oneself of the bigger picture of environmental problems and environmental law. The different pollution control regimes studied in this part are important to study in their own right but it is also valuable to reflect on how they fit into the larger jigsaw of environmental law.

FURTHER READING

Carolyn Abbot, *Enforcing Pollution Control Regulation: Strengthening Sanctions and Improving Deterrence* (Hart 2009).

Chris Hilson, *Regulating Pollution: A UK and EC Perspective* (Hart 2000).

Further Reading on Environmental Permitting (England and Wales) Regulations 2010:

DEFRA and DECC, *Explanatory Memorandum to the Environmental Permitting (England and Wales) Regulations 2010 No. 675*: <http://www.legislation.gov.uk/uksi/2010/675/pdfs/uksiem_20100675_en.pdf> accessed 7 February 2013. Note that this Explanatory Memorandum contains the Impact Assessment (IA) that assesses the projected costs and benefits of the EPRs over a ten year period (see the discussion on IAs in Section 3.3 of Chapter 2). The pro-forma for the IA now contains also questions on: whether enforcement of the proposed policy complies with the Hampton enforcement principles (discussed in Chapter 12); the monetized annual contribution of the policy to the reduction of emissions of greenhouse gases; and whether implementation of the policy will go beyond minimum EU requirements. The latter was answered negatively in the case of the EPRs.

DEFRA, *Environmental Permitting Guidance: Core Guidance*, version 3.1, last updated March 2010: <http://www.defra.gov.uk/publications/2011/06/16/p613560-ep2010-guidance> accessed 7 February 2013. The core guidance covers all key elements of the environmental permitting process, including a typology of different regulated facilities and facilities exempt from permitting, identification of the relevant regulator for each type of regulated facility, application procedures, standard permits, criteria for operator competence, public participation, enforcement, the charging regime, and appeals.

14

WATER POLLUTION

This chapter critically examines English as well as selected European Union (EU) law, which regulates the interlinked environmental challenges of protecting the quality and quantity of watercourses. The chapter deals with legal rules seeking to prevent and limit the pollution of rivers and other inland surface waters, such as lakes, as well as coastal areas and groundwater. One of the key challenges for water pollution law is to evolve into a more holistic, coherent, and integrated pollution control regime. In discussing this challenge this chapter refers to and critiques recent interesting attempts to develop environmental policy discourses of bioregionalism and ecofederalism, that is, attempts to map regulatory space on to 'natural' spaces.

The chapter is structured into five sections. Section 1 introduces both the concept of water quality within the natural environment and the discourse of bioregionalism that is increasingly popular (and also critiqued) in shaping environmental law regulation along the contours of the environmentally specific natural spaces, such as river basins, which it seeks to regulate. Section 2 sets out key provisions of the core piece of EU water legislation that shapes UK and English water pollution control law— the Water Framework Directive (2000/60/EC)– and also critiques its 'integrated' approach to water regulation in light of the bioregional and critical legal geography accounts of environmental regulation set out in Section 1. Section 3 illustrates the continuing importance of political space, the sphere of influence of public administration. It discusses the key tool of English water pollution control law— the environmental permitting system for water discharge and groundwater activities. This includes a discussion of English case law in relation to the main water pollution criminal offences. This case law is significant because whether water quality standards derived from river basin management plans (and translated into environmental permit conditions) actually lead to effective control of water pollution also depends on how courts interpret the scope of the water pollution offences that underpin the environmental permitting system. A discourse of bioregionalism must therefore acknowledge that there is no straightforward mapping of legal rules onto natural space, but that this 'mapping exercise' is mediated also by the interpretation of legal rules by public administrators and judges. Section 4 discusses two further important elements of an 'integrated' approach to water pollution control, the regulation of the supply of drinking water and the regulation of water abstraction. This final section further questions a bioregionalist approach to water regulation, since tackling water scarcity in some regions caused by climate change seems to require thinking in larger and different spatial categories than regional geographical land space.

In discussing legal rules for the prevention and control of water pollution, this chapter links to some key themes introduced in Parts I, II, and III of this textbook. First, the chapter highlights the significance of various definitions of environmental law. It adopts a descriptive definition of water pollution control law by discussing key EU Directives, UK statutes, and English case law for the regulation of the quantity and quality of water bodies. But the chapter also develops a critical analysis of English water pollution control law through reference to a purposive and jurisprudential definition of the subject. At first glance, a purposive definition of water law seems straightforward: it is the body of legal rules that seeks to protect water courses in order to protect public health and the environment. But underneath this basic definition lurk unresolved conflicts between different and competing purposes of the regulation of water resources depending on whether water is defined as a commodity, a public good, or an ecological resource, with the aims of water law consequently ranging from the efficient operation of markets in water, to the socially just supply of a public good by the welfare state or the effective conservation of a scarce natural resource. From a jurisprudential perspective, water law might be conceived of as a body of rules that is informed by a number of environmental principles (further discussed in Chapter 11), such as the polluter pays principle, the principle of sustainable development, and the principle that environmental damage should be rectified at its source.

Moreover, the chapter develops the idea of the social foundations of environmental law introduced in Chapter 1 of this textbook. Sections 1 and 2 thus suggest that environmental law does not simply reflect the political and economic orders of a particular society but also reflects how such orders organize and construct 'natural space'. Through the lens of critical legal geography literature, these sections criticize the development of bioregionalist environmentalist discourse—particularly salient in water pollution control—which advocates mapping legal rules onto natural spaces (such as the river basin) in order to achieve more effective environmental regulation.

Four caveats should be made before starting. First, this chapter does not deal with marine pollution—a topic in its own right and one in which public international law has a role to play. Second, we concentrate on the law of England in this chapter, and in particular how this has been shaped by EU law. With that said, while we note that many of the legal obligations involved are derived from EU law, national UK water policy is not entirely uniform, particularly because Scotland and Northern Ireland have different regulatory structures in relation to the water industry. For instance, the water industry has not been privatized yet in Scotland. Water supply and sewerage services are provided by Scottish Water—a public sector body accountable to the Scottish Parliament, but run like a private company. According to the Scotland Act 1998, water pollution is a matter for the Scottish Parliament. Similarly, under the Government of Wales Act 1998, responsibility for water pollution is a matter for the National Assembly for Wales. In Northern Ireland, responsibility for water quality matters lies with the Environment and Heritage Service of the Department of the Environment (NI). Third, while Section 4 touches on issues to do with flooding, water management, and other issues, the primary focus of this chapter is on water quality. Thus, for example, we do not discuss the important issue of regulating the water industry.

1 A HOLISTIC APPROACH TO WATER QUALITY, AND CHALLENGES IN DEVELOPING SUCH AN APPROACH

Before looking in detail at current legal regimes in relation to water pollution and quality, it is important to understand the importance of water quality, historical legal approaches to the issue, and the emergence of more recent regulatory discourses that argue for the need to take a bioregional approach to water quality. These three issues are considered in this first section.

1.1 REGULATING WATER QUALITY AS A DYNAMIC ISSUE

Water quality is a profoundly important issue not only because it raises questions about environmental quality but also because water is a necessity for life. It is thus not surprising that disputes over the collective use of water and water quality laws have a long pedigree. Water is neither a static nor a monolithic aspect of the environment.

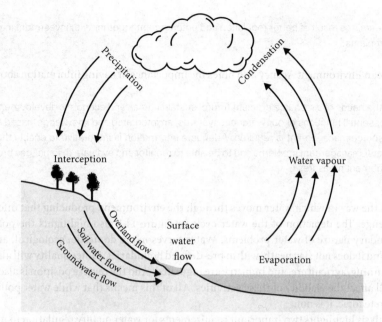

Figure 14.1 The hydrological cycle
Source: Northern Ireland Department for the Environment (DOENI).

Figure 14.1 is a powerful reminder that in the natural water cycle water is continuously transferred between land, sea, and atmosphere as rainfall replenishes rivers and the groundwater table with rivers finally discharging into coastal areas and oceans. Evaporation from the oceans then contributes to cloud formation. This is something we do learn at school but is easy to forget. It is important to remember because it means regulation of water quality does not involve regulating something static—rather, it concerns the regulation of something that both flows through the natural environment and works in a cycle. The regulation of water quality is thus complex, a point further fleshed out in the abstract from the European Environment Agency.

European Environment Agency, Europe's Environment—An Assessment of Assessments (EU, Sept 2011) 37, 41

Water issues are serious and worsening in many parts of Europe, making water management complex. While water is abundant in much of Europe, large areas are affected by water scarcity and droughts—particularly in Southern Europe and Central Asia with their severe lack of, and high demand for, water. Europe is also suffering from floods, with an increasing number of deaths, displacement of people and economic losses. Climate change is projected to exacerbate this, with more frequent and severe droughts or floods projected for many parts of Europe.

An estimated 120 million people in the pan-European region do not have access to safe drinking water or adequate sanitation, making them more vulnerable to serious water-related diseases. Despite progress over the past 15 years, especially those living in rural and remote areas in Eastern Europe, the Caucasus and Central Asia remain at risk. Water quality has improved in many parts of Europe over the past 20 years, the result of better regulation and enforcement together with investment in wastewater treatment plants.

The European Environment Agency also notes the importance of having information about water.

To meet the needs of a resource efficient future, sustain human and economic development and maintain the essential functions of our water ecosystems, an integrated and knowledge-based approach to water resource management is required. Adequate information is imperative to enable the identification of water management problems and to be able to monitor and evaluate the changes brought about by management measures.

Because of the way in which water moves through the environment, producing that information can be a challenge. The depiction of the water cycle in Figure 14.1 also highlights the polycentric and trans-boundary nature of water problems. Water serves many domestic, ecological, and industrial purposes and it does not stay neatly within pre-defined boundaries. Water quality will also be affected by how planning, agriculture, and industry are regulated. And the reverse position is also true—water quality will affect the viability of these activities. All of this means that while water pollution sounds like a discrete topic, it is not.

This analysis highlights two important requirements for water quality regulation to meet. The first is the need for the institutions governing water quality to relate logically to the bodies of water that they regulate. The second is the need for water regulation to be holistic. Historically, neither has been the case. In relation to the first issue, water regulation has primarily been created and implemented on a jurisdictional basis and this has long been a sticking point—particularly in international law.[1] In relation to the second issue, water pollution laws have developed in an *ad hoc* manner.

Thus, in England the common law developed the concept of riparian rights,[2] and many of the nuisance claims of the industrial era concerned water quality.[3] Legislation concerned with water quality was passed in the Victorian era,[4] and more recently an international human rights discourse has developed concerning the right to water. This is often derived from a constitutional right to life or a right to a clean environment. In India, for instance, federal and national courts have interpreted Article 21 of the Indian Constitution concerning a right to life as including the right to safe and sufficient water and sanitation.[5] The key point about these developments is that, until recently, much of this discourse was *ad hoc* and responsive to particular issues.

The EU was no exception. Water quality and water pollution issues were one of the first areas of EU regulatory activity in relation to the environment, but regulation tended to take the form of command and control regimes that regulated water quality in relation to particular bodies of water or particular types of water pollution problems.[6] As we shall see, a far more holistic approach is taken under Directive 2000/60/EC establishing a framework for Community action in the field of water policy.[7] However, before looking at that framework Directive, we need to understand what it means to take a

---

[1] Stephen McCaffrey, *The Law of International Watercourses* (2nd edn, OUP 2007).

[2] Joshua Getzler, *A History of Water Rights at Common Law* (OUP 2004).

[3] *Mason v Hill* (1832) 3 B & Ad 304; 110 ER 114 and *Stockport Waterworks v Potter* (1861) 7 H & N 160; 158 ER 433.

[4] Rivers Pollution Prevention Act 1876.

[5] For a general overview of this right, see Erik Bluemel, 'The Implications of Formulating a Human Right to Water' (2004) 31 Ecology LQ 957.

[6] Directive 75/440/EEC on the protection of surface waters for the abstraction of drinking water OJ [1975] L195/6 and Directive 76/160/EEC on the quality of bathing water [1976] OJ L31/1.

[7] OJ [2000] L327/1.

more holistic or bioregional approach to water regulation and what the challenges involved in such an approach are.

1.2 BIOREGIONALISM: FOREGROUNDING SPACE IN WATER REGULATION

An important aspect of environmental policy discourse in recent years has been a recognition that an understanding of space is important for designing regulatory regimes. Space matters in two ways. First, there are the natural spaces that are governed and constructed through legal rules. In the context of water pollution regulation, the key natural space in question is the river basin. Second, there are also political spaces relevant to the construction of legal rules, such as levels of government at which environmental regulatory powers are allocated. Water regulation is often enacted in multi-level governance regimes, where different levels of supranational or federal, state, and local government exercise regulatory powers in relation to the protection of the quality and quantity of water resources. Often these multi-level governance regimes are federal regimes in which both a central federal level of government can exercise powers in relation to water regulation, while individual states within the federation can also exercise regulatory powers.

In light of these developments, a particular environmental policy discourse has become influential, which suggests that the boundaries of natural rather than political space should drive legal regulation of the environment. On this view, water regulation should build on the natural space of the river basin, rather than the artificial and abstract category of the boundaries of the regulatory reach of regional offices of a state's public administration. This discourse can be described as bioregionalism. Dahlberg elaborates the idea further, defining it as re-embedding democratic governance in socio-natural systems. People, place, and nature are the key conceptual categories organizing this form of democratic governance. Regions are the primary unit of government within what Dahlberg calls ecological federalism.

Kenneth A Dahlberg 'Democratizing Society and Food Systems: Or How do we Transform Modern Structures of Power?' (2001) 18 Agriculture and Human Values 141, 145–46

[There is a need to] re-embed governance and politics in society by basing representative democracy on people, place, and nature.

[...]How shall we then combine such a re-balancing of power with place and nature? What is needed is an ecological federalism that will change our understanding of representation from that of individual human 'atoms' inhabiting geometrically defined 'territory' to also include representation of populations—including other living creatures—living in specific evolving habitats.

[...]In terms of including habitats in governance more generally, there are two different possible approaches. One is to change representational borders to better fit natural boundaries. This is what the 'bioregional' approach argues for, along with a radical decentralization of government. This is because it sees regional scale political units as the largest manageable political units – which would be made up of confederations of the communities therein. Regional boundaries would be based upon such 'natural' boundaries as watersheds or river basins. While raising important issues of scale and of how to include natural systems as part of governance, bioregionalism focuses only on lower levels, thus ignoring the full spectrum of hierarchy theory in ecology.

[...]Conceptually, we need to identify the central socio-natural systems that would be used in organizing each level of government. At the local level, these would likely include health, food, shelter, environment, economy, work, education, transportation, and security. Organizing government in terms of these systems will not solve all problems of coordination and bureaucratic politics; however, accompanied with broader systems training and thinking, it will encourage systemic rather than fragmented approaches to problems and will encourage the conceptual and political inclusion of natural processes and habitats in planning and decision making. In terms of the federal aspects, the relevant social, political, and natural systems and tasks at each level will need to be sorted out and analyzed in terms of power and structure. Building in democratic involvement at each level will be a central task. This means not only maintaining and strengthening the formal democratic procedures of governance, but trying to increase democratic structures and procedures within existing sectors: work, science and technology, education, health care, the media, etc. There is also a need to go beyond sectors (still based on functional specialization) to create new democratic systems.

Dahlberg defines bioregionalism as involving the mapping of 'regulatory space',[8] and in particular the boundaries of political and administrative power, onto natural space. Dahlberg further fleshes out his vision of bioregionalism by suggesting that it moves away from an anthropocentric approach to environmental regulation, by recognizing the right of other living creatures to be part of socio-natural systems. But Dahlberg does not question how notions of natural space become socially constructed. He does not alert us to the fact that what we understand as natural space is refracted through the lens of particular bodies of knowledge, such as environmental science, physical geography, and cartography that have developed within specific historical and socio-economic contexts, and thus are subject to challenge. Nor does he draw attention to the fact that natural space is not a fixed unit, but also subject to change. River basins, for instance, are not simply pre-given natural hydrological units but have been shaped through geological evolution of earth systems, such as the movement of glaciers as well as human interventions, such as farming systems.

The discourse of bioregionalism seeks to enhance the effectiveness of democratic environmental governance by closely matching the scope of legal rules to the contours of natural spaces, such as river basins, and by advocating decentralized environmental regulation that foregrounds the role of regions and local communities as the key political spaces for environmental regulation. This approach, however, can be criticized from the perspective of critical legal geography. Dahlberg's 'ecological federalism' does not critically examine how particular conceptions of natural and political space upon which 'effective' and 'ecological federalism' draws are socially constructed. Natural and political spaces seem to be pre-given and thereby pre-political. This assumption is squarely challenged in the critical legal geography literature that investigates intersections between law, space, and power. It links debates in critical legal studies with discussions in geography, starting from the idea that neither space nor law are pre-given and pre-political. Space is not 'objective' and does not exist, prior to, or separate, from political and economic relations. It acquires meaning through social action and is therefore relational. Hence, *critical* legal geography seeks to question reified, commonly accepted conceptions of space and their associated governance practices. For instance, the relationship between a particular territory and the individuals and resources it commands is not an inevitable, empirical fact, but often the outcome of specific policy choices. Critical legal geography therefore aims to render visible the social constructions of space drawn on by legal regulation as well as the spatial consequences of law. Blomley and Bakan further illustrate key ideas of a critical legal geography approach.

---

[8] Colin Scott, 'Analysing Regulatory Space: Fragmented Resources and Institutional Design' [2001] PL (2001) 329–53. See Chapter 12 for a further discussion.

Nicholas K Blomley and Joel C Bakan 'Spacing Out: Towards A Critical Geography of Law' (1992) 30 Osgoode Hall Law Journal 661–62, 669

One of the reasons for the apparent invisibility of space as an analytical category within legal studies rests with the modernist ascendancy of historical analysis within social theory. Certainly, critical studies within law have largely relied upon history in their attempts to argue against the closure of law. While this contributes to the invisibility of space, it also serves as an analogical basis for a *spatialization* of law. Legal actors can be understood not only as constructing historical representations, but also as defining and dividing *legal geographies*. Such geographies, we will argue, are of more than passing interest. Just as representations of history may buttress legal claims to rationality and closure, so may certain renderings of space. Further, just as such histories are contingent and contradictory, so are the geographies of law.

[...]

In this paper, we begin with the claim that legal thought and legal practice contain a number of representations—or geographies—of the multiple spaces of political, social, and economic life. Much as law relies in various ways on claims concerning history and time, it also simultaneously defines and draws upon a complex range of geographies and spatial understandings. While struggling to make sense of the complexity and ambiguity of social life, legal agents—whether judges, legal theorists, administrative officers, or others—represent and evaluate space in various ways. When we start looking, we discover that such representations are abundant and varied, touching all aspects of legal and social life, such as property, crime, contractual relations, intergovernmental relations, and so on. The construction of such spaces can be seen, for example, when legal actors designate boundaries between public and private spaces, make decisions concerning the autonomy of local governmental actors, or consider questions of personal mobility or spatial equality. Legal spaces are also relied upon implicitly on many other occasions. Legal interpretation, for example, with its encoded claims concerning the placement of the individual legal subject and the balance between universal and particularized legal knowledge, implies a claim about the situated contextuality of law. An assertion of legal closure constitutes not only a rejection of the historicity of social life but also its spatiality.

Blomley and Bakan outline that critical legal geography can contribute in various ways to a critical analysis of law, including environmental law, by questioning the particular representations of space that legal rules construct and draw on, including the constitutional concept of 'federalism'. We can extend this critique to the discourse of bioregionalism that works with an assumed, taken-for-granted, and essentialized understanding of natural spaces, such as ecosystems, river basins, and habitats. The discourse of bioregionalism reifies 'natural' spaces by treating them as physical, material, objective elements of the natural world. Critical legal geography suggests that what we consider at a particular point in time as a natural space is the result of a process of social construction and is therefore contestable.

An illustration of how these ideas can develop an analysis of water pollution control law is provided in Section 2. It critiques the focus on river basins as the main spatial category upon which the regulatory regime of the EU Water Framework Directive (2000/60/EC) is based. Moreover, a critical legal geography perspective can provide another angle on the themes discussed in various chapters in Parts IV and V of this textbook. These chapters illustrate that increasingly environmental regulation does not just draw on domestic legal rules but also on local as well as EU and international legal orders. Multi-level governance regimes, which sometimes take the form of constitutionally ordered federalist regimes, have become, therefore, an important feature of contemporary environmental law. Critical legal geography provides a fresh lens—different from that provided by political scientists—through which to question existing distributions of power at various levels of government in such regimes. In linking law and geography, legal rules and space, Blomley suggests that we should not think of space and legal rules as distinct, separate, clearly delineated concepts but should conceive of them as integral to and constitutive of each other.

Nicholas Blomley 'From "What" to "So What": Law and Geography in Retrospect' in J Holder and C Harrison (eds) Law and Geography, 5 *Current Legal Issues* (OUP 2003) 29

So far, I have tried to demonstrate the importance of space to those interested in law, and vice versa. But we need to push the analysis. If nothing else, my discussion thus far has relied upon a tripartite split, where 'law' affects 'space', both of which have a relation to something called 'society'. But on closer examination the relation may be a closer one: 'law' and 'geography' do not name discrete factors that shape some third pre-legal, a-spatial entity called society. Rather the legal and the spatial are, in significant ways, aspects of each other.

This becomes clear when we recognize the importance of law and space to order. The world is not given to us, but actively made through orderings which offer powerful 'maps' of the social world, classifying, coding, and categorizing. In so doing, a particular reality is created. Legal orderings, for example, are said to offer an 'ostensibly robust, plausibly coherent and functionally dependable image of social life and control'. Law allows us to distinguish 'citizen' from 'alien', 'public', from 'private', 'employee' from 'employer', 'wife' from 'husband', 'prisoner' from 'citizen', and so on. Similarly, space offers a powerful ordering framework. The boundary, which delineates and defines 'inside' with reference to the 'outside', whether at the scale of the State or the home, is a vital modality of ordering. Space comes with particular and deeply encoded classifications of appropriate behaviour. Behaviours and people that challenge such classifications, such as the homeless person who urinates in public, are deemed 'out of place'. Space and identity are also wedded: national and ethnic identities are often assumed to overlap.

But my central point here is that many spatial orderings are simultaneously legal orderings, and vice versa. Thus, 'employee' is to 'work-place' as 'wife' is to 'home'; 'property owner' is to 'land', as 'refugee' is to 'state territory', and so on. Both spatial and legal categories are mutually dependent. A prisoner without a prison, even a virtual one, is, of course, not a prisoner. A legal category such as 'citizen' is meaningless without the spatial category of 'territory'. In turn, land without an owner is an impossibility (at least within the West). The space of the 'home' entails particular legal subjects, such as the 'wife'. When we think about it, it becomes hard to isolate the 'legal' from the 'spatial'. Is a prison a spatial or a legal category? Both are integral; both are entangled.

We can also think of various examples of close links between spatial and legal categories in environmental regulation. For instance, the protected species is to habitat, as the controlled pollutant is to the nitrate sensitive area, and as the polluter is to contaminated land.

De Sousa Santos further analyses how legal governance can be understood in terms of spatial metaphors. He develops a symbolic cartography of law.

Boaventura de Sousa Santos 'Law: A Map of Misreading: Towards a Postmodern Conception of Law' (1987) 14 Journal of Law and Society 279, 282

In my view, the relations law entertains with social reality are much similar to those between maps and spatial reality. Indeed, laws are maps: written laws are cartographic maps; customary, informal laws are mental maps.

Understanding Maps

The main structural feature of maps is that in order to fulfil their function they inevitably distort reality. The great Argentinian writer Jorge Luis Borges has told us the story of the emperor who ordered the production of an exact map of his empire. He insisted that the map should be exact to the most minute detail. The best cartographers of the time were engaged in this important project. Eventually, they produced the map and, indeed, it could not possibly be more exact, as it coincided point by point with the empire. However, to their frustration, it was not a very practical map, since it was of the same size as the empire.

Santos adds to the analysis of space and legal governance three specific mechanisms through which the maps, including those maps that law creates, distort reality. These are scale, projection, and symbolization. Scaling a map involves decisions about how much detail to include. Projection means to distort the shapes and distances that are depicted on the map, for instance the shape of the polar regions is often distorted on maps. Symbolization involves the representation of selected features and details of reality in graphic symbols. Through these three different strategies, law operates at different legal scales. For instance, there are local, national, and international scales, which each contribute in their particular ways to legal governance. At an international scale of legal ordering, the legal map constructed is small-scale because it takes into its view only key elements of local legal orders. For example, from the perspective of a transnational corporation, an environmental dispute or disaster may appear as an entirely manageable event, for instance through a decision to relocate a polluting production facility.[9]

All of this may seem a little tangential to the topic of water pollution—but this is where the picture of the water cycle (Figure 14.1) becomes important. If we consider the characteristics of the water cycle, that water percolates through different spaces on land and underground rock strata and also interacts with the atmosphere, trying to figure out how to map regulatory space onto natural spaces becomes central to the legal control of water quality and quantity. Thus, the questions raised in the readings here become important.

FURTHER READING AND QUESTIONS

1. How would you start to identify the relations of power that are at stake in constructing the boundaries of natural and political space in a particular way?

2. What further arguments both for and against bioregionalism's emphasis on the region and local communities as the key political spaces through which to develop environmental regulation can you think of? Does the transboundary nature of water pollution not require at least the development, if not implementation of, environmental law at an international level?

3. A critical legal geography perspective can also add 'spatial justice' as a criterion for evaluating the distribution of increasingly scarce water resources among competing uses, such as supporting habitats, and use for human consumption and for agricultural and industrial purposes. See Andreas Philippopoulous-Mihalopoulous 'Spatial Justice: Law and the Geography of Withdrawal', (2010) 6(3) International Journal of Law in Context 201–16.

4. For a further discussion of legal geography and ideas of space see the Introduction to Part V. Also see Richard Ford, 'Law's Territory (A History of Jurisdiction)' in Nick Blomley (ed) *The Legal Geographies Reader: Law, Power and Space* (Blackwell 2001).

---

[9] Boaventura De Sousa Santos, 'Law: A Map of Misreading: Towards a Postmodern Conception of Law' (1987) 14 Journal of Law and Society 288.

2 GOVERNING THROUGH RIVER BASINS: THE EU WATER FRAMEWORK DIRECTIVE (2000/60/EC)

The starting point for understanding water quality and water pollution regulation in the EU (and thus England) is now Directive 2000/60/EC—the Water Framework Directive (WFD). Space is a key feature of the regulatory regime established under the EU WFD. This section provides an overview of the development of the Directive and its main features, how the Directive relates to ideas of space, how it relates to ideas of governance, its integration with other Directives, and its derogations. This is not a comprehensive overview of what is a fiendishly complex Directive but it provides a framework for understanding the Directive's main features and a starting point for making sense of its complexity.

It is also useful to note here that the WFD was transposed into English law through The Water Environment (Water Framework Directive) England and Wales Regulations 2003.[10] Moreover, DEFRA has given various directions to the Environment Agency (EA), such as The River Basin Districts Typology, Standards and Groundwater Threshold Values (Water Framework Directive) (England and Wales) Directions 2010.[11] This latter direction also completes the transposition of the related Directive 2008/105/EC (the Priority Substances Directive) in England. Further, DEFRA has issued a direction to the EA in relation to the classification of surface water and groundwater bodies, including the 'heavily modified' or 'artificial' derogations that excuse compliance with the water quality requirements of the WFD. Section 3, then, considers how the WFD is further implemented through the environmental permitting system in England and Wales.

2.1 THE WATER FRAMEWORK DIRECTIVE: OVERVIEW

As noted already, historically there were a range of Directives that regulated different aspects of water quality and water pollution in the EU. By the 1990s there was an increasing realization of the need for a more holistic approach to water quality and pollution issues.[12] What emerged out of that discourse was the WFD. The Directive came into force in 2000 and its implementation involves both a series of phased in obligations and the phasing out of other Directives. The Directive is one of the most comprehensive and ambitious pieces of recent EU environmental legislation. It is the first piece of EU water legislation that addresses both quality and quantity of water bodies in all twenty-seven EU Member States. Moreover, the Directive establishes legally binding targets for water quantity and quality in relation to a range of water bodies, such as inland surface, transitional,[13] coastal, and ground waters. It addresses both diffuse and point-source pollution.

Moreover, the Directive occupies a central position in EU water pollution control because it implements the environmental objectives of other so-called 'daughter' Directives, such as the 'Directive on environmental quality standards in the field of water policy' (2008/105/EC)[14] and the Directive on

---

[10] SI 2003/3242.

[11] <http://www.defra.gov.uk/environment/quality/water/legislation/water-framework-directive/> accessed 11 March 2013.

[12] European Commission, Communication from the Commission to the Council and the European Parliament: European Community Water Policy COM (1996) 59 final.

[13] Transitional water bodies are defined in Article 2(6) of the WFD as 'bodies of surface water in the vicinity of river mouths which are partly saline in character as a result of their proximity to coastal waters but which are substantially influenced by freshwater flows.'

[14] 2008/105/EC, OJ L 348/84.

Groundwater (2006/118/EC).[15] The Directive on Groundwater imposes an obligation upon Member States to take 'all measures necessary to prevent inputs into groundwater of hazardous substances'. Member States have to implement this *lex specialis* obligation through the WFD. It is stricter than the general obligation under the WFD to 'aim to reach' good chemical and ecological status in inland and coastal waters. In addition, measures taken under the WFD will help to implement a range of other EU water Directives, such as the 'Urban Waste Water Treatment Directive' (91/271/EEC)[16] and the 'Agricultural Nitrates Directive' (91/676/EEC).[17] The WFD also consolidates existing EU water legislation by repealing by 2013 various earlier water Directives.[18] Most importantly, the WFD occupies a central place in EU pollution control because its regulatory aims are of relevance to a range of other EU policies, such as those on fisheries, navigation, transport, energy, tourism, and regional policy, as well as, most importantly, the Common Agricultural Policy.[19]

Article 4(1)(a)(ii) WFD imposes an ambitious requirement upon Member States to 'aim to achieve' good surface water status, covering inland, coastal, and transitional waters by the end of 2015.[20] Good surface water status is composed of both good chemical status and good ecological status.[21] Article 4(1)(b)(ii) imposes a similar obligation upon Member States to 'aim to achieve' good ground water status by 2015, 'ensuring a balance between abstraction and recharging of groundwater'. The text of the WFD itself does not make it clear whether this obligation is merely a procedural or a substantive one, an obligation of means or actual results. Do Member States simply have to take all reasonable steps to achieve 'good status' for water courses by 2015 or do Member States incur the more onerous obligation of actually having to achieve 'good water status' as defined in outline in the WFD by 2015?

The text of the WFD seeks to enshrine ambitious water pollution control standards also through three further provisions. First, Article 10 states the following:

Article 10

The combined approach for point and diffuse sources

1. Member States shall ensure that all discharges referred to in paragraph 2 into surface waters are controlled according to the combined approach set out in this Article.
2. Member States shall ensure the establishment and/or implementation of:
   (a) the emission controls based on best available techniques, or
   (b) the relevant emission limit values, or
   (c) in the case of diffuse impacts the controls including, as appropriate, best environmental practices

   set out in:

   - Council Directive 96/61/EC of 24 September 1996 concerning integrated pollution prevention and control(19),

---

[15] OJ L 372/19.   [16] OJ L135/40.   [17] OJ L375/1.

[18] The Dangerous Substances Directive (2006/11/EC, [2006] OJ L64/52) and the Groundwater Water Directive (80/68/EEC, [1980] OJ L20/43), the Freshwater Fish Waters Directive (2006/44/EC, [2006] OJ L264/20) and the Shellfish Waters Directive (2006/113/EC, [2006] OJ L376/14) will be repealed.

[19] Ralf Boschek, 'The EU Water Framework Directive: Meeting the Global Call for Regulatory Guidance?' (2006) 41(5) Intereconomics 268–69. For instance, there is a Strategic Steering Group that seeks to develop a better integration of the policy fields of agriculture and water pollution control in the context of the 'Common Implementation System' set up under the WFD, discussed in section 2.3.

[20] Article 2(1) WFD, in the case of chemical status it also covers territorial waters.

[21] Article 2(18) WFD. 'Ecological status' is an additional criterion employed in the classification and standard setting for surface waters. 'Good ecological status' means that water courses that have been significantly affected by human activity can nevertheless sustain ecosystems.

> - Council Directive 91/271/EEC of 21 May 1991 concerning urban waste-water treatment(20),
> - Council Directive 91/676/EEC of 12 December 1991 concerning the protection of waters against pollution caused by nitrates from agricultural sources(21),
> - the Directives adopted pursuant to Article 16 of this Directive,
> - the Directives listed in Annex IX,
> - any other relevant Community legislation
>
> at the latest 12 years after the date of entry into force of this Directive, unless otherwise specified in the legislation concerned.
>
> 3. Where a quality objective or quality standard, whether established pursuant to this Directive, in the Directives listed in Annex IX, or pursuant to any other Community legislation, requires stricter conditions than those which would result from the application of paragraph 2, more stringent emission controls shall be set accordingly.

Article 10 article recognizes the importance of integrating other regulatory areas into water quality regulation. Second, Article 16(1) WFD requires Member States to take measures that progressively reduce intrinsically hazardous substances, such as heavy metals, and Member States must cease or phase out the discharge, emission, or loss of priority hazardous substances.[22] Third, Article 4(1)(a)(i) WFD imposes a 'non-deterioration' obligation upon Member States, which requires them to put measures in place that prevent deterioration in the existing quality of surface and ground waters. Failure to comply with this requirement may give rise to Commission infringement proceedings against a Member State under Article 258 TFEU.[23] Key to the system of establishing environmental standards under the WFD is the classification of water bodies.

Classification of water bodies by Member States is the first step in the implementation of the environmental standards under the WFD and is governed by Article 3 WFD. Classifications provide the baseline from which Member States' progress in improving quality and quantity of water bodies is assessed. Classifications also provide the reference point for applying the 'no-deterioration' principle referred to here. The test result for the parameter that scored the poorest result determines the overall classification of the water body. This stringency in the classifications required by the WFD should provide incentives for Member States to further enhance the quality of their water courses.

For surface waters, 'good status' describes 'overall status' of the water body. It has both an ecological and a chemical component. 'Ecological status' is assessed as 'high', 'good', 'moderate', 'poor', or 'bad'. 'High ecological status' is basically a pristine water body. For instance, a natural water body would be assessed as being of 'good ecological status' if it varies only a little from undisturbed natural conditions. 'Chemical status' of water bodies is only assessed on a 'good' or 'fail' basis. 'Ecological status' of water courses is assessed with reference to criteria such as what fish and plant life they support.[24] One of the problems, however, with these classifications is an absence of actual benchmarks to which they could be linked. For instance, in practice there are hardly any surface water courses in the UK that could be classified as of 'high ecological status', that is, as nearly pristine waters. In the absence of 'high ecological status' actually existing in a water body it is not quite clear how 'good ecological

---

[22] 'Priority hazardous substances' is the term now applied to what were called 'Black list substances' under the previous Dangerous Substances Directive (2006/11/EC, OJ L64/52). They are defined in Article 2(30) WFD as 'substances identified in accordance with Article 16(3) and (6) for which measures have to be taken in accordance with Article 16(1) and (8) WFD. Figure 14.2 provides a schematic overview of the different components that go into the classification of the overall status for a surface water body.

[23] William Howarth, 'Aspirations and Realities under the Water Framework Directive: Proceduralisation, Participation and Practicalities' (2009) 21 JEL 391, 410.

[24] See, for example, Annex V 1.1.1

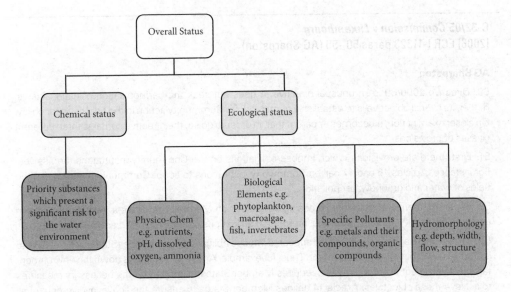

Figure 14.2 The components of overall status for surface water bodies

Source: Environment Agency, South East River Basin District, River Basin Planning: Working Together, at: <http://www.environment-agency.gov.uk/research/planning/33162.aspx.> 7.

status' should be determined. For ground water 'good status' is defined as having both a quantitative and a chemical component. Ground water is classified either as being of 'good' or 'poor status'. For Josefsson and Baaner this is problematic.

Henrik Josefsson and Lasse Baaner, 'The Water Framework Directive—A Directive for the Twenty-First Century?' (2011) 23(3) JEL 463, 484–85.

It is striking that 'The Water Framework Directive'—an extensive, supposedly collaborative effort joining social scientists and natural scientists—is so poorly designed. The Directive reflects the traditional method of aiming for ideal states, supported by the use of an obsolete understanding of ecology, to legitimise its pursuit of the pristine, ideal state.

The ecological variables of the norm of 'good ecological status' are established legally by a number of legal constructs: 'reference conditions', 'typology' of bodies of water, 'biological quality elements' and the 'one out—all out' principle. Inherent in these concepts are obsolete perceptions of environmental quality and of the functioning of ecosystems.

This comment once again highlights the challenges we saw in Section 1 of mapping legal space onto ecological space. Those challenges become also apparent in relation to the core of the WFD—river basin management.

Before turning to river basins, however, it is useful to briefly reflect on the nature of the WFD. We have only sketched its main features here and even from that sketch there is no doubt that it is a legally complex directive. AG Sharpston has elaborated on this point. The facts need not concern us.

C-32/05 *Commission v Luxembourg*
[2006] ECR I-11323 paras 50–55 (AG Sharpston)

AG Sharpston

50. Directive 2000/60 is an unusual directive. It does not seek the harmonisation of national laws. Rather, its overall objective is to establish a framework for Community action in the field of water policy. On closer examination, it becomes apparent that, in order to do so, the directive contains three different classes of provisions.

51. First, there are provisions which impose obligations on the Community institutions themselves. For instance, Articles 16 and 17 call on Community institutions to adopt Community measures in the fields of water and groundwater pollution.

52. Secondly, there are provisions imposing obligations on Member States vis-à-vis the Commission and the Community. Examples are the information obligations under Article 3(1) and Article 24(2).

53. Thirdly, there are provisions which appear to impose obligations on Member States with respect to individuals, with or without direct effect. Thus, for example, Article 4, which lays down the environmental objectives sought by the directive, requires Member States to implement the necessary measures to achieve these objectives. Article 14 obliges Member States to ensure the active involvement of all interested parties in the implementation of the directive.

54. In addition, different deadlines apply for the implementation of these various provisions.

55. The fact that the directive's provisions are far from homogeneous must in turn have implications for the way in which those provisions can or should be implemented at national level (some, indeed, may not require implementation at all). As the Court has elsewhere recognised, 'Community legislative practice shows that there may be great differences in the types of obligations which directives impose on the Member States and therefore in the results which must be achieved. Thus, some directives require legislative measures to be adopted at national level and compliance with those measures to be the subject of judicial or administrative review. Other directives lay down that the Member States are to take the necessary measures to ensure that certain objectives formulated in general and unquantifiable terms are attained, whilst leaving them some discretion as to the nature of the measures to be taken. Yet other directives require the Member States to obtain very precise and specific results after a certain period [...]'

The WFD is thus complex. This also becomes apparent from the conceptions of space that inform the working of the Directive, a point further discussed in Section 2.2.

2.2 THE WFD AND SPACE: GOVERNING THROUGH THE RIVER BASIN

In order to deliver its comprehensive and ambitious regulatory regime, the WFD relies on categories of natural and political space, in particular the river basin and a multi-level governance regime for the regulation of water pollution. In examining critically how the WFD regulates water pollution, it is therefore important to analyse further how the WFD constructs specific conceptualizations of the river basin and multi-level governance.

The key point here is that the WFD seeks to develop water pollution control by no longer administering legal rules for water pollution within the territory of artificially created administrative units, but within the territory of the natural hydrological unit of the river basin. A river basin is the area of land drained by a river and its tributaries, the latter being smaller rivers flowing into a larger river. Included in a river basin are often watersheds, such as mountains surrounding the river basin, confluences where rivers join each other, and the source of a river and its mouth where it flows into the sea or an ocean.[25] The WFD is therefore—like Integrated Pollution Control discussed in Chapter 17—informed by a holistic environmentalist discourse that seeks to achieve integrated management of the environment as an interconnected whole.

Preamble 13 to the Water Framework Directive states:

> There are diverse conditions and needs in the Community which require different specific solutions. This diversity should be taken into account in the planning and execution of measures to ensure protection and sustainable use of water in the framework of the *river basin. Decisions should be taken as close as possible to the locations where water is affected or used.* Priority should be given to action within the responsibility of Member States through the drawing up of program of measures adjusted to *regional and local conditions* (emphasis added).

Preamble 17 to the WFD further paints a picture of water courses being interconnected within a river basin. On the basis of this reasoning also an economic case is made for turning the river basin into the main regulatory unit:

> An effective and coherent water policy must take account of the vulnerability of aquatic ecosystems located near the coast and estuaries or in gulfs or relatively closed seas, as their equilibrium is strongly influenced by the quality of inland waters flowing into them. Protection of water status within *river basins* will provide economic benefits by contributing towards the protection of fish populations, including coastal fish populations (emphasis added).

Various features of the WFD further buttress the river basin as the key unit through which regulation occurs. First, as pointed out in Preamble 33 to the WFD, the legal measures taken under the WFD in order to realize its key objective of achieving 'good water status' are linked to each river basin:

> The objective of achieving good water status *should be pursued for each river basin*, so that measures in respect of surface water and groundwaters belonging to the same ecological, hydrological and hydrogeological system are coordinated [emphasis added].

Moreover, the importance of the river basin as 'natural space', and being the key unit through which the regulatory regime of the Directive is delivered, is affirmed by the fact that river basins take precedence also over the political space of the nation-state territory. Where a river basin transcends a nation-state's boundary the legal obligations of the WFD transcend nation-state boundaries and apply to the whole of the river basin as outlined also in Preamble 35 to the WFD. For river basins that transcend the jurisdiction of the WFD because they cover territory outside the EU, Preamble 35 envisages that EU Member States endeavour to co-ordinate water pollution control measures with the states outside the EU. Where river basins straddle the boundary of one or several EU Member States they will be designated according to Article 3(3) of the WFD as an international river basin.

The natural space of the 'river basin' is in particular operationalized through the creation of river basin *districts* and through river basin management plans which translate the general environmental objectives of the WFD into specific measures applicable to particular water courses. River basin districts are defined in Article 2(15) as the 'area of land and sea, made up of one or more neighbouring

---

[25] The WFD defines in Article 2(13) a river basin as 'the area of land from which all surface run-off flows through a sequence of streams, rivers and, possibly, lakes into the sea at a single river mouth, estuary or delta.'

river basins together with their associated groundwaters and coastal waters', which is identified under Article 3(1) as the main unit for the management of river basins. Article 3(1) WFD imposes a legal duty upon Member States to identify individual river basins within their national territory. Each river basin shall then be assigned to a river basin district.[26] Article 3(4) WFD clarifies that the river basin is the main unit through which water pollution control occurs by imposing a legal obligation upon Member States to ensure that the requirements of the WFD, in particular to achieve the environmental objectives spelt out in its Article 4, and thus all measures established in order to achieve water pollution control are co-ordinated for the whole of the river basin district.

Also, river basin management plans are central to affirming the natural space of the 'river basin'. Article 13 WFD requires Member States to ensure that a river basin management plan is produced for each river basin district lying entirely within their territory. These river basin management plans are one of the main regulatory tools through which the environmental objectives of the WFD are to be achieved. Annex VII WFD further specifies what should be contained in a river basin management plan. It should include a general description of the characteristics of the river basin district. For the two main types of water courses within a river basin district, surface and ground waters, it maps the location and boundaries of water bodies and provides an account of the current quality of the water body. Moreover, the river basin management plan includes a summary of the pressures on the water body generated, for instance, through human activity, such as through point source pollution, but also diffuse pollution, water abstraction and—in an attempt to achieve some integrated management of the environment—through land use that may adversely affect the water body. The river basin management plan also contains a list of the environmental objectives that have been established under Article 4 WFD for surface waters, ground waters, and protected areas.[27] Most importantly, the river basin management plan is a key tool for water pollution regulation because, according to Annex VII A Nr 7, it sets out a summary of the programme of measures adopted under Article 11 WFD, as well as measures taken to deal with particularly polluting so-called priority substances. The river basin management plan also has to provide a summary of the controls in place in the river basin for limiting point source discharges and water abstraction.

The first set of river basin management plans, copies of which had to be sent to the Commission,[28] had to be published by Member States by 2009. The UK is currently in the process of developing the next round of river basin management plans. While according to Article 18(2)(c) WFD the European Commission will include in its report on the implementation of the WFD an analysis of the river basin management plans submitted, its approval is not necessary for the adoption of river basin management plans in the EU Member States. The Commission can only make 'suggestions' for the improvement of future plans (Article 18(2)(c)). In the UK, the Secretary of State heading DEFRA has a discretion to approve or reject river basin management plans for river basins in England or to direct the EA to modify the plan (Regulation 14(1) of The Water Environment (Water Framework Directive) (England and Wales) Regulations 2003).[29] For river basins in Wales, the Welsh Assembly exercises this power. Preparation of these plans has been hampered by lack of data among national regulators and the vagueness of the legal obligations set out in the WFD, such as the requirements under Article 4 to achieve good surface and ground water status by 2015. For instance, in the river basin management plan for the South East River Basin District in the UK, the

[26] According to Article 3(1) 'coastal waters shall be identified and assigned to the nearest or most appropriate river basin district or districts'.

[27] Annex IV WFD clarifies what counts as a protected area. These can be areas designated for the abstraction of water intended for human consumption, or areas designated as bathing waters under the Bathing Water Directive (76/160/EEC, [1976] OJ L31/1). (See the new Bathing Water Directive 2006/7/EC, OJ L64/37.) Areas may also have been designated as protected areas for more ecocentric purposes, such as for the protection of habitats or species, for instance a Natura 2000 site designated under Directive 92/43/EEC, [1992] OJ L 206/7 and Directive 79/409/EEC, [1979] OJ L103/1.

[28] Article 15(1) WFD.   [29] SI 2003 No 3242.

majority of improvement measures to be taken under the plan will focus on *rivers* in the first river basin management cycle, because an understanding of why other surface waters, such as lakes, coasts, and estuaries, so far do not achieve 'good status' or 'potential' is only being developed. It is expected, however, that the quality and quantity of the data basis for future river basin management plans will improve since part of river basin management plans is the monitoring of the quality of water courses. As more and better data become available through the implementation of the first round of river basin management plans, the quality of subsequent river basin management plans is likely to improve. The purpose of the plan is to establish a programme of measures in order to ensure that all waters in the river basin achieve the objective of good water status by 2015. The extract from the river basin management plan further illustrates the difficulties of determining causes of pollution within the natural space of the river basin.

Environment Agency, Water for Life and Livelihoods, River Basin Management Plan, South East River Basin District (December 2009) at: http://www.environment-agency.gov.uk/research/planning/124978.aspx, 10

Reasons for not achieving good status or potential

This section takes a closer look at rivers. The majority of management actions in the first river basin management cycle will be applied to rivers. Reasons for not achieving good status or potential in other surface waters are being developed. The first course of action for lakes, coasts and estuaries is to develop a better understanding of the issues.

To identify what needs to be done to improve the environment, the reasons for not achieving good status need to be understood. The main reasons most frequently identified by Environment Agency staff using monitoring data and their knowledge and experience of individual water bodies are shown in table 3. Each relates to one or more pressures, which in turn impact on elements of the classification.

The reasons for failure include point source discharges from water industry sewage works, diffuse source pollution from agriculture, abstraction and a range of reasons due to physical modifications. The actions in this plan will increase the number of waters achieving good status or potential, for example through significant investment in improving discharges from sewage works and changes to land management practices. Even if good status is not completely achieved, they will also lead to improvements to the key elements impacted. The case study below describes a case like this for fish.

Table 3 Main reasons (where known) for not achieving good ecological status or potential

Reasons for failure	Key elements impacted
Point source water industry sewage works	ammonia, phosphate, dissolved oxygen
Physical modification flood protection and coastal erosion	fish, invertebrates, mitigation measures
Diffuse source agricultural	fish, invertebrates, phosphate, dissolved oxygen
Physical modification urbanization	fish, invertebrates, mitigation measures
Physical modification wider environment	fish, invertebrates, mitigation measures
Abstraction	hydrology
Physical modification land drainage	dissolved oxygen, fish, mitigation measures
Physical modification barriers to fish migration	fish
Diffuse source unknown	fish, invertebrates, phosphate, dissolved oxygen
Diffuse source mixed urban run-off	dissolved oxygen, invertebrates, phosphate

It is important to note that because classification involves a wider range of elements than previous monitoring schemes, and as many of the key pressures are complex and occur in combination, we often do not know the reason for a failure. For many water bodies, the reasons for failure are unknown, or it is uncertain whether there is a failure or whether pressures really are causing an impact. In these cases we will need to investigate, as discussed in 'Investigations – improving outcomes for 2015' in Section 5.

For groundwater quality, the main reasons for poor status are high or rising nitrate concentrations, with some failure for pesticides and other chemicals. The main reasons for poor quantitative status is that abstraction levels – mainly for drinking water – exceed the rate at which aquifers recharge. The plan identifies a range of actions to prevent deterioration and improve groundwater elements, as well as investigations to improve the confidence in groundwater classification.

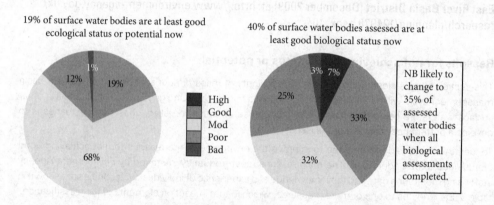

Figure 14.3 Map of ecological status/potential and biological status of surface water bodies in the South East River Basin District

Source: Environment Agency, Water for Life and Livelihoods, River Basin Management Plan, South East River Basin District, at: <http://www.environment-agency.gov.uk/research/planning/124978.aspx>, 10.

The plan also includes an inventory of the current quality of surface water bodies in the river basin, as depicted in Figure 14.3.

The plan openly acknowledges that 77% of water bodies in the South East River Basin District will not achieve good water status by 2015.[30] This further illustrates how ambitious the environmental targets of the WFD are. Finally, the river basin management plan for the South East River Basin District illustrates that the WFD sits at the heart of a pollution control regime, which includes a number of EU Directives. The plan prioritizes the achievement of water pollution control objectives for so-called 'protected areas' that have been designated under a range of other EU water pollution control Directives (some phased out by the Directive), such as the Bathing Water Directive (recreational waters), the Birds Directive (Natura 2000 sites), the Drinking Water Directive (drinking water protected areas), the

[30] Environment Agency, Water for Life and Livelihoods, River Basin Management Plan, South East River Basin District, December 2009, 27.

Freshwater Fish and Shellfish Directives (waters for the protection of economically significant aquatic species), the Habitats Directive (Natura 2000 sites), the Nitrates Directive (nitrate vulnerable zones), and the Urban Waste Water Treatment Directive (sensitive areas).[31] Moreover, the plan bears the imprint of an environmental policy discourse that emphasizes integrated, rather than media-specific, environmental management because it is subject to a strategic environmental impact assessment and an assessment under the Conservation of Habitats and Species Regulations 2010, in order to determine whether the river basin management plan is likely to have any significant effects on any Natura 2000 sites.

River basin management plans—a key regulatory tool through which the environmental objectives of the WFD are to be implemented—further valorize the natural space of the 'river basin' as the key unit through which the regulatory regime of the WFD is delivered. But various provisions in the WFD and regional implementation practices transform the meaning of the 'natural' spatial category of the 'river basin' and undermine in various ways the 'river basin' as the key regulatory unit.

First, Article 3(1) WFD enables the combination of small river basins with larger basins or the joining of neighbouring small basins into one river basin district. Hence, the WFD also defines river basin districts as units that may actually encompass a range of different river basins for the purposes of administrative expediency and 'economies of scale' in the administration of water pollution controls. Second, Article 3(6) WFD provides another opportunity to derogate from the idea of bioregionalism, that is, the mapping of regulatory space onto natural space. It enables Member States to 'identify an existing national or international body as competent authority for the purposes of this Directive'. While Member States are under a duty, according to Article 3(2) WFD, to nominate a competent authority that will implement the legal obligations imposed under the WFD in each river basin district, this does not have to be a newly created administrative unit. Hence, while the WFD goes some way to map the administrative unit of the 'river basin district' onto the natural space of the river basin, it also detracts from that because it enables Member States to maintain pre-existing administrative units set up for the implementation of water pollution control laws that do not correspond at all to the natural space of the river basin. Germany, for instance, has made wide use of Article 3(6) WFD. It relies mainly on co-ordination arrangements between existing state water authorities who retain their legislative and executive powers over water management.[32]

Third, the text of the WFD also enables fragmentation of the 'river basin' into smaller spatial categories, created also for administrative expediency. Article 13(5) WFD provides that 'river basin management plans may be supplemented by the production of more detailed programmes and management plans for sub-basin, sector, issue, or water type, to deal with particular aspects of water management'.

Fourth, national implementation practice starts to whittle away at the idea of mapping regulatory space onto natural space. The EA for England and Wales has adopted a 'catchment agenda' for implementing the WFD. A catchment is a smaller drainage basin than a river basin, that is, an area of land from which water from rainfall drains into a water course. The South East River Basin District Plan divides the river basin into nine catchments,[33] for the purposes of administrative expediency and in order to achieve its 'efficient' and 'cost-effective' implementation.[34] This 'catchment planning

---

[31] Environment Agency, River Basin Management Plan, South East River Basin District, 8.

[32] Timothy Moss, 'The Governance of Land Use in River Basins: Prospects for Overcoming Problems of Institutional Interplay with the EU WFD' (2004) 21 Land Use Policy 85–94, at 91.

[33] Environment Agency, Water for Life and Livelihoods, River Basin Management Plan, South East River Basin District, 34.

[34] Ibid, 58.

agenda' is further reinforced by the fact that the drafting of river basin management plans also takes account of Catchment Flood Management Plans and Catchment Abstraction Management Strategies.[35]

But other provisions in the WFD still pursue the bioregionalist discourse of mapping regulatory space onto natural space. In particular the WFD's idea of developing a notion of river basin democracy harks back again to the 'river basin' as the key spatial category that underpins the operation of the WFD. River Basin democracy means that the boundaries of political space—given meaning through the idea of democratic governance—become modelled on natural space, here the river basin. The legally non-binding Preamble 46 to the WFD highlights the importance of public participation in river basin management planning:

> To ensure the participation of the general public including users of water in the establishment and updating of river basin management plans, it is necessary to provide proper information of planned measures and to report on progress with their implementation with a view to the involvement of the general public before final decisions on the necessary measures are adopted.

Article 14 WFD imposes legal obligations upon Member States to consult citizens in relation to the drawing up of river basin management plans. Article 14(1) requires Member States in general terms to 'encourage the active involvement of all interested parties in the implementation of this Directive, in particular in the production, review, and updating of the river basin management plans'. Draft river basin management plans have to be made available to the public for comments at least one year before the beginning of the period to which the plan refers (Article 14(1) WFD). The consultation duty is phrased widely since it includes—upon citizens' request—a duty to give access to background documents and information that informed the development of the draft river basin management plan. 'Active involvement and consultation' of citizens is further facilitated through Article 14(2) WFD, because Member States are required to allow at least six months for the provision of comments.[36]

For drafting the South East District River Basin plan the EA conducted a public consultation exercise from 22 December 2006 to 22 June 2007. The EA has been pro-active in consulting about 500 citizens in the South East District River Basin area as part of its public consultation exercise.[37] This involved a discussion, through an electronic questionnaire, about how the public consultation for the drafting of the river basin management plan should be conducted. Responses to the survey were provided by general and very specialized environmental NGOs, such as the Campaign to Protect Rural England, Kent and the British Dragonfly Society, town councils, water companies, and representatives of industrial interests, such as the Quarry Products Association, as well as some anonymous respondents.[38] Responses to the questionnaire raised interesting issues about how the public consultations should be conducted. Queries were raised, for instance, about what procedures would be adopted for resolving conflicts in river basin district liaison panels. Moreover, should the responses from the various organizations involved in the public consultation process be 'weighted' in order to reflect their varying importance,

---

[35] Environment Agency, Water for Life and Livelihoods, River Basin Management Plan, South East River Basin District, 16, 17, 25.

[36] DEFRA and the Welsh Assembly government have provided guidance for river basin management planning in England and Wales (Water for Life and Livelihoods: A Framework for River Basin Planning in England and Wales), at: <http://www.environment-agency.gov.uk/research/planning/33244.aspx>.

[37] Environment Agency, Water for Life and Livelihoods, River Basin Management Plan, South East River Basin District, Annex L.

[38] Environment Agency, Water for Life and Livelihoods, River Basin Management Plan, South East River Basin District, at: <http://www.environment-agency.gov.uk/research/planning/33106.aspx> 3.

rather than to treat all responses to the public consultation exercise equally? The EA has created these liaison panels in each River Basin District with individuals representing water companies, ports, business and industry, the Consumer Council for Water, agriculture, other industry sectors specific to the district, environmental regulators, and NGOs. In the South East District the liaison panel includes representatives of businesses, planning authorities, environmental organizations, consumers, navigation, fishing and recreation bodies, and central, regional, and local government.[39]

But the way consultation has been carried out in practice further reflects the limits of scaling democratic governance to the natural space of the river basin. The EA has organized public consultation in relation to the drafting of river basin management plans at various levels. Its guidance 'Water for Life and Livelihoods: A Framework for River Basin Management Planning, the EA[40] outlines that stakeholders will be consulted at those levels of governance at which this appears necessary. At the national level this involves consultation with a group of stakeholder organizations. At river basin district level public consultation is facilitated through liaison panels. The EA envisages that the panels will help to encourage river basin district-wide action through their sectors, monitor overall progress, and prepare for the second cycle of River Basin Management Planning.[41] In addition, the EA draws on established consultation arrangements at catchment level and seeks to engage individuals and existing networks also at a local level. Maria Lee's extract further explains the operation of public participation provisions in the context of the WFD.

Maria Lee 'Law and Governance of Water Protection Policy' in Joanne Scott (ed)
Environmental Protection: European Law and Governance (OUP 2009) 43–45

One of the key governance techniques imposed on Member States through the Water Framework Directive is public participation. [...]

Public participation potentially fills many roles. In the context of vague objectives such as those in the Water Framework Directive, public participation goes with the recognition that many important decisions will be made at the implementation stage. The normal democratic credentials found in legislative processes (as controversial as they might be at EU level) do not provide adequate legitimacy for this exercise of discretion. More instrumentally, participation in implementation can keep Member States on the straight and narrow. Broad involvement can also contribute to a complex and multi-faceted decision, for which all the necessary knowledge and information is unlikely to be found in a single institution. In this respect, public participation fits nicely with the determination of the Water Framework Directive to generate information and knowledge to decision-makers that simply cannot be found in a single bureaucracy, however expert. The sheer complexity of river basin management demands external involvement.

[...] Although Article 14 applies to the Directive's provisions generally, the primary locus for public participation is around the River Basin Management Plan. Individuals are more likely to engage with the range of issues that are of concern to them the more concrete, the closer, and the more immediate proposals are. The river basin scale could to this extent be a barrier to broad participation. More positively, however, river basin management implies transboundary environmental regulation along ecologically relevant units. Whilst the Directive is silent on the subject, this should similarly imply transboundary participation, and potentially powerful ideas of 'European environmental citizenship'.

---

[39] Environment Agency, Water for Life and Livelihoods, River Basin Management Plan, South East River Basin District, 27.

[40] At: <http://www.environment-agency.gov.uk/research/planning/33244.aspx>, ch 3.

[41] Environment Agency, Water for Life and Livelihoods, River Basin Management Plan, South East River Basin District, 57–58.

[...] And in the UK, for example, whilst broader participation is discussed, the emphasis is very much on seeking consensus in relatively small 'liaison' groups. Support for the idea that technical expert discourse is alone sufficient for either legitimacy or effectiveness is however rare now in the EU. But putting this into practice is obviously enormously difficult and an ongoing process. The Water Framework Directive may even lead to two tiers of 'participation': 'active involvement' for a relatively narrow group of 'interested parties', which might include environmental and business interest groups; and a 'mere' opportunity to provide written comments for the more general public.

[...]

Finally, and more positively, the obligation in Annex VI to include in the River Basin Management Plan 'a summary of the public information and consultation measures taken, their results and the changes to the plan made as a consequence', is an important reason giving obligation. It not only concentrates the mind of the decision-maker but also allows public and peer scrutiny of participatory measures.

Maria Lee's analysis provides a critical take on the idea of scaling political space, here democratic governance, to natural space, such as the river basin. Her pragmatic evaluation of citizens being interested in matters that directly affect them suggests that the scale of the river basin is probably too large to ensure effective citizen involvement in river basin management planning. Her point is borne out by implementation practices of the EA in England and Wales, which has organized its public consultation in relation to the development and implementation of river basin management plans, also on the scale of catchments.[42] Howarth presents a sceptical view of the possibilities of public participation in river basin management planning.

William Howarth 'Aspirations and Realities under the Water Framework Directive: Proceduralisation, Participation and Practicalities' (2009) 21 Journal of Environmental Law 3 404, 406

Given the essentially voluntary character of participation, it would be logically impossible to 'compel' members of the public to engage in 'participation' on water management planning matters arising under the WFD. Nonetheless, the wording of the Directive comes as close to mandating Member States to ensure that public participation takes place, insofar as is reasonably possible and certainly fulfils the Aarhus requirements in this respect. The important questions are about how these obligations are translated into national law and how faithfully they are implemented in practice. The obligation to 'encourage' active involvement seems to suggest something beyond the ordinary elements of a consultation process, involving a 'potentially much deeper form of participation, although there is little compulsion here', perhaps indicating a shift towards a model of 'active citizenship' in which power is shared between a wide range of stakeholders. However, the obligation to encourage involvement falls short of a duty to ensure that this actually occurs and the WFD itself gives no further indication as to what kind of 'encouragement' is needed.

[...]

What the broad legal obligations on participation that have been recounted actually entail in practice is more difficult to interpret. A general concern is that the practical challenges of engaging the wider general public may mean that a narrower 'stakeholder' or representative approach to participation is needed. Beyond that, many of the issues needing to be resolved in implementing the WFD are readily

---

[42] Environment Agency, Water for Life and Livelihoods, River Basin Management Plan, South East River Basin District, 57.

capable of being placed in complex scientific or technical methodological contexts, which will have the effect of marginalising participants from outside a narrow community of expert stakeholders. As the issues become more specific and specialised, the pool of potential participants becomes progressively smaller, though the importance of decisions does not diminish, where, as often, 'the devil is in the detail'. The upshot of this is that, widespread 'participation' can mask the real distribution of influence in decision-making, where the most crucial decisions are eventually made by a handful of key players.

Howarth's discussion draws attention to the fact that the text of the WFD does not clarify exactly what steps Member States have to take to discharge the duty under Article 14(1) to 'encourage the active involvement of all interested parties in the implementation of this Directive, in particular in the production, review and updating of the river basin management plans'. The ECJ has further strengthened citizens' public participation rights in relation to river basin management planning by determining that Article 14 confers a right upon individuals to be actively involved in the implementation of the Directive within Member States.[43]

An ambitious interpretation of Article 14 WFD suggests that it establishes not merely public consultation, but participatory river basin democracy, which is based on a co-operative rather than adversarial approach to democratic decision-making.[44] This ambitious vision of participatory river basin democracy draws on 'social learning'. Social learning describes a particular approach to dealing with potential conflicts over water use by enabling participants to identify and understand the different cognitive frameworks through which stakeholders perceive various aspects of water regulation.[45] Where this vision of river basin democracy is implemented, the WFD turns into an interesting example of what has been labelled as 'experimentalist governance'.[46] This is another feature of the WFD that is discussed further in Section 2.3.

2.3 THE COMMON IMPLEMENTATION STRATEGY AS AN EXAMPLE OF EXPERIMENTALIST GOVERNANCE

In order to further capture the democratic nature of the governance regime established by the WFD it is important to discuss not just the provisions in relation to river basin democracy, but also the 'Common Implementation Strategy' (CIS) set up under the WFD. The CIS is a three tier EU-wide network of scientists, Member State representatives, and high-level water pollution control policy actors, the so-called water directors, who further flesh out in more specific detail the standards set out in the text of the WFD. It was set up in 2001 by the European Commission. The CIS reflects a principle of subsidiarity and has been considered as potentially further enhancing democratic governance in the implementation of the WFD through 'experimentalism'.

[43] C 32/05 *Commission v Luxembourg*, [2006] ECR I-11323, para 80.

[44] Joanne Tippett, Bradley Searle, Claudia Pahl-Wostl, and Yvonne Rees, 'Social Learning in Public Participation in River Basin Management—Early Findings from Harmonicop European Case Studies' (2005) 8 Environmental Science & Policy 287–99.

[45] Ibid, 292–93.

[46] Charles F Sabel and Jonathan Zeitlin 'Learning from Difference: The New Architecture of Experimentalist Governance in the EU' (2008) 14 ELJ 271–327.

Joanne Scott and Jane Holder 'Law and New Environmental Governance in the European Union' in Gráinne de Búrca and Joanne Scott (eds) *Law and New Governance in the EU and the US* (Hart Publishing 2006) 226–27, 236, 238

In practice, Member State implementation takes shape against the backdrop of the so-called Common Implementation Strategy (CIS). Nowhere mentioned in the directive, this provides an informal forum for Member State cooperation in implementation. The CIS provides for 'open co-operation' between the Member States, and between the Commission and the Member States, in the implementation of the WFD. It reflects a 'new partnership working method', involving scientific as well as political actors, creating networks of specialists from different Member States and different levels of governance. Against the backdrop of a dauntingly ambitious and complex framework directive, CIS provides for collaboration in implementation and in environmental problem solving.

With CIS, we find a dramatic and unexpected expression of new governance, nestling beneath the surface of Member State autonomy or sovereignty in implementation. The collaborative governance which this spawns is strongly imbued with the characteristics of experimentalism … it is committed to information sharing and the benchmarking of best practice. The Commission also deploys a 'scoreboard' approach, charting progress on implementation in respect of the WFD.

[…] With the Water Framework Directive (and CIS), the picture with regard to law is yet more complex and unsettled. Here we find elaborate collaborative processes, spanning sites and levels of governance. […] these processes appear to be neither constituted nor regulated by any recognisable *legal* act. An exhaustive reading of the treaties and of relevant legislation would give no hint of the existence or operation of CIS. Bearing in mind the formal sources of EU law, these processes seem to operate entirely beneath the legal radar, invisible to 'ordinary' as well as constitutional law. This lack of visibility may be attributed, at least in part, to the informal and voluntary nature of multi-level collaboration in CIS, and to the 'softness' of the instruments which ensue.

[…]Thus, we find with CIS a strange constellation; in formal terms a legal vacuum, but in material terms a high degree of formalisation and regularisation. In the light of this, it is possible to think of CIS as representing an example of what we might call *embedded constitutionalism*. The practice of governance has spawned a process of constitutionalisation from within, and a setting of expectations around certain core values; transparency, participation, accountability and the like. […] Experimentalism emerges as a key value in the immanent constitutionalisation of governance.

As pointed out in the extract, the CIS operates principally through legally non-binding soft law in the form of technical guidelines. It provides further input for Member States to define the general standards laid down in the WFD, but is also a tool for rendering Member States accountable to the Commission for the implementation of the WFD. Member States are required under CIS soft law to regularly submit reports to the Commission, such as copies of River Basin Management Plans and Interim Progress Reports about proposed measures to achieve compliance with the WFD.[47] The Commission then prepares its own report on a Member State's progress in implementing the Directive. The CIS develops 'benchmarks' for measuring a Member State's performance in implementing the WFD. Member States can therefore be compared to each other and against a 'best practice' standard.[48] Figure 14.4 provides an overview of the CIS organizational structure.

The CIS is managed by the *Water Directors* who are high level Member State representatives. They are the final decision-making forum with responsibility for developing water policy and steering

---

[47] Joanne Scott and Jane Holder, 'Law and New Environmental Governance in the European Union' in Gráinne de Búrca and Joanne Scott (eds) *Law and New Governance in the EU and the US* (Hart Publishing 2006) 230–31.
[48] Ibid, 231.

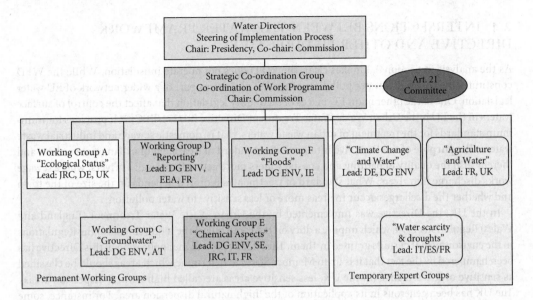

Figure 14.4 The CIS organizational structure

Source: Common Implementation Strategy for the Water Framework Directive (2000/60/EC) Work Programme, 2010–2012, 'Supporting the Implementation of the First River Basin Management Plans', at: <http://circa.europa.eu/Public/irc/env/wfd/library?l=framework_directive/implementation_documents/final_2010-2012/_EN_1.0_&a=d> 3.

implementation. The second tier of the CIS consists of the Strategic Coordination Group, which is chaired by the Commission, includes participants from each Member State, and co-ordinates the activities of the various working groups. The third tier of the CIS are working groups (WGs), which on average consist of thirty to forty members, including mainly staff from Member State Environmental Ministries or regulatory agencies as well as participants from European and international organizations and industry. NGOs, such as the World Wildlife Fund and the European Environmental Bureau, participate when they can contribute specific expertise.[49] For instance, the guidelines drafted by the WG on 'Ecological Status' sets out indicators and values for measuring water status, which should help to further define 'good' water status across the EU. For instance, a river classified in Sweden as being of 'good' water status should be comparable to a river of the same classification in Poland.

So far the discussion has suggested that the discourse of bioregionalism, the attempt to map regulatory space on to natural space, here the boundaries of the river basin, does not fully capture the nature of the regulatory regime established by the WFD for two reasons. First, as critical legal geography literature has pointed out, natural space is not a pre-given, unproblematic category but socially constructed. As discussed already, the text of the WFD itself and implementation practices of the EA transform the natural spatial category of the river basin, by providing for the combination of river basins and elements of river basins, such as catchments to be the scale at which the administration of the WFD is delivered. Second, public consultation in relation to the drafting of river basin management plans does not just occur at the scale of the river basin but also at national and local levels through established networks of stakeholder consultation. Hence, actual implementation practices by the EA also detract from the focus on the river basin as the key spatial category through which the Directive is implemented.

[49] Ibid, 228–29. For a further discussion of the Common Implementation Strategy, see also, The Common Implementation Strategy for the Water Framework Directive (2000/60/EC) Work Programme, 2010–12, 'Supporting the Implementation of the First River Basin Management Plans', at: <http://ec.europa.eu/environment/water/water-framework/objectives/implementation_en.htm>.

2.4 INTERSECTIONS BETWEEN THE WATER FRAMEWORK DIRECTIVE AND OTHER EU DIRECTIVES

As the analysis in Section 2.3 makes clear, the WFD does not operate in isolation. While the WFD constitutes the core of EU water pollution control, it also forms part of a wider network of EU water legislation. One of the other main EU pieces of secondary legislation that affect the control of surface waters in the EU is the Urban Waste Water Treatment Directive (91/271/EEC).[50] It provides for minimum standards for the treatment of urban waste waters, that is, domestic sewage and industrial waste waters. The purpose of the Directive is to raise the standard of treatment of urban waste waters, and thereby also the quality of bathing and coastal waters more generally, as well as rivers, where sewage works discharge into rivers. What standard of treatment is required depends on the size of the town and whether the discharges occur in areas more or less sensitive to water pollution.

In the UK, the Directive was implemented by the Urban Waste Water Treatment (England and Wales) Regulations 1994, which impose a duty on the EA to reflect the requirements of the Regulations in the environmental permits granted by them. The effectiveness of the application of this Directive has been hampered by the fact that it is up to Member States to determine which areas should be classified as sensitive or less sensitive (in the UK, less sensitive areas are called high natural dispersion areas). The UK has been generous in its application of the 'high natural dispersion area'. For instance, some estuarial waters have been classified as 'coastal', thus allowing lower levels of treatment to be applied.

This practice was successfully challenged in the case of *R v Secretary of State for the Environment, ex parte Kingston upon Hull City Council*.[51] The court held that the Secretary of State's decision to draw the boundaries of the estuary for the rivers Humber and Severn at the Humber and Severn road bridges, thus ensuring lower (and therefore cheaper) levels of treatment for treatment works along the rivers, had given undue consideration to costs. Costs should not have been taken into account, because the correct way of drawing the boundaries of the estuary was to carry out a genuine and rational assessment of what actually constituted the estuaries, which were redefined as a line between the two furthest points of land on each side of the river. The case further illustrates the limits of the assumptions of an environmentalist discourse of bioregionalism, that there is an unproblematic category of natural space, here 'the estuary', which can steer the implementation of environmental law. Instead, as argued in the critical legal geography literature, pre-existing relations of political power and economic conditions in the water industry contributed here to the social construction of the spatial category of 'the estuary'.

The WFD also intersects with the Habitats (Directive 92/43/EEC)[52] and Birds Directive (2009/147/EC).[53] Conservation sites with water-related features identified under these Directives will be designated as 'protected areas' under the WFD. Article 4(1)(c) WFD requires Member States to achieve compliance with the environmental objectives of the WFD at the latest fifteen years after the date of entry into force of the Directive, unless other deadlines are specified in the specific Community legislation under which the individual protected areas have been established.

Finally, it is worth noting that 'water damage' under the Environmental Liability Directive[54] is defined in Article 2(1)(b) to include:

> any damage that significantly adversely affects the ecological, chemical and/or quantitative status and/or ecological potential, as defined in Directive 2000/60/EC, of the waters concerned, with the exception of adverse effects where Article 4(7) of that Directive applies.

---

[50] [1990] OJ L 135/40.   [51] [1996] Env LR 248.
[52] [1992] OJ L 206/7, consolidated version.   [53] [2009] OJ L 20/7.
[54] Directive 2004/35/CE of the European Parliament and of the Council of 21 April 2004 on environmental liability with regard to the prevention and remedying of environmental damage [2004] OJ L143/56.

The WFD thus plays an important role in the implementation of the Environmental Liability Directive.[55]

2.5 DEROGATIONS UNDER THE WFD

Finally, it is important to note that while the text of the WFD thus seems to initially suggest that Member States have to implement ambitious water pollution control standards, closer analysis shows that they can take advantage of a number of derogations, which also limit the harmonization of water pollution control standards in the EU. Given the cross-border nature of water pollution, with pollutants being transported across nation-state boundaries through rivers, ground water bodies, and lakes that flow across national boundaries, this matters. Hence, a discourse of bioregionalism, that is, mapping a regulatory regime onto natural space, such as a river basin, is not necessarily associated with stringent environmental controls. The concern that the text of the WFD allows too much flexibility for Member States to qualify the general ambitious environmental objectives of the Directive[56] seems to be borne out by some Member States' implementation practices. For instance, in the UK, DEFRA and the Welsh Ministers have issued guidance to the EA in relation to the setting of water pollution control standards in river basin management plans,[57] which steer implementation practice towards the use of derogations provided for under the WFD also in order to ensure the 'cost-effective' implementation of the Directive.[58]

One of these powers of derogation for Member States relates to the classification of water bodies. According to Article 4(3)WFD Member States can designate some surface water bodies as 'artificial' or 'heavily modified'. An artificial water body is a body of surface water created by human activity, while a heavily modified water body is a body of surface water that has substantially changed in character due to physical alterations by human activity (Article 2(8)(9) WFD).This provision can be invoked if the water course has been created or modified for a particular use, such as water supply, flood protection, navigation, or urban infrastructure. Hence, by definition, water bodies classified as 'artificial' or as 'heavily modified' are not able to achieve natural conditions. The classification and objectives for these water bodies are determined with reference to 'ecological *potential*' rather than the more onerous standard of such water bodies having to achieve 'good ecological *status*' by 2015. The EA justifies these derogations in cost–benefit terms by suggesting that for some water bodies it may not be possible to achieve a near natural condition, because useful changes to the water body have been made, such as flood protection measures, changes in order to allow navigation, or changes to the water course that enable water to be held back for abstraction or power generation.

The wide use of the designation of waters as artificial or heavily modified in UK river basin management plans has been criticized and lead to litigation in the UK. The World Wildlife Fund-UK (WWF-UK) and the Angling Trust applied to the High Court for judicial review of the EA's river basin management plans. The claimants argued that the river basin management plans for England and Wales did not set specific enough targets or a sufficiently ambitious time frame for improving the poor ecological quality of English rivers. WWF-UK and the Angling Trust also suggested that the EA made excessive use of the power of derogation provided for under the WFD.[59] The action was withdrawn by these two environmental organizations in response to an announcement by DEFRA that a range of measures would be put in place in order to achieve a more ambitious approach to the drafting of the first round of river basin management plans. Among these were the establishment of ten pilot catchments where also 'enforcement action' would be considered in order to address pollution issues. WWF-UK and the Angling Trust also pressed their case for an earlier publication of the next round of draft river basin management plans,

---

[55] See Chapter 9 for an overview.   [56] Bill Howarth (n 23) 395.

[57] DEFRA and Welsh Ministers, River Basin Planning Guidance (2006), at: <http://archive.defra.gov.uk/environment/quality/water/wfd/documents/riverbasinguidance.pdf>, 33–34.

[58] Bill Howarth (n 23) 413.

[59] 'NGOs seek judicial review of water framework plans. ENDS Report No. 422, March 2010, 9.

in order for civil society groups to have greater scope for providing comments on the plans. DEFRA also committed to increasing the number of investigations of the quality of water bodies to be carried out for the first round of river basin management plans. The case presents an interesting example of how deeply EU environmental regulation can reach into national environmental politics.[60] While the legal provisions of the WFD are considered as not entirely clear, they were nevertheless a powerful lever for bargaining over implementation practices between two environmental NGOs and the ministry.

FURTHER READING AND QUESTIONS

1. The WFD has been criticized for failing to provide sufficiently developed economic tools for water regulation. Article 9 WFD provides for the recovery of costs for water services. What this really includes is unclear—recovery should include costs of environmental damage caused by water use, as well as adverse effects of over-abstraction of water through ground water bore-holes or from surface waters. For a further discussion, see Herwig Unnerstall, 'The Principle of Full Cost Recovery in the EU-Water Framework Directive—Genesis and Content' (2007) 19(1) Journal of Environmental Law 29–42.

2. Mireille Bogaart, 'The Co-Ordination of Water Quality Objectives and Carbon Reductions: the Possibilities for Less Stringent Obligations under the WFD and the IPPC Directive' (2009) 20(4) The Journal of Water Law 186–94. This article discusses the interesting conflict between commitments to the reduction of greenhouse gas emissions in the EU and legal requirements to improve water quality through the WFD and through the Directive on Industrial Emissions. This conflict arises because water treatment systems are often associated with significant carbon dioxide emissions.

3. Commission of the European Communities, Report from the Commission to the European Parliament and the Council on Implementation of the Water Framework Directive (2000/60/ EC) River Basin Management Plans, COM(2012) 670 final, at: <http://ec.europa.eu/ environment/water/water-framework/implrep2007/index_en.htm#third>.

4. For further discussion of the Directive, see Andrea Keessen, Jasper van Kempen, Marleen van Rijswick, Jan Robbe, and Chris Backes, 'European River Basin Districts: Are They Swimming in the Same Implementation Pool?' (2010) 22(2) JEL 197–221; PW Downs, Kenneth J Gregory, and Andrew Brookes 'How Integrated is River Basin Management?' (1991) 15(3) Environmental Management 299–309; Wendy Kenyon 'A Critical Review of Citizens' Juries: How Useful are they in Facilitating Public Participation in the EU Water Framework Directive?' (2005) 48 Journal of Environmental Planning and Management 3, 431–43; and Jens Newig, Claudia Pahl-Wostl, and Katja Sigel 'The Role of Public Participation in Managing Uncertainty in the Implementation of the Water Framework Directive', (2005) 15 European Environment 333–43.

5. For a further interesting discussion about the obligations under the WFD, particularly Article 4, see Jasper JH van Kempen, 'Countering the Obscurity of Obligations in European Environmental Law: An Analysis of Article 4 of the European Water Framework Directive' (2012) 24(3) JEL 499–533.

6. The European Commission has reviewed the WFD and in particular the first round of river basin management plans in its latest communication 'A Blueprint to Safeguard Europe's Water Resources.' It recommends the development of CIS guidance documents for the specification of ecological flows in rivers and water efficiency targets. See further *A Blueprint to Safeguard Europe's Water Resources, Communication from the Commission to the European Parliament, the Council, the European Economic and Social Committee and the Committee of the Regions, Brussels*, 14.11.2012, COM (2012) 673 final.

---

[60] Angling Trust, at: http://www.anglingtrust.net/news.asp?section=29&itemid=758.

3 ENVIRONMENTAL PERMITTING OF WATER DISCHARGE AND GROUNDWATER ACTIVITIES IN ENGLAND AND WALES

The discussion so far has been focused on how standards are created for water quality at the EU level. We might think of this as a 'top-down' analysis in that it focuses on how normative aspirations in relation to water quality are transformed into standards. But we also need to take a bottom-up approach. For those being regulated in England and Wales, their major experience of water pollution regulation will be through the permitting system. They will be operating under permits that will set conditions and those conditions will have been set within the framework of the WFD. A breach of a permit will possibly lead to prosecution.[61] Thus, for most of those being regulated, what is directly important is environmental permitting rather than the WFD itself. It should be noted that licensing of water discharge activities and ground water activities does not capture all activities that degrade water quality—this is because environmental permitting focuses on the individual point discharge of specific polluters, rather than diffuse water pollution in a given river basin. However, diffuse water pollution, such as nitrate run-offs from farmland, is a growing problem and, as such, permitting potentially detracts from the bioregionalist policy agenda of mapping 'regulatory space' onto 'natural space'.

Environmental permitting draws on the familiar technique of licensing, introduced in Section 3 of the Introduction to Part IV, in order to reduce the emission of pollutants from point sources. Within this section, Section 3.1 discusses key elements of environmental permitting in relation to water discharge activities and groundwater activities, while Section 3.2 discusses key case law in relation to the criminal offence that supports enforcement of the consent system. As noted in the Introduction to this part, the environmental permitting system is new. An important implication of this is that the understanding of this system is relatively thin. Thus, much of the case law that is discussed here relates to the old water pollution offence regime under the Water Resources Act 1991 and the previous legislation it replaced. Getting to grips with this case law in the updated legislative context of water pollution offences is once again a reminder of the challenges of the speed of legal change.[62]

3.1 KEY ELEMENTS OF THE CONSENT SYSTEM FOR WATER REGULATION

The EA for England and Wales is the 'competent authority' under Article 3(2) WFD for the implementation of the Directive in England and Wales. It grants permits under the Environmental Permitting (England and Wales) Regulations 2010 (EPRs). Core features of the EPRs are set out in Section 3 of the Introduction to Part IV. The central permitting requirement of the EPRs extends to require dischargers to obtain an environmental permit for 'water discharge activities' or 'groundwater activities'.[63]

Requirement for environmental permit

12.—(1) A person must not, except under and to the extent authorised by an environmental permit
—

---

[61] See Chapter 8.

[62] Elizabeth Fisher, Bettina Lange, Eloise Scotford, and Cinnamon Carlarne, 'Maturity and Methodology: Starting a Debate about Environmental Law Scholarship' (2009) 21 JEL 213, 228–31.

[63] Regulation 12(1) replaces the old offence under s 85 of the Water Resources Act (WRA) 1991, which has been repealed by Schedule 26(8)(2)(a) of the Environmental Permitting (England and Wales) Regulations 2010.

(a) operate a regulated facility; or

(b) cause or knowingly permit a water discharge activity or groundwater activity.

Schedule 21 sets out more particular details of permits required for water discharge activities. Paragraph 3 of Schedule 21 defines a 'water discharge activity' as follows:[64]

3.—(1) A 'water discharge activity' means any of the following—

(a) the discharge or entry to inland freshwaters, coastal waters or relevant territorial waters of any—

(i) poisonous, noxious or polluting matter,

(ii) waste matter, or

(iii) trade effluent or sewage effluent; [65]

(b) the discharge from land through a pipe into the sea outside the seaward limits of relevant territorial waters of any trade effluent or sewage effluent;

(c) the removal from any part of the bottom, channel or bed of any inland freshwaters of a deposit accumulated by reason of any dam, weir or sluice holding back the waters, by causing it to be carried away in suspension in the waters, unless the activity is carried on in the exercise of a power conferred by or under any enactment relating to land drainage, flood prevention or navigation;

(d) the cutting or uprooting of a substantial amount of vegetation in any inland freshwaters or so near to any such waters that it falls into them and failure to take reasonable steps to remove the vegetation from these waters;

(e) an activity in respect of which a notice under paragraph 4 or 5 has been served and has taken effect.

(2) A discharge or an activity that might lead to a discharge is not a 'water discharge activity'—

(a) if the discharge is made, or authorised to be made, by or under any prescribed statutory provision; or

(b) if the discharge is of trade effluent or sewage effluent from a vessel.

(3) In determining whether a discharge or an activity is a water discharge activity, no account must be taken of any radioactivity possessed by any substance or article or by any part of any premises.

Schedule 22 of the EPRs sets out details of permits required for groundwater activities. Paragraph 3 of Schedule 22 defines 'groundwater activity' as:

3.—(1) Subject to sub-paragraphs (2) and (3), 'groundwater activity' means any of the following—

(a) the discharge of a pollutant that results in the direct input of that pollutant to groundwater;

(b) the discharge of a pollutant in circumstances that might lead to an indirect input of that pollutant to groundwater;

---

[64] Some provisions of the Environmental Permitting (England and Wales) Regulations 2010 still refer to 'controlled waters'. This term retains the meaning it was given in s 104 of the Water Resources Act 1991. It refers to virtually all inland and coastal waters and includes four categories of water bodies. First, territorial waters, which refers to the sea within a line three miles out from the baseline from which the territorial sea is measured. Second, it includes coastal waters, which means the sea within this baseline. Third, it also comprises inland waters, such as rivers, streams, underground streams, canals, lakes, and reservoirs. Fourth, ground waters, that is, any waters contained in underground strata or in wells or boreholes.

[65] According to Regulation 2(1) EPR 2010, trade effluent has the meaning given in s 221 of the WRA 1991. It is defined in that section as any effluent from trade premises, which includes agricultural, fish farming, and research institutions, other than domestic sewage or surface water. Regulation 2(1) of the EPR 2010 defines 'sewage effluent' also in accordance with s 221 of the WRA 1991 as any liquid from sewage works other than surface water.

(c) any other discharge that might lead to the direct or indirect input of a pollutant to groundwater;

(d) an activity in respect of which a notice under paragraph 10 has been served and has taken effect;

(e) an activity that might lead to a discharge mentioned in paragraph (a), (b) or (c), where that activity is carried on as part of the operation of a regulated facility of another class.

Whereas Schedule 5 of the EPRs sets out the general procedure for applying for an environmental permit, including permits for water discharge and ground water activities, the procedures for obtaining such permits are further specified in Schedule 21 (for water discharge activities) and Schedule 22 (for groundwater activities). Thus, paragraph 7 of Schedule 22 of the EPRs spells out the procedure for applying for an environmental permit for groundwater activities specifically.

Applications for grant of environmental permit

7.—(1) This paragraph applies to an application for the grant of an environmental permit relating to—

(a) a discharge mentioned in paragraph 3(1)(a), (b) or (c); or

(b) an activity that might lead to such a discharge.

(2) When the regulator receives an application, it must ensure that all necessary investigations have been carried out to ensure that it grants any permit in accordance with paragraph 6.

(3) If it grants the permit, it must include conditions requiring all necessary technical precautions to be observed to ensure the objectives of paragraph 6 are achieved.

(4) A permit may not be granted—

(a) without examination of—

(i) the hydrogeological conditions of the area concerned,

(ii) the possible purifying powers of the soil and subsoil, and

(iii) the risk of pollution and alteration of the quality of the groundwater from the discharge, and

(b) without establishing whether the input of pollutants to groundwater is a satisfactory solution from the point of view of the environment.

(5) A permit may only be granted if the regulator has checked that the groundwater (and, in particular, its quality) will undergo the requisite surveillance.

Appeals can be lodged by the applicant to 'the appropriate authority' which is the Secretary of State for England, and the Welsh Ministers for Wales.

An appeal can be lodged for a refusal of consent. An appeal is a general re-hearing of the matter and the Secretary of State has the same powers as the Environment Agency originally had.

It is worth noting that paragraph 7(3) does not merely provide a power but imposes a duty upon the regulator to insert conditions in a consent limiting the discharge of water pollutants once it has decided that a permit will be issued. Regulation 31 of the EPRs 2010 provides a right of appeal to the Secretary of State or Welsh Minister in case an operator's application for a permit has been turned down. This right of appeal is for operators only, not for other interested parties, such as environmental NGOs.

In order to understand how the system of environmental permitting regulates water pollution activities, it is necessary to examine further the legal framework that guides regulator discretion in setting conditions in environmental permits. The regulator (here the EA) has a wide discretion in setting conditions in environmental permits, subject to general public law principles and statutory constraints. In relation to groundwater activities, paragraph 7(2) of Schedule 22 imposes a duty upon the EA to grant permits in accordance with the provisions of paragraph 6 of Schedule 22, which focuses on groundwater pollution.

> **Exercise of relevant functions**
>
> 6. For the purposes of implementing the Groundwater Directive, the Water Framework Directive and the Groundwater Daughter Directive, the regulator must, in exercising its relevant functions, take all necessary measures—
>
>   (a) to prevent the input of any hazardous substance to groundwater; and
>
>   (b) to limit the input of non-hazardous pollutants to groundwater so as to ensure that such inputs do not cause pollution of groundwater.

When setting conditions in discharge consents (as they were previously known), the EA also takes into account to what uses the receiving water will be put further downstream, the interaction between different discharges, which are, however, difficult to anticipate, in particular if the EA tries to limit pollutants to be allowed to be discharged under current environmental permits with a view to further pollution that may occur under permits to be issued at some time in the future. Moreover, the EA must take into account representations made by the public and interested parties (paragraph 1 of Schedule 5), as well as its general environmental protection duties laid down in ss 4–7 of the Environment Act 1995 and the EA's specific duties in relation to water pollution control set out in s 6(1) of the Environment Act 1995:[66]

> 6 (1) It shall be the duty of the Agency, to such extent as it considers desirable, generally to promote—
>
>   (a) the conservation and enhancement of the natural beauty and amenity of inland and coastal waters and of land associated with such waters;
>
>   (b) the conservation of flora and fauna which are dependent on an aquatic environment; and
>
>   (c) the use of such waters and land for recreational purposes;
>
> and it shall be the duty of the Agency, in determining what steps to take in performance of the duty imposed by virtue of paragraph (c) above, to take into account the needs of persons who are chronically sick or disabled. This subsection is without prejudice to the duties of the Agency under section 7 below.

It is not entirely clear how the old system of setting conditions in water discharge consents with reference to statutory water quality objectives contained in ss 82–84 of the Water Resources Act 1991 (WRA) will relate to the new legal framework created by the WFD and the EPRs. The WFD now sets its own water quality objectives, which are further specified in the river basin management plans. But the system of statutory water quality objectives under ss 82–84 of the WRA could still be used to

---

[66] Stuart Bell, Donald McGillivary and Ole Pedersen, *Environmental Law* (OUP 2013) 644.

implement the WFD. It is similar to the regulatory regime of the WFD. Section 82 WRA provides for the classification of stretches of water in relation to the standards it needs to reach. Under s 83 WRA, the Secretary of State then establishes a water quality objective for each stretch of controlled waters, which were taken into account when the EA set conditions in discharge consents. Standards established under s 83 WRA 1991 could now be those set out in river basin management plans. Section 84 WRA 1991 imposes a duty upon the EA to exercise its function, including the granting of discharge consents so as to achieve and maintain statutory water quality objectives at all times, at least as far as it is practicable to do so.

As set out in the Introduction to Part IV, the EPRs include provisions relating to the enforcement of all environmental permits. In light of the regulator's power to vary environmental permits, operators who discharge into water courses do not obtain a statutory *right* to discharge into a watercourse according to the terms of their original permit conditions but are subject to a flexible tool of regulation that enables the regulator to tighten water pollution control standards through a variation of the original permit, for instance in relation to new EU legislation, such as new Daughter Directives under the WFD, revised river basin management plans, or new installations discharging water pollutants starting up business in the vicinity of the water course. Beyond this, the regulator's powers to enforce the terms of environmental permits are extensive, including requiring operators to carry out clean-up operations where there has been breach of a permit (Regulation 36(3)(b)) or requiring operators to pay for steps taken by the regulator to remove a risk of serious pollution in relation to a permitted activity (Regulation 57(4) EPRs 2010). If the requirement to carry out clean-up operations is to the standard of restoring watercourses to high ecological status, that is, natural pristine conditions, they can prove financially onerous for operators.

To conclude, environmental permitting of water discharge and ground water activities is at the heart of water pollution control law in the UK. During environmental permitting, the focus shifts away from key elements of an environmentalist, bioregionalist discourse, a focus on natural space, aquatic ecosystems, and an integrated approach to water pollution control, to a focus on individual point discharges mainly from sewerage undertakers into surface waters. Section 3.2 considers the range of criminal offences in relation to water pollution provided under the EPRs.

3.2 WATER POLLUTION OFFENCES

Regulation 38, EPR 2010 extracted in the Introduction to Part IV, sets out a number of criminal offences that relate to behaviour right across the environmental permitting process.[67] Here we focus on the four offences that are pertinent to water pollution.[68] The construction of these offences is confusing for four reasons. First, Regulation 38 cross-refers to Regulation 12 of the EPRs. Second, these offences can overlap. Third, these offences are relatively new and thus a practice of applying them is yet to emerge. Fourth, some of the terminology of these new offences is similar to the offences under the former s 85(1) of the Water Resources Act 1991, which created very general offences where a person 'causes or knowingly permits any poisonous, noxious or polluting matter or any solid waste matter to enter any controlled waters'. However, other wording in Regulation 38 is different from this old provision. Thus, it is unclear how the new wording relates to the old wording (see further Section 3.3). As a starting point for dealing with this confusing picture, Table 14.1 unravels the relationship between Regulation 38 and Regulation 12.

---

[67] For example, Regulation 38(4)(a) concerns the failure to comply with a notice under Regulation 60(1) requiring information to be provided.

[68] For a wider discussion of the role of criminal law in UK environmental regulation, see Chapter 8.

Table 14.1 The relationship between Regulation 38 and Regulation 12

Regulation 38	Regulation 12
38(1)(a)—It is an offence for a person to contravene Regulation 12(1) [...]	12(1) A person must not, except under and to the extent authorised by an environmental permit— (a) operate a regulated facility; or (b) cause or knowingly permit a water discharge activity or groundwater activity.
Regulation 38(1)(b) It is an offence for a person to knowingly cause or knowingly permit the contravention of Regulation 12(1)(a).	12(1) A person must not, except under and to the extent authorised by an environmental permit— (a) operate a regulated facility [...]
Regulation 38(2): It is an offence for a person to fail to comply with or to contravene an environmental permit condition.	
Regulation 38(3): It is an offence for a person to fail to comply with the requirements of an enforcement notice or of a prohibition notice, suspension notice, landfill closure notice or mining waste facility closure notice.	

Note that the definition of 'water discharge activity' in paragraph 3(1)(a) of Schedule 21 further differentiates between the 'discharge *or* entry' of any poisonous, noxious or polluting matter etc to inland freshwaters, coastal waters or relevant territorial waters. This is different from the old s 85 offence, which referred only to polluting matter *entering* waters. As a result, there now seems to be both a specific offence of causing a *discharge* and a general offence of causing an *entry* of polluting matter into relevant waters. The term 'entry' covers both accidental and non-routine escapes of pollutants, possibly including run-off from agricultural land. Both the general and specific pollution offences require that the water discharge activity occurred otherwise than in accordance with a permit. It is also important to remember Regulation 40 which sets out defences for the Regulation 38 offences (see the Introduction to Part IV and Section 3.3.3). In all cases it should also be remembered that Regulation 38(6) provides that 'if an offence committed by a person under this regulation is due to the act or default of some other person, that other person is also guilty of the offence and liable to be proceeded against and punished accordingly, whether or not proceedings for the offence are taken against the first mentioned person'.

Overall, what can be seen is a set of pollution offences that overlap but that use quite distinct language. That language, particularly relating to 'knowingly', 'causing', and 'permitting', comes with baggage. As we shall see in Section 3.3, these terms have been subject to judicial interpretation in previous contexts. The question, of course, is whether the EPRs establish a very different context and thus require a different interpretation of these key terms.

3.3 THE PREVIOUS CASE LAW CONCERNING WATER POLLUTION OFFENCES

As can be seen in Section 3.2, the new EPR regime is a complicated one. As already noted, a further complication is that the wording of the offences under Regulation 38 is similar but not the same as the wording under the former s 85(1) of the Water Resources Act 1991 (the previous and well-litigated water pollution offence, set out already). This section considers some of the most significant features of the considerable body of case law concerning the former s 85 offence. We should stress at the outset that it is still not clear how exactly this body of case law will relate to the new EPR regime, but at the very least the cases here provide examples of how the judiciary interpreted these provisions. It is also clear that the recast water pollution offences within the EPRs are intended to capture most aspects of the old s 85 offence. We focus here on three issues from the existing case law: how the definition of pollution matter was interpreted under the previous Act; how 'causing' was defined; and how defences and the role of third parties were defined and interpreted.

Polluting matter

Regulation 3(1)(a) defines as 'water discharge activity' the 'discharge or entry to inland freshwaters, coastal waters or relevant territorial waters of any (i) poisonous, noxious or polluting matter, (ii) waste matter, or (iii) trade effluent or sewage effluent'. While there is a statutory definition of trade and sewage effluent in s 221 of the Water Resources Act 1991, and while waste matter is defined in Regulation 2 (1) of the EPRs,[69] there is no such definition of the terms 'poisonous, noxious or polluting matter'. These terms, however, were defined in the case of *R v Dovermoss Ltd* in the context of the old s 85 offence. The appellant, Dovermoss Ltd, caused slurry to be spread onto fields. The slurry spreading lead to high levels of ammonia in a source from which drinking water was abstracted. The appellant was convicted in the Crown Court of Carmarthen of polluting controlled waters contrary to s 85(1) WRA 1991. Dovermoss' appealed—inter alia—on the grounds that, while the levels of ammonia in the drinking water were higher than normal, they were within the levels required by the Drinking Water Quality Regulations. The ammonia should therefore not be considered as a polluting matter within the meaning of s 85(1) WRA 1991. The Court of Appeal allowed the appeal the extract from the *R v Dovermoss Ltd* case gives their statement in relation to the definition of 'polluting matter'.

R v Dovermoss Ltd Court of Appeal (Criminal Division)
[3 Feb 1995] Official Transcript 5, 6 (Stuart Smith LJ)

The next ground raises a point of law. It is submitted that the judge did not correctly define the words 'polluting matter' to the jury. There is no definition in the Act. The judge, after referring to Mr Dutton's evidence that the sample contained quite a lot of harmful and deleterious matter that affected the quality of the water, said:

'And that is really what "pollution" means; there is no particular definition of "pollution" other than it is that sort of material which, if introduced into the water, reduces the quality of the water. And pollution can do that to a greater or lesser degree, depending upon what the pollution is and how much of it there is.'

Mr Jones submits that the prosecution have to show that some harm has resulted to the water, such that it has a harmful effect on animal or plant life affected by the water or those who use it. Since the ammonia levels were lower than those permitted by the regulations, no such harmful effect was shown. We do not accept this submission. 'Pollute', 'pollutant' and 'pollution' are ordinary English words. The relevant definition of 'pollute' in the Oxford English Dictionary is: 'to make physically impure, foul or filthy; to dirty, stain, taint, befoul.' It is quite clear that it is intended to have a different meaning from 'poisonous or noxious matter', since these words appear in the section. 'Noxious' means harmful. We see no reason why the dictionary definition should not be adopted. It will, of course, be a question of fact and degree whether the matter does pollute the waters. Obviously, a very small quantity poured into a large watercourse may have no polluting effect at all. It is so diluted that it does not make it impure, foul or filthy. This is a question for the jury.

---

[69] 'Waste', except where otherwise defined, means anything that: (a) is waste for the purposes of the Waste Framework Directive, and (b) is not excluded from the scope of that Directive by Article 2(1) of that Directive.

> It appears to us that this case could equally well have been charged as a noxious matter since it is obvious that it was likely to cause harm. It is not necessary in such a case to establish actual harm. The likelihood or capability of causing harm to animal or farm life or to those who use the water is sufficient.

Polluting does not necessarily mean harmful and the judgment above raises themes similar to Mary Douglas' work, which was discussed in the Introduction to Part IV.

A broad approach to causation

Some of the most interesting case law under the previous water pollution offence regime related to the concept of causation. In general terms, the concept of 'causing' pollution under the old s 85(1) offence was construed quite broadly so as to define many actions as polluting (and criminal). The concept of cause does not play exactly the same role under the EPR regime. As set out in Table 14.1, the concept of 'cause' is relevant in two ways under Regulation 38. Thus, under Regulation 38(1)(a), it is an offence to contravene Regulation 12(1), which includes to *cause or knowingly permit* a water discharge activity or groundwater activity' without the authority of an environmental permit. Regulation 38(1)(b) introduces a second offence, which uses the concept of cause slightly differently (to '*knowingly* cause or knowingly permit the contravention of Regulation 12(1)(a)'), but this applies to the operation of 'regulated facilities' rather than to water discharge activities *per se*. In light of the similar construction of Regulation 38(1)(a) and the old s 85, the case law under the 1991 Act (and the previous legislation it replaced) gives a feeling for how the concept of 'cause' has been interpreted, and potentially for its application in the future, although the interaction between the two Regulation 38 offences is yet to be explored, and we now have both a general and specific water pollution offence (through the definition of a water discharge activity).

In *Alphacell v Woodward* [1972] A.C. 824 the appellants, Alphacell, ran a paper mill in Lancashire situated close to the bank of the river Irwell. One of their effluents was run into two settling tanks. One of the settling tanks had an overflow into the river, but its contents was prevented from overflowing direct into the river by two pumps, one operating automatically when the water reached a certain level and the other being switched on by hand as a standby. One day leaves blocked the pumps and water from the settling tank did flow into the nearby river. Alphacell was charged with causing polluting matter to enter the river contrary to s 2(1) of the Rivers (Prevention of Pollutions) Act 1951, which provides for a criminal offence for a person to 'cause or knowingly permit to enter a stream any poisonous, noxious or polluting matter'. This offence is similar to the one now spelt out in Regulation 38 of the EPR 2010, though narrower because it refers only to the entry of polluting matter, not also discharges, and concerns only 'streams' rather than inland freshwaters, coastal waters, or relevant territorial waters referred to in Regulation 38. Alphacell was convicted of the criminal offence under s 2 (1) of the Rivers (Prevention of Pollutions) Act 1951 and the Divisional Court dismissed its appeal. Alphacell appealed to the House of Lords on the grounds that they should have been acquitted since the overflow had taken place without their knowledge and without negligence on their part. The appellants argued that the operation of their factory was simply 'a' cause, but not 'the' cause and that this mattered because they did not consider s 2(1) of the Rivers (Prevention of Pollution) Act 1951 to create an 'absolute' offence that did not require *mens rea*. The House of Lords dismissed their appeal. It affirmed that there were two separate offences of causing and knowingly permitting a discharge and hence the 'knowing' requirement did not apply to the offence of causing water pollution.

Alphacell Ltd v Woodward
[1972] AC 824 (HL) 834–35, 839 (Lord Wilberforce in the House of Lords):

The subsection evidently contemplates two things—*causing*, which must involve some active operation or chain of operations involving as the result the pollution of the stream; *knowingly permitting*, which involves a failure to prevent the pollution, which failure, however, must be accompanied by knowledge. I see no reason either for reading back the word 'knowingly' into the first limb, or for reading the first limb as, by deliberate contrast, hitting something which is unaccompanied by knowledge. The first limb involves causing and this is what has to be interpreted. In my opinion, 'causing' here must be given a common sense meaning and I deprecate the introduction of refinements, such as *causa causans*, effective cause or *novus actus*. There may be difficulties where acts of third persons or natural forces are concerned but I find the present case comparatively simple.

In my opinion, this is a clear case of causing the polluted water to enter the stream. The whole complex operation which might lead to this result was an operation deliberately conducted by the appellants and I fail to see how a defect in one stage of it, even if we must assume that this happened without their negligence, can enable them to say they did not cause the pollution. In my opinion, complication of this case by infusion of the concept of mens rea, and its exceptions, is unnecessary and undesirable. The section is clear, its application plain. I agree with the majority of the Divisional Court, who upheld the conviction, except that rather than say that the actions of the appellants were *a cause* of the pollution I think it more accurate to say that the appellants caused the polluting matter to enter the stream.

Viscount Dilhorne further added policy reasons for an interpretation of the offence that defined causation widely without a requirement for *mens rea*, which seem to be if anything even more relevant in the context of contemporary water pollution control twenty-nine years after *Alphacell* was decided:

In this case it was argued that it was an essential ingredient of the offence that the appellants should—the case being dealt with as if there was no negligence—have intended the entry of the polluting matter into the river, that is to say, that they should have intended the commission of the offence. I cannot think that that was the intention of Parliament for it would mean that a burden of proof would rest on the prosecution that could seldom be discharged. Only if the accused had been seen tipping the polluting material into a stream or turning on a tap allowing a polluting liquid to flow into a stream or doing something of a similar character could the burden be discharged. Parliament cannot have intended the offence to be of so limited a character. Ordinarily all that a river authority can establish is that a discharge has come into a stream from a particular source and that it is of a polluting character. But the Act does not say that proof of that will suffice. If that were so, the Act would indeed create an absolute offence. It has also to be proved that the accused caused or knowingly permitted the pollution.

The question of when to limit a broad definition of 'causing' is particularly sharply raised when there is a clearly identifiable third party that is associated with the water pollution. Should a sewerage undertaker who is bound to receive into its sewers discharges from third parties be liable for water pollution? Paragraph 6 of Schedule 21 of the Environmental Permitting (England and Wales) Regulations (EPR) 2010 replaces the former offence in s 87 WRA 1991.[70] Paragraph 6 of Schedule 21 of the EPR 2010 defines causation broadly by explicitly stating in paragraph 6(2) that a discharging undertaker is considered to have caused a discharge of sewage effluent if the following three criteria are satisfied. First, that the matter that causes pollution is actually received by the discharging undertaker into

---

[70] According to paragraph 8(2)(c) of Schedule 26 s 87 of the WRA 1991 that specifically dealt with the liability of sewerage undertakers for their discharges has been repealed.

its sewers. Second, that the discharging undertaker was bound to receive the matter into its sewers. Third, that the discharge was not subject to an agreement under s 110A of the WIA 1991 between the sending and the receiving undertaker.[71] Sub-paragraph (5), however, makes it clear that a sewerage undertaker is not guilty of an offence under Regulation 38(1) if a third identified person 'caused or knowingly permitted' the discharge to be made into the sewer or works (Schedule 21, paragraph 6(5)(a)), or if it was a discharge without consent or in breach of consent conditions (paragraph 6(5)(a) of Schedule 21), or if the sewerage undertaker could not reasonably have been expected to prevent the discharge into the sewer or works (paragraph 6(5)(c) of Schedule 21).

Environmental Permitting (England and Wales) Regulations 2010, Schedule 21, para 6

Liability resulting from discharge of sewage effluent from public sewer

6.—(1) This paragraph applies for the purpose of determining liability for a water discharge activity that consists of a discharge of sewage effluent from a discharging sewer vested in a discharging undertaker.

(2) A discharging undertaker causes a discharge of sewage effluent if—
  (a) matter included in the discharge is received by the discharging undertaker into the discharging sewer or into any other sewer or works vested in it;
  (b) the discharging undertaker was bound (either unconditionally or subject to conditions which were observed) to receive the matter into the discharging sewer or other sewer or works; and
  (c) sub-paragraph (3) does not apply.

(3) This sub-paragraph applies if, before the discharging undertaker discharges the sewage effluent from the discharging sewer, the sending undertaker, under an agreement with the discharging undertaker under section 110A of the Water Industry Act 1991, discharges the sewage effluent through a main connection into—
  (a) the discharging sewer; or
  (b) any other sewer or works vested in the discharging undertaker.

(4) If sub-paragraph (3) applies, the sending undertaker causes the discharge if—
  (a) matter included in the discharge is received by the sending undertaker into a sewer or works vested in it; and
  (b) it was bound (either conditionally or subject to conditions which were observed) to receive that matter into that sewer or works.

(5) A sewerage undertaker is not guilty of an offence under regulation 38(1) in relation to a water discharge activity that consists of a discharge of sewage effluent from a sewer or works vested in it if—
  (a) the contravention is attributable to a discharge which another person caused or knowingly permitted to be made into the sewer or works;
  (b) the undertaker either was not bound to receive the discharge into the sewer or works or was bound to receive it there subject to conditions which were not observed; and
  (c) the undertaker could not reasonably have been expected to prevent the discharge into the sewer or works.

(6) A person is not guilty of an offence under regulation 38(1) in relation to a discharge which the person caused or knowingly permitted to be made into a sewer or works vested in a sewerage undertaker if that undertaker was bound to receive the discharge, either unconditionally or subject to conditions which were observed.

---

[71] Section 110A WIA 1991 provides a power for the Director General of Water Services to require a sewerage undertake to allow a main connection from a third party ('the sending undertaker') into its sewers.

The case of *National Rivers Authority v Yorkshire Water Services Ltd* [72]—though litigated under the previously applicable provisions of the Water Act 1989—is further support for a broad definition of causation by the judiciary in the case of discharges from sewerage undertakers, which is now clearly set out in paragraph 6(2) EPR 2010. The appellant, Yorkshire Water Services Ltd, owned and operated a sewage treatment works. Treated sewerage was discharged through an outlet pipe into a brook, which flowed into a nearby river. This discharge into the river was subject to a discharge consent issued by the NRA. Yorkshire Water Services, in turn, had issued several consents to companies who were discharging trade effluent into its sewers. These discharge consents contained various conditions, including the condition not to discharge the solvent iso-octanol, which is dangerous to river life. But a discharge of this substance was in fact made into Yorkshire Water Services sewers, with the iso-octanol finally and inevitably being discharged from Yorkshire Water's sewerage works into the nearby river, in excess of levels allowed in the Discharge Consent under which Yorkshire Water was discharging into the river. The case was finally heard by the then House of Lords which referred to *Alphacell v Woodward* and affirmed the reasoning in that case on causation.

National Rivers Authority v Yorkshire Water Services Ltd
[1995] 1 AC 452 (Lord Mackay of Clashfern)

In applying the words of the statute in the light of the decision of this House in Alphacell Ltd v. Woodward, I am of opinion that Yorkshire Water Services having set up a system for gathering effluent into their sewers and thence into their sewage works there to be treated, with an arrangement deliberately intended to carry the results of that treatment into controlled waters, the special circumstances surrounding the entry of iso-octanol into their sewers and works does not preclude the conclusion that Yorkshire Water Services caused the resulting poisonous, noxious and polluting matter to enter the controlled waters, notwithstanding that the constitution of the effluent so entering was affected by the presence of iso-octanol.

But the House of Lords allowed the appeal on the grounds that Yorkshire Water Services could avail itself of the defence in s 108(7) of the Water Act 1989—a defence similar to the one now spelt out in paragraph 6(5) of Schedule 21—even though it held that Yorkshire Water Services had caused poisonous, noxious, or polluting matter to enter controlled waters.

In further clarifying the definition of 'causation' the case law has attempted to distinguish between situations in which—even though there were intervening acts or omissions—the defendant is still considered to have been active enough to have 'caused' the pollution and scenarios where the defendant has been so passive that he or she is no longer considered to have caused the polluting discharge. In the first line of cases the courts have held the defendant liable to have 'caused' the water pollution even though there were intervening acts or omissions. In the first case, *CPC (UK) Ltd v NRA*, the appellant company CPC (UK) Ltd was convicted inter alia of having caused water pollution contrary to s 85(1) WRA 1991 but given absolute discharges as sentences because they has shown otherwise exemplary behaviour. CPC (UK) Ltd had used a cleaning liquid which was accidentally spilled from the company premises into a nearby river. When the company discovered the spillage it informed the NRA. The accidental spillage of the cleaning fluid was due to leaking pipes, which, in turn, was a defect that had occurred when the pipes were initially installed. The defendant company had the company premises fully surveyed before they bought them but the defect had not been picked up in the survey.

---

[72] [1995] 1 AC 444.

CPC (UK) Ltd v National Rivers Authority
[1994] WL 1060329, 3 (Lord Justice Evans)

Extract from the official court transcript:

The judgment of the House of Lords [in Alphacell] is authority for two propositions relevant to the present case. First, as the learned Recorder directed the jury, the operation of the factory by the appellants on the day in question was 'capable of being a cause'. Secondly, the question whether the appellants had caused pollution on the day in question was a question of fact and commonsense, to be decided by the jury. This approach has been adopted in two more recent judgments of the Queen's Bench Divisional Court, Wrothwel Ltd. v. Yorkshire Water Authority 26 October 1983: CSE (1984) Crim. L.R.45) and National Rivers Authority v. Yorkshire Water Services Ltd. (Q.B.D. (Crown Office List)) 15 November 1993.

The court further held that the defendant's act did not have to be the sole cause of the water pollution and held CPC UK Ltd liable of having caused here the water pollution. The case, however, leaves open the question of when the defendant's act is so remote that it can no longer be considered to be a cause of the water pollution. In a similar judgment in *Attorney-General's Reference (No 1 of 1994)*[73] the courts again decided that simply operating a sewerage system that was insufficiently maintained was enough for the defendant sewerage undertaker to have caused the water pollution. The court found that running the sewerage works in an unmaintained state was an active operation.

The issue of causation was discussed again in *Wychavon District Council v National Rivers Authority*.[74] In this case, Wychavon District Council appealed against the decision of the Vale of Evesham Magistrates' Court to convict the Council of an offence of causing sewage effluent to be discharged into controlled waters contrary to s 107(1)(c) of the Water Act 1989.[75] The water pollution was caused by a storm overflow adjacent to Evesham Hospital discharging raw sewage into the River Avon because a sewage pipe had become blocked. Wychavon District Council was charged because it was the agent for the statutory sewerage undertaker, Severn Trent Water Authority, and therefore had day-to-day responsibility for running the sewage system. It took the council two days to stop the sewage.

The question to be decided by the High Court was whether in law the appellant 'caused' the pollution by failing promptly to discover the source of the discharge of sewage effluent into the River Avon and thereafter failing to clear the blockage as soon as possible. The Magistrates' Court found that the appellant had not brought about the blockage and could not be said to have caused sewage effluent to enter the river merely by, as agents for the statutory undertaker, maintaining and operating the sewer. However, the appellant caused the overflow of sewage effluent to continue by failing, within a reasonable time, to discover and prevent the sewage effluent entering controlled waters. The main issue in this case was whether in failing to act promptly the appellant had caused the continuing pollution. The High Court referred again to *Alphacell v Woodward*.

Wychavon District Council v National Rivers Authority
[1993] 1 WLR 125, 136–37 (Watkins LJ)

The offence of causing polluting matter to enter a river requires, he said, a positive act by an accused and not merely a passive looking on. On neither material day was there in the present case, before

---

[73] [1995] 1 WLR 599.   [74] [1993] Env LR 330.
[75] Which became s 85 of the Water Resources Act 1991.

the act which cleared the blockage, any positive or active operation by the Council which in any way interfered with the continuous flow of sewage effluent into the river. As a matter of law, therefore, Mr. Tillyard said, the Council cannot in any sense be said to have caused the pollution

In my judgment, the facts found by the justices are not capable of establishing that the Council caused the pollution by creating a nuisance or otherwise. There is nothing to point to the performance by the Council of either a positive or a deliberate act such as could properly be said to have brought about the flow of sewage effluent into the River Avon. There are facts which, in my opinion, could point to inactivity amounting possibly to negligence. There are others which could amount to knowingly permitting sewage effluent to be discharged into controlled waters, but the Council was not charged with that. Whether, if they had been so charged, conviction would have followed, it is not, I think, right to comment upon here.

Accordingly, I would answer the question posed in the negative and quash the conviction.

The reasoning of *Wychavon DC v NRA* was also applied in the case of *National Rivers Authority v Welsh Development Agency* [1993] Env LR 407, though on the facts the case is much more convincing than *Wychavon* as an example of a situation where the defendant was simply passive and had not engaged enough in an active act or an underlying operation that lead to an assessment that the defendant had 'caused' the water pollution. The Welsh Development Agency (WDA) bought land for development as an Industrial Estate. It leased various units of that industrial estate to various tenants. The leases contained a clause that required tenants not to discharge any effluent into an adjacent stream. One day effluent was discharged from an unidentified factory unit on the estate into the stream. The WDA had designed, built, and maintained the drainage system. The NRA brought a prosecution against the WDA inter alia for causing trade effluent to be discharged into controlled water contrary to s 107(6) of the Water Act 1989. The Magistrates found that the WDA had not caused the discharge. The NRA's appeal to the High Court failed.

In the later case of *Environment Agency (formerly National Rivers Authority) v Empress Car Company (Abertillery) Ltd*[76] the House of Lords considered the question of what it meant to 'cause' something when the defence was that a third party vandal had been the direct cause of pollution. In a wide ranging and significant judgment Lord Hoffmann made the points given in the case extract.

Environment Agency (formerly National Rivers Authority) v Empress Car Company (Abertillery) Ltd
[1999] 2 AC 22, 29–30, 32–33, 34 (Lord Hoffmann)

The courts have repeatedly said that the notion of 'causing' is one of common sense. [...]

I doubt whether the use of abstract metaphysical theory has ever had much serious support and I certainly agree that the notion of causation should not be overcomplicated. Neither, however, should it be oversimplified. In the *Alphacell* case, at p. 834, Lord Wilberforce said in similar vein:

'In my opinion, 'causing' here must be given a common sense meaning and I deprecate the introduction of refinements, such as causa causans, effective cause or novus actus. There may be difficulties where acts of third persons or natural forces are concerned ...'

The last concession was prudently made, because it is of course the causal significance of acts of third parties (as in this case) or natural forces that gives rise to almost all the problems about the notion of

[76] [1999] 2 AC 22.

'causing' and drives judges to take refuge in metaphor or Latin. I therefore propose to concentrate upon the way common sense notions of causation treat the intervention of third parties or natural forces. The principles involved are not complicated or difficult to understand, but they do in my opinion call for some explanation. It is remarkable how many cases there are under this Act in which justices have attempted to apply common sense and found themselves reversed by the Divisional Court for error of law. More guidance is, I think, necessary.

The first point to emphasise is that common sense answers to questions of causation will differ according to the purpose for which the question is asked. Questions of causation often arise for the purpose of attributing responsibility to someone, for example, so as to blame him for something which has happened or to make him guilty of an offence or liable in damages. In such cases, the answer will depend upon the rule by which responsibility is being attributed. Take, for example, the case of the man who forgets to take the radio out of his car and during the night someone breaks the quarterlight, enters the car and steals it. What caused the damage? If the thief is on trial, so that the question is whether he is criminally responsible, then obviously the answer is that he caused the damage. It is no answer for him to say that it was caused by the owner carelessly leaving the radio inside. On the other hand, the owner's wife, irritated at the third such occurrence in a year, might well say that it was his fault. In the context of an inquiry into the owner's blameworthiness under a non-legal, common sense duty to take reasonable care of one's own possessions, one would say that his carelessness caused the loss of the radio.

Not only may there be different answers to questions about causation when attributing responsibility to different people under different rules (in the above example, criminal responsibility of the thief, common sense responsibility of the owner) but there may be different answers when attributing responsibility to different people under the same rule.

[...]What, therefore, is the nature of the duty imposed by section 85(1)? Does it include responsibility for acts of third parties or natural events and, if so, for any such acts or only some of them? This is a question of statutory construction, having regard to the policy of the Act. It is immediately clear that the liability imposed by the subsection is strict: it does not require mens rea in the sense of intention or negligence. Strict liability is imposed in the interests of protecting controlled waters from pollution. [...]

Clearly, therefore, the fact that a deliberate act of a third party caused the pollution does not in itself mean that the defendant's creation of a situation in which the third party could so act did not also cause the pollution for the purposes of section 85(1).

[...]While liability under section 85(1) is strict and therefore includes liability for certain deliberate acts of third parties and (by parity of reasoning) natural events, it is not an absolute liability in the sense that all that has to be shown is that the polluting matter escaped from the defendant's land, irrespective of how this happened. It must still be possible to say that the defendant caused the pollution.

Lord Hoffmann then turned to the authorities that had considered the role of foreseeability in determining whether something had been 'caused' by the defendant.

The question is whether the defendant caused the pollution. How is foreseeability a relevant factor to consider in answering this question?

[...]

therefore, will some acts of third parties (or natural events) negative causal connection for the purposes of section 85(1) and others not?

[...]In the sense in which the concept of foreseeability is normally used, namely as an ingredient in the tort of negligence, in the form of the question: ought the defendant reasonably to have foreseen what happened, I do not think that it is relevant. Liability under section 85(1) is not based on negligence; it is strict. No one asked whether Yorkshire Water Services Ltd ought to have foreseen that someone would put iso-octanol in their sewage. Likewise in *C.P.C. (U.K.) Ltd. v. National Rivers Authority* [1994] Env. L.R. 131 the defendant operated a factory which used cleaning liquid carried through PVC piping. The piping leaked because it had been badly installed by the reputable subcontractors employed by the previous owners of the factory. The Court of Appeal held that although the defendants were unaware of the existence of the defect and 'could not be criticised for failing to discover it,' the pollution had nevertheless been caused by their operation of the factory. So the fact that the negligent installation of the pipes had been unforeseeable was no defence. I agree with Lloyd L.J. that the question is not whether the consequences ought to have been foreseen; it is whether the defendant caused the pollution. And foreseeability is not the criterion for deciding whether a person caused something or not. People often cause things which they could not have foreseen.

The true common sense distinction is, in my view, between acts and events which, although not necessarily foreseeable in the particular case, are in the generality a normal and familiar fact of life, and acts or events which are abnormal and extraordinary. Of course an act or event which is in general terms a normal fact of life may also have been foreseeable in the circumstances of the particular case, but the latter is not necessary for the purposes of liability. There is nothing extraordinary or abnormal about leaky pipes or lagoons as such: these things happen, even if the particular defendant could not reasonably have foreseen that it would happen to him. There is nothing unusual about people putting unlawful substances into the sewage system and the same, regrettably, is true about ordinary vandalism. So when these things happen, one does not say: that was an extraordinary coincidence, which negatived the causal connection between the original act of accumulating the polluting substance and its escape. In the context of section 85(1), the defendant's accumulation has still caused the pollution. On the other hand, the example I gave of the terrorist attack would be something so unusual that one would not regard the defendant's conduct as having caused the escape at all.

In applying this foreseeability test Lord Hoffmann stated that the *Alphacell* case suggested that the overflow pumps of the tank becoming blocked by leaves was nothing out of the ordinary.

Lord Hoffmann's reasoning in *Empress* raises the question of when intervening acts are deemed sufficient enough to break the chain of causation. In *Environmental Agency v Biffa Waste Services, Eurotech Environmental Ltd*[77] the High Court made clear the point that a contractor acting on behalf of another company associated with a water pollution incident may also be considered as causing water pollution under s 85 WRA 1991 (paragraph 27). In this case one of the questions examined was whether the contractor Biffa, had acted as a mere agent for Severn Trent Water Authority (STW), whose sewers became blocked and lead to the pollution of a stream. On the facts of the case the court found insufficient evidence for Biffa to have acted as an independent contractor. Biffa was merely acting upon STW's instructions and therefore no prosecution could be brought against Biffa. The further question that arose in the case concerned whether Eurotech acted as an agent for Biffa, in helping to tanker away sewage and thus whether Biffa could be held vicariously liable for Eurotech's contribution to prolonging the water pollution. This was denied on the facts of the case (paragraph 30). The reasoning of *Empress* was further affirmed in *Environment Agency v Brock PLC*[78], in which the court found Brock liable for having caused water pollution by having done something to cause a leak, that was the pumping of leachate from a landfill site between different containers, which, once a leak developed, lead to the pollution of a nearby stream. The failure of the rubber seal in the pumping equipment was not held to be an extraordinary occurrence.

The offence of 'knowingly permitting' under Regulation 38 in connection with Regulation 12 of the Environmental Permitting (England and Wales) Regulations 2010 is more limited in scope than the offence of 'causing' a water discharge or a ground water activity. 'Knowingly permitting' covers

---

[77] [2006] EWHC 1102 (Admin).   [78] [1998] Env LR 607.

situations where the defendant may have been less active than is required for the offence of 'causing' water pollution. For instance, in *Wychavon District Council v the NRA*, the defendant could also have been charged with the offence of 'knowingly permitting' pollution once they were aware that pollution was occurring. The key issue in relation to the old s 85 'knowingly permitting' offence is what level of knowledge was required in order to commit the offence. In *Schulmans Incorporated Ltd v National Rivers Authority*,[79] constructive knowledge was held to be sufficient.

Finally, it should be noted that Regulation 38(6) EPRs 2010 replicates the former s 217(3) WRA 1991. It sheds light on the question of how intervening acts of third parties should be considered in terms of assessing whether a defendant has caused the water pollution. Regulation 38(6) introduces concurrent liability and provides that the intervening act of a third party does not nullify the criminal liability of a defendant who may still have been considered to have caused water pollution. Thus, in *Express Ltd v Environment Agency*,[80] a dairy owner was successfully prosecuted under the former s 217(3) WRA 1993 provision, though his only contribution to the water pollution was that he had allowed his premises to be used for cream to be transferred from an outside supplier to one of his customers. An accident occurred during one of these transfers leading to the pollution of a nearby brook through the spillage of cream. The dairy owner was still held liable because he had also failed to carry out a risk assessment and to ensure a safe system of transferring the cream.

Defences

It it has been noted here, and in the Introduction to Part IV, there are various defences to the offences set out in Regulation 38 EPRs 2010. In particular, Regulation 40 states that:

> It is a defence for a person charged with an offence under regulation 38(1), (2) or (3) to prove that the acts alleged to constitute the contravention were done in an emergency in order to avoid danger to human health in a case where—
>
> (a) the person took all such steps as were reasonably practicable in the circumstances for minimising pollution; and
>
> (b) particulars of the acts were furnished to the regulator as soon as reasonably practicable after they were done.

This bears a certain similarity to s 89(1) of the Water Resources Act, which allowed a defence in certain circumstances where the entry was 'caused [...] in an emergency in order to avoid danger to life or health'. Section 89(1) has been judicially considered in the *Express Ltd v Environment Agency* case. The wording of the two defences is different but the judicial approach in *Express Dairies* is interesting to note, particularly how Hale LJ considers the defence within the wide context of s 85(1). While the subject matter is similar to that in the *Express* case discussed already, the facts are very different.

Express Ltd (t/a Express Dairies Distribution) v Environment Agency
[2003] EWHC 448 (Admin) paras 5, 17–19, 20–25 (Hale LJ)

> The facts as found by the Justices were as follows, and I quote from paragraph 2 of the stated case:
>
> 'i) The vehicle registration number T822 KNN was coupled to a tanker trailer T520 that contained milk and was being used by Express Dairies Distribution on 1st February 2000 in the course of its business.

---

[79] [1993] Env LR D 1.   [80] [2005] Env LR 7.

ii) The vehicle was driven by Mr Kevin Pinches, an employee of Express Limited, on the M5 southbound.

iii) The trailer was built to the required British Standard but had an extra foot valve fitted to it, which exceeded the standard. The trailer was properly maintained and had passed the necessary tests.

iv) As a result of a tyre blow out on the trailer, part of the spray suppression system became detached hitting the under-run protection barrier (a legal requirement). The barrier became detached and sheared the delivery pipe, causing approximately 4,000 litres of milk to escape from the forward compartment of the milk tank.

v) Mr Pinches pulled on to the hard shoulder of the M5 southbound, just north of junction 4, where he stopped. At that point there are two drains approximately 100 metres apart which have no catch pit and feed into a culverted section of Battlefield Brook, controlled water within the meaning of the Water Resources Act 1991.

vi) The emergency services were alerted, including the Environment Agency, by the driver, who contacted his depot for advice and then operated the foot valve to stem the flow of escaping milk. The emergency services and the Environment Agency attended the scene.

ii) The milk from the tank entered Battlefield Brook and subsequently flowed to the pond at Silverdale.

viii) The Environment Agency deployed aerators and started aeration at approximately 6.00 pm in the pond at Silverdale.'

[...]The argument, as presented in the skeleton argument, was that the 'discharge' occurred in an emergency where there was a danger to life or health. The damage to the tanker constituted an emergency and the driver's response to that emergency caused the 'discharge'. It would have been life threatening to remain on the motorway with such an escape of milk, and hence the defence should apply.

Mr Gordon [for Express Dairies] accepts that the European Convention on Human Rights allows for offences of strict liability without any intent or negligence: see Salabiaku v France (1988) 13 EHRR 379, paragraph 27. But to do so, the provision must pursue a legitimate aim, be rationally connected to and proportionate to that aim, and he cites the well known case of de Freitas v Permanent Secretary of Ministry of Agriculture Fisheries, Lands and Housing [1999] 1 AC 69, PC, which adopted the test of proportionality derived from Canadian jurisprudence and applied in both South Africa and Zimbabwe at page 80G. He accepts that the offence under consideration here does pursue a legitimate aim.

He argues, however, that Parliament did recognise that blameworthiness might indeed be relevant to whether a person should ultimately be convicted of that offence, in other words that the lack of it could in some circumstances be a defence. On the Justices' construction, if a person deliberately brings about a discharge in order to save life, he will have a defence, whereas if he innocently brings about a discharge in circumstances where the discharge has begun but he is acting so as to avoid a danger to life or health, he will not, and that, he argues, might be seen as discriminatory for the purposes of Article 14. Thus he uses that to bolster his argument that if section 89(1) is capable of bearing the meaning contended for, it should be so interpreted.

He recognised in the oral argument before us that his written argument on section 89 suffered from the egregious entry of the concept of 'discharge'. As the offence with which we are concerned is the offence of causing an entry, the defence with which we are concerned, equally, is only concerned with causing an entry and not with the discharge which may or may not have taken place. The same problem may be said to affect the Justices' reasons under paragraph 6(iii) below, where they quote section 89:

'We find that this section is limited to situations in which the discharge occurs to preserve life or health, as in the example of the aeroplane which discharges fuel before making an emergency landing and so is not applicable to this case as the discharge was the result of the incident'.

Discharge is not involved in the offence under discussion. It is not, therefore, involved in the defence under discussion. We are not, therefore, concerned with why the milk was discharged from the tanker. The question is whether 'the entry is caused ... in an emergency in order to avoid danger to life or health'.

It is argued on behalf of the respondent that there has to be a purposive connection between causing the entry and the avoidance of danger to life or health, that is the entry has to be caused in order to save life or health. The words 'in order to' clearly do import a purpose, but that begs the question: at which point in the chain of causation of entry does the question why a particular act was being done have to be asked? If it is asked at the beginning of the chain, clearly the blow out was not caused in order to avoid danger to life or health. But the last element in the chain of causation, pulling into the side of the road where these drains into the brook happen to be, could well be said to have been for that very purpose.

It is pointed out for the respondents that there was no evidence of the driver's intention. He did not give evidence and we do not know whether that is why he pulled over onto the hard shoulder, but it is clear from the Justices' reasoning that they were content to assume that that was why he did so, and for the purpose of considering this argument, we similarly are prepared to make that assumption.

Causing entry is a much broader concept than discharging. As Lord Hoffman said, also in the Empress case, answers to questions of causation depend on why the question is being asked. In this case, it is being asked in order to provide a defence to an otherwise absolute offence. The context is that Parliament recognised that some of those acting in an emergency should be excused.

In my judgment, therefore, one is entitled to focus upon the chain of causation and ask whether the act which actually caused the entry was done in an emergency in order to save life or health. In this case, at least on the assumed facts, it clearly was. In other words, in my judgment, the facts of this case do fit within the language of the defence provided in section 89(1)(a) without the need for resort to the Human Rights Act as an aid to interpretation.

Note also the potential role of the Human Rights Act 1998 in the arguments of this case.

FURTHER READING AND QUESTIONS

1. For a discussion of the constructive knowledge requirement in the criminal water pollution control offence of 'knowingly permitting' a water discharge or groundwater activity, see David Wilkinson, 'Causing and Knowingly Permitting Pollution Offences: A Review' (1993) 4(1) Water Law 25.

2. See also the case *The Queen v RL, JF* [2008] EWCA Crim 1970, in which the Criminal Division of the Court of Appeal held that a prosecution for the s 85 WRA 1991 offence of causing water pollution could be brought not just against individuals, but also against unincorporated associations, in the particular case a golf club (paras 35–37).

3. The following cases address principles for the imposition of sanctions in the case of water pollution offences. The courts will take into account the seriousness of the offence, as well as aggravating and mitigating features (*R v Thames Water Utilities* [2010] Env LR 34, 601). Specific principles are set out in *R v Anglian Water Services Ltd* [2003] EWCA Crim 2243. Given the wide

definition of causation developed in the case law discussed here the courts have started to consider the question of 'culpability' when deciding on sanctions to be imposed for the strict liability offence of causing water pollution. In the case of *Dwr Cymru Cyfyngeoig v Flintshire Magistrates' Court* [2009] EWHC 2679, an unforeseen failure of a bearing in a motor operating parts of a sewerage treatment machinery lead to a discharge of sewage effluent in breach of consent conditions into the River Dee. Welsh Water's conviction of having caused the water pollution contrary to s 85 stood, but the imposition of a £2,500 fine was appealed on the grounds that given their limited culpability they should only have received an absolute or conditional discharge. The High Court refused the application holding that the magistrates had found limited rather than no culpability on the facts, and were therefore entitled to impose a small fine.

4 THE REGULATION OF DRINKING WATER AND WATER QUANTITY

Sections 2 and 3 have provided an overview of the most significant aspects of water quality regulation. They are not the only aspects of water regulation however, and this final section briefly discusses other regulatory regimes that touch on water quality and those that deal with water abstractions (concerning issues of water quantity). These different regimes also highlight the challenges involved in mapping legal space onto ecological space.

4.1 THE REGULATION OF THE SUPPLY OF DRINKING WATER IN ENGLAND AND WALES

Finally, the regulation of water quality through environmental objectives set through the WFD, national implementation through environmental permitting and the enforcement of water pollution control through criminal offences, affects the quality of both surface and groundwater bodies. But it is also necessary to discuss specific legal rules that complement this regulatory regime and seek to ensure that water is safe to drink. Their main anthropocentric purpose is to protect public health. The supply of drinking water in England and Wales is subject to legal obligations imposed by the EU Drinking Water Quality Directive (98/83/EC).[81] Article 1 of the Directive provides:

Objective

1. This Directive concerns the quality of water intended for human consumption.

2. The objective of this Directive shall be to protect human health from the adverse effects of any contamination of water intended for human consumption by ensuring that it is wholesome and clean.

According to Article 5 in connection with Annex I to the Directive these standards are further specified in the Directive for tap water with reference to forty-eight microbiological, chemical, and organoleptic parameters, the latter addressing colour, taste, and odour of drinking water. The Directive draws on World Health Organisation (WHO) guidelines for the setting of standards for

---

[81] [1998] OJ L 330/32.

drinking water quality. Article 7 of the Directive requires Member States to put in place programmes, including sampling, for the monitoring of the quality of water intended for human consumption. Moreover, Article 13 of the Directive requires Member States to ensure that consumers have adequate and up-to-date information on the quality of their drinking water. Article 9 of the Directive allows Member States to derogate from the standards for drinking water quality set by the Directive, but if they do so Member States have to set a maximum value to which derogated standards for their drinking water have to adhere. Moreover, this power for Member States is limited by the requirement that the lower standards must not constitute a potential danger to human health and there must be no other reasonable means available for maintaining the supply of drinking water in a particular area. Member States' power to derogate is also further limited by the fact that derogations shall be as short as possible and shall normally not last for more than three years. The purpose of the derogations is not to enable Member States to maintain drinking water quality standards lower than those prescribed in the Directive for the whole of the EU, but to gain time in order to put measures into place that will bring national drinking water quality up to EU standards. Member States' implementation efforts are also monitored by the Commission through reports on national drinking water quality that Member States have to provide to the Commission every three years (Article 13(3) Directive 98/83/EC).

The Drinking Water Quality Directive (98/83/EC) is implemented in the UK through provisions in the Water Industry Act (WIA) 1991 and secondary legislation. Section 67 WIA 1991 implements Article 1 of the Directive, which specifies that drinking water supplied in the EU must be 'wholesome'. This obligation is further defined in the Water Supply (Water Quality) Regulations 2000.[82] Regulation 27 of the Water Supply (Water Quality) Regulations 2000 (Amendment) Regulations 2007[83] impose further legal obligations on companies supplying drinking water by requiring them to use risk assessments in order to detect potential public health problems.

The Drinking Water Inspectorate (DWI) was established in 1990 to monitor water safety and quality. Section 70 of the WIA 1991 provides for a criminal offence of supplying water that is 'unfit for human consumption', with prosecutions to be brought by the Director of Public Prosecutions or the Secretary of State, whose prosecution powers have been delegated to the Chief Inspector of the Drinking Water Inspectorate. Section 70 WIA has been interpreted widely in *R v Yorkshire Water Services Ltd*,[84] which held that the offence can be made out simply by discolouration of the water, and hence without bacteriological contamination. Criminal offences in relation to the supply of drinking water 'unfit' for human consumption overlap with powers of prosecution under public nuisance provisions (see, for example, *R v South West Water Authority* [1991] LMELR 65).

4.2 THE REGULATION OF WATER QUANTITY

As indicated in the depiction of the natural water cycle at the beginning of the chapter, the protection of water quality and quantity are closely connected. A reduction in the quantity of water available often leads to a higher concentration of pollutants in a particular water course. The risk of flooding as well as a depletion of water bodies has increased due to man-made climate change. Droughts are no longer just an issue for Southern-Mediterranean countries in the EU, but also for Northern countries[85], including the UK, in particular its south east region.[86] The UK has thus only more recently

---

[82] SI 2000/3184.   [83] SI 2007/2734.   [84] [2002] Env LR 18.

[85] For instance, the Czech Republic, France, and Belgium have reported water scarcity problems. See the Third Follow-up Report to the Communication on water scarcity and droughts in the European Union, COM (2007) 414 final, at: <http://eur-lex.europa.eu/LexUriServ.do?uri=COM:2011:0133:FIN:EN:PDF>.

[86] See <http://www.defra.gov.uk/news/2011/05/20/water-companies-drier-climate/> for information about water companies' climate change adaptation reports, which outline actions—also in the context of their Water Resource

further developed statutory provisions that regulate the abstraction of water. This final section on the regulation of water abstraction and flooding also illustrates that the environmentalist policy discourse of bioregionalism is limited in framing water pollution law because climate change requires regulatory responses that transcend the natural space of the river basin.

Elements of the UK statutory regime dealing with water abstraction are contained in Part I of the Water Act 2003. In order to tackle water scarcity the Water Act (WA) 2003 introduces a range of new legal provisions. First, the WA 2003 places new general duties upon a range of participants in water regulation that seek to promote sustainable use of water resources. Second, the WA 2003 provides for new water resource planning tools, in particular through water resource management plans and drought plans. Third, the Act alters the balance of power between abstractors and regulatory authorities, by strengthening the role of the EA, the Secretary of State heading DEFRA, and the Welsh Assembly in controlling water abstraction through a number of specific provisions. Fourth, the WA 2003 strengthens the regulatory regime in relation to water abstraction through enhanced enforcement powers and penalties.

Section 72 WA 2003 amends section 6, so as to include in this duty a duty imposed upon the Environment Agency for England and Wales to secure the efficient use of water resources. Section 81 WA 2003 places a new duty on the Secretary of State and the Welsh Assembly to take appropriate steps to encourage water conservation. Moreover section 82 WA 2003 now imposes a very wide duty upon water undertakers to further water conservation when formulating or considering any proposals relating to any of their functions. Water conservation is further promoted through a new duty imposed upon all public authorities under section 83 WA 2003[87] to at least take into account, where relevant, the desirability of conserving water supplied to premises. Again the scope of this duty is drawn widely, applying to both their actual use of water but also to the exercise of their functions where these have an impact on water use. This may be relevant, for instance, for the procurement policies of local authorities as well as their housing and land use planning functions.

The general duties set out here, however, will only be effective if regulators can draw on regulatory tools that enable the implementation of these duties. Section 62 of the WA 2003 provides for water resource management plans and drought plans. These water resource management plans should ensure that water companies plan for demand for water also in the medium and long term and address the question of how this demand can be met. The Secretary of State or the Welsh Assembly can issue directions in relation to matters that the plan must address. Section 63 WA 2003 requires water undertakers to also develop drought plans. Drought plans must specify how water undertakers will continue to supply sufficient wholesome water during droughts while avoiding the use of drought orders or drought permits.[88] These powers for water resource planning are intended to be further strengthened through the Draft Water Bill 2012. Clause 24 of the Bill proposes an amendment of the relevant sections of the WIA 1991, so that drought plans would have to be developed in a five yearly cycle that aligns with the cycle of water resource management plans to be prepared by water companies (that is, undertakers). Clause 24 also contains a provision that would empower the Secretary of

Management Planning—for addressing anticipated increased water scarcity in the UK. Section 61 of the Climate Change Act 2008 provides a power for the Secretary of State heading DEFRA to direct water companies to prepare climate change adaptation reports.

[87] The WA 2003 provides for a wide statutory definition of public authority, including government departments (s 83(2)(b)), local authorities (s 83(2)(d)), and 'any other public body of any description' (s 83(2)(g)).

[88] Water companies can currently apply to the EA for a drought permit in the case of serious shortages of water supply due to exceptionally low rainfall. Applications for drought orders can be made in similar circumstances to the Secretary of State or the Welsh National Assembly. The effect of drought permits and orders is to allow a water company to compensate for water shortages through greater abstraction of water from existing or additional sources (Chapter 3 of Part 2 of the Water Resources Act 1991).

State in relation to water undertakers in England (and the Welsh Minister in respect of undertakers in Wales) to amend the time frame for water resource management plans through secondary legislation. Apart from these important water resource planning tools the WA 2003, however, also strengthens regulators' specific powers' in relation to abstraction.

Section 62 of the Water Act 2003 provides powers for the EA to control abstraction through much more specific provisions in abstraction licences. According to s 19(4) WA 2003, every new abstraction licence has to include the dates on which it takes effect and expires, but the WA 2003 stopped short of specifying a general length for abstraction licences. Hence, the EA will determine the duration of abstraction licences on a case-by-case basis also taking into account local circumstances. Three criteria will be considered in the case of applications for the renewal of abstraction licences: first, whether water resources in the area are sustainable and that the abstraction should not create adverse environmental impacts; second, that the water abstraction is really necessary; and, third, that there is efficient use of the abstracted water.[89] In addition, the preservation of scarce water resources is facilitated through the requirement that full licences[90] must state, and thus limit, the quantity of water authorized for abstraction. Abstraction licences do not confer absolute rights to water abstraction. The WA 2003 enables to manage abstraction flexibly. Section 10 WA 2003 provides a power for the Secretary of State for England and for the Welsh National Assembly to revoke orders made under s 33 of the WRA 1991 that grant rights to abstract water from inland waters or underground strata,[91] or orders made under local and private Acts, which provided exemptions from restrictions to abstract water. Finally, legal powers in relation to water abstraction have been further strengthened in the WA 2003 through a range of enforcement powers as well as stricter penalties that the new Environment Agency can deploy and new statutory rights of action.

Section 25 WA 2003 grants specific powers to the EA to revoke[92] or vary any abstraction licence, with a right of appeal to the Secretary of State for abstractors. The WA 2003 reduces the rights of compensation for existing abstraction licence holders in case the EA revokes or varies its licence. For licences that are revoked or varied and that have not been used for four years, s 25 of the WA 2003 removes the right to compensation. Section 27 WA 2003 also removes a right to compensation, in certain circumstances, for the revocation or variation of existing licenses where the abstraction of water under the licence is causing serious damage to the environment. In the case of new licences issued after the coming into force of section 19[93] of the WA 2003 there is no longer an entitlement to compensation if the licence variation occurred for the purpose of protecting water availability in the source of supply to which the licence relates (s 25(3)(a)).

4.3 REGULATING FLOODING

Climate change is also leading to stark fluctuations in water quantity through flooding. The Floods Directive 2007/60/EC[94] deals specifically with the assessment and management of flood risks. Article 4 requires Member States to carry out a preliminary assessment by 2011 in order to identify the risk of flooding. Member States also have to draw up flood risk maps by 2013. These maps must detail the

[89] Environment Agency, Managing Water Abstraction, June 2010, at: <http://cdn.environment-agency.gov.uk/geho0310bsbh-e-e.pdf>,12.

[90] This is only a discretionary power, not a requirement for the EA in the case of temporary or transfer abstraction licences.

[91] As defined in s 221(1) WRA 1991.

[92] It is unlikely, however, that the Environment Agency for England and Wales would revoke abstraction licences that are held for valid contingency planning purposes, referred to as 'sleeper licences' (Explanatory Notes to the Water Act 2003, 12).

[93] Which makes general provisions about form, contents and effects of water abstraction licences.

[94] Directive 2007/60/EC of the European Parliament and of the Council of 23 October 2007, on the assessment and management of flood risks, OJ L 277/27.

zones that are at risk of flooding. By 2015 flood risk management plans have to be set up (Article 7). According to Article 7(3) of the EU Floods Directive, the environmental objectives of the WFD have to be taken into account when flood risk management plans and coastal erosion plans are drawn up. The UK will seek to align the planning processes under the EU Floods Directive and the WFD.[95] The EU Floods Directive will be implemented also through Catchment Flood Management Plans, which are prepared by the EA, and Shoreline Management Plans, which are developed by local coastal authorities and the EA. It is intended that these Flood and Shoreline Management Plans can help to achieve the objectives of river basin management plans, rather than lower the status of a water body.[96]

Key elements of the regulatory regime in relation to preventing and dealing with flooding in England and Wales are contained in Part I of the Flood and Water Management Act 2010.[97] The Act also amends a number of existing provisions, for instance in the WRA 1991 in relation to flood management. The Act provides for legal obligations in response to various UK government and Welsh Assembly policy initiatives in relation to the recent severe floods in the UK, such as those in summer 2007.[98] The Act provides for adaptation to climate change by giving the EA a strategic oversight role in the management of flood and coastal erosion risks in England. These functions are exercised in Wales by the Welsh Ministers. The Act also requires county councils in England and local authorities in Wales to prepare and implement strategies in order to manage risks of flooding arising from ground, surface, and other water courses in their area.[99]

FURTHER READING AND QUESTIONS

1. While statutory provisions are nowadays key to water resource management, access to water can also be based on riparian rights as defined by the common law. Those who own land adjoining a river have the right to the 'ordinary use of water flowing past their land' (*Miner v Gilmour* [1858] XII Moore PC 131, 862, 870). For a further discussion, see Susan Wolf and Neil Stanley (eds) *Wolf and Stanley on Environmental Law*, 5th edition (2011 Routledge) 178–79. William Howarth and Simon Jackson, *Wisdom's of Law of Watercourses* (6th edn, Sweet & Maxwell 2011).

2. Do you think that water resource management plans are too narrow in scope and should be integrated into a wider conception of natural resource management plans that address land use, the protection of soil quality, and nature conservation?

---

5 CONCLUSION

This chapter has highlighted the significance of a developing environmental policy discourse that seeks to map legal rules, and more widely regulatory space, onto natural spaces. In the case of water

---

[95] Environment Agency, 'Water for Life and Livelihoods: River Basin Management Plan, Anglian River Basin District, (2009) 30.

[96] Ibid, 7.

[97] The Act received Royal Assent on 8 April 2010. It does not apply to Northern Ireland and most of the provisions of the Act do not apply to Scotland.

[98] Such as 'Future Water: the Government's Water Strategy for England', February 2008, at: <http://www.defra.gov.uk/publications/2011/06/16/pb13562-future-water/>. 'Making Space for Water: Taking Forward a New Government Strategy for Flood and Coastal Erosion Risk Management in England, March 2005, at: <http://archive.defra.gov.uk/environment/flooding/policy/strategy/index.htm> and the Government's Response to Sir Michael Pitt's Review of the Summer 2007 Floods, December 2008, at: <http://www.defra.gov.uk/environment/flooding/>.

[99] Explanatory Notes on the Act, compiled by DEFRA, 1.

pollution control law this means that the river basin is considered to be the main spatial category through which legal regulation is to be delivered. Part of this environmental policy discourse is also a developing concept of ecological federalism. While not very clearly defined, ecological federalism, in broad terms, seeks to address the question at which levels regulatory power should best be allocated in multi-level governance regimes in order to achieve effective environmental regulation, including water regulation. This chapter provided a critical perspective on this policy discourse through reference to a critical legal geography perspective, which questions the idea of natural space as pre-given and apolitical, and instead considers our ideas about what constitutes a natural space as constructed through specific economic and political relations. The chapter discussed the centrality of the river basin to the regulatory regime of the EU WFD and highlighted how the text of the Directive and the EA's implementation practices construct spatial categories above and below the scale of the river basin, by amalgamating smaller river basins into larger units and, more importantly in the UK, by focusing on the catchment level for implementing the WFD. The chapter then discussed how the environmental objectives of the WFD, as further specified in river basin management plans, are sought to be realized through programmes of measures spelt out in river basin management plans, and most importantly in England through environmental permitting of water discharge and ground water activities by the EA. Environmental permitting illustrates that natural spatial categories that are mobilized in water pollution control are mediated through political spaces, in particular the sphere of influence of public administrators in exercising discretionary powers to set conditions in relation to the discharge of water pollutants in environmental permits.

AIR POLLUTION AND
CLIMATE CHANGE

Various anthropogenic, and largely industrial, emissions into the air and atmosphere cause or contribute to a host of environmental problems, from local smog and acid rain to ozone depletion and climate change. However, the scientific understanding of these problems is complex and in a state of ongoing development—these problems are caused by natural as well as man-derived sources, and they involve pollutants travelling distances on prevailing winds as well as interacting unpredictably in the atmosphere. Like the science of air pollution issues, the law relating to these problems is complex and developing. This complicated legal picture exists both within and across jurisdictions, since air pollution environmental problems can be local but also related to the transboundary movements of pollutants, or the cumulative quantity of air pollutants internationally. Human activity in one part of the world can affect the environment and create problems elsewhere. Thus, a broad and overlapping patchwork of regulation exists to deal with air emissions, and this poses a challenge for legal analysis, particularly in evaluating how effectively different elements of the regulatory mix are operating in responding to air pollution problems.

In this chapter, 'air pollution' will be the general description used for those *anthropogenic* emissions into air that cause environmental problems, directly or indirectly. Such problems include the local and transboundary effects of pollutants on ambient air quality, climate change, and ozone depletion (the former two problems being the focus of this chapter). It should be noted that it is not only air emissions but also other human activity that contributes to these problems. A notable example of this, with respect to climate change, is change in land use (particularly tropical deforestation). Such activity contributes to air pollution indirectly, by removing a pre-existing 'sink' for greenhouse gas (GHG) emissions. However, the focus of the chapter is on emissions into the air and atmosphere from human activities, and how these are regulated or otherwise relevant to legal analysis. While this legal focus constructs a media-specific definition of the environment, this has been the approach of various regulatory regimes to date. It does however raise questions about what is the ideal regulatory architecture for dealing with air pollution problems.

Furthermore, particular understandings of environmental problems in turn determine the nature and possibilities of regulation that applies to them. How environmental problems—including air pollution problems—are constructed and understood is thus partly seen through the regulatory options adopted for dealing with them. This premise informs the structure of the chapter, which covers two categories of problems caused by anthropogenic air emissions—ambient air quality concerns and climate change[1]—and explores the legal and regulatory responses to these two environmental problems.

Having said that, 'air pollution' problems do not fit into a neat box. The edges of this topic are porous, reflecting Dryzek's point in Chapter 2 about the systemic complexity of environmental problems.[2] For example, regulation responding to ozone layer depletion has consequences for the global climate system and thus also for climate change regulation (this is particularly because the use of products encouraged to avoid ozone depletion in turn contributes to climate change effects); at the same time, ongoing pressures of climate change are raising new regulatory issues for protecting the ozone layer.[3] More broadly, air pollution problems are connected, and feed in, to wider systemic environmental processes and effects. This is illustrated by the tropical deforestation example already mentioned—climate change is caused by systemic climatic processes and responses, even if increased GHG emissions into the atmosphere are a primary cause. Accordingly, the law that relates to air pollution not only interconnects across the sections of this chapter but also with the law in other chapters of this book, including the regulation of water quality (Chapter 14), the integrated pollution prevention and control regime (Chapter 17), and planning and land use control (Chapter 18 and Part V generally). However, this legal complexity is not pure disorganization and reactivity; it reflects the nature of environmental problems and is an inevitable characteristic of environmental law. Intersections between and across legal regimes will be noted throughout the chapter, but as you go through the material for this and also for other topics, you should reflect on how coherent and complete these legal connections are, or might be.

UK law relating to air pollution, with a focus on English law, is introduced and structured in three sections in this chapter. Section 1 sets out the overarching themes of this area of law—this includes background on key air pollutants and guiding themes that characterize their regulation, as well as the challenges that a lawyer faces in making sense of air pollution as a UK 'environmental law' problem. Sections 2 and 3 map air pollution law by reference to two environmental problems that both shape and are also shaped by this area of law—ambient air quality and climate change. The chapter concludes by highlighting the main legal issues arising from the regulatory approaches to air pollution problems examined in the chapter, including the links between them and to other legal areas, and reflects on the most pressing questions and challenges that air pollution law poses for an environmental lawyer.

1 OVERARCHING THEMES

This section introduces some overarching themes that characterize air pollution law. These give background and set out recurring issues to keep in mind as you examine the different regulatory approaches to particular air pollution problems in the sections that follow.

1.1 ANTHROPOCENTRISM

Not only are environmental air pollution problems anthropogenic—in that they are caused by human activity—but the effects of air pollution on human health and social stability are key drivers for ambitious and broad regulatory action in this field of environmental law. From London's 1952 killer smog,

---

[1] Note that ozone layer depletion is not covered in detail in this chapter, but might be subject to a similar analysis.

[2] Section 2.2 of Chapter 2.

[3] World Meteorological Organisation, Global Ozone and Research Monitoring Project, *Scientific Assessment of Ozone Depletion: 2010* (Report No 52, Pursuant to Art 6 of the Montreal Protocol on Substances that Deplete the Ozone Layer).

which resulted in the death of thousands of people from respiratory illnesses, to the threats of sea level rises from climate change that could render some parts of urban environments uninhabitable, there is considerable motivation for action in regulating air pollution issues, which comes from the human instinct to survive and to preserve existing communities. Thus, as a result of the 1952 smog episode, the UK's Clean Air Acts of 1956 and 1958 were passed to restrict, and in some cases ban, the production of smoke, grit, and dust from various commercial, industrial, and domestic activities. Smog is caused by fog and smoke particles combining (smoke being caused largely by industrial activities as well as domestic fires), and it causes serious damage to human health, particularly since harmful pollutants such as sulphur dioxide (SO_2) and carbon monoxide (CO) are trapped in the area of fog and not dispersed by winds. Similarly, in relation to rising sea levels caused by climate change, ongoing rounds of negotiation under the UN Framework Convention on Climate Change (discussed in Section 3) interweave with scientific and journalistic reports concerning the impact of global warming on coastline communities, agitating for further action to protect threatened communities.

However, anthropocentrism cuts both ways in regulating air pollution. Human self-focus not only provokes efforts to tackle air pollution problems, but it also presents challenges for their regulation. Air pollution is a classic example of our propensity as 'independent rational, free-enterprisers' to 'foul our own nest'. Hardin thus explained the 'reverse' tragedy of the commons, as set out in Chapter 2.[4] Unregulated economic behaviour, in a socially stable environment, tends towards individual gain at the expense of collective resources. In this way, industry has (had) to be given very good reasons, such as serious and immediate health consequences, not to emit pollutants into the un-owned air in the course of its productive activity.

Added to this, there is a public perception problem with air pollution. Our focus on air pollution problems is not only self-centred but also blinkered. Historically, we have not worried about air pollution until we can really see it, or its effects, which means that regulation to date has been largely reactive and *ad hoc* in its development. This public perception problem is due to the fact that air pollution problems are often invisible in the air around us, particularly as they build up or as we live within them. In fact, the solution to some air pollution problems has been to *make them* invisible and hope that the problems go away. This occurred in the UK, between the 1930s and the 1970s, when a key and successful strategy used to clean up local air quality was the widespread introduction of taller chimneystacks for industrial installations, including power stations. Taller chimneys allowed pollution dispersal at higher levels in the atmosphere beyond the local vicinity of the polluting installation, and led to considerable improvement in (local) UK air quality.[5] However, the result was disastrous for environments further afield to which the industrial air emissions were carried. One of the most famous examples of this was the German and Scandinavian 'forest death' and poisoning of lakes that occurred in the 1960s and 1970s, which were partly caused by SO_2 emissions from UK coal-fired power stations being carried by prevailing winds to mainland Europe and reacting in the atmosphere to cause acid rain, which destroys plant life as well as the ecology of surface waters.[6]

The limits of human sight are matched by those of our foresight and imagination. An ongoing challenge, particularly for climate change regulation, is the reluctance of individuals, and particularly political processes, to act in relation to environmental problems that will be borne by future generations or even by us later in our own generation. There are many reasons for this, notably concern over economic stultification and disadvantage, as well as scientific uncertainty (and well-lobbied

---

[4] Section 2.1 of Chapter 2.

[5] This strategy was partly in response to the case of *Manchester Corp v Farnworth* [1930] AC 171 (HL). See Mark Wilde, 'Best Available Techniques (BAT) and Coal-Fired Power Stations: Can the Energy Gap be Plugged Without Increasing Emissions' (2007) 20 JEL 87, 91–93.

[6] OECD, *The OECD Programme on Long-range Transport of Air Pollutants—Measurements and Findings* (Organisation for Economic Co-operation and Development, Paris, 1977).

scepticism about scientific evidence), but there is a human story too. Quite simply, we are not very good at imagining future problems to fix, or putting the interests of our future selves or descendants before our own perceived present interests. For this reason, environmental ethicists impress the importance of the principle of inter-generational equity in formulating environmental policy and regulation.[7]

A related challenge to air pollution regulation posed by human self-focus arises from the fact that our air polluting activities impact on people in other parts of the world. Particularly when air-polluting activities in the UK have deleterious impacts on the environments of communities in other countries, and particularly on those in developing countries, considerations of ethics again arise. These include concerns of *intra*-generational equity, as it applies across communities. On one view, understanding such far-reaching environmental effects builds the case for action with respect to air polluting activities—such considerations were relevant in formulating the Convention on Long-Range Transboundary Air Pollution, considered in Section 2.2. However, the geographical distance between our polluting activities in the UK and their effects elsewhere also diminishes incentives for us, as an individual state and as a nation of individuals, to take action. This problem is well demonstrated by the seemingly intractable negotiations to control international GHG emissions under the UN Framework Convention on Climate Change.[8]

If nothing else, the international extent of the effects of air pollution highlights the *polycentricity* of air pollution problems.[9] For example, consider that global warming is driven by Western industrialization, which scientific evidence now indicates to be a likely cause of various environmentally damaging climate effects internationally (such as sea level rises and areas of prolonged drought, which have particularly adverse impacts in many developing countries).[10] This adds weight to the ethical argument that the UK has an obligation to contribute to international efforts to minimize GHG emissions, and so to organize UK regulatory efforts accordingly.[11] But it also implicates issues of international aid, international trade, economic sovereignty of nations, and socio-political governance in other countries in which we have no direct political involvement.[12] Climate change regulation, in particular, is very complicated to design, amend, defend, and implement, for all of these reasons.

1.2 THE AIR POLLUTION PROBLEM

Before considering further thematic issues that characterize UK air pollution law, this section sets out the main polluting air emissions, as well as their primary sources and environmental effects. It is important to note that there are no straightforward linear relationships between polluting air emissions and the environmental problems they cause, for at least two reasons. First, the causal chain between emissions and environmental problems is unpredictable. Polluting emissions, once in the atmosphere, move with prevailing winds and react with other elements in the atmosphere

---

[7] See Section 1.1 of Chapter 11.

[8] Daniel Bodansky, 'The Copenhagen Climate Change Conference: A Post-Mortem' (2010) 104 AJIL 230.

[9] See Section 2.1 of Chapter 2.

[10] Intergovernmental Panel on Climate Change, *Climate Change 2007: Synthesis Report—Contribution of Working Groups I, II and III to the Fourth Assessment Report of the Intergovernmental Panel on Climate Change* (IPCC, Geneva) 5–6. The report concluded that anthropogenic GHG emissions were very likely to have caused observed global average temperature increases, with other climate effects also likely caused according to varying degrees of probability (for example, sea level rises very likely, changes in wind patterns likely, increased risk of heat waves and drought more likely than not).

[11] See the Harris extract in Section 1.5.

[12] International law provides the main legal forum in which political interaction on environmental issues between states takes place, with international trade pressures and diplomacy providing other avenues. See further, Chapter 5. It remains to be seen whether increasing concern over this international environmental problem will increase political inter-involvement between nation-states.

and with each other, and do so in largely untraceable patterns, creating challenges in pinpointing precisely human causes for environmentally polluting effects. Second, some pollutants contribute to more than one environmental problem—for example, chlorofluorocarbons are both GHGs and ozone-depleting substances.[13] Legally however, they are regulated only as the latter. Thus, the legal regulation of these problems can be seen as shaping our definition and perception of these environmental problems, including their causes. In the same way, some of the pollutants described here are legally defined concepts, rather than strictly scientific ones, even though they draw on chemical terminology.

The following pollutants are the most common air emissions from human activity, which diminish air quality, cause climate change, and otherwise give rise to environmental problems. The list is not exhaustive, and the pollutants also interact with each other through atmospheric reactions, but it provides a basic working knowledge of the substances covered by air pollution regulation.

Sulfur dioxide and NO_x—acidifying, eutrophying, and reactive pollutants

Sulfur dioxide (SO_2) has long been a recognized problem of UK air pollution and a cause for environmental campaigning. SO_2 emissions are generated by the combustion of sulphur-containing fuels,[14] such as coal and petroleum, and metal smelting processes. They are thus produced by many industrial processes, including those in coal-fired power stations, as well as by transport (petrol-fuelled cars, buses etc).[15] NO_x refers to both nitrogen oxide and nitrogen dioxide (NO, NO_2), which are also generated during combustion processes, and arise particularly from traffic. Livestock farming is also a cause of NO_x.

SO_2 and NO_x cause acid rain and dry acid deposition when they are oxidized in the atmosphere (that is, when they react with water vapour and other atmospheric elements), to form sulphuric acid and nitric acid. 'Acid rain' refers to the process by which these acid pollutants are removed from the atmosphere by wet deposition—they 'rain' on soils, vegetation, and the built environment, as well as into freshwater river systems, causing the death of flora and fauna, degradation of soils, and corrosion of buildings and structures. Dry acidification occurs when the same compounds are directly taken up by vegetation and surfaces.

NO_x also reacts with other pollutants in the atmosphere to form toxic and otherwise health-harming compounds. For example, NO_x reacts with ammonia (NH_3), moisture, and other atmospheric compounds to form fine particulate matter (discussed further in the sub-section below on particulate matter), which is damaging to human health, particularly by impairing respiratory function. NO_x also reacts with volatile organic compounds (also discussed below) in the presence of sunlight to form ground-level ozone, which also poses serious health hazards to humans and plants. Ground-level ozone—unlike stratospheric ozone that protects humans from harmful concentrations of ultraviolet radiation by absorbing it and limiting how much reaches the earth's surface—is harmful to humans, primarily as a lung irritant, and also leads to vegetation degradation.

Further, NO_x reacts with other atmospheric elements to form nitrogen (N)-rich compounds that are deposited into freshwater and marine environments, giving rise to the problem of 'eutrophication'. Eutrophication occurs when the (nitrogen or phosphorous) nutrient balance in aquatic environments is disturbed.[16] When there is an increase in nitrogen in such environments, the result is leaching of

[13] Intergovernmental Panel on Climate Change/Technology and Economic Assessment Panel, *Special Report on Safeguarding the Ozone Layer and the Global Climate System: Issues Related to Hydrofluorocarbons and Perfluorocarbons* (2005) 5.

[14] 'Combustion' refers to any energy-producing reaction between a fuel and an oxidant (including air), usually at a high temperature.

[15] Note that SO_2 emissions are also generated naturally in volcano eruptions.

[16] It can also occur in land environments.

nitrogen into ground water systems, as well as vegetation changes in favour of N-tolerant species (such as algae) and away from those species that are reliant on oxygen in water (such as fish and shellfish). 'Algal blooms' in water environments are an example of eutrophication; these not only disrupt normal functioning of the aquatic ecosystem, but also affect human uses of water, from accessing drinking water, to fishing, to recreational enjoyment. This environmental problem is not only caused by atmospheric deposition of N-containing compounds,[17] but also by run-off from agricultural land (carrying N-rich fertilizers), animal waste from intensive livestock husbandry, aquaculture techniques, and discharge from sewage treatment plants. Air emissions are but one aspect of the environmental problem, demonstrating how environmental problems often involve interactions across environmental media, and thus require regulation that also captures these cross-media effects.[18]

Greenhouse gases (GHGs)

There is a suite of GHGs, which work together with clouds to intensify the sun's heat by trapping it in our atmosphere. This is a naturally occurring phenomenon—the 'greenhouse effect'—and it helps to maintain a constant habitable temperature on earth. Naturally occurring GHGs are water vapour, carbon dioxide, methane, and nitrous oxide. These gases become environmentally problematic when their concentrations increase sufficiently to change the balance of GHGs in the atmosphere, so amplifying the greenhouse effect and distorting the earth's climate system. 'Climate change' is the result, which is now occurring and threatens existing patterns of human habitation, as well as the broader stability of ecosystems. Despite heated controversy over the science of climate change, it is now recognized by the majority of the international scientific community that anthropogenic GHGs have been increasingly causing such atmospheric distortions since industrialization, which have resulted in problematic levels of global warming.[19]

Anthropogenic GHGs include carbon dioxide (CO_2), methane (CH_4), carbon monoxide (CO), ground level ozone (O_3), nitrous oxide (N_2O), and several fluorinated gases, including chlorofluorocarbons (CFCs), hydrofluorocarbons (HFCs), and sulphur hexafluoride (SF_6). Of these, CO_2 is the largest contributor to the greenhouse effect, while SF_6 is the most potent contributor. The main sources of the increasing atmospheric concentrations of these gases are again the combustion of fossil fuels, as well as land use change (particularly deforestation), livestock rearing, biodegradable landfill waste, the use of agricultural fertilizers, and the use of CFCs in refrigeration and fire retardant equipment. NO_x is also an 'indirect' GHG, due to its role in the production of ozone.

Note that not all of these GHGs are regulated by legal regimes that have been established to respond to climate change. As discussed in Section 3, the six major GHGs (CO_2, CH_4, N_2O, and three fluorinated gases) are included within the Kyoto Protocol regime, which sets binding emissions targets internationally, while the EU Emissions Trading Scheme currently covers only CO_2 (and some perfluororcarbons). Further, all these gases are not simply 'GHGs'. CFCs cause depletion of the atmospheric ozone layer, and CO_2 acts as an acidifying agent in the world's oceans. Due to increasing concentrations of CO_2 now dissolving in oceans, the role of oceans as carbon sinks looks set to have severe consequences for marine organisms and the food chain.[20] Changing wind patterns and higher temperatures caused

---

[17] Which include ammonia, an air emission from intensive livestock farming, and nitrous oxide (N_2O), as well as NO_x.

[18] See Chapter 14 for the water quality regulation targeted at the problem of eutrophication (focused on nitrate sensitive areas, particularly due to agricultural run-off), and Chapter 17 for integrated pollution control regulation that aims to address cross-media environmental problems holistically.

[19] See n 10 and accompanying text.

[20] See, for example, The Royal Society, *Ocean Acidification due to Increasing Atmospheric Carbon Dioxide* (Policy Document 12/05, June 2005).

by climate change are likely also to cause such effects and to compromise the ability of oceans to act as carbon sinks.[21] Similarly, N_2O also contributes to the eutrophication of aquatic environments, as discussed already. Thus, the interconnections between pollutants emitted into the air and various environmental problems demonstrate the complexity of those problems—both in understanding their causes, and then in thinking about how best to regulate them.

Heavy metal particulates

Cadmium, lead, and mercury are heavy metals that cause serious problems as air pollutants. These metals are emitted into the air by combustion processes—industrial activities, traffic, and energy production—and by the incineration of metal-containing waste (particularly batteries and electronic equipment). These heavy metals are very harmful to human health, causing kidney, lung, and bone problems (in the case of cadmium), and also acting as neurotoxins (lead and mercury). Air emissions containing these metals can harm human health via complex environmental pathways, in particular by deposition in topsoil in which food grows (which is then consumed by humans) or by contaminating water supplies. Such environmental effects can also be caused by air emissions containing heavy metal particulates that come from distant locations, transported by prevailing wind patterns.[22]

Particulate matter

Particulate matter refers to any matter in air that is very, very small. Measured in microns or nanometres, there is increasing evidence that dust particles of such small size can have significantly deleterious effects on human health, particularly in causing respiratory illnesses and lung cancers, irrespective of the chemical composition of the pollutant. Particulate matter can be emitted directly into the air, mainly from combustion processes, and can also form in the atmosphere through the reaction of pollutants, such as NO_x, NH_3, and volatile organic compounds. The science around the harmful effects of particulate matter is still developing, and regulatory responses to controlling it are evolving accordingly, particularly by increasingly focusing on smaller particulate matter. PM-10 (diameter of less than 10 microns) was first understood to be a problematic pollutant due to its ability to penetrate human tissue, and now PM-2.5 (diameter of less than 2.5 microns) is an increasing focus of scientific research and evidence as to its harmful effects.[23]

Benzene, polycyclic aromatic hydrocarbons, dioxins, and furans

These are aromatic organic compounds that are chemically related in their molecular structure. Many have toxic and carcinogenic effects, being able to alter DNA and even cause birth defects. These pollutants are present in fossil fuels, and as air pollutants they are caused by the incomplete combustion of carbon-based fuels (including coal and wood). Benzene is also widely used as an industrial solvent and is used in the production of plastics, synthetic rubber, and pharmaceutical drugs, amongst other things.

[21] See, for example, EU Commission, DG Environment News Alert Service, 'Climate Change: Reducing the Ocean Carbon Sink', 26 June 2008 (available at <http://ec.europa.eu/environment/integration/research/newsalert/pdf/113na5. pdf> accessed 7 February 2013).

[22] World Health Organisation, *Health Risks of Heavy Metals from Long-Range Transboundary Air Pollution* (2007, Germany).

[23] Commission Communication, 'The Clean Air for Europe Programme: Towards a Thematic Strategy for Air Quality', COM (2001) 245 final ('CAFE') 2–3; Soberans and others, 'Particulate matter Air Pollution induces hypermethylation of the p16 promoter via a mitochondrial ROS-JNK-DNMT1 pathway', (2012) Scientific Reports 2, 275.

Dioxin emissions (or polychlorinated dibenzodioxins) are also caused by waste incineration, metal smelting, applying sewage sludge to land, bleaching paper and fabric, and by reactions in the atmosphere, particularly above incineration facilities.

Persistent organic pollutants (POPs)

POPs are toxic pollutants that persist in the environment and are resistant to environmental degradation processes, existing in and passing through ecological chains and causing damage to the health of humans, animals, and plants. POPs bioaccumulate, that is, they bind to fatty tissues of living organisms, including humans, and they pass between generations and food chains, thus causing ongoing problems through systemic environmental effects. Well-known POPs are dichlorodiphenyltrichloroethane (DDT), polychlorinated biphenyls (PCBs), and dioxins (already mentioned). These enter the atmosphere as air emissions in various ways—many are or were used as pesticides, and PCBs enter the atmosphere from landfill sites and contaminated air in buildings. The harmful effects on human health of POPs are wide-ranging, causing cancer as well as neurological, reproductive and, immunity -related problems.

Volatile organic compounds (VOCs)

This final category of pollutants is a legal as well as a scientific category. Many organic compounds are highly reactive under normal atmospheric conditions. However, this category of compounds is also defined by particular regulatory contexts. For example, under the EU National Emissions Ceilings (NEC) Directive, VOCs are defined as 'all organic compounds arising from human activities, other than methane, which are capable of producing photochemical oxidants by reactions with nitrogen oxides in the presence of sunlight'.[24] This definition is shaped by the fact that the NEC Directive was primarily aimed at improving protection of the environment and human health against the risks of acidification, eutrophication, and ground-level ozone. Thus, the exclusion of methane is not on the grounds of its 'volatility' (it is a very volatile organic compound), but on the regulatory choice made as to the scope of this legislative initiative. This choice, in turn, shapes our understanding of the environmental problems addressed. By contrast, other compounds are understood in scientific terms to be VOCs—such as benzene, chlorofluorocarbons, and compounds found in paint and coatings—and these also cause a range of harmful health and environmental effects. These are subject to a variety of regulatory controls, each with their own definitions and scope as to the pollutants that they cover and why.[25]

1.3 REGULATORY COMPLEXITY (AND SUCCESS)

The complexity of air pollution problems set out in Section 1.2 is matched, unsurprisingly, by regulatory complexity. The seriousness of the problems caused by air pollution, particularly for human health,

---

[24] European Parliament and Council Directive 2001/81/EC of 23 October 2001 on National Emission Ceilings for certain atmospheric pollutants [2001] OJ L309/22 ('NEC Directive') art 3(k).

[25] For example, European Parliament and Council Directive 2004/42/CE of 21 April 2004 on the limitation of emissions of volatile organic compounds due to the use of organic solvents in certain paints and varnishes and vehicle refinishing products [2004] OJ L143/87 (note the wider definition of 'volatile organic compounds' in art 2(5), albeit that its application is limited due to the scope of the Directive); European Parliament and Council Regulation 1005/2009/EC of 16 September 2009 on substances that deplete the ozone layer [2009] OJ L286/1 (implementing through EU law the Montreal Protocol on the same subject, and regulating CFCs and related substances within a regime focused on ozone layer protection).

has led to a regulatory response best summed up as: 'throw everything at the problem'. Thus, a *wide range of regulatory strategies* has been adopted to deal with air pollution problems—from setting emission limit values, environmental quality standards, and process and product standards, to setting up market-based mechanisms. Further, these different regulatory measures have been changed or added to over time as air pollution problems have themselves changed or been better understood in scientific terms. In general, specific and UK-based regulation—applying to particular pollutants or particular polluting industries, such as lead in cars or alkali works—has over time been complemented or overtaken by more holistic and global approaches to dealing with air pollution problems.

The complexity of the UK legal map of air pollution regulation is also a product of the *jurisdictional layers* that intersect and inform it, bringing different regulatory focuses as well as different styles of governance. Thus, international and EU regulation both now contribute significantly to UK air pollution law, particularly to cater for the transboundary movements and interactions of air pollutants as well as the global problems of ozone depletion and climate change. Within EU law in particular, identifying and mapping air quality law is complicated by its interaction with other areas of EU law, relating to different regimes of environmental regulation as well as the law relating to competition matters and the internal market (discussed further in Section 2.2).

This multi-jurisdictional dimension to air pollution regulation brings further complicating factors beyond layering of legal obligations. This is because cross-border air pollution regulation must allow for *geographical and urban planning differences* that affect and drive air pollution (including the extent of urbanization, the location and concentration of industry, transport and housing, topography, and climate), as well as *human differences* (sensitivity to air pollutants). Regulating across jurisdictions also gives rise to *difficulties of information compatibility, collection, and exchange*, which are important in implementing air pollution controls and monitoring their effects in reducing air pollution levels. For this latter reason, Member States are under common legal obligations to share and exchange information on ambient air pollution levels and on pollutant emissions,[26] which are handled and published by the European Environment Agency, although some Member States do not have good records of providing this required data.

With this regulatory complexity also comes *considerable administrative and technical machinery* to monitor air pollution levels and to meet the informational and compliance demands of air quality regulation. Thus, throughout the EU, there are over 6000 monitoring stations that measure levels of ambient air pollutants. These monitoring stations must not only employ accurate techniques for reading emissions, but they must also be sufficiently representative to provide adequate air quality information (by collecting data from urban, suburban, and rural environments). They must also be classified according to the environmental causes in their areas for pollution readings (traffic, topography, industrial activity, domestic heating sources, population density, meteorological information, and local building structures all have an impact), in order that their results can be properly interpreted and understood. The methodologies required for these various aspects of monitoring air quality are scientifically complex and evolving. In light of this, keep in mind the administrative reality 'on the ground' as you read about various regulatory strategies that tackle air pollution in this chapter, particularly as to how administrative efficiencies (and inefficiencies) might be exploited (or perpetuated).

[26] Council Decision 97/101/EC of 27 January 1997 establishing a reciprocal exchange of information and data from networks and individual stations measuring ambient air pollution within the Member States [1997] OJ L35/14 ('EOI Decision') is the basis for the EEA's 'Airbase', which is a public air quality database system that draws from continuous monitoring of air pollutants throughout EU Member States. European Parliament and Council Regulation 166/2006/EC of 18 January 2006 concerning the establishment of a European Pollutant Release and Transfer Register [2006] OJ L33/1 is a different legal initiative, requiring annual reporting of environmental data on polluting emissions (to air, water, and land, as well as from waste generated) from industrial installations throughout the EU. The E-PRTR Regulation implements the international law UNECE PRTR Protocol under the Aarhus Convention: Kiev Protocol on Pollutant Release and Transfer Registers (2003; 2009).

All this regulatory complexity reflects the various challenges that need to be met in regulating air pollution problems. However, past experience indicates that these challenges can be met. There have been *significant regulatory successes* in improving air quality and reducing emissions of pollutants. Some key examples include the reversal of ozone layer depletion in light of measures taken under the Montreal Protocol to the 1985 Vienna Convention for the Protection of the Ozone Layer,[27] and the considerably improved air quality levels in the UK today since the days of intense city smogs, from Victorian times through to the mid-twentieth century. Air quality levels throughout the EU have also improved considerably since the 1970s, as the Commission has reported: 'air quality has been one of the great success stories of environmental policy, showing that it is really possible to de-couple economic growth from environmental degradation'.[28] In particular, problems of acid deposition are 'well on track' to being resolved.[29]

However, significant challenges in regulating air pollution problems remain, particularly due to increased transport movements within Europe and slow turnover of vehicles fleets,[30] and also in light of evolving scientific understanding of air pollution problems. Further, it should be noted that 'regulatory success' becomes more complicated when assessed beyond scientific measurements. Consider DuPuis's appraisal of air pollution regulation, and its successes, from a sociological perspective. The focus of the book is on US air pollution problems and policy, but the observations obtain equally in the UK and Europe.

E Melanie DuPuis (ed), *The Politics and Culture of Air Pollution: Smoke and Mirrors* (New York University Press 2004) 2–4

[This book understands] air pollution as part of a more social and political picture of the environment. [It emphasises] the existence of air pollution—and air pollution abatement policies—not as scientific models and measurements or economic values but as social 'artefacts': the products of social interactions and relationships, including inequalities, knowledge, power and politics. While science and economics provide crucial and substantial information about air pollution, only in combination with studies of the meaning of air pollution is it possible to paint the full social 'airscape' of air pollution policy.

[...]

Yet the past tells us that, at certain times and in certain places, pollution control policies were formed and polluted environments became cleaner. There was a time, after all, when only the urban elite neighbourhoods in the United States had access to running water in their homes... [I]n certain places at certain times dirty air has become cleaner. In some places the air was so thick with smoke that not only did thousands die prematurely but everyday practices became transformed: residents abandoned any thought of wearing lighter clothing, architects simplified building ornament to prevent the visible effects of acid erosion, and writers invented the 'mystery', wherein characters walked streets in search of answers behind a smoky veil.

[...]

[This book shows] that the 'fairer' and 'cleaner' options for some often imposed additional economic or pollution burdens on others... [E]nvironmental cleanup is a conflictual and contradictory process. The conflicts are not just between citizen breathers and industrial polluters but also between various visions of the city.

---

[27] UNEP, Montreal Protocol on Substances that Deplete the Ozone Layer (1987; 1989; and as subsequently amended).
[28] CAFE Communication (n 23) 2.
[29] Commission Staff Working Paper on the implementation of EU Air Quality Policy and preparing for its comprehensive review, SEC(2011) 342 final, 2.
[30] Ibid, 4.

Thus, air pollution regulation is not simply concerned with controlling excessive concentrations of pollutants in the air; it is a social construction that involves choices about what behaviour gets controlled, who bears the primary benefit and cost of this, and how much of a changed environment we, as a community, are happy to live in.

Overall, whether looking at air pollution as a social or a scientific phenomenon, it is clear that challenges remain. According to current environmental knowledge, the three key air pollution problems that need addressing today (in 2012–13) are: the ongoing challenges of climate change, problems of eutrophication caused by excess nutrient deposition, and urban air quality levels for ground-level ozone, particulate matter, and NO_2. How governments and societies choose to tackle those problems is another, and more difficult, question.

1.4 SCIENCE/LAW INTERSECTION

As has already been indicated, scientific uncertainty and evolving scientific knowledge have a significant role to play in air quality regulation. In particular, scientific knowledge meets law in two ways in regulating air pollution problems—influencing (1) the need for regulation, and (2) its form. First, evolving scientific knowledge leads to better understanding of air pollution problems and how they should be regulated. Thus, the case of PM-2.5 as a pollutant and understanding its effect on human health, discussed in Section 1.2, has led to the recent setting of further air quality standards to cover the pollutant under the Air Quality Framework Directive at EU level.[31] Similarly, the periodic scientific assessment reports of the Intergovernmental Panel on Climate Change internationally have justified and led to various agreements on climate change—the 1992 UN Framework Convention on Climate Change, its Kyoto Protocol in 1997, the Copenhagen Accord in 2009,[32] as well as the EU Emissions Trading Scheme (ETS).[33]

Second, scientific knowledge often shapes the form of, and even constitutes, air pollution regulation. In relation to climate change regulation again, the conceptualization of climate change as a problem that is caused by *total* global concentrations of GHGs sets up and explains the form of various regulatory strategies adopted. In particular, it allows trading systems and the flexibility mechanisms of the Kyoto Protocol.[34] These mechanisms aim to ensure an overall global reduction in emissions, but the precise location of these emission reductions is not critical.

In other cases, evolving scientific knowledge implements and fills in the substance of legal obligations within air pollution regulatory schemes. Thus, the air quality monitoring obligations prescribed by Chapter II of the Air Quality Framework Directive are substantiated by scientific assessment methodologies, including relevant 'modelling' and 'indicative measurements' of pollutant levels to be undertaken by Member States, with the scientific methods detailed in the Annexes to the Directive,[35] and aspects of these methods to be updated as scientific knowledge progresses.[36] In addition, acceptable environmental quality standards for PM-2.5, whilst prescribed as particular numerical concentrations in the Annexes of the Directive, are susceptible to review under the Directive, as scientific knowledge about the nature of the pollutant improves over time.[37]

---

[31] See Section 2.2.

[32] See Section 3.2.

[33] European Parliament Directive 2003/87 of 13 October 2003 establishing a scheme for greenhouse gas emission allowance trading within the Community [2003] OJ L275/32, as amended, art 14, Annex IV. See Section 3.3.

[34] See Sections 3.2 and 3.3.

[35] European Parliament and Council Directive 2008/50/EC of 21 May 2008 on ambient air quality and cleaner air for Europe [2008] OJ L152/1 ('AQFD'), arts 6, 8–11. On the role of modelling in environmental law, see Section 3.2 of Chapter 2.

[36] AQFD, art 5(2).

[37] ADFD, art 32. There is also provision for updating standards of other pollutants under the Directive.

Similarly, the central obligation of the EU ETS—that installations within the scheme must surrender allowances each year based on the amount of GHG emissions they have emitted (see further, Section 3.3)—can only work if there are accurate scientific methods for measuring those emissions. More broadly, the obligations on developed nations to meet binding GHG emissions reductions targets under the Kyoto Protocol can only be met if the GHG emissions of a relevant nation's activities can be properly measured. In fact, measuring these emissions is subject to ongoing scientific revision and some uncertainty and dispute. This demonstrates that apparently definitive legal obligations imposed to deal with air pollution problems—as for environmental problems more broadly—can be deceptively simple in their prescription when they are dependent on, and in reality constituted by, complicated scientific processes in their implementation.

1.5 NATURE OF 'LAW' IN AIR POLLUTION REGULATION

In light of the themes and particular environmental problems set out in Sections 1.1 to 1.4, the nature of the law studied in the area of air pollution control has particular characteristics. Overall, it is an area of considerable regulatory complexity involving:

- many different statutes and regulations—some overlapping, some adopting very different regulatory strategies;
- regulations and judicial determinations deriving from a range of jurisdictional levels and diverse public bodies;
- a dependence on scientific knowledge and assessment for its form and implementation; and
- relatively few judicial decisions, particularly in relation to air quality law.

On the final point, there are at least three reasons for the lack of judicial decisions in relation to air quality law. First, it takes time to understand the complex regulatory scheme of air quality regulation (now primarily contained in the EU Air Quality Framework Directive),[38] since it frequently evolves and is legally impenetrable without scientific data and knowledge to ascertain compliance with it. As the decision in *Janecek v Bayern* (discussed in Section 2.2) indicates, there are various avenues of legal redress available when air quality standards are breached, but these are not always obvious on the face of the legislation involved. This is related to the second reason for little litigation existing in relation to air quality law—key obligations to maintain healthy air quality levels rest on the state rather than on individuals. Where regulatory regimes impose air emission limits on individual operators, such as the IPPC regime or the EU ETS regime, there are more frequent challenges and legal disputes that lead to litigation. Where individuals are directly bound by air quality obligations, they have an interest in ensuring that these obligations are properly applied, particularly if they affect their economic interests adversely. Third, most air pollution 'law' happens at the level of administrative implementation of regulation and the actions of regulated actors in response to regulatory strategies. Where there is poor administrative practice involved in this implementation, then potential for public law disputes arises, otherwise law happens within the administrative state and 'on the ground', as is captured by a socio-legal approach to law rather than one focused on doctrine and judicial decisions.

Despite this administrative, scientifically-focused, and non-judicial character of much air pollution law, some scholars have argued that there are or should be uniform and unifying aspects of this

---

[38] See Section 2.2.

body of law, reflecting a jurisprudential conception of environmental law.[39] In particular, certain normative principles and values should inform the law relating to air pollution problems where there are transboundary aspects to the problems involved. Harris suggests that the regulation of global warming and climate change should be informed by values of international (social and distributive) justice and international environmental equity (IEE), even though these normative principles might in practice be shaped by political pragmatism.

PG Harris, 'The European Union and Environmental Change: Sharing the Burdens of Global Warming' (2006) 17 Colo J Entl L and Poly 309, 319–23

Ethical philosophers have endeavored to define what is fair and equitable in the context of [global climate change (GCC)], both within and between countries, and the United Nations' Intergovernmental Panel on Climate Change (IPCC) has also grappled with the question. In simple terms, equity means the quality of being fair, impartial, or even-handed in dealings with others. People will, of course, disagree about the precise definition or content of fairness and equity. Indeed, that disagreement has been much, or even most, of the focus of climate change negotiations over nearly the last two decades. In the final analysis, what constitutes a fair and equitable sharing of GCC burdens will be the result of political bargaining among the states and other influential actors, such as corporations and nongovernmental organizations (NGOs), [so that power will] play a role in determining which normative principles actually shape outcomes [...]

At the most basic level, fairness demands that Europe (among other developed parts of the world) act to limit and, ultimately, end the harm it causes by way of GCC, giving due consideration to the least well-off countries and people.

[...]

Various assessments of equity and fairness in the context of the GCC negotiations [reflect varying ethical philosophical approaches to equity]. For example, John Ashton and Xueman Wang have distilled the determination of what is fair and equitable in this context to five dimensions: (1) responsibility —who is to blame for GCC?; (2) equal entitlements—to what extent does agreement and action on climate change bring us 'towards such an equal entitlements world'; (3) capacity—those who are most able to act ought to do so; (4) basic needs—'the strong and well endowed should help the weak and less well endowed at least in meeting their basic needs ....Thus a fair climate change agreement would if possible help, and certainly not undermine, the efforts of the poorest countries to meet the basic needs of their people'; and (5) comparable effort—the requirements of some parties should not be more or less difficult to achieve than those of others [...] The upshot is that while debates about the precise content of IEE in the context of GCC continue, equity considerations are already being integrated into the GCC regime and the relevant policies of a number of major developed states, especially in Europe.

To appraise whether and how ideas of international environmental equity are in fact being incorporated into international and EU climate change policy and regulation, see Sections 3.2 and 3.3.

Sections 2 and 3 now address two different environmental problems of anthropogenic air pollution—ambient air quality and climate change—and set out two (overlapping and jurisdictionally layered) legal maps that relate to them. The goal of this mapping, in the face of rapidly developing, broad, and multijurisdictional measures relating to air pollution, is not purely descriptive, nor is it jurisprudential in the manner of Harris' analysis. Rather, mapping air pollution law allows us to see themes, to make links,

---

[39] Section 1.3 of Chapter 1.

and to identify contentious legal issues relating to air quality regulation. It also reveals how particular understandings of these air pollution problems shape the regulation that applies to them, and are shaped in turn by the legal construction of these regimes.

2 AMBIENT AIR QUALITY: LOCAL AND TRANSBOUNDARY AIR POLLUTION

This section covers the legal and regulatory approaches to dealing with ambient air quality problems. Ambient air quality concerns pollution levels in the outdoor environment, and particularly the effects of pollutants on human health and the environment at locations where air pollutants exist or otherwise settle back to ground level, interacting with the environment and contaminating the air that we breathe. Such polluting effects arise from both local and transboundary air emissions, with the main pollutants set out in Section 1.2. These include 'secondary pollutants', caused by polluting emissions reacting in unpredictable ways and at unpredictable locations in the atmosphere, such as ground-level ozone and particulate matter.

The sources of ambient air pollutants are largely anthropogenic and include growing industrial and energy production (particularly the burning of fossil fuels), construction, increasing road traffic, various other means of transport (trains, buses, heavy goods vehicles, planes, ships), waste sites (incinerators, landfills, hazardous waste sites), dry cleaning activities, and fires. Not only are the industrial activities that generate pollutants varied, but they represent different kinds of sources, from point sources and diffuse sources, to mobile sources and also natural sources. All this means that regulating individual activities or particular sources of air pollution is not sufficient to control air quality overall, although such targeted regulation can help (and is adopted). The nature of air quality problems means that different kinds of regulatory instruments are required, in order to account for the combined effects of all relevant pollutants in the ambient air and to limit total polluting emissions over a wide geographical area. These regulatory requirements also explain the reliance on *environmental quality standards* and *national pollutant emission ceilings* as key tools in regulating air quality levels in EU and UK environmental law today.

Note also that the EU is highly active in this area of environmental law, so that EU regulation now informs much UK and English air quality control. This is unsurprising given the transboundary nature and causes of air pollution—the EU clearly has competence under Article 191 TFEU to regulate this environmental issue.

2.1 HISTORY OF AIR QUALITY REGULATION

The history of UK air quality regulation is a long one, with air pollution controls known to exist in the thirteenth century.[40] They continued to be introduced over time, particularly in response to new industrial activities being carried out, which have caused serious public health and environmental problems through polluting emissions. Early air pollution controls were relatively simple and dealt with specific issues (such as burning coal) but regulating air quality has become more complicated in more recent times, as industrial processes have become more advanced and more numerous, and their polluting consequences more difficult technically to identify and control.

---

[40] Stuart Bell, Donald McGillivray, and Ole Pedersen, *Environmental Law* (8th edn, OUP 2013) ch 15.

The history of air quality controls is also a story of shifting regulatory strategies. As Wilde indicates in the following extract, analysing the history of evolving UK and EU air quality regulation shows the advantages and disadvantages of different regulatory techniques in dealing with air quality problems. Wilde's opening reference to the *Alkali Act* is to the first in a series of statutes that applied to industrial activities involving 'alkali works'—industrial processes that employed the 'Leblanc process' to create potash and soda ash, which are important chemicals in manufacturing glass, paper and textiles, and which generated very acidic emissions, causing serious acidification problems in the surrounding environment. This original narrow focus shows how early air quality regulation responded to identifiable and severe environmental problems by targeting specific industrial processes.

Mark Wilde, 'The New Directive on Ambient Air Quality and Cleaner Air for Europe'
(2010) 12 Env L Rev 282, 282–83

The Alkali Act 1863 was a groundbreaking piece of legislation which tackled, head-on, highly damaging acidic atmospheric emissions from an early chemicals industry. It established a professional inspectorate and imposed an ambitious emission limit on atmospheric emissions of hydrochloric acid from such plants. Indeed, provided one has the political will and the technical capability, stemming the flow of noxious emissions from exhausts and tailpipes is the obvious place to start when seeking to reduce pollution. Initially, the Act achieved spectacular results; as industry increased, however, the reductions were soon cancelled out by the proliferation of new plants.

This example neatly illustrates the shortcomings of an approach to pollution control that relies solely upon monitoring exhaust pipe emissions. Emission limits are of limited effect unless they are informed by data on the cumulative effect of emissions on the receiving media. The early emission limits placed on the alkali industry took no account of the growth of that particular industry, let alone the host of other polluting industries [outside the scope of Alkali regulation].

Air quality standards focus on the cumulative effect of pollutants from all sources in the atmosphere and, in this respect, form a vital element of any strategic response to the problem of atmospheric pollution. In the UK an early example of a strategic approach to air quality can been seen in the first Clean Air Act 1956, which empowered local authorities to declare smoke control areas. This approach was greatly expanded by the Environment Act 1995, which established the national air quality strategy under Part IV. This has provided the vehicle for adopting additional obligations on air quality imposed under European law.

At the European level there is a clear transboundary dimension to air quality [...] Airborne pollutants are no respecters of national borders and can be carried for hundreds, and even thousands, of miles. The EU [...] has been active in the field of atmospheric emissions since the 1970s, although its approach was somewhat piecemeal. Certain measures were not really environmental measures at all and were more concerned with harmonising technical standards in the interests of the common market; early tailpipe emission limits on motor cars are a classic example of this. Other measures focused on exhaust emissions from particular industrial sectors but did not form part of an integrated approach.

It was not until the 1990s that the EU instigated a strategy for improving European air quality as a whole.

Note that the historical approach to regulating acidifying pollutants from alkali works, whilst narrowly focused, was not *only* about limiting emissions. There were also some aspects of an integrated and cross-media approach to regulating these heavily polluting installations in Victorian times. However, this holistic aspect of air quality regulation fell out of favour during the twentieth century, before returning in a more comprehensive form in the current integrated pollution prevention and control (IPPC) regime. This indicates that regulatory approaches to environmental problems are cyclical rather than linear developments that evolve progressively over time.[41]

The other legal response to air quality problems historically was through the common law. Successful private nuisance actions changed the air polluting practices of heavy industry, but only in a manner that avoided damage to local, or relatively local, property interests due to the nature of the doctrine. An example of such a nuisance action is discussed in Chapter 6—*Halsey v Esso Petroleum Co Ltd*.[42] Beyond these limits, private nuisance actions can also *undermine* the improvement of overall air quality levels by contributing to longer-range air quality problems. This is because, particularly after the case of *Manchester Corp v Farnworth*, air pollution will not be an actionable nuisance if released higher into the atmosphere (via higher chimney stacks) and then carried further afield, so not harming local property interests. The result of higher chimney stacks being built on power stations and other UK industrial installations, from the 1930s onwards, was air pollution being carried to other countries by prevailing winds, including to northern European states, where the pollutants contributed to serious environmental harm.

The inadequacy of this common law response, as well as early regulatory strategies, in ensuring acceptable overall levels of ambient air quality led to a shift, from the late 1970s, to international developments on air quality regulation. Air quality control measures were adopted at both international and EU levels, focusing on transboundary air pollution, particularly with introduction of the 1979 Geneva Convention on Long-Range Transboundary Air Pollution (CLRTAP). The EU's motivation for instituting air quality controls was driven both by international legal developments and by internal market concerns. From the late 1970s, the EU (then European Community) began a piecemeal approach to tackling the most serious air pollution problems, introducing emissions standards for vehicles,[43] and also three Directives in the 1980s setting out minimum air quality standards for particular polluting substances.[44] This style of Directive—setting environmental quality standards for individual pollutants—has now been largely superseded by air quality standards being set under a single Air Quality Framework Directive, as discussed in the Section 2.2. Further, more comprehensive integrated pollution control regimes for large polluting industry were also subsequently introduced in EU law, as discussed in the Section 2.2 and in Chapter 17.

2.2 AIR QUALITY REGULATORY MAP

This section sets out the key features of the regulatory map that governs air quality in UK and English law today. This map is a complex one, reflecting what Bell & McGillivray call a 'mixed-regulation approach',[45] with a range of regulatory strategies and jurisdictional layers involved in tackling the problem of maintaining acceptable air quality levels. However, there are at least three distinctive features. First, this body of regulation is increasingly coherent, with more strategic and overarching approaches to air quality management being adopted rather than the *ad hoc* and reactive regulation of the past, as well as controls having a wide geographical coverage. Second, air quality regulation is increasingly detailed and flexible, to cater for evolving scientific understandings of the causes and

---

[41] Ben Pontin, 'Integrated Pollution Control in Victorian Britain: Rethinking Progress within the History of Environmental Law' (2007) 19(2) JEL 173. See also Section 1 of Chapter 17.

[42] [1961] 1 WLR 683.

[43] Council Directive 70/200/EEC of 20 March 1970 on the approximation of the laws of the Member States on measures to be taken against air pollution by emissions from motor vehicles [1970] OJ L76/1.

[44] Council Directive 80/779/EEC of 15 July 1980 on air quality limit values and guide values for sulphur dioxide and suspended particulates [1980] OJ L229/30; Council Directive 82/884/EEC of 3 December 1982 on a limit value for lead in the air [1982] OJ L378/15; Council Directive 85/203/EEC of 7 March 1985 on air quality standards for nitrogen dioxide [1985] OJ L87/1.

[45] Bell, McGillivray, and Pedersen (n 40) 577.

mechanisms that give rise to air quality problems, as well as difficulties in implementing air quality regulation. Third, the nature of the problem of polluted air quality—with its transboundary and unpredictable secondary atmospheric causes—makes certain regulatory approaches particularly suitable if overall air quality levels are to be controlled. Thus, air quality regulation involves: international as well as EU transboundary regulation; environmental quality standards (EQSs) to ensure that safe *overall* air quality levels are legally mandated; and national limits on polluting emissions. These regulatory approaches are supplemented by measures that apply specifically to the most heavily polluting substances and industries in order to control their emissions at source, so that there is, in the result, a multifaceted regulatory approach to controlling air quality.

Nonetheless, significant challenges for this body of regulation remain (as discussed in Section 1). In particular, the coherence of an EU-centred approach is undermined by the variability in geography, urbanization, levels and types of industrial activity, and population sensitivity throughout the EU's Member States. The success of controlling transboundary air pollution problems is also undermined by practical implementation difficulties, especially on exchange of information between Member States. However, there have been improvements in relation to the latter issue, particularly since Decision 97/101 on the exchange of information on air quality,[46] now subsumed within the Air Quality Framework Directive (AQFD), and with the co-ordinating and information-sharing role played by the European Environment Agency.[47] However, implementation problems remain, particularly since monitoring and air quality assessment obligations under the AQFD place onerous duties on Member States.

Overall, EU policy is the key driver of UK law relating to ambient air quality. That policy is currently set out in the Commission's 2001 Clean Air for Europe Programme (CAFE)[48] and the 2005 Thematic Strategy on Air Pollution (TSAP),[49] which was the first of the 6th Environment Action Programme's seven thematic strategies. The TSAP prescribed long-term air quality objectives for 2020,[50] with key priorities including the streamlining of different air quality directives into a single framework Directive and introducing new air quality standards for PM-2.5 (both done in 2008), tightening emission limit values from different sources,[51] and integrating air quality objectives into climate change and transport policies. CAFE also emphasized that both PM-2.5 and ground-level ozone were regulatory priorities for EU air quality law. In 2012–13, a policy review of the TSAP and CAFE was under consultation, with the 7th EU Environmental Action Programme (EAP) also in the pipeline. It is expected that there will be an updated EU Clean Air Package by the end of 2013, based on latest scientific knowledge and having at least the following priorities: updating the National Emissions Ceilings Directive,[52] expanding clean transport initiatives, and introducing other 'cost-effective' measures to meet the 6th EAP's objective 'to achieve levels of air quality that do not result in unacceptable

---

[46] EoI Decision (n 26).

[47] See n 26.

[48] See n 23.

[49] Commission, 'Thematic Strategy on Air Pollution' COM (2005) 446.

[50] For example, goals of a 47% reduction in loss of life expectancy through exposure to particulate matter, and a 43% reduction in areas or ecosystems exposed to eutrophication. Associated with these were quantified emissions reductions targets for particular pollutants: SO_2 emissions to decrease by 82%, NO_x emissions by 60%, primary PM-2.5 (particles emitted directly into the air) by 59% etc, measured against 2000-baseline levels. See ibid.

[51] This was achieved particularly through the 2010 Industrial Emissions Directive: see Chapter 17. More stringent emission limit standards for vehicles have also been introduced: European Parliament and Council Regulation 715/2007/EC of 20 June 2007 on type approval of motor vehicles with respect to emissions from light passenger and commercial vehicles (Euro 5 and Euro 6) [2007] OJ L171/1 (and a similar Regulation 595/2009/EC for heavy duty vehicles [2009] OJ L188/1); European Parliament and Council Directive 2009/33/EC of 23 April 2009 on the promotion of clean and energy-efficient road transport vehicles [2009] OJ L120/5.

[52] NEC Directive (n 24).

impacts on, and risks to, human health and the environment'. In setting these measures, action to reduce further air emissions linked to particulate matter, ground-level ozone, and nitrogen dioxide is a priority.[53]

While EU policy drives this area of environmental law, EU action still sits within a multi-jurisdictional regulatory effort to control air quality. Thus, before examining EU air quality legislation in detail, we analyse the international law aspects of air quality regulation, which are important both in driving EU action to improve air quality and in linking this action to broader international efforts, in relation to which the EU is itself a key player in promoting high environmental standards.

Air quality regulation in international law

The first big step in international law relating to transboundary air pollution came in the form of customary international law. In 1941, the *Train Smelter* arbitration established that 'no State has the right to use or permit the use of its territory in such a manner as to cause injury by fumes in or to the territory of another or the properties or persons therein, when the case is of serious consequence and the injury is established by clear and convincing evidence'.[54] The *Train Smelter* case concerned SO_2 emissions from smelting works in Canada that were causing crop and tree damage across the border in the US, due to acidifying emissions travelling from large, tall chimney stacks in British Columbia. However, this customary international law proved insufficient to control polluting transboundary emissions, particularly where there are difficulties in establishing clear and convincing evidence as to the sources of air pollution damage.

The primary international law control of transboundary polluting emissions today is now through a series of treaties—the 1979 Geneva Convention on Long-Range Transboundary Air Pollution (CLRTAP), and its various protocols. This Convention is a regional treaty, agreed under the auspices of the UN Economic Commission for Europe. Signatories include the EU and its Member States, eastern European states, as well as the US and Canada. EU states were amongst the first to sign and ratify the treaty, which was adopted in response to growing international concern over the transboundary movements of acidifying pollutants, particularly with the destruction of Scandinavian forests and lakes caused by polluting emissions coming from European locations thousands of kilometres away (including the UK).

The 1979 Convention does not set air quality standards directly, or set up liability rules for polluting states. Rather, contracting parties agree to 'endeavour to limit and, as far as possible, gradually reduce and prevent air pollution including long-range transboundary air pollution'.[55] Further, it contains important provisions on the sharing of information, collaborative research, monitoring, and consultation, with a view to developing policies to reduce discharges of air pollutants within the framework of the Convention. Subsequently, eight protocols have extended the Convention and targeted particular pollutants—including sulphur, nitrogen oxides, persistent organic pollutants, volatile organic compounds, ammonia, and toxic heavy metals—setting national emission limits and reduction targets for most of these pollutants, which signatory countries must meet across their respective geographic areas. These Protocols also set emission limit values (ELVs) for heavily polluting stationary sources, and require such stationary installations to adopt best available techniques (BATs), taking into account their technical characteristics, geographical location, and local environmental conditions.[56] Some of the Protocols also include ELVs for mobile sources, such as cars

---

[53] Commission Staff Working Paper (n 29) 4–8.
[54] *USA v Canada* (1941) 3 RIAA 1907, 1965.
[55] CLRTAP, art 2.
[56] 'BAT' is defined as 'the most effective and advanced stage in the development of activities and their methods of operation which indicate the practical suitability of particular techniques for providing in principle the basis for

and other forms of transport and mobile machinery,[57] or require emission reductions in relation to particular products.[58] An enhanced regulatory approach also adopted under some of the Protocols is an 'effects-based' approach, by which emission limits for pollutants are determined in view of their contribution to observable environmental problems, including photochemical pollution, acidification, and eutrophication, and their effects on human health and the environment.[59] Not all contracting parties to the original CLRTAP have signed and ratified each of the Protocols, although they all now bind the UK and EU.

The CLRTAP Protocols are revised as scientific knowledge about pollutants develops, and they also contain provisions for the ongoing carrying out of relevant scientific research and exchange of information and technologies. In light of such activity, the influential Gothenburg Protocol was recently renegotiated and updated in May 2012. The original 1999 Gothenburg Protocol to Abate Acidification, Eutrophication and Ground-level Ozone targeted sulphur, NO_x, VOCs, and ammonia, setting national emission reduction commitments for these pollutants, to be met by 2010. After its recent amendment, these commitments have been reviewed and updated with targets for 2020 and beyond, in addition to new provisions covering PM-2.5, which expressly includes black carbon (soot). The EU as a whole has now committed to reduce its emissions of SO_2, NO_2, ammonia, VOCs, and PM-2.5 by 59, 42, 6, 28, and 22%, respectively, against 2005 baseline levels. There are flexibility and assistance mechanisms for those states with poor air pollution records.

Two final aspects of the CLRTAP should be noted. First, this type of regulation, while focused on transboundary air pollution that damages air quality, links to climate change regulation. This is because several air pollutants that damage air quality and cause localized environmental damage also contribute to global warming. This was explicitly recognized in the recent updating of the Gothenburg Protocol where the climate-forcing characteristics of black carbon were acknowledged as a pressing problem, beyond its harmful consequences for human health as particulate matter. Its climate change effects provided additional justification for the inclusion of black carbon within the Protocol's PM-2.5 emission reduction commitments. The Protocol will thus produce dual benefits for these two different air pollution problems. This synergy between air quality and climate change regulation is not always so clearly recognized, but improving 'co-benefits' between air quality law and climate change regulation is an EU policy priority.

Second, beyond helping to establish the Convention in the first place, the EU plays a key role in the implementation and success of the CLRTAP. Thus, the Commission's Directorate-General for the Environment has a co-operation strategy with the CLRTAP, covering development of air pollution models and the maintenance of accurate inventories of air quality information (particularly through the European Environment Agency). The EU's research and monitoring efforts on air pollution are thus critical in directing and meeting international air quality commitments as well as developing and implementing EU air quality law.

---

emission limit values designed to prevent and, where that is not practicable, generally to reduce emissions and their impact on the environment as a whole', with this definition and further explanation contained in the Annexes of each Protocol.

[57] 1999 Gothenburg Protocol to Abate Acidification, Eutrophication and Ground-level Ozone, as amended in 2012.

[58] The 1998 Aarhus Protocol on Heavy Metals requires parties to phase out leaded petrol, and contains measures for reducing or managing heavy metal emissions from products such as batteries.

[59] This requires the determination of multi-pollutant, multi-effect 'critical loads' in relation to particular harmful effects. See, for example, 1988 Sofia Protocol concerning the Control of Emissions of Nitrogen Oxides or their Transboundary Fluxes (agreeing to negotiate a new instruments for NO_x adopting this approach, and to conduct further scientific research for his purpose: arts 2(3) and 6); 1994 Oslo Protocol on Further Reduction of Sulphur Emissions (art 2(1), subject to ongoing review of assessments of critical loads).

EU air quality regulation—Air Quality Framework Directive

Directive 2008/50/EC on ambient air quality and cleaner air for Europe (the Air Quality Framework Directive or AQFD)[60] is the latest milestone in EU air quality law. It both streamlines air quality law—in that it combines almost all previous EU Directives that constituted the framework for air quality management, including air quality standards and targets for particular pollutants[61]—and includes new and updated obligations in relation to PM-2.5.[62] The pollutants covered by the Directive are SO_2, NO_x, lead (Pb), carbon monoxide (CO), benzene, PM-10, PM-2.5, and ozone. Note that the Directive applies variable standards, as well as variable monitoring obligations, depending on the risks associated with particular pollutants (ground-level ozone and PM-2.5 have quite distinct regimes), geographical differences between and within Member States, and Member States' records in reaching air quality standards.

Core obligations of the AQFD

The AQFD has four main aspects, which require various types of interrelated Member State action on ambient air quality:

1. monitoring and assessment obligations;

2. mandatory environmental quality standards and targets;

3. obligations to introduce air quality plans; and

4. publicity and communication obligations.

Examples and key features of these four aspects are given here, although you will need to read the Directive in full to get a comprehensive view of its obligations.

First, the AQFD sets out a detailed regime for monitoring and assessing concentrations of pollutants in ambient air. It is only by collecting air pollution data that air quality standards can be met and implemented. However, since atmospheric pollution levels vary so greatly across the EU—due to differing geographical terrains, the locations of industrial, urban, and rural sites, and in light of different community practices as well as atmospheric reactions and weather movements—a vast web of measuring stations is required across the EU to ensure acceptable air quality levels overall. The AQFD requires Member States to establish 'zones or agglomerations' throughout their territory (Article 4), so that areas with relatively common air quality characteristics can be assessed together. The Directive seeks to minimize monitoring burdens by requiring intensive physical monitoring—obtaining air quality data from 'fixed measurements' taken at discrete sampling points—only in zones where threshold levels of pollutants are exceeded. For zones in which concentrations of relevant pollutants fall below the relevant threshold levels (as set out in Annex II of the AQFD), modelling or objective-estimation techniques are sufficient for generating required air pollution data in those areas (Articles 6(3) and (4)).

---

[60] See n 35.

[61] The previous framework Directive (96/62/EC) set basic principles for managing and assessing air quality levels in Member States, with four daughter directives providing specific air quality standards and targets, and numerical criteria and further detail for assessment obligations. The fourth of these daughter Directives—Directive 2004/107/EC relating to arsenic, cadmium, mercury, nickel, and polycyclic aromatic hydrocarbons in ambient air—remains outside the current AQFD, which otherwise merges all previous Directives, including the EoI Decision (n 26).

[62] Wilde indicates that the AQFD overall brings little substantive change, and argues that the failure to include ecological standards was disappointing: Mark Wilde, 'The New Directive on Ambient Air Quality and Cleaner Air for Europe' (2010) 12 Env LR 282, 290.

The role of scientific methods in establishing and meeting these measurement obligations in Chapter II of the Directive is central, from constituting the obligations—in setting assessment thresholds, requiring Member States to carry out modelling and estimation techniques, and using international scientific measurement methods as references (Article 8)—to being shaped by the Directive's requirements. In the latter sense, Article 7 and Annex III prescribe how sampling points for fixed measurements are to be located and installed. Note also that different assessment requirements apply for the various pollutants covered by the Directive. Thus, Article 6(5) provides additional assessment criteria for PM-2.5, and Articles 9 and 10 provide more stringent measuring obligations for ground-level ozone. In sum, these detailed assessment obligations impose intensive implementation obligations on Member States and require considerable scientific resources and infrastructure.

Second, the AQFD sets out a series of environmental quality standards (EQSs) and targets, which again vary for the different pollutants covered, in light of their respective risks to human and environmental health and current knowledge about how to control them, as well as the costs involved in doing this. Broadly, there is a sliding scale of air quality standards, with differing regulatory obligations and consequences associated with them, as set out in Table 15.1. The different standards are listed roughly in order of decreasing stringency (that is, increasing concentration limits of pollutants in numerical terms), albeit that some EQSs only apply to certain pollutants.

Table 15.1 Summary of AQFD air quality standards

Environmental Quality Standard	Regulatory Obligation/Consequence	Pollutants Covered
Long-term objective	All necessary measures not entailing disproportionate costs must be taken to ensure these are attained, by a currently undefined date (Article 17(1)) Non-derogation obligation where this EQS already met, so far as meteorological conditions and transboundary nature of ozone permits (Article 18)	Ozone
Critical level	Mandatory—EQS for the protection of vegetation, must complied with (Article 14)	SO_2, NO_x
National exposure reduction target	All necessary measures not entailing disproportionate costs must be taken with a view to attaining target (Article 15(1))	PM-2.5
Limit value	Mandatory—EQS for the protection of human health, shall not be exceeded; margins of tolerance apply; air quality plans required where exceedances, short term action plans may be drawn up if risk of exceedance (Articles 13, 16(2), 23, and 24(1)) Non-derogation obligation where this EQS already met (Article 12)	SO_2, NO_2, PM-10, Pb, CO, benzene, PM-2.5 (from 2015) SO_2, NO_2, PM-10, PM-2.5, Pb, benzene, CO

(Continued)

Table 15.1 (*Continued*)

Environmental Quality Standard	Regulatory Obligation/Consequence	Pollutants Covered
Exposure concentration obligation	Mandatory—EQS for the protection of human health, shall not be exceeded (Article 15(2))	PM-2.5
Target value	All necessary measures not entailing disproportionate costs must be taken to ensure this EQS not exceeded (Articles 16(1), 17) Air quality plans required to attain ozone target values where exceedances; short term action plans may be drawn up if risk of exceedance (Articles 17(2), 23, and 24(1))	PM-2.5 Ozone
Information threshold	Public to be informed if these pollutant levels reached (Article 19)	Ozone
Alert threshold	Public to be informed if these pollutant levels reached (Article 19); short-term action plan required if risk of exceedance (Article 24)	SO_2, NO_2, ozone

The precise numerical values for these different standards are set out in the Annexes to the Directives, and are subject to review as scientific knowledge develops. As you can see from Table 15.1, not all pollutants covered by the Directive have every type of EQS in the Directive associated with their management—the various kinds of EQSs are used as appropriate to control air quality problems known to be associated with a particular pollutant. Note also that the various EQSs have different averaging periods, which affects their level of stringency as well. Thus, a critical level averaged over a calendar year will allow more instances of exceedance than a limit value averaged over one hour, and in practice there are both annual and yearly standards to be reached for various pollutants. The margins of tolerance allowed for exceeding limit values also vary—they are invariably greater for hourly averages, and reduce to zero for yearly averages for some pollutants. Another factor that affects calculations as to whether EQSs are exceeded is that contributions to pollution levels from natural sources are not counted, if they can be evidenced (Article 20).[63]

For some pollutants covered by the Directive and in certain circumstances, extensions of time for attaining limit values are also available. Thus, for NO_2 and benzene, Member States that *cannot* (as opposed to *will not*) meet the required limit values in particular zones *may* postpone the limit value deadlines (1 January 2010), but not past 1 January 2015 (Article 22(1)). An extension of time is dependent on relevant air quality plans under Article 23 being established (which shall demonstrate how conformity with limit values will be achieved before the new deadline), and any exceedences of limit values not going beyond the maximum margins of tolerance set out in Annex XI. Extensions of time will not be accepted by the Commission beyond the time actually needed to comply, as indicated by evidence provided by Member States. Similar extensions of time are available for PM-10, where conformity with limit values (by 1 January 2005) cannot be achieved

---

[63] Similar allowances are made for winter sanding or salting of roads in calculating PM–10 levels: art 21.

due to 'site-specific dispersion characteristics, adverse climatic conditions or transboundary contributions', but not beyond 11 June 2011, although this was an exemption that was deemed to apply, rather than having been at the discretion of Member States to take up. Again, air quality plans must have been adopted, margins of tolerance applied, and all appropriate measures must be taken to meet any extended deadline (Article 22(2)).

The third feature of the AQFD, as seen in Table 15.1, is that is imposes obligations on Member States to introduce air quality management plans, both long-term and emergency plans, in relevant circumstances. Article 23 thus provides:

1. Where, in given zones or agglomerations, the levels of pollutants in ambient air exceed any limit value or target value, plus any relevant margin of tolerance in each case, Member States *shall ensure that air quality plans are established for those zones and agglomerations in order to achieve the related limit value or target value* specified in Annexes XI and XIV.

In the event of exceedances of those limit values for which the attainment deadline is already expired, the air quality plans shall set out appropriate measures, *so that the exceedance period can be kept as short as possible*. The air quality plans may additionally include specific measures aiming at the protection of sensitive population groups, including children.

Those air quality plans shall incorporate at least the information listed in Section A of Annex XV and may include measures pursuant to Article 24.

For more severe exceedances of limit values, Article 24 requires short-term action plans:

1. Where, in a given zone or agglomeration, there is a risk that the levels of pollutants will exceed one or more of the alert thresholds specified in Annex XII, Member States *shall draw up action plans indicating the measures to be taken in the short term in order to reduce the risk or duration of such an exceedance* [...]

However, where there is a risk that the alert threshold for ozone specified in Section B of Annex XII will be exceeded, Member States shall only draw up such short-term action plans when in their opinion there is a significant potential, taking into account national geographical, meteorological and economic conditions, to reduce the risk, duration or severity of such an exceedance [...]

2. The short-term action plans referred to in paragraph 1 may, depending on the individual case, provide for effective measures to control and, where necessary, suspend activities which contribute to the risk of the respective limit values or target values or alert threshold being exceeded. Those action plans may include measures in relation to motor-vehicle traffic, construction works, ships at berth, and the use of industrial plants or products and domestic heating. Specific actions aiming at the protection of sensitive population groups, including children, may also be considered in the framework of those plans.

Consider how drastic the measures adopted under an Article 24 short-term action plan could be–they might include traffic minimization, preventing heavily polluting vehicles on roads, or limiting certain construction works or the operation of industrial plants, at least in the short term to reduce pollution levels. However, such plans may be limited by other EU laws—as seen in the case of *Commission v Austria*, extracted below. Note also that, if relevant EQSs in the Directive are exceeded due to significant transboundary movement of air pollutants, or their precursor substances, then Member States are required to co-operate with each other, including by drawing up joint Article 23 air quality plans where appropriate (Article 25).

Fourth, the AQFD sets out publicity obligations, as also indicated in Table 15.1, in cases when information and alert thresholds are exceeded. In such cases, Member States shall take the necessary steps to inform the public by means of radio, television, newspapers, or the internet (Article 19). More broadly, Member States must make a range of air quality information available to the public, as Article 26 sets out:

> 1. Member States shall ensure that the public as well as appropriate organisations such as environmental organisations, consumer organisations, organisations representing the interests of sensitive populations, other relevant health-care bodies and the relevant industrial federations are informed, adequately and in good time, of the following:
>
> (a) ambient air quality in accordance with Annex XVI;
>
> (b) any postponement decisions pursuant to Article 22(1);
>
> [...]
>
> (d) air quality plans as provided for in Article 22(1) and Article 23 and programmes referred to in Article 17(2).
>
> The information shall be made available free of charge by means of any easily accessible media including the Internet or any other appropriate means of telecommunication [...]

These obligations reflect and reinforce access to environmental information obligations imposed on signatory states, including the EU and its Member States, by Article 4 of the Aarhus Convention.[64]

Implementing the AQFD

As can be seen from the nature and extent of the obligations under the AQFD, it places onerous compliance duties on Member States. This is one of the main perceived disadvantages of EQSs as a regulatory tool—they guarantee an optimal environmental outcome on their face, but they are technologically and administratively difficult to implement and enforce. Unsurprisingly, there has been variable implementation of the EU air quality controls across EU Member States, at least by the experience of precursor directives to AQFD.[65] The Commission reports that around one-sixth of environmental infringement cases relate to air quality, with the recent years having seen a marked increase in infringement cases in the air sector, including cases concerning PM-10 limit values not being met.[66] The UK, in particular, has been a serial offender in failing to meet mandatory EU limit values, particularly in heavily urbanized areas like central London.

Beyond Commission infringement proceedings, there is another powerful enforcement tool for getting Member States to fulfil their obligations under the AQFD. In *Janecek*, the ECJ found that the precursor provision to Article 24—Article 7(3) of Directive 96/62/EC—concerning the drawing up of short-term action plans was directly effective.

---

[64] See Section 3.1 of Chapter 7. The provisions of European Parliament and Council Directive 2007/2/EC of 14 March 2007 establishing an Infrastructure for Spatial Information in the European Community [2007] OJ L108/1 (INSPIRE) are also to be taken into account.

[65] Backes and others, 'Transformation of the first Daughter Directive on air quality in several EU Member States and its application in practice' (2005) 14 EELR 157.

[66] For the latest EU environmental infringement statistics, see: <http://ec.europa.eu/environment/legal/law/statistics.htm.> accessed 7 February 2013.

Case C-237/07 *Janecek v Freistaat Bayern*
(2008) ECR I-06221, paras 34–37, 39, 44, 46 (emphasis added)

34. [The issue is] whether an individual can require the competent national authorities to draw up an action plan in the case—referred to in Article 7(3) of Directive 96/62 [the precursor to Article 24 AQFD]—where there is a risk that the limit values or alert thresholds may be exceeded.

35. That provision places the Member States under a clear obligation to draw up action plans both where there is a risk of the limit values being exceeded and where there is a risk of the alert thresholds being exceeded. That interpretation, which follows from a straightforward reading of Article 7(3) [...] is, moreover, confirmed in the 12th recital in the preamble to the directive. What is laid down in relation to the limit values applies all the more with regard to the alert thresholds, in respect of which, moreover, Article 2—which defines the various terms used in the directive—provides that 'immediate steps shall be taken by the Member States as laid down in this Directive'.

36. In addition, the Court has consistently held that individuals are entitled, as against public bodies, to rely on the provisions of a directive which are unconditional and sufficiently precise [...]

37. As the Court of Justice has noted on numerous occasions, it is incompatible with the binding effect which Article 249 EC ascribes to a directive to exclude, in principle, the possibility of the obligation imposed by that directive being relied on by persons concerned. That consideration applies *particularly in respect of a directive which is intended to control and reduce atmospheric pollution and which is designed, therefore, to protect public health.*

[...]

39. It follows from the foregoing that the natural or legal persons directly concerned by a risk that the limit values or alert thresholds may be exceeded must be in a position to require the competent authorities to draw up an action plan where such a risk exists, if necessary by bringing an action before the competent courts.

[...]

44. [As to the content of the action plan, a]ccording to Article 7(3) [...], action plans must include the measures 'to be taken in the short term where there is a risk of the limit values and/or alert thresholds being exceeded, in order to reduce that risk and to limit the duration of such an occurrence'. It follows from that very wording that the Member States are not obliged to take measures to ensure that those limit values and/or alert thresholds are never exceeded.

[...]

46. It must be noted in this regard that, while the Member States thus have a discretion, Article 7(3) of Directive 96/62 includes limits on the exercise of that discretion which may be relied upon before the national courts [...], relating to the adequacy of the measures which must be included in the action plan with the aim of reducing the risk of the limit values and/or alert thresholds being exceeded and the duration of such an occurrence, taking into account the balance which must be maintained between that objective and the various opposing public and private interests.

In reading this case, be aware that Article 24 AQFD now has altered wording as to precisely when and why it requires the drawing up of short-term action plans (see the full text of Article 24 extract), so the outcome of *Janecek* does not now apply in exactly the same way. However, the overall point of the case remains—the mandatory provisions of the AQFD can provide a basis for individual legal action within Member States. Individual enforcement of the AQFD is thus an option that enhances the implementation possibilities of the Directive. It is also an option that individuals and NGOs may well be inclined to pursue, considering the deleterious consequences of poor air quality for human health. As seen in the ECJ's reasoning, this is one of the reasons bolstering the rationale for direct effect.[67] Note also that Member States have some discretion in formulating the content of the plans that they are required to draw up, but this is limited—any plans must still serve the purpose for which they are required: 'reducing the risk or duration' of the relevant exceedance.

Interactions with other regimes

As indicated at the outset of this section, the regulatory map dealing with air quality control is broader than the AQFD, albeit that it represents the central plank of EU air quality law, and has a significant effect in directing air quality law and policy in the UK. However, in light of the complexity of ambient air quality problems, a range of other regulatory strategies also contributes to reducing air quality problems, as examined further in the sub-sections that follow. Further, there is a range of other laws with which the AQFD overlaps in its application to environmental problems. These points of overlap can give rise to legal tensions, of two kinds in particular:

1. involving overlapping environmental regulation that works towards similar environmental outcomes in terms of improved air quality; or

2. involving other laws focused on different objectives, from English tort and property law to EU internal market law.

An example of the first kind of legal tension is the interaction between the AQFD and the Industrial Emissions control regime, which is examined further in the sub-section below on Industrial Emissions. An example of the second kind of legal tension is the interaction of the AQFD and EU internal market law. This was illustrated by the case of *Commission v Austria*, which concerned an alleged breach of Article 34 TFEU by the Austrian government by its ban on vehicles over 7.5 tonnes carrying certain goods (waste, rubble, building steel, and so on) on a section of the Austrian A1 motorway, which is a major European transport route. The measure had been introduced to improve air quality levels, and particularly to meet EU air quality standards for NO_2 in light of successively breached limit values. The Austrian government argued that its ban was adopted pursuant to the previous Air Quality Framework Directive. The Commission argued that the measure unlawfully restricted the free movement of goods.[68]

Case C-320/03 *Commission v Austria*
[2005] ECR I-9871 paras 66, 70–72, 73–77, 82–84

66. Clearly, by prohibiting heavy vehicles of more than 7.5 tonnes carrying certain categories of goods from travelling along a road section of paramount importance, constituting one of the main routes of land communication between southern Germany and northern Italy, the contested regulation obstructs the free movement of goods and, in particular, their free transit [...]

[...]

70. It is settled case-law that national measures capable of obstructing intra-Community trade may be justified by overriding requirements relating to protection of the environment provided that the measures in question are proportionate to the aim pursued [...]

71. In this case, it is undisputed that the contested regulation was adopted in order to ensure the quality of ambient air in the zone concerned and is therefore justified on environmental protection grounds.

72. In the first place, protection of the environment constitutes one of the essential objectives of the Community [...]

---

[67] But see, for example, *R (on the application of Clientearth) v Secretary of State for the Environment, Food and Rural Affairs* [2012] EWCA Civ 897.

[68] For more on this internal market law, see Section 5.2 of Chapter 4.

[...]

74. Secondly, more particularly concerning the protection of ambient air quality, it should be noted that, in Annex II, Directive 1999/30 [the former 'First Daughter Directive'] lays down limit values for nitrogen dioxide and oxides of nitrogen for the purpose of assessing that quality and determining at what point a preventive or corrective measure must be taken.

75. In that context, Directive 96/62 [former Air Quality Framework Directive] makes a distinction between the situation where there is a 'risk of the limit values being exceeded' and that where they have in fact been exceeded.

76. In respect of the first situation, Article 7(3) of that directive provides that Member States 'shall draw up action plans [...] in order to reduce that risk'. Those plans, the provision continues, may 'provide for measures to [...] suspend activities, including motor-vehicle traffic, which contribute to the limit values being exceeded'.

77. In the second situation, namely where it has been established that the levels of one or more pollutants exceed the limit values, increased by the margin of tolerance, Article 8(3) of Directive 96/62 provides that Member States 'shall take measures to ensure that a plan or programme is prepared or implemented for attaining the limit value within the specific time limit' [...]

[...]

82. However, the measures under [the relevant body of Austrian laws] cannot be described as a 'plan' or 'programme' within the meaning of Article 8(3) of Directive 96/62, since they are not in any way connected to a specific situation in which limit values have been exceeded. As for the contested regulation itself, adopted on the basis of [these Austrian laws], even if it could be described as a plan or programme, it does not, as the Commission has pointed out, contain all the information listed in Annex IV to Directive 96/62 [now Annex XV AQFD]...

83. In those circumstances, even if one were to concede that the contested regulation is based on Article 8(3) of Directive 92/62, it cannot be regarded as constituting a correct and full implementation of that provision.

84. The above finding does not, however, preclude the possibility that the obstacle to the free movement of goods arising from the traffic ban laid down by the contested regulation might be justified by one of the imperative requirements in the public interest endorsed by the case-law of the Court of Justice.

[The measure was ultimately found disproportionate and unlawful since other less restrictive means of restoring air quality had not been adequately explored.]

Again the relevant wording of the AQFD has changed, so this case needs to be read carefully in the context of current air quality law, but it does point to a difficult intersection between the Court's Article 34 TFEU jurisprudence and mandatory EU air quality requirements.[69] Consider the case if the Austrian government were to adopt a similar traffic ban to that in *Commission v Austria*, but now under an air quality plan that contained all relevant information required by Annex XV AQFD. Would the ban still infringe Article 34 TFEU if less restrictive measures have not been adequately explored and objectively discounted? If so, then the Directive's requirements would be constrained, if not undermined, by other aspects of EU law, which would not sit well with Article 11's integration principle: that environmental protection requirements must be integrated into *all* of the EU's policies and activities.

---

[69] This difficulty was reinforced by the subsequent decision in Case C-28/09 *Commission v Austria* (ECJ, 21 December 2011), in which the suite of road traffic measures subsequently introduced by the Austrian government on the same motorway (in an effort to be more justifiable in free movement terms whilst also meeting the requirements of the previous AQFD) were still found to be disproportionate.

National Emission Ceilings (NEC) Directive

Another important part of the UK air quality regulatory map is the regime of national emissions ceilings for various pollutants that applies within EU Member States which are, all signatories of the Gothenburg Protocol of the CLRTAP that contains explicit emissions ceilings requirements in relation to acidifying and eutrophying pollutants and ground level ozone precursors—SO_2, NOx, VOCs, and ammonia. This led to Directive 2001/81/EC on national emission ceilings for certain atmospheric pollutants (NEC Directive),[70] covering these four sets of pollutants. It set initial emission ceilings to be reached by 2010 and maintained thereafter—prescribing the *total* number of emissions for each pollutant from *any* source within the national geographical area,[71] with Member States to decide how those emissions are controlled and kept within the required overall limits. The next phase of these emission limit ceilings involves them being reset for a 2020 benchmark, with a view to achieving the overall goal of 'not exceeding critical levels and loads and of effective protection of all people against recognised health risks from air pollution'.[72] As indicated already, this Directive is likely to be updated soon.

Like EQSs, national emissions ceilings are regulatory tools that focus on environmental effects, by setting legal rules that match and are directly focused on desired environmental outcomes. In doing so, they again raise serious challenges of implementation and compliance monitoring. This is partly due to the uncertainties involved in modelling by Member States in their reporting of emissions to the Commission, albeit that a common international air pollution model has been used.[73] Member States have also found a range of challenges in meeting ceilings, from uncertainty in emission factors and unpredictable growth patterns, to flawed assumptions that abatement measures are universal and internal political resistance.[74]

Again, as seen in relation to the AQFD, the NEC Directive forms part of a bigger regulatory map, overlapping with other environmental regimes,[75] but also with other non-environmentally focused legal regimes. In relation to the latter, there are interactions with other areas of EU law in particular, which limit the means by which ceilings can be reached. An example of this was seen in the case of *Commission v Netherlands*, where an NO_x emissions trading scheme was found to be an unlawful state aid under Article 107 TFEU, even though set up to meet the requirements of the NEC Directive.[76] The conflict between laws is less intractable here, since the NEC Directive does not prescribe any particular means by which the ceilings are met, although it does show how that EU policy priorities need to be carefully reconciled.[77]

Industrial emissions—regulating emissions at source

As a further regulatory approach to tackling the air quality problem, the EU Directive on Industrial Emissions (IED) regulates air pollution emissions at source, controlling pollutants emitted by

---

[70] See n 24.

[71] Excluding international maritime traffic and aircraft emissions, other than take-off and landing: art 2.

[72] NEC Directive, art 1.

[73] AEA Energy & Environment, 'Evaluation of National Plans submitted under the National Emissions Ceilings Directive 2001/81/EC: Synthesis Report', March 2008, available at <http://ec.europa.eu/environment/air/pollutants/pdf/evaluation_synthesis_report.pdf> accessed 7 February 2013.

[74] Ibid.

[75] Beyond air quality control, there are other measures designed to tackle acidification, eutrophication, in particular in water regulation: for example, Council Directive 91/676/EEC of 12 December 1991 concerning the protection of waters against pollution caused by nitrates from agricultural sources [1991] OJ L375/1.

[76] Case C-279/08 P *Commission v Netherlands* (ECJ, 8 September 2011).

[77] Furthermore, the legal issues associated with these overlapping policy areas are not straightforward to resolve. Thus, at first instance in *Commission v Netherlands*, the Netherlands scheme was found to be lawful due to its environmental rationale: Case T-233/04 *Netherlands v Commission* [2008] ECR II-591.

individual heavily polluting installations, mainly with emission limit values (ELVs) that are imposed and monitored through permits.[78] The IED is a rationalizing Directive, which combined and updated seven previous EU Directives that regulated industrial emissions in different ways.[79] The Directive covers a range of large installations—from those covered by the integrated pollution prevention and control (IPPC) regime,[80] to large combustion plants (LCPs are power stations with a thermal input over 50 MW), waste incineration plants, and installations the production processes of which generate titanium dioxide (particularly paint production) or VOCs (from the use of organic solvents). The Directive contains various Chapters that regulate polluting emissions from these different types of installations in different ways. For example, for LCPs and waste incineration plans, chimneystacks of sufficient height to safeguard human health and the environment are required, and for some LCPs, minimum rates of desulphurization must be met.[81]

However, the IED broadly requires that the large industrial installations within its scope meet certain ELVs in their operation, for various pollutants. These ELVs not only cover emissions into the air—they certainly include atmospheric emissions, but the Directive is intentionally focused on controlling polluting emissions in an integrated way, covering pollution of all environmental media.[82] Further, these ELVs are calculated in different ways. For IPPC installations, a BAT ('best available techniques') standard informs the ELVs that apply, setting up a dynamic technology-driven standard.[83] For the installations covered by the Directive's other chapters (LCPs, waste incinerators, and so on), numerical limits are set in the Annexes as the relevant ELVs. These prescribed values are still connected to BAT, in that they have been determined on the basis of clean industrial technologies and in some cases may be more stringent than ELVs negotiated on a sectoral basis under the IPPC regime. The IED also contains flexibility mechanisms and derogations, which are a pragmatic response to various factors, including: more heavily polluting technologies having been permitted historically (transitional arrangements only),[84] varying local economic and environmental conditions,[85] the particular technical and economic characteristics of an installation,[86] emergency situations,[87] or the testing of new technologies.[88]

Beyond flexibility in the legal ELV standards, there might also be flexibility in their implementation or enforcement. Because ELVs are included as permit conditions for each relevant installation, their enforcement depends on regulatory practices and the relationships of regulators with regulated industry. However, the scientific aspect of enforcement is less prone to uncertainty, since measuring emissions from a single installation does not rely on modelling, fixed measurements over a wide geographic area, or unpredictable environmental elements or atmospheric reactions take into

---

[78] European Parliament and Council Directive 2010/75/EU Directive on industrial emissions (integrated pollution prevention and control) [2010] OJ L334/17 ('IED').

[79] Directive 2008/1/EC concerning integrated pollution prevention and control; Directive 78/176/EEC on titanium dioxide industrial waste; Directive 82/883/EEC on the surveillance and monitoring of titanium dioxide waste; Directive 92/112/EEC on the reduction of titanium dioxide industrial waste; Directive 1999/13/EC on reducing emissions of volatile organic compounds (VOCs); Directive 2000/76/EC on waste incineration; Directive 2001/80/EC on the limitation of emissions of certain pollutants from large combustion plants (LCP Directive). All of these Directives cease to have effect from 7 January 2014, except the LCP Directive, which is replaced from 1 January 2016.

[80] See Section 2 of Chapter 17.

[81] IED, arts 30, 30(1), and 46(1).

[82] The IPPC Chapter of the IED (Chapter II) does this in the most holistic way, taking into consideration cross-media effects of emissions in setting ELVs (art 14(1)(a)), whereas the other IED Chapters tend to have discrete measures dealing with emissions into air, water and soil, and waste emissions.

[83] See Section 2.1 of Chapter 17.

[84] For example, transitional national plans or agreed limited life times for some LCPs: IED, arts 32 and 33.

[85] For example, art 15(4).

[86] For example, art 59(2) and (3) (note that BAT must still be complied with).

[87] For example, art 30(6).

[88] For example, art 27.

account (as in the case of EQSs under the AQFD). This is one of the advantages of ELVs as a regulatory tool—they are capable of relatively accurate monitoring at the source of the relevant emission.

As already indicated, the IED regime can intersect with other areas of air quality law in legally uncertain ways. In *Rockware Glass*,[89] the Court of Appeal considered how the IPPC regime fits with EQSs set under the Air Quality Framework Directive (AQFD). In this case, the IPPC permit of Quinn Glass Limited—a glass manufacturer, which planned to build the largest glass container factory in Europe at a site at Elton, near Ellesmere Port—was being challenged by a competitor, Rockware Glass Limited. Rockware Glass argued that Chester City Council, in granting the permit, had acted unlawfully, particularly in failing to apply properly the concept of BAT in setting emission limit values for NO_x in the permit's conditions. Quinn Glass responded that the relevant ELVs did not need to be set any more strictly to meet the required IPPC BAT standard. This was particularly considering that the AQFD's EQSs for NO_x in the surrounding air and area would be met if the specified ELVs were respected—this demonstrated that an acceptable level of pollution was being released in the vicinity. The Court of Appeal rejected this argument.

R (Rockware Glass Limited) v Quinn Glass Ltd and Chester CC
[2006] EWCA Civ 992 paras 30–31, 33–37 (Buxton LJ)

30. The implications of [Quinn's] argument are fundamental. That is because [...] if it is correct the argument renders otiose the whole of the rest of this case, and indeed renders otiose most of the structures set up by the United Kingdom to operate the IPPC regime. That is because under this argument the only question that the regulator need ask himself is whether a proposed installation will raise the local EQS above the permitted level. There was therefore no need for [Chester City Council's employee] Mr Hosker to go through the process of investigation that he described in his evidence and certainly no need for him to include the annually reducing levels of permitted emissions. The only question that the court could ask itself when reviewing his work was whether EQS had been met. The errors that the judge considered that he had made were, all of them, irrelevant.

31. That was the basic version of this argument. Perhaps a subset of it was that the Directive also called for a balance between level of protection and cost. There could be no justification for requiring an installer to incur extra costs on more protection, such as, in the present case, protection that would reduce levels of emission below [the level in the contested permit], if the existing installation before that protection already met EQS.

[...]

33. I find the argument wholly unconvincing, both when one considers the general pattern of environmental protection and when one considers the detail of the legislation. As to environmental protection in general, there is a clear, obvious and centrally important distinction between the overall requirements of air quality and management on the one hand, and on the other the precautionary requirements imposed on installations of a particular sort that have been identified as potentially causing environmental problems. The latter are subject to strict and detailed regimes, which of course share the general aspirations of community environmental protection as a whole, but which address particular cases in detail.

34. That is particularly so of the national legislation and guidance that fills out the broader IPPC guidance... To put it bluntly, those who for their commercial purposes introduce potentially polluting operations have to be closely controlled, and cannot freeload on non-polluting local citizens by simply claiming that the EQS to which we all contribute has not yet been damaged [...]

---

[89] *R (Rockware Glass) v Quinn Glass Ltd and Chester CC* [2007] Env LR 3 (CA).

That is why detailed controls that do not refer to EQS are provided for in the IPPC Directive. When pressed on this point, [counsel for Quinn] was reduced to saying that the detailed controls were only machinery to enable a simple answer to be given to the single question of whether EQS was to be breached. If that were indeed their sole purpose, they are puzzlingly elaborate.

35. There are two other structural questions relevant to this argument. First the argument assumes that EQS levels are a datum or mark of Community approval. That is not so. […] [T]hey are minimum requirements […]

36. Second, the regime argued for by Quinn would be hopelessly impracticable. [Counsel for Quinn] pointed to the provisions for continued monitoring of installations and said that action could be taken against his client's plant if EQS were breached in the longer term. But that raises the question: action against whom? The point about EQS is that we are all in it together. If three more glassworks appear in Ellesmere Port, so that EQS is breached, which of them is to be required to take measures to reduce the EQS level to that which is acceptable? It is precisely for that sort of reason that the Community legislation sets limits, more stringent than the general environmental limits, plant by plant.

37. Against that background, it is hardly surprising that when we look at the terms of the legislation there is absolutely nothing in it that support Quinn's argument.

Rockware Glass shows that there are other regulatory regimes that complement the AQFD and also contribute to reducing ambient air pollution, which work in different ways and which also focus on limiting and preventing pollution at source. The IPPC regime has its own limitations in how far it can go in preventing air pollution from heavy industrial activity,[90] but it contributes something different from, and in most cases more environmentally ambitious than, the AQFD. *Rockware* also shows that having a multifaceted approach to regulating air quality does not mean having a neatly integrated and linked approach. Rather, there are many different ways to tackle the problem of air quality, and their points of overlap can give rise to difficult legal questions.

English air quality law

English law relating to ambient air quality largely involves implementation of the EU law obligations. Thus, the Environmental Permitting Regulations 2010 implement the requirements of the IED, and make the Environment Agency primarily responsible for its required permitting activities.[91] The NEC Directive is implemented via the National Emissions Ceiling Regulations 2002.[92] The EQSs under the AQFD are transposed into English law by the Air Quality Standards Regulations 2010,[93] which, like the NEC Regulations, simply put an obligation on the Secretary of State to ensure that Directive's various EQS requirements are met.

In terms of monitoring and assessment, DEFRA runs a series of monitoring networks for different pollutants throughout the UK,[94] with over 300 monitoring stations that involve both automatic and

---

[90] See Chapter 17.

[91] Or those of its precursor Directives. At the point of writing, as DEFRA was consulting on the transposition of the IED in England and Wales. See Section 2.2 of Chapter 17 for how the Environmental Permitting Regulations 2010 implement the Integrated Pollution Prevention and Control Chapter of the IED, and the Introduction to Part IV for discussion of the Regulations more generally.

[92] SI 2002/3118.

[93] SI 2010/1001.

[94] DEFRA's UK-AIR website provides information on these networks and makes collected data on pollutants available to the public: <http://uk–air.defra.gov.uk> accessed 7 February 2013.

non-automatic fixed measurement techniques.[95] These measurements rely on monitoring methods approved by the Environment Agency, and are supplemented by modelling where appropriate. Some of the networks are run by external bodies, such as the King's College London Environmental Research Group, which runs the London Air Quality Network, recording levels of pollutants across more than a hundred sites in London's boroughs and surrounding areas, as well as conducting supplementary modelling work.[96] Each year, DEFRA submits to the EU Commission collated data from these networks to determine compliance with the AQFD. DEFRA also maintains a separate emissions inventory—the National Atmospheric Emissions Inventory—recording emissions from a range of sources (e.g. industrial installations, mobile transport sources), using these both to meet CLRTAP reporting requirements and to feed data into air pollution models.[97]

As already discussed, the UK government has not always managed compliance with the AQFD's air quality standards, and has taken advantage of the available time extensions under the Directive for meeting PM-10 and NO_2 limit values. However, meeting these standards will be challenging in some of the UK's forty-three zones and agglomerations, particularly by roadsides in London and other major cities. The extended deadline for PM-10 (until June 2010) has now expired and areas of Greater London still exceed the limit values (in 2012–13). The UK government, with support from the London mayor, has adopted short-term measures to reduce the risk of the limit value being exceeded. However, if these measures do not result in sufficiently improved air quality in London, the Commission looks set to bring enforcement proceedings against the UK.[98] On extensions to NO_2 limit value deadlines, the UK government is also in a difficult position. This is firstly because it has not even applied for an extension of time for the worst offending zones (which may not comply with NO_2 standards until 2020 or 2025, including central London), and is thus in breach of the Directive.[99] In addition, the Commission has objected to time extensions requested for twelve out of twenty-four UK zones, and shortened the time of compliance with NO_2 limit values for four others.[100] By 1 January 2010 (the ordinary compliance deadline), only four of the UK's forty-three zones met the required limit values for NO_2.

Beyond these measures directly implementing EU law, there are other powers and laws for regulating air quality in the UK and England, which aim to improve air quality levels generally and thus also contribute to meeting EU air quality standards. Thus, the UK has a National Air Quality Strategy (NAQS), required under s 80 of the Environment Act 1995, which sets out a plan for meeting the UK's international and EU commitments.[101] Further, there are local measures required under the Air Quality (England) Regulations 2000.[102] These require local authorities to carry out regular reviews and assessments of air quality against standards and objectives prescribed in the regulations and to make action plans if air quality is found to breach the regulations for designated 'air quality management areas' (AQMAs). This local air quality management (LAQM) might seem to involve a minor piece of secondary legislation tacked on at the end of this topic, but it plays an important role in implementing air quality

---

[95] Automatic monitoring involves pollutant concentrations being measured and data collected from individual sites by modem. Non-automatic monitoring involves physical collection and chemical analysis of samples taken at sites.

[96] See London Air: <http://www.londonair.org.uk/LondonAir/Default.aspx> accessed 7 February 2013.

[97] See the NAEI website: <http://naei.defra.gov.uk> accessed 7 February 2013.

[98] Commission Decision on the notification by the United Kingdom of Great Britain and Northern Ireland of an exemption from the obligation to apply the daily limit value for PM10 in zones UK0001 and UK(GIB) (11 March 2011), C(2011) 1592 final.

[99] As conceded by the UK government in *R (Clientearth) v Secretary of State for the Environment, Food and Rural Affairs* [2011] EWHC 3623 (Admin), [2012] 1 CMLR 47.

[100] Commission Decision on the notification by the United Kingdom of Great Britain and Northern Ireland of a postponement of the deadline for attaining the limit values for NO2 in 24 air quality zones (25 June 2012), C(2012) 4155 final.

[101] DEFRA, *Air Quality Strategy for England, Scotland, Wales and Northern Ireland*, July 2007 ('NAQS').

[102] SI 2000/928 (as amended by SI 2002/3043), made under Part IV of the Environment Act 1995.

law, albeit that its role in complementing national air quality strategies and monitoring efforts is not altogether clear. LAQM was set up to provide a supplementary means of maintaining national air quality levels in a small number of 'pollution hotspots', beyond the reach of national efforts. In practice, by 2010, 58% of local authorities had declared AQMAs, some over their entire areas. This puts a considerable administrative burden on local authorities, and has led to some concern that monitoring and assessment efforts at local and national levels are being inefficiently duplicated, and that the role of local authorities in ensuring air quality standards needs to be clarified.[103]

Finally, there are also other legal mechanisms and powers to deal with air quality problems in UK and English law. There is the common law of nuisance, as examined in Section 2.1, as well as the Clean Air Act 1993 and its powers to introduce smoke control areas (prohibiting smoke from chimneys or the use of unauthorized fuel) where there are problematic smoke emissions from domestic or industrial sources. Otherwise, other national and local regulations can help to minimize air pollution levels, from traffic regulations[104] and vehicles standards, to climate change policy and planning controls.[105] The current NAQS proposes considering further measures such as a national road pricing scheme, low emission zones, increasing the uptake of low emission vehicles, retrofitting HGVs with diesel particulate filters, and reducing emissions from ships.[106]

FURTHER READING AND QUESTIONS

1. For further reading on regulating air pollution in international law, see Phoebe Okowa, *State Responsibility for Transboundary Air Pollution in International Law* (OUP 2000).

2. Various CLRTAP Protocols include obligations that heavily polluting installations should adopt 'best available techniques' (BATs). This is a concept and regulatory process standard that you will learn much more about in Chapter 17. Take one of the Protocols, say the 1998 Aarhus Protocol on Persistent Organic Pollutants (POPs), and examine the concept of BAT set out in Annex V. Do you think this imposes an onerous obligation? What exceptions to BAT exist? Is this the same kind of standard that forms the central regulatory obligation of the EU Integrated Pollution Prevention and Control regime, as set out in the Industrial Emissions Directive (see Chapter 17, Section 2)?

3. Compare the requirement for short-term action plans under Article 24(1) of the AQFD, with its precursor provision under Directive 96/62—Article 7(3), which provided that 'Member States shall draw up action plans indicating the measures to be taken in the short term where there is a risk of the limit values and/or alert thresholds being exceeded, in order to reduce that risk and to limit the duration of such an occurrence'. How does the new wording of Article 24 change the obligation on Member States? How might this affect the result in *Janecek*?

4. Section 2.2 considered how the AQFD intersects with other legal regimes, including the IPPC Chapter of the Industrial Emissions Directive. Consider how the AQFD and IED interact beyond the IPPC Chapter, in relation to large combustion plants, waste incinerators, and

---

[103] IHPC, *Review of Local Air Quality Management: A Report to DEFRA and the Devolved Administrations*, March 2010, 3–4. Available at <http://archive.defra.gov.uk/environment/quality/air/airquality/local/documents/laqm-report.pdf> accessed 7 February 2013.

[104] Bell, McGillivray, and Pedersen (n 40) 578–9.

[105] On climate change policy synergies, see NAQS (n 101) 36–39. For planning and air quality control, see the National Planning Policy Framework and general planning law principles, discussed in Chapter 18.

[106] NAQS (n 101) 44–49. Note also the measures no longer being considered, including product standards for domestic boilers and a switch away from coal to gas and oil for domestic combustion: ibid, 45.

> installations using organic solvents. On the interaction between the EU air quality law and regulation of large combustion plants, see M Wilde, 'Best Available Techniques (BAT) and Coal-Fired Power Stations: Can the Energy Gap be Plugged Without Increasing Emissions?' (2008) 20(1) JEL 87 (note this article was written prior to the revised AQFD).

3 CLIMATE CHANGE

3.1 CLIMATE CHANGE AND THE LAW

The climate change problem

The climate change problem was set out in Section 1.2, in terms of its basic pollutants and mechanisms. Whilst there has been considerable dispute over scientific knowledge in relation to climate change, there is now an accepted body of science that supports the view that climate change is a global environmental problem with irreversible and potentially catastrophic climate effects, which is being caused and exacerbated by anthropogenic GHG emissions.[107] International, EU, and UK policy-makers accept this view and it frames the regulatory options that have been pursued in response at all these jurisdictional levels. A key feature of this scientific understanding of the problem, which provides the assumed starting point for climate change-related regulation, is that the *total* concentration of anthropogenic GHGs in the global atmosphere is the relevant cause of the amplified greenhouse effect and thus global warming. Accordingly, while international efforts to reduce emissions are required, in light of the scale of response needed to deal with the problem, no particular GHG emitter or emission is required to be controlled, nor is any particular carbon sink to be preserved. As a result, various regulatory options are available to policy-makers, including trading schemes and financial incentives to preserve and manage forests, which are intended to be taken up by a large number of nations, operators, and individuals, but do not prescribe direct and targeted land use controls or individual liability for causing climate change.

Further, the regulatory approaches adopted to deal with climate change can in turn frame and define the very problem of climate change. For example, by focusing regulatory efforts on pricing GHG emissions (and pricing sinks that absorb such emissions), the climate change problem is broadly shaped as a financial cost of human activity and industrialization. It may be that this financial cost is found to be unaffordable in global terms, and so cannot simply be paid off to solve the problem, but the climate change problem also has ecological, socio-political, and ethical dimensions that are not easily captured through regulatory strategies that focus solely on financial metrics and market mechanisms. As the regulatory responses to climate change are set out in this section, keep in mind the extent to which they reflect the climate change problem in all these different dimensions.

What is climate change law?

On one view, 'climate change law' includes more than the sum total of discrete regulatory responses adopted to deal with the climate change problem. Due to the global and also deeply socially embedded nature of the problem and its causes, the law that actually relates to climate change is very wide-ranging, as Peel considers.

---

[107] See n 10.

Jacqueline Peel, 'Climate Change Law: The Emergence of a New Legal Discipline'
(2008) 32 MULR 922, 978

Not only does climate change have an integral international dimension, but it is also a problem that requires the integrated efforts of governments from the local to the national levels, ideally working across environmental sectors such as pollution control, water management and biodiversity conservation. Moreover, in a governance system that aspires to be democratic and participatory, recognising a diverse range of interests in, and responses to, climate change is essential, even though this is likely to give rise to conflicting perspectives on the appropriate content of regulatory measures. Finally, environmental regulatory analysis increasingly reveals that complex environmental problems such as climate change necessitate complex regulatory systems embracing more than one type of legal mechanism [giving rise to challenges of regulatory coordination, which also extend to the interaction between climate change law and other regulatory fields] [...]

[...] At the international level, coordination between the climate change regime and bodies dealing with issues of human rights and global trade looms as an issue of future significance. Domestically, we are increasingly seeing the penetration of climate change considerations into a variety of legal areas such as insurance law, corporate law, planning law, taxation law and energy law.

Peel's point about the broad range of laws that apply to, and which can affect, the problem of climate change is a good one, and you should keep in mind how the air quality regimes examined in Section 2 and in other chapters of this book—including pollution control, planning, nature conservation, and environmental impact assessment—also constitute regulatory responses to the climate change problem, and how well they integrate with the bespoke regulatory responses considered in this section.

Beyond the regulatory response to climate change by governments, scholarly analysis to date has also focused on the prospects of *climate change litigation* as a legal response to climate change, both to deter climate change-causing behaviour (judged to be unreasonable, a wrong, or otherwise unlawful) and to right past wrongs, that is, actions that have caused harm to others by contributing to climate change. Climate change litigation might also be seen as a 'gap filler', where regulatory responses are weak or not yet dealing effectively with the climate change problem. Peel also discusses the nature of this litigation, as a key component of what she sees as the 'new legal discipline' of climate change law.

Jacqueline Peel, 'Climate Change Law: The Emergence of a New Legal Discipline'
(2008) 32 MULR 922, 955–957

[C]ases brought in an effort to abate current greenhouse emissions from activities such as coal mines and coal-fired power stations have already made a significant contribution to the development of climate change law in Australia and abroad. The turn to the courts is largely a consequence of inaction on climate change at the national level (at least until the end of 2007), which led environmental groups and others to explore non-legislative solutions such as litigation to the problem of global warming. Climate change litigation (seeking redress for damage arising from human activities said to be causing climate change) may take a range of forms.

[...]

> [...] [W]hile recognising the different nature of the actions brought and the role of particular legislation and policies in determining outcomes, there is a need to look for 'common features' in the case law, identifying 'issues, principles and approaches that apply across the climate law domain',[108] [particularly for developing a legal culture more aware of the need to factor climate change considerations into environmental decision-making.]

Despite Peel's suggestion that a turn to the courts is a key plank of climate change law, there are at least two problems with this, from a legal perspective. First, there will be serious problems of causation and adducing scientific proof if an action requires proof that harm has been caused by climate change-inducing activities. This is because climate change consequences, which might involve coastal erosion or flooding, can rarely be attributed to single or even discretely identifiable anthropogenic sources of GHG emissions—relevent emissions may have occurred in many locations across multiple jurisdictions and they may also take some time (decades or longer) to cause the relevant harm.

Second, identifying or defining 'climate change litigation' is not straightforward, as Peel acknowledges. This is because climate change cases can occur in a range of jurisdictions, and involve a range of legal questions—from negligence claims to public and constitutional law disputes—with climate change issues both central and peripheral to a particular case. In short, there is a range of legal cultures and contexts in which 'climate change cases' may arise and this suggests that looking for common features or principles is methodologically problematic.[109] In EU law, for example, there are cases challenging various aspects of the EU emissions trading scheme, which involve issues of EU law (such as the principles of equal treatment and proportionality), as well as interpretive questions relating to the particular details of the scheme itself, which also invoke broader constitutional questions of EU law. These are not legal issues that are easily translatable into other legal contexts, and they relate more to EU law than particular features of climate change or climate change litigation more broadly. Having said that, some scholars maintain that there are lessons to be learned from climate change litigation across legal contexts and jurisdictions. Osofsky highlights how the jurisdiction-specific nature of courts and tribunals can play an important role in grounding, or 'rescaling', legal aspects of the otherwise inherently multi-jurisdictional problem of climate change.

Hari M Osofsky, 'Conclusion: Adjudicating Climate Change Across Scales' in William CG Burns and Hari M Osofsky (eds), *Adjudicating Climate Change: State, National and International Approaches* (CUP 2009) 378–79

> The tribunals adjudicating climate change litigation and the laws that they are relying upon generally are constituted at specific, fixed scales [...]
>
> The fluidity in the scales of this litigation comes not from the tribunals themselves then, but rather from the multiscalar nature of the problem of climate change and regulatory efforts to address it. These "fixed" entities, in their stability, provide a framework in which contestation across scales can take place. The aim of this litigation is not to shift the scales of the tribunals and what law they can consider, but rather to rescale aspects of regulating greenhouse gas emissions and impacts.

---

[108] Citing Tim Bonyhady, 'The New Australian Climate Law' in Tim Bonyhady and Peter Christoff (eds), *Climate Law in Australia* (Federation Press 2007) 13.

[109] As debated in papers at the British Academy, *Roundtable Workshop an Climate Change Litigation, Policy and Mobilization* (April 2012, London).

Whatever the merits of this scholarly debate, climate change litigation to date has been limited and fragmented. Sections 3.2, 3.3, and 3.4 now examine in more detail the regulatory responses to climate change, which represent direct legal and governance responses to the climate change problem.

3.2 INTERNATIONAL CLIMATE CHANGE POLICY AND REGULATION

The central plank of the international climate change regime is the UN Framework Convention on Climate Change (UNFCCC), which *encourages* stabilization of GHG emissions by industrialized countries at levels that will not cause dangerous climate effects, and establishes a core principle of 'common but differentiated responsibilities'. This principle recognizes that developed countries are principally responsible for the current high levels of atmospheric GHG emissions after over 150 years of industrial activity, and places heavier regulatory and financial burdens on those nations for dealing with the problem. The subsequent Kyoto Protocol *requires* such action, imposing binding GHG emissions reductions on developed nations, amongst other things. However, Kyoto's initiative and progressive spirit are at risk of falling into abeyance as its first commitment period has ended (2008–12), and the next phase of international climate change obligations fails in significant respects to be clearly defined or agreed (at the time of writing).

UN Framework Convention on Climate Change (UNFCCC)

The first Intergovernmental Panel on Climate Change report on the problem of global warming, which was prepared in 1990 by an international collaborative scientific effort under the auspices of the UNEP and WMO, led to the adoption of the UNFCCC at the Rio Conference on Environment and Development in 1992.[110] The scientific case setting out the problem of climate change thus drove and framed the regulatory response at the international level. This can be seen in the Convention's core objective in Article 2, which places scientific facts at the core of the commitment made by signatory states:

> The ultimate objective of this Convention and any related legal instruments that the Conference of the Parties may adopt is to achieve, in accordance with the relevant provisions of the Convention, stabilization of greenhouse gas concentrations in the atmosphere *at a level that would prevent dangerous anthropogenic interference with the climate system*. Such a level should be achieved within a time frame sufficient to allow ecosystems to adapt naturally to climate change, to ensure that food production is not threatened and to enable economic development to proceed in a sustainable manner.

It is not surprising then that the IPCC has continued to play a key role in determining what constitute such 'dangerous anthropogenic interferences' with the climate system and in informing subsequent policy and regulatory developments concerning climate change at the international level. Thus, the IPCC's subsequent three reports (in 1995, 2001, and 2007 respectively) have informed ongoing climate negotiations, contributing relevant scientific information and methodologies for obligations under the Kyoto Protocol,[111] and the fourth assessment report being a central aspect of negotiations for the 2009 Copenhagen Accord, discussed further below. The fifth IPCC assessment report is expected in 2014.

---

[110] UN Framework Convention on Climate Change (adopted 9 May 1992, ratified 21 March 1994) 1771 UNTS 107 ('UNFCCC').

[111] United Nations, Kyoto Protocol to the United Nations Framework Convention on Climate Change (adopted 11 December 1997; ratified 16 February 2005) Kyoto Protocol, arts 3 and 5 ('KP').

As its name suggests, the UNFCCC is a framework convention—it sets out overall goals, principles, and the direction of international regulation, rather than comprehensive detailed commitments. In terms of principles, as indicated already, the Convention establishes the principle of 'common but differentiated responsibilities'. This manifests in the two Annexes, which list those developed nations that will be required to 'take the lead in combating climate change and the adverse effects thereof'.[112] Other general principles feature the need to protect the climate system for future as well as present generations, sustainable development, a version of the precautionary principle,[113] the promotion of an open economic system, and the need to consider special circumstances of developing countries.[114]

In terms of commitments, Article 4(1) of the Convention requires all parties—developed and developing—to *report* national anthropogenic emissions; to undertake mitigation programmes; to take climate change into account in their social, economic, and environmental policies and actions; and to cooperate in research and information sharing in relation to the climate system and climate change, including technology development and transfer. Further, Article 4(2) establishes differentiated responsibilities for developed country parties, requiring in particular the 41 'Annex I parties' to adopt policies and measures to *limit* emissions and enhance GHG sinks and reservoirs. Articles 4(3) and 4(4) go a step further, requiring Annex II parties (a subset of Annex I countries) to finance developing countries in meeting their obligations under the Convention, including funding technology transfer, as well as assisting developing nations to meet some costs of adapting to climate change.

Kyoto Protocol

The Kyoto Protocol, signed in 1997 and ratified in 2005, is a protocol to the UNFCCC. In particular, it derives from and expands on the Convention's Article 4(2) obligations on Annex I developed nations. The core provisions and obligations of the Protocol are set out here.

United Nations, Kyoto Protocol to the United Nations Framework Convention on Climate Change (1997; 2005)

Article 3

1. The Parties included in Annex I shall, individually or jointly, ensure that their aggregate anthropogenic carbon dioxide equivalent emissions of the greenhouse gases listed in Annex A do not exceed their assigned amounts, calculated pursuant to their quantified emission limitation and reduction commitments inscribed in Annex B and in accordance with the provisions of this Article, with a view to reducing their overall emissions of such gases by at least 5 per cent below 1990 levels in the commitment period 2008 to 2012 [...]

[...]

3. The net changes in greenhouse gas emissions by sources and removals by sinks resulting from direct human-induced land-use change and forestry activities, limited to afforestation, reforestation and deforestation since 1990, measured as verifiable changes in carbon stocks in each commitment period, shall be used to meet the commitments under this Article of each Party included in Annex I [...]

[...]

10. Any emission reduction units, or any part of an assigned amount, which a Party acquires from another Party in accordance with the provisions of Article 6 or of Article 17 shall be added to the assigned amount for the acquiring Party.

---

[112] UNFCCC, art 3(1).
[113] Ibid, art 3(3).
[114] Ibid, art 3.

11. Any emission reduction units, or any part of an assigned amount, which a Party transfers to another Party in accordance with the provisions of Article 6 or of Article 17 shall be subtracted from the assigned amount for the transferring Party.

12. Any certified emission reductions which a Party acquires from another Party in accordance with the provisions of Article 12 shall be added to the assigned amount for the acquiring Party.

13. If the emissions of a Party included in Annex I in a commitment period are less than its assigned amount under this Article, this difference shall, on request of that Party, be added to the assigned amount for that Party for subsequent commitment periods.
[...]

Article 4

1. Any Parties included in Annex I that have reached an agreement to fulfil their commitments under Article 3 jointly, shall be deemed to have met those commitments provided that their total combined aggregate anthropogenic carbon dioxide equivalent emissions of the greenhouse gases listed in Annex A do not exceed their assigned amounts.
[...]

Article 6

1. For the purpose of meeting its commitments under Article 3, any Party included in Annex I may transfer to, or acquire from, any other such Party emission reduction units [ERUs] resulting from projects aimed at reducing anthropogenic emissions by sources or enhancing anthropogenic removals by sinks of greenhouse gases in any sector of the economy, provided that:

   (a) Any such project has the approval of the Parties involved;

   (b) Any such project provides a reduction in emissions by sources, or an enhancement of removals by sinks, that is additional to any that would otherwise occur; [and]

   (d) The acquisition of emission reduction units shall be supplemental to domestic actions for the purposes of meeting commitments under Article 3 [...]
[...]

Article 12

1. A clean development mechanism is hereby defined.

2. The purpose of the clean development mechanism shall be to assist Parties not included in Annex I in achieving sustainable development and in contributing to the ultimate objective of the Convention, and to assist Parties included in Annex I in achieving compliance with their quantified emission limitation and reduction commitments under Article 3.

3. Under the clean development mechanism:

   (a) Parties not included in Annex I will benefit from project activities resulting in certified emission reductions; and

   (b) Parties included in Annex I may use the certified emission reductions [CERs] accruing from such project activities to contribute to compliance with part of their quantified emission limitation and reduction commitments under Article 3, as determined by the Conference of the Parties serving as the meeting of the Parties to this Protocol [...]

[...]

5. Emission reductions resulting from each project activity shall be certified by operational entities to be designated by the Conference of the Parties serving as the meeting of the Parties to this Protocol, on the basis of:

(a) Voluntary participation approved by each Party involved;

(b) Real, measurable, and long-term benefits related to the mitigation of climate change; and

(c) Reductions in emissions that are additional to any that would occur in the absence of the certified project activity.

6. The clean development mechanism shall assist in arranging funding of certified project activities as necessary.

[...]

Article 17

The Conference of the Parties shall define the relevant principles, modalities, rules and guidelines, in particular for verification, reporting and accountability for emissions trading. The Parties included in Annex B may participate in emissions trading for the purposes of fulfilling their commitments under Article 3. Any such trading shall be supplemental to domestic actions for the purpose of meeting quantified emission limitation and reduction commitments under that Article.

The overall result of these provisions, for the 2008–12 compliance period, should be a reduction of 5.2% in global GHG emissions below 1990 levels,[115] although parties have varying reduction commitments, as Annex B sets out, reflecting their different capacities to reduce emissions. Thus, Iceland is in fact allowed to increase its GHG emissions during this period by 10%, whereas the EU and its Member States (as at 1994) were required to reduce emissions by 8% by 2012 as against a 1990 baseline. Note that Article 3's binding emission reduction obligations apply to only thirty-nine of the UNFCCC's Annex I parties, being those parties that have ratified the Protocol, which includes the EU (then European Community).[116] Further, Annex I parties are required to meet their reduction commitments through a variety of policies and measures, such as those listed in Article 2(1) and as appropriate for national circumstances. However, Annex I parties are to pursue limitation of emissions from aviation and shipping fuel by working through the International Civil Aviation Organization and the International Maritime Organization, respectively (Article 2(2)).

For meeting these binding reduction commitments, the Protocol allows a range of methods and flexibility mechanisms, all possible due to the understanding of the climate change problem as one that can be met by emissions reductions (or absorptions) in any location globally.[117] Thus, Article 4 provides that emissions reductions obligations can be aggregated by agreement, so that combined emissions in an aggregated group are not to exceed the sum total of the assigned amounts for its constituent countries. The EU adopts such an aggregated arrangement with its Burden Sharing Agreement, discussed in the following section. There are then three flexibility mechanisms provided by the Protocol. First, its 'Joint Implementation' provision in Article 6 allows Annex I parties to benefit from emission reductions activities undertaken by other Annex I parties by the transferral of

---

[115] This covers the six GHGs set out in Annex A of the Protocol: CO_2, CH_4, N_2O, SF_6, and two groups of gases: hydrofluorocarbons and perfluorocarbons. Note that this 5.2% reduction is calculated on the basis of *all* Annex I parties ratifying the Protocol, which to date has not occurred, with the US notably failing to ratify (along with the delayed ratification of Australia in 2008, and the withdrawal of Canada from the Protocol in December 2012).

[116] In total, there are 191 parties to the Kyoto Protocol, including non-Annex I parties.

[117] Note reductions obligations can be met by creating carbon sinks: KP, art 3(3).

'emission reduction units', or ERUs, which can only be issued for such activities that are additional to existing projects and practice in the transferring state.

Second, the 'Clean Development Mechanism' in Article 12 allows Annex I parties to benefit from emissions reductions projects in developing countries, which are thus tied into the scheme. Annex I countries get credit for financing projects in developing countries that result in 'certified emission reductions' (CERs), so long as these are also additional to those that would have otherwise occurred in those countries (such as cleaner energy production methods, or reforestation in developing countries). Third, Article 17 provides that *emissions trading* is allowed between Annex I parties, which can sell any surplus of their Annex B assigned amounts if they come in under their target emissions reductions, and also trade any ERUs or CERs. As a result, the Kyoto Protocol scheme is designed to reduce GHGs by 5.2% from 1990 levels and no further—the financial incentives of the scheme do not encourage deeper emissions reductions overall.

Another crucial aspect to ensuring that the Annex I parties meet their emissions targets is accurate measuring and reporting of parties' GHG emissions. To this end, Articles 5, 7, and 8 of the Protocol establish annual reporting requirements and procedures for reviewing the data submitted.[118] The methodologies to be adopted in measuring emissions rely on IPCC guidance (Article 5). Note, however, that there might be adjustments to these methodologies over time, as well as to particular annual emissions data submitted, as better environmental knowledge and techniques develop, demonstrating that scientific uncertainty characterizes but also potentially undermines the Kyoto scheme. Further, the administrative architecture required internationally for all the Protocol's monitoring, reporting, and certification procedures is considerable and somewhat at odds with its regulatory 'flexibility'. The framework Convention's Conference of the Parties (COP), and its numerous subsidiary bodies, thus has a sizeable job in elaborating the details of, and ensuring compliance with, the obligations of the Kyoto Protocol, as well as negotiating next steps under the Convention itself.

Beyond meeting the Annex B emissions reductions targets, Article 10 of the Protocol places an obligation on *all* parties to formulate national and regional plans to mitigate climate change and to facilitate adaptation, reaffirming Article 4(1) UNFCCC, and also to engage in a variety of cooperative practices to improve responses to climate change internationally, again following the UNFCCC's provisions. The real issue for the Kyoto Protocol is what comes next. Kyoto was intended to be a first step along a route to more stringent emissions reduction targets, for more countries. One of the main sticking points preventing such regulatory progress is the increasingly contested distinction between developed (Annex I) parties and non-listed developing countries in the framework Convention. Some of the emerging and ever strengthening economies of the world—in particular, China, India, South Africa, and Brazil—are not subject to emissions reductions commitments under Kyoto (not being Annex I parties), and their rapid industrialization threatens not only to undermine the reductions achieved by Annex I parties but also to exacerbate the climate change problem globally. The (ethical) argument made by such rapidly developing countries is that they should not be denied opportunities to industrialize and grow, as Western nations have done in the past; and thus should not be subject to similar emissions reductions constraints. On the other hand, Annex I parties cannot see how the climate change problem can be tackled, in scientific terms, without such heavily polluting nations controlling their emissions. At the same time, the least developed nations of the world remain vulnerable to the worst effects of climate change, often due to their geographical locations (African and island nations in particular) and their limited financial resources for adapting to a changing climate.

---

[118] The subsequent Marrakesh Accord adds further compliance and monitoring procedures.

Post-Kyoto negotiations

Article 3(9) of the Kyoto Protocol provides that Annex I parties shall agree commitments for subsequent periods (that is, from 2012), and that negotiations for these commitments were to begin by 2005. Such negotiations did indeed begin but, in light of the tensions outlined already, successive COP meetings—particularly in Bali (COP 13, 2007), Copenhagen (COP 15, 2009), Cancun (COP 16, 2010), and Durban (COP 17, 2011)—proved almost intractable in efforts to decide on binding emissions reductions commitments post-2012 and related financial obligations to assist developing nations in mitigating and adapting to climate change. These COP negotiations have instead resulted in a series of non-binding political agreements, which amount to 'soft law' at best, and which edge ever closer to, but have not yet made, the next legally binding climate change treaty. Some progress has been made by these COP soft law agreements, which include the Bali Road Map, Copenhagen Accord, Cancun Agreements, and Durban Platform for Advanced Action.[119] These agreements reflect a stronger focus on international efforts to *adapt* to climate change impacts, and also establish a range of new mechanisms and bodies to promote climate change action, particularly in developing nations through finance, technology transfers, and capacity-building support provided by wealthier nations.

In this vein, there is now a Technology Mechanism (and associated Climate Technology Centre) established to assist the development of adaptation and mitigation-related technology and its transfer between countries; a Green Climate Fund for providing long-term finance for developing countries in limiting their GHG emissions and adapting to climate change impacts; an associated 'REDD-plus' mechanism to incentivize developing nations to curb deforestation and forest degradation and to enhance the function of forests as carbon sinks; and the establishment of an Adaptation Committee to coordinate international adaptation efforts. In 2012–13, these mechanisms are at relatively embryonic stages and the levels of funding for them from developed nations remain subject to ongoing negotiation.

Progress has also been made on negotiating post-2012 GHG emissions reductions commitments. Under the 2009 Copenhagen Accord, Annex I parties agreed to submit (non-binding) economy-wide emissions reductions targets for 2020, while developing nations agreed to submit nationally appropriate mitigation programmes.[120] Many of the Annex I targets submitted were tactical or conditional commitments, for example, the EU agreed to a 2020 target of cutting emissions by 20% against a 1990 baseline, or otherwise to a more stringent 30% target as part of a global agreement in which developing countries also 'contribute adequately according to their responsibilities and respective capabilities'. These commitments have since been formally 'acknowledged' under the UNFCCC,[121] but developing a post-Kyoto international agreement on climate change mitigation remains contentious and legally unresolved.

At the time of writing, negotiations for a post-2012 legal framework were focused on three issues. First, the Durban COP in 2011 agreed that the Kyoto Protocol would extend seamlessly into a second commitment period from 2013, with a wider and more specific group of GHGs covered.[122] At the Doha round of COP 18 (December 2012), the legal mechanism for this continuation of Kyoto was agreed, with the extended commitment period set at eight years. However, only some developed nations,

---

[119] For full details, see the UN Kyoto Protocol website: <http://unfccc.int/2860.php> accessed 7 February 2013.

[120] Decision -/CP.15, Copenhagen Accord, UN Climate Change Conference 2009, Copenhagen, paras 4 and 5 ('Copenhagen Accord').

[121] UNFCCC Subsidiary Bodies for Scientific and Technological Advice and Implementation, 'Compilation of economy-wide emission reduction targets to be implemented by Parties included in Annex I to the Convention', 34th Session (Bonn, June 2011).

[122] Including nitrogen trifluoride and the species of hydrofluorocarbons and perfluorocarbons listed in the Fourth IPCC Assessment Report.

including the EU, have accepted new carbon cutting targets during this extended period of the Kyoto Protocol. Second, after the Doha conference, there is now a commitment to set up a 'pathway' to assist the most vulnerable populations with protection against 'loss and damage' caused by gradual climate change effects. Third, the Durban Platform for Advanced Action includes an agreement to negotiate by 2015 a new global climate change treaty with more radical emissions reductions targets, which would commence in 2020. COP 18 in Bonn (May 2012) launched the Ad Hoc Working Group on the Durban Platform for Enhanced Action to take forward negotiations for this 2020 treaty. No doubt negotiations for this global agreement will be highly contested, but they will occur against a background of scientific evidence that there is little time left to prevent irreversible climate change. The Copenhagen Accord stated that 'deep cuts in global emissions are required according to science, and as documented by the IPCC Fourth Assessment Report with a view to reduce global emissions so as to hold the increase in global temperature below 2 degrees Celsius'.[123] In 2011, the view of the International Energy Agency was that global GHGs would need to peak no later than 2017 to have a chance of staying below a 2 degree Celsius rise.[124] However, it is noteworthy that, at the Doha round of COP 18, the parties also launched a 'robust process' to review the long-term temperature goal of the UNFCC by 2015.

3.3 EU CLIMATE CHANGE POLICY AND REGULATION

EU climate change policy overall

Of the international players involved in climate change negotiations, the EU has been a leader in agitating for progressive policies that will limit global emissions, decarbonize economies, and take all possible measures to limit global warming to less than 2 degrees Celsius above pre-industrial average global temperatures. The EU has not only signed and ratified the UNFCCC and Kyoto Protocol,[125] along with its Member States, but it has also unilaterally committed to cutting its emissions by at least 20% against 1990 levels by 2020. It may go even further in its commitments if a new global treaty is agreed, as indicated in Section 3.2. Further, it has set out a 'roadmap' for achieving a low carbon economy by 2050, aiming to reduce domestic emissions by 80 to 95% in that time.[126]

In signing up to the Kyoto commitments, the fifteen EU Member States at the time (pre-2004 EU states) agreed to aggregate their emissions, as Article 3 of the Protocol allows. Thus, the EU had a target of reducing GHG emissions by 8% overall by the end of 2012, but the burden for reaching this overall EU target was differently distributed throughout the fifteen Member States involved, as established under a Burden Sharing Agreement,[127] illustrated in Figure 15.1.

Member States that have joined the EU since 2004 are not within this 'emissions bubble' and must meet their required emissions reductions as UNFCCC Annex I parties under the Kyoto Protocol independently. In a 2011 report, the European Environment Agency reported that the EU-15 was on track to meet its Kyoto target (although Austria, Italy, and Luxembourg were not on track to meet their EU burden sharing targets), and all other EU Member States were on track to meet their 2012 targets.[128]

---

[123] Copenhagen Accord, para 2.

[124] IEA, *World Energy Outlook* (Nov 2011).

[125] Council Decision 94/69/EC of 15 December 1993 concerning the conclusion of the United Nations Framework Convention on Climate Change [1993] OJ L 33/11; Council Decision 2002/358/EC of 25 April 2002 concerning the approval, on behalf of the European Community, of the Kyoto Protocol to the United Nations Framework Convention on Climate Change [2002] OJ L130/1.

[126] Commission Communication, 'A Roadmap for Moving to a Competitive Low Carbon Economy in 2050', COM(2011) 0112 final.

[127] Council Decision 2006/944/EC of 14 December 2006 determining the respective emission levels allocated to the Community and each of its Member States under the Kyoto Protocol [2006] OJ L358/87.

[128] EEA, *Greenhouse Gas Emission Trends and Projections in Europe 2011: Tracking Progress Towards Kyoto and 2020 Targets* (Luxembourg, 2011).

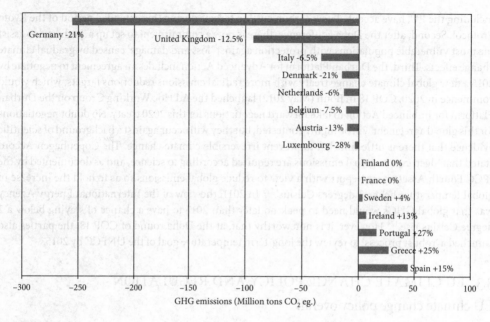

Figure 15.1 EU Burden Sharing Agreement for the 2008–12 Kyoto Protocol compliance period
Source: The Air Pollution and Climate Change Secretariat, Sweden.

In order to reach these Kyoto emissions reductions obligations, and to go even further in mitigating climate change, the EU has implemented a wide range of policies and regulatory tools. The most recent and ambitious of these were set out in the EU's 2008 'Climate and Energy Package', which has resulted in the following measures:[129]

- the Renewable Energy Directive, which sets binding national renewable energy targets, requiring EU Member States collectively to lift the proportion of their total energy consumption derived from renewable energy sources to 20% by 2020, with individual Member States required to meet varying targets as appropriate to their circumstances;[130]

- an Effort Sharing Decision, which sets differential caps for Member State emissions from sectors that fall outside the EU emissions trading scheme (discussed in the following sub-section), amounting overall to a 10% cut in those emissions, against a 2005 baseline, by 2020;[131]

- the Carbon Capture and Storage Directive, which establishes a legal framework for environmentally safe geological storage of CO_2 'to contribute to the fight against climate change'.[132]

In addition, the EU has a raft of measures to support energy efficiency, working towards a 20% increase in energy efficiency by 2020, through primary energy savings. Regulatory measures working towards

[129] The 2009 amendments to the EU ETS, discussed in the following sub-section, were also part of this package.
[130] European Parliament and Council Directive 2009/28/EC of 23 April 2009 on the promotion of the use of energy from renewable sources [2009] OJ L140/16.
[131] European Parliament and Council Decision 406/2009/EC of 23 April on the effort of Member States to reduce their greenhouse gas emissions to meet the Community's greenhouse gas emission reduction commitments up to 2020 [2009] OJ L140/136.
[132] European Parliament and Council Directive 2009/31/EC of 23 April 2009 on the geological storage of carbon dioxide [2009] OJ L140/114, art 1.

this goal include Directive 2010/31/EU on the energy performance of buildings,[133] and ecodesign and energy labelling requirements for energy-related products.[134] The 2011 Energy Efficiency Action Plan is the latest initiative to keep this EU policy strategy on track, setting out more ambitious measures for the energy saving potential of buildings, transport, the public sector, and for incentivizing more competitive and innovative EU industry to promote energy efficiency.[135] This Action Plan led to Directive on energy efficiency,[136] which amongst other things requires Member States to set 'indicative national energy efficiency targets' for 2020 (taking into account various considerations including the EU's 2020 absolute energy consumption targets as well as certain national factors), to establish long-term strategies to renovate the national stock of commercial and residential buildings (both public and private) and to establish national energy efficiency obligation schemes. Further, Member States must: ensure that energy customers either have individual energy meters or are billed based on actual use, conduct mandatory energy audits for large companies, ensure high energy efficiency standards for public sector buildings and operations, and require investigation into and encourage the potential for national heating and cooling plans for developing high-efficiency energy co-generation and efficient district heating and cooling (requiring also appropriate strategic urban planning). The Directive may also lead to mandatory national energy efficiency targets being imposed if insufficient progress is made towards the EU 20% energy savings goal by 2014.

In addition to these various complementary measures and policies that work towards mitigating climate change, the EU also has an evolving policy framework for *adapting* to the impacts of climate change in a more strategic way. A 2009 EU White Paper has set the policy foundation for building and improving EU resilience to climate change impacts.[137]

EU emissions trading scheme (ETS)

However, the 'jewel in the crown' of the EU's progressive and internationally leading climate change policy is the EU emissions trading scheme (ETS).[138] It is important to note that the ETS is facilitative. Its operation does not guarantee that the EU or its Member States will meet their international obligations or EU targets for reducing GHG emissions, nor is it the only measure designed to achieve these goals, as the previous sub-section highlighted. However, it does set up a mechanism for incentivizing reductions in emissions, at least in theory, and for flexibly shifting emissions obligations to operators and Member States that are best placed to achieve them.

The EU scheme is a 'cap and trade' style ETS.[139] It sets an overall cap for GHG emissions across those European states that are subject to the scheme—all twenty-seven EU Member States plus Iceland, Liechtenstein, and Norway—and also allows relevant polluters to trade their emissions in order to stay within the relevant cap. The ETS commenced in January 2005, with a phased introduction that

---

[133] [2010] OJ L153/13.

[134] European Parliament and Council Directive 2009/125/EC of 21 October 2009 establishing a framework for the setting of ecodesign requirements for energy-related products [2009] OJ L285/10; European Parliament and Council Directive 2010/30/EU of 19 May 2010 on the indication by labelling etc of the consumption of energy by energy-related products [2010] OJ L153/1.

[135] Commission Communication, 'Energy Efficiency Plan 2011', COM (2011) 109 final. This also complements the Europe 2020 Strategy's flagship initiative for a resource efficient Europe (COM (2011) 21), which is also relevant in the context of waste regulation (see Chapter 16).

[136] European Parliament and Council Directive 2012/27/EU of 25 October 2012 on energy efficiency [2012] OJ L315/1. This replaced the Cogeneration Directive (2004/8/EC) and the Energy Services Directive (2006/32/EC).

[137] Commission, 'White Paper: Adapting to Climate Change: Towards a European Framework for Action' COM(2009) 147/4.

[138] Stavros Dimas, EU Environment Commissioner, 'Climate Change—International and EU Action' (Climate Change Conference Speech, Prague, 31 October 2008), accessible at: <http://europa.eu/rapid/pressReleasesAction.do?reference=SPEECH/08/570&format=HTML&aged=0&language=EN&guiLanguage=en> accessed 7 February 2013.

[139] See Section 4.2 of Chapter 12, for the regulatory theory underlying different types of ETSs.

allowed Member States and industries to familiarize themselves with (and accept) the scheme initially, and to prepare for it administratively (Phase I lasted three years). Subsequent phases constrained further the conditions under which GHGs can be traded on the EU ETS market so as to improve environmental outcomes. Phase II of the scheme ran for five years, from 2008 to 2012, and Phase III commenced in 2013. Here, the basic features of the EU ETS scheme are outlined.

Initially the EU ETS covered only CO_2 emissions and some N_2O and perfluorocarbon emissions, emitted from certain processes undertaken by large installations, as set out in Annex I of the ETS Directive.[140] These Annex I industrial processes include power stations, oil refineries, iron and steel works, and factories making cement, glass, paper, and bricks, but not all heavily polluting sectors are covered. This differential application led to the entire scheme, when it was introduced, being challenged for its lawfulness in the EU courts. In the *Arcelor* case, representative industry from the steel sector claimed that the scheme infringed the general EU law principle of equal treatment, since it did not (in Phases I and II) apply to the chemical and non-ferrous metal sectors, amongst others. The ECJ agreed that the scheme applied in a discriminatory way in relation to directly competitive sectors but that the inequality was justified on the basis of ensuring the effectiveness of the scheme and in light of the administrative reality of getting it off ground.[141]

The 'cap' and 'trade' elements of the scheme are designed through specific provisions of the ETS Directive. The scheme's *cap* on emissions, in Phases I and II, was set through individual Member State national allocation plans (NAPs, which in combination formed the 'EU' cap). Each Member State NAP had to set out the total quantity of emissions to be allocated to relevant installations within that Member State, with allocation based on 'objective and transparent criteria'.[142] The Commission could reject a NAP, 'on the basis that it is incompatible with the criteria listed in Annex III or with Article 10', providing reasons. In terms of the allocation of emissions to individual installations within Member States, in Phase I at least 95% of allocations were made free of charge, and in Phase II, at least 90%. This setup created significant problems with many Member States in their NAPs over-allocating (largely free) allowances to protect national industries. As a result, the Commission tried to rein states in and to limit NAPs centrally using their power to reject NAPS, in an effort to reduce the overall EU cap by 10% during Phase II. Legal disputes resulted, with ECJ finding that this action, whilst perhaps well motivated in terms of constraining the market to improve environmental outcomes, was beyond terms of the ETS Directive as formulated at the time.[143] The Commission had overreached its powers.

In terms of the *trade* aspect of the EU ETS, the Directive contains a number of core obligations that establish the market and make the trading system work. In short, installations covered by the scheme are required to obtain permits to operate, and to surrender *tradable* allowances each year equivalent to their total actual emissions, as a condition of their permit.

---

[140] European Parliament and Council Directive 2003/87/EC of 13 October 2003 establishing a scheme for greenhouse gas emission allowance trading within the Community (as amended by Directive 2009/29/EC) [2003] OJ L275/32; [2009] OJ L140/63 ('ETS Directive').

[141] Case C-127/07 *Société Arcelor Atlantique et Lorraine* [2008] ECR I–09895. This was a preliminary reference action from the French Conseil d'Etat, with a direct challenge to the scheme by Arcelor under art 263 TFEU failing for want of standing (Case T-16/04 *Arcelor v Parliament and Council* [2010] ECR II-00211—an interesting EU law standing case). Note that, in Phase III, more sectors and processes have been included in the scheme, including some from the chemicals and non-ferrous metals sectors.

[142] Including requiring Member State NAP caps on emissions to be 'consistent' with Kyoto Protocol obligations and the technological potential of activities covered (ETS Directive, arts 9, 10, Annex III).

[143] Particularly in relation to Eastern European accession states (recently transitioned market economies and some with energy security issues linked to dependency on Russian gas): for example, Case T-183/07 *Poland v Commission* [2009] ECR II–3395; Case T-263/07 *Estonia v Commission* [2009] ECR II-3463; Case T-369/07 *Latvia v Commission* (General Court, 22 March 2011).

European Parliament and Council Directive 2003/87/EC of 13 October 2003 Establishing a Scheme for Greenhouse Gas Emission Allowance Trading Within the Community [2003] OJ L275/32 (as amended by Directive 2009/29/EC) ('ETS Directive')

Article 4

Greenhouse gas emissions permits

Member States shall ensure that, from 1 January 2005, no installation carries out any activity listed in Annex I resulting in emissions specified in relation to that activity unless its operator holds a permit issued by a competent authority in accordance with Articles 5 and 6 [...]

Article 6

Conditions for and contents of the greenhouse gas emissions permit

1. The competent authority shall issue a greenhouse gas emissions permit granting authorisation to emit greenhouse gases from all or part of an installation if it is satisfied that the operator is capable of monitoring and reporting emissions [...]

2. Greenhouse gas emissions permits shall contain the following:

   (a) the name and address of the operator;

   (b) a description of the activities and emissions from the installation;

   (c) a monitoring plan...;

   (d) reporting requirements; and

   (e) an obligation to surrender allowances... equal to the total emissions of the installation in each calendar year, as verified in accordance with Article 15, within four months following the end of that year.

Article 12

Transfer, surrender and cancellation of allowances

1. Member States shall ensure that allowances can be transferred between:

   (a) persons within the [Union];

   (b) persons within the [Union] and persons in third countries, where such allowances are recognised in accordance with the procedure referred to in Article 25 [...]

3. Member States shall ensure that, by 30 April each year, the operator of each installation surrenders a number of allowances [...] equal to the total emissions from that installation during the preceding calendar year as verified in accordance with Article 15, and that these are subsequently cancelled.

4. Member States shall take the necessary steps to ensure that allowances will be cancelled at any time at the request of the person holding them.

Article 16

Penalties

[...]

2. Member States shall ensure publication of the names of operators... who are in breach of requirements to surrender sufficient allowances under this Directive.

> 3. Member States shall ensure that any operator [...] who does not surrender sufficient allowances by 30 April of each year to cover its emissions during the preceding year shall be held liable for the payment of an excess emissions penalty. The excess emissions penalty shall be EUR 100 for each tonne of carbon dioxide equivalent emitted for which the operator or aircraft operator has not surrendered allowances.[144] Payment of the excess emissions penalty shall not release the operator or aircraft operator from the obligation to surrender an amount of allowances equal to those excess emissions when surrendering allowances in relation to the following calendar year.

In order to have sufficient allowances to meet their GHG emissions in any given year, Annex I installations can do one of four things: (1) reduce their emissions; (2) use their allowances granted by or bought from the relevant state entity administering the scheme; (3) buy allowances from other installations within the EU ETS market; or (4) buy CERs or ERUs through the linked CDM and Joint Implementation mechanisms of the Kyoto Protocol.[145] Linking into this wider Kyoto emissions trading market was done in legal terms through the 2004 Linking Directive,[146] although Article 11a of the ETS Directive put limits on how many of these external credits can be used to meet EU ETS allowance requirements.

Other problematic issues that characterized Phase II of the ETS were both structural and administrative. In structural terms, particularly due to the parameters for setting NAPs, Member States that were generally on track to meet their Kyoto emissions targets had no strong incentive in Phase II to reduce permitted emissions beyond current levels. This was partly due to the problems caused by some states over-allocating emissions in their NAPs, as noted already, which resulted in generally low carbon prices. Another structural issue is a broader one of EU law, with inconsistent legal signals being sent on the setting up of supplementary trading schemes by Member States. Article 24 of the ETS Directive seems to encourage such regulatory initiatives, however they can fall foul of other EU law, particularly state aid rules, as the Netherlands found in its efforts to set up a NO_x trading scheme, outlined in Section 2.2. In terms of administrative issues, the EU ETS proved bureaucratically cumbersome, particularly with different allowance registries operating across all thirty European states in the scheme. This also allowed fraudulent exploitation of the scheme, with criminals using the varying VAT-taxable status of allowances across EU states to make significant financial gains through carbon trading. Further, there were technological problems, with cyber attacks leading to the theft of allowances electronically and resultant distortions in the system.

From 2013, Phase III of the EU ETS sees some considerable changes, with the ETS Directive having been substantially amended (by Directive 2009/29/EC), reflecting both a natural progression of the ETS and learning from the lessons of Phases I and II. Bogojević describes the key features of the new ETS, particularly on shifting EU power in controlling the scheme.

Sanja Bogojević, 'The EU ETS Directive Revised: Yet Another Stepping Stone' (2009) 11 Env LR 279, 280

The revised EU ETS Directive attempts to remedy the inconsistencies in the emissions trading market by creating a more harmonised emissions trading system. This includes centralising the setting of the

---

[144] To increase in accordance with the EU consumer prices index, from January 2013.
[145] See Section 3.2.
[146] European Parliament and Council Directive 2004/101/EC of 27 October 2004 amending Directive 2003/87/EC in respect of the Kyoto Protocol's project mechanisms [2004] OJ L338/18. Note that the EU ETS was operational before the Kyoto Protocol was in force.

cap on emissions, allocation rules, and codifying monitoring, verification and reporting requirements in regulations [...] adopted by the European Commission. The centralisation in the revised Directive has given rise to questions about whether the new amendments are in fact part of a 'Commission coup', in which regulatory power is concentrated within the European Commission instead of leaving it in the hands of the Member States. Labelling the revised Directive a legal document that simply imposes strict centralised governance would, however, be an oversimplification of the EU ETS. Alongside the centralisation of the cap, a major revision of the EU ETS is the shift from 'grandfathering' to auctioning of emission allowances, which will be managed by the Member States. From this perspective, allocation of power under the trading scheme is balanced between the European Commission and the Member States rather than tipped either way [...]

Overall, the revised EU ETS Directive is 'meatier' than its predecessor in the sense that it is a more detailed legal text, which seeks to respond to the lessons learned from previous phases of emissions trading in the EU. This does not mean that the revised text is final or complete. Creating a well-functioning emissions trading market in the EU is declared to be a 'learning by doing' process, which takes time and experience to finalise. From this perspective, the revised Directive may fulfil the ambition of 'refining' and 'improving' certain aspects of the EU ETS but in reality it is just yet another stepping stone in the complex process of establishing a successful emissions trading system within an EU and global context.

Note that the legal implications of the EU ETS, and its construction, are not just concerned with improving the regulatory structure of the scheme in order to promote environmental outcomes. They also concern matters of EU constitutional law and how power and competence are attributed between the EU and its Member States.

In Phase III, as Bogojević indicates, there are now various centralized aspects of the EU ETS. There is a Commission-imposed single EU-wide emissions cap, which takes as its starting point the total NAP allocations at the mid-point of the Phase II period, and is then reduced each year by 1.74% (Article 9). Centralized administration for the trading of allowances is established in the form of a single EU registry (Article 19), and the Directive allows for centralized procedures for monitoring and verifying the emissions of Annex I installations (Articles 14, 15). The revised ETS Directive also has provisions relating to insider fraud and market manipulation (Article 12(1a)).

Beyond centralization, Phase III sees more industries and gases included in the scheme, with the notable addition of the aviation industry. All airlines that take off or land in an EU Member State are now subject to the scheme, and must surrender allowances each year corresponding to the amount of emissions they produce (calculated by a complicated formula, that depends roughly on fuel used and distance travelled by an airline's flights).[147] There has been strenuous resistance to the inclusion of aviation within the scheme on various grounds, including the detrimental financial impact on the airline industry, and concerns about how the Chicago Convention and other international law norms that regulate international aviation sit legally with this expansion of the EU ETS. This latter concern resulted in a high profile decision of the ECJ, ultimately upholding the lawfulness of aviation's inclusion within the scheme, which required the Court to reason in detail about the relationship between international law and EU law in this case.[148]

In terms of auctioning and allocating allowances, Phase III also sees significant changes. Within the overall EU cap, Member States will be allocated allowances based on their historical usage (88% allocated this way), poor economic conditions (10% allocated to poorer states under a 'solidarity

---

[147] ETS Directive, arts 12(2a) and 14(3); Annexes 1 and 4(B). Note there is a one year deferral scheme for flights into and out of the EU until autumn 2013 to encourage a global market-based approach to regulating aviation GHGs.

[148] Case C-366/10 *Air Transport of America* (CJEU, 21 December 2011).

mechanism'), and good emissions reduction records (2% to reward performing states).[149] European states in the scheme will then allocate their allowances at the national level. All allowances are to be auctioned nationally, with some exceptions. There is discretion for free allocations for some industries (such as district heating), new market entrants, and for those making products (not sectors) that are at risk of carbon leakage (Articles 10a and 10b).[150] Carbon leakage occurs when there is, in fact, an increase in CO_2 emissions in states outside the ETS due to emissions reductions by Member States under strict EU climate policy (in effect, more products will be made offshore and imported into the EU due to the environmental costs of making them in the EU, doing nothing to reduce GHG emissions globally). As for the sale proceeds of auctioned allowances, Member States are to invest at least 50% of auction revenue in projects combating climate change (Article 10(3)).

On one view, all this change to the EU ETS looks like problems being fixed, and the scheme getting ever closer to the theoretical model of a cap-and-trade ETS, which will lead to quantifiable GHG emissions reductions. However, on a broader analytical view, the picture is not quite so simple. The following extract reflects on emissions trading schemes, taking into account the experience of the EU ETS as well as other environmental ETSs, considering their rationales, successes, and challenges, from the perspective of regulatory theory in particular. This connects to the analysis in Chapter 12 of ETSs, and provides one legal approach to evaluating the EU ETS. Consider, in particular, which of the challenges highlighted by Baldwin are reflected in the experience and construction of the EU ETS to date.

Robert Baldwin, 'Regulation Lite: the Rise of Emissions Trading' (2008) 2 Regulation and Governance 193, 196–98, 201–4

Despite their potential advantages, emissions trading mechanisms raise a series of contentious issues. They are not free from difficulties, and a brief review of emissions trading's main alleged weaknesses and areas of contention will show how much emissions trading still needs to be justified [...]

[...]

2.1. Targeting and objectives

A first issue with emissions trading concerns the objectives to be pursued. A trading process, in itself, offers no benefit to, say, the environment. It does not reduce greenhouse gas emissions. What it does do is to provide a way for a given target to be achieved at lowest cost [...]

It should be noted here that, in meeting targets with a trading device, much depends on the mode of defining emissions and distributing allowances [...]

[...]

Additionally, implementation timescales were tight in the EU ETS and a complex set of allocation rules had to be worked to. As a result, it can be argued, powerful interests were able to exploit their informational advantages to keep the constraining effects of the ETS at bay [...]

[...]

[149] ETS Directive, art 10.

[150] The Commission is to set 'benchmarks' for such allocations across sectors under art 10a (set by reference to the best performers in a sector), and to make proposals under art 10b, in light of the procedures set out in those Articles. Note that Eurofer sought to annul the Commission's Decision 2011/278/EU determining transitional Union-wide rules for harmonized free allocation of emission allowances pursuant to art 10a, arguing that the benchmark for the hot metal sector was set at a technically unachievable level. Its action was dismissed for want of standing: Case T-391/11 *Eurofer v Commission* (General Court, 4 June 2012).

The message to be drawn from the EU ETS is that if allowances are distributed at no cost, there are serious incentives to distort emissions projections so as to create windfalls. One answer to this problem is to allocate allowances by means of auctions.

Baldwin then goes on to make similar arguments about other aspects of ETSs that disincentivize cost-effective strategic decisions to abate emissions, including uncertainty in regulatory structures susceptible to change, markets that are not robust, transaction costs, poor information flows, and enforcement challenges, particularly in light of market players coming from a range of jurisdictions with emissions/operations that require accurate verification for the system to work.

2.3. Is emissions trading fair?

A fundamental problem with market-based systems of distribution is that such systems have an inherent bias in favor of those parties who possess wealth and they tend to remove power from those who lack resources. The results of trading may be claimed to be cost-effective but this does not ensure fairness.

[...]

Post Kyoto, a key issue is the development effect of trading systems [...] The charge [...] is that historically based allocations allow currently high emitters to impose environmental damage on other countries and to lock the less developed nations into lower levels of development. The linked concern is that in the early years of trading, the mechanism allows existing industrialized users to meet their targets at lowest cost and to avoid making reductions in home emissions. When, however, developing countries become faced with emissions targets themselves, the cheapest forms of emissions abatement will have been exhausted and only more expensive high-tech forms will be left—at which time industrialized countries will be unwilling to invest abroad. In short, industrialized countries will have gained preferential use of lowest cost abatement methods and reaped a competitive advantage while suppressing development.

[...]

2.4. Is emissions trading accountable and transparent?

It has been argued [...] that emissions trading combines democratic accountability with a market mechanism and that trading focuses public attention on decisions about aggregate emissions reductions. In this regard, it is claimed that emissions trading can offer more democratic accountability than the rule-making processes of traditional command regulation. Skeptics, however, argue that trading systems have a special complexity that does not facilitate access, [making] citizen participation in emissions trading programs more difficult than in traditional regulation and render[ing] such programs highly vulnerable to industry lobbying.

Baldwin's piece focuses on certain key analytical issues that are particularly important to regulation scholars, such as whether regulation is effective (including cost-effective) in achieving desired outcomes, and whether transparent and accountable in governance terms. He also considers whether ETSs are fair in terms of equal treatment and distributive justice, which echoes some of the philosophical concerns of Harris in Section 1.5. However, while Baldwin's piece is a sweeping review of many ideas relating to ETSs, it should be noted that the wide range of literature on these regulatory schemes varies in scholarly focus and analytical outlook. Thus, Bogojevic highlights how such variety in scholarly approaches in fact tells us different things about ETSs.

Sanja Bogojević, 'Ending the Honeymoon: Deconstructing Emissions Trading Discourses'
(2009) 21(3) JEL 443, 444–45

It is often understood that emissions trading schemes try to solve the problem of the overexploitation of commons and, in [this context], commons in air. Beyond this initial remark, scholars present different views as to what the underlying principle of emissions trading is or ought to be. I argue that these different perspectives can be set out in the following three models: the *Economic Efficiency, Private Property Rights* and *Command-and-Control* models. According to the *Economic Efficiency Model* emissions trading has the role of a 'profit-centre'; in the *Private Property Rights Model* these trading schemes form part of a certain world-view in which citizens, via private property rights, defend and manage commons independently of governmental programs; while in the *Command-and-Control Model* emissions trading is regarded as 're-regulation' [...]

[These] models demonstrate that emissions trading can be viewed through different lenses, each lens setting out a different framework through which to construct emissions trading schemes. This means that the way in which emissions trading is portrayed frames the way in which we think about these trading schemes, and subsequently influences the way in which legislation, upon which emissions trading schemes are based, is constructed. In other words, when we discuss and conceptualise emissions trading schemes, we in fact refer to a set of diverse regulatory strategies, each based on a different understanding of the role of the market, the state, and emissions allowances.

[...] By highlighting certain legal implications that follow from the different understandings and portrayals of emissions trading—and more precisely, the different roles of the market, the state, and emissions allowances—the models show that the underlying themes in emissions trading literature evolve around complex legal dilemmas such as how to allocate regulatory power and to whom in regard to common resources.

In short, the jewel in the crown of the EU's climate change policy is not a straightforward legal phenomenon or success story, despite the moves to press ahead with its expansion and evolution in coming years. As Baldwin highlights, change and uncertainty in the regulatory regime can undermine its effectiveness. Further, the practical problems and legal challenges associated with the regime indicate that it will remain a complicated form of legal control within the EU, sitting within a wider body of EU climate change regulation that is ever-growing and evolving, which itself sits against a backdrop of problematic international climate change policy and politics.

3.4 UK CLIMATE CHANGE POLICY AND REGULATION

In addition to this complex body of international and EU climate change law and policy, the UK itself has an extensive and progressive set of laws and policies that relate and respond to climate change issues. These partly implement EU and international obligations but also go further, as the UK government aims to 'demonstrate UK leadership internationally, signalling we are committed to taking our share of responsibility for reducing global emissions'.[151] The existence of a separate Whitehall Department for Energy and Climate Change (DECC) demonstrates how seriously the UK government takes this policy arena, but also indicates that it is seen as a challenge beyond the environmental policy sphere (DECC was borne out of a merger of cross-departmental policy units, including the

---

[151] DEFRA, *The Contribution that Reporting of Greenhouse Gas Emissions Makes to the UK Meeting its Climate Change Objectives* (Nov 2010) 10.

climate team from DEFRA and the energy unit from the former Department for Business Enterprise and Regulatory Reform) and one that is closely associated with business, economic activity, and energy policy.

Implementing the EU ETS Directive

In terms of implementing EU climate change law, a key aspect of this is seen in the Greenhouse Gas Emissions Trading Scheme Regulations,[152] which implement the EU ETS Directive.[153] There are three particularly notable features of these Regulations. First, they implement the permitting requirements of the ETS Directive *outside* the integrated administrative scheme of the Environmental Permitting Regulations 2010 (EPRs).[154] The reason for keeping ETS permits outside the scope of the EPRs is probably one of administrative convenience, since a different set of installations is covered by the ETS regime.[155] Second, the sanction for failing to surrender sufficient allowances is a blanket fine, which the regulator has no discretion in imposing and which can amount to a substantial sum. Civil penalties for excess emissions emitted after 1 January 2008 are calculated at €100 per tonne of reportable emissions.[156] Third, they contain significant extra-judicial appeal mechanisms.

On appeals under the ETS Regulations, various decisions made by the Environment Agency within the scheme of the Regulations can be appealed on their merits, from the refusal of permits and the conditions with which they are granted, to the Agency's determination of reportable emissions for individual installations and decisions on excluded installations.[157] Under Phase II of the ETS, such appeals were mostly determined by the Secretary of State, and Schedule 2 of the 2005 Regulation set up an intricate appeal mechanism for this purpose. It allowed for the appointment of a separate person to hold a hearing, and for representations to be made by the appellant (and where applicable the regulator) at any such hearings, which could be heard (partly) in private.[158] At the end of the hearing, the person holding the hearing had to make a report in writing to the Secretary of State, including his or her conclusions and recommendations or reasons for not making any recommendation in relation to the appeal. This report was shared with the parties but was not publicly available. This quasi-judicial process, albeit that it might be judicially reviewed on points of law, raised questions about its compatibility with Article 6 of the European Convention of Human Rights.[159] This was particularly since the proceedings and their conclusion might not have been publicly accessible or available, thus limiting opportunities for judicial review by interested parties other than the appellant installation and Environment Agency. Notably, this appeal procedure

---

[152] Greenhouse Gas Emissions Trading Scheme Regulations 2012 SI 2012/3038 ('ETS Regulations'). These apply throughout the UK.

[153] Phases I and II of the ETS were implemented through previous sets of GHG ETS Regulations, in 2003 (SI 2003/3311) and 2005 (SI 2005/925).

[154] See Section 3 of Introduction to Part IV.

[155] While many UK installations within the EU ETS also fall under the IPPC regime, which are covered by the EPRs (see Section 2.2 of Chapter 17), the EU ETS covers a distinct grouping, particularly with the recent inclusion of the aviation industry.

[156] ETS Regulations, Regulations 41, 42 and 54. For a recent example of a large fine levied under these regulations, in 2010, ExxonMobil was fined €3.3 million by SEPA for failing to surrender allowances for previously undeclared but reportable CO_2 emissions. Note there is a lower fine for failure to surrender allowances for emissions that are subsequently reported as a correction: reg 54(5) and (6).

[157] ETS Regulations, reg 73.

[158] Interested third parties might also have the opportunity to make representations, although they might not have known about the hearing unless it was wholly or partly heard in public.

[159] Article 6 ECHR—implemented through the Human Rights Act 1998—provides that, in the determination of his or her civil rights and obligations, everyone is entitled to a *fair and public hearing* within a reasonable time by an *independent and impartial tribunal* established by law. Judgment shall be *pronounced publicly by the press* and the public may be excluded from all or part of the trial in only limited circumstances in the public interest. Cf *Alconbury* [2001] UKHL 23: see Section 2.2 of Chapter 18.

has been removed under Phase III of the ETS, and all appeals are now to be heard by the First-Tier Tribunal and, in some cases, the Planning Assessment Commission, under regulation 75.

UK climate change initiatives

Beyond implementing the EU ETS, the UK government has introduced a host of initiatives in relation to limiting UK GHG emissions. These initiatives seek to fulfil EU and international emissions reductions commitments but also reflect unilateral and even more ambitious UK climate change policy. A range of sectoral reforms and initiatives is examined here, but a central legal plank of the UK government's climate change policy is the Climate Change Act 2008. This is a remarkable statute, in at least three aspects. First, it sets demanding and binding GHG emission reduction commitments—to reduce GHG emissions overall by 80% by 2050. Second, despite this, it is unclear what sanctions there can be for a future government in failing to meet its own legislated emissions reduction targets.[160] Third, there is a powerful role for the independent Climate Change Committee (CCC) in advising government in relation to various matters in the Act. It is also a unique statute—no other EU Member State (or arguably nation) has a similar long-term climate statute. The basic mechanism of the Act is that it requires the relevant Secretary of State (currently for Energy and Climate Change) to set and meet five yearly 'carbon budgets', which set emissions caps for the relevant period so as to make progress towards achieving the Act's 2050 target of reducing the GHGs emissions covered by the Act (CO_2, CH_4, NO_2, HFCs, PFCs, and SH_6). The Act's basic obligations are extracted here.

Climate Change Act 2008[161]

1 The target for 2050

(1) It is the duty of the Secretary of State to ensure that the net UK carbon account for the year 2050 is at least 80% lower than the 1990 baseline.

[...]

4 Carbon budgets

(1) It is the duty of the Secretary of State—

  (a) to set for each succeeding period of five years beginning with the period 2008–2012 ('budgetary periods') an amount for the net UK carbon account (the 'carbon budget'), and

  (b) to ensure that the net UK carbon account for a budgetary period does not exceed the carbon budget.

  [...]

5 Level of carbon budgets

(1) The carbon budget—

  (a) for the budgetary period including the year 2020, must be such that the annual equivalent of the carbon budget for the period is at least 34% lower than the 1990 baseline;

---

[160] Note also that there are limits on the extent to which this duty can bind the current government: *R (People & Planet) v HM Treasury* [2009] EWHC 3020 (Admin). Cf *R (Hillingdon LBC) v SS for Transport* [2010] EWHC 626 (Admin), [2010] JPL 976 (see Section 2.1 of Chapter 11).

[161] As amended by Climate Change Act 2008 (2020 Target, Credit Limit and Definitions) Order SI 2009/1258.

(b) for the budgetary period including the year 2050, must be such that the annual equivalent of the carbon budget for the period is lower than the 1990 baseline by at least the percentage specified in section 1 (the target for 2050);

(c) for the budgetary period including any later year specified by order of the Secretary of State, must be such that the annual equivalent of the carbon budget for the period is—

(i) lower than the 1990 baseline by at least the percentage so specified, or

(ii) at least the minimum percentage so specified, and not more than the maximum percentage so specified, lower than the 1990 baseline.

[...]

10 Matters to be taken into account in connection with carbon budgets

(1) The following matters must be taken into account—

(a) by the Secretary of State in coming to any decision under this Part relating to carbon budgets, and

(b) by the Committee on Climate Change in considering its advice in relation to any such decision.

(2) The matters to be taken into account are—

(a) scientific knowledge about climate change;

(b) technology relevant to climate change;

(c) economic circumstances, and in particular the likely impact of the decision on the economy and the competitiveness of particular sectors of the economy;

(d) fiscal circumstances, and in particular the likely impact of the decision on taxation, public spending and public borrowing;

(e) social circumstances, and in particular the likely impact of the decision on fuel poverty;

(f) energy policy, and in particular the likely impact of the decision on energy supplies and the carbon and energy intensity of the economy;

(g) differences in circumstances between England, Wales, Scotland and Northern Ireland;

(h) circumstances at European and international level;

(i) the estimated amount of reportable emissions from international aviation and international shipping for the budgetary period or periods in question.

[...]

13 Duty to prepare proposals and policies for meeting carbon budgets

(1) The Secretary of State must prepare such proposals and policies as the Secretary of State considers will enable the carbon budgets that have been set under this Act to be met.

(2) The proposals and policies must be prepared with a view to meeting—

(a) the target in section 1 (the target for 2050), and

(b) any target set under section 5(1)(c) (power to set targets for later years).

(3) The proposals and policies, taken as a whole, must be such as to contribute to sustainable development.

There is also some flexibility under the Act, so that the GHGs that it covers might be amended by Order.[162] Similarly, the relevant baselines, budgetary periods, and percentage reduction targets for emissions might be altered, if significant developments are made in scientific knowledge about climate change or in EU or international policy.[163] For now, the targets for the carbon budgets until 2027 have been set.

	First Carbon budget (2008–12)	Second Carbon budget (2013–17)	Third Carbon budget (2018–22)	Fourth Carbon budget (2023–27)
Carbon budget level (million tonnes carbon dioxide equivalent ($MtCO_2e$))	3,018	2,782	2,544	1,950
Percentage reduction below base year levels	23%	29%	35%	50%

Figure 15.2 UK Carbon Budget GHG Emissions Targets 2008–27
Source: The Carbon Plan, 3

Further provisions of the Act set out:

- a requirement for limits on use of 'carbon units' that may be used to meet emissions reductions targets (particularly international credits purchased through Kyoto's Clean Development Mechanism or Joint Implementation provision), and a duty on the Secretary of State to have regard to the need for UK domestic action on climate change in meeting the targets and carbon budgets of the Act (ss 11 and 15);

- an obligation on Government to report to Parliament on its proposals and policies for each carbon budget period,[164] and to make annual statements on the net carbon account for each year (ss 14 and 16);

- additional measures to reduce GHG emissions, including: powers to introduce domestic ETSs through secondary legislation (ss 44, 45, and 46), guidance to develop effective corporate reporting of GHG emissions (s 85),[165] and charges for single-use carrier bags (s 77); and

- a duty on government to produce climate change impact reports and adaptation plans every five years (Part 4).

As for the role of the CCC, this is an independent, expert advisory body with extensive powers set up under Part 2 of the Act. The CCC has various duties but the extent of the CCC's power can

---

[162] Climate Change Act 2008, s 24.
[163] Ibid, ss 2, 6, and 23.
[164] Currently, see HM Government, *The Carbon Plan: Delivering our Low Climate Future*, 2 December 2011. By 31 December 2012, the Government needs also to have included international aviation and shipping emissions in the Act or explained to Parliament why not: Climate Change Act 2008, s 30.
[165] From April 2013, all UK listed companies are required to report carbon emissions in their annual reports to Companies House (the UK being the first country internationally to take this compulsory step).

really be seen in the extent to which the Secretary of State 'must obtain, and take into account, the advice of the Committee on Climate Change' in doing various things under the Act.[166] These include: setting, amending target percentages for, and otherwise altering, carbon budgets (ss 7, 9, and 22), or altering the overall 2050 target or baseline year (s 3). This role of the CCC arguably gives same insight into the legal consequences for the government in failing to meet the Act's obligations. If, for example, for reasons of political expediency, the UK government were minded to alter (and perhaps make less ambitious) the reduction targets of the Act, any such action would be judicially reviewable as being ultra vires if not done by taking into account the advice of the CCC. The CCC, with its detailed work in assessing the state of the UK economy and the potential for decarbonizing the living habits and infrastructure of UK society, thus provides a check and lock on the environmental goals of the Act, and a constraint on the discretion of the government in setting climate change policy.[167]

In addition to the Climate Change Act, the UK government has embraced a full and detailed agenda of climate change initiatives. A full and up-to-date picture of all UK climate-related action requires a close look over DECC's website, since policy and regulatory reform in this area is fast-moving and politically contentious. Overall, the policies of the UK government reflect its approach to climate change as a 'whole economy' problem, for which there is no simple regulatory solution, but fundamental reform required across all sectors, particularly energy production, residential, industry, and transport. The scale of the challenge to 2050 is set out starkly in the following image extracted from the CCC's 2008 report on Building a Low-Carbon Economy.

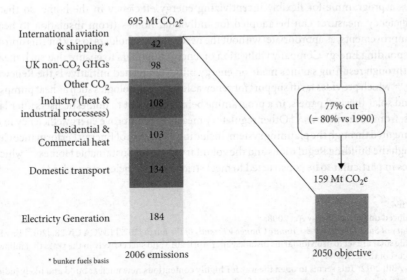

Figure 15.3 Cutting GHG emissions by 80% by 2050: the sectoral challenge

Source: UK National Atmospheric Emissions Inventory (2008), extracted from *Building a Low-Carbon Economy* 38.

---

[166] Note that there is also a significant role for 'national authorities', which comprise the UK Secretary of State, the Welsh and Scottish Ministers, and the relevant Northern Irish department, in making representations under the Act that the Secretary of State must take into account.

[167] See Section 2.2 of Chapter 11.

The strategic overview of the initiatives planned to achieve this drastic cut in GHG emissions by 2050 is set out in the government's Carbon Plan,[168] with detailed figures and targets of how these reform packages across sectors will lead to an 80% reduction against a 1990 baseline. At the time of writing, the key initiatives in place or in the pipeline include, in relation to *energy production*, a Renewables Obligation (RO) on electricity suppliers, requiring them to source a minimum and annually increasing amount of their energy from renewable sources, thereby financing large-scale renewable energy production in the process (with a view to meeting the UK's EU target of 15% of energy production from renewables by 2020). This mandatory requirement is supported by a financial mechanism and incentive in the form of Renewables Obligation Certificates (ROCs). ROCs are issued to electricity generators for renewable energy they generate, and suppliers then purchase these from generators of renewable energy (on top of the wholesale energy price). Suppliers must surrender sufficient ROCs each year to meet their required targets—for any shortfall, they must pay a buy-out price, which accumulates in a fund that is recycled back only to those suppliers that have complied with the scheme.

In addition to the RO, subsidies for small-scale renewable energy production are provided through feed-in-tariffs (FITs) for solar photovoltaic, wind, and other forms of microgeneration.[169] The setting of FITs, which guarantee payments to individuals or businesses who generate their own electricity and feed any unused energy back into the grid, is a good example of how frequent change to these schemes causes legal problems. In adjusting the FIT rates for solar energy production in late 2011, so as to keep the scheme affordable, the government introduced retrospective changes that were found to be ultra vires and thus unlawful.[170] Further, there is also a plan for overall reform of the UK electricity market to make it more robust for the future, including by embedding low carbon energy production into its structure.[171]

In terms of reducing GHG emissions from *residential* sources, the 'Green Deal' introduced in 2012 establishes a programme for flexibly incentivizing energy efficiency in the home, so that bespoke energy efficiency measures can be adopted for individual homes (from insulation to heating and lighting improvements, as appropriate) without the need for householders to pay for this upfront. There is a corresponding Energy Company Obligation on energy suppliers to ensure that such measures are financed through resulting savings made on energy bills.[172] A related initiative is the Renewable Heat Incentive,[173] which provides tariff support for renewable heat technologies such as heat pumps, biomass boilers, and solar thermal panels, in a programme being rolled out to domestic users after large-scale heat users, from 2012 onwards.[174] Other regulatory measures to improve energy efficiency in the home are implemented through the planning system, including by the use of Energy Performance Certificates and through the Building Regulations and the voluntary Code for Sustainable Homes,[175] which require new homes in particular to be constructed to meet strict energy efficiency standards.

---

[168] See n 164.

[169] Introduced under the Energy Act 2008.

[170] *Secretary of State for Energy & Climate Change v Friends of the Earth* [2012] EWCA Civ 28, [2012] Env LR 25. FITs for large scale solar are set to drop for farms installed after April 2013 and successively in the years that follow (to reflect the falling cost of the technology).

[171] Energy Bill 2012. This seems to open the way for highly contentious new nuclear build and likely judicial review challenges: cf *R (Greenpeace) v Secretary of State for Trade and Industry* [2007] EWHC 311, [2007] Env LR 29 (see Section 2.2 of Chapter 11).

[172] The Energy Act 2011 introduced the Green Deal and corresponding ECO, which offer greater benefits to poorer households and areas.

[173] Introduced under the Energy Act 2008.

[174] Note that in its support for biomass boilers in particular, the Renewable Heat Incentive (RHI) can conflict with the Clean Air Act 1993 (see p 635). Accordingly, in 2012, DEFRA was seeking to limit eligibility for RHI payment to biomass boilers that keep their emissions below certain levels.

[175] DCLG, *Improving the Energy Efficiency of our Homes and Buildings: Energy Certificates and Air-Conditioning Inspections for Buildings* (1 March 2008); The Building Regulations 2010 SI 2010/2214, pt 6; DCLG, *Code for Sustainable Homes: Technical guide—2010* (11 November 2010).

Targeted regulatory efforts, beyond the EU ETS, to reduce GHG emissions by *industry* include three key measures: the Climate Change Levy (CCL), Climate Change Agreements (CCAs), and the CRC Energy Efficiency Scheme.[176] The CCL is a tax on the use of energy by industry, commerce, and the public sector, which aims to promote energy efficiency.[177] All revenue raised is returned to business in two ways—through a cut in employers' national insurance contributions, and through funding energy efficiency and low carbon technologies. CCAs are agreements that energy intensive industries can choose to enter, comprising a sectoral agreement alongside an individual agreement for particular installations, with the goal of reducing emissions or improving energy efficiency. Meeting the terms and targets of CCAs qualifies relevant industrial installations for a 65% discount from the CCL, set to increase to 80% from April 2013. The scheme has been extended until at least 2023.

Finally, the CRC Energy Efficiency Scheme sets up an emissions reporting and trading scheme under the Climate Change Act. Large public and private organizations, which are not within the EU ETS or subject to a CCA, qualify for the scheme.[178] From 2010/11 onwards, qualifying organizations are obliged to monitor and report their energy use each year,[179] and from 2011/12 to purchase and surrender allowances equivalent to their reported CO_2 emissions each year.[180] Participating organizations are ranked in league tables according to their energy performance, with proceeds from the selling of allowances redistributed to participants in proportions that correspond to their league table positions, setting up financial as well as reputational incentives to improve energy performance. In 2012, the CRC scheme was reviewed in order to simplify the scheme, which had been onerous and difficult to implement. The government announced a range of modifications to the scheme, including the abolition of the performance league tables, although the aggregated energy use and emissions data of participants will continue to be published.

FURTHER READING AND QUESTIONS

1. Consider the extract by Peel at the start of Section 3.1. Do you agree that it is necessary to think of climate change law in the expansive terms presented by Peel and as a 'new legal discipline'? What legal analytical advantages or disadvantages might this perspective bring?

2. Does the Kyoto Protocol's Clean Development Mechanism allow UNFCCC Annex 1 parties an easy option for meeting their emissions reductions obligations under Annex B of the Protocol? Note Article 6(1)(d) of the Protocol and the fact that it was meant to be a first step, not a complete regulatory solution to the problem of global warming.

3. What challenges does the EU ETS face in Phase III from 2013? Are these legal challenges, or other types of challenges?

4. Read Case C-366/10 *Air Transport of America* (CJEU, 21 December 2011). Are you convinced that including aviation in the EU ETS complies with all relevant rules of international law, including the Kyoto Protocol? Might the arguments in the case look different from the perspective of a public international lawyer? For further reading on this case, see Sanja Bogojevic, 'Legalising

---

[176] Note the Carbon Plan sets out a range of further initiatives to reduce GHG emissions, particularly from the transport and agriculture sectors and from waste generation and management. See n 164.

[177] Finance Act 2000, s 30, schs 6 and 7.

[178] Organizations are sufficiently large if their total half-hourly electricity consumption is over 6000 megawatt-hours (MWh) once electricity used for transport and domestic accommodation has been excluded. They include schools and local authorities, supermarkets, water companies, and all central government departments.

[179] CRC Energy Efficiency Scheme Order 2010 SI 768/2010.

[180] The CRC Energy Efficiency Scheme (Allocation of Allowances for Payment) Regulations 2012 SI 2012/1386.

Environmental Leadership: A Comment on the CJEU's Ruling in C–366/10 on the Inclusion of Aviation in the EU Emissions Trading Scheme', (2012) 24(2) JEL 345.

5. For further reading and a sceptical view of the economic regulatory model of the EU ETS, see G Winter, 'The Climate is no Commodity: Taking Stock of the Emissions Trading System' (2010) 22(1) JEL 1.

6. Do you think that the UK's Climate Change Act 2008 is a powerful piece of legislation? Does it represent a legal guarantee of environmentally progressive climate change policy in the UK until 2050 (in which case, what does this say about its nature in constitutional terms), or is it more symbolic in its legal effect?

7. For a case that considers air pollution problems through a human rights lens, see *Marangopoulos Foundation for Human Rights v Greece*, Complaint No 30/2005, European Committee of Social Rights. This case concerns Article 11 of the European Social Charter, which grants to everyone the right 'to benefit from any measures enabling him to enjoy the highest possible standard of health attainable'. This Charter falls under the auspices of the Council of Europe, so the decision shows environmental law operating in another distinct forum, in which all of the international and EU regimes considered in this chapter (EU air quality control, climate change law, IPPC regulation) are drawn on to find that Greece was in violation of its Charter obligations in relation to air pollution conditions for people living in lignite mining areas.

4 CONCLUSION

This chapter has set out and analysed the law that applies to air pollution problems, focusing on ambient air quality and climate change regulation in particular. Overall, it can be seen that different aspects of these environment problems shape the law that applies to them. For example, the history of industrialization and developing awareness about its air polluting effects are reflected in a deeper UK legal history relating to local air pollution problems. By contrast, emerging and urgent scientific and political developments concerning GHG-induced climate change have resulted in a recent and international regulatory response, involving regulatory strategies that could not work for localized air quality regulation. In these two examples, the mix of relevant jurisdictions, level of scientific certainty, the types of regulatory strategy, and legal 'experience', ranges widely.

At the same time, legal regimes also construct air pollution problems in various ways. For example, in regulating ambient air quality, evolving scientific knowledge has led to amended regulation and thus a new understanding of the air pollution problem. This can be seen in relation to developments in the AQFD 2008 in regulating PM-2.5 and ground-level ozone. Some scientific responses to the AQFD have judged it to be too soft in setting particulate matter quality standards and thus misrepresenting the environmental problem that the regulation seeks to address.[181]

In the result, the complex legal map that relates to air pollution problems, which involves a range of regulatory strategies, is not simply an *ad hoc* confusion of poorly coordinated legislation. Rather, different aspects of air pollution regulation have been introduced and designed to cater for different types—and legal constructions—of air pollution problems. And whilst these regulatory approaches do overlap, and do not always integrate well, their variety and frequent amendment shows that no single approach to air pollution problems is adequate to deal with those problems. Thus, for example,

---

[181] KCL London Air Quality Network, *Report 14: Air Quality in London 2006–07*, 2.

limiting point source emissions is not enough to control air pollution problems, since cumulative impacts get missed.[182] Nor is it sufficient simply to set environmental quality standards for pollutants in the ambient air, as under the AQFD, since there are technical difficulties in achieving, implementing, and enforcing these standards, and such standards do not necessarily encourage controlling pollution at source.

At the same time, other regulatory measures that target the *prevention* of polluting air emissions by controlling their source or generation increasingly complement environmental quality standards, reflecting the principle of rectification at source.[183] This is seen in the market in emission rights introduced under the EU emissions trading scheme—capping and putting a price on carbon dioxide emissions sets up a financial incentive to reduce and discourage their production. Measures that prevent air pollution emissions at source are also seen in regulatory controls that are 'designed in', which prevent polluting emissions from arising at all so that implementation problems are removed. Prominent examples are regulations that restrict the concentration of lead and sulphur in petroleum products;[184] or which incentivize the design of vehicles to minimize polluting emissions and promote fuel efficiency;[185] or which restrict the use of hazardous elements in electronic and other products or require energy efficient product design.[186] The latter example is in fact not readily identified as 'air pollution' regulation, demonstrating that air pollution problems are the result of chains of actions and industrial processes. A holistic and preventive approach to air pollution problems thus involves a combined regulatory effort with other pollution control regimes, from waste and water pollution regulation to industrial integrated pollution control, as well as environmental regulation that controls product design and the use of resources. To that extent, this chapter has provided an overview of the regulation that applies specifically to air pollution problems, but it does not represent *all* regulation that deals with, or is required to deal with, such problems.

[182] Although the IPPC regime sets up a more sophisticated form of emission limit regulation than simply limiting air emissions from stationary sources, incorporating the evolving BAT standard designed to promote innovative and ever-improving pollution-reduction technology for large-scale industry, at least in theory. See Section 2 of Chapter 17.

[183] See Section 1.1 of Chapter 11.

[184] European Parliament and Council Directive 98/70/EC of 13 October 1998 relating to the quality of petrol and diesel fuels [1998] OJ L350/58; Council Directive 1999/32/EC of 26 April 1999 relating to a reduction in the sulphur content of certain liquid fuel [1999] OJ L121/13.

[185] See n 51.

[186] See, for example, European Parliament and Council Directive 2011/65/EU of 8 June 2011 on the restriction of the use of certain hazardous substances in electrical and electronic equipment (recast) [2011] OJ L174/88; European Parliament and Council Directive 2006/66/EC of 6 September 2006 on batteries and accumulators and waste batteries and accumulators [2006] OJ L266/1; European Parliament and Council Directive 2009/125/EC of 21 October 2009 establishing a framework for the setting of ecodesign requirements for energy-related products [2009] OJ L285/10.

16

WASTE REGULATION

Waste regulation concerns a different kind of environmental problem from those considered elsewhere in this textbook. Essentially, this is because the very notion of 'waste', which can give rise to very serious environmental and health problems, is a legally constructed one. Unlike air quality control and water pollution regulation, which focus on harms to particular (albeit interconnecting) environmental media, or climate change regulation, which deals with an environmental problem largely defined by developing scientific knowledge, waste regulation is focused solely on an identified *pollution source*, which is defined and characterized in legal terms. We all have a sense of what waste is—it is the material we put in the rubbish bin, or see (or don't see) at a landfill site, or walk past littering the footpath, a park, or a river. This everyday understanding of waste shows why it is an environmental issue, but what exactly makes a substance waste and the distinction between waste and non-waste are very difficult lines to draw, as this chapter will show. And they are legal lines to draw. Thus, the definition of 'waste' is a critical legal question—it is only by classifying material as waste that the body of regulation examined in this chapter is triggered, from waste management licensing, to hazardous waste controls, to transfrontier waste shipments regulation.

The main reason why there is such complexity around defining materials as waste is that objects no longer wanted by one person might still be useful to another. For example, I may no longer want an old winter coat. Will it be waste if I put it in the bin? Yes. What about if I put it in a clothing recycling bin? Maybe. If I cut it up into pieces and make a patchwork quilt out of the fabric? I don't think so (does it matter that I destroyed the coat?) What if I give it to a grateful friend? No. What if I sell it to a second hand clothing store? Well now I'm getting something in return for it, so that cannot be waste. It is this kind of spectrum of dealings with no longer wanted items that the definition of waste has to navigate, against a backdrop of EU and UK government policy that encourages and seeks to incentivize the recycling and re-use of materials, and extending the lifecycles of natural resources generally. In that process of navigation, there is a big role for policy in shaping and complicating the scope of the area of law, through its legally constructed definition of waste. However, waste policy also pursues a range of goals, which can operate in tension. Thus, while waste prevention and extending resource life-cycles are priorities, so is minimizing environmental harm from waste materials and dealings involving them. The tension in balancing these policy goals pervades the regulatory structure of EU waste law, and influences how the concept of waste is interpreted (particularly judicially) and thus legally construed.

The chapter is structured in three sections. Section 1 considers the problem of waste and the different ways in which it can be conceptualized and understood, before examining the legal solutions that have developed to define waste in EU and UK law. Section 2 then considers EU waste law and policy, which centres around the Waste Framework Directive (WFD) 2008 (which replaced earlier framework Directives) as the main legal instrument in this area, containing amongst other things the core legislative definition of waste. Section 2 also considers the 'daughter' EU waste Directives that sit under the WFD and relate to certain forms of waste management and different waste streams, like packaging and electronic waste, as well as EU rules on waste shipments. Section 3 then considers waste regulation in UK law, with a focus on English law. Much of this UK law and policy is now driven by EU developments, although the UK has some measures to deal with waste problems beyond transposed EU rules, and the administration of waste law at national and local levels is a significant operation in its own right, requiring a vast infrastructure and network of industry operators.

1 THE WASTE PROBLEM: DEFINING WASTE

1.1 THE PROBLEM OF WASTE

In general, we commonly think of waste as trash, rubbish, refuse, litter—the objects that we no longer want, which are thrown away, dirty, and at the end of their useful lives. However, on closer reflection, waste has multiple meanings. It is a notion that carries meaning beyond physical objects to convey negative ideas of the decaying, misuse, or squandering of valuable things—wasting time, financial resources, opportunities, space, and youth. In our everyday lexicon and in political rhetoric, such negative connotations and associations are strong and emotive.

When thinking about objects that are waste—the subject of this area of environmental law—again there are differing conceptions of waste, but the negative ideas associated with waste in general also resonate throughout this legal area, reflected particularly in the difficulty that courts have had in adopting a legal definition of waste that recognizes its more positive potential. The four extracts given here reflect varying conceptions of objects as waste—from presenting such waste as a major problem to be fixed to a concept that need not exist at all. The first extract sets the scene for the EU's waste management policy, and it conceptualizes waste as a widespread social problem, with serious environmental consequences.

European Commission, *Being Wise with Waste: the EU's Approach to Waste Management* (Publications Office of the European Union, 2010) 2–3

Waste is an issue that affects us all. We all produce waste: on average, each of the 500 million people living in the EU throws away around half a tonne of household rubbish every year. This is on top of huge amounts of waste generated from activities such as manufacturing (360 million tonnes) and construction (900 million tonnes), while water supply and energy production generate another 95 million tonnes. Altogether, the European Union produces up to 3 billion tonnes of waste every year.

All this waste has a huge impact on the environment, causing pollution and greenhouse gas emissions hat contribute to climate change, as well as significant losses of materials—a particular problem for the EU which is highly dependent on imported raw materials.

The amount of waste we are creating is increasing and the nature of waste itself is changing, partly due to the dramatic rise in the use of hi-tech products. This means waste now contains an increasingly complex mix of materials, including plastics, precious metals and hazardous materials [some 100 million tonnes is hazardous, containing heavy metals and other toxins] that are difficult to deal with safely.

EU waste management policies aim to reduce the environmental and health impacts of waste and improve Europe's resource efficiency [...] Proper waste management is a key element in ensuring resource efficiency and the sustainable growth of European economies.

[...]

Whether it is re-used, recycled, incinerated or put into landfill sites, the management of household and industrial waste comes at a financial and environmental cost. First, waste must be collected, sorted and transported before being treated which can prove expensive and result in greenhouse gas emissions and pollution of air, soils and water.

Girling see waste as being less a problem that needs controlling or fixing through environmental policy, but more as an inevitable part of life, the costs and regulation of which are highly complex matters.

Richard Girling, *Rubbish! Dirt on Our Hands and the Crisis Ahead* (Transworld Publishers 2005) i–iii

Waste is as necessary to life as air and water. Just to be born into our own bodies is to create lifelong problems of disposal. Waste, after all, is what life itself becomes when it's over [...] To create, or to *be*, rubbish is as basic a freedom as speech, education, or water. Without the freedom to write bad books for the pulping plant, there would be no good ones to be kept in the library. There is no apple without a core; no nourishment without the consequent flush of the cistern; no shelf-life without a sealed and stackable pack; nothing made or grown without its necessary margin of scrap. The economics of waste are often the negative image of what we might expect. Even in basic terms of energy and materials, 'excessive' packaging may save more than it costs. Local authorities with apparently good recycling records may depend for their green credentials on energy from garbage incinerators, or low-grade compost used in landfills. 'Green' initiatives by governments may be a shade so dark that they are indistinguishable from black.

The third extract shows that waste is a complicated phenomenon for another reason—waste itself can be seen as a resource. This is because what is waste to one person has potential to be a useful object to another. As Girling puts it, 'rubbish is in the eye of the beholder'; 'one man's waste [...] is another man's bounty'.[1]

DEFRA, *Government Review of Waste Policy in England 2011*, 6

Waste is a resource. It is clear that for too long we have worried about how to dispose of waste, but not enough about how to minimise it, or the use we can make of it. At a time of material resource pressure—even scarcity in some areas—we need to consider waste more fully within broader material flows and sustainable material use.

Taking this line of thinking even further, waste might not be seen as a resource to maximize, but as something to be prevented altogether. The Zero Waste Charter takes this approach, promoting 'zero waste', which supports the prevention of waste by maximizing and extending the use of primarily materials and products, as well as maximizing its value once produced through recovering and recycling. These priorities—prevention then recovery—reflect the direction of current EU and UK

---

[1] Richard Girling, *Rubbish! Dirt on Our Hands and the Crisis Ahead* (Transworld Publishers 2005) 356, 365.

waste policy, as encapsulated by the waste hierarchy in Section 2.2. This extract also makes clear that it is not 'waste' itself that is the direct pollutant of the environment, but what is done with it—it is a *source* of pollution or a *pollution risk*.

Zero Waste Alliance UK, *Zero Waste Charter*, presented to UK Parliament 18 June 2002

Zero Waste is a new concept [that] entails re-designing products and changing the way waste is handled so that products last longer, materials are recycled, or, in the case of organics, composted. Waste is in the process of being designed away.

The immediate imperatives behind the drive for Zero Waste are environmental. There is a new awareness of the dangers to human health of waste landfills and incinerators. Landfills are major producers of methane, and polluters of water tables. Incinerators produce greenhouse gases, and are a source of heavy metals, particulates and dioxins. Zero Waste strikes at the cause of this pollution.

It also lightens the ever growing pressure on the world's forests, soils, and mineral resources by making more with less. Doubling the life of a car saves the 15 tonnes of materials required to make a new one. Recycling paper gives wood fibres six lives rather than one. Increasing the productivity of resources in this way also leads to major savings in energy. Zero Waste will play a central role in cutting CO_2 emissions and sequestering carbon in the soil.

However, the prevention of waste altogether—through maximizing resource use or clever and efficient product design—or its recycling into new materials may be a utopic goal, a direction of policy and behavioural travel, rather than a realistic future outcome. This is because patterns of past waste-generating behaviour are part of, and arguably essential to, urban living, leaving indelible environmental marks that are kept conveniently out of sight of everyday life. The extract from Nagle presents this picture through an anthropological analysis of waste problems that have built up over time, through a study of 'Fresh Kills', now closed but in its time the biggest landfill site in the world, which serviced Manhattan and its surrounds in New York City. Not all places rely so heavily on landfill for waste disposal—some rely more in incineration, particularly European states where available land is scarcer—but the UK has also been heavily dependent on landfill historically.

Robin Nagle, 'The History and Future of Fresh Kills' in *The Filthy Reality of Everyday Life*, (Profile Books 2011) 190, 192, 198–99

[A] landfill seems a lowly and unlikely commons. But it serves, in the sense of a resource set aside by the community for its shared use, to enhance the greater good. Without a functioning landfill or some other way of ridding itself of debris, no metropolis can survive.

[...]

Trash invites a willing ignorance that is nicely revealed in our vehemently vague language of discard. We don't 'put' it away, which would imply that we save it for later use. Rather, we 'throw' it away, and the 'away' is comfortably undefined—but it is often a landfill. As the last stop for our discards, landfills force commonality on our material traces, whether or not such commonality existed before. They hold startlingly accurate records of the people who form them, and unlike the people, they endure [...]

[...]

Since its inception, Fresh Kills has [...] allowed the citizens of New York to live at breakneck speed without having to change consumption habits or consider that the 'away' is a real place [...]

[...]

Often a landfill can be forgotten once it is covered over and turned into something else—a golf course, say, or a park. But landfills like Fresh Kills are too big to ignore, and so they pose a continual cognitive dissonance. They betray the lie of the 'away'. They confront us with part of the real physical cost of the way we organise our material lives.

Nagle also makes clear that landfills are not simply sources of pollution; they too have their useful value, beyond being a vital 'commons' for a city. This is partly because the nature of a landfill will change over time—it is itself an evolving environment.

In New York, street-side trash collecting was legislated in the 1650s, but it happened only sporadically, and much waste was simply dumped along the city's shore. This proved a popular solution to the problem of too much trash and too little space. Even in the 1600s, real estate was a hot commodity in New York, and much of urban life centred on the downtown waterfront [...] In Manhattan, below City Hall, 33 per cent of the land is built on 'street sweepings, ashes, garbage, ballast from ships, dirt and rubble from excavated building sites, and other forms of solid waste dumped along the shore.' [para 188]

[...]

From its start until its closure, [Fresh Kills] represented not only the prevalent solid-waste disposal technologies of the day, but it also helped advance the science of landfill design[...] Today, as Freshkills Park, it continues to be a centre of significant innovation as environmentalists work to build an ecology rich with plant and animal life. [para 198]

In conclusion, the conceptualization of waste is far from straightforward—waste is a resource, a problem, a phenomenon reducible to zero. It is an essential part of life, but an opportunity for adopting new social behaviours and industrial practices. The legal definition of waste, now examined in Sections 1.2 and 1.3, grapples with these different aspects of conceptualizing waste and also draws lines favouring one approach over another, albeit not very cleanly. Defining waste is a legal exercise in determining what kind of material is (and should be) classified as waste, and what waste policy then directs should be done with it. If you keep in mind the bigger conceptual problems involved in identifying waste and appreciating its fate explored in this section, this will help you to understand the legal ambiguities and tensions in this area of law.

1.2 THE EU LAW SOLUTION TO DEFINING WASTE

The EU law approach to defining waste is central to EU waste law, and it also provides the main authoritative source for UK law on this legal issue. This is due to the overarching role of the EU Waste Framework Directive (WFD) as the basis for all waste law and regulation, in EU and UK law alike. As Scotford has written elsewhere:[2]

[The WFD] acts as a framework for [EU] waste legislation... It sets the agenda for [EU] waste regulation through its statement of waste policy. It establishes regulation applying to all waste. It ensures the compatibility of [EU] waste instruments, particularly by establishing a *common definition of waste*. It covers the field of waste, ensuring that there are no regulatory loopholes in targeting the polluting effects of waste within the [EU].

---

[2] Eloise Scotford, 'Trash or Treasure: Policy Tensions in EC Waste Regulation' (2007) 19(3) JEL 367, 373.

Thus, the Directive's central concept of 'waste' is the trigger for the application of EU and Member State waste law prescriptions and regulatory controls. It is only if there is a subject or object that is identifiable as Directive 'waste' that the laws that comprise this area of environmental law—examined further in Sections 2 and 3—come into operation. Identifying waste in this way is an exercise in legal construction, and is defined in Article 3(1) WFD as follows:[3]

waste means any substance or object which the holder discards or intends or is required to discard.

Unsurprisingly, this legal definition resembles the everyday understanding of waste—as something that we discard or throw away, usually into the rubbish bin. However, in breaking down the definition and interpreting its seemingly simple terms, much legal complexity has been found. As a starting point, the Commission has issued guidance on interpreting various aspects of the WFD, including the tripartite aspect of discarding included in the Article 3(1) definition.

EU Commission, *Guidance on the Interpretation of Key Provisions of Directive 2008/98/EC on Waste* (DG Environment, June 2012) 10–12

The key term of the waste definition is 'discard', used in three alternatives ('any substance or object (1) which the holder discards or (2) intends or (3) is required to discard'), without providing definitions or clarification on the exact meaning of these.

However, the first alternative is describing an action or activity of the holder of the substance or the object, the second describes an intention of the holder, and the third a legal obligation (see examples below). These three alternatives are not always easy to distinguish [...]

For a number of every-day situations, the allocation of a holder's actions and activities to one of the three 'discarding' alternatives and thus the classification of a substance or object as a waste is an easy task. For example, an item thrown in a dustbin is discarded, and is thus considered waste. On the other hand, for a number of cases and in a very wide range of circumstances, there remains uncertainty.

[...]

1.1.2.2 Practical examples for the three alternatives of 'discarding'

Discard:

- An item is thrown into a waste bin;
- A company transfers material to a waste collector.

Intention to discard:

- In its decommissioning plan in the event of future closure, an operating site indicates that it will send off-site for appropriate disposal or recovery any of its stock of raw materials that cannot be returned;
- The holder of leftover quarried stone which has been stored for an indefinite length of time to await possible use discards or intends to discard that leftover stone.

---

[3] European Parliament and Council Directive 2008/98/EC of 19 November 2008 on waste [2008] OJ L312/3 (Waste Framework Directive or '2008 WFD'), art 3(1). Note that there have been other legal constructions of waste, particularly in UK law, which have relied on exclusive and inclusive definitions, presumptions, and lists of substances, which are now obsolete in light of this WFD definition. See David Pocklington, *The Law of Waste Management* (2nd edn, Sweet & Maxwell 2011) 24.

Requirement to discard:

- Any oil containing PCBs above 50 ppm must be discarded under the provisions of EU PCB/PCT Directive 96/59/EC and is therefore to be considered waste;
- Stockpiles of banned pesticides must be discarded and therefore be managed as waste.

As the guidance itself suggests, there remains uncertainty in many cases as to the existence of waste. This is because, as Section 1.1 demonstrated, even our everyday or social understandings of waste are far from straightforward, and they can evolve over time. The various ways of thinking about waste are again played out in the context of this legal definition, which, for all its deceptive simplicity, has been the cause of much confusion over its interpretation. This confusion has not been simply due to competing understandings of waste but also the differing *purposes* of waste policy and regulation, which have changed over time and which in turn give rise to differing understandings of what should be characterized and thus legally regulated as waste.

At the heart of the complexity concerning the definition of waste in EU law is a tension between regulating waste as an *environmental harm* and treating it as a *potentially valuable resource*. This tension reflects the history of EU waste regulation, which has been marked by a series of evolving WFDs, starting in 1975 with a Directive focused primarily on regulating the disposal of waste with a view to minimizing environmental harm in this process,[4] before a considerable amendment of the Directive in 1991,[5] which introduced a wider set of regulatory controls over materials that are waste, and also changed the Directive's focus to encourage the recycling and recovery of waste. In particular, a waste hierarchy was introduced, which prioritized the prevention and recovery of waste over its disposal.[6] The current WFD, introduced in 2008 to replace the previous versions, is a further iteration of the Directive again, adjusting further the direction of EU waste regulation and policy, with a central aim of maximizing resource use more broadly (as discussed in Section 2.1). Throughout these legislative changes, the core definition of waste has remained largely unchanged, but the regulatory and policy context in which it operates has shifted. The EU law conception of waste has thus also altered in the process, taking it from a concept that is focused on environmental harm to one that is focused on the productive potential of waste and resources more generally. How this changing conception is reflected in the legal interpretation of the Article 3(1) definition of waste has, however, been doctrinally contentious. The following extract shows why the concept of discarding is important to the definition of waste but also why and how it causes interpretive problems in the context of the Directive, in which the term 'discard' is undefined.

Eloise Scotford, 'Trash or Treasure: Policy Tensions in EC Waste Regulation' (2007) 19(3) JEL 367, 370, 375–76

The inherent probability that unwanted (waste) items will become polluting through disposal, is reflected in the Directive's definition of 'waste', which turns on identifiable actions of discarding materials. The *actions* of the holder of material are targeted because the environmental and health dangers posed by waste, as distinct from other, materials stem from their holder no longer wanting them, and no longer having any (self-)interest in their use or existence. The holder may thus be inclined to dispose of such

---

[4] Council Directive 75/442/EEC of 15 July 1975 on waste [1975] OJ L194/39.

[5] Council Directive 91/156/EEC of 18 March 1991 amending Directive 75/442/EEC of 18 March 1991 on waste [1991] OJ L78/32; later codified in European Parliament and Council Directive 2006/12/EC of 5 April 2006 on waste [2006] OJ L114/9 ('2006 WFD').

[6] 2006 WFD, art 3.

materials carelessly, not wanting to pay the costs of disposal (or recovery). Unwanted materials that are finally disposed of (to whatever environmental standard) will likely have a polluting effect on the environment.

[...]

The term 'discard' is central to this definition, and is undefined. This omission has given rise to significant problems in interpreting the Directive. It is submitted that, while undefined, the verb 'discard' importantly identifies waste as an *action-based concept*, rather than a substance-based concept. Thus the question of what 'discard' means is a question of what actions (with respect to substances and objects) are to be caught by the definition of waste. This action-focused understanding of waste reflects waste's inherent risk as a pollutant... As an action, what 'to discard' means, short of final disposal, can be frustratingly unclear.

Confusion over the meaning of 'discard' stems partly from the fact that discarded material might be either disposed of *or recovered*, since these are the two permissible fates of waste prescribed by the Directive [as examined further below]. Any uneasiness generated by the idea that materials might be both discarded *and* recovered can be removed by appreciating that the discarding of materials is a necessary prerequisite for their disposal or recovery as waste [...]

Current debate surrounding the meaning of 'discard' is concerned with the extent to which it is to be given 'an extended meaning, going beyond the concept of getting rid of unwanted materials, to cover the situation where materials are [re-used, or stored, sold or otherwise transferred for beneficial re-use]' [...] The difficult issue here is discerning between when materials have been discarded even though they are later reused, and when materials are reused (or perhaps simply 'used') *rather than discarded*. In the first case, the regulatory provisions of the Directive will apply; in the second, they will not.

The sub-sections here examine the evolving EU case law that has attempted to deal with this question of when materials are discarded, particularly where they might yet be put to further productive use. Keep in mind that some of the earlier cases discussed are being decided before significant changes were made to the WFD in 1991, or as they are being introduced, and they are thus responding to a changing regulatory context.

EU definition of waste: early case law and *ARCO Chemie*

In *Walloon Waste*, the European Court of Justice said the following about the nature of waste:[7]

With respect to the environment, it is important to note that waste is *matter of a special kind*. Accumulation of waste, even before it becomes a health hazard, constitutes a *danger to the environment*, regard being had in particular to the limited capacity of each region or locality for waste reception.

This special status of waste, as a latent risk to the environment, has informed much of the Court's reasoning about the definition of waste. Seeing waste as a problem first and foremost, rather than a potential resource, has been the predominant approach of the Court. However, as outlined already, this gives rise to a tension in defining waste within the context of the WFD, which is increasingly concerned with preventing waste and encouraging its re-use. This tension has resulted in an increasingly complicated

---

[7] Case C-2/90 *Commission v Belgium (Walloon Waste)* [1992] ECR I-4431, para 30. This case is discussed further in Section 5.2 of Chapter 4, and Section 1.3 of Chapter 11.

and often confusing body of case law. As Carnwath LJ stated in *R (OSS) Group v Environment Agency*, 'a search for logical coherence in the [CJEU] case-law is probably doomed to failure'.[8] His Honour went on to state that the 'fundamental problem is the court's professed adherence to the [WFD] definition', without adequately explaining or interpreting the terms of that definition or otherwise applying it in inappropriate circumstances.

However, the case law to date has presented a series of decisions about the definition of waste, which highlight points of controversy relating to this legal concept, and which show at the very least the arguments that have *not* worked in seeking to characterize materials as waste or non-waste. The earliest of these key cases was *Vessoso and Zanetti*, a preliminary reference from the Italian courts, arising out of criminal proceedings against haulage contractors charged with transporting substances on behalf of third parties without prior authorization. The criminal charges depended on the substances being characterized as waste. The preliminary reference raised two questions: (1) whether waste is to be understood as excluding substances and objects that are capable of economic reutilization; and (2) whether the holder disposing of a substance or object must intend to exclude any further economic re-use by others for the substance or object to be waste. Note that this case concerned the original 1975 incarnation of the WFD. The original WFD was less focused on the recycling, recovery, and prevention of waste, and its definition of waste was also slightly different—'any substance or object which the holder *disposes of* or is required to dispose of pursuant to the provisions of national law in force' (with no reference to 'intention' to dispose of). In spite of these differences, the judicial interpretation of 'waste' in *Vessoso* has not only remained good law, but it predicted the direction of things to come.

Joined Cases C-206 & C-207/88 *Criminal Proceedings against Vessoso and Zanetti* [1990] ECR I-1461

The [recitals in the former Waste Directive preambles] stress the importance of encouraging the recovery of waste and the use of recovered materials in order to conserve natural resources. Furthermore, the [Directives] provide that waste disposal is to be understood as including the transformation operations necessary for the recovery, reuse or recycling of waste. Finally, [the Directives] require Member States to take appropriate steps to encourage the prevention, recycling and processing of waste, the extraction of raw materials and possibly energy therefrom and any other process for the reuse of waste. It is clear from those various provisions that a substance of which its holder disposes may constitute waste within the meaning of [the former WFD] even when it is capable of economic reutilization.

[...]

[The Directive definition of waste] refers generally to any substance or object of which the holder disposes, and draws no distinction according to the intentions of the holder disposing thereof. Moreover, [it also specifies] that waste also includes substances or objects which the holder 'is required to dispose of pursuant to the provisions of national law in force'. A holder may be required by a provision of national law to dispose of something without necessarily intending to exclude all economic reutilization thereof by others.

The result in *Vessoso* was upheld even after the change of wording of the definition of waste with the 1991 amendments to the Directive (dispose became 'discard', 'intention to discard' was also included), and its broader shift to a system of EU waste regulation focused on waste recovery as well as, and in preference to, waste disposal. Thus, in the subsequent *Tombesi* case, under the revised definition of waste, it was

---

[8] *R (OSS Group Ltd) v Environment Agency* [2007] EWCA Civ 611, [2008] Env LR 8, para 55.

again held that 'waste' covered all objects and substances discarded by owners, even if they have a commercial value and are collected on a commercial basis for recycling, reclamation, or re-use.[9]

In cases that followed on the meaning of waste, Advocates-General made various suggestions to the Court for 'short-cuts' or tests to qualify and give more detail to the Article 3(1) definition. Thus, in *Tombesi* itself, AG Jacobs had suggested a 'by-pass' approach to the definition, so that any materials could be presumed to be waste if they were subject to an Annex IIA or IIB disposal or recovery operation (the Annexes to the WFD set out non-exhaustive lists of such waste operations, which are regulated by the Directive, as discussed in Section 2.3).[10] Conversely, materials *not* subject to any of these operations would not be waste. In *Interenvironment Wallonie*, AG Jacobs tried a different approach, arguing that, in distinguishing between waste recovery and the processing of non-waste materials, it is relevant to consider whether a substance will be put directly to continued use in its existing form. For by-products and residues of certain industrial operations, such continued use would occur if the material, and the subsequent process to which it was to be put, met normal health and environmental requirements applicable to non-waste products and processes (an 'environmental criterion').[11] This approach was echoed by the related arguments of AG Alber in *ARCO*, who argued that waste materials that have been recovered or reprocessed should *no longer* be considered as waste—so that their use does not need control or authorization—if they no longer pose a 'danger typical of waste' and their use does not pollute the environment any more than an equivalent raw material.[12] All of these suggestions were avoided or rejected by the Court of Justice, which has instead prioritized the system of supervision and control established by the Directive, keeping the definition of waste as broad as possible.[13]

As a result, these early cases still left unresolved the difficult issue of what 'discard' means. This is the key question of construction on which the definition of waste turns, and the landmark *ARCO* decision in 2000 was meant to clarify this issue once and for all. In the first extract from *ARCO*, consider the Court's general approach to this question of interpretation, including the interpretive role for the precautionary and preventive principles in the Court's reasoning.

Joined Cases C-418/97 & C-419/97 *ARCO Chemie Nederland v Minister Van Volkshuisvesting* [2000] ECR I-4475 paras 36–40 (emphasis added)

It follows that the scope of the term waste turns on the meaning of the term discard. The Court has held that that term must be interpreted in light of the aim of the directive. In that regard, the third recital in the preamble to [the 1991 Waste Framework Directive] states that the essential objective of all provisions relating to waste disposal must be the protection of human health and the environment against harmful effects caused by the collection, transport, treatment, storage and tipping of waste. It should further be pointed out that, pursuant to Article 130r(2) of the EC Treaty (now, after amendment, [Article 191(2) TFEU]), Community policy on the environment is to aim at a high level of protection and is to be based, in particular, on the precautionary principle and the principle that preventive action should be taken. It follows that the concept of waste *cannot be interpreted restrictively*.

---

[9] Joined Cases C-304/94 & 330/94 & 342/94 & 224/95 *Criminal Proceedings against Tombesi* [1997] ECR I-3561. For related cases, in which national legislation seeking to exempt recoverable materials from classification as waste has been found to be incompatible with WFD, see: Case C-422/92 *Commission v Germany* [1995] ECR I-1097; Case C-103/02 *Commission v Italy* [2004] ECR I-9127.

[10] Ibid, Opinion of AG Jacobs, 24 October 1996, para 55.

[11] Case C-129/96 *Inter-Environment Wallonie ASBL v Region Wallonne* [1997] ECR I-7411, Opinion of AG Jacobs, 24 April 1997, paras 80–81.

[12] Joined Cases C-418/97 & C-419/97 *ARCO Chemie Nederland v Minister Van Volkshuisvesting* [2000] ECR I-4475, Opinion of AG Alber, 8 June 1999, para 109.

[13] These alternative tests were rejected in *ARCO*: ibid, paras 49, 65–67.

On this purposive analysis, the Court draws on both the preventive and precautionary princi-ples to find that the environmental purpose of the WFD requires a wide definition of waste that will catch as many 'discarded' items as possible within its regulatory and supervisory scope. It is, however, far from clear that either principle should have led to this interpretive outcome, for at least three reasons. First, both principles have open and not obviously overlapping meanings. As indicated in Section 1.1 of Chapter 11, prevention tends to be association with preventing known environmental risks, and precaution with preventing unknown or uncertain risks. Second, it is not obvious that the idea of preventing waste, or of avoiding uncertain risks that might be associated with it, leads to a broad definition of waste, which may, through an increased regulatory burden, in fact discourage efforts to develop innovative production processes that maximize the use of resources and thereby prevent waste. As Lee and Stokes put it, the 'broad brush approach [to the definition of waste] simultaneously serves to undermine the Directive's auxiliary aim of encourag-ing the re-use and recycling of waste'.[14]

Third, the notion of prevention—which is more apt in the context of waste problems (mostly dealing with certain environmental risks and harms)—is a layered concept, itself capable of multiple meanings. As Scotford explains in the following extract, the WFD does not simply require *any* prevention of waste and its harmful consequences, but prioritizes the prevention of waste being generated at all, which has consequences for thinking about the definition of waste purposively in this regulatory context. Note also the role of the principle of rectification at source in thinking about the prevention of waste, which is not a principle mentioned by the ECJ in *ARCO*, but is reflected in the principles of proximity and self-sufficiency in the WFD and supported elsewhere in the Court's case law as central to the regulation of waste in EU law.

Eloise Scotford, 'Trash or Treasure: Policy Tensions in EC Waste Regulation' (2007) 19(3) JEL 367, 370–71

2.1.1.1 Layers of prevention
In theory, the inherent probability that unwanted items will become polluting through disposal can be prevented in two ways:

1. By regulating the circumstances of that disposal, either by imposing environmental standards for final disposal methods or by discouraging disposal in favour of reuse, recycling or other waste recovery.

2. By influencing people's actions, so that they do not 'want' to get rid of materials so readily.

This latter strategy concerns *waste prevention or reduction*, and aims to minimise the amount of material that becomes waste in the first place, and maximise the use of resources. The former strategy concerns true *waste regulation*, which aims to prevent pollution but not waste production, and policies on waste disposal and recovery will influence its precise form. Both these strategies reflect layers of the preventive principle,[15] intervening at different points in the hierarchy of pollution: waste prevention corresponds with preventing pollution at source, while waste regulation represents efforts to prevent pollution further down the pollution stream (minimising polluting points of impact). In posing different approaches to the waste problem, there is potential for these strategies to operate in tension.

---

[14] Robert Lee and Elen Stokes, 'Rehabilitating the Definition of Waste: Is it Fully Recovered?' (2008) 8 YEEL 162, 162–63.
[15] See further, Section 1.1 of Chapter 11.

The Directive embraces both strategies. In particular, Article 3 [now Article 4, examined further below in Section 2.2], which sets out the general waste policy to be adopted by Member States, fleshes them out and places them in an order of priority (the waste hierarchy), which prioritises waste prevention over waste regulation. The hierarchy reveals the principles of prevention and rectification at source working in tandem to generate EC waste policy, mandating that Member States regulate and prevent causes of pollution as far upstream as possible.

The ECJ's conclusion in *ARCO* that waste must not be interpreted restrictively did not end there however. The Court went on to articulate that whether a substance is to be classified as waste due to an act of discarding 'must be determined in the light of all the circumstances, regard being had to the aim of the directive and the need to ensure that its effectiveness is not undermined'.[16] And the Court gave a list of indicators that might constitute evidence of acts of discarding, as set out here.

Joined Cases C-418/97 & C-419/97 *ARCO Chemie Nederland v Minister Van Volkshuisvesting* [2000] ECR I-4475 paras 65–6, 69, 71, 83–4, 86–7 (emphasis added)

65. Just as the concept of waste is not to be understood as excluding substances and objects which are capable of economic reutilisation, it is not to be understood as excluding substances and objects which are capable of being recovered as fuel in an environmentally responsible manner and without substantial treatment.

66. The environmental impact of the processing of that substance has no effect on its classification as waste [...]

[...]

69. [A]lthough the method of treating a substance has no impact on its nature as waste, it may serve to *indicate* the existence of waste. If the use of a substance as fuel is a common method of recovering waste, that use may be evidence that the holder has discarded or intends or is required to discard that substance within the meaning of Article 1(a) [now Article 3(1)] of the directive.

[...]

71. As to what is commonly regarded as waste, that element, too, is irrelevant in view of the express definition of waste in Article 1(a) of the directive, but it may also serve to indicate the existence of waste.

[...]

83. [Other] circumstances may constitute evidence that the holder has discarded the substance or intends or is required to discard it within the meaning of Article 1(a) of the directive.

84. That will be the case, in particular, where the substance used is a production residue, that is to say a product not in itself sought for use as fuel.

[...]

86. The fact that the substance is a residue for which no use other than disposal can be envisaged may also be regarded as evidence of discarding. That fact gives the impression that the holder of the substance acquired it for the sole purpose of discarding it, either because he wishes to or because he is required to, for example under an agreement concluded with the producer of the substance or with another holder.

87. The same will apply where the substance is a residue whose composition is not suitable for the use made of it or where special precautions must be taken when it is used owing to the environmentally hazardous nature of its composition.

---

[16] Joined Cases C-418/97 & C-419/97 *ARCO Chemie Nederland v Minister Van Volkshuisvesting* [2000] ECR I-4475 ('ARCO'), para 88.

This reasoning contains a number of problematic aspects. First, the approach of the Court under-mines an action-based concept of waste (focused on acts of discarding) with an objective appraisal of substances in light of their particular characteristics and methods of treatment. Elsewhere this approach has been roundly rejected by the Court, including within the reasoning of *ARCO* itself, introducing apparent contradictions into its reasoning on the definition of waste. One explanation for this is the Court being concerned that its approach to defining waste is workable in practice. Second, the Court does not draw any distinction between substances that a holder 'discards or intends or is required to discard'—the objective factors it sets out are suggested to indicate any or all of these aspects of the definition, thereby unhelpfully failing to elucidate the purpose of the 'intention to discard' ele-ment of the definition, added in 1991.[17] Third, this extract suggests that materials—residues—that are not the primary products of a production process will be difficult to keep out of classification as waste. The limitations of this point have since been addressed by further ECJ case law and an amendment to the Directive to deal with by-products that are not waste.[18] But it highlights again the different pur-poses of the Directive operating in tension—waste regulation and supervision are taking precedence over recognizing that materials may have flexible and continuing types of productive use.

EU definition of waste: reforms of the 2008 Directive

In light of this confusion in the case law, the revised 2008 WFD aimed, amongst other things, to simplify the definition of waste. It did not do this by way of wholesale reform—the same definition of waste remains in Article 3(1) with its undefined central requirement of discarding. However, the Directive now contains other provisions that inform the definition of waste. Thus, Article 2 sets out a series of exceptions from the scope of the Directive,[19] which in effect take certain materials out of the definition of waste.

Article 2: Exclusions from the Scope

1. The following shall be excluded from the scope of this Directive:

    (a) gaseous effluents emitted into the atmosphere;

    (b) land (in situ) including unexcavated contaminated soil and buildings permanently connected with land;

    (c) uncontaminated soil and other naturally occurring material excavated in the course of construc-tion activities where it is certain that the material will be used for the purposes of construction in its natural state on the site from which it was excavated;

    (d) radioactive waste;

    (e) decommissioned explosives;

    (f) faecal matter, if not covered by paragraph 2(b), straw and other natural non-hazardous agricultural or forestry material used in farming, forestry or for the production of energy from such biomass through processes or methods which do not harm the environment or endanger human health.

[17] Commission guidance on interpreting the Directive suggests that this objective test relates only to the second alternative in the definition of waste (intention to discard), so that the holder's intention is to be inferred from his or her actions having regard to the factors identified by the Court, although this is not what the Court explicitly says in *ARCO* (cf Case C-9/00 *Palin-Granit Oy* [2002] ECR I-3533, para 25). See Commission, *Guidance on the Interpretation of Key Provisions of Directive 2008/98/EC on Waste* (D-G Environment, June 2012) ('WFD 2008 Guidance') 10.

[18] See the sub-section on the by-product exception: below at p 680.

[19] Exceptions existed under previous framework Directives but these were amended in deliberate and significant ways under the 2008 WFD.

These exceptions exist for different reasons—some because of the existence of other, extensive regimes of environmental control (gaseous effluents);[20] some respond to case law that has clarified the scope of waste (particularly in by-products cases, examined in a following sub-section below) or produced unsatisfactory results in practice (unexcavated contaminated soil);[21] and some are arguably due to lobbying by industry (agriculture and forestry, construction, nuclear).[22] On radioactive waste, bespoke regulations exist at both EU and Member State levels.

Article 2(2) goes on to exclude from the scope of the Directive certain materials *to the extent that* they are covered by other EU legislation—including, waste waters, animal by-products and carcasses, and mining waste.[23] In the *Thames Water* case, the ECJ made clear that such exclusions will only apply where the other relevant legislation covers the same terrain as the WFD—that is, it must contain precise provisions relating to the management of the relevant waste and ensure a level of protection at least equivalent to that under the WFD.[24]

The 2008 WFD also shapes the definition of waste through Articles 5 and 6, which relate specifically to by-products and the end-of-waste, and which are examined further in the sub-sections that follow, after first considering the nature of the 'holder' of waste. Beyond this, however, the 2008 Directive has done little to undo the complicated case law of the Court of Justice. This can be seen in the Commission's 'non legally binding' guidelines accompanying the 2008 Directive, which largely endorse all the previous EU case law relating to the definition of waste.[25]

EU definition of waste: 'holder' of waste

The issue of who is a 'holder' of waste may seem obvious, but it is another complicated and also important aspect of the definition of waste, for two reasons. First, the actions of the holder of waste constitute the relevant act of discarding, as Article 3(1) provides. Second, the Directive also seeks to cover and regulate a number of actors within the waste chain, who are at various times 'holders' of waste, so as to extend responsibility for waste management (including the costs of taking care of and managing waste) to as many people as possible. Thus, Article 3(6) of the Waste Directive defines a 'waste holder' as:

> the waste producer *or* the natural or legal person who is in possession of the waste.

The extension of this definition beyond the person physically possessing or 'holding' the waste to the producer of the waste broadens the definition to match its discarding core—the person who first discarded the material creates the waste and remains in the frame for its management. To ensure

---

[20] Which are regulated as air pollution and industrial emissions: see Chapters 15 and 17.

[21] This is a partial reversal of the much criticized decision in Case C-1/03 *Criminal Proceedings against Van de Walle* [2004] ECR I-7613, discussed further in the sub-section below.

[22] Ludwig Krämer, *EU Environmental Law* (7th edn, Sweet & Maxwell 2012) 341–42.

[23] There is separate EU legislation covering these areas: European Parliament and Council Regulation 1774/2002/EC of 3 October 2002 laying down health rules concerning animal by-products not intended for human consumption [2002] OJ L273/1; Council Directive 91/271/EEC of 21 May 1991 concerning urban waste-water treatment [1991] OJ L135/40; European Parliament and Council Directive 2006/21/EC of 15 March 2006 on the management of waste from extractive industries [2006] OJ L102/15.

[24] Case C-252/05 *R (Thames Water Utilities) v Bromley Magistrates' Court* [2007] 1 WLR 1945. Note this case is no longer good law in its application of this exception to *national* legislation, which is not possible after the 2008 amendments to the Directive.

[25] WFD 2008 Guidance (n 17) 9–12.

a complete system of waste management control, Article 3(5) defines a 'waste producer' even more widely as:

anyone whose activities produce waste (original waste producer) *or* anyone who carries out pre-processing, mixing or other operations resulting in a change in the nature or composition of this waste.

As the following case extract from *Commune de Mesquer* shows, the Court of Justice has interpreted this definition widely in order to extend the liability provisions of the Directive to a range of actors. The Court's reliance on the polluter pays principle in *Commune de Mesquer* draws on the precursor to Article 14 of the Directive–Article 15 of the WFD, which applied at the relevant time. Article 14 imposes responsibility for the costs of waste management on waste holders in the following way, notably extending liability to *original* waste producers and in some cases to the *product* producers:

Article 14: Costs

1. In accordance with the polluter pays principle, the costs of waste management *shall* be borne by the original waste producer or by the current or previous waste holders.

2. Member States *may* decide that the costs of waste management are to be borne partly or wholly by the producer of the product from which the waste came and that the distributors of such product may share these costs.

The 2006 Directive version was worded slightly differently, requiring the 'cost of disposing of waste' to be imposed on the current waste holder and/or previous waste holders or product producers.[26] In light of this former provision, which applied at the relevant time, the Court in *Commune de Mesquer* had to determine who constituted a relevant holder of waste. This was a case involving the largest ever oil spill off the French coast, and the legal question concerned who was responsible for the clean-up costs. On the facts, the petroleum company Total International Ltd had chartered a ship—the Erika—to transport oil from France to Italy, where it was to be received by buyer ENEL. En route, the ship ran aground off the coast of France, dumping its oil and causing considerable damage to the French coastline. The French authorities sought to sue Total for the clean-up costs, using the WFD to do so by arguing, firstly, that the spilled oil was waste, and secondly, that Total was a relevant holder of that waste, even though at the time of the accident the oil was in possession of the shipping company.

Case C-188/07 *Commune de Mesquer v Total France SA and Total International Ltd*
[2008] ECR I-4501 paras 73–78 (emphasis added)

73. The Court has held [in *Van de Walle*], in the case of hydrocarbons spilled by accident as the result of a leak from a service station's storage facilities which had been bought by that service station to meet its operating needs, that those hydrocarbons were in fact in the possession of the service station's manager. The Court thus found that, in that context, the person who, for the purpose of his activity, had the hydrocarbons in stock when they became waste could be regarded as the person who 'produced' them

---

[26] 2006 WFD, art 15.

within the meaning of [the Directive]. Since he is at once the possessor and the producer of that waste, such a service station manager must be regarded as its holder within the meaning of [the Directive].

74. In the same way, in the case of hydrocarbons spilled by accident at sea, it must be held that the *owner of the ship* carrying those hydrocarbons is in fact in possession of them immediately before they become waste. In those circumstances, the shipowner may thus be regarded as having produced that waste within the meaning of [the Directive], and on that basis be categorised as a 'holder' within the meaning of [the Directive].

75. However, that directive does not rule out the possibility that, in certain cases, the cost of disposing of waste is to be borne by one or more previous holders.

76. [...] [T]he question which arises is whether the person who sold the goods to the final consignee and for that purpose chartered the ship which sank may also be regarded as a 'holder', a 'previous' one, of the waste thus spilled. The referring court is also uncertain whether the producer of the product from which the waste came may also be responsible for bearing the cost of disposing of the waste thus produced.

77. On this point, Article 15 of Directive 75/442 [now Article 14] provides that certain categories of persons, in this case the 'previous holders' or the 'producer of the product from which the waste came', may, in accordance with the 'polluter pays' principle, be responsible for bearing the cost of disposing of waste. That financial obligation is thus imposed on them *because of their contribution to the creation of the waste* and, in certain cases, to the consequent risk of pollution.

78. In the case of hydrocarbons accidentally spilled at sea following the sinking of an oil tanker, the national court may therefore consider that the *seller of the hydrocarbons and charterer of the ship carrying them* has 'produced' waste, if that court, in the light of the elements which it alone is in a position to assess, reaches the conclusion that that seller-charterer contributed to the risk that the pollution caused by the shipwreck would occur, in particular if he failed to take measures to prevent such an incident, such as measures concerning the choice of ship. In such circumstances, it will be possible to regard the seller-charterer as a previous holder of the waste [...]

This case shows the extent to which the Court of Justice will go to further the environmental protection aims of the Directive. One reason that the Court needed to go to such lengths to find that Total was a 'previous holder' of the waste was that the producer of the product from which the waste came (the oil refiner) was a different company in the Total corporate group, which sold the fuel oil on to Total International for the purposes of this transaction.

Note also the previous case on which *Mesquer* relied—*Van de Walle*—in which it was held that an owner of a petrol station had 'discarded' waste involuntarily when petrol leaked from underground storage tanks, thus being identified as a relevant holder of the waste.[27] Again this case shows that the Directive has been interpreted to attach responsibility for waste management on a large number of people, particularly by relying on the polluter pays principle to interpret the terms of the Directive. Not only is the definition of waste 'holder' in the Directive widely framed and layered, but it is also construed broadly in light of the harm prevention aims of the Directive, and is then further supported by the imposition of waste management responsibility on other related actors in the waste chain. The waste management obligations of the Directive are explored further in Section 2.3.

---

[27] Case C-1/03 *Criminal Proceedings against Van de Walle* [2004] ECR I-7613, discussed further below in the subsection on spills (p 688). While aspects of *Van de Walle* (in particular, on whether the accidentally spilled petrol can in fact constitute waste) have been overturned by the 2008 WFD, the point that a holder of waste can be an involuntary participant remains good law.

EU definition of waste: by-product exception

As the analysis of *ARCO* showed, the ECJ, in casting the net of waste control widely, was reluctant to exempt residues of production processes from the definition of waste. However, this legal position became more and more fraught as businesses and individuals sought to find productive uses for materials that were not the primary products of the (primarily industrial and agricultural) processes in which they were engaged. Such efforts furthered the key waste prevention goal of EU waste policy, and the doctrinal question was whether the definition of waste should be interpreted so as to recognize and incentivize these efforts. The ECJ subsequently qualified its position in *ARCO* and found that the definition should be so interpreted, developing a new aspect of its waste doctrine in *Palin Granit*, extracted here. In this case, a large quantity of leftover rock from granite quarrying was being stored on site pending further use. This further use had not yet been organized but would most likely involve constructing harbours or breakwaters and it would be done by third parties, not the quarry operators themselves.

Case C-9/00 *Palin Granit Oy*
[2002] ECR I-3533 paras 32–38 (emphasis added)

32. [I]n *ARCO Chemie Nederland*, the Court pointed out the importance of determining whether the substance is a production residue, that is to say, a product not in itself sought for a subsequent use. As the Commission observes, in the case at issue in the main proceedings the production of leftover stone is not Palin Granit's primary objective. The leftover stone is only a secondary product and the undertaking seeks to limit the quantity produced. According to its ordinary meaning, waste is what falls away when one processes a material or an object and is not the end-product which the manufacturing process directly seeks to produce.

33. Therefore, it appears that leftover stone from extraction processes which is not the product primarily sought by the operator of a granite quarry falls, in principle, into [a waste] category [...]

34. One counter-argument to challenge that analysis is that goods, materials or raw materials resulting from a manufacturing or extraction process, the primary aim of which is not the production of that item, may be regarded *not as a residue but as a by-product* which the undertaking does not wish to 'discard', within the meaning of the first paragraph of Article 1(a) of Directive 75/442 [now Article 3(1) WFD], but intends to exploit or market on terms which are advantageous to it, in a subsequent process, without any further processing prior to reuse.

35. Such an interpretation would not be incompatible with the aims of Directive 75/442. There is no reason to hold that the provisions of Directive 75/442 which are intended to regulate the disposal or recovery of waste apply to goods, materials or raw materials *which have an economic value as products* regardless of any form of processing and which, as such, are subject to the legislation applicable to those products.

36. However, having regard to the obligation [...] to interpret the concept of waste widely in order to limit its inherent risks and pollution, the reasoning applicable to by-products should be confined to situations in which the *reuse of the goods, materials or raw materials is not a mere possibility but a certainty, without any further processing prior to reuse and as an integral part of the production process*.

37. It therefore appears that, in addition to the criterion of whether a substance constitutes a production residue, a second relevant criterion for determining whether or not that substance is waste for the purposes of Directive 75/442 is the *degree of likelihood that that substance will be reused*, without any further processing prior to its reuse. If, in addition to the mere possibility of reusing the substance, there is also a financial advantage to the holder in so doing, the likelihood of reuse is high. In such circumstances, the substance in question must no longer be regarded as a burden which its holder seeks to 'discard', but as a genuine product.

38. In the case at issue, the Finnish Government correctly points out that the only foreseeable reuses of leftover stone in its existing state, for example in embankment work or in the construction of harbours and breakwaters, necessitate, in most cases, potentially long-term storage operations which constitute a burden to the holder and are also potentially the cause of precisely the environmental pollution which Directive 75/442 seeks to reduce. The reuse is therefore not certain and is only foreseeable in the longer term, with the result that the leftover stone can only be regarded as extraction residue which its holder 'intends or is required to discard' within the meaning of Directive 75/442

Thus, *Palin Granit* set out a 'by-product exception' to the definition of waste, stepping away from the reasoning in *ARCO* to recognize multiple stages in lifecycles of products, which should be kept out of the ambit (and burden) of waste regulation. The Court remains true to the supervisory purpose of the Directive, whilst promoting waste prevention, by limiting the exception through a tripartite proviso—re-use must be certain, require no further processing of the material, and form an 'integral part of the production process'. However, these criteria themselves required interpretation and application, which can be problematic.

First, the test of 'certainty' is ambiguous on the reasoning and result of *Palin Granit* itself. The result of the case indicates that the test of certainty is strict—certainty will not be established unless there is an identifiable re-use guaranteed *in the short-term*, at the point at which waste classification falls to be determined (in this case, the point at which the rock became leftover). However, the Court's reasoning also suggests a more flexible certainty test—'likelihood of re-use', which can be shown by a combination of the *possibility* of re-use along with a *financial advantage* to the holder in so doing. This allows certainty to be shown in cases where there is every intention and likelihood that a secondary product will be re-used, even though the precise circumstances of that re-use cannot be shown at the very moment of the product's creation. This more flexible approach is significant as it allows markets in secondary products to develop and holders of by-products to engage every effort to find subsequent uses for them, rather than forcing holders of such substances to be licensed as waste operators in the window before they confirm uses for secondary products from their production processes. The argument against this more flexible certainty test is that anything less than absolute certainty of re-use creates a loophole for unscrupulous operators to exploit to avoid waste regulation by claiming that they plan to re-use waste materials without having any real intention to do so. However, a sham intention fails the certainty of re-use criterion, even if it might be difficult to detect and implement in practice.

Subsequent cases have continued to grapple with this issue of certainty of re-use,[28] and they have also dealt with other elements of the *Palin Granit* by-product proviso. Thus, in *Commission v Spain*,[29] the ECJ found that an agricultural practice whereby pig slurry was spread on agricultural land for use as a soil fertilizer did not involve waste. The Commission had argued that the spreading of livestock effluent in this way on over 200 farms in a region of Catalonia constituted waste, in light of concerns that run-off from this widespread practice was causing serious nitrate pollution problems in a local Spanish aquifer. The slurry would be more tightly controlled though the management responsibilities imported by waste regulation. The Court found otherwise, developing the *Palin Granit* proviso in two respects:

- The Court found that certainty of re-use could be demonstrated through use by *third parties* (here, other farmers who were purchasing the slurry as fertilizer).

[28] For a strict application of the certainty test, see Case C-114/01 *AvestaPolarit Chrome Oy* [2003] ECR I-8725. For cases that continue to endorse the more flexible approach to certainty in this context, see Case C-176/05 *KVZ retec GmbH v Austria*, para 62; Cases C-194/05, C-195/05 and C-263/05 *Commission v Italian Republic* [2007] ECR I-11661, para 39.

[29] Case C-121/03 *Commission v Spain* [2005] ECR I-7569.

- The Court phrased the 'integral part of the production process' criterion slightly differently, requiring instead that the slurry be used as 'part of the continuing process of production'. This different form of words seems to widen the by-product exception, making it less awkward to apply to uses of secondary products in subsequent production processes which are unrelated to the primary processes that generated the relevant products—subsequent uses can thus continue on from, without being integral to, the original production processes involved. Note also that the Court uses the term 'production process' very loosely in relation to this by-product exception, applying it to livestock farming and crop growing in *Commission v Spain*.

This close analysis of the wording in *Palin Granit* may seem pedantic, but the determination of by-products is a crucial point at which the distinction between waste and non-waste must be determined. It gives rise to difficult borderline cases of waste classification, which show the core purposes underlying the definition of waste in tension. The complexity of this case law led the Commission to issue an Interpretive Communication on Waste and By-Products in 2007.[30] This is mainly a restatement of ECJ case law, but it also contains a useful illustrative list of non-waste by-products for particular waste streams in its Annex. Beyond this, the by-product case law to date will remain useful in interpreting the now codified version of the *Palin Granit* exception in Article 5 of the 2008 WFD.

Article 5: By-products

1. A substance or object, resulting from a production process, the primary aim of which is not the production of that item, may be regarded as not being waste referred to in point (1) of Article 3 but as being a by-product only if the following conditions are met:

   (a) further use of the substance or object is certain;

   (b) the substance or object can be used directly without any further processing *other than normal industrial practice*;

   (c) the substance or object is *produced* as an integral part of a production process; and

   (d) further use is lawful, i.e. the substance or object fulfils all relevant product, environmental and health protection requirements for the specific use *and will not lead to overall adverse environmental or human health impacts*.

2. On the basis of the conditions laid down in paragraph 1, measures may be adopted to determine the criteria to be met for specific substances or objects to be regarded as a by-product and not as waste referred to in point (1) of Article 3. Those measures, designed to amend non-essential elements of this Directive by supplementing it, shall be adopted in accordance with the regulatory procedure with scrutiny referred to in Article 39(2).

Not only do the pre-2008 cases considered in this section assist in interpreting the Article 5(1) criteria, but the Commission's Guidance to interpreting the 2008 WFD also gives some direction. On the basic issue of whether the primary aim of a production process is the production of a substance or object, the Guidance suggests that where the production of the material concerned is 'the result of a technical

---

[30] Commission, *Communication on the Interpretive Communication on Waste and By-Products* COM(2007) 59 final.

'choice', it cannot be a production residue and is considered an intended product.[31] Indications that a material is the result of a technical choice include: if the manufacturer could have produced the primary product without producing the relevant substance, or the production process was modified to give the substance specific characteristics.

Certainty of further use

The Commission's guidance draws on the existing case law (for example, storage for an indefinite time is not certain), but also offers indicative circumstances as to when certainty of further use might be shown:[32]

- Existence of contracts between the material producer and subsequent user.
- A financial gain for the material producer.
- A solid market (sound supply and demand) existing for this further use.
- Evidence that the material fulfils the same specifications as other products on the market.

By contrast, certainty of further use is unlikely in the following circumstances:

- There is no market for the material.
- Only part of the material is to be used, with the rest to be disposed of (should be initially treated as waste).
- The financial gain for the waste holder is nominal compared to the cost of waste treatment.

Even these indicators can be contentious—for example, a solid market might not be shown if it is embryonic but it may be desirable that it develops so as to prevent waste generation. The Commission acknowledges that certainty of further use may be difficult to prove definitively in advance, and that all will depend on the facts.[33]

Used directly without any further processing other than normal industrial practice

The new qualification that further processing may be allowed if it constitutes 'normal industrial practice' opens up the possibility that, as more sophisticated production cycles are developed, which may involve transferring secondary products to third parties for further use, these may not be regulated as waste even if further processing of the products is involved. For now, the Commission sees this criterion as allowing the same kinds of processing that raw materials might require—material being filtered, washed, or dried, modified as to size or shape, or combined with other materials—in order to be used in production processes. This should not be an avenue for disguised waste processing, such as decontamination operations.[34]

Produced as an integral part of a production process

The Commission guidance suggests that this is a cumulative condition that might limit what is understood as 'normal industrial practice' in the previous condition. It requires asking how integrated the tasks for preparing the material for further use in the main production process are. However, it also requires the scope of 'production' to be defined—the more broadly this is defined, the more secondary

---

[31] WFD 2008 Guidance (n 17) 15.
[32] Ibid, 16–17.   [33] Ibid.   [34] Ibid, 17–18.

products with further uses might be included as part of the production process. A significant change here is the requirement that substances be *produced* as an integral part of a production process, rather than used as an integral part of such a process, as *Palin Granit* suggested, (and which *Commission v Spain* reworded to get around its restrictive effect).

Further use is lawful and will not lead to overall adverse environmental or human health impacts

The requirement that further use be lawful seems a bit redundant in light of the fact that otherwise applicable laws will continue to apply to the use of any secondary products. However, the new overall condition that further use must not lead to adverse environmental or human health impacts does add something substantive. This is a necessary rather than a sufficient condition,[35] but it does import an objective element into the application of the by-product exception, which is at odds with the pre-2008 WFD case law,[36] and with the idea of discarding—an action-based concept—being at the core of the definition of waste.

Note that Article 5(2) also introduces a role for comitology in developing more specific by-product criteria for particular substances or objects. This suggests a reason, and also a potential solution, for the intractability of the general waste tests and doctrines developed to date in relation to by-products. At a certain point, the detail of the particular substances involved and their potential uses are important. Whereas one set of secondary products might be particularly valuable for further use, another might be more difficult to put to further use without considerable processing and decontamination, and the risks of the by-product exception being abused might be accordingly greater.

EU definition of waste: end-of-waste

Along with by-products, determining the point at which waste materials cease to be waste has been a contentious legal area. Establishing end-of-waste status is particularly important for businesses that use former waste materials in their production processes, such as paper mills using recycled paper in the making of new paper products or manufacturing plants using reclaimed oils as fuel to power their facilities. Are these operators using waste materials, so that they need to be licensed and subject to the control of waste regulation, or are they using recovered materials and prolonging their productive lifecycles as (non-waste) resources? Establishing the end-of-waste is also important for meeting recycling targets, which the UK is required to do under EU law (see Section 2.3)—it is only if a waste material has been relevantly recovered or recycled and is no longer waste that it will count towards these targets. The Directive's definition of waste has caused serious difficulties in answering these questions since, as AG Colomer stated in *Commission v Italy*, 'discarding' tests are awkward to apply where waste is recovered or re-used.[37] In the English courts, Carnwath LJ put the problem thus:[38]

> The subjective 'intention to discard' may be a useful guide to the status of the material in the hands of the original producer. However, it is hard to apply to the status of the material in the hands of someone who buys it for recycling or reprocessing; or who puts it to some other valuable use. In no ordinary sense is such a person 'discarding' or 'getting rid of' the material. His intention is precisely the opposite.

---

[35] Cf the 'environmental criterion' suggested by AG Jacobs in *Inter-Environment Wallonie ASBL v Region Wallonne* (n11).

[36] In *ARCO*, the Court held that the 'environmental impact of the processing of that substance has no effect on its classification as waste', although its reasoning on this was somewhat contradictory, as discussed above.

[37] Case C-486/04 *Commission v Italy* [2006] ECR I-11025, Opinion of AG Ruiz–Jarabo Colomber, 20 May 2006, para 53.

[38] *R(OSS Group Ltd) v Environment Agency* [2007] EWCA Civ 611, para 55. See further discussion of this case in Section 1.3.

The Court of Justice sought to grapple with this issue in *ARCO*. That case was in fact a set of joint cases—*ARCO* and *Epon*—referred to the Court on the issue of when waste materials ceased to be waste. In *ARCO*, the materials involved were secondary materials ('LUWA bottoms') extracted from catalysts in a chemical production process, which had a high enough calorific value to be used as a fuel. They caused no adverse effects on the environment when burnt as fuel and were rendered inert by that process, acting no differently from fuel oil. The Netherlands authorities treated the LUWA bottoms as waste in authorizing their use as fuel in cement manufacture. In *Epon*, the materials were pulverized wood chips from the construction and demolition sector contaminated with toxic substances, which the relevant Dutch authorities authorized an electricity generating company to use as fuel (not waste) in one of its power stations. Both of these authorization decisions were challenged at the national level. The reasoning of the ECJ in these cases, as extracted above, and focused on elaborating the definition of waste in general terms by adhering strictly to the test of discarding. The Court did not need to make findings on the facts of these cases, which were submitted to the Court by way of preliminary reference. However, the facts raised issues as to both waste generation (whether by-products were involved) and, if the materials at issue were found to be waste, when they ceased to be waste. On the latter point, the Court went so far as to suggest that:[39]

> [E]ven where waste has undergone a *complete* recovery operation which has the consequence that the substance in question has acquired the same properties and characteristics as a raw material, that substance may none the less be regarded as waste if, in accordance with the definition in Article 1(a) of the Directive, its holder discards it or intends or is required to discard it.
>
> The fact that the substance is the result of a complete recovery operation [...] is only one of the factors to be taken into consideration for the purpose of determining whether the substance constitutes waste and does not as such permit a definitive conclusion to be drawn in that regard.

In relation to the toxically contaminated woodchips, the Court found that merely sorting and pulverizing them for use as fuel was not sufficient to deprive them of waste classification, when this 'does not have the effect of transforming those objects into a product analogous to a raw material, with the same characteristics as that raw material and capable of being used in the same conditions of environmental protection'.[40] This suggests a basis on which an end-of-waste point might be identifiable, but the Court did not directly say so. The 2008 WFD seeks to address this vexed end-of-waste issue more directly.

Article 6: End-of-waste status

1. Certain specified waste shall cease to be waste within the meaning of point (1) of Article 3 when it has undergone a recovery, including recycling, operation and complies with specific criteria to be developed in accordance with the following conditions:

   (a) the substance or object is commonly used for specific purposes;

   (b) a market or demand exists for such a substance or object;

   (c) the substance or object fulfils the technical requirements for the specific purposes and meets the existing legislation and standards applicable to products; and

---

[39] *ARCO* (n 16) paras 94–95 (emphasis added).
[40] Ibid, para 96.

> (d) the use of the substance or object will not lead to overall adverse environmental or human health impacts.
>
> The criteria shall include limit values for pollutants where necessary and shall take into account any possible adverse environmental effects of the substance or object.
>
> 2.The measures designed to amend non-essential elements of this Directive by supplementing it relating to the adoption of the criteria set out in paragraph 1 and specifying the type of waste to which such criteria shall apply shall be adopted in accordance with the regulatory procedure with scrutiny referred to in Article 39(2). End-of-waste specific criteria should be considered, among others, at least for aggregates, paper, glass, metal, tyres and textiles.
>
> [...]
>
> 4. Where criteria have not been set at Community level under the procedure set out in paragraphs 1 and 2, Member States may decide case by case whether certain waste has ceased to be waste taking into account the applicable case law. They shall notify the Commission of such decisions n accordance with Directive 98/34/EC [...] laying down a procedure for the provision of information in the field of technical standards and regulations [...] where so required by that Directive.

Article 6 is framed differently from Article 5 in that it *requires* specific end-of-waste criteria to be developed through EU comitology procedures in order for the Directive to give precise legal direction on this issue. This picks up on the idea that the solution to a lot of difficulties with the definition of waste will be found in considering particular waste streams in detail. In formulating end-of-waste criteria for particular waste streams, the provisions of Article 6(1) must be complied with, including an overriding requirement that the waste in question has undergone a 'recovery' operation. 'Recovery' is defined in Article 3(15) as:

> any operation the principal result of which is waste serving a useful purpose by replacing other materials which would otherwise have been used to fulfil a particular function, or waste being prepared to fulfil that function, in the plant or in the wider economy. Annex II sets out a non-exhaustive list of recovery operations.

According to Annex II, recovery operations include recycling processes, using material as a fuel, reclaiming chemicals, various forms of land treatment, and storage pending recovery operations. Recital 22 to the Directive also provides that 'for the purposes of reaching end-of-waste status, a recovery operation may be as simple as the checking of waste to verify that it fulfils the end-of-waste criteria.' However, it is important to keep in mind that a material must be classified as waste in the first place before it can be subject to a recovery operation, and there is a key distinction between recovery and re-use (not involving waste) and preparation for re-use (involving waste). These different operations are prioritized by the Directive, as examined in Section 2.2.

As to Article 6(1)'s further criteria, the Commission's WFD 2008 Guidance indicates that (a) and (b) are related and that they might be shown by:[41]

> • The existence of firmly established market conditions related to supply and demand.
>
> • A verifiable market price being paid for the material.
>
> • The existence of trading specifications or standards.

---

[41] WFD 2008 Guidance (n 17) 23.

As suggested already, the requirement that an established market exists may be problematic for emerging or volatile markets involving recycled products. Article 6(1)(c) requires compliance with the technical specifications or standards that apply to virgin materials for the same purpose. According to the Commission guidance, Article 6(1)(d) requires comparing the use of the material under relevant. However, it also product and waste legislation, accounting for the fact that adverse environmental or health effects may also be caused by virgin/comparable materials requires considering whether the relevant product legislation is sufficient to minimize adequately the environmental or human health impacts, which seems odd to the extent that it requires waste regulation to fill the gap of product regulation in relation to environmental problems, but only for material that was formerly waste. Overall, the approach seems to be to catch materials that would create *greater* environmental risks if released from the waste regime.

At the time of writing the EU had introduced one Regulation through the process in Articles 6(1) and 6(2)—Regulation 333/2011 establishing criteria determining when certain types of scrap metal cease to be waste.[42] An interesting feature of this Regulation is that it establishes Conformity Assessment Bodies, Environmental Verifiers, as well as 'independent external verifiers' from other Member States, who are involved in checking that the specific criteria are met in practice. For recovered scrap metal imported into the EU, its end-of-waste status is to be demonstrated by the importer issuing a 'statement of conformity'.

However, where the EU has not developed criteria under Article 6(1) for specific waste streams, Member States are to make end-of-waste decisions on a case-by-case basis in accordance with 'applicable' case law (and not the criteria in Article 6(1)). Relevant case law at the EU level has been inconclusive to date. The UK courts have been more forthcoming, as Section 1.3 shows—for now this constitutes the 'applicable' case law to guide UK businesses and regulators. However, the UK must notify the Commission of any end-of-waste criteria that constitute 'technical regulations' (which do not include single case decisions),[43] for these to be checked against the Article 6(1) criteria and internal market rules, and potentially to trigger EU harmonization measures.[44]

The final contentious issue in establishing end-of-waste is determining the precise point at which waste ceases to be waste. On this, the Commission guidance offers the following:[45]

The moment when a material or substance reaches EoW [end-of-waste] is simultaneous with the completion of the recovery and recycling processes [...]

Generally speaking, the point of completion of a recovery operation may be considered to be the moment where a useful input for further processing, not representing any waste-specific risks to health and the environment, becomes available. Specific legislation on EoW criteria may determine a particular point where waste becomes non-waste.[46]

In short, the ongoing legal ambiguities relating to end-of-waste again reflect the fundamental tension in the definition of waste between recognizing and incentivizing waste prevention and maintaining a robust supervisory system in relation to waste materials. The 2008 WFD has improved this legal

[42] Council Regulation 333/2011/EU of 31 March 2011 establishing criteria determining when certain types of scrap metal cease to be waste under Directive 2008/98/EC [2011] OJ L94/2.

[43] For the definition of technical regulations, see European Parliament and Council Directive 98/34/EC of 22 June 1998 laying down a procedure for the provision of information in the field of technical standards and regulations [1998] OJ L204/37, art 1.

[44] Ibid, arts 8–10.

[45] WFD 2008 Guidance (n 17) 25. Cf Case C-444/00 *R (Mayer Parry Recycling) v Environment Agency* [2003] ECR I-6163.

[46] Thus, under the scrap metal end-of-waste Regulation 333/2011, transfer of possession from one holder, who produced the EoW material, to another holder is a legal condition for reaching the EoW status.

situation to a certain degree, and should do so further over time as new EU end-of-waste criteria are issued for more waste streams.

EU definition of waste: spills

An awkward extension of the definition of waste has been to cover material that is unintentionally spilled. Acts of discarding (even intended or required) are difficult to identify in cases of accidentally spilled material, but the following extract shows how the Court of Justice has managed to stretch the logic of the waste definition to cover such cases. The case, *Van de Walle*, was a preliminary reference from a Belgian case in which the senior staff of Texaco Belgium and Texaco were prosecuted for abandoning waste as the result of an accidental leak of hydrocarbons (petrol) from underground storage tanks at a service station.

Case C-1/03 *Criminal Proceedings against Van de Walle*
[2004] ECR I-7613 paras 47, 49, 52–3.

47. It is clear that accidentally spilled hydrocarbons which cause soil and groundwater contamination are not a product which can be re-used without processing. Their marketing is very uncertain and, even if it were possible, implies preliminary operations would be uneconomical for their holder. Those hydrocarbons are therefore substances which the holder did not intend to produce and which he 'discards', albeit involuntarily, at the time of the production or distribution operations which relate to them.

[...]

49. If hydrocarbons which cause contamination are not considered to be waste on the ground that they were spilled by accident, their holder would be excluded from the obligations which Directive 75/442 [now 2008 WFD] requires Member States to impose on him, in contradiction to the prohibition on the abandonment, dumping or uncontrolled disposal of waste.

[...]

52. The same classification as 'waste' within the meaning of Directive 75/442 applies to soil contaminated as the result of an accidental spill of hydrocarbons. In that case, the hydrocarbons cannot be separated from the land which they have contaminated and cannot be recovered or disposed of unless that land is also subject to the necessary decontamination. That is the only interpretation which ensures compliance with the aims of protecting the natural environment and prohibiting the abandonment of waste pursued by the Directive [...]

53. Since contaminated soil is considered to be waste by the mere fact of its accidental contamination by hydrocarbons, its classification as waste is not dependent on other operations being carried out which are the responsibility of its owner or which the latter decides to undertake. The fact that soil is not excavated therefore has no bearing on its classification as waste.

The decision seems to assume the operation of the WFD before determining if, in fact, it applies (that is, if there is waste in the first place) and it overlooks the fact that some Member States, such as the UK, have bespoke contaminated land regimes.[47] However, it shows the concerned effort of the ECJ to extend the regulatory scope of the WFD and to promote its environmental protection purposes.

Van de Walle has now been partly overturned in light of the Article 2(1)(b) 2008 WFD, which excludes from the scope of the Directive 'land (in situ) including unexcavated contaminated soil and buildings permanently connected with land'. However, the general reasoning that accidental spills of

---

[47] Not to mention the EU's Proposal for a Framework Directive for the protection of soil: COM(2006) 232 final. See also Chapter 21 for analysis of the UK contaminated land regime. Note that not all Member States have such laws.

material can constitute waste has not been overturned, and this has been applied in subsequent cases, including *Commune de Mesquer* (discussed already) in which the ECJ found that oil unintentionally spilled at sea constituted waste, and *Thames Water*, where it relied on the same reasoning to find that sewage escaping from faulty pipes amounted to waste.[48]

EU definition of waste: hazardous waste

Some waste materials are further classified as 'hazardous'. The main consequence of this classification is the application of more restrictive waste management controls. Article 3(2) of the 2008 WFD defines 'hazardous waste' as:

> waste which displays one or more of the hazardous properties listed in Annex III.

Annex III includes and defines the following properties that render waste hazardous: explosive, oxidizing, highly flammable, irritant, harmful, toxic, carcinogenic, corrosive, infectious, mutagenic, sensitizing, and ecotoxic. For example:

> 'Oxidizing': substances and preparations which exhibit highly exothermic reactions when in contact with other substances, particularly flammable substances [...]
>
> 'Harmful': substances and preparations which, if they are inhaled or ingested or if they penetrate the skin, may involve limited health risks [...]
>
> 'Toxic': substances and preparations (including very toxic substances and preparations) which, if they are inhaled or ingested or if they penetrate the skin, may involve serious, acute or chronic health risks and even death

Thus, there needs to be identifiable waste, as examined in this chapter so far, but the relevant substance or object must also display certain chemical or physical criteria that will require technical assessment in order for hazardous waste to exist.

Note also the role of Article 7's 'Waste List' in relation to hazardous waste. The Waste List is a list of categorized waste materials, updated by technical experts through a comitology process—it has existed since 2000 as the 'European Waste Catalogue' (EWC).[49] Inclusion of a material as waste in the List does not mean that it is waste in all circumstances—Article 3(1) must still be satisfied. The List includes hazardous waste, including the limit values of concentrations of hazardous substances. While the 'list of waste shall be binding as regards determination of the waste which is to be considered hazardous waste' (Article 7(1)), Article 7(2) makes clear that the List does not dictate authoritatively what constitutes hazardous waste, since a Member State 'may consider waste as hazardous waste where, even though it does not appear as such on the list of waste, it displays one or more of the properties listed in Annex III'.[50] In such a case, the Member State must inform the Commission, which may lead to an amendment of the List. The purpose of the List, or the EWC, is to provide a common coding system for classifying waste material across the EU, and also to set out those waste materials that will always be hazardous waste ('absolute entries' in the EWC).

---

[48] Case C-252/05 *R (Thames Water Utilities) v Bromley Magistrates' Court* [2007] 1 WLR 1945.

[49] Commission Decision 2000/532/EC of 3 May 2000 [2000] OJ L226/3.

[50] This confirms the reasoning in Case C-318/98 *Criminal Proceedings against Fornasar and Ors* [2000] ECR I-4785.

1.3 THE UK LAW SOLUTION TO DEFINING WASTE

The definition of waste in UK law is found in various places—in a range of statutes as well as in a body of case law—all of which derive from or relate to the EU definition of waste.

Defining waste in UK law: the statutory response

There are various UK statutory definitions of waste since a range of legislative instruments implements the WFD—covering different Directive obligations and also increasingly involving separate implementation across the devolved administrations. Section 3.2 examines this implementation picture in more detail, but there are three main pieces of waste legislation in the UK and/or England that define waste. First, Part II of the Environmental Protection Act 1990 (EPA), as amended, incorporates the WFD definition of waste in s 75(2) as follows:

'Waste' means anything that is waste within the meaning of Article 3(1) of Directive 2008/98/EC of the European Parliament and of the Council on waste.

Part II of the EPA ('Waste on Land'), which sets out key waste offences and waste collection and recycling obligations, also relies on the concept of *controlled waste* as the subject of many waste obligations. This limits the broader definition of waste to 'household, industrial and commercial waste or any such waste', but it still relies on the EU waste definition as its core element.[51] Second, the Environmental Permitting Regulations 2010, which implement the WFD permitting obligations, define waste in Regulation 2(1) as:

'waste', except where otherwise defined, [...] means anything that—

a) is waste within the meaning of Article 3(1) of the Waste Framework Directive; and

b) is not excluded from the scope of that Directive by Article 2(1), (2) or (3).

Third, the Waste (England and Wales) Regulations 2011, which implement the balance of the WFD's obligations, do not set out a separate definition of waste but provide that '[t]erms which are used but not defined in these Regulations and are used in the Waste Framework Directive have the same meaning as in that Directive'.[52] The variation between these definitions essentially reflects the scope of waste control involved rather than any difference in the basic definition of waste—all rely on the Article 3(1) definition. None however seeks to define the problematic discarding element of this definition in any more detail.

The Government has attempted to elucidate these statutory waste definitions through guidance. When the current Directive definition was first introduced in 1994,[53] the government also issued a guidance document—Circular 11/94—addressing various ambiguities that the simple 'discard' definition left open-ended.[54] This Circular has now been superseded by the case law of the European courts discussed in Section 1.2, as well as amendments to the Directive itself, but it was an important source of legal guidance for some time.

---

[51] EPA, s 75(4); Controlled Waste (England and Wales) Regulations 2012 SI 2012/811.

[52] The Waste (England and Wales) Regulations 2011 SI 2011/988, reg 3(2).

[53] The Waste Management Licensing Regulations 1994 SI 1994/1056.

[54] Department of the Environment, *Environmental Protection Act 1990: Part II Waste Management Licensing, The Framework Directive* (London: Her Majesty's Stationery Office, 1994), Annex 2.

The role of UK regulatory guidance on the definition of waste has continued to be important and also contentious. Guidance has diverged as between UK regulators, and senior judges have called for DEFRA and the Environment Agency to 'join forces in providing practical guidance for those affected [by waste regulation]'.[55] While the Environment Agency has no discrete guidance on the definition of waste generally, it has published technical guidance on hazardous waste in collaboration with the Scottish and Northern Ireland environment agencies.[56] It also runs (again collaboratively) a 'Waste Protocols Project' for determining the end-of-waste status for certain waste streams, setting out what is required to produce a 'fully-recovered, non-waste, quality product' within those waste streams.[57] Under Article 6(4) of the 2008 WFD, these protocols need to be reported to the Commission as technical standards (which may lead to EU harmonization).

In 2012, DEFRA produced new guidance on the definition of waste, following consultation in light of the 2008 WFD.[58] This guidance is 'national' guidance on the definition of waste, developed after consultation and in collaboration with the Welsh Government, the Department of the Environment in Northern Ireland, the Environment Agency, and the Northern Ireland Environment Agency.[59] It takes into account the changes brought in by the 2008 WFD, the Commission's guidance on the 2008 WFD, as well as the case law of the European and UK courts. It is certainly an ambitious and relatively comprehensive document (although the sixty-nine pages prove the point that this is a difficult legal issue). An interesting feature of this guidance is that it is divided into two parts: (1) a practical guide for businesses and other organizations who need to comply with waste regulation (Part 2); and (2) detailed legal guidance on the definition of waste (Part 3). The exercise of turning the complicated law on the definition of waste into something simple for non-legal experts in Part 2 is understandable in its motivation but nonetheless a real challenge. Consider the user-guide 'flow chart' in Figure 16.1 provided for determining whether a substance is waste (all questions must be answered). Do you think this (Figure 16.1) is a legally accurate and/or practically helpful picture? Keep this picture in mind as you read through the UK judicial developments on the definition of waste in the following sub-section.

Defining waste in UK law: the judicial response

In seeking to address the ambiguities in the definition of waste, the UK (primarily English) courts have waxed and waned between a restrictive and broad approach to the definition of waste, often reacting to Court of Justice decisions. Thus, in *Mayer Parry Recycling*,[60] Carnwath J found that certain scrap metal did not need to be treated as waste where it did not require a recovery operation before re-use. By contrast, scrap metal that required a recovery operation under Annex IIB of the Directive was waste until the operation was complete. This approach—echoing AG Jacob's *Tombesi* by-pass—was no longer good law after *ARCO*. Taking a restrictive approach again, this time in light of *ARCO*, the High Court in *Castle Cement* found that waste solvents remained waste until they were burnt as fuel, even if processed for subsequent use as fuel for cement production through a highly technical process and thereby replacing primary materials in a subsequent production

---

[55] *R(OSS) v Environment Agency* (n 8) para 68.

[56] Technical Guidance WM2, *Hazardous Waste: Interpretation of the Definition and Classification of Hazardous Waste*; (Environment Agency, NIEA, SEPA; 2nd edn, 2011, as amended). See also <http://www.environment-agency.gov.uk/business/topics/waste/32200.aspx> accessed 6 February 2013.

[57] <http://www.environment-agency.gov.uk/business/sectors/142481.aspx> accessed 6 February 2013.

[58] DEFRA, *Guidance on the Legal Definition of Waste and its Application* (August 2012).

[59] Note that the Scottish regulator or government was not involved and Scotland maintains its own guidance on the definition of waste.

[60] *Mayer Parry Recycling v Environment Agency* (1999) 1 CMLR 963.

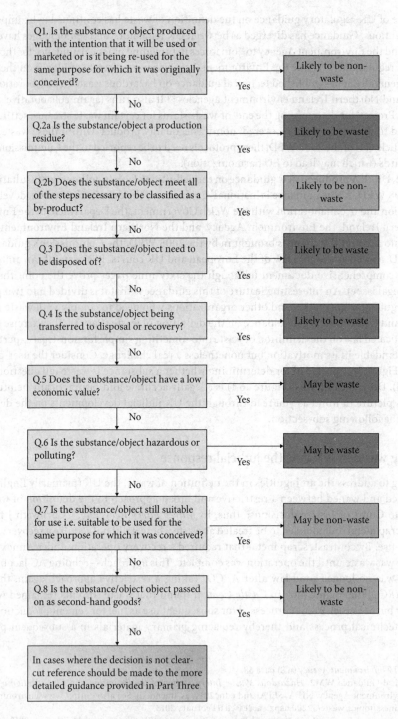

Figure 16.1 Has the substance or object become waste criteria?
Source: Guidance on the legal definition of waste and its application, DEFRA, 2012, 17.

process.[61] Stanley Burton J was particularly influenced by the harmful nature of the solvent-derived fuel in the case and the potential application of the (then) Waste Incineration Directive to cement kilns that co-incinerated waste.

However, more recent approaches of UK courts have moved on, building a body of doctrine that goes beyond the doctrine of the EU courts, as the following four extracted cases demonstrate. The progression of these cases shows incremental and pragmatic reasoning that seeks to resolve the problems and unanswered ambiguities of Court of Justice reasoning on the definition of waste. In doing so, they adopt a more nuanced approach to resolve the issue of waste classification on complicated facts and thereby seek to fulfil the purposes of the Directive in a balanced way, giving more equal weight to the waste prevention as well as environmental harm minimization aims of waste regulation.

The first case—*R(OSS) v Environment Agency*—concerned whether lubricating oil, not used as fuel originally, which became waste and was recovered for subsequent use as fuel, could be burnt as anything other than waste. This was a concern for the claimants since their products—recycled fuel oil—risked being caught by the former Waste Incineration Directive, in a way that would require their customers to have waste permits to use them. The Environment Agency argued that waste status of OSS's recycled fuel oil could only be lost on burning the fuel (by the customer), and the High Court at first instance agreed, following Stanley Burton J's reasoning in *Castle Cement* and relying on the ECJ's overly inclusive approach to waste, which was primarily concerned with controlling the use of waste materials, even where that use posed no more risk to human health or the environment than equivalent natural products. However, on appeal, Lord Justice Carnwath (as he then was) found the jurisprudence of the ECJ unsatisfactory, at least as it related to the issue of when material ceased to be waste, and sought to inject a healthy dose of common sense into the legal interpretation of 'waste'.

R (OSS Group Ltd) v Environment Agency
[2007] EWCA Civ 611 paras 60–65 (Carnwath LJ) (emphasis added)

60. Lord Reed's judgment in the *Scottish Power* case seems to me an impressively thorough example of the required approach. The particular case concerned the use by Scottish Power of 'waste derived fuel' ('WDF') (treated sewage sludge obtained from Scottish Water) as an alternative to coal. The judgment contains a painstaking review of the European case-law. [The judgment contains] an exhaustive enumeration of the indicators which can found in the cases. On the facts of the particular case, the judge held that the product had not ceased to be waste, essentially for three reasons:

i) The WDF could not on the evidence be used under the same conditions of environmental protection as the coal which would otherwise be used;

ii) The operation which took place at the sludge treatment centre neither fell within any of the categories listed in Annex IIB [of the Directive setting out types of recovery operations], nor was it analogous to any such operation:

'It is clear that the sewage sludge is not recycled; and there is no distinct substance reclaimed from the sludge by extracting moisture from it and forming it into pellets. If one asks what is recovered from the sludge, the answer is, energy; and if one asks how it is recovered, the answer is, by burning.'

iii) The project for the sludge treatment centre was driven principally by Scottish Water's need to establish a new means of disposal, to replace disposal into the sea (to comply with the Directive on urban waste water).

---

[61] *Castle Cement v Environment Agency* (2001) 2 CMLR 19.

61. That can be contrasted with the decision of the Administrative Law Division of the Dutch Council of State, given on 14th May 2003, *Icopower BV v Secretary of State* ('Icopower'). The case concerned the transport to Sweden of 'energy pellets', produced in the following way (as described in the judgment):

'The appellant collects industrial waste products. These waste products consist of a mixture of paper, cardboard, untreated wood, plastic foil, textiles, possibly mixed with a limited percentage organic leftover substances (canteen waste) and/or glass, stone and cans. After acceptance a pre-selection takes place and the leftover substances are homogenised and reduced in size on a shredder, after which the ferro-metals are separated from the rest of the substances. After that low calorific fractions are separated from high calorific ones in a screen drum. Hereafter a separation takes place of non-ferro-metals and different components. The remaining flow, called 'fluff' by the appellant, is brought into the correct humidity degree, homogenised and pressed into energy pellets. The energy pellets are sold to electricity and heat-producing plants where they are used as (additional) fuels in these installations'.

62. The court noted that the pellets were produced with the sole aim of their use as fuel; that it was not claimed that they contained pollutants such as heavy metals; and that they were used in the same way as regular fuels, with no special precautionary measures being needed to protect the environment. On this basis it concluded that the energy pellets were 'equivalent to regular fuels' and that, applying the reasoning of the *ARCO* judgment, they could not be characterised as waste under Article 1(a).

63. Although we are not called upon to decide the correctness of that decision, I see no reason to doubt it. It seems to me a practical and common sense approach to the issue, which is consistent with the letter and spirit of the Directive and with the case-law. It is also consistent with the objective of encouraging the recovery of waste materials for uses which replace raw materials. It *should be enough that the holder has converted the waste material into a distinct, marketable product, which can be used in exactly the same way as an ordinary fuel, and with no worse environmental effects*. It cannot be said that such a material is being 'discarded' in any ordinary sense of the term, and there is nothing in the objectives of the Directive which requires any fictitious assumption to that effect. The energy pellets would perhaps have failed DEFRA's [suggested] test, because they were not 'hardly distinguishable' from the alternative fuels. But, as I have said, I do not think such a general test can be extracted from [the European case law]. Nor do I see any reason for it. The objectives of the Directive do not include mimicry.

Conclusions

64. I return to the rival formulations of the 'end of waste test'. The Agency's [suggested test—if the intended end-use is combustion, the materials remain waste until that is completed, regardless of any prior treatment –] is in my view too narrow. If it were correct it would have provided a complete answer to the *ARCO* [case]. The mere fact that the materials in both cases were destined for combustion would have been enough to ensure their continuing categorisation as waste. However, that was not the court's view. Such test is contradicted directly by the court's answer to the first question in *ARCO*, and indirectly by the assumptions underlying the other answers. For the same reason, I would disagree respectfully with the [trial judge's] answer to the appeal question. To the extent that Stanley Burnton J adopted the same approach in *Castle Cement* [...], I would also disagree with that part of his reasoning, although the decision may have been justifiable on its own facts [...]

65. I have not disregarded the Agency's concerns [...] about the practical difficulties of applying a wider test, in particular of determining an appropriate comparator. However, I am not convinced that the difficulty is as great as they suggest. In most cases, as in *Scottish Power* and *Icopower*, the nature of the potential alternatives will be reasonably clear. In any event, as the ECJ has acknowledged, such difficulties are inherent in the imprecise nature of the Article 1(a) definition.

As Lee and Stokes note, *OSS* was a landmark case in English law on waste.

Robert Lee and Elen Stokes, 'Rehabilitating the Definition of Waste: Is it Fully Recovered?' (2008) YEEL 162, 179–80

The impact of the Court of Appeal's decision in *OSS Group v Environment Agency* is far-reaching. It effectively rejects the excessively broad approach of the ECJ in favour of a more commonsensical treatment of notions of 'waste' and 'discarding', and in so doing exhibits greater coherence with aims of re-using and recycling waste materials for other purposes. By highlighting the implications of the ECJ's habitual focus on inferring from the holder an intention to discard, Carnwath LJ illustrates how widening the definition of waste to give effect to the protective aims of the Directive can at the same time undermine the Directive's capacity to motivate the re-incorporation of waste into the economic cycle [...] *OSS Group v Environment Agency* [...] underlines the resounding capacity of the definition of waste to create markets in the re-use of waste materials—a capacity which has been largely untapped by the ECJ jurisprudence. Contrary to patterns emerging from the EC case law, the UK Court of Appeal in *OSS Group v Environment Agency* has demonstrated a willingness to adopt a more flexible approach in accord with a wider waste strategy.

The significance of *OSS* in elucidating the definition of waste in English law is also highlighted by Carnwath J's decision in *OSS* not to refer the case to the European courts:[62]

I would have doubts about the appropriateness of a further reference in this area of the law. I would hesitate to describe the matter as "acte clair", in the traditional sense. But that is not because of lack of opportunity for the Court to provide clarification if it had wished to do so. *ARCO* itself, in which the Court had the assistance not only of the Advocate-General and the Commission, but of five intervening states, would have been an ideal opportunity. One must assume that the decision not to do so was deliberate. Any lack of clarity is inherent in the imprecision of the test which the court has declared.

Subsequent English cases have followed the common sense approach of *OSS* in considering the definition of waste, both concerning the issue of end-of-waste and the classification of waste in the first place. Thus, in *Environment Agency v Thorn International*, the Administrative Division of the High Court held that old household electrical equipment, bought and repaired by Thorn for resale, was not waste at all, despite being discarded by householders.[63] The Court distinguished the legal question at issue in this case from that in *ARCO* and *OSS* where a narrower issue was at stake (whether items that were undoubtedly waste had ceased to be waste). In this case, by contrast, the Court had no problem in finding that, even if the electrical equipment should have been regarded as waste at an earlier stage (when discarded by consumers), it was not by the time it was selected for repair by Thorn. The electrical goods were being retained for use for their original purpose, and they were being repaired and refurbished for such re-use rather than processed into new forms for further use. This is the very sort of activity that pursues the preventive purpose of the Directive. Further, the Court found that this conclusion 'applied the Directive according to its purpose to prevent hazardous materials harming either the environment or those humans who came into contact with them.'[64]

A similarly pragmatic approach to classifying materials as waste was seen in the subsequent case of *Inglenorth*, where demolition materials (containing 'solid breeze blocks, large and small pieces of

---

[62] *OSS* (n 8) para 69.
[63] *Environment Agency v Thorn International UK Ltd* [2008] EWHC 2595.
[64] Ibid, para 27.

concrete, tiles, pieces of brick, clay pipe and clay') were moved from one garden centre to another, allegedly to be used by the garden centre owner of both sites to build and fix a car park. The material was not toxic or a danger to the public, and it covered an area approximately 28 metres long, 3.5 metres wide, and 1.5 metres high, when deposited on a track adjacent to the second garden centre site. The owner did not have a waste management licence, and did not need one if he was not using or depositing waste. However, if he was depositing waste, then he would need a permit, and the transporter of the waste was also under obligation to make sure this was done (as explained in more detail in Section 3.3). Sir Anthony May explained the problem in the case as follows.

Environment Agency v Inglenorth
[2009] EWHC 670 para 5 (Sir Anthony May)

5. The question which this case [...] raises is exemplified in most respects by the following example: if I get a lorry driver to deliver hardcore from a demolition site to my drive when I am going to use the hardcore to mend my drive, or it may be as a subbase for a concrete slab in the garage that I am constructing, is the hardcore as delivered to me waste and do I need a licence to receive it and does the lorry driver commit an offence by delivering it when I have no licence and does he have to warn me about the need for having a licence. Those are not the exact facts [...] but they raise, in my view, the essential question which is whether the hardcore so delivered for that purpose was waste. The common sense answer [...] is that it was not because the hardcore is material which I am going to use, not material which I am going to discard. I am not going to discard it, I am not going to throw it away or get rid of it.

The Environment Agency argued in response that the WFD and its implementing UK legislation are 'not always instruments of common sense'.[65] In particular, subsequent use of materials must be *immediate* in order for it to avoid being 'discarded' and thus classified as waste. This issue is similar to that in *PGO*, considered in Section 1.2, concerning whether the storage of materials at a site pending further use might undermine the certainty of their re-use, albeit that shorter time frames were involved in *Inglenorth* and the materials were to be used by the same person (that is, third party users did not need to be found by the waste holders for the materials to be re-used). The High Court found that:

33. [...] Immediate use cannot be taken literally. As for example, if material is deposited at a site intending it to be used straight away for building operations, if it is not used straight away, because, for instance, the weather is bad and prevents building operations; or other and different material is required to be delivered first before this material can be used; or machinery has to be brought on to the site before it can be used and there is some delay before it is brought to the site; any of these examples would not, depending on the facts, prevent the material from being reused immediately, if that is the expression that needs to be addressed. The distinction in my judgment must be between depositing the material for storage pending proposed reuse and depositing it for use more or less straight away without it being, in any sensible use of the word, stored. Depending always on the facts, hardcore which is going to be used next week for current building operations is not being stored.

This judgment shows the Court adopting a common sense approach to the definition of waste, following Carnwath J's lead in *OSS*. The reasoning also prioritizes a waste prevention purpose, in keeping materials that are to be re-used out of the supervisory (and costly) control of waste regulation.

---

[65] *Environment Agency v Inglenorth* [2009] EWHC 670, para 6.

However, just when you might think you are getting to grips with this difficult legal area, a more recent case has confined *Inglenorth* to its facts and tempered the narrower approach to defining waste in these English cases with a healthy dose of pragmatism in the other direction. While the prevention of waste and re-use, or extended use, of materials should be encouraged, this should not be to the point of allowing unscrupulous waste practices. A particular risk—and common form of waste crime, as seen in Section 3.3—is the dumping of waste materials under the guise of storing them on land pending use, or their use as 'landscaping'. The judgment in the following case can be understood as trying to minimize this risk, thus promoting again the harm minimization purpose of the Directive, and picking up the reasoning in *PGO* that storage of unwanted materials for a period of time on land can be a useful indicator that they are waste.

R v W and ors
[2010] EWCA Crim 927 paras 2–4, 33–34 (Court of Appeal)

2. The prosecution arose from the deposit at a farm of a large quantity of materials, extracted principally from neighbouring farm land in the course of construction on that land of new hotel premises. The materials consisted in large measure of soil and subsoil excavated during the works [...] The Respondents, TJC and PAC, are the owners of the farm onto which the materials were deposited; the Respondent W is the manager of the site. The prosecution claimed that they were able to identify at least 648 lorry loads of materials amounting to some 9126 tonnes that had been deposited onto the land owned by TC and PC and managed by W. It was common ground that no waste management licence under the Act had been obtained in respect of these activities. The Crown's case was that the materials constituted 'controlled waste' within the meaning of the [Environmental Protection Act 1990]. There was evidence that the Respondents had been paid some £20,000 to £25,000 to receive the materials onto their land.

3. The defence case that was to be presented, and which was known to the judge when he made his ruling, was that the receipt of the material was for the purpose of creating an area of hard standing for the extension of the farm facilities and the construction of a new farm building [a cattle shed] on top of it. It appeared from the Crown evidence that the materials had in fact been used to create a horizontal platform of some 100 x 60 metres, extending outwards in a wedge form from the naturally sloping land, with a vertical elevation of about 15 metres at its highest point [...]'

4. [T]he farm is set in an area of substantial scenic beauty in a Special Area of Conservation, within the highest category of such designation in European Union terminology. [...]

[...]

33. [W]e do not take the view that the question of immediate re-use of the relevant material can be entirely determinative of the status of the material regardless of other considerations. Sir Anthony May's example [in *Inglenorth*] of hardcore delivered for the immediate invisible repair of a domestic driveway may be one thing, but (by way of further example) the piling up of hardcore and subsoil, which was waste in the hands of the party who extracts it from the land, for the construction an intrusive artificial ski-slope on someone else's land may well be another. [S]uch material may well remain as waste which has to be disposed of in some manner notwithstanding an immediate intention of the recipient to re-use it. 'The term "discard" must be interpreted in the light of the aims of the [Directive] ...' and '... material which was originally waste needs to continue to be so treated until acceptable recovery or disposal has been achieved': see again per Carnwath LJ in *OSS*, paras 14(iv) and 56.

34. We conclude [...] that excavated soil which has to be discarded by the then 'holder' is capable of being waste within the Act and, in any individual case, ordinarily will be. Having become waste it remains waste unless something happens to alter that. Whether such an event has happened is a question of fact for the jury. The possibility of re-use at some indefinite future time does not alter its status: see

Palin Granit, and indeed *ARCO*. Actual re-use may do so (*Inglenorth*), but only if consistent with the aims and objectives of the Act and of the Directive: the principal ones of which are the avoidance of harm to persons or to the environment, as set out in the recitals to the Directive. Which of those aims and objectives are relevant to an individual case will depend on the cases presented by the parties. In this case, for example, the main concern maintained by the Crown is for the environment around the village where the Respondents' farm lies (as a Special Area of Conservation) and visual amenity in the area generally. Matters which, in our judgment, are readily capable of assessment by a jury in deciding whether any material in issue is in fact 'waste'.

In stating that the 'principal' aims of the WFD are the avoidance of harm to the environment and person, the Court of Appeal seems to be overstating the position, in light of the different aims of the Directive, which can be very difficult to reconcile, as this case shows. What this case really demonstrates is that the issue of whether matter is waste essentially is a matter of fact—disguised dumping as non-waste will not avoid the control of waste regulation, whereas extending the lifecycles of materials in genuine efforts to maximize resource use is properly outside the scope of the WFD. Thus, the Court of Justice is right when it says that discarding 'must be determined in the light of all the circumstances',[66] but it has left it to Member State courts to figure out *how* it so depends.

FURTHER READING AND QUESTIONS

1. For further reading on the legally fraught definition of waste, see David Wilkinson, 'Time to Discard the Concept of Waste', (1999) 1 Env LR 172; Stephen Tromans, 'EC Waste Law—A Complete Mess?' (2001) 13 JEL 133; Ilona Cheyne, 'The Definition of Waste in EC Law' (2002) 14 JEL 61. Note how old these articles now are, showing the protracted and longstanding nature of the legal debate over the definition of waste.

2. Consider the objective factors set out by the ECJ in *ARCO* for determining when there has been an act of discarding or an intention to discard. Do any of these factors help to clarify or improve the WFD definition of waste? (On this see DEFRA's guidance on the definition of waste (n 58) 36–43.) Give reasons if you do not think that the factors suggested by the Court are particularly useful. Can you think of a better doctrinal approach for reasoning about the definition of waste? Why do you think the Court reasoned as it did?

3. Why do you think there has been such legal difficulty in deciding whether secondary products are waste? What are the relevant policy tensions involved in this legal issue? See further, Eloise Scotford, 'Trash or Treasure: Policy Tensions in EC Waste Regulation', (2007) 19(3) JEL 367.

4. Consider the following sets of facts and determine whether you think they involve 'waste' materials, for the purposes of the 2008 Waste Framework Directive:

   a. A mine operator plans to use some leftover rock and sand residue from mining operations to fill in mine galleries once they have been exhausted (to provide structural support for the ground above). The operator provides guarantees as to the identification and actual use of those substances within the mine. The remainder of the rock and sand residue is to be processed into aggregate material for use in the construction industry. (See Case C–114/01 *AvestaPolarit Chrome Oy* [2003] ECR I-8725.)

---

[66] *ARCO* (n 16), para 88.

b. Petroleum coke is produced in an oil refinery intentionally, or in the course of producing other petroleum fuels. The coke is certain to be used as fuel to meet the energy needs of the refinery itself, as well as those of other industrial operators. (See Case C-235/02 *Saetti and Frediani* [2004] ECR I-1005.)

c. Waste Solutions Ltd operates a landfill site. It is planning to screen and sort waste that arrives at its landfill site more closely, in order to separate out food and garden waste, for this to be used in a new biomass power plant to be built on the site rather than being sent to landfill. Biomass power plants are still emerging as proven technologies, and they involve using either heat or chemical reactions to convert biological material—such as food and plant material—into energy.

5. Consider how *R(OSS) v Environment Agency* sits with Article 6 of the 2008 WFD, and consider how DEFRA has dealt with this case and the issue of waste-derived fuel in its guidance on the definition of waste (n 58) 56–59.

6. Consider again the facts of *Environment Agency v Inglenorth*. Why do you think that the Environment Agency was so keen to get this case within the scope of waste law? What kind of purpose for waste regulation does the Agency's approach reflect? How can you reconcile this decision with *R v W*?

7. For a complex set of EU and English litigation revisiting the vexed issue of whether accidentally spilled material constitutes waste, in the context of sewage that had overflowed onto land through faulty pipes, see Case C-252/05 *R(Thames Water Utilities) v Bromley Magistrates' Court* [2007] 1 WLR 1945; *R(Thames Water) v Bromley Magistrates* [2008] EWHC 1763 (Admin); and the cases preceding both. What key aspect of the latter case has been overturned by Article 2(2) of the 2008 WFD? As a postscript to these cases, and after eight years of litigation in this waste prosecution, the matter returned to Bromley Magistrates Court, which in 2011 convicted Thames Water of fifteen waste offences and fined the company over £200,000 in relation to the spilled sewage.

8. For other cases on the definition of waste in the UK courts, see *Cheshire County Council v Armstrong's Transport (Wigan) Ltd* [1995] Env LR 62 and *Meston Technical Services v Warwickshire County Council* [1995] Env LR 380. Are these cases still good law in light of the 2008 WFD? Do these cases illuminate any further Article 3(1) WFD's reference to 'intention' to discard?

2 EU WASTE REGULATION FRAMEWORK

2.1 THE EU WASTE FRAMEWORK DIRECTIVE: ITS FUNCTIONS, POLICY TENSIONS, AND FUNDAMENTAL OBLIGATIONS

As set out in Section 1.2 of the WFD has had several incarnations since its initial introduction as a Directive concerned primarily with the disposal of waste in 1975. The Directive has essentially retained three functions over this time—a framework function (setting core obligations and concepts for a range of EU waste legislation); a policy-directing function (directing EU and Member State waste policy); and a regulatory function (prescribing obligations in relation to materials that are waste). Legal problems with these Directives, particularly since the 1991 amendments, have largely centred on the definition of waste and its tortured interpretation in light of the tension in the Directive between its *policy priority* of preventing the generation of waste and its *regulatory control* of materials that are waste. Section 1 showed how this tension between the different functions of the Directive has played out in the cases concerning the definition of waste.

The 2008 Directive sought to resolve these fundamental problems and also to simplify and consolidate EU waste law. It is a consolidation of the pre-existing framework Directive as well as the previously supplementary Waste Oils and Hazardous Waste Directive[67]—the current WFD has thus expanded considerably to include measures relating to these areas as well. However, the 2008 Directive also represents a next stage in EU waste law, as Scotford critically analyses.

Eloise Scotford, 'The New Waste Directive – Trying to Do it All … An Early Assessment' (2009) 11(2) Env LR 75, 76, 79–80

The new Directive was intended to clarify, simplify and re-orient its framework provisions, so as both to fix the perceived problems of past waste regulation and to reflect the new life-cycle, resources-focused approach to waste policy set out in the Commission's Sixth Environment Action Programme. However, the latter objective undermines the former [...] The Directive is now a legislative instrument of a different order to its predecessor, in terms of both its scale and ambition, and with this comes increased legal complexity.

[...]

While the tension in Community waste policy between waste prevention and waste regulation is not new, [...] it takes on an added dimension in the new Directive. Article 1 introduces an objective for the Directive, which demonstrates the breadth of the Directive's environmental and health protection ambitions: it aims to protect the environment and human health, not just by preventing and reducing the adverse impacts of waste, but also by 'reducing the overall [environmental and human health] impacts of resource use and improving the efficiency of such use'. Here lies a new source of the unclear messages about the goals of Community waste policy. No longer is the Waste Directive merely about waste and minimising the adverse impacts of waste generation and management (including through encouraging waste prevention); it is now also about minimising the adverse environmental and health impacts of resources generally, as they are productively used throughout their life-cycles.

' [...]

[T]he approach of the new Directive might be defended thus: while it is concerned with casting the waste net widely, it is then focused on releasing it quickly. Once environmental standards are met and re-use/recyclate markets present themselves, waste status ends, thereby promoting both waste 'minimisation' (rather than prevention) as well as uncompromising environmental standards. This is the result that the Directive wants to achieve, with its vision of a 'European recycling society', in which resources are encouraged to take their place. This vision reflects the Commission's determination to modernise its thinking about waste, viewing it as a 'valued resource' rather than an 'unwanted burden'. But the point remains that the casting of the regulatory net has consequences (of cost and perception in particular) and it is possible that the new Directive will blunt its regulatory potential by the scale of its environmental protection ambition. It is one thing to see waste as a resource; quite another to see all resources as waste.

Thus, rather than resolving the policy tensions of the previous WFD, the 2008 Directive gives them new life with its ambitious new Article 1 objective and an agenda to build a society in which resource use is maximized in all possible ways, before being waste and also once becoming waste. The objective is a laudable one in terms of natural resources and waste policy, but it comes at a cost of doctrinal clarity for this discrete

---

[67] Directives 91/689/EEC and 75/439/EEC, which were repealed with effect from 12 December 2010.

area of environmental law, which fundamentally depends on being able to draw the line between what is waste and what is not. Some improvements in drawing this line have been introduced with the Directive, particularly with the introduction of Articles 5 and 6 on by-products and end-of-waste, as examined in Section 1.2. However, at the time of writing, we await decisions by the CJEU on defining waste under the 2008 WFD to see whether or not it brings any further clarification to this vexed legal issue.

The structure of the 2008 WFD can be roughly broken down into policy-directing and regulatory measures, reflecting its functions, which are further explored in Sections 2.2 and 2.3. In terms of the fundamental waste obligations of the WFD, these are found in Articles 13 and 36.

Article 13

Protection of Human Health and the Environment

Member States shall take the necessary measures to ensure that waste management is carried out without endangering human health, without harming the environment and, in particular:

(a) without risk to water, air, soil, plants or animals;

(b) without causing a nuisance through noise or odours; and

(c) without adversely affecting the countryside or places of special interest.

Article 36

Enforcement and Penalties

1. Member States shall take the necessary measures to prohibit the abandonment, dumping or uncontrolled management of waste.

These are general and overriding obligations on Member States, which they must implement through waste policy and more detailed measures, and Member States can be found to be in breach of them, including the more general environmental provisions of Article 13, as seen in *Commission v Italy*. This case concerned a serious waste problem that had built up in the Italian city of Naples, which relied primarily on insufficient landfill or illegal abandonment to deal with its waste. As the ECJ held, the result of inadequate waste infrastructure over a period of time could amount to an infringement of Article 13, which, whilst it left a margin of discretion for Member States to adopt appropriate measures, was still binding as to the result to be achieved.

Case C-297/08 *Commission v Italy*
[2010] ECR I-1749 para 97

97. [I]n principle, it cannot be inferred directly from the fact that a situation is not in conformity with the objectives laid down in Article 4(1) of Directive 2006/12 [now Article 13 WFD] that the Member State concerned has necessarily failed to fulfil its obligations under that provision, that is to say, to take the requisite measures to ensure that waste is disposed of without endangering human health and without harming the environment. However, if that situation persists and, in particular, if it leads to a significant deterioration in the environment over a protracted period without any action being taken by the competent authorities, this may be an indication that the Member States have exceeded the discretion conferred on them by that provision.

On the facts in this case, at the relevant time:

103. [T]he waste littering the public roads totalled 55 000 tonnes, adding to the 110 000 tonnes to 120 000 tonnes of waste awaiting treatment at municipal storage sites [...] Furthermore, [...] the local inhabitants, exasperated by such accumulation, have taken the initiative of igniting fires in the piles of refuse, which is harmful both for the environment and for their own health [...]

106. [Further, the accumulation] of such large quantities of waste along public roads and in temporary storage areas [...] has therefore undoubtedly given rise to a 'risk to water, air or soil, and to plants or animals' within the meaning of Article 4(1)(a) of Directive 2006/12. Moreover, such quantities of waste inevitably cause 'a nuisance through noise or odours' within the meaning of Article 4(1)(b), especially when the waste remains uncovered in streets and along roads over a protracted period.

107. Moreover, given the lack of availability of sufficient landfills, the presence of such quantities of waste outside appropriate, approved storage facilities is likely to affect 'adversely ... the countryside or places of special interest' within the meaning of Article 4(1)(c) of Directive 2006/12.

This case unsurprisingly also involved a breach of Article 36 (ex-Article 4(2)).

2.2 EU WASTE POLICY

Waste policy has had a long history in the EU, leading to the earliest version of the WFD being introduced in 1975. From the first commitment of EU Member States to a Community environmental policy in 1972, through all the EC and EU Environmental Action Programmes since 1973, waste prevention and minimizing environmental harm associated with waste management have been Community and now Union policy priorities.[68] Current EU policy initiatives push the waste prevention priority even further, as waste problems in many Member States remain pressing, and they are largely found in the Thematic Strategy on Waste Prevention and Recycling,[69] which was introduced in 2005 under the 6th Environmental Action Programme (EAP) (the 7th EAP is on the near horizon).[70] Today, EU waste policy also relates to wider strategic efforts to maximize natural resources and regulate their use through whole 'lifecycle' approaches, rather than simply concentrating on end-of-pipe measures that focus on waste materials alone.[71] This broader policy approach is reflected in Article 1 of the 2008 WFD.

However, within the WFD itself, there are various measures that set out the shape and direction of EU waste policy through legal prescription. The key WFD provision for this purpose is Article 4. Article 4(1) provides that the waste hierarchy set out in Figure 16.2 'shall apply as a priority order in waste prevention and management legislation and policy'. This implies that the hierarchy applies to EU and Member State waste policy alike and, moreover, that it is mandatory. The idea of policy being legally binding is counter-intuitive to English lawyers but it is common enough in EU law, reflecting both the framework and policy-directing function of this Directive (and EU Directives and many

---

[68] See Ludwig Krämer, *EU Environmental Law* (7th edn, Sweet & Maxwell 2012) 329.

[69] Commission Communication, 'Taking sustainable use of resources forward–A Thematic Strategy on the prevention and recycling of waste', COM(2005) 666 final.

[70] European Parliament and Council Decision 1600/2002/EC of 22 July 2002 laying down the Sixth Community Environment Action Programme [2002] OJ L242/1.

[71] Commission Communication, 'Thematic Strategy on the sustainable use of natural resources', COM(2005) 670 final; Commission Communication, 'Integrated Product Policy–Building on Environmental Life-Cycle Thinking', COM(2003) 302 final; Commission Communication on the Sustainable Consumption and Production and Sustainable Industrial Policy Action Plan, COM(2008) 397 final.

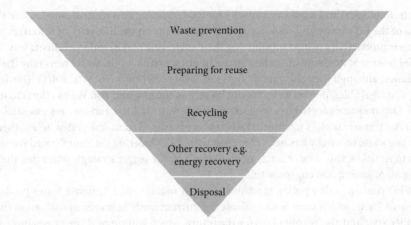

Figure 16.2 The Waste Hierarchy—Article 4(1) Waste Framework Directive 2008

Treaty provisions generally), and also the blurred relationship between law and policy in environmental law.[72]

All these hierarchy terms—'preparing for re-use', 'recovery', and so on—are defined in Article 1 (and further explored in Section 2.3), so that the waste policy direction set by Article 4 is highly prescriptive. Note that the top level and priority of the hierarchy—waste prevention—does not in fact involve waste, encapsulating the ongoing tension that this chapter has highlighted in the definition and regulation of waste. The WFD, as the central legal instrument for EU and UK waste law, encourages waste prevention as a priority whilst only having regulatory control over materials that are classified as 'waste'.

Despite the mandatory formulation of the hierarchy, Article 4(2) allows some exceptions to its order. Thus it provides (with emphasis added):

> When applying the waste hierarchy referred to in paragraph 1, Member States shall take measures to encourage the options that deliver the *best overall environmental outcome*. This may require specific waste streams *departing from the hierarchy where this is justified by life-cycle thinking* on the overall impacts of the generation and management of such waste.
>
> Member States shall ensure that the development of waste legislation and policy is a fully transparent process, observing existing national rules about the consultation and involvement of citizens and stakeholders.
>
> Member States shall take into account the *general environmental protection principles of precaution and sustainability, technical feasibility and economic viability, protection of resources as well as the overall environmental, human health, economic and social impacts*, in accordance with Articles 1 and 13.

The reasons for these exceptions are several—different waste streams demand different treatment to maximize resources and to control environmental risks,[73] Member States may be at different stages in

---

[72] See Section 2 of Chapter 11. Cf Krämer (n 68), 335 (finding that Article 4's hierarchy can be a legal 'recommendation' only).

[73] For example, the UK government considers that the use of anaerobic digestion for certain organic waste, such as food waste, to generate energy is a better overall environmental outcome than recycling such waste: *Anaerobic Digestion Strategy and Action Plan for England* (DECC & DEFRA, 2011) para 23.

terms of technological and economic capacity for implementing new waste strategies, and the overall direction of the EU's waste and resource strategy is to focus on the lifecycles of resources and maximizing their productivity (whilst minimizing their environmental harm) in a holistic way. These reasons give Member States more discretion in the implementation of the waste hierarchy than appears at first glance, although they also muddy the clear legal prescription in Article 4(1). The difficulty of meeting that legal obligation on its terms can be seen in the England and Wales efforts to implement Article 4. One measure adopted has been to require all waste holders and carriers essentially to tick a box on waste transfer notices (completed when waste is passed from one person to another) to indicate that the waste hierarchy has been complied with.[74] Considering the complicated considerations involved in Article 4, this style of implementation misses the bigger strategic point that the Article is requiring Member States to engage with.

The WFD contains other policy measures. Thus, it requires that Member States produce Waste Management Plans, which must both evaluate the current waste management situation throughout the Member State and also set out plans for the future, which will support the provisions and obligations of the Directive. Article 28 sets out the matters that the plan must include, including information on site identification for disposal and recovery installations, and the need for new waste infrastructure and collection schemes. Thus, waste planning overlaps with urban planning and there needs to be a synergy between the two at the national level. Members of the public, relevant authorities, and stakeholders are to have the opportunity to participate in this waste planning process.[75]

Further, the WFD requires that Member States, between themselves, establish an integrated and adequate network of disposal installations, and installations for the recovery of mixed municipal waste collected from private households,[76] to allow the EU to become self-sufficient in waste disposal and limited recovery operations, and to enable Member States to work towards that aim individually (Article 16). This *self-sufficiency principle* is supported by a *proximity principle*, which requires that disposal (or limited recovery) of waste occurs at 'one of the nearest appropriate installations, by means of the most appropriate methods and technologies, in order to ensure a high level of protection for the environment and public health'.[77] These principles reflect the broader Treaty environmental principle of 'rectification at source'.[78] The policy directions of these principles give rise to some legal complexity, since some movement of waste between Member States is allowed under EU law (particularly for recovery under the Waste Shipments Regulation—see further Section 2.5).[79] However, it is clear that it is possible for Member States to infringe Article 16's requirement of maintaining an adequate network of waste infrastructure.[80] Thus, in the infringement case concerning Naples urban waste problems discussed in Section 2.1, Italy was also found to be in breach of Article 16 (ex-Article 5 under the 1991 WFD) for failing to have sufficient installations to enable it to dispose of its urban waste close to the place where that waste is produced. Planned incinerators had not yet been built and its one legal landfill site in the region could not cope with the volume of local waste, much of which was transported to Germany or other regions of Italy.

---

[74] The Waste (England and Wales) Regulations 2011 SI 2011/988, regs 12 and 35(2)(d).

[75] 2008 WFD, art 31.

[76] Including where this collection also covers such waste from other producers: 2008 WFD, art 16(1). The network of such installations is to take into account best available techniques.

[77] 2008 WFD, art 16(3).

[78] TFEU, art 191(2).

[79] Article 16(1) attempts to reconcile the overlap with the Waste Shipments Regulation by allowing Member States to protect their installation network by preventing incoming waste shipments for recovery and preventing outgoing shipments in some cases. At base, waste is a good that is protected by free movement rules unless there is a good environmental protection reason to counter this: see Section 2.5.

[80] See also Case C-494/01 *Commission v Ireland* [2005] ECR I-3331.

Two final waste policy-directing measures in the WFD are an encouragement to Member States to adopt producer responsibility measures (such as requiring acceptance of returned products, paying for their subsequent management as waste, and designing products to reduce environmental impacts),[81] and the requirement now for waste *prevention* planning. Waste prevention is defined in Article 3(12) as:

'prevention' means measures taken before a substance, material or product has become waste, that reduce:

(a) the quantity of waste, including through the re-use of products or the extension of the life span of products;

(b) the adverse impacts of the generated waste on the environment and human health; or

(c) the content of harmful substances in materials and products;

Since the Directive does not directly regulate material that is not yet waste, it is not surprising that one of its key measures for promoting the top priority of the waste hierarchy is to require Member States themselves to develop programmes for preventing waste. Article 29 thus requires Member States to draw up Waste Prevention Programmes, which aim to 'break the link between economic growth and the environmental impacts associated with the generation of waste' and must include qualitative and quantitative benchmarks for the waste prevention measures adopted.[82] Member States that fail to implement their own Waste Prevention Programmes may have that fact published by the European Environment Agency.[83] As with Waste Management Plans (which may be integrated in the same document), the general public, stakeholders, and relevant authorities are to be involved in drawing up waste prevention plans.[84] Waste prevention planning is supported by Article 11(1)'s requirement for Member States to 'take measures, as appropriate, to promote the re-use of products and preparing for re-use activities'.

This summary of the policy-directing measures of the WFD is not the final story. The WFD represents a stage in an ever-changing area of EU policy and law, and the Directive contains suggestions of further EU measures to come, setting the scene of future waste policy. These include measures on biowaste,[85] EU benchmarks for waste prevention,[86] an EU product ecodesign policy addressing the generation of waste and the presence of hazardous materials,[87] and further 'support measures' at the EU level to change current consumption patterns.[88]

2.3 EU WASTE TREATMENT AND MANAGEMENT OBLIGATIONS

In terms of the regulatory function of the Directive, there are a range of obligations placed on Member States, waste holders, and waste producers in relation to materials that are classified as waste. Article 15 sets out the basic waste management obligation on Member States:

---

[81] 2008 WFD, art 8. See also arts 14(2) and 15(3). These are Member State measures beyond existing EU producer responsibility schemes: see Section 2.4.

[82] Annex 4 also sets out the EU's 'wish-list' of waste prevention measures that Member States must consider adopting in their plans: art 29(2).

[83] 2008 WFD, art 30(2).

[84] 2008 WFD, art 31.

[85] Article 22 requires Member States to encourage environmentally safe treatment and use of bio-waste, as well as its composting and digestion, with a suggestion of EU measures to come.

[86] 2008 WFD, art 29(4).

[87] 2008 WFD, art 9(a).

[88] 2008 WFD, art 9(b).

> Member States shall take the necessary measures to ensure that any original waste producer or other holder *carries out the treatment of waste himself* or *has the treatment handled by a dealer or an establishment or undertaking* which carries out waste treatment operations or arranged by a private or public waste collector in accordance with Articles 4 and 13.

Waste treatment operations

In terms of the treatment of waste that must be carried out under Article 15, there are two types of waste treatment that might be undertaken—disposal and recovery operations. As explained in Section 1.2, *recovery operations* are those 'the principal result of which is waste serving a useful purpose by replacing other materials which would otherwise have been used to fulfil a particular function, or waste being prepared to fulfil that function, in the plant or in the wider economy', with Annex II setting out an illustrative list. Recovery operations include 'recycling' operations, by which waste materials are 'reprocessed into products, materials or substances whether for the original or other purposes'.[89] Recovery operations are to be distinguished from *re-use*, which sits higher in the waste hierarchy, and defined in Article 3(13) as:

> any operation by which products or components that are *not* waste are used again for the same purpose for which they were conceived.

However, preparing objects for such re-use may still involve waste materials. Thus, there is also a definition of *preparing for re-use* in Article 3(16), but note that this still requires material that is waste in the first place (and so would not cover a case like *Inglenorth* above). It provides:

> 'preparing for re-use' means checking, cleaning or repairing recovery operations, by which products or components of products that have become waste are prepared so that they can be re-used without any other pre-processing.

Disposal, by contrast, which sits at the bottom of the waste hierarchy, means:

> any operation which is not recovery even where the operation has as a secondary consequence the reclamation of substances or energy. Annex I sets out a non-exhaustive list of disposal operations. (Article 3(19))

Beyond Article 15, there are two key obligations on Member States in relation to carrying out waste treatment (recovery and disposal) operations:

Article 10

Recovery

1. Member States shall take the necessary measures to ensure that waste undergoes recovery operations, in accordance with Articles 4 and 13.

2. Where necessary to comply with paragraph 1 and to facilitate or improve recovery, waste shall be collected separately if technically, environmentally and economically practicable and shall not be mixed with other waste or other material with different properties.

[...]

---

[89] 2008 WFD, art 3(17).

Article 12

Disposal

Member States shall ensure that, where recovery in accordance with Article 10(1) is not undertaken, waste undergoes safe disposal operations which meet the provisions of Article 13 on the protection of human health and the environment.

Read together, these two provisions require that recovery operations be carried out as a priority, in accordance with the waste hierarchy and the overriding environmental protection obligation of Article 14. Note that Article 12 does not say 'where recovery in accordance with Article 10(1) *cannot be* undertaken', arguably leaving some room for Member States to recover waste less than they possibly can. However, Article 4 still applies.

The key waste management obligation that applies to any establishment or undertaking intending to carry out waste treatment is that they are required to obtain a *permit*, in accordance with the conditions and specifications in Article 23. Permits must thus include, inter alia, the type of waste that can be treated by the relevant operator, the method to be used and safety measures to be undertaken, monitoring and control requirements, and site closure and after-care provisions, as necessary.[90] Permits must be refused where the permitting authority 'considers that the intended method of treatment is unacceptable from the point of view of environmental protection, in particular when the method is not in accordance with Article 13'.[91] Exemptions from the permitting requirement are allowed for disposal of non-hazardous waste at the place of production and recovery operations,[92] but only where Member States have laid down general rules for the relevant activity, which are designed to ensure that Article 13 is complied with and that best available techniques are used for any disposal operations covered.[93]

A significant issue in practice relating to waste treatment is how 'energy-from-waste' (EfW) operations are classified and regulated. The 2008 WFD introduced a new limit as to when such operations can be classified as recovery operations. Thus, Annex II provides that incineration facilities dedicated to the processing of municipal solid waste are only recovery operations where their energy efficiency is equal to or above a certain numerical value calculated by an energy efficiency formula.[94] This is supported by the definition of 'disposal' in Article 12, which envisages that EfW activities can be disposal operations in some cases. More broadly, within EU law, there is ambiguity over the EU's priorities with respect to waste incineration—whether it is to be seen as the least preferred method of waste recovery or even a method of waste disposal, as the WFD suggests, or rather as a valuable source of renewable energy. Other Directives support the latter position—such as the Industrial Emissions Directive, which exempts certain waste incineration operations from its controls[95]—as does EU policy on renewable energy, which has ambitious renewable energy targets and sees incinerating waste as one means to achieving them (along with biomass plants).[96]

[90] Note that the EU may establish technical minimum standards for some treatment operations under art 27.
[91] 2008 WFD, art 23(3).
[92] 2008 WFD, art 24.
[93] 2008 WFD, art 25.
[94] Article 23(4) further provides that a condition of any permit covering incineration or co-incineration with energy recovery is that the recovery must take place with a high level of energy efficiency.
[95] European Parliament and Council Directive 2010/75 of 24 November 2010 on industrial emissions (integrated pollution prevention and control) [2010] OJ L334/17 (IED), art 42.
[96] See further, Krämer (n 68) 332. On EU renewable energy policy, see Section 3.3 of Chapter 15.

The final innovation introduced by the 2008 WFD in relation to waste treatment operations are recycling targets to be met by Member States, in an effort to move towards a 'European recycling society'. Article 11(2) thus requires Member States to 'take the necessary measures designed to achieve' targets of 50% recycling by weight at least of household paper, metal, plastic, and glass by 2020, and 70% recycling by weight of non-hazardous construction and demolition waste by 2020. Article 11(1) also requires separate collection systems to be set up for at least paper, metal, plastic, and glass by 2015, except where not technically, environmentally, and economically practicable.

Waste management operations

In contrast to waste treatment operations, waste management operations are a broader set of operations relating to waste, which are also subject to regulatory control. Waste management is defined in Article 3(9) as:

> the collection, transport, recovery and disposal of waste, including the supervision of such operations and the after-care of disposal sites, and including actions taken as a dealer or broker.

The Court of Justice has clarified that the concept of transporting waste on a professional basis 'covers not only those who, in the course of their business as carriers, transport waste produced by others, but also those who, whilst not professional carriers, nevertheless in the course of their own business activity, transport waste which they have produced'.[97]

Operators involved in waste management (other than waste treatment operators) are required to be registered with the relevant national authorities.[98] They are also to be subject to periodic inspections. All waste management operators are required to keep detailed records of the waste that they handle and its characteristics, as specified in Article 35. By these obligations, the Directive aims to monitor the waste cycle from the time it is produced, including monitoring the conditions of collection and transportation.

Note that waste management responsibilities are extended through the polluter pays principle in Article 14, according to which the costs of waste management are to be borne by the original waste producer or current or previous waste holders. Member States may also decide that they are to be borne by the producer or distributors of the products from which the waste came.[99]

In relation to management of hazardous waste, the Directive contains more stringent controls. Thus, while the regulatory provisions that apply to waste generally also cover hazardous waste, extra provisions guarantee the traceability of hazardous waste and introduce a ban on the mixing and diluting of hazardous waste.[100] Mixing of hazardous waste with other waste or substances may, however, be allowed where the undertaking has a waste management permit, the operation conforms to best available techniques and Article 13 is respected, with no increased adverse impacts on human health or the environment.[101] Note also, with respect to the management of waste oils, that extra provisions are included in Article 21, which shifts the focus from waste oil regeneration to separate collection at the European level.

---

[97] Case C-270/03 *Commission v Italy* [2005] ECR I-5255, para 23.

[98] As are any waste treatment operators exempted from permitting requirements: art 26. The Directive does not allow any exceptions to the obligation of registration according to the type or quantity of waste being handled: ibid.

[99] See further Section 1.2.

[100] 2008 WFD, arts 17, 18(1) and 35.

[101] 2008 WFD, art 18(2).

2.4 DAUGHTER EU WASTE DIRECTIVES

Under the WFD sit a number of 'daughter' Directives, which regulate different forms of waste management as well as different waste streams. In terms of waste management, the two key Directives in the past have been the Landfill and Waste Incineration Directives. The latter is now subsumed within the Industrial Emissions Directive. Further, there is a series of Directives that deal with particular waste streams, from animal waste and batteries to packaging waste and end-of-life vehicles,[102] many of which are cast as producer responsibility Directives.

Waste management directives: incineration and landfill

From 2014, waste incineration and co-incineration plants are regulated under the Industrial Emissions Directive (IED).[103] The IED is discussed in detail in Chapter 17, and it includes a chapter on waste incineration control, which essentially requires waste incineration operators to hold a permit that imposes emission limit values for various pollutants, requires certain chimney stack heights to minimize local air pollution problems and requires minimization of residues and the recovery of heat produced in incineration processes, amongst other things.[104] In addition, waste incineration plants of a certain size, along with large waste disposal sites, are regulated as IPPC installations under Part II of the IED, which requires the adoption of best available techniques that allow a high level of protection of the environment as a whole.[105]

Landfill waste disposal sites, by contrast, are regulated under the Landfill Directive, which has had a considerable impact in the UK, as a country historically heavily on reliant on landfill for disposal. The Directive defines 'landfill' broadly to cover:[106]

a waste disposal site for the deposit of the waste onto or into land (i.e. underground), including:

- internal waste disposal sites (i.e. landfill where a producer of waste is carrying out its own waste disposal at the place of production), and
- a permanent site (i.e. more than one year) which is used for temporary storage of waste, but excluding:
- facilities where waste is unloaded in order to permit its preparation for further transport for recovery, treatment or disposal elsewhere, and
- storage of waste prior to recovery or treatment for a period less than three years as a general rule, or
- storage of waste prior to disposal for a period less than one year [...]

The Directive has two primary functions—it sets targets for reducing the amount of biodegradable municipal waste (BMW) sent to landfill, and it imposes regulatory controls in relation to landfill sites. In terms of targets, the Directive requires a 50% reduction of BMW waste in landfill from 1990 levels by 2009, and a 65% reduction by 2016. The UK has four-year reprieve to meet these deadlines

---

[102] See Krämer (n 68) 355–63.

[103] The former Waste Incineration Directive (Directive 2000/76/EC on waste incineration) is repealed as of 7 January 2014.

[104] IED (n 95).

[105] Ibid, Annex I, para 5. On IPPC controls, see further, Chapter 17.

[106] Council Directive 99/31/EC of 26 April 1999 on the landfill of waste [1999] OJ L182/1, art 2(g). See *Blackland Park Exploration Ltd v Environment Agency* [2004] Env LR 33 for a case in which identifying a legal landfill was not a straightforward matter.

as a Member State that has relied so extensively on landfill in the past, but it is doing well enough in meeting these targets.

As for the regulatory control of landfill sites, the Landfill Directive requires that landfill operators hold a permit, which contains obligations specific to the site to ensure appropriate operating methods, capacity and also aftercare provisions, making operators responsible into the future, including by monitoring and maintaining the site for as long as it may present an environmental hazard and having adequate financial resources to cover any costs associated with this.[107] All costs associated with running a landfill site are 'covered by the price to be charged by the operator for the disposal of any type of waste in that site'.[108] The Directive also contains more general obligations relating to landfill sites, which are classified into three types—for non-hazardous waste, for hazardous waste, and for inert waste. There is a ban on mixing different classifications of waste in landfills, as well as a total ban on used tyres, other flammable items, clinical waste, liquids, and some hazardous wastes (to prevent problems of fires and toxic liquids leaching into the surrounding soil and groundwater).[109] Article 6 requires that waste must be treated before disposal (including sorting and compacting) and meet waste acceptance criteria, in accordance with Annex II.

Producer responsibility regimes

There is a series of Directives that seek to control waste problems through a lifecycle approach, by setting recovery targets for materials in certain waste streams and imposing obligations on producers of products that become waste. These include the Packaging Waste Directive (PWD),[110] the End-of-Life Vehicles Directive (ELV Directive),[111] and the WEEE Directive (applying to electronic and electrical waste). These Directives all have slightly different features, but in general they set out target percentages for recovering waste derived from particular products, with producers of the relevant products responsible for the cost of this and for ensuring that certain waste-minimizing features are designed into the products themselves. Thus, under the PWD, there are target ranges of packaging waste recovery and recycling, which must be met by 2008, and Member States must set up systems for the collection of packaging waste and the re-use or recovery of packaging waste collected. Despite serious implementation problems for this Directive, with target dates being postponed repeatedly, these obligations are now, to a considerable extent, overtaken by the general recycling targets in the 2008 WFD. The other main innovation of the PWD was the requirement that only packaging complying with the 'essential requirements' set out in Annex II of the Directive can be placed on the EU market, with the Commission to promote European standards for some packaging features.

Subsequent producer responsibility Directives have become more sophisticated in their lifecycle approach, setting up more complicated schemes but also imposing further obligations on producers. Thus, under the ELV Directive, costs incurred in transferring a vehicle to a facility for destruction are to be met by the vehicle manufacturer, with 95% of vehicle waste to be recovered and re-used by 2015 (85% by 2006), but slightly lower recycling targets. Vehicle manufacturers are also encouraged to minimize the use of hazardous substances in their car design (with some substances, such as mercury and cadmium, banned since 2003 in most cases) and to design cars to facilitate recycling and recovery. The WEEE Directive goes so far as to put obligations on some retailers and distributors to take back waste from electrical and electronic equipment (WEEE) from household consumers free

---

[107] Ibid, arts 8, 9, and 13.
[108] Ibid, art 10.
[109] Ibid, arts 5 and 6.
[110] European Parliament and Council Directive 94/62/EC of 20 December 1994 on packaging and packaging waste [1994] OJ L365/10.
[111] European Parliament and Council Directive 2000/53/EC of 18 September 2000 on end-of-life vehicles [2000] OJ L269/34.

of charge. Manufacturers are also encouraged to cooperate to promote design of EEE that facilitates recovery and re-use, and particularly to follow the ecodesign requirements of Directive 2009/125.[112] Again, there are recycling targets for different categories of WEEE, which producers must ensure are met. Producers must also finance the collection, treatment, recovery, and environmentally sound disposal of WEEE—although the nature of this obligation varies depending on how the waste was collected, when the relevant products were produced and whether the waste came from private households or elsewhere. The WEEE Directive has proved very problematic to implement,[113] and a new version of the Directive was passed, in force from August 2012,[114] which aims to be more workable in practice and to sit better with other related EU legislation, including the Regulation on Registration, Evaluation, Authorization and Restriction of Chemicals ('REACH regulation').[115]

2.5 WASTE SHIPMENTS REGULATION

The 'shipment of waste' refers to all movements of waste materials, whether by ship or other means of transport. In the EU, such movements will be for some form of waste treatment—disposal or recovery—since this is the obligatory fate of all waste material. The reasons for waste shipments range from environmentally protective to environmentally risky. Thus, some shipments are made to send waste to a better recovery facility or to a place where they will replace natural resources in production cycles. However, other shipments are made because local waste treatment infrastructure is inadequate or to send hazardous waste elsewhere to minimize local environmental harms. The 2008 WFD has something to say on such movements of waste, through its principles of proximity and self-sufficiency, which require disposal and some recovery of waste at one of the 'nearest appropriate installations' to the place of waste production.[116] This picture is further complicated in the EU since waste is a good, whether recyclable or not, in relation to which free movement rules apply throughout the single market.[117] On top of this, there are strict international controls for waste shipments, particularly for protecting developing nations from being dumping grounds for toxic waste from industrialized countries.[118] As a result, the regulation of waste shipments has many considerations to balance and the EU regulatory system in place is complicated. The international aspects of waste shipments—shipments in and out of the EU—are not covered in the chapter, which focuses on the EU Waste Shipments Regulation (WSR),[119] as it applies to waste shipments between EU Member States.

The WSR has been in effect since 2007,[120] but its Annexes of waste lists ('green' and 'amber' listed waste) are subject to frequent amendment, being updated in light of international developments and

---

[112] European Parliament and Council Directive 2009/125/EC of 21 October 2009 establishing a framework for the setting of ecodesign requirements for energy-related products [2009] OJ L285/10.

[113] See, for example, *Waste Recycling Group v Phillips Electronics UK Ltd* [2010] EWHC 2064 (Ch).

[114] European Parliament and Council Directive 2012/19/EU of 4 July 2012 on waste electrical and electronic equipment (WEEE) [2010] OJ L197/38. This Directive sits alongside European Parliament and Council Directive 2011/65/EU of 8 June 2011 on the restriction of the use of certain hazardous substances [2011] OJ L174/88.

[115] European Parliament and Council Regulation 1907/2006/EC of 18 December 2006 [2006] OJ L396/1.

[116] See Section 2.2.

[117] Case C-2/90 *Commission v Belgium (Walloon Waste)* [1992] ECR I-4431, para 28.

[118] Basel Convention on the Control of Transboundary Movement of Hazardous Wastes and their Disposal (in force 1992); Organisation for Economic Cooperation and Development, *Decision on the Control of Transboundary Waste* C(2001) 107/final; Bamako Convention on the Ban of the Import Into Africa and the Control of Transboundary Movement and Management of Hazardous Wastes Within Africa (in force 1998).

[119] European Parliament and Council Regulation 1013/2006/EC of 14 June 2006 on shipments of waste [2006] OJ L190/1 ('WSR').

[120] EU waste shipment controls have existed since the mid-1980s (Directive 84/631 [1984] OJ L326/31), with major legislative revisions in 1993 (Regulation 259/93 [1993] OJ L30/1) and then the 2006 WSR, in light of the international Basel Convention coming into force and regulatory controls being tightened up to minimize shipments of environmentally harmful waste.

scientific and technical decisions as to which waste is appropriate for shipment between countries. The basic obligations of the WSR for shipments between Member States are that:

- Green-listed non-hazardous waste (Annex III) destined for *recovery* is allowed to circulate freely within the EU, subject to notification and documentation requirements when shipments involve mixed green waste or are over a certain size.[121]

- Any waste destined for *disposal*, or amber-listed hazardous waste (Annex IV) destined for *recovery*, is subject to a system of prior written notification and consent. By this process, the proposed sender of waste must notify the local competent authority of the planned shipment, providing relevant information and financial guarantees. The local competent authority then notifies the competent authorities of the place of destination and transit, with a thirty day period of objection then triggered from the date that the destination authority acknowledges the notification. During that thirty day period, the competent authorities of destination and dispatch must give a decision, either consenting to the shipment (this can be with conditions) or objecting to it on a number of allowable grounds, as set out in Articles 11 and 12. These grounds include: the proposed shipment would not comply with the principles of proximity or self-sufficiency in the WFD; the proposed shipment would not comply with national legislation in the destination Member State relating to environmental protection, public order, public safety, or health protection; the notifier or consignee has been delinquent in the past; or, in some cases, the proposed recovery facility in the destination Member State employs lower treatment standards than in the home Member State.

The finer details of the WSR require close reading of the lengthy Regulation, but one other feature to note is that the classification of wastes into hazardous (amber) and non-hazardous (green) lists is not done by means of the definition of hazardous waste in the WFD. Rather, the WSR relies heavily on the classification of hazardous waste under the Basel Convention on the control of transboundary movements of hazardous waste.[122] This is because the WSR partly seeks to implement that international system of transboundary waste shipment. However, the Basel and EU lists and classifications of hazardous waste do not correspond exactly, introducing further complexity into this area of law.

FURTHER READING AND QUESTIONS

1. For the EU's interpretive guidance on the 2008 WFD, see EU Commission, *Guidance on the Interpretation of Key Provisions of Directive* 2008/98/EC on Waste (D-G Environment, June 2012). Note that it is explicitly 'not legally binding'.

2. In what ways does the 2008 WFD improve the legal definition of waste, if any? In what ways does it make it (more) complicated?

3. Having now studied the provisions of the 2008 WFD in some detail, do you think the Directive is more concerned with maintaining high environmental standards or with promoting the prevention of waste and re-use of unwanted products? Does this need to be a binary distinction of purposes? Does the objective in Article 1 assist in elucidating the terms and function of the Directive?

---

[121] 2008 WFD, arts 3(2), 18. In exceptional cases, green waste may be subject to more stringent control if it displays hazardous characteristics: WSR, art 3(3).

[122] Above n 118.

4. Do you think the result in *Environment Agency v Inglenorth* (considered in Section 1.3) is consistent with the scheme of the 2008 WFD, taking into account particularly its definition of 'preparing for re-use'?

5. For further commentary on the 2008 WFD, see Hazel Nash, 'The Revised Directive on Waste: Resolving Legislative Tensions in Waste Management?' (2009) 21(1) JEL 139.

6. The interaction of various aspects of EU waste law can get very complicated. Case C-176/05 *KVZ retec GmbH v Austria* [2007] ECR I-01721 provides a good example, involving the overlap between the WFD, WSR, and Regulations on animal waste. Has the result of this case changed with the 2008 WFD and its Article 2(b) and (c) exclusions?

7. On the interaction between waste shipments regulation and free movement rules, read Case C-203/96 *Dusseldorp* [1998] ECR I-4075. Would this case be decided differently in light of the 2006 WSR, and Article 12 in particular? Why do you think the Netherlands government wanted to prevent the export of waste oil filters to Germany? Overall, what scope do Member States have to take unilateral environmental protection measures that restrict the free movement of waste within the EU, whether on the basis of Article 36 TFEU, the *Cassis de Dijon* doctrine, or Article 193 TFEU? (See Chapter 4 for a refresher on these EU free movement rules.)

3 WASTE REGULATION IN UK/ENGLISH LAW

3.1 THE LANDSCAPE OF UK WASTE REGULATION: HISTORICALLY AND TODAY

In UK law historically, environmental problems caused by waste were not dealt with by bespoke waste regulation. Rather, general public health controls dealt with waste problems and, from 1947, the planning system sought to control some of the problems associated with waste accumulation and treatment through consents for use of land. It was not until the 1970s that the UK introduced two particular measures that were the foundation of modern UK and also EU waste law. First, the Deposit of Poisonous Wastes Act 1972 set up a licensing system for the disposal of hazardous wastes. Then Part I of the Control of Pollution Act 1974, introduced a similar system for the disposal of most non-hazardous wastes ('controlled waste'). These systems of licensing for waste disposal inspired the first EU WFD in 1975, which also focused on the disposal of waste and regulating its operation through licensing in order to minimize environmental harms. Since then, the EU has built considerably on this idea in regulatory and policy terms, as we saw in Section 2, and UK waste regulation has accordingly been largely dictated by EU developments ever since.

The next major step change in UK waste law, corresponding with the introduction of the 1991 WFD,[123] was the introduction of Part II of the Environmental Protection Act 1990 (in force in stages from 1992). Part II changed the focus of UK waste control from waste disposal to waste management, extending licensing and registration requirements to all those involved in the handling of waste, including those importing, producing, storing, transporting, trading in, recovering, or disposing of waste. A duty of care was imposed on all those involved in the waste chain (s 34, discussed in Section 3.3), so that individual handlers of waste could not exonerate themselves of responsibility by passing waste on to another without first determining that that person was an appropriate waste operator. And the administrative responsibilities for managing and regulating waste were also recast by the

---

[123] Council Directive 91/156 [1991] OJ L192/1.

EPA 1990, dividing responsibilities for waste collection, treatment, and disposal (which rest with local authorities as Waste Collection and Disposal Authorities) from those of regulating waste operations (which from 1996 have rested with the Environment Agency, and previously regional Waste Regulation Authorities).

The EPA 1990 was subsequently amended in several ways—boosting strategic waste planning for waste and waste minimization measures,[124] and repealing its waste licensing provisions, which are now covered by the Environmental Permitting (England and Wales) Regulations 2010, discussed in Section 3.2. A key provision in terms of strategic planning was section 44A, which required the Secretary of State for the Environment to prepare a National Waste Strategy for England and Wales. In combination with a planning policy relating to waste and more specialized waste plans,[125] and waste plans for the other devolved administrations, this Strategy fulfilled the WFD requirement for the UK to have a waste management plan.[126] The old section 44A requirement is now covered by the Waste (England and Wales) Regulations 2011, which requires the preparation of a waste management plan and also waste prevention programme. The current waste plan for England is the *Waste Strategy for England 2007* (WS 2007, supplemented now by the *Government Review of Waste Policy in England 2011*), which both analyses the current state of waste control in England and suggests directions for the future. Key objectives of the WS 2007 are putting more emphasis on waste prevention and re-use, exceeding landfill diversion targets for biodegradable municipal waste as well as increasing diversion of non-municipal waste from landfill, investing in infrastructure for that purpose and for managing hazardous waste, increasing recycling and energy recovery, and reducing GHG emissions from waste management. The Strategy sets targets for waste in England—to reduce the amount of waste not re-used, recycled, or composted (ideally by 45% by 2020), as well as target recycling and recovery rates for household and municipal waste (which match and go beyond those in Article 11 WFD).[127]

In implementing waste policy since the EPA 1990, there has been a range of measures introduced to seek to minimize waste and encourage its recycling—from the landfill tax (discussed further in Section 3.2), to the now defunct Landfill Allowance Trading Scheme,[128] to the recent measures requiring separate collection of materials for recycling.[129] Some of these measures implement EU waste regulation directly, whereas other legislative provisions and innovations are more generally geared towards meeting the UK's strategic waste policy goals. A final notable feature of UK waste law today is its increasingly devolved nature. Each of the devolved UK administrations has its own waste management plan, and even the core waste offences (examined in Section 3.3) have divergent aspects for Scotland. Further, the particular legislative measures adopted to implement EU legislation differ across the different UK administrations.

---

[124] By the Environment Act 1995 and Clean Neighborhoods and Environment Act 2005 in particular.

[125] National planning policy relating to waste is found in the *Planning Policy Statement 10: Planning for Sustainable Waste Management* (Office of the Deputy Prime Minister, 2005), to be replaced in due course (2013 or soon thereafter) by an integrated National Waste Management Plan for England. As for more specialized waste plans, the Waste and Emissions Trading Act 2003 requires the government to prepare a strategy for reducing the amount of biodegradable waste that goes to landfill (ss 17–20); see also the joint industry and *Government Anaerobic Digestion Strategy and Action Plan for England* (DECC and DEFRA 2011).

[126] 2008 WFD, art 28.

[127] The 2011 Waste Review adds other planned waste developments, including new voluntary responsibility deals to drive waste prevention and recycling, providing technical support to councils and business for 'recycling-on-the-go' schemes, increasing the frequency and quality of rubbish collections, scrapping the landfilling of wood waste, and scrapping bin fines and taxes while strengthening powers to deal with repeat fly-tipping offenders.

[128] Waste and Emissions Trading Act 2003; The Landfill Allowance and Trading Scheme (England) Regulations 2004 SI 2004/3212 (and subsequent amending regulations).

[129] The Waste (England and Wales) (Amendment) Regulations 2012 SI 2012/1889.

3.2 IMPLEMENTING EU WASTE LAW IN UK LAW

In light of the history of UK waste regulation, UK devolution, and the depth and breadth of EU waste regulation, it is unsurprising that the implementation of EU waste law presents a fragmented and complex legal map of English and UK law.[130] Thus, the WFD itself is implemented in England and Wales through at least the following measures: aspects of the EPA 1990 (as amended); the Environmental Permitting (England and Wales) Regulations 2010 (EPRs), Schedule 9 (discussed further here); and the Waste (England and Wales) Regulations 2011.[131] The EPRs in particular are a key means for implementing EU waste licensing controls, and they also implement the Landfill Directive (in Schedule 10).[132] The hazardous waste aspects of the WFD are implemented through the Hazardous Waste (England and Wales) Regulations 2005 (as amended).[133] Beyond this, the EU producer responsibility schemes are implemented throughout the UK by the Producer Responsibility Obligations (Packaging Waste) Regulations 2007 (as amended),[134] the End-of-Life Vehicles (Producer Responsibility) Regulations 2005,[135] and the Waste Electrical and Electronic Equipment Regulations 2006.[136] And the Waste Shipments Regulation is implemented through the United Kingdom Transfrontier Shipment of Waste Regulations 2007.[137] On top of these legislative measures, DEFRA and the Environment Agency issue a range of guidance documents on the implementation of EU law. Thus, there is guidance on the definition of waste (as discussed in Section 1.3), on the application of the waste hierarchy,[138] and a number of further guidance documents relating to the 2008 WFD are planned.[139] The Environment Agency's end-of-waste 'quality protocols' are a good example of detailed guidance documents filling in the gaps of ambiguous EU law to show how this aspect of the definition of waste is implemented in English law (see Section 1.3).

The remainder of this section highlights three aspects of EU waste law implementation that are particularly notable. This is not an exhaustive analysis but it gives a sense of the kinds of issues that national courts and regulators need to deal with in interpreting and applying EU waste obligations, as implemented through UK or English law.

Permitting for waste—the integrated administration of pollution control

The primary mechanism for controlling waste in this jurisdiction is through a system of licences or permits. The basic permitting obligations derive from EU law, and they are implemented in English and Welsh law through two statutory mechanisms: the Environmental Permitting (England and Wales) Regulations 2010 (EPRs), and Part II of the Environmental Protect Act 1990 (EPA). These

---

[130] For a detailed account of EU waste law implementation, see Pocklington (n 3) ch 5.

[131] SI 2011/988.

[132] Repealing the former Landfill (England and Wales) Regulations 2002 SI 2002/1559.

[133] SI 2005/894.

[134] SI 2007/871.

[135] SI 2005/263.

[136] SI 2006/3289. The WEEE Directive is also partly implemented through the EPRs, and its new 2012 version is likely to require new transposing legislation.

[137] SI 2007/1711. Although the WSR, as an EU Regulation, does not need independent implementation in the UK, these UK-wide Regulations also serve to implement international waste shipment controls. The *UK Plan for Shipments of Waste* is also part of this implementation—a legally binding statutory policy document issued by DEFRA and the devolved administration governments that, amongst other things, bans all shipments of waste to and from the UK for disposal, save in enumerated exceptional circumstances.

[138] DEFRA published guidance for English businesses on the waste hierarchy in 2011, which was already under review in 2012, with a revised guidance document expected after consultation in 2012–13.

[139] See <http://www.defra.gov.uk/environment/waste/legislation/eu-framework-directive> accessed 6 February 2013.

two statutory schemes establish various waste offences for failing to hold and breaching required waste permits, and they overlap to some extent, although the EPA regime goes further than enforcing permitting requirements and is considered in detail in Section 3.3. The EPRs set out the scheme under which waste permits can be obtained and the conditions on which they can be issued.[140] A comprehensive account of this permitting scheme, which is administratively streamlined with other permitting regimes in England and Wales, is set out in Section 3 of the Introduction to Part IV. This section highlights particular features of the EPR regime that are specific to waste law.

The basic requirement to obtain a permit under the EPRs is found in regulation 12(1):

> A person must not, except under and to the extent authorised by an environmental permit—
>
> (a) operate a regulated facility [...]

A regulated facility is defined in regulation 8 to include a 'waste operation', which regulation 2 defines as the 'disposal or recovery of waste'. Note that paragraph 3 of Schedule 2 sets out those waste operations that are exempt from EPR permitting obligations (as allowed under Articles 24 and 25 of the 2008 WFD):[141]

> 3.—(1) For the purpose of the definition of 'exempt waste operation', the requirements are—
>
> (a) that a waste operation—
>
>   (i) falls within a *description in Part 1 of Schedule 3*, and
>
>   (ii) satisfies the general and specific conditions specified in Part 1 of that Schedule in relation to the description;
>
> (b) subject to sub-paragraph (2) and paragraph 9(10) of this Schedule—
>
>   (i) that the waste operation is registered, and
>
>   (ii) an establishment or undertaking is registered in relation to it; and
>
> (c) that the *type and quantity of waste submitted to the waste operation, and the method of disposal or recovery, are consistent with the need to attain the objectives mentioned in Article 4(1) of the Waste Framework Directive.*

Part 1 of Schedule 3 then sets out in considerable detail the types of waste uses, treatments, and disposal and storage operations that count as 'exempt waste operations'. As to the requirement in paragraph 3(1)(c), the Court of Appeal confirmed in *O'Grady Plant and Haulage Ltd v Tower Hamlets LBC* that any exemption does not exempt an operator from the basic environmental objectives of the 2008 WFD.[142]

For those waste operations that do in fact require a permit, Schedule 9 then includes detailed provisions on how waste operations are to be licensed under the EPRs, in a way that incorporates the requirements of the 2008 WFD. Thus, in exercising its permitting functions under the EPRs, the Environment Agency must do so to implement Article 13 WFD, to ensure that the waste hierarchy in Article 4 WFD is applied to the generation and treatment of waste by a waste operation, and to ensure that the WFD's Article 23 permitting requirements are met (Schedule 9(4)).

---

[140] This was formerly provided for by Part II EPA 1990 and the Waste Management Licensing Regulations 1994.

[141] See Section 2.3.

[142] [2011] EWCA Crim 1339; [2011] Env LR 30 (note that this case related to an equivalent exemption regulation in the former Waste Management Licensing Regulations).

Recall that failure to hold or comply with a required permit as a waste operator is a criminal offence, as regulation 38 provides:

(1) It is an offence for a person to—

    (a) contravene regulation 12(1); or

    (b) knowingly cause or knowingly permit the contravention of regulation 12(1)(a).

(2) It is an offence for a person to fail to comply with or to contravene an environmental permit condition.

The EPRs also cover the permitting of landfill and waste incineration operations, with detailed provisions set out in Schedules 10 and 13. Overlapping permitting requirements under the EPRs are dealt with by regulation 8(4).

Criminalizing EU waste obligations in national law

This discrete aspect of implementing EU waste law picks up on the themes and analysis in Chapter 8, and explores further the contentious issue of how EU law norms can shape national criminal law. Waste law is one of the areas of English and UK national law in which criminal offences are used prevalently—waste offences support the EPR licensing regime and also exist as a separate regime beyond EU law implementation, as examined in Section 3.3. However, the proper extent of EU law competence becomes contentious when criminal offences are directed by EU legislation.[143] This issue is explored through an illustrative case here—*R v KV*—which is a challenge to the breadth of EU waste shipment obligations as transposed by UK regulations, the breach of which gives rise to criminal sanctions. The case concerned the lawfulness of regulation 23 of the United Kingdom Transfrontier Shipment of Waste Regulations 2007, which provide that a person commits an offence if, in breach of the EU Waste Shipments Regulation, he or she transports specified waste destined for recovery in a country not sanctioned to receive it under international law. A ground of the challenge concerned the proportionality of the strict liability nature of this offence considering the potential breadth of its application to potential 'persons' involved in transporting waste (for example, arrangers, freight forwarders, persons who transport the waste to port for export, the operator of any port facility, shipping company, and so on).

R v KV
[2011] EWCA Crim 2342 paras 40–41 (Court of Appeal)

40. In general there is no issue of proportionality under EU law with respect to strict liability offences [...] The defendants point out that there are none of the standard defences in the UK Regulations to the commission of an offence under regulation 23, which one would expect if regulation 23 was a strict liability offence: cf. Environmental Protection Act 1990, s. 33(7) [...]

41. [...] Assuming that this is an offence involving strict liability, it does not, in our judgment, fail for disproportionality for that reason. Sentence in a court in England or Wales is at large and discretionary; there is ample power in the court to avoid imprisonment, or indeed serious punishment, if a defendant has genuinely offended entirely without fault. The theoretical possibility of a transporter of waste being duped into transporting it without any means of knowing he is doing so would exist also if the offence

---

[143] As Case C-176/03 *Commission v Council (Environmental Crime)* [2005] 3 CMLR 20 decided, EU law can direct that criminal sanctions are required to make EU environmental law effective, but substantive interference with national criminal justice systems is beyond EU competence.

were limited in the way contended for by the defendants to physical crossing of the last Member State boundary. For both environmental and public health reasons, the handling of waste is very closely managed under EU Regulation 1013/2006 and [relevant] international instruments [...] That involves imposing considerable duties of supervision and enquiry on those who handle such material.

The legal detail of the transboundary waste shipment regime involved in this case is less important than the balance struck by the courts in maintaining the strict liability of EU waste shipment offences but taking advantage of the flexible criminal justice procedures of the English courts.

Landfill tax

The UK landfill tax is a measure that partly implements the 2008 WFD's polluter pays principle in Article 14(1)—'the costs of waste management shall be borne by the original waste producer or by the current or previous waste holders'. But it goes further than requiring waste holders to bear the costs of waste management, since the tax is not correlated with the direct costs of landfill management and the revenue raised goes to the UK treasury rather than to landfill operators. The tax is charged in addition to waste disposal costs that are also included in landfill gate fees. While the tax might be understood as meeting the broader social costs (externalities) associated with landfilling waste, the landfill tax is really an economic instrument to incentivize the prevention of waste, or at least to promote its recovery over disposal. Thus, the UK landfill tax is a measure that implements the WFD waste hierarchy (Article 4) and also seeks to meet the landfill diversion targets in the Landfill Directive. It is also a measure that assists in meeting the UK government's carbon budgets (and thus EU and international emission reduction targets),[144] since landfills are a significant source of GHG emissions.

The landfill tax was established by Part III of the Finance Act 1996. The tax is levied at two rates—for 'active' waste and for inactive or inert waste, with the latter charged at a lower rate. Rates also increase annually in accordance with a 'landfill tax escalator', which has been revised upwards in the last decade. Thus, while the government in 2002 planned to escalate the rate by £3 per tonne each year to reach a rate of £35 per tonne, by 2009 the rate for active waste was at £40 per tonne and the escalator had increased to £8 per tonne per year. The rate in the tax year 2012/13 is £64 per tonne and the government's current goal is to reach a rate of £80 per tonne in the tax year 2014/15, which will not be reduced in future years.[145] The rate for inert waste has been frozen at £2.50 per tonne since 2008. Those disposing of waste at landfill can get some tax relief by contributing to approved environmental bodies under the Landfill Communities Fund, which funds environmental projects. Overall, the landfill tax has become a significant cost to business as well as to local authorities, and is now the primary financial driver for reducing landfill activity.

In terms of its legal mechanism, the landfill charge itself is imposed by section 40 of the Finance Act 1996, set out here along with subsequent sections that explain key terms.

40. Charge to tax

(1) Tax shall be charged on a taxable disposal.

(2) A disposal is a taxable disposal if—

    (a) it is a disposal of material *as waste*,

    (b) it is made by way of landfill,

---

[144] See Section 3.4 of Chapter 15.   [145] HM Treasury, Budget 2010.

(c) it is made at a landfill site, and

(d) it is made on or after 1st October 1996.

(3) For this purpose a disposal is made at a landfill site if the land on or under which it is made constitutes or falls within land which is a landfill site at the time of the disposal.

[...]

64. Disposal of material as waste

(1) A disposal of material is a disposal of it as waste if the person making the disposal does so with the intention of discarding the material.

(2) The fact that the person making the disposal or any other person could benefit from or make use of the material is irrelevant.

(3) Where a person makes a disposal on behalf of another person, for the purposes of subsections (1) and (2) above the person on whose behalf the disposal is made shall be treated as making the disposal.

[...]

65. Disposal by way of landfill

(1) There is a disposal of material by way of landfill if—

(a) it is deposited on the surface of land or on a structure set into the surface, or

(b) it is deposited under the surface of land.

(2) Subsection (1) above applies whether or not the material is placed in a container before it is deposited.

(3) Subsection (1)(b) above applies whether the material—

(a) is covered with earth after it is deposited, or

(b) is deposited in a cavity (such as a cavern or mine)

Various challenges to levying of the ever-increasing landfill tax have been brought in the courts, which have involved the construction of these statutory provisions, including revisiting legal controversies over the definition of waste, as implicated by the provisions. In *Commissioners of Customs & Excise v Parkwood*, the Court of Appeal considered the construction of s 40 in light of a case where a landfill operator had purchased recycled waste material for use at its landfill site for road-making and landscaping purposes. The landfill operator, Parkwood, was assessed to landfill tax on the recycled material 'deposited' on its site. Parkwood successfully challenged this assessment.

Commissioners of Customs & Excise v Parkwood Landfill Ltd
[2002] EWCA Civ 1707 paras 21–23 (Aldous LJ)

21. The crux of the dispute between the parties does not turn upon construction of the word 'disposal'. It depends upon what is a taxable disposal. Is it a disposal made at one time?

22. I am of the view that the natural meaning of s 40(2) requires a disposal which is a taxable disposal to satisfy the conditions in sub-ss (a), (b), (c) and (d) at the same time. Those subsections use the word 'it' to refer back to the 'disposal' which suggests that the disposal has to be made at a landfill site by way of landfill and also to be a disposal of material as waste.

23. The tax is a landfill tax, not a landfill and recycling tax. The tax is to be paid when waste material is disposed by way of landfill in a landfill site: not on waste material (eg fines) which has been recycled (eg into blocks) which may be used in a landfill site (eg to build a wall or hard standing). The disposal referred to in s 40(2) is a particular disposal.

As a result, Parkwood was not liable to pay landfill tax on the recycled material used at its site, which had relevantly ceased to be waste through a recycling operation prior to its use by Parkwood.[146] This reasoning and outcome were supported in the subsequent case of *Commissioners for HMRC v Waste Recycling Group (WRG)*, in which it was a case of *re-use* of inert waste materials by a landfill site operator for covering over active waste (as it was required to do as under its landfill licences to prevent waste being blown away or creating unpleasant smells) and for road-building on site. WRG had received the relevant inert waste, and obtained title to it, through a number of avenues, sometimes directly at the landfill site, and in other cases at transfer stations and 'amenity sites' that it operated to receive waste from local authorities and the public (for sorting and distributing waste to either recycling or landfill). In some cases, WRG paid for the inert material, in other cases it was paid to receive it, and in other cases again it received or made no payment. The issue was whether WRG was liable to pay landfill tax on the inert materials that it used for necessary functions on its landfill sites.

Commissioners for HMRC v Waste Recycling Group
[2008] EWCA Civ 849 paras 33–36 (The Chancellor of the High Court)

33. [I]t is clear that, assuming there to have been a disposal at all, the disposal relevant for the purposes of s.40(2)(a) was made by WRG on its own behalf. So the question posed by s.64(1) is whether WRG then intended to discard the materials. The word 'discard' appears to me to be used in its ordinary meaning of 'cast aside', 'reject' or 'abandon' and does not comprehend the retention and use of the material for the purposes of the owner of it. I agree with counsel for WRG that s.64(2) does not apply in such circumstances because there is, at the relevant time, either no disposal or no disposal with the intention of discarding the material.

34. It follows from this conclusion that the relevant intention may well not be that of the original producer of the materials. There is no principle that material once labelled as 'waste' is always 'waste' just because the original producer of it threw it away. That is not the relevant time at which the satisfaction of the conditions imposed by s.40(2) is to be considered. Recycling may indicate a change in the relevant intention but is not an essential prerequisite; re-use by the owner of the material for the time being may do likewise. Thus although the passing of title is not conclusive, it is, in my view, of greater relevance than [the Tribunal and court below] were prepared to attribute to it.

35. It may be that the economic circumstances surrounding the acquisition of the materials in question by the ultimate disposer of them will cast light on his intention at the relevant time. They cannot, as I see it, affect the decision on this appeal because the use of the relevant materials by WRG is clear and such use is conclusive of its intention at the relevant time by whatever means and on whatever terms WRG acquired them.

36. In my view, the materials used by WRG for daily cover and building roads were not the subject matter of a taxable disposal as defined in s.40(2).

---

[146] Cf *Commissioners of Customs & Excise v Darfish Ltd* [2000] All ER (D) 361.

The reasoning in this case revisits the meaning of 'discard' and demonstrates that the definition of waste, in its application, can manifest in a variety of regulatory and statutory contexts, which will affect its meaning (here the timing of the discarding was critical) and thus whether there is waste for the purposes of the particular regulatory scheme involved. This follows the approach of Carnwath J in *OSS*,[147] where he adopted a common sense approach of looking beyond the initial act of discarding to consider the regulatory purpose at the point that the legal classification as waste fell to be determined. The result in *WRG* also echoes the reasoning in *Inglenorth*, also examined in Section 1.3, in that it seeks to exempt from waste material that is being put to productive use, even if initially discarded, thus furthering the waste prevention aim of EU waste law. But consider again the qualified reasoning in *R v W*,[148] where it was held that 'having become waste [material] remains waste unless something happens to alter that'. Is this a justified approach in the context of the landfill tax? Or does *WRG* show that the legal analysis as to waste classification is more nuanced and differently focused in this regulatory context?

3.3 WITHIN AND BEYOND EU LAW: UK WASTE OFFENCES AND CIVIL SANCTIONS

Waste offences

Since the introduction of the EPA 1990, there has been a suite of four offences that form the backbone of the UK legal regime for prosecuting waste offences, which range from fly-tipping to any form of mishandling of waste. Along with ex-section 85 of the Water Resources Act 1991 (now regulations 12(1)(b) and 38 EPRs), these are the most litigated offences in the UK courts dealing with environmental crime. However, unlike the former section 85 water pollution offence, these EPA waste offences have not been repealed with the introduction of the EPRs (and their newly fashioned criminal offences relating to pollution). As a result, we are left with a set of EPA offences that overlap with the EPRs offences for failing to obtain or breaching a waste operation licence, but also criminalize a wider range of actions relating to waste. The extent of serious waste crime in the UK should not be underestimated —it is largely financially motivated in light of the costs of treating and dealing with waste lawfully (particularly in light of the landfill tax), and the Environment Agency devotes considerable resources to investigating and prosecuting waste crime.[149]

Environmental Protection Act 1990, sections 33–34 (England and Wales version)

33 Prohibition on unauthorised or harmful deposit, treatment or disposal etc. of waste

(1) [A] person shall not—

    (a) deposit controlled waste or extractive waste, or knowingly cause or knowingly permit controlled waste or extractive waste to be deposited in or on any land unless an environmental permit authorising the deposit is in force and the deposit is in accordance with the permit;

---

[147] See Section 1.3.
[148] Ibid.
[149] Local authorities prosecute less serious waste crime, and note that there are more minor litter offences in pt IV EPA, as well as offences relating to the collection of waste in ss 46–47, which local authorities are also responsible for prosecuting.

(b) submit controlled waste, or knowingly cause or knowingly permit controlled waste to be submitted, to any listed operation[150] (other than an operation within subsection (1)(a)) that—

(i) is carried out in or on any land, or by means of any mobile plant, and

(ii) is not carried out under and in accordance with an environmental permit.

(c) treat, keep or dispose of controlled waste or extractive waste in a manner likely to cause pollution of the environment or harm to human health.

[...]

34 Duty of care etc. as respects waste

(1) [I]t shall be the duty of any person who imports, produces, carries, keeps, treats or disposes of controlled waste or, as a dealer or broker, has control of such waste, to take all such measures applicable to him in that capacity as are reasonable in the circumstances—

(a) to prevent any contravention by any other person of section 33 above;

(aa) to prevent any contravention by any other person of regulation 12 the Environmental Permitting Regulations or of a condition of a permit granted under those Regulations;

(b) to prevent the escape of the waste from his control or that of any other person; and

(c) on the transfer of the waste, to secure—

(i) that the transfer is only to an authorised person or to a person for authorised transport purposes; and

(ii) that there is transferred such a written description of the waste as will enable other persons to avoid a contravention of that section or regulation 12 of the Environmental Permitting Regulations or any condition of an environmental permit and to comply with the duty under this subsection as respects the escape of waste.

There are some exceptions to these offences—no waste offence under section 33(1)(a) or (b) will be committed in relation to exempt waste operations or household waste that is kept, treated, or disposed of within the curtilage of a domestic property.[151]

Meaning of deposit

Whilst early case law provided that a 'deposit' in section 33(1)(a) meant the act of leaving waste in its final place of disposal,[152] in *Thames Waste Management Limited v Surrey County Council*, the Court of Appeal gave deposit a broader and more nuanced construction, considerably widening the potential application this offence.[153] On the facts, a prosecution under section 33(1)(a) was brought in relation to a pile of waste that was left uncovered on a waste disposal site over a bank holiday weekend, causing strong odours in the surrounding residential area. A condition of the defendant's waste disposal licence was that any deposit of waste should be covered over. The defendant argued that the meaning of deposit could not be stretched to cover this situation and that the charge should properly have been brought as one of breaching a waste licence condition (which it also denied). Rose LJ held that the case was properly brought under section 33(1)(a), since this offence overlapped with that of breaching a licence (an offence

---

[150] Defined in s 33(13) as an operation listed in Annex I or II of the 2008 WFD.

[151] EPA, ss 33(1A), (2).

[152] *Leigh Land Reclamation Ltd v Walsall Metropolitan BC* (1991) 155 JP 547.

[153] *Thames Waste Management Limited v Surrey County Council* [1997] Env LR 148.

now brought under the EPRs and which can be charged simultaneously), and that 'the word "deposit" takes its flavour from its context'. In this case, it was significant that it was 'inherent [...] that "waste had been deposited otherwise than in accordance with the licence"'. Overall,[154]

> although clearly 'deposit' is a putting down, it has also [...] to be construed, unless the context otherwise required, in a broad sense. The context in the present case does not, in my judgment, otherwise require. A continuing state of affairs is in my judgment capable of being embraced within the meaning of the word 'deposit'.

Whilst deposit generally has a broad meaning and can relate to ongoing activities throughout waste management processes, the context can also in some cases narrow the meaning of deposit, along the lines suggested by Rose LJ in *Thames Management*. In *Milton Keynes DC v Fuller*,[155] victims of fly-tipping on their land who were forced to move waste in order to gain access to their property had not committed a waste offence by depositing waste. The Court found that, in determining whether there is an unlawful deposit, 'each case has to be decided on the particular facts that are raised and found', leaving room for an offence still to be found in some cases where a defendant moves illegally deposited waste off their land.

Knowledge and causation

A significant feature of these offences is that they are all strict liability offences except where knowledge is required—where persons *knowingly cause* or *knowingly permit* a deposit of waste or its submission to a treatment operation without a permit.[156] However, an element of strictness has still been imported into these knowledge requirements, which have been broadly construed by the courts. Thus, knowledge only of the relevant deposit is required (not of breach of a permit condition),[157] and constructive knowledge is enough. Knowledge can be inferred from the circumstances if a deposit of waste is obvious. This might even be inferred in circumstances where the defendant simply operated a licensed waste disposal site, inviting waste deposits to be made in or on its land, with no further evidence of knowledge as to a particular deposit or permit breach.[158] Bell, McGillivray and Pedersen suggest that this effectively makes landfill operators strictly liable for breaches of environmental permit conditions.[159]

As for the requirement of causation, this is also broadly construed, with reasoning in sub-sections 33(1)(a) and (b) cases relying on water pollution cases and their easily satisfied 'strict liability' form of causation. Assistance can thus been derived from those water pollution cases, examined in detail in Chapter 14,[160] whilst remembering that this is still a different statutory context, so that arguments for different interpretations on causation might be made.

General pollution offence

Unlike the offences under sub-sections 33(1)(a) and (b), under which liability can be avoided if an environmental permit sanctions the action in question, sub-section 33(1)(c) covers a wider range of

---

[154] Ibid, 155–56.
[155] *Milton Keynes DC v Fuller* [2011] Env LR 31.
[156] Note that s 33(5) EPA provides that where controlled waste is carried in and deposited from a motor vehicle, the person who controls the use of the vehicle shall, for the purposes of s 33(1)(a), be treated as knowingly causing the waste to be deposited whether or not he or she gave any instructions for this to be done.
[157] *Shanks & McEwan (Teeside) Ltd v Environment Agency* [1999] QB 333, 342.
[158] Ibid, 346.
[159] Stuart Bell, Donald McGillivray, and Ole Pedersen, *Environmental Law* (8th edn, OUP 2013), 697.
[160] See Section 3.3 of Chapter 14.

situations—from fly-tipping through to any handling of waste at all that is likely to give rise to environmental pollution or harm to human health. Pollution of the environment is defined broadly in section 29(3) as:

> pollution of the environment due to the release or escape (into any environmental medium) from—
>
> (a) the land on which controlled waste or extractive waste is treated,
>
> (b) the land on which controlled waste or extractive waste is kept,
>
> (c) the land in or on which controlled waste or extractive waste is deposited,
>
> (d) fixed plant by means of which controlled waste or extractive waste is treated, kept or disposed of,
>
> of substances or articles constituting or resulting from the waste and capable (by reason of the quantity or concentrations involved) of causing harm to man or any other living organisms supported by the environment.

This is a very useful catch-all provision for regulators but it also means that virtually any harm done to the environment by waste can be prosecuted.

Defences

There are two defences in section 33(7)—one relating to acts done in an emergency to avoid danger to human health, and one exonerating a defendant where they have acted with due diligence. The framing of the emergency defence—requiring the taking of all steps as were reasonably practicable for minimizing pollution and harm and informing details of the incident to the Environment Agency as soon as practicable—corresponds to the defence also available for water pollution offences, and so case law relating to the latter should also be instructive here.[161] The due diligence defence has been construed by the courts to require a high level of diligence—routine waste collection practices and relying on assurances of others as to the holding of required permits is not enough.[162] Specified inquiries and inspections of individual waste loads must be made.

Section 34 duty of care

This 'duty of care' is not to be confused with that in tort law—it is a regulatory crime provision that places an obligation on all operators in the waste chain to check that waste controls are being complied with in the treatment, transport, import, and storage of waste. It adds another layer of waste management control to ensure that holders of waste cannot turn a blind eye to rogue or delinquent operators to whom they might transfer, or from whom they might receive, waste.[163] The duty reinforces the waste permitting system, as well as the waste offences in section 33(1). It also requires holders of waste to prevent its 'escape' (whether the waste is in their control or under the control of another), and to transfer waste only with a sufficiently detailed written description to enable others to avoid breaching the duty of care. The one limit on these requirements is that those in control of waste are only required 'to take all such measures […] as are reasonable in the circumstances', but considering the extent of measures required under the due diligence defence in section 33(7), what is 'reasonable' in the circumstances is relatively onerous. An example of a prosecution brought under section 34 is the *Inglenorth* case extracted in Section 1.3, which involved proceedings brought against carriers of waste between

---

[161] See Section 3.3 of Chapter 14.

[162] *Durham County Council v Peter Connors Industrial Services* [1993] Env LR 197; *Environment Agency v Short* [1998] Env LR 300.

[163] Again there is an exception for occupiers of domestic properties in relation to household waste produced on the property, although they have a duty to transfer household waste to authorized persons: ss 34(2), (2A).

two garden centre sites. The case ultimately turned on the definition of waste, because there can be no offence if there is no waste. As for the definition of an 'escape' of waste, *Gateway Professional Services v Kingston Upon Hull CC* held that there is a distinction between a deliberate dumping of waste and an escape—the former needs to be prosecuted under sub-section 33(1)(a).[164]

Remedies

The sanctions for breaches of these criminal offences include criminal sanctions but also a range of other remedies. In terms on criminal sanctions, section 33(8) provides that the maximum penalty for a breach of section 33(1) in cases of summary conviction is twelve months imprisonment or a £50,000 fine or both, or in cases of indictment, five years' imprisonment or an unlimited fine or both. Conviction under section 34 carries only the prospect of a fine. Magistrates and Crown courts have been criticized for handing down inadequate criminal sanctions for waste offences, in terms of deterrence and reflecting the severity of the crimes involved. However, the 2008 case of *R v Kelleher* might indicate that judicial views are changing. In this case, the Court of Appeal upheld fourteen and twenty-two month prison sentences against defendants who had committed egregious fly-tipping offences.[165] The Court observed that commercial fly-tipping was a serious problem, and that the incidents in this case had been carefully planned and had taken place over a period of time, even though no prolonged environmental harm was caused.

However, there is a range of other remedies and powers that might be employed for waste crime. Thus, under section 33B, a sentencing court can make compensation orders to cover any clean-up costs incurred by the Environment Agency, local authority, or occupier of land in removing the waste involved or reducing its environmental consequences.[166] A court can also order the forfeiture of a waste offender's vehicle if used in the commission of the waste offence (section 33C). Other judicial remedies that might flow from a criminal conviction are an order of the Crown court to confiscate money made through waste crime under the Proceeds of Crime Act 2002, or a successful civil liability claim under section 73(6) EPA in relation to any property damage or personal injury caused by a deposit of controlled waste in contravention of section 33(1) (except where the person suffering the damage was wholly at fault or had voluntarily assumed the risk).

Civil sanctions for waste obligations

Beyond the section 33 and 34 EPA waste offences, it should be noted that England and Wales have introduced a regime of flexible civil sanctions for other waste offences. This regime was established by the Regulatory Enforcement and Sanctions Act 2008 (RESA), and is discussed in more detail in Chapter 8. RESA civil sanctions provide an alternative to criminal prosecution of offences, and are imposed by the regulator to allow more flexible enforcement, with the sanctions available ranging from fixed and variable monetary penalties to enforcement undertakings and various notices to cease activities and restore harm.[167] In 2012–13, civil sanctions had been made available for a number of waste offences, including those under the Packaging Waste Regulations 2007, the Hazardous Waste Regulations 2005, and the Transfrontier Shipment of Waste Regulations 2007. Enforcement undertakings offered and accepted in relation to breaches of the Packaging Waste Regulations have been particularly popular, with delinquent parties giving undertakings to the Environment Agency to do things ranging from

---

[164] *Gateway Professional Services v Kingston Upon Hull CC* [2004] Env LR 42.

[165] *R v Kelleher* [2008] EWCA Crim 3055.

[166] See s 59 EPA for the powers of the Environment Agency and local authorities to require the clean-up of waste on land.

[167] Section 34A EPA also allows fixed penalty notices to be issued for certain s 34 offences, as an alternative to prosecution.

making donations to environmental charities to financing projects for minimizing food and packaging waste. (You might consider the social and political consequences of such pledged donations, which are procured and approved by an independent government agency.) The Environment Agency will only accept such undertakings, in lieu of prosecution, if satisfied that the prospective defendant has also taken sufficient action to ensure the offending conduct does not recur.

3.4 INTERACTION BETWEEN WASTE REGULATION AND ENGLISH PLANNING LAW

Waste law overlaps with a number of other areas of environmental law, and with planning law in particular. Planning law has an important role to play in controlling use of land, as Chapter 18 examines, and that includes strategic siting and amenity concerns associated with environmentally sensitive land use operations such as waste management. There are two main ways in which planning law affects and controls waste management operations. First, through planning policy: there is a planning policy document, Planning Policy Statement 10,[168] which sets out national guidance for creating a network of waste management facilities in a way that supports the waste hierarchy and promotes sustainable waste management, for identifying suitable sites and for determining planning applications for waste facilities. This final aspect picks up the second way in which planning law controls waste management—by requiring planning consent.

Paragraph 3(1) of Schedule 9 of the Environmental Permitting Regulations 2010 provides that no environmental permit should be given for a waste operation under the EPRs if use of the site requires planning permission (or development consent as a major infrastructure project under the Planning Act 2008) and no such consent is in force. Thus, a waste management facility cannot operate without planning permission, where this is required. And in many cases it will be required. Section 55(3)(b) of the Town and Country Planning Act 1990 provides that the deposit of refuse or waste materials on land involves a material change in its use (which requires planning permission) when the area of the deposit is extended or its height is extended beyond the level of adjacent land. Further, the building of any structure or plant for waste treatment purposes (including waste recovery and processing as well as deposit and disposal) can amount to 'development' that requires planning permission, and some waste management practices may also amount to a material change in the use of land.

As for considerations that planning authorities may take into consideration when deciding development applications and/or devising appropriate planning conditions, a (practically difficult) line needs to be drawn between those considerations that are related to planning and amenity, and those that concern pollution control more broadly. The latter function is to be carried by the regulatory authority (Environment Agency or local authority) that is responsible for deciding and issuing environmental permits under the EPRs. However, a planning authority should not delegate all environmental and pollution control responsibility to the environmental permitting authorities; it still has an important role to play in deciding how particular parcels of land are to be used within the context of their surroundings and local community. This is made clear by paragraph 122 of the National Planning Policy Framework (NPPF) extracted in Chapter 18. That is the general principle but following it in individual cases can be complicated, as cases such as *Harrison v Secretary for Communities and Local Government and Cheshire West and Chester Council* demonstrate.[169] A further issue in these planning

---

[168] See n 125. Note that this is to be replaced by an integrated National Waste Management Plan for England in 2013 or soon thereafter.

[169] [2009] EWHC 3382 (note that the wording of Planning Policy Statement 23 [10]—the precursor to NPPF [122]—was slightly different in this case). See Sections 5.3 and 5.5 of Chapter 18.

cases is whether EU waste policy should carry extra weight in deciding whether and how to approve waste management-related applications. In *Thornby Farms v Daventry DC*, the Court of Appeal struggled to determine how Article 13 (ex-Article 4) of the WFD should be taken into consideration in the planning decision-making process, considering that it is expressed in mandatory terms. Rather than finding that it carried more weight than other material considerations (as the court below had held)[170], the Court of Appeal held that there may be cases in which the Article 13 obligation could be breached by a planning decision-maker if there is a plain and flagrant disregard for its environmental protection objective.[171] Reflecting the themes covered in Chapter 11, this is an interesting case where the line between law and policy is challenged through the legalizing of policy concerns at the EU level.[172]

FURTHER READING AND QUESTIONS

1. Do you think that the legislative picture of waste law in the UK is coherent and easy to follow? If not, what consequences do you think this might have?

2. Read waste review and government documents on the implementation of the *National Waste Strategy—Government Review of Waste Policy in England 2011* (DEFRA, 2011) and other waste review documents at http://www.defra.gov.uk/environment/waste/review/. What do these tell you about the waste pollution problem in England today?

3. Do the waste offences in sections 33 and 34 of the Environmental Protection Act 1990 impose strict liability? Do these offences perform an important function in environmental law beyond the offences relating to waste operations now contained in the Environmental Permitting Regulations 2010?

4. Do you think that the accidental escape of sewage from the sewerage network amounts to a 'deposit' of waste? This legal question is one of several that had to be navigated in the *Thames Water Utilities* litigation—see *R (on the application of Thames Water Utilities Ltd) v Bromley Magistrates' Court)* [2009] Env LR 13, and Section 1.3.

5. For a good example of the difficult interaction of planning law and waste regulation, revisit the *R v W* case in Section 1.3—consider the extra facts set out in paragraphs 4–5 of the judgment. How are planning and pollution control regimes working together in this case? Are they working well?

6. For the overlap of waste regulation with contaminated land powers and water pollution control, see Stuart Bell, Donald McGillivray, and Ole Pedersen, *Environmental Law* (8th edn, OUP 2013) 710–11.

---

4 CONCLUSION

This chapter has considered the extensive body of EU and UK waste law that relates to waste. A considerable part of the chapter was devoted to the definition of waste, since this is a matter of complex legal construction that both reflects the deep tensions in waste policy and acts as a trigger for this body of environmental law to be engaged. Once material is classified as waste, then it and the operations to which it is subject (and the land on which such operations take place) will then be subject to a range

---

[170] *R (Murray) v Derbyshire CC* [2002] Env LR 28. See also *R v Bolton MBC; ex p Kirkman* [1998] Env LR 719 on this issue.

[171] *Thornby Farms v Daventry DC* [2002] EWCA Civ 31, para 53.

[172] See Section 1.4 of Chapter 11.

of controls, through the environmental permitting system, the criminal justice system, and also the planning system. Current waste statistics in the UK suggest that improvements have been made by this body of law and the concerted and binding EU and UK policy that sits behind it, but that there is still some way to go in making individuals and businesses aware of the waste that they generate and to change their behaviours to minimize the production of waste and its environmentally harmful nature. One future direction for the regulation of waste management that seems likely is the increasing control of waste materials according to individual waste streams—this more targeted approach to waste regulation assists in reducing ambiguity around the definition of waste and is encouraged by the life-cycle approach of EU waste policy that qualifies the waste hierarchy in Article 4 of the 2008 WFD. Another likely future direction is an increasing emphasis on product design and producer responsibility, targeting problems of waste at their very source—the point at which the materials that eventually become waste are made. In encouraging and requiring manufacturers to extend the usable lives of their products and to remove environmentally harmful elements for when they become waste, the EU and UK may not be heading to a 'zero-waste' society but there is certainly a strong regulatory focus on waste prevention. The more that environmental policy heads down this route, waste law is left with something of a paradox as to its existence: if the ultimate goal of waste law is that waste does not exist, this also limits the very application of waste law itself.

17

INTEGRATED POLLUTION CONTROL

This Chapter considers a regime of pollution control different from those discussed in Chapters 14, 15, and 16. Rather than focusing on discrete environmental media (water, land, or air), or an individual source of pollution (e.g. waste), integrated pollution control attempts to alter pollution law quite radically by moving away from the idea that the natural environment consists of distinct environmental media and separate pollution problems. This fragmented conception of the natural environment has traditionally been mirrored in media-specific environmental law, with separate legal rules being developed for the control of pollution for water, air, and land, as Chapters 14, 15, and 16 show. Bold reforms, however, in recent decades have moved away from this traditional position to view and regulate environmental problems more holistically. Overall, this chapter illustrates the point made in Chapter 1, that the act of defining 'the environment' also shapes the legal rules that seek to protect it. At the same time, the act of regulating 'the environment', in turn, serves to construct our understandings of the environment itself. A particular focus of this chapter is to interrogate the extent to which integrated forms of pollution control regulation truly reflect an integrated view of the environment, and to consider the limits of the current 'integrated' regulatory strategy for framing and conceptualizing environmental problems.

Integrated Pollution Control (IPC), as a form of environmental regulation, was developed in the EU in the early 1990s, following an early UK lead. In contrast to media-specific legal regimes, IPC takes a holistic view of the environment, which acknowledges that ecosystems draw on interconnected and interdependent elements of the living and non-living environment. A wetland, for instance, relies for its continued existence on abiotic factors, such as rocks and sunshine, as well as water and soil for the survival of its fish and birds. IPC involves setting and enforcing environmental legal standards that take this integrated nature of the environment into account. In this way, IPC shares features with Environmental Impact Assessment (EIA), discussed in Chapter 19, which aims to assess the impact of projects on all dimensions of the environment (that is, air, water, and land quality). Moreover, IPC shares with EIA an emphasis on the prevention of pollution, seeking to do more than simply mitigating the effects of pollution that has already occurred.

This chapter critically assesses the incorporation of holistic understandings of the natural environment into environmental law. First, it traces the elusive policy idea of holistic environmental regulation and decision-making and draws attention to the early emergence of ideas of integrated pollution control in Victorian environmental law in Britain. Second, the chapter maps the application of holistic understandings of the natural environment through IPC regimes in both the EU and the UK. In doing so, it also illustrates the significance of descriptive, purposive, and jurisprudential definitions of pollution control law. While it is necessary to engage with the descriptive detail of the legal IPC rules in force, it is also important to understand from a purposive perspective the policy goals that these legal rules seek to implement in practice. In addition, IPC demonstrates legal complexity when understood jurisprudentially, as explored in Section 3 of this chapter. Thus, by questioning how the technology standards on which current IPC regulation relies contribute to the development of a coherent and consistent body of environmental law, the chapter suggests that a critical analysis of IPC reveals difficulties in tying down the meaning of its legal obligations. These difficulties might be interpreted as a shift towards 'procedural' environmental governance, but they might also be indicative of a more fundamentally unsettling indeterminacy of pollution control law.

1 THE HISTORY OF IPC AS AN ENVIRONMENTAL POLICY IDEA

Contemporary IPC regimes are a reaction to fragmented and reactive forms of controlling pollution through law. As the name suggests 'integrated pollution control' (IPC) seeks to integrate what were previously fragmented systems of pollution control. Traditionally, there have been separate legal rules that regulate the pollution of water, air, and land. For instance, the first wave of EU environmental legislation developed in the 1970s and 1980s focused on specific environmental media. There were various Directives for the control of pollutants in watercourses, such as the Dangerous Substances Directive,[1] the Groundwater Directive,[2] and the Shellfish Directive.[3] Then there were Directives focused on air pollution, such as the Large Combustion Plant Directive,[4] and more specific Directives relating to particular air pollutants.[5] Alongside this, pollution on land was subject to various legal controls at the UK level,[6] as well as EU waste regulation.[7]

Moreover, it is important to remember that environmental laws are often administered by public officials within an institutional environment. Within this administrative context, a media-specific approach to environmental regulation is not surprising given that it reflects the tendency of officials to break down environmental problems into smaller chunks that are assigned to different parts of public organizations, which can marshal specialist expertise in relation to air, water, or land pollution.[8] But a media-specific approach to environmental regulation is fundamentally flawed in that it fails to recognize that, in practice, environmental media are interconnected. A media-specific approach has led not only to fragmented regulation, but also to 'end of pipe' regulation. End of pipe regulation refers to measures that control the (inevitable) pollution caused by some industrial or other environmentally harmful process, including pollution abatement technology that is installed after production process technology has been put in place. Examples of such technology include the installation of a fabric filter in a chimneystack to remove dust emissions or the operation of a water treatment plant at an installation's site in order to treat emissions into a watercourse or the public sewer. End of pipe regulation is reactive; it fails to promote cleaner production technologies; and it usually just shifts pollution from one environmental medium to another. Thus, for example, limiting dust emissions from a factory chimney through a filter (such as a fabric filter or an electric precipitator) generates a filter cake that still needs to be disposed of, probably to landfill.

By contrast, 'holism' in environmental regulation seeks to depart from a fragmented and reactive approach to controlling pollution. At its most general, it seeks to ensure that legal rules reflect the

---

[1] Directive 86/280/EEC on limit values and quality objectives for discharges of certain dangerous substances included in List 1 of the Annex to Directive 76/464/EEC [1986] OJ L181/16.

[2] Directive 80/68/EEC [1980] OJ L020/43.   [3] Directive 79/923/EEC [1979] OJ L281/47.

[4] Directive 88/609/EEC [1988] OJ L336/1.

[5] E.g. Council Directive 82/884/EEC on a limit value for lead in the air [1982] OJ L378/15.

[6] Deposit of Poisonous Wastes Act 1972; Control of Pollution Act 1974, Part 1.

[7] Council Directive 75/442/EEC on Waste [1975] OJ L194/39.

[8] Jane Holder and Maria Lee, *Environmental Protection, Law and Policy* (2nd edition, CUP 2007) 355.

physical characteristics of the natural environment that is being regulated. Legal rules should mirror 'the laws of nature', and thus they should be more effective. But it is important to recognize that attempting to create environmental law in the image of 'nature' is mediated by social factors. As discussed in Chapter 1, how we think about nature is socially constructed. There are many different ways of perceiving nature.[9] Moreover, social structures, such as the form that regulatory and regulated organizations take, will mediate how and to what extent environmental law can mirror 'nature'.

The extracts from Cullinan and Elliot suggest that the policy idea of holistic environmental governance is elusive, particularly as various commentators attribute different regulatory consequences to it. While Cullinan argues that holism in environmental governance involves questioning reliance on market mechanisms (as well as traditional legal concepts), Elliott suggests, in the context of US environmental regulation, that greater reliance on economic incentive based environmental regulation, including trading schemes, is an element of the pursuit of holistic environmental governance.

Cormac Cullinan, *Wild Law: A Manifesto for Earth Justice* (Green Books 2011) 26–27, 29, 30–31

I gradually formed a working hypothesis in my mind that the prospects of a governance system being successful could be increased by designing it in a way that took account of the attributes of what was being governed. Over time I began unconsciously to embroider this rudimentary hypothesis with scraps of ideas picked up from here and there. One such idea was the conscious recognition that the way in which most governance systems rely on economic considerations and the functioning of markets to guide human behaviour is often highly inappropriate. Making certain decisions in this way virtually guarantees that from a long-term perspective, bad or sub-optimal decisions will result. This is so even if market distortions are corrected by full cost accounting that, for example, ensures that the costs of pollution are borne by the polluter and incorporated into the prices of commodities.

[...] [R]eforming our governance systems will require us to entirely reconceptualise our *idea* of law from a biocentric or Earth-centred perspective. Reforming national legislation and entering into new international agreements will be insufficient unless these are done on the basis of a new understanding that the essential *purpose* of human governance systems should be to support people to play a mutually enhancing role within the community of life on Earth. This requires us first to recognise that at the moment the governance systems of most countries and of the international 'community' actually facilitate and legitimise the exploitation and destruction of Earth by humans. [...] [I] argue that in order to change completely the purpose of our governance systems, we must develop coherent new theories or philosophies of governance ('Earth jurisprudence') to supplant the old. This Earth jurisprudence is needed to guide the realignment of human governance systems with the fundamental principles of how the universe functions [...] Giving effect to Earth jurisprudence and bringing about systemic changes in human governance systems will also require the conscious fostering of wild law.

[...]

Wild law expresses Earth jurisprudence. It recognises and embodies the qualities of the Earth system within which it exists. As an approach it seeks both to foster passionate and intimate connections between people and nature and to deepen our connection with the wild aspect of our own natures. It tends to focus more on relationships and on the processes by which they can be strengthened, than on end-points and 'things' like property... Wild law opens spaces within which different and unconventional approaches can spring up, perhaps to flourish, perhaps to run their course and die.

[9] See further, Chapter 20.

Donald Elliott, 'Toward Ecological Law and Policy' in M Chertow and D Esty (eds) *Thinking Ecologically: The Next Generation of Environmental Policy* (Yale UP 1997) 170–71, 173–74

Most of today's environmental law violates the basic principles of ecology. Nature teaches the connectedness of all activities, but most current-generation law regulates separate pollutants with little consideration of ecosystems as a whole. The continuums of nature generally adapt gradually, but today's environmental law makes sharp distinctions between safe and unsafe, attainment versus non attainment areas, permissible versus impermissible levels of pollution.

[...]

Ordinances to control smoke, or to manage wastes, have existed in big cities like London and Chicago for hundreds of years. Although science increased public awareness of environmental pollution and the urgency for dealing with it in the 1960s, what is really distinctive about the 'environmental law' created in the United States in the 1970s and 1980s are the legal techniques used for combating pollution. [T]he existing legal system for regulating pollution in the United States consists of the following elements:

- pollutant-by-pollutant, or industry-by-industry, regulation carried out by government under federal statutes after lengthy administrative proceedings and court challenges;

- minimum standards set by administrative agencies at the federal level limiting the amount of pollution that may be put into the air, water or land;

- requirements that the states translate federal goals into facility-specific legal requirements for individual factories or other sources of pollution;

- establishment of legal rights for environmentalists and other citizen groups to sue to enforce pollution laws.

[...]

There are serious divisions and disagreements about what direction legal policies and institutions for environmental regulation should take over the long run. On the one hand, some argue that the basic premises for [environmental regulation today have been mistaken], and that we should return to a market-based system of environmental protection, perhaps through an improved system of property rights... The desire for more responsive, more efficient, and less expensive environmental law led by government is real, but the public wants better and smarter environmental regulation, not a return to the unregulated markets of the nineteenth century. At the other extreme from the market theorists are visionaries who would redraft our environmental laws from scratch in a new 'unified' or 'organic' statute.

[...] [In my view] we are not yet ready to commit ourselves to any of these sweeping reforms, but that we must adopt an 'evolutionary strategy' to environmental reform in which we continue to experiment with all of the innovative ideas—just as nature rarely commits itself to a single strategy, but maintains diversity and experimentation.

Elliott's extract highlights some themes that are also relevant in contemporary debates about holistic environmental regulation in the EU including questioning the ability of centralized political powers to set pollution control standards, the importance of 'learning' in the design of environmental regulation, and the search for 'cost-effectiveness' in the application of environmental controls. These themes are discussed further in Section 3. In order to trace the meaning of 'holistic' environmental decision-making and its manifestation and implementation through integrated pollution control, Pontin examines the historical roots of the system in the UK.

Ben Pontin, 'Integrated Pollution Control in Victorian Britain: Rethinking Progress within the History of Environmental Law' (2007) 19 (2) JEL 173, 187–89

In tracing IPC [now reflected in Part I of *Environmental Protection Act 1990* and subsequent EU-inspired reforms] back to Victorian-era legislation enacted between 1863 and 1881 addressed to the problem of chemical industry pollution, [known as the Alkali Acts, this article] challenges the modernity of this leading regulatory concept, highlighting levels of sophistication in environmental law and policy during the early stages of industrialisation which many scholars today around the world would consider inconceivable.

[...]

The earliest Alkali Act was concerned exclusively with regulating acid gas emissions to the atmosphere from a single, nascent chemical industry process (the 'Leblanc process'). However, Parliament was soon alerted to the impact of controlling atmospheric emissions on land and water, to which the pollutants were simply transferred. [Accordingly, the 1881 Act] imposed a duty on alkali works deploying the Leblanc process to use bpm [best practicable means] to control pollution to air, land and water

[...]

[However, as a form of multi-media control, the 1881 Act had a number of shortcomings.] First, multi-media control under the 1881 Act was narrow in scope: it was confined, tentatively, to Leblanc works and processes, leaving the mandate of the Alkali Inspectorate in respect of other registered works and processes to lie with air pollution alone. Second, even in respect of Leblanc processes, it is unclear whether the Inspectorate got fully to grips with its expanded responsibilities. On the contrary, the annual reports of the Inspectorate in the aftermath of the 1881 Act coming into force continued to focus on air pollution, with generally less attention to disposal of waste to land, and barely any mention of discharges to water. Third, and perhaps most fundamental, there is little evidence that the Inspectorate took a holistic view of the environment, or indeed was obliged to under the 1881 Act. The Act appears to have required application of bpm to minimise pollution of each environmental medium taken individually, rather than the present-day concern with optimal (or most practicable) allocation of pollution to the environment as a whole.

[...]

The post-Victorian era in this context brought neither progress nor even stagnation in alkali regulation; during this time, regulatory law took steps backwards, as early innovation unravelled.

Ben Pontin's analysis does not just provide an insight into the early origins of integrated pollution control in Britain, it also highlights two further key themes relevant to IPC as a legal phenomenon. First, Pontin identifies a 'constraint theory' as one model (of three) for understanding the historical development of environmental law—under this model, historical legislation and regulatory interventions establish 'a crude precedent for piecemeal and uncoordinated development of the law', which serves as a constraint on subsequent regulatory innovation. This model applies also to contemporary IPC regimes. It suggests that specific environmental laws cannot be understood in isolation, but—in defining the subject descriptively—they have to be mapped in context, taking into account how one particular environmental law, or pollution control regime, such as IPC, relates to other environmental laws, such as waste regulation or even urban planning law. Earlier environmental laws in particular can limit later environmental law. This 'constraint' model chimes with an important critique of contemporary IPC pollution control regimes. IPC regimes are held back from fully realizing their potential also because they have to fit in with existing older, media-specific environmental legal regulation. This point is further explored in Section 2.2.

Second, Pontin argues that legal regulation of the chemical industry in Britain is best understood in cyclical terms—'cycle theory' is his third model for understanding the history of environmental law, according to which the law is understood to have developed in relatively discrete cycles, with periods of innovation giving way to periods of decline. This analytical framework draws attention to a further critique of environmental law, including IPC regimes. Cyclical developments of environmental law question the idea that environmental law progresses in a rational, linear manner towards an ever more sophisticated and effective body of legal rules. More fundamentally, this highlights the significance of the socio-political contexts in which environmental law is developed for understanding why it takes the form that it does—a point raised in Chapter 2. In this way, Pontin sees the social foundations of IPC controls through an historical analysis of specific interest group politics, such as the inclination of members of the House of Lords in Victorian Britain to limit damage to the natural environment. For Pontin, changes in this political environment serve to explain the decline of IPC control during the twentieth century.

2 EU AND UK INTEGRATED POLLUTION CONTROL

The policy idea of holistic environmental regulation discussed in Section 1 has found expression in both EU and UK pollution control law in recent decades. On the back of innovative UK regulatory practice, the UK proposed an initiative for an EU-wide Directive on Integrated Pollution Prevention and Control. This led to the Commission publishing, in 1993, a formal proposal for the IPPC Directive.[10] The UK's role in instigating this legal development was remarkable given the fact that, in the 1970s and 1980s, the UK had been considered by other EU Member States as a laggard in terms of environmental protection. This was partly because of the UK's 'tall chimney stack' policy, which meant that the UK exported its air emissions to other regions, including Scandinavia,[11] and also because of its reliance on fast flowing rivers and an extensive coastline for the dispersion of water pollutants. However, as seen in Section, the UK also had an historical investment in IPC.

This section discusses the formal legal rules that constitute the regime of integrated pollution control in the EU as well as the laws that implement the EU regime in the UK. This integrated EU pollution control regime is one of significant scope, covering a wide range of mainly industrial, but also intensive, agricultural installations, and thus major polluters, albeit that it is limited to the most polluting of these institutions. In examining this wide-ranging regime of integrated industrial pollution control through a descriptive lens, this section also pursues a critical purpose. When reading through the materials presented here, you should consider the extent to which the legal rules implement the idea of 'integrated' and 'holistic' environmental decision-making.

2.1 EU INTEGRATED POLLUTION CONTROL: THE DIRECTIVE ON INDUSTRIAL EMISSIONS (2010/75/EU)

History and structure of Directive 2010/75

The EU regime for integrated control of industrial emissions started with the Integrated Pollution Prevention and Control Directive (IPPC Directive),[12] which was introduced in 1996 and twice substantially amended before being codified in January 2008 into a consolidated text (Directive 2008/1/EC).[13] The IPPC Directive was then superseded in 2010 by the current Industrial Emissions

---

[10] COM (1993) 0423.   [11] See further, Chapter 15.

[12] Council Directive 96/61/EC concerning integrated pollution prevention and control [1996] OJ L257/26.

[13] Council Directive 2008/1/EC concerning integrated pollution prevention and control [2008] OJ L24/8. All references to the former IPPC Directive are to this consolidated 2008 version, unless otherwise stated.

Directive (IED), which retains the core provisions of the IPPC Directive in its Chapter II. The basic structure of the IED, and the IPPC Directive before it, is to require large-scale industrial installations to obtain permits in order to operate. Note that, under the IED, this structure now applies to a wider range of installations than those that fell within the IPPC regime—the IED thus integrates pollution control regulation in another way, by bringing into a single Directive a number of pollution control regimes that regulate emissions from large-scale industrial installations. These include the former IPPC regime, as well as sectoral regimes controlling emissions from waste incineration, large combustion plants, and industrial processes involving solvents and titanium dioxide.[14] Emissions from these different heavy industrial activities are now all regulated in the various Chapters of the IED (Chapters II–VI), with slightly varying regimes of control for each, reflecting partly historical differences of approach in regulating these regimes. However, Chapter I contains common provisions that set up the basic permitting scheme of the Directive as well as setting out an overall objective of the Directive in Article 1:

> This Directive lays down rules on integrated prevention and control of pollution arising from industrial activities.
>
> It also lays down rules designed to prevent or, where that is not practicable, to reduce emissions into air, water and land and to prevent the generation of waste, in order to achieve a high level of protection of the environment taken as a whole.

This chapter focuses mainly on the installations that come within the scope of Chapter II of the IED—these installations are set out in Annex I,[15] and are subject to IPC regulation in its broadest sense. Thus, permits for these installations are to be issued on the basis of considering and minimizing the 'integrated' pollution effects of a relevant installation on the environment, usually through the imposition of conditions attaching to the permit that impose bespoke emission limit values on individual installations. Chapter II contains a range of regulatory features that pursue this position, which are examined in the following sub-section. The core of these regulatory features is the 'best available techniques' (BAT) standard, which is used as a basis for imposing pollution limits on installations, according to the 'best' technology available in the relevant sector. By contrast, the other IED chapters generally impose fixed numerical limits on polluting emissions for the installations that they regulate, where these emission limit values are set through technological appraisal relevant to the sector covered and also guided by the Article 1 objective already outlined.

En route to creating this wide-ranging industrial emissions pollution regime, the IPPC Directive was amended twice, as already noted, and these amendments now shape the overall structure of the IED. A first set of amendments to the initial IPPC Directive embedded public participation in the IPC regulatory process. These changes occurred mainly through the Public Participation Directive,[16] which

---

[14] The IED replaces the former IPPC Directive as well as six sectoral pollution control Directives: Directive 1999/13/EC on the limitation of emissions of volatile organic compounds due to the use of organic solvents in certain activities and installations [1999] OJ L85/1; Directive 2000/76/EC on the incineration of waste [2000] OJ L332/91; Directive 2001/80/EC on the limitation of emissions of certain pollutants into the air from large combustion plants [2001] OJ L309/1; as well as three Directives related to the Titanium dioxide industry (Directive 78/176/EEC [1978] OJ L54/19); Directive 82/883/EEC [1982] OJ L378/1; Directive 92/112/EEC [1992] OJ L409/11).

[15] Annex I to the IED lists the type of installations, above a specific capacity threshold, to which the obligations of Chapter II of the Directive apply. These include installations involved in the energy industries, the production and processing of metals, the mineral and chemical industries, waste management activities, pulp and paper production, textiles, tanning, organic solvent surface treatments, intensive pig and poultry farming, large dairies, food processing plants, and slaughterhouses.

[16] Directive 2003/35/EC providing for public participation in respect of the drawing up of certain plans and programmes relating to the environment [2003] OJ L156/17.

required Member States to ensure that citizens are given 'early and effective opportunities' to partici-pate in IPPC permitting. This amendment also added the requirement that members of the public be consulted in relation to draft IPPC permits, thus seeking to increase opportunities for citizens to influ-ence pollution control permitting by involving them at a stage when licence conditions relating to the operation of installations can still be changed. Before this amendment, citizens could only comment on permit applications. However, this change did not deal with the practice of draft licences being already fully negotiated between an operator and the relevant licensing authority, and in practical terms thus finalized, before being made available for public consultation. The IED has subsequently dealt with this issue—paragraph 1(d) of Annex IV imposes a duty on Member States to inform the public of draft deci-sions taken in relation to permits. Paragraph 2 of Annex IV also imposes a duty on Member States to give members of the public access to the background reports and advice relied on in the drafting of pollution permit decisions.[17] Moreover, the Public Participation Directive introduced a provision, now found in Article 25 of the IED, which imposes a duty on Member States to ensure that, in accordance with the relevant national legal system, citizens have access to courts or another independent or impartial body, to challenge decisions taken under the IED.[18] Note that the provision leaves significant discretion to Member States to flesh out the scope of this right.

The second amendment to the initial 1996 IPPC Directive related to its interaction with climate change regulation. Thus, the EC Directive establishing a scheme for greenhouse gas (GHG) emission allowance trading (Emissions Trading Scheme (ETS) Directive)[19] removed the power of Member State competent authorities to impose emission limit values in IPPC permits for those greenhouse gases that are traded under the ETS Directive, at least for installations covered by both Directives.[20] This highlights potential problems in linking the EU IED regime to other forms of pollution control law (such as climate change regulation), a theme further discussed in Section 2.3.[21] Note, however, that Preamble 10 to the IED reaffirms Member States' powers under Article 193 TFEU 'to maintain or introduce more stringent pro-tective measures', including greenhouse gas emission requirements, beyond the IED permitting process as long as such measures are compatible with the Treaties and have been notified to the Commission.

The final key change to the consolidated IPPC Directive occurred through the introduction of the new IED itself. The new Directive was intended to address several shortcomings that had been identi-fied in the implementation of the previous versions of the IPPC Directive.

Report from the Commission to the Council and the European Parliament, Report of the Commission on the Implementation of Directive 96/61/EC Concerning Integrated Pollution Prevention and Control COM(2005) 540 final, 2–5

The IPPC Directive has applied to new installations since 30 October 1999, which was the deadline for transposition. For existing installations, the final deadline to achieve full compliance with the Directive is 30 October 2007, unless an installation is subject to a 'substantial change' before that date.

---

[17] In accordance with the provisions of the Directive 2003/4/EC on Public Access to Environmental Information [2003] OJ L41/26, and the Aarhus Directive.

[18] This implements the access to justice aspects of the Aarhus Directive: see Chapters 7 and 10.

[19] Directive 2003/87/EC establishing a scheme for greenhouse gas emission allowance trading within the Community [2003] OJ L275/32.

[20] See now IED, Article 9. Note that Art 9(1) provides an exception so that IED permits might include emission limit values for a greenhouse gas where this is 'necessary to ensure that no significant local pollution is caused'. Moreover, Article 9(2) provides that Member States may choose not to impose energy efficiency requirements in IED permits in relation to combustion or other units emitting carbon dioxide for those activities covered by the ETS Directive.

[21] See also the discussion of climate change regulation in Chapter 15.

Delays in transposition

Generally, the IPPC Directive has been transposed with considerable delays. At the end of 2004, all EU 15 Member States had finally transposed the Directive, but with some remaining gaps in the legislation of some Member States.

The Commission has checked the transposition of all old Member States. The legislation of new Member States is being checked. A number of shortcomings have been identified in the large majority of Member States […]

Different approaches to transposition

A number of different approaches have been used by the various Member States in order to transpose the Directive. A considerable number of Member States already had integrated permitting systems in place. Some Member States (for instance France and Sweden) only made relatively small changes to their pre-existing national legislation. This has also led to a considerable diversity in the exact approaches used to transpose the IPPC Directive. In many of these Member States some elements of the pre-existing systems still dominate. Other Member States (such as Portugal, Spain and Greece) without a pre-existing integrated permitting system in place usually developed new legislation as well as new integrated permitting systems and procedures, following the provisions of the Directive more precisely. Some of them, however, appear to be late in establishing a fully operational permitting system.

Limited number of IPPC permits issued

Member States reported (for the period until the end of 2002) around 45,000 installations falling under the scope of the IPPC Directive. During the first reporting period, 5545 installations were granted permits for substantial changes (4750) or as new (795) installations. This represents approximately 13% of all installations […] [Despite these numbers constituting only partial data, they], point to significant variations between Member States concerning the numbers of permits issued. For example, Italy, Spain and Portugal each reported less than 10 permits granted for 'substantial changes' in existing installations, whereas several other Member States reported much higher permitting levels for such types of installations. Greece did not provide data on the number of permits issued.

[…]

Determination of permit conditions based on BAT

The situation varies considerably among Member States. Certain Member States have developed guidance documents to assist competent authorities, while others have not published such specific documents. Certain Member States have established sectoral legislation based on BAT. The large majority of Member States indicate that the BAT Reference Documents (BREFs) published by the Commission pursuant to Article 16(2) of the Directive on the exchange of information on BAT are taken into account generally and in specific cases when determining BAT. However, this is not systematically addressed in all of the relevant legislation

[…]

Compliance with permit conditions

Most Member States have established procedures to check compliance with permit conditions, generally through on-site inspections. The frequency for such inspections, as well as the use of 'self-monitoring' carried out by the operators or by non-administrative bodies (e.g. accredited laboratories), vary among Member States. The requirement for operators to regularly inform the competent authorities of the results of the monitoring of releases has been introduced in most Member States. Procedures for regular inspections are still being developed in certain Member States. Procedures and frequencies vary considerably among Member States. For instance, inspections are carried out in Sweden on average every two years for each installation, France has developed an annual programme of inspections, and, in Spain, competent authorities carry out inspections on their own initiative. The number of enforcement actions (administrative or criminal) varies considerably across the Member States. For instance, the Netherlands reported 310 enforcement actions and France 148 successful prosecutions

[...]

Reporting of emission limits values

Compared with the data on representative emission limit values reported previously by Member States, it is difficult to draw firm conclusions on increasing or decreasing trends in these values. The comparison of reported emission limit values, with the objective of verifying their expected convergence, is in most cases not possible due to the different ways used by Member States to express these limit values in permits (e.g. over different time periods or with different statistical requirements for compliance)

In response to these concerns about the effectiveness of the former IPPC Directive, the Commission published, in December 2007, a proposal for a Directive on Industrial Emissions, which was revised and finally adopted in November 2010 on the basis of Article 192 TFEU (ex-Article 175 TEC).[22] Industry representatives were not in favour of a recast IPPC Directive and had argued for simply better enforcement of the existing IPPC Directive. The new IED pursues environmental objectives, addressing the fact that there had been insufficient reductions in emissions from IPPC installations, particularly due to the fact that the BAT standard under the previous IPPC Directives had not been fully implemented.

However, it is important to note that the IED also pursues economic objectives, in particular it aims to achieve a greater level playing field among industrial operators in the EU. Significant differences in implementation of BAT among EU Member States had lead to a distortion of competition because operators face stricter environmental standards in some Member States than in others. Further, the attempt to promote greater integration of pollution control should also implement the European Commission's 'Better Regulation' agenda. The IED should save regulated installations money through simplified, 'one stop' regulation through the BAT standard. Moreover, electronic reporting by Member States on progress in implementing the Directive should save money. However, the Commission's view is that the largest savings will come from changing implementation practices at Member State level.

Thus, there are high hopes for the IED. Even though it does not radically restructure the former IPPC Directive, its provisions sharpen in many respects the IPPC regulatory framework as well as extending its scope to incorporate other schemes for regulating industrial emissions. Having considered the background to the IED, we now consider the integrated nature of the pollution control measures under the IED.

How is industrial pollution control 'integrated' under the IED?

Industrial pollution control is integrated in at least four ways in the IED. These various forms of integration have different dimensions and spheres of application, but they are, in combination, generally

[22] COM(2007) 844 final.

geared towards developing a common system of pollution control across the EU for comparable large industrial installations, in a way that minimizes polluting effects in the environment, understood in a holistic way. In setting out these four different integrating aspects of the IED, this sub-section first considers the two features that apply to all industrial installations regulated under the IED, before considering two more detailed integrating measures that apply to Chapter II installations alone.

The first integrating feature of the IED has already been set out—it is seen in the Article 1 objective for the Directive. This provides that the IED, as a whole, has the objective of regulating for the integrated prevention and control of pollution arising from the industrial activities covered by the Directive, and in a manner that prevents or, where that is not practicable, reduces emissions into air, water, and land and prevents the generation of waste 'in order to achieve a high level of protection *of the environment taken as a whole*'. Hence, when a purposive approach to the interpretation of the Directive is adopted, *all* of its provisions should be interpreted in the light of the overriding integration aim of the Directive.

The second feature of the IED that seeks to limit the fragmentation of pollution control can be seen in Article 5(2) :

> Member States shall take the measures necessary to ensure that the *conditions* of, and the *procedures for* the granting of, the permit are *fully coordinated* where more than one competent authority or more than one operator is involved or more than one permit is granted, in order to guarantee an effective integrated approach by all authorities competent for this procedure (emphasis added).

Article 5(2)'s 'full coordination' obligation has both procedural and substantive aspects, which pursue integration of pollution control in two different but interrelated ways. In procedural terms, the Directive requires a single, unified permitting procedure for installations covered by the Directive. Note however that it does not require Member States to establish a single permitting authority or provide a single environmental permit. When the Commission proposal for the original 1996 IPPC Directive was discussed, some Member States, such as Germany that has a strong tradition in media-specific environmental regulation, opposed the suggestion that Member States should set up unified permitting authorities or issue single permits. In Germany, separate permits for air and water pollution are still issued for IPPC installations (those now regulated under Chapter II of the Directive) under the Federal Emission Control Law (the 'Bundesimmissionsschutzgesetz') and the Water Framework Law (the 'Wasserhaushaltsgesetz'). By contrast, one single environmental permit can be issued in England for industrial installations and air, water, and land pollution control expertise is combined in one single regulator—the Environment Agency (EA).[23]

In light of the fact that the IED does not require the establishment of a single, integrated environmental regulator, it is particularly problematic that it does not further define what is meant by a 'full co-ordination' of the authorization procedure for installations covered by it. This has implications for the substantive dimensions of Article 5(2) IED, in requiring Member States to 'fully coordinate' BAT conditions as well as the procedure for the grant of the permit where more than one competent authority is involved in the permitting process. There will be variation across Member States in the extent to which permitting officials in different environmental regulatory authorities really talk to each other when issuing separate parts of a permit for integrated industrial emissions control.

---

[23] Since the introduction of the Environmental Permitting (England and Wales) Regulations 2007: discussed further in Section 2.2. From 1 April 2013, however, the Environment Agency for Wales will be part of a separate regulatory agency, 'Natural Resources Wales', which will also comprise the former Countryside Council for Wales and the Forestry Commission Wales, at: <http://www.environment-agency.gov.uk/aboutus/145716.aspx>.

Implementation practice, potentially beyond the control of the formal law, thus determines the limits to 'integration' of pollution control under the IED.

The integration of pollution control is further promoted through the obligations that apply to installations under Chapter II. Two aspects of these obligations are considered here: (1) the application process for a permit, which frames the permitting process so as to set a higher bar for environmental protection in a holistic sense; and (2) the process for granting permits, which involves designing and attaching conditions to permits that are approved. It should be noted that, in both these processes, the BAT standard plays a central role. BAT is not considered in detail here but analysed in detail further below for the contribution it makes to integrated pollution control under the IED.

In relation to the process for applying for a permit under Chapter II, Article 12(1)(g) requires Member States to ensure that the operator of an Annex I installation includes a description of the proposed technology and techniques for preventing and, where that is not possible, reducing emissions from the installation. Moreover, Article 12(1)(i), along with Article 11(b), seeks to promote integrated pollution prevention and control through the application of adopting the 'best available techniques' technology standard.

Article 12: Applications for permits

1. Member States shall take the necessary measures to ensure that an application for a permit includes a description of the following:

   (a) the installation and its activities;

   (b) the raw and auxiliary materials, other substances and the energy used in or generated by the installation;

   (c) the sources of emissions from the installation;

   (d) the conditions of the site of the installation;

   (e) where applicable, a baseline report in accordance with Article 22(2);

   (f) the nature and quantities of foreseeable emissions from the installation into each medium as well as identification of significant effects of the emissions on the environment;

   (g) the proposed technology and other techniques for preventing or, where this is not possible, reducing emissions from the installation;

   (h) measures for the prevention, preparation for re-use, recycling and recovery of waste generated by the installation;

   (i) further measures planned to comply with the general principles of the basic obligations of the operator as provided for in Article 11;

   (j) measures planned to monitor emissions into the environment;

   (k) the main alternatives to the proposed technology, techniques and measures studied by the applicant in outline.

   An application for a permit shall also include a non-technical summary of the details referred to in the first subparagraph

2. Where information supplied in accordance with the requirements provided for in Directive 85/337/EEC or a safety report prepared in accordance with Directive 96/82/EC or other information produced in response to other legislation fulfils any of the requirements of paragraph 1, that information may be included in, or attached to, the application.

Article 12 is in three ways more onerous for permit applicants—in terms of promoting integrated pollution control—than was Article 6 under the former IPPC Directive. First, and most importantly, Article 12(1)(k) of the IED now requires operators in every case to document in their application various alternative technologies that they have considered before settling on the specific technology and techniques that form the basis of the application. This seeks to promote further the integrated prevention and control of pollution, because it seeks to avoid operators committing themselves at an early stage of planning a new installation, or substantially changing an existing installation, to one particular production and pollution abatement technology, for instance on economic or technical grounds. Instead—and similar to the technique of environmental impact assessment—operators should consider the various options that are available for running their industrial process and abating pollution from it. Reference to alternative technologies in the operator's application also enables the regulator to discuss which amongst a range of options best reflects an integrated approach to pollution prevention and control. Article 6(1)(j) of the former IPPC Directive, by contrast, only required the operator to describe 'the main alternatives, if any, studied by the applicant in outline'. The qualification that the alternatives to the operator's proposed process technology have to be only studied 'in outline' has, however, been retained. This weakens the requirement to engage in a serious consideration of the environmental consequences of different process technologies and to select the best one on environmental grounds.

Second, Article 12(1)(e) of the IED tightens up provisions for preventing and remedying pollution of land and groundwater from an installation. Member States now have to ensure that operators provide in their application, where applicable, a baseline report in accordance with Article 22(2). This baseline report assesses the state of soil and groundwater contamination at the site at the start of operations, in order to enable a quantified comparison with the conditions of the site once activities cease. This baseline report will also help to determine the potential legal obligations of the operator under Article 22(3), including restoring the site to its former state, as described in the baseline report, once an industrial operation ceases, as well as mitigating significant future risks to human health and the environment. Third, Article 6(g) of the former IPPC Directive required only 'where necessary, measures for the prevention and recovery of waste generated by the installation'. Article 12(1)(h) of the IED now requires operators in all cases also to describe in an application measures for the re-use of waste and recycling.

The final provision in the IED that seeks to implement an integrated approach to pollution control concerns how permits are actually granted. Thus, Article 14 (1)(a) requires that conditions in permits consider cross-media effects.

Article 14: Permit conditions

1. Member States shall ensure that the permit includes all measures necessary for compliance with the requirements of Articles 11 and 18.
2. Those measures shall include at least the following:
3. (a) emission limit values for polluting substances listed in Annex II, and for other polluting substances, which are likely to be emitted from the installation concerned in significant quantities, having regard to their nature and *their potential to transfer pollution from one medium to another* (emphasis added).

When a national regulator, such as the EA in England, considers what conditions to impose in the environmental permit, the effects of these conditions on emissions into all three environmental media—air, water, and land, that is, the environment as a whole—have to be considered. Thus, conditions in the permit, for instance those limiting the release of SO_2 into air, should not be set in isolation from conditions seeking to limit emissions into water or land from an installation. The potential knock-on effects of limiting pollution into one environmental medium onto another medium should be taken into account, in order to avoid a mere shifting around of pollutants from one environmental medium to another. The problem, however, is that the IED does not spell out a methodology for taking cross-media effects of pollution into account. Article 13 simply suggests that the Commission shall organize an exchange of information between Member States, industry, and environmental NGOs about what constitutes the 'best available techniques' (BATs) in order to achieve integrated pollution prevention and control. This should also address 'cross-media effects' (Article 13(2)(b)). The fact that the IED itself does not provide for a methodology for determining cross-media effects of pollutants is particularly problematic in light of the fact that considering such cross-media effects requires making difficult trade-off decisions, involving relative pollution effects in relation to watercourses, air, or land. Whether one course of action is more acceptable than another thus depends not only on sufficient knowledge about the long-term environmental consequences of these options, but also on the values placed on better air quality relative to better water or land quality. As discussed in Chapter 2, the application of law to environmental problems often involves uncertainty in scientific environmental knowledge as well as establishing and considering values that will be attributed to different aspects of environmental quality.

The limits of integration of pollution control under the IED

As already suggested, while the IED is in many ways a step forward in integrating industrial pollution control, in other ways its integrating efforts remain limited. The limits of pollution control integration in the IED can be seen in four ways. First, as explained already, the Directive does not impose a requirement upon Member States to issue one single permit for emissions to all three environmental media from an installation by a single, integrated regulatory authority. It simply imposes a requirement for an integrated permitting procedure under which (in some cases media-specific) regulatory authorities should co-ordinate the imposition of licence conditions. Second, when setting conditions in permits for Annex I installations under Chapter II, derogations from the BAT standard (which are partly determined by considering holistic effects on the environment) are allowed. The construction of the BAT standard, and derogations from it, are considered in the following sub-section.[24]

Third, the policy idea of 'integrated pollution control' in the Directive on IED is also limited, because it does not implement a fully integrated control of *all* the environmental impacts of products produced by installations covered by the Directive. There is an attempt to integrate different media that are directly affected, rather than to implement full life cycle analysis to control the products produced by installations.[25] For instance, the Directive currently does not provide explicit powers for

---

[24] Note that some derogations are limited in that environmental regulators must take into account applicable emission limit values set out in the Annexes to the Directive as a minimum standard (art 15(4)(b)). Even though these fixed limits set a minimum standard, not all have been devised by taking their cross-media impacts into account. A number of these emission limit values have been transferred from the media specific Directives that the IED replaced, such as the Solvents Directive, the Large Combustion Plant Directive and the Waste Incineration Directive, with the latter two mainly focusing on air pollutants.

[25] As European policy currently encourages: European Commission, 'Communication from the Commission to the Council and the European Parliament—Integrated Product Policy—Building on Environmental Life-Cycle Thinking', COM(2003) 302 final.

national regulators to impose conditions which would control, for instance, environmental effects associated with the transportation of the goods produced by an installation or otherwise minimize the environmental impacts of these goods along the commercial chain, when they are handled by retailers and final consumers. The focus is still on integrated pollution control of emissions from the production process only.

Fourth, integrated pollution prevention and control through the IED is limited because it does not make express provision for a wider conception of 'integration' of pollution controls as envisaged in Article 11 TFEU (ex Article 6 TEC).

Article 11 TFEU

Environmental protection requirements must be integrated into the definition and implementation of the Union policies and activities, in particular with a view to promoting sustainable development.

This is despite the fact that the legally non-binding Preamble 45 to the IED suggests that the Directive seeks to promote the application of Article 37 of the Charter of Fundamental Rights of the EU. This requires that 'a high level of environmental protection and the improvement of the quality of the environment must be integrated into the policies of the Union and ensured in accordance with the principle of sustainable development'.

In the context of the IED, 'integration' as defined in Article 11 TFEU could be implemented by providing powers for regulatory authorities to consider environmental considerations as an integral part of a range of other EU policies that impact on installations, rather than seeing them as pursuing competing purposes. For instance, operators of installations may argue against proposed permit conditions in negotiations with regulators on the grounds that they are incompatible with public health, or health and safety protection, as well as maintaining employment. An expansive definition of Article 11 TFEU would provide powers for the regulator to reject operator arguments that are based on a conception of a conflict between environmental and other EU policies, including economic policies seeking protection of employment. The regulator could reject such arguments on the grounds that economic arguments will only be considered in the context of the development of cleaner production processes. However, a legal framework to require such decision-making is not yet in place. The legal implications of Article 11 TFEU are currently more modest, being primarily concerned with overarching questions of EU competence. But it could be argued that this integration principle, enshrined in the Treaty, should be used to *interpret* the terms of the IPPC Directive, including its permit granting provisions, to impose legal obligations on regulators as already suggested.[26]

IPC under Chapter II IED: the key obligation to employ BAT

In order to evaluate further the extent to which the IED promotes an 'integrated' approach to pollution prevention and control, it is necessary to examine the key legal obligation—a technology standard—that the Directive requires Member States to ensure is complied with at Annex I installations. This BAT technology standard is the key tool through which Chapter II of the Directive seeks to implement an integrated approach to pollution control.

---

[26] See further, Chapter 11.

Article 11

General principles governing the basic obligations of the operator

Member States shall take the necessary measures to provide that installations are operated in accordance with the following principles:

(a) all the appropriate preventive measures are taken against pollution;

(b) the best available techniques are applied;

(c) no significant pollution is caused;

(d) the generation of waste is prevented in accordance with Directive 2008/98/EC;

(e) where waste is generated, it is, in order of priority and in accordance with Directive 2008/98/EC, prepared for re-use, recycled, recovered or, where that is technically and economically impossible, it is disposed of while avoiding or reducing any impact on the environment;

(f) energy is used efficiently;

(g) the necessary measures are taken to prevent accidents and limit their consequences;

(h) the necessary measures are taken upon definitive cessation of activities to avoid any risk of pollution and return the site of operation to the satisfactory state defined in accordance with Article 22.

In contrast to Article 3(1)(a) of the former IPPC Directive, there is now greater emphasis on operators having to comply with the BAT technology standard in order to fulfil their general obligations under the Directive. Article 3(1)(a) required installations to apply the best available techniques only as a qualification of the general duty to take all the appropriate preventative measures against pollution. However, the obligation to apply 'the best available techniques' is now a separate and distinct obligation under Article 11(b) of the IED. What does this requirement to employ 'the best available techniques' actually mean?

Setting the BAT Standard

Article 3

Definitions

For the purposes of this Directive the following definitions shall apply:

[...]

(10) 'best available techniques' means the most effective and advanced stage in the development of activities and their methods of operation which indicates the practical suitability of particular techniques for providing the basis for emission limit values and other permit conditions designed to prevent and, where that is not practicable, to reduce emissions and the impact on the environment as a whole:

(a) 'techniques' includes both the technology used and the way in which the installation is designed, built, maintained, operated and decommissioned;

(b) 'available techniques' means those developed on a scale which allows implementation in the relevant industrial sector, under economically and technically viable conditions, taking into consideration the costs and advantages, whether or not the techniques are used or produced inside the Member State in question, as long as they are reasonably accessible to the operator;

(c) 'best' means most effective in achieving a high general level of protection of the environment as a whole (emphasis added).

Hence, the BAT technology standard is considered as a tool to achieve protection of the environment as a whole, and thus integrated pollution prevention and control. The meaning of the 'best available techniques' standard is further spelt out through so-called Best Available Techniques Reference Documents (BREFs). These are further defined in Article 3 (11) and (12) of the Directive on Industrial Emissions (2010/75/EU) IED:

(11) 'BAT reference document' means a document, resulting from the exchange of information organised pursuant to Article 13, drawn up for defined activities and describing, in particular, applied techniques, present emissions and consumption levels, techniques considered for the determination of best available techniques as well as BAT conclusions and any emerging techniques, giving special consideration to the criteria listed in Annex III;

(12) 'BAT conclusions' means a document containing the parts of a BAT reference document laying down the conclusions on best available techniques, their description, information to assess their applicability, the emission levels associated with the best available techniques, associated monitoring, associated consumption levels and, where appropriate, relevant site remediation measures

Annex III, extracted here, sheds further light on the definition of 'best available techniques'.

Annex III

Criteria for determining best available techniques

1. the use of low-waste technology;
2. the use of less hazardous substances;
3. the furthering of recovery and recycling of substances generated and used in the process and of waste, where appropriate; comparable processes, facilities or methods of operation which have been tried with success on an industrial scale;
4. technological advances and changes in scientific knowledge and understanding;
5. the nature, effects and volume of the emissions concerned;
6. the commissioning dates for new or existing installations;
7. the length of time needed to introduce the best available technique;
8. the consumption and nature of raw materials (including water) used in the process and energy efficiency;
9. the need to prevent or reduce to a minimum the overall impact of the emissions on the environment and the risks to it;
10. the need to prevent accidents and to minimise the consequences for the environment;
11. information published by public international organisations.

The BREF document drafting process

BAT reference documents (BREFs) are drawn up through an exchange of information that is organized by the European Commission, as prescribed by the process set out in Article 13.

Article 13

BAT reference documents and exchange of information

1. In order to draw up, review and, where necessary, update BAT reference documents, the Commission shall organise an exchange of information between Member States, the industries concerned, non-governmental organisations promoting environmental protection and the Commission

2. The exchange of information shall, in particular, address the following:

   (a) the performance of installations and techniques in terms of emissions, expressed as short- and long-term averages, where appropriate, and the associated reference conditions, consumption and nature of raw materials, water consumption, use of energy and generation of waste;

   (b) the techniques used, associated monitoring, cross-media effects, economic and technical viability and developments therein;

   (c) best available techniques and emerging techniques identified after considering the issues mentioned in points (a) and (b).

3. The Commission shall establish and regularly convene a forum composed of representatives of Member States, the industries concerned and non-governmental organisations promoting environmental protection.

   The Commission shall obtain the opinion of the forum on the practical arrangements for the exchange of information and, in particular, on the following:

   (a) the rules of procedure of the forum;

   (b) the work programme for the exchange of information;

   (c) guidance on the collection of data;

   (d) guidance on the drawing up of BAT reference documents and on their quality assurance including the suitability of their content and format.

   The guidance referred to in points (c) and (d) of the second subparagraph shall take account of the opinion of the forum and shall be adopted in accordance with the regulatory procedure referred to in Article 75(2)

4. The Commission shall obtain and make publicly available the opinion of the forum on the proposed content of the BAT reference documents and shall take into account this opinion for the procedures laid down in paragraph 5.

5. Decisions on the BAT conclusions shall be adopted in accordance with the regulatory procedure referred to in Article 75(2).

6. After the adoption of a decision in accordance with paragraph 5, the Commission shall without delay make the BAT reference document publicly available and ensure that BAT conclusions are made available in all the official languages of the Union.

7. Pending the adoption of a relevant decision in accordance with paragraph 5, the conclusions on best available techniques from BAT reference documents adopted by the Commission prior to the date referred to in Article 83 shall apply as BAT conclusions for the purposes of this Chapter except for Article 15(3) and (4).

Article 13 thus sets out this exchange of information in seven paragraphs, and in much more detail than the four paragraphs of Article 17 of the former IPPC Directive. For the first time, the subject matter of this information exchange is now spelt out in the text of the actual legislative instrument (in Article 13(2)). Under the previous IPPC Directive, the process of the information exchange on BAT had been informally developed by the Commission in conjunction with Member States, representatives of industry, and environmental NGOs. In fact, the text of the IPPC Directive did not even refer to BAT reference documents. Hence, Article 13(3) of the IED enhances the transparency of the BREF drafting process. The text of the Directive itself now also recognizes the existence of the Information Exchange Forum (IEF), a body composed of representatives of the Member States, industries concerned, and NGOs promoting environmental protection, which had been set up informally by the Commission when BREF writing started under the initial 1996 IPPC Directive. The forum is assigned particular tasks, including advising the Commission on its rules of procedure. This is a significant step. By recognizing the existence of the IEF explicitly in the text of the Directive, this paves the way for holding the IEF accountable for its contribution to the BREF writing process. It moves towards the legalization of BREF drafting in accordance with standards of principles of administrative law and good administrative practice.

Article 13 of the IED introduces a network approach to defining the BAT technology standard. The work of this network is co-ordinated by the European IPPC Bureau, based in Seville, Spain, and has therefore been called the 'Sevilla Process'. The European Commission has invested significant resources in this process. The information exchange network consists in fact of two branches. First, so-called Technical Working Groups (TWGs), which include representatives of regulatory authorities or national environmental ministries in theory from all of the twenty-seven EU Member States, and in practice from those who actually participate, as well as representatives for trade associations and individual large corporations from the sectors covered by the IED and representatives of environmental NGOs. Second, there is the IEF—now recognized in Article 13(3) of the IED Directive, which consists of higher ranking political representatives for the different Member States as well as representatives of industry and environmental NGOs. It is chaired by the European Commission. More information about the network and the type of substantial BAT Reference (BREF) guidance documents that it publishes can be found on the website of the European IPPC Bureau: <http://eippcb.jrc.es>.

The important point to note is that international environmental standard-setting networks, such as those established under Article 13 IED, modify the role that the nation-state, and public authorities more specifically, play in the development of environmental law. International networks, which straddle a public–private divide by involving government representatives as well as representatives of private regulated installations and environmental NGOs, now contribute to the setting of environmental standards that are ultimately enforced by nation-states. But the legitimacy of standard-setting by these international networks of limited visibility has been questioned. In particular, are they sufficiently accountable to citizens? These issues matter also in light of the fact that the composition of the network raises difficult issues about how procedurally to balance the power of the various participants in the network. For instance, environmental NGOs do not participate on an equal footing with Member State and industry representatives given their limited resources. It has also been criticized that support for the work of the European IPPC Bureau in Seville has been provided mainly by northern and western European Member States who have seconded staff from their national environmental authorities for specified periods to the Bureau and whose representatives have been particularly active in the so-called TWGs. Hence, it has been suggested that northern and western European Member States have been more influential in environmental standard-setting through the BREF documents than southern and new central and eastern European Member States. Similarly, large industrial operators have been more prominent in the TWGs and have usually greater influence on shaping their trade associations' approaches to environmental standard-setting than small- and medium-sized operators. Article 13(3)(a) of the Directive provides some opportunity to tackle these issues by tasking the IEF—the body that oversees the BREF drafting process—with advising the Commission on the rules of procedure that should govern the work of the IEF.

But it is not only these procedural balance of power issues that have been criticized; the very nature of the environmental standard-setting process through the Article 13 network has also been questioned.

It is unclear how, in practice, tensions between technical and political aspects of the work of the network should be reconciled. While the TWGs seek to focus on engineering and environmental science expertise when setting out options for what constitute 'the best available techniques' for a particular sector of industry, they also become drawn into a political negotiation process in which interests of the different participants, in particular Member States and industry representatives, are asserted. BAT standards spelt out in BREF conclusions have been criticized for representing the mean, or at worst lowest common denominator, of what technical experts consider possible. The network sought to address this through an institutional design that distinguishes between two levels of decision-making, that of the TWGs, which is meant to focus on technical issues, and that of the IEF, which is tasked with considering wider political and policy issues in BAT standard setting. But this attempt to delineate clearly technical and political elements in environmental standard-setting breaks down in practice.

Against this contentious background of the practical and socio-political reality of the BREF drafting process since the introduction of the IPPC Directive, the IED introduces a major innovation in relation to the drafting process. Firstly, Article 13(5) requires that BAT conclusions have to be adopted in accordance with the regulatory comitology committee procedure referred to in Article 75(2). The comitology committee consists of representatives of the Member States and is chaired by the Commission. According to Article 13(5), it has a crucial role: it decides on the adoption of BAT conclusions. The BAT conclusions constitute the nub of the BAT reference document (Article 3(12)). They crystallize a whole range of available techniques that were considered by the TWG down to a select number of key techniques considered as BATs.

Moreover, the BAT conclusions will link particular technologies to 'associated emission levels' and thus give fairly clear guidance to national permitting officials as to what level emission limit values should be set in environmental permits for installations covered by Chapter II of the IED. This important task of making final decisions on the legally non-binding BREF guidance documents is a task now in the hands of the Commission and the Member States, which is different from the situation under the previous IPPC Directives. With there being no legislative requirement for the approval of BAT conclusions, in practice the IEF approved BAT conclusions. Now, under the regulatory comitology committee procedure, industry influence on the approval of BAT conclusions has been removed.

Further, the approval of BAT conclusions is now potentially more transparent than under the previous IPPC Directives, because there are some rights of access to the Commission proposal for the approval of a BAT conclusion and other Commission documents considered in the deliberations of the regulatory comitology committee.[27] It is, however, unclear whether this will lead to more environmentally stringent BAT conclusions. It may be that this more formal decision-making process, and

---

[27] Council Decision 1999/468/EC laying down the procedures for the exercise of implementing powers conferred on the Commission [1999] L184/23 ('Comitology Decision' as amended by Council Decision 2006/512/EC), Articles 7(2) and (3); Regulation (2001/1049/EC) regarding public access to European Parliament, Council and Commission documents. These previous Council Decisions have now been superseded by a new Comitology Regulation: Regulation (EU) No. 182/2011 of the European Parliament and of the Council of 16 February 2011, laying down rules and general principles concerning mechanisms for control by Member States of the Commission's exercise of implementing powers, [2011] OJ L 55/13. According to art 2(2) (iii) and art 13(c) of the Regulation the so-called examination procedure will apply to the adoption of BREF documents under the IED. Under the new Comitology Regulation the Commission's implementing powers are curtailed in various ways. First, according to art 11, the European Parliament and the Council have a right of scrutiny and can contest the draft implementing act on the grounds that it exceeds the implementing powers provided for in the basic act. Second, art 3(4) of the new Regulation steers the Commission towards adopting implementing acts based on a consensus in the Comitology Committee. Third, art 3(7) provides for an opportunity to review the Comitology Committee's decision before an Appeal Committee. Fourth, art 13(1)(c) provides that the implementing Act may not be adopted in the absence of an opinion of the Comitology Committee.

the greater role for the BREF documents in defining BAT, will increase lobbying activity—directed at DG Environment, in relation to preferred views about what constitutes BAT—on the part of representatives of Member States, industry, and environmental NGOs.

BAT enhanced under the IED

In comparison to the former IPPC Directive, the IED also seeks to tighten up and harmonize the definition of BAT by enhancing the role of the BREF documents in the permitting process in five key ways. First, according to Article 14(3), 'BAT conclusions shall be the reference for setting the permit conditions'. Under the previous IPPC Directive, BREF documents were merely one factor to be taken into account in setting emission standards in national permits. Second, according to Article 15(3), competent authorities in the Member States now have to ensure that emissions from IPPC installations do not exceed the emission levels associated with the best available techniques as laid down in the BAT conclusions of BREFs. Third, under Article 14(1)(d)(ii), it will now be more transparent if a regulatory authority has set emission standards in a particular installation permit that are different from those recommended in the BAT conclusion. Member State authorities now have to ensure that operators provide results of emission monitoring at installations which 'allow a comparison with the emission levels associated with the best available techniques' (Article 15(3)(b)). Fourth, the IED seeks to strengthen the BAT standard for delivering better environmental protection by giving greater prominence to 'emerging techniques.' An 'emerging technique' is defined in Article 3(14) as:

> a novel technique for an industrial activity that, if commercially developed, could provide either a higher general level of protection of the environment or at least the same level of protection of the environment and higher cost savings than existing best available techniques

This definition shows that the value of emerging techniques is considered not just for their environmental protection but also for their cost-saving potential. Such emerging techniques must now be acknowledged and incorporated into the BAT standard in various ways. Thus, Article 19 requires Member States to ensure that their regulatory authorities are informed of developments in BAT and of the publication of any new or updated BAT conclusions. This information shall also be made available to the public. Article 21(3) requires Member State authorities to reconsider permit conditions and if necessary to update them within four years of the publication of BAT conclusions. The application of emerging techniques in BAT permitting is also further supported through the fact that Article 15(5) enables Member State regulatory authorities to grant temporary derogations of up to nine months from compliance with the BAT standard in order to enable the testing and use of emerging techniques. These provisions show that reference to 'emerging techniques' renders the BAT standard dynamic, thus promoting the Commission's goal to encourage operators to go beyond mere 'regulatory compliance' in designing and operating their industrial processes.

In terms of the BREF drafting process, Article 13(2)(c) suggests that the Sevilla process shall yield information not only about 'the best available techniques' at the relevant time, but also about emerging techniques. Hence, Article 3(11) defines a BAT reference document as containing information about any emerging techniques in the relevant sector, as well as BAT conclusions. Since some of the existing BREF documents to date have been considered as not sufficiently focused upon the 'best' element of the 'best available techniques' standard, the IED's focus on 'emerging techniques' seeks to ensure that the latest technological developments (rather than a low common denominator in existing techniques) informs the standard setting process under the Directive.

Furthermore, Article 27(1) asks Member States 'where appropriate, to encourage the development and application of emerging techniques, in particular for those emerging techniques identified in BAT reference documents'. Article 27(2) requires the Commission to set up guidance to assist Member States in the development and application of emerging techniques. These legal obligations to pay attention to the development of 'emerging techniques' are backed up through enforcement provisions. Article 72(1) of the IED requires Member States in their reports to the Commission about the implementation of the Directive to provide information also about progress made with the development and application of emerging techniques.

The fifth way in which the IED serves to enhance the BAT standard is through stronger powers to enforce the legal obligation to operate facilities in accordance with the 'best available techniques' standard. Article 23 sets out detailed provisions on environmental inspections, which were developed also by reference to Recommendation 2001/331/EC on minimum criteria for environmental inspections.[28] Article 23(2) requires Member States to set up a national, regional, or local plan for inspections of IPPC installations. Moreover, Article 23 makes provision for routine and non-routine inspections, with the latter addressing serious environmental incidents, though the inspection regime is a risk-based regime that seeks to target limited inspection resources to those installations that pose the greatest environmental risks. The fairly detailed prescriptions of Article 23 on enforcement further illustrate Joanne Scott's view of the IPPC Directive as a significant intervention into the 'procedural lives' of EU Member States, discussed further in Section 3.2.

Derogations from the BAT standard

While it is clear that the legal obligation to operate IPPC installations in compliance with BAT has been strengthened through the IED, it is also important to point out powers for regulators to derogate from the BAT standard.

Article 15(4)

By way of derogation from paragraph 3, and without prejudice to Article 18, the competent authority may, in specific cases, set less strict emission limit values. Such a derogation may apply only where an assessment shows that the achievement of emission levels associated with the best available techniques as described in BAT conclusions would lead to disproportionately higher costs compared to the environmental benefits due to:

(a) the geographical location or the local environmental conditions of the installation concerned; or

(b) the technical characteristics of the installation concerned.

This power of derogation, however, is subject to two main qualifications. First, the emission limit values set by the regulatory authority that derogate from the BAT standards under subparagraph (a) must not exceed any applicable emission limit values set out in the Annexes to the IED. Second, the regulatory authority is still subject to the overriding legal obligation to ensure that no significant pollution is caused and that a high level of protection of the environment as a whole is achieved. Further, this power to derogate from the BAT standard can be circumscribed with Article 15(4) giving

---

[28] Recommendation 2001/331/EC providing for minimum criteria for environmental inspections in the Member States [2001] OJ L–118/41.

the Commission power to establish criteria for derogating under Article 15(4) that curtail Member States' powers to derogate from the BAT standard.

Moreover, Article 14(4) also grants significant powers to Member State regulatory authorities to set stricter permit conditions than those achievable by the use of the best available techniques as described in relevant BAT conclusions. Member States can also set out further rules guiding the discretion of regulatory authorities to set such stricter rules. This goes further than Article 10 of the previous IPPC Directive, which qualified the power of Member State authorities to set standards stricter than BAT, so that it could only be exercised in cases where there was a risk of breach of an environmental quality standard. The powers to set stricter standards according to Article 14(4) of the IED is additional to those of Article 18 to set permit standards at a level stricter than BAT in order to ensure compliance with an environmental quality standard.

As a final point, the IED's derogation provisions raise some unresolved questions about the BAT standard, in particular whether it is a sector-wide or site-specific standard. Article 3(10)(b) of the IED defines 'available techniques' as those that can be implemented 'in a relevant industrial sector' and BREF documents set out BAT standards for whole industrial sectors, such as the iron and steel, the pulp and paper, or the cement and lime industries. While various provisions in the IED (Preamble 43; Annex III, n. 7) allow a distinction to be made between BAT standards for existing and new installations, and thus refer to the BAT standard with reference to particular installations, the Directive otherwise seeks to provide for sector-wide technology standards, which—at least in theory—should be stricter than site-specific standards because they do not take into account idiosyncratic factors of technical and cost considerations that are specific to the site, but seek to enshrine a standard of average performance in a sector that also takes into account those installations that achieve high levels of environmental protection. But Article 15(4)(a) and (b) seems to detract from this by allowing permitting authorities to take site-specific factors into account, such as the technical characteristics of the installation, its geographical location, and the local environmental conditions, when defining the BAT technology standard for an installation. There is thus a tension in the IED. On the one hand, the IED seeks to avoid the lowering of BAT standards through their adaptation to the specifics of particular installations, which can detract from the pursuit of high environmental standards, due to a history of low investment in environmental protection at a site, technical difficulties in complying with environmental protection standards, or the benefits of a relatively unpolluted surrounding environment that does not call for stringent environmental standards. On the other hand, the Directive also contains provisions that allow site-specific factors to be taken into account through the setting of emission limit values in permits for BAT determinations, such as in Article 15(4).

To conclude, the IED seeks to implement an integrated, holistic approach to pollution control in the EU through the BAT technology standard. The extracts here from the Directive itself have pointed to the limits of the integration of pollution control across all three environmental media, air, water, and land. In order to further assess the Directive's success in implementing a system of integrated pollution control, it is necessary to examine how it has been implemented in the UK and in England and Wales in particular.

FURTHER READING QUESTIONS

1. Do you think that the process for writing BREFs under Article 13 of the IED should be spelt out in more detail in the text of the Directive? What do you consider as the advantages and disadvantages of approving BAT conclusions through a regulatory Comitology Committee?

2. In what ways could there be greater harmonization and centralization of the environmental standard-setting process under the IED? Would this promote higher levels of environmental protection in the EU Member States?

3. For further reading on the IED and the history of its introduction, see Andrew Farmer, 'Revising IPPC: Incremental Change Rather than a Radical Overhaul of EU Industrial Emissions Policy', (2008) 10(4) Env LR 258; Bettina Lange, 'The EU Directive on Industrial Emissions: Squaring the Circle of Integrated, Harmonised and Ambitious Technology Standards?' (2011) 13 Env LR 199.

2.2 ENVIRONMENTAL PERMITTING IN ENGLAND AND WALES

The UK is an important Member State to consider for examining the implementation of the EU regime on integrated pollution prevention and control. The UK is a highly industrialized country and 4000 out of 52,000 installations covered by the previous IPPC Directive are situated in the UK alone.[29] Moreover, at least in terms of formal procedures enshrined in its national system of integrated pollution control, the UK has been ambitious in its approach to integrating pollution controls, if not necessarily a 'best practice' leader in terms of substantive BAT standards.

In the latter respect, the UK has progressively introduced innovative integrated permitting procedures. Thus, the PPC (England and Wales) Regulations 2000,[30] which were a core element of the UK implementation of the IPPC Directive initially, as well as the now applicable Environmental Permitting (England and Wales) Regulations 2010 (EPRs)[31] are examples of a more far-reaching definition of 'integration' than the EU integrated pollution prevention and control regime necessarily envisages. They integrate both the administrative and substantive obligations of pollution control, as explained in the Introduction to this part. The UK, as well as two other EU Member States, seized the opportunity when implementing the IPPC Directive to combine licensing of IPPC installations and most large waste management facilities, through one single permit and permitting procedure. A full integration of all PPC and waste management licensing was achieved through the Environmental Permitting (England and Wales) Regulations 2007.[32] Further licensing regimes, such as those relating to water discharge activities, as well as radioactive substances, were brought within a single procedure of environmental permitting through the 2010 EPRs. Clause 26(7) of the draft Water Bill 2012 will enable the extension of the scope of the environmental permitting regime for England and Wales to include water abstraction and impounding licences, as well as flood defence consents.

Moreover, the majority of IPPC installations and those with the most significant environmental impacts (approximately 3600) are subject to permitting by the EA for England and Wales (soon to be the regulator for England alone),[33] or the Scottish Environment Protection Agency (SEPA) for installations based in Scotland. These environment agencies, which were set up through the Environment Act 1995, combine within a single regulator expertise in relation to the control of pollution to land, water, and air for these heavily polluting installations. More specifically, the integrated pollution control system in England and Wales distinguished between three types of installations, so called 'Part A(1) and (2)' processes as well as 'Part B' processes.[34] Part A(1) processes are the most polluting

---

[29] European Commission Directorate General Environment, *Monitoring of Permitting Progress for Existing IPPC Installations*, Final Report, March 2009, Entec UK Limited, 11.

[30] SI No 1973. [31] SI No 675. [32] SI No 3538.

[33] <http://www.environment-agency.gov.uk/business/topics/permitting/default.aspx>.

[34] Regulation 2(1) in connection with Paragraph 1 of Part 1 of Schedule 1 of the EPRs 2010.

installations that generate cross-media impacts. They are those covered by Annex I of the former IPPC Directive and are regulated by the EA.[35]

Part A(2) and B processes are less complex installations. Part B activities are those that generate emissions only to air and thus are considered to raise fewer cross-media effects than installations that have point discharges to all three environmental media, air, water, and land. But this distinction of Part B processes flows from a narrow definition of cross-media impacts, since air pollutants alone also have cross-media impacts, for instance when they get deposited in a water course and, as in the case of NO_x and SO_x, acidify water courses.[36] The environmental permitting authority and regulator for Part A(2) and B processes is the relevant local authority. So far about 400 permits have been issued for Part A(2) processes and 22,000 for Part B processes, also reflecting the smaller size of Part B processes.[37]

The UK system of IPC was first developed in the UK through Part I of the Environmental Protection Act 1990. In fact, the EU initiative for the initial IPPC Directive (96/61/EC) was a response also to the UK IPC regime. The Commission wanted to avoid the situation that EU Member States might develop their own national IPC systems, thereby undermining a level-playing field of competitive conditions for industrial installations across the whole of the EU. IPC was then further developed in the UK, because once the IPPC Directive came into force in 1996 it created legal obligations for the UK to implement its provisions in national law. The UK (other than Northern Ireland) thus implemented the former IPPC Directive through the Pollution Prevention and Control (PPC) Act 1999 (PPC Act). This is a basic framework Act that consists of only seven sections. Its main operative provision is s 2, which empowers the Secretary of State to issue regulations that implement the EU IPPC regime in the UK.

PPC Act 1999, section 2

Regulation of polluting activities

The Secretary of State may by regulations make provision for any of the purposes listed in Part I of Schedule 1 [which includes, amongst other matters relevant to regulating polluting activities, the making of provisions that implement the former IPPC Directive]; and Part II of that Schedule has effect for supplementing Part I.

[...]

(4) Before making any regulations under this section, the Secretary of State shall consult—

  (a) the Environment Agency if the regulations are to apply in relation to England or Wales;

  (b) the Scottish Environment Protection Agency if the regulations are to apply in relation to Scotland;

  (c) such bodies or persons appearing to him to be representative of the interests of local government, industry, agriculture and small businesses respectively as he may consider appropriate; and

  (d) such other bodies or persons as he may consider appropriate.

[...](6) The power to make regulations under this section shall be exercised by statutory instrument.

[...]

---

[35] EPRs 2010, Regulation 32.   [36] See further, Chapter 15.

[37] Further information about regulation of polluting installations by local authorities can be found at: <http://archive.defra.gov.uk/environment/quality/pollution/ppc/localauth/pubs/guidance/manuals.htm>.

(8) No regulations to which this subsection applies shall be made (whether alone or with other regulations) unless a draft of the statutory instrument containing the regulations has been laid before, and approved by a resolution of, each House of Parliament [...]

(9) Subsection (8) applies to—

   (a) the first regulations to be made under this section which apply in relation to England;

   (b) the first regulations to be made under this section which apply in relation to Wales;

   (c) the first regulations to be made under this section which apply in relation to Scotland;

   (d) regulations under this section which create an offence or increase a penalty for an existing offence;

   (e) regulations under this section which amend or repeal any provision of an Act.

Note that s 2(4)(c) of the PPC Act 1999 specifies a requirement to consult sections of civil society, with business and local government interests being granted a specific right to be consulted before the passing of Regulations under the PPC Act. Environmental NGOs and individual citizens, such as those living in the vicinity of large polluting industrial installations, are treated differently—they are subsumed into the general category of 'other bodies or persons' under s 2(4)(d).

Section 2(9) of the PPC Act 1999 refers to the possibility of *different* regulations existing for England, Wales, and Scotland. Section 2(8) of the PPC Act 1999 requires such regulations—in the form of draft statutory instruments—to be laid before and approved by both Houses of Parliament. The relevant Welsh ministers, however, have chosen not to exercise their powers and have so far adopted the same Regulations to those that apply in England. As s 2 allows, the PPC Act 1999 was further fleshed out through the Pollution Prevention and Control (England and Wales) Regulations 2000,[38] which were replaced by the Environmental Permitting (England and Wales) Regulations 2007, as set out already, which have now been superseded by the 2010 EPRs, which came into force on 6 April 2010. Note however that, at the time of writing, the new IED provisions have not yet been implemented into the law of England and Wales and into its EPR scheme. The precise form of implementing the IED was being consulted on in 2012, but it is likely that the permitting and other requirements of the IED will be incorporated into the existing EPRs, largely by way of amended schedules.

Note that the EPRs do not apply in Scotland and Northern Ireland, where the SEPA and the chief inspector of the NIEA still issue PPC permits, which are not administratively integrated within a broader range of pollution permitting regimes as they are in England and Wales. Thus, there are different PPC Regulations applicable in Northern Ireland and Scotland, the Pollution Prevention and Control Regulations (Northern Ireland) 2003,[39] and the Pollution Prevention and Control (Scotland) Regulations.[40] Again, these regulations may change with the implementation of the IED within those jurisdictions, but the point remains that the devolution of environmental regulation in the UK provides a further limit to the administrative integration of pollution control.

Thus, for England and Wales alone, Regulation 8(1)(a) of the EPRs 2010 includes an 'installation' (which includes an installation covered by Annex 1 of the former IPPC Directive) within the definition of 'regulated facility', which triggers the core EPR permitting requirement under Regulation 12. For further information on the basic permitting requirements and core mechanisms of the Regulations, see Section 2.1. Schedule 7 of the EPRs (England and Wales) 2010 then makes further provision in relation to Annex I (or Part A) installations. Schedule 7, paragraph 3 accordingly requires the regulator to implement an integrated approach.

---

[38] SI No 1973.   [39] SR 46.   [40] SSI 2000/323.

Environmental Permitting Regulations 2010, Schedule 7

Exercise of Regulator's Functions: General

3. The regulator must exercise its functions under these Regulations for the purpose of achieving a high level of protection of **the environment taken as a whole** by, in particular, preventing or, where that is not practicable, reducing emission into the air, water and land (emphasis added).

Regulations 25 and 27 grant 'rule-making authorities', such as the EA, the power to prepare and apply standard rules to 'standard facilities', which include installations covered by the former IPPC Directive. 'Standard facilities' share characteristics in relation to environmental hazards across any industry sector. The EA can develop standard rules because Article 17 of the IED provides a power for Member States to develop 'general binding rules' for activities listed in Annex I to the Directive, which take the place of individual permit conditions. Such standard rules must also reflect an integrated approach and seek a high level of protection for the environment as a whole.

The Explanatory Memorandum issued by DEFRA and DECC to accompany the EPRs also highlights that environmental permitting is not just about standard setting but is closely connected to the enforcement of environmental standards. DEFRA and DECC suggest that integrated, single permitting for sites also means that the EA will move to single, common inspections. It is not entirely clear whether this will lead to a reduced number of individual inspections for a site. The main purpose is to cut down on un-coordinated site visits by inspectors associated with different pollution control regimes.[41] The Explanatory Memorandum adds—clearly meant as reassurance—that the new environmental permitting regime does not change the EA's role as a regulator (without clarifying precisely the nature of that role).[42] The 'better regulation' agenda looms large in the Explanatory Memorandum, which puts integrated pollution control in an economic context by pointing to 'savings in the cost of compliance, due to more integrated thinking resulting in innovative and therefore cheaper compliance'.[43] Thus, in 2010, we can see a drift in the policy idea of 'integrated' pollution control from its origins in ecosystem-focused thinking and James Lovelock's Gaia hypothesis to a concern with financial costs.

While the EPRs spell out mainly the procedural dimensions of the IPPC regime in England and Wales,[44] the EA has also developed 'technical guidance' notes that contribute to a substantive definition of what constitute BATs for the different industry sectors covered by the IPPC Directive (and the EPRs in England and Wales). These national BAT guidance documents take into account, but sometimes also deviate from, the EU-wide BREF documents. An example of an EA sector guidance note, here for Iron and Steel installations, can be found at: <http://www.environment-agency.gov.uk/static/documents/Business/IPPC_S2.01June04.pdf>. Sector guidance notes for England and Wales provide a further adaptation of EU BREF documents to UK conditions, rather than a replication of the latter.

The EA also provides 'regulatory guidance' which clarifies (for Agency staff and applicants alike) the Agency's interpretation of key terms such as 'operator' and 'installation', and the application of key aspects of the permitting process, such as 'setting standards for environmental protection' and 'determinations involving sites of high public interest': <http://www.environment-agency.gov.uk/business/topics/permitting/36419.aspx>. There are also 'horizontal guidance' documents issued by the EA, which address generic issues of concern to all sectors under the EPRs. These include how to

---

[41] Explanatory Memorandum to the Environmental Permitting (England and Wales) Regulations 2010 No. 675, at: http://www.defra.gov.uk/environment/quality/permitting/.

[42] Ibid, 57.   [43] Ibid, 29.   [44] See further, Introduction to this part, Section 3.

carry out environmental risk assessments, how to prevent accidents, as well as how to justify and carry out cost–benefit analysis for control measures. Copies of these 'horizontal guidance' documents can be found at: <http://www.environment-agency.gov.uk/business/topics/permitting/36414.aspx>. In addition to the EA's guidance, DEFRA provides 'policy guidance' such as its 'Core Guidance' on the Environmental Permitting (England and Wales) Regulations 2010 referred to in the Further Reading and Questions at the end of this section. All of these guidance notes are not legally binding but are factors to be taken into account by the EA or other relevant regulators when a specific installation is granted a permit under the EPR regime, albeit that they are very persuasive in practice.

Finally, under Regulation 46 of the EPRs, in connection with Schedule 24, paragraph 1(1)(d), the regulator must maintain a public register of all environmental permits issued in England and Wales. You can search the register online and see examples of environmental permits at: <http://www2.environment-agency.gov.uk/epr/search.asp>.

To conclude, the implementation of the EU IED in the UK reveals a picture of significant legal complexity with different layers of statutory legal obligations, various sets of Regulations (which are yet to be updated to implement the IED rather than the former IPPC Directive), and a range of different technical guidance and policy documents fleshing out pollution control obligations. Overall, this detracts from the transparency and legal certainty of this pollution control regime.

FURTHER READING AND QUESTIONS

Further reading on integrated pollution prevention and control:

1. Bettina Lange, 'From Boundary Drawing To Transitions: The Creation of Normativity under the EU Directive on Integrated Pollution Prevention and Control' (2002) 8(2) ELJ 246, which analyses how transitions from a 'social' to a 'legal' sphere contribute to the construction of normativity in regimes of integrated pollution prevention and control.

2. Marc Pallemaerts, 'IPPC: Re-regulation or De-regulation?' (1996) 5(6) European Environmental Law Review 174.

3. Neil Emmott and Nigel Haigh, 'Integrated Pollution Prevention and Control: UK and EC Approaches and Possible Next Steps', (1996) 8(2) JEL, 301 provides an early commentary on the IPPC Directive (96/61/EC) by comparing it with the UK IPC system under Part I of EPA 1990.

4. Martina Doppelhammer, 'More Difficult than Finding the Way Round Chinatown? The IPPC Directive and its Implementation' (2000) 9(7) European Environmental Law Review 199; (2000) 9(8) 246.

5. Specify different possible meanings of 'integration' in relation to pollution control regimes and assess the extent to which the EU Directive on Industrial Emissions (2010/75/EU) and the environmental permitting regime in England and Wales are truly 'integrated' pollution control regimes.

6. How does the IED seek to prevent pollution?

7. Do you think that the activities of the network under Article 13 of the IED contribute to the legitimacy and accountability of environmental regulators in environmental standard setting? See also: Bettina Lange 'Thinking About Procedure: Understanding Legitimacy in EU Environmental Governance Networks' in Olaf Dilling, Martin Herberg, and Gerd Winter (eds), *Transnational Administrative Rule-Making: Performance, Legal Effects, and Legitimacy* (Hart Publishing 2010) 41–76.

8. Read Section 5.3 of Chapter 18 and note in particular the following four cases, the latter two of which are extracted in Chapter 18:

- *Gateshead MBC v Secretary of State for the Environment* [1995] Env LR 37.
- *R v Bolton MBC Ex p. Kirkman* [1998] Env LR 719.
- *Hopkins Developments Ltd v First Secretary of State and North Wiltshire DC* [2007] Env LR 14.
- *Harrison v Secretary for Communities and Local Government and Cheshire West and Chester Council* [2009] EWHC 3382.

Do the decisions in these cases promote 'integrated' pollution control in the UK? Do you think that one of the limits to integrating environmental knowledge from a planning and a pollution control perspective is the need to preserve public law decision-making powers of distinct environmental regulators, such as planning and pollution control authorities? Or are there other issues at play?

9. You are advising 'Megaplant', a company that wants to build and operate a new thermal power station in the UK. Their environmental consultants have told them that the fitting of a state of the art scrubber at the power station will cost £2 million. There is also another type of scrubber that could be fitted—this is older technology that has been in use at thermal power plants for the last fifteen years and is still used by most existing power plants in the UK. This type of scrubber would cost £1.5 million to install. The management of 'Megaplant' is considering installing the older scrubber in their new plant given that the company incurred significant financial losses last year due to the acquisition of an ailing small combined heat and power plant. Megaplant seeks your advice on which scrubber technology would likely to be considered as BAT under the IED Directive.

2.3 A WEB OF REGULATION: THE INTERRELATIONSHIP BETWEEN IPPC AND OTHER POLLUTION CONTROL REGIMES

In order to understand the scope and nature of 'best available techniques' as a technology standard and the extent to which it implements the policy idea of 'holistic' and 'integrated' pollution prevention and control, it is necessary to examine how the IED and national IPC regimes interact with other existing pollution control law. This also matters because, in practice, numerous questions about the application of the IED result from conflicts and overlaps with other pollution control laws. The IED also interacts with a wide range of other pollution control regimes.

This sub-section provides a typology of different legal interactions between the IED and other pollution control regimes. It refers only to a selection of the pollution control regimes with which the IED interacts as illustrative examples of these typologies. Overall, interactions between the IED and other pollution control regimes both provide opportunities and give rise to problems for achieving environmental protection outcomes.

Overlapping pollution control regimes that limit the environmental protection potential of the IED

The first type of interaction between the IED and other EU Directives is fairly clear in legal terms but potentially limits the environmental protection potential of the IED. An example of this type of interaction is the relationship between the IED and the ETS Directive, briefly discussed already. As set out here, Article 9(1) of the IED states that a permit shall not include an emission limit value for direct emissions of greenhouse gases (GHGs) from installations that are covered by both the ETS Directive and the IED, unless such an emission limit value would be 'necessary to ensure that no significant local pollution is caused'.[45] This loss of power for regulatory authorities to set emission limit values for GHGs emitted from industrial installations is significant,[46] firstly, because the IED applies to energy, minerals, iron and steel industries, and waste incinerators, which through their combustion processes are very significant emitters of carbon monoxide and dioxide, two key GHGs. Secondly, a large number of installations are covered by both the IED and the ETS Directive.[47] Moreover, GHG emissions can also be reduced through energy efficiency measures applied to combustion processes. Whereas Annex III of the IED considers energy efficiency as one of the criteria for determining what constitutes 'the best available techniques' for an installation, Article 9(2) enables Member State regulatory authorities not to impose requirements relating to energy efficiency in relation to burners or other units emitting CO_2 at an installation for those installations that are covered by both Directives.

However, it is questionable whether the IED really does prevent Member States from setting ELVs for GHGs in permits.[48] This view relies on the idea that the amendment of the IPPC Directive (96/61/EC) through the ETS Directive in Article 9(3) only prohibits Member States to impose ELVs under the IPPC Directive and its successors, including the IED, but not under other national legislation or rules. This reading of Article 9(1) of the IED is further supported by the primary EU law provision in Article 193 TFEU, which expressly preserves powers for Member States to maintain or introduce more stringent protective measures, which must be compatible with the Treaties. But whether such residual powers for Member States are available also depends on whether EU environmental secondary legislation has fully harmonized the field of regulating CO_2 emissions. If there has been such harmonization (which an ETS might well represent), then there is no room for more stringent action by Member States. Moreover, given the fact that national emission limit values will not *necessarily* be more stringent than actual emissions emitted under a trading scheme where the price for the GHGs allowance is high, as will be explained further, Member States may not be able to rely on Article 193 TFEU in any case.

This issue has been further clarified through the legally non-binding Preamble 10 of the Directive on Industrial Emissions, which now explicitly states in general terms that, in accordance with Article 193 TFEU, Member States can maintain or introduce more stringent protective measures, also in relation to GHG emission requirements, as long as these measures are compatible with the EU Treaties and have been notified to the Commission. Preamble 9 adds a further clarification of the interface between the IED and the ETS Directive that the permit for an installation covered by the ETS Directive shall not include an emission limit value for direct emissions of the greenhouse gases specified in Annex I to that Directive unless this is necessary for preventing significant local pollution.

The consequences of this interface between the IED and the ETS Directive for environmental protection, and in particular for tackling climate change, are not clear, but the possibility of weakening environmental protection is opened up. Installations covered by the IED that emit CO_2 are now free to purchase emission allowances under the EU ETS to cover their GHG emissions and thus to potentially emit *more* GHG emissions than they could have emitted if they would have been subjected to a

[45] Regulators maintain powers to impose emission limit values for GHGs where an installation is exempted from the EU Emissions Trading regime: IED, art 9(4).

[46] This change occurred first through an amendment of the first IPPC Directive (96/61/EC) [1996] OJ L257/26 by the Emissions Trading Directive (2003/87/EC) [2003] OJ L275/32.

[47] See ETS Directive, Annex I, as amended by Directive 2009/29/EC [2009] L140/63.

[48] David Wyatt and Richard Macrory, Legal Advice, 'Does the EU's proposed Directive on Industrial Emissions (IPPC) preclude Member States from Imposing Emission Limits for CO_2 under National Rules other than those implementing the proposed Directive?', at: <http://www.europolitique.info/pdf/gratuit_fr/269819-fr.pdf>.

stringent emission limit value for GHGS under the IED in their environmental permit. Given the fact that in Phase I and II of the EU ETS prices for emission allowances have been very low, this is a real risk. However, if prices for GHG emission allowances go up in the EU, this may be an incentive for operators of installations to reduce their GHG emissions, potentially below the limit that a fixed BAT technology standard would have set.

The wider point to note here is that the interface between a traditional 'command and control' regulatory regime imposed through the IED and a flexible, economic incentive regulatory regime, such as the ETS established under the ETS Directive, leads to a lack of control for regulators in reducing GHG emissions. Chapter 2 flagged up the importance of uncertainty in knowledge about environmental problems in environmental law. The interaction between the IED and the ETS Directive extends uncertainty in knowledge about environmental problems to lack of knowledge about the impact of market based regulatory tools.

This type of problematic interface would have become even more significant if the UK's and Netherlands' push for the establishment of an EU-wide emissions trading regime in NO_x and SO_x had been successful. Such a trading regime would have taken these two further key air pollutants out of the ambit of the IED and again opened up the possibility of potentially fewer reductions of polluting emissions through a market based regulation. Such an extension of EU-wide emissions trading, however, had been opposed by industry. The Commission has now decided not to go ahead with an EU-wide scheme. But the problematic interface persists in relation to national ETSs and the obligations of the IED.

For instance, the UK had already established a national ETS for NO_x and SO_x in 2007 to meet the obligations of the former Large Combustion Plant Directive.[49] The IED seems to allow Member States to achieve compliance with its legal obligations for large combustion plants through national emissions trading, for example, in NO_x and SO_x. The IED enables Member States to put in place 'transitional national plans' that cover specified air pollutants, but only for the time period from 1 January 2016 to 30 June 2020. Once a transitional national plan covers a large combustion plant, Article 32(2) exempts it from the provisions of Article 30 IED for specified air pollutants,[50] but only for the time period from 1 January 2016 to 30 June 2020.

But a number of procedural prescriptions are in place that will limit the uncertainty that the introduction of a trading instrument will introduce the achievement of a reduction in specific air pollutants. First, Article 32(2) IED requires that emissions of SO_x, NO_x, and dust from large combustion plants that applied to installations through permit conditions until December 2015 must be at least maintained, and that—as a minimum—these emissions should comply with the requirements of the previous Large Combustion Plant Directive and previous IPPC Directive.[51] Second, Article 32(3) further clarifies that, if Member States choose to implement the provisions of the IED on large combustion plants through a national emissions trading scheme for NO_x and SO_x, it has to be a 'cap and trade' system.[52] Article 32(3) requires that the transitional national plan shall set a ceiling, which defines the maximum total annual emissions for all the plants covered by the plan. The minimum cap has to be set at the level of the emission limit values specified for major air pollutants in the previous Large

---

[49] Directive 2001/80/EC on the limitation of emissions of certain pollutants into the air from large combustion plants [2001] OJ L309/1.

[50] Article 30 IED requires that large combustion plants comply with the *emission limit values* set out in Part I of Annex V to the Directive.

[51] Moreover, according to art 32(2) IED, 'Combustion plants with a total rated thermal input of more than 500 MW firing solid fuels, which were granted the first permit after 1 July 1987, shall comply with the emission limit values for nitrogen oxides set out in Part 1 of Annex V'.

[52] See further, Chapter 12.

Combustion Plant Directive.[53] Pressure for emission reductions is also maintained through the provision that plant closures or the withdrawal of plants from the regulatory scheme, for instance through capacity reduction, shall not lead to an increase of emissions available for the remaining plants covered by the plan. Fourth, transitional national plans have to be fairly specific because Article 32(3) further requires that, for each pollutant, the plan must specify a cap which defines the maximum total annual emissions for all of the plants covered by the plan, taking into account the thermal input of each plant, its actual annual operating hours, and its fuel use.

Overlapping pollution control regimes where the IED takes precedence to increase levels of environmental protection

In a second type of interaction between the pollution control regime under the IED and other pollution control regimes, the provisions of the Directive may take precedence over the environmental standards of other pollution control regimes, thereby leading to better environmental protection. An example of this is the interaction between the legal rules that implement integrated pollution prevention and control under the IED in the UK, in particular under the Environmental Permitting (England and Wales) Regulations 2010 ('EPRs'), and the contaminated land regime under Part II A of the Environmental Protection Act 1990 (EPA 1990). DEFRA's Core Guidance for the EPRs suggests that if a regulated facility is polluted (including its land) as a result of activities regulated under integrated pollution prevention and control, powers to take enforcement action under Part IIA of EPA 1990 are displaced by enforcement powers under the EPRs.[54] Once an environmental permit for an installation, including installations covered by the IED, has been surrendered, the regulator can further consider remediation of the land. The requirements for remediation imposed by the environmental permitting regime will usually be higher than those required under Part IIA of EPA 1990.[55]

Overlapping pollution control regimes where the IED takes precedence to potentially lower levels of environmental protection

There is a third type of overlap between IPC and other EU environmental Directives. In this scenario the IPC regime takes precedence, with the possibility to detract from environmental protection objectives set out in other EU environmental Directives. An example of this type of overlap arose in the joint ECJ cases of *Stichting Natuur en Milieu and Others v College van Gedeputeerde Staten van Groningen* (C-165/09) and *College van Gedeputeerde Staten van Zuid-Holland* (C-166/09 and C-167/09).[56] These cases arose at the time when the former consolidated IPPC Directive was still in force, but the ECJ's reasoning in the cases is still relevant for understanding the relationship between the IED and other EU environmental protection directives.

In these cases, permissions to construct power stations in various locations in the Netherlands were challenged, on the grounds that on the basis of scientific evidence it was likely that the Netherlands would breach its obligations to comply with overall emissions ceilings for NO_x and SO_x under the EU

---

[53] According to Article 32(3) IED, the ceiling for emissions for the years 2019 and 2020 shall be set with reference to the emission limit values set out in Part 1 of Annex V of the Directive. The upper limits for the years 2017 and 2018 shall be set in such a way that there is a continuous 'linear' decrease of the upper limit for emissions over the whole period of the transitional plan from 2016 until 2019. Hence, for the years 2017 and 2018 Member States have more flexibility in that they are simply required to provide for 'a linear decrease' of the ceilings for the time period from 2016 to 2019, leaving open how much that decrease will be in each specific year.

[54] DEFRA (2013) Environmental Permitting Guidance, Core Guidance March 2013, para A 1.7.

[55] Ibid para A1.7, 79.   [56] [2011] 3 CMLR 21; [2012] Env LR 2.

National Emissions Ceiling Directive (NEC Directive).[57] Two Dutch environmental organizations and four citizens argued before a Dutch court that Article 9 of the IPPC Directive required the Dutch public authorities to have rejected the permit applications, or at least to have imposed limits in relation to NO_x and SO_x in the permits for these new power stations.[58] The cases were referred through the preliminary reference procedure to the ECJ. The ECJ held that Article 9(1), (3), and (4) of the former IPPC Directive did not require national authorities to impose emission limits for NO_x and SO_x in permits for new power stations, as long as the overall programmatic environmental objectives for the reduction of NO_x and SO_x laid down in the NEC Directive were met. The ECJ found that the old consolidated IPPC Directive was concerned with the imposition of *specific qualitative requirements*, which related to concentrations of polluting substances that had to be achieved within a particular environmental medium, such as air.[59] In contrast to this, the NEC Directive was concerned with the establishment of general, programmatic aims for NO_x and SO_x for Member States.

Moreover, the NEC Directive was not listed in Annex II of the IPPC Directive as one of the Directives that were to be considered during the permitting of an IPPC installation. The ECJ also held that the NEC Directive could not be considered as 'other Community legislation', which had to be considered in the IPPC permitting process, because such 'other Community legislation' had to contain emission limit values. The NEC does not provide for such specific emission limit values; it simply sets upper limits for Member States for the total emissions of four key air pollutants.[60]

Hence, the ruling in the case retains significant discretionary powers for national authorities to allow them to decide how they will achieve compliance with EU environmental protection directives, in particular where these—such as the NEC Directive in this case—do not provide for specific emission limit values for installations. The Netherlands, for instance, had established a national NO_x trading scheme in order to achieve the objectives of the NEC Directive. For SO_x, a binding and enforceable memorandum of understanding was concluded between the national and provincial Dutch public authorities and all the electricity companies concerned. This memorandum of understanding required all signatories to comply with an emission limit for the Dutch energy sector as a whole for the period from 2008 to 2019.[61]

In contrast to the first type of overlap discussed here, in this second type of overlap EU environmental legislation does not explicitly detract from the power of the national permitting authority to impose conditions to restrict the emission of certain pollutants (though note that since Phase III of EU ETS, NO_x gases are now also traded as GHGs and thus the Dutch national authorities can no longer impose emission limit values in relation to NO_x in permits granted under the IED, unless this is necessary in order to ensure that no significant local pollution is caused). But, in practice, a similar situation arises as in the first overlap. The ECJ decided in joint cases C-165/09, C-166/09, and C-167/09 that the national permitting authority was not required to use Article 9 of the then old IPPC Directive to impose clear and specific emission limit values in relation to NO_x and SO_x on new installations. Other measures taken by the Netherlands to achieve a reduction in NO_x and SO_x emissions may have been more effective in improving air quality than emission limit values imposed in the IPPC permits for the thermal power stations. But they may also have been less effective, and the view of the environmental organizations here was that a traditional 'command and control' tool was more apt than flexible, co-operative tools to reduce emissions in light of scientific evidence that the Netherlands was likely not to meet its national emission targets under the NEC.

---

[57] 2001/81/EC; [2001] OJ L 309, 22. For further discussion of the NEC Directive, see Chapter 16.

[58] *Stichting Natuur en Milieu and Others v College van Gedeputeerde Staten van Groningen* (C-165/09) and *College van Gedeputeerde Staten van Zuid-Holland* (C-166/09 and C-167/09), para 38.

[59] Ibid, para 62.   [60] Ibid, para 65.   [61] Ibid, para 27.

Overlapping environmental regulation where the IED takes precedence with no effect on environmental protection

There is a fourth type of interaction between the IED and other environmental legislation. This is mainly procedural and involves legal powers under the IED taking precedence as *lex specialis* without significant effect on the level of environmental protection achieved. An example of this is the interaction between the IED and EA powers under the EPRs, on the one hand, and the statutory nuisance regime under Part III of EPA 1990, on the other hand.[62] Statutory nuisances are regulated by local authorities but, unless the Secretary of State or the Welsh ministers have granted consent, a local authority may not start proceedings in respect of a statutory nuisance where enforcement action against the nuisance could be taken under the EPRs.[63] While statutory nuisances can be prosecuted as a criminal offence under s 80(4) EPA 1990, the EA can employ significant enforcement powers under the EPRs, such as prosecution for a criminal offence under Regulation 38(2) for operating in breach of the conditions of an environmental permit. Perhaps even more effectively in terms of bargaining 'in the shadow' of these legal provisions, which can have a significant impact on the operator's commercial interests, the EA has powers to revoke or suspend the environmental permit under Regulations 22(1) and 37(1) of the EPRs. If activities occur on sites regulated under the IED that are not covered by the EPRs, local authority powers in relation to statutory nuisance can still be used without the consent of the Secretary of State or the Welsh ministers. Moreover, citizens retain powers to bring private prosecutions under s 82 EPA 1990 in relation to statutory nuisance occurring at installations covered by the IED.[64]

Overlapping EU and 'gold plated' national pollution control regulation

Finally, there is a fifth type of interaction between the IED and other environmental legislation involving national implementation of law that imposes potentially more onerous obligations than required under the Directive. Various examples of this exist in the UK context. First, the EPRs go further in their procedural definition of integrated pollution prevention and control than the IED requires. As well as the waste regulation incorporated by the EPRs (England and Wales) 2007, water discharge activities, ground water activities, and the regulation of radioactive substances are now included in the single permitting system operated by the EA.

However, the courts may be more reluctant to give expression to national legal provisions that go further than EU law requires. In *R (on the application of Edwards and another (Appellant)) v Environment Agency and others (No. 2) (Respondents)*,[65] the publicity requirements of the then applicable PPC (England and Wales) Regulations 2000 went further than the former IPPC Directive required, because they applied to existing installations and required publication of formal supplementary inquiries as well as the further information obtained through such inquiries. The House of Lords rejected an appeal that sought to quash a PPC permit on grounds of procedural unfairness because the national courts were under no duty to impose the wider interpretation of the PCC regulations, as long as the requirements of the IPPC Directive were complied with. The House of Lords also rejected a wide interpretation of the PPC Regulations on the policy ground that a requirement imposed upon

---

[62] See further, Chapter 9 for discussion of statutory nuisances.
[63] Section 79(10) Environmental Protection Act 1990. See DEFRA (2013) Environmental Permitting Core Guidance, A.1.19.
[64] It is likely that these powers will remain the same for the UK regulator now that the IED has been passed.
[65] [2008] UKHL 22.

the EA to disclose its internal working documents for further public consultation would create a risk of never-ending public participation processes.

This case may still hold some relevance. Although the IED has extended access to information for members of the public in comparison to the previous IPPC Directive, the EPRs provide for a broad range of detailed obligations, which are imposed upon the regulator in relation to the inclusion of information in a public register. For instance, paragraph 1(1)(i) of Schedule 24 of the EPRs provides an open-ended obligation according to which 'all other information given to the regulator in compliance with' an environmental permit condition, an enforcement notice, a suspension notice, as well as closure notices for landfill sites and mining waste facilities, or notices issued under Regulation 60 of the EPRs (which enables regulators to obtain information about emissions from a site), shall be placed on the public register. Paragraph 1(1)(j) adds to this that 'every report published by the regulator relating to an assessment of the environmental consequences of the operation of an installation' shall also be placed on the public register.

3   THE NATURE OF ENVIRONMENTAL LEGAL OBLIGATIONS UNDER IPC

3.1   IS THE 'BEST AVAILABLE TECHNIQUES' STANDARD INDETERMINATE?

From a jurisprudential perspective, a critical analysis of the IED, and the BAT standard in particular, raises questions about the nature of integrated pollution control law. The questions raised in Section 2.2 about the interpretation of the BAT technology standard already indicate that it can be difficult to pin down what constitutes BAT in general terms or for a specific installation. This criticism may not be answered by simply perfecting techniques of legal interpretation and the development of further case law in relation to IPPC, of which there is little so far. This raises the question of whether 'indeterminacy' may be a characteristic of the BAT technology standard. But, as the extracts from Endicott and Yablon show, there is not necessarily agreement on how we define 'indeterminacy' in law.

Timothy Endicott, *Vagueness in Law* (OUP 2000), 7–9, 20, 202–3

Linguistic Indeterminacy

No person shall take or possess, in the County of Lanark or the Regional Municipality of Ottawa-Carleton, any bullfrog unless the tibia thereof is five centimetres or more in length. (Regulation under the Ontario Game and Fish Act, O. Reg. 694/81).

We can think of cases in which liability for catching bullfrogs in Ottawa is indeterminate, that is, cases in which the law does not determine whether an offence has been committed. What if a bullfrog has one tibia longer than 5 cm and one shorter? What if the length of a tibia is pushed over 5 cm by a rare growth? [...]

Countless indeterminacies appear in linguistic formulations of legal rules: lexical ambiguities (does 'person' include a company?), syntactical ambiguities (does the person have to be in Ottawa? does the bullfrog?), uncertainty as to whether 'take' adds anything to 'possess', and so on.

Bullfrog hunters and their lawyers might face further legal indeterminacies that do not arise from the language of the regulation: if there is an unresolved conflict between the bullfrog regulation and another rule, or if the power to make the regulation or the procedures by which it was promulgated or enforced are suspect, or if it is unclear whether proof of some mental state is required for conviction, or whether principals are liable when agents take bullfrogs. And the lawyers and the bullfrog hunters may face further uncertainties that are neither linguistic nor legal, such as whether the authorities will exercise their discretion to prosecute, whether a particular witness will make it to court, and so on.

Those non-linguistic indeterminacies arise because life and legal systems are complicated. But people can choose their words, and it would be reassuring to think that linguistic indeterminacy, at least, could be eradicated by careful use of language. Perhaps the drafters of the bullfrog regulation set out to do this by avoiding imprecise terms like 'adult bullfrog' or 'large bullfrog'. What does their failure to eliminate linguistic indeterminacy show about law and language? Indeterminacy seems pervasive and obdurate.

[...]

I will argue that, when the concessions to determinacy are accounted for, every claim about indeterminacy that we will see is consistent with what Hart said about language: 'There will indeed be plain cases ... to which general expressions are clearly applicable ... but there will also be cases where it is not clear whether they apply or not.'

[...]

When is Vagueness a Deficit in the Rule of Law?

Vagueness in the law is not necessarily a deficit in the rule of law [...] If we return to Raz's organizing principle - that people must be able to use the law as a guide—then it is tempting to keep on insisting that vagueness is always a deficit, because there are ways in which people really cannot guide themselves by a vague rule (where they *could* guide themselves by a similar precise rule).

[...]

To make sense of the organizing principle of the ideal, we need to distinguish between using the law as a guide, and using the law to dictate an outcome in every possible case

[...]

Vagueness is a deficit when it lends itself to arbitrariness [...] to abandoning the reason of the law. Authorities can use vagueness to exempt their actions from the reason of the law, or even to make it impossible to conceive of the law as having any reason distinguishable from the will of the officials. Then vagueness is a deficit in the rule of law.

In this extract, Endicott defines 'indeterminate law' as law the meaning of which is vague. But does Endicott's discussion of the vagueness of legal *rules* shed any light on the nature of the BAT technology *standard*? Technology standards may be considered as one of the most precise legal prescriptions. In contrast to the rule against bullfrog taking and possession referred to at the beginning of Endicott's extract, the IED *defines* the various terms that make up BATs concept. Usually BAT norms are also further defined through specific reference conditions, such as the temperature and gas pressure under which a particular emission limit value for say an air pollutant has to be met. Such a detailed definition of the environmental standard means that the standard is to some degree determinate and 'closed'. If the standard is set out in purely general terms, it is indeterminate or 'open'.

The following may be considered as an example of a determinate BAT standard: a condition in an environmental permit requires the operator to install any one of the fixed number of known abatement technologies referred to in the conclusion of the BREF document for Iron and Steel plants in order to abate emissions from a coke oven. The emission limit value imposed in such a permit would be 20 mg/nm^3 of NO$_x$ emissions. The meaning of this emission limit value is further rendered precise in the permit through reference to a particular *validated measurement methodology* by which compliance with this standard will be assessed and the *reference conditions* (that is, the particular pressure and temperature of the stack gases) under which this standard has to be achieved. Moreover, the *guidance* provided by the Secretary of State and the environmental regulators, such as the EA, on what constitutes BAT, may further close the meaning of BAT. Such detailed definition of the standard means that there is some determination (or 'closure') of a standard that, if set out in purely general terms, would be indeterminate (or 'open').

Further, in order to understand whether the BAT standard is indeterminate, it is important to go beyond an abstract, legal theoretical consideration of environmental law, and to consider the determinacy and indeterminacy of environmental law as an empirical issue. One legal rule, in its application to various fact scenarios, may generate both closed and open norms, depending on the precise situation to which it applies. Thus, in some industry sectors controlled by the IED, the list of technologies that are considered as BAT may be left open or there may be no agreement in the first place on what constitutes BAT, there may simply be 'split views' in TWGs. There may also be *no* agreement on what constitutes a validated measurement method for a particular pollutant and the range of permissible emissions of this pollutant may be very wide, providing limited closure of the technology standard. Hence, there may in fact be *variation* in the *degree of determinacy* of a legal rule. Most importantly, understanding indeterminacy of law as an empirical issue brings to the fore another important definition of indeterminacy, which considers it not simply as vagueness in law, but as arising from the fact that legal rules by themselves often cannot explain the behaviour of legal actors, and thus legal outcomes.

Charles Yablon, The Indeterminacy of the Law: Critical Legal Studies and the Problem of Legal Explanation' (1985) 6 *Cardozo Law Review*, 917–20, 931

A central assertion of the Critical Legal Studies theorists is that the law—or more specifically, the relationship between authoritative doctrinal materials (like statutes, cases, etc.) and the actions of legal decision makers—is loose or 'indeterminate.' They reject the notion that legal doctrine can ever compel determinate results, in a deductive sense, in concrete cases. In so doing, Critical theorists seek to associate legal indeterminacy with the feeling, familiar to most law students and practising lawyers, that doctrine can be utilized to argue any side of any legal issue. [...] [T]his perception—that every case can be argued both ways within the doctrinal system—appears to be inconsistent with another equally familiar phenomenon. Lawyers can, and often do, 'determine,' in the sense of 'predict,' the results of concrete cases, and they do so largely through an analysis and application of doctrinal principles.

[...]The Critical claim that the law is indeterminate need not, and should not be viewed merely as a dispute about the extent to which law is predictable. Indeed, such a claim need not at all deny the existence of predictive, or even causal relationships between legal doctrine and concrete legal results. Rather, the Critical claim of legal indeterminacy may be understood as a declaration that doctrine can never be an adequate *explanation* of legal results.

[...] the inadequacy of doctrinal explanation leads to the emphasis in Critical theory on the motivations of decision makers and the explanation of legal results in terms of underlying social and political structures.

If doctrines and policies cannot explain judicial results, what can? [...] Since Critical theorists are well aware that doctrines and policies exist to justify any legal result, the decision maker's *choice* of any particular doctrine becomes the fundamental event that requires explanation.

This is true even if the decision maker believes herself to be constrained by doctrinal rules and does not recognize that she has made such a choice at all. If the judge believes herself constrained by the Parol Evidence Rule, it is the source of that belief which requires explanation. That explanation cannot be provided by the Parol Evidence Rule itself, but may perhaps be provided by an analysis of her attitude toward the Rule-her *motive* in concluding that that rule was applicable, and not some other.

Yablon's analysis provides a framework for capturing the vagueness of the BAT technology standard in the IED. But his categorical insistence on the indeterminacy of the 'law in the books' needs to be qualified by reference to an analysis of the 'law in action' that is nuanced enough to recognize different degrees of indeterminacy in the 'law in action'. Particularly in relation to the BAT technology standard, this includes variation in openness and closure of the standard. In the IED, the BAT technology standard is defined in a fairly open-ended way, also because it is a dynamic technology standard that is subject to change.

Yablon suggests that, from a critical legal studies perspective, legal arguments are ultimately arguments over the nature of political and social activity. If the text of the IED is limited in tying down the meaning of the BAT technology standard and thus on its own terms cannot explain why regulators and regulated installations implement particular BAT standards, the question arises whether economic arguments are at the heart of what amounts to BAT, even if the text of the Directive does not suggest that economic considerations should weigh more strongly in BAT determinations than environmental considerations. Can cost considerations in the application of the BAT standard 'close' the meaning of BAT? The IED is fairly transparent in importing economic considerations directly into the legal text, even though references to cost considerations in BAT determinations do not further 'close' the BAT standard in the legal text but, if anything, further open up the possibility of different environmental standards being considered as 'BAT'. During the *practical* application of the BAT standard, however, cost considerations are often important determining factors in the choice of environmental standards. They contribute to 'closing' the BAT standard and thus rendering it less indeterminate.

Article 3(10)(b) of the IED defines 'available' techniques as those that are 'developed on a scale which allows implementation in the relevant industrial sector, under economically and technically viable conditions, taking into consideration the costs and advantages'. There is no definition of 'costs' in the IED and hence it is unclear whether they include costs to the environment and the regulator or refer only to costs for operators. The Commission communication, 'On the Road to Sustainable Production', suggests that pollution reduction benefits to society should be considered as counterbalancing costs to operators.[66] Moreover, the text of the IED does not provide for a procedure or methodology for determining costs, that is, whether they should include installation and maintenance costs or capital investment costs only and how costs should be taken into account in BAT determinations.[67] Government guidance seems to suggest that costs should only be a secondary factor to be taken into account in the determination of BAT:[68]

[66] Communication of 19 June 2003 from the Commission to the Council, the European Parliament, the European Economic and Social Committee, and the Committee of the Regions: 'On the Road to Sustainable Production. Progress in implementing Council Directive 96/61/EC concerning integrated pollution prevention and control' COM(2003) 354 final, 15.

[67] Previous UK national guidance suggested that cost considerations should include operation and capital costs. DEFRA Environmental Permitting Guidance: The IPPC Directive, March 2010, version 3.0, 20.

[68] Ibid, 20.

> Once the options have been ranked, that which minimises environmental impact from the installation will be BAT unless economic considerations render it unavailable

There are further specific provisions in the IED that refer to costs; such as Article 15(4), which allows competent authorities in the Member States to derogate from BAT if this would lead to disproportionately high costs compared to the environmental benefits to be gained. This derogation only applies where the disproportionately higher costs are caused by the geographical location or the local environmental conditions of the installation concerned or its technical characteristics. But it is clear that in balancing the 'best' and the 'available' elements of the BATs technology standard regulators have considerable discretion. The Directive seems to construct BAT standard setting as a trade-off between economic and environmental considerations.

A 2005 case of the English courts, *R (on the application of Rockware Glass Ltd) v Chester CC*,[69] tipped the balance of this trade-off decision towards environmental considerations. This case was decided under the former IPPC Directive, but its arguments and findings about the BAT standard are also relevant for BAT determinations under the IED. The applicant—Rockware Glass Ltd—was a glass manufacturer and commercial competitor of Quinn, another glass manufacturer who, in March 2005, had obtained a PPC permit from Chester City Council for the operation of a new glass container manufacturing plant projected to be the biggest glass plant in Europe. Rockware Glass Ltd launched a successful judicial review application in the High Court against Chester City Council for the PPC permit to be quashed, though the quashing order was stayed pending the appeal to the Civil Division of the Court of Appeal. In particular, Rockware challenged the NO_x emission limit imposed in this permit for a new installation, considering it to be too low. The permit granted by Chester City Council required Quinn to reduce its NO_x emissions from its new plant over time as follows:

- 1000 mg/nm3 by the end of year one of operations;
- 900 mg/nm3 by the end of year two;
- 750 mg/nm3 by the end of year three;
- 500 mg/nm3 by the end of year four, that is, 2009.

The Court found these staged emission limit values to be unlawful since the national Sector Guidance Note (SG) 2 for glass manufacturing processes clearly stated that staged emission limits were only available for *existing* processes, while *new* installations such as Quinn's had to comply from the start of its operations with the 500 mg/nm3 limit for NO_x.[70]

The first key legal issue in the case was the relationship between air quality standards imposed by the EU Air Quality Framework Directive and the emission limit values required under the IPPC Directive. Quinn argued that Chester City Council should only have regard to the question whether local air quality standards—as required under the Air Quality Directive—were breached through the emission limit for NO_x in Quinn's PPC permit. The Court of Appeal rejected this argument, which is extracted and analysed in detail in Section 2.2 of Chapter 15. The Court's reasoning emphasizes the importance of environmental considerations, beyond mere compliance with EU air quality standards, as central to a definition of what constitute the BATs in an integrated pollution prevention and control regime, to the detriment of cost arguments. A key legal issue examined in the case concerned the question what constituted BAT for the glass container manufacturing process. Whilst the extract here has shown that environmental pollution reduction was the priority concern in setting BAT standards, there were more detailed aspects of setting this standard that involved questions over the proper

---

[69] [2006] EWCA Civ 992.
[70] *R (on the application of Rockware Glass Ltd) v Chester CC* [2006] EWCA Civ 992, para 55.

relevance of economic considerations. More specifically, the particular issue was whether Quinn was legally required to install secondary catalytic reduction (SRC) that would reduce NO_x emissions to below 500 mg/nm3 at his installation, also given the extra costs of these secondary abatement measures. On this point, the extract gives the findings of the Court of appeal in *R (on the application of Rockware Glass Ltd) v Chester CC* at first instance.

R (on the application of Rockware Glass Ltd) v Chester CC
[2006] EWCA Civ 992, paras 48–50 (Buxton LJ)

Now SG2 is merely guidance: but there should be reasons shown for departing from it. Even using the cross-fire furnaces that Quinn have installed, it is perfectly possible to achieve the SG2 level of NOX of 500 mg per cubic metre now, and not just by 2009. That can be done by the installation of secondary adjustments to the system. That is asserted in the affidavit of a Mr Kitson, filed on behalf of Quinn, in which he sets out the circumstances in which Quinn is in the process of applying for a new permit to take the place of the one that stands quashed. He says this in paragraph 4.5:

'The new IPPC application proposes the installation of secondary catalytic reduction-denox system. This is intended to reduce the NOX emissions from the plant to below 500 mg/m3 and it is intended that the new IPPC permit would contain a limit of 500 mg/m3 for NOX.'

49 Quinn objects to doing that because it says it will cost them money; apparently calculated, as far as we can see from the papers, at a figure of 67p per tonne produced, or a cost increase of some 3%. Quinn's objection to being asked to take that step reverted to the claim that I have rejected, that they cannot be required to do anything if emissions in the area as a whole remain below currently stated minimum EQS values. But if BAT in terms of emission standards is properly applied, no rational reason was advanced, indeed no other reason at all was advanced, for departing from the SG2 guidance that BAT is that which reduces emissions to or below 500. We know that such technology is available in this case and indeed is currently being installed.

50 I would therefore not interfere with the judge's declarations, whilst noting that the future course for the regulator in this case should be guided by the provision of SG2 as explained in the preceding paragraphs.

The Court of Appeal suspended the quashing order until Chester City Council had decided on the new PPC permit for which Quinn had applied. Quinn's new application provided for the installation of secondary catalytic reduction to its burners that would bring NO_x emissions down to less than 500 mg/nm3. Contrary to what counsel for Rockware Glass had argued, the Court of Appeal held that the short-term deferment of the quashing order for the first PPC permit was not incompatible with the court's obligations to give full expression to EU law, here the obligation to give full effect to the IPPC Directive in national law.[71]

So, what light does the Rockware case shed on the indeterminacy of the BAT standard? The legal provisions of the former IPPC Directive and UK law by themselves cannot completely account for the result in this case. Economic considerations did contribute to the 'closure' of the BAT standard here. Note that the Court of Appeal did not require Quinn to implement pollution prevention fully, which would have been achieved through the installation of the more modern oxyfuel process for glass manufacture, referred to in Sector Guidance Note 2 as BAT.[72] Given that Quinn had simply gone ahead and built the plant with its burners without first seeking planning permission from Chester

[71] *R (on the application of Rockware Glass Ltd) v Chester CC* [2006] EWCA Civ 992, paras 75–76.
[72] SG 2, October 2006, para 3.51.

City Council, or indeed providing an Environmental Impact Assessment for the development,[73] Lord Justice Buxton found that it would have been disproportionate to require Quinn to install the new technology if secondary measures for the existing cross-fire burners could bring the NO_x emissions down to the required 500 mg/m3. Buxton LJ also referred in his judgment to the fact that Quinn had taken on a substantial number of employees.

Qualitative empirical research about the approach of UK and German regulators' approach to BAT decision-making suggests—as in the case of Quinn—that operators and sometimes regulators consider costs as a key issue in the determination of BAT. While sometimes low in visibility, cost considerations are highly significant and pervasive for achieving BAT definitions.[74] Cost arguments would not necessarily have to be raised explicitly but could also be couched in terms of what is technically feasible at a particular installation or what is environmentally desirable to achieve. Further, cost considerations are pervasive in the determination of BAT also because they are considered cumulatively at three different levels. First, costs of techniques are considered when the EU BREF documents are drafted for the various sectors covered by the IED. Second, costs are again taken into account when EU Member States draw up national guidance notes or pass technical rules, such as the 'Technical Instruction Air' (TA Luft) in Germany, or draw up sector permitting plans as in the UK. Third, costs are considered at the local level when BAT is determined for a specific installation. While the presumption is that a BAT technique for an installation would be one of the techniques listed in the national Technical Guidance Note, there may be deviations from this in exceptional circumstances. Such deviations, however, would require a specific justification and reasons for why a lower cost option was chosen and how standards at the installation could be raised through an improvement programme.[75]

3.2 DOES THE DIRECTIVE ON INDUSTRIAL EMISSIONS PROVIDE FOR 'PROCEDURAL' AND 'REFLEXIVE' ENVIRONMENTAL STANDARDS?

Further examination of the legal provisions of the IED from a jurisprudential perspective raises the question of whether the Directive's contribution to developing the integrity of environmental law lies in the prescription of *procedures* for environmental standard setting, rather than in the definition of specific *substantive* environmental standards. In other words: can the provisions of the IED be considered as illustrative of new forms of EU governance and 'procedural' or 'reflexive' law in particular?

Karl-Heinz Ladeur, 'Chapter 13: Coping with Uncertainty: Ecological Risks and the Proceduralization of Environmental Law in G Teubner, L Farmer, and D Murphy (eds) *Environmental Law and Ecological Responsibility: The Concept and Practice of Ecological Self-Organisation* (1994 John Wiley & Sons 1994) 325, 328–29

Administrative regulation and flexibilization

[...] All this is to say that the regulatory perspective of the state must be adapted to a second-order proceduralization. This is a version of proceduralization that both presupposes and assists the processes

---

[73] In *R (on the application of Ardagh Glass Ltd) v Chester City Council* [2010] EWCA Civ 172 the Court of Appeal found that it was proportionate and thus lawful for Chester City Council to consider in exceptional circumstances retrospectively an EIA and grant retrospectively planning permission for Quinn's glass manufacturing process.

[74] Bettina Lange (2008) *Implementing EU Pollution Control: Law and Integration*, ch 7.

[75] Ibid, ch 8.

of search and learning at the level of the enterprise. The first step towards the proceduralization of risk management can already be seen in the imposition of a set of predetermined legal standards. This is not satisfactory because it can create perverse effects, through the costs it imposes on the product development process, without effectively creating more safety [...] (See generally, Gaines, 1990: 289; Shapiro, 1990: 39; Magat, 1982.) At the same time, the effect of this uncertainty on the innovation processes of firms is incalculable... Would it not be more useful to operate beyond the traditional forms of intervention on a second order level, with presumptions for (or against) enterprises according to their procedural level of environmental management (as a kind of self-definition and self-observation of dynamic enterprises?) Procedure could be the basis for the confidence that risk information is being generated in a reasonable way, and thus turn administrative control away from the imposition of tests and towards the evaluation of the risk management of the enterprise itself.

[...]

Science and regulation

These considerations should have made it clear why the problem of environmental law cannot simply be solved by substituting a reference to science for the loss of practical experience. In fact, to do so is misleading, because the openness of science suggests an endless search for safety, unless this is specifically prevented by pragmatic, administrative rationality [...] The perverse result of the existing practice of co-ordination between administration and science, is that it tends to undermine confidence in scientific expertise which has to shoulder the responsibility which administration rejects. The main responsibility in risk management should, on the contrary, belong to administration. Risk strategies must be able to rely on a certain confidence, in the same way that the traditional control strategies based on experience were able to. They are not designed according to a normal deductive logic, but to one of plausibility and for this reason they must contain a potential for self-observation and revision (Dubucs, 1987). Accordingly, they should be reinforced by a procedural rationality which allows the planning and modelling of a variety of operations and options. By stressing the experimental character of scientific modelling as *one* element of a complex operational strategy, it is possible to lay open the provisional character of its knowledge base as the best *available* knowledge, as well as the need to formulate stop rules which accept the time dependency and the limited nature of decisions made under conditions of undecidability (Dupey, 1988)

Karl-Heinz Ladeur discusses the proceduralization of environmental law in the specific context of the development of risky new products and with reference to systems-theory as developed by Niklas Luhmann and further applied to an analysis of legal regulation by Günther Teubner. Proceduralization refers here to environmental regulators merely setting frameworks for pollution reduction activities, which are then developed and managed by private enterprises themselves. Given the fact that the actual pollution abatement technologies that provide the reference point for BAT determinations are developed by mainly private industrial operators, Ladeur's understanding of 'proceduralization' captures one element of the nature of the BAT standard under the IED. While the public administration becomes involved in the setting of the BAT standard, this involvement may be understood, according to Ladeur, mainly in procedural terms. Scientific knowledge about what constitutes the BATs is generated to a considerable extent by private regulated installations themselves.

But, more specifically with reference to integrated pollution control, Joanne Scott develops the idea of 'procedural environmental law' in the context of EU multi-level governance and in relation to the initial IPPC Directive (96/61/EC),[76] by focusing on 'flexibility in implementation' as one of its characteristics.

---

[76] Scott's work refers to the IPPC Directive (96/61/EC), and not the subsequent consolidated IPPC Directive (2008/1/EC) or the Directive on Industrial Emissions (2010/75/EU). However, the points made in the extract here concern procedural provisions of the EU regime of integrated pollution prevention and control that have not changed substantially.

Joanne Scott, 'Flexibility, "Proceduralization", and Environmental Governance in the EU' in G de Burca and J Scott (eds) *Constitutional Change in the EU: From Uniformity to Flexibility?* (Hart Publishing 2000), 259, 265–66, 270–71

[This chapter focuses] upon what may be called the 'flexibility in implementation' approach [to environmental governance in the EU], and exemplifies this model by reference to the Directive on Integrated Pollution Prevention and Control (IPPC). [It] argues that while the flexibility in implementation model is characterized by an endorsement of substantive differentiation in environmental standards in the EU, it is nonetheless (relatively) prescriptive in establishing *procedures* according to which Member State implementation is to be achieved [...] Viewed from any one of a number of theoretical perspectives—be it 'responsive regulation', systems theory or deliberative politics—the Community's (procedurally constrained) flexibility in implementation model emerges as having much to commend it. It nonetheless raises important practical, legal and normative questions.

Joanne Scott then further fleshes out the meaning of 'proceduralization' through reference to 5 values:

Flexibility: facilitating differentiated responses to environmental problems, *decentralisation* of responsibility for environmental problem solving within a framework of multi-level governance; public/private partnerships implying intense *participation* for non-governmental actors, including industrial and environmental associations and citizens groups; *reflexivity* pointing to the importance of continuous learning and adjustment of solutions, at all levels, in the light of new information and experience; and *deliberation* between different groups and levels and spheres of government, implying a more consensual approach to decision-making, albeit against a backdrop of the contestability of the relevant knowledge base.

[...]

The Directive's interest in promoting reflexivity in environmental decision-making is apparent from a number of provisions of the Directive. First and foremost is the obligation incumbent upon operators of industrial installations to include a wide range of information in their permit application, thus seeking to expand the knowledge base according to which governmental decisions are adopted. Also important in this respect is the plethora of information exchange mechanisms established, the emphasis upon monitoring and the dissemination of the results thereof, and the necessity of periodically revisiting permitting decisions adopted, even in the absence of substantial changes to the plants concerned

Joanne Scott identifies multi-level governance in the EU as a further driver for the proceduralization of environmental law. Substantive environmental standards may not always be best set at the EU level, but may require some adaptation to local environmental conditions. Hence the contribution of various levels of governance, EU, national, regional, and local should be considered in the environmental standard-setting process. More simply, difficulties to come to agreements on common environmental standards among the twenty-seven EU Member States—many of which have strong and divergent traditions of national approaches to pollution control—can be a further driver for the adoption of EU procedural environmental law, a first step towards greater convergence in EU environmental governance.

Ladeur locates the development of procedural environmental law in the limits of the legal system to intervene successfully into the social systems of a regulated facility. Environmental law thus takes on a more modest role in simply outlining procedures for environmental regulation without prescribing substantive outcomes, thereby seeking to promote self-reflection and correction by regulated facilities in line with the general regulatory goals specified by the regulator. Procedural law can be criticized—from a functional perspective—as weak environmental law. In relation to the EU regime of integrated pollution prevention and control, 'flexibility in implementation' has meant in practice not just necessary divergence in the implementation of its obligations in the different Member States, but significant shortcomings in Member States to fully implement the obligations of the previous IPPC Directives. Thus, in a number of Member States, conditions in PPC permits fell short of BAT standards specified in the EU BREF documents. The IED has limited, to some extent, flexibility in environmental standard setting. It has done so by integrating six sectoral pieces of EU legislation into the new integrated pollution prevention and control regime under the IED and through its greater emphasis on BREF documents and in particular BAT conclusions as the basis for permit conditions. But it has not gone as far as making BREF documents legally binding.

Scott, however, draws attention to the fact that also procedural prescriptions involve significant exercise of public powers by the EU institutions and therefore should comply with EU constitutional legal principles, such as subsidiarity and proportionality, and—it should be added—with EU administrative law doctrines, such as the rule against unlawful delegation of decision-making powers,[77] the protection of legitimate expectations as well as assessments of manifest error in decision-making (including in the application of the precautionary principle).[78] The implementation of the IED is thus embedded in a wider constitutional and administrative law context, which curtails the exercise of public power. The interesting point that emerges here is that while technology standards are usually understood as fairly specific, substantive environmental standards, the IED provides for a technology standard that is set out in general environmental and administrative legal procedural terms. While this form of procedural environmental regulation may be hailed as a new, innovative, and experimental form of environmental governance, it can also be criticized for 'hollowing out' environmental standards and it draws on the old established 'command and control' regulatory technique of licensing industrial installations through permits. More fundamentally, the dichotomy between 'procedure' and 'substance' needs to be questioned since it goes to the heart of how integrated pollution control under the IED is analysed from a jurisprudential perspective. As discussed in Section 2.3, in practice the 'procedural' BAT standard under the IED does interact with various substantive EU and national environmental standards, sometimes in problematic ways. Procedural standards under the IED thus provide the framework that is filled in by substantive standards, some of which are set out in other EU or national environmental legislation.

FURTHER READING AND QUESTIONS

1. Identify those provisions of the Directive on Industrial Emissions (2010/75/EU) that in your view promote learning about environmental problems and standard setting, amongst regulators as well as the regulated, thus promoting reflexive environmental governance.

2. How in your view could elements of reflexive governance in the IED be strengthened?

3. What factors that shape environmental regulators' behaviour, apart from cost considerations, may contribute to closure of BAT norms in practice?

4. For a further discussion of variation in openness and closure of the BAT standard under the EU regime on integrated pollution prevention and control, see Bettina Lange, *Implementing EU*

---

[77] Case 5/56, *Meroni & Co, Industrie Metallurgiche SpA v High Authority* [1958] ECR 133.
[78] On the application of the precautionary principle by EU institutions, see further, Chapter 11.

Pollution Control: Law and Integration (CUP 2008) and Bettina Lange, 'Searching for the Best Available Techniques Open and Closed Norms in the Implementation of the European Union Directive on Integrated Pollution Prevention and Control', (2006) 2(1) International Journal of Law in Context 67. For further discussion of the implementation of the previous IPPC Directives in different EU Member States see also Eberhard Bohne, *The Quest for Environmental Regulatory Integration in the European Union: Major Accident Prevention* (Kluwer Law International 2006).

4 CONCLUSION

This chapter has critically examined attempts to promote holistic environmental decision-making through the legal rules framing integrated pollution prevention and control at both the EU and UK national level. While the policy idea of holistic environmental governance is elusive, it becomes clearer when traced through specific pollution regimes at particular points in time. The idea that environmental law should reflect 'the laws of nature' is often considered as a characteristic of second wave environmental regulation, although it had appeal even long before the first wave of modern environmental regulation in the 1960s and 1970s. Since then, integrated pollution control has evolved considerably, both technically and in the ambition of its scope. From a jurisprudential perspective, and particularly on a closer analysis of the BAT technology standard—the key regulatory tool of contemporary regimes of integrated pollution control—this evolutionary process raises difficult and very interesting questions about the determinacy and procedural nature of integrated pollution control obligations.

PART V

ENVIRONMENTAL LAW, ENVIRONMENTAL PROBLEMS, AND LAND

INTRODUCTION

In this final part of the textbook, we look at the operation of a variety of environmental law regimes that relate to land. Chapter 19 provides an overview of planning law. As shall be seen, planning law is not just about environmental problems. However, in England, it not only has a major impact on how environmental problems are conceptualized but is also the regime through which many environmental law problems are addressed. This can particularly be seen in relation to environmental impact assessment, nature conservation, and land contamination. These three regimes are then examined in Chapters 19, 20, and 21 respectively. While each area involves at least one specific legal regime, planning law plays an important role in how these regimes operate. Finally, Chapter 22 considers the EU regime for genetically modified organisms, which has an increasing relevance for managing land and regulating environmental problems that relate to it.

Three important themes run through all the chapters in Part V. The first is the significance of legal culture in understanding the nature of land and the relationships of individuals to land. The second is the way in which the level of governance involved shapes our understanding of land and ecology. Following on from this, the third theme is the influential role of devolution and EU governance in relation to environmental problems, land, and environmental law.

One caveat should be made before starting. There is considerable overlap between these chapters and other parts in this book. For example, the line between pollution control and planning is often blurred and problems of land contamination are directly related to issues to do with pollution control. Moreover, how land is conceptualized and the role of EU governance are also relevant to pollution control.

1 ENVIRONMENTAL REGULATION AND RIGHTS TO LAND—LEGAL CULTURE ACROSS PRIVATE AND PUBLIC LAW SPHERES

The chapters in this part require a broader reflection of the legal relationship between the individual and land. This is because each chapter is concerned with how a governing authority regulates what occurs on land, and particularly what occurs on private land. Further, the regulatory regimes involved overlay, and extend beyond, the private relationships that are the subject of land law and which are protected by it. Thus, for example, planning law and nature conservation involve legislative regimes that place limits on what property right holders can do with property. Likewise, Part IIA of the Environmental Protection Act 1990 creates a liability regime for land contamination that can impose liabilities upon those who caused the contamination as well as current landowners. As a result, the operation of these regimes interacts with—and effectively reshapes—ideas of private property and understandings of what limits can be placed on the use of property. (Before reading the chapters in this part, it may be useful to reread at least Chapters 6 and 7.)

With that said, the dominant legal paradigm still sees the relationship between individuals and land from the perspective of individual private rights in land. In this way, the regimes examined in this part are embedded in discourses about what is the legitimate role of the state in regulating private property.

Nicole Graham, *Lawscape: Property, Environment and Law* (Routledge 2011) 183

Environmental regulation, where it requires and/or prohibits specific land use practices, is regarded as antithetical to one of the basic principles or rights of private property, the right of exclusion. It is not simply the right to exclude the physical presence of others, but any interference with the control of the property, including state regulations about land use.

Thus, private rights are privileged in planning law processes, particularly in the context of appeals and enforcement. Likewise, Section 2.2 of Chapter 6 showed how the Sites of Special Scientific Interest (SSSI) regime (examined in Chapter 20) has given rise to a challenge under Article 1 of the 1st Protocol of the ECHR, which is concerned with vindicating individual rights to private property.[1]

However, the chapters in Part V all show that there is a tension between individual rights in private property and the public interest in environmental protection. There is no easy way to resolve this tension and the different regimes examined manage it in different ways. Moreover, this tension highlights the need for a more nuanced understanding of land and property. This more nuanced understanding can be achieved by returning to the point in Chapter 2 that *values* shape our understanding of environmental problems. The same is true of how we understand land and territory. And the values that frame our understanding of land are invariably embedded in legal and socio-political culture. We can see this by interrogating the paradigm model of private interests in land, as Blomley does by considering what can be learnt from the classic English children's book *The Tale of Peter Rabbit* by Beatrix Potter. As some of us may remember, Peter is a young rabbit who creeps into Mr McGregor's garden after his mother told him not to.

Nicholas Blomley, 'The Boundaries of Property: Lessons from Beatrix Potter' (2004) 48 Canadian Geographer 91, 93–94

Peter then enjoys some vegetables until Mr McGregor discovers him and chases him from the garden. Peter, who loses his coat in the ensuing furor, returns home, where he is sent to bed in disgrace. Peter Rabbit is partly a moral tale, which teaches children to obey their parents. It also teaches children to obey the boundary. Peter Rabbit, in that sense, is a didactic tale of law, property and space. [...]

In this sense, Peter Rabbit offers us a clear example of what Joseph Singer (2000) has identified as the privileged understanding of property, which assumes a single owner, entitled to a consolidated bundle of rights (use, exclusion and alienation). The boundary is clearly important to this dominant model—which, in honour of Beatrix Potter, I will name the McGregor model—and seems to have a number of distinguishing characteristics:

- A determinate location and meaning: Both rabbits and gardeners are supposed to know where the boundary is and what it means. This lack of ambiguity is said to be one of the advantages of the boundary as a communicator (cf Sack 1986).

---

[1] *R (Trailer & Marina (Leven) Ltd) v Secretary of State for the Environment, Food & Rural Affairs* [2004] EWCA Civ 1580, [2005] 1 WLR 1267.

- Spatially defined rights: Mr McGregor's rights are imagined as effectively absolute within the boundaries and non-existent beyond the boundary. There are similarities to notions of state sovereignty, where the state is assumed to have absolute, indivisible authority over the territory within its boundaries (Whitaker 1999).

- The boundary as separator: The boundary divides Mr McGregor from other owners or the state. These others are viewed as potentially threatening; thus, Mr McGregor is charged with defending his boundaries.

- A 'separative self' (Nedelsky 1990): This celebrates the individual autonomy of Mr McGregor and views relations with others as secondary, even a threat to the formation of the self. Owner's activities are self-regarding: they legitimately concern only Mr McGregor.

Peter Rabbit is more of a tale about theft and trespass than environmental law, but Blomley's McGregor model is a useful starting point for seeing how ideas about land are bundled up with ideas about the ownership of land that are multifaceted.

Furthermore, they are contestable ideas about ownership of land. The four features of the McGregor model are all challenged by the regimes of environmental law in this part. First, determinate locations of pieces of property often do not work well in relation to environmental problems, which can extend in geographical terms across private property boundaries or even be geographically indeterminate in some cases. Thus, there is no reason why the boundaries of nature conservation enclaves (Chapter 20) will accord with the boundaries of private ownership. Second, the spatially defined rights of a property owner over his or her territory might be at odds with what is understood as required for environmental protection purposes by the state. Consider, for example, the way in which planning law and the SSSI regime prevented the building of the sacrificial sea wall in *Boggis v Natural England*,[2] thus constraining an owner's rights to develop his land as he pleased. Third, planning law shows that landowners are not separated from others by the boundary of their land. Thus, it will often require an owner to change their 'development' because of the impacts it will have outside the boundaries of their property. Those impacts may be on direct neighbours but they also may affect a neighbourhood or an enclave or a species protected under nature conservation law.[3] Fourth, and as already seen in the Graham extract, environmental law can be understood as a threat to private property rights and to the individual autonomy of the property-owning individual.

Another related scholarly perspective on the socio-political appreciation of relationships between individuals and land has been developed in recent years by law and geography scholars studying the interrelationships between law and ideas of place.[4] This scholarship was discussed in Chapter 14 and, just as it is relevant to water, it is relevant here. The chapters in Part V also reflect issues of power, particularly in relation to genetically modified organisms and contaminated land. As you study these regimes, you should ponder the type of power relations involved in each regime. Planning is a good example of this. Likewise, in nature conservation, there is an ongoing attempt to find more private solutions to species and habitats problems, particularly in light of the tension between private property and state intervention discussed already.[5] However, in most cases, there is a significant role for governing authorities, who exert considerable influence and power in regulating the environment, thereby partly constructing the environmental 'space' involved. This important role of state authorities leads on to the second theme that runs through the chapters in this part—governance—discussed in Section 2.

---

[2] [2009] EWCA Civ 1061. See Section 3.1 of Chapter 20.
[3] *Morge v Hampshire County Council* [2011] UKSC 2, [2011] 1 All ER 744.
[4] See Chapter 14 as well.   [5] See Chapter 22.

Overall, in legal terms, the relationship between private property and public law is central to the chapters in this part and it reflects a nuanced and socially embedded aspect of UK legal culture that determines the nature of the relationship between individuals and land. Lawyers, scholars, and students should thus avoid over-simplifying ideas about land as matching those dictated by land law or as simple legal ideas in any respect. Environmental law itself tells an important part of the social, political, and legal story of the (property) relationship between individuals and land.

2 GOVERNING LAND MANAGEMENT

A second feature of Chapters 18, 19, 20, 21, and 22 is the complex nature of governance arrangements over environmental problems that concern land. In particular, a significant number of governing authorities regulate these areas of environmental law. Nature conservation thus involves both specialist and generalist institutions in the regulatory process. Further, these institutions exist at the local, devolved, national, and EU institutional levels. Thus, to understand planning law, one must understand local–central governmental relations, and environmental impact assessment gives rise to legal questions about what type of legal obligations are imposed on an EU Member State.[6] The EU regime for genetically modified organisms also raises questions about the powers that Member States have to take unilateral action in relation to environmental policy.[7] Accordingly, all these chapters raise issues about the role of the state in regulating environmental problems. These issues were also discussed in Chapters 2, 3, 4, and 7.

The chapters in this part also highlight the interrelationship between the relevant governing authorities and how ecological space is defined. Layard and Holder explain this within the context of EU law.

Antonia Layard and Jane Holder, 'Seeking Spatial and Environmental Justice for People and Places within the European Union' in Andreas Philippopoulos-Mihalopoulos (ed), *Law and Ecology: New Environmental Foundations* (Routledge 2011) 171

Environmental law is spatially situated. Its 'stuckness' ensures that the qualities of each site are as significant to environmental regulation as the nature of the regulated activity itself. Each determination must ultimately be made *in situ*, evaluating how activities and uses impact upon humans, other species, habitats or ecosystems. This spatial understanding of environmental law patterns EU environmental law in particular. We see it, for example, in Natura 2000, with its network of protected sites, conceived of as a series of pan-European ecological places. Similar place-making underpins the use of spatial units as the foci for public governance, particularly the river basin management at the heart of the 2000 Water Framework Directive and the focus on individual European seas that underpins the 2007 Marine Strategy Framework Directive. It is inherent in the drawing of nitrogen vulnerable and 'air quality management zones' where environmental obligations are imposed differently either side of the line.

Note that Layard and Holder are highlighting the role of pollution regimes, in relation to land-focused regimes of environmental law specifically. In these cases, our understanding of ecosystems and the

---

[6] Case C-201/02 *Wells* [2004] ECR I-723.
[7] Case C-439/05 *Land Oberösterreich and Republic of Austria v Commission* [2007] ECR I-7141. See Section 4.3 of Chapter 22.

environment adopts a European scale rather than a national or local one. Thus, Natura 2000 is a EU wide ecological network (see further Chapter 20) and the Water Framework Directive charaterises and regulates river basins that cross national boundaries throughout the EU (see Chapter 14). The point is that it is not just Peter Rabbit slipping under the boundary but the state as well. Thus, governing authorities involved in regulating environmental problems and land management are also reorienting the understanding of ecological space through overlapping and fluid jurisdictional boundaries.

One result of having such fluid jurisdictional boundaries in the regulation of environmental problems relating to land is that individuals might not have an obvious sense of where their legal rights and grievances should properly lie. Considering that public participation (see Chapter 7) and rights of access to justice (see Chapter 10) are very important in environmental law, this uncertainty can create practical as well as legal difficulties. Hilson conceptualizes this legal uncertainty in broader conceptual terms.

Chris Hilson, 'Greening Citizenship: Boundaries of Membership and the Environment' (2001) 13 JEL 335, 348

Just as the lack of widespread European identity may be problematic as far as general EU citizenship is concerned so the lack of a widespread European environmental identity may create problems for arguments about membership in relation to EU environmental citizenship. It may well be the case that environmental identity remains very much national in focus. As long as people perceive the EU as consisting not of one European environment, but of several separate ones, there will be difficulties in persuading the courts and others of the need to broader membership. But, equally, if environmental identity has begun to shift beyond the local and the national so that people have multiple environmental identities, then there is a need for law and policy to reflect that shift.

Beyond such environmental existential concerns for individuals as legal actors, it also needs to be appreciated that different levels of governance in relation to environmental problems generate complexity for the environmental lawyer because they interact with each other. Thus, for example, Chapter 20 examines how EU and UK regimes for nature conservation intertwine. Some of the most interesting academic work on this type of governance interaction is by Osofsky. In the extract here she discusses the Deepwater Horizon spill in the Gulf of Mexico in 2010.

Hari Osofsky, 'Multidimensional Governance and the BP Deepwater Horizon Oil Spill' (2011) 63 Florida Law Review 1077, 1079

From a purely physical perspective, the BP Deepwater Horizon oil spill is overwhelming. Deepwater drilling itself pushes the limits of our technical capabilities, and containing a spill at that depth proved extremely difficult. Nearly five million barrels of oil spilled into the ocean and an unprecedented 1.8 million gallons of dispersants were used. The full impacts of the spill on ecosystems and human health will only become clearer over the passage of many years.

However, the governance challenges that the spill represents are equally daunting. The regulatory aftermath of the spill takes place at the intersection of two legal regimes: one governing offshore activities and the other addressing oil spills and other disasters. Both of these regimes crosscut every level of governance, from international to sublocal, and involve multiple actors at each of these levels. The overlapping, but fragmented, applicable law creates conflicts over who controls which aspects of the drilling and the emergency response, and when top-down and bottom-up approaches are appropriate.

In addition, the technological difficulty requires a high level of involvement by the responsible private actors (BP and, at times, the companies with which it subcontracted) in the governmental response, even as the government also sues some of those corporations.

Thus, in thinking about the various layers of governance regimes that apply to particular environmental problems, we cannot keep them analytically separate. The interactions between them are also important.

3 A WORD ON DEVOLUTION

The final theme to highlight in Chapters 18, 19, 20, 21, and 22 concerns their focus, as in most chapters of this textbook, on the law as it relates to England. This focus ensures a depth of understanding that is to be encouraged in environmental lawyers. But the narrow focus on English law comes at a cost—the devolution process since 1998 has had an important impact on all environmental law and to ignore it completely is to ignore a fundamental feature of environmental law in the UK. Indeed, the impact of devolution can be seen in all the areas covered by this textbook, and particularly in the chapters in this part, since devolution has led to obvious differences between the devolved regions in relation to land management. Chapter 3 addressed issues of devolution in UK environmental law in some detail and it is important to remember devolution processes have been asymmetrical, topic-specific, and ongoing. Recent developments seen in this part have been particularly significant. Thus, for example, while in the 1990s delegated legislation implementing EU environmental impact assessment regulation covered both England and Wales, since 2011 it now only covers England, further fragmenting the UK environmental law picture (which still implements a common EU legal framework) as a result.

Devolved UK environmental law will lead to the creation of different understandings of place and ecological space in the different regions of the UK as different regimes become embedded in different regional histories throughout the UK. Pedersen makes the points well in analysing the idea of environmental justice in the UK.

Ole W Pedersen, 'Environmental Justice in the UK: Uncertainty, Ambiguity and the Law'
(2011) 31 LS 279, 294

Thus, while the UK Government and the devolved administrations are paying attention to environmental justice as a concept, this is arguably done in a vague and unstructured fashion. For instance, research from Scotland looking into the usage of the phrase 'environmental justice' in the Scottish Parliament indicated that it was used in a wide range of connections including: the use of genetically modified crops; spreading of sewage sludge; environmental courts; climate change; specific road constructions in Glasgow; testing of depleted uranium weapons at Dundrennan; the EU's Common Agricultural Policy; and smoke-free public places.

The research from Scotland moreover highlights the fact that environmental justice has different connotations across the UK. In England and Wales, where most of the empirical environmental justice work has been carried out, environmental justice has numerous implications, ranging from access of ethnic minorities to countryside areas and implementation of the Aarhus Convention, to the correlation between income and proximity to pollution. In Scotland, environmental justice has been placed in a context of historical injustices associated with land ownership and the feudal land tenure system in Scotland. This historical context does not seem to have formed part of environmental justice deliberations in other parts of the UK. In Northern Ireland, environmental justice has received very little attention compared to the rest of the UK. Despite appreciation of social inequality in Northern Ireland, such agendas are yet to be linked to environmental issues to the same extent as in England, Wales and Scotland. Instead, environmental justice concerns have been raised primarily along procedural lines, for instance in relation to public participation in development control. One reason for the difference in prominence of environmental justice across the UK is likely to be the relatively strong environmental NGO community, which is particularly present in England, Wales and Scotland. Here, as noted above, groups like FoE and FoES have played an important role in shaping environmental justice debates. Another factor is that, for many years, environmental issues have played a relatively minor role in Northern Irish politics due to the Troubles.

In other words, regional politics within the devolved UK regions will come to shape environmental law in those areas. Peel and Lloyd provide one example of this.

Deborah Peel and Michael Gregory Lloyd, 'A Coastal and Marine National Park for Scotland: A Tactical or Strategic Affair?' (2009) 14 International Planning Studies 293, 306–07

Devolution potentially offers a different perspective on the development of marine policy in Scotland. On the one hand, it has served to provide the opportunity to develop legislation to establish Scotland's first two terrestrial parks. This may, in part, be seen as policy catch-up. National park credentials potentially offer a way to provide a universally recognized (through differentiated) spatial designation to put Scotland on a standing with other nation states. It was initially anticipated, for example, that the opportunity to designate a Coastal and Marine National Park could provide yet another way of showcasing the unique qualities of Scotland's marine environment. This suggests that there was a strong perception that national park status might be used to 'kite-mark' or brand the marine environment as a way to ensure that it achieves international recognition. In practical terms, it was anticipated that this could help advance coastal and marine tourism potential, for example. On the other hand, as the story unfolded, devolution appears to have accentuated the spatial fragmentation and inter-scalar tensions surrounding the management and planning for the marine environment. [...]

Following Feeny et al.'s (1996) examination of institutional relations in complex arenas, such as the marine, where different interests and property rights prevail, the policy objective of advancing the reality of a Coastal and Marine National Park in Scotland has clearly been the subject of competing political and policy ambitions. Here, the different missions of individual agencies and communities of interest have advanced particular agendas at different times. It is evident that there are very complex interactions among the different resource users of the marine environment. In effect, the policy idea of the park has had to navigate a perceived legacy of government failure around the management of the marine resource. Against this, from an environmental perspective, there is often a countervailing view of market failure and the consequential tragedy of the marine commons. This suggests that the ability to create effective institutional arrangements for the marine and coastal environment will depend not only on established patterns of behaviour of the regulatory authorities involved, but the ability and capacity to convince minds, change cultures, and to mobilize support for a new form of collective and participative action. For now, however, the Coastal and Marine National Park as an individual policy measure has clearly been submerged by a lack of political support and the weight of strategic argument.

Peel and Lloyd thus highlight the importance of understanding the governing context in order to appreciate and evaluate the regulation of environmental problems. We could not agree more.

4 CONCLUSION

This introduction highlights how the chapters in Part V present and interrogate difficult issues concerning the interrelationship between law, governance, and our understanding of the natural environment. These issues show how legal problems and questions about land management adopt and assume particular constructions of the environment and reflect certain socio-political ideas and arguments in the process. These issues are thus an important part of the legal story in understanding why environmental problems relating to land management are often so complex and the disputes to which they give rise so intractable.

All this may give the impression that the chapters in this part are not particularly legally focused. Do not be deceived. The different areas covered in this part are some of the most legislative and doctrinally complex areas of environmental law. Thus, Chapter 18 provides an introduction to the complex legislative regime of planning law and Chapter 20 gives an overview of the many different legislative regimes that exist in relation to nature conservation. In all these areas, a dense body of case law can also be evidenced. Moreover, as is obvious from our discussion here, this is an area in which many levels of governance are involved. Thus, in Chapters 19 and 20, a major theme of environmental impact assessment and nature conservation is how EU and national law interact. Therefore, these last five chapters require readers to concentrate on the law and concentrate hard! With that said, the themes in this introduction should not be forgotten.

18

PLANNING LAW

Planning law is the law that regulates what form the built environment should take. As such, it inevitably plays a central and guiding role in English environmental law. This is particularly because planning law is the starting point for regulating most 'development' and it is 'development' that is often at the core of environmental problems, in terms of environmental protection challenges and also more generally as a site for disputes over the use, exploitation, and creation of our 'environment'. How planning law regulates development will thus significantly affect how environmental problems are understood and addressed, in both normative and practical terms. Normatively, planning law operates on assumptions about what should be the nature and form of our surroundings. Or to put it another way—'behind every theory of planning law is a theory of environmental quality'.[1] Planning law thus plays a powerful role in shaping our understanding and expectations of the form that environmental protection should take.

From a practical perspective, because the planning regime is the starting point for development, it shapes how environmental problems are understood. Moreover, while other legal regimes may regulate particular environmental problems, they often do so adjacent to, and or in combination with, the planning system. Indeed, we shall we see that the regulatory approaches to issues such as contaminated land, environmental impact assessment, and nature conversation are heavily dependent on the operation of the planning regime.

Environmental lawyers thus must understand planning law. With that said, planning law is a subject in its own right with its own area of practice and, significantly, its own textbooks.[2] It is also a subject that interacts with other areas of legal practice and scholarship, including housing law, heritage law, and building control regulation. Thus, a single chapter cannot do justice to the subject and environmental lawyers and scholars must acknowledge that their engagement with planning law is not a wholesale one. To be an environmental lawyer is not to be a planning lawyer. The converse is also true. In light of all this, it needs to be stressed that this chapter is an *introduction* to planning law, which aims to highlight the most important elements of the planning system that environmental lawyers should know and understand.

The structure of the chapter is as follows. First, it gives a brief overview and history of planning law. Conceptually, planning law can be understood as having two distinct parts—the creation of 'plans' (broadly defined) and a process of 'planning'. From its history, it can be seen that the foundations of the major features of our current planning system were laid in the wake of World War II. Second, the chapter gives an overview of planning law and sets out some of its major themes. This is

---

[1] To paraphrase Carol Harlow and Richard Rawlings, *Law and Administration* (3rd edn, CUP 2009) 1.

[2] There is a list of further reading at the end of this chapter.

needed because the different aspects of the planning regime are so interrelated (as well as intricate and wide-ranging) that delving into it without a broader framework is liable to cause confusion. Three main themes of planning law can be identified: the relationship between central and local government; the interaction between private rights and the public interest, particularly through dispute settlement mechanisms, which play a significant role in planning law; and the normative nature of planning regimes. Sections 3, 4, 5, and 6 then consider the four main aspects of the English planning regime: central government policy and local development frameworks; the concept of 'development' and the requirement for planning permission; the consideration of planning permission; and, finally, enforcement and dispute resolution.

Six important points should be made at the outset. First, as already stressed, this is an introduction to planning law and in that spirit the chapter is not overly cluttered with the many statutory provisions relevant to planning law (although you will be pointed to the key legislative provisions where relevant). It is also an introduction that focuses on the main relationships between planning and environmental law. For example, compulsory purchase, which plays an important role in planning law and can play a role in environmental disputes, is not covered here. Thus, environmental lawyers need to be wary of confining themselves to limited aspects of planning law.

Second, much of this chapter addresses 'environmental protection' rather than 'environmental problems' as the focus of inquiry, because the interface between planning and environmental law is primarily between planning law and laws, policies, or strategies for environmental protection. But the point in the first paragraph of this chapter should be kept in mind—planning plays a more overarching role in how environmental problems are understood and addressed.

Third, planning law plays an important role in a number of other chapters in this book, particularly in relation to contaminated land (Chapter 21) and environmental impact assessment (Chapter 19). This chapter is thus fundamental for a large part of your environmental law study. Fourth, it is useful to note that, besides the environmental assessment regimes considered in Chapter 19, there is little EU law that relates directly to planning law. Indeed, under Article 192(2) TFEU, Union competence in relation to planning depends on unanimous Member State voting for its exercise. With that said, EU Directives concerning environmental assessment (Chapter 19), waste (Chapter 16), and nature conservation (Chapter 20) are all highly relevant to planning regimes. Fifth, planning law is primarily administrative law, and readers might find it useful to re-read Chapter 7 before reading this chapter.

Finally, planning law is in a constant state of flux. At the time of writing, the Coalition government were undertaking a major process of reform. As that is the case, a visit to the companion website for this chapter and/or the website for the Department of Communities and Local Government is essential.

1 PLANNING: A CONCEPTUAL OVERVIEW AND HISTORY

Planning and planning law permeates our lives in a way that no other subject in environmental law does. The houses that we reside in, the areas in which we live, and the places in which we work, relax, and shop are nearly always shaped by planning law. However, the ubiquitous nature of planning law does not make it any easier to understand. Indeed, its ever-present and pervasive nature makes it difficult to capture in a big picture, which this chapter aims to do but while focusing on those aspects of planning law that most significantly interrelate with environmental issues. To give some grounding to this challenging but also inherently partial exercise, it is useful to consider what land use planning is about, and to examine the history of our current planning framework. A brief study of both reveals the various and varying dimensions of the subject.

1.1 DEFINING PLANNING

As already noted, planning law is the law of land use planning. To understand planning law, a student or lawyer thus needs to understand what 'land use planning' is. For most students, lawyers, and scholars, vague images of maps and plans will drift into their heads, but, as Hall and Tewdwr-Jones make clear, the concept of planning is far more complicated.

Peter Hall and Mark Tewdwr-Jones, *Urban and Regional Planning*
(5th edn, Routledge 2011) 1, 3

Whether you go the Oxford English Dictionary or the American Webster's, there you find that the noun 'plan' and the verb 'to plan' have several distinct meanings. In particular, the noun can either mean 'a physical representation of something' – as for instance a drawing or a map; or it can mean 'a method for doing something'; or 'an orderly arrangement of parts of an objective'. The first meaning, in particular, is quite different from the others: when we talk about a street 'plan' of London or New York, we mean something quite different from when we talk about our 'plan' to visit London or New York next year. But there is one definition that combines the others and blurs the distinction, as when we talk about a 'plan' for a new building. This is simultaneously a physical design of that building as it is intended to be, and a guide to realizing our intention to build it. And it is here that the real ambiguity arises.

The verb 'to plan', and the nouns 'planning' and 'planner' that are derived from it, have in fact only the second, general group of meanings: they do not refer to the art of drawing up a physical plan or design on paper. They can mean either 'to arrange the parts of, or 'to realize the achievement of, or, more vaguely, 'to intend'. The most common meaning of 'planning' involves both the first two of these elements: planning is concerned with deliberately achieving some objective, and it proceeds by assembling actions into some orderly sequence. One dictionary definition, in fact, refers to what planning does; the other, to how planning does it.

After considering the complexity of these different definitions, Hall and Tewdwr-Jones conclude that:

To summarize, then: planning as a general activity is the making of an orderly sequence of action that will lead to the achievement of a stated goal or goals. Its main techniques will be written statements, supplemented as appropriate by statistical projections, mathematical representations, quantified evaluations and diagrams illustrating relationships between different parts of the plan. It may, but need not necessarily, include exact physical blueprints of objects.

In relation to urban planning, they note that it is an area of study that is multidisciplinary, multi-objective, and multi-dimensional. None of this will be new to environmental law scholars, students, and lawyers—it is the same set of challenges that we saw discussed in Chapter 2.

Hall and Tewdwr-Jones' distinction between 'plan' as a noun and verb, and the complex interplay between these senses of the term, is a good starting point for lawyers. This is because the law of planning can be understood as encapsulating: the law of plans, the laws relating to the planning process, and the interrelationship between both. Yet, that is not enough to understand the subject. Its history is also significant, as considered in Sections 1.2 and 1.3.

1.2 PLANNING LAW PRIOR TO 1947

The roots of contemporary planning law in England lie in the nineteenth century and its framework is primarily a product of post-World War II Britain. That history is fascinating in itself (see further Section 1.4), but here there is room only for a brief sketch.

The nineteenth century and early twentieth century

The starting point for understanding planning law is the range of urban problems caused by industrialization from the early nineteenth century onwards. Chapter 3 set out McLaren description of those problems,[3] and in cities in particular, there were three glaring and interrelated problems. First, there was a problem of mass poverty. Second, there was a problem of almost unimaginably poor housing conditions, where families were squeezed into sub-standard housing.[4] Third, there were serious problems of public health—there were very high mortality rates and the nineteenth century was marked by waves of epidemics.[5]

At the start of the nineteenth century, while local government was a significant power in England, central government had a marginal role to play in public life. However, the need for a collective response to these different problems resulted in some of the first centralized regulatory responses, such as the Poor Laws of 1832 and the Public Health Act 1842.[6] This administrative experimentalism was controversial, particularly as it raised questions about the role and nature of central government as well as its relation to local government.[7] Yet, despite these reforms, the urban problems remained and, by the late nineteenth century, it was becoming apparent that the problems were wide-ranging and not discrete.

Peter Hall, *Cities of Tomorrow: An Intellectual History of Urban Planning and Design in the Twentieth Century* (3rd edn, Blackwell Publishing 2002) 46–47

The problem was the giant city itself. The perception of it was the source of multiple social evil, possible biological decline, and potential political insurrection. From 1880 to 1900, perhaps 1914, middle-class society—the decision-makers, the leader-writers, the pamphleteers, the activists—was running scared. Much of this fear was grotesquely exaggerated, some of it deliberately so by practiced self-publicists. But the underlying reality was horrific enough, and it stemmed from poverty. The rich might through revolution, have given to the poor; it would not have done anyone much good, for there was all too little to go around. That poverty had been endemic since the beginnings of society, but in the countryside it could be more or less hidden; once concentrated in the city, it was revealed [......]

The difference then lay in the fact of concentration, whereby some thousands of the rich and some millions of the middle classes were brought into close contact with millions of the poor and very poor. In this sense industrialization and urbanization, as the Marxists always say, did create a new set of social relationships and a new set of social perceptions.

---

[3] John McLaren, 'Nuisance Law and the Industrial Revolution: Some Lessons From Social History' (1983) 3 OJLS 155. See Chapter 3.

[4] This is vividly discussed in Peter Hall, *Cities of Tomorrow: An Intellectual History of Urban Planning and Design in the Twentieth Century* (3rd edn, Blackwell Publishing 2002) ch 2.

[5] The most famous of these was Edwin Chadwick, *Report on the Sanitary Condition of the Labouring Population of Great Britain* (Edinburgh UP 1964).

[6] Oliver MacDonagh, 'The Nineteenth Century Revolution in Government: A Reappraisal' (1958) 1 Historical Journal 52 and David Roberts, *Victorian Origins of the British Welfare State* (Yale UP 1960).

[7] Joshua Toulmin Smith, *Local Government and Centralisation* (John Chapman 1851).

This new set of social relationships and social perceptions resulted in a focus on planning for all rather than simply dealing with poor housing and poor health conditions in a reactive or welfare-focused response. The new focus on planning manifested in two different ways. First, in intellectual and political terms—from the late nineteenth century, there were social movements that saw the need to re-plan cities. These included the middle class Radical movement, the Arts and Craft Movement, and many interrelated strands of socialism. Influential writers of these movements include the artists William Morris and John Ruskin. Pinder discusses some of these approaches.

David Pinder, *Visions of the City* (Edinburgh UP 2005) 31–32

[T]hese approaches emphasised spatial concerns, asserting the importance of changing urban space as a means of constructing a different and better future. Both also came to have a profound impact on the discourses and practices of modern planning, and on the spatial and social landscape itself.

As Pinder highlights, they proposed:

'restorative Utopias', in so far as they responded to the upheaval of the modern city by projecting a new spatial form that was intended to restore and shore up values about urban settlement, community, order and harmony. Aspects of this approach find voice in [William] Morris's dream. In thinking about how the foul and dark urban spaces of industrial capitalism might be replaced by a garden landscape that would provide the setting for a new civilisation, he was joined by numerous critics who also opposed the disorder associated with urban expansion and industrialisation [...] However, [this] strand of utopianism [...] did not see itself as anti-urban as such. Rather, it claimed to be opposed to the current state of cities as it looked towards a different mode of urban living, one that would be more integrated with the country and closer to nature. In recoiling from aspects of the crowded city with its dirt and noise and uproar, it searched for an alternative urbanism that still valued aspects of city life.

An important feature of this search for an alternative urbanism was that it moved 'beyond merely a negative critique of the nineteenth century metropolis'.[8] Rather, a group of thinkers and planners emerged who 'showed how modern techniques of construction create a new mastery of space from which innovative urban forms could be built'.[9] Such new urban forms and spaces were not neutral but 'expressed the ideals of co-operation and social justice'.[10] These progressive thinkers included Le Corbusier (Continental Europe) and Frank Lloyd Wright (USA) but, in England, the most significant thinker was Ebenezer Howard. Howard is universally understood to be one of the most significant figures in planning, particularly due to his development of the idea of 'garden cities'—cities that were 'vehicles for a progressive reconstruction of capitalist society into an infinity of co-operative commonwealths'.[11]

The second turn towards planning was legislative in nature. Thus, while legislation throughout the latter nineteenth century was focused on public health and improving sanitary conditions of housing, the first Planning Act was passed in 1909,[12] giving power to local government to develop planning schemes, although the focus was still on sanitary conditions. The 1909 Act also strengthened the inspection powers of local authorities and allowed them to close down houses as unfit for

---

[8] Robert Fishman, *Urban Utopias in the Twentieth Century* (MIT Press 1982) 12.
[9] Ibid.
[10] Ibid, 14.
[11] Hall (n 4) 88.
[12] Housing, Town Planning Etc Act 1909.

human habitation with an appeal to a Local Government Board, rather than to a court as had been the case under previous legislation. It was the exercise of this power that gave rise to the case of *Local Government Board v Arlidge*,[13] which is generally recognized as one of the seminal cases in English administrative law.

Local Government Board v Arlidge
[1915] 1 AC 120 (HL), 131–32 (Viscount Haldane LC)

The Facts

Under Section 17 of the 1909 Act, Hampstead Borough Council made an order prohibiting a house Mr Arlidge was the assignee of a lease on to be used for human habitation until it was fit for purpose. Mr Arlidge appealed to the Local Government Board, who held a public inquiry and confirmed the order. Mr Arlidge sought a quashing of that order for breach of natural justice. The House of Lords, found the Board was under no legal duty to observe it.

The HL

Stringent powers of inspection were given to both the local authority and the Local Government Board. In the case of an appeal, the procedure as to everything, including costs, was to be such as the Board might by rules determine. The Board was to have power to make such order on any appeal as it should think equitable [...] The rules were to provide that the Board should not dismiss any appeal without having first held a public local inquiry. [...]

My Lords, it is obvious that the Act of 1909 introduced a change of policy. The jurisdiction, both as regards original applications and as regards appeals, was in England transferred from Courts of justice to the local authority and the Local Government Board, both of them administrative bodies, and it is necessary to consider what consequences this change of policy imported.

My Lords, when the duty of deciding an appeal is imposed, those whose duty it is to decide it must act judicially. They must deal with the question referred to them without bias, and they must give to each of the parties the opportunity of adequately presenting the case made. The decision must be come to in the spirit and with the sense of responsibility of a tribunal whose duty it is to mete out justice. But it does not follow that the procedure of every such tribunal must be the same. In the case of a Court of law tradition in this country has prescribed certain principles to which in the main the procedure must conform. But what that procedure is to be in detail must depend on the nature of the tribunal. In modern times it has become increasingly common for Parliament to give an appeal in matters which really pertain to administration, rather than to the exercise of the judicial functions of an ordinary Court, to authorities whose functions are administrative and not in the ordinary sense judicial. Such a body as the Local Government Board has the duty of enforcing obligations on the individual which are imposed in the interests of the community. Its character is that of an organization with executive functions. In this it resembles other great departments of the State. When, therefore, Parliament entrusts it with judicial duties, Parliament must be taken, in the absence of any declaration to the contrary, to have intended it to follow the procedure which is its own, and is necessary if it is to be capable of doing its work efficiently.

In other words, new administrative institutions were emerging to deal with collective issues such as housing and planning, and these were understood to operate differently from courts. As the

---

[13] [1915] 1 AC 120.

constitutional scholar AV Dicey noted about *Arlidge*, it was a case that deserved 'the most careful attention of all students interested in the development of the English system of government'.[14] While *Arlidge* was essentially a planning case, its focus on process highlights a fundamental theme that we will see throughout planning law—the importance of procedure and its relationship to individual rights.

1.3 THE TOWN AND COUNTRY PLANNING ACT 1947 AND BEYOND

The 1909 Act was not a comprehensive scheme of planning and, as Cullingworth and Nadin explain here, by the 1940s, its drawbacks were becoming obvious.

Barry Cullingworth and Vincent Nadin, *Town and Country Planning in the UK* (14th edn, Routledge 2006) 22–23

The prewar system of planning was defective in several ways. It was optional on local authorities; planning powers were essentially regulatory and restrictive; such planning as was achieved was purely local in character; the central government had no effective powers of initiative, or of coordinating local plans [...]

By 1942, 73 per cent of the land in England and 36 per cent of the land in Wales had become subject to interim development control, but only 5 per cent of England and 1 per cent of Wales was actually subject to operative schemes [...] there were several important towns and cities as well as some large country districts for which not even the preliminary stages of a planning scheme had been carried out. Administration was highly fragmented and was essentially a matter for the lower-tier authorities: in 1944 there were over 1,400 planning authorities [...]

The new conception of town and country planning [behind the 1947 Act] underlined the inadequacies [...] Large cities were no longer to be allowed to continue their unchecked sprawl over the country-side. The explosive forces generated by the desire for better living and working conditions would no longer run riot. Suburban dormitories were a thing of the past. Overspill would be steered into new and expanded towns which could provide the conditions people wanted, without the disadvantages inher-ent in satellite suburban development. When the problems of reconstructing blitzed areas, redevelop-ing blighted areas, securing a 'proper distribution' of industry, developing national parks, and so on, are added to the list, there was a clear need for a new and more positive role for the central government, [and] a transfer of powers from the smaller to the larger authorities, a considerable extension of these powers [...]

The Town and Country Planning Act 1947 brought all development under control by making it subject to planning permission. Planning was to be no longer merely a regulative function. Development plans were to be prepared for every area in the country. These were to outline the way in which each area was to be developed or, where desirable, preserved. In accordance with the wider concepts of planning, powers were transferred from district councils (DCs) to county councils. The smallest planning units thereby became the counties and the county boroughs. Coordination of local plans was to be effected by the new Ministry of Town and Country Planning.

The Town and Country Planning Act 1947 was only one of a number of new pieces of legislation. There was also the National Parks and Access to the Countryside Act 1949, the Distribution of Industry Act

[14] AV Dicey, 'The Development of Administrative Law in England' (1915) 31 LQR 148, 148.

1945, and the New Towns Act 1946. The first of these is discussed in Chapter 20 as it relates to nature conservation.[15]

The Town and Country Planning Act, as amended, is the blueprint for our contemporary planning system and its key features—the requirement that 'development' needs planning permission, the co-ordinating role of central government, and the role of local development plans—can all be seen in the contemporary planning system. However, this legislation did not remain static and it has been subject to ongoing amendment, with legislative consolidations in 1962, 1971, and most recently in 1990 (although almost immediately it was subject to amendment by the Planning and Compensation Act 1991). Likewise, there has been ongoing amendment of delegated legislation in relation to permitted development and other issues within the planning regime. These amendments occurred for a range of reasons and, in this regard, it is important to remember the multiple concerns of planning law. For example, in 1990, issues relating to heritage conservation were excised and put into the Planning (Listed Buildings and Conservation Areas) Act 1990. Likewise, issues relating to compensation for property owners are a long-standing theme that has influenced the development of planning law.[16]

Reform has continued apace since 1990. The Planning and Compulsory Purchase Act 2004 overhauled the system for the creation of local plans by introducing 'local development frameworks', further discussed in Section 3.2. The 2004 Act also introduced 'regional spatial strategies', which (at the time of writing) are in the process of being abolished by the Coalition Government.

The Planning Act 2008 then introduced a new framework for dealing with major infrastructure projects. Layard describes the various circumstances that led up to this reform.

Antonia Layard, 'Planning and Environment at the Crossroads' (2002) 14 JEL 401, 401–02

The flashpoints of current planning concerns are disparate with agitated critics often at loggerheads with each other. Business, for instance, is concerned with the delays and bureaucracy planning applications entail. The mammoth public inquiry for Heathrow's Terminal 5, taking 524 days over four years, is cited as a prime example of red tape holding up enterprise and investment. Pressure groups, in contrast, are concerned with access to the planning system. In particular, though they welcome simplification to the process, campaigners maintain that it is unacceptable for applicants to be able to appeal a refusal of permission when interested third parties are unable to complain if permission is granted, even if statutory consultees had objected to the development, it departs from the development plan or the local authority is granting permission to itself. Objectors believe a third-party right of appeal must be introduced to remove the planning system's pro-development bias and redress the balance between developers and the community. The government meanwhile is concerned with the complexity, uncertainty, delays and lack of community engagement.

The 2008 Act addresses these problems by creating a new framework for 'nationally significant infrastructure projects', including requiring the creation of national policy statements concerning infrastructure development. The Act thus identifies a series of types of development and creates a separate planning process for them. 'Nationally significant infrastructure projects' are defined in s 14 of the Act and include a range of large scale projects including construction or alteration of gas reception facilities, airport-related and other transport developments, harbour facilities, dams

---

[15] Section 2.4 of Chapter 20.

[16] For a discussion of this see Barry Cullingworth and Vincent Nadin, *Town and Country Planning in the UK* (14th edn, Routledge 2006) 196–200.

construction and alteration, and water treatment facilities. The Secretary of State has the power to amend this list.[17]

The 2008 Act introduced a range of reforms, including a framework for imposing Community Infrastructure Levies,[18] but the main purpose of the Act is to develop a more coherent approval system for major projects and to incorporate debate and consultation earlier into the process, which should ensure a quicker consideration of consent for these projects. To put it another way, the aim of the Act is to placate the different sides of the debate highlighted by Layard. To establish this more coherent process for infrastructure projects, the regime under the Act has a number of aspects. First, there is a set of separate guidance documents for local authorities, due to the fact that these projects need to be treated differently by them. A revision of these documents is currently being consulted on.[19] Second, there are twelve national policy statements that prescribe government policy on infrastructure projects. These are produced by a range of different government departments, depending on the kind of infrastructure involved. Third, the Act created a new institutional regime for dealing with the projects it covers. Originally, the Act set up an independent Infrastructure Planning Commission (IPC) but this was abolished by the Localism Act 2011 in April 2012 and its activities are now delegated by the Secretary of State to the Planning Inspectorate. McCracken, commenting before the demise of the IPC, noted the following about the Act.

Robert McCracken, 'Infrastructure Planning Commission: Challenge or Opportunity' [2009] 13 Supp (The show must go on) JPEL 7, 9

Three characteristics stand out. The first is that the new system is front loaded. Much more is expected before applications are submitted. The second feature is the amount of important detail to be supplied by delegated legislation and guidance. The third feature is the great degree of discretion given to the IPC. Much will depend on the culture which develops within the Commission.

This last point is particularly significant in light of the functions of the IPC now being taken up by the Planning Inspectorate. How the decision-making culture will develop in that new administrative context will be interesting to see (and determinative of national infrastructure planning in the UK).

More recently, the Localism Act 2011 has implications for planning law, although it is also relevant to a wide swathe of other local government activity. As noted already, the 2011 Act abolished the IPC and it also abolishes regional spatial strategies (discussed further here). While the 2011 Act does not otherwise make major adjustments to the planning law framework, it does add extra features that adjust the balance of the system in incremental but not insignificant respects. First, the Act introduces a new regime of neighbourhood forums that can create neighbourhood plans and neighbourhood development orders.[20] Second, it introduces rights of community organizations (established to further the social, economic, and environmental well-being of individuals in a community) to develop land through 'community right to build orders',[21] as well as opportunities for local groups to purchase

---

[17] Planning Act 2008 s 14(3).

[18] Ibid, Part 5.

[19] Department of Communities and Local Government, *Planning Act 2008: Consultation on Proposed Changes to the Suite of Guidance Documents for the Major Infrastructure Planning Regime* (April 2012).

[20] Localism Act 2011, Part 6, ch 3, introducing ss 61E–Q of the TCPA 1990 and ss 38A–C of the Planning and Compulsory Purchase Act 2004.

[21] Localism Act 2011, s 116(3), introducing Schedule 4C TCPA 1990.

interests in assets of community value.[22] Third, and significantly, it grants to neighbours rights to be consulted in the *formulation* of development applications.[23] Overall, however, the reforms are not as dramatic as the name of the Act would suggest. Layard makes this point well.

Antonia Layard, 'The Localism Act 2011: What is "Local" and How Do We (Legally) Construct It?' (2012) 14 Env L Rev 134, 143–44

Analysing the legal provisions demonstrates that the Localism Act is as much about philosophy as concrete change [...]

Ultimately, despite its catchy title and the frequent assumptions that the philosophy of localism is self-evident, based on the fact that locals know best and care most about their locality, in practice the Act has no single, coherent approach.

The philosophy of localism is not an end-point in the process of planning reform. As we shall see in Section 3.1, central government policy continues to play a significant, albeit often changing, role in planning law. Central government planning policy has undergone substantial revision over the years and, as we write this textbook, more reforms are occurring, and are proposed, in relation to the planning system as a whole, which adjust again the respective roles for local and central government in planning law. Most of these reforms are driven by concerns about ensuring economic growth and they involve central government directing the course of planning development, overlaid across a strong 'localism' agenda (in political terms at least). The mixed messages at the political level essentially show that both local and central government play important roles in the planning system and the interrelationship between the two requires careful legal analysis.

FURTHER READING AND QUESTIONS

1. What are the implications for developing a legal framework for planning if we understand 'plan' as both a verb and a noun?

2. The literature on planning is a rich and exciting one and the work highlighted here only touches the surface. On the history of planning law, two very good works are Barry Cullingworth and Vincent Nadin, *Town and Country Planning in the UK* (14th edn, Routledge 2006); Peter Hall and Mark Tewdwr-Jones, *Urban and Regional Planning* (5th edn, Routledge 2011).

2 THE LEGAL FRAMEWORK FOR PLANNING: A VERY BRIEF SKETCH

The discussion in Section 1 was primarily concerned with setting the overall scene for planning law and, as is already clear, it has many different legal, political, and historical strands. This section now focuses on the current planning framework. As already stressed, that framework is complex. The section gives a quick overview of the whole regime, before we consider in more detail the legal issues relevant to environmental protection that arise at each step of the planning process. A firm grasp of the overall picture is needed at the outset since different aspects of the planning regime are so interrelated that it is not possible to describe one part of it without referring to other parts.

---

[22] Localism Act 2011, Part 5, ch 3.
[23] Ibid, s 122, introducing TCPA 1990, ss 61W–Y.

2.1 THE BASIC FRAMEWORK

The basic legislative framework for planning is governed by the Town and Country Planning Act 1990 (TCPA), as amended. The TCPA is accompanied by a detailed and intricate body of delegated legislation, including the Town and Country Planning (Use Classes) Order 1987 and Town and Country Planning (General Permitted Development Order) 1995 (as amended).

The planning regime can broadly be understood as consisting of four interrelated parts: the creation of policy and plans; the requirement to seek planning permission; consideration and determination of a planning application; and rights of appeal and methods of enforcement of planning decisions. The first of these parts concerns the creation of plans, while the remaining aspects relate to the process of planning.

The creation of policy and plans occurs at both the central and local government level. At the central government level, there is the new National Planning Policy Framework as well as circulars and other forms of guidance. While none of these documents are strictly legally binding, they play a fundamental guiding role in shaping the normative expectations and decision-making outcomes of planning law. At the local level, there are local development frameworks (an evolution from local development plans), which include a range of other guidance documents, such as local plans and supplementary planning documents. These documents provide an important source of normative expectation about what the planning regime should achieve as well as practical guidance.

Turning to the process of planning, Lord Bingham describes the requirement for planning permission for development.

South Bucks District Council v Porter
[2003] UKHL 26, [2003] 2 AC 558 paras 10–11 (Lord Bingham)

10. Over the past 60 years there has been ever-increasing recognition of the need to control the use and development of land so as to prevent inappropriate development and protect the environment. This is, inevitably, a sensitive process, since it constrains the freedom of private owners to use their own land as they wish. But it is a very important process, since control, appropriately and firmly exercised, enures to the benefit of the whole community.

11. It is unnecessary for present purposes to do more than identify the rudiments of the current planning regime, now largely found in the Town and Country Planning Act 1990. The cornerstone of this regime, regulated by sections 55-106B in Part III of the Act, is the requirement in section 57(1) that permission be obtained for the carrying out of any development of land as defined in section 55. Applications are made to, and in the ordinary way determined in the first instance by, local planning authorities, which are local bodies democratically-elected and accountable. The responsibility of the local community for managing its own environment is integral to the system [...]

However, that responsibility is not unfettered and is governed by a legislative regime. The most significant aspect of that regime is in s 70(1)–(2) TCPA, which states:

(1) Where an application is made to a local planning authority for planning permission—
  (a) subject to sections 91 and 92, they may grant planning permission, either unconditionally or subject to such conditions as they think fit; or
  (b) they may refuse planning permission.

(2) In dealing with such an application the authority shall have regard to the provisions of the development plan, so far as material to the application, and to any other material considerations.

Particular attention should be paid to subsection (2) and the idea of 'material considerations'. As we will see, local authorities, central government, Planning Inspectors, and the courts have all contributed to the understanding of this key concept in the determination of planning applications.

Another significant source of considerations relevant to the determination of a planning application is s 38(6) of the Planning and Compulsory Purchase Act 2004, which states:

> (6) If regard is to be had to the development plan for the purpose of any determination to be made under the planning Acts the determination must be made in accordance with the plan unless material considerations indicate otherwise.

Moreover, as shown in Section 5 of Chapter 19, in cases of development applications where an environmental assessment is required, the Town and Country Planning (Environmental Impact Assessment) Regulations 2011 require that:

> 3(4) The relevant planning authority or the Secretary of State or an inspector shall not grant planning permission or subsequent consent pursuant to an application to which this regulation applies unless they have first taken the environmental information into consideration, and they shall state in their decision that they have done so.

These considerations are not exhaustive and highlight that the determination of a planning application is a complex exercise. Further, the initial determination of a planning application, usually by a local planning authority, is not the end of the planning process, as Lord Bingham explains.

South Bucks District Council v Porter
[2003] UKHL 26, [2003] 2 AC 558 paras 11–12 (Lord Bingham)

> 11. [. . .] But the local planning authority's decision is not final. An appeal against its decision lies to the Secretary of State, on the merits, which will be investigated by an expert, independent inspector empowered to hold an inquiry at which evidence may be received and competing interests heard before advice is tendered to the Secretary of State. The final decision on the merits rests with the Secretary of State, a political office-holder answerable to Parliament. The courts have no statutory role in the granting or refusing of planning permission unless, on purely legal grounds, it is sought to challenge an order made by the local planning authority or the Secretary of State: in such event section 288 of the Act grants a right of application to the High Court. In addition, there exists the general supervisory jurisdiction of the High Court, which may in this field as in others be invoked to control decisions which are made in bad faith, or perversely, or unfairly or otherwise unlawfully. But this is not a jurisdiction directed to the merits of the decision under review.
>
> 12. The second crucial instrument of control provided by the Act is the enforcement notice, which local planning authorities are empowered to issue by section 172 where it appears to them that there has been a breach of planning control and that it is expedient to issue a notice. Once the notice has taken effect, it amounts to a mandatory order to do what the notice specifies as necessary to remedy the breach (section 173). Failure to comply may be penalised, on summary conviction, by a substantial fine, and on conviction on indictment by an unlimited fine (section 179(8)). Persistent non-compliance may give rise to repeated convictions (section 179(6)). The coercive effect of an enforcement notice may be reinforced by a stop notice, which the local planning authority may (save in the case of buildings used as dwelling houses) serve if they consider it expedient that any relevant activity should cease before the expiry of the period for compliance (section 183). Failure to comply may be visited with the

same penalties as on non-compliance with an enforcement notice (section 187(2)), and persistent non-compliance may give rise to repeated convictions (section 187 (1A)). Again, however, the local planning authority's decision on enforcement is not final: a right of appeal to the Secretary of State lies against an enforcement notice (section 174). On appeal the merits of the planning situation may be fully explored and an application for planning permission may be made (section 174(2)(a)). In this instance also the control regime is entrusted to democratically-accountable bodies, the local planning authority and the Secretary of State. The role of the court is confined to determining a challenge on a point of law to a decision of the Secretary of State (section 289), and to its ordinary supervisory jurisdiction by way of judicial review.

There are three things to note from this account. First, it is interesting that such a detailed descriptive account of the planning regime is found in the case law. Such discussions by judges are not uncommon and highlight the importance of understanding and analysing the legislative regime for resolving legal disputes under it. This may seem a truism—but it is particularly important to remember in this chapter. Planning law is not about the application of free-floating principle but essentially involves paying careful attention to the detail of planning legislation.

Second, local authorities, central government, the Planning Inspectorate, and the courts all have a role to play in planning law. Authority over planning does not rest in the hands of any one institution but of many, and the interrelations between them shape the law, as we will see here. The final thing to highlight again is that, from a legal perspective, planning law is quintessentially administrative law. Lord Bingham, by using touchstones such as democracy, accountability, and review, is characterizing planning law in administrative law terms.

2.2 MAJOR CONCEPTUAL THEMES

Before engaging in the legal framework for planning in more detail, it is useful to take a step back and consider some of the conceptual themes that run through planning law, many of which have already emerged in the discussion so far. Identifying conceptual themes for planning law is trickier than one might expect. The very brief history and sketch of the planning law framework in Section 2.1 show that the story of the development of planning law in England and Wales is really a story with multiple narratives. Some of those narratives, such as insanitary housing and conservation, have become separate regulatory areas (housing law, heritage law), but others remain features of planning law. The dynamic and multi-faceted nature of planning law can be seen in planning theory. As Campbell and Fainstein note, there are many themes and issues that have preoccupied, and which continue to preoccupy, planning theorists.

Scott Campbell and Susan S Fainstein, 'Introduction: The Structure and Debates of Planning Theory' in Scott Campbell and Susan Fainstein (eds), *Readings in Planning Theory* (2nd edn, Blackwell Publishing 2003) 12–13

A generation ago, the engaging debates of planning theory involved the conflicts between comprehensive versus incremental planning, objectivity versus advocacy, centralization versus decentralization, top-down versus bottom-up leadership, and planning for people versus planning for place. These debates from the adolescence of planning theory now seem a bit tired and bypassed. It is not that they have been conclusively resolved, but rather that the field is so broadly scattered that each pole lives on. This current eclecticism reflects the fragmentation of planning itself. Nevertheless, these debates were arguably necessary for the intellectual development of the field, and the young planning theorist still needs to read and understand these controversies.

Campbell and Fainstein go on to note that a continuing theme in planning has been the idea of planners as servants of the public interest, despite postmodern insights into the plurality of that concept:

[I]n end, the question of the public interest is the leitmotiv that holds together the defining debates of planning theory. The central task of planners is serving the public interest in cities, suburbs, and the countryside. Questions of when, why, and how planners should intervene—and the constraints they face in the process—all lead back to defining and serving the public interest, even while it is not static or fixed. The restructured urban economy, the shifting boundaries between the public and private sectors, and the changing tools and available resources constantly force planners to rethink the public interest. [. . .] This constant rethinking is the task of planning theory.

Rethinking the public interest is also somewhat the task of planning lawyers, who find themselves confronted with planning regimes that continually shift and lurch from one reform to another. Overall, however, three themes can be seen to endure in planning law—the respective roles of central and local government; the role of dispute settlement, particularly in negotiating the interaction of private and public interests; and the normative nature of planning regimes. Some of these themes may be 'tired and bypassed' for planning theorists, but as we will see over the course of this chapter, they are centre stage for planning lawyers.

Local and central government

The first theme to note is that of the relationship between central and local government. The significance of local government in the planning system has been touched on already, including identifying local authorities as primary planning decision-makers and in our discussion of the Localism Act 2011. However, central government also has an important role in planning law, also seen already. As the extract from Loughlin in Chapter 3 highlights,[24] the relationship between local and central government has been both juridified and politicized over time. That can be seen very clearly in planning law where the relationship between the two layers of government has become more regulated by policy, legislation, delegated legislation, and case law. Thus, for example, Section 3.1 covers a body of cases concerning the powers of local planning authorities in light of national policy. The Localism Act 2011 is just a further step in the trend of negotiating planning powers between central and local government and, while the philosophy of localism is one of giving power back to localities, the 2011 Act does this through creating new and additional regulatory frameworks, such as neighbourhood forums. Layard explains the implication of this.

Antonia Layard, 'Law and Localism: the Case of Multiple Occupancy Housing'
(2012) 32 LS 551, 557–58

While the advent of the Localism Act does little to change the basic framework of planning law and policy so that local authority planning powers remain intact, the Act creates a profound new role for legally

---

[24] Section 3.2 of Chapter 3.

constructed neighbourhoods. It is for this reason that the Government has claimed that the Localism Act has introduced 'radical' reforms to the planning system 'taking power away from officials and putting it into the hands of those who know most about their neighbourhood—local people themselves'.

Yet as studies of scale illustrate, it is unrealistic to think of these distinctions as truly separate. In practice, difficult planning questions about hostels for the homeless or waste incinerators require a coordinated approach that does not necessarily prioritise neighbourhood preferences from the bottom up. While the Localism Act constructs the neighbourhood scale as significant in land use decision-making, empowering local residents to influence what development goes where, it does not yet provide a convincing answer as to how to resolve conflicts between the neighbourhood and local authority level. Both are constructed as 'local'.

In other words, law is constructing our understanding of what is 'local'. How these updated 'localism' features of the planning regime will operate in practice will be interesting to see.

In light of this primarily conceptual discussion, the tension between central and local government manifests itself in various ways in planning law. On the one hand, it is local authorities that primarily consider planning applications in light of local development frameworks, and thus the authority to grant planning permission rests with them. As such, Lord Bingham is correct when he states 'the responsibility of the local community for managing its own environment is integral to the system'. On the other hand, central government also has a key role in the determination of planning applications. First, central government produces policy guidance documents that shape and limit local authority. Second, both the operation of the Planning Act 2008 and the 'call in' procedure under s 77 TCPA allow central bodies to decide planning applications. Finally, as noted by Lord Bingham, the decision of a local planning authority in relation to a development application can be appealed to the Secretary of State. All these features of the planning regime are considered here but they reinforce that the central–local government relationship is integral to planning law. From an environmental protection perspective, this relationship is significant because it determines which body makes decisions about planning and the limits placed on their power.

Dispute settlement, rights, and the public interest

A second important theme in planning law is dispute settlement. Decisions about planning inevitably involve conflicts about how land will be used and developed and those conflicts need to be resolved. We saw glimpses of this in Lord Bingham's description of the planning system, which indicated that inherent in planning law is a conflict between different forms of interests and, in particular, between private rights and the public interest. Moreover, as we saw in *Arlidge*,[25] planning is polycentric in nature, which means that traditional bi-polar adjudicative frameworks are not well suited to resolving the disputes to which planning gives rise. In light of this, from very early on, other forums for dispute settlement (such as inquiries) have been developed in the planning context.

Indeed, the role of inquiries—independent hearings that report to a Minister—became a central feature in planning law by the 1920s. This development occurred in a rather *ad hoc* manner. *Arlidge* was thus the first, but not the last, word on the issue and anxieties over planning inquiries, particularly in relation to compulsory purchase issues, became a major focus in the 1920s and 1930s. Lord Hewart, who was Lord Chief Justice of England, published *The New Despotism* in 1929 in which he

[25] *Arlidge* (n 13).

censured many different aspects of the emerging administrative state.[26] He declared that inquiries were 'in practice nugatory' and could not be 'of much value' to a Minster in forming their conclusion.[27] He then went on to note that:

> All great constitutional lawyers have recognized that it is the rule, or supremacy, of the law, administered by independent judges, that is the basis of all our constitutional liberties, and it is this characteristic of the British Constitution which, above all, makes that Constitution admired throughout the civilized world.[28]

Hewart's attack on inquiries thus reflected concerns with constitutional law. For him, inquiries did not offer equivalent protection to that provided by the judicial process. Hewart's book was a catalyst for the Donoughmore Committee's report on Minister's Powers in 1932.[29] The Donoughmore report drew a distinction between planning inquiries that were 'of a judicial nature' and more *ad hoc* inquiries, but still found it difficult to characterize definitively such processes. In light of this, and consistent with the rest of the report, the committee did not set down any procedure for how such inquiries should operate.[30]

By the 1950s, there was again a rumbling disquiet, particularly in light of the dramatic growth of tribunals and inquiries in other areas.[31] The Franks Committee on Tribunals and Enquiries was set up and reported in 1957. Harlow and Rawlings provide an excellent analysis of the Committee's conclusions on inquiries.

Carol Harlow and Richard Rawlings, *Law and Administration* (3rd end, CUP 2009) 574–75

The post-war Franks Committee followed Donoughmore in focusing on planning and land inquiries, numerically the commonest form of inquiry. Once again the hybrid character of inquiries was emphasised:

The intention of the legislature in providing for an inquiry or hearing in certain circumstances appears to have been twofold: to ensure that the interests of citizens most closely affected should be protected by the grant of statutory right to be heard in support of the objections, and to ensure that thereby the Minster should be better informed about the facts of the case. [Reports on the Committee on Tribunals and Enquiries, Cmnd 218 (1957) 269]

Inquiries were not to be classified as 'purely administrative because of the provision of a special procedure preliminary to the decision', which involved the testing of an issue, 'often partly in public'. They were not on the other hand purely judicial, 'because the final decision cannot be reached by the application of rules and must allow the exercise of a wide discretion in the balancing of public and private interest':

If the administrative view is dominant the public inquiry cannot play its full part in the total process, and there is a danger that the rights and interest of the individual citizens affected will not be sufficiently protected. In these cases it is idle to argue that Parliament can be relied upon to protect the citizen, save exceptionally

---

[26] Lord Hewart, *The New Despotism* (Ernest Benn Ltd 1929). [27] Ibid 51. [28] Ibid 52.
[29] Committee on Ministers' Powers, *Report of Committee of Ministers' Powers* (Cmd 4060, 1932).
[30] Harlow and Rawlings (n 1) 573–74.
[31] Patrick Devlin, 'The Common Law, Public Policy and the Executive' [1956] CLP 1.

> [...] [I]f the judicial view is dominant there is the danger that people will regard the person before whom they state their case as a kind of judge provisionally deciding the matter, subject to an appeal to the Minister. [Reports of the Committee on Tribunals and Enquiries, Cmnd 218 (1957) 272–74]

The 'judicial view' also tended to place emphasis on protecting the rights of the individual. The Franks Committee resulted in the Tribunals and Inquiries Act 1958, which, in line with the Committee's conclusions, required that tribunals and inquiries should be regulated by the principles of openness, fairness, and impartiality.[32]

This discussion may appear a little tangential for environmental lawyers, but there are two important points to take from it. First, the history of planning law has been closely entwined with the history of administrative law. The Franks Committee was a critical step in the history of administrative law and the problems encountered by the Committee in categorizing processes as 'judicial' and 'administrative' have been an ongoing theme in administrative law (explored further). If environmental problems are bound up in planning law, they are also bound up in administrative law.

Second, implicit in the discussion over the evolving nature of inquiries is a distinction between individual rights and the collective interest. As Griffith highlights, this was a major theme in the Franks report.

John Griffith, 'Tribunals and Inquiries' (1959) 22 MLR 125, 126

> The Franks Report began by making some rather formal passes through the air without striking anything except poses—a little unreal though not altogether lacking in charm, as if the drafters thought there was a lot of stuff always said at this point, to be got out of the way and set down. I mean passages like the need 'to seek a new balance between private right and public advantage, between fair play for the individual and efficiency of administration,' 'the procedures by which the rights of individual citizens can be harmonised with wider public interests,' 'finding a right relationship between authority and the individual' [...]

This set of issues has remained relevant and recent reforms to planning processes largely represent variations on this set of themes. Thus, for example, the Planning Act 2008 creates a separate framework in relation to 'nationally important infrastructure projects'. Hence, while there has been a great deal of reform and change in planning law, certain themes remain constant.

In particular, how to balance private rights and the public interest is an ongoing concern of planning law. This issue was put into sharp focus by the introduction of the Human Rights Act 1998 (HRA), in light of the duties of states under Article 6 of the European Convention of Human Rights (ECHR). Article 6 provides that:

> In the determination of his civil rights and obligations [...] everyone is entitled to a fair and public hearing within a reasonable time by an independent and impartial tribunal established by law.

In *Bryan v UK*,[33] the European Court of Human Rights held that Article 6 applied to the determination of planning applications, but that Article 6 had not been breached because, on the facts of *Bryan*, the

---

[32] Committee on Administrative Tribunals and Enquiries, *Report of the Committee on Administrative Tribunals and Enquiries* (Cmnd 218, 1957).

[33] [1995] 21 EHRR 342.

Planning Inspector's decision had been subject to the full supervisory jurisdiction of a court empowered to carry out judicial review in relation to such planning decisions. The same issue was subsequently the first HRA case to be heard by the House of Lords. In *Alconbury*, the House found that 'call in' powers under s 77 and appeal powers under s 78, which result in the Secretary of State determining planning applications, did not result in a breach of Article 6 for lack of an independent body to determine the individual 'civil' rights at issue in planning cases (the Secretary of State, like the planning inspector in *Bryan*, was not relevantly independent and impartial). This is because the Court had full supervisory jurisdiction in relation to the minister's decision, again due to its powers to conduct judicial review of administrative decisions.[34] In coming to this conclusion, a number of the law Lords discussed the nature of the planning system. Lord Clyde's analysis is given here.

R (Alconbury) v Environment Secretary
[2001] UKHL 23 para 139 (Lord Clyde)

139. The general context in which this challenge is raised is that of planning and development. The functions of the Secretary of State in the context of planning may conveniently be referred to as 'administrative', in the sense that they are dealing with policy and expediency rather than with the regulation of rights. We are concerned with an administrative process and an administrative decision. Planning is a matter of the formation and application of policy. The policy is not matter for the courts but for the Executive. Where decisions are required in the planning process they are not made by judges, but by members of the administration. Members of the administration may be required in some of their functions to act in a judicial manner in that they may have to observe procedural rules and the overarching principles of fairness. But while they may on some occasions be required to act like judges, they are not judges and their determinations on matters affecting civil rights and obligations are not to be seen as judicial decisions. Even although there may be stages in the procedure leading up to the decision where what used to be described as a quasi-judicial character is superadded to the administrative task, the eventual decision is an administrative one. [...]

Moreover the decision requires to take into account not just the facts of the case but very much wider issues of public interest, national priorities. Thus the function of the Secretary of State as a decision-maker in planning matters is not in a proper sense a judicial function, although certain qualities of a judicial kind are required of him.

This analysis is resonant of Lord Bingham's. Planning is characterized as an administrative–democratic process and the need for adjudicative rights is downplayed. At the same time, it needs to be remembered that planning law involves interference with private property rights. Thus, the distinction between private rights and the public interest shapes the nature and form of dispute settlement over planning decisions, as well as planning law more generally.

The normative nature of planning regimes

The final theme to note in relation to planning law is that it has an inherently normative dimension. Each exercise in planning law reform is an exercise in promoting, at the very least, a vision of good public decision-making, and at the most, a vision of society. The former can be seen in Lord Bingham's

---

[34] Paul Craig, 'The Human Rights Act, Article 6, and Procedural Rights' [2003] PL 753.

and Lord Clyde's judgments here. The latter can be seen in the discussion of Pinder in Section 1.2. Likewise, historically there have been debates in planning over whether a 'top-down' or 'bottom-up' approach is best.

From a legal perspective, this means that the legal regime at any particular time will reflect normative visions of good decision-making and good societies. This is evidenced in Layard's discussion of the Localism Act 2011. Of course, at any specific point in time, planning law is unlikely to reflect only one vision of decision-making or society. Thus, for example, McAuslan in 1980 recognized the importance of ideology in planning law but identified three different ideologies at play: those of the public interest, private property, and public participation.

Patrick McAuslan, *The Ideologies of Planning Law* (Pergamon Press 1980) 265

The previous two chapters have discussed the general governmental context in which the law and administration of land use planning and control operate. The context explains and supports the ideological orientation of the law, and in turn has received support from that ideological orientation. Both context and law place the emphasis on the ideology of public interest rather than, and at the expense of, the ideology of public participation. The government itself operates in a society which is based on recognition of the institution of private property and a market for property [...]

McAuslan's general conclusion was that, due to the dominance of the other two ideologies, public participation had little room to operate. But note that McAuslan's analysis reflects the time at which he was writing. Changes to the planning system and administrative law (Chapter 7) have strengthened participation and also introduced shifting ideas of the public interest. Yet his general argument, and the tensions that he identifies, remain, as seen already with the influence of Article 6 ECHR.

However, concepts of private property, public participation and public interest are not the only normative values underpinning planning law. Thus, since the early 1990s, the concept of sustainable development has been understood to be a 'core principle' underpinning planning.[35] The Planning and Compulsory Purchase Act 2004 requires those exercising functions in relation to local development documents to do so 'with the objective of contributing to the achievement of sustainable development'.[36] And, under the new National Planning Policy Framework (NPPF), the 'purpose of the planning system is to contribute to the achievement of sustainable development'.[37] Chapter 11 discusses in more detail the definition of sustainable development in the context of the NPPF, as well as more broadly, and it is important to remember that the NPPF approach to sustainable development, as far as it can be identified, is not the only 'definition' of sustainable development to be found in law and policy.[38] However, the multi-pronged nature of sustainable development is useful as a vehicle for reflecting the many goals of planning law and, in the NPPF, there are twelve 'core land use planning principles' identified.

---

[35] Office of the Deputy Prime Minister, *Planning Policy Statement One: Delivering Sustainable Development* (2005) paras 2–3.

[36] Section 39(1).

[37] Department for Communities and Local Government, *National Planning Policy Framework* (2012) para 6.

[38] See Section 2.3 of Chapter 11.

Department for Communities and Local Government, *National Planning Policy Framework* (2012) para 17

17. Within the overarching roles that the planning system ought to play, a set of core land-use planning principles should underpin both plan-making and decision-taking. These 12 principles are that planning should:

- be genuinely plan-led, empowering local people to shape their surroundings, with succinct local and neighbourhood plans setting out a positive vision for the future of the area. Plans should be kept up-to-date, and be based on joint working and co-operation to address larger than local issues. They should provide a practical framework within which decisions on planning applications can be made with a high degree of predictability and efficiency;

- not simply be about scrutiny, but instead be a creative exercise in finding ways to enhance and improve the places in which people live their lives;

- proactively drive and support sustainable economic development to deliver the homes, business and industrial units, infrastructure and thriving local places that the country needs. Every effort should be made objectively to identify and then meet the housing, business and other development needs of an area, and respond positively to wider opportunities for growth. Plans should take account of market signals, such as land prices and housing affordability, and set out a clear strategy for allocating sufficient land which is suitable for development in their area, taking account of the needs of the residential and business communities;

- always seek to secure high quality design and a good standard of amenity for all existing and future occupants of land and buildings;

- take account of the different roles and character of different areas, promoting the vitality of our main urban areas, protecting the Green Belts around them, recognising the intrinsic character and beauty of the countryside and supporting thriving rural communities within it;

- support the transition to a low carbon future in a changing climate, taking full account of flood risk and coastal change, and encourage the reuse of existing resources, including conversion of existing buildings, and encourage the use of renewable resources (for example, by the development of renewable energy);

- contribute to conserving and enhancing the natural environment and reducing pollution. Allocations of land for development should prefer land of lesser environmental value, where consistent with other policies in this Framework;

- encourage the effective use of land by reusing land that has been previously developed (brownfield land), provided that it is not of high environmental value;

- promote mixed use developments, and encourage multiple benefits from the use of land in urban and rural areas, recognising that some open land can perform many functions (such as for wildlife, recreation, flood risk mitigation, carbon storage, or food production);

- conserve heritage assets in a manner appropriate to their significance, so that they can be enjoyed for their contribution to the quality of life of this and future generations;

- actively manage patterns of growth to make the fullest possible use of public transport, walking and cycling, and focus significant development in locations which are or can be made sustainable; and

- take account of and support local strategies to improve health, social and cultural wellbeing for all, and deliver sufficient community and cultural facilities and services to meet local needs.

Included in these twelve principles are many aspirations that highlight that planning plays a multi-faceted role in regulatory and also social terms. There are many hopes and expectations in relation to what planning law can achieve.

Moreover, there are other statutory obligations that impose duties on those making planning decisions. Thus, for example, s 40(1) of the Natural Environment and Rural Communities Act 2006 requires the following:

> Every public authority must, in exercising its functions, have regard, so far as is consistent with the proper exercise of those functions, to the purpose of conserving biodiversity.

This section is discussed in more detail in Chapter 20.[39]

The fact that planning law has a range of normative goals, many of which are not purely environmental, means that planning law is an object of frustration for those environmental lawyers who understand environmental law purposively. If the object of planning law is understood to be environmental protection alone, then it is a deeply problematic area of law. This can be seen in the extract from the Royal Commission of Environmental Pollution's (RCEP) report on Environmental Planning.

Royal Commission on Environmental Pollution, *Environmental Planning* (Cm 5459, 2002) 3–4

We have considered the requirements for environmental sustainability. We have concluded that present planning procedures in the UK do not have the coherence and effectiveness needed to meet those requirements [...] Dramatic changes in land use are in prospect in the countryside. Much needs to be done to reinvigorate urban areas. To reduce emissions of greenhouse gases, radical changes will be needed in the ways the UK obtains and uses energy. At the same time, extensive adaptations are likely to be necessary to cope with the changes in weather patterns and rises in sea level which now appear inevitable. It will be necessary to find more efficient ways of using other natural resources, especially water and minerals. The solutions to these problems will require new policies in many fields, and will certainly pose major challenges for the planning and regulation of land use. The town and country planning system needs to be modified and extended so that it can facilitate successful responses to a changing world [...]

One reform recommended by the RCEP was the need for strong institutional connections between planning and environmental protection regulators. The Commission also concluded that 'regulatory and planning systems are unlikely to contribute to sustainable development unless there is strong commitment to that overall goal extending across all sectors'. In that regard they stated:

We see a pressing need for:

- clearer policies and objectives for the environment;
- statutory recognition of the central role of town and country planning in protecting and enhancing the environment;
- rationalising the overall system for environmental planning by introducing integrated spatial strategies covering all aspects of sustainable development;

---

[39] See Section 2.1 of Chapter 20. See also Conservation of Habitats and Species Regulations 2010 (as amended), Regulation 9(4), discussed in Section 5.4.

- ensuring that strategies cover all forms of land use;
- much improved availability of information about the environment;
- further steps to engage a wider range of people in decisions about setting and achieving environmental goals.

The RCEP's aspirations are admirable, and some their recommendations led to reform. But, as we shall we see, the reconciliation of environmental protection goals with other aspects of the planning regime is not a straightforward exercise.

FURTHER READING

1. From the description in Section 2.1, sketch your own model of the planning law system. For more detailed discussions of planning law, see the list of textbooks at the end of this chapter.

2. On top-down or bottom-up approaches see Jane Jacobs, *The Death and Life of Great American Cities* (The Modern Library 1993) criticizing the top-down planning approach to planning in New York in the 1960s.

3. Lord Hoffmann's very thoughtful judgment in *R (Alconbury) v Environment Secretary* [2001] UKHL 23 is well worth a careful read. In particular, note how he conceptualizes different aspects of the planning process and distinguishes between what is involved in a planning application and planning enforcement.

4. Consider again the twelve principles set out in paragraph 17 of the National Planning Policy Framework extracted here. How reconcilable are these principles?

---

3 CENTRAL GOVERNMENT POLICY AND LOCAL DEVELOPMENT FRAMEWORKS

The discussion so far provides a very rough overview of the planning regime. In this section and Sections 4, 5, and 6 we provide a more careful analysis of the four most significant aspects of planning law for environmental lawyers: central government policy–local development frameworks; what constitutes 'development' and the process of applying for planning permission; the planning application determination process; and finally, enforcement, appeals, and judicial review. It is important to remember that none of this analysis is comprehensive as the system is simply too complex to be easily captured in one chapter.

Chapter 11 discusses the role of policy in environmental law at length. Here we consider the role of both central government and local government policy in planning law. That role is a significant one and understanding planning law requires understanding the many different roles that policy plays within it. In reading this chapter , you may find it useful to return to the discussion in Chapter 11 on the different ways in which law and policy interact.

3.1 CENTRAL GOVERNMENT POLICY

Central government planning policy guidance has long been a feature of the planning system. Broadly speaking, there are four different types of policy document in the planning context: planning policy;

planning circulars; 'Dear Chief Planning Officer' letters; and National Policy Statements under the Planning Act 2008, which relate to specific aspects of large scale infrastructure. This section deals with each of these separately, as each type of document raises distinct issues. With that said, there is also much in common between these documents and the general discussion in Chapter 11 about the role of policy is relevant to them all.

National Planning Policy Framework

The first, and most significant, of these policy documents is the National Planning Policy Framework (NPPF), discussed briefly already, which was introduced in 2012. This fifty-seven-page document replaced over 1000 pages of guidance that had been encapsulated in a series of planning policy statements (PPSs),[40] which had, in turn, replaced planning policy guidance (PPG) documents. While the length and content of these different documents has varied over the years, the idea behind them has not changed.

Mark Tewdwr-Jones, 'Plans, Policies and Inter-governmental Relations: Assessing the Role of National Planning Guidance in England and Wales'
(1997) 34 Urban Studies 141, 142

Although there has never been a 'national physical plan' in England and Wales, central government has always provided a clear approach in determining and promoting planning policy to be operated across the various spatial areas. Rather than developing a statutory national physical plan, the government has preferred to rely on a system of discretion rather than prescription, a process where central government sets down the legal framework and broad policy for local government to interpret.

In other words, the purpose of such policy documents is *not* to map out in detail where development should take place. Rather, these documents provide a framework for the exercise of discretion both in creating local planning documents and in making planning decisions. These documents are a mixture of normative prescription and general practical guidance.

While these policy documents have no legal footing (they are not required by any planning statute), they have played an important role in limiting discretion. The NPPF states that:

The National Planning Policy Framework constitutes guidance for local planning authorities and decision-takers both in drawing up plans and as a material consideration in determining applications.[41]

This gives the NPPF a similar status to previous planning policy documents and in Chapter 11 *R v Derbyshire CC, ex p Woods* is discussed in considering the legal relevance of such planning documents.[42] We also see another example of juridical consideration of these documents in relation to the now defunct *PPS 23: Planning and Pollution Control* in Section 5.2.

---

[40] Note some PPSs's in relation to waste and minerals still remain at the time of writing.
[41] Para 13.
[42] [1998] Env LR 277. See Section 2.3 of Chapter 11.

Planning circulars

The second category of central government policy documents involves planning circulars, which give guidance in relation to specific issues. These also have no statutory basis but are often understood as quasi-legislative in nature as they provide quite specific guidance about how decisions should be made. Thus, for example, Circular 15/92 provides guidance on the publicity of planning applications and Circular 3/09 provides guidance on the awards of costs in proceedings under the different Planning Acts. In some cases, a circular expands on a particular legislative reform. For example, Circular 08/10: Changes to Planning Regulations for Dwelling houses and Houses in Multiple Occupation provides an explanation for changes brought in by The Town and Country Planning (Use Classes) (Amendment) (England) Order 2010.

As these few examples highlight, Planning Circulars are not about 'broad policy' but are more about providing guidance for discretion in the practical and working aspects of the planning regime, primarily in relation to procedure and the interpretation of new legislative reforms. This is not to say that the issues they address do not relate to matters of broad policy or that they are not contentious, but that the nature of these circulars is quite distinct from the NPPF.

These Circulars are heavily replied upon by local planning authorities and by planning inspectors, and they will often be referred to by judges in sketching the legal context for a decision.[43] Yet, the legal role of such documents is different from the central government planning policy documents mentioned already.

R (Enstone Uplands and District Conservation Trust) v West Oxfordshire District Council DC
[2009] EWCA Civ 1555, para 36 (Sullivan LJ)

The Facts

It was arguing that a local planning authority had failed to take into account a 'material consideration' in granting planning permission which was para 93 of Circular 11/95 'Use of Conditions in Planning Permission'. The relevant part of para 93 stated that 'a permission personal to a company is inappropriate because its shares can be transferred to other persons without affecting the legal personality of the company.'

The Court

36. [...] it is important to bear in mind that circular 11/95 is not an enactment; it contains advice as to good practice. Whether the advice in the circular has or has not been followed may very well be a good indicator as to whether a condition is or is not lawful; but failure to follow the advice does not necessarily result in unlawfulness. Specifically, the fact that circular 11/95 advises that a personal condition is inappropriate if the person is a company does not mean a) that the imposition of such a condition is necessarily unlawful (rather than unwise or undesirable because it may be ineffective as a means of controlling the impact of a permitted use; or b) that, if such a condition is unlawfully imposed, the permission as a whole is unlawful since the condition may not go to the root of the permission.

---

[43] For example, *Loader v Secretary of State for Communities and Local Government* [2011] EWHC 2010 (Admin), [2012] Env LR 8. Note this decision was appealed but the appeal was dismissed. See *Loader, R (on the application of) v Secretary of State for Communities and Local Government & Ors* [2012] EWCA Civ 869.

Circulars are thus more about 'good practice' than about the normative aspirations of the planning system.

'Dear chief planning officer' letters

Alongside circulars is a series of letters to chief planning officers. These tend to be very short. They often announce new developments, such as the introduction of new policy and legislation or the removal of old legislation and policy. The documents are descriptive of developments and provide little substantive guidance.

This is not to say that the documents are uncontroversial and do not give rise to legal issues. Consider the case of *Cala Homes (South) Limited v Secretary of State for Communities & Local Government* and note in particular the way in which a letter from executive government announcing future legislative developments gives rise to quite nuanced legal issues.

Cala Homes (South) Limited v Secretary of State for Communities & Local Government
[2011] EWCA Civ 639 paras 26–27 (Sullivan LJ)

The Facts

After the Secretary of State's attempt to revoke Regional Strategies by executive action was found invalid the Chief Planner sent a letter to all local planning authorities stating that 'However, the Secretary of State wrote to Local Planning Authorities and to the Planning Inspectorate on 27 May 2010 informing them of the Government's intention to abolish Regional Strategies in the Localism Bill and that he expected them to have regard to this as a material consideration in planning decisions'. The claimant brought an action for judicial review arguing, among other things, that the Secretary of State was 'engaging in a transparently unlawful attempt to subvert the application of the statutory framework for the taking of planning decisions, and to thwart the effect of the judgment of Sales J. in the first proceedings, by asking decision-makers to take into account, when acting under the extant legislation, the Government's proposal to seek changes to that legislation in the future'. In the Divisional Court Justice Lindbolm found that Secretary of State was entitled to advise authorities that the proposed revocation of Regional Strategies was to be regarded as a material consideration.

The CA

26. If the Chief Planning Officer's letter had advised local planning authorities to ignore the policies in the regional strategies, or to treat them as no longer forming part of the development plan, or to determine planning applications otherwise than in accordance with them because the Government proposed to abolish them, or if it had told decision-makers what weight they should give to the Government's proposal, then such advice would have been unlawful. *Laker Airways Ltd. v Department of Trade* [1977] 1 QB 643, is an example of policy guidance which was unlawful because it was contrary to the statutory objectives laid down for the Civil Aviation Authority by section 3 of the Civil Aviation Act 1971: see per Lord Denning at p. 704 A-F. As Lindblom J explained in paragraphs 58–62 of his judgment, it is necessary to look at what the Chief Planner's letter actually said. It expressly stated that the effect of the decision of Sales J was 'to re-establish regional strategies as part of the development plan', and said that decision-makers should have regard to the proposed abolition of regional strategies as a material consideration in planning decisions. No doubt the letter could have said more, but it must be remembered that the letter was addressed to the Chief Planner's fellow professionals: the Planning Inspectorate and the Chief Planning Officers of the Local Planning Authorities in England. The Chief

Planner did not need to remind those to whom he sent the letter that re-establishing regional strategies as part of the development plan meant that planning applications had to be determined in accordance with the regional strategies unless material considerations indicated otherwise.

27. The advice that decision-makers 'should still have regard to the letter of 27th May 2010 in any decisions they are currently making' might well have been misleading if it had been addressed to a less expert audience. Mr. Mould accepted that in the great majority of cases, the letter dated 27th May 2010 will be of no relevance whatsoever because regional policy will not be in issue at all, or will at best be of marginal significance. The Planning Inspectors and Chief Planning Officers who received the letter would have been well aware of this, and would have sensibly interpreted the letter as referring only to those decisions in which, in their judgment, regional policy was a significant issue. The letter says nothing about the weight to be given to the proposed abolition of regional strategies. Given the very early stage that the proposal has reached in the legislative process, and the fact that revocation of any individual regional strategy will be subject to the SEA [Strategic Environmental Assessment] process, many Planning Inspectors and Chief Planning Officers may well consider that they should give little, if any, weight to the proposed abolition of regional strategies in the decisions that they are currently taking. That position will change if the proposal progresses, or fails to progress, through the legislative and environmental assessment process, but those responsible for taking planning decisions are familiar with the general proposition that the weight to be given to emerging policy is contingent on its progress towards finality: see para. 52 of the judgment of Lindblom J. In summary, the Chief Planner's letter dated 10th November 2010 might have been better and more fully expressed, but what it did say was not unlawful.

This reasoning not only reflects a complex interaction between the legislative and executive regimes but also considers the audience for these types of documents. Sullivan LJ's judgment shows that the 'Dear Chief Planning Officer' has a very particular audience.

Planning Act 2008 and National Policy Statements

The final group of central government policy documents to note are the new National Policy Statements (NPSs) for Nationally Significant Infrastructure Projects. An important point to note about NPSs is that they are produced by a range of different government departments, depending on the topic.

In Chapter 11, there is mention in passing of the new framework for NPSs by Carnwath LJ in *R (Hillingdon LBC) v Secretary of State for Transport*.[44] In that case, Carnwath LJ was emphasizing that there is a statutory framework for NPSs to which it is important to have regard. That framework—which prescribes how these statements are created, and the nature of their content—can be found in Part 2 of the Planning Act 2008. In particular, s 13 sets out the means by which NPSs can be legally challenged, which is by way of judicial review—a provision that reflects the fact that NPSs can be controversial in nature.

In terms of their legal relevance, s 104 requires the Secretary of State to have regard to NPSs in the determination of applications relating to large infrastructure projects. Their function is thus similar to local development frameworks, discussed in Section 3.2. The NPPF also makes clear that '[n]ational policy statements form part of the overall framework of national planning policy, and are a material consideration in decisions on planning applications.'[45] As NPS documents are new, we are yet to see any sustained examples of them being judicially considered.

---

[44] [2010] EWHC 626 (Admin). See extract in Section 2.1 of Chapter 11.
[45] Department for Communities (n 37) para 3.

3.2 LOCAL DEVELOPMENT FRAMEWORKS

The creation of planning policy is not the province of central government alone. Under planning legislation, local planning authorities must also develop their own policies. As with central government policy, these policies also have legal significance, although in the case of local development plans, that relevance is regulated by statute.

The creation of local development frameworks

Historically, local planning policy was in the form of 'local development plans' but, by the late 1990s, the process of creating such plans had become ossified and overly complicated. The Planning and Compulsory Purchase Act 2004 overhauled the process by replacing local development plans with 'local development frameworks' and also set out a new procedure for creating such frameworks. The procedure is explained by Carnwath LJ in the *Barratt Developments Plc v The City of Wakefield Metropolitan District Council* case.

Barratt Developments Plc v The City of Wakefield Metropolitan District Council
[2010] EWCA Civ 897 paras 5–7 (Carnwath LJ)

5. The Planning and Compulsory Purchase Act 2004, supplemented by the Town and Country Planning (Local Development)(England) Regulations 2004, provides the statutory framework for the preparation of the Local Development Framework ('LDF'), of which the Core Strategy forms part. These documents form part of the 'development plan' for the area, in accordance with which development applications must be decided unless material considerations indicate otherwise (s 38(3)(6)).

6. The judge set out in some detail the procedural requirements for preparation of the Core Strategy. I need only pick out the key points:

i)   The authority must have regard among other things to:

a) national policies and advice contained in guidance issued by the Secretary of State and [...]

iii) it must contain a reasoned justification of the policies (reg 13(1)).

iv) Before it is adopted it must be submitted for independent examination by a planning inspector on behalf of the Secretary of State, to determine (inter alia) whether it satisfies these requirements and 'whether it is sound' (s 20(5)).

v)   Any person who makes representations seeking to change the plan must be given an opportunity to appear before and be heard by the inspector (s 20(6)).

vi) The inspector must make recommendations and give reasons for those recommendations (s 20(7)).

vii) The authority can only adopt the strategy, whether as originally prepared or with modifications, in accordance with recommendations of the inspector (s 23).

7. It is to be noted that the procedure does not include a formal planning inquiry in the traditional sense. Collins J described what I understand to be the ordinary format for such an open hearing:

'... this is not a traditional planning inquiry. It is, as its title suggests, an examination. Inspectors are encouraged to make it relatively informal, and it can be, and frequently is, I understand, carried out by means of discussion. Although formal evidence can no doubt be given and tested if the Inspector decides that that is essential for the purpose of reaching the necessary result, that would be rare, and generally speaking it is dealt with on the basis of written documents being presented, and then discussion between the interested parties and the Inspector based upon those written documents.' (*Persimmon Homes (North East) Ltd v Blyth Valley BC* [2008] EWHC 1258 (Admin) para 49)

The procedures under the 2004 Act have been adjusted by amendment but the distinct nature of the procedure remains. The overall aim of the local development framework (which can include local plans and supplementary planning documents) is that local planning policy is easily accessible.

As indicated above, local development documents must also be developed with the 'objective of contributing to the achievement of sustainable development' (s 39(2)). The NPPF expands on this (note that we also extracted paragraph 14 (which also relates to decision-taking) in Section 2.3 of Chapter 11).

Department for Communities and Local Government, *National Planning Policy Framework* (2012) paras 14–16 (emphasis in the original)

14. At the heart of the National Planning Policy Framework is a **presumption in favour of sustainable development**, which should be seen as a golden thread running through both plan-making and decision-taking.

For **plan-making** this means that:

- local planning authorities should positively seek opportunities to meet the development needs of their area;

- Local Plans should meet objectively assessed needs, with sufficient flexibility to adapt to rapid change, unless:

  - any adverse impacts of doing so would significantly and demonstrably outweigh the benefits, when assessed against the policies in this Framework taken as a whole; or

  - specific policies in this Framework indicate development should be restricted [...]

15. Policies in Local Plans should follow the approach of the presumption in favour of sustainable development so that it is clear that development which is sustainable can be approved without delay. All plans should be based upon and reflect the presumption in favour of sustainable development, with clear policies that will guide how the presumption should be applied locally.

16. The application of the presumption will have implications for how communities engage in neighbourhood planning. Critically, it will mean that neighbourhoods should:

- develop plans that support the strategic development needs set out in Local Plans, including policies for housing and economic development;

- plan positively to support local development, shaping and directing development in their area that is outside the strategic elements of the Local Plan; and

- identify opportunities to use Neighbourhood Development Orders to enable developments that are consistent with their neighbourhood plan to proceed.

The framework for Neighbourhood Development Orders was introduced by the Localism Act 2011.[46]

---

[46] See Section 1.3.

The legal relevance of local development frameworks

As seen in Section 2.1, the legal relevance of local development frameworks is on a statutory footing due to s 38(6) of the Planning and Compulsory Purchase Act 2004. This section replaces the old s 54A TCPA, which had slightly different wording. The NPPF makes clear the significance of the local development plan.

Department for Communities and Local Government, *National Planning Policy Framework* (2012) paras 11–12

11. Planning law requires that applications for planning permission must be determined in accordance with the development plan unless material considerations indicate otherwise.

12. This National Planning Policy Framework does not change the statutory status of the development plan as the starting point for decision making. Proposed development that accords with an up-to-date Local Plan should be approved, and proposed development that conflicts should be refused unless other material considerations indicate otherwise. It is highly desirable that local planning authorities should have an up-to-date plan in place.

All of this raises the question of what it means to decide something 'in accordance with the development plan' and, not surprisingly, this has been litigated on a number of occasions. Recently, the Supreme Court considered this issue in relation to a case that arose under a similar Scottish provision. Lord Reed's judgment focuses on how a local planning authority must construe a development plan.

Tesco Stores Ltd v Dundee City Council (Scotland) [2012] UKSC 13 paras 17–19, 21–22 (Lord Reed JSC)

17. It has long been established that a planning authority must proceed upon a proper understanding of the development plan: see, for example, *Gransden & Co Ltd v Secretary of State for the Environment* (1985) 54 P & CR 86, 94 per Woolf J, affd (1986) 54 P & CR 361; *Horsham DC v Secretary of State for the Environment* (1991) 63 P & CR 219, 225-226 per Nolan LJ. The need for a proper understanding follows, in the first place, from the fact that the planning authority is required by statute to have regard to the provisions of the development plan: it cannot have regard to the provisions of the plan if it fails to understand them. It also follows from the legal status given to the development plan by section 25 of the 1997 [Scottish] Act. The effect of the predecessor of section 25, namely section 18A of the Town and Country (Planning) Scotland Act 1972 (as inserted by section 58 of the Planning and Compensation Act 1991), was considered by the House of Lords in the case of *City of Edinburgh Council v Secretary of State for Scotland* 1998 SC (HL) 33, [1997] 1 WLR 1447. It is sufficient for present purposes to cite a passage from the speech of Lord Clyde, with which the other members of the House expressed their agreement. At p 44, 1459, his Lordship observed:

'In the practical application of sec 18A it will obviously be necessary for the decision-maker to consider the development plan, identify any provisions in it which are relevant to the question before him and make a proper interpretation of them. His decision will be open to challenge if he fails to have regard to a policy in the development plan which is relevant to the application or fails properly to interpret it.'

18. In the present case, the planning authority was required by section 25 to consider whether the proposed development was in accordance with the development plan and, if not, whether material

considerations justified departing from the plan. In order to carry out that exercise, the planning author-ity required to proceed on the basis of what Lord Clyde described as 'a proper interpretation' of the relevant provisions of the plan. We were however referred by counsel to a number of judicial dicta which were said to support the proposition that the meaning of the development plan was a matter to be determined by the planning authority: the court, it was submitted, had no role in determining the meaning of the plan unless the view taken by the planning authority could be characterised as perverse or irrational. That submission, if correct, would deprive sections 25 and 37(2) of the 1997 Act of much of their effect, and would drain the need for a 'proper interpretation' of the plan of much of its meaning and purpose. It would also make little practical sense. The development plan is a carefully drafted and considered statement of policy, published in order to inform the public of the approach which will be followed by planning authorities in decision-making unless there is good reason to depart from it. It is intended to guide the behaviour of developers and planning authorities. As in other areas of administra-tive law, the policies which it sets out are designed to secure consistency and direction in the exercise of discretionary powers, while allowing a measure of flexibility to be retained. Those considerations point away from the view that the meaning of the plan is in principle a matter which each planning authority is entitled to determine from time to time as it pleases, within the limits of rationality. On the contrary, these considerations suggest that in principle, in this area of public administration as in oth-ers (as discussed, for example, in *R (Raissi) v Secretary of State for the Home Department* [2008] QB 836), policy statements should be interpreted objectively in accordance with the language used, read as always in its proper context.

19. That is not to say that such statements should be construed as if they were statutory or contractual provisions. Although a development plan has a legal status and legal effects, it is not analogous in its nature or purpose to a statute or a contract. As has often been observed, development plans are full of broad statements of policy, many of which may be mutually irreconcilable, so that in a particular case one must give way to another. In addition, many of the provisions of development plans are framed in language whose application to a given set of facts requires the exercise of judgment. Such matters fall within the jurisdiction of planning authorities, and their exercise of their judgment can only be challenged on the ground that it is irrational or perverse (*Tesco Stores Ltd v Secretary of State for the Environment* [1995] 1 WLR 759, 780 per Lord Hoffmann). Nevertheless, planning authorities do not live in the world of Humpty Dumpty: they cannot make the development plan mean whatever they would like it to mean.

Lord Reed then referred to *R v Derbyshire County Council, ex p Woods*, which was extracted in Chapter 11.[47] After discussion of a number of other cases, he noted:

21. A provision in the development plan which requires an assessment of whether a site is 'suitable' for a particular purpose calls for judgment in its application. But the question whether such a provision is concerned with suitability for one purpose or another is not a question of planning judgment: it is a question of textual interpretation, which can only be answered by construing the language used in its context. In the present case, in particular, the question whether the word 'suitable', in the policies in question, means 'suitable for the development proposed by the applicant', or 'suitable for meeting identified deficiencies in retail provision in the area', is not a question which can be answered by the exercise of planning judgment: it is a logically prior question as to the issue to which planning judgment requires to be directed.

22. It is of course true, as counsel for the respondents submitted, that a planning authority might misconstrue part of a policy but nevertheless reach the same conclusion, on the question whether the proposal was in accordance with the policy, as it would have reached if it had construed the policy

---

[47] See Section 2.3 of Chapter 11.

correctly. That is not however a complete answer to a challenge to the planning authority's decision. An error in relation to one part of a policy might affect the overall conclusion as to whether a proposal was in accordance with the development plan even if the question whether the proposal was in conformity with the policy would have been answered in the same way. The policy criteria with which the proposal was considered to be incompatible might, for example, be of less weight than the criteria which were mistakenly thought to be fulfilled. Equally, a planning authority might misconstrue part of a policy but nevertheless reach the same conclusion as it would otherwise have reached on the question whether the proposal was in accordance with the development plan. Again, however, that is not a complete answer. Where it is concluded that the proposal is not in accordance with the development plan, it is necessary to understand the nature and extent of the departure from the plan which the grant of consent would involve in order to consider on a proper basis whether such a departure is justified by other material considerations.

Lord Reed is here highlighting a number of different ways in which a local development plan might be construed. A further issue is how a plan affects what is understood to be a 'material' consideration.

Bromley LBC v Secretary of State for Communities and Local Government
[2007] EWHC 2480 (Admin) para 18 (Mole QC J)

The Facts

Claimants argued that a 'material consideration' could not be something already considered in a plan. In this case, the plan set up policies for limiting development on Metropolitan Open Land (MOL).

The HC

18. It is agreed by counsel that Mr Brown appears to be right to submit that there is no direct authority for the proposition that in order to be a 'material' consideration, capable of indicating a determination other than in accordance with the development plan, the consideration in question must not have been one that was taken into account in the adoption of that development plan. But I suspect that the reason for that may be because it is a proposition that is sufficiently obvious not to require any authority. In my judgment it would strike at the basic principle of the primacy of the development plan if it were open to a decision maker to refuse to decide in accordance with the development plan on the basis of a consideration that had been fully taken into account in the decision to adopt that plan. [...] If it is evident that a consideration had indeed been taken into account in the adoption of the plan, it seems to me that no reasonable Inspector could properly conclude that the identical consideration was material or, alternatively, if it was material, that any weight should be put upon it. To take an example relevant to this case; suppose the Council, on the basis of the need to meet a shortfall in housing provision, judged that site A, rather than site B, be taken out of the MOL, allocated for housing and drafted the MOL boundaries in the development plan accordingly. In my judgment the decision maker would go wrong in law if, on the basis of an unchanged need, he were to decide that site B rather than site A was better allocated for housing. The decision maker would be substituting his own planning judgment for that reflected in the development plan. He would be failing to recognise the priority required by statute to be given to that plan.

But, of course, that all depends upon the considerations being the same as those already taken into account. Once a circumstance has changed and the consideration is not quite the same, or there are other new relevant circumstances to take into account, the significance or otherwise of the differences becomes a matter of the Inspector's judgment with which the court will not interfere unless the judgment is *Wednesbury* unreasonable. Of course the Inspector may also go wrong in law if he fails to give his mind to whether or not the consideration that is said to be "material" really is significantly different from one that has already been taken into account in the adoption of the plan.

As with the judicial consideration of central government policy here, the approach to s 38(6) is nuanced. Policy is not a set of rigid rules and judges need to probe quite carefully in their legal analysis to determine its legal effects. Again, referral back to both Chapters 7 and 11 might be useful for readers.

FURTHER READING AND QUESTIONS

1. The full text of the NPPF and other policy documents can be found on the Department of Communities and Local Government website at <http://www.communities.gov.uk/planning andbuilding/planningsystem/> accessed 27 September 2012. Local Framework Documents can be found on local planning authority websites. Read through these briefly and consider the amount of detail in them and how helpful they would be in directing and shaping discretion.

2. Besides the issues identified here, consultation on the development of policy can also be legally controversial. See Chapter 11 for a discussion of this, particularly in relation to *R (Hillingdon LBC) v Secretary of State for Transport* [2010] EWHC 626 (Admin).

3. In light of the discussion in Section 3.1 on central government policy, what can you conclude about the legal nature of high-level government policy in planning law? Consider this issue in light of the discussion in Sections 2.1 and 2.2 of Chapter 11.

---

4 DEVELOPMENT AND APPLYING FOR PLANNING PERMISSION

As highlighted in Section 2.1, 'development' requires planning permission. This section considers the nature of development as well as the process of applying for planning permission. As will be seen, the question of what constitutes development is not simply a technical issue. How that term is defined fundamentally regulates the scope of planning law.

4.1 'DEVELOPMENT' AND THE SCOPE OF PLANNING LAW

Section 57(1) TCPA states that 'planning permission is required for the carrying out of any development of land'. Section 55 states:

(1) Subject to the following provisions of this section, in this Act, except where the context otherwise requires, 'development,' means the carrying out of building, engineering, mining or other operations in, on, over or under land, or the making of any material change in the use of any buildings or other land.

(1A) For the purposes of this Act 'building operations' includes—

(a) demolition of buildings;

(b) rebuilding;

(c) structural alterations of or additions to buildings; and

(d) other operations normally undertaken by a person carrying on business as a builder.

As is clear from this definition, there are two different types of 'development'—operational development and 'change of use' development. As s 55(1A) makes clear, building operations include all types of building works and thus operational development has a wide definition. Development where there is understood to be a 'material change of use' is primarily governed by delegated legislation—The Use Classes Order 1987 categorizes different activities, or uses of land, into different classes. Something is a 'change of use' under the Order only if it is a change from one class listed to another. Further, some legislation specifically provides that some activities will amount to a change of use, for example, the turning of one dwelling house into two.[48]

There is a complex body of case law that has built up concerning whether different operations and different activities amount to development, particularly in the context of planning enforcement. Any planning law textbook has at least one dense chapter dedicated to the topic. This is not surprising. Whether something is classified as development or not will determine whether it is governed by planning law. For those thinking about planning law from an environmental law perspective, these cases are less significant. In most cases where there is an environmental problem, there is also clearly development—usually 'operational development'. However, because the issue of what development is relates to the legal scope of planning law, it is not something environmental lawyers can ignore. The *Chas Storer Limited v Secretary of State for Communities and Local Government, Hertfordshire CC* case highlights the complexity of determining whether something amounts to a 'change of use' and thus falls within the scope of planning law.

Chas Storer Limited v Secretary of State for Communities and Local Government, Hertfordshire CC
[2009] EWHC 1071 paras 41, 48–49 (Stephen Morris QC)

The Facts

The Appellant (Chas Storer) operated a waste collection and processing site which had historically mainly collected and processed paper. The local planning authority served an enforcement notice alleging that a 'material change of use' had occurred as the site was now accepting 'co-mingled waste' and the notice imposed requirements restricting the type of materials the site could accept, hours of operation, and the number of lorry movements. The appellant appealed to a Planning Inspector who upheld the finding of change of use and imposed similar restrictions. The Appellant appealed to the Administrative Court arguing that as the Inspector had found that the material change of use only related to the acceptance of co-mingled waste then the restrictions placed on the activity could not related to anything else.

The HC

41. [...] In my judgment, paragraph 7.45 is, in its own terms, clear. There the Inspector found that it was the receipt and bulking of co-mingled waste which constituted, or gave rise to, the material

---

[48] s 55(3)(a) TCPA 1990.

change of use. He further found that, absent the addition of co-mingled waste, the increase in vehicle movements and in the hours of operation since 1996 would not have given rise to a material change of use. This is the clear sense of the entire paragraph. Moreover examination of individual passages within the paragraph lead to the same conclusion. Both these findings appear from the two sentences *'Nevertheless if this were the whole story I do not believe there would have been a material change of use, notwithstanding what is likely to have been a fairly large increase in throughput and vehicle movements. It is the change in the nature of the materials which is telling'*. Whilst, in the next two sentences of paragraph 7.45, he accepted that the co-mingled waste was only partially responsible for the overall increase in activity on the Site and that handling of other materials also caused noise concerns, he then went on to single out the particularly adverse effects of co-mingled waste in the following terms: *'But the co-mingled material is a new type of waste with a specific character which is likely to have impacts from noise during handling, as has been experienced locally. There are also other effects, mainly the increased presence of vermin.'* He then concluded that *'overall... there has been a material change of use'*. His final sentence is *'Given the significance which I attribute to the co-mingled waste this is likely to have occurred by the end of 2003'*. [...]

In the next several paragraphs, the Judge goes on to consider a number of arguments put by each side concerning the text, and thus the meaning, of the Inspector's decision.

48. For these reasons, in my judgment, the Inspector's findings and conclusion on the nature of the material change are found at paragraph 7.45. Paragraph 7.45 clearly stated that it was the addition of co-mingled waste that constituted or gave rise to the material change of use. I do not consider that the material change of use was found to be any wider than that. At no point in the Decision Letter did the Inspector state that the material changes of use included the increased vehicle movements and hours of operation. To reach such a conclusion would fly in the face of the clear findings in paragraph 7.45, not only that the material change of use was the addition of co-mingled waste, but also that the increase in vehicle movements and hours of operation on their own would *not* have constituted a material change of use.

49. On the basis of this finding, increases in vehicle movements and hours of operation between 1996 and 2006 did not constitute or form part of the material change of use and thus did not amount to development. It follows that such activities at those increased levels remained lawful use. The Inspector was not entitled to impose requirements which went beyond what was necessary to confine relevant activities to lawful use.

This case is one of many, and it highlights three important points. First, again, the meaning of development will determine what is governed by planning law. On the facts here, since the vehicle movements and hours of operation were lawful, the enforcement notice could not regulate them. Second, the question of what constitutes a material change of use is very fact-specific and these cases turn on the precise circumstances involved. Third, the reasoning shows a highly textualist approach to the planning inspector's decision—an approach that characterizes much planning law argument and reasoning.

4.2 THE PROCESS OF APPLYING FOR PLANNING PERMISSION

If planning permission is required, then a planning application must be submitted to the local planning authority. Before this is done, there are often pre-application discussions with the planning authority. It also may be at this stage that the EIA regime will be relevant (see further Chapter 19).

Before determining a planning application, the planning authority is under a duty to publicize the application. Under s 65 TCPA, the Secretary of State is given power to pass orders setting out the requirements for the publicizing of planning applications. These requirements are set out in the Town and Country Planning (General Development Procedure) Order 1995, which creates three different types of publicity requirement depending on the nature of the development involved.[49] Development that is accompanied by an environmental statement (again, see the EIA requirements in Chapter 19) or involves a departure from the local development plan requires the most significant form of publicity. Circular 15/92 also provides guidance on the publicity of planning applications. It makes clear that, while publicity is important, it should not be at the cost of slowing down the process too much.

From an academic perspective, there has been considerable focus on the importance of public participation in planning law (see, for example, McAuslan in Section 2.2). This is not surprising—as seen in Section 2.3 of Chapter 7, environmental lawyers understand public participation as an important aspect of ensuring environmental protection. From a planning law perspective, obligations of participation are understood in administrative law terms. Consider the *R (Gavin) v Haringey LBC* case.

R (Gavin) v Haringey LBC
[2003] EWHC 2591 (Admin) paras 23, 25–31 (Richards J)

23. Article 8(4) of the Town and Country Planning (General Development Procedure) Order 1995 provides:

'In the case of an application for planning permission which is not a paragraph (2) application, if the development proposed is a major development the application shall be publicised by giving requisite notice -

(a) (i) by site display in at least one place on or near the land to which the application relates for not less than 21 days, or

(ii) by serving the notice on any adjoining owner or occupier,

and

(b) by local advertisement.' [. . .]

25. It is common ground that there was a failure to comply with article 8(4), though there is a dispute about the extent of the failure. The council accepts that it failed to comply with (b) in that, although a notice was placed in the *Haringey Independent*, that newspaper did not circulate in the area of the site. It submits, however, that it complied with (a), in that it served notice in accordance with the alternative in (a)(ii) on the adjoining owners and occupiers - indeed it went beyond that, by sending written notices to the occupiers of properties in the area even though, like the claimant, they were not strictly 'adjoining' the application site. The claimant, on the other hand, contends that there was a failure to comply with (a) as well.

26. The claimant's case on (a) is that the council had a discretion whether to proceed by way of displaying a site notice or by way of serving notices on adjoining owners or occupiers. Any statutory discretion has to be exercised in accordance with the spirit and purpose of the enabling statute and in particular for reasons relevant to the achievement of the statutory purpose: *R v Tower Hamlets LBC, ex p Chetnik* [1988] 1 AC 858 at 872-873. The purpose of the publicity provisions is to secure notification of persons likely to be interested in the planning application. Consideration must therefore be given to whether that

[49] Note also the pre-publicity requirements introduced by the Localism Act 2011—see s 122 of that Act, which introduced s 61W into the TCPA 1990.

purpose is best achieved in an individual case by site notices or by the service of notices on adjoining owners and occupiers. In an urban context the former may be more appropriate, given that those likely to be interested will extend beyond those immediately adjoining the site. In the present case, however, the evidence is that the council simply followed its practice of serving notices on adjoining owners and occupiers rather than using site notices. Accordingly there was a failure to give proper consideration to the exercise of the statutory discretion.

27. I have substantial doubts as to whether article 8(4)(a) imposes on a local planning authority an obligation to consider which of the two methods is best calculated to give notice of the application to those likely to be interested in the application. On the face of it, either of those methods is equally valid in every case: the relevant judgment has already been made by the Secretary of State, who, in making the 1995 Order, has formed the view that the purpose of ensuring that sufficient notice is given will be sufficiently achieved by a combination of (a) either of those methods plus (b) local advertisement.

28. Neither Mr Stephenson for the council, however, nor Mr Goatley for Wolseley has advanced that line of argument. Mr Stephenson's submission, adopted by Mr Goatley, is simply that the council's practice, which it followed in this case, was to serve notices on adjoining owners and occupiers rather than to use site notices, and that the adoption of such a practice has not been shown to be unlawful.

29. I am inclined to accept that, if and to the extent that it is incumbent on a local planning authority to make a discretionary judgment between the two alternatives in article 8(4)(a), it is permissible to decide to adopt a general practice rather than to assess each individual case separately, subject always to a willingness to consider any reasons advanced for departing from the practice in an individual case. It appears that the council had a practice of serving notices on adjoining owners and occupiers, and there is no suggestion that any reasons were advanced for departing from the practice in this case. So I would reject the claimant's case based on a failure to consider which method to use in the individual case. There still remains a question whether the practice itself was lawful. The difficulty about that issue is the lack of evidence about the adoption of the practice or the reasons for it. The court has so little to go on that I would if necessary fall back on acceptance of Mr Stephenson's submission that the claimant has failed to establish that the practice followed in this case was unlawful.

30. I do not consider, however, that a decision on the disputed issue under article 8(4)(a) is strictly necessary. In circumstances where the claimant did not otherwise receive notification of the planning application, the admitted failure to comply with article 8(4)(b) would have been a sufficient reason for quashing the grant of planning permission if there had been a timely challenge. If there was a failure to comply with article 8(4)(a) as well, it would be a point to put in the balance when considering the exercise of discretion to grant or withhold relief; but in my judgment it would not carry much additional weight and would not materially affect the outcome of the balancing exercise in the circumstances of the case as a whole. I therefore propose to say no more about it.

31. I should make clear that, in concluding that the failure to comply with article 8(4)(b) would have been a sufficient reason for quashing the grant of planning permission, I am satisfied that the claimant was substantially prejudiced by the failure. He would have been in a position to make representations of substance in opposition to the proposed development, in respect of matters such as loss of amenity, visual intrusion, type of use (eg the range of goods permitted to be sold by retail), hours of operation, traffic and car parking spaces. Such representations would have gone both to the principle of planning permission and to the conditions to be imposed if permission were granted. They might not have been successful, but they were of sufficient substance that he could legitimately complain of the denial of an opportunity to make them. The case for relief would have been reinforced by the fact that a substantial number of other residents would appear to have been unaware of the planning application and would also have objected to it if they had been notified.

Richards J is thus simultaneously allowing the Council considerable discretion but also ensuring that it meets its obligation. As with other aspects of planning law, the balance to be struck is a nuanced one.

There are a number of other procedural aspects to the process of applying for planning permission, and two in particular are important to note. First, in some cases a planning authority is required to consult with other specialist bodies. This obligation is set out in Article 10 of the Town and Country Planning (General Development Procedure) Order 1995, which contains a long table listing when consultation is required with various bodies. For example, Natural England must be consulted in specific cases where nature conservation issues are implicated in a planning application. Second, under s 77 TCPA the Secretary of State may 'call in' a planning application, taking it out of the hands of the local planning authority to consider and determine it him or herself, although this power is used very rarely and primarily for cases of national significance.

5 THE PLANNING APPLICATION DETERMINATION PROCESS: WHAT IS RELEVANT FOR A DECISION-MAKER TO CONSIDER?

The process of determining a planning application is fiendishly complex and this section focuses only on the concept of 'material considerations', which is the key device for determining what local authorities (and other planning decision-makers) are required to consider in determining applications. This concept was outlined in Section 2.1, and this section examines examples of where environmental issues are taken into account as, or as aspects of, relevant material considerations, and briefly discusses the role of planning conditions. In determining planning applications, the environmental impact assessment regime and contaminated land issues may also be relevant. These are considered in Chapters 19 and 21 respectively.

5.1 THE CONCEPT OF 'MATERIAL CONSIDERATIONS'

As we have already seen, s 70(2) TCPA requires that those determining planning applications shall have regard to 'the provisions of the development plan, so far as material to the application, and to any other material considerations'. The role of development plans was considered in Section 3.2. Central government policy documents, discussed in Section 3.1, are also relevant material considerations. However, we are yet to explore what a 'material consideration' is. The starting point for understanding the nature of a material consideration is the analysis in *Stringer v Minister of Housing and Local Government*. The facts of the case are not relevant.

Stringer v Minister of Housing and Local Government
[1970] 1 WLR 1281, 1294–95 (QB) (Cooke J)

It may be conceded at once that the material considerations to which the Minister is entitled and bound to have regard in deciding the appeal must be considerations of a planning nature. I find it impossible, however, to accept the view that such considerations are limited to matters relating to amenity. So far as I am aware, there is no authority for such a proposition, and it seems to me to be wrong in principle. In principle, it seems to me that any consideration which relates to the use and development of land is capable of being a planning consideration. Whether a particular consideration falling within that broad class is material in any given case will depend on the circumstances. However, it seems to me that in considering an appeal the Minister is entitled to ask himself whether the proposed development is compatible with the proper and desirable use of other land in the area. For example, if permission is sought to erect an explosives factory adjacent to a school, the Minister must surely be entitled and bound to consider the question of safety. That plainly is not an amenity consideration. The broad nature of the duties of planning authorities in dealing with an application is indicated in the judgment of Widgery J. in *Fitzpatrick Developments Ltd. v. Minister of Housing and Local Government* (unreported) May 24, 1965. Widgery J. said:

'It is the duty of the local planning authority in the first instance, and the Minister if the matter comes to him by way of appeal, to plan the area concerned, and an essential feature of planning must be the separation of different uses or activities which are incompatible the one with the other.' [...]

It seems to me that all considerations relating to the use and development of land are considerations which may, in a proper case, be regarded as planning considerations. [...]

I find it equally difficult to accept that the local planning authority and the Minister on appeal must have regard only to the public interest as opposed to private interests. It is, of course, true, as Salmon J pointed out in the *Buxton* case [1961] 1 QB 278 , that the scheme of the legislation is to restrict development for the benefit of the public at large. But it seems to me that it would be impossible for the Minister and local planning authorities to carry out their duties as custodians of the public interest if they were precluded from considering the effect of a proposed development on a particular use of land by a particular occupier in the neighbourhood. The public interest, as I see it, may require that the interests of individual occupiers should be considered. The protection of the interests of individual occupiers is one aspect, and an important one, of the public interest as a whole. The distinction between public and private interests appears to me to be a false distinction in this context.

This reasoning shows that the discretion of the decision-maker (whether it be a local planning authority, the Secretary of State, or a Planning Inspector) in determining a planning application is considerable. Moreover, it can be seen that public and private interests are entangled in that process of consideration. It is also important to remember that ministerial policy will be a relevant material consideration in determining planning applications, and it will embed many different aspirations about urban development. Or to put the matter another way—the issue of 'material considerations' is the legal site where the normative aspects of planning law come to be applied. In practice, determining planning applications is a very messy and very issue-specific process in which many different factors can come into play.

5.2 MATERIAL CONSIDERATIONS AND ENVIRONMENTAL PROTECTION ISSUES: THE GENERAL RELATIONSHIP

Many material considerations will not be directly relevant to environmental law, beyond relating to environmental problems broadly understood to include disputes over use of land. More narrowly, environmental protection can be a material consideration in planning decision-making. This was made explicit by paragraph 8 of the now defunct *Planning Policy 23: Planning and Pollution Control* (2004):

Any consideration of the quality of land, air or water and potential impacts arising from development, possibly leading to an impact on health, is capable of being a material planning consideration, in so far as it arises or may arise from any land use.

Beyond this, a considerable number of detailed PPSs existed in relation to environmental protection issues. These included: *Planning and Climate Change—Supplement to Planning Policy Statement 1; PPS 9: Biodiversity and Geological Conservation; PPS 10: Planning for Sustainable Waste Management;* as well as *PPS 23: Planning and Pollution Control (including Annexes).* Of these, only PPS 10 remains, although this is also to be replaced.[50] In the place of these multiple planning policy documents is the NPPF. While the Framework is generally relevant to environmental law, paragraphs 109–25 are directly concerned with the protection of the natural environment and deal with a range of issues, including air quality issues (paragraph 124), light pollution (paragraph 125), nature conservation and biodiversity (paragraphs 117–18), and noise pollution (paragraph 123). There is no longer a statement similar to paragraph 8 of PPS 23. Rather, the NPPF states the following.

Department for Communities and Local Government, National Planning Policy Framework (2012) para 109

The planning system should contribute to and enhance the natural and local environment by:

- protecting and enhancing valued landscapes, geological conservation interests and soils;

- recognising the wider benefits of ecosystem services;

- minimising impacts on biodiversity and providing net gains in biodiversity where possible, contributing to the Government's commitment to halt the overall decline in biodiversity, including by establishing coherent ecological networks that are more resilient to current and future pressures;

- preventing both new and existing development from contributing to or being put at unacceptable risk from, or being adversely affected by unacceptable levels of soil, air, water or noise pollution or land instability; and

- remediating and mitigating despoiled, degraded, derelict, contaminated and unstable land, where appropriate.

These different goals are fleshed out in further detail in the following paragraphs of the framework. We look at the policy regarding the interrelationship between planning law and biodiversity and land contamination regulation in Chapters 20 and 21 respectively. Here, three case studies of the interrelationship between the determination of a planning application and other aspects of environmental law are considered. All these examples relate to policy and legislation that has now been amended or replaced (in the various ways considered so far in this chapter), but the legal issues that they highlight remain.

5.3 PLANNING AND POLLUTION REGULATION

The interrelationship between the determination of a planning application and pollution control regulation has been a significant issue in practice. From the perspective of planning law, the relevant question is whether pollution is a 'material consideration' and, if so, whether the fact that a specialist regulator regulates pollution problems is also a 'material consideration'. The short answer is yes, and yes. The long answer is more complicated. The NPPF is the starting point for understanding this relationship.

---

[50] PPS 10 is to be replaced in due course (in 2013 or soon thereafter) by an integrated National Waste Management Plan for England. See further, Section 3.4 of Chapter 16.

Department for Communities and Local Government, *National Planning Policy Framework*
(2012) paras 120, 122

120. To prevent unacceptable risks from pollution and land instability, planning policies and decisions should ensure that new development is appropriate for its location. The effects (including cumulative effects) of pollution on health, the natural environment or general amenity, and the potential sensitivity of the area or proposed development to adverse effects from pollution, should be taken into account. [...]

122. In doing so, local planning authorities should focus on whether the development itself is an acceptable use of the land, and the impact of the use, rather than the control of processes or emissions themselves where these are subject to approval under pollution control regimes. Local planning authorities should assume that these regimes will operate effectively. Equally, where a planning decision has been made on a particular development, the planning issues should not be revisited through the permitting regimes operated by pollution control authorities.

Paragraph 122 is a rewording of the former paragraph 10, PPS 23.

Office of the Deputy Prime Minister, *Planning Policy Statement 23: Planning and Pollution Control* (2004) para 10 (now defunct)

10. The planning and pollution control systems are separate but complementary. Pollution control is concerned with preventing pollution through the use of measures to prohibit or limit the release of substances to the environment from different sources to the lowest practicable level. It also ensures that ambient air and water quality meet standards that guard against impacts to the environment and human health. The planning system controls the development and use of land in the public interest. It plays an important role in determining the location of development which may give rise to pollution, either directly or from traffic generated, and in ensuring that other developments are, as far as possible, not affected by major existing, or potential sources of pollution. The planning system should focus on whether the development itself is an acceptable use of the land, and the impacts of those uses, rather than the control of processes or emissions themselves. Planning authorities should work on the assumption that the relevant pollution control regime will be properly applied and enforced. They should act to complement but not seek to duplicate it.

In the past, paragraph 10 has been the focus of judicial consideration due to the difficult reality of the apparently simple principle that the planning and pollution regimes are 'complementary'. In practice, the regimes will interrelate in their application to a development or installation that is subject to controls under both. While PPS23 no longer exists, the spirit of paragraph 10 lives on in the NPPF (although you should note the differences) and the problems highlighted by the two cases extracted here remain.

Hopkins Developments Ltd v First Secretary of State
[2006] EWHC 2823 (Admin) paras 11–15 (George Bartlett QC)

The Facts

Hopkins Development Ltd applied to North Wiltshire District Council for planning permission for a concrete plant and associated development. Hopkins Development Ltd appealed to the Planning Inspector who dismissed the appeal, for a number of reasons including that the general surroundings would suffer form an increase in dust. Hopkins Development Ltd appealed under s 288 of the TCPA claiming that the Inspector had misunderstood the law on pollution control and that the Inspector should have concluded that the relevant pollution regime would have provided sufficient protection from the dust. As such, the impact of dust was not a justification for refusing planning permission.

The HC

11. The relationship between the planning and pollution control regimes has been the subject of consideration by the Court of Appeal in *Gateshead Metropolitan Borough Council v Secretary of State for the Environment* (1994) 71 P & CR 350 and *R v Bolton Metropolitan Borough Council, ex p Kirkman* [1998] JPL 787. They establish the proposition that the impact of air emissions from a proposed development is capable of being a material planning consideration but in considering that issue the planning authority is entitled to take into account the pollution control regime. Thus in appropriate cases planning authorities can leave pollution control to pollution control authorities, but they are not obliged as a matter of law to do so. PPS23 reflects this. [...]

12. It is clear that the inspector had in mind this passage from paragraph 10. It was relied on by the appellant, and the inspector recorded this at paragraph 8 of his decision. Mr Wadsley [for Hopkins Development Ltd], however, points to the first sentence of paragraph 11 of the decision, where the inspector said:

'PPS23 advises that it is important for planning authorities to consider properly the loss of amenity from emissions in the planning process in its wider context and not just from the narrow perspective of statutory nuisance.'

13. The reference is to paragraph 1.8 of Annex 1 to PPS23, and this begins: 'With reference to pollution that causes statutory nuisance...'. While on the face of it the fact that the inspector referred to the quite different regime of statutory nuisance is surprising, it does not seem to me to be sufficient to point to the conclusion that, when in the next sentence of paragraph 11 the inspector referred to the pollution control regime under the 1999 Act, he was confusing the two regimes. In any event I do not see that, in the ultimate analysis, this point could be determinative in view of the way in which the inspector was asked to consider the proposed mitigation measures and the fact that he did so and reached a conclusion that was based upon them. As appellant the claimant had placed reliance on the fact that the mitigation measures, which it described in its representations in the appeal, had satisfied the EHO [environmental health officer]. Thus the inspector could assume, as he was being asked to assume, that these were the measures that would be applied under the pollution control regime. He considered them, and in paragraph 9 he explained why, despite them, he took the view that there would be significant dust emissions from the proposed plant. His conclusion in paragraph 11 that the amenities of the area and of local residents and land users would be seriously harmed by dust was based on this assessment. Thus he did what paragraph 10 of PPS23 said that he should do—he focussed on whether the development itself was an acceptable use of the land and the impacts that it would have, rather on than the control of the processes or emissions themselves. In approaching the matter in this way, in my judgment, he acted in accordance with the law.

14. The alternative way in which Mr Wadsley puts his case in relation to dust is to say that, in view of the existence of the pollution control regime, the conclusion that dust would cause serious harm to the amenities was *Wednesbury* unreasonable.[51] Under the 2000 Regulations the council in issuing a

---

[51] See Section 4.1 of Chapter 10 for an explanation of this term.

permit would have to impose conditions to ensure that the plant was operated in such a way that no significant pollution was caused; and pollution includes emissions which impair or interfere with amenities. It was therefore not open to the inspector to conclude, assuming, as he had to assume, that the pollution control regime would be properly applied and enforced, that dust emissions from the plant would or might seriously impair the amenities of the area.

15. This is an argument that is superficially attractive. But it is dependent on the underlying assumption that, in relation to the likely impact of pollutants to which the 2000 Regulations apply, primacy must be accorded to the judgment of the regulator above that of the planning authority. I can see no basis for such an assumption, and it does not appear to me that the passage from paragraph 10 of PPS23 that I have quoted above provides support for it. It would effectively mean that, unless it was clear to the planning authority that the plant could never achieve a permit (cf *Gateshead* per Glidewell LJ at 359), the potential impact of pollutants could never enter into its consideration of whether planning permission should be granted. The thrust of paragraph 10 is that planning authorities should focus on the impacts rather than the control of emissions, not that they must subordinate their judgment on the impacts to those of the pollution control authority. I therefore reject Mr Wadsley's contention that it was not open to the inspector to conclude that the impact of dust would be seriously adverse.

This is quite a strong judgment and the implications of it are discussed here in a more recent case.

Harrison v The Secretary of State for Communities and Local Government
[2009] EWHC 3382 (Admin) paras 21–22 (McKenna J)

21. The thrust of the decision in *Hopkins* therefore, a decision which of course is persuasive but not binding on me, is that the planning decision maker was entitled to reach his own conclusions as to the impact of the proposed development on amenity and whether the site under consideration was the appropriate location for the proposed development. The fact that the impact might be capable of being regulated under a pollution control regime did not necessarily mean that the only possible option available to an Inspector was to leave everything to that regime. If the planning decision maker considered that there might be adverse consequences because of the effects of the proposed development on amenity and/or issues as to the appropriateness of locating the development of the site in question, he was entitled to have regard to such matters as material considerations in making his decision on the planning merits of the proposed development.

22. This approach to my mind accords with a fair reading of PPS 23 paragraph 10 [...]

The overall point of these judgments is that while planning and pollution regimes should theoretically be kept separate, in reality they overlap in terms of subject matter and the considerations that planning authorities and regulators need to take into account. How precisely they overlap will be specific to the facts of any individual case and no definitive generalizations can be drawn as to matters that are the sole province of planning authorities and those that are considered by environmental regulators alone.

As a result, in some cases, a single planning application may require a range of different forms of consent from different authorities, particularly where there is an environmental protection aspect involving issues to do with nature conservation, waste, or other pollution problems. This situation has led to criticisms and a number of reports, including recently the Penfold Review on Non-Planning Consents. A small extract from that report is included here.

Adrian Penfold, *Penfold Review of Non-Planning Consents: Final Report* (URN 10/1027 July 2010) i

A well functioning planning system is vital to ensuring that the right decisions about development are made for the right reasons. What is apparent from the findings of my interim report is that 'non-planning consents'—those consents that have to be obtained alongside or after, and separate from, planning permission in order to complete a development—can also have a serious impact on how efficiently and effectively the end-to-end development process operates. The complexity of the non-planning consents landscape and its interaction with the planning system impose additional costs and generate additional risk for businesses. Together, they are a sizeable factor in determining the investment climate in the UK and, therefore, in delivering sustainable development and economic growth. They also play an essential part in achieving wider Government goals such as tackling climate change, delivering well-functioning infrastructure and promoting the health and well-being of local communities.

The report was not only concerned with pollution consents but also listed building consents, the work of Natural England (the regulator that deals with nature conservation matters), and traffic orders. The report went on to make a number of recommendations to assist in streamlining the planning and permitting processes and, in November 2011, the Department for Business, Innovation and Skills published a document discussing how they would implement the review.[52] Since then, DEFRA is also considering the relationship between planning and pollution control in light of the Coalition government's 'Red Tape Challenge'.

Besides those developments, the Penfold review is also interesting for the light it casts on how planning interacts with the rest of the regulatory landscape. This can be seen in the comment from Penfold, writing after the publication of the review.

Adrian Penfold, 'The Relationship Between Planning Permission and Non-Planning Consents: Unfinished Business?' [2010] (13 Supp) JPEL 27, 28, 42

My view has however changed during the course of the review and when undertaking research for this paper. I now believe that there is no going back to that rose-coloured past where each department and area of regulation had its role and protected it assiduously. The scope of planning, both in policy formulation and development control, is unlikely to be seriously reduced; in fact it is more likely to continue to grow. However, the logical implications of the increase in scope have not been followed through in the structure and organisation of the consent landscape, creating tensions and inefficiencies which will at some point need to be addressed. The increased scope of planning doesn't appear to have been accompanied by any increase in its authority, particularly in relation to other consent regimes [...]

In the same paper, he later commented:

Planning's growing scope, in terms of subject matter and the depth of detail now routinely considered as part of the process, is a fact of life. There have been many calls for that increased scope to somehow be drawn back, or at the least for its growth to be stopped or limited. That is a policy option but I believe

---

[52] Department for Business, Innovation and Skills, *Implementation of the Penfold Review* (November 2011) <http://www.bis.gov.uk/assets/biscore/better-regulation/docs/i/11-1413-implementation-of-penfold-review.pdf> accessed 27 September 2012.

> that the drivers of that growth in scope remain, ie European Directives, public expectation, a culture of risk aversion amongst local planning authorities and applicants, the pressure to consider issues in the round coming from the sustainability agenda etc.

Penfold's point is that we cannot pretend that the relationship between planning law and any other regulatory priorities can be anything but complicated. That can clearly be seen in *Hopkins* and *Harrison*. The two other examples given here prove the same point.

5.4 PLANNING AND NATURE CONSERVATION

The second example of the interface between the determination of a planning application and other areas of environmental law deals with nature conservation. As can been seen in Chapter 20, there is a range of different nature conservation regimes that impose responsibilities and duties on planning authorities. The particular example considered here concerns the now repealed Conservation (Natural Habitats, & c) Regulations 1994 (the Habitats Regulations). Regulation 3(4) of those Regulations stated:

> (4) [. . .] every competent authority in the exercise of any of their functions, shall have regard to the requirements of the Habitats Directive so far as they may be affected by the exercise of those functions.

The Conservation of Habitats and Species Regulations 2010 (as amended), which replaced the 1994 Regulations, contain a similar duty in Regulation 9(5), although competent authorities now 'must have regard to' (compare to 'shall have regard to' in Regulation 3(4)) the requirements of the Habitats Directive. The 2010 Regulations as they apply to protected sites are discussed in more detail in Chapter 20, but here we provide an extract from a Supreme Court case in which the nature of the obligation in Regulation 3(4) in relation to protected species under the Habitats Directive was considered. While the Regulation provides quite a detailed framework for planning authorities in relation to protected sites, the framework for protected species is less so.

Interestingly in this case, different Justices came to different views on both the nature of the planning process and the nature of the obligation in Article 3(4). Parts of the judgments of Lord Brown and Lord Kerr (dissenting) are extracted here.

Morge v Hampshire CC
[2011] UKSC 2 paras 26–31 (Lord Brown JSC) paras 57–58, 76–82 (Lord Kerr JSC, dissenting)

The Facts

Planning permission was granted by Hampshire County Council (CC) for a roadway for rapid transport buses between Fareham and Gosport. Morge sought judicial review arguing that the CC had not taken into account the impact of the development on several species of bats protected under the Habitats Directive. Two issues were raised in the appeal to the Supreme Court. First, what was the proper interpretation of article 12 (1)(b) of the Habitats Directive 92/43/EEC. Second, how should Regulation 3 (4) of the Conservation (Natural Habitats, &c.) Regulations 1994 (the Habitats Regulations) operate in relation to local planning authorities. The extracts below involve this latter issue.

Lord Brown

26. Article 12(1) requires member states to 'take the requisite measures to establish a system of strict protection for the animal species listed in Annex IV(a) in their natural range'. Wisely or otherwise, the UK chose to implement the Directive by making a breach of the article 12 prohibition a criminal offence. Regulation 39 of the 1994 Regulations (as amended) provides that: '(1) a person commits an offence if he ... (b) deliberately disturbs wild animals of any such species [that is, a European protected species]'. It is Natural England, we are told, who bear the primary responsibility for policing this provision.

27. It used to be the position that the implementation of a planning permission was a defence to a regulation 39 offence. That, however, is no longer so and to my mind this is an important consideration when it comes to determining the nature and extent of the regulation 3(4) duty on a planning authority deliberating whether or not to grant a particular planning permission.

28. Ward LJ [in the Court of Appeal] dealt with this question in paragraph 61 of his judgment as follows:

'61. The Planning Committee must grant or refuse planning permission in such a way that will 'establish a system of strict protection for the animal species listed in Annex IV(a) in their natural range ... If in this case the committee is satisfied that the development will not offend article 12(1)(b) or (d) it may grant permission. If satisfied that it will breach any part of article 12(1) it must then consider whether the appropriate authority, here Natural England, will permit a derogation and grant a licence under regulation 44. Natural England can only grant that licence if it concludes that (i) despite the breach of regulation 39 (and therefore of article 12) there is no satisfactory alternative; (ii) the development will not be detrimental to the maintenance of the population of bats at favourable conservation status and (iii) the development should be permitted for imperative reasons of overriding public importance. If the planning committee conclude that Natural England will not grant a licence it must refuse planning permission. If on the other hand it is likely that it will grant the licence then the planning committee may grant conditional planning permission. If it is uncertain whether or not a licence will be granted, then it must refuse planning permission.'

29. In my judgment this goes too far and puts too great a responsibility on the Planning Committee whose only obligation under regulation 3(4) is, I repeat, to 'have regard to the requirements of the Habitats Directive so far as [those requirements] may be affected by' their decision whether or not to grant a planning permission. Obviously, in the days when the implementation of such a permission provided a defence to the regulation 39 offence of acting contrary to article 12(1), the Planning Committee, before granting a permission, would have needed to be satisfied either that the development in question would not offend article 12(1) or that a derogation from that article would be permitted and a licence granted. Now, however, I cannot see why a planning permission (and, indeed, a full planning permission save only as to conditions necessary to secure any required mitigating measures) should not ordinarily be granted save only in cases where the Planning Committee conclude that the proposed development would both (a) be likely to offend article 12(1) and (b) be unlikely to be licensed pursuant to the derogation powers. After all, even if development permission is given, the criminal sanction against any offending (and unlicensed) activity remains available and it seems to me wrong in principle, when Natural England have the primary responsibility for ensuring compliance with the Directive, also to place a substantial burden on the planning authority in effect to police the fulfilment of Natural England's own duty.

30. Where, as here, Natural England express themselves satisfied that a proposed development will be compliant with article 12 , the planning authority are to my mind entitled to presume that that is so. The Planning Committee here plainly had regard to the requirements of the Directive: they knew from the Officers' Decision Report and Addendum Report (see para 8 above and the first paragraph of the Addendum Report as set out in para 72 of Lord Kerr's judgment) not only that Natural England

had withdrawn their objection to the scheme but also that necessary measures had been planned to compensate for the loss of foraging. For my part I am less troubled than Ward LJ appears to have been (see his para 73 set out at para 16 above) about the UBS's conclusions that 'no *significant* impacts to bats are anticipated' — and, indeed, about the Decision Report's reference to 'measures to ensure there is no significant adverse impact to [protected bats]'. It is certainly not to be supposed that Natural England misunderstood the proper ambit of article 12(1)(b) nor does it seem to me that the planning committee were materially misled or left insufficiently informed about this matter. Having regard to the considerations outlined in para 29 above, I cannot agree with Lord Kerr's view, implicit in paras 75 and 76 of his judgment, that regulation 3(4) required the committee members to consider and decide for themselves whether the development would or would not occasion such disturbance to bats as in fact and in law to constitute a violation of article 12(1)(b) of the Directive.

31. Even, moreover, had the Planning Committee thought it necessary or appropriate to decide the question for themselves and applied to article 12(1)(b) the less exacting test described above rather than Ward LJ's test of imperilling the bats' conservation status, there is no good reason to suppose that they would not have reached the same overall conclusion as expressed in paras 74 and 75 of Ward LJ's judgment (see para 16 above). [...]

Lord Kerr

57. As legislative provisions go, regulation 3 (4) of the Conservation (Natural Habitats, &c.) Regulations 1994 (the Habitats Regulations) is relatively straightforward. Its terms are uncomplicated and direct [...]

58. In plain language this means that if you are an authority contemplating a decision that might have an impact on what the Directive requires, you must take its requirements into account before you reach that decision. Of course, if you know that another agency has examined the question and has concluded that none of those requirements will be affected, and if you are confident that such agency is qualified to make that judgment, this may be sufficient to meet your obligation under the regulation. What lies at the heart of this appeal is whether the regulatory committee of Hampshire County Council, when it came to make the decision whether to grant the planning permission involved in this case, either had regard itself to the requirements of the Habitats Directive or had sufficient information to allow it to conclude that some other agency, in whose judgment it could repose trust, had done so and had concluded that no violation arose. [...]

76. The critical issue on this appeal, therefore, is whether there is any evidence that the regulatory committee considered at all the duty that it was required to fulfil under regulation 3 (4) of the 1994 Regulations.

77. In addressing this question I should immediately say that I agree with Lord Brown on his analysis of the nature of the requirement in article 12 (1) (b) of the Habitats Directive. As he has observed, a number of broad considerations underlie the application of the article. It is designed to protect species (not specimens of species) and its focus is on the protection of species rather than habitats, although, naturally, if major intrusion on habitats is involved, that may have an impact on the protection of the species. Not every disturbance will constitute a breach of the article. The nature and extent of the disturbance must be assessed on a case by case basis.

78. The European Commission's guidance document of February 2007 contains a number of wise observations as to how the application of the article should be approached. While the word 'significant' has not been employed in article 12 (1) (b), a 'certain negative impact likely to be detrimental must be involved'. In making any evaluation of the level of disturbance, the impact on survival chances, breeding success or reproductive ability of the affected species are all obviously relevant factors. Like Lord Brown, I am sanguine about Mr Cameron QC's formulation of the test as one involving the question

whether there has been 'a certain negative impact likely to have been detrimental to the species, having regard to its effect on the conservation status of the species'. And also like Lord Brown, I consider that the Court of Appeal pitched the test too high in saying that disturbance must have 'a detrimental impact on the conservation status of the species at population level' or constitute a threat to the survival of the protected species.

79. Trying to refine the test beyond the broad considerations identified by Lord Brown and those contained in the Commission's guidance document is not only difficult, it is, in my view, pointless. In particular, I do not believe that the necessary examination is assisted by recourse to such expressions as *de minimis*. A careful investigation of the factors outlined in Lord Brown's judgment (as well as others that might bear on the question in a particular case) is required. The answer is not supplied by a pat conclusion as to whether the disturbance is more than trifling.

80. Ultimately, however, and with regret, where I must depart from Lord Brown is on his conclusion that the regulatory committee had regard to the requirements of the Habitats Directive. True it is, as Lord Brown says, that they knew that Natural England had withdrawn its objection. But that cannot substitute, in my opinion, for a consideration of the requirements of the Habitats Directive. Regulation 3 (4) requires every competent authority to have regard to the Habitats Directive in the exercise of its functions. The regulatory committee was unquestionably a competent authority. It need scarcely be said that, in deciding whether to grant planning permission, it was performing a function. Moreover the discharge of that function clearly carried potential implications for an animal species for which the Habitats Directive requires strict protection.

81. Neither the written material submitted to the committee nor the oral presentation made by officers of the council referred to the Habitats Directive. The reference to Natural England's consideration of the Habitats Regulations, if it was properly understood, could only have conveyed to the committee that that consideration had been for a purpose wholly different from the need to protect bats. It could in no sense, therefore, substitute for a consideration of the Habitats Directive by the committee members whose decision might well directly contravene one of the directive's central requirements. It is for that reason that I have concluded that those requirements had to be considered by the committee members themselves.

82. It may well be that, if Natural England had unambiguously expressed the view that the proposal would not involve any breach of the Habitats Directive and the committee had been informed of that, it would not have been necessary for the committee members to go behind that view. But that had not happened. It was simply not possible for the committee to properly conclude that Natural England had said that the proposal would not be in breach of the Habitats Directive in relation to bats. Absent such a statement, they were bound to make that judgment for themselves and to consider whether, on the available evidence the exercise of their functions would have an effect on the requirements of the directive. I am afraid that I am driven to the conclusion that they plainly did not do so.

Lord Walker, Lady Hale, and Lord Mance agreed with Lord Brown and their judgments are also well worth reading. While much of the analysis turns on the wording of the old 1994 Regulations, the opinions of each judge are underpinned by different assumptions about what it means for a planning authority to 'have regard' to an issue, which remains relevant under the 2010 Habitats Regulations.

5.5 PLANNING AND WASTE MANAGEMENT

The final example we examine of the overlap between planning law and other areas of environmental law concerns waste management. In so far as waste management is a form of pollution control, this example overlaps with the discussion in Section 5.3. However, waste management is subject to additional specific planning as well as pollution controls.[53] The overlap between planning and waste management controls was the issue that arose in *Horner*. There are two interesting things to note in this decision. First, the waste regulation regime is a complex web in itself, as discussed further in Chapter 16. Second, the focus in this case is on the concept of 'Best Practicable Environmental Option' and the role it plays in shaping the discretion of the planning authority.

R (Horner) v Lancashire CC & Anor
[2007] EWCA Civ 784 paras 74–80 (Auld LJ)

The Facts

Horner challenged a planning permission for a unit for handling animal waste derived fuel. One of her arguments was that the planning authority had not complied with its duties as a local planning authority under the Waste Management Licensing Regulations 1994 ('the 1994 Waste Regulations'), in not taking account of the principles of Best Practical Environmental Option ('BPEO') derived from a national waste plan, known as the National Waste Strategy 2000 and the Council's local waste plan, both in part an implementation of EU obligations under the Waste Framework Directive, as amended, 75/442/EEC.

The CA

74. The issue on this ground is, as I have said, limited to the question of relevance to the Judge's consideration of the BPEO principles whether specific consideration of it by the Council would have made any difference. It goes to the question whether any failure of process by the Council in relation to the BPEO principle rendered its decision unlawful so as to deprive him of jurisdiction, as a matter of law or by way of discretion to uphold the decision.

75. The jurisdiction challenge is based largely on observations of this Court in paragraphs 107–113 of *Derbyshire Waste* [*Ltd v Blewett [2004] EWCA Civ 1508*], in which it declined to interfere with the decision of the judge below, Sullivan J, in holding that even if the local planning authority had not been obliged to comply with BPEO methodology, its consideration of its principles was so inadequate as to render the grant of planning permission unlawful. In that case, unlike this, there was no local waste management plan.

76. I had better summarise what the Court's observations in *Derbyshire Waste* amounted to. In doing so, I emphasise that they were not—and could not logically have been—limited to landfill cases:

   i)   it is not a pre-condition of the grant of planning permission by a local planning authority that it meets the BPEO principles;

   ii) it is sufficient for the authority to keep them in mind as important, but not overriding, considerations while having regard to all material planning considerations;

   iii) there are two levels at which local planning authorities should consider BPEO, first in the making of their local waste plans, and, second, when considering individual planning applications;

   iv) in the context of an individual planning application a local planning authority cannot normally be expected to have the resources to conduct a full and well-informed evaluation normally required of it in its waste -planning capacity, in particular, in the preparation of a local waste management plan;

[53] See further Chapter 16, and Section 3.4 in particular.

v) the required intensity of consideration of BPEO principles on individual planning applications, in the sense of specific reference to and application of them, should normally depend on whether there is a regional and/or local waste management plan and what it says;

vi) where there is no regional or local waste management plan, a local planning authority, when considering waste planning applications with BPEO considerations must, as a matter of law and can reasonably be expected to, undertake some BPEO analysis;

77. The Court in *Derbyshire Waste* thus did not purport to lay down any hard and fast rule as to what would or would not pass the test of legality as a matter of generality even where, as in the case before it, there was no local waste management plan. It follows that it is a highly insecure basis upon which to found an argument of illegality for want of consideration of BPEO considerations, as Mr Tromans has attempted in this case, where there is a local waste management plan to which the Council had regard, as the Judge noted in paragraphs 106, 107 and 111 of his judgment. (see paragraphs 59 and 61 above).

78. More importantly, the Judge, in paragraphs 109–112, found that the Council effectively considered all the relevant factors going to the achievement of the 1994 Waste Regulations' objectives. Mr Tromans has not suggested to the Court any factor relevant to the BPEO hierarchy or proximity principles or any realistically useful line of enquiry open to the Council additional to those discussed by the Judge in those paragraphs.

As with the cases discussed already, the obligations on the local planning authority require a nuanced and multi-faceted approach to decision-making. In *Horner*, Auld LJ went on to compare the obligation to consider BPEO with the obligations in relation to environmental impact assessment. This analysis is extracted here and should be read in light of Section 6.1 of Chapter 19 and the decision of the House of Lords in *Berkeley v Secretary of State For The Environment*.[54]

79. As Miss Patterson emphasised, there is an important distinction to be drawn between an EIA assessment and consideration of BPEO principles where either or both are required. In *Berkeley*, Lord Hoffmann, with whom the other Law Lords agreed, indicated at paragraphs 7 and 8 that an EIA has a two-fold purpose, first to produce an assessment that could be weighed in the planning balance, and second, to help to inform the public of the substantive issues in the case. The BPEO principles do not have that dual role; they are relevant, albeit importantly, to the balance of planning considerations in the decision-making process, namely as to whether the grant of permission would be 'in line' with the relevant waste objectives. A judge, when considering the lawfulness of a planning permission against the exercise of the local planning authority's balance of material planning considerations, is, in my view, entitled, subject to *Wednesbury* constraints, to form a view as to whether in the circumstances, given the balance of material considerations in play or that should have been in play, the omission or inadequate consideration by the authority of BPEO as one of them would not have made any difference. If, as here, a judge holds that it would not, given the paucity of practicable lines of enquiry open to it, that, in my view, is a relevant consideration to his decision that the permission is legally valid.

80. Accordingly, in my view, the appeal under this ground should also be dismissed.

In comparing the obligations under the waste and environmental assessment regimes, Auld LJ is highlighting the differences between them. The obligation to consider BPEO is not the same as the obligation to adhere to the environmental impact assessment regime. Likewise, as his analysis makes clear, both obligations must be integrated into administrative law concepts and doctrine.

[54] [2001] 2 AC 603 (HL).

Hopkins, Harrison, Morge, and *Horner* are just four examples of many cases in which planning authorities integrate environmental protection issues into their consideration of planning applications. As can be seen from all of these cases, the process of integration is not legally simple and depends very much on the nature of each environmental regime involved.

5.6 THE GRANT OF PLANNING PERMISSION AND THE USE OF CONDITIONS

As is clear from s 70(1) TCPA, in considering a planning application, local planning authorities have three options—they may refuse planning permission; they may grant unconditional planning permission; or they may grant planning permission subject to conditions. As is clear from the wording of the Act, the local planning authority has considerable discretion in imposing conditions and again this is a well-litigated issue that takes up considerable space in a planning textbook. Lord Collins discusses the law on the point. The case concerns a compulsory purchase order and so the facts are not relevant. The issue is when, and how, planning conditions can be imposed.

R (Sainsbury's Supermarkets Ltd) v Wolverhampton City Council
[2010] UKSC 20 paras 44–46 (Lord Collins JSC)

44. In *Pyx Granite Co Ltd v Ministry of Housing and Local Government* [1958] 1 QB 554 (reversed on other grounds [1960] AC 260) Lord Denning said (at p 572) in relation to what is now section 70(1)(a) of the 1990 Act: 'Although the planning authorities are given very wide powers to impose "such conditions as they think fit," nevertheless the law says that those conditions, to be valid, must fairly and reasonably relate to the permitted development.' Pyx Granite had the right to quarry in two areas of the Malvern Hills. The company required permission to break fresh surface on one of the sites. Conditions attached to the planning permission relating to such matters as the times when machinery for crushing the stone could be used and the control of dust emissions were held valid. The facts do not appear fully in the judgments, but it seems that the equipment was on the part of the land under the control of the company which was not the land in respect of which the application for permission related, but they could properly be regarded (for the purposes of the Town and Country Planning Act 1947, section 14) as 'expedient … in connection with' the permitted development. Lord Denning said, at p 574: 'It would be very different if the Minister sought to impose like conditions about plant or machinery a mile or so away.'

45. Lord Denning's formula that 'the conditions must [be] fairly and reasonably [related] to the development' was approved in *Newbury District Council v Secretary of State for the Environment* [1981] AC 578 , 599 (Viscount Dilhorne), 607 (Lord Fraser of Tullybelton), 618 (Lord Scarman), 627 (Lord Lane). Viscount Dilhorne said, at p 599:

'It follows that the conditions imposed must be for a planning purpose and not for any ulterior one, and that they must fairly and reasonably relate to the development permitted. Also they must not be so unreasonable that no reasonable planning authority could have imposed them…'

As Lord Hoffmann said in *Tesco Stores Ltd v Secretary of State for the Environment* [1995] 1 WLR 759, 772, as a general statement this formulation has never been challenged. See eg *Grampian Regional Council v Secretary of State for Scotland* 1984 SC (HL) 58, 66. In the Newbury case itself it was held that the Secretary of State was entitled to come to the conclusion that a condition imposed by a local authority requiring the removal of existing substantial buildings was not sufficiently related to a temporary change of use for which permission was granted.

46. The effect of the adoption of the *Pyx Granite/Newbury* formula was to put severe limits on the powers of planning authorities: *Tesco Stores Ltd v Secretary of State for the Environment* [1995] 1 WLR 759, 772–723. Conditions requiring off-site roadway benefits were held to be unreasonable in, for example, *Hall & Co Ltd v Shoreham-by-Sea Urban District Council* [1964] 1 WLR 240 (ancillary road condition held to be *Wednesbury* unreasonable (*Associated Provincial Picture Houses Ltd v Wednesbury Corpn* [1948] 1 KB 223)); *Bradford Metropolitan City Council v Secretary of State for the Environment* (1986) 53 P & CR 55 (where it was suggested that it would make no difference if they were included in a section 106 agreement); cf Westminster Renslade Ltd v Secretary of State for the Environment (1983) 48 P & CR 255 (not legitimate to refuse a planning application because it did not contain provisions for the increase of the proportion of car parking space subject to public control: the absence of a benefit not a reason for refusing planning permission where the benefit could not have been lawfully secured by means of a condition).

Thus, while the discretion to impose conditions is wide, it is not unfettered.

It should also be noted that under ss 106–106B TCPA, the planning authority may enter into an agreement with the party seeking planning permission which imposes a planning obligation. This is a major area of planning practice and can result in those who are granted planning permission being required to build extra infrastructure in the area or to make financial contributions to support the needs of the community. Lord Hoffmann explains the logic of these provisions.

Tesco Stores Ltd v Secretary of State for the Environment
[1995] 1 WLR 759 (HL) 776–77 (Lord Hoffmann)

The new section 106 of the Town and Country Planning Act 1990 says in express terms that agreements under that section may require a developer to pay sums of money. [...] Parliament has therefore encouraged local planning authorities to enter into agreements by which developers will pay for infrastructure and other facilities which would otherwise have to be provided at the public expense. These policies reflect a shift in Government attitudes to the respective responsibilities of the public and private sectors. While rejecting the politics of using planning control to extract benefits for the community at large, the Government has accepted the view that market forces are distorted if commercial developments are not required to bear their own external costs.

Note that there is also delegated legislation governing the process (Town and Country Planning (Modification and Discharge of Obligations) Regulations 1992) and, as with other areas, there is policy guidance. In light of this, a question arises concerning the extent of discretion that planning authorities have under ss 106–106B. Circular 5/2005 sets out guiding principles. Amongst other things, it lays down principles for when planning obligations should be sought.

Office of the Deputy Prime Minister, *Circular 5/2005 Planning Obligations* (2005) para B5

The Secretary of State's policy requires, amongst other factors, that planning obligations are only sought where they meet *all* of the following tests. The rest of the guidance in this Circular should be read in the context of these tests, which must be met by all local planning authorities in seeking planning obligations.

A planning obligation must be:

(i)   relevant to planning;

(ii) necessary to make the proposed development acceptable in planning terms;

(iii) directly related to the proposed development;

(iv) fairly and reasonably related in scale and kind to the proposed development; and

(v) reasonable in all other respects.

The Circular also makes clear that planning permission cannot be 'bought or sold'. In short, the planning obligations regime makes the exercise of granting planning permission more complicated and its operation requires the exercise of greater discretion on the part of the planning authority.

Finally, in relation to planning conditions, it should be remembered that the Planning Act 2008 introduced a mechanism by which planning authorities can charge a Community Infrastructure Levy,[55] This is a levy that local authorities can impose on new developments in their area to fund infrastructure projects. This obviously overlaps with s 106 agreements but is more explicit in its aim and structured in its application.

FURTHER READING AND QUESTIONS

1. Consider whether the following would amount to a 'material consideration' for the purposes of s 70(2) TCPA:

   a) the fact that the developer had been in jail;

   b) the fears of the local residents that the development might create environmental or some other kind of risks. You might find it useful to have regard to *Gateshead MBC v Secretary of State for the Environment* [1994] Env LR 11 (QB); *Newport BC v Secretary of State for Wales* [1998] Env LR 174 (CA) (costs case). With that said, historically the discretion on the issue was often limited by PPSs. For example, see *T Mobile v First Secretary of State* [2004] EWCA Civ 1763, [2005] Env LR 18.

2. As is clear from the cases extracted in this section, the consideration of planning permission is a highly fact- and context-specific matter and decisions are enmeshed in a web of policy. As Auld LJ indicates in *Horner*, in these circumstances, one must be wary not to create hard and fast general principles. Thus, the only way really to understand case law relating to planning permission is to read a variety of cases. Another example of a case concerning 'material considerations' and environmental issues is *Barbone & Anor (On Behalf of Stop Stansted Expansion) v Secretary of State for Transport* [2009] EWHC 463 (Admin) (expansion of Stansted).

3. Would the reasoning of the judges in *Morge* have been different if the relevant provision had been Regulation 9(5) of the Conservation of Habitats and Species Regulations 2010 and not Regulation 3(4) of the 1994 Regulations?

---

[55] (n 20).

6 ENFORCEMENT, APPEALS, AND JUDICIAL REVIEW

The final aspects of planning law to consider are planning enforcement and appeals. As with all other aspects of the planning system, these are complicated processes, and a small section cannot do them justice. This section thus sketches out the major features of enforcement, appeals, and judicial review as they relate to planning decisions.

6.1 PLANNING ENFORCEMENT

For the practising planning lawyer, enforcement is nearly always the starting point for engaging with planning law. Enforcement occurs when a local planning authority serves an enforcement notice in relation to development that is not authorized. The enforcement process is complex but there are two important features to note. First, it is not a criminal offence to carry out development without planning permission. However, it is a criminal offence not to comply with an enforcement notice. Thus, enforcement really is enforcement—it is the major means by which compliance with the planning regime is ensured. As a practical result, much of the case law concerning the planning regime takes place in the context of enforcement. The second important point to note is that the focus of enforcement is on the rights of those who are served with an enforcement notice. This is a natural (and legal)[56] consequence of the fact that failure to comply with an enforcement notice will result in a criminal offence being committed. In broader terms, however, it results in a 'rights' flavour to the area of the law. Lord Justice Carnwath explains the enforcement procedure. The facts of the case are not relevant.

North Dorset District Council v Trim
[2010] EWCA Civ 1446, [2011] 1 WLR 1901 para 12 (Carnwath LJ)

12. Under the 1990 Act as amended, a breach of condition notice may be served where planning permission has been granted subject to conditions and any of the conditions is not complied with (s 187A(2)). The notice may be served on the person carrying out the development or the person having control of the land ('the person responsible'). It must specify the steps to be taken, or activities required to cease, in order to comply with the conditions. If the notice is not complied with in the time allowed, the person responsible is guilty of an offence (s 187A(9)). The offence may be charged by reference to a day or a longer period, and there may be subsequent charges for continued failure to comply following a first offence (s 187A(10)).

Note that the current enforcement procedure was in fact designed to be simpler and more straightforward than the system before the 1991 Act. However, as Purdue has wryly noted, '[i]n the case of technicality and complexity it could be said that like the poor they will always be with us'.[57] In part, that is inevitable due to the fact that, in cases involving the possible limitation of individual rights, proper procedure becomes important. There is a time limit on enforcement however. Section 171B states:

(1) Where there has been a breach of planning control consisting in the carrying out without planning permission of building, engineering, mining or other operations in, on, over or under land, no enforcement

---

56 ECHR, arts 6–7, Protocol 7, arts 2–4.
57 Michael Purdue, 'Reform of the Enforcement of Planinng Control: A Forgotten Cause?' [2008] JEPL 434, 434.

action may be taken after the end of the period of four years beginning with the date on which the operations were substantially completed.

(2) Where there has been a breach of planning control consisting in the change of use of any building to use as a single dwellinghouse, no enforcement action may be taken after the end of the period of four years beginning with the date of the breach.

(3) In the case of any other breach of planning control, no enforcement action may be taken after the end of the period of ten years beginning with the date of the breach.

This of course provides some certainty for land owners and after a period of time an owner can apply for a certificate of lawful use (s 191) if there has been no enforcement action in the described time frames. The Supreme Court has recently considered these provisions in relation to the situation where an owner conceals the development.

The Supreme Court *Secretary of State for Communities and Local Government and another v Welwyn Hatfield Borough Council*
[2011] UKSC 15 paras 1–2, 7–8, 54–56 (Lord Mance JSC)

The Supreme Court

1. In July 1999 Mr Beesley, the second respondent, bought 22 acres of open land in the Green Belt on the outskirts of Northaw, Potters Bar. In October 1999 he applied for and in March 2000 obtained planning permission to construct a hay barn for grazing and haymaking. Upon a further application made in January 2001, this was in October 2001 revoked and in December 2001 replaced by a second planning permission for the same barn, re-sited differently. Each planning permission was subject to the condition that 'The building hereby permitted shall be used only for the storage of hay, straw or other agricultural products and shall not be used for any commercial or non agricultural storage purposes'.

2. Between January and July 2002, with the assistance of his builder father-in-law, Mr Beesley constructed a building which was to all external appearances the permitted barn, with walls in profiled metal sheeting, a roller-shutter door, two smaller doors and eight roof lights. Internally it was a dwelling house with full facilities, including garage, entrance hall, study, lounge, living room, toilet, storeroom, gym and three bedrooms, two of them with en suite bathrooms, and connected to mains electricity, water and drainage and a telephone line. On 9 August 2002 Mr Beesley and his wife moved in and there they lived continuously for four years. Welwyn Hatfield Borough Council, the appellant, in whose area the property lies, remained unaware throughout that the building was or was being used as a dwelling house.

After the requisite time, Mr Beesley applied for planning permission and it was refused. He appealed and a planning inspector granted a certificate of lawful use. The LPA sought judicial review and Collins J overturned the decision. The Court of Appeal then overturned his decision:

7. [...] However, Mummery LJ expressed puzzlement at

'the total absence of argument from the council, or the Secretary of State, about the effect of Mr Beesley's reprehensible conduct in obtaining planning permission by deception and in failing to implement it' (para 43).

He added (para 45) that

'it is very difficult to believe that Parliament could have intended that the certificate procedure in section 191 should be available to someone who has dishonestly undermined the legislation by obtaining a planning permission which would never have been granted if the council had been told the truth'.

8. The council now appeals to the Supreme Court. [and in doing so] seeks to raise a new point, picking up Mummery LJ's remarks in terms of a principle of public policy. Neither Mr Beesley nor the Secretary of State has objected to this new second point being argued. However, both dispute that public policy can have any role in the relevant statutory scheme […]

54. Whether conduct will on public policy grounds disentitle a person from relying upon an apparently unqualified statutory provision must be considered in context and with regard to any nexus existing between the conduct and the statutory provision. Here, the four-year statutory periods must have been conceived as periods during which a planning authority would normally be expected to discover an unlawful building operation or use and after which the general interest in proper planning control should yield and the status quo prevail. Positive and deliberately misleading false statements by an owner successfully preventing discovery take the case outside that rationale. […]

55. If the owner of an unauthorised house were to bribe or by menaces coerce a planning authority officer into turning a blind eye to unlawful development for four years, it is inconceivable that the building owner could then rely on the four year period, even though the owner would not have to (and surely would not) mention anything but his four year period of occupation in his attempt to bring himself within the literal language of the sections. It is true that the council would then be able to show that a criminal offence had been committed (in the case of a bribe under the Public Bodies Corrupt Practices Act 1889, section 1 and in the case of menaces probably under the Theft Act 1968, section 21, since the purpose of 'gain' includes under section 34(2)(a) 'keeping what one has'). However, if a planning authority were to discover an unauthorised development or use, and the property owner were, in order to avoid enforcement action within the four years, falsely to assure the planning authority that the four years had not expired, and that he intended to remove or cease the development or use before they did, and so succeed in avoiding enforcement action during the four years, I very much doubt whether the owner could thereafter rely upon sections 171B and 191(A), merely because no criminal offence had been committed.

56. Here, Mr Beesley's conduct, although not identifiably criminal, consisted of positive deception in matters integral to the planning process (applying for and obtaining planning permission) and was directly intended to and did undermine the regular operation of that process. Mr Beesley would be profiting directly from this deception if the passing of the normal four-year period for enforcement which he brought about by the deception were to entitle him to resist enforcement. The apparently unqualified statutory language cannot in my opinion contemplate or extend to such a case.

The right of an owner thus has limits. What is striking about this case is that, as Mummery LJ points out, the issues were not raised earlier. This case is also a reminder that planning law must both act as an ex ante and post hoc regulatory regime.

6.2 APPEALS AND THE PLANNING INSPECTORATE

A significant feature of the planning regime is that under s 78 TCPA, an applicant for planning permission has a right of appeal to the Secretary of State. This procedure emerged out of the use of inquiries, which was discussed in Section 2.2. This appeal is on the merits so that all aspects of the decision—factual and legal—get remade. The actual hearing of the appeal is more often than not done by a planning inspector from the Planning Inspectorate, to which the Secretary of State delegates their powers.[58] Appeals can be made and heard through written representations, at a hearing or at

---

[58] Schedule 6 TCPA 1990 and The Town and Country Planning (Determination of Appeals by Appointed Persons) (Prescribed Classes) Regulations 1997.

an inquiry. There is a complex body of procedures for these processes in delegated legislation and policy.[59]

The procedure and powers of the Planning Inspectorate represent a unique legal phenomenon and one that has been under-analysed. On the one hand, such institutions are administrative bodies; on the other hand, they are akin to a court in their operation, with a triad-like relationship existing between the different adjudicative players.[60] Likewise, while the decisions of planning inspectors do not amount to formal precedent, they are still used as guides by local planning authorities. The procedure for hearings and inquiries is very flexible and can veer between the inquisitorial and the adversarial. The role of third parties in the process also varies considerably, with only major inquiries really guaranteeing them a role. Moreover, while these planning appeals on the merits can be understood as non-legal, they take on a very legal nature, both in form and vocabulary. Thus, in inquiries, parties will often have formal legal representation and the most successful arguments will be grounded in a subtle appreciation of the law. Likewise, while the Planning Inspectorate operates independently of the Secretary of State, the power of appeal is legislatively entrusted to the Secretary of State.

Appeals under s 78 are thus highly ambiguous in nature and the ambiguity is intensified by the fact that planning appeals often involve conflicts between private rights and the public interest. Thus, for example, the right of the individual to develop their land will need to be decided in light of the public interest in the amenity of the local area. Further, different parties will have different expectations about the nature of the appeal process and there will often be challenges to the process and procedure involved. However, the courts have made clear that they do not wish to see an over-judicialization of planning appeals, as can be seen in *Bushell* (also discussed in Chapter 7 and 11).

Bushell v Secretary of State for The Environment
[1981] AC 75 (HL) 97 (Lord Diplock)

To 'over-due judicialise' the enquiry by insisting on observance of the procedures of the court of justice which professional lawyers alone are competent to operate effectively in the interests of their clients would not be fair. It would, in my view, be quite fallacious to propose that at an enquiry of this kind the only fair way of ascertaining matters of fact and expert opinion is by the oral testimony of witnesses who are subjected to cross-examination on behalf of parties who disagree with what they have said. Such procedure is peculiar to litigation conducted in courts that follow the common law system of procedure; it plays no part in the procedure of courts of justice under legal systems based upon the civil law, including the majority of our fellow member states of the European Community; even in our own Admiralty Court it is not availed of for the purpose of ascertaining expert opinion on questions of navigation—the judge acquires information about this by private enquiry of assessors who are not subject to cross-examination by the parties. So refusal by an Inspector to allow a party to cross-examine orally at a local enquiry a person who has made statements of facts or has expressed expert opinions is not unfair per se.

When fairness requires an Inspector to permit a person who has made statements on matters of fact or opinion, whether expert or otherwise, to be cross-examined by a party to the enquiry who wishes to dispute a particular statement must depend on all circumstances. In the instant case, the question arises in connection with expert opinion upon a technical matter. Here the relevant circumstances in considering whether fairness requires that cross-examination should be allowed include the nature

---

[59] The Planning Inspectorate, *Procedural Guidance: Planning Appeals and Called In Planning Applications* (PINS 01/2009, April 2010).

[60] Martin Shapiro, *Courts: A Comparative and Political Analysis* (University of Chicago Press 1981). See Section 1 of Chapter 10.

of the topic upon which the opinion is expressed, the qualifications of the maker of the statement to deal with that topic, the forensic competence of the proposed cross-examiner, and, most important, the Inspector's own views as to whether the likelihood of cross-examination will enable him to make a report which will be more useful to the minister in reaching his decision than it otherwise would be is sufficient to justify any expense and inconvenience to other parties to the enquiry which would be caused by any resulting prolongation of it.

This has echoes of *Arlidge* and, while a hearing or inquiry will appear court-like, it is not a judicial process and a planning inspector operates with considerable discretion.

The final thing to note is that, under rule 19(1) of the Town and Country Planning Appeals (Determination by Inspectors) (Inquiries Procedure) (England) Rules 2000, a planning inspector is to 'notify his decision [...] and his reasons for it in writing'.[61] The nature of this obligation to give and publicize reasons has been considered judicially.

South Buckinghamshire DC v Porter (No 2)
[2004] UKHL 33, [2004] 1 WLR 1953 para 36 (Lord Brown)

36. The reasons for a decision must be intelligible and they must be adequate. They must enable the reader to understand why the matter was decided as it was and what conclusions were reached on the 'principal important controversial issues', disclosing how any issue of law or fact was resolved. Reasons can be briefly stated, the degree of particularity required depending entirely on the nature of the issues falling for decision. The reasoning must not give rise to a substantial doubt as to whether the decision-maker erred in law, for example by misunderstanding some relevant policy or some other important matter or by failing to reach a rational decision on relevant grounds. But such adverse inference will not readily be drawn. The reasons need refer only to the main issues in the dispute, not to every material consideration. They should enable disappointed developers to assess their prospects of obtaining some alternative development permission, or, as the case may be, their unsuccessful opponents to understand how the policy or approach underlying the grant of permission may impact upon future such applications. Decision letters must be read in a straightforward manner, recognising that they are addressed to parties well aware of the issues involved and the arguments advanced. A reasons challenge will only succeed if the party aggrieved can satisfy the court that he has genuinely been substantially prejudiced by the failure to provide an adequately reasoned decision.

This obligation to give reasons is not only important in itself, but as can be seen from Lord Brown's judgment, it also acts as a substantive constraint on discretion. It amounts to firm guidance as to how an Inspector should reason their decision.

6.3 THE ROLE OF COURTS

As is clear from the wealth of case law considered in this chapter, courts have a significant role to play in planning law. That role has both a common law and statutory basis. The common law basis—through administrative law judicial review doctrine—is considered in Section 4 of Chapter 7, and thus will not be discussed in detail here. However, two things are worth noting. First, common law

---

[61] SI 2000/1625.

judicial review has a very important role to play in planning law because the statutory grounds of review of planning decisions, while wide, operate only in certain circumstances. For third parties in particular, judicial review often provides the only means of challenging planning decisions (appeals under s 78 only being available to the applicant for planning permission). Second, in light of the evolution of judicial review, there is arguably little difference in substance between review under a planning statute and common law judicial review, as Carnwath LJ highlights.

E v Secretary of State for Home Department
[2004] EWCA Civ 49, [2004] QB 1044 para 42 (Carnwath LJ)

42. Thus, in spite of the differences in history and wording, the various procedures have evolved to the point where it has become a generally safe working rule that the substantive grounds for intervention are identical. (The conceptual justifications are another matter; see, for example, the illuminating discussion in Craig *Administrative Law* 5th Ed pp 476ff). The main practical dividing line is between appeals (or review procedures) on both fact and law, and those confined to law. The latter are treated as encompassing the traditional judicial review grounds of excess of power, irrationality, and procedural irregularity.

Note also that statutory review of planning decisions has more than one basis. Thus, s 113 of the Planning and Compulsory Purchase Act 2004 allows for review of local plans. Further, the most significant statutory basis for review of planning appeals is s 288 TCPA. Review of an appeal under s 288 can only relate to a question of law and the nature of that review is explained here.

South Cambridgeshire DC v Secretary of State for Communities and Local Government
[2008] EWCA Civ 1010 para 15 (Scott Baker LJ)

15. It is necessary to make the following general observations about s.288.

(i)   A decision may only be challenged on ordinary administrative law grounds. *Seddon Properties Ltd v Secretary of State* (1978) P + CR 26.

(ii)   Interpretation of policy is the matter for the decision maker. Where the interpretation is one that the policy is reasonably capable of bearing there is no basis for intervention by the court. *R v Derbyshire County Council ex parte Woods* [1997] JPL 958.

(iii) The weight to be attached to material considerations and matters of planning judgment are within the exclusive jurisdiction of the decision maker. *Tesco Stores Ltd v Secretary of State* [1995] 1WLR 759.

(iv)   A decision letter must be read in good faith, and references to polices must be taken in the context of the general thrust of the reasoning. The adequacy of the reasons is to be assessed by reference to whether the decision in question leaves room for general doubt as to what the decision maker has decided and why. *South Somerset District Council v Secretary of State* [1993] 1PLR 80 and *Clarke Homes Ltd v Secretary of State* (1993) 66 P + CR 263.

(v)   There is no obligation on the decision maker to refer to every material consideration, only the main issues in dispute. *Bolton Metropolitan Borough Council v Secretary of State* (1995) 71 P + CR 309.

(vi) Reasons can be briefly stated, the degree of particularity depending on the nature of the issues falling for decision. The reasoning must not give rise to substantial doubt as to whether there was error of law, but such an inference will not readily be drawn. *South Bucks District Council v Porter* (No.2) [2004] UKHL 33.

We have already seen many of these principles discussed and applied in the cases in this chapter. It is important to note that they not only regulate the nature of review but also the nature of the planning decision-making process. One of the most significant principles is the concept that 'the weight to be attached to material considerations and matters of planning judgment are within the exclusive jurisdiction of the decision maker'. This is expanded on in the extract from *Tesco Stores Ltd v Secretary of State for the Environment*.

Tesco Stores Ltd v Secretary of State for the Environment
[1995] 1 WLR 759 (HL) 780 (Lord Hoffmann)

The law has always made a clear distinction between the question of whether something is a material consideration and the weight which it should be given. The former is a question of law and the latter is a question of planning judgment, which is entirely a matter for the planning authority. Provided that the planning authority has regard to all material considerations, it is at liberty (provided that it does not lapse into *Wednesbury* irrationality) to give them whatever weight the planning authority thinks fit or no weight at all. The fact that the law regards something as a material consideration therefore involves no view about the part, if any, which it should play in the decision-making process.

This distinction between whether something is a material consideration and the weight it should be given is only one aspect of a fundamental principle of British planning law, namely that the courts are concerned only with the legality of the decision-making process and not with the merits of the decision. If there is one principle of planning law more firmly settled than any other, it is that matters of planning judgment are within the exclusive province of the local planning authority or the Secretary of State.

Inherent in this reasoning are complex ideas about deference and institutional competence, which were discussed in Chapter 7.[62] Simply stated, and as demonstrated by nearly everything in this chapter, the types of boundaries discussed by Lord Hoffmann—between what constitutes a material consideration and the weight to be attached to it, between the respective roles of planning authorities and courts, between law and merits—are essential to planning law but also difficult to determine in practice.

FURTHER READING AND QUESTIONS

1. For further discussion of the nature of the planning inspectorate, see Carol Harlow and Richard Rawlings, *Law and Administration* (3rd edn, CUP 2009) 582–88.

2. The Planning Inspectorate's website is a useful source of information. See <http://www.planning-inspectorate.gov.uk/> accessed 26 September 2012.

---

[62] See Section 4.2 of Chapter 7.

3. Many of the cases extracted in this chapter are examples of common law judicial review or judicial review under s 288. For examples of review of local development framework documents under s 113 of the 2004 Act, see *Capel Parish Council v Surrey CC* [2009] EWHC 350 (Admin) (review of Waste Plan Development Plan Documents) and *Barratt Developments Plc v Wakefield MDC* [2010] EWCA Civ 897 (affordable housing requirements laid down in a core Strategy). Note the heavily fact-dependent nature of these cases.

7 CONCLUSION

An annoying refrain in this chapter has been that planning is complicated and that a nuanced approach is always needed in deciding and evaluating planning applications. It is particularly frustrating for a student who is seeking to master a subject swiftly and concisely. But the point of this chapter has been to highlight that students need to be wary of taking such an approach. The planning system is complex, it is polycentric, it has many normative aims, it involves a wide array of institutions, and it must reconcile a range of public interests and private rights. It is also an example of administrative law in practice. As we see in the other chapters in Part V (and in the Part IV on pollution control), the planning system is also complicated by the ways in which it interacts with other environmental law regimes. Moreover, it is a system undergoing constant change and, by the time you are reading this, the regime may have evolved once again. Thus, as stressed at the outset, this chapter is an introduction, and only an introduction. It has attempted to sketch out the major features of the planning process and its relationship to environmental protection, and to highlight the major themes of the subject.

FURTHER READING AND QUESTIONS

1. For those wishing to understand more about the planning process, see either Robert Duxbury, *Telling & Duxbury's Planning Law and Procedure* (15th edn, OUP 2012) or Victor Moore and Michael Purdue, *A Practical Approach to Planning* (12th edn, OUP 2012).

2. Note that the access to justice aspects of planning law are touched on in Chapter 10. In light of the material covered in this chapter, consider what types of forums and routes third parties may have to challenge planning decisions. See *Ashton v Secretary of State for Communities and Local Government, Coin Street Community Builders Ltd* [2010] EWCA Civ 600 extracted in Section 2.4 of Chapter 10.

19

ENVIRONMENTAL
IMPACT ASSESSMENT

Environmental impact assessment (EIA) is a decision-making tool by which the potential environmental impact of a project can be assessed so that assessment can be taken into account in making
a decision about whether that project can go ahead, and if so, on what basis. Since 1985 there has
been an EU Directive (the EA Directive) requiring an EIA to be carried out for all public and private
projects that are 'likely to have a significant effect on the environment'[1] before they are granted development consent by a public authority. In England the Directive has been implemented into the town-
planning regime as delegated legislation.[2] While, as Chapter 18 made clear, EIA is not the only (and
arguably still not the most important) means by which environmental impacts are taken into account
in planning, it has given rise to some of the most thought provoking environmental law litigation in
recent years that raises questions about the nature of environmental law obligations and the role of
the courts in enforcing them.

This chapter is an overview of the EIA legal regime in the EU and how it has been implemented into
English law. EIA is a very different type of decision-making technique from those used in other areas
of environmental law. It is fundamentally concerned with the *process* by which decisions are made.
From a legal perspective, this feature of it, as well as the fact that the obligation to carry out EIA is in
an EU Directive, has given rise to a range of legal issues that can be broadly understood as falling into
three overlapping categories.

First, there are those issues relating to the fact that EIA is a process that carries great symbolic
weight. As de Sadeleer notes, there is a belief that EIA is forcing 'truly revolutionary changes upon
traditional administrative processes' in that it gives 'rise to a dynamic which informs administrators,
project initiators, and third parties and provides them with an opportunity to require fuller integration of environmental concerns into the decision-making process'.[3] The nature of that dynamic is
open to question however and while EIA has been heralded as an important step in the development
of environmental law there is often very little agreement over its nature or purpose. EIA is often
simultaneously understood as technocratic, participatory, or a form of civic science. Whichever view
is taken will affect the type of legal obligations placed on decision-makers and the type of rights of
individuals that are recognized.

---

[1] Originally Council Directive of 27 June 1985 on the assessment of the effects of certain public and private projects
on the environment 85/337/EEC OJ [1985] L175/40 and now Directive 2011/92/EU on the assessment of the effects of
certain public and private projects on the environment (codification) OJ [2012] L28/1.

[2] Now the Town and Country Planning (Environmental Impact Assessment) (England) Regulations 2011.

[3] Nicolas de Sadeleer, *Environmental Principles: From Political Slogans to Legal Rules* (OUP 2002) 87.

The second category of legal issues to do with EIA arises due to the novel nature of the obligations that it imposes. The obligation to carry out an EIA is set out in a Directive. Article 288 TFEU states that 'A directive shall be binding as to the result to be achieved, upon each Member State to which it is addressed, but shall leave to the national authorities the choice of form and methods'. The challenge in the implementation of EIA is that the 'result to be achieved' is the 'form and methods' of EIA not a particular result. Furthermore, the fact that the EA Directive does not create individual rights in the conventional sense raises questions about whether the Directive has direct effect as that term is understood traditionally.[4]

The third category of legal issues that the EA Directive raises includes those concerned with the integration of EIA into English administrative law. The role of national courts is to police whether a decision-maker has properly adhered to the EIA regime in a given circumstance. This form of independent review is an essential aspect of EIA but it is also difficult. Administrative decision-making in this area is discretionary and complex, and expert decision-makers are operating in circumstances of scientific uncertainty and political controversy. How the courts review EIA decision-making is driven by two different factors—how the EIA process is conceptualized and how the courts understand what their role should be in enforcing it.

Beyond these legal issues it is also important to remember that EIA is being applied in the context of environmental disputes. Different views over how communities should develop are frequently at the heart of EIA legal disagreements but while those views often drive conflict and disagreement they do not always have an obvious legal manifestation. The socio-political aspects of environmental disputes should not be forgotten. Moreover, while a useful decision-making tool, EIA also has its limits, particularly in circumstances of scientific uncertainty.

This chapter is structured as follows. The first section is an overview of EIA. The second section is a brief analysis of the historical development of EIA. The third section is an overview of the EA Directive and the fourth section is an analysis of how it has been interpreted by the CJEU. The fifth and sixth sections look at its implementation in England and the way in which it has been interpreted by the courts. The final section is an analysis of the Strategic Environmental Assessment (SEA), a similar assessment technique that applies to certain programmes and policies.

As always, there are four important caveats before we start. First, this chapter provides an introduction to EIA and a list of more specialist texts can be found at the end of this chapter. Second, it should be noted that there is some confusion in terminology in this area. The EA Directive is actually the 'Environmental Assessment Directive' but is commonly referred to as the EIA Directive. Furthermore, the term EIA is used by some commentators to refer to only the actual assessment process and by others to the process by which projects are chosen to be assessed, assessed, and then a final decision is made about that project. We use the latter terminology in this chapter. Third, to understand EIA in England there is a need to understand the planning system. Chapter 18 should thus be read before reading this chapter. Fourth, the 2003 amendments to the EA Directive have resulted in it giving rise to a number of legal issues concerning the Aarhus Convention on Access to Information, Public Decision Making and Access to Justice in Environmental Matters. These issues are discussed in Section 2.4 of Chapters 7 and Section 2.3 of 10. In particular, a discussion of Article 11 of the EA Directive can be found in the latter chapter.

---

[4] Case 26/62 *NV Algemene Transport en Expeditie Onderneming van Gend en Loos v Netherlands Inland Revenue Administration* [1963] ECR 1.

1 ENVIRONMENTAL IMPACT ASSESSMENT: AN OVERVIEW

As we shall see in this chapter, EIA as we currently understand it originated in the US with the National Environmental Policy Act 1969. Since then, many different types of EIA process have developed in jurisdictions across the world (including at the international level). Likewise, many variations on the traditional idea of EIA have also been developed including forms of policy assessment, social impact assessment, and fauna impact statements. Thus, in Section 7 we will look at the concept of strategic environmental assessment. In light of all these developments it is not surprising that EIS has developed as a separate discipline and the dense amount of technical detail about EIA can at times be overwhelming. It is thus valuable to start with a few general comments about EIA. We then consider the nature and purpose of EIA and its limitations.

1.1 EIA AS A PROCESS

EIA refers to a systematic decision-making process in which information is collected about the possible environmental impacts of a project and, on the basis of that information, the potential impact of that project on the environment is then assessed. That assessment is then taken into account into the decision about whether a project should proceed, and if so whether the environmental impacts should be prevented or mitigated in some way. The systematic and formalized nature of EIA distinguishes it from the ad hoc way in which environmental impacts are considered by planning authorities as a 'material consideration' (see Chapter 18). Indeed EIA is understood to proceed by a series of steps. We identify the four most significant steps for lawyers to be aware of.

The first is *screening*, which involves making a decision about what activities should be subject to an EIA. As we will see, screening decisions have given rise to the most litigation. This is because, for developers, screening is a considerable financial and administrative burden, which may result in a project being delayed or stopped, while for those wishing to challenge a project, the EIA process is often the most obvious means by which their concerns can be raised and debated. Screening can be carried out in many different ways. In the EU, screening is done through a mixture of identifying a list of types of projects that should be subject to EIA and also, in some cases, requiring a decision about whether they 'are likely to have significant effects on the environment'.

The next step is the making of a decision about what impacts of a project should be assessed. This is known as *scoping*. Thus, for example, assessment could focus on both the building and operation of a mine or just the operation of it. Likewise, assessment may focus on local environmental impacts and/or global environmental impacts. The scope of an assessment can be fixed by legislation or it can be determined in relation to each individual project. While historically scoping has been downplayed in the EU context, it has become increasingly important. This is not surprising—the scope of an assessment will play an important role in determining what is, and what is not, considered by decision-makers.

The third step is the process of assessment, which involves *preparing an environmental impact statement* (EIS). These are also known as environmental statements (ES) under the EA Directive. For those working in the field, this involves a series of many different steps including: describing the project and environmental base line, identifying and predicting impacts from a project, evaluating their significance, and assessing whether those impacts can be mitigated or other alternatives can be considered. Each of these steps involves different methods, different technical skills, and different uncertainties. While the general framework for these activities is set out in the EA Directive, law regulates few of these processes directly. Furthermore, judges have tended to be deferential in reviewing the assessment process.

Alongside the third step is the fourth step of *public participation* where members of the public have the right to see the EIS and comment on it. This has always been a significant feature of the EIA process, and is more so now in light of the reforms to the EIA process due to the Aarhus Convention (see Section 2.4 of Chapter 7). The role of the public is both symbolically and practically important and we will see the legal significance of this in how the courts have interpreted the Directive.

The fifth and final step in EIA is the *making of a decision* about whether a project should go ahead, and if so on what basis. An EIS needs to be taken into account at this stage it does not formally dictate what the final decision will be. With that said, if an EIS identifies serious concerns about a project then it is less likely that that project will be given permission to proceed. Likewise, decision-makers can decide to impose conditions on a project in light of the EIS.

As this makes clear, EIA is a very well thought-out process consisting of a number of decision-making steps. With that said, EIA is not a formula and it will require the considerable exercise of discretion in its operation. Thus, for example, screening will require the consideration of numerous factors as will the assessment of an EIS. In most jurisdictions, EIA is an administrative process, although it will normally be the developer who will prepare an EIS (often using consultants).

1.2 THE NATURE AND PURPOSE OF EIA

The discussion so far has focused on EIA as a process. It is not a process that occurs in a vacuum however. EIA operates within particular institutional contexts and regard must be had to surrounding social and political values. This is not only in regards to how it operates, but more importantly to what is understood to be its role and nature. Integrating EIA into decision-making maybe a groundbreaking step for environmental protection but there is actually very little agreement about the nature of that step. Among commentators, EIA is understood to have a number of different purposes and to vary considerably in its nature. These differences are reflected in the extracts from Benson, Saarikoski, and Carpenter.

John F Benson, 'What Is the Alternative? Impact Assessment Tools and Sustainable Planning' (2003) 21 Impact Assessment and Project Appraisal 261, 262

For most authors, EIA is seen as a rational and systematic process, perhaps also as holistic, proactive, anticipatory and integrated, bur firmly located in the 1960s' demand for systematic and rational approaches to environmental planning. The 'idealised model' for EIA that appears in many texts has uncertain origins, but seems to be based on NEPA [National Environmental Policy Act] and the rationalist model. Despite this, there has been remarkably little written about the conceptual and theoretical basis of EIA [...]

At the rationalist end of the spectrum of behavioural decision-making theories, decision-makers are assumed to be acting in an objective and value-free manner and basing their decisions on a systematic and largely technical assessment of the evidence. Such 'rationalism' can be traced to Weber and neo-classical economics. Administration and decision-making processes become systematised and routinised, and rules are used to ensure uniformity, which sounds remarkably like a summary of EIA under EU Directives.

Heli Saarikoski, 'Environmental Impact Assessment (EIA) as Collaborative Learning Process' (2000) 20 Environmental Impact Assessment Review 681, 682

EIA has lost its credibility as a process driven by experts in which the public can only react to ready-made reports such as environmental impact statements. The emerging view of EIA holds that participation is not just a supplementary part of the assessment; rather EIA is a collective process where different actors—affected citizens, interest groups, authorities, and experts—can deliberate and exchange their views of the goals and their knowledge on the impacts of the proposed developments.

Recent developments in resource management and alternative dispute resolution, among other fields, have emphasized public policy making as a public learning process. Forester draws on Reich in arguing that our interests are fundamentally shaped by social processes in which people deliberate and probe the interests of other parties as well as their own interests. The intersubjective nature of interests and values leads Forester to propose a notion of public dispute resolution processes not as interest-based bargaining, but as democratic public spheres "in which citizens can speak and listen, argue and negotiate, come into conflict, and yet act together too". In this kind of civic discovery, people can come to see their own interests and concerns of others and those of others in a new light, to recognize previously unrecognized values, and redefine problems and their solutions. In the context of natural resource management, Lee, and Daniels and Walker hold that the complexity and controversial nature of these decision-making situations require a collaborative learning approach, where different parties define the problems, frame issues, generate alternatives, debate choices, and at the same time sort out their own and others' values, orientations, and priorities.

Richard A Carpenter, 'Keep EIA Focused' (1999) 19 Environmental Impact Assessment Review 111, 111

Environmental impact assessment (EIA) means predicting the consequences of 'man's activity on the interrelations of all components of the natural environment' [U.S. National Environmental Policy Act, Sec. 101(a)]. That such consequences, as described by bio-geo-physical science, might subsequently lead to effects in social, economic, and cultural matters is obvious. These secondary considerations, however, should not be elevated to an equivalent command of the always-limited funds and personnel that are available for EIA. Professional practitioners, the readers of *EIA Review*, must be vigilant and guard against the dilution of the EIA, which is a specialized decision aid, one among many.

Carpenter goes on to note that topics which are 'vaguely defined, value dependent, non-quantifiable, time consuming, and analysis resistant' must not 'subvert the completion of the fundamental natural science assessment'.[5]

These three perspectives are an illustration of the variation in views over the role and nature of EIA. Benson understands it in bureaucratic terms, Saarikoski in deliberative terms, and Carpenter in scientific terms. These differences of opinion are not just at the theoretical level but translate into practice. Thus, for example Carpenter and Saarikoski have very different views on what actors should be involved in the EIA process. For Carpenter they will be primarily scientists while for Saarikoski

---

[5] Richard A Carpenter, 'Keeping EIA Focused' (1999) 19 Environmental Impact Assessment Review 111, 112.

they will be also members of the community. Likewise, each author describes the role and nature of public participation and information collection differently. Most EIA regimes will have both, but these can be understood in many different ways. Thus, for example, public participation may be a form of information provision, interest representation, or deliberative problem-solving. Likewise, the collection of information as part of the EIA process may serve a number of different purposes, including assessing the impact of a project and aiding the process of deliberation. This means that information may need to come in a variety of forms so as to be comprehensible and useful to the different actors involved in the EIA process.

What is also clear from these extracts is that, despite its technical nature, EIA is not a neutral set of procedures but rather a social practice embedded in environmental politics. Assessing the environmental impact of a project must be seen against a background of socio-political conflict over that project. Likewise, the divergences of opinion over its nature and purpose reflect environmental values and politics. As O'Riordan notes:

> If one sees EIA not so much as a technique, rather as a process that is constantly changing in the face of shifting environmental politics and managerial capabilities, one can visualise it as a sensitive barometer of environmental values in a complex environmental society.[6]

EIA was developed as part of environmentalism in the 1960s and 1970s and cannot be separated from the conflicts and debates that were discussed in Chapter 2. Understandings of EIA are complicated because environmental problems are both physically and socio-politically messy.

An important question that you may be thinking is what the implication of all of this is for the practice and study of environmental law. These variations may be intellectually interesting, but it is not immediately obvious how they will legally manifest themselves. The reality is that they do have an important impact on the role and nature of law. EIA regimes vary considerably from jurisdiction to jurisdiction; not just in technical detail but in what is understood to be the role and nature of EIA and this will have implications for legal rights and remedies. If EIA is understood in Saarikoski's deliberative terms then interested third parties will arguably have greater participatory rights than if EIA is conceptualized in Carpenter's more scientific terms. Likewise, if a decision that was part of an EIA process is judicially reviewed what is understood to be *Wednesbury* unreasonable or even a relevant or irrelevant consideration will be different under the three models described here. To make matters more complicated, different legal actors in a particular regime may hold very differing beliefs about the role and nature of EIA and a legal conflict may in essence be over that point. An important question that an environmental lawyer needs to ask in dealing with a legal dispute over EIA is thus what the different parties involved in the process understand the role and nature of EIA to be. Answering such a question will not lead to the resolution of a legal dispute but it will give a lawyer a greater insight into why there is a dispute in the first place.

1.3 PROBLEMS AND LIMITS OF EIA

Before moving to the legal aspects of EIA, it should be made very clear that EIA is a very limited tool for decision-making and it is not a magic wand for dealing with disputes concerning the environmental implications of development. The problems with EIA are many but can largely be understood as falling into three categories.

---

[6] Timothy O'Riordan, 'EIA from the Environmentalist's Perspective' (1990) 4 VIA 13.

The first category is the subset of issues that arise because of the limits of scientific knowledge. One of the reasons why EIA is viewed as useful is because it acts as a way of collecting, collating, and interpreting information. The problem however is that the information base is often deficient and there is no realistic means of improving it. Problems of scientific uncertainty were discussed in Section 3.4 of Chapter 2 and are particularly acute in EIA as it is a form of prediction.

David P Lawrence, 'The Need for EIA Theory Building' (1997) 17 Environmental Impact Assessment Review 79, 87–88

Uncertainty occurs when environmental conditions and impacts are indeterminate, and probabilities cannot be ascertained. Two subsets of uncertainty are ignorance (do not know what we should know) and indeterminacy (understanding not possible, because causal chains or networks are open). Uncertainty is inherent in EIA. It is evident in definitions of problems and opportunities, in planning visions, ends, and means, in the planning environment (present and future), in value judgments and related decision areas. There must be uncertainty when determining the quantities of residuals, land, and resources consumed, when predicting the environmental management and controls of the future, when translating controlled rates of emission into ambient environmental quality, and when estimating and valuing impacts on receptors.

Factors contributing to uncertainty include: time and resource limitations; lack of theory; inadequate baseline data; oversimplified models; novelty of the technology, materials, or setting; inherent variations in complex systems; and control and replication problems [...]

EIA usually involves complex processes and systems, which generate counterintuitive, acausal behaviour, are characterized by multiple interactions and feedback/feedforward loops, involve diffused authority and are often irreducible. Surprise is inherent to complex systems. Surprise-generating mechanisms include: logical tangles (which lead to paradoxical conclusions); catastrophes (where a small change can lead to discontinuous shifts); chaos (deterministic randomness); incompatibility (output transcends rules); irreducibility (behaviour cannot be decomposed into parts); and emergence (self-organized patterns). In a complex environment, reductionism, prediction, and control will be severely constrained. Surprises should be expected. A flexible, precautionary approach will be needed with provision for evolution, change, and various combinations of reversible, irreversible, deterministic, and stochastic processes.

A scientific, positivistic approach will not be generally appropriate for the trans-scientific, messy problems often encountered in EIA. A less analytical, more holistic, approach will be required. A new scientific paradigm, which incorporates concepts such as complexity, nonlinearity and emergence, is more appropriate.

Lawrence's description makes very clear the quite insurmountable problems that those involved in the EIA process have in assessing environmental impacts. Scientific uncertainty is not just a problem at the margins but one that seriously limits the utility of EIA, particularly if EIA is understood in the terms of Carpenter.

This leads to the second set of problems with EIA—that there is a danger that too much faith is placed on it as a decision-making tool and in particular its ability to predict future impacts. This is not only problematic because it encourages too much weight to be given to an EIS (and what maybe the flawed information in it) but also because it distorts what is important in the decision-making process. Consider the comments of Tribe in relation to impact analysis tools and other forms of assessment that are akin to EIA.

Laurence H Tribe, 'Technology Assessment and the Fourth Discontinuity: The Limits of Instrumental Rationality' (1972–73) 46 S Cal L Rev 617, 627

Moreover analysis is often intended not only to aid the decision-maker in choosing a course of action, but also to help him in *persuading others* of the justifiability and wisdom of his choice. The usefulness of analysis in such advocacy is drastically reduced whenever it does not at least *appear* to point objectively and unambiguously toward a particular alternative. Thus, the users of policy-analytic techniques are under constant pressure to reduce the many dimensions of each problem to some common measure in terms of which 'objective' comparison seems possible - even when this means squeezing out 'soft' but crucial information merely because it seems difficult to quantify or otherwise render commensurable with the 'hard' data on the problem. Thus, because policy-analytic techniques prove most powerful when the various dimensions of a question are reduced to a common denominator, or at least to smoothly exchangeable attributes, the continuing tendency that accompanies analytic techniques is to engage in such reduction whenever possible, with the result not only that 'soft' variables tend to be ignored or understated but also that *entire problems tend to be reduced to terms that misstate their underlying structure and ignore the 'global' features that give them their total character.*

Tribe is highlighting two problems. First, because of the emphasis given to analysis in EIA only things that are subject to analysis get taken into account. This problem is made more acute because in regards to public decision-making, 'a decision made by the numbers (or by explicit rules of some other sort) has at least the appearance of being fair and impersonal' and thus promoting the rule of law.[7] Second, what this also means is that EIA has an important but not necessarily constructive role in 'framing' an environmental problem. If EIA is understood to be the major way in which an environmental problem is characterized and it only characterizes it in terms of the specific physical impact of an activity then other implications of the decision may be ignored. EIA can thus actually be quite a counterproductive (and very resource intensive) way of addressing environmental disputes.

A third problem with EIA is that, as already highlighted, the EIA process does not dictate a particular outcome. Faith in EIA is faith in the assumption that by requiring decision-makers to consider the environmental impacts of projects they will make decisions that avoid those impacts. This assumption however ignores the reality of administrative decision-making. In a 1973 article the American environmental lawyer Joseph Sax stated that the 'redemptive quality of procedural reform is about nine parts myth and one part coconut oil' in expressing his frustration with the wishful thinking that underlay the US EIA regime.[8] He went on to note that, in his experience, there were numerous problems with the EIA process that meant it failed to influence decision-makers. In the main, these were problems to do with the fact that, by itself, EIA could not change the nature, interests, or agenda of decision-making institutions. Different and more powerful legal and political forces were required.

The issue of the effectiveness of EIA has been an ongoing matter of debate. More recently, Jay and others came to the following conclusions.

[7] Theodore Porter, *Trust in Numbers: The Pursuit of Objectivity in Science and Public Life* (Princeton UP 1995) 8.
[8] Joseph Sax, 'The (Unhappy) Truth About NEPA' (1973) 26 Oklahoma L Rev 239.

Stephen Jay, Carys Jones, Paul Slinn, and Christopher Wood, 'Environmental Impact Assessment: Retrospect and Prospect' (2007) 27 Environmental Impact Assessment Review 287, 298

There is no doubt that, especially in more mature EIA systems, EIA has made a difference to patterns of development through design modifications, institutional learning, and stakeholder involvement. The quality of decisions involving EIA has improved as a result of the increased use of modification or mitigation, the use of more stringent conditions upon permissions and, occasionally, the non-implementation of potentially environmentally damaging proposals which might previously have been approved.

However, there has been growing dissatisfaction over the fact that EIA's influence over development decisions is relatively limited and that it appears to be falling short of its full potential. Even its most immediate aims of ensuring that the likely environmental consequences of developments are properly taken into account and ameliorated where necessary are only being met to a limited degree. The achievement of its substantive aim, contributing to more sustainable patterns of activity, although difficult to assess, appears to be even more elusive. This may be partly because this aim is ill-defined in itself but it also betrays a failure to incorporate into EIA systems any clear rationale for working to such an end.

What can be seen here is not just that the aim of EIA is ill defined but, rather, that many different aims might exist. As the question of effectiveness can only be considered in light of the purpose to be achieved then the assessment of the effectiveness of EIA will always be difficult.

FURTHER READING

1. An excellent and thorough overview of EIA can be found in John Glasson, Riki Therivel, and Andrew Chadwick, *Introduction to Environmental Impact Assessment* (4th edn, Routledge 2011). A very detailed account of different techniques in EIA can be found in Peter Morris and Riki Therivel, *Methods of Environmental Impact Assessment* (3rd edn, Routledge 2009).

2. For those wishing to read further about the theoretical aspects of EIA see Jane Holder, *Environmental Assessment: The Regulation of Decision-Making* (OUP 2004) 22–29.

2 THE HISTORICAL DEVELOPMENT OF EIA

The discussion in Section 1 makes clear that underpinning the process of EIA are different normative assumptions about good decision-making. Those assumptions have not come from nowhere and understanding the history of EIA is an important part of understanding the process itself. That history can be seen to have three overlapping aspects: the emergence of the concept in the US; its proliferation in numerous other jurisdictions; and its evolution into other types of environmental assessment techniques—each are briefly considered here.

2.1 THE UNITED STATES

EIA originated with the National Environmental Policy Act 1969 (NEPA) in the US. NEPA was passed in the context of the flourishing of environmental politics in the 1960s and in light of environmental controversies over the environmental impact of cities, industrial activity, and tourist activities. It, along with other statutes of the time was 'action forcing', in that it required the Federal government to take action in the face of a perceived environmental crisis. In passing the Act the Congress declared their intention to be, among other things, to 'encourage productive and enjoyable harmony between man and his environment'.[9] Under 42 USC §4332(2)(c) (also known as s 102) federal agencies are required to:

include in every recommendation or report on proposals for legislation and other major Federal actions significantly affecting the quality of the human environment, a detailed statement by the responsible official on—

(i) the environmental impact of the proposed action,

(ii) any adverse environmental effects which cannot be avoided should the proposal be implemented,

(iii) alternatives to the proposed action,

(iv) the relationship between local short-term uses of man's environment and the maintenance and enhancement of long-term productivity, and

(v) any irreversible and irretrievable commitments of resources which would be involved in the proposed action should it be implemented.

The Act also set up a Council of Environmental Quality (CEQ) that developed further guidelines for EIA.[10]

EIA, as already noted, was about the process by which decisions were made. The concept of procedure and process were not in any way new to US administrative law as the Administrative Procedure Act 1946 placed great emphasis on administrative decision-making acting in accordance with various procedures and processes.[11] NEPA however, represented a very different approach to thinking about process.

Robert L Rabin, 'Federal Regulation in Historical Perspective' (1986) 38 Stan L Rev 1189, 1287

The primary thrust of NEPA—which underscores its distinctive character—was its reliance upon an internal management technique that owed a greater debt to organization theory than to administrative law. Under the most optimistic scenario, the routinization of an impact statement requirement would necessitate specialized administrative personnel and the establishment of new channels of communication and information-flow within an agency. If these bureaucratic operating procedures were conscientiously pursued, a traditionally mission-oriented agency could exhibit a new sensitivity in defining its organizational goals.

The question of course was what that 'new sensitivity' was and, as already seen, there was considerable variation on this point. Despite this underlying ambiguity, NEPA was a very symbolic statute and it still occupies a revered place in American environmental law.

---

[9] 42 USC § 4331.   [10] 40 CFR § 1500.   [11] 5 USC § 551 ff.

William H Rodgers Jr, 'The Most Creative Moments in the History of Environmental Law: the What "Whats"' (2000) U III L Rev 1, 31

The most admired of all the environmental laws is the NEPA. It is admired for its form, its structure, and its robustness. It is praised for its eloquence of formulation and for the cleverness in the way it was attached to existing agency mandates. It has been emulated by a hundred other initiatives. It is celebrated for any number of paradigm shifts—from simple public policy evaluation to impact assessment to comprehensive rationality to ecological experimentation to public participation to integrated decision-making.

Rodgers concludes that it is the 'Magna Carta' of American environmental law but what is interesting about Rodgers' comments is that he recognizes that NEPA is actually often identified with many different types of revolution.

The most significant of those revolutions was legal and the reason for this was very simple.

Harold Leventhal, 'Environmental Decision-Making and the Role of the Courts' (1974) 122 U Pa L Rev 509, 515, 517–18

Given the premise of the Act, it is clear that the review required to safeguard its objective must be conducted by an institution that is 'independent' in the sense that it is not caught up in the agency's mission as its reason for being and basis for succeeding. There are three possible forums for review that meet this requirement: Congress, superagencies in the executive branch, and the courts.

Congress, Leventhal noted, was under extreme time constraints and, while the CEQ did have a role in issuing guidelines, any supervisory function it had was largely informal. The role of supervising and enforcing EIA processes fell to the courts, and in particular generalist courts with no specialist expertise in environmental matter. He noted:

Review to ensure balance, coupled with restraint on the part of the reviewer, requires a generalist who can penetrate the scientific explanation underlying the decision just enough to test its soundness. A specialist whose attention was directed exclusively to environmental issues would tend to intrude his own judgment on the issues, thereby co-opting the discretion of the agency.

Leventhal's analysis is insightful in that it recognizes that for EIA to work there must be a review process. It cannot be self regulating. As Leventhal's comments also suggest, the court in carrying out such judicial review must balance restraint and activism. Different variations on this balance will be seen in both the CJEU and English courts approach to EIA. It has also been a major theme in US case law and NEPA has given rise to thousands of cases.

An important question to ask is whether NEPA has been a success. The reality is that it is not an easy one to answer. Consider the summary of a report into NEPA on its twenty-fifth anniversary in 1997.

Kathleen McGinty, 'Foreword', The National Environmental Policy Act: A Study of Its Effectiveness After Twenty-five Years (Council of Environmental Quality, Executive Office of the President 1997) iii

Overall, what we found is that NEPA is a success — it has made agencies take a hard look at the potential environmental consequences of their actions, and it has brought the public into the agency decision-making process like no other statute. In a piece of legislation barely three pages long, NEPA gave both a voice to the new national consensus to protect and improve the environment, and substance to the determination articulated by many to work together to achieve that goal. To that end, NEPA charges CEQ and all federal agencies with achieving 'productive harmony' among our environmental, economic, and social objectives. NEPA directs federal agencies to open their doors, bring the public in, and offer genuine opportunities for participation and collaboration in decision-making.

Despite these successes, however, NEPA's implementation at times has fallen short of its goals. For example, this NEPA Effectiveness Study finds that agencies may sometimes confuse the purpose of NEPA. Some act as if the detailed statement called for in the statute is an end in itself, rather than a tool to enhance and improve decision-making. As a consequence, the exercise can be one of producing a document to no specific end. But NEPA is supposed to be about good decision-making—not endless documentation.

The Study finds that agencies sometimes engage in consultation only after a decision has—for all practical purposes—been made. In such instances, other agencies and the public at large believe that their concerns have not been heard. As a result, they may find themselves opposing even worthy proposed actions. This may in turn lead to agencies seeking 'litigation-proof' documents, increasing costs and time but not necessarily quality. In such cases, potential cost savings are also lost because a full range of alternatives has not adequately been examined. Other matters of concern to participants in the Study were the length of NEPA processes, the extensive detail of NEPA analyses, and the sometimes confusing overlay of other laws and regulations.

McGinty's comments highlight the mixed success of EIA that Jay and others noted. On the one hand, it has clearly placed environmental protection on the agenda in the planning of projects, but it has not always done so in a particularly meaningful way, and while there has been a concern to comply with EIA procedure it has not always been for the right reasons. In particular, the avoidance of litigation has seemingly taken primacy over improving environmental quality.

2.2 THE PROLIFERATION OF EIA IN A RANGE OF JURISDICTIONS

Very quickly after the creation of NEPA other jurisdictions introduced EIA into their environmental law including Canada (1973); Australia (1974); West Germany (1975); and France (1976).[12] By the 1990s EIA was also being promoted at the international level. In 1991 the UN Economic Commission for Europe's Espoo Convention on Environmental Impact Assessment in a Transboundary Context was signed. Principle 17 of the Rio Declaration on Environment and Development in 1992 also stated that:

Environmental impact assessment, as a national instrument, shall be undertaken for proposed activities that are likely to have a significant adverse impact on the environment and are subject to the decision of a competent authority.

Major international lending organizations now required those states borrowing funds to carry out EIA. EIA thus went from being a novel decision-making practice to being part of the modus operandi of decision-making that had possible impacts on the environment.

[12] Christopher Wood, *Environmental Impact Assessment: A Comparative Review* (2nd edn, Prentice Hall 2003).

In this process of transplantation and translation the concept of EIA did not remain static. EIA took on many different forms and variations and what was included in the EIA process varied from jurisdiction to jurisdiction. Furthermore, the introduction of EIA led to the development of other forms of assessment including social impact assessments, sustainability assessments, and regulatory impact statements.

Carys Jones and others, 'Environmental Assessment: Dominant or Dormant' in Jane Holder and Donald McGillivray (eds), *Taking Stock of Environmental Assessment: Law, Policy and Practice* (Routledge 2007) 21–22

This proliferation of other forms of impact assessment reflects the recognized value of a structured and consistent approach to evaluating environmental, and other, aspects when taking decisions. Thus, Sadler regarded EA as largely being successful as a policy instrument because it had developed to include new areas and impacts. However, Benson considered that EA was too limited in application to answer fully the broad questions involved in considering the full effects of human activities in sustainability terms. Sadler saw the future of EA as being part of a framework, linking it in an integrated way to other instruments such as lifecycle analysis, environmental auditing and environment accounting, and sustainability approaches such as the principles espoused in Agenda 21.

These different views echo the different perspectives on EIA seen already. They also highlight the way in which the promotion of EIA has been part of larger trends in environmental law and public administration.

2.3 STRATEGIC ENVIRONMENTAL ASSESSMENT

One particular variation on EIA to note is SEA. We will look at the EU regime in Section 7 but here it is useful to understand the differences between SEA and EIA. A major limitation of EIA as a tool for assessing environmental impacts is that it only applies to particular projects rather than to the more general activities of developing policy, passing legislation, and developing sectoral policy. These more general activities will directly influence what projects are even possible and what projects will be seen as acceptable. Thus, if there is a general policy in a jurisdiction that hydroelectric dams should be built it becomes very difficult when considering whether an individual dam project should be stopped because of the environmental impacts. The development of SEA has been a response to this. Versions of SEA were developed in the 1970s but it was in the late 1980s that a series of practices were given the label of SEA.

SEA and EIA share similar foundations in that both are systematic processes that require information, although SEA is more ambitious in that it is being promoted as a means by which to re-orientate public decision-making. The SEA process however is quite distinct from that of EIA. First, a comprehensive SEA regime should apply to all strategic decision-making and require the decision-maker to identify both the objects of their strategic decision-making (for example, better transport) and their SEA objectives. The decision-maker must then identify the most environmentally sustainable alternatives, achieving their strategic objective by carrying out assessments of different alternatives and consulting on them. Such a process, by its very nature is less quantitative than EIA and far more focused on identifying and debating alternatives.

Daniel McClusky and Elsa Joao, 'The Promotion of Environmental Enhancement in Strategic Environmental Assessment' (2011) 31 Environmental Impact Assessment Review 344, 345.

The principal aims of the SEA process are as follows: to help decision makers integrate environmental and sustainability considerations into strategic actions; to enhance environmental protection; to promote public participation in the decision-making process; and to increase government and local authority transparency. In addition to these aims, one of the functions of the SEA process is to identify positive environmental impacts of a strategic action and enhance them, which may refer to enhancing for example biodiversity, ecosystems (as well as soils, water or air), landscape character, green spaces and cultural or historical heritage.

Thus, just as with EIA, there are many normative assumptions underpinning SEA and there is not clear agreement over its nature and purpose or what exactly it entails.

Thomas B Fischer and Kim Seaton, 'Strategic Environmental Assessment: Effective Planning Instrument or Lost Concept?' (2002) 17 Planning, Practice & Research 31, 31

Throughout the 1980s and 1990s, strategic environmental assessment (SEA) attracted increasing attention from planners, politicians, academics and other interested parties worldwide. However, it is probably fair to say that during the same period it lost much of its original clarity. At the end of the 1980s, SEA was portrayed as an extension of project environmental impact assessment (EIA) principles to the levels of policies, plans and programmes, originally mainly in spatial and land-use planning. By the end of the 1990s, however, the term SEA was used in an interchangeable manner for a wide range of different kinds of assessments, ranging from policy assessment for complex multi-sectoral systems to the assessment of large projects. In particular, SEA's promotion as an instrument for supporting decision making for sustainable development necessitated the consideration of a much wider range of issues than solely the biophysical environment. Further, whilst some SEAs have dealt mainly with spatial alternatives, others have considered comprehensive policy options. Procedural characteristics have also varied greatly, with some SEAs based on EIA procedural stages, while others do not appear to have had any clearly defined procedure at all. In addition, the optimal level of integration into the underlying policy, plan and programme, that is, the place in the decision-making hierarchy, is usually unclear. The role of the sector of SEA application has also not been clearly defined.

Fischer and Seaton illustrate that disagreements over the nature and purpose of SEA have a number of different dimensions. A significant aspect of those disagreements is how to integrate SEA into existing decision-making structures. This process of integration is a far greater challenge in relation to SEA because it must apply more widely than EIA does. We will see this in Section 7.

FURTHER READING

1. For further discussion of NEPA case law see an excellent US environmental law textbook such as Robert Percival and others, *Environmental Regulation: Law, Science and Policy* (6th edn, Wolters Kluwer 2009).

2. Some early and classic examples of US court reviewing decisions in relation to NEPA can be found in *Calvert Cliffs' Coordinating Committee, Inc. v US Atomic Energy Commission* 449 F 2d

1109 (DC Circuit 1971); *National Resources Defense Council v Morton* 458 F 2d 827 (DC Circuit 1972); and *Vermont Yankee Nuclear Power Corporation v Natural Resources Defense Council* 435 US 519 (1978).

3. For a discussion of EIA in the international context see Neil Craik, *The International Law of Environmental Impact Assessment* (CUP 2008).

4. For a discussion of SEA see Riki Therivel, *Strategic Environmental Assessment in Action* (2nd edn, Routledge 2010). For a discussion of its theoretical aspects see Olivia Bina, 'A Critical Review of the Dominant Lines of Argumentation on the Need for Strategic Environmental Assessment' (2007) 27 Environmental Impact Assessment Review 585.

3 THE ENVIRONMENTAL ASSESSMENT DIRECTIVE IN THE EU

Ideas for an EU Directive on EIA were originally developed in the mid-1970s. Investigations by the Commission into a harmonized EIA scheme began in 1975 and the Commission put forward its first draft of the Directive to the Council in 1980. As in the US, EIA was promoted as a revolutionary form of decision-making that gave expression to the policy of prevention—that environmental problems should be rectified before they occur. There was strong opposition to the Directive from a number of Member States, including the UK. While EIA was accepted in practice there was a concern it would lead to an over rigid system and the growth of litigation seen in the US.

Council Directive 85/337/EEC of 27 June 1985 on the assessment of the effects of certain public and private projects on the environment[13] was passed under what was then Articles 100 and 235 TEC.[14] While the fundamental motivation for the Directive was environmental protection one of the bases for harmonization was the common market competence (then Article 100 TEC) and thus the harmonizing of this area of environmental regulation was a means of maintaining the common market by ensuring competition was not distorted by different Member States having different EIA regimes. The Directive was amended by Council Directive 97/11/EC of 3 March 1997,[15] so as to address what was perceived to be one of the many weaknesses of the Directive, including that: it did not apply to enough projects; trans-boundary effects were not properly considered; and the information provided by the developer needed to be more comprehensive. The Directive was amended again by Directive 2003/35/EC of the European Parliament and of the Council of 26 May 2003,[16] so as to ensure that the Directive was consistent with the Aarhus Convention on Access to Information, Public Participation and Access to Justice in Environmental Matters.[17] Finally, Directive 2009/31/EC[18] amended the Annexes I and II of the EA Directive, by adding projects related to the transport, capture, and storage of carbon dioxide (CO_2). The Directive, and its amendments, has now been codified in Directive 2011/92/EU on the assessment of the effects of certain public and private projects on the environment.[19] It is interesting to note that this codification was under Article 192(1) TFEU.

---

[13] [1985] OJ L175/40. [14] Now 115 and 358 TFEU (see Chapter 4 for details). [15] [1997] OJ L73/5.
[16] [2003] OJ L156/17. [17] See Chapters 7 and 10. [18] [2009] OJ L140/114. [19] [2012] OJ L28/1.

3.1 THE BASIC OBLIGATION

The basic obligation under the EA Directive is set out in Article 2(1) which states:

> Member States shall adopt all measures necessary to ensure that, before consent is given, projects likely to have significant effects on the environment by virtue, *inter alia*, of their nature, size or location are made subject to a requirement for development consent and an assessment with regard to their effects. These projects are defined in Article 4.

This basic obligation is important in that it guides how the Directive is interpreted and what is understood to be its purpose. When in doubt in interpreting the Directive one should always return to Article 2(1), and it shall be seen here that the Court uses it as the starting point for their approach to the Directive. It should also be noted that for an EIA to be required the effects that a project has on the environment need not be adverse. Rather the test is that of the *significance* of the impacts.

Article 3 sets out in very general terms that an environmental impact assessment will identify, describe, and assess in an appropriate manner, in light of each individual case, and in accordance with Articles 4–12, the direct and indirect effects of a project on human, animal and plant life, the natural environment, and cultural heritage. Article 1(2) defines a 'project' in the following terms:

> — the execution of construction works or of other installations or schemes,
> — other interventions in the natural surroundings and landscape including those involving the extraction of mineral resources;

'Development consent' is also defined in that provision as:

> the decision of the competent authority or authorities which entitles the developer to proceed with the project;

The Directive allows Member States to integrate EIA into existing procedures.[20]

3.2 SCREENING

The first step of EIA is a screening process in which the public authorities of Member States must consider whether a particular project should be subject to EIA. Article 2(1) is supplemented by Article 4. As shall be shown, the meaning of Article 4 has been heavily litigated before the CJEU and it was also substantially amended in 1997 to address many of the concerns raised by that litigation.[21] After 1997 Article 4(2)–(4) now states:

> 2. Subject to Article 2 (4), for projects listed in Annex II, the Member States shall determine whether the project shall be mad subject to an assessment in accordance with Articles 5 to 10. Member States shall make that determination through:
>   (a) a case-by-case examination;

---

[20] Article 2(2).
[21] Case C-133/94 *Commission v Belgium* [1996] ECR I-2323; Case C-392/96 *Commission v Ireland* [1999] ECR I-5901.

or

(b) thresholds or criteria set by the Member State.

Member States may decide to apply both procedures referred to in (a) and (b).

3. When a case-by-case examination is carried out or thresholds or criteria are set for the purpose of paragraph 2, the relevant selection criteria set out in Annex III shall be taken into account.

4. Member States shall ensure that the determination made by the competent authorities under paragraph 2 is made available to the public.

Annex III refers to a range of selection criteria relating to the characteristics, location, and potential impact of a project. Characteristics of the project include its size, its cumulation with other projects, the use of natural resources, the production of waste, pollution and nuisances, and the risk of accidents. The location of projects includes the environmental sensitivity of geographical areas having regard to issues such as existing land use, the relative abundance, quality and regenerative capacity of natural resources in the area, and the absorption capacity of the area. Characteristics of the impact to consider include its extent, its trans-frontier nature, its magnitude and complexity, its probability, and its duration, frequency, and reversibility.

Article 4 divides projects into two categories—Annex I and Annex II projects. Annex I projects definitely require an EIA, while Member States must consider whether an Annex II project does or does not require one. Annex I lists a range of projects that obviously will have a significant impact on the environment. These include (but are not limited to) crude oil refineries, nuclear power stations, installations solely designed for the permanent storage or final disposal of radioactive waste, integrated chemical installations; motorways, and trading ports. Annex II lists the range of the projects that, depending on the circumstances, are likely to have a significant impact on the environment. These include projects that are part of agriculture, silviculture, aquaculture, extractive industries, the energy industry, the production and processing of metals, the mineral industry, the chemical industry, the textile, leather, wood and paper industry, the rubber industry, tourism and leisure, and other projects including change and extension of projects lists in Annex I or Annex II.

In terms of screening, Annex II projects have been the source of the most controversy, whether it is in relation to the creation of thresholds, or the operation of discretion in considering a particular project. This is not surprising for two reasons. First, the guiding question for Article 4(2) (whether a project is likely to have a significant impact upon the environment) does not yield any straightforward answers as it is predictive, discretionary, and value laden. Second, for developers, the question of whether an EIA, is or is not, required is important for financial reasons. Developers bear the main costs of doing an EIA and so being required to carry out an EIA will be an important factor in assessing the viability of a development. Likewise, because of this, there is a strong incentive on the part of developers to litigate the issue.

The Directive does provide for a number of very limited exceptions where an EIA does not apply, including in relation to projects for national defence purposes[22] and projects 'the details of which are adopted by a specific Act of national legislation'.[23] Article 2(4) also provides for a procedure by which Member States can exempt specific projects. Among other things, it requires the Member State to inform the Commission of the exemption prior to granting consent.

[22] Article 1(3). See Case C-435/97 *WWF v Autonome Provinz Bozen* [1999] ECR I-5613.
[23] Article 1(4). See Case C-287/98 *Luxembourg v Linster* [2000] ECR I-6917 for an interpretation of this.

3.3 SCOPING

The next possible step of EIA is that of scoping in which a decision is made by a public authority about what environmental impacts should be taken into account in an environmental statement (ES). Scoping is very much about framing what is the environmental problem that needs to be assessed and, as we have already seen, how an EIS frames a problem is vitally important to what gets examined. Thus, for example, in building a large power station there may be serious environmental impacts from carrying in construction machinery to the location at which the power station will be built but it is not obvious that these issues of transport should be considered in an EIS.

Before 1997 there was no scoping requirement in the Directive and even now the requirement on Member States is not strictly mandatory. Article 5(2) of the Directive requires Member States to 'take all necessary measures' to ensure that if a developer requests an opinion about what information should be supplied that it is given to them. Likewise, the Directive also empowers competent authorities to give such opinions even if the developer has not requested such information. Scoping has generally been encouraged and the Commission has developed guidelines on the topic.[24]

3.4 THE INFORMATION REQUIRED

Whether or not there is an explicit scoping process the information to be considered as part of an EIA will vary from project to project. There is no prescribed form for an ES although the Directive does provide some guidance of what should be included. Article 5(1) of the Directive requires that Member States:

> [...] shall adopt the necessary measures to ensure that the developer supplies in an appropriate form the information specified in Annex IV inasmuch as:
>
> (a) the Member States consider the information is relevant to a given stage of the consent procedure and to the specific characteristics of a particular project or type of project and of the environmental features likely to be affected [...]

The information listed in Annex IV includes the following: a description of the project; alternatives; aspects of the environment likely to be affected; preventive and reductive measures; difficulties encountered in complying the information; and a non-technical summary. Article 5(1) gives some flexibility to Member States in deciding what information a developer must supply. However Article 5(3) states:

> The information to be provided by the developer in accordance with paragraph 1 shall include at least:
>
> (a) a description of the project comprising information on the site, design and size of the project,
>
> (b) a description of the measures envisaged in order to avoid, reduce and, if possible, remedy significant adverse effects,
>
> (c) the data required to identify and assess the main effects which the project is likely to have on the environment,
>
> (d) an outline of the main alternatives studied by the developer and an indication of the main reasons for his choice, taking into account the environmental effects,
>
> (e) a non-technical summary of the information referred to in points (a) to (d).

[24] Commission, *Guidance on EIA Scoping* (Office of Official Publications of the European Communities 2001).

3.5 CONSULTATION AND PUBLIC PARTICIPATION

In the original Directive, Article 6 set out the rights of consultation and participation although it did not amount to a very stringent obligation. Primarily it required Member States to inform the public and give them a chance to give their opinion but little more. In regards to matters of consultation, the Directive was amended by Directive 97/11/EC and more importantly by Directive 2003/35/EC to bring it in line with the Aarhus Convention (see Section 2.4 of Chapter 7 and Section 2.3 of Chapter 10), and the end result is that there is now a far greater obligation placed on Member States to consult the relevant authorities and to ensure that the public are given opportunities to participate. Article 6(1) now states:

> 1. Member States shall take the measures necessary to ensure that the authorities likely to be concerned by the project by reason of their specific environmental responsibilities are given an opportunity to express their opinion on the information supplied by the developer and on the request for development consent. To this end, Member States shall designate the authorities to be consulted, either in general terms or on a case-by-case basis. The information gathered pursuant to Article 5 shall be forwarded to those authorities. Detailed arrangements for consultation shall be laid down by the Member States.

This requirement also applies to scoping.[25] Article 7 also sets out requirements for informing and consulting other Member States if a project is likely to have significant trans-boundary environmental effects.

Articles 6(2)–(6) set out the main requirements for public participation.

> **Article 6**
>
> [...]
>
> 2. The public shall be informed, whether by public notices or other appropriate means such as electronic media where available, of the following matters early in the environmental decision-making procedures referred to in Article 2(2) and, at the latest, as soon as information can reasonably be provided:
>
> (a) the request for development consent;
>
> (b) the fact that the project is subject to an environmental impact assessment procedure and, where relevant, the fact that Article 7 applies;
>
> (c) details of the competent authorities responsible for taking the decision, those from which relevant information can be obtained, those to which comments or questions can be submitted, and details of the time schedule for transmitting comments or questions;
>
> (d) the nature of possible decisions or, where there is one, the draft decision;
>
> (e) an indication of the availability of the information gathered pursuant to Article 5;
>
> (f) an indication of the times and places where and means by which the relevant information will be made available;
>
> (g) details of the arrangements for public participation made pursuant to paragraph 5 of this Article.
>
> 3. Member States shall ensure that, within reasonable time-frames, the following is made available to the public concerned:
>
> (a) any information gathered pursuant to Article 5;
>
> (b) in accordance with national legislation, the main reports and advice issued to the competent authority or authorities at the time when the public concerned is informed in accordance with paragraph 2 of this Article;

---

[25] Article 5(2).

(c) in accordance with the provisions of Directive 2003/4/EC of the European Parliament and of the Council of 28 January 2003 on public access to environmental information (1), information other than that referred to in paragraph 2 of this Article which is relevant for the decision in accordance with Article 8 and which only becomes available after the time the public concerned was informed in accordance with paragraph 2 of this Article.

4. The public concerned shall be given early and effective opportunities to participate in the environmental decision-making procedures referred to in Article 2(2) and shall, for that purpose, be entitled to express comments and opinions when all options are open to the competent authority or authorities before the decision on the request for development consent is taken.

5. The detailed arrangements for informing the public (for example by bill posting within a certain radius or publication in local newspapers) and for consulting the public concerned (for example by written submissions or by way of a public inquiry) shall be determined by the Member States.

6. Reasonable time-frames for the different phases shall be provided, allowing sufficient time for informing the public and for the public concerned to prepare and participate effectively in environmental decision-making subject to the provisions of this Article.

Under Article 1(2) the public is defined as 'one or more natural or legal persons and, in accordance with national legislation or practice, their associations, organizations or groups' and the 'public concerned' is defined as:

the public affected or likely to be affected by, or having an interest in, the environmental decision-making procedures referred to in Article 2(2). For the purposes of this definition, non-governmental organisations promoting environmental protection and meeting any requirements under national law shall be deemed to have an interest.

These definitions are taken from the Aarhus Convention.

These amendments are highly significant in that by creating far more stringent public participation requirements they are arguably transforming the nature and purpose of EIA to make it more deliberative and participatory. Thus, in considering the models discussed in Section 1, the amendments required by 97/11/EC and 2003/35/EC are making EIA far more like Saarikoski's model than those described by Benson and Carpenter. There are now duties on Member States to ensure public consultation occurs as early as possible in the environmental decision-making process, and in a way that allows for real consultation with a wide section of the public. Likewise, as seen here, it requires third parties to have remedies and rights of appeal in cases where there has been a possible breach of the Directive. For some, these amendments might not be enough in that the public do not play a substantive role in decision-making and the stringency of the obligations will depend on how administrators and courts interpret them. With that said, these amendments have considerable symbolic importance and, as already seen, such symbolism is particularly important in regards to EIA.

3.6 DECISION-MAKING AND CHALLENGES TO DECISIONS

Article 8 of the Directive states that:

The results of consultations and the information gather pursuant to Articles 5, 6, and 7 must be taken into consideration in the development consent procedure.

This is important in that it not only requires information to be taken into account but also the outcomes of any consultation or participation process. The competent authority must also inform the public and any relevant Member States of the content of the decision and other details.[26]

Article 11 (ex Article 10a)

1. Member States shall ensure that, in accordance with the relevant national legal system, members of the public concerned:

   (a) having a sufficient interest, or alternatively,

   (b) maintaining the impairment of a right, where administrative procedural law of a Member State requires this as a precondition,

   have access to a review procedure before a court of law or another independent and impartial body established by law to challenge the substantive or procedural legality of decisions, acts or omissions subject to the public participation provisions of this Directive.

2. Member States shall determine at what stage the decisions, acts or omissions may be challenged.

3. What constitutes a sufficient interest and impairment of a right shall be determined by the Member States, consistently with the objective of giving the public concerned wide access to justice. To this end, the interest of any non-governmental organisation meeting the requirements referred to in Article 1(2), shall be deemed sufficient for the purpose of subparagraph (a) of this Article. Such organisations shall also be deemed to have rights capable of being impaired for the purpose of subparagraph (b) of this Article.

4. The provisions of this Article shall not exclude the possibility of a preliminary review procedure before an administrative authority and shall not affect the requirement of exhaustion of administrative review procedures prior to recourse to judicial review procedures, where such a requirement exists under national law.

   Any such procedure shall be fair, equitable, timely and not prohibitively expensive.

5. In order to further the effectiveness of the provisions of this article, Member States shall ensure that practical information is made available to the public on access to administrative and judicial review procedures.

Article 11 is again a direct product of the Aarhus Convention and the case law in relation to it is discussed in Section 2.3 of Chapter 10. The failure of the original Directive to address access to justice issues did not aid the promotion of the public participation aspects of the Directive because many (although not all) national administrative law regimes would only recognize that those with directly affected private rights had the right to challenge the decision.

3.7 IMPLEMENTATION AND ENFORCEMENT

As must be clear from above, the EU framework for EIA does give considerable latitude to Member States and is open to different interpretations about the nature of the process that it requires. What obligations the EA Directive actually entails can only be assessed by looking at how the Directive

---

[26] Article 9.

is implemented, interpreted, and enforced. The case law of the CJEU and the English courts will be considered further but here it is useful to make some general comments about how the EA Directive has been implemented and enforced. A useful starting point is the Commission's comments about the EA Directive from their annual review concerning the monitoring of the application of EU Law.

Commission of the European Communities, *Situation in the Different Sectors: Accompanying 28th Annual Report on Monitoring the Application of EU Law* (2010) SEC(2011) 1093 final, 185

Due to its large scope of application, the EIA Directive can generate a relatively high number of complaints. However, given the essentially procedural character of the obligations laid down by the Directive, only a small number of complaints lead to infringement cases. The majority of the infringement cases concern bad (incomplete or incorrect) transposition of the Directive's provisions or failure of the Member States to apply the screening mechanism (article 4(2) and Annex III of the Directive).

As we can see from this, screening is a major focus of implementation issues. The Directive has also been subject review in 2009.

Commission of the European Communities, *On the Application and Effectiveness of the EIA Directive* COM(2009) 378 final, para 3.1

Implementation and case-law show that, when establishing thresholds, MS often exceed their margin of discretion, either by taking account only of some selection criteria in Annex III or by exempting some projects in advance. In addition, although the trend is on the increase, EIAs carried out in the various MS vary considerably (from fewer than 100 to 5 000), even when comparing MS of a similar size. The levels at which thresholds have been set has clear implications for the amount of EIA activity. Furthermore, there are still several cases in which cumulative effects are not taken into account, while problems remain when it comes to eliminating "salami slicing" practices, especially for big investment plans. These features could jeopardise the legitimacy of the Directive and undermine efforts to establish common screening standards.

As noted in Section 1, screening is one the most important aspects of EIA because it is the process by which it is decided which projects are governed by the regime. The difference between subjecting 100 and 5,000 projects to the regime is a very large one! The Commission has recently put forward proposals for revising the Directive. See the companion website for details.

The reasons for these differences in practice in Member States are many. In part they are due to the divergent opinions over the nature and purpose of EIA as seen in Section 1. In part they are due to the differing commitments on the part of Member States to this sort of environmental protection, and in part they are due to the operation of quite distinct legal, administrative, and political cultures. All these points are highlighted in the extract from a study comparing the implementation of the EA Directive in France and the UK.

John Glasson and Caroline Bellanger, 'Divergent Practice in a Converging System? The Case of EIA in France and the UK' (2003) 23 Environmental Impact Assessment Review 605, 622

The comparison between France and the UK does reveal variations in practice in terms of the application of minimum requirements and in approaches to additional 'best practice' features. The French practice tends to focus more on biophysical features, using an environmental science expert-based approach. The UK practice takes a wider spread of impacts and is somewhat more consultative in approach.

[...]

The national characteristics of MSs [Member States], their culture, history, legal and administrative frameworks and political and social dynamics, can provide major barriers to harmonisation. The Anglo-French comparison has highlighted a number of underlying factors. The French attitude to the environment, and general levels of environmental awareness, appear less conducive to effective EIA. Institutional factors are also significant. EIA in France is much more of a 'top-down' administrative process than in the UK. This is partly a reflection of the organisation of government and the distribution of power in the two countries. It may also reflect the fact that France already had an administrative EIA system in place well before the introduction of the EC Directive and was somewhat suspicious of the attempt to standardise using an 'Anglo-Saxon' model. The nature and perceptions of practitioners in the 'EIA markets' in the two countries are also revealing. In France, the EIA practitioners tend to be engineers and scientists and the approach is more technological/science-based than in the UK. French practitioners are 'experts', and there is little scope for the involvement of the public and pressure groups. The whole approach in France appears more secretive, and the very act of gaining access to EISs is a challenge in itself! The facts that the survey of French practitioners gave a much higher ranking to the role of lawyers in the EIA process, and also to the view that EIA was a bureaucratic burden, are indicative also of the nature of the French EIA system.

Glasson and Bellanger's comments emphasize the very deep rooted nature of these differences. Disparate approaches to the implementation of the EA Directive are not superficial but reflect fundamental divergences over issues of legal and administrative culture. Glasson and Bellanger do go on to suggest a shift towards regulatory convergence, and the Commission has encouraged such convergence through publishing guidance for Member States on both screening and scoping.[27] With that said, harmonization should not be taken as a given and the Commission in their 2009 review also noted differences in public participation procedures as well as concerns about the quality of ESs and the EIA process. They also raised issues about how it interrelated with other EU environmental law regimes. As noted above, this report may pave the way for future reforms.

---

[27] See <http://ec.europa.eu/environment/eia/eia-support.htm> accessed 28 September 2012. Documents to note are Commission of the European Communities, *Guidance on EIA Screening* (Office of Official Publications of the European Communities 2001); Commission of the European Communities, *Guidance on EIA Scoping* (Office of Official Publications of the European Communities 2001).

4 THE CJEU AND THE DIRECTIVE

As already seen in this chapter, integral to EIA is the process of reviewing whether a decision-maker has complied with the EIA process. As in the US, and despite the fact that in developing the Directive there was a desire to avoid litigation, the courts have had a significant role to play in determining whether Member State authorities are acting in accordance with the Directive. The case law of the CJEU is considered here, followed by the English case law. The CJEU has considered the EA Directive numerous times in the context of actions brought pursuant to Articles 258, 263, and 267 TFEU.[28] The vast majority of this case law has been concerned with the actions of Member States. There have been some challenges to Article 263 concerning the responsibilities of Community institutions in relation to the Directive but these have been mainly decided on other grounds such as standing.[29] The general thrust of the CJEU's jurisprudence, as with nearly all its jurisprudence in relation to the implementation of Directives, has been to ensure that the Directive is properly implemented and applied. As noted in the introduction, this has not always been straightforward because the 'result' in Article 288 terms is the 'forms and methods'. Three aspects of that case law are considered here: those issues concerned with how the Directive should be generally interpreted; those matters concerned with the discretion that Member States have in relation to the screening process; and those issues concerning the direct effect of the Directive. It should be noted that this is not an exhaustive analysis—the Court has interpreted many different aspects of the Directive. Likewise, the interaction between the Aarhus Convention and the Directive are discussed in Section 2.4 of Chapter 7 and Section 2.3 of Chapter 10.

4.1 WIDE SCOPE AND BROAD PURPOSE

The general approach of the CJEU is to interpret EU law purposively and no more is this true that in regard to the EA Directive. In the *Aannemersbedrijf P K Kraaijeveld BV and Others v Gedeputeerde Staten Van Zuid-Holland (Dutch Dykes)* case the CJEU[30] stressed that the 'wording of the Directive indicates that it has a wide scope and a broad purpose'. In that case it meant that the expression 'canalization and flood-relief works' should include dyke reinforcement activities. In particular the concern in interpreting the Directive is to ensure that works that by reason of their nature, size, or location, are likely to have significant effects on the environment, are subject to an impact assessment. In other

---

[28] See Chapter 4 for an explanation of these proceedings.

[29] Case C-325/94P *An Taisce & WWF v Commission* [1996] ECR I-3727; Case C-321/95 P *Stichting Greenpeace Council v Commission* [1998] ECR I-1651.

[30] Case C-72/95 *Aannemersbedrijf P K Kraaijeveld BV and Others v Gedeputeerde Staten Van Zuid-Holland* [1996] ECR I-5403, paras 31 and 39.

words Member States must adhere to the obligation set out in Article 2(1) of the Directive. The Court put the matter succinctly in *WWF v Autonome Provinz Bozen* where they stated:

> Consequently, whatever the method adopted by a Member State to determine whether or not a specific project needs to be assessed, be it by legislative designation or following an individual examination of the project, the method adopted must not undermine the objective of the Directive, which is that no project likely to have significant effects on the environment, within the meaning of the Directive, should be exempt from assessment, unless the specific project excluded could, on the basis of a comprehensive assessment, be regarded as not being likely to have such effects.[31]

This purposive approach can be seen in a number of other cases and a starting point for legal analysis should always be Article 2(1).[32] Further examples of this in relation to screening will be seen in Section 4.2.

Article 2(1) is not only relevant to screening. It can also be seen in how the Court generally interprets the Directive as can be seen in the *R (Wells) v Secretary of State for Transport, Local Government and the Regions* case.

Case C-201/02 *R (Wells) v Secretary of State for Transport, Local Government and the Regions* [2004] ECR I-723, paras 44–47

Facts

In 1947 planning permission had been granted for quarrying at a certain site. In 1991 (by which time quarrying had not been carried on for a number of years) the owners sought registration of the old permission under the Planning and Compensation Act 1991. The permission was registered but was required to be subject new planning conditions. The question for the ECJ was whether the approval of a new set of conditions and/or reserved matters on the existing permission was a 'development consent' for the purposes of the EIA Directive.

The ECJ

44. In the main proceedings, the owners of Conygar Quarry were obliged under the Planning and Compensation Act 1991, if they wished to resume working of the quarry, to have the old mining permission registered and to seek decisions determining new planning conditions and approving matters reserved by those conditions. Had they not done so, the permission would have ceased to have effect.

45. Without new decisions such as those referred to in the previous paragraph, there would no longer have been consent, within the meaning of Article 2(1) of Directive 85/337, to work the quarry.

46. It would undermine the effectiveness of that directive to regard as mere modification of an existing consent the adoption of decisions which, in circumstances such as those of the main proceedings, replace not only the terms but the very substance of a prior consent, such as the old mining permission.

---

[31] Case C-435/97 *WWF v Autonome Provinz Bozen* [1999] ECR I-5613, para 45.
[32] For example, Case C-392/96 *Commission v Ireland* [1999] ECR I-5901, para 72, Case C-87/02 *Commission v Italy* [2004] ECR I-5975, para 44; Case C-117/02 *Commission v Portugal* [2004] ECR I-5517, para 82.

47. Accordingly, decisions such as the decision determining new conditions and the decision approving matters reserved by the new conditions for the working of Conygar Quarry must be considered to constitute, as a whole, a new consent within the meaning of Article 2(1) of Directive 85/337, read in conjunction with Article 1(2) thereof.

This decision has important implications for what does, and what does not, require consent in national planning systems. It is also has implications for when screening should occur. This is significant in the UK because of the existence of 'outline planning permission',[33] which allows planning permission to be granted with some issues (for example, landscape, layout, and scale) being left for consideration at a reserved matters stage.[34] Outline planning permission is particularly significant for big projects involving multiple developers and buildings. The question is at what stage the need for an EIA should be considered.

Case C-508/03 *Commission v United Kingdom*
[2006] ECR I-3969, paras 95–106

95. By its second complaint, the Commission in essence contends that the national rules at issue, under which an assessment may be carried out only at the initial outline planning permission stage, and not at the later reserved matters stage, incorrectly transpose into domestic law Articles 2(1), 4(2), 5(3) and 8 of Directive 85/337, as amended.

96. The Commission argues that, where national law provides for a consent procedure comprising more than one stage, Directive 85/337, as amended, requires that an assessment may in principle be carried out at each stage in that procedure if it appears that the project in question is likely to have significant effects on the environment.

97. The Commission contends that, in so far as the national rules at issue in the present case preclude an assessment at the later reserved matters stage, they do not satisfy that requirement.

98. In its view, those rules allow some projects to escape assessment although they are likely to have significant effects on the environment.

99. The United Kingdom Government contends, on the other hand, that Article 2(1) of that directive makes it clear that a project must be subject to an assessment 'before consent is given'. Since that 'consent' is given when outline planning permission is granted (and not when the reserved matters are subsequently approved), the rules at issue correctly transpose Articles 2(1), 4(2), 5(3) and 8 of Directive 85/337, as amended.

100. As to those submissions, it should be noted that Article 1(2) of that directive defines 'development consent' for the purposes of the directive as the decision of the competent authority or authorities which entitles the developer to proceed with the project.

101. In the present case, it is common ground that, under national law, a developer cannot commence works in implementation of his project until he has obtained reserved matters approval. Until such approval has been granted, the development in question is still not (entirely) authorised.

102. Therefore, the two decisions provided for by the rules at issue in the present case, namely outline planning permission and the decision approving reserved matters, must be considered to constitute, as a whole, a (multi-stage) 'development consent' within the meaning of Article 1(2) of Directive 85/337, as amended.

---

[33] Section 92 TCPA 1990.
[34] Town and Country Planning (Development Management Procedure) (England) Order 2010.

103. In those circumstances, it is clear from Article 2(1) of Directive 85/337, as amended, that projects likely to have significant effects on the environment, as referred to in Article 4 of the directive read in conjunction with Annexes I and II thereto, must be made subject to an assessment with regard to their effects before (multi-stage) development consent is given (see, to that effect, Case C-201/02 *Wells* [2004] ECR I-723, paragraph 42).

104. In that regard, the Court stated in *Wells*, at paragraph 52, that where national law provides for a consent procedure comprising more than one stage, one involving a principal decision and the other involving an implementing decision which cannot extend beyond the parameters set by the principal decision, the effects which a project may have on the environment must be identified and assessed at the time of the procedure relating to the principal decision. It is only if those effects are not identifiable until the time of the procedure relating to the implementing decision that the assessment should be carried out in the course of that procedure.

105. In the present case, the rules at issue provide that an environmental impact assessment in respect of a project may be carried out only at the initial outline planning permission stage, and not at the later reserved matters stage.

106. Those rules are therefore contrary to Articles 2(1) and 4(2) of Directive 85/337, as amended. The United Kingdom has thus failed to fulfil its obligation to transpose those provisions into domestic law.

This again is a purposive interpretation—the point is that Member States must always have in mind their Article 2(1) obligation.

An implication of these cases is that Article 2(1) doesn't only have implications for how the Directive is interpreted but also for Member State decision-making in relation to projects likely to have a significant effect on the environment. This, as we shall see in Section 4.3, means that giving legal effect to the Directive in Member States' legal systems can have important implications.

One word of caution before moving on. The purposive interpretation of the Court does have limits, particularly pragmatic ones. This can be seen the case of *Mellor*,[35] discussed in Section 4.2. Likewise, it can be seen in the interpretation of different aspects of the Directive.[36] These limits are implicit in Article 2(1) in that the focus of the Court's purposive interpretation is upon ensuring that Member States comply with the duty in Article 2(1) not on the Directive writ large.

4.2 SCREENING AND THRESHOLDS

The most litigated issue before the CJEU has been what type of projects should be subject to an EIA. For reasons already highlighted this is not surprising. The legal issues in relation to screening largely fall into two categories. First, as with the *Dutch Dykes* case, there are issues to do with how particular terms in the Directive should be interpreted.[37]

Second, there are those questions concerning what the extent of Member State discretion in screening is. In particular, can a Member State exclude whole classes of projects listed in Annex II from the screening process if they don't think any of those projects will have a significant effect on the environment? The issue also arose in the *Dutch Dykes* case extracted here, which was before the 1997 amendments.

---

[35] Case C-75/08 *R (Mellor) v Secretary of State for Communities and Local Government* [2009] ECR I-3799.
[36] Case C-216/05 *Commission v Ireland* [2006] ECR I-787.
[37] See also Case C-133/94 *Commission v Belgium* [1996] ECR I-2323, paras 27–28.

**Case C-72/95 *Aannemersbedrijf P K Kraaijeveld BV and Others v
Gedeputeerde Staten Van Zuid-Holland***
[1996] ECR I-5403, paras 52–53

52. In a situation such as the present, it must be accepted that the Member State concerned was entitled to fix criteria relating to the size of dykes in order to establish which dyke projects had to undergo
an impact assessment. The question whether, in laying down such criteria, the Member State went
beyond the limits of its discretion cannot be determined in relation to the characteristics of a single
project. It depends on an overall assessment of the characteristics of projects of that nature which
could be envisaged in the Member State.

53. Thus a Member State which established criteria or thresholds at a level such that, in practice, all
projects relating to dykes would be exempted in advance from the requirement of an impact assessment would exceed the limits of its discretion under Articles 2(1) and 4(2) of the directive unless all
projects excluded could, when viewed as a whole, be regarded as not being likely to have significant
effects on the environment.

Thus, Member States can use thresholds in providing guidance to decision-makers but they cannot
exclude whole classes of projects. The starting point for understanding a Member State's obligation
is always Article 2(1). The *Dutch Dykes* case also illustrates that in cases where what is at issue is the
screening process in relation to a particular project then if that activity is excluded but does not have
a significant effect on the environment that does not mean that the threshold is a valid one. It must
be the case that all projects that fall below that threshold would not have a significant impact on the
environment. The higher the threshold the more difficult this will be to establish. Moreover, to make
matters more complicated, while thresholds tend to relate to the size of projects, that is only one
aspect of a project that will influence the environmental effect of that project. Location and nature are
also important, as are the cumulative effects of projects.[38] This latter issue is particularly important
because one possible way of avoiding the obligations of a Directive is to 'salami slice' a project into
smaller projects—none of which on their own are likely to have a significant effect but together do.

The need to consider these other effects was confirmed with the amendments to Article 4 in 1997.[39]
After its amendment Article 4(2) still allows for the use of thresholds but Annex III of the Directive
now provides far greater guidance on the factors that are required to be considered in the screening
process. A Member State cannot simply comply with the Directive by putting in place a set of rules
that list when a project is, or is not, deemed to be likely to significantly affect the environment. Rather,
a Member State must be constantly guided by Article 2(1) and they 'must adopt all measures necessary
to ensure that' projects that should be subject to an ES are so. There must be an active consideration of
whether a specific project is likely to significantly affect the project. A national decision-maker cannot
say the reason why a project that falls into Annex II does not need to be subject to an ES is because
national rules say it doesn't. Rather, the required approach is that a decision-maker must, by a consideration of all the factors listed now in Annex III, determine whether a particular project is not likely
to significantly affect the environment.

None of this means that Member States cannot lay down rules or set thresholds but that they will
exceed the 'margins of their discretion' if such thresholds exclude projects that are likely to have a
significant effect on the environment. From a practical perspective this means that the role of such
thresholds will be limited. It also means that from the perspective of thinking about EIA as a process,

---

[38] Council Directive 97/11/EC [1997] OJ L73/5. Also see C-392/96 *Commission v Ireland* [1999] ECR I-5901.
[39] See Section 3.2.

what the CJEU is emphasizing is the active exercise of discretion as opposed to the engagement with a formulaic course of action. Thinking of EIA in process terms is not to say that there is no discretion on the part of Member States, but the opposite. Such discretion exists and the Directive requires it to be exercised. The 'end' in Article 288 TFEU terms is the explicit and careful consideration of environmental impacts in specific projects. This can be seen in the *Abraham v Région Wallonne* case.

Case C-2/07 *Abraham v Région Wallonne*
[2008] ECR I-1197, paras 29–40

29. By its second question the national court asks, in essence, whether works relating to the infrastructure of an existing airport whose runway is already more than 2 100 metres in length fall with the scope of point 12 of Annex II, read in conjunction with point 7 of Annex I, to Directive 85/337, in its original version.

30. Pursuant to point 12 of Annex II in the version prior to Directive 97/11, 'modifications to development projects included in Annex I' constitute projects subject to Article 4(2). Point 7 of Annex I refers to the 'construction [...] of airports [...] with a basic runway length of 2 100 m or more'.

31. Société de développement et de promotion de l'aéroport de Liège-Bierset, TNT Express Worldwide and the Kingdom of Belgium submit that it necessarily follows from that wording that only modifications to the 'construction' of an airport with a runway length of 2 100 metres or more are covered and not modifications to an existing airport.

32. The Court has frequently pointed out, however, that the scope of Directive 85/337 is wide and its purpose very broad (see, to that effect, Case C-72/95 *Kraaijeveld and Others* [1996] ECR I-5403, paragraph 31, and Case C-435/97 *WWF and Others* [1999] ECR I-5613, paragraph 40). It would be contrary to the very objective of Directive 85/337 to exclude works to improve or extend the infrastructure of an existing airport from the scope of Annex II on the ground that Annex I covers the 'construction of airports' and not 'airports' as such. Such an interpretation would indeed allow all works to modify a pre-existing airport, regardless of their extent, to fall outside the obligations resulting from Directive 85/337 and would, in that regard, thus deprive Annex II to Directive 85/337 of all effect.

33. Consequently, point 12 of Annex II, read in conjunction with point 7 of Annex I, must be regarded as also encompassing works to modify an existing airport.

34. That interpretation is in no way called into question by the fact that Directive 97/11 has replaced point 12 of Annex II to Directive 85/337 with a new point 13, which expressly designates 'any change or extension of projects listed in Annex I or Annex II, already authorised, executed or in the process of being executed ...' as a project subject to Article 4(2) of Directive 85/337, as amended by Directive 97/11, whereas point 12 of Annex II merely referred to 'modifications to development projects included in Annex I'. The new wording adopted by Directive 97/11, the fourth recital in the preamble to which makes reference to experience acquired in environmental impact assessment and stresses the need to introduce provisions designed to clarify, supplement and improve the rules on the assessment procedure, merely sets out with greater clarity the meaning to be given here to the original wording of Directive 85/337. The Community legislature's amendment cannot, therefore, warrant an *a contrario* interpretation of the directive in its original version.

35. In addition, the fact that the works at issue in the main proceedings do not concern the length of the runway is not relevant to the question whether they fall within the scope of point 12 of Annex II to Directive 85/337. Point 7 of Annex I to Directive 85/337 makes a point of defining the term 'airport' by reference to the definition given in Annex 14 to the Chicago Convention of 7 December 1994 on International Civil Aviation. Under that annex, an aerodrome is 'a defined area on land or water (including any buildings, installations and equipment) intended to be used either wholly or in part for the arrival, departure and surface movement of aircraft'.

36. It follows that all works relating to the buildings, installations or equipment of an airport must be considered to be works relating to the airport as such. For the application of point 12 of Annex II, read in conjunction with point 7 of Annex I, to Directive 85/337, that means that works to modify an airport with a runway length of 2 100 metres or more thus comprise not only works to extend the runway, but all works relating to the buildings, installations or equipment of that airport where they may be regarded, in particular because of their nature, extent and characteristics, as a modification of the airport itself. That is the case in particular for works aimed at significantly increasing the activity of the airport and air traffic.

37. Finally, it is appropriate to remind the national court that, although the second subparagraph of Article 4(2) of Directive 85/337 confers on Member States a measure of discretion to specify certain types of projects which will be subject to an assessment or to establish the criteria and/or thresholds applicable, the limits of that discretion are to be found in the obligation set out in Article 2(1) of the directive that projects likely, by virtue inter alia of their nature, size or location, to have significant effects on the environment are to be subject to an impact assessment (*Kraaijeveld and Others*, paragraph 50).

38. Thus, a Member State which establishes criteria and/or thresholds taking account only of the size of projects, without also taking their nature and location into consideration, would exceed the limits of its discretion under Articles 2(1) and 4(2) of Directive 85/337.

39. It is for the national court to establish that the competent authorities correctly assessed whether the works at issue in the main proceedings were to be subject to an environmental impact assessment.

40. The answer to the second question must therefore be that point 12 of Annex II, read in conjunction with point 7 of Annex I, to Directive 85/337, in their original version, also encompasses works to modify the infrastructure of an existing airport, without extension of the runway, where they may be regarded, in particular because of their nature, extent and characteristics, as a modification of the airport itself. That is the case in particular for works aimed at significantly increasing the activity of the airport and air traffic. It is for the national court to establish that the competent authorities correctly assessed whether the works at issue in the main proceedings were to be subject to an environmental impact assessment.

We have included the factual analysis in this extract because it provides a useful illustration of how the CJEU's reasoning works in practice. Again the way in which Article 2(1) dominates the reasoning can be seen.

This case concerns how discretion is exercised in relation to Article 4(2). An associated issue is how a Member State must show that they have undertaken screening. In particular, must they give reasons? This question arose in the *R (Mellor) v Secretary of State for Communities and Local Government* case. Note how the Court integrates this question with their previous case law as well as emphasizing the role of the individual in being able to challenge a decision.

Case C-75/08 *R (Mellor) v Secretary of State for Communities and Local Government*
[2009] ECR I-3799, paras 51–61

51. It is thus clear from the objectives of Directive 85/337 that the competent national authorities, when they receive a request for development consent for an Annex II project, must carry out a specific evaluation as to whether, taking account of the criteria set out in Annex III to that directive, an EIA should be carried out.

52. Thus the Court, in its judgment of 10 June 2004 in *Commission* v *Italy*, cited above, found that the Italian Republic had failed to fulfil its obligations under Directive 85/337, since it was clear from all the evidence which had been submitted to the Court that the competent authorities had not carried out 'screening' of the need for an assessment, provided for in Italian legislation to ensure application of Article 4(2) and (3) of Directive 85/337.

53. In that judgment, the obligation arising from Article 4(2) of Directive 85/337 to ensure that a project does not require an assessment before deciding to dispense with such an assessment was at issue.

54. As there was nothing in the evidence in the case-file submitted to the Court to indicate that such an evaluation had taken place in the course of the administrative consent procedure for a bypass project, the Court held that a failure to fulfil obligations resulting from Directive 85/337, as alleged by the Commission, was established.

55. The Court pointed out, moreover, in paragraph 49 of that judgment, that the determination by which the competent authority takes the view that a project's characteristics do not require it to be subjected to an EIA must contain or be accompanied by all the information that makes it possible to check that it is based on adequate screening, carried out in accordance with the requirements of Directive 85/337.

56. It does not follow, however, from Directive 85/337, or from the case-law of the Court, in particular, from that judgment, that a determination not to subject a project to an EIA must, itself, contain the reasons for which the competent authority determined that an assessment was unnecessary.

57. It is apparent, however, that third parties, as well as the administrative authorities concerned, must be able to satisfy themselves that the competent authority has actually determined, in accordance with the rules laid down by national law, that an EIA was or was not necessary.

58. Furthermore, interested parties, as well as other national authorities concerned, must be able to ensure, if necessary through legal action, compliance with the competent authority's screening obligation. That requirement may be met, as in the main proceedings, by the possibility of bringing an action directly against the determination not to carry out an EIA.

59. In that regard, effective judicial review, which must be able to cover the legality of the reasons for the contested decision, presupposes in general, that the court to which the matter is referred may require the competent authority to notify its reasons. However where it is more particularly a question of securing the effective protection of a right conferred by Community law, interested parties must also be able to defend that right under the best possible conditions and have the possibility of deciding, with a full knowledge of the relevant facts, whether there is any point in applying to the courts. Consequently, in such circumstances, the competent national authority is under a duty to inform them of the reasons on which its refusal is based, either in the decision itself or in a subsequent communication made at their request (see Case 222/86 *Heylens and Others* [1987] ECR 4097, paragraph 15).

60. That subsequent communication may take the form, not only of an express statement of the reasons, but also of information and relevant documents being made available in response to the request made.

61. In the light of the foregoing, the answer to the first question is that Article 4 of Directive 85/337 must be interpreted as not requiring that a determination, that it is unnecessary to subject a project falling within Annex II to that directive to an EIA, should itself contain the reasons for the competent authority's decision that the latter was unnecessary. However, if an interested party so requests, the competent administrative authority is obliged to communicate to him the reasons for the determination or the relevant information and documents in response to the request made.

4.3 THE DIRECT EFFECT OF THE DIRECTIVE

Implicit in the analysis in Section 4.2 is the fact that Article 2(1) must have direct effect and the CJEU has clearly ruled that this is indeed the case.[40] The problem was that when they did this in the mid 1990s, the legal obligations in the EA Directive did not accord with what was traditionally understood as the test for direct effect. Historically there was a presumption that for a provision to have direct effect it must normally give rise to an individual right.[41] There are, however, no conventional individual rights given under the EA Directive except the provisions of Article 6 in relation to public participation. Second, the Directive gives considerable discretion to Member States, which was again is contrary to the traditional principles of direct effect that states that provisions only have direct effect when they are negative, precise, and unconditional.[42]

The assertion by the Court that obligations in the EA Directive did have direct effect attracted considerable attention from lawyers and academics. Some saw it as a variation on direct effect[43] and others thought it was 'not direct effect in the traditional sense and it would perhaps be as well to find another formula to avoid confusion'.[44] Others still saw the reasoning as problematic.[45] This discussion about direct effect was overlapping with other developments in direct effect doctrine more generally.[46] What can be seen in the *Luxembourg v Linster* case is that the EA Directive is a focal point for a more general discussion by the Advocate General about the legal effect of Directives.

Case C-287/98 *Luxembourg v Linster*
[2000] ECR I-6917, Opinion of AG Leger, paras 63–68, ECJ, 31–39

The Facts

The government of Luxembourg starting proceedings to appropriate the land of the Linsters for the building of a motorway, the authorisation of which had been granted by the legislature who had decided that an ES was not necessary. The Linsters argued in defence that an ES was necessary and the building of the motorway was in breach of Art 5(1) and 6(2) of the directive.

AG Leger

63. Where the direct effect of a directive is not clear cut, the Court's case-law attempts to preserve the full effectiveness of the Community rules by other means, which seek both to attain that objective and not to call into question the nomenclature of Community measures given in Article 189 [now Article 288 TFEU] of the Treaty.

64. In short, where one of the parties to proceedings before a national court seeks recognition of a right under a directive which has not been transposed and cannot have direct effect in domestic law,

---

[40] Case C-72/95 *Aannemersbedrijf P K Kraaijeveld BV and Others v Gedeputeerde Staten Van Zuid-Holland* [1996] ECR I-5403.

[41] Case 8/81 *Becker v Finanzamt Munster-Innenstadt* [1982] ECR 53.

[42] *van Gend en Loos* (n 4).

[43] Jan Jans, *European Environmental Law* (Europa Law Publishing 2000) 174.

[44] David Edward, 'Foreword', in Jane Holder (ed), *The Impact of EC Environmental Law in the United Kingdom* (Kluwer International 1997) xiv.

[45] Derek Wyatt, 'Litigating Community Environmental Law—Thoughts On the Direct Effect Doctrine' (1998) 10 JEL 8, 18.

[46] For example, Case C-194/94 *CIA Security International SA v Signalson SA* [1996] ECR I-2201; Case C-443/98 *Unilever Italia SpA v Central Food SpA* [2000] ECR I-7535.

it appears that it is not possible for the ability to plead substitution to result in application of the directive. In that situation, the party concerned can only opt for a solution which enables him to derive the appropriate consequences from the directive's precedence over domestic law, without guaranteeing him full application of Community law. The two ways in which the directive can be pleaded seek to give the individual the means of invoking, by differing means and to differing extents, the relevant provisions of the directive, either by influencing the interpretation of domestic law or by using it as a basis for an action for reparation.

65. It is therefore possible now to talk of 'minimum enforceability' where the 'greater enforceability' provided by recognition of direct effect cannot operate.

66. Those judgments, however, fall into the same category, since they derive from actions brought by parties relying directly on rights introduced for their benefit by a directive. The solutions adopted by the Court of Justice in that regard result from the finding, after close analysis of the content of the provisions in question, that they cannot have direct effect.

67. It seems to me that a case such as that before the court making the present reference is of a different nature and therefore calls for a different solution. In the proceedings before that court, the intention of the parties is to challenge the rule which it is sought to apply to them, relying on Directive 85/337 in support of their claim, rather than to seek the Directive's direct application. The main proceedings correspond to the logic of the ability to plead exclusion'.

68. In other words, it is for the Linsters less a question of relying on a subjective (individual) right which they seek to enforce than of applying to the national court for review of whether domestic law is in accordance with the relevant Community law, a process which may result in invalidation of the national rule.

I would point out in this connection that in the judgment in *Verbond van Nederlandse Ondernemingen*, cited above, as in the judgments which refer to it, the Court has indicated that '...the individual invokes a provision of a directive before a national court in order that the latter shall rule whether the competent national authorities...have kept within the limits as to their discretion set out in the directive'.

The ECJ

31. With regard to the right of a national court, responsible for reviewing the legality of a procedure for the expropriation in the public interest of property belonging to private individuals, to take account of a directive which has not been fully transposed, notwithstanding the expiry of the time-limit laid down for that purpose, in order to review whether certain formalities laid down by that directive have been complied with, it should be recalled that, according to the third paragraph of Article 189 [now Art 249] of the Treaty, A directive shall be binding, as to the result to be achieved, upon each Member State to which it is addressed, but shall leave to the national authorities the choice of form and methods.

32. In that regard the Court has held in a number of cases that it would be incompatible with the binding effect conferred on directives by that provision to exclude, as a matter of principle, any possibility for those concerned to rely on the obligation which directives impose. Particularly where the Community authorities have, by directive, imposed on Member States the obligation to pursue a particular course of conduct, the effectiveness of such an act would be diminished if individuals were prevented from relying on it in legal proceedings and if national courts were prevented from taking it into consideration as a matter of Community law in determining whether the national legislature, in exercising its choice as to the form and methods for implementing the directive, had kept within the limits of its discretion set by the directive (see Case 51/76 *Verbond van Nederlandse Ondernemingen v Inspecteur der Invoerrechten en Accijnzen* [1977] ECR 113, paragraphs 22, 23 and 24, *Kraaijeveld and Others*, cited above, paragraph 56, and Case C-435/97 *WWF and Others v Autonome Provinz Bozen and Others* [1999] ECR I-5613, paragraph 69).

33. As regards, more specifically, the limits of the discretion set by Directive 85/337, the Member States are required, under Article 2 thereof, to adopt all measures necessary to ensure that projects likely to have significant effects on the environment are made subject to an assessment with regard to their effects before consent is given.

34. Construction of a motorway is a project falling within a class in Annex I, which means that, in accordance with Article 4(1) of the Directive, it must be the subject of an assessment.

35. Article 5 of the Directive requires the Member States to adopt the necessary measures to ensure that the developer supplies information, the minimum items of which are specified in Article 5(2). Under Article 6(2), they must ensure that there is public access to the request for consent to carry out the project and to the information supplied by the developer, and that members of the public have the opportunity to express an opinion before the project is initiated.

36. It is true that Article 5(1) of the Directive allows the Member States some discretion in implementing the Community provision at national level since it states that the Member States are to adopt the necessary measures to ensure that the developer supplies the required information where they consider, first, that the information is relevant to a given stage of the consent procedure and to the specific characteristics of a particular project or type of project and, second, that a developer may reasonably be required to compile that information.

37. However, this discretion, which a Member State may exercise when transposing that provision into national law, does not preclude judicial review of the question whether it has been exceeded by the national authorities (see, in particular, *Verbond van Nederlandse Ondernemingen*, cited above, paragraphs 27, 28 and 29, and *Kraaijeveld and Others*, cited above, paragraph 59).

38. It follows that the provisions of the Directive may be taken into account by national courts in order to review whether the national legislature has kept within the limits of the discretion set by it.

39. The answer to the first question must therefore be that a national court, called on to examine the legality of a procedure for the expropriation in the public interest, in connection with the construction of a motorway, of immovable property belonging to a private individual, may review whether the national legislature kept within the limits of the discretion set by the Directive, in particular where prior assessment of the environmental impact of the project has not been carried out, the information gathered in accordance with Article 5 has not been made available to the public and the members of the public concerned have not had an opportunity to express an opinion before the project is initiated, contrary to the requirements of Article 6(2) of the Directive.

What can be seen in this case is a focus on what the Member State's obligations are as opposed to what rights have been created. This is not to render the earlier case law irrelevant but, rather, as the Advocate General recognizes, there are now two different categories of direct effect cases—substitution cases, which are the more traditional direct effect cases, and exclusion cases into which the EIA cases fall. The extract from Lenz and others considers the latter.

Miriam Lenz, Dora Sif Tynes and Lorna Young, 'Horizontal What? Back to Basics' (2000) 25 European L Rev 509, 517

What then unites the cases in which this check [the traditional test for direct effect] is dispensed with? It has been suggested that the common thread is the fact that what the applicants were seeking was the mere dis-application of a conflicting national provision, rather than the direct application of a Community measure. The decisions in these cases revolved around the margin of appreciation left to a Member State when implementing Community law. Exceeding this discretion will thus lead to the setting aside of a national measure; for example in *Kraaijeveld* a construction project had to be reassessed as to its potential environmental impact. The question in these cases therefore seems to have been not whether the directive had direct effect as such, but rather the more basic issue of whether the supremacy of Community law called for the subordination of the contradictory national provision.

Thus, the case law on the direct effect of the EA Directive reflects a more general shift in thinking about EU law obligations. The comments of Edward, then a judge of the CJEU, makes this point well.

David Edward, 'Direct Effect: Myth, Mess or Mystery' in Jolande Prinssen and Annette Schrauwen (eds) *Direct Effect: Rethinking a Classic of EC Legal Doctrine* (Europa Publishing 2002) 13

The analysis should always start with the obligation, an obligation on whom, to do what and by when. If you start from there, you will arrive at a coherent result. But the questions then to be solved are not the same in each case. In some cases the question is, does the individual have the right to sue for performance of the obligation? In other cases the question is, does the Community have the right to enforce the obligation? And there may be a series of different problems to which the same apparent reasoning is applied.

As I have said, I do not think that, put in that way, the questions at issue are materially different in a great many cases from questions that arise in national law. 'Direct effect' (using that expression in a broad way) provides us with criteria for selecting or rejecting the norms to be applied for clarifying the scope of judicial competence.

The importance of Article 4(3) of the TEU should also be stressed here. Obligations on Member States exist not only because of the Directive itself but because of the obligation on Member States to ensure the fulfilment on their obligations under the Treaty.

Another issue concerning direct effect raised by the EA Directive is whether a challenge by a third party to the decision of a public decision-maker not to require an ES amounts to a form of horizontal direct effect and therefore is not allowed. This has been the subject of legal argument in national courts[47] and was addressed by the CJEU in *Wells*. The CJEU also addressed the issue of what responsibility a Member State has on remedying breaches of EU law. The facts were explained in Section 4.1.

Case C-201/02 *R (Wells) v Secretary of State for Transport,*
Local Government and the Regions
[2004] ECR I-723, paras 56–58, 63–70

56. As to that submission, the principle of legal certainty prevents directives from creating obligations for individuals. For them, the provisions of a directive can only create rights (see Case 152/84 *Marshall* [1986] ECR 723, paragraph 48). Consequently, an individual may not rely on a directive against a Member State where it is a matter of a State obligation directly linked to the performance of another obligation falling, pursuant to that directive, on a third party (see, to this effect, Case C-221/88 *Busseni*

---

[47] For example, *R v Durham County Council, ex p Huddleston* [2000] 1 WLR 1484 (CA).

[1990] ECR I-495, paragraphs 23 to 26, and Case C-97/96 *Daihatsu Deutschland* [1997] ECR I-6843, paragraphs 24 and 26).

57. On the other hand, mere adverse repercussions on the rights of third parties, even if the repercussions are certain, do not justify preventing an individual from invoking the provisions of a directive against the Member State concerned (see to this effect, in particular, Case 103/88 *Fratelli Costanzo* [1989] ECR 1839, paragraphs 28 to 33, *WWF and Others*, cited above, paragraphs 69 and 71, Case C-194/94 *CIA Security International* [1996] ECR I-2201, paragraphs 40 to 55, Case C-201/94 *Smith & Nephew and Primecrown* [1996] ECR I-5819, paragraphs 33 to 39, and Case C-443/98 *Unilever* [2000] ECR I-7535, paragraphs 45 to 52).

58. In the main proceedings, the obligation on the Member State concerned to ensure that the competent authorities carry out an assessment of the environmental effects of the working of the quarry is not directly linked to the performance of any obligation which would fall, pursuant to Directive 85/337, on the quarry owners. The fact that mining operations must be halted to await the results of the assessment is admittedly the consequence of the belated performance of that State's obligations. Such a consequence cannot, however, as the United Kingdom claims, be described as inverse direct effect of the provisions of that directive in relation to the quarry owners. [...]

63. The United Kingdom Government contends that, in the circumstances of the main proceedings, there is no obligation on the competent authority to revoke or modify the permission issued for the working of Conygar Quarry or to order discontinuance of the working.

64. As to that submission, it is clear from settled case-law that under the principle of cooperation in good faith laid down in Article 10 EC the Member States are required to nullify the unlawful consequences of a breach of Community law (see, in particular, Case 6/60 *Humblet* [1960] ECR 559, at 569, and Joined Cases C-6/90 and C-9/90 *Francovich and Others* [1991] ECR I-5357, paragraph 36). Such an obligation is owed, within the sphere of its competence, by every organ of the Member State concerned (see, to this effect, Case C-8/88 *Germany* v *Commission* [1990] ECR I-2321, paragraph 13).

65. Thus, it is for the competent authorities of a Member State to take, within the sphere of their competence, all the general or particular measures necessary to ensure that projects are examined in order to determine whether they are likely to have significant effects on the environment and, if so, to ensure that they are subject to an impact assessment (see, to this effect, Case C-72/95 *Kraaijeveld and Others* [1996] ECR I-5403, paragraph 61, and *WWF and Others*, cited above, paragraph 70). Such particular measures include, subject to the limits laid down by the principle of procedural autonomy of the Member States, the revocation or suspension of a consent already granted, in order to carry out an assessment of the environmental effects of the project in question as provided for by Directive 85/337.

66. The Member State is likewise required to make good any harm caused by the failure to carry out an environmental impact assessment.

67. The detailed procedural rules applicable are a matter for the domestic legal order of each Member State, under the principle of procedural autonomy of the Member States, provided that they are not less favourable than those governing similar domestic situations (principle of equivalence) and that they do not render impossible in practice or excessively difficult the exercise of rights conferred by the Community legal order (principle of effectiveness) (see to this effect, inter alia, Case C-312/93 *Peterbroeck* [1995] ECR I-4599, paragraph 12, and Case C-78/98 *Preston and Others* [2000] ECR I-3201, paragraph 31).

68. So far as the main proceedings are concerned, if the working of Conygar Quarry should have been subject to an assessment of its environmental effects in accordance with the requirements of Directive 85/337, the competent authorities are obliged to take all general or particular measures for remedying the failure to carry out such an assessment.

69. In that regard, it is for the national court to determine whether it is possible under domestic law for a consent already granted to be revoked or suspended in order to subject the project in question to an assessment of its environmental effects, in accordance with the requirements of Directive 85/337, or alternatively, if the individual so agrees, whether it is possible for the latter to claim compensation for the harm suffered.

70. The answer to the third question must therefore be that under Article 10 EC the competent authorities are obliged to take, within the sphere of their competence, all general or particular measures for remedying the failure to carry out an assessment of the environmental effects of a project as provided for in Article 2(1) of Directive 85/337.

Again we can see here that the CJEU is seeking to ensure the effectiveness of the Directive. They emphasize that the main responsibility for EIA is on the public decision-maker and that, notwithstanding the principle of procedural autonomy, there is a duty on the Member State to remedy a breach of EU law. This second point is particularly important because it requires national courts to provide remedies in situations such as these even when the national law does not traditionally require it.

FURTHER READING AND QUESTIONS

1. Consider the following fact situations. Would such implementation held to be a breach of Article 2(1) and Article 4(2) by the CJEU?

   a. Member State X requires all underground mining projects (listed in Annex II) to be subject to an EIA.

   b. In Member State Y, marinas are only required to be subject to assessment if they exceed seventy berths. The Member State says this threshold has been based on a series of scientific studies showing there is no significant environmental impact below that threshold.

   c. In Member State Z decision-makers are required to consider whether any project is likely to have a significant impact on the environment. There has been no transposition of Annex I or II but there has been a transposition of Annex III.

2. For further discussion of the concept of rights in EU law see Chris Hilson and Tony Downes, 'Making Sense of Rights: Community Rights in EC Law' (1999) 24 European L Rev 121; and Sacha Prechal and Leigh Hancher, 'Individual Environmental Rights: Conceptual Pollution in EU Environmental Law?' (2002) 2 YEEL 89.

---

5 EIA IN ENGLAND

EIA has been part of English law since 1988 and the development of the legal and administrative framework for EIA has been closely interrelated. In particular, court decisions have had a powerful impact on how EIA has been understood in England. In this section we consider the Town and Country Planning (Environmental Impact Assessment) Regulations 2011 (the EIA Regulations) and in Section 6 how the Court has interpreted and applied the Directive. It should also be noted that the Infrastructure Planning (Environmental Impact Assessment) Regulations 2009 (as amended) apply to nationally significant infrastructure projects. Those Regulations are beyond the scope of this chapter.[48]

---

[48] See Section 1.3 of Chapter 18 for a discussion of the regime for nationally significant infrastructure projects.

In England the EA Directive was primarily implemented into law as part of the planning regime in 1988.[49] The original regulations (and their 1999 replacement)[50] have now been superseded by the 2011 Regulations. The 2011 Regulations apply to England only. All Regulations were passed under s 2(2) of the European Communities Act 1972.[51]

The central obligation of the Regulations is set out in Regulation 3(4). It states:

> 3(4) The relevant planning authority or the Secretary of State or an inspector shall not grant planning permission or subsequent consent pursuant to an application to which this regulation applies unless they have first taken the environmental information into consideration, and they shall state in their decision that they have done so.

'An application to which this regulation applies' is defined in Regulation 3(1):

> (a) to every application for planning permission for EIA development received by the authority with whom it is lodged on or after the commencement of these Regulations;
>
> (b) to every application for planning permission for EIA development lodged by an authority pursuant to regulation 3 or 4 (applications for planning permission) of the General Regulations on or after that date;
>
> (c) to every subsequent application in respect of EIA development received by the authority with whom it is lodged on or after the commencement of these Regulations; and
>
> (d) to every subsequent application in respect of EIA development lodged by an authority pursuant to regulation 11 of the General Regulations on or after the commencement of these Regulations;

Regulation 2 defines both EIA development and EIA application.

> 'EIA application' is:
>
> (a) an application for planning permission for EIA development; or
>
> (b) a subsequent application in respect of EIA development;
>
> 'EIA development' means development which is either—
>
> (a) Schedule 1 development; or
>
> (b) Schedule 2 development likely to have significant effects on the environment by virtue of factors such as its nature, size or location;

Schedules 1 and 2 accord with Annexes 1 and 2 of the Directive. With that said, note that the 2011 Regulations refer to categories of 'development' not 'projects' as the Annexes of the Directives do. This is because, as we saw in Section 4.1 of Chapter 18, planning law's scope is defined by what a 'development' is.[52]

The general EIA process has already been described in relation to the Directive but it is worth noting in brief a few features of how EIA operates alongside the planning process. The first is that there are three different ways in which a development may be subject to the EIA process.

---

[49] It should be noted that the Directive does apply to some projects that don't require consent under this regime and they need to be addressed separately.

[50] Town and Country Planning (Assessment of Environmental Effects) Regulations 1988 and Town and Country Planning (Environmental Impact Assessment) (England and Wales) Regulations 1999.

[51] Although note 71A TCPA 1990.   [52] s 55 TCPA 1990.

1. A developer may decide themselves that a development is an EIA development and submit an EIA as part of the process.[53] This is particularly likely in cases where a development falls squarely into the categories in Schedule 1.

2. A planning authority may undertake a 'screening opinion'[54]

3. The Secretary of State may also direct whether a development is an EIA development.[55]

Developers can request screening opinions and screening directions[56] and the Regulations set out a procedure for the consideration of both opinions and directions.[57] Planning authorities can also 'screen' developments where it 'appears to them' 'an application which is before them for determination is a Schedule 1 application or a Schedule 2 application' and there has been no screening opinion or direction.[58] In considering a Schedule 2 development, the factors in Schedule III (which mirrors Annex III of the Directive) must be have had regard to. The discretion of the planning authority and the Secretary of State in regards to screening will be clearly governed by the Directive and the CJEU's case law. As screening is also heavily contested, it has given rise to a considerable body of case law in the English courts as well. This will be discussed further in Section 6.

The bulk of the regulation provides a framework for regulating the EIA process including the procedures for scoping,[59] publicity,[60] and a range of different types of developments, including the review of old mining and minerals permissions (ROMPS)[61] and activities having significant transboundary effects. Of particular note is Regulation 31, which deals with unauthorized development.[62]

> 31. The Secretary of State or an inspector shall not grant planning permission or subsequent consent under section 177(1)(1) (grant or modification of planning permission on appeals against enforcement notices) in respect of unauthorised EIA development unless the Secretary of State or inspector has first taken the environmental information into consideration, and shall state in the decision that they have done so.

This is significant because, as we saw in Chapter 18, the consideration of the validity of development is often in the context of enforcement. The failure to apply for planning permission thus does not mean that a development carrying out an EIA development can escape the obligations under the Directive. The Regulation is thus integrating the Directive into the planning regime.

As the Regulations are integrated into the planning system then the operation of the Regulation is primarily dependent on the discretion of local planning authorities (LPAs). Studies by researchers have show that this does not always occur as it should. The late Joe Weston carried out a number of very thoughtful studies on this issue and extracted here are conclusions from one of his most recent studies before he died.

Joe Weston, 'Screening for Environmental Impact Assessment Projects in England: What Screening?' (2011) 29 Impact Assessment and Appraisal 90, 96.

> From the examination of planning application documents provided on local authority websites it has been found that very many LPAs (the majority in this sample) are simply not applying the EIA Regulations where they should be and, even where projects are being screened for EIA, the tests for significance

---

[53] Regulation 4(2)(a).   [54] Regulation 4(2)(b).   [55] Regulation (3)–(4).
[56] Regulation 5.   [57] Regulations 5–6.   [58] Regulation 7.
[59] Part 4.   [60] Part 5.   [61] Part 10.   [62] Part 11.

that are applied are poorly justified and in some cases in conflict with the rulings of important court judgements [sic].

The reasons for this will be varied and we can easily claim, as is often argued in papers like this, that there is a need for more training and education in EIA. We have in fact had 22 years in which to teach the rudiments of screening and apparently have still not managed to reach the right people. Most, if not all, planning courses in universities include EIA as a part of the programme and continuous professional development courses are on offer all over the country on an almost continuous basis. [...]

A further explanation for the findings from this research could simply be a deep level of incompetence within English LPAs and an inability to recognize their statutory duties and the need to properly record and make public the results of their screening decisions. Perhaps, though, there is another, more deep-seated, reason why so many LPAs are not screening projects for EIA. When EIA was first introduced into the UK planning system there was a good deal of resistance from planners who argued that they had always considered the environmental implications of projects in their decision-making. Indeed, the first decade or so of implementation of the EIA Directive in the UK was marked by a minimalist approach. These research findings, both in the absence of evidence of screening and the poor application of screening criteria, suggest that the culture of 'resistance' or 'disownment' remains strong. The fact that in some cases LPAs were asking for reports on individual environmental impacts and yet not asking for a full EIA suggests that the avoidance 'if at all possible' culture, found in the 2000 study, is an important, and often neglected, factor in assessing the effectiveness of EIA.

Weston's analysis is a reminder that there is a need to not just study law in books but also how it is applied in practice. Weston's ultimate conclusion was that studies such as these highlight the need to re-theorize EIA.

FURTHER READING

1. For a further discussion of the implementation of the Directive in the EU see Jane Holder, *Environmental Assessment: The Regulation of Decision-Making* (OUP 2004).

---

6 THE EA DIRECTIVE IN THE ENGLISH COURTS

The EA Directive has been the subject of considerable litigation in the English courts. In this section we consider some different aspects of that case law, focusing particularly on cases concerning screening and the substantive review of discretion. However, before reviewing these cases, we need to understand the general approach of the English courts to the Directive.

6.1 THE GENERAL APPROACH

Before 2000, it is fair to say that the approach of the English courts to interpreting and implementing the EA Directive was minimalist.[63] The turning point in the case law was the House of Lords' decision in *Berkeley v Secretary of State for the Environment*.[64] That case concerned challenge to planning

---

[63] *R v Poole BC, ex p Beebee* [1991] JPL 643 (QB); *R v Secretary of State for the Environment ex parte Marson* [1998] Env LR 761 (CA).

[64] [2001] 2 AC 603.

permission for a controversial apartment development on the site of Fulham Football Club, which was situated on the banks of the River Thames. The challenge was on the grounds that there had been a failure to consider whether an ES was needed. The judge at first instance held that no ES was required. The Court of Appeal held that an ES should have been required but that as the preparation of the EIA would not have had any impact on the outcome of the decision, as the environmental issues had already been properly discussed, then the Secretary of State's decision should be upheld. The case was appealed to the House of Lords.

Berkeley v Secretary of State for the Environment and Others
[2001] 2 AC 603, 608 (Lord Bingham), 615–17 (Lord Hoffmann)

Lord Bingham

For reasons given in more detail by Lord Hoffmann, I do not in any event agree that there was substantial compliance with the requirements of the Directive and the Regulations in this case. It is quite true that consideration was given, over many years, to various schemes for developing this site and that the scheme for which permission was given was the subject of detailed, careful and informed consideration and wide consultation. But the cornerstone of the régime established by the Regulations is provision by the developer of an environmental statement as described in Schedule 3 to the Regulations, setting out (among other things) the data necessary to identify and assess the main effects which the development was likely to have on the environment. The developer provided no document which, in my view, met that requirement.

Lord Hoffmann

[...] I said in *Reg. v. North Yorkshire County Council, Ex parte Brown* [2000] 1 A.C. 397, 404; [1999] 2 W.L.R. 452, 458, that the purpose of the Directive was 'to ensure that planning decisions which may affect the environment are made on the basis of full information.' This was a concise statement, adequate in its context, but which needs for present purposes to be filled out. The Directive requires not merely that the planning authority should have the necessary information, but that it should have been obtained by means of a particular procedure, namely that of an EIA. And an essential element in this procedure is that what the Regulations call the 'environmental statement' by the developer should have been 'made available to the public' and that the public should have been 'given the opportunity to express an opinion' in accordance with article 6.2 of the Directive. As Advocate General Elmer said in *Commission of the European Communities v Federal Republic of Germany* (Case C-431/92) [1995] ECR I-2189, 2208-2209, para 35:

It must be emphasised that the provisions of the Directive are essentially of a procedural nature. By the inclusion of information on the environment in the consent procedure it is ensured that the environmental impact of the project shall be included in the public debate and that the decision as to whether consent is to be given shall be adopted on an appropriate basis.

The directly enforceable right of the citizen which is accorded by the Directive is not merely a right to a fully informed decision on the substantive issue. It must have been adopted on an appropriate basis and that requires the inclusive and democratic procedure prescribed by the Directive in which the public, however misguided or wrongheaded its views may be, is given an opportunity to express its opinion on the environmental issues. In a later case (*Aannemersbedrijf P K Kraaijeveld BV v Gedeputeerde Staten van Zuid- Holland* (Case C-72/95) [1996] ECR I-5403, 5427, para 70), Advocate General Elmer made this point again:

'Where a member state's implementation of the Directive is such that projects which are likely to have significant effects on the environment are not made the subject of an environmental impact assessment, the citizen is prevented from exercising his right to be heard.

Perhaps the best statement of this aspect of an EIA is to be found in the UK government publication 'Environmental Assessment: A Guide to the Procedures' (HMSO, 1989), p 4:

The general public's interest in a major project is often expressed as concern about the possibility of unknown or unforeseen effects. By providing a full analysis of the project's effects, an environmental statement can help to allay fears created by lack of information. At the same time it can help to inform the public on the substantive issues which the local planning authority will have to consider in reaching a decision. It is a requirement of the Regulations that the environmental statement must include a description of the project and its likely effects together with a summary in non-technical language. One of the aims of a good environmental statement should be to enable readers to understand for themselves how its conclusions have been reached, and to form their own judgments on the significance of the environmental issues raised by the project.

A court is therefore not entitled retrospectively to dispense with the requirement of an EIA on the ground that the outcome would have been the same or that the local planning authority or Secretary of State had all the information necessary to enable them to reach a proper decision on the environmental issues. Although section 288(5)(b), in providing that the court 'may' quash an ultra vires planning decision, clearly confers a discretion upon the court, I doubt whether, consistently with its obligations under European law, the court may exercise that discretion to uphold a planning permission which has been granted contrary to the provisions of the Directive. To do so would seem to conflict with the duty of the court under article 10 (ex article 5) of the EC Treaty to ensure fulfilment of the United Kingdom's obligations under the Treaty. In classifying a failure to conduct a requisite EIA for the purposes of section 288 as not merely non-compliance with a relevant requirement but as rendering the grant of permission ultra vires, the legislature was intending to confine any discretion within the narrowest possible bounds. It is exceptional even in domestic law for a court to exercise its discretion not to quash a decision which has been found to be ultra vires: see Glidewell LJ in Bolton Metropolitan Borough Council v Secretary of State for the Environment (1990) 61 P & CR 343, 353 Mr Elvin was in my opinion right to concede that nothing less than substantial compliance with the Directive could enable the planning permission in this case to be upheld.

9. Substantial compliance

The case upon which Mr Elvin relied for the submission that substantial compliance would do was Commission of the European Communities v Federal Republic of Germany (Case C-431/92) [1995] ECR I-2189. In that case the Federal Republic had failed to transpose the Directive into its domestic law by the stipulated date and had given consent to the construction of a power station without an EIA. It had however followed the procedures required by its own Bundesimmissionsschutzgesetz or Federal Pollution Protection Law. In enforcement proceedings under article 169 of the EC Treaty, the Commission conceded that, in complying with domestic procedures, the developer had in fact supplied all the information required by article 5(2) and Annex III of the Directive. It also conceded that the information had been made available to the public and that the public had been given an opportunity to express an opinion in accordance with Article 6. Advocate General Elmer considered and rejected the other points on which the Commission continued to maintain that there had been a failure to comply. He said, at p 2207, para 33, that 'the procedure followed in this specific case complied with all the requirements of the Directive'.

Commission v Germany (Case C-431/92) in my opinion establishes that an EIA by any other name will do as well. But it must in substance be an EIA. Can this be said of the procedure followed in the present case?

[...] I do not accept that this paper chase can be treated as the equivalent of an environmental statement. In the first place, I do not think it complies with the terms of the Directive. The point about the environmental statement contemplated by the Directive is that it constitutes a single and accessible compilation, produced by the applicant at the very start of the application process, of the relevant environmental information and the summary in non-technical language. It is true that article 6.3 gives member states a discretion as to the places where the information can be consulted, the way in which the public may be informed and the manner in which the public is to be consulted. But I do not think it allows member states to treat a disparate collection of documents produced by parties other than the developer and traceable only by a person with a good deal of energy and persistence as satisfying the requirement to make available to the public the Annex III information which should have been provided by the developer.

Lord Hope, Lord Hutton, and Lord Millett all agreed with both Lord Bingham and Lord Hoffmann.

Berkeley represented a watershed in the approach of English courts to EIA. This is for three reasons. First, the concept of 'substantial compliance' was a significant adjustment to the traditional principles of judicial review.[65] An obvious consequence of it is that it creates opportunities for challenging decisions and since *Berkeley* there has been a dramatic growth in judicial review challenges. The second important aspect of the *Berkeley* decision is that EU law principles became the starting point for analysing EIA. Lord Hoffmann's decision is an explicit and authoritative example of this approach. Since *Berkeley* English courts have been far more willing to consider the CJEU's EIA case law and, as such, the obligation set out in Article 2(1) of the Directive has been taken more seriously. Thus, while *Berkeley* was not a case about screening, its emphasis on Article 2(1) meant English courts would review the screening process more vigorously.

The third reason why *Berkeley* is such a significant decision is that Lord Hoffmann stated explicitly why the EIA process was important. He expanded his analysis in *R v North Yorkshire County Council, ex p Brown*,[66] where he characterized EIA primarily in terms of information provision. In *Berkeley* he, as Steele notes, emphasizes that 'the citizen has a right to be involved quite independently of whether the decision-maker believes that the citizen will be able to enhance the process or add anything of value'.[67]

Berkeley is essentially a case about the role that national courts play in implementing the EA Directive. What the case is not directly about is the nature of review. This issue has arisen far less in the cases, but it is important to think about because very different approaches can be taken to it. This can be seen in the Privy Council decision of *Belize Alliance of Conservation Non-Governmental Organizations v The Department of the Environment, Belize Electric Company Limited*[68] (the BACNGO

---

[65] See Section 4 of Chapter 7. But also see the judgment of Lord Carnwath in *Walton v Scottish Ministers* [2012] UKSC 44.

[66] [2000] 1 AC 397 (HL).

[67] Jenny Steele, 'Participation and Deliberation in Environmental Law: A Problem Solving Approach' (2001) 21 OJLS 415, 420.

[68] [2004] UKPC 6, [2004] Env LR 38.

case), which concerned an appeal from the Belize Court of Appeal. In that case Lord Hoffmann and Lord Walker took very different approaches to reviewing both the procedure and substance of EIA.

Belize Alliance of Conservation Non-Governmental Organizations v The Department of the Environment, Belize Electric Company Limited
[2004] UKPC 6, paras 12–13, 67–73 (Lord Hoffmann), 118–121 (Lord Walker)

The Facts

The Belize Alliance of Conservation Non Governmental Organisations (BACNGO) challenged the Belize government's decision to grant planning permission to BECOL for the building of a hydro-electric dam for which an EIA had been conducted. One of their arguments was that the EIA was inadequate because it contained factual errors in relation to the geology of the dam's region and because the government had asked for more information from the developer which the public had not had a chance to be consulted about. The Belize Court of Appeal did not accept their arguments and BACNGO appealed to the Privy Council.

Lord Hoffmann (for the majority)

12. [...] What each system [of EIA] attempts in its own way to secure is that a decision to authorise a project likely to have significant environmental effects is preceded by public disclosure of as much relevant information about such effects as can reasonably be obtained and the opportunity for public discussion of the issues which are raised.

13. What these systems also have in common is that they distinguish between the procedure to be followed in arriving at the decision and the merits of the decision itself. The former is laid down by statute and is binding upon the decision-making authority. The latter is entirely within the competence of that authority. As Linden JA said with reference to the Canadian legislation in *Bow Valley Naturalists Society v Minister of Canadian Heritage* [2001] 2 FC 461, 494 (in a passage quoted by the Chief Justice in this case):

'The Court must ensure that the steps in the Act are followed, but it must defer to the responsible authorities in their substantive determinations as to the scope of the project, the extent of the screening and the assessment of the cumulative effects in the light of the mitigating factors proposed. It is not for the judges to decide what projects are to be authorized but, as long as they follow the statutory process, it is for the responsible authorities'. [...]

67. The Chief Justice and the Court of Appeal were impressed with the thoroughness of the EIA in its survey of archaeological remains, wild life and plants. The possibility of unknown ruins, the birds, animals and plants at risk, were clearly identified. The proposals for mitigation show a studied avoidance of any attempt to gloss over the potential environmental damage.

68. Regulation 7 provides that 'the scope and extent of the [EIA] shall be determined by the DOE [Department of the Environment]'. It is for the DOE to approve the terms of reference (regulation 16) and decide whether the EIA complies with those terms. It is for the DOE to decide whether it is necessary to require further work or studies or supply further information. It appears to their Lordships to follow that the question of whether the EIA complies with Act and regulations, both in respect of providing the material for public discussion and of providing a proper basis for decision-making, is primarily entrusted to the DOE. The decision to accept the EIA should therefore not be set aside except on established principles of administrative law: compare Sullivan J in *R v Rochdale Metropolitan Borough*

Council, ex p Milne [2001] Env LR 406, 433. For that purpose it is necessary for the appellants to show that the DOE acted irrationally or in such a way as to frustrate the purpose which an EIA is intended to serve.

69. The ground upon which the appellants submit that they can satisfy this demanding requirement is that the DOE postponed consideration of matters which should have been contained in the EIA. But, as their Lordships have observed, that only raises the question of what should have been in the EIA. Both the Chief Justice and the Court of Appeal cited with approval the remarks of Cripps J in the Land and Environment Court of New South Wales in *Prineas v Forestry Commission of New South Wales* (1983) 49 LGRA 402, 417:

I do not think the [statute] ... imposes on a determining authority when preparing an environmental impact statement a standard of absolute perfection or a standard of compliance measured by no consideration other than whether it is possible in fact to carry out the investigation. I do not think the legislature directed determining authorities to ignore such matters as money, time, manpower etc. In my opinion, there must be imported into the statutory obligation a concept of reasonableness ... [P]rovided an environmental impact statement is comprehensive in its treatment of the subject matter, objective in its approach and meets the requirement that it alerts the decision maker and members of the public ... to the effect of the activity on the environment and the consequences to the community inherent in the carrying out or not carrying out of the activity, it meets the standards imposed by the regulations. The fact that the environmental impact statement does not cover every topic and explore every avenue advocated by experts does not necessarily invalidate it or require a finding that it does not substantially comply with the statute and the regulations.

70. Their Lordships also respectfully adopt these observations. It is not necessary that an EIA should pursue investigations to resolve every issue. This is not only common sense but contemplated by the terms of the Belize legislation itself. Thus regulation 5(f) says that an EIA should include an indication of 'gaps in knowledge and uncertainty which may be encountered in computing the required information" and regulation 19(b), prescribing the form of an EIA, says it should contain a summary which highlights the 'conclusions, areas of controversy and issues remaining to be resolved'.

71. Environmental control in Belize is an iterative process which does not stop with the approval of the EIA. The Act expressly provides for an approval subject to conditions (section 20(7)), as was granted in this case. An EIA is required to include a monitoring plan and the NEAC [National Environmental Appraisal Committee] is required to consider the need for a 'follow up programme'. It is therefore in their Lordships' opinion wrong to approach an EIA as if it represented the last opportunity to exercise any control over a project which might damage the environment.

72. The appellants placed reliance upon the decision of Harrison J in *R v Cornwall County Council, ex parte Hardy* [2001] Env LR 25. Their Lordships express no views upon the correctness of this decision as a matter of English (or perhaps European) law; it turned upon the interaction between the two European directives: the Directive on environmental assessments (85/337/EEC) and the Habitats Directive (92/43 EEC). The latter Directive provides for the strict protection of a certain species of bat. The developer wanted to fill in some mineshafts in which there was reason to believe that the bats might be living. The planning authority gave permission on condition that, before the shafts were filled, a survey should be undertaken to find out whether any bats were there. The judge decided that this was unreasonable. The terms of the Habitats Directive made it imperative that before planning permission was granted, an environmental assessment should have been undertaken, including a bat survey. A condition that such a survey be undertaken later ('when the same requirements for publicity and consultation do not apply') was not enough: para 62.

73. Their Lordships would only observe that the statutory background to this decision was altogether different from that which exists in Belize. In the present case, they consider it to be impossible to say that the EIA was inadequate to meet the requirements of the relevant legislation.

Lord Walker dissenting (Lord Steyn agreeing with him)

[...] 118. In this most unsatisfactory state of affairs a few essential points are clear. The geology in the EIA was seriously wrong, as both Mr Fabro and Dr Merritt now accept. The predominantly sandstone bedrock is probably capable of providing a satisfactory foundation for a dam but only if the new geological information is taken into account in the design. Under the EPA and the Regulations the design of such an important public works project was required to be included in the EIA, and should have been the subject of public consultation and public debate before approval, and before work started on the project. Instead there are to be changes in the design (a fact recently acknowledged by Dr Merritt and deposed to by the Inspector of Mines) but the nature of the changes has been withheld from the public. The appellant's case is, as Mr Clayton submitted and as I would accept, stronger than that of the successful appellant in *Berkeley v Secretary of State for the Environment* [2001] 2 AC 603. In that case all the relevant information was (one way or another) in the public domain, but only if the public embarked on a 'paper chase' (see at page 617). Here not even the most protracted and determined paper chase could have got at the true facts.

119. I would therefore have allowed the appeal and quashed the DoE's decision (embodied in the decision letter of 5 April 2002) to grant environmental clearance for the project. I would have done so on the ground that the EIA was so flawed by important errors about the geology of the site as to be incapable of satisfying the requirements of the EPA and the Regulations. These flaws were, on Mr Fabro's own evidence, known to him at the time of the decision. I would in the absence of a satisfactory undertaking grant an injunction restraining BECOL from continuing work on the project unless and until a corrected EIA is prepared for public consultation, and secures recommendation by NEAC and approval by the DoE.

120. In eloquent supplementary submissions made to the Board on behalf of the DoE the Attorney-General drew attention to what he called the economic and demographic realities of the case. Belize is a small country (its total population is about 250,000) and it has very limited economic resources. It needs foreign direct investment, and delay in the Chalillo dam project might, the Attorney-General said, mean that the project never went ahead. Its loss would be a grave blow to the country. He submitted that even if the EIA had identified the bedrock as sandstone, the design of the dam would not necessarily have been different. The Attorney-General also mentioned Mr Fabro's affidavit of 3 December 2003 and conceded that it might be inconsistent with the terms of his exchange of correspondence (letters of 30 May and 10 June 2003) with Mr Garel of BACONGO.

121. The Attorney-General's submissions call for respectful attention but they do not alter my view of what should be the outcome of the appeal. Belize has enacted comprehensive legislation for environmental protection and direct foreign investment, if it has serious environmental implications, must comply with that legislation. The rule of law must not be sacrificed to foreign investment, however desirable (indeed, recent history shows that in many parts of the world respect for the rule of law is an incentive, and disrespect for the rule of law can be a severe deterrent, to foreign investment). It is no answer to the erroneous geology in the EIA to say that the dam design would not necessarily have been different. The people of Belize are entitled to be properly informed about any proposals for alterations in the dam design before the project is approved and before work continues with its construction.

This case of course does not concern the EA Directive and English law. With that said, it is a useful case for understanding the challenges for courts in reviewing the EIA process. Lord Hoffmann's judgment is in a similar vein to his judgment in *Berkeley* in that his starting point for analysis is the nature of the EIA process. He also extends his analysis by considering EIA case law from other Commonwealth jurisdictions (Canada and Australia). Second, this case contains an excellent discussion about what the scope of judicial review should be. The different approaches of Lord Hoffmann and Lord Walker are quite striking. Lord Hoffmann stresses that the role of the Court is not to engage in factual review while Lord Walker sees that, in certain circumstances, it is. Both are taking different approaches to what their task should be. Lord Hoffmann is more concerned with procedure while Lord Walker is concerned with the methodological integrity of the decision.

Since *Berkeley* the case law concerning EIA has grown exponentially and the lower courts have constantly revisited the question of what should be the nature of the court's review in this area of law. As will be seen, it is an issue that is not yet resolved and nor is it likely to be. Section 6.2 considers the case law concerning screening and Section 6.3 discusses the case law in relation to environmental statements.

6.2 SCREENING

As already noted, screening is one of the most controversial aspects of EIA. This is due to its discretionary nature, the uncertain nature of prediction, and the fact that the outcome of a screening decision has serious consequences for developers and the wider public alike. If an ES is required there will be extra costs for the developers and the opportunity for the public to know and discuss the environmental consequences of a development. If no ES is required, the developer will have fewer costs but members of the public may be aggrieved because the opportunity for knowledge and discussion is lost.

The English courts have divided screening into two different steps. The first step is to consider whether a particular development is a Schedule I or Schedule II development. In *R (Goodman) v Lewisham LBC*[69] that step was conceptualized as a question of law and thus 'if the authority reaches an understanding of those expressions that is wrong as a matter of law, then the court must correct that error'.[70] The court's approach to the second step in screening however is not the same. The second step in screening only applies to Schedule II developments and requires a decision-maker to determine whether a Schedule II development is likely to have a significant impact on the environment.

R (Jones) v Mansfield District Council
[2003] EWCA Civ 1408 paras 14–18 (Dyson LJ)

The Facts

The applicant challenged planning permission for the development of an industrial development claiming that the local planning authority had erred in law by concluding that no EIA was required because the project would was not likely to have a significant impact on the environment. The administrative court concluded that the decision that an EIA was not required was lawful. That decision was appealed.

The CA

14. The judge said (para 7) that the question whether the development 'would be likely to have significant effects on the environment by virtue of factors such as its nature, size or location' was a matter for decision by the local planning authority, subject to review on *Wednesbury* grounds. The correctness of this proposition does not seem to have been in issue before the judge, and it was not challenged in the grounds of appeal. During the course of oral argument, Carnwath LJ raised the point with counsel, and

---

[69] [2003] EWCA Civ 140, [2003] Env LR 28, extracted in Section 4.3 of Chapter 7.
[70] Ibid, para 8.

suggested that the question might be one for the court to decide as a question of primary fact. In the course of his reply, Mr Wolfe embraced this suggestion, and submitted, but very briefly and without developing the point, that the decision of the council was not subject to a *Wednesbury* review, but to a full appeal on the facts and the law. It is unfortunate that the point was the subject of only the most exiguous argument. In these circumstances, I do not propose to deal with it at any great length.

15. In my judgment, the judge was right. The decision of the highest authority that he cited in support of his view was *Berkeley v Secretary of State for the Environment* [2001] 2 AC 603, at 610G-H and 614G-615A. It is true that neither of these passages provides explicit support for the judge's conclusion. In the first, Lord Hoffmann said that, in the absence of a direction by the Secretary of State pursuant to regulation 2(2), the question whether an application is or is not a Schedule 2 application 'is left to be determined in the first instance by the opinion of the local planning authority'. In the second passage, he said in relation to a direction under regulation 2(2): 'if no reasonable Secretary of State could have considered that the club's application was a Schedule 2 application, the judge would of course have been entitled to rule that no EIA could have been required'. As I have already stated, regulation 2(2) provides that 'Where the Secretary of State gives a direction which includes a statement that in his opinion proposed development would be likely ....', that statement is determinative. There is no corresponding express reference to the role of the local planning authority. But as Lord Hoffmann said, in the absence of a direction by the Secretary of State under regulation 2(2), it is for the local planning authority to determine whether an application is a Schedule 2 application.

16. It is right to say that Lord Hoffmann did not deal specifically with the role of the court in any challenge to a decision by a local planning authority. But it would be very surprising if the nature of the court's reviewing function were to differ according to whether the decision as to whether the application is a Schedule 2 application is made by the local planning authority or the Secretary of State. The question that is left to be determined in the first instance by the local planning authority is the same as the question that is determined by the Secretary of State pursuant to regulation 2(2). I do not consider that the use of the word 'opinion' in regulation 2(2) indicates that there is any difference. The fact that the decision of the local planning authority may be overridden by a formal direction of the Secretary of State does not justify or require a different role for the court in the two cases. Accordingly, I would hold that what Lord Hoffmann said in relation to challenges to decisions by the Secretary of State applies equally to challenges to decisions by local planning authorities.

17. Whether a proposed development is likely to have significant effects on the environment involves an exercise of judgment or opinion. It is not a question of hard fact to which there can only be one possible correct answer in any given case. The use of the word 'opinion' in regulation 2(2) is, therefore, entirely apt. In my view, that is in itself a sufficient reason for concluding that the role of the court should be limited to one of review on *Wednesbury* grounds.

18. I note that in *Aannemersbedriijf P K Kraaijeveld v Gedeputeerde Staten Van Zuid-Holland* [1997] 3 CMLR 1, the ECJ said:

'[59] The fact that in this case the Member States have a discretion under Articles 2(1) and 4(2) of the directive does not preclude judicial review of the question whether the national authorities exceeded their discretion (see, in particular, VERBOND VAN NEDERLANDSE ONDERNEMINGEN). [60] Consequently where, pursuant to national law, a court must or may raise of its own motion pleas in law based on a binding national rule which were not put forward by the parties, it must, for matters within its jurisdiction, examine of its own motion whether the legislative or administrative authorities of the Member State remained within the limits of their discretion under Article 2(1) and 4(2) of the directive ...'

It seems to me that this passage (particularly the reference to administrative authorities having a 'discretion') supports the view that I have just expressed. I take the word 'discretion' to mean an exercise of judgment, rather than discretion in the strict sense.

Review of the question of whether a project is likely to have a significant impact on the environment is thus on the deferential grounds of *Wednesbury* unreasonableness and it is interesting how Dyson LJ relied on both the nature of the decision and EU law to reach such a conclusion. Moreover, *Goodman* and *Jones* are not focusing so much on laying down guidance for what the decision-maker should be doing but, rather, are concerned with how the courts should approach their task. This is not to say the decisions will not have an impact on administrative decision-making but that they will do so in an indirect way.

Here is a more recent example of the Court of Appeal considering the question of whether something 'is likely to have a significant effect'.

R (Bateman) v South Cambridgeshire DC
[2011] EWCA Civ 157 paras 16–19 (Moore-Bick LJ)

16. Some support for the view that the expression 'is likely to have' should be construed as 'may possibly have' is to be found in paragraph 51 of the opinion of Advocate General Kokott in *Mellor*. She said:

'If it is obvious that there are no significant effects on the environment, such a screening can be sufficiently documented by a single sentence. If, on the other hand, certain possible environmental effects have already been raised, more extensive statements are needed to show that those effects have been properly considered. The case-law on the obligation to state reasons under primary law offers guidance here. According to that case-law, there must be a sufficient demonstration of the reasons why legal and factual aspects which have already been raised in the procedure do not show that there is a *possibility* of significant effects on the environment.' (Emphasis added.)

17. Mr. McCracken was inclined to accept in the light of that passage and of paragraphs 44-45 of the court's judgment in *Landelijke Vereniging tot Behoud van de Waddenzee v Staatssecretaris Van Landbouw, Natuurbeheer en Visserij* [2004] ECR I-7405, [2005] 2 CMLR 31 concerning the Habitats Directive (Directive 92/43/EEC) that 'likely' in this context means 'possible', but it is fair to say that there is nothing in the judgment of the court in *Mellor* which directly bears on the point. In my view something more than a bare possibility is probably required, though any serious possibility would suffice.

18. In support of his submission as to the meaning to be given to the word 'significant' in this context Mr. Drabble referred us to the checklist in the European Commission's Guidance on EIA Screening published in 2001, which suggests that a useful simple check as to whether an effect is significant is to ask oneself whether it is one that ought to be considered and to have an influence on the decision whether to grant development consent. However, in *R v St. Edmundsbury Borough Council ex parte Walton* [1999] Env. L.R. 879 Hooper J. (as he then was) expressed the view that the council's decision not to require an environmental statement under the forerunner of the current regulations, the Town and Country Planning (Assessment of Environmental Effects) Regulations 1988, was not *Wednesbury* unreasonable, even though, if one were prepared, it might consider that the development was likely to have effects that were sufficiently serious to justify a refusal of planning permission. Accordingly, Mr. McCracken Q.C. submitted that there is no inconsistency in the present case between deciding that the development will not have significant environmental effects and calling for detailed assessments of increased traffic movements, landscape effects and noise.

19. For my own part, I do not think that one should attempt to place too rigid an interpretation on the word 'significant' in this context, [...] for reasons which will become apparent it is not necessary to reach a final decision on either of these questions in the present case. I would therefore prefer not to place a gloss of my own on the words used in the Regulations and leave it to planning authorities to decide on a case by case basis whether the development under consideration is likely to have a

significant effect on the environment, as that expression is to be understood in the light of the developing case law of the European Court.

Note here both the reliance on CJEU case law and the way in which the question of what is a 'significant effect' becomes a legal question.

That latter fact is inevitable and means that the courts have also been required to consider a number of issues in relation to screening where their review is somewhat more intensive. One example of this is where a court is required to review a screening decision on the ground that it was based on inadequate information. This again was addressed in *Jones*.

R (Jones) v Mansfield District Council
[2003] EWCA Civ 1408 paras 38–39 (Dyson LJ)

38. [...] [T]he question whether a project is likely to have significant effect on the environment is one of degree which calls for the exercise of judgment. Thus, remedial measures contemplated by conditions and/or undertakings can be taken into account to a certain extent (see *Gillespie*). The effect on the environment must be 'significant'. Significance in this context is not a hard-edged concept: as I have said, the assessment of what is significant involves the exercise of judgment.

39. I accept that the authority must have sufficient information about the impact of the project to be able to make an informed judgment as to whether it is likely to have a significant effect on the environment. But this does not mean that all uncertainties have to be resolved or that a decision that an EIA is not required can only be made after a detailed and comprehensive assessment has been made of every aspect of the matter. As the judge said, the uncertainties may or may not make it impossible reasonably to conclude that there is no likelihood of significant environmental effect. It is possible in principle to have sufficient information to enable a decision reasonably to be made as to the likelihood of significant environmental effects even if certain details are not known and further surveys are to be undertaken. Everything depends on the circumstances of the individual case.

Dyson LJ is recognizing that 'significance' is not a 'hard edged' concept and thus discretionary, he is also requiring that a decision-maker has 'sufficient' information on which to base their decision. For a court to assess this they must engage in more intensive review than required under the *Wednesbury* unreasonableness standard.[71]

Another area where courts have engaged in more intensive review is assessing whether a planning authority can take into account possible mitigation measures in screening, usually resulting in a decision that no ES is required. This issue has been the subject of considerable litigation and also arose in the *Jones* case already extracted.

Bellway Urban Renewal Southern v Gillespie
[2003] EWCA Civ 400 paras 29–37 (Pill LJ) para 46 (Laws LJ)

The Facts

The Secretary of State granted planning permission for the redevelopment of a gasworks for residential housing and community developments. A condition of planning permission was that a site investigation

---

[71] *Younger Homes (Northern) Ltd v First Secretary of State* [2003] EWHC 3058 (Admin).

would be carried out to determine ground contamination and a remediation scheme set up to be super-vised by the local authority. The development was an 'urban development' project and so fell into Schedule II but the Secretary of State concluded that no ES was required because the condition above meant the project was not likely to have a significant impact on the environment. At first instance the judge (Richards J) held that the Secretary of State had erred in law by not requiring an ES. The devel-oper appealed and the Court of Appeal dismissed the appeal.

Pill LJ

29. In *World Wildlife Fund & ors v Autonome Provinz Bozen & ors* [2001] 1 CMLR 149, the European Court of Justice stated, at paragraph 37, that 'the criteria or thresholds mentioned in Article 4(2) of the Directive are designed to facilitate examination of the actual characteristics of any given project in order to determine whether it is subject to the requirement to carry out an assessment'. Underlining the objective of the Directive, the Court stated at paragraph 45 that no project likely to have significant effects on the environment should be exempt from assessment 'unless the specific project excluded could, on the basis of a comprehensive assessment, be regarded as not being likely to have such effects'. 'All the elements of the project relevant to the environmental impact assessment' must also be laid down in detail if a legislative Act is to be relied on to grant consent (paragraph 59).

30. In *British Telecommunications*[72], the site to be developed was of archaeological interest and the relevance of a mitigation strategy was considered. Elias J stated:

'73. ... There is no doubt that it is for the planning authority to decide in the first instance whether or not there are likely to be significant effects on the environment such as to warrant an environmental statement. Can they conclude that there would be significant effects, save for the fact that they have required (or at least will require) the developer to take mitigating steps whose effect is to render such effects insignificant? In my judgment they cannot. Paragraph 3 of Schedule 2, [the reference must be intended to be to para-graph 2 of Schedule 3 of the 1988 Regulations] which sets out the information required (and in turn reflects Article 5 of the Directive read with Appendix IV) requires amongst other things that there is a description of the measures envisaged to "avoid, reduce and if possible remedy" adverse effects. The purpose is surely to enable public discussion to take place about whether the measures will be successful, or perhaps whether more effective measures can be taken than those proposed to ameliorate the anticipated harm. In my opin-ion, therefore, the question whether or not there are likely to be significant environmental effects should be approached by asking whether these would be likely to result, absent some specific measures being taken to ameliorate or reduce them. If they would, the environmental statement is required and the mitigating measures must be identified in it.

'74. In this case it is clear that there would be potentially highly significant effects on the archaeology, unless measures are directed to eliminate them. Accordingly, [the officer] erred in law in taking these meas-ures into account when deciding that no significant effect was likely ....'

31. In *Lebus*[73], the proposed development was the erection of an egg production unit. The issue was as to the relevance of proposed pollution control measures and management techniques to the screen-ing decision.

32. Commenting on *British Telecommunications*, Sullivan J stated:

'Whilst each case will no doubt turn upon its own particular facts, and whilst it may well be perfectly reason-able to envisage the operation of standard conditions and a reasonably managed development, the underly-ing purpose of the Regulations in implementing the Directive is that the potentially significant impacts of a development are described together with a description of the measures envisaged to prevent, reduce and,

---

[72] *British Telecommunications Plc v Gloucester City Council* [2001] EWHC 1001 (Admin).
[73] *R (Lebus) v South Cambridgeshire DC* [2002] EWHC 2009 (Admin), [2003] Env LR 17.

where possible, offset any significant adverse effects on the environment. Thus the public is engaged in the process of assessing the efficacy of any mitigation measures.

It is not appropriate for a person charged with making a screening opinion to start from the premise that although there may be significant impacts, these can be reduced to insignificance as a result of the implementation of conditions of various kinds. The appropriate course in such a case is to require an environmental statement setting out the significant impacts and the measures which it is said will reduce their significance.'

33. Sullivan J described the approach of the Council in *Lebus* and concluded:

'... In so far as one can discern the Council's reasoning, it was erroneous on the two grounds set out above: it was no answer to the need for an EIA to say the information would be supplied in some form in any event, and it was not right to approach the matter on the basis that the significant adverse effects could be rendered insignificant if suitable conditions were imposed. The proper approach was to say that potentially this is a development which has significant adverse environmental implications: what are the measures which should be included in order to reduce or offset those adverse effects?'

34. In his judgment in the present case, Richards J underlined, at paragraph 75, and in my view correctly underlined, Sullivan J's statement that each case will turn upon its own particular facts and that 'it may well be perfectly reasonable to envisage the operation of standard conditions and a reasonably managed development'. I do, however, agree with Mr Lindblom's submission that the judgment as to whether an EIA is required is a judgment different from and to be made before an assessment of the procedures appropriate if an EIA is held to be required.

35. I also find persuasive the submissions on behalf of the Secretary of State to Richards J in the present case, though their relevance to the test actually applied by the Secretary of State will need to be considered. As summarised by the judge (paragraph 61), they were:

'On the information before him the Secretary of State was entitled to form the judgment that a development carried out in accordance with the stated remediation strategy was unlikely to give rise to significant effects. He was entitled to take the view that the outstanding details of the remediation works and the elements of uncertainty were not such as to affect that judgment or to create a likelihood of significant effects. In other words this was a case where the Secretary of State was reasonably satisfied that the boundary would not be crossed.'

36. When making his screening decision, the Secretary of State was not in my judgment obliged to shut his eyes to the remedial measures submitted as a part of the planning proposal. That would apply whatever the scale of the development and whether (as in *BT*) some harm to the relevant environmental interest is inevitable or whether (as is claimed in the present case) the development will actually produce an improvement in the environment. As stated in *Bozen*, it is the elements of the specific project which must be considered and all the elements of the project relevant to the EIA. In making his decision, the Secretary of State is not required to put into separate compartments the development proposal and the proposed remedial measures and consider only the first when making his screening decision. If the judges in the cases cited took a contrary view, I respectfully disagree, though it appears to me that both Sullivan J in *Lebus* and Richards J in the present case did not require all remedial or mitigating measures to be ignored.

37. The Secretary of State has to make a practical judgment as to whether the project would be likely to have significant effects on the environment by virtue of factors such as its nature, size or location. The extent to which remedial measures are required to avoid significant effects on the environment, and the nature and complexity of such measures, will vary enormously but the Secretary of State is not as a matter of law required to ignore proposals for remedial measures included in the proposals before him

when making his screening decision. In some cases the remedial measures will be modest in scope, or so plainly and easily achievable, that the Secretary of State can properly hold that the development project would not be likely to have significant effects on the environment even though, in the absence of the proposed remedial measures, it would be likely to have such effects. His decision is not in my judgment pre-determined either by the complexity of the project or by whether remedial measures are controversial though, in making the decision, the complexity of the project and of the proposed remedial measures may be important factors for consideration. [...]

Laws LJ

46. I would express my reasons for dismissing the appeal very shortly as follows. Where the Secretary of State is contemplating an application for planning permission for development which, but for remedial measures, may or will have significant environmental effects, I do not say that he must inevitably cause an EIA to be conducted. Prospective remedial measures may have been put before him whose nature, availability and effectiveness are already plainly established and plainly uncontroversial; though I should have thought there is little likelihood of such a state of affairs in relation to a development of any complexity. But if prospective remedial measures are not plainly established and not plainly uncontroversial, then as it seems to me the case calls for an EIA. If then the Secretary of State were to decline to conduct an EIA, as it seems to me he would pre-empt the very form of enquiry contemplated by the Directive and Regulations; and to that extent he would frustrate the purpose of the legislation. [...]

The guidance given in *Gillespie* has been applied in other cases.[74] As is clear from the opinions in *Gillespie* and in the cases cited by Pill LJ, review for assessing whether a decision-maker can take into account a mitigation measure in concluding that no ES is required is reasonably intensive. This is not surprising, as it is a more a matter of statutory interpretation than of pure discretion, but again it complicates the issue of how courts actually judicially review this aspect of the screening process.

These cases are only a few of the examples that have arisen in relation the EA Directive in English courts in relation to screening. Many other examples could be given, particularly focusing on specific aspects of the Regulations. What can be seen here is the general approach—one grounded in English administrative law principles and EU law doctrine.

6.3 THE ADEQUACY OF THE ENVIRONMENTAL STATEMENT

The issue of whether an ES is adequate has been less litigated than decisions about screening. With that said, there is considerable overlap in approach because Regulation 3(4) forbids a planning authority in relation to an 'EIA development' to grant planning permission without first taking 'the environmental information into consideration'.[75] Thus, while the adequacy of an ES is separate from whether there was adequate information for a screening decision,[76] as shall be seen, the courts have approached both questions in a similar way. As well, it is important to note that, as already seen in the *BACNGO* case, different judges may take different approaches to what the nature of their review should be.

There are very few cases where there is a direct judicial review challenge to the methodological quality of an ES. This is not surprising as clearly such issues would be beyond both the legal and

---

[74] *R (CATT) v Brighton and Hove CC* [2007] EWCA Civ 298, [2007] Env LR 32.
[75] *R v Cornwall County Council, ex p Hardy* [2001] Env LR 25 (QB).
[76] *R (Orchard) v Secretary of State for the Home Department* [2003] EWCA Civ 37, [2004] Env LR 12.

technical competence of the Court. What is often a subject of argument is that there was not enough information on which to base a proper ES.

R v Cornwall County Council, ex p Hardy
[2000] WL 1421266 (QB) paras 67–69, 71–73 (Harrison J)

The Facts

Cornwall County Council granted planning permission for the extension of a landfill site after considering an ES. The EIA process had highlighted that the development had implications for a number of species included horseshoe bats which were listed under the Habitats Directive. English Nature had stated more investigation of these bats was needed before permission should be granted. The Council had made investigation a condition of the permission.

The HC

67. Applying those principles to the facts of this case, if the nature conservation aspects relating to the bats, badgers and liverwort did not involve 'significant adverse effects', there would be no requirement for the environmental statement to contain the measures envisaged to deal with them and no duty on the respondent to consider those measures before granting planning permission. Similarly, if those nature conservation aspects did not amount to 'main effects' there would be no requirement for the environmental statement to contain the data to assess them and no duty on the respondent to consider that data before granting planning permission. It is therefore necessary to consider whether the respondent could rationally conclude that those nature conservation aspects did not amount to 'significant adverse effects' or 'main effects'

68. The non-technical summary of the environmental statement stated that there would be no significant adverse environmental effects which should prevent the proposal from gaining planning permission, and the site assessment summary, when dealing with nature conservation, stated that no protected species would be affected. That was, of course, information supplied by the environmental consultants responsible for compiling the environmental statement. However, the Director of Planning also advised the Planning Committee in his report that there were no significant nature conservation issues and he advised them that there was no significant conflict with Structure Plan policy ENV5 which provides that development should not adversely affect to a significant degree any protected species or its habitat.

69. It is difficult, however, to see how the Planning Committee could have accepted that advice in the light of their acceptance of the advice from English Nature and Cornish Wildlife Trust that further surveys should be carried out to ensure, inter alia, that bats would not be adversely affected by the development […].

71. Having decided that those surveys should be carried out, the Planning Committee simply were not in a position to conclude that there were no significant nature conservation issues until they had the results of the surveys. The surveys may have revealed significant adverse effects on the bats or their resting places in which case measures to deal with those effects would have had to be included in the environmental statement. They could not be left to the reserved matters stage when the same requirements for publicity and consultation do not apply. Having decided that the surveys should be carried out, it was, in my view, incumbent on the respondent to await the results of the surveys before deciding whether to grant planning permission so as to ensure that they had the full environmental information before them before deciding whether or not planning permission should be granted.

72. I appreciate that the advice of English Nature and of the Cornish Wildlife Trust was that the surveys should be carried out before the development started rather than before planning permission was granted. However, that advice was not, in my view, consistent with the requirements of the Directive and the Regulations, however understandable the reasons for the advice may have been, because the results of the surveys could have contained information which, under the Regulations, would have to be in the environmental statement which had to be considered by the respondent before deciding whether to grant planning permission. If it is thought that bats are, or may be, present within the area to be filled, the fact that they are itinerant creatures cannot excuse a failure to ascertain their presence as part of the environmental statement before planning permission is granted because that is the time at which the information has to be provided. The technical difficulty of carrying out the survey in the woodland area was not a matter relied upon by the Director of Planning in the body of his report, nor was it relied upon by Mr Straker on behalf of the respondent and, in any event, as Mr McCracken suggested, there could, if necessary, be a 'minded to grant' resolution to overcome that aspect.

73. In my judgment, the grant of planning permission in this case was not lawful because the respondent could not rationally conclude that there were no significant nature conservation effects until they had the data from the surveys. They were not in a position to know whether they had the full environmental information required by Regulation 3 before granting planning permission.

It may be argued that *Hardy* is not a representative case. Lord Hoffmann taking a very different approach in *BACNGO* suggested that it turned on the fact that the bats were recognized under the Habitats Directive and some commentators have suggested that the courts have become more deferential since it.[77] Yet the question of standard of review is not a settled one as evidenced by the differing approaches of Lord Walker and Lord Hoffmann in *BACNGO*.

Another example can be seen in *Bowen-West v Secretary of State for Communities and Local Government*.

Bowen-West v Secretary of State for Communities and Local Government
[2012] EWCA Civ 321, paras 7–8, 10–11, 27–42 (Laws LJ)

The Facts

The appellant, a local resident, appealed against planning permission granted to Augean plc to dispose of low level radioactive waste ('LLW') at a hazardous waste landfill site known as the East Northamptonshire Resource Management Facility for a limited period of time. Augean plc had also decided to seek planning permission for further use of the site (up to 2026). The challenged planning permission was thus part of a larger proposed project

The CA

7. There is no contest but that the third respondents' application of 21 July 2009 was for Environmental Impact Assessment (EIA) development, so that an Environmental Statement was required under the regulations. An Environmental Statement was accordingly prepared, but it addressed the environmental effects of the current proposal in isolation. The central question we have to decide is whether the

---

[77] Martin Edwards, 'Case Comment: Environmental Impact Assessment: Significant Adverse Effects' [2004] JPEL 178.

Secretary of State deciding on appeal whether to allow the July 2009 application was bound to treat the intended further proposals as involving or constituting 'indirect, secondary or cumulative effects' of the existing proposal within the meaning of paragraph 4 of Part I of Schedule 4 to the Regulations. An Environmental Statement has to include (see paragraph 2.1(a) of the Regulations):

'...such of the information referred to in Part I of Schedule 4 as is reasonably required to assess the environmental effects of the development.'

8. Paragraph 4 of Part I of Schedule 4 stipulates:

'... description of the likely significant effects of the development on the environment, which should cover the direct effects and any indirect, secondary, cumulative, short, medium and long-term, permanent and temporary, positive and negative effects of the development, resulting from:(a)the existence of the development...'

[...]

10. The appellant's principal case, in briefest outline, is that the current development for which planning permission was granted by the Secretary of State in May last year is 'demonstrably but Phase 1 of a much larger scheme and will lead to a "foot in the door" for major further planning permissions on the same site for the same use' (see paragraph 1 of the appellant's principal skeleton). That being so, the appellant says that the deputy judge ought to have concluded that the Secretary of State had erred in failing to treat the intended further proposals as involving 'indirect secondary or cumulative effects' and ought, accordingly, to have held that those effects should have been assessed within the EIA process.

11. There is a further ground of appeal. The appellant says that the deputy judge was also in error in applying the conventional Wednesbury standard of review (*Associated Provincial Picture Houses v Wednesbury Corporation* [1948] 1 QB 223) as a test of the legality of the Secretary of State's view as to the proper scope of the required EIA. It is submitted that the law of the European Union requires a more intensive judicial scrutiny. [...]

27. I turn then to what I regard as the main question: whether the Secretary of State should have concluded that the largest scheme involved indirect, secondary or cumulative effects of the July 2009 proposal?

28. First and foremost, this is, in my judgment, an issue of fact. Whether it is such or not has been at the centre of the argument to which we listened yesterday and today. But it is clear, as I see the matter, that it is indeed a matter of fact or of judgment: clear from the judgment of Sullivan LJ with whom Jacob LJ and Sir Mark Waller agreed in the case of *Brown v Carlisle County Council*: see paragraph 21. Sullivan LJ said in terms:

'The answer to the question—what are the cumulative effects of a particular development—will be a question of fact in each case.'

It is clear also from the words of the regulation itself: 'such information as it reasonably required' and 'a description of the likely significant effects'. These formulations import, as it seems to me, the application of a measured judgment to the evidence. This is not contradicted by the learning, of which Mr Drabble reminded us yesterday, which shows that the term 'likely' in the regulation means 'possible': see *R(Bateman) v South Cambs DC & Ors* [2011] EWCA Civ 157.

29. Whether or not the appellant is right to submit that European Union law requires a more intrusive judicial scrutiny of the Secretary of State's assessment of the matter than is given by the conventional *Wednesbury* approach (Ground 2)—and I will return to that—it must surely be the case that the views

of the Inspector and the Secretary of State as the primary judges of fact are entitled to very considerable weight.

30. More deeply perhaps, Mr Drabble submitted on this part of the case that the question whether the effects of the larger scheme are cumulative effects of the smaller is itself one of law. This, with respect to Mr Drabble, is in my judgment a mistake. It entails a suggested rule to the effect, broadly, that in any case where it is intended to continue or supplant a limited scheme with a larger one, the effects of the latter are to be treated as the cumulative effects of the former. There is in my judgment nothing in the Regulations nor indeed the Directive to suggest that the European legislature or domestic legislature implementing the Directive contemplated an approach that could be categorised by so rigid a rule. It seems to me that the texts are all consistent with the proposition that what are and what are not indirect, secondary or cumulative effects is a matter of degree and judgment.

31. Relying on *R(Goodman) v LB Lewisham* [2003] Env.LR 644, paragraph 8, Mr Drabble submitted yesterday that the Secretary of State has to get the legal meaning of 'cumulative effects' right. If this is anything more than a statement of the obvious proposition that the meaning of a text is for the court to ascertain, then it is to restate the supposed rule: which, in my judgment, is no rule.

32. I should next point up the fact that some of the principal authorities relied on by the appellant as demonstrating the breadth of the EIA provisions are not about the scope of the EIA to be undertaken in a case where, as here, an Environmental Statement admittedly falls to be made. Rather, they address the question whether an EIA is required at all. They are 'screening' rather than 'scoping' positions. This is so of *Kraaijeveld, Commission v Spain, Ecologistas* and also *Swale Borough Council ex parte RSPB* [1991] 1 PLR 6, to which reference was made in the written argument. It is in this type of case, screening cases, that the courts have been concerned, energetically concerned, to put a stop to the device of using piecemeal applications as a means of excluding larger developments from the discipline of EIA. That approach cannot simply be read across to a case which is not about screening at all, but rather about the appropriate scope of an EIA.

33. At the heart of this case, it seems to me, is the proposition that the issues arising here are not comparable with those that arose in these screening decisions. In a case such as the present as I have indicated, we are dealing with what is quintessentially a matter of judgment, just as *Sullivan J* (as he then was) held was the case in relation to whether a park and ride scheme was an integral part of a larger scheme: see *R(Davies) v SSCLG* [2008] EWHC (Admin) 2223. A like question as regards the relation between a specific proposal for a freight distribution centre and the overall proposed development of Carlisle Airport arose in Brown's case to which I have already referred. There, there was an inextricable link between the two by virtue of the effect of an agreement made under section 106 of the Town and Country Planning Act 1990. The deputy judge in our case cited Sullivan LJ's judgment in *Brown* extensively. For present purposes, it is enough, with respect, to set out the holding from the headnote in the Environmental Law Reports as follows. This is to be found at page 47 of the appeal bundle:

'It was difficult to see how the commitment in the s.106 agreement to bring forward the "airport works" could, on the one hand have been adequate to ensure that the "development as a whole" could be regarded as policy compliant for the purposes of the Development Plan, but on the other hand, insufficient to make the airport works part of the cumulative effects of the development for the purposes of the EIA Regulations. Whilst submissions had been made that the airport works were "inchoate", and so were not required to be assessed at that stage, the difficulty was that they had been sufficiently detailed for assessment of the economic and other advantages which would result. The grant of planning permission had been unlawful as there had been a failure to comply with reg.3(2) of the 1999 Regulations.'

I agree with the observations of the deputy judge distinguishing Brown. At paragraphs 39 and 40 of his judgment (to which I have already referred) he said this: '39. There is no doubt that the Brown decision (whilst clearly a scoping case) is distinguishable on its facts, since (paragraph 21) the s.106 Agreement ensured that the Freight Distribution Centre could not lawfully be developed in isolation; it could only be developed if its cumulative effects included the carrying out of the airport works. In other words, the airport works were integral to the permitted development; hence the question (paragraph 25), which had not been addressed, and to which there was only one rational response.

40. In the present case, the permitted developments can go ahead irrespective of the future proposals. That was the finding of the Inspector, who said that this was a "stand-alone proposal". It is not in truth one integrated development such as the Carlisle Airport development in Brown…' Then the deputy judge referred to *Ecologistas* and *Commission v Spain*.

34. I should next say a word about the effect of the grant of the present planning permission as a precedent, a 'foot in the door': an expression used by Sullivan LJ in *Brown*: see paragraph 39 of the judgment in that case. It is said it was a foot in the door for the larger intended scheme. As I have shown, the Inspector and the Secretary of State accepted that there would be some precedent effect.

35. The grant of planning permission may, in my judgment, be said to concede the principle of disposing of LLW on this site or adjacent to it, but only to the extent or on the scale allowed by the permission. If the larger application proceeds, the issue of disposal of LLW of the magnitude thereby contemplated will be open and undecided. It will certainly not be foreclosed nor in my judgment prejudiced by the current permission. It seems to me that the Secretary of State was entitled to conclude at paragraph 4 of the decision letter (which I have read) that:

'There is nothing to support the Council's claim that permission in this case would frustrate the aims of the Environmental Impact Regulations and the Directive.' It is noteworthy that if the larger scheme is in due course applied for, it will as a whole (including that part of it which is in effect the present scheme) be the subject of an EIA; and thereby it seems to me the purpose of the Directive will be fulfilled. In Commission v Spain, the court said this (paragraph 47):'…the Directive's fundamental objective is that, before consent is granted, projects likely to have significant effects on the environment by virtue, *inter alia*, of their nature, size or location should be made subject to a mandatory assessment with regard to their effects.' That is precisely what will happen if the larger scheme is in due course applied for. The third respondent's case to the inquiry moreover included this passage accepted by the Inspector: '2.5 The appeal proposal is not piecemeal development or a development which can only properly be considered as part of a larger whole, as alleged in NCC's additional reasons for refusal (a) and (b)… both of which have been rejected in the PINS ruling. It is not inevitably part of a more substantial development. If permitted, the development will be implemented regardless of the outcome of any further planning application. There is no cumulative or in-combination situation that would arise between the two proposals, even if any implementation of a subsequent permission occurred prior to the expiry in 2013 of the one now sought, which seems unlikely. In any event, the subsequent application would require assessment on the full effects of the extension to the landfill area and the extension of time for the already permitted area so that any cumulative effects would be considered then. At present, it is not possible to carry out that exercise.'

36. Given all these considerations and for these reasons, I for my part would acquit the Secretary of State of any Wednesbury error in judging that the EIA here need not encompass the third respondent's wider prospective scheme. I do not accept that the Inspector and the Secretary of State made, as is suggested, an impermissible leap from the view that this was a stand-alone project to the conclusion that, therefore, no EIA of the larger scheme was necessary. Account was taken of the relationship between the scheme in hand and the larger scheme; of the relevance of precedent; of the want of detail of the future scheme; of the fact that the current scheme could properly be dealt with on its own merits.

37. If one looks for a meaning of the term 'indirect, secondary or cumulative effects', it is perhaps worth emphasising that the grant of a further planning permission—here for the larger scheme—surely

cannot of itself be such an effect. The putative 'cumulative effects' on Mr Drabble's argument can only be what are the direct effects of the larger scheme itself or perhaps some effect factually arising from the current and larger scheme together. But all such effects would be examined if the larger scheme is gone into.

38. Thus I would not merely acquit the Secretary of State of a Wednesbury error. I consider, so far as the facts of the matter appear to me, that his conclusion was correct.

39. I turn to Ground 2. It is in the circumstances (if my Lords agree with my conclusions on the first ground) strictly unnecessary to embark upon the debate about the appropriate intensity of review. I will deal with it shortly. *R(Goodman) v LB Lewisham* [2003] EWCA Civ 140, paragraph 9; *Jones v Mansfield DC* [2004] ELR 391, paragraphs 14 to 15 and *R(Blewett) v Derbyshire CC* [2003] EWHC Admin 2775, paragraphs 32 and 33, all indicate, as it seems to me, that the conventional Wednesbury approach applies to the court's adjudication of issues such as arise here, if I am right in holding that such issues are a matter of fact and judgment.

40. In *R(BugLife) v Medway Council and Ors* [2011] EWHC Admin 746, His Honour Judge Thornton QC opined that the courts might visit the question whether European Union law required them to apply a proportionate standard. For my part, I do not see that there is any true question of proportionality arising in the present case. We are not concerned with the exercise of a discretion and therefore we are not concerned with assessing whether a response to a particular aim is or is not proportionate. We are concerned with a fact-finding exercise. There is nothing, as it seems to me, in the jurisprudence of the Court of Justice to show that the conventional English law approach is inapt. Paragraph 48 of *Ecologistas* perhaps suggests, though I accept it does not state, the contrary. Paragraph 39 of *Abraham & Ors*, C-2/07, which is a screening not a scoping decision, does not in my judgment assist the appellants. Mr Drabble has relied in a supplementary skeleton argument on other authority of the Court of Justice. However *Commission v Germany* C-431/92 and *Commission v Spain* are infringement cases in which the Court of Justice must inevitably make all judgments of fact and law. Kraaijeveld in the circumstances takes the matter no further.

41. I am inclined to accept Mr McCracken's submission for the third respondents that the Court of Justice is of course concerned to see that the law is properly applied in the Member States, but in the present context that is achieved by the Wednesbury standards.

42. In the circumstances, I see no reason, even assuming if it were open to us to do so, to seek to move the law from where it presently stands in this area. This, in any case, would not be the case in which to do so.

What can be seen is the application of cases already discussed in this section. Likewise, we can see regular and comfortable reliance on CJEU cases. We can also see how questions of fact and questions of law become entangled.

FURTHER READING AND QUESTIONS

1. Do you think the English EIA regulations have a different nature and purpose than the EA Directive? In particular consider the wording of Regulation 3(4).

2. How applicable is Lord Hoffmann's reasoning in the *BACNGO* case to English case law? In particular consider how important it was for his conclusions that EIA in Belize is an iterative process.

3. Consider the following hypothetical screening decisions. Do you think the court would interfere and if so why?

a) Planning Authority A decides that a motorway service area does not require an ES to be conducted because it falls below the 5 hectare threshold set by the regulations. A local resident argues that it should be subject to an ES because it is ugly, will create noise pollution, and will encourage other developments in the area.

b) Planning Authority C grant planning permission to a tanning factory (the floor space being above the threshold) without requiring an ES. They state that the reason why it doesn't need one is because a condition of the planning consent is that the developer guarantees to put in place an environmental management system and to clean up any contamination.

4. In *Cooper v HM Attorney General* [2010] EWCA Civ 464, [2011] 2 WLR 448 there was a failed attempt to bring an action against the Court of Appeal on the basis of a breach of EU law and the case of Case C-224/01 *Köbler v Republik Osterreich* [2003] ECR 1-10239. The case makes interesting reading, particularly in relation to how the CJEU's case law has evolved.

5. On the issue of the EA Directive and the difficulties it imposes on granting retroactive planning permission see *Ardagh Glass Ltd v Chester CC* [2010] EWCA Civ 172, [2011] 1 All ER 476.

6. On the application of *Mellor* and the duty to give reasons see *R (Friends of Basildon Golf Course) v Basildon DC* [2010] EWCA Civ 1432, [2011] Env LR 16.

7. It has always been the case that legal arguments about the EA Directive were raised alongside grounds of judicial review and legal challenges in planning law. It is increasingly common for there to be grounds of challenge under different environmental law Directives in the same case raising a question about how they interact. See *R (Edwards) v Environment Agency* [2008] UKHL 22, [2008] 1 WLR 1587 (IPPC) and Case C-43/10 *Nomarchiaki Aftodioikisi Aitoloakarnanias* (CJEU 11 September 2012). For a recent case in which there is a drawing on different EU Directives in the interpreting of the EA Directive see *R (Loader) v Secretary of State for Communities and Local Government* [2012] EWCA Civ 869 [2012] 3 CMLR 29.

7 STRATEGIC ENVIRONMENTAL ASSESSMENT (SEA)

SEA was discussed in Section 2.3 and we now turn to consider the SEA Directive and how it has been applied in England. The SEA Directive was only passed in 2001 and the time limit for implementation was 2004. As such, the Directive has been in operation for a much shorter period than the EA Directive. That should give pause for thought because, as we saw in Section 6 it took both the CJEU and the English courts at least a decade to really begin to develop a body of doctrine around the SEA Directive. To put that another way, it is still early days.

7.1 THE STRATEGIC ENVIRONMENTAL ASSESSMENT DIRECTIVE

The idea of developing SEA in the EU was originally debated in the 1970s when an EA Directive was proposed. It was not until the 1990s, and in particular the Fifth Action Programme on the Environment, that proposals for an SEA Directive became more concrete. The SEA Directive[78] was

---

[78] European Parliament and Council Directive 2001/42/EC on the assessment of the effects of certain plans and programmes on the environment OJ [2001] L197/30.

passed in 2001 under Article 175(1) TEC (now Article 192(1) TFEU)[79] and reflects the principles in Article 191(2) and Article 11 TFEU. The latter is particularly important because SEA is a very explicit example of the attempts to integrate environmental considerations into more mainstream decision-making. Article 1 of the Directive states:

> The objective of this Directive is to provide for a high level of protection of the environment and to contribute to the integration of environmental considerations into the preparation and adoption of plans and programmes with a view to promoting sustainable development, by ensuring that, in accordance with this Directive, an environmental assessment is carried out of certain plans and programmes which are likely to have significant effects on the environment.

The Directive however is relatively narrow in its scope.

Unlike the EA Directive where the concept 'project' is very broad, the SEA Directive relates to 'plans and programmes'. These are defined in Article 2:

> (a) 'plans and programmes' shall mean plans and programmes, including those co-financed by the European Community, as well as any modifications to them:
> — which are subject to preparation and/or adoption by an authority at national, regional or local level or which are prepared by an authority for adoption, through a legislative procedure by Parliament or Government, and
> — which are required by legislative, regulatory or administrative provisions;

Article 3 provides that:

> **Article 3**
>
> 1. An environmental assessment, in accordance with Articles 4 to 9, shall be carried out for plans and programmes referred to in paragraphs 2 to 4 which are likely to have significant environmental effects.
>
> 2. Subject to paragraph 3, an environmental assessment shall be carried out for all plans and programmes,
>
> (a) which are prepared for agriculture, forestry, fisheries, energy, industry, transport, waste management, water management, telecommunications, tourism, town and country planning or land use and which set the framework for future development consent of projects listed in Annexes I and II to Directive 85/337/EEC, or
>
> (b) which, in view of the likely effect on sites, have been determined to require an assessment pursuant to Article 6 or 7 of Directive 92/43/EEC.
>
> 3. Plans and programmes referred to in paragraph 2 which determine the use of small areas at local level and minor modifications to plans and programmes referred to in paragraph 2 shall require an environmental assessment only where the Member States determine that they are likely to have significant environmental effects.
>
> 4. Member States shall determine whether plans and programmes, other than those referred to in paragraph 2, which set the framework for future development consent of projects, are likely to have significant environmental effects.

---

[79] See Section 3.1 of Chapter 4 for a discussion.

> 5. Member States shall determine whether plans or programmes referred to in paragraphs 3 and 4 are likely to have significant environmental effects either through case-by-case examination or by specifying types of plans and programmes or by combining both approaches. For this purpose Member States shall in all cases take into account relevant criteria set out in Annex II, in order to ensure that plans and programmes with likely significant effects on the environment are covered by this Directive.

Annex II sets out the criteria that Member States are to take into account in this screening process, although it should be noted that these criteria would mean most plans and programmes under Article 3(2)–(4) would require an SEA. While the scope of the Directive is narrower we can see that the structure of it is similar to the screening provisions under the EA Directive. The SEA Directive set out clear categories and discretionary categories for when an environmental assessment is required.

If an SEA is required then an environmental assessment should be carried out and an environmental report be prepared.[80] Article 5(1) requires:

> 1. Where an environmental assessment is required under Article 3(1), an environmental report shall be prepared in which the likely significant effects on the environment of implementing the plan or programme, and reasonable alternatives taking into account the objectives and the geographical scope of the plan or programme, are identified, described and evaluated. The information to be given for this purpose is referred to in Annex I.

Note here that 'reasonable alternatives' are explicitly required to be taken into account. Preparation of an environmental report includes a consultation process (including in relation to transboundary environmental effects).[81] As with EIA, a decision-maker must not only take into account the report but also the outcomes from the consultation processes. An important aspect of the SEA process is that it must be 'carried out during the preparation of a plan or programme and before its adoption or submission to the legislative procedure'.[82] In other words, an SEA cannot be an afterthought. Alongside the Directive, the Commission has also published guidelines similar to those they have published for the EA Directive.[83]

The CJEU has considered the interpretation of the Directive on a number of occasions. As with the EA Directive, most of these cases concern screening. It is fair to say the approach of the Court in these cases is less purposive than in relation to the EA Directive. In part this is probably to do with the fact that there is no equivalent provision to Article 2(1) of the EA Directive in the SEA Directive. It also may reflect the fact that the Directive is narrower in its aspirations. One recent example of the CJEU's approach to interpretation can be seen here.

**Case C-567/10 *Inter-Environnement Bruxelles ASBL, Pétitions-Patrimoine ASBL v Région de Bruxelles-Capitale*
(CJEU 22 March 2012) paras 24–31, 33, 36–42**

> 24. By its second question, which it is appropriate to consider first since it concerns the very concept of plans and programmes, the national court asks the Court whether the condition set out in Article 2(a) of Directive 2001/42 that the plans and programmes envisaged in that provision are those 'which are

---

[80] Articles 3(1) and 5.   [81] Articles 6–7.   [82] Article 4(1).

[83] Commission, *Implementation of Directive 2001/42/EC on the assessment of the effects of certain plans and programmes on the environment* from <http://ec.europa.eu/environment/eia/sea-support.htm> accessed 2 October 2012.

required by legislative, regulatory or administrative provisions' must be interpreted as being intended to apply to plans and programmes, such as the land development plans at issue in the main proceedings, which are provided for by national legislation but whose adoption by the competent authority would not be compulsory.

25. According to the applicants in the main proceedings, a mere literal interpretation of that provision, which would exclude from the scope of Directive 2001/42 plans and programmes that are only provided for by legislative, regulatory or administrative provisions, would entail the dual risk of not requiring the assessment procedure for land development plans which normally have major effects on the territory concerned and of not ensuring uniform application of the directive in the Member States' various legal orders, given the differences existing in the formulation of the relevant national rules.

26. The Belgian, Czech and United Kingdom Governments submit, on the other hand, that it is apparent not only from the wording of Article 2(a) of Directive 2001/42 but also from the directive's *travaux préparatoires* that the European Union legislature did not intend to make administrative and legislative measures that are not required by rules of law subject to the environmental impact assessment procedure established by the directive.

27. The European Commission considers that, where an authority is subject to a legal obligation to prepare or adopt a plan or programme, the test of being 'required' within the meaning of Article 2(a) of Directive 2001/42 is met. That is prima facie so, in its view, in the case of the plans that must be adopted by the Brussels-Capital Region.

28. It must be stated that an interpretation which would result in excluding from the scope of Directive 2001/42 all plans and programmes, inter alia those concerning the development of land, whose adoption is, in the various national legal systems, regulated by rules of law, solely because their adoption is not compulsory in all circumstances, cannot be upheld.

29. The interpretation of Article 2(a) of Directive 2001/42 that is relied upon by the abovementioned governments would have the consequence of restricting considerably the scope of the scrutiny, established by the directive, of the environmental effects of plans and programmes concerning town and country planning of the Member States.

30. Consequently, such an interpretation of Article 2(a) of Directive 2001/42, by appreciably restricting the directive's scope, would compromise, in part, the practical effect of the directive, having regard to its objective, which consists in providing for a high level of protection of the environment (see, to this effect, Case C-295/10 *Valčiukienė and Others* [2011] ECR I-0000, paragraph 42). That interpretation would thus run counter to the directive's aim of establishing a procedure for scrutinising measures likely to have significant effects on the environment, which define the criteria and the detailed rules for the development of land and normally concern a multiplicity of projects whose implementation is subject to compliance with the rules and procedures provided for by those measures.

31. It follows that plans and programmes whose adoption is regulated by national legislative or regulatory provisions, which determine the competent authorities for adopting them and the procedure for preparing them, must be regarded as 'required' within the meaning, and for the application, of Directive 2001/42 and, accordingly, be subject to an assessment of their environmental effects in the circumstances which it lays down. [...]

Question 1

33. By its first question, the Cour constitutionnelle asks whether the total or partial repeal of a plan or programme falling within Directive 2001/42 must be subject to an environmental assessment within the meaning of Article 3 of that directive. [...]

36. It is to be noted first of all, as the national court has, that Directive 2001/42 refers expressly not to repealing measures but only to measures modifying plans and programmes.

37. However, given the objective of Directive 2001/42, which consists in providing for a high level of protection of the environment, the provisions which delimit the directive's scope, in particular those setting out the definitions of the measures envisaged by the directive, must be interpreted broadly.

38. In this regard, it is possible that the partial or total repeal of a plan or programme is likely to have significant effects on the environment, since it may involve a modification of the planning envisaged in the territories concerned.

39. Thus, a repealing measure may give rise to significant effects on the environment because, as has been observed by the Commission and by the Advocate General in points 40 and 41 of her Opinion, such a measure necessarily entails a modification of the legal reference framework and consequently alters the environmental effects which had, as the case may be, been assessed under the procedure prescribed by Directive 2001/42.

40. It is to be recalled that, when the Member States draw up an environmental report within the meaning of Article 5(1) of Directive 2001/42, they must take into consideration, in particular, information concerning 'the relevant aspects of the current state of the environment and the likely evolution thereof without implementation of the plan or programme' within the meaning of point (b) of Annex I to the directive. Therefore, inasmuch as the repeal of a plan or programme may modify the state of the environment as examined at the time of adoption of the measure which is to be repealed, it must be taken into consideration with a view to scrutiny of the subsequent effects that it might have on the environment.

41. It follows that, in light of the characteristics and the effects of the measures repealing that plan or programme, to regard those measures as excluded from the scope of Directive 2001/42 would be contrary to the objectives pursued by the European Union legislature and such as to compromise, in part, the practical effect of the directive.

42. On the other hand, it must be made clear that, in principle, that is not the case if the repealed measure falls within a hierarchy of town and country planning measures, as long as those measures lay down sufficiently precise rules governing land use, they have themselves been the subject of an assessment of their environmental effects and it may reasonably be considered that the interests which Directive 2001/42 is designed to protect have been taken into account sufficiently within that framework.

The approach of the Court is purposive, but that purpose is limited by both the scope of the Directive and the nature of SEA itself. This can also be seen in relation to Article 3(2)(b).

Case C-177/11 *Syllogos Ellinon Poleodomon kai Chorotakton v Ypourgos Perivallontos* (CJEU 21 June 2012) para 24

24. The answer to the question referred is therefore that Article 3(2)(b) of the SEA Directive must be interpreted as meaning that the obligation to make a particular plan subject to an environmental assessment depends on the preconditions requiring an assessment under the Habitats Directive, including the condition that the plan may have a significant effect on the site concerned, being met in respect of that plan. The examination carried out to determine whether that latter condition is fulfilled is necessarily limited to the question as to whether it can be excluded, on the basis of objective information, that that plan or project will have a significant effect on the site concerned.

In other words the operation of the SEA Directive in this context requires action under the Habitats Directive.

7.2 STRATEGIC ENVIRONMENTAL ASSESSMENT IN ENGLAND

The SEA Directive was implemented into English law with the Environmental Assessment of Plans and Programmes Regulations 2004 (separate Regulations exist for Wales, Northern Ireland, and Scotland). Guidance on the Regulations can be found on the Department of Communities and Local Government website.[84] As stressed already, the implementation of the SEA Directive is in early days. One particular issue has been that the revocation of regional strategies under the Localism Act 2011,[85] in light of Case *C-567/10 Inter-Environnement Bruxelles AS* discussed already, does require a SEA to be carried out.

The Regulations have begun to give rise to litigation, although that litigation tends to be fact specific and revolved around issues such as the revision of the Core Strategies.[86] One example can be seen here—a recent case from Scotland that reached the Supreme Court. In 2001 a non-statutory regional partnership (NESTRANS) was set up and in 2003 published a regional transport strategy (known as the MTS). Among the scheme described and costed in the report was a 'western peripheral route' (WPR) around Aberdeen. The WPR was announced and proved controversial. The route was reconfigured and in 2005 the final version of the project was announced and it now included a trunk road (known as Fastlink). Lord Reed considered the case law of the CJEU on the SEA Directive in detail and then applied it to the facts.

Walton v Scottish Ministers
[2012] UKSC 44 paras 59–62, 64–66 (Lord Reed JSC)

59. In the present case, the WPR was subject to an EIA; and there is no longer any complaint that that assessment failed to meet the requirements of the EIA Directive. The question whether there also required to be an SEA depends upon whether the decision to construct the Fastlink as part of the WPR was a modification of a 'plan' or "programme" as defined in article 2(a) of the SEA Directive, and was therefore itself such a plan or programme; and, if so, whether it set the framework for future development consent of a project listed in article 3(2)(a) (there being no dispute that the WPR is such a project). The reasoning of the Court of Justice and the Advocate General in such recent cases as *Terre Wallone ASBL v Région Wallone and Inter-Environnement Wallonie ASBL v Région Wallone* ((Joined Cases C-105/09 and C-110/09) [2010] I-ECR 5611 BAILII: [2010] EUECJ C-105/09, and *Inter-Environnement Bruxelles ASBL, Pétitions-Patrimoine ASBL and Atelier de Recherche et d'Action Urbaines ASBL v Région de Bruxelles-Capitale* (Case C-567/10) [2012] 2 CMLR 30 suggests that these questions are to some extent inter-related.

60. In determining whether the Fastlink decision was a modification of a 'plan' or 'programme' as defined in article 2(a), the first question is whether, as Mr Walton contends, the MTS (or the local transport strategies which it comprised) was a plan or programme within the meaning of that provision.

61. It might be argued with some force that none of these documents has been shown to have been 'required by legislative, regulatory or administrative measures' as stipulated by the second indent of article 2(a), even according the term 'required' the width of meaning given to it in *Inter-Environnement Bruxelles* at para 31. It might also be argued that NESTRANS, at least, was not an 'authority' within

---

[84] *A Practical Guide to the Strategic Environmental Assessment Directive*, March 2006 available at: <http://www.communities.gov.uk/publications/planningandbuilding/practicalguidesea> accessed 2 October 2012.

[85] See Section 1.3 of Chapter 18.

[86] *St Albans City & District Council v Secretary of State for Communities and Local Government* [2009] EWHC 1280 (Admin) and *Cala Homes (South) v Secretary of State for Communities and Local Government* [2011] EWCA Civ 639.

the meaning of the first indent, since it was established voluntarily and did not exercise any statutory functions. On the other hand, it might be argued that the documents 'set the framework for future development consent of projects', as explained by Advocate General Kokott in her opinion in *Terre Wallone* at points 64–65, and were therefore likely to have significant effects on the environment. In those circumstances, it might be argued that a purposive interpretation of the directive would bring the documents within its scope.

62. For reasons which I shall explain, it does not appear to me to be necessary to reach a concluded view on these questions. It is sufficient to say that it appears to me to be arguable that the MTS, or the local transport strategies which formed its constituent parts, formed a plan or programme within the meaning of the directive. The question whether the decision to construct the Fastlink constituted a modification to a plan or programme can be considered on the hypothesis that the MTS (or its constituent documents) comprised such a plan or programme. [...]

64. Proceeding on the hypothesis that the MTS (or its constituent documents) constituted a plan or programme, the next issue which requires to be considered is whether the Fastlink constituted a modification to that plan or programme within the meaning of article 2(a). In my view it did not.

65. As I have explained, the MTS proposed that the local roads authorities should construct a WPR which would, on completion, become part of the trunk road network. In March 2003 the Ministers took over responsibility for designing and constructing the WPR, as the authority responsible for trunk roads. In doing so, the Ministers assumed responsibility for a specific development. In the terminology of the EIA and SEA Directives, that development could aptly be described as a 'project', defined in article 1 of the EIA Directive as meaning, in the first place, 'the execution of construction works or of other installation or schemes'. It could not readily be regarded as a plan or programme subject to the SEA Directive (assuming that to have been temporally applicable): the Ministers did not assume responsibility for the preparation of a document setting the framework for future development consent of projects.

66. The subsequent decision to enlarge the project, so as to provide a trunk road connection [which was what Fastlink was] between Stonehaven and the WPR as previously envisaged, was taken by the Ministers primarily in order to relieve congestion on the A90 and anticipate the need to increase the capacity of that road. In taking that decision, the Ministers modified a project: they did not modify the legal or administrative framework which had been set for future development consent of projects. It is therefore not the SEA Directive which would apply, but other EU legislation such as the EIA Directive, as the Commission explained in its guidance document, *Implementation of Directive 2001/42 on the Assessment of the Effects of Certain Plans and Programmes on the Environment* (2003), para 3.9.

FURTHER READING AND QUESTIONS

1. For an excellent overview of SEA see Riki Therivel, *Strategic Environmental Assessment in Action* (2nd edn, Routledge 2010).

2. The operation of the SEA Directive was reviewed by the Commission. Commission, *Report from the Commission on the Application and Effectiveness of the Directive on Strategic Environmental Assessment (Directive 2001/42/EC)* COM(2009) 469.

3. The consultation procedure under Article 6 of the Directive has also been subject to consideration by the CJEU. See Case C-474/10 *Department of the Environment v Seaport (NI) Ltd* (CJEU, 20 October 2011). A thoughtful discussion of the case can be found in Sharon Turner, 'The Strategic Environmental Assessment Directive: A Potential Lever for Independent Environmental Regulation in Northern Ireland' (2012) 24 JEL 357.

4. Further examples of the SEA Directive being considered by the English courts can be found at *Save Historic Newmarket Ltd v Forest Heath District Council* [2011] EWHC 606 (Admin); *Heard v Broadland District Council* [2012] EWHC 344 (Admin); and *Cogent Land LLP v Rochford City Council* [2012] EWHC 2542.

8 CONCLUSION

This chapter has been an introduction to EIA. It has examined the nature and purpose of EIA, the way in which it has developed, the EU EIA regime, and the challenges that EIA has created for the CJEU and for English courts. As stated at the beginning of this chapter, the challenges created by EIA largely fall into three categories. First, there are those challenges created by the fact that EIA is characterized as a revolutionary process. There is, however, not always agreement over the nature and purpose of that process and that can be seen in the variations in EIA regimes and in commentators' understandings of them. Second, there are those challenges involved in implementing the EA Directive into national law. The CJEU has been required to provide guidance on how Member States should conduct screening which ultimately limits Member State discretion. Likewise, while the CJEU has concluded that the Directive has direct effect it has only been able to do so by adjusting traditional direct effect doctrine. Finally, EIA has created a number of challenges for national courts in carrying out judicial review of EIA decision-making. The most significant challenge in this regard has been establishing what the appropriate standard of review is. It is perhaps this last question which will prove to be a constant source of litigation far into the future.

FURTHER READING

1. Stephen Tromans, *Environmental Impact Assessment* (2nd edn, Bloomsbury Professional 2012) provides an excellent and detailed analysis of both the EIA Directive and the SEA Directive.

2. John Glasson, Riki Therivel, and Andrew Chadwick, *Introduction to Environmental Impact Assessment* (4th edn, Routledge 2011) is a thorough non-legal discussion of EIA.

3. A very detailed account of different techniques in EIA can be found in Peter Morris and Riki Therivel, *Methods of Environmental Impact Assessment* (3rd edn, Routledge 2009).

4. A thoughtful scholarly account of EIA can be found in Jane Holder, *Environmental Assessment: The Regulation of Decision-Making* (OUP 2004).

NATURE CONSERVATION

Nature conservation is one of the most paradoxical subjects in environmental law. On the one hand, it is the area of law that often first comes to mind when one thinks of environmental law. It gives rise to terrible jokes such as: environmental law is 'concerned with the birds and the bees'. On the other hand, it is a topic that students often struggle with, and in particular struggle to be interested in! This is because nature conservation law is effectively a series of different legislative regimes containing a vast array of different statutory provisions. There are few overarching legal ideas or principles and this is an area where you really need to study legislative regimes in detail.

Saying this may appear an off-putting start—who wants to learn about something that others find dull? However, we highlight this paradox for two reasons. First, it is important to appreciate that the dense legislative landscape of nature conservation presents an intellectual challenge for those who wish to understand this area. This is particularly when that legislative landscape is not subject to easy rationalization. And so, if you do not expect to find a neat framework of legal obligations that relate to nature conservation, then you will find this area of environmental law less disappointing. Second, once you get past the legislative complexity, it really is an interesting area of law—nature conservation laws reveal a lot about what we value in our natural environment and how we value it. The big picture is still lurking there in the detail, and mastering the detail will put you in a position to critique its broader implications as well as to understand it.

The chapter is structured as follows. The first section considers the different aspects of nature conservation as an environmental problem. In particular, it is important to appreciate the following: that there are many different reasons for wanting to conserve nature; the limits of scientific knowledge in understanding the natural environment; and that decision-making in relation to nature conservation is profoundly polycentric. The second section provides a brief overview of the relevant international, EU, and national nature conservation regimes that apply in England. In relation to these, both the legislative and institutional landscapes are complex. Sections 3 and 4 consider two of the most significant of these regimes—the Sites of Special Scientific Interest (SSSI) Framework under the Wildlife and Countryside (WC) Act 1981 and the linked regimes of the EU Birds Directive[1] and Habitats Directive.[2] The final section briefly reflects on the ongoing attempts to reform nature conservation law.

As always, we have three important caveats. First, this is a highly technical area of law and this chapter does not replace a good detailed textbook on specific nature conservation regimes. For this purpose, please see the further reading list at the end of the chapter. Second, our primary focus in the

---

[1] Directive 2009/147/EC of the European Parliament and of the Council of 30 November 2009 on the conservation of wild birds [2010] OJ L20/7. Note this is the codified version of Directive 79/409/EEC as amended.
[2] Council Directive 92/43/EEC of 21 May 1992 on the conservation of natural habitats and of wild fauna and flora [1992] OJ L206/7.

chapter is upon those regimes that protect areas of land (by what we call the 'enclave technique'), as this form of ecosystem protection not only aligns neatly with environmental law more broadly, but has also been highly contentious in operation. Thus, this chapter does not cover in great detail individual wildlife regimes (such as schemes for hunting or protecting birds and other species), or issues to do with other forms of landscape designation, nor does it cover the important issue of the interface between agriculture and environmental protection. Third, this is an area where the law is undergoing quite fast paced change (see Section 5 and the Conservations of Habits and Species (Amendment) Regulations 2012) and thus a visit to our companion website is encouraged. Finally, we appreciate that the label 'nature conservation law' itself has serious limitations. 'Nature' is a vague concept and the purpose of the laws discussed in this chapter is not always conservation. We use the label because, despite these problems, it has been a popular term historically and any other term has similar, or other, limitations.

1 NATURE CONSERVATION AS AN ENVIRONMENTAL PROBLEM

It is generally recognized that industrialization and urbanization since the nineteenth century have led to a degradation of the natural environment worldwide. As a response, a body of law has emerged in most jurisdictions that, for our purposes, we can call 'nature conservation law'. Broadly speaking, nature conservation law is comprised of those laws concerned *specifically* with protecting the natural environment. We say 'specifically' because nearly all environmental law can be understood as protecting the natural environment in some way. At the same time, it needs to be acknowledged that nature conservation laws may also pursue other purposes than simply protecting the environment (such as the management of a species for hunting).

Before considering nature conservation law in detail, it is important to have some understanding of nature conservation as a problem. This returns us to the discussion in Chapter 2 and, in particular, three important issues—the different ways in which we value nature, the challenges in assessing damage to the natural environment, and the polycentric nature of environmental problems.

1.1 ENVIRONMENTAL VALUES AND PROTECTING THE NATURAL ENVIRONMENT

There are many different reasons that a society may wish to protect nature. Thus, in Chapter 2, we saw ecocentric and anthropocentric views of environmental protection, but even that distinction is a crude one, as it doesn't fully capture all the ways in which nature is valued.[3] For example, Eckersley identifies animal liberation, resource ecology, and preservationism as different ways to 'value' the environment.[4] These modes of thought have developed over time and often in response to each other.

In discussing nature and its value, scholars often focus on ecocentric understandings of nature. Eckersley explains the main features of this perspective.

[3] Timothy O'Riordan, *Environmentalism* (2nd edn, Pion 1983).
[4] Robyn Eckersley, *Environmentalism and Political Theory: Towards an Ecocentric Approach* (UCL Press 1992) ch 2.

Robyn Eckersley, *Environmentalism and Political Theory: Towards an Ecocentric Approach* (UCL Press 1992) 46

[An ecocentric perspective offers] a more encompassing approach than any of those so far examined in that it (i) recognizes the full range of human interests i the nonhuman world (ie, it incorporates yet goes beyond the resource conservation and human welfare ecology perspectives); (ii) recognizes the interests of the nonhuman community (yet goes beyond the early preservationist perspective); (iii) recognizes the interests of future generations of nonhumans; and (iv) adopts a holistic rather than an atomistic perspective (contra the animal liberation perspective) insofar as it values populations, species, ecosystems, and the ecosphere as well as individual organisms.

The scholarly focus on ecocentrism in relation to nature conservation is not surprising. If nature is to be valued, then valuing it for its own sake makes a certain sense. Yet, ecocentric perspectives fit uneasily into mainstream socio-political discourses and legal discourses. This is because those discourses are primarily anthropocentric in nature. Take, for example, Dworkin's description of the fish, which was the focus of the US Supreme court decision in *Tennessee Valley Authority v Hill*.[5] That decision involved the interpretation and operation of US endangered species legislation.

Ronald Dworkin, *Law's Empire* (Fontana 1986) 21

The conservationists discovered that one almost finished TVA dam, costing over one hundred million dollars, would be likely to destroy the only habitat of the snail darter, a three-inch fish of no particular beauty or biological interest or general ecological importance.

Dworkin's analysis is not an ecocentric perspective. For him, the fish has no purpose—there is no argument that it should exist for its own sake. His view is not uncommon. Eckersley notes: that the greatest concentration of ecocentric activists can usually be found in organizations, campaigns, or movements that promote the protection of wilderness.[6]

There are two implications of this. The first is that such activist organizations tend to operate most strongly in jurisdictions where there are large tracts of wilderness, such as Australia and the US. Second, those organizations tend to be understood as socially radical. Yet, while ecocentrism may not be mainstream, it does not mean that nature is not valued. Rather, it is to say that mainstream policy and legal discourses about nature conservation are overwhelmingly anthropocentric. Nature is valued for the benefits that it provides to humans. This perspective can be seen in the two extracts given here. The first concerns the Millennium Ecosystem Assessment, an international exercise and body that developed out of international discourses concerning biodiversity, including the UN Convention on Biodiversity (CBD).

Millennium Ecosystem Assessment, *Ecosystems and Human Well Being: Synthesis* (Island Press 2005) © World Resources Institute, v

The assessment focuses on the linkages between ecosystems and human well-being and, in particular, on 'ecosystem services.' An ecosystem is a dynamic complex of plant, animal, and microorganism

---

[5] 437 US 153 (1978).   [6] Eckersley (n 4) 46.

communities and the nonliving environment interacting as a functional unit. The MA [Millennium Assessment] deals with the full range of ecosystems—from those relatively undisturbed, such as natural forests, to landscapes with mixed patterns of human use, to ecosystems intensively managed and modified by humans, such as agricultural land and urban areas. Ecosystem services are the benefits people obtain from ecosystems. These include *provisioning services* such as food, water, timber, and fiber; *regulating services* that affect climate, floods, disease, wastes, and water quality; *cultural services* that provide recreational, aesthetic, and spiritual benefits; and *supporting services* such as soil formation, photosynthesis, and nutrient cycling [...] The human species, while buffered against environmental changes by culture and technology, is fundamentally dependent on the flow of ecosystem services.

The language of 'ecosystem services' can also be seen in the following assessment of nature conservation issues in England, published at the time that a similar ecosystem assessment exercise was underway in the UK.[7]

Natural England, *State of the Natural Environment 2008* (Natural England 2008) 297

England's natural environment is important for its intrinsic value, but it is also vital for the ecosystem services it provides. These include not only easily valued services such as flood defence, clean water and carbon sequestration, but also the less tangible and equally important cultural, aesthetic, health and wellbeing benefits. The evidence for these non-valued services is accumulating and we have provided case studies in this report.

Taking this approach even further, an ad hoc Natural Capital Committee was established in 2012,[8] which reports to Cabinet via the Economic Affairs Committee, with the aim of advising government on where, when, and how natural assets are being used unsustainably and how it should prioritize action in light of economic valuations of natural environmental 'assets'.[9]

While these two extracts put forward anthropocentric understandings of nature conservation, it can also be seen that there are many different anthropocentric reasons for protecting nature. Indeed, at least fifteen different reasons for valuing nature can be seen in the extracts from Dworkin, Natural England, and the Millennium Ecosystem Assessment (see if you can spot them all).

There is one obvious, and also one less obvious, implication of this state of affairs. The obvious implication is that societies will create different nature conservation regimes to protect nature for different reasons in divergent ways. Thus, if a species is being protected because it is endangered, that will result in a different type of legal regime from protecting an area of wilderness because of its beauty. This variety of reasons to protect nature, and thus different ways of doing so, will be seen throughout this chapter.

The less obvious implication of the way in which values operate in relation to nature conservation law is that different reasons for protecting nature will also frame our understanding of nature differently. For example, if what is valued is beauty, then nature conservation regimes will frame our understanding of nature by identifying and protecting what is beautiful. That is a different framing of

---

[7] UK National Ecosystem Assessment, *The UK National Ecosystem Assessment Technical Report* (UNEP-WCMC, 2011).

[8] In light of the Government's Natural Environment White Paper, *The Natural Choice: Securing the Value of Nature* (TSO 2011).

[9] See <http://www.defra.gov.uk/naturalcapitalcommittee/> accessed 3 February 2013.

nature from what we see in the Convention on Biological Diversity, which (and as its name suggests) focuses on biological diversity, a concept that it defines in the following terms.

Convention on Biological Diversity

Article 2

'Biological diversity' means the variability among living organisms from all sources including, inter alia, terrestrial, marine and other aquatic ecosystems and the ecological complexes of which they are part; this includes diversity within species, between species and of ecosystems.

All of this is an explanation as to why 'nature conservation' is too crude a label for this area of the law. For the lawyer, it also means that each regime must be analysed carefully for not only what it protects and why it protects it, but also for how nature is conceptualized by it.

1.2 SCIENTIFIC ASSESSMENT AND NATURE CONSERVATION

To know that there is a nature conservation problem and to address that problem, scientific information is needed about the natural environment. As this is the case, a major aspect of promoting biodiversity has involved creating frameworks for the collection and dissemination of environmental information. For example, Chapter 40 of Agenda 21 sets out a programme to do exactly this—as part of that programme, 'State of the Environment' reporting has become a regular exercise in jurisdictions across the world.[10]

Within the EU and England and Wales, there are a number of mechanisms for reporting on the state of the natural environment. Two extracts from such reports are set out here.

European Environment Agency, *The European Environment—State and Outlook 2010: Synthesis* (EEA 2010) 50–51, 53

Quantitative data on the status and trends of European biodiversity are sparse, both for conceptual and practical reasons. The spatial scale and level of detail at which ecosystems, habitats and plant communities are discerned is to a certain extent arbitrary. There are no harmonised European monitoring data for ecosystem and habitat quality, and the results of case studies are difficult to combine. Reporting under Article 17 of the Habitats Directive has recently improved the evidence base, but only for the listed habitats.

Species monitoring is conceptually more straightforward, but resource-intensive and necessarily very selective. Around 1700 vertebrate species, 90000 insects and 30000 vascular plants have been recorded in Europe. This figure does not even include the majority of marine species, or bacteria, microbes and soil invertebrates. Harmonised trend data cover only a very small fraction of the total number of species—they are largely limited to common birds and butterflies. Again, Article 17 reporting under the Habitats Directive provides additional material for target species.

---

[10] United Nations, *Agenda 21: The United Nations Programme of Action from Rio* (1992) <www.un.org/esa/dsd/agenda21/> accessed 19 September 2012.

The data for common bird species suggest a stabilisation at low levels during the last decade. Populations of forest birds have declined by around 15% since 1990, but from 2000 onwards numbers appear stable. Farmland bird populations declined dramatically in the 1980s, mainly due to agricultural intensification. Their populations have remained stable since the mid-1990s, albeit at a low level. General farming trends (such as lower input use, increased set-aside and share of organic farming) and policy measures (such as targeted agri-environment schemes) may have contributed to this. Grassland butterfly populations, however, have declined by a further 50% since 1990, indicating the impact of further intensification of agriculture on the one hand and abandonment on the other.

The conservation status of the most threatened species and habitats remains worrying despite the now established Natura 2000 network of protected areas. The situation appears worst for aquatic habitats, coastal zones and nutrient-poor terrestrial habitats, such as heaths, bogs, mires and fens. In 2008, only 17% of the target species under the Habitats Directive were considered to have a favourable conservation status, 52% an unfavourable status, and the status of 31% was unknown.

These aggregated data, however, do not allow conclusions about the effectiveness of the protection regime of the Habitats Directive, since time series are not yet available and habitat restoration and species recovery may require more time. Also, no comparison can currently be made between protected and unprotected areas within the species' ranges. For the Birds Directive, however, studies indicate that the bird conservation measures in Natura 2000 have been effective.

The cumulative number of alien species in Europe has been increasing steadily since the beginning of the 20th century. Out of a total of 10000 established alien species, 163 have been classified as the worst invasives because they have proved to be highly invasive and damaging to native biodiversity in at least part of their European range. While the increase may be slowing down or levelling off for terrestrial and freshwater species, this is not the case for marine and estuarine species.

Note how the legal frameworks in this analysis—the Habitats and Birds Directive (examined in Section 4)—provide important benchmarks for what should be measured and how it should be measured. Indeed, decisions about what is to be reported on, and what indicators are to be used, are crucial aspects of this type of reporting, and it is important to remember that such decisions will involve value judgments and frame our understanding of nature in different ways.

The next extract comes from Natural England's *State of the Environment Report 2008*, which reports on the decade up until 2008. Note the different focus from the *European Environment—State and Outlook 2010: Synthesis* extract. The report considers landscape protection and there is no explicit discussion of EU legal frameworks.

Natural England, *State of the Natural Environment 2008* (Natural England 2008) 297–98

There has been a levelling off in the past decade in the long-term decline of a number of indicator species including farmland birds and butterflies. However, the trend for some groups is still downwards. For example, the flora, birds and butterflies most associated with our woodland are all continuing to decline. There has been a particular decline in specialist species—those species that have very specific habitat requirements—revealed in the monitoring of birds, bumblebees and butterflies. For example, the specialist grassland edge Duke of Burgundy butterfly has declined by 50% in the last ten years.

Wetland and freshwater habitats continue to give us particular concern. Our open waters are perhaps in the worst condition of all habitats, even where legally protected. Wetland species are suffering with, for example, eels declining by 90% since the mid-1980s and water voles the most rapidly declining mammal. There have been major declines in populations of breeding wading birds on unprotected lowland wetland grasslands, notably the snipe which is down by 90% in some regions. Coastal habitats such as saltmarshes are declining due to coastal squeeze and pollution.

However, some of the trends over the last ten years show that there has been real improvement. There have been major increases in heathland birds, for example nightjar, woodlark and Dartford warbler—and the last of these has increased its range by over 100% due to milder winters. Some wetland birds have shown massive increases (for example gadwall, whooper swan), the recovery of the otter has continued, and four bat species are increasing significantly.

For our landscapes, whilst some 20% are showing signs of neglect, existing character has been maintained in 51%, and enhanced in 10%.

The last ten years have seen a major increase in opportunities to enjoy the natural environment by giving a right of access to mountain, moor, heath, down and registered common land. There is a growing body of evidence relating to the benefits of access to and engagement with the natural environment—specifically in terms of individuals' health and wellbeing—and this is increasingly being recognised in public policy. However, there is a complex relationship between provision of opportunities for access and engagement with the natural environment and resulting behaviours.

These are only two of many examples of such reports. Thus, the EEA and Natural England also produce reports on more specific topics and other institutions produce their own reports—see the further reading section at the end of the chapter.

It is very easy in reading these reports to get the impression that the statistics they provide are utterly definitive and easily obtainable. But it is important to remember the EEA's statement that 'quantitative data on the status and trends of European biodiversity are sparse, both for conceptual and practical reasons'. Indeed, scientific uncertainty is a particularly pertinent problem in understanding nature conservation. The natural environment is an open-ended and iterative system and ecology is still a relatively new discipline compared with other areas of science. There are very real practical problems collecting data about species—no species of animal is simply going to come when you whistle and line up neatly to be counted. This is illustrated in the extract from an Australian merits review decision, which concerned the impact of building a road through a gorge on the habitat of the Giant Burrowing Frog. The legal issues need not concern us. What is interesting are the many uncertainties concerning whether the frog was in the gorge and whether the road would have an impact on the frog. Webb and York are two experts appearing before the court.

Leach v Director General of National Parks and Wildlife Service
[1993] NSWLEC 191 (Stein J) NSW Crown Copyright

Upon an examination of the available material relevant to the Giant Burrowing Frog (Heleioporus australiacus) and the knowledge of the frog in this particular habitat, one is driven to the conclusion that there is a dearth of knowledge. We know with reasonable certainty that the call of a male frog was heard by Dr York and Mr Daly in 1992. We know that it is likely that there is a population of the frogs in the area. Webb, an expert on the frog, says that the amphibian is known to move great distances from breeding areas when foraging for food at night. While its prime habitat appears to be a gorge or creek environment, the Giant Burrowing Frog may forage wider afield into drier areas. It is not surprising therefore that its call was heard in an area some distance from the gorge. Dr York's statement that the degradation of the gorge habitat leads to the conclusion that it is not prime habitat for the species is open to question and is not self evident to me. Dr York does, however, make the point in his report (Ex M1) that the nature and extent of the population of the Giant Burrowing Frog in the study area are unknown. Notwithstanding, he says that it is possible to make a reasonable assessment of the possible impacts of the road because of the known habitat requirements. Dr York sees a very small loss of foraging habitat and no loss or interference with access to food or breeding patterns.

Garry Webb disagrees with a number of conclusions of Dr York. He accepts that the species is notoriously difficult to find but is critical of the limited reptile and amphibian survey, which is certainly inadequate to determine the regional significance of its presence at Bomaderry Creek. Since it is listed as a rare and vulnerable species, Mr Webb says that its conservation should be given a high priority. I accept his opinion. The frog is known in only a small number of locations in the Shoalhaven region. Apart from the present case, only two sightings have been made—at Jervis Bay and 15km south-east of Bowral in 1963. Its distribution is obviously patchy and its recent listing by the Scientific Committee understandable.

In the opinion of Mr Webb the road would present an insurmountable barrier to the dispersion of frogs at favourable times and divide suitable habitat into small isolates. He doubts the relevance of any of the proposed mitigating factors to frogs and knows of no study which supports the efficacy of underpasses for frogs. (In this regard Mr Webster handed up a beautifully presented booklet entitled *Amphibienschutz* from Baden-Wurttemberg. Its photographs include frogs and highway underpasses. Unfortunately the text is in German, and notwithstanding my ancestry, I am unable to comprehend its import).

Mr Webb also opines other potential impacts on the Giant Burrowing Frog. However, he concludes his report by emphasising the inadequacy of the data to quantify the extent and size of the population in the area 'nor to assess the potential impact of the proposed road'. In his view there has been an inadequate survey, an inadequate assessment of potential habitat and an inadequate assessment of the impact of the development on the survival of the population of the Giant Burrowing Frog. Again, I accept and prefer his opinion.

Furthermore, collecting meaningful data about the natural world cannot be done quickly. Deep understanding of ecosystems can only be developed over a long period of time by a group of dedicated scientists with institutional support.

Tim Clutton-Brock and Ben C Sheldon, 'The Seven Ages of Pan' *Science* (5 March 2010) 1207, 1207–08. Reprinted with permission from AAAS.

Imagine yourself as a latter-day Jane Goodall, establishing your camp on the edge of the rainforest, eager to document the behavior and ecology of a previously unstudied ape. As months pass, the animals stop scrambling away as soon as they see you and you can catch occasional glimpses of them as they feed. Stick at it for a year or two and, if you are lucky, you will be able to recognize individuals and spot interesting new behavior patterns. But to understand the network of social relationships between individuals, you need to know their ages, kin relations, and relative dominance rank. That will take at least one decade or, more likely, two. However, other important questions will take three or four decades of systematic data collection: how and why groups increase or decline in size; how genetic differences interact with environmental factors to affect breeding success and survival; how population density is regulated. During all this time you will need to withstand the vicissitudes of funding, political disturbances, and the demands of your career and family.

For long-lived species, the time scale outlined above is no exaggeration. After Jane Goodall started to study the chimpanzees at Gombe in 1960, it took her and her collaborators 50 years to obtain the data required to fully describe the life histories of chimpanzees—a quantitative Seven Ages of Pan—and answer important questions [...]

Compared to primates, many other mammals are relatively easy to catch and mark and (with the exception of elephants) have shorter life spans. As a result, some studies now provide records of the full life histories of several thousand individuals spanning multiple generations and offer opportunities to investigate biological questions that are not yet accessible in primates. Multigenerational pedigrees that can be used to assess the relative contributions of genotype and environment to individual differences now exist for an increasing number of birds and mammals, and modern genomic approaches have also started to yield new insights. However, their application requires the existence of extensive phenotypic and ecological data, and there are no short-cuts to obtaining these data.

It is particularly important to keep this last sentence in mind. Data collection relating to the natural environment is a long and intensive process. This fact, and the scientific uncertainties involved, is in the background in all policy decisions and legal issues relating to nature conservation.

1.3 POLYCENTRISM, CONFLICT, AND NATURE CONSERVATION

Chapter 2 considered how environmental problems are polycentric. Nature conservation issues are particularly polycentric in that they involve an interrelated web of different interests across society, as illustrated by Reid's discussion. Reid also highlights how nature conservation measures are highly specific to particular areas.

Colin T Reid, 'The Privatisation of Biodiversity? Possible New Approaches to Nature Conservation Law in the UK' (2011) 23 JEL 203, 223–24

Biodiversity conservation is distinctly different from many elements of environmental law, especially control of emissions, because of the nature of what is to be conserved. Although for emissions controls there are often very localised impacts to be considered as well, in many cases what counts is the overall quality of a fairly large unit, such as a groundwater reservoir, river basin or the global atmosphere. This enables an approach to be taken that can easily accommodate trade-offs within overall limits set at a broad level and thereby allow for a less coordinated approach to the specific action taken to achieve emission reductions. The same is not true for biodiversity. Not only must each species and habitat be considered individually, as opposed to the way in which greenhouse gases can be grouped together as the focus of control, but the measures needed are site specific and can only be effective if a whole network of sites is similarly protected. Greatly enhanced protection for whales is of no benefit to red squirrels. The most wonderful measures conserving a forest are of no benefit to migratory wading birds, and protecting the birds' winter feeding grounds is of no benefit if their summer breeding habitat is destroyed or the places where they stop and feed on their migration routes are no longer able to support them. Moreover, if we are to help species cope with the challenge of rapid climate change, conservation efforts must be directed not just as those areas of value today but at those that will provide a home for species as their current habitat ceases to be suitable. Conservation effort therefore cannot work as a collection of distinct and essentially fungible units, but must proceed in a coherent and coordinated manner, creating networks of ecosystems and mixing strictly protected areas as 'biodiversity citadels' within a generally supportive context which will enable these to remain in good health.

Also implicit in Reid's analysis is that nature conservation issues often involve profound socio-political conflict. This is due to the factors highlighted by Reid here and also the roles of the different values discussed in Section 1.1. Nature conservation decisions also often require choices to be made between competing and irreconcilable uses of land. Pristine wilderness cannot be maintained if a road is to be built through that wilderness. Bird wading grounds cannot exist if a car park is built over them. Decisions thus need to be made about what is important and those decisions will nearly always be contentious because they involve picking winners and losers (in environmental, social, and economic senses).

FURTHER READING AND QUESTIONS

1. For further reading about anthropocentric and ecocentric perspectives of the natural environment, see Linda Kalof and Terre Satterfield (eds), *The Earthscan Reader in Environmental Values* (Earthscan 2005).

2. The recent HM Government, *The Natural Choice: Securing the Value of Nature* (Cm 8082, June 2011) is an important example of government policy on the natural environment. Read it and consider how nature is framed and valued.

3. There is a range of different sources of information about the state of the natural environment, including biodiversity. The European Environment Agency (<www.eea.europa.eu/> accessed 19 September 2012) is a particularly good source for EU-related information. For the UK, see the Joint Nature Conservation Committee's Biodiversity in Your Pocket indicators (<http://jncc.defra.gov.uk/> accessed 19 September 2012). These sources are regularly updated. Reports are also produced by other bodies from time to time, for example, Environmental Audit Committee Report, *Halting Biodiversity Loss* (2007–08 HC 743).

4. For a history of the development of ecology and the nature conservation movement in the UK, see Peter Ayres, *Shaping Ecology: The Life of Arthur Tansley* (John Wiley & Sons 2012). The essays in Norman Maclean (ed), *Silent Summer; The State of Wildlife in Britain and Ireland* (CUP 2010) are also useful.

---

2 NATURE CONSERVATION LAW—THE BIG PICTURE

This section now turns to the legal landscape of nature conservation law. In brief, nature conservation regimes exist at the UK, EU, and international levels. At the national level, even before the devolution process of the late 1990s, there were variations in nature conservation regimes between the different UK regions. Our focus here is upon the English regimes, which involve three main pieces of legislation—National Parks and Access to the Countryside (NPAC) Act 1949, the Wildlife and Countryside Act (WC) 1981 (as amended), and the Natural Environment and Rural Communities (NERC) Act 2006. The NPAC Act puts in place a framework for creating National Parks, local nature reserves, and national nature reserves. The WC Act implements international obligations in relation to endangered species and also now the SSSI regime. NERC, amongst other things, sets up Natural England. Note also the Marine and Coastal Access Act 2009, which puts into place a framework for Marine Conservation Zones (MCZs). There are numerous other pieces of legislation protecting particular species[11] and we shall see, in Section 4, that the Habitats Directive has been implemented through delegated legislation.[12]

---

[11] Protection of Badgers Act 1982 and Conservation of Seals Act 1970.
[12] Conservation of Habitats and Species Regulations 2010 SI 2010/490 (as amended).

At the EU level there are two key Directives—the Birds Directive[13] and the Habitats Directive.[14] The Environmental Liability Directive (see Section 3 of Chapter 9) is also relevant as 'environment damage' under the Directive includes damage to species and habitats covered by the EU nature conservation Directives (Article 2(1)).

At the international level, there is a range of different conventions that protect nature. Historically, these regimes were regional in nature,[15] protected particular species,[16] or did both.[17] However, over the last several decades, more 'global' regimes have also developed, such as and the World Heritage Convention (which also protects cultural heritage)[18] and the Convention on Biological Diversity (CBD)[19]

While this description makes clear that nature conservation law is a field crowded with legal documents, it gives very little feeling for the nature of the legal obligations that these legal frameworks create, or how they operate and interrelate in practice. This section gives a brief overview of these features, firstly considering the major aspects and techniques of legal frameworks in this area. It then sketches the range of different frameworks that are relevant in England, starting with the international regimes. This may give the impression that nature conservation law is a 'top-down' development where international law has been the catalyst. As will become clear, that is not the case.

2.1 NATURE CONSERVATION LAW—MAJOR FEATURES AND TECHNIQUES

Any legal regime to protect nature involves creating frameworks for identifying what should be protected and providing legal tools for how it should be protected. In identifying *what* should be protected, some nature conservation regimes, particularly those protecting species, explicitly identify the species that are to be protected.[20] However, most regimes will need to set out the rationale for protection and to create a process by which areas and/or species can be identified and classified as worthy of protection. This process is usually administrative in nature. The precise process involved can vary however. Thus, as we will see, there are differences between the notification process under s 28(1) of the WC Act 1981 and the designation processes of Special Protection Areas (SPA) and Special Areas of Conservation (SACs) under the Birds and Habitats Directives. The latter regimes involve quite complex identification processes, where species to be protected are set out in the Annexes of these Directives and then the designation processes involve EU as well as Member State institutions. In all cases, the identification process has a scientific and technical aspect but it is important to remember that the process is not value-free—this is due both to scientific uncertainty and to the fact that any legal regime is based on a legal prescription of what should be protected.

The second part of any nature conservation regime concerns *how* something should be protected— the 'operational' aspect of a nature conservation regime. Generally speaking, there are four main legal

---

[13] (n 1).   [14] (n 2).

[15] African Convention on the Conservation of Nature and Natural Resources 1968 1001 UNTS 3; Convention on the Conservation of European Wildlife and Natural Habitats (Bern Convention) 1979 ETS 104.

[16] Convention on International Trade in Endangered Species of Wild Fauna and Flora (CITES) (1973) 993 UNTS 243; International Convention for the Regulation of Whaling (Whaling Convention) (1949) 161 UNTS 72.

[17] Convention for the Protection of the Marine Environment of the North Atlantic (OSPAR Convention) 1992 2354 UNTS 67.

[18] Convention concerning the Protection of the World Cultural and Natural Heritage, 16 November 1972 (in force since 17 December 1975) 11 ILM 1358.

[19] Convention on Biodiversity 1760 UNTS 79, 31 ILM 818 (1992).

[20] For example, Protection of Badgers Act 1982.

techniques used in protecting nature. These techniques exist on a spectrum between those legal techniques that focus on particular species to those that are more wide-ranging. First, there are criminal offences for harming, taking, or trading in a particular protected species and/or licensing regimes that limit the taking of species. The 1973 Convention on International Trade in Endangered Species of Wild Fauna and Flora (CITES)[21] is an example of this type of regime, as it bans international trade in particular plants and animals and related products. This technique most obviously comes to mind when thinking about nature conservation law but it is the second technique—the enclave technique— that dominates contemporary nature conservation law.

Under the enclave technique, it is not only a species that is protected but a habitat, landscape, or ecosystem. The word 'enclave' has come to denote an area or population that is distinct from all around it. As a legal technique in nature conservation law, the enclave technique is concerned with identifying an area in which legal controls are placed on various activities.

The dominance of the enclave technique in nature conservation law is for two different reasons. First, to protect a species, their habitat must be protected. This is the reason why the Birds Directive has a SPA designation process (see further, Section 4). The second reason for the dominance of the enclave technique is that many nature conservation regimes have focused on protecting not just particular flora or fauna but landscapes and ecosystems. Natura 2000 and SSSIs are two examples of this (examined in Sections 3 and 4), and village greens[22] and national parks[23] are also examples of enclaves. There is considerable variation in what occurs within an enclave and, in most cases, human activity is not stopped completely but is either managed or limited. Further, areas around an enclave will also need to be protected.

The third legal technique for protecting nature is the integrating of nature conservation into other areas of decision-making. This is inevitable because other areas of decision-making, such as transport policy, energy policy, and planning, have major impacts upon nature conservation. Thus, we will see here the way in which different nature conservation regimes affect planning law. Section 40(1)–(3) of the Natural Environment and Rural Communities Act 2006 is also important to note in this regard.

Natural Environment and Rural Communities Act 2006

Section 40 (1)–(3)

(1) Every public authority must, in exercising its functions, have regard, so far as is consistent with the proper exercise of those functions, to the purpose of conserving biodiversity.

(2) In complying with subsection (1), a Minister of the Crown, government department or the National Assembly for Wales must in particular have regard to the United Nations Environmental Programme Convention on Biological Diversity of 1992.

(3) Conserving biodiversity includes, in relation to a living organism or type of habitat, restoring or enhancing a population or habitat. [...]

While this provision looks promising, in practice, this obligation has not been as significant as more specific nature conservation obligations that exist. Thus in *R (Buglife, The Invertebrate Conservation Trust) v Thurrock Thames Gateway Development Corporation*[24] the Court focused far more closely

---

[21] 993 UNTS 243.
[22] Commons Act 2006 and Commons Registration Act 1965. See Section 2.3 of Chapter 6.
[23] NPAC Act 1949. See Section 2.4.   [24] [2009] EWCA Civ 29, [2009] Env LR 18.

on the now defunct *Planning Policy Statement 9: Biodiversity and Geological Conservation*, which then existed and was a more detailed discussion of how biological conservation should be taken into account in planning decisions. In light of the repeal of PPS 9, and the introduction of the National Planning Policy Framework (NPPF),[25] this raises a question about whether s 40 will have greater significance in the future.

The final set of legal techniques to note are a set of emerging governance techniques that involve both public and private actors. As we shall see, there has always been a significant role for the voluntary sector in nature conservation— wildlife trusts being a good example of this—but in recent years there has been an increased focus on the use of more novel regulatory techniques. Much of this is still in development. Reid highlights the potential for using conservation easements, biodiversity offsets, and payments for ecosystem services,[26] as well as the context in which such measures are being proposed.

Colin T Reid, 'The Privatisation of Biodiversity? Possible New Approaches to Nature Conservation Law in the UK' (2011) 23 JEL 203, 230–31.

Although extensive legal controls have been introduced, the current approach to conservation based on the central role of public authorities is not achieving its objective of maintaining biodiversity, far less reversing the serious decline in recent decades. [...] The failure of the present law may be attributable not so much to any inherent weaknesses but more to that fact that conservation measures have been left to stand on their own against a tide of other pressures that prioritise economic development and human convenience over the need to protect the health of the biosphere on which we all depend. Yet, especially at a time of austerity in public finances, there is clearly an attraction in adopting a new approach that relies less on public authorities and 'command and control' and places more responsibility in the hands of the private sector. This would match the deregulation and privatisation approach that has been taken in other areas of environmental law, as well as giving greater effect both to current political ideas of transferring responsibility from central government and to the ethos of stewardship and shared responsibility that is part of building a more sustainable society.

It should be noted that these four legal techniques for nature conservation are not mutually exclusive. Thus, the enclave technique and the integrating technique will often be used together. Likewise, the emergence of new governance techniques in this area does not necessarily negate a role for the state.

2.2 INTERNATIONAL LAW FRAMEWORKS

International law frameworks for protecting nature have existed since the late nineteenth century and, as noted already, there is a range of different regimes in this area. As Bowman, Davies, and Regdwell point out, these regimes have been becoming increasingly sophisticated and institutionally embedded, both at the international and national levels.[27] This is particularly in relation to regimes protecting specific species, such as the Whaling Convention.[28]

---

[25] See Section 3.1 of Chapter 18.
[26] Colin T Reid, 'The Privatisation of Biodiversity? Possible New Approaches to Nature Conservation Law in the UK' (2011) 23 JEL 203.
[27] Michael Bowman, Peter Davies, and Catherine Redgwell, *Lyster's International Wildlife Law* (2nd edn, CUP 2010) ch 22.
[28] 161 UNTS 72.

It is also the case that a number of national and EU nature conservation laws originate from international law regimes. For example, the Control of Trade in Endangered Species (Enforcement) Regulations 1997 implements CITES. The Bern Convention on the Conservation of European Wildlife and Natural Habitats[29] was a powerful catalyst for the EU Birds and Habitats Directives. The UK SSSI regime is used as means of implementing the Convention on Wetlands of International Importance especially as Waterfowl Habitat (Ramsar Convention).[30] Furthermore, international law and policy discourses about nature conservation have a powerful framing effect. We have seen this in relation to the idea of 'ecosystem services' already.

With that said, the role of international law should not be overplayed. This is particularly so in relation to the CBD, the most high profile international law regime in this area, as Harrop explains.

Stuart R Harrop, '"Living In Harmony With Nature"? Outcomes of the 2010 Nagoya Conference of the Convention on Biological Diversity' (2011) 23 JEL 117, 119

The CBD is an example of a 'hard' international law that possesses a 'soft' nature. The obligations in the text are for the most part textually diluted or heavily qualified leaving extensive discretion to Member States in the manner of their implementation. The result is a purportedly normative hard law that operates in the manner of an aspirational, policy-oriented soft instrument. The compromises in the original negotiations of the CBD that created these circumstances resulted in part because the issue of biodiversity protection requires erosion of a country's sovereignty over its natural resources and in so doing clashes with a number of political, social and economic interests. It also imposes costs on states that give security to politically distant generations of beneficiaries but with no obvious returns in the characteristically short-term political future. In consequence, the CBD's provisions are largely 'expressed as overall goals and policies' rather than obligations.

This is not to say that international law is irrelevant but that each international agreement must be understood in its own terms. In some cases, international regimes will create significant obligations that are observed in practice (such as CITES); in other cases, the regimes will be more aspirational and have a soft law nature (such as the CBD).[31]

2.3 EU LAW AND POLICY

There is a number of small EU initiatives that reflect international nature conservation regimes,[32] but, as noted in Section 2.2, there are two Directives that are understood as the centre piece of EU nature conservation law—the Birds Directive and the Habitats Directive.[33] The Birds Directive encompasses 'all species of naturally occurring birds in the wild state in the European territory of the Member States to which the Treaty applies',[34] and places duties on Member States to protect those species and their habitats.[35] These include duties to prohibit or regulate the sale of certain species,[36] or the hunting of them.[37] Annex 1 of the Directive identifies particular species that are subject to 'special conservation measures', including the creation of 'special protection areas'.[38] The Directive thus regulates

---

[29] See n 15.   [30] 996 UNTS 243.   [31] See Section 4.3 of Chapter 5.

[32] Regulation 338/97 on the protection of species of wild fauna and flora by regulating trade therein [1997] OJ L61/1 reflects the CITES regime.

[33] European Parliament and Council Directive 2009/147/EC on the conservation of wild birds [2009] OJ L20/7; Council Directive 92/43/EEC on the conservation of natural habitats and of wild fauna and flora [1992] OJ L206/7.

[34] Article 1.   [35] Articles 2–3.   [36] Article 6.   [37] Articles 7–8.   [38] Article 4.

species directly and also makes use of the enclave technique. The enclave technique has been the most significant and controversial aspect of the implementation of the Directive in the UK and will be considered in detail in Section 4.

The Habitats Directive is a more ambitious Directive that provides a framework for protecting not only the habitats of particular plant and animal species but also natural habitat types. Besides requiring Member States to take measures to 'establish a system of strict protection' for the species that it covers (Articles 12–13), it also provides a staged framework for the creation of special areas of conservation (SACs), with a view to building a network of representative habitats across the EU. The SAC designation process involves a number of steps. As we shall see in Section 4, designation does not stop activity taking place in either a SPA or a SAC, but it does require assessment of impacts before potentially damaging activity can take place (and places limits on activities that are found to be damaging to the ecological integrity of the relevant enclave site). As Directives, these regimes need to be implemented into UK law, and how this has occurred is examined in Section 4.

However, EU involvement in nature conservation is not limited to these two key Directives. The sites identified under the Birds and Habitats Directives are understood to create the Natura 2000 network. As of January 2011, this network was made up of 26, 106 sites[39] covering 949, 910 km². Most of those sites are designated under the Habitats Directive. Bryan discusses the nature of the Natura 2000 network.

Sharon Bryan, 'Contested Boundaries, Contested Places: The Natura 2000 Network in Ireland' (2012) 28 Journal of Rural Studies 80, 82

The network does not necessarily entail the crude and rigid imposition of boundaries. It constitutes, to some extent, an attempt to reconstruct nature conservation in a less bounded manner, dislodging it from the shackles of a strict nature–society dichotomy. The old 'fortress conservationist' or 'fences and fines' narrative in other words, has been replaced with a desire for a more integrated approach where human–nature relations are no longer seen as necessarily detrimental to biodiversity and are sometimes acknowledged as essential to its conservation. The practice of nature conservation is thus taken out of 'reserves' (or at least the *sole* preserve of the reserve) and into new milieus as new actors (farmers, hunters, foresters, landholders etc) are enrolled in the process. A new emphasis on site management by humans, rather than strict protection from humans, signifies an important policy paradigm shift in European nature conservation policy. In practice, however, designations can lead to a suite of potential, and at times extensive land-use restrictions. While the network contains a myriad of 'nature parks' across Europe, its contours simultaneously by-pass and slice through private, public and commonly-held lands. [...] With Natura 2000 we are understood to be 'living with nature'. It is an approach that promises new conceptualisations of the nature–society relationship.

However, in spite of its attempts to be more integrative, Natura 2000 remains a top-down, 'science-first' [...] conservation initiative. Leibenath notes how the Birds and Habitats Directives are 'based on a merely ecological–technical approach towards conservation'. The entire designation process, for example, begins with lists of species and habitat types considered worthy 'of Community interest' as decided by networks of pan-European ecological experts. From European right down to local levels, the dominance of a techno-scientific discourse permeates all aspects of Natura 2000. Its underlying methodology is premised on the supremacy of expert knowledge systems and the authority of science is continually appealed to in the event of disputes at EU, national and local levels. In such expert-led,

---

[39] See <http://ec.europa.eu/environment/nature/natura2000/barometer/docs/n2000.pdf> accessed 19 September 2012. Note statistics refer to SCIs not SACs. See Section 4 for details.

technocratic fora, there is little room for other ways of knowing or relating to nature. The Habitats Directive states that the habitats and species under its auspices form part of a common European heritage, but as ask Pinton asks, 'whose heritage, that of scientists, ecological activists, rural populations, city dwellers, all Europeans?'.

Bryan is highlighting that the enclave technique can take many forms and the top-down 'science-first' approach will be seen further in Section 4.

Alongside these developments, the EU also has a Biodiversity Strategy, which is described by the Commission here. Note here again the language of 'ecosystem services'.

Commission, Our Life Insurance, 'Our Natural Capital: An EU Biodiversity Strategy to 2020' COM(2011) 244 final, 2, 4

The EU mandate

In March 2010, EU leaders recognised that the 2010 biodiversity target would not be met despite some major successes, such as establishing Natura 2000, the world's largest network of protected areas. They therefore endorsed the long-term vision and ambitious headline target proposed by the Commission in its Communication 'Options for an EU vision and target for biodiversity beyond 2010'.

2050 vision

By 2050, European Union biodiversity and the ecosystem services it provides—its natural capital— are protected, valued and appropriately restored for biodiversity's intrinsic value and for their essential contribution to human wellbeing and economic prosperity, and so that catastrophic changes caused by the loss of biodiversity are avoided.

2020 headline target

Halting the loss of biodiversity and the degradation of ecosystem services in the EU by 2020, and restoring them in so far as feasible, while stepping up the EU contribution to averting global biodiversity loss. [...]

The 2020 Biodiversity strategy includes six mutually supportive and inter-dependent targets that respond to the objectives of the 2020 headline target. They will all help to halt biodiversity loss and the degradation of ecosystem services, with each seeking to address a specific issue: protecting and restoring biodiversity and associated ecosystem services (targets 1 and 2), enhancing the positive contribution of agriculture and forestry and reducing key pressures on EU biodiversity (targets 3, 4 and 5), and stepping up the EU's contribution to global biodiversity (target 6). Each target is broken down into a package of actions designed to respond to the specific challenge addressed by the target.

These strategies build on Natura 2000 but have also led to the type of integrated governance techniques discussed in Section 2.1. As a result, there is a rich discourse about nature conservation in the EU.

2.4 NATURE CONSERVATION LAW—UK DERIVED FRAMEWORKS

Nature conservation law has not only been an international or EU phenomenon. While there is very little common law protection of nature, English and UK legislation protecting certain species can be traced back to the late nineteenth century. These legislative developments reflect the strong middle-class interest in nature conservation, as discussed in Section 1.1 of Chapter 3. Historically, legislation tended to be species-based.[40] It was also devolved legislation from a relatively early stage, and, by the late 1940s, different approaches in Scotland, England, and Wales could be seen. More recent legislative and executive devolution has resulted in further divergences between these regions. This chapter focuses upon the English position.

While nature conservation in England has a long history, the blueprint for the modern framework stems from the report of the Huxley Committee in 1947,[41] which argued both for an explicit nature conservation regime and a specialist institution for overseeing such a regime. This report led to the NPAC Act 1949 being passed. That Act created the Nature Conservancy Council (and early forerunner of Natural England) and set up frameworks for the creation of local nature reserves, national nature reserves, National Parks, SSSIs, and Areas of Outstanding National Beauty (AONB). This range of different enclaves reflected the fact that an area might be protected for different reasons and activity in an enclave might be subject to different controls. A number of these regimes, and the SSSI regime in particular, were overhauled by the WC Act 1981, which also created a regime of marine nature reserves. The 1981 Act has since been substantially overhauled by the CROW Act 2000 and NERC 2006. The different protection regimes introduced by these Acts are briefly outlined here.

The SSSI regime will be discussed in detail in Section 3, but here it is worth noting that it is a very pure expression of the Huxley Committee's aims in that the core of the regime concerns identifying and protecting sites that are of 'scientific interest'. As of September 2012, there were 4100 SSSIs in England covering 8% of the land area. Over 70% of those sites are also SACs, SPAs, or Ramsar sites. A number of them are also national nature reserves or local nature reserves. Thus, there is considerable overlap between the different enclave designations. This reflects the fact that a similar site can be valued for different reasons, but it does not mean that the different designations have the same purpose.

National Parks are governed by Part II of the NPAC Act. Unlike in other jurisdictions, national parks in England are not areas of land that are preserved public tracts of land but rather areas that are designated a national park by reason of:

(a) their natural beauty, and
(b) the opportunities they afford for open-air recreation, having regard both to their character and to their position in relation to centres of population.[42]

In other words, the purpose of national parks is not primarily nature conservation but more concerned with balancing the protection of beauty and the provision of recreation opportunities. With that said, s 5(1) NPAC Act 1949 does refer to the purpose of Part II as also being 'conserving and enhancing the natural beauty, wildlife, and cultural heritage of the areas' designated as national parks. There are ten national parks in England and much of the land within them is privately owned.

---

[40] For example, Wild Birds Protection Act 1880.
[41] *Conservation of Nature in England and Wales* (Cmd 7122, 1947).
[42] NPAC Act 1949, s 5(2).

Each national park is governed by a Park Authority.[43] These authorities act as local planning authorities for areas inside the national park.[44]

AONBs were originally designated under the NPAC Act but the framework for them is now set out in Part IV of the CROW Act. The basis for designation is as follows:

(1) Where it appears to [Natural England] [...] that an area which is in England but not in a National Park is of such outstanding natural beauty that it is desirable that the provisions of this Part relating to areas designated under this section should apply to it, [Natural England] may, for the purpose of conserving and enhancing the natural beauty of the area, by order designate the area for the purposes of this Part as an area of outstanding natural beauty.[45]

AONBs are thus partly defined by how they relate to the statutory definition of national parks. There are currently thirty-three AONBs in England. The following duty is placed on public bodies in relation to AONBs:

In exercising or performing any functions in relation to, or so as to affect, land in an area of outstanding natural beauty, a relevant authority shall have regard to the purpose of conserving and enhancing the natural beauty of the area of outstanding natural beauty.[46]

Relevant authorities are defined very broadly to include most public decision-makers.[47] AONBs do not have their own governing authorities but they do require management plans.[48] Their designation also has implications for planning law (see Section 2.6).

The NPAC Act also created regimes for national nature reserves (NNR) and local nature reserves (LNR). The NERC Act redefined the definition of a 'nature reserve' in relation to NNRs.

NPAC Act 1949

Section 15

(1) In this Part, 'nature reserve' means—

    (a) land managed solely for a conservation purpose, or

    (b) land managed not only for a conservation purpose but also for a recreational purpose, if the management of the land for the recreational purpose does not compromise its management for the conservation purpose.

(2) Land is managed for a conservation purpose if it is managed for the purpose of—

    (a) providing, under suitable conditions and control, special opportunities for the study of, and research into, matters relating to the fauna and flora of Great Britain and the physical conditions in which they live, and for the study of geological and physiographical features of special interest in the area, or

    (b) preserving flora, fauna or geological or physiographical features of special interest in the area, or for both those purposes.

(3) Land is managed for a recreational purpose if it is managed for the purpose of providing opportunities for the enjoyment of nature or for open-air recreation.

---

[43] The National Park Authorities (England) Order 1996 SI 1996/1243.   [44] TCPA 1990 s 4A.
[45] CROW Act, s 82(1).   [46] Ibid, s 85(1).   [47] Ibid, s 85(2).   [48] Ibid, s 89.

The key thing to note is that NNRs are 'managed'. About two-thirds of NNRS are managed by Natural England and other public authorities or NGOs manage the remainder. About 30% of NNRs are owned by Natural England, 50% leased, and the rest are held under Nature Reserve Agreements.[49] There are currently 224 NNRs in England. LNRs follow the same regime structure to that of NNRs but the power of designation and management lies with local authorities.[50] The basis of designation is also similar, although the focus is on 'interests of the locality'.[51] There are approximately 1500 LNRs in England. Some LNRs and NNRs are also SSSIs.

The WC Act 1981 also created a regime for marine nature reserves (MNRs),[52] but only three of these have ever been designated. In 2009, the Marine and Coastal Act 2009 was passed, which created a new body—the Marine Management Organisation—which had a number of wildlife licensing powers transferred to it,[53] as well as powers to create marine conservation zones.[54]

It also needs to be remembered that international and EU designations require UK implementation. Thus, alongside the enclave designations outlined here are also SPAs, SACs, Ramsar sites, and World Heritage sites. As already indicated, to make matters more complicated, there is considerable overlap. Thus, all land-based SPAs and SACs are also SSSIs. This does not mean that SPAs and SACs are the same as SSSIs,[55] nor that the regimes of protection are the same. Further, these regimes do not operate in isolation from other aspects of environmental law. As discussed further in Section 4.4, there is a complex legal interaction between planning law and SSSIs and SPAs and SACs in particular.

This overview provides a flavour for the complexity of nature conservation regimes in England. However, it is not an exhaustive analysis and there are also other forms of landscape designation and protection, such as limestone pavement orders.[56] We have also not described the many frameworks for licensing the taking and killing or different species of wildlife.[57] In short, these different regimes create a web of different mechanisms for managing land and its natural features.

2.5 THE INSTITUTIONAL LANDSCAPE

For that web to operate, there needs to be a range of institutions. And the legal and institutional landscape for nature conservation is a crowded one, with local, regional, devolved, UK, EU, and international bodies all being involved in nature conservation.

At the international level, a number of conventions create institutional frameworks that are crucial to their operation. Thus, institutions such as the International Whaling Commission,[58] the World Heritage Committee,[59] and the Ramsar Secretariat[60] all have significant roles in implementing their relevant conventions. There are also a range of other NGOs, and public and private institutions such as the International Union for Conservation of Nature (IUCN). These institutional frameworks are examples of the autonomous institutional arrangements discussed in Section 5 of Chapter 5.

At the EU level, DG Environment plays a leadership role in relation to Natura 2000 and the Birds Directive and the Habitats Directive.[61] In the UK, the main government department overseeing

---

[49] NPAC Act 1949, s 16.   [50] Ibid, s 21.
[51] Ibid, s 21(4), although note this is in relation to management agreements and acquisition.
[52] WC Act 1981, s 36.   [53] Marine and Coastal Access Act 2009, Chapter 2.   [54] Ibid, s 116.
[55] See *R (Fisher) v English Nature* [2004] EWCA Civ 663, [2004] 4 All ER 861 for a discussion of the relationship.
[56] WC Act 1981, s 34.   [57] See Further Reading at the end of the chapter.
[58] <http://iwcoffice.org/convention> accessed 25 September 2012.
[59] <http://whc.unesco.org/en/comittee> accessed 12 September 2012.
[60] <www.ramsar.org> accessed 12 September 2012.
[61] <http://ec.europa.eu/environment/nature/index_en.htm> accessed 12 September 2012.

nature conservation policy and law is DEFRA, but this is an area in which specialist public bodies also have a role to play. In England, the independent body Natural England (previously English Nature and before that the Nature Conservancy Council) provides most of the specialist input in this area. The Joint Nature Conservancy Committee (JNCC) is the national statutory advisor. The situation is further complicated by the fact that nature conservation regimes will have implications for planning and other areas of decision-making, discussed in Section 2.6 and seen throughout this chapter.

Besides its teeming nature, there are two interesting things to note about this institutional landscape. The first is that national institutions whose remit primarily concerns nature conservation have largely been set up as independent scientific bodies. This reflects not only the importance of scientific expertise in this area but also the legacy of the Huxley Committee, which stressed the need for scientific institutions. Bodies such as Natural England and JNCC also have statutory footings. Thus, Natural England was constituted under Part 1 of the NERC Act 2006. Its purpose is set out in Section 2 of that Act:

(1) Natural England's general purpose is to ensure that the natural environment is conserved, enhanced and managed for the benefit of present and future generations, thereby contributing to sustainable development.

(2) Natural England's general purpose includes—

(a) promoting nature conservation and protecting biodiversity,

(b) conserving and enhancing the landscape,

(c) securing the provision and improvement of facilities for the study, understanding and enjoyment of the natural environment,

(d) promoting access to the countryside and open spaces and encouraging open-air recreation, and

(e) contributing in other ways to social and economic well-being through management of the natural environment.

(3) The purpose in subsection (2)(e) may, in particular, be carried out by working with local communities.

This is certainly aspirational and inspirational. The JNCC was also put a statutory footing by that Act. Section 33 states:

(1) The UK conservation bodies and the joint committee have the functions conferred on them by this Part for the purposes of—

(a) nature conservation, and

(b) fostering the understanding of nature conservation.

(2) Each of them must, in discharging their functions under this Part, have regard to—

(a) actual or possible ecological changes, and

(b) the desirability of contributing to sustainable development.

The second important thing to note about the institutional landscape of nature conservation is the important role played by the voluntary sector.

Hadrian Cook and Alex Inman, 'The Voluntary Sector and Conservation for England: Achievements, Expanding Roles and Uncertain Future' (2012) 112 Journal of Environmental Management 170, 173

Around 500 UK charities provide some form of environmental service; these range from local to national importance to those with largely local functions. Armed with a level of legal recognition, responsibilities and a remit for conservation management, environmental charities became enmeshed with the array of national government statutory bodies and local government roles, including the management of nature reserves. In the case of WT, WFWT and RSPB or of the county wildlife trusts they also operate as campaigning organisations. Lacking both governmental and democratic remits, mass membership confers legitimacy and they are regularly consulted as a part of the statutory process. Larger NGOs, by dint of mission, may display limited remits and questions may be asked in respect of smaller charities regarding their ability to embrace a wider vision, or more problematically they might appear on the outside as 'single-issue' groups.

The term 'governance' also implies not only 'steering' but also a distribution rather than a concentration of power (Pierre and Peters, 2000). It is at once compatible with communitarian activity and local democracy, while permitting relations that are hierarchical as well as horizontal and include the commercial sector.

The historical account enables us to distinguish four NGO functions:

- that of ownership for protection against development
- that of practical management for conservation
- that of campaigning and advising, and finally
- as a vehicle for public engagement at many levels

These functions provide alternatives to state ownership or to the more problematic issues around the regulation of economic or other activity on private land. There is also the question of 'job substitution', perhaps of local authority employees, perhaps of contract workers in the private sector.

This is an area of activity that does not yield easily to traditional legal analysis, involving as it does a range of governance arrangements, which raise the types of questions seen in Chapter 13. Thus, a study of the legal frameworks for decision-making alone, while challenging in itself, also provides an incomplete picture of nature conservation law.

2.6 PLANNING

The final thing to note in this overview of nature conservation law is that, while each of the regimes discussed in Section 2.5 provides a framework for managing activity in protected areas, an important aspect of how nature conservation regimes work in England is the way in which they interact with, and are even implemented through, the planning system. Some of the details of this interaction are considered further but here it is worth noting that 'development',[62] whether within or near protected areas will clearly have impacts on habitats within those areas. As that is the case, local planning authorities will need to consider those impacts as part of the planning process. There are some explicit legislative provisions that govern this.[63] In particular, Regulation 9(3) of the Conservation

---

[62] TCPA 1990, s 55 (1).

[63] TCPA, s 4A (national parks are planning authorities); Conservation of Habitats and Species Regulations 2010, Regulations 9(1), 9(3) and 9A, as amended.

of Habitats and Species Regulations 2010 (as amended by the Conservation of Habitats and Species (Amendments) Regulations 2012) requires that a:

> competent authority [see section 4.4 for a definition], in exercising any of their functions, must have regard to the requirements of the Habitats Directive so far as they may be affected by the exercise of those functions.

This obligation is distinct from the duty in Regulation 9(1) that states that the Secretary of State, nature conservation bodies, 'must exercise their functions under the enactments relating to nature conservation so as to secure compliance with the requirements of the Habitats Directive'. In other words there is a more general, and flexible, obligation under Regulation 9(3) that will apply to local planning authorities, while 9(1) imposes a far more stringent obligation on the Secretary of State and nature conservation bodies. A new Regulation 9A also sets out specific obligations in relation to 'wild bird habitat'. Regulation 68 also makes clear that the assessment provisions of the Regulations apply to the granting of planning permission (see Section 4.4). These provisions highlight the way in which EU obligations must interrelate with the powers of national bodies and much of the details of these Regulations is concerned with regulating the detail of that interrelationship.[64] It is also interesting to note that the 2012 amendments were due to DEFRA deciding that the original 2010 Regulations did not amount to a proper implementation of the Directives.[65]

There are also general duties such as s 40 NERC Act 2006 and s 28G WC Act 1981 (discussed further). Planning policy guidance also exists. Before March 2012, this was found in *PPS 9: Biodiversity and Geological Conservation*, but it is now found in paragraphs 118 and 119 of the NPPF, which since March 2012 guides all planning development decisions in England.

Department of Communities and Local Government, *National Planning Policy Framework* (March 2012) paras 118–19

118. When determining planning applications, local planning authorities should aim to conserve and enhance biodiversity by applying the following principles:

- if significant harm resulting from a development cannot be avoided (through locating on an alternative site with less harmful impacts) adequately mitigated, or, as a last resort, compensated for, then planning permission should be refused;

- proposed development on land within or outside a Site of Special Scientific Interest likely to have an adverse effect on a Site of Special Scientific Interest (either individually or in combination with other developments) should not normally be permitted. Where an adverse effect on the site's notified special interest features is likely, an exception should only be made where the benefits of the development, at this site, clearly outweigh both the impacts that it is likely to have on the features of the site that make it of special scientific interest and any broader impacts on the national network of Sites of Special Scientific Interest;

---

[64] See *Elliott v Secretary of State for Communities and Local Government* [2012] EWHC 1574 (Admin) for how institutionally complicated this duty can be in its application. This case concerned the Regulations before they were amended.

[65] <http://www.defra.gov.uk/rural/protected/chsr2010/> accessed 13 December 2012.

- development proposals where the primary objective is to conserve or enhance biodiversity should be permitted;
- opportunities to incorporate biodiversity in and around developments should be encouraged;
- planning permission should be refused for development resulting in the loss or deterioration of irreplaceable habitats, including ancient woodland and the loss of aged or veteran trees found outside ancient woodland, unless the need for, and benefits of, the development in that location clearly outweigh the loss; and
- the following wildlife sites should be given the same protection as European sites:
  - potential Special Protection Areas and possible Special Areas of Conservation;
  - listed or proposed Ramsar sites; and
  - sites identified, or required, as compensatory measures for adverse effects on European sites, potential Special Protection Areas, possible Special Areas of Conservation, and listed or proposed Ramsar sites.

119. The presumption in favour of sustainable development (paragraph 14) does not apply where development requiring appropriate assessment under the Birds or Habitats Directives is being considered, planned or determined.

The framework defines European Sites as including:

candidate Special Areas of Conservation, Sites of Community Importance, Special Areas of Conservation and Special Protection Areas, and is defined in regulation 8 of the Conservation of Habitats and Species Regulations 2010.[66]

The relative newness of this document means that it has little operational history but it shows the tension between wishing to provide a simple overarching principle for the area (conserve biodiversity) and the need for planning authorities to navigate the range of different UK, EU, and international obligations.

From a practical perspective, local planning authorities will consult with Natural England as part of the planning process.[67] In *Morge*,[68] extracted in Chapter 18, the Supreme Court placed great weight on that consultation process (albeit in the context of species protection under Articles 12–16 Habitats Directive, and not the protection of European sites). This relationship reinforces the image of Natural England as an independent scientific body. The respective roles of planning authorities and Natural England in planning applications concerning SACs and SPAs (Article 3–11 Habitats Directive) are a bit more nuanced.[69]

FURTHER READING AND QUESTIONS

1. Imagine a country called Utopia with a similar landscape to England but no nature conservation laws. Think about how and why you might create regimes and what they might protect.

---

[66] Department of Communities and Local Government, National Planning Policy Framework (March 2012) 52.
[67] As required for SSSIs under s 28I WC Act. See also Town and Country Planning (General Development Procedure) Order 1995 SI 1995/419, art 10(u).
[68] *Morge v Hampshire County Council* [2011] UKSC 2, [2011] 1 All ER 744.   [69] See Section 4.4.

Try to draft in outline what a regime might look like if it were created for one of the following purposes:

a) to preserve pristine wilderness;

b) to promote biodiversity;

c) to ensure ecosystems are not degraded by recreational, agricultural, and tourism activities.

2. For more detailed discussion of such different regimes, see the further reading section at the end of the chapter.

3. Further examples of EU policy documentation on nature and biodiversity can be found at <http://ec.europa.eu/environment/nature/index_en.htm> accessed 19 September 2012.

3 SITES OF SPECIAL SCIENTIFIC INTEREST

This section and Section 4 examine how 'enclaves' are protected by the SSSI regime, the Birds Directive, and Habitats Directive. As explained in the introduction, our focus on enclaves is due to their significant implications for environmental law (being the law that applies to environmental problems), as well as their being the most controversial aspect of nature conservation law. Sections 3 and 4 do not to provide an exhaustive account of these regimes but rather aim to provide an overview of how sites are designated under these regimes, and how they are protected.

We touched upon the SSSI regime under the WC Act 1981 (as amended) in Section 2 and saw that SSSIs cover a substantial part of the physical landscape in England (8% in 2012). This regime applies to private land and is not concerned with stopping *any* activity occurring on land but managing the activity that does occur. This section considers the notification process for SSSIs, and the level of protection granted (including the interaction with the planning system).

3.1 BASIS OF NOTIFICATION

As discussed already, the SSSI regime has historical roots in post-war Britain and in the belief that nature had a scientific value. Indeed, that belief was enshrined in the very idea of a 'site of *special scientific* interest'. Section 28 of the WCA 1981 expands a little on this definition. It states:

(1) Where [Natural England] are of the opinion that any area of land is of special interest by reason of any of its flora, fauna or geological or physiographical features, it shall the duty of [Natural England] to notify that fact–

　(a) to every local planning authority in whose area the land is situated;

　(b) to every owner and occupier of any of that land; and

　(c) to the Secretary of State.

(2) [Natural England] shall also publish a notification of that fact in at least one local newspaper circulated in the area in which the land is situated

(3) A notification under subsection (1) shall specify the time (not being less than three months from the date of giving the notification) within which, and the manner in which, representations or objections with respect to it may be made; and [Natural England] shall consider any representation or objection duly made.

(4) A notification under subsection (1)(b) shall also specify—

    (a) the flora, fauna, or geological or physiographical features by reason of which the land is of special interest, and

    (b) any operations appearing to [Natural England] to be likely to damage that flora or fauna or those features, and shall contain a statement of [Natural England] views about the management of the land (including any views [English Nature] may have about the conservation and enhancement of that flora or fauna or those features).

There are three important things to note about s 28. First, the key criterion for a SSSI is relatively broad—'special interest by reason of any of its flora, fauna or geological or physiographical features'. Thus, a SSSI protects not only animals and plants but also areas of geological interest, and the definition is sufficiently broad that SACs, SPAs, and Ramsar sites can easily be designated SSSIs (as already noted). Guidelines exist on the selection of SSSIs, originally developed by the Nature Conservancy Council (a predecessor of Natural England), and there are separate guidelines for biological[70] and geological SSSIs,[71] which are highly technical in nature.

Second, a SSSI notification not only outlines natural features of interest but also how they should be protected and managed. This is important because the notification notice will list those activities that require consent from Natural England. Finally, s 28 sets out an administrative process and the remainder of the section sets out the further procedures for notification. Notification thus creates an ongoing relationship between Natural England, a land-owner, and public bodies.

In light of the consequences of notification, which in particular limit the landowner's rights to use land, it is not surprising that the decision of Natural England (or its predecessors) to notify a site as a SSSI has been subject to judicial review. Indeed, litigation over SSSIs is primarily about the notification process in light of the range of legal consequences that follow once a site is notified. Two very different examples of challenges to notifications are given here.[72]

R (Fisher) v English Nature
[2004] EWCA Civ 663, paras 126–130 (Wall LJ)

The Facts

The appellants challenged the notification of Breckland Farmland as a SSSI in 2000. They did so on a range of grounds including that English Nature had confused the designation process under the Habitats Directive and SSSI notification. Lightman J rejected their grounds as did the Court of Appeal. In dismissing the appeal Wall LJ noted that he found himself 'inexorably and repeatedly coming back to two points'.

The CA

126. [...] The first was that this is an application for judicial review of a decision made by a specialist body, and thus only susceptible to challenge on the limited grounds provided by judicial review. The second was the point [that] ...... -

---

[70] <http://jncc.defra.gov.uk/page-2303> accessed 19 September 2012.
[71] <http://jncc.defra.gov.uk/page-2317> accessed 19 September 2012.
[72] See also *R (Aggregate Industries UK Ltd) v English Nature* [2002] EWHC 908 (Admin); [2003] Env LR 3.

what the Appellants have not done is to explain how English Nature could ever reasonably take the view that an area of land was not of special scientific interest by reason of the birds it supports when in their opinion it is of European significance for those birds.

127. The only answer to this question provided by the appellants was that this had been English Nature's view in 1994, and they had been wrong to change it in 2000. But once it is established, as the [High Court] judge found (and, in my judgment, as the evidence manifestly bears out) that English Nature's change of stance had been adopted after careful consideration and was rational, then the simple fact of the matter is that on the post 2000 criteria, the Breckland Farmland manifestly is an SSSI [...]

128. The rest, in my judgment, follows inexorably. English Nature reasonably formed the opinion that the area of land was of special interest by reason of its internationally important population of stone-curlew. This led to the duty to notify under section 28(1) of the 1981 Act. There is nothing in the process of consultation, or in English Nature's consideration of the objections, to which objection can be taken. The process is thus rational and procedurally fair, and at the end of it, having listened to and considered the objections, English Nature remained of the same opinion and confirmed the notification. At this level, the case, it seems to me, is very simple, and is a straightforward application of English Nature's statutory responsibilities to the facts of a particular case.

129. Speaking for myself, I do not think that there is anything in the point that the judge misdirected himself by criticising the appellants for not mounting a formal challenge to the decision to notify. I tend to agree with the appellants that a challenge to that decision might well, within the structure imposed by section 28 of the 1981 Act have been met with the judicial retort that it was premature, and that the appellants should wait until confirmation (if it occurred) before mounting a challenge. I regard the consultation / objection process as being of considerable importance. That process had to be properly carried out. But the resultant question, in my judgment, is unaffected. Was the Decision one which it was properly open to English Nature to make on all the information available to them? In my judgment, the answer to that question is plainly yes.

130. However careful and sophisticated the argument to the contrary, it seems to me that the words contained in section 28(1) of the 1981 Act are very clear. The Breckland Farmland is an area of land, and on any construction of the language it is 'of special interest by reason of its...fauna' (its population of stone-curlew).

Wall LJ is highlighting the importance of scientific judgement. While judicial review of these types of decisions is often described as deferential this should not be thought of as a judge engaging in no form of review. Wall LJ's approach is not particularly deferential and he scrutinizes both the reasoning and procedure of English Nature. He also emphasizes the importance of the statutory framework—procedurally and in the way in which it de-limits the powers of English Nature. The significance of that framework can be seen in the *Boggis v Natural England* case in which an eroding cliff area had been designated a SSSI due its special scientific interest from a geological perspective. A nearby landowner had built a 'sacrificial seawall' to stop the erosion and, in a legal dispute with the local authority and English Nature over the seawall, had challenged the notification of the cliff as a SSSI. In the Court of Appeal, there were two arguments.

Boggis v Natural England
[2009] EWCA Civ 1061, paras 11–18 (Sullivan LJ)

11. Mr Jones [for Mr Boggis] submitted that English Nature had approached both the notification and the confirmation of the SSSI on the basis that 'the process of exposure' of the cliffs was a geological

feature of special interest. He submitted that English Nature was wrong to do so because 'the act of exposure was not a geological feature'. Had English Nature approached the notification and confirmation of the SSSI on that basis it would have been in error, but when Mr Jones was asked to identify those passages in the Notification the Supporting Information Supplementing the Notification Package, and the Report ('the documents') on which he relied in support of this submission, he was unable to identify any passage which might have suggested that English Nature thought that the act, or process, of exposure of the cliffs was a geological feature.

12. The documents understandably refer to the fact that exposure of the cliffs was taking place, and would continue to take place, as a result of 'continuing coastal processes', not least because English Nature was concerned to take coastal erosion into account when drawing the boundary of the SSSI. However, the geological features of special interest were said to be: the 'Pleistocene vertebrate palaeontology and Pleistocene/Quaternary of East Anglia at Easton Bavents', referred to for convenience during the hearing as 'the fossils' and 'the sediments' respectively. The Report said that the sediments were 'of national importance for the stratigraphical and palaeo-environmental study of the Lower Pleistocene in Britain', and continued:

'These geological features include exposures of the three major elements of the Norwich Crag Formation; the Crag itself (Chillesford Church Member), the Baventian Clay (Easton Bavents Member) and the Westleton Beds (Westleton Member).' (Report para. 1.3.1) (emphasis added)

13. Thus, English Nature was not saying that the act or process of exposure was a geological feature, it was saying that the geological features of special interest were not confined to the sediments behind the cliff face, but included the exposure. A geological exposure, as in the case of an exposed cliff or quarry face, is a geological feature. At the risk of stating the obvious, it is readily understandable that among the reasons why such a geological feature might be of special interest would be the fact that it is exposed. As the Report explained:

'As the cliff face has eroded geologists have been able to study the new sections in order to gather valuable scientific data, identify how the geological sequence is changing and use this environmental information to correlate the site more widely with other sites in the GCR and those outside of Great Britain. A three-dimensional picture of the landscape and associated depositional environments can then also be developed. Palaeo-environmental information derived from the site contributes to our understanding of how the environment responded to changes in climate.'

14. Recognition that the geological features of special interest were not confined to the sediments, but included the exposure at the cliffs (not the act or process of the cliffs' exposure) disposes of the alternative submission advanced by Mr Jones: that if the act of exposure of the cliffs is not the geological feature of special interest, that feature must be the sediments and the fossils, and allowing nature to take its course will result in their destruction, not their conservation. In this respect, reliance was placed by both the Respondents and the Interested Party on the duty imposed by section 28G (2) of the 1981 Act on all public bodies, including English Nature, when the exercise of their functions is likely to affect the flora, fauna etc. in any SSSI :

'to take reasonable steps, consistent with the proper exercise of [their] functions, to further the conservation and enhancement of the flora, fauna or geological or physiographical features by reason of which [the SSSI] is of special scientific interest.'

15. In his submissions on behalf of the Interested Party, Mr Balogh also referred to the definition of 'nature conservation' in section 131(6) of the *Environmental Protection Act 1990* (the 1990 Act):

'In this part "nature conservation" means the conservation of flora, fauna or geological or physiographical features.' In my view, the definition of 'nature conservation' in section 131(6) of the 1990 Act does not, for the purposes of this appeal, add anything of substance to the duty under section 28G(2) of the 1981 Act to further the conservation and enhancement of the geological features by reason of which this SSSI was designated.

16. The submission that English Nature's approach, to allow natural processes (in this case coastal erosion) to proceed freely, would result in the destruction rather than the conservation of those geological features is based upon two misconceptions:

i) that the geological features in question are confined to the sediments and did not include the exposure; and ii) that 'conservation' in this context means preservation of the status quo.

17. The Report explained why allowing natural processes to take their course would conserve the exposure:

'The key management principle for coastal geological sites is to maintain exposure of the geological interest by allowing natural processes to proceed freely. Inappropriate construction of coastal defences can conceal rock exposures and result in the effective loss of the geological interest. In addition, any development which prevents or slows natural erosion can have a damaging effect. Erosion is necessary to maintain fresh geological outcrops. Reducing the rate of erosion usually results in rock exposures becoming obscured by vegetation and rock debris [...] Conserving the geological exposures and the geomorphological features is not about preventing erosion but allowing their continued evolution.'

18. Even if it is assumed that 'conservation' in section 28G(2) means 'preservation', allowing nature to take its course will 'preserve' the exposure, while hindering those processes would harm it because that which is obscured will cease to be exposed. It is therefore, unnecessary to consider in any detail the meaning of 'conservation' in section 28G(2), but since the Interested party has sought guidance on this aspect of the appeal, I will deal with the issue. There is no definition of 'conservation' in the 1981 Act, and the parties were not able to point to a definition in any other enactment. Mr Balogh referred to the Convention Concerning the Protection of the World Cultural and National Heritage adopted by the General Conference of UNESCO on 16th November 1972, and to dictionary definitions. The former is, understandably, expressed in such general terms as to be of no material assistance, and the latter are of no assistance because we are not concerned with the meaning of 'conservation' in isolation or in the abstract, but with the meaning of 'conservation' in a particular statutory context: nature conservation. Whatever may be the meaning of conservation in other contexts, one would have thought that allowing natural processes to take their course, and not preventing or impeding them by artificial means from doing so, would be a well recognised conservation technique in the field of nature conservation. 'Conservation' is not necessarily the same as 'preservation', although in some, perhaps many, circumstances preservation may be the best way to conserve. Whether that is so in any particular case will be a matter, not for the lawyers, but for the professional judgement of the person whose statutory duty it is to conserve.

Note the importance of the wording of the SSSI documentation and the way in which Sullivan LJ points out the importance of the *specific* statutory context. While it might be argued that *Boggis* is not really concerned with nature conservation, it is a reminder of the importance of reading the legislation and notification documents carefully.

Besides these cases, in Section 2.2 of Chapter 6 we also consider the reasoning in the case of *R (Trailer & Marina (Leven) Ltd) v Secretary of State for the Environment, Food & Rural Affairs* [2004] EWCA Civ 1580, [2005] 1 WLR 1267 in which a challenge was also brought under the HRA in relation to the changing SSSI regime and its effect on landowner rights.

3.2 PROTECTING SSSIS

These consequences of notifying a SSSI primarily concern the duties of landowners and others in relation to how the site is managed. Historically, the SSSI regime depended on what can be fairly described as a system of voluntary self-regulation on the part of landowners. Landowners were required to notify the Nature Conservancy Council but, after a period of time, they could continue to carry out the activity they wished to carry out. This did not go unnoticed.

Southern Water Authority v Nature Conservancy Council
[1992] 1 WLR 775 (HL), 778 (Lord Mustill)

It needs only a moment to see that this regime is toothless, for it demands no more from the owner or occupier of an SSSI than a little patience. Unless the council can convince the Secretary of State that the site is of sufficient national importance to justify an order under section 29—as we have seen, a task rarely accomplished—the owner will within months be free to disregard the notification and carry out the proscribed operations, no matter what the cost to the flora etc. on the site. In truth the Act does no more in the great majority of cases than give the council a breathing space within which to apply moral pressure, with a view to persuading the owner or occupier to make a voluntary agreement.

Not surprisingly, under this regime, SSSIs were being degraded at an alarming rate. That situation changed with amendments to the WC Act introduced by both the CROW Act 2000 and the NERC Act 2006, which put in place a more rigorous framework for managing SSSIs. It also provided a mechanism for de-notifying SSSIs, which reflected the fact that some SSSIs have degraded so significantly as to be no longer worthy of notification.[73] Owners are now subject to the duty in s 28E:

28E. (1) The owner or occupier of any land included in a site of special scientific interest shall not while the notification under section 28(1)(b) remains in force carry out, or cause or permit to be carried out, on that land any operation specified in the notification unless—

  (a) one of them has, after service of the notification, given Natural England notice of a proposal to carry out the operation specifying its nature and the land on which it is proposed to carry it out; and

  (b) one of the conditions specified in subsection (3) is fulfilled. [...]

(3) The conditions are—

  (a) that the operation is carried out with Natural England's written consent;

  (b) that the operation is carried out in accordance with the terms of an agreement under section 16 of the 1949 Act, section 15 of the 1968 Act, or section 7 of the Natural Environment and Rural Communities Act 2006;

  (c) that the operation is carried out in accordance with a management scheme under section 28J or a management notice under section 28K.

This regime means that Natural England can stop activities happening on SSSIs. The details of the nature of consent required are set out in the Act, as is a framework for management schemes.[74] There

---

[73] Section 28D.   [74] Section 28J.

are avenues for appeal to the Secretary of State in relation to both consent decisions and management schemes.[75]

Section 28G also imposes a general duty on Ministers of the Crown, the National Assembly of Wales, local authorities, statutory undertakers, and a range of other public bodies and officials 'to further the conservation and enhancement of the flora, fauna or geological or physiographical features by reason of which the site is of special scientific interest'.[76] This section reflects the way in which decision-making by public bodies, particularly planning authorities, can have an impact on SSSIs.[77] Section 28I requires such bodies to give notice to Natural England 'before permitting the carrying out of operations likely to damage any of the flora, fauna or geological or physiographical features by reason of which a site of special scientific interest is of special interest'.[78] This requirement applies to planning applications and also to pollution permitting decisions (see Part IV), and s 28I goes on to set out the process that the relevant public body must follow in consulting Natural England and taking into account its advice.[79]

Most significantly, s 28P gives the SSSI regime teeth by creating a series of offences. The two most significant are:

(1) A person who, without reasonable excuse, contravenes section 28E(1) is guilty of an offence and is liable on summary conviction to a fine not exceeding £20,000 or on conviction on indictment to a fine.

(2) A section 28G authority which, in the exercise of its functions, carries out an operation which damages any of the flora, fauna or geological or physiographical features by reason of which a site of special scientific interest is of special interest—

(a) without first complying with section 28H(1), or

(b) (if it has complied with section 28H(1)) without first complying with section 28H(4)(a), is, unless there was a reasonable excuse for carrying out the operation without complying, guilty of an offence and is liable on summary conviction to a fine not exceeding £20,000 or on conviction on indictment to a fine.

These are quite significant offences,[80] but it should be noted that much of the force of the SSSI regime derives from the way in which the legislative framework creates a relationship between Natural England, landowners, and public bodies. That is nicely captured in the introduction to Natural England's guidance to SSSI landowners.

Natural England, *Sites of Special Scientific Interest: A Brief Guide for Land Owners and Occupiers* (Natural England 2012) 3

The responsibility for protecting SSSIs is shared by many, but as an owner or occupier you play the most important role in shaping the condition of your site. At Natural England we understand that the

---

[75] Sections 28F and 28L.   [76] Section 28G(2).

[77] *Britannia Assets (UK) Ltd v Secretary of State for Communities & Local Government (Rev 1)* [2011] EWHC 1908 (Admin), [2011] All ER (D) 45. See the Inspector's decision ibid, para 72.

[78] Section 28I(2). Note also s 28H, which requires public bodies to notify Natural England if their own operations are likely to damage SSSI features.

[79] It must wait twenty-eight days for response, take NE advice into account in determining the relevant application and attaching any conditions, and give notice to NE if its advice is not followed along with reasons.

[80] Note the defences, including in cases of emergency, in s 28P(4). Also note the offences in s 28P(6) and s 28P(6A), which impose duties on individuals in relation to SSSIs.

land you own or manage fulfils a range of needs beyond its value for nature conservation. Our network of Land Management Advisers understand your wider needs and have a wealth of expertise that can help you look after the natural features of your site within its everyday working context.

Thus, the provisions relating to the creation of management agreements and schemes are the focus of the day-to-day administration of SSSIs. Landowners do get something out of these arrangements, as they can be paid for the costs of positive site management and forgone income.[81] However, in establishing such agreements and schemes, Natural England retains strong regulatory oversight in relation to SSSIs, in light of the offences described here, and also through its power to compulsorily acquire land on which SSSIs are being poorly managed.[82]

The final thing to note is that SSSIs clearly have implications for planning and planning will have implications for SSSIs. In this regard, it is important to remember that the duty set out in s 28G applies to planning authorities. In considering planning applications, planning authorities must consult Natural England and take into account nature conservation matters as set out here, including in light of relevant provisions of the NPPF (since 2012). We do not know yet how the NPPF will change practice from the previous position under PPS 9, but it is useful to note that this issue has not been greatly litigated where a SAC or SPA is not involved. When it is, it tends to turn heavily on the specific facts.[83] Finally, in cases where planning permission has been granted for a particular development, that permission acts a defence to any s 28P proceedings.[84] This might seem quite harsh—that the planning system trumps nature conservation—but it is not necessarily the case when one considers the duties on planning decision-makers to take nature conservation matters into consideration. This defence aims to give certainty to those who obtain planning permission.

> **FURTHER READING**
>
> 1. A great wealth of information can be found about SSSIs on Natural England's website (<http://www.naturalengland.org.uk/> accessed 19 September 2012). You can search the location of SSSIs and access information about reasons for notification and what operations require consent.
>
> 2. Examples of how SSSIs have given rise to legal issues in planning cases can be seen in *Persimmon Homes Teesside Ltd v R (Lewis)* [2008] EWCA Civ 746, [2009] 1 WLR 83 and *Britannia Assets (UK) Ltd v Secretary of State for Communities & Local Government (Rev 1)* [2011] EWHC 1908 (Admin), [2011] All ER (D) 45.

4 EU LAW: SPAS AND SACS

We now turn to the designated protection areas under the Birds Directive (SPA) and Habitats Directives (SACs). In doing so it is important to remember that the Birds Directive and the Habitats Directive not

---

[81] For example, WC Act s 28M. See also DEFRA, *Guidelines on Management Agreement Payments and Other Related Matters* (2001).

[82] WC Act, s 28N.

[83] For example, *R (Buglife, The Invertebrate Conservation Trust) v Thurrock Thames Gateway Development Corporation* [2009] EWCA Civ 29, [2009] EWCA Civ 29, [2009] Env LR 18.

[84] WC Act, s 28P(4) (only for planning decisions where merits have been considered, not in cases of automatic permission under the Town and Country Planning (General Permitted Development) Order 1995.

only provide protection through enclaves but also directly regulating species. That is not our focus, but it is important to keep in mind. The designation process for SPAs and SACs is quite different but, since 1992, the level of protection under both regimes has been governed by Article 6 of the Habitats Directive. It is important to remember that SPAs and SACs are only one aspect of each of these Directives.

4.1 BIRDS DIRECTIVE—SPECIAL PROTECTION AREAS

Article 4(1) states:

> The species mentioned in Annex I shall be the subject of special conservation measures concerning their habitat in order to ensure their survival and reproduction in their area of distribution.
>
> In this connection, account shall be taken of:
>
> (a) species in danger of extinction;
>
> (b) species vulnerable to specific changes in their habitat;
>
> (c) species considered rare because of small populations or restricted local distribution;
>
> (d) other species requiring particular attention for reasons of the specific nature of their habitat.
>
> Trends and variations in population levels shall be taken into account as a background for evaluations.
>
> Member States shall classify in particular the most suitable territories in number and size as special protection areas for the conservation of these species in the geographical sea and land area where this Directive applies.

As is clear from this Article, the basis of designation of a special protection area is scientific. The CJEU has reinforced this point on a number of occasions, particularly as Member States have sought to rely on Article 2, which allow Member States to take account of 'economic and recreational requirements' alongside 'ecological, scientific and cultural requirements' in taking the 'requisite measures' to maintain the population of species to which the Directive applies.

Case C-44/95 *R v Secretary of State for the Environment, ex p Royal Society for the Protection of Birds*
[1996] ECR I-3805 paras 23–27

> 23. It must be noted first that Article 4 of the Birds Directive lays down a protection regime which is specifically targeted and reinforced both for the species listed in Annex I and for migratory species, an approach justified by the fact that they are, respectively, the most endangered species and the species constituting a common heritage of the Community (see Case C-169/89 *Van den Burg* [1990] ECR I-2143, paragraph 11).
>
> 24. Whilst Article 3 of the Birds Directive provides for account to be taken of the requirements mentioned in Article 2 for the implementation of general conservation measures, including the creation of protection areas, Article 4 makes no such reference for the implementation of special conservation measures, in particular the creation of SPAs.
>
> 25. Consequently, having regard to the aim of special protection pursued by Article 4 and the fact that, according to settled case-law (see in particular Case C-435/92 *APAS v Préfets de Maine-et-Loire and de la Loire Atlantique* [1994] ECR I-67, paragraph 20), Article 2 does not constitute an autonomous derogation from the general system of protection established by the directive, it must be held (see paragraphs

17 and 18 of *Santoña Marshes*)—that the ecological requirements laid down by the former provision do not have to be balanced against the interests listed in the latter, in particular economic requirements.

26. It is the criteria laid down in paragraphs (1) and (2) of Article 4 which are to guide the Member States in designating and defining the boundaries of SPAs. It is clear from paragraphs 26 and 27 of Santoña Marshes that, notwithstanding the divergences between the various language versions of the last subparagraph of Article 4(1), the criteria in question are ornithological criteria.

27. In view of the foregoing, the answer to the first question must be that Article 4(1) or (2) of the Birds Directive is to be interpreted as meaning that a Member State is not authorized to take account of the economic requirements mentioned in Article 2 thereof when designating an SPA and defining its boundaries.

Designation must thus be on ornithological criteria alone and Member States cannot refuse to designate because of the economic or political implications. As a consequence, if scientific evidence exists indicating that an area should be a SPA, then a Member State may have a duty to designate it as such. This is an issue that has arisen in a number of cases in light of NGOs collecting and collating data about bird habitat sites.

Case C-235/04 *Commission v Spain*
[2007] ECR I-5415, paras 13–15, 20, 23–27

13. The Commission takes the view that the Kingdom of Spain has not classified as SPAs territories sufficient in size and in number having regard to the areas of importance for the conservation of birds identified in the ornithological list published in 1998 ('the IBA 98').

14. The Spanish Government objects to the use of the IBA 98. That inventory, it submits, does not have the same value as the *Inventory of Important Bird Areas in the European Community* published in 1989 ('the IBA 89') since, because it was neither commissioned nor supervised by the Commission, the accuracy of its results is not guaranteed.

15. [The Spanish government argues] [t]he IBA 98 was drawn up exclusively on the initiative of the Sociedad Española de Ornitología (Spanish Ornithological Society; 'SEO/BirdLife') which decided unilaterally to amend the IBA 89 in order to increase the number and size of the areas to be protected in Spain. No public authority having responsibility for environmental matters supervised the drawing-up of that list to ensure the precision and accuracy of its data. The increase in number and above all in size of new areas requiring to be protected in the IBA 98 in comparison with the IBA 89 is therefore impossible to justify or check. [...]

20. According to the Commission, the IBA 98 relies on the best documented and most accurate references available to define the areas most appropriate to the survival and reproduction of bird species in accordance with Article 4(1) and (2) of Directive 79/409. The IBA 98 is based on balanced ornithological criteria such as population size, bird diversity and the risks to which the species are exposed on an international scale, allowing identification of the places most likely to ensure conservation of the species listed in Annex I to Directive 79/409 and of the migratory species not listed in that annex. [...]

23. As a preliminary point, it must be borne in mind that Article 4 of Directive 79/409 lays down a regime which is specifically targeted and reinforced both for the species listed in Annex I and for the migratory species, an approach justified by the fact that they are, respectively, the most endangered species and the species constituting a common heritage of the European Community (Case C-191/05 *Commission v Portugal* [2006] ECR I-6853, paragraph 9, and case-law cited). Furthermore, it is clear from the ninth recital in the preamble to that directive that the preservation, maintenance or restoration

of a sufficient diversity and area of habitats is essential to the conservation of all species of birds. The Member States are therefore required to adopt the measures necessary for the conservation of those species.

24. For that purpose, the updating of scientific data is necessary to determine the situation of the most endangered species and the species constituting the common heritage of the Community in order to classify the most suitable areas as SPAs. It is therefore necessary to use the most up-to-date scientific data available at the end of the period laid down in the reasoned opinion.

25. In that regard, it should be recalled that the national lists, including the IBA 98 drawn up by SEO/BirdLife, revised the first pan-European study carried out in the IBA 89 and provide more exact and up-to-date scientific data.

26. In view of the scientific nature of the IBA 89 and of the absence of any scientific evidence adduced by a Member State tending particularly to show that the obligations flowing from Article 4(1) and (2) of Directive 79/409 could be satisfied by classifying as SPAs sites other than those appearing in that inventory and covering a smaller total area, the Court has held that that inventory, although not legally binding, could be used by the Court as a basis of reference for assessing whether a Member State has classified a sufficient number and size of areas as SPAs for the purposes of the abovementioned provisions of Directive 79/409 (see, to that effect, Case C-3/96 *Commission v Netherlands* [1998] ECR I-3031, paragraphs 68 to 70, and Case C-378/01 *Commission v Italy* [2003] ECR I-2857, paragraph 18).

27. It must be held that the IBA 98 provides an up-to-date list of the areas of importance for the conservation of birds in Spain which, in the absence of scientific proof to the contrary, constitutes a basis of reference permitting an assessment to be made as to whether that Member State has classified areas of a sufficient number and size as SPAs to protect all the bird species listed in Annex I to Directive 79/409 and the migratory species not listed in that annex.

Note here the Court is allowing the possibility of Spain being able to produce other evidence, but Spain cannot simply ignore the IBA 98 on the grounds that a public authority did not produce it.

4.2 HABITATS DIRECTIVE

The designation process of SACs under the Habitats Directive is quite different than for SPAs, reflecting as it does the more ambitious goals of the Habitats Directive and Natura 2000. The designation process was originally time-limited, but the process is still ongoing throughout the EU, particularly due to enlargement. The designation process, as set out in Article 4, consists of a number of steps

1. On the basis of the criteria set out in Annex III (Stage 1) and relevant scientific information, each Member State shall propose a list of sites indicating which natural habitat types in Annex I and which species in Annex II that are native to its territory the sites host. For animal species ranging over wide areas these sites shall correspond to the places within the natural range of such species which present the physical or biological factors essential to their life and reproduction. For aquatic species which range over wide areas, such sites will be proposed only where there is a clearly identifiable area representing the physical and biological factors essential to their life and reproduction. Where appropriate, Member States shall propose adaptation of the list in the light of the results of the surveillance referred to in Article 11.

The list shall be transmitted to the Commission, within three years of the notification of this Directive, together with information on each site. That information shall include a map of the site, its name, location, extent and the data resulting from application of the criteria specified in Annex III (Stage 1) provided in a format established by the Commission in accordance with the procedure laid down in Article 21.

2. On the basis of the criteria set out in Annex III (Stage 2) and in the framework both of each of the five biogeographical regions referred to in Article 1 (c) (iii) and of the whole of the territory referred to in Article 2 (1), the Commission shall establish, in agreement with each Member State, a draft list of sites of Community importance drawn from the Member States' lists identifying those which lost one or more priority natural habitat types or priority species.

Member States whose sites hosting one or more priority natural habitat types and priority species represent more than 5 % of their national territory may, in agreement with the Commission, request that the criteria listed in Annex III (Stage 2) be applied more flexibly in selecting all the sites of Community importance in their territory.

The list of sites selected as sites of Community importance, identifying those which host one or more priority natural habitat types or priority species, shall be adopted by the Commission in accordance with the procedure laid down in Article 21.

3. The list referred to in paragraph 2 shall be established within six years of the notification of this Directive.

4. Once a site of Community importance has been adopted in accordance with the procedure laid down in paragraph 2, the Member State concerned shall designate that site as a special area of conservation as soon as possible and within six years at most, establishing priorities in the light of the importance of the sites for the maintenance or restoration, at a favourable conservation status, of a natural habitat type in Annex I or a species in Annex II and for the coherence of Natura 2000, and in the light of the threats of degradation or destruction to which those sites are exposed.

5. As soon as a site is placed on the list referred to in the third subparagraph of paragraph 2 it shall be subject to Article 6 (2), (3) and (4).

The first stage is thus the drawing up of a list of sites by a Member State. As with SPAs, the basis for identification of sites at this stage is purely scientific. This can be seen in the *R v SS for Transport and the Regions, ex p First Corporate Shipping* case, where the issue was whether Member States could take into account economic and social considerations at Stage 1 of the SPA designation process.

Case C-371/98 *R v SS for Transport and the Regions, ex p First Corporate Shipping*
[2000] ECR I-9253, paras 12–16, 19–25

12. It should be noted that the question of interpretation referred for a preliminary ruling relates only to Stage 1 of the procedure for classifying natural sites as SACs laid down by Article 4(1) of the Habitats Directive.

13. Under that provision, on the basis of the criteria set out in Annex III (Stage 1) together with relevant scientific information, each Member State is to propose and transmit to the Commission a list of sites, indicating which natural habitat types in Annex I and native species in Annex II are to be found there.

14. Annex III to the Habitats Directive, which deals with the criteria for selecting sites eligible for identification as sites of Community importance and designation as SACs, sets out, as regards Stage 1, criteria for the assessment at national level of the relative importance of sites for each natural habitat type in Annex I and each species in Annex II.

15. Those assessment criteria are defined exclusively in relation to the objective of conserving the natural habitats or the wild fauna and flora listed in Annexes I and II respectively.

16. It follows that Article 4(1) of the Habitats Directive does not as such provide for requirements other than those relating to the conservation of natural habitats and of wild fauna and flora to be taken into account when choosing, and defining the boundaries of, the sites to be proposed to the Commission as eligible for identification as sites of Community importance. [...]

19. It should be noted that the first subparagraph of Article 3(1) of the Habitats Directive provides for the setting up of a coherent European ecological network of SACs to be known as 'Natura 2000', composed of sites hosting the natural habitat types listed in Annex I and habitats of the species listed in Annex II, to enable them to be maintained or, where appropriate, restored at a favourable conservation status in their natural range.

20. Moreover, Article 4 of the Habitats Directive sets out the procedure for classifying natural sites as SACs, divided into several stages with corresponding legal effects, which is intended in particular to enable the Natura 2000 network to be realised, as provided for by Article 3(2) of the directive.

21. In particular, the first subparagraph of Article 4(2) prescribes that the Commission is to establish, on the basis of the lists drawn up by the Member States and in agreement with each Member State, a draft list of sites of Community importance.

22. To produce a draft list of sites of Community importance, capable of leading to the creation of a coherent European ecological network of SACs, the Commission must have available an exhaustive list of the sites which, at national level, have an ecological interest which is relevant from the point of view of the Habitats Directive's objective of conservation of natural habitats and wild fauna and flora. To that end, that list is drawn up on the basis of the criteria laid down in Annex III (Stage 1) to the directive.

23. Only in that way is it possible to realise the objective, in the first subparagraph of Article 3(1) of the Habitats Directive, of maintaining or restoring the natural habitat types and the species' habitats concerned at a favourable conservation status in their natural range, which may lie across one or more frontiers inside the Community. It follows from Article 1(e) and (i), read in conjunction with Article 2(1), of the directive that the favourable conservation status of a natural habitat or a species must be assessed in relation to the entire European territory of the Member States to which the Treaty applies. Having regard to the fact that, when a Member State draws up the national list of sites, it is not in a position to have precise detailed knowledge of the situation of habitats in the other Member States, it cannot of its own accord, whether because of economic, social or cultural requirements or because of regional or local characteristics, delete sites which at national level have an ecological interest relevant from the point of view of the objective of conservation without jeopardising the realisation of that objective at Community level.

24. In particular, if the Member States could take account of economic, social and cultural requirements and regional and local characteristics when selecting and defining the boundaries of the sites to be included in the list which, pursuant to Article 4(1) of the Habitats Directive, they must draw up and transmit to the Commission, the Commission could not be sure of having available an exhaustive list of sites eligible as SACs, with the risk that the objective of bringing them together into a coherent European ecological network might not be achieved.

25. The answer to the national court's question must therefore be that, on a proper construction of Article 4(1) of the Habitats Directive, a Member State may not take account of economic, social and cultural requirements or regional and local characteristics, as mentioned in Article 2(3) of that directive, when selecting and defining the boundaries of the sites to be proposed to the Commission as eligible for identification as sites of Community importance.

Note again the purposive approach of the Court in interpreting the Directive.

At Stage 2, the Commission prepares a list of sites of Community importance (SCIs).[85] In doing so, they should rely on the criteria in Annex III of the Directive. The matters that can be taken into account at this stage have also been considered by the Court.

Case C-226/08 *Stadt Papenburg v Bundesrepublik Deutschland*
[2010] ECR I-131, paras 27–33

27. The first subparagraph of Article 4(2) of the Habitats Directive provides that, on the basis of the criteria set out in Annex III (Stage 2) to that directive, the Commission is to establish, in agreement with each Member State, a draft list, drawn from the Member States' lists, of SCIs for each of the biogeographical regions referred to in Article 1(c)(iii) of the directive.

28. Annex III to the Habitats Directive, which relates to the criteria for selecting sites eligible for identification as SCIs and designation as special areas of conservation, lists, so far as concerns Stage 2 in that annex, criteria for assessing the Community importance of the sites included on the national lists.

29. Those assessment criteria were defined on the basis of the objective of conserving the natural habitats or the wild fauna and flora listed respectively in Annex I or Annex II to the Habitats Directive, and of the objective of coherence of Natura 2000, namely the European ecological network of special areas of conservation which is provided for in Article 3(1) of the Habitats Directive.

30. It follows that the first subparagraph of Article 4(2) of the Habitats Directive, as such, does not provide for requirements other than those relating to the conservation of natural habitats and wild fauna and flora or to the setting up of the Natura 2000 network to be taken into account when the Commission, in agreement with each of the Member States, draws up a draft list of SCIs.

31. If, in the phase of the classification procedure that is governed by the first subparagraph of Article 4(2) of the Habitats Directive, the Member States were permitted to refuse to give their agreement on grounds other than environmental protection, the achievement of the objective referred to in Article 3(1) of the Habitats Directive would be put in danger, namely the setting up of the Natura 2000 network, which is composed of sites hosting the natural habitat types listed in Annex I to the directive and habitats of the species listed in Annex II and which must enable the natural habitat types and the species' habitats concerned to be maintained or, where appropriate, restored at a favourable conservation status in their natural range.

32. That would, in particular, be the case were the Member States able to refuse to give their agreement on the basis of economic, social and cultural grounds and regional and local characteristics as referred to in Article 2(3) of the Habitats Directive, a provision which, moreover, as was stated by the Advocate General in point 38 of her Opinion, does not constitute an autonomous derogation from the general system of protection put in place by that directive.

33. The answer to the first question is therefore that the first subparagraph of Article 4(2) of the Habitats Directive must be interpreted as not allowing a Member State to refuse to agree on grounds other than environmental protection to the inclusion of one or more sites in the draft list of SCIs drawn up by the Commission.

The final step of the designation process is that Member States must designate the selected sites as SACs and, in so doing, protect them in accordance with the terms of the Directive.

---

[85] Article 4(2).

4.3 LEVEL OF PROTECTION—ARTICLE 6 HABITATS DIRECTIVE

Before 1993, Article 4(4) the Birds Directive placed a duty on Member States to protect SPAs and allowed little leeway to Member States to derogate from that duty.[86] Article 6 of the Habitats Directive was grounded in a different approach and Article 7 of that Directive replaces Article 4(4) of the Birds Directive with Article 6. In other words, Article 6 of the Habitats Directive now governs both SACs and SPAs.

Article 6

1. For special areas of conservation, Member States shall establish the necessary conservation measures involving, if need be, appropriate management plans specifically designed for the sites or integrated into other development plans, and appropriate statutory, administrative or contractual measures which correspond to the ecological requirements of the natural habitat types in Annex I and the species in Annex II present on the sites.

2. Member States shall take appropriate steps to avoid, in the special areas of conservation, the deterioration of natural habitats and the habitats of species as well as disturbance of the species for which the areas have been designated, in so far as such disturbance could be significant in relation to the objectives of this Directive.

3. Any plan or project not directly connected with or necessary to the management of the site but likely to have a significant effect thereon, either individually or in combination with other plans or projects, shall be subject to appropriate assessment of its implications for the site in view of the site's conservation objectives. In the light of the conclusions of the assessment of the implications for the site and subject to the provisions of paragraph 4, the competent national authorities shall agree to the plan or project only after having ascertained that it will not adversely affect the integrity of the site concerned and, if appropriate, after having obtained the opinion of the general public.

4. If, in spite of a negative assessment of the implications for the site and in the absence of alternative solutions, a plan or project must nevertheless be carried out for imperative reasons of overriding public interest, including those of a social or economic nature, the Member State shall take all compensatory measures necessary to ensure that the overall coherence of Natura 2000 is protected. It shall inform the Commission of the compensatory measures adopted.

Where the site concerned hosts a priority natural habitat type and/or a priority species, the only considerations which may be raised are those relating to human health or public safety, to beneficial consequences of primary importance for the environment or, further to an opinion from the Commission, to other imperative reasons of overriding public interest.

Articles 6(1) and 6(2) place relatively straightforward duties upon Member States to protect areas. We say 'relatively' because, as we saw in cases like *Morge*,[87] what is 'significant' is not always self-evident. The duty in Article 6(2) has been interpreted purposively by the CJEU.

Case C-404/09 *Commission v Spain*
(CJEU, 24 November 2011) paras 126–128, 142

The Facts

The Commission brought an enforcement action against Spain in relation to their failure to prevent mining operations having an adverse impact upon an SPA which was the habitat for a population of capercaillie.

---

[86] Case C-57/89 *Commission v Germany* [1991] ECR I-883.   [87] *Morge* (n 68).

The CJEU

126. Concerning [...] the complaint that [...] the Kingdom of Spain did not comply with Article 6(2) of the Habitats Directive, it should be recalled that an activity complies with that provision only if it is guaranteed that it will not cause any disturbance likely significantly to affect the objectives of that directive, particularly its conservation objectives (see, to that effect, Case C-241/08 *Commission* v *France* [2010] ECR I-1697, paragraph 32).

127. Moreover, by virtue of Article 6(2) of the Habitats Directive, the protective legal status of SPAs must guarantee the avoidance therein of the deterioration of natural habitats and the habitats of species as well as significant disturbance of the species for which those areas have been classified (see, in particular, Case C-535/07 *Commission* v *Austria* [2010] ECR I-0000, paragraph 58 and case-law cited).

128. It follows that this complaint is well founded only if the Commission demonstrates to a sufficient legal standard that the Kingdom of Spain has not taken the appropriate protective measures, consisting in preventing the operational activities [...] from producing deteriorations of the habitats of the capercaillie and disturbances of that species likely to have significant effects having regard to the objective of that directive consisting in ensuring the conservation of that species. [...]

142. Moreover, in order to establish a failure to fulfil obligations within the meaning of Article 6(2) of the Habitats Directive, the Commission does not have to prove a cause and effect relationship between a mining operation and significant disturbance to the capercaillie. Since Article 6(2) and (3) of the Habitats Directive are designed to ensure the same level of protection, it is sufficient for the Commission to establish the existence of a probability or risk that that operation might cause significant disturbances for that species (see, to that effect, *Commission* v *France*, paragraph 32, and Case C-2/10 *Azienda Agro-Zootecnica Franchini and Eolica di Altamura* [2011] ECR I-0000, paragraph 41).

Article 6(2) cannot be read in isolation however—it must be read alongside Article 6(3), which places a duty of 'appropriate assessment' upon a Member State. That duty has been given a precautionary interpretation by the CJEU, as seen in the *Landelijke Vereniging tot Behoud van de Waddenzee, Nederlandse Vereniging tot Bescherming van Vogels v Staatssecretaris Van Landbouw, Natuurbeheer en Visserij* case, in which the Court also interpreted the concept of 'plan or project'.

Case C-127/02 *Landelijke Vereniging tot Behoud van de Waddenzee, Nederlandse Vereniging tot Bescherming van Vogels v Staatssecretaris Van Landbouw, Natuurbeheer en Visserij* [2004] ECR I-7405, paras 38–45

38. The answer to the second question must therefore be that Article 6(3) of the Habitats Directive establishes a procedure intended to ensure, by means of a preliminary examination, that a plan or project which is not directly connected with or necessary to the management of the site concerned but likely to have a significant effect on it is authorised only to the extent that it will not adversely affect the integrity of that site, while Article 6(2) of the Habitats Directive establishes an obligation of general protection consisting in avoiding deterioration and disturbances which could have significant effects in the light of the Directive's objectives, and cannot be applicable concomitantly with Article 6(3) [...]

39. According to the first sentence of Article 6(3) of the Habitats Directive, any plan or project not directly connected with or necessary to the management of the site but likely to have a significant effect thereon, either individually or in combination with other plans or projects, is to be

subject to appropriate assessment of its implications for the site in view of the site's conservation objectives.

40. The requirement for an appropriate assessment of the implications of a plan or project is thus conditional on its being likely to have a significant effect on the site.

41. Therefore, the triggering of the environmental protection mechanism provided for in Article 6(3) of the Habitats Directive does not presume—as is, moreover, clear from the guidelines for interpreting that article drawn up by the Commission, entitled 'Managing Natura 2000 Sites: The provisions of Article 6 of the "Habitats" Directive (92/43/EEC)'—that the plan or project considered definitely has significant effects on the site concerned but follows from the mere probability that such an effect attaches to that plan or project.

42. As regards Article 2(1) of Directive 85/337, the text of which, essentially similar to Article 6(3) of the Habitats Directive, provides that 'Member States shall adopt all measures necessary to ensure that, before consent is given, projects likely to have significant effects on the environment ... are made subject to an assessment with regard to their effects', the Court has held that these are projects which are likely to have significant effects on the environment (see to that effect Case C-117/02 *Commission v Portugal* [2004] ECR I-0000, paragraph 85).

43. It follows that the first sentence of Article 6(3) of the Habitats Directive subordinates the requirement for an appropriate assessment of the implications of a plan or project to the condition that there be a probability or a risk that the latter will have significant effects on the site concerned.

44. In the light, in particular, of the precautionary principle, which is one of the foundations of the high level of protection pursued by Community policy on the environment, in accordance with the first sub-paragraph of Article 174(2) EC, and by reference to which the Habitats Directive must be interpreted, such a risk exists if it cannot be excluded on the basis of objective information that the plan or project will have significant effects on the site concerned (see, by analogy, inter alia Case C-180/96 *United Kingdom v Commission* [1998] ECR I-2265, paragraphs 50, 105 and 107). Such an interpretation of the condition to which the assessment of the implications of a plan or project for a specific site is subject, which implies that in case of doubt as to the absence of significant effects such an assessment must be carried out, makes it possible to ensure effectively that plans or projects which adversely affect the integrity of the site concerned are not authorised, and thereby contributes to achieving, in accordance with the third recital in the preamble to the Habitats Directive and Article 2(1) thereof, its main aim, namely, ensuring biodiversity through the conservation of natural habitats and of wild fauna and flora.

45. In the light of the foregoing, the answer to Question 3(a) must be that the first sentence of Article 6(3) of the Habitats Directive must be interpreted as meaning that any plan or project not directly connected with or necessary to the management of the site is to be subject to an appropriate assessment of its implications for the site in view of the site's conservation objectives if it cannot be excluded, on the basis of objective information, that it will have a significant effect on that site, either individually or in combination with other plans or projects.

This last sentence is quite cryptic as a legal test but the practical manifestations of it can be seen quite clearly in the *Nomarchiaki Aftodioikisi Aitoloakarnanias v Ipourgos Perivallontos* case. The Court is essentially saying that Member States cannot find that there will be no significant effects on the integrity of a European site without adequate information about those effects. Article 6(3) is thus less concerned with assessment and more with the adequacy and quality of information.

Case C-43/10 *Nomarchiaki Aftodioikisi Aitoloakarnanias v Ipourgos Perivallontos*
(CJEU, 11 September 2012) paras 106, 110–117

106. By its eleventh question, the referring court seeks, in essence, to ascertain whether Directive 92/43 must be interpreted as precluding consent being given to a project for the diversion of water not directly connected with or necessary to the conservation of a SPA, but likely to have a significant effect on that SPA, in the absence of information or of reliable and updated data concerning the birds in that area. [...]

110. In that regard, it must be recalled that Article 6(3) of Directive 92/43 provides for an assessment procedure intended to ensure, by means of a prior examination, that a plan or project which is not directly connected with or necessary to the management of the site concerned but likely to have a significant effect on it is authorised only to the extent that it will not adversely affect the integrity of that site (see Case C-127/02 *Waddenvereniging and Vogelbeschermingsvereniging* [2004] ECR I-7405, paragraph 34, and Case C-304/05 *Commission v Italy* [2007] ECR I-7495, paragraph 56).

111. With regard to the concept of 'appropriate assessment' within the meaning of Article 6(3) of Directive 92/43, it should be noted that the directive does not define any particular method for the carrying out of such an assessment (*Commission v Italy*, paragraph 57).

112. The Court has, however, held that that assessment must be organised in such a manner that the competent national authorities can be certain that a plan or project will not have adverse effects on the integrity of the site concerned, given that, where doubt remains as to the absence of such effects, the competent authority will have to refuse development consent (see Commission v Italy, paragraph 58).

113. With regard to the factors on the basis of which the competent authorities may gain the necessary level of certainty, the Court has stated that it must be ensured that no reasonable scientific doubt remains, and those authorities must rely on the best scientific knowledge in the field (see *Waddenvereniging and Vogelbeschermingsvereniging*, paragraphs 59 and 61, and *Commission v Italy*, paragraph 59).

114. Furthermore, knowledge of the effects of a plan or a project in the light of the conservation objectives relating to a given site is an essential prerequisite for the application of Article 6(4) of Directive 92/43, since, in the absence thereof, no condition for application of that derogating provision can be assessed. The assessment of any imperative reasons of overriding public interest and that of the existence of less harmful alternatives require a weighing up against the damage caused to the site by the plan or project under consideration. In addition, in order to determine the nature of any compensatory measures, the damage to the site must be precisely identified (see, to that effect, *Commission v Italy*, paragraph 83, and *Solvay and Others*, paragraph 74).

115. In the light of the foregoing, it cannot be held that an assessment is appropriate where information and reliable and updated data concerning the birds in that SPA are lacking.

116. That said, where the development consent given to a project is annulled or revoked because that assessment was not appropriate, it cannot be ruled out that the competent national authorities may gather *a posteriori* reliable and updated data on the birds in the SPA concerned and that they may appraise, on the basis of that data and an assessment thereby supplemented, whether the project for the diversion of water adversely affects the integrity of that SPA and, where necessary, what compensatory measures must be taken to ensure that the execution of the project will not jeopardise protection of the overall coherence of Natura 2000.

117. Consequently, the answer to the eleventh question is that Directive 92/43, and in particular Article 6(3) and (4) thereof, must be interpreted as precluding development consent being given to a project for the diversion of water which is not directly connected with or necessary to the conservation

of a SPA, but likely to have a significant effect on that SPA, in the absence of information or of reliable and updated data concerning the birds in that area.

Note the way in which the Court emphasizes the importance of information. Article 6(3) is thus a duty for decision-makers to inform themselves.

In cases where there is likely to be a negative impact on a SPA or SAC, and this is then established by adequate information, Article 6(3) effectively prevents the project or plan from going ahead. However, Article 6(4) allows that 'imperative reasons of overriding public interest, including those of a social or economic nature' can be a reason for a project or plan still to proceed, so long as there are no alternative solutions for the plan or project (which may include doing nothing)[88] and that compensatory measures are taken so as to ensure that the overall coherence of Natura 2000 is protected. The Court has considered what constitute 'imperative reasons of overriding public interest' on a number of occasions and the *Solvay and Others v Région Wallonne* case is an example of their approach. Note in particular the way in which the Court relates the operation of Article 6(4) to Article 6(3).

Case C-182/10 *Solvay and Others v Région Wallonne* (CJEU, 16 February 2012) paras 71–79

71. By its sixth question, the referring court essentially asks whether Article 6(4) of the Habitats Directive must be interpreted as meaning that the creation of infrastructure intended to accommodate the management centre of a private company may be regarded as an imperative reason of overriding public interest, such reasons including those of a social or economic nature, within the meaning of that provision, capable of justifying the implementation of a plan or project that will adversely affect the integrity of the site concerned.

72. Article 6(4) of the Habitats Directive provides that if, in spite of a negative assessment carried out in accordance with the first sentence of Article 6(3) of the directive, a plan or project must nevertheless be carried out for imperative reasons of overriding public interest, including those of a social or economic nature, and there are no alternative solutions, the Member State is to take all compensatory measures necessary to ensure that the overall coherence of Natura 2000 is protected (see Case C-304/05 *Commission v Italy* [2007] ECR I-7495, paragraph 81).

73. Article 6(4) of that directive must, as an exception to the criterion for authorisation laid down in the second sentence of Article 6(3), be interpreted strictly (see Case C-304/05 Commission v Italy, paragraph 82).

74. Moreover, it can apply only after the implications of a plan or project have been studied in accordance with Article 6(3) of the Habitats Directive. Knowledge of those implications in the light of the conservation objectives relating to the site in question is a necessary prerequisite for the application of Article 6(4), since, in the absence of those elements, no condition for the application of that derogating provision can be assessed. The assessment of any imperative reasons of overriding public interest and that of the existence of less harmful alternatives require a weighing up against the damage caused to the site by the plan or project under consideration. In addition, in order to determine the nature of any compensatory measures, the damage to the site must be precisely identified (see Case C-304/05 *Commission v Italy*, paragraph 83).

75. An interest capable of justifying, within the meaning of Article 6(4) of the Habitats Directive, the implementation of a plan or project must be both 'public' and 'overriding', which means that it must be

---

[88] Commission, Guidance Document on Article 6(4) of the Habitats Directive 92/43/EEC (January 2007).

of such an importance that it can be weighed up against that directive's objective of the conservation of natural habitats and wild fauna and flora.

76. Works intended for the location or expansion of an undertaking satisfy those conditions only in exceptional circumstances.

77. It cannot be ruled out that that is the case where a project, although of a private character, in fact by its very nature and by its economic and social context presents an overriding public interest and it has been shown that there are no alternative solutions.

78. In the light of those criteria, the mere construction of infrastructure designed to accommodate a management centre cannot constitute an imperative reason of overriding public interest within the meaning of Article 6(4) of the Habitats Directive.

79. The answer to Question 6 is therefore that Article 6(4) of the Habitats Directive must be interpreted as meaning that the creation of infrastructure intended to accommodate a management centre cannot be regarded as an imperative reason of overriding public interest, such reasons including those of a social or economic nature, within the meaning of that provision, capable of justifying the implementation of a plan or project that will adversely affect the integrity of the site concerned.

Article 6(4) also carves out a role for the European Commission. At the very least, the Commission must be notified of any reliance on this exception and, where the site hosts a priority natural habitat site or a priority habitat site,[89] the Commission has control over whether there might exist any 'other imperative reasons of overriding public interest' that could justify a development. An opinion from the Commission can be sought on this; otherwise the exception to Article 6(3) is more limited in cases involving priority species, applying only where there are reasons 'relating to human health or public safety, [or] to beneficial consequences of primary importance for the environment'. The Commission has produced a guidance document on the Article 6(4) procedure,[90] as well as over eighteen opinions in relation to Article 6(4).[91]

In a thoughtful article, Krämer makes the following comment about the role of the Commission in the Article 6(4) procedure.

Ludwig Krämer, 'The European Commission's Opinions under Article 6(4) of the Habitats Directive' (2009) 21 JEL 59, 62, 67, 84

As a general remark, it can be observed that the Habitats Directive tries to ensure that habitats which come under its Article 6 are not significantly affected by plans or projects. Therefore, such plans or projects shall normally not be authorised (Article 6(3)). The provisions of Article 6(4), which provide for compensatory measures, constitute an exception to those of Article 6(3) and must therefore be interpreted restrictively. [...]

The binding provision in Article 6(4) of the Habitats Directive to ask for a Commission Opinion is clearly the institution of a Community procedure, even if this procedure is not elaborated in detail. [...]

Commission Opinions under Article 6(4) of the Habitats Directive are at the cross-point between ecological and economic/social considerations. Article 6(4) is a legal provision which tries to ensure a balance between diverging interests.

---

[89] These are SACs that host threatened habitats or species that are primarily represented within the geographical scope of the EU, and are listed in the Directive's Annexes.

[90] (n 88).

[91] <http://ec.europa.eu/environment/nature/natura2000/management/opinion_en.htm> accessed 26 September 2012.

In this article, Krämer stresses the importance of making opinions public and concludes by noting that '[t]ransparency and public discussion are a very effective means to preserve, protect and improve the quality of the environment'.[92]

This point, and the procedure under Article 6, is a reminder that assessment and discourse are integral to *how* nature is protected. Nature conservation requires management in a polycentric context where there are competing interests in relation to the use of land. In such a situation, nature conservation is never simply going to involve the application of a series of rigid legal commands.

4.4 NATIONAL IMPLEMENTATION

The Habitats Directive was originally implemented in England, Wales, and Scotland by the Conservation (Natural Habitats, & c.) Regulations 1994 but in 2010 those Regulations were replaced by the Conservation of Habitats and Species Regulations 2010, which also apply in England, Wales, and Scotland, although the Regulations provide a more specific differentiated regime that reflects devolution. It is also important to note that the 2010 Regulations have been subject to two amendments already. The 2012 amendments being quite substantial. Thus, for example, the wording of Regulations 9 and 9A discussed in Section 2.6 has been changed. The reason for these reforms go back to 2005, when the CJEU found the UK government to have infringed EU law by failing to implement the Habitats Directive properly in a number of different ways.[93] Reid and Woods make an interesting comment in relation to that judgment.

Colin T Reid and Michael Woods, 'Implementing EC Conservation Law'
(2006) 18 JEL 135, 149

The UK Government may feel slightly hard done by in that its transposition of the Directive was criticised by the Commission and the Court, both for being too general and for being too specific. On the one hand the imposition of a general obligation on the relevant authorities to exercise existing powers so as to secure compliance with the Directive was seen as insufficient to provide clear and precise implementation On the other, the attempt to give greater clarity to a prohibition on all indiscriminate means of killing species by banning the specific methods which might actually be used, was seen to risk leaving loopholes and gaps in the law [...] This 'belt and braces' approach to implementation may seem quite sensible when applying overarching obligations within an existing complex system of legislation in which it is perhaps difficult to 'cover all the angles'. It will not always be easy to strike the middle ground that provides a 'precise legal framework . [...] such as to ensure the full and complete application of the Directive and allow harmonised and effective implementation'. However, the ECJ appears concerned to ensure that a sufficient degree of focused transposition is undertaken by Member States through the comprehensive application of clearly stated duties that avoid undue speculation on the part of 'end-users' of the legislation.

The need for 'focused transposition' is a reminder of the legal complexity of EU law. Different legal obligations require different means of transposition and place distinct obligations on a range of different bodies.

---

[92] Ludwig Kramer 'The European Commission's Opinions under Article 6(4) of the Habibats Directive' (2009) 21 JEL 59, 85.

[93] Case C-6/04 *Commission v UK* [2005] I-ECR 9017.

The 2010 Regulations set out a range of different duties and obligations, including that public that bodies 'must have regard to the requirements of the Directives' in exercising any of their functions, as set out in Regulation 9(3) (see Section 2.6). Our focus here is on the more specific duties that relate to SPAs and SACs. In this regard, the protection offered by Article 6 of the Habitats Directive is implemented through Part 6 of the 2010 Regulations, which provides a set of quite detailed procedures. For our purposes, the most significant is Regulation 61(1)–(6), which states:

61. (1) A competent authority, before deciding to undertake, or give any consent, permission or other authorisation for, a plan or project which—

(a) is likely to have a significant effect on a European site or a European offshore marine site (either alone or in combination with other plans or projects), and

(b) is not directly connected with or necessary to the management of that site,

must make an appropriate assessment of the implications for that site in view of that site's conservation objectives.

(2) A person applying for any such consent, permission or other authorisation must provide such information as the competent authority may reasonably require for the purposes of the assessment or to enable them to determine whether an appropriate assessment is required.

(3) The competent authority must for the purposes of the assessment consult the appropriate nature conservation body and have regard to any representations made by that body within such reasonable time as the authority specify.

(4) They must also, if they consider it appropriate, take the opinion of the general public, and if they do so, they must take such steps for that purpose as they consider appropriate.

(5) In the light of the conclusions of the assessment, and subject to regulation 62 (considerations of overriding public interest), the competent authority may agree to the plan or project only after having ascertained that it will not adversely affect the integrity of the European site or the European offshore marine site (as the case may be).

(6) In considering whether a plan or project will adversely affect the integrity of the site, the authority must have regard to the manner in which it is proposed to be carried out or to any conditions or restrictions subject to which they propose that the consent, permission or other authorisation should be given.

Regulation 7(1) provides:

For the purposes of these Regulations, 'competent authority' includes—

(a) any Minister of the Crown (as defined in the Ministers of the Crown Act 1975(I)), government department, statutory undertaker, public body of any description or person holding a public office;

(b) the Welsh Ministers; and

(c) any person exercising any function of a person mentioned in sub-paragraph (a) or (b).

This is a wide definition, which can also encompass private companies carrying out public functions, such as acting as a statutory undertaker.[94] Regulation 68 makes clear that these assessment

---

[94] *R (Akester) v Department for Environment, Food and Rural Affairs* [2010] EWHC 232 (Admin), [2010] Env LR 33, paras 85–86.

provisions apply in a variety of planning contexts, including the grant of planning permission. However, the Regulations do not only apply in a planning context—Regulation 61(1) makes clear that their assessment requirements also apply in relation to consents given in other regulatory contexts (such as pollution control permits), as well as plans or projects undertaken by competent authorities themselves. This latter requirement was at issue in the *Akester* case. This case involved a ferry company (Wightlink) introducing new larger ferries on the route between the Isle of Wight and Lymington, which did not require planning permission or any other regulatory consent. Concerns had been raised, including by Natural England, that the larger ferries would have an impact upon nearby SPAs. The ferry company was a statutory harbour authority and thus found to be a 'competent authority' for the purposes of the Regulations. The question then was whether the introduction of larger ferries constituted a 'plan or project', in which case there was a duty on Wightlink to carry out an appropriate assessment.

R (Akester) v Department for Environment, Food and Rural Affairs
[2010] EWHC 232 (Admin) paras 69–79, 81 (Owen J)

69. It is submitted on behalf of the claimants that the introduction of the W class was plainly a 'plan' or 'project' within the meaning of the directive. The Lymington Harbour Commissioners and Natural England take the same view; and DEFRA now accepts that on the specific facts a 'plan' or 'project' is involved. But Wightlink continue to maintain that the introduction of the W class ferries did not amount to a 'plan' or 'project' within the meaning of the directive.

70. Neither 'plan' nor 'project' is defined in the Habitats Directive; but the interpretation and application of the terms were considered in the *Waddenzee* case. It concerned mechanical fishing for cockles by means of trawls or dredges in the form of metal cages dragged over the seabed by a vessel. The leading edge of the cage consisted of a metal plate, 1m in width which served to scrape the upper 4–5 cms of the seabed into the cage. The metal plate was fitted with a nozzle from which a powerful jet of water emerged, and which pulverised the seabed so that a mixture of water, sand, cockles and other organisms entered the cage, the sieved contents of the cage then being sucked on board hydraulically. The court held that mechanical cockle fishing was an activity '*within the concept of 'project' as defined in the second indent of Article 1(2) of Directive 85/337'*, namely an intervention in the natural surroundings and landscape, and that such a definition of project was relevant to defining the concept of plan or project as provide for in the Habitats Directive (.....

71. Mr Richard Drabble QC, who appeared for Wightlink, argued that *Waddenzee* was decided on its own facts, and that the decision offers no general conclusion as to how the term 'project' is to be interpreted. I accept that the question is inevitably fact sensitive, but nevertheless consider that *Waddenzee* is of assistance in three respects. First it provides confirmation as to the breadth of approach to be adopted in interpreting Article 6(3), secondly it provides guidance as to the test to be applied in determining whether a proposal amounts to a 'plan' or 'project' within the meaning of the directive; and thirdly the decision is based on an analogous factual situation.

72. As to the first, recitals in the preamble to an EC measure may be used to confirm the interpretation to be given to an operative provision, see *Case 107/80 Adorno v Commission* [1981] ECR 1469 at 1484–1485; and the 10th recital to the directive make it clear that the terms 'plan or project' should be given a wide interpretation in that it states that:

'... *an appropriate assessment must be made of any plan or program likely to have a significant effect on the conservation objectives of a site which has been designated.'*

That is also reflected in the guidance given by the Commission in *Managing Natura 2000 Sites* at paragraph 4.3:

'*In as much as Directive 92/43/EEC does not define "plan" or "project", due consideration must be given to general principles of interpretation, in particular the principle that an individual provision of Community law must be interpreted on the basis of its wording and of its purpose and the context in which it occurs*'

73. The guidance continues with the advice (at paragraphs 4.3.1, 4.3.2) that both the words 'project' and 'plan' should be given a '*very broad*' definition and meaning.

74. In *Waddenzee* the court made it clear that Article 6(3) should be interpreted in the light of its broad objective, namely a high level of protection of the environment, and in particular that the authorisation criteria laid down in its second sentence '*integrates the precautionary principle*', which it described as being one of the foundations of the high level of protection pursued by Community policy (see in particular paragraphs 44 and 58).

75. As to the second, *Waddenzee* provides guidance as to the test to be applied to determine whether a proposal amounts to a 'plan' or 'project' within the meaning of the directive. A plan or project will be caught by Article 6(3), in the sense that it will trigger the requirement for an appropriate assessment of its environmental impact, if it '*is likely to have a significant effect*' on the site. The test by reference to which the requirement of an appropriate assessment will be invoked, is expressed in a variety of ways in *Waddenzee*. The phrase used at paragraph 40 is '*being likely to have a significant effect on the site*'; at paragraph 41, and by reference to the Commission guidance *Managing Natura 2000 Sites*, '*mere probability that such an effect attaches to that plan or project*'; at paragraph 43 '*a probability or a risk that the latter …the plan or project) will have significant effects on the site concerned*'; and at paragraph 45 '*if it cannot be excluded … that it will have a significant effect on that site*'. But I am satisfied, bearing in mind the requirement to interpret Article 6(3) by reference to the precautionary principle, that the proper approach is that the requirement for an appropriate assessment is triggered unless the risk of significant adverse effects can be excluded.

76. Mr Drabble submitted that it would be an incorrect approach to Article 6(3) to conclude that just because an action could potentially have an impact on the environment or on a European site, then it should be considered to be to be a 'plan or project'. But in my judgment that it precisely the effect of Article 6(3), an interpretation supported by the decision in *Waddenzee*

77. As to the third I am satisfied that the facts in *Waddenzee* provide a very close parallel. In *Waddenzee* the intervention with the natural surroundings was the effect of the dredging operation on the seabed, both by the plate at the leading edge scraping the top 4–5 cms into the cage, and by the disturbance of the seabed by the powerful jet of water from the nozzle attached to the leading edge. Similarly the operation of the W class has the potential to interfere with the natural surroundings in that by their size and displacement, means of propulsion and steering, and the fact that they operate in narrow channels and at certain states of the tide in very shallow water, the vessels may disturb the bed and banks of the river and cause erosion to the mudflats and salt-marshes within the protected sites. Mr Drabble argued that *Waddenzee* is to be distinguished on the basis that the intervention in the natural surroundings was a direct effect of the dredging operations, whereas any effect of the use of the ferries is indirect. But in my judgment that is not a distinction of significance. The question is whether the activity gives rise to a risk of adverse effects on the protected sites, whether directly or indirectly.

78 In his written advice to Wightlink to which I have referred at paragraph 53 above, Mr Drabble further argued that if the claimants' contention that the introduction of the W class is a plan or project within the ambit of the Habitats Directive is accepted, then that '*would mean that every time a shipping line employed different or larger vessels in any port, there would be a requirement to consider whether an appropriate assessment had first to be carried out*'. But that argument is flawed in that it is not the introduction of the vessels that triggers the requirement to consider whether an appropriate assessment

has to be carried out, but rather the possible effect of the operation of such vessels on the protected sites.

[...]

81. I am entirely satisfied that the introduction of the W class ferries on the Lymington to Yarmouth route was a project within the ambit of Article 6(3). On 12 February 2009 Natural England gave formal advice to Wightlink, Lymington Harbour Commissioners, New Forest District Council and the Marine and Fisheries Agency (see paragraph 49 above) in which it advised in terms that *'cannot be ascertained that the introduction of the "W class" ferries will not have an adverse effect on the Natura 2000 Interest.'* In my judgment a decision maker considering at that point whether the proposed introduction of the W class ferries was a plan or project within the meaning of the Habitats Directive and the Habitats Regulations would have been bound to conclude that the risk of significant adverse effects on the protected sites could not be excluded, and that in consequence the requirement for an appropriate assessment was triggered.

Owen J's approach is not only purposive, but he also draws on the how the courts have interpreted the duties created by other EU Directives. In his analysis, the question of what is a 'plan or project' is closely related to the potential for impact. This case raises similar issues as those seen in Chapter 19 in relation to how English courts have incorporated CJEU case law concerning the Environmental Assessment Directive. There are thus interesting parallels between this and cases such as *Berkeley v Secretary of State for the Environment.*[95]

The willingness of the courts to engage in purposive interpretation can also be seen in *Feeney v Oxford City Council*, which involved a challenge to Oxford City's Core Strategy for allegedly failing to comply with the Habitats Regulations 2010. In preparing the Core Strategy, the Council had prepared two Habitats Regulation Assessments (HRA). The court considered not only the duty under Regulation 61 but also that under Regulation 102(1) which states:

102.—(1) Where a land use plan—

(a) is likely to have a significant effect on a European site or a European offshore marine site (either alone or in combination with other plans or projects), and

(b) is not directly connected with or necessary to the management of the site, the plan-making authority for that plan must, before the plan is given effect, make an appropriate assessment of the implications for the site in view of that site's conservation objectives.

In this case, the judge reviewed the legislative framework and the Court of Justice case law and came to the following conclusion.

Feeney v Oxford City Council
[2011] EWHC 2699 (Admin) (Stephen Morris QC sitting as a Deputy High Court Judge)
paras 27–28, 88–93

27. Once an appropriate assessment has been made, in my judgment, the true construction of regulations 61(5) and 102(4), Article 6.3 2nd sentence and the two ECJ cases is as follows:

(1) The competent authority is required to *take account* of the conclusions in that appropriate assessment.

---

[95] [2001] 2 AC 603.

(2) It is *then* required to *ascertain* whether or not the plan or project will 'adversely affect the integrity' of the relevant Site; this is a matter for its judgment/assessment. Strictly, in my judgment, this is a stage distinct from the stage of 'appropriate assessment': see the words "in the light of the conclusions in the appropriate assessment in Article 6.3 and regulation 61(5)". So, for example, the competent authority's appropriate assessment might find that there will or might be harm, but yet the authority could subsequently ascertain, as result of measures or action taken after the appropriate assessment, that there would be no harm; this is plainly envisaged by the reference, in Article 6.4, to 'alternative solutions'.

(3) The competent authority may only agree to the plan or project if the competent authority concludes (or ascertains) that it *will not* adversely affect the integrity of the relevant Site; if it does so conclude, then the competent authority has a discretion whether or not to agree to the plan.

28. Thus, on the one hand, whether or not there is "adverse effect" is a matter of judgment for the competent authority; on the other hand, there is a legal obligation on the authority *not* to approve the plan or project unless it has concluded that there will be no adverse effect

After considering the arguments of the parties, the judge then considered the facts before him.

88. In my judgment, in adopting the Core Strategy in its final form, the Council did ascertain and conclude that the Core Strategy *in that form* would not cause harm to the Oxford Meadows SAC. The adoption, in the Core Strategy, of the qualifying wording as recommended by the Joint Statement, ensures that no such harm can or will arise. Thus, the proper interpretation of the Core Strategy as adopted is that, with the qualifying wording in place, there is no uncertainty as to harm. On this basis, the claim under Issue 1 has no real prospect of success.

89. The key to this issue is to understand that the 'land use plan' (or 'plan or project') which is being agreed or approved by the Council, under regulations 102(4) (and 61(5)), is the Core Strategy as a whole and in its final form; it is not, narrowly and specifically, the Northern Gateway development CS6 in its current form as set out within the Core Strategy. The fallacy in the Claimant's argument is that it is directed towards the latter. I accept that it cannot be said that the Northern Gateway development CS6 *in its particular present form* will not cause harm to the SAC. However that was not the relevant land use plan (or project or plan) which the Council approved on 14 March 2011.

90. The Core Strategy in its final form includes the 'safeguard' of the qualifying wording. Since there is a safeguard built into and within the Core Strategy as adopted to ensure that there will be no harm in the future, then the adoption of the Core Strategy *as so qualified* will, necessarily, not cause harm. As Mr Crean QC put it in his skeleton argument, 'the Core Strategy explicitly excludes development where it cannot be demonstrated that it will not have an adverse effect on the Oxford Meadows SAC'.

91. The task of the competent authority is one of making certain, or ensuring, *prospectively* that no harm will arise in the future: see *Waddenzee*, and paragraph 24 above. I accept that there is no express statement, either in the Core Strategy itself, or by the Inspectors or by the Council in adopting the Core Strategy that 'with the safeguard in place, I am satisfied that there will be no harm to the SAC'. Nevertheless this is the effect of the terms of the Core Strategy in its final adopted form. As explained in the passage from the Joint Statement set out in paragraph 57 above, and in the Inspectors' conclusions, the very purpose of the inclusion of paragraph 3.4.43 of the qualifying wording was to guarantee that there cannot be an adverse effect in the future; 'ensuring that the plan is compliant' means certainty as to absence of harm. This point was expressly made by Mr. Sloman in his written response made for the full Council meeting (and also recorded in the April 2011 version of the HRA).

92. This conclusion is supported by the following further factors. *First*, a core strategy is a high level strategic document and the detail falls to be worked out at a later stage. Subsequent appropriate assessment of specific proposals is plainly envisaged by, and indeed necessitated under, the regime. Each

appropriate assessment must be commensurate to the relative precision of the plans at any particular stage and no more. There does have to be an appropriate assessment at the Core Strategy stage, but such an assessment cannot do more than the level of detail of the strategy at that stage permits. Adv. Gen. Kokott expressly recognises this at §49 of her Opinion in *Commission v UK*. *Secondly*, if the use of a "safeguard" condition such as the present was impermissible, proposals would have to be ruled out altogether at the core strategy stage, and there could be no scope for subsequent appropriate assessment at a later stage, as specifically envisaged by Adv. Gen. Kokott. If the Claimant's argument were correct, a core strategy could never be approved, where, as is likely, the specific detail of future particular development is not known. No core strategy could ever involve detailed consideration of the impact on SAC of specific development proposals. In this way, the Council cannot be criticised for not making an appropriate assessment at a site specific level; there are currently no detailed proposals. *Thirdly*, I do not accept the Claimant's allegation that the Council failed to have regard to the precautionary principle. The HRA itself expressly refers (at page 2) to the precautionary principle. Further the entire approach of the Council in introducing and approving the qualifying wording, in the context of possible concerns raised by Natural England and BBOWT [Buckinghamshire, Berkshire, and Oxfordshire Wildlife Trust], was based upon advance consideration of future possibilities. *Fourthly*, following the close of oral argument, the Council provided, and the Claimant did not dispute, a number of examples of core strategies having been approved subject to conditions, of which three have been made expressly subject to conditions as a 'safeguard' to address potential harm to SACs under the Habitats Regulations. Moreover, in the specific context of the Habitats Regulations, it is noteworthy that, in the *Lewis* case, the scheme in issue was approved but only subject to conditions which had been specifically suggested by Natural England and the RSPB to address their concerns in relation to the particular sites. There was no suggestion that such prospective, safeguarding, conditions were impermissible under regulation 48(5) of the 1994 Regulations as improperly qualifying the conclusion of 'no adverse effect'.

93. As to the Claimant's argument concerning Article 6.4, the derogation under Article 6.4 deals only with matters of public interest and arises only if there is both a negative appropriate assessment *and* no alternative solutions. Here, in practice, the qualifying wording was an alternative solution - and that could be, and was, properly approved under Article 6.3 and at a stage *after* the appropriate assessment.

This reasoning shows a careful consideration of the intricate 2010 Regulations as well as a purposive interpretation of the Directive.

This case, along with *Akester*, highlights that Article 6 of the Habitats Directive has serious implications for a range of activities and it is not surprising that it has been a controversial provision. There have been arguments from some quarters that the UK government, in implementing the Habitats Directive, has 'gold plated' it, that is, they had gone above and beyond the legal duties of EU law implementation. In particular, these concerns have related to the perception that the Directive has limited commercial port development (many SPAs and SACs being along coasts). The extract from Morris paints a more complicated picture.

Roger KA Morris, 'The Application of the Habitats directive in the UK: Compliance or Gold Plating?' (2011) 28 Land Use Policy 361, 368

Davidson (2006b) emphasised in his summary that actual evidence to support assertions of 'gold plating' was often lacking. This new analysis [in this article] supports the Davidson findings. There are grounds for believing that the UK Government, like those of other Member States, has sought to minimise the impacts of the Directive but European case law and direct challenges to its legislative framework have contributed to more restrictive implementation. There is also evidence that both Government and its regulators have sought pragmatic approaches that have subsequently encountered unforeseen problems. Approaches such as the DETR guidance (1998) and the omission of the Humber Estuary from the original SAC series are illustrative of this changing regulatory environment.

Analysis of port development proposals also shows that the Habitats Directive has not been solely responsible for limiting economic growth in the ports sector, although it may have slowed down some capacity upgrades. Projects such as Felixstowe South and Bathside Bay have been equally constrained by the need to address transport infrastructure issues. Recent shortages in customers have also affected the short-term viability of these projects and consequently the economic impact of delay may not be as severe as critics have suggested. There may even have been savings because new capacity would have been under-utilised in the short to medium term, making funding a major issue too.

The Habitats Directive has established a common template for assessment of nature conservation impacts and has required competent authorities to justify particular judgements. This challenges people and organisations that have been used to much less rigorous or onerous processes and consequently there will be inevitable voices of dissent. This dissent has been highlighted by antipathy towards the Directive and allegations of 'gold plating'. The final test of the Habitats Directive's influence lies in the degree to which the decline in biological diversity is halted in Europe.

Morris is once again reminding us of the polycentric and conflict-bound nature of nature conservation problems as well as the multi-level and multi-dimensional nature of administrative decision-making. The conservation of nature is always taking place in the context of a range of different human activities, for which it also has implications.

FURTHER READING AND QUESTIONS

1. There is a range of different guidance documents produced by both the European Commission and the UK government bodies concerning the way in which the Birds and Habitats Directives operate. DEFRA's website is particularly useful. See <http://www.defra.gov.uk/habitats-review/implementation/process-guidance/guidance/sites/> accessed 19 September 2012.

2. For further discussion of the role of the Commission in decisions about compensatory measures under Article 6(4), see Donald McGillivray, 'Compensating Biodiversity Loss: The EU Commission's Approach to Compensation under Article 6 of the Habitats Directive' (2012) 24 JEL 417.

3. There will be cases where there is more than one competent authority under the 2010 Habitats Regulations. This situation is regulated by Regulation 65. Regulation 65(2) states:

Nothing in regulation 61(1) […] requires a competent authority to assess any implications of a plan or project which would be more appropriately assessed under that provision by another competent authority.

The legal effect of this was considered in *Cornwall Waste Forum St Dennis Branch v Secretary of State for Communities and Local Government* [2012] EWCA Civ 379, in which arguments concerning legitimate expectations were raised. The case is an interesting example of how environmental law regimes can raise quite tricky issues of administrative law.

5 A NOTE ON REFORM

Nature conservation law is always under revision due to new information about the natural environment coming to light, as well as changing perceptions over its value. Three examples of such legal revision processes are given here. Note that each of these processes of review has a very different purpose and a different focus. The concept of comprehensive reform of nature conservation law is thus elusive. As this is a dynamic area of law, a visit to our companion website is also strongly advised.

The first example is a process of review instigated by the last Labour government. In 2009, the Labour government commissioned a review of England's wildlife and ecological network. That review did not report until after the change of government in 2010, and its main finding is set out here.

John H Lawton and others, Making Space for Nature: a Review of England's Wildlife Sites and Ecological Network (2010), vi

We propose that the overarching aim for England's ecological network should be to deliver a natural environment where: Compared to the situation in 2000, biodiversity is enhanced and the diversity, functioning and resilience of ecosystems re-established in a network of spaces for nature that can sustain these levels into the future, even given continuing environmental change and human pressures.

In the Foreword to the Review, John Lawton, the Chair of the review group stresses that:

The report argues that we need a step-change in our approach to wildlife conservation, from trying to hang on to what we have, to one of large-scale habitat restoration and recreation, under-pinned by the re-establishment of ecological processes and ecosystem services, for the benefits of both people and wildlife. We are not proposing a heavy, top-down set of solutions. It is a long-term vision, out to 2050, and defines a direction of travel, not an end-point. This vision will only be realised if, within the overall aims, we work at local scales, in partnership with local people, local authorities, the voluntary sector, farmers, other land-managers, statutory agencies, and other stakeholders. Private landowners, land managers and farmers have a crucial role to play in delivering a more coherent and resilient wildlife network.

Lawton also commented on the Review when writing in the Environmental Law Review.

John Lawton, 'Making Space for Nature' (2011) 13 Env L Rev 1, 4–5

The evidence demonstrates that the SSSI series, important as it is, clearly does not in itself comprise a coherent and resilient ecological network. Perhaps this should not come as a surprise since SSSIs were not designated with this aim in mind; they were selected simply to be representative of particular kinds of habitat and assemblages of species. Looking across all three Tiers of wildlife sites, the evidence demonstrates that only attribute (1) is substantially met; in all other cases there are serious shortcomings in the network. Notably, many of England's wildlife sites are too small - for example, the median area of an SSSI is only 25.5 ha (small sites can only support small total populations of vulnerable species, making chance extinctions more likely); losses of certain habitats have been so great that the area remaining is no longer enough to halt the additional loss of species without concerted efforts (for instance, 97 per cent of flower-rich meadows and grasslands were lost in England and Wales between 1930 and 1984, and the losses continue); with the exception of Natura 2000 sites and SSSIs, most of England's semi-natural habitats important for wildlife are generally insufficiently protected and under-managed; many of the natural connections in our countryside have been degraded or lost, leading to isolation of sites (so that if species are lost from a site - for instance, after a hard winter or a fire - the lost species are unable to recolonise it); and too few people have easy access to wildlife.

So, what to do? The essence of what needs to be done to enhance the resilience and coherence of England's ecological network can be summarised in four words: *more, bigger, better* and *joined*

There are five key approaches which encompass these, and also take account of the land around the ecological network. We need to:

(a) improve the quality of current sites by better habitat management;

(b) increase the size of current wildlife sites;

(c) enhance connections between, or join up, sites, either through physical corridors, or through 'stepping stones';

(d) create new sites; and

(e) reduce the pressures on wildlife by improving the wider environment, including through buffering wildlife sites.

This is an ambitious agenda and one that recognizes the limits of ecological protection offered by the current regimes. The Government responded to the review in 2011,[96] and the developments since then have also reflected the agenda set out in HM Government, *The Natural Choice: Securing the Value of Nature*.[97] One of the reforms that the Review has led to is the creation of new Nature Improvement Areas, which were selected after a national competition. These are locally-led nature conservation projects that receive public funding for their activities.[98]

A second, different process of legal reform was instigated by the Treasury in 2011, and this led the Government to publish the *Report of the Habitats and Wild Birds Directives Implementation Review* in March 2012.[99] This report recommended streamlining the operation of these EU nature conservation regimes, particularly in relation to major infrastructure projects.[100] In 2012, a Major Infrastructure and Environment Unit and a Major Infrastructure and Habitats Group were in the process of being set up.[101] A key theme of these reforms is the need to 'facilitate' infrastructure projects. How this reform of a central plank of (EU) nature conservation law develops will be interesting to see. Draft DEFRA guidance on Article 6(4) of the Habitats Directive is a product of a recent consultation process.[102]

A third process of (possible) reform is the project of the Law Commission of England and Wales under its eleventh Programme of Law Reform relating to 'wildlife law'. In 2012, the Law Commission published a lengthy and carefully considered consultation paper looking at the reform of certain aspects of wildlife law. The Commission describes the scope of this law reform project in the following way.

Law Commission, *Wildlife Law: A Consultation Paper* (Law Com No 206, 2012), para 1.20

The project encompasses consideration of the species-specific provisions allowing for the conservation, control, protection and exploitation of wildlife present within England and Wales. It covers,

[96] DEFRA, *Government Response to the Making Space for Nature Review* (PB13537 June 2011), <http://www.defra.gov.uk/publications/files/pb13537-lawton-response-110607.pdf> accessed 20 September 2012.

[97] (Cm 8082, June 2011).

[98] Further information can be found at <http://www.naturalengland.org.uk/ourwork/conservation/biodiversity/funding/nia/default.aspx> and <http://www.defra.gov.uk/environment/natural/whitepaper/nia/> accessed 20 September 2012.

[99] <http://www.defra.gov.uk/publications/files/pb13724-habitats-review-report.pdf> accessed 20 September 2012.

[100] <http://www.defra.gov.uk/publications/2012/12/11/pb13840-habitats-iropi-guide-1211/> accessed 13 December 2012.

[101] <http://www.defra.gov.uk/habitats-review/implementation/infrastructure-projects/mieu/> accessed 20 September 2012.

[102] <http://www.defra.gov.uk/consult/2012/08/07/habitats-directive-iropi/> accessed 20 September 2012.

therefore, the species-specific protection afforded to wild birds and other animals under part 1 of the Wildlife and Countryside Act 1981, the species protection provisions in the Conservation of Habitats and Species Regulations 2010, and Acts covering individual species (or limited groups of species). The project also includes consideration of Acts dedicated to welfare protection, such as the Animal Welfare Act 2006 and the Wild Mammals (Protection) Act 1996. Control provisions, such as those for invasive species, are included in scope, as are Acts providing for the exploitation of certain species.

That sounds as though it covers quite a lot, but, as the Law Commission explicitly notes, what are not covered are the level of species protection, general schemes for animals, and the protection of wildlife outside territorial waters. They are also not considering habitats protection, as the Commission explains in the following way.

Law Commission, *Wildlife Law: A Consultation Paper* (Law Com No 206, 2012) para 1.24

The legislative provisions on habitats are excluded from the project. The purpose of the project is to reform the law relating to wildlife. While the protection of wildlife is, of course, inextricably linked to the protection of habitats, the project would become a significantly more extensive review of environmental law were we to include both habitat and wildlife legislation.

SSSIs are also not directly included as their focus is not only upon wildlife. Within this remit, the Law Commission is making a number of proposals in their consultation paper. The most interesting, from the perspective of environmental lawyers, is the argument for a rationalisation and simplification.

Law Commission, *Wildlife Law: A Consultation Paper* (Law Com No 206, 2012) paras 5.19–5.20

5.19 [...] many of the problems with the legal regime arise because the governing provisions are strewn across various enactments. This makes it difficult for individuals to discover the exact legislative regime that applies to a particular species (or even to know where they should look).

5.20 A single statute for wildlife management would have definite benefits. It would allow for increased consistency (where different terms have been used to mean the same thing in different statutes). It would also mean that there is a comprehensive statute for those interested in wildlife law, rather than users having to trawl through the myriad of existing statutes.

The argument for simplification and rationalization is deeply appealing. As we saw in Section 2, this is an area that is eye watering in its legislative complexity. But the analysis in this chapter also raises a number of questions about how easy such a process of rationalization would be. Three problems are particularly significant. The first is whether rationalization can occur if the focus is only upon one aspect of nature conservation law (species but not their habitats). With that said, it is profoundly difficult to cover all areas of the subject.

The second problem is the multi-level nature of nature conservation regimes. It is not just that these regimes are developed in different contexts but that the legal obligations embedded in these regimes are the product of quite different legal cultures. Thus, we saw the very purposive way in which the obligations under the Habitats and Birds Directives—EU law obligations—have been interpreted. Likewise, this is an area in which devolution has a significant role to play.

The third problem is that while different nature conservation regimes do overlap, they protect different things for different reasons. The SSSI regime is ultimately driven by a different logic (protecting scientifically interesting natural features) from that of the Natura 2000 network (preserving an EU ecological network through selecting and conserving representative examples of different habitat types). Rationalization of all of nature conservation law would thus result in abandoning specific and finely-tuned nature conservation goals.

The idea of rationalizing reform also raises an interesting question about what such reform of the labyrinthine body of nature conservation law can, and should, amount to. The web of legislation and the fact that the different reforms identified here are occurring at the same time is evidence of the fact that reform is unlikely to identify *the* foundational principles of this area of environmental law. The laws in this area are all too much creations of environmental policy, particular principles, and environmental legislation for there to be a single foundation of them. Yet, that does not mean that some kind of basic re-organization is possible. As a first step, however, this is an area of law that could benefit from some sustained reflection on how it is mapped and understood.

FURTHER READING

1. A more detailed overview of these reform developments can be found in Lynda Warren, 'New Approaches to Nature Conservation in the UK' (2012) 14 Env L Rev 44.

2. The problems of reform and consolidation are not only seen in England. Australia has also had challenges in reforming this area of law. See *Report of the Independent Review of the Environmental Protection and Biodiversity Conservation Act 1999* (October 2009) <http://www.environment.gov.au/epbc/review/publications/pubs/final-report.pdf/> accessed 20 September 2012.

---

6 CONCLUSIONS

This chapter has provided an overview of many legislative frameworks. It can be easy in setting out and navigating this kind of overview to forget that underlying those frameworks are environmental problems that have both socio-political and scientific aspects. Indeed, a key reason for the legal complexity in this area concerns the fact that nature conservation is not a simple or straightforward environmental problem. Societies value nature for different reasons, while our understandings of ecosystems is still incomplete, and the management of the natural environment is a highly polycentric affair. The law of nature conservation is thus messy for a reason.

FURTHER READING

This chapter has only provided an overview of this area of law. For more detailed analysis of particular aspects of nature conservation law, the following three texts are particularly useful:

• Colin Reid, *Nature Conservation Law* (3rd edn, Thomson Reuters 2009).

- Michael Bowman, Peter Davies and Catherine Redgwell, *Lyster's International Wildlife Law* (2nd edn, CUP 2010).

- Alexander Gillespie, *Conservation, Biodiversity and International Law* (Edward Elgar 2011).

In addition, the websites of the JNCC (<*jncc.defra.gov.uk/*> accessed 20 September 2012) and Natural England (www.naturalengland.org.uk/ accessed 20 September 2012) have useful information about the different nature conservation regimes in England.

THE LAW RELATING TO
LAND CONTAMINATION

At first glance, the environmental law topic of 'the law relating to land contamination' seems straightforward—the environmental problem appears discrete (a specific piece of land is contaminated) and the necessary response rather obvious (the removal of the contaminant from the land). Yet the problem of land contamination and the laws relating to it are the most paradigmatic examples of the complexities of environmental law. Rather, than a discrete environmental problem, land contamination is more a microcosm that encapsulates the polycentric, scientific, and socio-political difficulties we see in all environmental problems (Chapter 2). In particular, land contamination is both a problem to do with pollution and with land use. Moreover, it is a problem with a temporal dimension—'contamination' has occurred in the past.

The legal framework in the UK for dealing with land contamination is also anything but simple. While there is a dedicated 'contaminated land' regime it is a last resort and its provisions are relatively rarely used. Rather, the vast majority of land contamination issues are dealt with through the planning system or through other forms of voluntary action. With that said, the contaminated land regime 'frames' how the problem of land containuiation is understood in England. What is meant by this is that the definition of contaminated land contained in that regime provides the starting point for deciding whether a legal response is needed in any other context.

The aim of this chapter is to provide an overview of both the problem of land contamination and the legal frameworks that relate to it. In Section 1, the concept of 'land contamination' and the multifaceted nature of land contamination are examined and it is shown that land contamination is simultaneously an environmental health issue, a scientific and engineering problem, a socio-political problem, a commercial problem, a planning problem, and a legal problem.

In Section 2, an overview is given of how contaminated land is addressed in England. A brief overview is given of the different legal frameworks and then the definition of 'contaminated land' is examined and it is shown how it plays a role in different contexts. In Sections 3 and 4 the two most significant frameworks for dealing with land contamination are discussed in detail—the planning system and Part IIA of the Environmental Protection Act 1990. In Section 5, the overall framework for addressing land contamination is reflected upon.

Five points should be noted before starting. First, because terms such as 'contaminated land' and 'land affected by contamination' are legal terms with legal meanings, the phrase 'land contamination' is used here to refer to the general problem of land that may be contaminated. To put it another way— be careful with your terminology!

Second, we do not deal with all aspects of the contaminated land regime. Thus, we do not focus on the pollution of controlled waters or more specialized issues such as radioactive contamination, nor on the details of how the regime operates in the devolved regions. All these issues are important in practice, but the purpose of this chapter is to aid readers in understanding the logic of the regime and we feel that is best done by focusing on its core features.

Third, land contamination is an area dominated by guidance. As that is the case, there is a danger than any discussion of land contamination simply becomes a watered down version of these documents. The approach in this chapter is to highlight some key features of this guidance and to highlight the very real intellectual challenges in this area. There is thus an expectation that readers will look at these other documents separately.

Fourth, besides overlaps with waste law (see Chapter 16), there are no EU laws directly related to land contamination although the Commission did propose a Soil Framework Directive in 2006.[1] With that said, there is a Soil Thematic Strategy overseen by DG Environment that publishes studies and other publications in this area.[2] The difficulties in achieving harmonization between Member States in this area are very much due to the complexity of land contamination problems.

Fifth, it should be noted that Part IIA operates in both Wales and Scotland but not Northern Ireland. In Northern Ireland the Waste and Contaminated Land (Northern Ireland) Order 1997 has been enacted but is not yet in force. That Order is similar to Part IIA. All of this means that while the focus in this chapter is upon England, our general discussion is relevant to the devolved regions.

Finally, this chapter must be read alongside the chapters on planning law (Chapter 18), waste law (Chapter 16), and statutory liabilities and remedies (Chapter 9). In particular, it must be appreciated that the relationship between waste law and land contamination is a very close one. That relationship is touched upon in Section 1.2 of Chapter 16.

1 LAND CONTAMINATION: AN OVERVIEW

Land contamination usually refers to a situation where a past activity on land has left in soil (and sometimes ground water) something that is understood as a threat to present activities on that land. This definition highlights three important features of land contamination.

First, to describe something as 'contaminated' is to connote that a *threat exists* because of something that has been *added to* land (or to ground water). As seen in Chapter 2, whether something is a 'threat' is not a question of simple objective fact. Not only are there scientific uncertainties involved but what is a threat depends on what we value. Second, the act of contamination is a *past* event. In some cases, it will be in the recent past but in most cases contamination will have occurred many years ago. More significantly, it may have occurred at a time when the act of contamination was not understood as problematic in that it was not perceived to be creating a threat and/or it was not illegal. The past nature of land contamination makes it distinct from waste law (see Chapter 16). Waste law as a form of pollution control is usually about ex ante control of activities so as to stop contamination in the future. In contrast, the laws of land contamination deal with it in a post hoc manner.

Third, land contamination is about the contamination *of land*. This is a tautology but an important one to note. In essence what it means is that land contamination is about the contamination of property. In many cases this will be private property but in some cases it will be property owned by the state. The important point to note is that land contamination is closely tied up with ideas of property ownership and transfer and the value of land will depend on whether land is deemed to be contaminated. It is also the case that land contamination regulatory regimes will also limit what can occur on

---

[1] COM(2006) 232 final.
[2] <http://ec.europa.eu/environment/soil/three_en.htm> accessed 28 September 2012.

land. It is for this reason that land contamination has one of the highest profiles of all environmental law regimes in commercial environmental law. This will be seen throughout this chapter. The final important thing to note in regards to the fact that land contamination is about land is that as an environmental problem it is primarily a matter of concern for those in the locality of the contamination or those who own property. Land contamination thus does not have the global profile of other environmental problems such as climate change. This does not mean that it is a non-contentious issue however.

Overall, then, what can be seen is that even the definition of land contamination has a number of facets. Land contamination can be understood as an environmental and health problem; a scientific and engineering problem; a socio-political problem; a property development problem; and a legal problem. Each of these different ways of understanding the problem of land contamination highlight different complexities and thus it is useful to discuss each in turn. What is also important to note is that these different ways of conceptualizing the problem of land contamination are not mutually exclusive.

1.1 LAND CONTAMINATION AS AN ENVIRONMENTAL AND HEALTH PROBLEM

For most environmental lawyers, land contamination will be largely understood as an environmental and public health problem. The 'threats' it creates are thus risks to environmental quality and human health, usually from chemicals, or other substances involved in manufacture, being left on land. This may be because such substances were stored on the land, were by-products of the manufacturing process, or were waste.

Many different practices since industrialization may have led to land contamination. Gasworks, oil refineries, petroleum storage, heavy engineering works, railway depots, abattoirs, chemical manufacture, waste disposal, military related activities, scrap yards, laboratories, textile manufacture, glass making, printing works, and food processing are just a few of the commonly cited examples of practices than can lead to land contamination. Some of these activities will have happened on a large scale but others will have been occurring on smaller sites.

Once there is land contamination human exposure to it can occur in a variety of different ways including direct skin contact, inhalation, contamination of drinking water, and/or the uptake of contaminants by plants grown in contaminated soil. There are many different problems that can arise from exposure to historical land contamination—both chronic and acute. As we shall see here, this is an issue over which considerable scientific uncertainty exists.

Historically, land contamination was also an issue that was paid relatively little attention due to the fact that the focus was on a range of other health problems caused by industrialization. By the 1960s and 1970s there was a shift in focus and increasing attention was being paid to the problems of toxic exposure due to both the rise of the environmental movement and works such as Rachel Carson's *Silent Spring* (see Section 3 of Chapter 2).[3] The specific issue of land contamination only began to gain a significant high profile in the 1970s in the US with the discovery that residential homes had been built on, or close to, hazardous waste sites. The most famous of these was Love Canal in Niagara, New York. The extract from Szasz explains the story of Love Canal in terms of how it was reported by the press. The extract is useful because it highlights how land contamination is not a discrete health problem.

---

[3] Rachel Carson, *Silent Spring* (Houghton Mifflin 1962).

Andrew Szasz, *EcoPopulism: Toxic Waste and the Movement for Environmental Justice*
(University of Minnesota Press 1994) 42–43

Decades earlier, Hooker Chemical had dumped toxic chemical waste, 'thousands of drums' of it, into Love Canal, a partially completed and abandoned navigation channel. In 1952, the canal was covered up. A year later, Hooker sold the land to the Niagara Falls Board of Education. A school was built. Developers built homes and 'unsuspecting families' moved in. In the 1970s, after heavy rains, chemical wastes began to seep to the surface, both on the school grounds and into people's yards and basements. Federal and state officials confirmed the presence of eighty-eight chemicals, some in concentrations 250 to 5,000 times higher than acceptable safety levels. Eleven of these chemicals were suspected or known carcinogens; others were said to cause liver and kidney ailments.

The sense that this was a disaster was conveyed explicitly: a 'calamity that has been steadily and silently building up for a long time' was now 'seeping ... coming out of the ground' into people's lives. More subtly, the reports conveyed the ominousness of the events at Love Canal by showing visuals that seemed to signify 'normalcy,' but undermining or reversing, signifying the opposite, through voice-over narration. Some examples: A boy bicycles along a quiet suburban street while the narrator says, 'There have been instances of birth defects and miscarriages among families." Kids play on a community playground while the narrator reports the New York Health Department's recommendation that pregnant women and small children evacuate.

What this extract highlights in particular is the apparent 'invisibility'[4] of the health problems created by land contamination. An English example of a land contamination incident is given by Barnes, Litva, and Tuson.

Geoffrey J Barnes, Andrea Litva, and Shirley Tuson, 'The Social Impact of Land Contamination: Reflections on the Development of a Community Advocacy and Counselling Service Following the Weston Village Incident' (2005) 27 Journal of Public Health 276, 277

The Weston village contamination incident made national headlines in 2000. A long-standing community close to Runcorn, Weston was an old-fashioned company town, a largely working-class community of some 500 houses, with village shop, post office, primary school and church and many people employed in the large ICI plant nearby. Then within a few days of the millennium, ICI revealed to the community that the toxic chemical, hexachlorobutadiene (HCBD), had been identified seeping from a former sandstone quarry that had been used for the disposal of chemical waste a few decades earlier. This chemical is a waste product of the chlorine industry and has been linked to kidney damage in animal based studies. A few weeks later the chemical was detected at levels considered a risk to health in 21 houses adjoining the quarries (although some distance from the main part of the village) and most of the people occupying these houses were evacuated to local hotels, whilst health concerns were investigated. ICI designated the whole of Weston village as its communication zone and so the whole village came to be associated with the incident and stigmatized. Colourful headlines followed in the national press including 'Village in the Shadow of Death' in the *News of the World* and 'Village of the Damned' in the *Guardian*. A BBC Panorama documentary also focused on the incident. Clinical tests carried out on people who lived in houses affected by HCBD identified abnormalities in kidney function, which were thought likely to have been caused by prolonged HCBD exposure. Follow-up tests carried out

[4] Michael Edelstein, *Contaminated Communities: Coping With Residential Toxic Exposure* (2nd edn, Westview Press 2004) 9.

10 months after the exposure ended, found that results for most had returned to normal suggesting that ending exposure had been beneficial. Epidemiological studies carried out by the Small Area Statistics Unit suggested that the whole wider Runcorn area had elevated rates of kidney disease. However, rates in Weston did not appear to be particularly elevated compared with other areas in the Borough.

Both these examples are where large amounts of waste were disposed of on a particular site. But as noted already, land contamination can also occur on sites where industrial activity was, and is carried out, due to accidents, the way materials were stored, and/or local pollution. It is also the case that contamination can occur through non-industrial processes. Thus, burial sites and agricultural land can also be found to be contaminated.

1.2 A SCIENTIFIC AND ENGINEERING PROBLEM

As already noted, the threats from land contamination are by no means certain. The complexity of uncertainty is discussed in Chapter 2 and it is a very real issue in regards to land contamination. The uncertainties in regards to land contamination can largely be divided into two different groups—those uncertainties concerned with establishing whether a particular contaminant is an environmental or health hazard as a matter of scientific possibility, and those uncertainties concerned with establishing whether a particular contaminant on a particular piece of land did, or could, cause harm. Each is dealt with in turn here.

The first set of uncertainties relate to establishing whether any particular contaminant is understood to be a health or environmental hazard. The problems with establishing such proof are described by Cranor.

Carl F Cranor, *Toxic Torts: Science, Law and the Possibility of Justice* (CUP 2006) 11

Carcinogens, reproductive toxicants, and neurotoxicants are invisible, undetectable intruders that can have long latency periods (eg, from a few months to more than forty years for cancer), rarely leave signature diseases, often operate by means of unknown, complex, subtle molecular mechanisms and, when they materialize into harm, injure humans in ways that researchers might not discover for years. The results can be catastrophic for affected individuals. Understanding the properties of such substances and assessing any risks they pose, requires even more subtle scientific expertise and studies than for other areas of inquiry. And they usually must be conducted on the frontiers of existing scientific knowledge.

The problems posed by the properties of molecular invaders are exacerbated by the effort, difficulties, costs, and time it takes to establish toxicity effects. Scientific studies for determining risks and harms can be comparatively insensitive (human epidemiological studies), not fully understood (animal studies used for inferring toxicity effects on humans), in their infancy (some short term tests that hold some promise), or yet to be developed (molecular or DNA techniques that might aid etiological investigations). Often researchers must assemble various kinds of evidence, most of which taken individually will not be decisive by itself, in order to identify a substance as toxic to humans.

The second set of uncertainties concern whether a particular site of land contamination is a health or environmental problem. In this regard, these are uncertainties in relation to whether there is contamination at a site and whether that contamination is significant enough to cause a health or environmental problem. In relation to the former, there is no exhaustive survey of land in which all its previous uses are recorded. Indeed, the previous uses of pieces of land often represents a form of 'lost knowledge'—a concept explored by Frickel, who discusses how there was little knowledge about sites converting from industrial to non-industrial uses in the city of New Orleans.

Scott Frickel, 'On Missing New Orleans: Lost Knowledge and Knowledge Gaps in Urban Hazardscape' (2008) 13 Environmental History 643, 644–45

Yet well over half of our sample sites (59.4 percent) had converted to various nonindustrial uses, be they commercial sites such as restaurants or grocery stores; public and quasi-public uses such as parks, public housing, or churches; or private residences. These are not the endpoints that research on brownfields and environmental justice typically capture, in large part because places like playgrounds or restaurants tend not to be listed on federal and state hazard inventories, nor do they tend to appear hazardous to people living nearby. Yet nonindustrial uses together represent the dominant conversion pattern among the sites in our sample.

These former industrial sites, and whatever contaminants that may remain behind, represent lost knowledge of various sorts: community knowledge about daily life in and around the facilities and about the people who worked inside or played nearby; managerial knowledge about the social organization of industrial production in those places; technical knowledge about the materials used there, how they were transformed and where they went; geographic knowledge about the spatial distribution of those now-relict wastes; and not least, chemical knowledge about how substances change over time and in interaction with air, soil, water, and living organisms [...]

While it is rarely missed, lost knowledge matters. Because people (and bureaucracies) tend to make decisions on the basis of what they know, rather than what they do not know, lost knowledge limits the possibilities of social action. It is in this sense that lost knowledge can forestall even well-meaning efforts to understand, for example, the relationship between environmental hazards and public health in New Orleans, as our second study illustrates.

If there is no knowledge about the previous use of the site, no data about contaminants on it, and the health effects of a contaminant are not unique to that contaminant then establishing whether a particular piece of land is contaminated and that contamination is leading to health and environmental problems can be very difficult.

Moreover, even if a contaminant is found on a particular site, whether it is causing an environmental or public health problem is hard to establish. Part of the problem, as noted by Cranor, is that the health effects from contaminants are generic. Another aspect of this form of uncertainty is that collecting health data on such effects so as to identify clusters is not routine. Moreover, even if a cluster of particular health effects is identified, it is not irrefutable proof they are caused by that particular contaminant. If a contaminant is identified, as it was at Love Canal, the research then carried out is often being done in less than ideal circumstances. The extract from Steegmann discusses the science carried out in the wake of that controversy.

A Theodore Steegmann Jr, 'History of Love Canal and SUNY at Buffalo's Response: History, The University Role, and Health' (2001) 8 Buffalo Environmental Law Journal 173, 181–82, 189

Science here was a long way from the clinic and laboratory, with all of their securities. It was rough, fast field work at a low level toxic exposure site—a situation designed to promote borderline results and disagreements. Allan Mazur's 1998 book *A Hazardous Inquiry* offers this outsider's analysis. 'The scientific study of Love Canal looks more like a prizefight than a search for truth. Some commentators on this and other technical controversies have given up the notion of objectivity regarding scientific expertise, as no different than any other resource that can be used to win political goals.' Had Mazur been there, he would probably have seen not so much a prize fight, but rather a search for truth in the face of adversity.

Steegmann goes on to describe in detail the analysis carried out and it is a riveting read. At the end of his article he makes a number of conclusions.

Lessons for the scientific community are as follows:

1. Be prepared. If you get a call for help tomorrow, what exactly will you do?
2. Go to the community. Talk to people, and make yourself listen.
3. Be constructive in your criticisms of colleagues' work. Be sure you do not confuse laboratory or clinical settings with field data gathering. Recognize that you may be defensive.
4. Science is the art of the possible. If you have only 500 households in your sample, deal with it. If your tools do not match the task, make new tools.
5. Use parsimony. Trust the voles. Multidisciplinary work is more likely to resolve ambiguity than specialized effort.

Steegmann's rather curious reference to the voles is a reference to the fact that in the Love Canal area studies had shown a lower number of meadow voles than expected, and that the voles that were there had shorter lives and liver problems. This study was an academic study not directly connected to the controversy, and Steegmann's point is the importance of gathering knowledge from a range of different scientific fields. Overall, Steegmann highlights how trying to establish whether a particular contaminant is causing a problem puts significant pressure on scientific processes. It also puts pressure on any approach which depends on 'proof of the facts' before making decisions.

The scientific and engineering problems to do with land contamination do not end there however. Even if a health and environmental problem is identified the necessary action to be taken is by no means clear. The process of clean-up usually takes the form of somehow removing the soil or water in which the contaminant is contained or isolating the contaminant so it cannot be a threat. That might sound simple but it can be quite a feat of engineering in practice. Because of this, clean-up is expensive and that raises questions about the *extent* of clean-up. Those questions are complicated by scientific uncertainty. Moreover, the process of clean-up can itself carry its own environmental and public health risks. The Corby litigation discussed in Sections 3.2 and 3.4 of Chapter 6 is an example of this. It was the process of clean-up which actually caused the harm.

1.3 A SOCIO-POLITICAL PROBLEM

As must be becoming clear from the discussion in this chapter so far, land contamination is a controversial issue. An initial reason for this is that land contamination problems arise because land previously used for industrial uses is now being used for residential uses, but most of those who live on residential land have an expectation that residential land is 'safe'. This can be seen in Szasz's discussion of Love Canal, where media depicted the threat of land contamination as a threat to unsuspecting families.

Highlighting that at the heart of land contamination issues is a conflict between industrial and non-industrial use is only the beginning however. Edelstein highlights three particular features of land contamination. These features, he notes, distinguish land contamination from natural disasters. They also explain why the conflict between industrial and residential land use is so controversial.

Michael Edelstein, *Contaminated Communities; Coping With Residential Toxic Exposure* (2nd edn, Westview Press 2004) 16–18

Technological Failure. First, toxic disaster is technological in origin, implying that the technological control over nature that enables us to enjoy a high standard of living has failed [...]

Human Causality. Contrast perceptions of victims of the 1977 Johnstown Pennsylvania, flood with those of residents of the Love Canal neighbourhood, whom I interviewed two years later. The first disaster was seen as 'an act of God,' the latter as stemming from corporate greed and government corruption [...] [W]hen victims realize that a disaster is humanly caused, they are likely to develop attributions of responsibility causing feelings of distrust and anger toward the perceived agents of harm. [...]

Involuntariness. It follows from these causal characteristics that central to the impact of contamination is its involuntary nature. All three critical elements of voluntary risk are violated: victims lack awareness, volition, and the opportunity to evaluate their risk. We do not expect to consent to participate in natural events, yet we hold dear the belief that, with events of a social origin, we have the right to choose to be involved. We are likely to blame those who have subjected us to undesired conditions and thus further deprived us of our volition.

Edelstein's analysis thus highlights that the type of exposures that land contamination can give rise to tensions issues with relationships within society.

The complexity of these issues is further magnified by the uncertainties concerning the consequences of exposure. None of this is to say that the risk of harm does not exist but that the risk of harm can be difficult to establish, and that further complicates controversy. Indeed, land contamination controversies are classic examples of 'risk society politics' in that they often become debates over how risks should be distributed within a society where that debate is complicated by uncertainty.[5] This type of politics and controversy can manifest itself in many different ways. Three particular features of land contamination disputes are useful to note here—the psychological impact of land contamination on those who are potentially exposed to a threat, the distrust that that group has towards others, and the nature of the disputes.

The first consequence of the social complexity of land contamination—the psychological impact of land contamination—is considered in by Barnes, Litva, and Tuson.

Geoffrey J Barnes, Andrea Litva, and Shirley Tuson, 'The Social Impact of Land Contamination: Reflections on the Development of a Community Advocacy and Counselling Service Following the Weston Village Incident' (2005) 27 Journal of Public Health 276, 277

The Weston incident possessed all the 'fright factors' highlighted by the DOH [Department of Health] in its document on risk perception. ICI, facing damaging media stories almost daily, responded rapidly by offering to purchase the houses of almost all owner-occupiers in the village who wanted to leave. However, this appeared to cause more problems than it solved. Although some were undoubtedly

[5] Ulrich Beck, *Risk Society: Towards A New Modernity* (Sage Publications 1992). See Section 4.1 of Chapter 13 for a discussion of this work.

relieved to be given a way out, others decided to move because they saw ICI's action as a sign that things were much worse than they were being told. Others were worried that ICI's offer could be withdrawn, leaving them with houses that could potentially be without any value, and others who were determined to stay became isolated and increasingly depressed as neighbours moved away. Within months large parts of the village resembled a ghost town.

As a number of sociologists working on the topic of land contamination have highlighted, these types of reaction are particularly due to the fact that what was understood as a 'safe' place (one's home) is suddenly revealed to be a potential threat.[6]

Related to this, and also highlighted by these studies, is the second important socio-political aspect of land contamination to note—there is often severe mistrust between involved parties. This distrust often relates to particular groups in land contamination disputes as the extract from Eiser and others explains.

J Richard Eiser and others, '"Trust me, I'm a Scientist (Not A Developer)": Perceived Expertise and Motives as Predictors of Trust in Assessment of Risk from Contaminated Land' (2009) 29 Risk Analysis 288, 295–96

[O]ur findings indicate that, within the specific context of land contamination, independent scientists are a highly trusted potential source of information. Developers, on the other hand, are actively distrusted, as perceived both by individuals who believed they lived close to contamination and those who did not. (In fact, there were several locations of more or less severe contamination within most of the sample areas.) Perceived exposure to contamination had remarkably little effect on trust in the different sources, apart from the council, which was more distrusted by those who saw themselves as exposed, presumably because they saw the council as failing to protect them from any risk [...]

Subsequent analyses offer insight into these differences between levels of trust for the different sources. The council and developers were both distrusted, despite coming runners-up to scientists in perceived knowledge of risks, that is, expertise. [...] These two sources were seen as particularly lacking in openness and shared interests (with residents) and most likely to underestimate or underplay any risks. Conversely, residents' groups and friends and family (as well as local media, to a slightly lesser extent) are quite highly trusted despite not being seen as particularly expert. This appears to be because these sources are seen as scoring highly on openness and shared interests, and showing a more precautionary bias in interpretation and communication.

What is particularly interesting in this analysis is that land contamination often highlights that different groups in society (developers, residents, councils) will have different interests and this leads to distrust. Yet, as we see, nearly all these groups are involved in decisions involving land contamination.

As this is the case, then land contamination controversies often result in the destabilizing of communities as explained by Shriver and Kennedy.

---

[6] Kai Erikson, *A New Species of Trouble: The Human Experience of Modern Disasters* (WW Norton & Co 1994) and Edelstein (n 4).

Thomas E Shriver and Dennis K Kennedy, 'Contested Environmental Hazards and Community Conflict Over Relocation' (2005) 70 Rural Sociology 491, 492

The majority of the existing research conducted on environmental hazards emphasizes what Freudenburg and Jones (1991) have aptly referred to as 'corrosive communities,' in which residents engage in hostile debates and attempt to assign blame. From this perspective, ecological damages are coupled with disruptions to the social fabric of the impacted communities. Several important characteristics associated with contaminated communities emerge from the literature and serve as a basis for framing the present study. A common feature of contaminated communities is the emergence of competing factions. In many technological hazard cases, multiple groups emerge within the community to promote a set of claims regarding environmental risks. In some communities citizen groups emerge to challenge the local power structure, while in other cases the community groups are pitted against one another.

Following on from this, the third socio-political complexity to note is the role of the state. Edelstein describes that role in the US context, but it is also applicable in any context where a land contamination problem is identified.

Michael Edelstein, *Contaminated Communities; Coping With Residential Toxic Exposure* (2nd edn, Westview Press 2004) 161–62

With the discovery and announcement of contamination, toxic victims suddenly find themselves in a complex institutional context made up of the various local, state, and federal agencies having jurisdiction over their contamination incident. This is an unfamiliar life context for most people, one for which they lack experience. Their lives are essentially captured by agencies on which they become dependent on clarification and assistance. Technical experts and lawyers, from government and industry, now dictate the terms defining such core issues as safety and risk and whether they will be helped to find safe water or to relocate [...]

Effectively, toxic victims become 'disabled,' to use Ivan Illich's term, as suddenly they are dependent on professionals to expertly handle various areas of life formerly governed by their own naive wisdom [...]

[...] The dilemma is that there is rarely a quick fix for contamination; often there is no real fix at all, at least on the time scale of the human life span. [...]It is much easier to identify and label contamination than to remove it. The gap between identification and recognized solution is key to contamination's consequences.

The controversial nature of land contamination thus lies as much in the regulatory response to it than in the inherent problem itself and the same issues seen already to do with trust, involuntariness, and technological failure are as inherent in the remediation process as in the initial act of land contamination. This creates serious challenges for fashioning a legal response to the problem of land contamination.

1.4 A COMMERCIAL AND PROPERTY DEVELOPMENT PROBLEM

The third aspect of land contamination to note is that it is also a commercial and property development problem. As noted already, land contamination directly relates to the value of property. In many other countries, issues to do with land contamination have resulted in the abandonment of land. In the UK, that is less of an option, due to both the limited amount of land and the historic commitment to the idea of not building on the green belt. In such circumstances, land must be re-used. Indeed, as the extract from Catney and others explains, it is the need to re-use land for housing that has been a catalyst for placing contaminated land on the environmental law agenda.

Philip Catney and others, 'Dealing with Contaminated Land in the UK Through "Development Managerialism"' (2006) 8 Journal of Environmental Policy and Planning **331, 333**

In order to achieve the government's aim of developing a larger proportion of housing in existing urban areas, greater attention needed to be given to the contamination problem. The de-industrialization of the 1980s revealed just how much land in the UK was subject to some form of industrial contamination. Following the identification of the need to accommodate 4.4 million extra households in England between 1991 and 2016, the issue of remediating that contaminated land became unavoidable. As part of its drive to regenerate the inner cities and to protect the countryside, the government initially set a target that 60 per cent of new homes should be built on brownfield land by 2008. The Barker Review (2004), established by the Treasury to examine the constraints upon the long-term supply of housing in the UK, supported this orientation. The report argued that the government needs to encourage the redevelopment of brownfield and contaminated land in order to increase housing supply and to reduce house price inflation. Thus, if the government's longer-term economic and social goals are to be achieved, the issue of contaminated land must be addressed.

In light of this context, Catney and others argue, dealing with land contamination has largely been understood as requiring 'development manageralism'. They explain the term in the following way.

Philip Catney and others, 'Dealing with Contaminated Land in the UK Through "Development Managerialism"' (2006) 8 Journal of Environmental Policy and Planning **331, 332**

'Development managerialism' reflects a politico-administrative perspective which: (i) while recognizing that contamination poses health and environmental problems, frames the issue primarily in economic terms, as an obstacle to economic progress and urban (re)development; and (ii) structures the palliative response primarily through the existing administrative apparatus of planning. The emphasis within the discourse is on minimizing urban blight, protecting economic interests and harnessing market-led development processes to bring contaminated land back into productive use. Cost effectiveness has been a recurrent theme in how the UK government has sought to deal with the problem. While in some other countries the issue has been treated primarily as an environmental and a health matter— contaminated land must be dealt with comprehensively in order to protect the public and to return the environment to a benign state—the UK's approach has been more pragmatic.

This is a fundamentally different way to understand the issue of land contamination from the perspectives in Section 1.3. From this perspective, land contamination is a barrier to another social goals— the provision of housing and the avoidance of urban waste lands. It is not that the threats from land contamination are ignored but that those threats are see in a broader context.

1.5 A LEGAL PROBLEM

The final aspect of land contamination to note is that it is also a problem with no easy legal solution. Contamination is often a product of property owners carrying out activities in the past on their own land which at the time they were carried out were legal. From a private law perspective this raises tricky conceptual questions concerning retroactive liability and the rights of property owners. From a more practical perspective, there is the problem that those that caused the contamination will in many cases no longer exist, being companies that operated many decades ago.

The case of *Cambridge Water*[7] (see Section 6.2 of Chapter 6) is a classic example of the problems of retroactive liability for land and water contamination. What could be seen there was how conventional principles of tort liability discouraged the imposition of liability in that case. These concepts are not the only barrier to developing legal responses to the problem of land contamination however.

William Howarth, '"Poisonous, Noxious or Polluting": Contrasting Approaches to Environmental Regulation' (1993) 56 MLR 171, 172

Undeniably, the concepts of property, possession and fault have profound limitations in the environmental context. If the object of environmental laws are to prevent environmental damage, then there is no compelling reason why land ownership or possession should provide a defence to causing such harm, nor is there any overriding reason why lack of these interests on the part of a complainant should provide a bar to legal redress. Similarly, with the concept of fault, there can be few conceivable instances where a person embarks upon a course of action with the sole motive of environmental vandalism. Rather, the problem is that environmental harm is the unintended, but increasingly unacceptable, by-product of environmentally unsustainable lifestyles and the industrial and other production processes that are needed to continue them. In law, the concept of fault tends to be understood as an individual rather than a collective predicate and for that reason the attribution of fault to society as a whole, or even a particular branch of industrial activity, is conceptually difficult to bring within general legal cognisance.

Whilst the limitations of the concepts of property, possession and fault in the environmental context are well recognised, the invocation that environmental protection requires 'an activist, intrusive role to be played by the executive arm of government' begs the question as to what precisely is required to be done. Even if the view is conceded, that the role of the law in environmental protection is most effectively exercised through the executive arm of government, the task of translating broadly, and often imprecisely, formulated environmental goals into the precise detail required for effective regulatory law, and providing for appropriately constituted regulatory authorities properly empowered to oversee its adherence, remains a fundamental challenge to law and legal systems.

Howarth's point is that environmental problems such as contaminated land result in the creation of public law regimes with a heavy administrative aspect. Yet, the problem remains of how to operate such a regime in light of the fact that what is being dealt with has occurred in the past. Likewise, the fact that land contamination is simultaneously a health and environmental problem; a scientific and engineering problem; a socio-political problem; and a property development problem also makes the crafting of any legal regime very difficult as it needs to accommodate these different complexities.

[7] *Cambridge Water v Eastern Counties Leather plc* [1994] 2 AC 264.

One example of this can be seen in the US with the Comprehensive Environmental Response, Compensation, and Liability Act 1980 (CERCLA), which created an incredibly broad liability regime that caught the creators of hazardous waste, transporters of such waste, and the owners and operators of a site in a liability net. Because of the way issues of land contamination gained a public profile in the US, CERCLA was also largely seen as being related to the problem of the management of hazardous waste both in the past and the future. As Lazarus explains, CERCLA was quite a radical development in US environmental law.

Richard J Lazarus, _The Making of Environmental Law_ (University of Chicago Press 2004) 109–10

After CERCLA became law, liability for environmental contamination was no longer just someone else's problem. It became everyone's problem, and the impact of this change was immediate and far-reaching. It generated a huge demand for environmental lawyers to represent those concerned about their potential exposure. It also made public and private entities more aware of the implications of not taking every possible measure to guard against liability based on future activities.

On the one hand, the regime was understood as a success as it, as Lazarus notes, shaped corporate behaviour to ensure that contamination did not occur again. On the other hand, however, the wide-sweeping liability of CERCLA paired with high remediation costs also meant that the application of the statute was deeply controversial and resulted in some sites being abandoned. A government fund, Superfund, did remediate these 'orphan sites' but this response differs greatly from the 'development managerialism' seen already.

Moreover, in light of the multifaceted nature of land contamination problems, the interpretation of the statute has been far from straightforward.

Stephen Breyer, _Breaking the Vicious Circle: Towards Effective Risk Regulation_ (Harvard UP 1993) 39–40

Consider, for example, CERCLA section 121(d), which says that EPA must clean up toxic waste sites to a condition that 'at a minimum [...] assures protection of human health and the environment.' The section goes on to specify that the 'clean' site must also meet any other legal standard that is either (1) 'applicable' or (2) 'relevant and appropriate.' It adds that such standards must include the 'goals established under the Safe Drinking Water Act,' but only if those goals are 'relevant and appropriate under the circumstances'.[25]

This language sounds reasonable. The instruction to EPA to apply all 'applicable' standards is perhaps redundant, for an 'applicable' standard, by definition, applies. But what harm can a redundant instruction do? Moreover, concern about applying potentially unknown other standards such as Safe Drinking Water Act goals, is mitigated by the qualifying phrase 'relevant and appropriate.'[26]

Nonetheless, such specific statutory language can create administrative difficulties, if applied to cleaning up a toxic waste dump like the _Ottati & Goss_ site in southern New Hampshire. Safe Drinking Water Act goals often express ideal conditions that few actual drinking water systems can meet. Typical statutory goals, for example, may include 'no carcinogens,' a goal that, if taken literally, means not a single molecule of aflatoxin, red dye no. 2, or benzene, or, for that matter, not the tiniest microscopic particle of pepper, spinach, or mushroom.

[25] 42 USC §9621(d)(1), (2)(A); emphasis added.

[26] See Environment Protection Agency, 'National Oil and Hazardous Substances Pollution Contingency Plan,' 55 Fed. Reg. 8666 (1990); Lawrence E. Starfield, 'The 1990 National Contingency Plan—More Detail and More Structure, but Still a Balancing Act,' 20 *Envtl. Law Rep.* 10222 (1990).

Breyer goes not to note that in such circumstances the regulating agency (the US Environmental Protection Agency (EPA)) develops rules and guidance to flesh out the goals and these can aim at a very high level of protection, which can be incredibly costly to achieve.[8] On the other hand, the EPA has also been criticized for not enforcing CERCLA properly.[9] We will see the importance of statutory interpretation in the next sections.

FURTHER READING AND QUESTIONS

1. For an excellent interdisciplinary analysis of a land contamination problem see 'Special Issue: Toxic Risk and Governance: The Case of Hexachlorobenzene' (2009) 90 Journal of Environmental Management 1567–1662, which contains a number of articles that examine a contaminated site in Sydney, Australia. Jonathan Harr's non-fiction account of a tort liability action concerning groundwater contamination *A Civil Action* (Vintage Books 1995) is a stunningly good account of the complexities of litigation in this area.

2. How easy would it be for you to discover the prior uses of the land that you grew up on?

3. For a discussion of the history of the US Comprehensive Environmental Response, Compensation and Liability Act 1980 see John Hird, *Superfund: The Political Economy of Environmental Risk* (John Hopkins UP 1994).

4. Are the socio-political aspects of land contamination relevant to lawyers?

---

2 LAND CONTAMINATION: A LEGAL OVERVIEW

The discussion so far might appear to be a long winded analysis of the problem of land contamination, but without understanding the complexity of land contamination problems there can be no understanding of the difficulties in developing a legal response to the problems it creates. Any legal response will be shaped by, and will shape, the different issues highlighted in Section 1. Thus, while the focus of this chapter now turns to the legal frameworks for land contamination in the UK none of the discussion in Section 1 should be forgotten.

---

[8] Stephen Breyer, *Breaking the Vicious Circle: Towards Effective Risk Regulation* (Harvard UP 1993) 11–19.
[9] Craig Collins, *Toxic Loopholes: Failures and Future Prospects for Environmental Law* (CUP 2010) ch 4.

2.1 THE LEGAL FRAMEWORKS FOR LAND CONTAMINATION IN THE UK

The current contaminated land regime in the UK is relatively new and has only been in operation since 2000, with Part IIA of the Environmental Protection Act 1990 coming into operation (although the amendments were made in 1995). Before then there was no established regime for land contamination, although land contamination was dealt with in an ad hoc way through the planning system. Bell and Etherington provide a pithy history of how the Part IIA regime developed.

Stuart Bell and Laurence Etherington, 'The Role of Consultation in Making Environmental Policy and Law' (1999) 8 Nott LJ 48, 57–58

The issue of how to deal with 'contaminated land' was first identified within Government as a potentially significant one for the United Kingdom during the late 1980's in a Report by a House of Commons Select Committee on the Environment on *Toxic Waste*. Following the realisation that there may be problem, the Parliamentary Select Committee on the Environment produced a report on Contaminated Land in 1989 which attempted to identify the scale of this problem and concluded that the existing law was not sufficient to deal with it. Following further consultation, the Committee's recommendation that the *caveat emptor* rule be abolished in relation to contamination was included in the Environmental Protection Act 1990 by section 143, which provided for a set of public registers identifying contaminated sites. These rules would have attempted to correct imperfections as to market information. However, the Registers proposals were flawed in a number of respects, including: by merely identifying past uses of land (as well as arguably identifying the wrong uses) they failed to identify land which was actually contaminated, rather than merely potentially contaminated; they made no provision for removal of sites from Registers which proved not to be contaminated or were 'cleaned up'; and they identified problems without clearly identifying their extent and who was responsible for rectifying them. Land would therefore be 'blighted' but with no incentives to do anything about it. The crucial issue, which was not addressed, was liability for and recovery of the costs of remediation. Criticism and resistance to the Registers proposals from a variety of sources (and articulated, at least in part, through responses to two consultation exercises) resulted in their abandonment and a wholesale review of wider areas of policy and law. This included liability for clean up, cleanup standards and when cleanup would be required, as well as considering information dissemination. The policy review lead to proposals in the policy document Framework for Contaminated Land in 1994 and which were crystallised as a new legal regime in Part IIA of the Environment Act, which provides a comprehensive (and complex) set of rules which seek to deal with: the identification of contaminated land; identification of cleanup requirements; and allocation and apportionment of liability for these clean up requirements, as well as dissemination of information.

Bell and Etherington note that the development of contaminated land was shaped by numerous consultation exercises. Besides those noted here, there were a number of others including the 'wide ranging'[10] consultation exercise concerning *Paying for our Past*,[11] which focused on questions of how liability should be structured.

The end result was the Part IIA regime, which was introduced into the Environmental Protection Act 1990 by the Environment Act 1995 but which did not come into force until 2000. This meant that

---

[10] Stuart Bell and Laurence Etherington, 'The Role of Consultation in making Environmental Policy and Law' (1999) 8 Nott LJ 48, 58.

[11] Department of the Environment, *Paying for Our Past* (March 1994).

there were five years during which lawyers and commentators were trying to predict how Part IIA would operate in practice.

Part IIA provides a framework for defining contaminated land, identifying it, apportioning liability in relation to the cost of remediation, and remediating it. The most significant aspects of the regime will be discussed in Section 4, but here it is worth noting five significant aspects of it. The first is that while the regime is often described as being a liability regime it is more akin to an administrative regime as the bulk of Part IIA sets out the administrative processes that local authorities (LAs) must follow in relation to contaminated land.

The second significant aspect of the regime is that Part IIA explicitly empowers the Secretary of State to issue statutory guidance in relation to various aspects of Part IIA. Statutory guidance was first issued in 2000 and revised in 2006 and 2012. This guidance was very detailed and the 2006 version was over 200 pages long. It was also accompanied by non-statutory guidance produced by DEFRA and a number of documents produced by the Environment Agency. Likewise, Annex 1 of *PPS23: Planning and Pollution Control* provided further guidance to planning authorities about how to deal with land contamination in the planning process (see Section 3). In April 2012 the 2006 statutory guidance was replaced with new statutory guidance that was sixty-seven pages long. In March 2012, PPS23 was also replaced with the National Planning Policy Framework (NPPF). The Environment Agency's Model Procedures for the Management of Land Contamination (CLR 11) are still in operation, however. The Environment Agency has also developed a Contaminated Land Exposure Assessment (CLEA) framework that sets out the methodology (and provides software) for establishing whether long-term exposure to a contaminant on a site might be problematic. The new statutory guidance and the NPPF will be discussed further, but here it is important to note that these documents arguably represent a new era in how Part IIA will operate.

The third aspect to note of Part IIA is that at the heart of the regime lies a focus on risk assessment.

DEFRA, Environmental Protection Act 1990: Part 2A. Contaminated Land Statutory Guidance (2012) para 1.3 (emphasis added)

1.3 Part 2A provides a means of dealing with unacceptable risks posed by land contamination to human health and the environment, and enforcing authorities should seek to find and deal with such land. Under Part 2A the starting point should be that land is not contaminated land unless there is reason to consider otherwise. *Only land where unacceptable risks are clearly identified, after a risk assessment has been undertaken in accordance with this Guidance, should be considered as meeting the Part 2A definition of contaminated land.*

Thus, as we shall in Section 2.2, land is only 'contaminated land' for the purposes of Part IIA if it fulfils these requirements. This is a relatively narrow definition of land contamination. The guidance goes onto set out the objectives of Part 2A.

DEFRA, Environmental Protection Act 1990: Part 2A. Contaminated Land Statutory Guidance (2012) para 1.4

1.4 The overarching objectives of the Government's policy on contaminated land and the Part 2A regime are:

(a) To identify and remove unacceptable risks to human health and the environment.

(b) To seek to ensure that contaminated land is made suitable for its current use.

(c) To ensure that the burdens faced by individuals, companies and society as a whole are proportionate, manageable and compatible with the principles of sustainable development.

While these objectives are expressed perhaps more crisply than in previous statutory guidance, they do reflect the fundamental logic of Part IIA since its inception. In particular, the design of the regime counteracted some of the concerns that had arisen from the US experience (see Section 1.5). What is clear from this is that Part IIA is not about the clean-up of all land contamination.

The fourth feature to note of Part IIA is that it is both explicitly and practically a regime of last resort.

DEFRA, Environmental Protection Act 1990: Part 2A. Contaminated Land Statutory Guidance (2012) para 1.5

1.5 Enforcing authorities should seek to use Part 2A only where no appropriate alternative solution exists. The Part 2A regime is one of several ways in which land contamination can be addressed. For example, land contamination can be addressed when land is developed (or redeveloped) under the planning system, during the building control process, or where action is taken independently by landowners. Other legislative regimes may also provide a means of dealing with land contamination issues, such as building regulations; the regimes for waste, water, and environmental permitting; and the Environmental Damage (Prevention and Remediation) Regulations 2009.

In other words, the expectation is that problems of land contamination are expected to be dealt with in other ways. In particular, the vast majority of land contamination problems will be dealt with under the planning system and this is discussed in Section 3.

Fifth, despite the fact that Part IIA is a regime of last resort, it does play a significant role in how land contamination is 'framed' as a problem in the UK. The concept of 'framing' denotes the way in which a problem is understood and in so doing 'tacitly define[s] the horizons of possible and acceptable action'[12]. This is because:

problems that have been framed with particular causal explanations can also, in principle, be controlled by addressing the perceived causes. At the same time, framing is by its nature also an instrument of exclusion. As some parts of an issue come within a problem frame, other parts are left out as irrelevant, incomprehensible, or uncontrollable.[13]

As we have seen, there are many different ways to frame land contamination. In the UK it has been framed as a problem of ensuring ongoing land use and in thinking about issues of liability and responsibility the focus has remained on pragmatic responses to land contamination issues. This approach embodies the idea of 'development managerialism' discussed already and is very different to how the problem was framed and understood in the US. The most significant aspect of this framing process is the definition of 'contaminated land' in Part IIA. Thus, an important starting point in thinking about

---

[12] Expert Group on Science and Governance, *Taking European Knowledge Society Seriously* (European Commission 2007) 73–75.

[13] David Winickoff and others, 'Adjudicating the GM Food Wars: Science, Risk and Democracy in World Trade Law' (2005) 30 Yale J Int'l L 81, 94. Also discussed in Section 2.1 of Chapter 22.

land contamination across all legal regimes is to understand that definition and how it frames the rest of legal activity in relation to land contamination.

2.2 THE PART IIA DEFINITION OF 'CONTAMINATED LAND'

Section 78A(2) of the Environmental Protection Act 1990 states:

'Contaminated land' is any land which appears to the local authority in whose area it is situated to be in such a condition, by reason of substances in, on or under the land, that—

(a) significant harm is being caused or there is a significant possibility of such harm being caused; or

(b) pollution of controlled waters is being, or is likely to be, caused;

and, in determining whether any land appears to be such land, a local authority shall, subject to subsection (5) below, act in accordance with guidance issued by the Secretary of State in accordance with section 78YA below with respect to the manner in which that determination is to be made.

It is also useful to set out s 78A(4)–(5).

(4) 'Harm' means harm to the health of living organisms or other interference with the ecological systems of which they form part and, in the case of man, includes harm to his property.

(5) The questions—

    (a) what harm or pollution of the water environment is to be regarded as 'significant',

    (b) whether the possibility of significant harm or of significant pollution of the water environment being caused is 'significant',

    (c) whether pollution of controlled waters is being, or is likely to be caused,

shall be determined in accordance with guidance issued for the purpose by the Secretary of State in accordance with section 78YA below.

There are four particular things to note about this definition. First, it requires a judgment to be made by the local authority. Second, harm is not only caused to humans but also to ecological systems and property. Third, the definition requires not only that a substance is on, or under, land, but that 'significant harm is being caused or there is a significant possibility of such harm being caused'. This is where risk assessment will have a role a play. Fourth, the definition explicitly recognizes the role of statutory guidance. The nature of that role will be considered in more detail in Section 4.1 but here we turn to that guidance for a more detailed understanding of the definition of 'contaminated land'.

As already noted, the operation of that definition is dependent on risk assessment and the statutory guidance provides guidance in relation to this.

DEFRA, Environmental Protection Act 1990: Part 2A. Contaminated Land Statutory Guidance (2012) paras 3.1–3.4

3.1 Part 2A takes a risk-based approach to defining contaminated land. For the purposes of this Guidance, 'risk' means the combination of: (a) the likelihood that harm, or pollution of water, will occur as a result of contaminants in, on or under the land; and (b) the scale and seriousness of such harm or pollution if it did occur.

3.2 All soils contain substances that could be harmful to human or environmental receptors, although in the very large majority of cases the level of risk is likely to be very low. In conducting risk assessment under the Part 2A regime, the local authority should aim to focus on land which might pose an unacceptable risk.

3.3 Local authorities should have regard to good practice guidance on risk assessment and they should ensure they undertake risk assessment in a way which delivers the results needed to make robust decisions in line with Part 2A and this Guidance.

3.4 Risk assessments should be based on information which is: (a) scientifically-based; (b) authoritative; (c) relevant to the assessment of risks arising from the presence of contaminants in soil; and (d) appropriate to inform regulatory decisions in accordance with Part 2A and this Guidance.

Closely connected to the concept of risk is the concept of 'contaminant linkage'.

**DEFRA, Environmental Protection Act 1990: Part 2A. Contaminated Land
Statutory Guidance** (2012) paras 3.8–3.9

3.8 Under Part 2A, for a relevant risk to exist there needs to be one or more contaminant-pathway-receptor-linkages [sic]—'contaminant linkage'—by which a relevant receptor might be affected by the contaminants in question. In other words, for a risk to exist there must be contaminants present in, on or under the land in a form and quantity that poses a hazard, and one or more pathways by which they might significantly harm people, the environment, or property; or significantly pollute controlled waters. For the purposes of this Guidance:

(a) A 'contaminant' is a substance which is in, on or under the land and which has the potential to cause significant harm to a relevant receptor, or to cause significant pollution of controlled waters.

(b) A 'receptor' is something that could be adversely affected by a contaminant, for example a person, an organism, an ecosystem, property, or controlled waters. The various types of receptors that are relevant under the Part 2A regime are explained in later sections.

(c) A 'pathway' is a route by which a receptor is or might be affected by a contaminant.

3.9 The term 'contaminant linkage' means the relationship between a contaminant, a pathway and a receptor. All three elements of a contaminant linkage must exist in relation to particular land before the land can be considered potentially to be contaminated land under Part2A, including evidence of the actual presence of contaminants. The term "significant contaminant linkage", as used in this Guidance, means a contaminant linkage which gives rise to a level of risk sufficient to justify a piece of land being determined as contaminated land. The term 'significant contaminant' means the contaminant which forms part of a significant contaminant linkage.

The Guidance makes clear that the consideration of risks should only be in relation to the current use of land that the guidance defines as both including the current official use, any temporary use which would be allowed within the boundaries of the planning permission, and any likely informal use such as children playing on the land.[14] This is significant because it means that the definition of

---

[14] Para 3.5.

'contaminated land' is intimately connected with the use the land is put to. Thus, land may be 'contaminated land' for one use and not another.

The Guidance makes a number of general comments about risk assessment including the processes it involves and that LPAs may need to rely on outside expertise.

DEFRA, Environmental Protection Act 1990: Part 2A. Contaminated Land Statutory Guidance (2012) paras 3.12–3.13

3.12 The process of risk assessment involves understanding the risks presented by land, and the associated uncertainties. In practice, this understanding is usually developed and communicated in the form of a 'conceptual model'. The understanding of the risks is developed through a staged approach to risk assessment, often involving a preliminary risk assessment informed by desk-based study; a site visit and walkover; a generic quantitative risk assessment; and various stages of more detailed quantitative risk assessment. The process should normally continue until it is possible for the local authority to decide: (a) that there is insufficient evidence that the land might be contaminated land to justify further inspection and assessment; and/or (b) whether or not the land is contaminated land.

3.13 For land to proceed to the next stage of risk assessment there should be evidence that an unacceptable risk could reasonably exist. If the authority considers there is little reason to consider that the land might pose an unacceptable risk, inspection activities should stop at that point.

Evidence is thus required although, as we saw in Section 1.2, land contamination is an area in which a range of different uncertainties operates. The Guidance does also refer to scientific uncertainty but sees its scope as relatively limited.

DEFRA, Environmental Protection Act 1990: Part 2A. Contaminated Land Statutory Guidance (2012) paras 3.31–3.32

3.31 All risk assessments of potentially contaminated land will involve uncertainty, for example due to scientific uncertainty over the effects of substances, and the assumptions that lie behind predicting what might happen in the future. When building an understanding of the risks relating to land, the local authority should recognise that uncertainty exists. The authority should seek to minimise uncertainty as far as it considers to be relevant, reasonable and practical; and it should recognise remaining uncertainty, which is likely to exist in almost all cases. It should be aware of the assumptions and estimates that underlie the risk assessment, and the effect of these on its conclusions.

3.32 The uncertainty underlying risk assessments means there is unlikely to be any single "correct" conclusion on precisely what is the level of risk posed by land, and it is possible that different suitably qualified people could come to different conclusions when presented with the same information. It is for the local authority to use its judgement to form a reasonable view of what it considers the risks to be on the basis of a robust assessment of available evidence in line with this Guidance.

Besides these more general comments the Guidance also provides guidance on what is a 'significant harm' and what is a 'significant possibility of significant harm', which considers a range of different categories. Two examples are provided here. The first is the general discussion in relation to what is a 'significant harm to human health'.

DEFRA, Environmental Protection Act 1990: Part 2A. Contaminated Land Statutory Guidance (2012) paras 4.4–4.6

4.4 Conditions for determining that land is contaminated land on the basis that significant harm is being caused would exist where: (a) the local authority has carried out an appropriate, scientific and technical assessment of all the relevant and available evidence; and (b) on the basis of that assessment, the authority is satisfied on the balance of probabilities that significant harm is being caused (i.e. that it is more likely than not that such harm is being caused) by a significant contaminant(s).

4.5 The following health effects should always be considered to constitute significant harm to human health: death; life threatening diseases (e.g. cancers); other diseases likely to have serious impacts on health; serious injury4; birth defects; and impairment of reproductive functions.

4.6 Other health effects may be considered by the local authority to constitute significant harm. For example, a wide range of conditions may or may not constitute significant harm (alone or in combination) including: physical injury; gastrointestinal disturbances; respiratory tract effects; cardio-vascular effects; central nervous system effects; skin ailments; effects on organs such as the liver or kidneys; or a wide range of other health impacts. In deciding whether or not a particular form of harm is significant harm, the local authority should consider the seriousness of the harm in question: including the impact on the health, and quality of life, of any person suffering the harm; and the scale of the harm. The authority should only conclude that harm is significant if it considers that treating the land as contaminated land would be in accordance with the broad objectives of the regime as described in Section 1.

This last sentence is recognizing that some non-scientific factors may have a role to play in the determination of whether something is causing significant harm. The overarching objectives have been extracted already and among them we saw 'that the burdens faced by individuals, companies and societies as a whole are proportionate, manageable, and compatible with the principles of sustainable development'.

A similar reference can be seen in relation the discussion concerning what is a 'significant possibility of significant harm to human health'. Likewise, it is clear that scientific uncertainty should only be considered in the confines of risk assessment.

DEFRA, Environmental Protection Act 1990: Part 2A. Contaminated Land Statutory Guidance (2012) paras 4.10–4.12, 4.16

4.10 In assessing the possibility of significant harm to human health from the land and associated issues, the local authority should act in accordance with the advice on risk assessment in Section 3 and the guidance in this section.

4.11 The term 'possibility of significant harm' as it applies to human health, for the purposes of this guidance, means the risk posed by one or more relevant contaminant linkage(s) relating to the land. It comprises:

(a) The estimated likelihood that significant harm might occur to an identified receptor, taking account of the current use of the land in question.

(b) The estimated impact if the significant harm did occur i.e. the nature of the harm, the seriousness of the harm to any person who might suffer it, and (where relevant) the extent of the harm in terms of how many people might suffer it.

> 4.12 In estimating the likelihood that a specific form of significant harm might occur the local authority should, among other things, consider:
>
> (a) The estimated probability that the significant harm might occur: (i) if the land continues to be used as it is currently being used; and (ii) where relevant, if the land were to be used in a different way (or ways) in the future having regard to the guidance on 'current use' in Section 3.
>
> (b) The strength of evidence underlying the risk estimate. It should also consider the key assumptions on which the estimate of likelihood is based, and the level of uncertainty underlying the estimate. [...]
>
> 4.16 The decision on whether the possibility of significant harm being caused is significant is a regulatory decision to be taken by the relevant local authority. In deciding whether the possibility of significant harm being caused is significant, the authority is deciding whether the possibility of significant harm posed by contamination in, on or under the land is sufficiently high that regulatory action should be taken to reduce it, with all that would entail. In taking such decisions, the local authority should take account of the broad aims of the regime set out in Section 1 of this Guidance.

The Guidance also provides similar guidance in relation to ecological system effects and property effects.

Overall, what can be seen is that the definition of 'contaminated land' is primarily in the Statutory Guidance not in the legislation. Moreover, as DEFRA notes, the process of determining what is contaminated land is a 'regulatory process'. It requires the exercise of administrative discretion and is not directly concerned with the imposition of liability.

2.3 THE 'FRAMING POWER' OF THE PART IIA DEFINITION

Land contamination does not manifest itself with little labels popping out of the ground telling the world there is a land contamination problem on a particular site. As is implicit in the definition of contaminated land under Part IIA, such land has to be identified. Part of the significance of Part IIA and the associated Statutory Guidance is that they provide a methodology for identifying what is contaminated land and public and private actors in other contexts can use that methodology. This is important because land contamination may become a legal issue in many different ways. It is useful to note four such ways here, and in each context the framing significance of the definition of land contamination in Part IIA can be seen.

The first way is through scandal and controversy akin to that seen in relation to Love Canal and Weston village. A recent example is concerns about land contamination at a housing estate in Motherwell, Scotland where local residents are worried about the possible health effects of historic contamination.[15] The important point is that the statutory definition of 'contaminated land' will play an important role in identifying whether officially there is a problem and thus whether a regulatory response is needed.[16] This is particularly important where the threats are so uncertain, and the dispute polarized.

---

[15] 'New test fears over Motherwell "toxic homes"' <http://www.bbc.co.uk/news/uk-scotland-glasgow-west-14312166> accessed 28 July 2011 and Graham Miller, 'Resident's search to find truth about Motherwell contamination' Wishaw Press, 25 July 2012 <http://www.wishawpress.co.uk/wishaw-news/local-wishaw-news/wishaw-news/2012/07/25/resident-s-search-to-find-truth-about-motherwell-contamination-76495-31464567/> accessed 29 September 2012.

[16] For details see <http://www.northlanarkshire.gov.uk/index.aspx?articleid=17546> accessed 29 September 2012.

The second way that land contamination arises as a legal issue is through the planning system and the development of land. This will be discussed in more detail in Section 3 but the important point to note here is that land contamination becomes an issue when planning permission is applied for to develop the land. We saw in Section 4.1 of Chapter 18 that in s 55 of the Town and Country Act 1990 'development' refers to both building work and also the change of use. In these circumstances, if land contamination is identified, then the developer will have the burden of remediating the land as part of their planning permission. As a developer also reaps the economic benefits of development then there is a fair chance that they will be willing to do so. From this perspective, land contamination and its remediation becomes part of the mainstream development process. Land contamination is thus not a scandal but rather a 'fact' of developing land and the requirement of remediation has a routine aspect to it. Part II not only provides the definition of 'contaminated land' but it also provides an important extra incentive to developers to comply with the planning system. This is in two ways. First, Part IIA is detailed enough (particularly with the statutory guidance) to make clear what is a problem. Second, the liability regime means that developers may find themselves liable under the Part IIA regime if they do not deal with the land contamination issues. Dealing with contaminated land in the planning system thus must always be seen as operating in the shadows of Part IIA.

The third way that land contamination becomes a legal issue is through Part IIA itself. The framing power of the definition of contaminated land is obvious here. Under Part IIA land is identified by a local authority (or for special sites, the Environment Agency) as 'contaminated land' and is placed on the contaminated land register. As we shall see, this has only occurred in a relatively small number of cases. The important implication for being placed on this register is that the question of liability for remediation then arises. That liability can be significant.

Finally, the combined effect of all of the above means that land contamination will be an important issue for commercial practice. Failure to deal with land contamination problems can result in reputational risks to a company or liability. Likewise, remediation will be a feature of the planning process. What this means is that land contamination has become an important issue for commercial transactions, particularly the buying and selling of land or the buying and selling of companies that own land. For this reason land contamination is an issue for transactional environmental law.[17] Lee and Vaughan explain the different roles of the lawyer in transactions here.

Robert G Lee and Steven Vaughan, 'The Contaminated Land Regime in England and Wales and the Corporatisation of Environmental Lawyers' (2010) 17 International Journal of the Legal Profession 35, 38, 52–53

A strong orientation towards the transaction, transactionalism, is said to be a dominant feature of modern client/lawyer relationships. Four suggested roles of lawyers in transactions are presented here; they are not mutually exclusive and it is likely that certain elements of each of these roles may be found in all major transactional work. The four roles depict the transactional lawyer as follows: as transaction costs engineer; as reputational intermediary; as enterprise architect; or as the reducer of regulatory costs. Reflecting on these roles, the first two involve a limited role in the transaction in which the environmental lawyer facilitates the deal, largely by acting as an honest broker in eliminating informational asymmetries. In contrast, the second two roles are far more pro-active and involve the structuring of the transaction itself to accommodate the issues thrown up by environmental regulation.

[17] See Section 6.5 of Chapter 6 on private law.

Lee and Vaughan then go on to analyse these different roles in the context of the contaminated land regime. Their overall point is that Part IIA has seen an increased role for environmental lawyers in transactional work because it increased the potential for liability and the costs associated with the development of land. Lee and Vaughan consider each of these roles in turn, but an important further point in their analysis is that a client's understanding of land contamination as a legal issue will vary from client to client.

> The degree of caution exhibited by the client in relation to contaminated land risk [...] does vary from client to client and must be factored into any work. For some clients, the Part 2A regime is a common facet of deals (where, for example, the client is an established property developer); for others, less so. As the regime has unfolded over the last eight years and certain clients have become accustomed to the lack of active enforcement of the provisions of Part 2A, this has led, in some areas, to an acceptance of the risks which the contaminated land regime presents. Here, much depends on the type and nature of the client. So-called 'trade' clients, actively involved in some form of industry, may be more willing to accept site contamination risks than, say, private equity houses, which, because they will look to repackage the business and sell it in a reasonably short time frame, will wish to stay clear of risk. Moreover, as we have seen, the geographical centre of business interest may make a difference. It seems that clients based primarily in the US have certain difficulties in translating the fear of Superfund style liabilities into the realities of Part 2A. These attitudinal variations, within the client base over time, have led to additional changes in the nature of the practices of the environmental lawyers engaged by particular clients.

Lee and Vaughan's analysis includes extracts from a number of interviews that they conducted and it is well worth a careful read. The important point to appreciate is that Part IIA is playing a role in these transactional contexts, albeit a varied one.

The fact that land contamination arises as a legal issue in different ways further complicates land contamination as a problem. In some instances land contamination is about conflict and scandal, in other cases it is about day-to-day property transactions and development. In other circumstances still, it is a commercial issue. The important point to note is that, in all these cases, the definition of land contamination in Part IIA is framing our understanding of the problem.

FURTHER READING AND QUESTIONS

1. Can you think of other ways Part IIA could have defined 'contaminated land'? What are the advantages and disadvantages of the other definitions that you can think of?

2. Consider whether the following situations would result in the land in question being found to be 'contaminated' under the Part IIA regime. Do look at the Statutory Guidance when considering each problem.

   a) A former gasworks site where large amounts of heavy metals are in the soil is concreted over and a warehouse is built on the site.

   b) A housing estate has been built on a former household rubbish dump, the contents of which were unknown. There is no evidence that a health risk has been created but the residents of the housing estate suffer from mental distress in knowing about the existence of the rubbish dump.

   c) The existence of a certain chemical on residential land stops the lawn growing on that land.

3. The significant role that contaminated land plays in property transaction can be seen in litigation. Thus, for example, *Lambson Fine Chemicals Ltd v Merlion Capital Housing Ltd* [2008]

EWHC 168 (TCC), [2008] Env LR 37 concerned a claim that a written misrepresentation had been made concerning the extent of contamination of a property. The court found it had not. As Thornton notes:

the case provides an illuminating example of the complexities of investigating contaminated sites, structuring deals with appropriate documentation and the importance of parties' knowledge. The critical issue of securing evidence of such knowledge in allocating and apportioning remediation liabilities is particularly evident, albeit that such knowledge was absent in the case itself.[18]

4. Further examples of land contamination issues leading to commercial litigation can be seen in *Esso Petroleum Co Ltd v Rickford Ltd* [2006] EWHC 556 (Ch) (covenants in contracts for future use) and *BAL 1996 Ltd v British Alcan Aluminium Plc* [2006] Env LR 26 (QBD) (TCC) (indemnity for litigation concerning land contamination).

3 LAND CONTAMINATION AND THE PLANNING SYSTEM

What Section 3 has highlighted is that land contamination can become a legal issue in a number of ways. That makes it difficult to discuss in a textbook because a focus on the formal legal regimes can be very misleading. With that said those frameworks should not be ignored and in this, and Section 4, how land contamination is dealt with under the planning and Part IIA regimes is discussed.

From a planning law perspective, land contamination is an issue both in regards to the creation of plans and for planning permission. Between 2004 and 2012 *Planning Policy Statement 23—Annex 2—Planning and Pollution Control: Development of Land Affected by Contamination*—set out detailed guidance for planning authorities about the contaminated land regime and how it interacted with the planning system. There are two interesting things to note about that guidance. First, it described land contamination as 'land affected by contamination' and not 'contaminated land'. This was due the fact that the Part IIA definition depends on what the current use of land is, while planning law needs to assess future uses. Second, with that said, the Part IIA definition still framed the understanding of land contamination and when land contamination required a legal response. Thus, the discussion was still in terms of linkages and receptors.

PPS 23 was replaced by the NPPF in March 2012. The following provisions now apply to land contamination.

Department of Communities and Local Government, National Planning Policy Framework (2012) paras 120–21

120. To prevent unacceptable risks from pollution and land instability, planning policies and decisions should ensure that new development is appropriate for its location. The effects (including cumulative effects) of pollution on health, the natural environment or general amenity, and the potential sensitivity of the area or proposed development to adverse effects from pollution, should be taken into account. Where a site is affected by contamination or land stability issues, responsibility for securing a safe development rests with the developer and/or landowner.

---

[18] Justine Thornton, 'Case Comment: Contaminated Land Investigations and Misrepresentation' (2009) 21 JEL 237.

121. Planning policies and decisions should also ensure that:

- the site is suitable for its new use taking account of ground conditions and land instability, including from natural hazards or former activities such as mining, pollution arising from previous uses and any proposals for mitigation including land remediation or impacts on the natural environment arising from that remediation;

- after remediation, as a minimum, land should not be capable of being determined as contaminated land under Part IIA of the Environmental Protection Act 1990; and

- adequate site investigation information, prepared by a competent person, is presented.

It is hard to know what the practical effect of these new paragraphs will be but at the very least it would encourage reliance on the Part IIA statutory guidance.

What this guidance does highlight is that land contamination is one issue among a number that local planning authorities (LPAs) LPAs are dealing with in considering planning permission. This is consistent with the idea of 'development managerialism' seen in Section 1.4 in that the issue of land contamination is being subsumed into the more wide-ranging issue of the efficient re-use of land in the UK. That, of course, can be problematic as can be seen in the two cases here. What these cases illustrate is that where land contamination arises as an issue it cannot be easily ignored.

R (Technoprint plc) v Leeds City Council
[2010] EWHC 581 paras 47–52 (Wyn Williams J)

Facts

The Claimants challenged the grant of planning permission to demolish a workshop and build 12 flats on the site on a number of different grounds including the way the issue of land contamination had been addressed in the planning application process.

The HC

47. Drainage matters and contaminated land were also identified by Mr Smith as a main issue in his Delegation Report. On 15 November 2007 Ms Rosie Bartlett, a technical officer employed by the [LPA], sent a memo to Mr Smith [the LPA case officer dealing with the application] in which she wrote:

'The applicant has not provided any information relating to land contamination issues in support of the above application.

The applicant has not demonstrated that the site would be suitable for the proposed use. As the end use is residential and therefore sensitive, we require the submission of at *least* a Phase I (desk study) report to support the application. Depending on the findings of the Phase I report, it may be appropriate for the applicant to also submit a Phase II (site investigation) report and remediation statement. For example, if a site has previously been used as a petrol filling station or gas works (i.e. a previous use that is potentially contaminating) we would require more information to be provided at the application stage.

[...]

I would recommend that you obtain the information outlined above prior to granting permission....'

48. Evidently the [developer] obtained a Phase I report. On 28 November 2007 Ms Bartlett recommended that the [developer] be asked for a Phase II report and, if necessary, a remediation statement in support of the planning application.

49. There is no evidence that Mr Smith asked the [developer] to provide a second report and, certainly, no such report was obtained. On 5 February 2008 Mr Smith emailed Ms Bartlett as follows:-

'I was writing up this application for approval and had (perhaps mistakenly) thought that there were no objections from Can I condition a Phase II submission?' Contaminated Land in your response dated 28 Nov 07.

The same day Mr Smith and Ms Bartlett spoke together and she then responded to the effect that since the application needed to be determined by Thursday she had recommended conditions although she would have preferred a site investigation up front.

50. The [LPA] has offered no explanation why the application had to be determined 'by Thursday.' I assume that it was on that day that the time limit for determining the application was due to expire. Nonetheless on the strength of this exchange the planning permission granted was made subject to no less than 6 conditions relating to the topic of land contamination.

51. The delegation report deals with this issue very shortly. Mr Smith wrote:-

'Conditions have been placed to deal with the submission of further phase II studies and remediation of the site. This has been conditioned as agreed by the contaminated land consultation.'

This was a very cryptic summary of what had transpired.

52. In my judgment, it was unreasonable for planning permission to be granted when so many issues relating to potential land contamination were unresolved. I appreciate that solutions can usually be found to overcome problems associated with land contamination. It does seem to me, however, that a reasonable local planning authority would have demanded much more information from the Interested Party before deciding to grant permission rather than grant permission subject to conditions when the extent of any potential problem was simply unknown. To repeat, land contamination was not identified as some peripheral issue in this case; it was identified as one of the main issues for consideration.

The second case involves a previous industrial estate in relation to which planning permission for parking and residential housing was granted. The grant of planning permission was challenged and one of the grounds of that challenge was that the Council failed to have regard to the fact that the land in question is likely to be contaminated, and that it acted unreasonably in failing to impose a condition requiring a site investigation and a scheme of remediation to be carried out before the development permitted may be begun. Note, in particular, the heavy reliance on both the old *PPS 23* and the Part IIA regime in the judge's reasoning. We extract here also the barrister's argument because it is useful to see how different arguments were put to the Court. In reading this case you might find it useful to refer back to Chapter 18.

R (Gawthorpe) v Sedgemoor DC
[2012] EWHC 2020 (Admin) paras 17–34 (John Howell QC sitting as a Deputy High Court Judge)

17. When consulted on the application, the advice of the Council's Environmental Health Officer was recorded in the Officer's report (which was considered by the Planning Committee at their meetings in April and May 2010). It was as follows, so far as relevant:

- 'The site of the proposed development is located on the same site as a former works and industrial units and the land therein and close thereto may be contaminated.

- The applicant should carry out detailed site investigation, in line with current UK guidance, to determine the nature, extant and level of contamination, both in the soil and underlying geology and the application should not be determined until the results are known and the associated risks assessed.

- In cases were contamination is shown to exist, a detailed scheme showing the appropriate remedial measures to remove risks to future site users should be submitted and approved before planning permission is granted.'

18. This advice appears to have replicated the Environmental Health Officer's advice in respect of the application which was subsequently granted planning permission in 2009. In that grant the advice was then included as a note to the applicant, not as a condition imposed on the grant of planning permission. Why no condition was then imposed has not been explained.

19. The advice given by the Environmental Health Officer reflected the guidance by the Secretary of State in Annex 2 to PPS 23. That advice recognises, as Miss Thomas pointed out, that the primary responsibility to deal with contamination issues is that of the developer. But the advice given (at paragraph [2.33]) is that, where development is proposed on land that is or may be affected by contamination, an assessment of risk should be carried out by the applicant for the local planning authority before the application is determined; that any existing or new unacceptable risks should be identified and proposals made to deal with them effectively as part of the development process; and that local planning authorities should satisfy themselves that intending developers have addressed effectively the issue of potential contamination in bringing forward their proposals.

20. The further advice (at paragraph [2.49]) is that:

'In determining applications, the local planning authority will need to be satisfied that development does not create or allow the continuation of unacceptable risk from the condition of the land in question.'

It is also stated (at paragraph [2.59]) that, where it is satisfied the development proposed will be appropriate having regard to the information currently available about contamination of any of the site and the proposed remediation measures and standards, the local planning authority shall grant planning permission subject to any conditions requiring such further investigations and remediation (including verification as would be necessary, reasonable and practicable).

21. In this case, the Officer's report recommended planning permission should be granted. It proposed no condition relating to contamination. It contained no explanation why the Planning Officer thought that that recommendation in the absence of such a condition was appropriate in the light of the Environmental Health Officer's advice and the Secretary of State's policy.

22. There is no explanation in the evidence about what consideration, if any, was given to this issue by members of the Planning Committee at their meetings in April and May 2010; why this advice was not followed, or why a condition requiring investigation and any necessary remediation before the development was begun was not recommended or imposed.

23. Mr Atkinson has filed two witness statement. In neither statement does he suggest that he considered the question of contamination prior to the grant of planning permission.

24. It appears that the preliminary site investigations and analysis have, in fact, been carried out subsequently. A report on these investigations, dated July 2011, states that it is not possible to make more than preliminary comments on the likelihood of remnant contamination of the site. But it states there is a risk posed by remnant hydrocarbon contaminates on the site and that it is likely that it will be necessary to consider either further environmental assessment or remedial measures to remove the risk.

25. On 8 June 2012, the owner of the land, EE Lane & Sons (Holding) Ltd, entered into a unilateral undertaking under section 106 of the Town and Country Planning Act 1990 that development under both the 2009 and 2011 planning permissions would not be begun until a site investigation had been

carried out; any necessary remediation scheme had been prepared and approved by the Council; and any necessary remediation scheme works had been carried out or complied with to the Council's satisfaction.

ii. submissions

26. On behalf of the Claimant, Mr Leader submitted (i) that the site's potential contamination was a material planning consideration which the local planning authority was bound to take into account; (ii) that it had failed to do so or had failed to give any reasons why the Environmental Health Officer's advice had not been followed, supported as it was by the Secretary of State's planning guidance, and (iii) that it was unreasonable to grant planning permission without imposing a condition addressing the need for a site investigation and possible remedial matters in the circumstances. Mr Leader accepted that the unilateral undertaking now belatedly entered into provides at least the same protection as the condition which he contends should have been imposed. In those circumstances, he realistically accepted that it would be futile to quash the planning permission on this ground alone but he invited me to grant a declaration that the decision to grant planning permission was flawed.

27. On behalf of the Council, Miss Megan Thomas did not suggest that the views of the Council's Environmental Health Officer did not relate to a material planning consideration. However, she submitted that members had had regard the views of the Environmental Health Officer, as they must be assumed to have read the report in which they were contained, and that it cannot be said that they were acting unreasonably in granting planning permission without imposing any condition dealing with contamination. She submitted (i) that members were entitled to place some reliance on the fact that any developer of the site would strive to avoid any potential and future claims from homeowners arising from any adverse effects of contamination and (ii) that there were alternative statutory means open to the Council under Part IIA of the Environmental Protection Act 1990 to secure decontamination of the land if contamination was found and judged harmful, and that (in accordance with the advice in Circular 11/95) a condition should not be imposed which would duplicate other controls. She also submitted that the fact that the owner's agents had tried to make contact with the Environmental Health Officer before the Committee considered the reports in April and May 2010 was a relevant background fact, although she accepted there was no evidence to show that members were aware of that fact.

iii. Whether the grant of planning permission was flawed

28. I accept that the Claimant has not shown that the Committee failed to have any regard to what the Environmental Health Officer had advised. I am prepared to assume that they did indeed read the report written for them by the Planning Officer, and read it with care.

29. But that, of course, does not mean that the Committee acted reasonably in resolving that delegated planning permission should be granted, without complying with the Secretary of State's guidance or imposing any condition in respect of that matter.

30. Miss Thomas relied on paragraph 22 of Circular 11/95 which advises that a condition that duplicates the effect of other controls will normally be unnecessary, and one whose requirements conflicts with the requirements of other controls would be unreasonable.

31. Part IIA of the Environmental Protection Act 1990 instituted a regime under which local authorities are responsible for causing their area to be inspected from time to time for the purpose of identifying contaminated land, and for the relevant enforcing authority in respect of such land to serve remediation notices on appropriate persons. Requiring a developer to investigate whether a site is contaminated and to carry out remediation before any development is begun is plainly not regarded by the Secretary of State, however, as conflicting with the advice in paragraph 22 of Circular 11/05. On the contrary, in paragraph [2.12] of Annex 2 to PPS 23, the Secretary of State stated that in his view Part IIA of the 1990 Act 'is not directed to assessing risks in relation to the future use of the land that would require

a specific grant of planning permission. This is primarily a task for the planning system, which aims to control development and land use in the future'.

32. Indeed, even in Circular 11/95, the Secretary of State had given more specific advice about contaminated land, indicating that conditions may be imposed in order to ensure that the development propose of the site would not expose future users or occupiers of the site to risks associated with contaminants present. In particular, the advice at paragraph 75 of that Circular was:

'In cases where there is only a suspicion that the site might be contaminated, or where the evidence suggests there may be only slight contamination, planning permission may be granted subject to conditions that the development will not be permitted to start until a site investigation and assessment have been carried out and that the development itself will incorporate any remedial measures shown to be necessary.'

33. That advice was, it appears, strengthened by PPS 23, which was issued in 2004. That advice also makes plain that merely relying on a developer's own self-interest to secure remediation (if required) before development is carried out is insufficient in the view of the Secretary of State. In his view, planning authorities are expected to exercise the powers of development control vested in them to deal with contamination issues.

34. It is plain that no reasons have been given why the Planning Committee or Mr Atkinson decided to proceed contrary to the advice of the Environmental Health Officer and the guidance of the Secretary of State. Planning authorities are obliged to give summary reasons for their grant of planning permission. Those which I have set out above do not address this issue. No complaint is made about that by Mr Leader, on behalf of the claimant. But, in my judgment, the circumstances are such that no reasonable planning authority would have proceeded to grant planning permission without a condition addressing the contaminated land issues in the face of the advice of the Secretary of State and their own Environmental Health Officer absent a good reason for so doing. None has been shown in response to this claim. Accordingly, in my judgment, the decision to grant planning permission was unlawful and I will so declare.

PPS 23 no longer exists so it will be interesting to see whether similar approaches will be taken in the future. These two cases may also give the impression that the courts are activist in relation to the treatment of land contamination in the planning system, but in other cases the courts have been far more deferential.[19] One obvious reason for this is the perceived technical expertise needed in this area. With that said, what is interesting about the two judgments here is how much they focus on the importance of process. The problem in these cases was that an issue was identified but the nature of the decision-making processes did not reflect the seriousness of that issue.

FURTHER READING AND QUESTIONS

1. Another example of a challenge to how the issue of land contamination was dealt with as part of the planning application process can be seen in *R (Bedford) v Islington LBC* [2002] EWHC 2044 (Admin), [2003] Env LR 463. See also *Dowmunt-Iwaszkiewicz v First Secretary of State* [2004] EWHC 2537 (Admin); *R (Villa Ria Trading) v First Secretary of State, Slough BC* [2006] EWHC 3326 (Admin).

2. For a further discussion of land contamination in the planning context see Ben Pontin and Chris Willmore, 'Displacing Remedies from Environmental to Planning Law: The Enforcement of Contaminated Land Legislation in Britain' (2006) 6 YEEL 97.

[19] *R (Bedford) v Islington LBC* [2002] EWHC 2044 (Admin), [2003] Env LR 463.

4 PART IIA OF THE ENVIRONMENTAL PROTECTION ACT 1990 IN FURTHER DETAIL

We have already discussed Part IIA in outline but we now turn to considering various aspects of it in more detail. The approach in this section is thus to highlight three key features of the regime. First, we consider the role of policy guidance. Second, we discuss how the regime sets up an administrative system for identifying contaminated land and serving remediation notices. Finally, the system creates a regime for apportioning responsibility for remediation. It should be remembered that this chapter is just an introduction to the regime. To understand the regime in detail a careful reading of the legislation, policy guidance, and a specialist textbook is needed (see the Further Reading section at the end of this chapter).

4.1 THE ROLE OF *STATUTORY* GUIDANCE

We have seen that policy plays a significant role in much of environmental law.[20] As we have already seen, Part IIA is no exception. What is distinctive about the role of policy under Part IIA is that it is *statutory* in nature.

DEFRA, Environmental Protection Act 1990: Part 2A. Contaminated Land Statutory Guidance (2012) paras 1.1 and 1.3

1.1 This statutory guidance ('this Guidance') is issued by the Secretary of State for Environment, Food and Rural Affairs in accordance with section 78YA of the Environmental Protection Act 1990 ('the 1990 Act'). […] This Guidance applies only in England […]

1.3 This Guidance is legally binding on enforcing authorities, and relevant sections of Part 2A which form the basis of this Guidance are mentioned in specific Sections of this Guidance below. This Guidance has been subject to Parliamentary scrutiny under the negative resolution parliamentary procedure, in accordance with section 78YA of the 1990 Act. The Environment Agency and other relevant bodies in the land contamination sector have been consulted in relation to this Guidance, as required by section 78YA(1) of the 1990 Act, and a full public consultation was held between December 2010 and March 2011. This Guidance should be read in accordance with Part 2A.

The practical consequence of this is that reference must be had to both Part IIA and the guidance. Etherington has described the Statutory Guidance in relation to Part IIA as 'hard guidance'. He explains a number of different reasons for its utilization.

Laurence Etherington, 'Mandatory Guidance' for Dealing With Contaminated Land: Paradox or Pragmatism' (2002) 23 Stat LR 203, 207–08, 220–21, 224–25.

[W]hilst Part IIA comprises a lengthy and complex addition to the statute book, the essential detail of this new regime is provided through a number of supplementary rules. A wide variety of rule-types are used, which cover almost the whole spectrum of those available to the legislator:

(1)   Primary Legislation

(2)   Regulations in the form of Statutory Instruments

---

[20] See Section 2 of Chapter 11 in particular.

(3) 'Hard' Guidance [under s. 78YA]

(4) 'Soft' Guidance

(5) Site Specific Guidance from the Environment Agency

(6) Departmental Circular covering the Statutory Guidance

(7) Orders made by the Secretary of State

(8) Directions given by the Secretary of State

(9) Local Authorities' Inspection Strategies

(10) Scientific and Technical Standards

Rule-types (1) and (2) are Hard law, whilst the remainder are Soft Law (with the possible exception of (3), which is uncertain and discussed in detail below). There are three types of central government guidance—(3), (4) and (6); guidance produced by government agency—(5); ministerial decrees—(7) and (8); local government policy—(9); and technical standards—(10), which are produced from a variety of sources. The complexity of this system of rule-types is obvious (and a further element of the system is constituted by private agreements which are afforded special status so that they are the most important rules in many situations). The structure of the rules in terms of sanctions follows a pattern commonly used for environmental issues: administrative law provisions deal with matters substantively, imposing duties upon the enforcing authorities and providing them with powers to require remedial works to be carried out. If these requirements are not complied with, there are criminal law procedures and sanctions, as well as administrative powers to carry out works and civil law remedies to secure repayment for them, or to secure compliance with requirements.

As Etherington notes in his excellent survey, much of this is reminiscent of planning law. What is unique in the Part IIA regime is the use of 'hard guidance' under section 78YA, and Etherington goes on to consider its use in particular. Here are some of his conclusions.

It seems that the rationale for using Hard Guidance in relation to Part IIA was to provide additional elements of flexibility in both the rule-making procedure and in the resulting rules. Additional flexibility in the procedure allowed controversial policy decisions—such as mitigating retrospective liability, whilst protecting the public purse—to be deferred, so that acceptance of the policy, and of the implementing rules, by powerful interests could be secured incrementally over a number of stages, whilst discussions with these interests ensured that serious errors—both technical and of political judgment—were avoided. [...]

The use of Hard Guidance is one way of alleviating concerns where those governed by the rules might not be happy with discretionary decision-making by the selected decision-maker. This could result from differing cultural perspectives of matters (such as risk, and differing values, regarding matters such as the balance between economic development and the need for ecological protection). One example of these is lawyers seeing problems as resulting from gaps in the rules, thus seeking legalisation, whilst others might perceive too many rules as the source of the problem.

Part IIA's complexity, and the process by which it was produced, bears all the hallmarks of rule 'formalism' by lawyers. A significant amount of detail in the rules consists of attempts to deal with every conceivable possibility, and one can find many examples in the drafts following consultation exercises where some unusual situation has been directly addressed—having been 'missed' in earlier drafts. The process of formalism is not surprising given the subject-matter of the rules, the consultation procedures carried out, and, more importantly, the extent to which lawyers were 'players' in those consultation procedures. As well as the natural inclination for lawyers to seek certainty through legalization (exacerbated by the imposition of retrospective liability), a further stimulus for seeking certainty was the nature of the main regulator: local authorities.

Etherington was writing in the early days of the regime. As we have seen, the statutory guidance both grew and shrunk between now and then. The 2012 statutory guidance provides less technical detail than the 2006 guidance and focuses more upon setting out the decision-making processes that a LPA must engage in. With that said, the document still places a considerable limitation on the discretion of local authorities. This is both due to its explicit aims (discussed already in Section 2.1) and the quite definitive use of language. The guidance now reads far more as a set of supplementary rules (akin to delegated legislation) and less as technical guidance documents that provided a 'thicker' account of the regime. How practice will change in relation to contaminated land (both in regards to Part IIA and otherwise) will be interesting to see.

4.2 IDENTIFICATION OF CONTAMINATED LAND

We discussed the definition of 'contaminated land' in Section 2.2. Part IIA and the Statutory Guidance also set out a process by which such land is identified as contaminated by local authorities.

Part IIA places a duty on local authorities to inspect its area 'from time to time' for the purposes of 'identifying contaminated land'.[21]

DEFRA, Environmental Protection Act 1990: Part 2A. Contaminated Land Statutory Guidance (2012) paras 2.2–2.4

2.2 This Guidance recognises that there are two broad types of 'inspection' likely to be carried out by local authorities: (a) strategic inspection, for example collecting information to make a broad assessment of land within an authority's area and then identifying priority land for more detailed consideration; and (b) carrying out the detailed inspection of particular land to obtain information on ground conditions and carrying out the risk assessments which support decisions under the Part 2A regime relevant to that land. This Guidance refers to the former as 'strategic inspection' and the latter as 'detailed inspection'. [...]

2.3 The local authority should take a strategic approach to carrying out its inspection duty under section 78B(1). This approach should be rational, ordered and efficient, and it should reflect local circumstances. Strategic approaches may vary between local authorities.

2.4 The local authority should set out its approach as a written strategy, which it should formally adopt and publish to a timescale to be set by the authority. Strategies produced in accordance with previous versions of this Guidance should be updated or replaced to reflect this Guidance. The authority may choose to have a separate strategy document and/or to include its strategy as part of a wider document.

Part IIA also sets out a procedure for a special site designation[22] and the Contaminated Land (England) Regulations 2006 provides a list of land which is required to be designated as a special site.[23] This includes, for example, certain controlled waters, land contaminated due to waste acid tars, petroleum refining, land within a nuclear site, land on which chemical or biological weapons were manufactured, and land owned by the Ministry of Defence. The designation of a contaminated land site as a 'special site' means that it will be managed by the Environment Agency.

---

[21] Section 78B(1).   [22] Sections 78C and 78D.
[23] Contaminated Land (England) Regulations 2006, Regulation 2.

If land is determined to be contaminated land (or a special site) then the local authority is under a duty to serve a remediation notice.[24] That notice should be served on an 'appropriate person' and the notice must specify 'what that person is to do by way of remediation and the periods within which he is required to each of the things so specified'.[25] The question of who is an 'appropriate person' is dealt with in the next section but there is considerable detail in the Act, Regulations and guidance about the remediation process including recovery of the costs of remediation once an 'appropriate person' has been identified. Section 78P(1)–(2) states:

(1) Where, by virtue of section 78N(3)(a), (c), (e) or (f) above, the enforcing authority does any particular thing by way of remediation, it shall be entitled, subject to sections 78J(7) and 78K(6) above, to recover the reasonable cost incurred in doing it from the appropriate person or, if there are two or more appropriate persons in relation to the thing in question, from those persons in proportions determined pursuant to section 78F(7) above.

(2) In deciding whether to recover the cost, and, if so, how much of the cost, which it is entitled to recover under subsection (1) above, the enforcing authority shall have regard—

(a) to any hardship which the recovery may cause to the person from whom the cost is recoverable; and

(b) to any guidance issued by the Secretary of State for the purposes of this subsection.

The Statutory Guidance provides quite detailed guide on this Section. The main guiding principles are set out here.

DEFRA, Environmental Protection Act 1990: Part 2A. Contaminated Land Statutory Guidance (2012) paras 8.5–8.7

8.5 In making any cost recovery decision, the enforcing authority should have regard to the following general principles:

(a) The authority should aim for an overall result which is as fair and equitable as possible to all who may have to meet the costs of remediation, including national and local taxpayers.

(b) The 'polluter pays' principle should be applied with a view that, where possible, the costs of remediating pollution should be borne by the polluter. The authority should therefore consider the degree and nature of responsibility of the relevant appropriate person(s) for the creation, or continued existence, of the circumstances which lead to the land in question being identified as contaminated land.

8.6 In general the enforcing authority should seek to recover all of its reasonable costs. However, the authority should waive or reduce the recovery of costs to the extent that it considers this appropriate and reasonable, either: (i) to avoid any undue hardship which the recovery may cause to the appropriate person; or (ii) to reflect one or more of the specific considerations set out in the statutory guidance in sub-sections 8(b), 8(c) and 8(d) below. In making such decisions, the authority should bear in mind that recovery is not necessarily an 'all or nothing' matter (i.e. where reasonable, appropriate persons can be made to pay part of the authority's costs even if they cannot reasonably be made to pay all of the costs).

---

[24] Section 78E(1).   [25] Section 78E(1).

8.7 In deciding how much of its costs it should recover, the enforcing authority should consider whether it could recover more of the costs by deferring recovery and securing them by a charge on the land in question under section 78P. Such deferral may lead to payment from the appropriate person either in instalments (see section 78P(12)) or when the land is next sold.

The more specific considerations relate to charities, social housing landlords, trusts, and circumstances where there are threats of business closure and insolvency. The impact of these types of factors will be discussed by Lees in Section 5.

Part IIA also gives a right given to appeal to the Secretary of State a remediation notice (s 78L), the process of which is fleshed out in the Regulations. The Act also gives a local authority or the Environment Agency powers to carry out remediation in certain cases (s 78N). It is also the case that they must keep a register of remediation notices alongside other information (s 78R). All this gives the Part IIA regime a very administrative feel—it is essentially a regime for administering the problem of land contamination. However, that process of administering also involves apportioning liability and it is that process of apportionment that has been the most high profile aspect of the regime.

4.3 DETERMINING WHO IS AN 'APPROPRIATE PERSON'

Under Part IIA, liability for remediation is placed on the legal actor who is determined to be the 'appropriate person'. Who is an appropriate person is set out in s 78F.

(1) This section has effect for the purpose of determining who is the appropriate person to bear responsibility for any particular thing which the enforcing authority determines is to be done by way of remediation in any particular case.

(2) Subject to the following provisions of this section, any person, or any of the persons, who caused or knowingly permitted the substances, or any of the substances, by reason of which the contaminated land in question is such land to be in, on or under that land is an appropriate person.

(3) A person shall only be an appropriate person by virtue of subsection (2) above in relation to things which are to be done by way of remediation which are to any extent referable to substances which he caused or knowingly permitted to be present in, on or under the contaminated land in question.

(4) If no person has, after reasonable inquiry, been found who is by virtue of subsection (2) above an appropriate person to bear responsibility for the things which are to be done by way of remediation, the owner or occupier for the time being of the contaminated land in question is an appropriate person.

(5) If, in consequence of subsection (3) above, there are things which are to be done by way of remediation in relation to which no person has, after reasonable inquiry, been found who is an appropriate person by virtue of subsection (2) above, the owner or occupier for the time being of the contaminated land in question is an appropriate person in relation to those things.

(6) Where two or more persons would, apart from this subsection, be appropriate persons in relation to any particular thing which is to be done by way of remediation, the enforcing authority shall determine in accordance with guidance issued for the purpose by the Secretary of State whether any, and if so which, of them is to be treated as not being an appropriate person in relation to that thing.

(7) Where two or more persons are appropriate persons in relation to any particular thing which is to be done by way of remediation, they shall be liable to bear the cost of doing that thing in proportions determined by the enforcing authority in accordance with guidance issued for the purpose by the Secretary of State.

(8) Any guidance issued for the purposes of subsection (6) or (7) above shall be issued in accordance with section 78YA below.

(9) A person who has caused or knowingly permitted any substance ("substance A") to be in, on or under any land shall also be taken for the purposes of this section to have caused or knowingly permitted there to be in, on or under that land any substance which is there as a result of a chemical reaction or biological process affecting substance A.

This section is very different from classic liability regimes and is again administrative in nature. The Statutory Guidance provides a detailed analysis of how to apply this section, particularly in relation to the exclusion and apportionment of responsibility. In thinking about these issues it is important to keep in mind the following.

DEFRA, Environmental Protection Act 1990: Part 2A. Contaminated Land Statutory Guidance (2012) para 7.4

7.4 For some land, the process of determining liabilities will consist simply of identifying either a single person (either an individual or a corporation such as a limited company) who has caused or knowingly permitted the presence of a single significant contaminant, or the owner of the land. The history of other land may be more complex. A succession of different occupiers or of different industries, or a variety of substances may all have contributed to the problems which have made the land "contaminated land" as defined for the purposes of Part 2A. Numerous separate remediation actions may be required, which may not correlate neatly with those who are to bear responsibility for the costs. The degree of responsibility for the state of the land may vary widely. Determining liability for the costs of each remediation action can be correspondingly complex

Some of that complexity can be seen in the following cases. The first is an example of how the question of 'caused or knowingly permitted' can be difficult to establish. In the *Circular Facilities (London) Ltd v Sevenoaks DC* case we can see the factual difficulties in making such a determination.

Circular Facilities (London) Ltd v Sevenoaks DC
[2005] EWHC 865 (Admin) paras 30–43 (Newman J)

The Facts

CFL developed land in the early 1980s for residential purposes. After finding the land to be contaminated for the purposes of Part IIA due to buried organic matter, the Council served a remediation notice on CFL. CFL did not place the matter on the land but a report that identified the contamination was handed to the council when CFL owned the land and was developing it in March 1980. The report had been carried out in 1978 when the land was owned by a Mr Scott (who had not placed the material on the land). Mr Ketteringham who was the controlling mind of CFL claimed to know nothing of the report.

The HC

30. Mr Smith, counsel for CFL (who did not appear below), submitted that three issues arose on the appeal:

(1) The validity of the Judge's finding that CFL knew of the presence of buried organic material or gases between 1979 and 1985.

(2) Whether, assuming that there was knowledge of the contents of the report, such knowledge was sufficient for CFL to be found to have knowingly permitted the substances to be in or on the land.

(3) Whether the Judge was right to conclude that the policy of the Act was to make developers liable.

31. I have the advantage in this court of a copy of the closing submissions on behalf of the Council made by Mr Lewis.

32. Paragraph 18 of those submissions is in the following terms:

'The Appellant "knowingly permitted" the "substance" (the organic material and gas) to be "in … or under" the land at Well Close, The Appellant completed its purchase of the land at Well Close on 12 November 1979, see para 16 of Mr Ketteringham's evidence at page 78 of Bundle A. Contrary to what Mr Ketteringham asserts at para 19 of his evidence on page 79 of Bundle A, the Appellant knew of the presence of the organic material and the generation of gas, having submitted to the Council (or having had submitted on its behalf by Mr Scott, Mr Ketteringham's "agent" or "unofficial partner") the soil investigation report (dated 7 July 1978) on 28 March 1980, see date stamp at page 103 of Bundle A. The presence of "black organic matter" in the trial pits dug on the land is confirmed on pages 104 to 106 of Bundle A and the report refers to "gases bubbling through" water in Trial Pit 3 on page 105. The report dictated the use of piled foundations for the houses constructed by the Appellant on the land and those foundations were duly provided. It is implausible to suggest that Mr Ketteringham did not have personal knowledge of the contents of the report. In any event, it is clear that his relationship with his agent/partner Mr Scott was such as to fix him with knowledge of the contents of the report.'

33. Mr Lewis repeated the submission in this court and submitted that it was clear that the Judge must have concluded that Mr Ketteringham did know of the presence of organic material and the generation of gas. The difficulty in this court and the difficulty with his submission to the court below was that Mr Ketteringham had denied personal knowledge, but the submission of Mr Lewis was couched in terms that, whilst it was contrary to what Mr Ketteringham asserts, '… the Appellant knew of the presence of the organic material'. Significantly he did not submit that Mr Ketteringham knew, but CFL knew. So formulated, it begs the question as to how CFL knew if the Judge had concluded that Mr Ketteringham personally had no such knowledge. According to the submission, the contention that Mr Scott had submitted the report was relied upon for the argument. But the Judge made no finding about who submitted the report to the Council. Further, Mr Scott was not Mr Ketteringham's agent, but CFL's agent. It is not clear that the unofficial partners were Mr Ketteringham and Mr Scott.

34. It was open to Mr Lewis to submit that it was 'implausible' to suggest that Mr Ketteringham did not have personal knowledge of the contents of the report, but it was for the Judge to reach a conclusion of fact on the balance of probabilities as to whether he did know or did not know. Whilst the Judge referred to a number of factors which were relevant to a conclusion in this regard, in no part of his judgment did he find what Mr Ketteringham did know or did not know. Had he found that Mr Ketteringham had the requisite knowledge, the company would be taken as having the same knowledge because he was the controlling mind of the company. Neither does the Judge set out adequate reasons for the conclusion reached by him that '[…] the company […] must have been aware of the organic material […]'. True it is that he referred to the informal partnership with Mr Scott, the use of Mr Scott as an agent

of the company and to his views as to what he believed to be the risks of the company investing in the development and the need in connection therewith to assess the soil investigation report. But, that said, it is not clear in whom the judge concluded the requisite knowledge was reposed as a result of those considerations. It was incumbent upon the Judge to disclose his chain of reasoning, in particular if it led to a conclusion of fact contrary to the evidence of Mr Ketteringham. If the Judge's conclusion was that Mr Ketteringham must have known, despite the evidence he had given to the clear effect that he did not, and, as a result, the Judge regarded him as mistaken in this regard, then he should have said so.

35. But in my judgment the lack of clarity goes deeper. The reference to Mr Scott as agent or partner probably derives from the last sentence in paragraph 18 of the submissions he had received from Mr Lewis. That submission, with respect, was misconceived. According to the evidence, Mr Scott was the agent of CFL and not the agent of Mr Ketteringham. Whilst circumstances can arise in which a principal is fixed with the knowledge of an agent, it is by no means straightforward to assert that, if the principal fixed with the knowledge of his agent is also the controlling mind of a company, the company is to be regarded as fixed with the imputed knowledge or constructive knowledge of its controlling mind. However, on a proper analysis, the evidence pointed to Mr Scott being the agent of CFL and, in that event, his knowledge could, according to the circumstances, be imputed to CFL even though Mr Ketteringham did not know. Nor again is it entirely clear that, even if Mr Scott and Mr Ketteringham were to be regarded as within a personal partnership relationship, CFL should be fixed with the knowledge imputed through that relationship. That being an alternative submission advanced by Mr Lewis, and having regard to the terms of the judgment, it is impossible to discern whether the Judge found that Mr Scott's knowledge was to be imputed to Mr Ketteringham and, therefore, to CFL or whether he was finding that Mr Ketteringham did personally know but was mistaken in his recollection.

36. More than this, as it was recognised in argument by Mr Lewis, the relevance of Mr Scott's agency was, on the evidence, his capacity as an agent for CFL appointed by Mr Ketteringham. In the circumstances of this case, it may have been arguable, if investigated, that according to the law of agency the knowledge of Mr Scott, as it seems the court is likely to have concluded existed, could, as a matter of law, in certain circumstances, be imputed to CFL. In particular, in this regard, the phrase 'directing mind and will' can, according to authority, be the directing mind and will of a company which reposes in different persons in respect of different activities. See *El Ajou v Dollar Land Holdings plc and Another* [1994] 2 All ER 685, in particular the judgment of Hoffmann LJ.

37. Having regard to the way in which the matter was argued, this basis of imputing knowledge to CFL was not considered and not investigated in the evidence with a view to it forming a basis for the dismissal of the appeal.

38. I accept the force of the submissions advanced for CFL that if the Judge was rejecting Mr Ketteringham's evidence to the effect that he did not know of the organic matter or gases at the material time then he should have made a clear finding in that regard giving his reasons for his conclusion. I agree that it is not clear from the judgment on what basis the Judge concluded that CFL and/ or Mr Ketteringham had knowledge of the contents of the report. I accept the submission that if the Judge came to the conclusion that because the report was available on the planning register and was available therefore to CFL that that in itself was insufficient to impute knowledge of the contents of the report to CFL.

39. In my judgment it was incumbent upon the Judge to state whether or not he found, as a fact, that Mr Scott knew of the contents of the soil report and, if so, what legal conclusion that gave rise to. If the Judge was to impute Mr Scott's knowledge to CFL then the legal basis for so doing should have been explored and disclosed. If the Judge found that Mr Scott submitted the report to the Council he should have said so.

40. In view of the above, I have reached the conclusion that this appeal must be allowed. This court, on a statutory appeal such as this, has the power to consider whether there should be a re-trial. In my judgment the underlying ambit of the evidence and applicable legal principle, when fully explored and considered, could give rise to a legitimate conclusion that CFL was an appropriate person to be served with a remediation notice. That being the case and there having been expenditure by the Council of money by way of remediation, I would be minded, in the exercise of my discretion, to conclude that there should be a re-trial. It is no answer to proceedings such as this, which inevitably involve the reviewing of matters which occurred many years ago, to simply exclude judicial inquiry long after the event. I agree that in the context of Magistrates' Courts proceedings, without the benefit to be gained from disclosure obligations, that trials on matters as historic as this, without reference to adequate documentation, giving rise to complex principles of law, present a demanding set of proceedings for a district judge to resolve. Nevertheless, having weighed all these considerations, it seems to me that, subject to any specific representations from the parties, the matter should be re-tried.

41. follows that it is not necessary for me to deal with the other grounds of appeal which were urged before me but, for the purposes of clarification, I should say something about the argument advanced on the basis that the meaning to be attributed to 'knowingly permitted' required some knowledge of the potential harm from the substances in the land. Mr Smith submits that the court should not construe the section, in particular section 78F subsection (9), as rendering a person liable as having knowingly permitted a substance to be on the land, if the relevant person is not aware of the possibility that a chemical reaction or process could lead to the land being contaminated. He submits there must be some knowledge of the potential harm to which the presence of the substance in the soil could give rise.

42. In this regard, he refers to particular paragraphs in the circular, Annex 2, which have the status of guidance and thus do not dictate the meaning of the provisions.

43. In my judgment this argument simply cannot stand in the face of the express terms of subsection (9) of section 79F. By the terms of the section, a person needs only to have knowledge of a substance (in this case organic material) and the statute provides that in that event, having knowingly permitted that substance, referred to as 'substance A', to be in, on or under the land that person:

'... shall also be taken for the purposes of this section to have caused or knowingly permitted there to be in, on or under that land any substance which is there as a result of a chemical reaction or biological process affecting substance A'.

In my judgment there is no basis for limiting the ambit of the section to exclude responsibility to those who do not know of the potentiality for the chemical reaction or biological process which can affect substance A. The knowledge of the substance is taken to be the knowledge of the substance generated by the process.

There are two interesting points to note about this case. First, the question of 'caused or knowing permitted' is largely a question of fact, which can be difficult to determine because 'contamination' occurred so far in the past and the relevant people are often dead (as was the case with Mr Scott). Second, 'knowingly permitted' will include developers, which is why Part IIA will provide an extra incentive to developers to comply with planning conditions that relate to remediation.

The *R (National Grid Gas Plc) v The Environment Agency* case is perhaps the most high profile example of a challenge to determining who is an 'appropriate person'. The question of who 'caused or knowingly permitted' land to be contaminated in this case is a very different one from the *Circular Facilities (London) Ltd v Sevenoaks DC* one and relates to the transfer of ownership of companies. Also note that this case was extracted and discussed in Section 1.4 of Chapter 11.

R (National Grid Gas Plc) v The Environment Agency
[2007] UKHL 30 [2007] 1 WLR 1780 paras 9–16, 19–23 (Lord Scott)

9. The actual polluters of the Bawtry site had been, first, two private companies, namely, the Bawtry and District Gas Company ('B&DGC') and the South Yorkshire and Derbyshire Gas Company ('SY&DGC'). The B&DGC had purchased the Bawtry site in about 1912 and constructed on the site a gas works which became operational in about 1915. In 1931 the B&DGC was amalgamated with the SY&DGC and the amalgamated company continued gas production at the Bawtry site. The gas industry was nationalised by the Gas Act 1948 after which the site was owned and controlled by the EMGB. However gas production at the site was discontinued shortly after nationalisation and in 1965 the site was sold to Kenton Homes Ltd. In 1966 the site, still undeveloped for housing purposes, came into the ownership of Kenneth Jackson Ltd, which company applied for and obtained planning permission to build houses on the site. The 11 residences already referred to were then built. Seven of them were, for a time, owned by the Secretary of State for Defence but subsequently all 11 passed into private ownership.

10. As is explained in para 30 of Forbes J's judgment (at first instance), it is not known exactly when the coal tar residues were buried at the site. It is probable that most of this happened when the site was in private ownership before nationalisation, but some part may have happened while the site was owned by the EMGB.

11. Section 17(1) of the Gas Act 1948 provided that:

'... all property, rights, liabilities and obligations which, immediately before [the appointed vesting date] were property, rights, liabilities and obligations of an undertaker [eg B&DGC and SY&DGC] ... shall on the vesting date vest by virtue of this Act and without further assurance in such Area Board as may be determined by order of the Minister'.

Thus the Bawtry site passed into the ownership of the EMGB subject to the liabilities of the B&DGC and the SY&DGC 'immediately before' the vesting date.

12. According to evidence given to Forbes J, it was not, in the mid 1960s when the EMGB sold the site or previously, considered dangerous to leave coal tar residues under the land, provided they were properly contained. The conveyance of the site by the EMGB to Kenton Homes Ltd in 1965 described the site as including 'the underground tanks installed on part thereof' (see para 31 of Forbes J's judgment).

13. By the Gas Act 1972 the Area Gas Boards were abolished and their property, rights, liabilities and obligations were transferred to the British Gas Corporation (the 'BGC') which remained in state ownership. So the BGC became subject to any liabilities of the EMGB arising out of its previous ownership of the Bawtry site or inherited under section 17(1) of the 1948 Act from B&DGC and SY&DGC.

Privatisation

14. Privatisation of the gas industry was effected by the Gas Act 1986. A 'successor company', in the event British Gas plc, was formed, public subscription in this new company was invited by the Government (the advertised enthusiasm of 'Sid' played a prominent part as did, of course, a formal prospectus) and the transfer to the successor company, British Gas plc, of the BGC's assets and liabilities was effected by section 49 of the 1986 Act. Section 49(1) said that on a transfer date to be nominated by the Secretary of State -

'...all the property, rights and liabilities to which the [BGC] was entitled or subject immediately before that date shall...become by virtue of this section property, rights and liabilities of...[the successor company]...'

15. Members of the public, individual as well as corporate, encouraged by the advertisements and prospectus to which I have referred, subscribed for shares in British Gas plc on the basis of the statutory scheme whereunder the company in which they were investing would take over the assets and liabilities of the BGC as they stood 'immediately before' the transfer date. The proceeds of the subscription enriched the Treasury and, thereby, the public at large.

16. After a series of corporate re-organisations in the 1990s, the part of British Gas plc's undertaking concerned with the transportation and storage of gas devolved on Transco. It is worth emphasising that the Bawtry site formed no part of the assets transferred to British Gas plc. The site had been sold for housing over 20 years earlier by the EMGB. And the liabilities created by the Environmental Protection Act 1990 did not exist in 1986 when British Gas plc was floated. [...]

19. It is clear that B&DGC and SY&DGC would, if they had still been in existence, have been appropriate persons for section 78F purposes. Both were polluters. But both have long since been dissolved. The EMGB, too, a third polluter, would have been an appropriate person, but it was dissolved after the 1986 privatisation of the gas industry. It seems likely that Kenton Homes Ltd and Kenneth Jackson Ltd would have been aware of the presence of the coal tar under the ground of the Bawtry site and that it would have been arguable that they had 'knowingly permitted' the coal tar to remain there. But both these companies have been dissolved, the former in 1983, the latter in 1993. The present owners and occupiers of the 11 residences would be appropriate persons but, as I have said, the Agency has decided not to pursue them. But how can it sensibly be said that Transco is an appropriate person, it being common ground that Transco neither caused nor knowingly permitted the coal tar to be buried at the Bawtry site and that British Gas plc, Transco's progenitor, came into existence some 20 years after the Bawtry site had been sold for housing?

20. The argument for the Agency, advanced by Mr Pleming with success before Forbes J, was that 'person' in section 78F, as in the phrase 'person ... who caused or knowingly permitted ... ' should be construed so as to include every person who became by statute the successor to the liabilities of the actual polluters ie B&DGC, SY&DGC and the EMGB. This is, in my opinion, a quite impossible construction to place on the uncomplicated and easily understandable statutory language. The emphasis in section 78F, both in subsection (2) and in subsection (3), is on the actual polluter, the person who '...caused or knowingly permitted...'. The suggested construction makes nonsense, also, of the language of the statutory provisions under which, upon nationalisation in 1948, the liabilities of the private gas undertakers were transferred to the state owned Area Boards and, upon privatisation in 1986, the liabilities of the state owned Area Boards were transferred to British Gas plc. Both in section 17(1) of the 1948 Act and in section 49(1) of the 1986 Act the assets and liabilities transferred were expressly limited to those existing 'immediately before' the transfer date. The notion that that language can encompass a liability created by Parliament in 1995 by the amendment of the 1990 Act seems to me, with the greatest respect, unarguable. Parliament is, of course, sovereign and can impose what liabilities it sees fit on whom it chooses. But very careful statutory language would be needed to impose on a company innocent of any polluting activity a liability to pay for works to remedy pollution caused by others to land it had never owned or had any interest in.

21. Mr Pleming told your Lordships on a number of occasions that Parliament had enacted the 1990 Act (with its 1995 amendment) on the principle that the polluter should pay and that innocent owners or occupiers of contaminated land should not have to pay. I have no doubt that that was so and have no quarrel with that principle. But Transco was not a polluter and is no less innocent of having 'caused or knowingly permitted' the pollution than the innocent owner or occupiers of the 11 residences.

22. Mr Pleming argued, also, that since British Gas plc was the transferee and so had the benefit of the assets of the EMGB, which might be taken as including the proceeds arising from the sale of the Bawtry site, it was right and fair that British Gas plc's successor, Transco, should bear any liabilities relating to that site. An immediate answer is that the liabilities imposed on British Gas plc by the 1986

Act were the liabilities existing immediately before the date of transfer and that those liabilities could not include liabilities coming into existence, some nine years later, under the 1995 amendment of the 1990 Act. But an additional answer is that the Agency's attempt to cast the burden of paying for the remediation works on to Transco falsifies the basis on which the investing public were invited to subscribe for shares in British Gas plc. The investing public (including Sid) were entitled to believe that the liabilities of the new company, identified in the prospectus that accompanied the flotation, were, as section 49(1) of the 1986 Act said, limited to those existing immediately before the date of transfer. They would have subscribed for shares in that belief and the Treasury would have benefited accordingly from the representations that had been made by government to the investing public. I find it extraordinary and unacceptable that a public authority, a part of government, should seek to impose a liability on a private company, and thereby to reduce the value of the investment held by its shareholders, that falsifies the basis on which the original investors, the subscribers, were invited by government to subscribe for shares. And I can see no reason to suppose that Parliament intended to produce that result.

23. Mr Pleming invited your Lordships, pursuant to *Pepper v Hart* [1993] AC 593, to peruse the Parliamentary record in order to establish whether Parliament intended 'the person' in section 78F to bear the extended meaning contended for by the Agency. Your Lordships did peruse the record, de bene esse, but, to my mind, there is little, if anything, to assist Mr Pleming's argument. In any event, while recourse to Hansard may be permissible to assist in resolving an ambiguity in the statutory language, I can find no relevant ambiguity in section 78F. *Pepper v Hart* provides no authority for recourse to Hansard in order to alter plain and unambiguous statutory language.

The other judgments, particularly Lord Neuberger's are also useful to read. What can be seen in all judgments is an attempt to understand the nature of the liability regime created by Parliament. Thus, the decision is not about defining 'appropriate person' broadly or narrowly but about understanding how the concept actually operates in the real world of property transfer and company acquisition. Particularly interesting to note about the judgments are the references to shareholders.

The third example relates to the challenges involved in apportioning liability. This can be seen in the *R (Redland Minerals Ltd) v of State for Environment, Food and Rural Affairs* case relating to a challenge of a remediation notice.

R (Redland Minerals Ltd) v of State for Environment, Food and Rural Affairs
[2010] EWHC 913 (Admin), paras 34–38 (Sales J)

The Facts

Redland Minerals Ltd (RML) brought judicial review proceedings against a remediation notice under s78E of the Environmental Protection Act 1990. That notice, based on an Inspector's report, identified RML as an 'appropriate person' under Part IIA and thus liable for remediation on the basis that RML had caused bromide and bromate to contaminate the soil on the relevant site. RML sought judicial review in relation to one of the remediation measures and on them being not excluded from liability. Sales J confirmed the legality of the remediation measure and considered the issues of the apportionment of liability between it and Crest who developed the site for residential purposes and who purchased the site from Redland in 1983 after carrying out a site investigation report which identified the contamination but not the full extent of it. The issue of apportionment of liability between the two is considered below.

The HC

34. I turn then to Redland's final ground of challenge which is apportionment of liability by the Secretary of State in the remediation notice as between Redland and Crest. This related both to bromide and bromate. The inspector dealt with this at paragraphs 961 to 976 of the inspector's report. In particular he said at paragraph 962:

'If the Secretary of State were to agree that both Redland and Crest caused bromate to be in, on or under the land at SLC, it would be necessary to apportion the costs of any bromate related remedial action between the two. Whilst there is no direct evidence of the relative quantities of bromate that are referable to them, Redland and Crest carried out very different operations on the land and controlled it for significantly different periods of time. In the circumstances, it would be unfair to apportion the costs of remediation equally and, in the absence of a more appropriate suggestion, Crest's proposal that the costs should be split 85% (Redland) to 15% (Crest) seems reasonable, as this broadly reflects the relative duration of periods when the site was under their control. In this respect, Crest's rounding up to the nearest 5% is favourable to Redland.'

35. After the inspector produced his report, the Secretary of State gave the parties an opportunity to make further representations. Redland put in representations on the question of apportionment which raised an argument relating to the way in which Crest's actions had caused contaminants to be flushed into the soil at a faster rate. Redland said this:

'The failing of Crest's (and thus the Inspector's analysis) is that it is based simply on time alone. However, the flux calculation presented on behalf of Redland (which was in principle accepted by the Inspector at paragraph 903) showed that the removal of the hardstanding by Crest and other matters for which Crest were responsible had the effect of introducing a 4-fold increase in the rate of downward migration in comparison to the situation while the premises was in Redland's ownership. As a result, the level of Crest's liability should be proportionately increased to account for the increased acceleration of the contaminant. A note is attached as Appendix 1 to these submissions from Leslie Heasman, Redland's witness at the inquiry, which indicates the effect of increasing Crest liability either 4-fold or by double see paragraphs 1–4). The parties' liability for the bromate linkage should either be 40.60, Crest: Redland (if increased by a factor of 4) or 25.75, Crest: Redland (if doubled). [...]

Second, and in any event, in the same way as is the case for the bromate SPL, the increased speed of flow caused by Crest's actions should also apply to the bromide SPL so that the proportionate liability should be either 83.17, Crest: Redland (if increased by a factor of 4) or 71:29, Crest: Redland (if doubled). The relevant calculations are included at Appendix 1, at paragraphs 5 and 6.'

The Secretary of State dealt with this aspect of the notice at paragraphs 40 to 43 of the decision letter which stated:

40. The Secretary of State supports the Inspector's recommendation that Crest should bear 15% of the liability for bromate contamination and 55% of the liability for bromide with the remaining 85% (bromate) and 45% (bromide) being allocated to Redland. In reaching his conclusions, the Secretary of State has paid careful attention to the general principles and specific approaches described in Part 6 of Section D of the Statutory Guidance (which are referred to in IR/961 and also above in paragraph 15). .

41. In IR962 the Inspector looks to attribute liability for the bromate significant pollutant linkage on the basis of the quantities of bromate for which the two parties were responsible. This is consistent with the general principles of the Statutory Guidance. However, achieving this is not straightforward as it is not possible to measure the quantities involved accurately.

42. The Secretary of State notes the Inspector's comment in IR962 that Crest and Redland undertook very different operations whilst in control of St Leonard's Court. The qualitative contribution of these operations

to the bromate contamination of the site is set out at length at various places in the IR. However, the complexity of this case does not very easily lend itself to a simple quantitative method which transparently captures all these arguments. In the circumstances, the Secretary of State believes that the period for which the two parties were in control of the site provides (see again IR962) an appropriate mechanism for apportionment and produces a result which is consistent with the broader facts of this case. Therefore the Secretary of State agrees that the division of liability for bromate should be Crest 15% and Redland 85% as described in IR962.

43. The Secretary of State also agrees with the Inspector's conclusion that the apportionment of liability for bromate (above) should form the basis of the apportionment of liability for bromide (IR966). This is because the same arguments which determine the apportionment of liability for bromate also apply to bromide (with the exception of the issue of degradation which does not arise). However, as noted by the Inspector, the apportionment of liability for bromide is affected by the additional consideration of the partial application of the "sold with information" exclusion test discussed at paragraphs 36 — 39 above.'

36. The critical part of the Secretary of State's reasoning is in paragraph 42. Mr Reed complains that the reasoning here is defective because it does not properly grapple and deal with the points on causation made by Redland. I reject that complaint. It is clear from reading the whole of the inspector's report and the whole decision letter that different causation mechanisms in relation to the contamination of the site were very much in the Secretary of State's mind. It is also relevant to refer to my judgment yesterday refusing permission to Crest to challenge the remediation notice which deals with the way in which Crest had contributed to the presence of contaminants in the site by demolition of the buildings and the hardstanding there. These were matters plainly taken into account by both the inspector and the Secretary of State.

37. Against that background it is in my view clear that the point made by the Secretary of State in his decision that there was no simple causative mechanism in this case, which could lead clearly to any particular apportionment of liability between Crest and Redland was a valid one. Rather a broad evaluative judgment on causation was required. Redland had caused all the bromide and bromate to be on the land in the first place and allowed them to filter down to the lower strata during its long period in control of the site. Crest had brought no contaminants onto the site but had accelerated the way in which the contaminants already in the land were flushed down to the lower levels.

38. As the Secretary of State fairly observed at paragraph 42 of the decision letter:

'... the complexity of this case does not very easily lend itself to a simple quantitative method which transparently captures all these arguments.'

He therefore indicated, in sufficiently clear terms, that he did not accept Redland's proposed quantitative method and agreed with the broader evaluative judgment on causation responsibility made by the inspector. There is, in my view, no arguable defect in this reasoning and I refuse permission in relation to this ground as well.

Again what can be seen in this case is the importance of the factual matrix.

FURTHER READING AND QUESTIONS

1. For a discussion that compares the contaminated land regime to the environmental liability directive see Maria Lee, '"New" Environmental Liabilities; The Purpose and Scope of the Contaminated Land Regime and the Environmental Liability Directive' (2009) 11 Env L Rev 264.

2. For further reading on the issue of who exactly is liable see Daniel Lawrence and Robert Lee, 'Permitting Uncertainty: Owners, Occupiers, and Responsibility for Remediation' (2003) 66 MLR 261. For an interesting conceptual discussion of the issues see Jenny Steele, 'Remedies and Remediation: Foundational Issues in Environmental Liability' (1995) 58 MLR 615.

3. Consider the following problem. Number 62–68 Town Rd is a 2 hectare property located in an inner city residential area in a large English city. Between 1860 and 1966 it was owned by the Mad Hatter Company, which operated a hat factory on the site. Numerous chemicals were, and still are, used in hat manufacture for varnishing and stiffening hats. As well, until the early 1900s mercury nitrate was used by the Mad Hatter Company in the manufacture of hat felt on the Town Rd site. In 1966 the Mad Hatter Company was bought by Hats R Us plc which continued to run a hat factory on the site. A fire destroyed the factory in 1980. The clearing up of the site was contracted to Dodgy & Son. After the fire, the property was no longer used as a hat factory but as a warehouse for hats, including hats that were faulty and factory seconds. Hats R Us plc was declared insolvent in 2008 and the administrators have now put the property up for sale. The property includes all contents of the warehouse including the faulty goods and factory seconds, which have no market value. A survey of the land also reveals that many fire-damaged drums of a hat stiffening chemical (ABC) have been buried in a large pit at the rear of the property. The presumption is that the drums were buried on the property by Dodgy & Son in 1980. The representatives of Hats R Us plc claim to have no knowledge of these drums.

Ritzy Residences plc is interested in purchasing the property for developing the property into luxury residences. Advise Ritzy Residences about the potential environmental law liabilities and regulatory responsibilities to which it may be exposed if it purchases the land, as well as the legal issues that may arise if it seeks planning permission for residential housing.

5 REFLECTIONS

An issue that has been left out of the analysis is whether the overall legal framework discussed in Section 4 actually addresses the problem of land contamination. Answering that question is more difficult than it looks for two reasons. First, any opinion on this will depend upon how land contamination is understood as a problem. The socio-political perspectives discussed in Section 1.3 will deeply influence views about the acceptability and effectiveness of the current regime. One thing is very clear however—the UK legal response depends on the definition of contaminated land in Part IIA and how it is defined in guidance. As we have seen, the new policy guidance gives it quite a narrow interpretation.

The reason why it is difficult to assess the effectiveness of the legal regimes for land contamination in England is that much of what is occurring is not formally legally documented or easily accessible. It is occurring in the private sector or in relation to individual planning permissions. Before, however, considering this bigger picture it is important to note what action has actually occurred pursuant to Part IIA.

Environment Agency, Dealing with Contaminated Land in England and Wales. A Review of Progress from 2000–2007 with Part 2A of the Environmental Protection Act (2009) 3

This is our second statutory report on the state of *contaminated land* for England and our first report for Wales, which we have to produce under Part 2A of the Environmental Protection Act 1990. The report gives an overview of the progress made in identifying and remediating *contaminated land* since Part 2A was introduced in 2000 (England) and 2001 (Wales) until 31 March 2007. We have prepared the report using information we have collected from local authorities in England and Wales. We also used our own information on *special sites* which we regulate under Part 2A. A summary of the key findings follows:

- Land contamination in England and Wales is mainly dealt with through the planning system. Local authorities estimate that around 10 per cent of contaminated sites are dealt with under Part 2A.

- All local authorities have produced strategies for inspecting their areas for *contaminated land*.

- By the end of March 2007, most local authorities in England and Wales had inspected less than 10 per cent of their areas for *contaminated land*. The cost of inspecting sites in England and Wales, including sites determined as *contaminated land*, designated *special sites* and sites that did not need to be determined, is around £30 million.

- By the end of March 2007, 781 sites had been determined under Part 2A, including 35 designated *special sites*. Of the 746 *contaminated land* (non-special) sites, local authorities reported that 144 had been completely remediated.

- From the start of Part 2A until the end of March 2007, we were asked to inspect, or oversee the inspection of, 144 potential *special sites* in England and Wales at a cost of around £4 million. Inspections are ongoing for 59 sites, of those we inspected, 35 became designated *special sites*, five of which have been fully remediated. Up to the end of March 2007 remediating *special sites* has cost in the region of £7.3 million.

- Local authorities in England and Wales report that the remediation of most *contaminated land* sites starts more than one year after the site has been determined and that the time it takes to remediate sites can range considerably between a number of months to many years. Costs reported for remediating *contaminated land* and *special sites* until the end of March 2007 are around £20.5 million, with costs anticipated to rise to around £62 million for all sites currently determined under Part 2A.

- Where sites have been remediated, this has mainly been through excavation and off-site disposal of material. Local authorities report that this is also the most common way proposed for treating sites that have not yet been remediated.

- Local authorities in England and Wales ranked the definition and identification of *contaminated land* and risk assessment as the most helpful aspects of Part 2A. They also ranked risk assessment, funding associated with implementing Part 2A and apportioning liability as the least helpful aspects of the Contaminated Land Regime.

These numbers are not small but they are not large either. Vaughan reflects on this report.

Steven Vaughan, 'The Contaminated Land Regime: Still Suitable for Use?' [2010] JPEL 142, 155–56

With 781 determinations of 'contaminated land' out of a possible 33,500 sites in a seven-year period Pt 2A hardly smacks of regulatory success. However, this article shows the Pt 2A regime is complex and complicated on a variety of levels and cannot be so easily taken at face value. Currently, we have a knowledge gap both in the context of the extent of the 'problem' (the number of sites which would fall within the definition of 'contaminated land') and in terms of the limited expertise (legal and technical) of the primary regulators under Pt 2A. At the same time, determining current liability for historic acts (in situations where properties have had multiple owners or occupiers over decades, or longer) presents a variety of evidential challenges as to the allocation of responsibility for remediation. Regulators additionally lack both the resources and, in certain areas, the inclination to actively enforce the regime. Even where the appetite to enforce does exist, the lack of clear guidance (both in the context of soil guideline values and in terms of little judicial interpretation of certain concepts in the regime) acts as a further disincentive to enforce for those already afraid of legal action by potential corporate members of a liability class.

This being said, there are indications that Pt 2A has delivered to some small extent. Perhaps not in the context of formal enforcement action, but in how it has acted as a knowledge driver on the issue of the impacts of our industrial heritage and as a remediation driver (albeit via planning controls, some voluntary action and contract-linked clean ups). Following the start made by the Environment Agency (who, in 2008, considered options for modernisation of the regime), there is currently within Defra the appetite and the ability to review Pt 2A and consider the potential for reform. The challenge (or, rather, one of the many varied and difficult challenges) would be in drafting a revised regime which, on a consensus basis, is viewed as more effective, more suitable for use, than Pt 2A by the multitude of stakeholders with an interest in contaminated land inspection, assessment and remediation. This article has sought to suggest that any regime that is going to result in much more direct regulatory intervention will need to overcome the twin problems of diffusion of regulatory resources and operational complexity.

That reform is still in the process of gestation as this is being written, but Vaughan's overall point is an important one. Part IIA has resulted in behavioural change. Vaughan was, of course, writing before the issuing of the new guidance. Whether that new guidance will see a further evolution in behaviour remains to be seen.

Lees takes a different perspective and focuses on how local authorities have interpreted the liability provisions of the regime. In particular she focuses on the role of environmental principles in the interpretation of the regime.

Emma Lees, 'Interpreting the Contaminated Land Regime: Should the "Polluter" Pay?' (2012) 14 Env L Rev 98, 101–02, 105, 106–07

The perception surrounding the Contaminated Land Regime is that it has achieved very little and has been described as a 'classic case of regulatory failure'. One barrier to more effective use of this legislation is cost. Over 140 local authorities ranked the 'funding of implementing' the regime as one of the three least helpful aspects of the provisions. Yet there is nothing in the regime itself that demands that local authorities should always be burdened with excessive costs. The search for contaminated land is certainly expensive, but the bulk of the cost is to be found in the cost of remediation. The totality of this cost, in most cases, need not be the responsibility of the enforcing authority.

There is no doubt, however, that under the current regime, the Environment Agency and local authorities do bear the brunt of the cost where there is no Class A person. The explanation for this lies in

> the interpretation of the provisions of the regime and particularly the Guidance. There are two keys aspects of the regime which, it is suggested here, are being misinterpreted. First, local authorities are giving a broad interpretation to the meaning of 'hardship' [section 78P]. Secondly, there seems to be something of a misapprehension that there is a presumption against recovery from Class B persons. [...]
>
> These factors mean that the contaminated land regime is not achieving as much as it could. Only 10 per cent of land (to March 2007) had been surveyed by local authorities to determine whether it was contaminated or not. We are 90 per cent of the way from even knowing the scale of the contamination problem because local authorities cannot afford to look for, or more worryingly to find, contaminated land.

Lees goes on to note that much of this situation arises from decision-makers giving primacy to the polluter pays principle.

> There is evidence [...] that some of the enforcing authorities are elevating the status of the 'polluter pays' principle within the regime from one amongst a number of relevant legal principles to the status of *primus inter partes*. Placing liability for remediation or costs onto Class A persons is justified by the fact that they are 'polluters'—but a similar liability for Class B persons is not justified because they are not polluters. Rather they are 'innocent owner-occupiers'. However, this conclusion does not necessarily follow from the statutory guidance.

Once again Lees was writing before the introduction of the new statutory guidance. Her analysis is a reminder that a regime such as Part IIA cannot be seen in isolation from the rest of environmental law or from assumptions about when, and when not, it is acceptable for a public body to impose liability on a private actor. The tendencies she has emphasized will arguably become even more common place with the greater focus in the new guidance upon the 'burdens faced by individuals' under Part IIA.

6 CONCLUSION

There is a temptation to think that land contamination as a simple legal problem just about creating regimes for cleaning up 'dirty' land. Compared to dealing with issues such as climate change, that seems a refreshingly easy thing to do. But, as has been made clear in this chapter, land contamination is a multifaceted problem that arises as a legal issue in a number of contexts. Moreover, the legal framework in the UK is a counter intuitive one. Part IIA may be explicitly about contaminated land but most land contamination issues will be dealt with in other contexts. With that said, the definition of contaminated land under Part IIA frames how land contamination is understood in the UK. That gives environmental lawyers much to think about and in thinking about it there needs to be a careful consideration of guidance, how the different systems interact and the role of the private sector. It also must be remembered that the framing power of Part IIA derives from the liability regime under that Part. Moreover, what have been described are the basics of the regime—there are many specifics in relation to particular issues not covered in this chapter. Thus, while contamination may be about dirt it is anything but simple.

FURTHER READING

1. The most thorough evaluation of Part IIA can be found in Stephen Tromans and Robert Turrall-Clarke, *Contaminated Land* (2nd edn, Sweet & Maxwell 2007).

2. Guidance documents in relation to contaminated land can also be found on DEFRA's and the Environment Agency's websites.

GENETICALLY MODIFIED
ORGANISMS

This chapter examines the legal regulation of the potential risks that arise from the use of genetically modified organisms (GMOs) in agriculture. Genetic modification can be understood as occurring when

the genetic material of an organism (either DNA or RNA) is altered by use of a method that does not occur in nature and the modification can be replicated and/or transferred to other cells or organisms. Typically, genetic modification of micro-organisms involves the removal of DNA, its manipulation outside the cell and reinsertion into the same or another organism. The aim of GM is often to introduce a new or altered characteristic to the target organism[1]

The chapter focuses mainly on European Union (EU) and UK law. It deals with the legal rules that control the potential risks arising from the particular characteristics of the GMO that has been produced rather than the process of genetic modification itself. Thus, at issue here are the regulation of genetically modified food, feed for animals, plants, such as GM crops, as well as seeds. Examples of such products are GM potatoes, GM soy feed, GM carnations, and GM seeds for a range of crops, such as rice and wheat.[2] The chapter also illustrates wider themes in environmental law. First, GMO regulation shows that environmental law is not a discrete subject with clearly defined legal subject boundaries, a point introduced in Chapter 1. While GMO regulation seeks to prevent and minimize damage to the environment from the release of GMOs into the environment, the law also serves a range of other purposes, such as to protect animal and public health, to ensure consumer choice between conventional, organic, and GM agricultural products, and to maintain an integrated EU market in GM food and feed stuffs. Hence, environmental law in relation to GMOs overlaps with food and public health as well as EU and international economic law.

Second, this chapter also highlights the importance of legal and political cultures for understanding why environmental law takes the form it does and how it is implemented, a theme

[1] Advisory Committee on Genetic Modification, 4th and Final Report, December 2003 at: <http//www.hse.gov.uk/aboutus/meetings/committees/sacgmcu/gm-rep4.pdf>, para 2 accessed 11 March 2013.

[2] The chapter does not deal with the legal regulation of transgenic agricultural animals. The Commission adopted on 19 October 2010 a five year moratorium on the cloning of farm animals, the use of cloned farm animals, and the sale of food products from such animals, for further information see <http://europa.eu/rapid/pressReleasesAction.do?reference=IP/10/1349> accessed 11 March 2013. The current UK Government, however, is not opposed to farm animal cloning and considers the promotion of new bio-technologies in the farming sector as important, see: <http://www.defra.gov.uk/food-farm/animals/cloning/> accessed 11 March 2013.

discussed in the Introduction to Part II and Chapter 3. A key problem for the legal regulation of GMOs in the EU has been the widely divergent cultural attitudes to transgenic agriculture and its regulation. While in France, Austria, Greece, and Poland citizens have opposed transgenic agriculture, this is much less so the case in the Netherlands, Spain, and Denmark. Difficulties in achieving agreement between those Member States who support GM agriculture and those who oppose it have lead to delays and blockages of EU wide authorizations for transgenic agricultural products.

Third, this chapter illustrates that environmental law is increasingly transnational in character, a theme further discussed in Chapters 5, 12, and 13 in relation to international environmental law, regulatory strategy and governance. In order to solve a specific environmental problem it is necessary to find and interpret legal provisions from different legal systems that interact in complex ways. For instance, international trade law limits legal competencies of the EU and its Member States in relation to GMO regulation, while EU law limits Member States' legal powers in relation to GMO agriculture. From a governance perspective the interaction between different legal systems raises questions about whether power is appropriately distributed between various GMO regulators, operating at local, regional, national, supranational, and international levels. What vision of ecological federalism do multi-level environmental governance regimes, here the regime for GMO regulation, establish? This theme is also further discussed in relation to the management of water quality in Chapter 14.

This chapter develops an analysis of these three key themes through four sections. The first provides a flavour of the controversial public policy debates about transgenic agriculture that have partly shaped environmental law in relation to GMOs, but that legal rules on GMOs do not always fully respond to. The second section discusses briefly the international legal frameworks that have influenced how GMO regulation is carried out in the EU. The third section focuses on the EU regulatory framework for transgenic agricultural products, critiquing in particular the science dominated EU administrative authorization procedures. Section 4 examines the main English legal provisions for the regulation of transgenic agricultural products. It should be stressed that this chapter is not an exhaustive analysis of GMO regulation but an introduction to its major themes and how it operates in EU law.

1 PUBLIC POLICY CONTROVERSIES GIVING RISE TO GMO REGULATION

Transgenic agriculture is a highly controversial area of risk regulation characterized by emotive public discourses both for and against it. Comparable perhaps to the regulation of water, environmental law in relation to transgenic agriculture seeks to maintain the most fundamental resources for the survival of human populations: soil and food. Moreover, environmental law in relation to transgenic agriculture also affects conventional and organic agriculture, and therefore is crucial to how societies achieve food security and tackle the persisting problem of hunger, in particular in developing countries. Legal regulation of agricultural GMOs thus intersects with the protection of the fundamental human right to life. In this section we provide an overview of why GMOs have proved so controversial and how debates over GMOs in the EU have developed.

1.1 THE NATURE OF GMO CONTROVERSIES

GMOs are controversial in the EU. They did not start out that way, however, as the extract from Levidow, Carr, Wield, and von Schomberg explains.

Les Levidow, Susan Carr, David Wield and Rane von Schomberg 'European Biotechnology Regulation: Framing the Risk Assessment of a Herbicide-Tolerant Crop' (1997) 22 Science Technology and Human Values 472, 473–4

Of all the GMOs released in field trials by the early 1990s, approximately half were crops that had an inserted gene for herbicide resistance. Even before commercialization, these products have been drawn into the broader conflict over how to conceptualize GMOs: as environment-friendly products or as self-reproducing pollutants. Herbicide-resistant crops have been heralded as a means for farmers to reduce herbicide usage, but they have also been attacked for perpetuating dependence on herbicides. The risk debate has served as a proxy for contending models of sustainable agriculture, especially in the United States.

Biotechnologists portray herbicide-resistant crops as safe and products on grounds that the inserted gene confers a precise resistance to a less-persistent herbicide. According to ICI Seeds, herbicide-resistant crops will reduce dependence on herbicides by reducing the quantities used; such crops will offer greater choice to farmers, by allowing them to defer herbicide applications until after the seedlings have emerged. On this basis, herbicide-resistant crops have been greeted as the ultimate solution to the problem of weeds resistant to herbicides.

However, this R&D agenda has been denounced for perpetuating dependence on chemical herbicides, regardless of whether or not their quantities are reduced. Environmentalist critics have warned that an inadvertent spread of the herbicide-resistance genes to weedy relatives or sheer selection pressure through herbicide sprays could result in the emergence of new herbicide resistant weeds. The development of such weeds would require yet new products to remedy the problems of previous ones. This scenario has been called a 'genetic treadmill'; by analogy to the chemical 'pesticide treadmill' products to remedy the problems of previous of pesticide-resistant pests.

GMOs thus mean different things for different groups. This concerns not only the role GMOs play in agriculture but also the science behind GMOs.

Sheila Jasanoff, 'Biotechnology and Empire: The Global Power of Seeds and Science' (2006) 21 Osiris 273, 275–76

Still in its infancy more than three decades after its first experimental successes in western laboratories, so-called green biotechnology has rapidly become a global industry promising enormous benefits to the world's poor. Its proponents claim it has the capacity to overcome nature, making plants that can resist drought, ward off insects, and with the ability to produce micronutrients engineered into their genes, even transcend the 'normal' dividing line between food and pharmaceuticals. Biotechnology by some definitions is as old as 'second nature,' the first successful prehistoric attempts by human societies to harness nature's growth to serve their basic needs for food, fuel, clothing, and shelter. Under another definition, the one I use here, biotechnology is much newer. It is the name given to an array of manipulative techniques based on alterations of the cellular and subcellular structures of living things enabled by the 1953 discovery of the structure of DNA. These techniques include, most notably, not only genetic engineering, gene splicing, but also operations such as cell fusion and cell culturing carried out at levels of structure significantly smaller than the whole organism.

Thus, biotechnology has been understood both as a continuation of past practices and as a new body of science. A further complication is that there are considerable scientific uncertainties in relation to the health and environmental effects of GMOs. We discussed scientific uncertainty in Chapter 2, but here it is useful to note how scientific uncertainty pervades questions over the environmental and public health impact of GMOs. In particular, much of the uncertainty arises from the newness of GMOs—there is simply not enough information about them. The risks from GMOs have thus been described as uncertain risks.

Marjolein van Asselt and Ellen Vos, 'Wrestling with Uncertain Risks: EU Regulation of GMOs and the Uncertainty Paradox' (2008) 11 J of Risk Research 281–82

The notion uncertain risks refers to possible, new, imaginable hazards, with which society has no or limited experience. It is uncertain whether the particular activity, product or phenomenon constitutes a risk to humans and/or the environment, because causalities are complex, the possible multiple effects are heterogeneous and extend to the long-term and/or the global scale and risk perceptions clash. The use of genetically modified organisms is an example of uncertain risks. As Lang and Hallman (2005) phrase it: 'the potential for risk in using [GMO] [...] remains just that—potential. There has yet to be an event that would allow institutions and experts to move [it] [...] from an uncertain risk to a quantifiable hazard'. Scientific or historic proofs of harmful consequences are lacking, but suspicions cannot be fully refuted either. Notwithstanding efforts to develop comprehensive frameworks we are convinced that uncertain risks pose different governance challenges. Uncertain risks need to be sharply distinguished from traditional, simple risks which can be calculated by means of statistics on frequencies and actual impacts. Approaches, tools, routines, procedures and structures that work quite well in the regulation of simple risks are not just inadequate, but may even hamper responsibly dealing with uncertain risks. In the case of uncertain risks, basic, seemingly simple, questions as to whether there is a 'real' risk or whether there is 'enough' safety cannot be answered by science. The presence of uncertainty challenges, or at least complicates, the role of experts as risk assessors.

Thus, what is clear from this discussion is that GMOs raise issues over both their use and scientific nature. It is also the case that there is a range of different ways that GMOs can be 'framed' and conceptualized. Jasanoff explains how this occurs.

Sheila Jasanoff, 'In the Democracies of DNA: Ontological Uncertainty and Political Order in Three States' (2005) 24 New Genetics and Society 139, 141

It is widely recognized by now that public problems do not simply appear on policy agendas, as if placed there through the direct imprint of exogenous events. Rather, they are framed in particular ways by cultural commitments that predispose societies, no less than the individuals within them, to fit their experiences into specific types of causal narratives. These narratives are grounded in longstanding institutional practices and ways of knowing that enable societies at once to conceptualize and find solutions to newly perceived threats to their security or well-being. Even the most technical issues are interpreted in the context of established, but varied, social approaches to defining and coping with public problems. These insights, largely derived from studies of domestic policy and politics, acquire added significance when translated into a comparative framework. By exposing underlying sources of variation, cross-cultural comparisons can help explain why national publics are more or less inclined to accept particular forms of technological change. At the same time, by grounding risk perception and regulatory behavior in the deeper matrix of political culture, comparative work resists dismissing the opposition to biotechnology as nothing more than an unreasoning fear of novelty, grounded in the public's ignorance of scientific facts.

What this also means is that regulation will have a role to play as Jasanoff goes on to explain.

[Regulatory] institutional frameworks constitute in effect an apparatus of collective sense-making through which national governments and publics interpret what biotechnology both promises and threatens. More specifically, national regulatory approaches help to position the ontological novelties created by biotechnology either on the side of the familiar and manageable or on the side of the unknown and perhaps insupportably risky. Public responses to biotechnology are thus shown to be embedded within robust and coherent political cultures rather than being ad hoc and contingent expressions of concern that vary unpredictably from issue to issue.

1.2 GMO DISCOURSE IN THE EU

The regulatory regime for GMOs will be discussed in Section 3, but here we provide an overview of the general public debate concerning GMOs in the EU. In light of what has been discussed in Section 1.1, it is not surprising that in the EU perceptions of governments and citizens about the advantages and disadvantages of transgenic agriculture diverge widely, particularly between different Member States.[3] French citizens have been particularly vocal in opposing transgenic agriculture. The extract from Bonny provides an overview of the types of concerns French citizens have about GMO agriculture, concerns also held by some other EU citizens.

Sylvie Bonny 'Why are Most Europeans Opposed to GMOs? Factors Explaining Rejection in France and Europe' (2003) 6(1) Electronic Journal of Biotechnology 50, 53–54

At the end of the 90's, debate on GMOs (authorization, importation, labelling, impact, etc.) was situated in a context strongly influenced by food safety issues (BSE, listeriosis, etc.) that had been widely publicized. Furthermore, the movement criticizing the various excesses of the agricultural and food system, that had previously been a fairly minority affair, grew as problems of pollution and safety came to the forefront. Now, GMOs were perceived as a strengthening of the highly industrialized agriculture that is precisely a target of much criticism in western Europe today, particularly in France.

[…] In France GMOs have been strongly opposed by various NGOs, groups and associations. Initially these consisted essentially of ecologist organizations (Greenpeace, Friends of the Earth, etc.) and groups of various tendencies (i.e. Ecoropa, the Natural Law Party), as well as supporters of the Green political parties and organic agriculture associations. This movement progressively expanded from environmentalist circles towards groups active in the economic domain including, for example a farmer's union—the Confédération Paysanne—, antiglobalisation organizations (ATTAC), LETS, etc. Finally, small circles of associations were created for the very purpose of fighting against GMOs. The impact of these associations has been strong, owing to the dynamism of their action which gave them extensively publicity: numerous strongly-worded press communiqués, the repeated mass dissemination of alerts and warnings, petitions, leaflets, standard letters to send to elected representatives or agro-food firms, lawsuits, demonstrations, and so on. In particular, these groups took advantage of the new

---

[3] Several EU Member States, such as Hungary, Austria, Poland, France, Germany, Greece, Italy and, Luxembourg, have instituted 'safeguard measures' to prohibit the cultivation, marketing, or import of GM products already approved under EC legislation. There are bans on the cultivation of GM crops in five EU countries and no cultivation in sixteen others. No majority could be found among Member States to approve draft Council decisions to have the various national bans on GMO cultivation suspended (Mihail Kritikos 'Traditional Risk Analysis and Releases of GMOs into the European Union: Space for Non-scientific Factors?' (2009) 34(3) ELR, 431.

communication technologies: multi transmission of information via automatic mailing lists, electronic forums, extremely well documented web sites used extensively by many as sources of information, etc. The endless reuse and circulation of certain information (sometimes very partial or biased) on the internet gave it credibility due to multiple repetition that ended up making it seem reliable (since it was frequently mentioned, it was corroborated).

[...] On the other hand the firms involved have often maintained a more traditional type of communication, strongly influenced by their usual clientele—the upstream agricultural sector, not the public at large. Moreover, until 1997-98 they often underestimated suspicion of GMOs, considering it to be the product of irrational and somewhat residual fears that would progressively disappear as more information became available. But their promotion of the advantages of GMOs did not convince the public.

Opposition to transgenic agriculture in the EU has also been documented by the latest public opinion survey, conducted by the European Commission in 2010.[4] Fifty-four per cent of Europeans hold the view that GM food is not good for themselves or their family, though there is variation between Member States. Eighty per cent of survey respondents in Latvia and 78% in Greece agreed with the statement that GM food is not good, but in Ireland only 39% of the interview respondents agreed and in the UK 40%, with public opinion divided in the UK, the Netherlands, and the Czech Republic.[5] Fifty-nine per cent of European citizens do not consider GM food as 'safe for their health'. In the southern Mediterranean countries of Greece (85%) and Cyprus (83%) this view is held most strongly. While there are differences between Member States, in no Member State were there more respondents who considered GM food safe for their health than those who disagreed.[6] There is also concern among European citizens about the environmental impacts of transgenic agriculture: less than a quarter (23%) hold the view that 'GM food does no harm to the environment'. A majority of 53% consider GM food to have adverse environmental consequences. Concern about the environmental impacts of GM agriculture was particularly strongly expressed in Greece and Sweden (74% thought that GM food harmed the environment). But in the Czech Republic (41%) and Slovakia (35%) there was support for the idea that GM food does not harm the environment.[7] Not surprisingly then, a majority of 61% of European citizens hold the view that the 'development of GM food should not be encouraged'.[8] An important point about these different views on biotechnology is that they are quite complex, as Mayer and Stirling show.

Sue Mayer and Andy Stirling, 'GM Crops: Good or Bad?' (2004) 5 EMBO Reports 1021, 1021

[A] wide range of research into public attitudes to GM food and crops shows that people typically have a wider and more varied appreciation of the risks than is usually included in a scientific approach.

[4] Eurobarometer 73.1 Report, Biotechnology, Conducted by TNS Opinion & Social on request of European Commission Survey co-ordinated by Directorate General Research, Fieldwork conducted, January to February 2010, published October 2010, at: <http://ec.europa.eu/public_opinion/archives/ebs/ebs_341_en.pdf> accessed 11 March 2013. The survey ascertained the views of a representative sample of citizens in the current twenty-seven EU Member States, EFTA countries (Switzerland, Norway, Iceland) and two candidate countries, Turkey and Croatia.
[5] Eurobarometer 73.1. Report, 2010 Biotechnology, 20. It seems that the European Commission is also facing an uphill battle in convincing the European public that biotechnology is an innovative potential growth sector in the EU. European citizens are sceptical about the benefits of GM food for the economy. On average 50% of Europeans disagreed with the statement that GM food 'is good for their national economy' (Eurobarometer, 73.1., Report 2010 Biotechnology, 19).
[6] Ibid, 28.   [7] Ibid, 30.   [8] Ibid, 31.

The overall picture indicates a diversity of public perspectives, which makes it difficult to apply a single general idea of 'the public'. However, certain common themes arise. One is that people typically consider GM food and crops in their wider social context. Their judgements are based as much on expectations about institutional interests and organizational behaviour as on scientific or technical information. As a result of recent experiences, which are epitomized by—but not limited to—the bovine spongiform encephalopathy (BSE) episode in the UK, people tend to be less confident that industry and governments will necessarily act in the 'public interest'. This applies to all of the interested parties, including NGOs. What distinguishes the latter is not that the public simply accepts their arguments, but that the public appreciates the general role of NGOs as critical and dissenting voices. An analysis of public attitudes to biotechnology in Europe found that 'NGOs, especially environmental ones, were […] appreciated for their capacity and willingness to ask difficult questions and raise issues which would not be raised otherwise. But they were perceived as biased, just like other actors. The difference was that, compared to firms and governments, they were expected to take into account wider societal and environmental interests. But it was also recognized that NGOs have their own vested interests, such as raising funds and membership'.

This relates back to Jasanoff's discussion about framing in Section 1. Her constructivist perspective suggests that the ideas we generate about the advantages and disadvantages of transgenic agriculture are powerful because they not only shape how we think but also how we act in the world. Participants in debates about transgenic agriculture and its legal regulation approach the subject from different analytical and normative points of view associated with different disciplines, cultures, and interests, often shaped by the organizations we belong to. Communication in the sense of reaching understanding and taking decisions becomes problematic. This is a wider symptom of the challenge of interdisciplinarity in environmental law.[9]

FURTHER READING AND QUESTIONS

1. How can agricultural GMOs give rise to environmental problems? In what way is transgenic agriculture different from or similar to other environmental problems that are legally regulated? Why does transgenic agriculture evoke strong emotional responses? See also Bettina Lange, 'Getting to Yes: Structuring and Disciplining Arguments For and Against Transgenic Agricultural Products in European Union (EU) authorisations' in Brad Jessup and Kim Rubinstein (eds), *Environmental Discourses* (CUP 2012).

2. What conceptions of science and technology underpin arguments for and against transgenic agriculture? For further discussion see Thomas Bernauer *Genes, Trade, and Regulation: The Seeds of Conflict in Food Biotechnology* (Princeton University Press 2003) and Julia Black 'Regulation as Facilitation: Negotiating the Genetic Revolution' (1998) 61 MLR, 621. This was written before the new EU regulatory framework came into force, but nevertheless provides an interesting argument for an 'integrationist' approach towards risk-regulatory decision-making in relation to GMOs, that questions the 'neutrality', 'objectivity', and 'universality' of scientific knowledge from a constructionist perspective and calls for 'translators and interpreters' that can help to improve communication about risks and their management in relation to GMOs. See also Michael Cardwell 'Public Participation in the Regulation of Genetically Modified Organisms: A Matter of Substance or Form?' (2010) 12(1) Env L Rev 12.

---

[9] WTO, *European Communities—Measures Affecting the Approval and Marketing of Biotech Products: Reports of the Panel* WR/DS291/R, WT/DS293/R (29 September 2006) paras 7.1751–1760.

2 INTERNATIONAL LAW AND GMOS

Section 3 will further analyse the current EU GMO authorization procedures. Before that, in this section we will outline how international law has shaped discourses over GMOs. We consider both international trade law and the Cartagena Protocol on Biosafety. What can be seen in both cases is that international law not only limits and shapes the legal powers that the EU and nation-states as signatories to various Agreements and Conventions have in regulating GMOs. On a more subtle level it structures what counts as a valid legal argument in order to oppose or support trade in transgenic agricultural products.

2.1 THE WTO AND THE *BIOTECH* DECISION

In Chapter 5 we discussed the World Trade Organisation (WTO) regime. The most significant of the Agreements in relation to GMOs is the Sanitary and Phytosanitary (SPS) Agreement. Indeed in the noughties a dispute settlement panel was required to consider whether aspects of the EU GMO regulatory regime complied with the Agreement. The background of this EC-Biotech dispute is explained here. The starting point is the very different approaches taken then by the US (the product approach) and the EU (the process approach).

David Winickoff and others, 'Adjudicating the GM Food Wars: Science, Risk, and Democracy in World Trade Law' (2005) 30 Yale J.L. Int'l L. 81, 87–89

The 'products approach' to regulating GMOs assumes that no untoward risk occurs merely from applying this technology to agricultural production. GMOs are subjected to stricter rules only when the end products are not substantially equivalent to their conventional counterparts. In contrast, the 'process approach' rests on the idea that genetic engineering itself may entail novel and unique risks to human health or the environment. Whereas the United States has embraced the products approach to GM agriculture, the European Union and its member states have tended to adopt the more precautionary process approach. [...] The inherent tensions between these two divergent regulatory philosophies first produced open conflict in the 1990s, when the 'genetic modification of dietary staples such as corn and soybeans ... caused strong trade frictions' in transatlantic relations.

[...]By 1998, public opposition to GM crops and food was growing across Europe, whereas in the United States the issue had caused little such public controversy. European concerns about the risks of genetic modification to human health and to the environment resulted in both increased demand for consumer choice and in an ongoing ethical discourse regarding genetic tampering with nature. In discussions about new imports of GM crops, a number of EU member states expressed concern at the levels of uncertainty surrounding such products and the potential harmful effects of such crops. At a meeting of the EU Council of Environment Ministers in June 1999, France, Denmark, Greece, Italy, and Luxembourg stated that they would block new authorizations of GMOs until Directive 90/220/EEC was revised and legislation had been put in place to cover labeling and traceability. Austria, Belgium, Finland, Germany, The Netherlands, Spain, and Sweden did not go as far, but stated they would take a "thoroughly precautionary approach" in dealing with new GMO authorizations.

As a result of this change in policy, EU member states granted no new approvals of GMOs after 1998, giving rise to the charge of a de facto European moratorium.

[...]Under the WTO's dispute resolution process, the United States, Canada, and Argentina first called for consultations concerning Europe's alleged moratorium on GM crop imports on May 14, 2003. [...]

In their formal requests for a panel, the complaining member states cited three measures that, they argued, adversely affect exports of agricultural and food products in violation of WTO law:

(1) 'a moratorium on the approval of products of agricultural biotechnology' in which 'the EC has suspended consideration of applications for, or granting of, approval of biotech products under the EC approval system';

(2) blockage under existing EC legislation of all 'applications for placing [further] biotech products on the market'; and

(3) the maintenance by EC member states of national marketing and import bans on biotech products even though those products have biotech products even though those products have already been approved by the EC for import and marketing in the EC.

The dispute did also involve arguments in relation to the Technical Barriers to Trade Agreement,[10] but the main focus was upon the SPS Agreement.[11] The report of the Dispute Settlement Panel was only issued after lengthy and complex proceedings in which there was the submission of a large quantity of material, extensive fact finding, and the putting forward of many different arguments by the parties including *amicus curiae* briefs. The final report ran to over 1000 pages not including annexes.

Much of the reasoning of that report need not concern us but one important part of the report to note was the Panel's discussion of Article 2.2 and Article 5.1 (see Chapter 5). They recognized that Article 5.1 and Article 2.2 were related, but they also recognized that they operated independently of each other.[12] This conclusion was inevitable because they found that a number of the different EU actions challenged were not measures (to which Article 5.1 only applies). The practical result was that Article 5.1 was not seen as interchangeable with Article 2.2. Following on from this, the Panel understood the requirement for a risk assessment as part of a reasoning process that a Member State had to undertake—the risk assessment requirement being central to this.[13] This is not to say that the Member State itself had to undertake the risk assessment,[14] but that the reasoning involved in a risk assessment was essential to justifying a measure. This is, of course, consistent with how the requirements of the SPS Agreement have been understood,[15] but in light of this the continuing emphasis on risk assessment in the EU GMO regulatory regime should come as no surprise.

2.2 THE CARTAGENA PROTOCOL ON BIOSAFETY

The Cartagena Protocol on Biosafety was negotiated within the framework of a public international environmental law instrument, the UN Convention on Biological Diversity, which entered into force in 1993. It is therefore considered as an environmental counterweight to the trade focused WTO agreements. The legal significance of the Protocol for GMO regulation is not entirely clear. Its Preamble states that the Protocol does not imply 'a change in the rights and obligations of a Party under any existing international agreement', but also that this statement 'is not intended to subordinate this Protocol to other international agreements'.[16] In the EC-Biotech dispute the WTO Panel suggested

---

[10] At: <http://www.wto.org/English/docs_e/legal_e/17-tbt_e.htm> accessed 11 March 2013.

[11] At: <http://www.wto.org/English/tratop_e/sps_e/sps_e.htm> accessed 11 March 2013.

[12] Ibid, paras 7.1751–60.   [13] Ibid, paras 7.3019–7.3021.   [14] Ibid, para 7.3024.

[15] Elizabeth Fisher, 'Beyond the Science/Democracy Dichotomy: The World Trade Organisation Sanitary and Phytosanitary Agreement and Administrative Constitutionalism' in Christian Joerges and Ulrich Petersmann (eds), *Constitutionalism, Multilevel Trade Governance and Social Regulation* (Hart 2006).

[16] Maria Lee, *EU Regulation of GMOs: Law and Decision Making for a New Technology* (Edward Elgar 2008) 228.

that the Cartagena Protocol can be used to interpret provisions of WTO agreements.[17] The Protocol can also be considered as an example of 'international standards, guidelines and recommendations of an international organization' referred to in Annex A of the SPS Agreement with which SPS measures should comply according to Article 3.2. of the SPS Agreement. Preambles 13 of Directive 2001/18/EC and 43 of Regulation 1829/2003/EC—the two core pieces of EU legislation that establish EU GMO authorization procedure—expressly state that they take into account the legal requirements of the Cartagena Protocol on Biosafety.

The Protocol regulates 'living modified organisms' (LMOs) through a requirement of 'advance informed agreement' in the case of exports and imports of LMOs. This advanced informed agreement must be based on a risk assessment which has been carried out 'in a scientifically sound manner [...] and takes into account recognised risk assessment techniques' (Articles 10 and 15 of the Cartagena Protocol). Within nine months (270 days) the country into which import of GMOs is proposed must let the notifier of the import know whether it permits the import and upon which conditions (Article 10). The Protocol does not require advance informed agreement for LMOs for GM food and feed but enables Parties to the Protocol to regulate GM food and feed through domestic regulation that is consistent with the objectives of the Protocol. Moreover, while Article 15 of the Cartagena Protocol requires a risk assessment to be carried out as part of the Party's decision-making process under the advanced informed agreement procedure, Article 26 of the Protocol also allows the Parties to take into account 'socio-economic considerations arising from the impact of living modified organisms on the conservation and sustainable use of biological diversity, especially with regard to the value of biological diversity to indigenous and local communities'; though taking into account such socio-economic considerations have to be in compliance with the international legal obligations of the Parties. The Cartagena Protocol thus provides space for the consideration of a wider range of concerns beyond purely scientific evidence.

2.3 REFLECTING ON THE ROLE OF INTERNATIONAL LAW

It is useful in proceeding further to reflect on the discussion so far. In doing so you might also find it useful to refer back to Chapter 5. Criticisms of international law as unduly restricting a full debate about the advantages and disadvantages of transgenic agriculture through its narrow focus on scientific knowledge also suggest that international law may therefore suffer from a legitimacy and accountability deficit, a point introduced in Chapter 5. But as Lee points out the WTO regime may also enhance accountability of risk regulatory choices, by requiring Northern, Western countries—who are especially powerful when combined in a regional trading bloc such as the EU—to consider the impact of their regional and national legal restrictions on trade in transgenic agricultural products upon the agricultural economies of other, including developing, countries.[18]

Evaluating the scope of these potential legitimacy and accountability deficits of international environmental law is by no means straightforward, also given the fact that some of the power brokering between states is hidden from view, though a greater understanding of this is key to understanding the social foundations of environmental law. It is clear that the negotiation of international agreements and their interpretation by the WTO dispute resolution fora is embedded in a wider context of international power relations. Not only are states with large, powerful, and rich economies the most frequent litigants before the WTO's formal dispute resolution bodies,[19] they are often also able to choose whether or not to submit to the rulings of the WTO dispute resolution fora. They may be able to cope with trade retaliatory measures from states

---

[17] EC Biotech case, WTO, European Communities—Measures Affecting the Approval and Marketing of Biotech Products: Reports of the Panel WR/DS291/R, WT/DS293/R (29 September 2006) para 7.55.
[18] Lee (n 16) 206.   [19] Ibid.

in whose favour the Panel or Appellate Body (AB) ruled. But while the dispute resolutions of the WTO Panel and its AB are important, they are only a small part of settling international trade standards and an analysis of power relations between states becomes more complex when probing into the dynamics of these committee negotiations. International trade law is also interpreted by the various committees established under WTO agreements, a feature not dissimilar to the committee system in EU governance, discussed further in Chapter 13. For instance, states have to notify trade restrictive measures they want to adopt to committees under the SPS and TBT Agreements. This also enables consultation with other states.[20] It has been suggested that exchange of good practices, standard setting, and thus further interpretation of the loosely worded, general provisions of WTO agreements in the SPS Committee can actually enhance accountability by requiring signatories, such as the EU, to justify its regulatory choices and their potential impact on international trade, including exports from developing countries.

FURTHER READING AND QUESTIONS

1. '[...] risk assessment is not a singular concept but it has to vary with context, processes of public deliberation and review are essential components of risk assessment, especially for low certainty, low consensus technologies such as GMOs and most especially in relation to the transfer of technological products across national borders' (Laurence Busch, Robin Grove-White, Sheila Jasanoff, David Winickoff, and Bryan Wynne, Amicus Curiae Brief in the Case of EC: Measures Affecting the Approval and Marketing of Biotech Products (WT/DS291, 30 April 2004)). Do you agree?

2. For further analysis of GMOS and international trade, see Joseph Murphy and Les Levidow, *Governing the Transatlantic Conflict over Agricultural Biotechnology: Contending Coalitions, Trade Liberalisation and Standard Setting* (Routledge 2006) and Han Somsen (ed), *The Regulatory Challenge of Biotechnology: Human Genetics, Food and Patents* (Edward Elgar 2007).

3. Andrew Lang and Joanne Scott, 'The Hidden World of WTO Governance', (2009) 20(3) Eur. J. Int'l L. 575. This article provides a fascinating insight into the workings of two WTO committees, the Services Council, and the SPS Committee, which are understood to promote regulatory learning through the building of interpretative communities. Richard Steinberg 'The Hidden World of WTO Governance: A Reply to Andrew Lang and Joanne Scott' (2009) 20(4) Eur. J. Int'l Law 1063. This article takes issue with Scott's and Lang's argument on the basis of a realist perspective, which suggests that the interests of states and the power politics resulting from these are key to understanding what goes on in WTO committees, in contrast to Lang's and Scott's constructivist perspective. See also Andrew Lang and Joanne Scott 'The Hidden World of WTO Governance: A Rejoinder to Richard H. Steinberg' (2009) 20(4) Eur. J. Int'l L. 1073.

4. For a discussion of the SPS Agreement, see Joanne Scott *The WTO Agreement on Sanitary and Phytosanitary Measures: A Commentary* (OUP 2007). This provides a detailed, comprehensive legal commentary. See also Joseph McMahon and Margaret A Young, 'The WTO's Use of Relevant Rules of International Law: An Analysis of the Biotech Case' (2007) 56 ICLQ 907.

---

[20] Ibid, 207.

3 CORE ELEMENTS OF THE EU LEGAL FRAMEWORK FOR THE AUTHORIZATION OF GMOS

We now turn to the focus of this chapter—the EU. In this section we provide an overview of the regulatory regimes, the role of science, the multi-level governance aspects of these regulatory regimes, and attempts at reforming them.

3.1 AN OVERVIEW OF THE EU GMO REGIMES

The cornerstones of this new EU regulatory framework are the Deliberate Release Directive 2001/18/EC,[21] which had to be implemented by Member States by 17 October 2002, the Food and Feed Regulation 1829/2003/EC,[22] which came into force on 18 April 2004, and the Labelling Regulation 1830/2003/EC.[23] All three pieces of legislation implement the type of precautionary approach discussed by Winickoff in Section 3. This approach is not surprising considering the uncertainties already discussed.

While Directive 2001/18/EC deals with the deliberate release of GMOs into the environment, either for the purposes of a field trial or more large scale commercial cultivation and the placing of products derived from GMOs or containing GMOs on the EU market, Regulation 1829/2003/EC regulates the placing onto the EU market of GMO food and feed products. There are some similarities, but also differences between the authorization procedures established under Directive 2001/18/EC and Regulation 1829/2003/EC. In practice most applications for the authorization of agricultural GMOs proceed under Regulation 1829/2003/EC. The Commission has facilitated this through its 'one door–one key' procedure, which is meant to reduce administrative burdens on biotech applicant companies. If authorization for a GMO is sought both for release, that is, cultivation, and its use in food or feed, such as in the case of GM maize for instance, then the entire application can be lodged under Regulation 1829/2003/EC with the criteria of Directive 2001/18/EC being applied to the authorization of those activities, such as cultivation, to which Directive 2001/18/EC applies without two separate applications, one under Directive 2001/18/EC and another one under Regulation 1829/2003/EC, having to be lodged.

Both the authorization procedure under Directive 2001/18/EC and Regulation 1829/2003/EC foreground scientific knowledge, and in particular a risk assessment of the GMO during the first phase of decision-making (see Figure 22.1), as the main basis upon which decisions about authorizations are taken. The Regulation and the Directive, however, do not establish an entirely technocratic system of risk regulatory decision-making, because they also allow wider considerations to be taken into account in a second, subsequent risk management phase. The Commission has defined risk management as 'the process of weighing policy alternatives in the light of the results of a risk assessment' in the Explanatory Memorandum attached to the proposal for Regulation 178/2002/EC.[24] In this phase, political as well as ethical considerations can be taken into account, with Article 7(1) of Regulation 1829/2003/EC enabling 'other legitimate factors relevant to the matter under consideration' to be considered.[25] The *risk assessment* phase is carried out by scientifically competent national and supranational bodies, such as the European Food Safety Authority (EFSA). The *risk management* phase is handled by political actors, such as the Commission, Member States, and comitology Committees, which take decisions on how to best manage the risks that have been identified and assessed during the risk assessment phase. Risk

---

[21] [2001] OJ L106/1.   [22] [2003] OJ L268/1.   [23] [2003] OJ L268/24.

[24] Mihail Kritikos, 'Traditional risk analysis and releases of GMOs into the European Union: space for non-scientific factors?' (2009) 34(3) ELR, 405, 421.

[25] Ibid, 421.

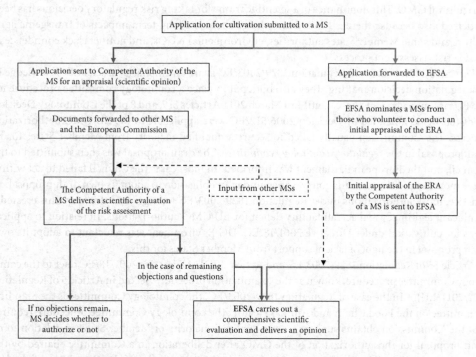

Figure 22.1 A representation of the risk assessment processes under Directive 2001/18/EC and Regulation EC 1829/2003

Source: GHK Consulting, 2011. *Evaluation of the EU legislative framework in the field of cultivation of GMOs under Directive 2001/18/EC and Regulation (EC) No 1829/2003, and the placing on the market of GMOs as or in products under Directive 2001/18/EC*. Jarvis, A; Conway, M *et al* for DG SANCO, European Commission.

management consists of the actual decision on authorization applications, the imposition of conditions in authorizations, and the establishment of national safeguard measures. It also includes the more practical issues of post-release monitoring, as well as inspections and labelling.

The text of Directive 2001/18/EC and Regulation 1829/2003/EC distinguishes between a risk assessment and management phase in risk regulatory decision-making. The legislation therefore seems to be an example of environmental law contributing to 'boundary work' on the science–politics interface, an idea discussed in Chapter 2 with reference to Bruno Latour's work. In the context of biotechnology 'boundary work' captures the idea that, while revolutionary biotechnological innovations allow the manipulation of what is 'natural' and 'cultural', the creation and maintenance of key social demarcations between what is 'natural' and 'cultural', what is 'scientific' and what is 'political', what is 'fact' and what is 'interest' are key to maintaining social, and as suggested here, legal orders.[26] Such boundary work, however, is precarious. Paragraph C.2.6. of the guidance on how to carry out an environmental risk assessment in Annex II of Directive 2001/18/EC suggests that risk management strategies should be taken into account in the assessment of risks. Moreover, in practice the Commission has mainly based its decisions during the risk management phase on the risk assessment[27] The Commission usually does not disagree with EFSA's scientific opinions on a specific

[26] Sheila Jasanoff, *Designs on Nature: Science and Denmocracy in Europe and the United States* (Princeton UP 2005) 26.
[27] Kritikos (n 24) 424.

agricultural GMO. This dominance of a scientific frame for taking risk regulatory decisions has been criticized also because there is limited knowledge about the long-term impacts of transgenic agriculture and some Member States authorities, environmental NGOs, and notifiers lack confidence in the EU risk assessment process.

Directive 2001/18/EC and Regulation 1829/2003/EC share an emphasis on scientific knowledge in risk regulation decision-making. They also both put in place a comitology committee procedure for the EU risk management phase. Until 1 of March 2011 Articles 5, 7, and 8 of the Comitology Decision 1999/468/EC as amended by Decision 2006/512/EC were applicable to the EU GMO authorization process. The Commission usually failed to secure a qualified majority from Member States for its draft proposal in the *regulatory comitology committee*. The draft proposal was then submitted to the Council, and the European Parliament was informed. In most cases the Council failed to act within three months, and the Commission was then under an obligation to adopt its own draft proposal. In practice, most authorizations under Regulation 1829/2003/EC were granted this way. This created a significant legitimacy and accountability deficit for EU GMO authorizations. In relation to applications for cultivation under Directive 2001/18/EC, DG Environment was reluctant to adopt its own draft proposal in the light of lack of support from Member States for this.

Article 35 of Regulation 1829/2003/EC and Article 30(2) of Directive 2001/18/EC refer to the comitology Committee procedure, known as the 'examination procedure' set out in Article 5 of Regulation (182/2011/EU).[28] In the case of Regulation 1829/2003/EC, the comitology Committee is the Standing Committee on the Food Chain and Animal Health. The comitology Committee procedure requires that the Commission obtains support from a qualified majority of Member States in relation to its draft proposal for the authorization of the GMO after deliberation in a Committee chaired by the Commission and composed of representatives of the Member States. If the Committee delivers a positive opinion, the Commission has to adopt the draft decision unless there are exceptional circumstances or new points to consider that could justify non-adoption of the measure (Article 5(2) Regulation 182/2011/EU). If the Committee delivers a negative opinion on the Commission draft decision for authorization of the GMO, the Commission can not adopt the decision. The Commission then can only re-submit the draft to the Committee for a second round of discussion, or put an amended draft to the Committee or submit its original proposal for the implementing act to the Appeal Committee (Article 5(3) Regulation 182/2011/EU). If the comitology Committee does not deliver an opinion, because it does not form a qualified majority either for or against the Commission draft decision, the Commission then has the freedom to decide whether to still adopt or to reconsider its draft decision, unless the act is considered to concern the protection of the health or safety of humans, animals, or plants (Article 5(4)(a) Regulation 182/2011/EU). Member States thus retain significant influence over the adoption of implementing acts by the Commission, and in contrast to the previously applicable regulatory comitology procedure the Commission is no longer under a duty to adopt its own draft decisions in the face of Member States' opposition.

While it remains to be seen how the new 'examination procedure' under Article 5 of Regulation (182/2011/EU) will work in practice in the context of GMO authorizations, it may further strengthen the technocratic elements of EU-level risk decision-making in relation to transgenic agricultural products in the risk management phase. It has removed the additional layer of politicized decision-making in the Council that existed under the previous regulatory comitology decisions.[29] Moreover, Article 3(4)

---

[28] European Parliament and Council Regulation (EU) 182/2011 of 16 February 2011, laying down rules and general principles concerning mechanisms for control by Member States of the Commission's exercise of implementing powers (182/2011) [2011] OJ L55/1.

[29] Maria Weimer 'What Price Flexibility?—The Recent Commission Proposal to Allow for National "Opt-Outs" on GMO Cultivation under the Deliberate Release Directive and the Comitology Reform Post-Lisbon' (2010) 1(4) European Journal of Risk Regulation 351, 345.

of the new comitology Regulation (182/2011/EU) envisages a process of deliberation and negotiation around the actual content of the Commission's draft decision, rather than just hard bargaining around fixed preferences, by enabling the chairperson to present amended drafts to the Committee during several meetings and a requirement upon the chair of the committee to build consensus in relation to draft implementing acts. While Regulation 1829/2003/EC and Directive 2001/18/EC share the comitology Committee procedure in the risk management phase they also have distinct features, which are further discussed in this section.

Regulation 1829/2003/EC

Authorizations under Regulation 1829/2003/EC and Directive 2001/18/EC start through an application being submitted to a competent authority in an EU Member State. In the case of Regulation 1829/2003/EC in the UK this is the Food Standards Agency (FSA). It acts, however, only as a 'letter box' for accepting applications which are directly forwarded to the European Food Safety Authority (EFSA).

Applications lodged under Regulation 1829/2003/EC are decided through one EU level decision-making procedure, since authorizations for GM food and feed clearly raise issues of the integrated EU market in food and feed stuffs.[30] According to Article 1(a) the Regulation seeks to provide for 'a high level of protection of human life and health, animal health and welfare, environment and consumer interests in relation to genetically modified food and feed, whilst ensuring the effective functioning of the internal market'. In contrast to this Directive 2001/18/EC focuses on the protection of human health and the environment. It is questionable whether the absence of a clear hierarchy of purposes in Regulation 1829/2003/EC and its adoption on the basis of various TFEU articles[31] allows the trade-off of environmental, animal, and human health protection against the building of an internal market in GM foods and feed stuff.

Authorization procedures under Regulation 1829/2003/EC are overseen by DG Health and Consumers (Sanco) in the Commission and EFSA's scientific opinion is at the heart of authorizations.[32] The extract from a summary of a scientific opinion of EFSA gives a flavour of its analysis.

Opinion of the Scientific Panel on Genetically Modified Organisms on an application (reference EFSA-GMO-NL-2004-02) for the placing on the market of insect-tolerant genetically modified maize 1507, for food use, under Regulation (EC) No 1829/2003 from Pioneer Hi-Bred International/Mycogen Seeds, Question No EFSA-Q-2004-087) Opinion adopted on 19 January 2005, (2005) 3(3) The EFSA Journal 182, 1–3, 18

This document provides an opinion of the Scientific Panel on Genetically Modified Organisms (GMO Panel) of the European Food Safety Authority (EFSA) on 1507 maize, genetically modified to provide protection against specific lepidopteran pests. The maize also contains a gene providing tolerance to the herbicide glufosinate. In delivering its opinion the Panel considered the application, additional information provided by the applicant and comments submitted by the Member States. Further information from other applications for placing 1507 maize on the market under current regulatory procedures were taken into account where appropriate, as were comments from the Member States.

---

[30] Before Regulation 1829/2003/EC came into force GM food was regulated through the European Parliament and Council Regulation (EC) 258/97 of 27 January 1997 concerning novel foods and novel food ingredients [1997] OJ L43/1 (Novel Foods Regulation).

[31] TFEU, arts 43, 114, and 168(4)(b).

[32] EFSA has published guidance on how risk assessments of food and feed from genetically modified plants should be conducted (EFSA Journal 2011; 9(5): 2150).

[…] 1507 maize was assessed with reference to its intended use employing the appropriate principles as described in the 'Guidance Document of the Scientific Panel on Genetically Modified Organisms for the Risk Assessment of Genetically Modified Plants and Derived Food and Feed'. The scientific assessment included examination of the DNA inserted into 1507 maize and the nature and safety of the target proteins produced by the transgenic plants with respect to toxicology and allergenicity. Furthermore, a comparative analysis of agronomic traits and composition was undertaken and the safety of the whole food was evaluated. A nutritional and an environmental assessment, including monitoring plan, were both undertaken. 1507 maize has been developed for protection against specific lepidopteran pests such as the European corn borer (Ostrinia nubilalis) and Sesamia spp. and for tolerance to the herbicide glufosinate. Insect resistance is achieved by production of a truncated Cry1F protein from Bacillus thuringiensis ssp. aizawai and tolerance to the herbicide is conferred by a phosphinothricin-Nacetyltransferase (PAT) from Streptomyces viridochromogenes. Maize embryos were transformed by particle bombardment to transfer a DNA fragment containing these two genes. As a result of the genetic modification, the 1507 event contains an insert bearing both cry1F and pat genes, under the control of the maize ubiquitin and the 35S promoters, respectively.

[…]While these sequences may have resulted from the transformation process (insertional events), there were no indications that these additional fragments would result in the transcription of new RNA other than the mRNAs transcribed from the cry1F and pat genes. In the unlikely event that this does occur, bioinformatics analysis showed that any resulting peptides or proteins would have no homology to known toxins or allergens. Analysis of DNA sequences flanking both ends of the insert shows that they correspond to maize genomic DNA. Analysis of kernel chemical composition from field trials in South America and Europe showed that 1507 maize was substantially equivalent to its non-GM comparator. Furthermore, appropriate animal feeding trials indicated that 1507 maize is nutritionally equivalent to its non-GM comparator.

Application EFSA-GMO-NL-2004-02 only concerns food uses for 1507 maize. Therefore, there is no requirement for scientific information on possible environmental effects associated with the cultivation of the GM maize. The GMO Panel agrees that unintended environmental effects due to the establishment and spread of GM maize will not be different from those of maize bred traditionally. The monitoring plan provided by the applicant is in line with the intended uses for the GMO. In conclusion, the GMO Panel considers that the information available for 1507 maize addresses the outstanding questions raised by the Member States and considers that 1507 maize will not have an adverse effect on human and animal health or the environment in the context of its proposed use. This scientific opinion corresponds to the risk assessment report requested under Article 6(6) of Regulation (EC) No 1829/2003 and will be part of the overall opinion as required by Regulation (EC) No 1829/2003.

[…]

As initial steps in the administrative procedures and risk assessment, EFSA made the valid application available to the Member States and the Commission and consulted nominated risk assessment bodies of the Member States, including the national Competent Authorities within the meaning of Directive 2001/18/EC following the requirements of Article 6(4) Regulation (EC) No 1829/2003, to request their comments on the safety assessment of the genetically modified food. The Member State bodies had three months after the date of receipt of the request (until 3 December 2004) within which to make their opinion known. All comments were evaluated by the GMO Panel and taken into consideration for the further risk assessment. Comments on risk management issues, such as co-existence of different agronomic systems were excluded from further considerations.

Conclusions and recommendations

[…]

The GMO Panel has assessed information provided on molecular inserts within the transgenic event, on the safety of the proteins expressed and on the potential for risks associated with any changes to the nutritional, toxicological and allergenic properties of 1507 maize. Analysis of the chemical composition of the maize and field trial data were also used to assess the potential for changes to safety, nutritional as well as agronomic parameters. No data have emerged to indicate that maize line 1507 is any less safe than its non-GM comparators. The GMO Panel considers that 1507 maize will have similar impacts as other comparable non-GM maize cultivars on the environment. The only adverse effect identified was the possibility that resistance to Bt toxin might evolve in corn borers exposed to 1507 maize following cultivation for some years. The Panel accepts the monitoring plan developed by the applicant to monitor specifically for resistance in corn borers and recommends that cultivation should be accompanied by appropriate risk management strategies to minimise exposure of both target and non-target insects to Bt toxins. In addition, the Panel accepts in principle the general surveillance plan submitted by the applicant. The GMO Panel is therefore of the opinion that there is no evidence to indicate that placing of maize line 1507 and derived products on the market is likely to cause adverse effects on human or animal health or the environment in the context of its proposed use. The GMO Panel is of the opinion that, based on the outcome of the risk assessment, no specific conditions or restrictions should be imposed on the placing of 1507 maize on the market for food use. No specific conditions or restrictions for food use and handling, including post-market monitoring requirements regarding the use of 1507 maize for human consumption, are regarded as necessary. Furthermore, there is no need for specific conditions for the protection of particular ecosystems/environment and/or geographical areas.

This extract from a summary of EFSA's scientific opinion illustrates that applications are assessed for the nutritional, toxicological, and allergenic properties of the transgenic agricultural product and an analysis of its agronomic traits is carried out. Moreover, the precision of the process of changing the DNA of the maize plant is assessed, and in particular whether DNA fragments generated during the process of transforming the maize DNA may have toxic or allergenic effects. This analysis matters also in light of criticisms that genetic engineering is less precise than often suggested and that therefore DNA fragments created during the process of genetic manipulation of a plant may have adverse environmental consequences.

In order to assess the safety of the GMO product EFSA also establishes whether the GM maize plant and food can be considered as equivalent to non-GM maize plants and food. Field trials are referred to as relevant evidence here; and there is also a terse statement about animal feeding studies, which have in practice been quite controversial, because there is disagreement about what type of animals allow comparison to humans when assessing the nutritional safety of the GM product. There is also debate about the length for which these studies need to be conducted. Similarly brief is the assessment of the monitoring plan provided by the applicant. Member States and environmental NGOs during public consultation phases have criticized monitoring plans as not being detailed enough. The limitations of current practice, in relation to post market environment monitoring (PMEM) plans, is also highlighted in the EPEC report.

EPEC (for DG SANCO European Commission), Evaluation of the EU Legislative Framework in the Field of Cultivation of GMOs Under Directive 2001/18/EC and Regulation (EC) No 1829/2003, and the Placing on the Market of GMOs as or in Products Under Directive 2001/18/EC (March 2011) 55

PMEM plans provide risk managers with the information for decision making and developing risk management strategies post-authorisation. If a flow of new GMO approvals was seen, pressure for improvement in the quality and content of PMEM plans would rapidly develop. Currently the main issue with the monitoring of GMO cultivation, according to the majority of Member States, is that PMEM plans do not meet the objectives of the legislation. Member States highlighted deficiencies in the content, guidelines, definition of baselines and borderline between case specific and general surveillance (GS). General surveillance is mandatory for cultivated GMOs in order to help identify unanticipated adverse effects. Case specific monitoring is required after placing on the market where there is scientific evidence of a potential adverse effect linked to the genetic modification.

The methods used for general surveillance and quality and availability of networks are also judged inadequate by consultees There is a risk that existing general surveillance will be unable to cope if approvals for GM cultivation increase in the future. Inadequate general surveillance networks will also affect the availability of good quality data for PMEM plans for future GM cultivation approvals.

Thus, the main challenge for improving GMO post market environmental monitoring in Europe is to better coordinate and manage data access, data analysis and knowledge transfer/sharing for the dual (and interrelated) purposes of improving PMEM plans and post-authorisation monitoring and surveillance. This can be done by:

i. improving the content of PMEM plans;

ii. promoting greater harmonisation and standardisation of data access and analysis;

iii. providing better guidelines; and

iv. improving or creating new surveillance networks.

In its scientific opinion, EFSA clearly defines its role as only being concerned with risk assessment, considering issues of co-existence between GM, conventional, and organic agriculture, raised in some MS comments, as risk management issues that are beyond its jurisdiction, though EFSA expresses in its conclusion a clear view that no conditions need to be imposed in the authorization, arguably an issue of risk management. The main risk identified is that pests, such as the corn borer, may become resistant to the BT toxin expressed by the GM maize plant, which is meant to repel the corn borer and thus save on insecticide in the cultivation of GM maize. The magnitude or likelihood of that risk is, however, not specified. Finally, it seems slightly unsettling that in its conclusion EFSA does not suggest that GM maize is just as safe as conventional maize products, but concludes—less reassuringly—that 'no data have emerged to indicate that maize line 1507 is any less safe than its non-GM comparators'. Article 2(12) of Regulation 1829/2003/EC, however, defines 'conventional counterpart' as non-GM food or feed 'for which there is a well-established history of safe use' and Article 9(3) of Regulation 1829/2003/EC requires that authorizations should evaluate the safety in use of the food.

Directive 2001/18/EC

Directive 2001/18/EC as amended by Directive 2008/27/EC authorizes the release of GMOs, thus including their cultivation or their placing onto the market. The Directive was adopted on the basis of Article 114 TFEU (ex 95 EC) which deals with the approximation of laws in order to promote the establishment and functioning of the internal market, here through the creation of a level playing field through harmonized rules on GMO regulation in the EU. Until the reorganization of administrative responsibilities for GMO regulation within the Commission in 2010, DG Environment dealt with authorizations under Directive 2001/18/EC, which are now also handled by DG Sanco.

According to Article 13 of Directive 2001/18/EC, the authorization procedure begins in an EU Member State through a manufacturer or importer of GMO agricultural products submitting an application to the national competent authority of the Member State in which the GMOs are to be released or placed onto the market. In the UK, this is the Department for Environment, Food and Rural Affairs (DEFRA). In contrast to Regulation 1829/2003/EC there is a stronger national dimension to this authorization procedure. The national competent authority is required to prepare a national assessment report in relation to the application that includes a risk assessment, which mainly examines the environmental risk assessment submitted by the applicant, who has an interest in the authorization of the application. Member States retain important national decision-making powers. If the competent national authority rejects the application, this is the end of the matter. The applicant, however, can try to obtain authorization in another EU Member State. If the national competent authority of another EU Member State provides a positive assessment report of the application, this report will be forwarded to the Commission, which will then inform the other EU Member States and give them an opportunity to comment on the application. If other Member States do not object to the application, the national competent authority to which the application was submitted can grant the application according to the so-called *standard decision-making procedure* under Article 15 of Directive 2001/18/EC.

In case other EU Member States or the Commission raise objections, the more complex so-called *community decision-making procedure* under Article 18 of Directive 2001/18/EC applies. In practice, the Commission usually does not raise objections to authorization applications since its official policy is to enable consumer choice between conventional, organic, and GM agricultural products. The community decision-making procedure triggers the comitology procedure under Article 30(2) Directive 2001/18/EC, discussed here. This authorization procedure applies to commercial releases or the placing on the market of GMOs and proceeds under Part C of Directive 2001/18/EC. Article 2(4) Directive 2001/18/EC defines 'placing onto the market' as making the GMO available to other persons. This does not have to be for financial consideration.

There is also a simplified, mainly national, authorization procedure for 'Part B' releases for the purpose of researching GMOs, for example, through field trials.[33] Authorizations granted for Part B releases are only valid in the territory of the Member State that granted the consent while Part C releases for commercial purposes generate consents that are valid throughout the entire EU territory. In practice, applications, for instance by research institutes, for field trials have declined since 2006—perhaps also due to direct action protests, including destruction of GM crops, by anti-GM activists. Applications for Part B releases are increasingly concentrated in just a few Member States. The decline in information gathered about the environmental impacts of GMO releases across a variety of geographical locations in the EU through field trials is problematic, since it reduces the knowledge available for assessing environmental impacts in relation to Part C releases.

3.2 SCIENTIFIC DISCOURSE AS A LIMITED FORM OF COMMUNICATION IN EU GMO AUTHORIZATIONS

Having set out the key elements of the EU legal procedures for authorizing agricultural GMOs, this section examines actual authorization practices, which have been criticized as being unduly dominated by a scientific discourse. Law, and in particular administrative authorizations, can be understood as a form of communication.[34] The particular challenge for EU GMO authorizations is that they have to grapple with highly divergent points of view, interests, and disciplinary perspectives. In comparison to air and water pollution control as well as contaminated land problems, there seems to have been greater resistance among citizens, and some institutional political actors, to consider transgenic agriculture purely as a scientific issue, which can be mainly understood and regulated by expert risk assessments. Moreover, the legitimacy of risk-regulatory decision-making has been

---

[33] Applications for Part B releases in England are decided by DEFRA.
[34] David Nelken, *Law as Communication* (Dartmouth 1996).

hampered by weak provisions for national and EU-level public participation in EU GMO authorizations. Boundary work not just at the 'science–politics' but also at the 'emotion–rationality' interface has therefore become precarious. EU GMO authorizations seek to keep at bay strong emotive reactions of EU citizens to transgenic agriculture, also by appealing to trust in science, scientific experts, and regulatory procedures. The legal regulation of GMOs therefore also points to the limits of the functionalist response that seeks to restore confidence of citizens and Member States in science based authorization procedures through the 'right' risk communication.

A recent independent consultant's report, commissioned by the Commission, highlights further practical problems with risk assessments in EU GMO authorizations. Among these are a lack of consistency among assessments between different Member State authorities and an absence of sufficient resources both for Member State competent authorities and EFSA.[35] In the light of this scepticism about risk assessments, what role can and do non-scientific considerations play in EU GMO authorizations according to law, policy, and actual practices of institutional actors?

Mihail Kritikos, 'Traditional Risk Analysis and Releases of GMOs into the European Union: Space for Non-Scientific Factors?' (2009) 34(3) ELR 405, 418–19

A qualitative analysis of the public comments submitted to the SNIF database in the frame of 23 Pt C notification procedures signifies a plurality of reservations about the overall effect of the commercialisation of genetic engineering and the release of its products into the natural and agricultural environment. Almost all the critical comments express concerns about the potential risks posed by the notified products to human health and to environmental safety and originate both from members of the public and from independent experts and specialised civil society organisations. A considerable amount however is of non-scientific nature due to the fact that the manifestations of the risks and benefits of genetic engineering acquire socioeconomic forms. These public comments include, inter alia, concerns about fairness, distribution of technological risks and benefits and consumer choice, the potential economic risks of the industrial capture of both biosafety research and biotechnology patenting, the potential dependence of local farmers on international GM-grain suppliers and industrial expertise, the effects of the commercial application of agricultural biotechnology upon organic dairying, the sustainability of rural economies and livelihoods, the preservation of traditional agronomic practices and the safeguarding of the existence of small farm units. The wealth of concerns regarding the effects of GMO releases and the apparent open ended character of the risk assessment framework notwithstanding, the examination of online documents submitted to the SNIF database, at the level of risk assessment, suggests that the GMO Panel (or alternatively the Commission and/or the national authorities) has not taken, either implicitly or explicitly, non-expert inputs into consideration. For instance, in the case of the safety assessment of the notified commercial release of maize DAS-59122-7, the GMO Panel viewed the issue of costs-benefits, the possible contributions to sustainable development and to the society in general, ethical questions and the assessment of potential socioeconomic effects as falling outside its remit. In all its responses, the Panel approaches non-scientific public comments and lay concerns as external to the established expert control evaluation paradigm. As one member of the EFSA GMO Panel has noted: 'Examining ethical and socio-economic concerns is beyond our competencies and capacities. This is a policy task for the Member States and for the Commission at the level of risk management.'

---

[35] EFSA has published guidance on how risk assessments of food and feed from genetically modified plants should be conducted: (2011) 9(5) EFSA Journal 2150.

Kritikos' analysis highlights that actual authorization practices have further enhanced the significance of scientific discourses referred to in the text of the EU legislation by turning them into the dominant form of communication about the potential advantages and disadvantages of transgenic agricultural products. Similar to the discussion in Chapter 17 about the indeterminacy of the BAT standard under systems of integrated pollution prevention and control, this section suggests that discursive practices are key to understanding the application of environmental law. They matter, in particular, when the formal legal framework does not fix the meaning of key concepts such as 'risk' and 'adverse effects' in Directive 2001/18/EC.

This points to a gap between the Commission's 'good governance' rhetoric of participative, inclusive, and deliberative decision-making and the reality of EU risk regulation of GMOs. This is indicative of wider, unresolved controversies about appropriate models of risk regulation, a theme further discussed in Chapter 12 on regulatory strategy and Chapter 13 on governance.

3.3 EU GMO AUTHORIZATIONS AS A MULTI-LEVEL GOVERNANCE REGIME

EU GMO authorizations are the outcome of a multi-level governance regime that involves strong central powers for the EU supranational actors, and also thereby limits debate about the advantages and disadvantages of agricultural GMOs in particular in relation to Member States' and their citizens' views. This section outlines what legal powers remain with Member States in relation to GMO regulation. It highlights that the Court of Justice of the EU, including both the Court of Justice and the General Court, has been key to further shaping the distribution of power between EU supranational institutions and Member States as envisaged in primary and secondary EU law. It has thereby fleshed out a particular vision of 'ecological federalism' (see Chapter 14) that underpins the current EU regulatory regime for agricultural GMOs.

One of the most significant decisions can be seen here. The case involved Land Oberösterreich (Province of Upper Austria) attempting to rely on Article 114(5) TFEU (then Art 95(5)) to derogate from Directive 2001/18 due to the fact that it then did not allow the cultivation of GMOs. Article 114(5) is extracted in Chapter 5 and you may find it useful to read before reading the judgment in this extract. The main issue before the CJEU was whether Land Oberösterreich had a right to be heard.

Joined Cases C-439/05 and C-454/05 P, *Land Oberösterreich and Another v Commission of the European Communities*
[2007] ECR I—714, paras 31–35, 37–41, 43–44

31. As regards the procedure laid down in Article 95(5) EC, the introduction of new national provisions must be based on new scientific evidence relating to the protection of the environment or the working environment by reason of a problem specific to that Member State arising after the adoption of the harmonisation measure (see, to that effect, *Denmark* v *Commission*, paragraph 57).

32. The requirement that new scientific evidence must be adduced in support of the request may, in this respect, lead the Commission, as part of its assessment of the merits of that request, to have recourse to outside experts in order to obtain their views on that evidence, and those views will serve as a basis for the final decision.

33. Thus, the Commission itself acknowledged that it was not in a position, in the present case, to assess alone the scientific evidence in the Müller report and stated that, as a consequence, it had to request an opinion from EFSA before taking a decision under Article 95(5) EC.

34. It must be ascertained whether, as the appellants submit, the right to be heard should have been applied in such a case or whether, as was held in *Denmark* v *Commission*, the right to be heard did not apply as regards Article 95(4) EC.

35. In that respect, the principle of the right to be heard, whose observance is ensured by the Court, requires a public authority to hear interested parties before adopting a decision which concerns them (Case C-315/99 P *Ismeri Europea* v *Court of Auditors* [2001] ECR I-5281, paragraph 28, and *Denmark* v *Commission*, paragraph 45).

[...]

37. However, it is not apparent, first, from the wording of Article 95(5) EC, that the Commission is required to hear the notifying Member State before it takes its decision to approve or reject the national provisions in question. Taking into consideration the specific features of that procedure, the Community legislature merely laid down, in Article 95 EC, the conditions to be fulfilled in order to obtain a Commission decision, the period within which the Commission must issue its decision to approve or reject and possible extensions to that period.

38. Next, the procedure laid down in Article 95(5) EC, like indeed the one laid down in Article 95(4) EC, is initiated, as set out in paragraph 29 of this judgment, not by a Community or national institution but by a Member State, and the Commission's decision is taken only in response to that initiative. In its request, the Member State is at liberty to comment on the national provisions it asks to have adopted, as is quite clear from Article 95(5) EC, which requires the Member State to state the grounds on which its request is based.

39. Furthermore, the Commission must be able, within the prescribed period, to obtain the information which proves necessary without being required to hear the notifying Member State before it takes its decision (see, concerning the procedure laid down in Article 95(4) EC, which is subject to the same time-limits as those applicable to the procedure laid down in Article 95(5) EC, Denmark v Commission, paragraph 48).

40. It must be emphasised that, according to the second subparagraph of Article 95(6) EC, national derogating provisions are deemed to have been approved if the Commission does not take a decision within a specified period. In addition, under the third subparagraph of Article 95(6) EC, no extension of that period is allowed if the matter is not complex and where there is a danger for human health.

41. The authors of the Treaty intended, in the interest of both the notifying Member State and the proper functioning of the internal market, that the procedure laid down in that article should be swiftly concluded. That objective would be difficult to reconcile with a requirement for prolonged exchanges of information and observations.

[...]

43. Finally, in the light of the specific features of the procedure laid down in Article 95(5) EC, the similarities of that procedure with the one laid down in Article 95(4) EC and the common objective of those two paragraphs, which is to enable Member States to obtain derogations from harmonisation measures, there is no need to adopt a solution different from that adopted in respect of Article 95(4) EC. Consequently, the Commission is not required to observe the right to be heard before taking a decision under Article 95(5) EC (see, to that effect, as regards Article 95(4) EC, Denmark v Commission, paragraph 50).

44. The Court of First Instance was therefore correct to hold that the right to be heard should not apply to the procedure laid down in Article 95(5) EC.

The outcome of the case *Land Oberösterreich and Another v Commission of the European Communities* is not surprising. The Court followed an entirely defensible interpretation of Article 114(5) and affirmed what, simply through the provisions of the Treaty article, is a very limited power for Member States to derogate from EU environmental harmonization measures. But more specific criticisms of the Court's approach can be raised. In particular, the case *Land Oberösterreich v Commission* highlights three shortcomings of the EU multi-level governance regime for agricultural GMOs. First, arguments about the appropriate distribution of power between the EU and other levels of governance are not necessarily conducted explicitly but clothed in the language of procedural EU administrative law. Austria and the region of Upper Austria contested the Commission's refusal to approve its safeguard measure under Article 114 (5) on the grounds that the Commission had not provided them with an opportunity to rebut the Commission's view that Austria's scientific evidence, compiled in the so-called Müller report, was insufficiently new and did not indicate an environmental problem *specific* to Austria.

Second, the case leaves EFSA's role as centrally collating 'objective', 'universal' scientific knowledge untouched. It thereby shapes a multi-level governance regime that grants significant powers to EU supranational actors through forced consensus science. It is questionable whether this gives sufficient expression to Article 30(1) of the General Food Regulation 178/2002/EC, which imposes a duty upon EFSA to 'exercise vigilance in order to identify at an early stage any potential source of divergence between its scientific opinions and the scientific opinions issued by other bodies carrying out similar tasks' with a view to achieve co-operation and resolution of the divergences in view of Article 30(4). The Advocate General, on behalf of the Court, went quite far as a judicial actor to scrutinize the scientific evidence that Austria supplied in order to apply for its safeguard measure.

Joined Cases C-439/05 and C-454/05 P, *Land Oberösterreich and Another v Commission of the European Communities*
[2007] ECR I—7141, para 123 (AG Sharpston)

123. It is easily verifiable that of the 115 references cited in the Müller report completed in April 2002, only 22 date from that year or from 2001, the year in which Directive 2001/18 was adopted, and that fewer than half of those appear to be of a scientific nature. The appellants have made no claim that the 2001 or 2002 scientific references were decisive or even significant as regards the conclusions presented. And, since the issue is whether the evidence Austria presented to justify its request was new, the fact that other new evidence may subsequently have come to light cannot affect the validity in law of the Commission's decision, having regard to the evidence on the basis of which it was taken and the time at which it was taken.

The strong affirmation by the case of centrally EFSA determined, objective, scientific knowledge as key to adjudicating questions about the allocation of regulatory powers between EU supranational institutions and Member States seems further flawed in light of the fact that the meaning of the scientific data was mediated by the ordinary language of legal provisions. In order to determine whether Austria could rely on the safeguard measure of Article 114(5) TFEU the Court had to determine whether Austria had supplied new evidence that showed that there was an environmental problem *specific* to Austria. Austria argued that EFSA, by referring also to the French language version of the term, had given it a narrower interpretation than the legislative provision of Article 114(5) had intended. The more difficult test that EFSA had in fact applied was whether Austria had supplied scientific evidence that showed there was an environmental problem 'unique' to Austria, which had appeared after Directive 2001/18/EC had come into force and had to be now remedied through a safeguard measure. 'Unique' required that the environmental problem could only be found in one Member State while 'specific' meant that an environmental problem could be specific to more than one region in the EU. While the AG held that the Commission had misinterpreted Article 114(5) on the basis of this linguistic mistake, which led EFSA to apply the wrong test to the scientific data submitted by Austria, the Court found that the Commission had not erred in law in its interpretation of Article 114(5). In the end, however, this difference in opinion between the Advocate General and the Court did not matter, because both found that the conditions laid down in Article 114 TFEU for Member States to take advantage of the safeguard measure were cumulative. Since, Austria clearly had not provided 'new' scientific evidence it could not rely on Article 114 and hence the question whether any of the other cumulative conditions of Article 114 had been fulfilled became moot.

Third, the case *Land Oberösterreich* affirms an EU multi-level governance regime in which—para-doxically—issues that are not centrally harmonized at the EU level, such as the issue of co-existence, cannot provide the basis for national safeguard measures derogating from centralized EU authoriza-tions. Co-existence refers to the fact that wind and insects can carry pollen over distances. Cultivation of GM crops therefore poses the risk of contamination of conventional or organic crops with GM material. The Commission has not legislated on this issue of co-existence yet, but has only drawn up legally non-binding guidelines.[36] Austria argued that the Commission ignored its argument that it should be allowed to establish GM free zones because the Commission had not solved yet the issue of co-existence. The Advocate General, however, and the Court following the AG's opinion rejected this argument by drawing a potentially artificial line between 'environmental management' and 'socio-economic issues of agricultural management'.

Joined Cases C-439/05 and C-454/05 P, *Land Oberösterreich and Another v Commission of the European Communities*
[2007] ECR I-7141, paras 117–18 (AG Sharpston)

117. The appellants have argued, on the basis of EFSA's statement that it 'was not asked by the Commission to comment on the management of co-existence of GM and non-GM crops', that EFSA and the Commission ignored the central issue raised by Austria in its request.

118. It seems to me, however, that the Commission correctly sought to distinguish between the environmental issues with which Article 95(5) EC and Directive 2001/18 are concerned and the socio-economic issues of agricultural management, which fall outside the scope of the legislation. In setting out its terms of reference, EFSA stated that it was 'not requested to comment on information that does not impact on risk to human health and the environment, in particular that relating to the management of co-existence.' Its opinion clearly did—properly—consider the environmental issues, in particular concerning gene flow, but—equally properly—did not comment on those other issues.

In light of the fact that in the Common Agricultural Policy (CAP) farmers are clearly recognized as central to managing the environmental aspects of farming, this distinction is puzzling. Moreover, recent reforms of the CAP have exactly sought to overcome traditional perceptions of a distinction between economic and environmental aspects of farming, also in the light of the sustainable develop-ment principle.

The Court interpreted narrowly again in a further case the scope of Member States' powers in the EU multi-level governance regime for GMOs to derogate from EU GMO authorizations. Case C-165/08 *Commission v Poland*[37] came before the Court through legal action taken by the Commission under Article 258 TFEU (ex Article 226 ECT) against Poland for breach of EU law. The Commission alleged that the Polish Law on Seeds from June 2003 was in breach of Articles 22 and 23 of Directive 2001/18, as well as Articles 4(4) and 16 of Directive 2002/53.

---

[36] Commission Recommendation of 13 July 2010 on guidelines for the development of national co-existence meas-ures to avoid the unintended presence of GMOs in conventional and organic crops, [2010] OJ C200/01.
[37] [2009] ECR I-6843.

One of the key legal issues in the case argued before the Court was the question of whether Directive 2001/18/EC had already completely harmonized the law in the EU in relation to ethical issues pertaining to the authorization of GMOs, as the Commission suggested, or whether the provisions on ethical objections to GMOs in Directive 2001/18/EC were only rudimentary. Poland relied on the latter point also suggesting that the law in relation to ethical issues of GMOs had not been fully harmonized because Directive 2001/18/EC was mainly concerned with the protection of human health and the environment. Hence, Poland suggested that Member States could therefore rely directly on Article 36 TFEU (Article 30 TEC) in order to justify measures restricting trade in transgenic agricultural products on ethical grounds. Poland also relied upon Article 29(1) of Directive 2001/18, which grants a power to the Commission to consult the European Group on Ethics in Science and New Technologies 'on ethical issues of a general nature without prejudice to the competence of Member States', in order to argue that Directive 2001/18/EC expressly preserved the competence of the Member States to regulate ethical issues related to GMOs.

Poland's attempt to widen the meaning of the term 'ethical objections' to GMOs, by arguing that the introduction of GM agriculture in opposition to the majority of Polish people was 'unethical', was unsuccessful. The Court, however, left open the possibility that ethical objections in terms of religious concerns may justify national restrictions on GMOs.

Case C-165/08 *Commission of the European Communities v Republic of Poland*
[2009] ECR I-6843, paras 30–31, 50–52, 54–55, 57–58

30. In the present case, the adoption of the contested national provisions was inspired by the Christian and Humanist ethical principles adhered to by the majority of the Polish people.

31. In that connection, the Republic of Poland goes on to put forward a Christian conception of life which is opposed to the manipulation and transformation of living organisms created by God into material objects which are the subject of intellectual property rights; a Christian and Humanist conception of progress and development which urges respect for creation and a quest for harmony between Man and Nature; and, lastly, Christian and Humanist social principles, the reduction of living organisms to the level of products for purely commercial ends being likely, inter alia, to undermine the foundations of society. [...]

50. Without disputing that the prohibitions laid down in the contested national provisions would infringe Directives 2001/18 and 2002/53 if it were to be confirmed that they are intended solely to regulate trade in genetically modified seed varieties and their inclusion in the common catalogue of varieties of agricultural plant species, the Republic of Poland contends that that is not the position in the present case. In so far as those national provisions pursue ethical objectives which are unrelated to the objectives which characterise those directives, namely the protection of the environment and of human health, and free circulation, they are actually outside the scope of those directives, which means that the obstacles to the free circulation of GMOs to which they give rise, potentially in breach of Article 28 EC, may in some circumstances be justified under Article 30 EC.

51. In that connection, however, the Court considers that, for the purposes of deciding the present case, it is not necessary to rule on the question whether—and, if so, to what extent and under which possible circumstances—the Member States retain an option to rely on ethical or religious arguments in order to justify the adoption of internal measures which, like the contested national provisions, derogate from the provisions of Directives 2001/18 or 2002/53.

52. In the present case, it is sufficient to hold that the Republic of Poland, upon which the burden of proof lies in such a case, has failed, in any event, to establish that the true purpose of the contested

national provisions was in fact to pursue the religious and ethical objectives relied upon, which for the Commission is a matter of doubt. [...]

54. As regards, more specifically, the justification based on the protection of public morality relied on by the Republic of Poland in the present case, it must be held, first, that the relevant evidentiary burden is not discharged by statements as general as those put forward by that Member State during the pre-litigation procedure and consisting in references to fears regarding the environment and public health and to the strong opposition to GMOs manifested by the Polish people, or even to the fact that the administrative regional assemblies adopted resolutions declaring that the administrative regions are to be kept free of genetically modified cultures and GMOs.

55. Clearly, in those circumstances, public morality is not really being invoked as a separate justification, but as an aspect of the justification relating to protection of human health and the environment, which is precisely the concern of Directive 2001/18 in the present context (see, to that effect, Case C-1/96 *Compassion in World Farming* [1998] ECR I-1251, paragraph 66). [...]

57. Secondly, and as regards the more specifically religious or ethical arguments put forward by the Republic of Poland for the first time in the defence and rejoinder submitted to the Court, it must be held that that Member State has failed to establish that the contested national provisions were in fact adopted on the basis of such considerations.

58. The Republic of Poland essentially referred to a sort of general presumption according to which it can come as no surprise that such provisions were adopted in the present case. First, the Republic of Poland relies on the fact that it is well known that Polish society attaches great importance to Christian and Roman Catholic values. Secondly, it states that the political parties with a majority in the Polish Parliament at the time when the contested national provisions were adopted specifically called for adherence to such values. In those circumstances, according to that Member State, it is reasonable to take the view that the Members of Parliament, who do not, as a general rule, have scientific training, are more likely to be influenced by the religious or ethical ideas which inspire their political actions, rather than by other considerations, in particular, those linked to the complex scientific assessments relating to the protection of the environment or of human health.

A further important plank in the EU multi-level governance regime that allocates significant regulatory powers to the EU central level are the powers of the Commission to enforce compliance with EU law in relation to GMOs by the Member States.[38] The case of *Commission of the European Communities v France* (Case C-121/07)[39] confirms, on the basis of the earlier judgment in Case C-304/02 *European Commission v France*[40], that the Commission has powers to impose both proportionate lump sum and periodic penalty payments in relation to Member States' failure to implement fully and accurately EU law in relation to GMOs under Article 260 TFEU (ex Article 228 TEC).

Article 260 TFEU (ex Article 228 ECT) comes into play when Member States fail to comply with an earlier judgment, issued by the ECJ under Article 258 TFEU, that finds a Member State in breach of EU law. The proportionate lump sum payment seeks to punish the Member State for failing to comply with the original ECJ judgment under Article 258 TFEU (ex Article 226 ECT). The periodic penalty payment will be imposed for the duration of time that the Member State continues to be in breach

---

[38] A number of Member States had not fully implemented EU GMO regulation as documented in the following infringement proceedings C–416/03 *Commission v Hellenic Republic* ECR 275; C–421/03 *Commission v Republic of Austria* [2004] ECR 275; C–422/03 *Commission v Kingdom of the Netherlands* [2004] ECR 275; C–417/03 *Commission v Kingdom of Belgium* [2004] ECR275; C–423/03 *Commission v Republic of Finland* [2004] ECR 75; C–419/03 *Commission v French Republic* [2004] ECR 275; C–420/03 *Commission Against Federal Republic of Germany* [2004] ECR 275.

[39] [2009] Env LR 23.   [40] [2005] ECR I-6263.

of EU law. The clock starts to tick from the time of the first judgment issued under Article 258 TFEU (ex Article 226 ECT) with which the Member State failed to comply. In the case of *Commission of the European Communities v France* (Case C-121/07) the lump sum imposed on France was 10 million Euros for a four year delay to implement Directive 2001/18/EC into French law. The Commission's application for a periodic penalty payment, however, was rejected, since France had complied with its legal obligations to implement Directive 2001/18/EC by the deadline specified in the reasoned opinion issued by the Commission under Article 258 TFEU.

3.4 REFORM OF THE EU GMO AUTHORIZATION PROCEDURES

Given the limited responsiveness of the current EU legal regulatory regime for agricultural GMOs and continuing pressures to comply with international trade law given that GMO authorizations are still delayed, France took the initiative in 2008 when it held the EU Council Presidency to start a discussion about the reform of the current EU GMO authorization procedures.[41] The Commission then engaged in wide consultation with stakeholders about the direction of the reforms. Both DG Environment and DG Sanco commissioned independent consultant reports that gathered survey evidence from Member States' competent authorities, environmental NGOs, EFSA, research institutes, and business interests.[42] The Commission went, finally, for a reform option that grants greater powers to Member States to restrict the cultivation of GMOs on their territory. This should help to resolve conflicts between the Commission and EU Member States. It remains to be seen though whether greater powers for Member States, which can be exercised at the national, regional, or local level, in relation to the cultivation of GMO crops will make them more responsive to their citizens' concerns in relation to transgenic agriculture. In addition, while the Environment Council conclusions from December 2008 addressed a whole range of shortcomings in the current EU regulatory regime for agricultural GMOs, the Commission's legislative reform proposal focuses only upon the reform of the most serious bottleneck in authorizations: the cultivation of GM crops.

European Commission, Brussels, 13.7.2010, COM(2010) 375 final, 2010/0208 (COD) Proposal for a Regulation of the European Parliament and of the Council amending Directive 2001/18/EC as regards the possibility for the Member States to restrict or prohibit the cultivation of GMOs in their territory paras 5–6, 8–9

(5) Experience has shown that cultivation of GMOs is an issue which is more thoroughly addressed by Member States, either at central or at regional and local level. Contrary to issues related to the placing on the market and the import of GMOs, which should remain regulated at EU level to preserve the internal market, cultivation has been acknowledged as an issue with a strong local/regional dimension. In accordance with Article 2(2) TFEU Member States should therefore be entitled to have a possibility to adopt rules concerning the effective cultivation of GMOs in their territory after the GMO has been legally authorised to be placed on the EU market.

---

[41] See the Environment Council's conclusions from 4 December 2008 at: <http://www.consilium.europa.eu/uedocs/cms_Data/docs/pressdata/en/envir/104509.pdf> accessed 11 March 2013.

[42] See, for example, Evaluation of the EU Legislative Framework in the Field of Cultivation of GMOs under Directive 2001/18/EC and Regulation (EC) No 1829/2003, and the Placing on the Market of GMOs as or in Products under Directive 2001/18/EC, Final Report, EPEC, for DG Sanco European Commission, Main Report, March 2011, at: <http://ec.europa.eu/food/food/biotechnology/evaluation/index_en.htm> accessed 11 March 2013.

(6) In this context, it appears appropriate to grant to Member States, in accordance with the principle of subsidiarity, more freedom to decide whether or not they wish to cultivate GMO crops on their territory without changing the system of Union authorisations of GMOs and independently of the measures that Member States are entitled to take by application of Article 26a of Directive 2001/18/EC to avoid the unintended presence of GMOs in other products.

[...]

(8) According to the legal framework for the authorisation of GMOs, the level of protection of human/animal health and of the environment chosen in the EU cannot be revised by a Member State and this situation must not be altered. However Member States may adopt measures restricting or prohibiting the cultivation of all or particular GMOs in all or part of their territory on the basis of grounds relating to the public interest other than those already addressed by the harmonised set of EU rules which already provide for procedures to take into account the risks that a GMO for cultivation may pose on health and the environment. Those measures should furthermore be in conformity with the Treaties, in particular as regards the principle of non discrimination between national and non national products and Articles 34 and 36 of the Treaty on the Functioning of the European Union, as well as with the relevant international obligations of the Union, notably in the context of the World Trade Organisation.

(9) On the basis of the subsidiarity principle, the purpose of this Regulation is not to harmonize the conditions of cultivation in Member States but to grant freedom to Member States to invoke other grounds than scientific assessment of health and environmental risks to ban cultivation of GMOs on their territory.

[...]

Article 1

Modification of Directive 2001/18/EC

In Directive 2001/18/EC, the following Article shall be inserted with effect from the date of entry into force of this Regulation:

'Article 26b

Cultivation

Member States may adopt measures restricting or prohibiting the cultivation of all or particular GMOs authorised in accordance with Part C of this Directive or Regulation (EC) No 1829/2003, and consisting of genetically modified varieties placed on the market in accordance with relevant EU legislation on the marketing of seed and plant propagating material, in all or part of their territory, provided that:

(a) those measures are based on grounds other than those related to the assessment of the adverse effect on health and environment which might arise from the deliberate release or the placing on the market of GMOs; and,

(b) that they are in conformity with the Treaties.

By way of derogation to Directive 98/34/EC, Member States that intend to adopt reasoned measures under this Article shall communicate them to the other Member States and to the Commission, one month prior to their adoption for information purposes'.

The proposed Regulation devolves legal decision-making powers back to Member States in relation to the cultivation of GM crops that have been authorized under Part C of the Deliberate Release Directive (2001/18/EC) or under the Food and Feed Regulation (1829/2003/EC). Hence, the law relating to the cultivation of GM crops will be less harmonized than it was under Directive 2001/18/EC and Regulation 1829/2003/EC before the proposed amendments.

The key legal issue, however, raised by the proposed Regulation is the question of what the scope of Member States' powers really is in restricting the cultivation of GMO crops, given the fact that Article 26(b) requires such measures to be in conformity with the Treaties, and thus how, amongst others, the proportionality principle will curtail Member States' freedom to restrict cultivation.

The Commission hopes that the proposed Regulation will solve the current inter-institutional deadlock between itself and the Council. In the past the Council currently did not authorize Commission proposals for cultivation, leaving the Commission to approve its own proposals for authorization. Moreover, in several cases the Council has refused to approve Commission applications to disallow some Member States' anti-GMO cultivation measures, although the Commission considered, on the basis of FEFSA's opinion, these national safeguard measures to be lacking in scientific justification.[43] If the proposed Regulation is adopted Member States may be more willing to approve applications for the authorization of cultivation of GM crops, because they retain powers to restrict the cultivation of such crops in their own territory. This matters, since there have been several applications for authorization pending[44]Moreover, the Commission hopes that the proposed Regulation will decrease the number of Member States wanting to put in place safeguard measures under Directive (2001/18/EC) itself.

Most importantly, the proposed Regulation will enable the broadening—at least in the Member States—of the debate about the advantages and disadvantages of transgenic agriculture. Article 26(b) enables Member States to take measures based on grounds unrelated to the assessment of the adverse effect on health and the environment, and thus in the Commission's understanding of this phrasing on grounds that are unrelated to EFSA's centralized scientific risk assessment. This enables Member States to base measures on socio-economic grounds, for instance.

FURTHER READING AND QUESTIONS

1. 'The dichotomy between scientific and democratic risk regulatory decision-making needs to be questioned'. Critically discuss this statement and outline how the democratic legitimacy of the current EU GMO authorization procedures could be enhanced.

2. Read Case C-552/07 *Commune de Sausheim v Pierre Azelvandre* [2009] ECR I-00987. How does this case promote transparency in the activities of national administrations in relation to the authorization of GMOs?

3. Consider the implications of Case C-442/09 *Bablok and Others v Freistaat Bayern* ECJ (6 September 2011) for the scope of the GMO definition under Regulation 1829/2003/EC.

4. Do you think that the ECJ judgment in Joined Cases C-58/10 to C-68/10 *Monsanto SAS and Others v Ministre de l'Agriculture et de la Peche* ECR (8 September 2011) clarifies in what circumstances Member States can avail themselves of the safeguard procedure under Article 23 of Directive 2001/18/EC and when a Member State has to rely on Article 34 of Regulation 1829/2003/EC?

5. See Sheila Jasanoff, *Designs on Nature* (Princeton UP 2005). This is a classic in the field that provides a comprehensive comparative account of GMO regulation in the US and the EU. While it examines the EU legal regulatory framework before Regulation 1829/2003/EC came into force, its theoretical contribution is still relevant.

---

[43] 'GMO's in a Nutshell' at <http://ec.europa.eu/food/food/biotechnology/qanda/d1_en.htm> accessed 11 March 2013.

[44] Sara Poli, 'The Commission's New Approach to the Cultivation of Genetically Modified Organism' (2010) 1(4) European Journal of Risk Regulation 339, 341.

6. Other useful references include: Patrycja Dambrowska, *EU Governance of GMOs* (Hart Publishing 2010); Les Levidow and Claire Marris, 'Science and Governance in Europe: Lessons from the Case of Agricultural Biotechnology' (2010) 28(5) Science and Public Policy 345; N Thayyil, 'Deliberative Turning from a Law-Science Cul-de-Sac: Speculations Regarding Community Transgenic Regulation' (2008) Yearbook of European Environmental Law 153; Nico Krisch, 'Pluralism in Postnational Risk Regulation: The Dispute over GMOs and Trade' (2010) 1(1) Transnational Legal Theory' 1; and Tamara K Hervey, 'Regulation of Genetically Modified Products in a Multi-Level System of Governance: Science or Citizens?' (2001) 10 Review of European Community and International Environmental Law 321.

7. The Advocate General in the Joined Cases C-439/05 and C-454/05 *P Land Oberoberösstereich and Republic of Austria v European Commission* [2007] ECR I-07141 stated: 'Having regard to the stress laid by the appellants on the precautionary principle, I would add that, relevant though the principle may undoubtedly be when assessing new evidence concerning a new situation, no amount of precaution can actually render that evidence or that situation new. The novelty of both situation and evidence is a dual criterion which must be satisfied before the precautionary principle comes into play' (para 134). Do you agree?

8. 'Adjudication of cases concerning the distribution of powers between the EU and Member States can provide an opportunity for the Court to develop EU procedural administrative law. The Court missed that opportunity in Joined Cases C-439/05 and C-454/05 *P Land Oberösstereich* by relying too much on the previous decision in *Denmark v Commission* (C-3/00) [2003] ECR I-2643) and by emphasizing the importance of quick administrative decisions. The Court failed to develop the content of the right to be heard from a more principled and democratic perspective'. Critically discuss this statement.

9. Case C-236/01 *Monsanto Agricoltura Italia SpA and Ors v Presidenza del Consiglio dei Ministri and Ors* [2003] ECR I-08105 concerns earlier, no longer applicable legislation for GM foods, the Regulation No 258/97 concerning novel foods and novel food ingredients. The case, however, is interesting for its wider conclusions about Member States' residual powers to impose safeguard measures in derogation of EU authorizations. What standards for scientific knowledge does the case require for such knowledge to become the basis for national safeguard measures? Should these standards differ depending on whether the cultivation of GMOs or their consumption as food stuffs is concerned? Compare the standards imposed for scientific knowledge in the Monsanto case with those established in the *Land Oberösterreich* case.

10. 'EU supranational actors currently wield too much power in the EU multi-level governance regime for agricultural GMOs. Both the assessment and management of potential risks arising from agricultural GMOs are best carried out by national, regional, or local actors in the EU'. Do you agree? Why?

11. Does the proposed new Article 26(b) of Directive 2001/18/EC comply with international trade law, in particular the SPS Agreement?

4 THE UK LEGAL FRAMEWORK FOR AGRICULTURAL GMOS

In order to fully understand the EU multi-level governance regime it is important to examine national, here English, legal provisions for the regulation of agricultural GMOs. While EU Member States have a legal obligation to implement the provisions of Directive 2001/18/EC into their national law, various

Member States, either on a national or regional level, have adopted GMO regulation that goes further than the requirements of Directive 2001/18/EC.[45] Hence, from a legal perspective the compatibility of such national or regional GMO regulation with EU law is a key issue. In contrast to Directive 2001/18/EC, Regulation 1829/2003/EC does not really raise issues of the correct formal legal transposition of EU law into national law since its provisions are directly applicable in the legal systems of the Member States, but more stringent national or regional regulation of GM food and feed products may still be in breach of EU law. In the case of the UK Directive 2001/18/EC and Regulation 1829/2003/EC having been fully implemented, the UK has not imposed stricter requirements in breach of EU law. In practice though it is mainly English law for the authorization of Part B releases under Directive 2001/18/EC that matters since no GM crops are currently commercially grown in the UK.[46] Also legal measures implementing Regulation 1829/2003/EC matter because GM soy is being used in the UK for animal feed and some GM food products are being sold.[47]

4.1 IMPLEMENTATION OF DIRECTIVE 2001/18/EC

The main primary legislation, which regulates the release and placing onto the market of GMOs in the UK, is Part VI of the Environmental Protection Act 1990 (EPA). Part VI only provides a general framework of regulation that is fleshed out in more detail through secondary legislation.[48] It grants legal powers and imposes duties upon the Secretary of State heading DEFRA to control the deliberate release and placing onto the market of GMOs in England, including powers to implement Directive 2001/18/EC. The main purpose of the regime under Part IV, according to section 106 EPA 1990, is to prevent or minimize any damage to the environment that may arise from the escape or release from human control of genetically modified organisms.

Mirroring Directive 2001/18/EC, a risk assessment is at the heart of the regulatory controls imposed by Part VI EPA 1990 (s 108(1) EPA 1990). But section 108(1) also seems to go beyond Directive 2001/18/EC because anybody who imports, acquires, releases, or places onto the market GMOs will also be required to provide a risk assessment even if he or she does not require a consent under s 111(1)(a) EPA 1990. Given the wording of section 109(2)(b) the Act only seems to tolerate a low level of risk:

> A person who proposes to import or acquire genetically modified organisms:
>
> (b) shall not import or acquire the organisms if it appears that, despite any precautions which can be taken, there is a risk of damage to the environment being caused as a result of their importation or acquisition.'

Section 111(1) EPA 1990 implements the requirement for a consent from Directive 2001/18/EC into English law by prohibiting the importation, acquisition, release, or placing onto the market of GMOs unless authorized by a consent granted by the Secretary of State. In granting consents, the Secretary of

---

[45] See, for example, the provisions in *Oberösterreich* discussed in Section 4.3.

[46] In 2012 two experimental field trials of GM potatoes and of GM wheat began. Genewatch UK, 'GM Crops and Food in Britain and Europe' at: <http://www.genewatch.org/sub-568547> accessed 20 November 2012. Department for Environment, Food and Rural Affairs (DEFRA), 'Genetic Modification (GM)' at: <http://www.defra.gov.uk/environment/quality/gm/> accessed 20 November 2012.

[47] <http://www.defra.gov.uk/environment/quality/gm/> accessed 11 March 2013.

[48] Stephen Tromans, 'Promise, Peril, Precaution: The Environmental Regulation of Genetically Modified Organisms' (2001) 9(1) Indiana J. Global Legal Stud 187, 189–90.

State is advised by a scientific independent committee, set up under section 124 EPA 1990, called the Advisory Committee on Releases into the Environment (ACRE).[49] ACRE plays an important role in the national administrative decision-making process. It provides opinions on all Part B and C applications for experimental or commercial release. The Committee advises on risks to human health and the environment. Apart from providing expert opinions on specific applications, ACRE has also developed national guidance on environmental risk assessment in relation to GMOs and best practice in the design of post-market monitoring plans.[50] Section 111(8) EPA 1990 grants a power to the Secretary of State to impose conditions on the consent or indeed refuse an application for consent. Section 111(10) provides a power to revoke or vary a consent. These powers of the regulator are further strengthened through the provisions in section 109, which impose a range of general duties upon those who deal with GMOs. Among these is a duty to identify the risks of damage to the environment and to cease any activities if it appears that, despite the precautions that could have been taken, there is a risk of damage to the environment.

It is interesting to note, though, that Part VI EPA 1990 provides more specific and explicit provisions in order to prevent damage to the environment from GMOs than Directive 2001/18/EC. Preamble 16 to Directive 2001/18/EC states that Member States retain their powers to address potential damage caused by GMOs. But national provisions must not conflict with the EU Environmental Liability Directive, which addresses damage caused by GMOs. Section 112(5) EPA 1990 strengthens post-release monitoring. It provides for an implied condition in consents that the consent holder should 'take all reasonable steps to keep himself informed [...] of any risks there are of damage to the environment being caused' as a result of the GMOs being released or marketed. Section 109(3)(c) imposes a specific technology standard in order to prevent damage occurring to the environment from GMOs. It requires persons keeping GMOs to use 'the best available techniques not entailing excessive cost for keeping the organisms under his control and for preventing any damage to the environment being caused as a result of his continuing to keep the organisms'. Section 112 (7) provides for an implied condition that consent holders 'shall take all reasonable steps' to keep themselves informed of 'developments in the techniques which may be available in his case for preventing damage to the environment being caused'. Moreover, section 120 EPA 1990 grants the court the power to order a defendant who committed an offence under Part VI EPA 1990 to remedy harm caused to the environment by GMOs. Under section 121 EPA 1990 the Secretary of State can also take such action him or herself where an offence has been committed under section 118 EPA 1990, with the option of recovering the costs of doing so from the person convicted of an offence under Part VI EPA 1990.

Finally, the powers granted to the Secretary of State under Part VI EPA 1990 are backed up through a range of enforcement provisions, that also fulfil the UK's obligations to provide for sanctions in national law in order to ensure compliance with Directive 2001/18/EC. According to section 110 EPA 1990 the Secretary of State can serve a prohibition notice on any person proposing to import, acquire or release, or place on the market or actually keep GMOs if he or she is of the opinion that any such activity would involve a risk of causing damage to the environment. Section 114(1) EPA 1990 provides a power for the Secretary of State to appoint inspectors for the enforcement of Part VI EPA 1990 who have a range of powers at their disposal, such as rights of entry and powers of inspection (section 115(3)(d)) and to require the production of information (section 115(3)(h)). Section 118 EPA 1990 provides for a range of offences, including handling GMOs in contravention of the duties imposed under section 108 EPA 1990 or a consent imposed under section 111 EPA 1990, as well as offences for

[49] Further information about ACRE can be found at: <www.defra.gov.uk/acre/> accessed 10 October 2012.
[50] Christopher Rogers, 'Co-existence or Conflict? A European Perspective on GMOs and the Problem of Liability' (2007) 27 Bulletin of Science, Technology and Society 234.

contravening prohibition notices or obstruct inspectors in their enforcement work. The standard penalties apply, according to section 118(3)(a) on summary conviction a fine of up to £20,000 or imprisonment up to six months, or both. According to section 118(3)(b) on conviction on indictment there is an unlimited fine provision and imprisonment up to five years, or both. For some offences under Part VI EPA 1990 a conviction on indictment can only lead to an unlimited fine and imprisonment for up to two years or both (section 118(4)(b)).

Since Part VI EPA 1990 was drafted before Directive 2001/18/EC came into force the Regulations made under the Act, the Genetically Modified Organisms (Deliberate Release) Regulations 2002,[51] provide for further implementation of Directive 2001/18/EC into English law.[52]

For instance, Regulation 32(4) provides that the power for the Secretary of State under section 110 EPA 1990 to issue prohibition notices is in accordance with the safeguard clause of Article 23(2) Directive 2001/18/EC. Member States do not have power to unilaterally issue prohibition notices but have to inform the Commission of the proposed restrictions on the release or marketing of a GMO for which consent has already been granted. The Commission will then decide with the aid of a comitology Committee—as referred to under Article 30(2) of Directive 2001/18/EC—whether the Member State can invoke the safeguard measure, such as a prohibition notice. Regulation 21(1) of the Genetically Modified Organisms (Deliberate Release) Regulations 2002 further provide that the Secretary of State must consult the Health and Safety Executive (HSE), the main government agency dealing with health and safety issues in the UK, in relation to any decisions about consents to release GMOs that invoke matters of the protection of public health.

4.2 IMPLEMENTATION OF REGULATION 1829/2003/EC

Since an EU Regulation creates immediate legal effect in the legal systems of all EU Member States, not much formal legal provision is required in order to implement the provisions of Regulation 1829/2003/EC into English law. In England Regulation 1829/2003/EC is implemented through the Genetically Modified Food (England) Regulations 2004, as well as the Genetically Modified Animal Feed (England) Regulations 2004.[53] The Genetically Modified Food (England) Regulations 2004 were passed under the UK Food Safety Act 1990 and came into force on 4 October 2004. They are short and mainly provide for the enforcement and administration of Regulation 1829/2003/EC in England in accordance with Article 45 of Regulation 1829/2003/EC, which requires Member States to put in place 'effective, proportionate and dissuasive' penalties in order to ensure compliance with provisions of the Regulation. For instance, Regulation 5 and Schedule Part I provide that if a GM food is marketed in contravention of the prohibition spelt out in Article 4(2) of Regulation 1829/2003/EC—that GM food has to be authorized before being placed onto the market—it can be removed from sale through a magistrate's order and destroyed. Moreover the operator of the food business can be prosecuted

---

[51] SI 2002/2443.

[52] The Regulations came into force on 17 October 2002 and replaced the earlier Genetically Modified Organisms (Deliberate Release) Regulations 1992 (SI 1992/3280). Under devolution arrangements in the UK, separate Regulations apply for Scotland and Wales, The Genetically Modified Organisms (Deliberate Release) (Scotland) Regulations 2002 (SI 2002/541) and The Genetically Modified Organisms (Deliberate Release) (Wales) Regulations 2002 (SI 2002/3188). The powers and duties assigned to the Secretary of State in relation to the regulation of agricultural GMOs in England are carried out in Wales by the National Assembly for Wales and by the Scottish Parliament in relation to Scotland. But the UK government and devolved administrations have established joint arrangements for assessing applications for the release of GMOs. This involves consultation with the Advisory Committee on Releases to the Environment (ACRE), the Health and Safety Executive, and the Food Standards Agency, and, as appropriate, the statutory nature conservation bodies, such as English Nature.

[53] Similar Regulations implement Regulation 1829/2003/EC in Northern Ireland, Scotland, and Wales.

for an offence. Similarly, the requirement spelt out in Article 9(3) of Regulation 1829/2003/EC, that authorization holders shall inform the Commission of any new scientific and technical information that may influence the safety evaluation of the GM food product, is further implemented in English law through regulation 5 and Part II of the Schedule of the Genetically Modified Food (England) Regulations 2004. In case of breach of Article 9(3) of the Regulation, regulation 5 and Schedule Part II provide a power to remove the affected product from sale and for it to be destroyed. It is also an offence to fail to notify such new information. Moreover, regulation 7 enables authorized officers to rely on enforcement powers under the Food Safety Act 1990 if the food operator is in breach of a specified Community provision, that is, Regulation 1829/2003/EC. Finally, regulation 3 establishes the UK Food Standards Agency (FSA) as the national competent authority, which EFSA has to consult when it carries out safety assessments under Regulation 1829/2003/EC. The FSA, in turn, is advised by the independent UK Advisory Committee on Novel Foods and Processes (ACNFP).

5 CONCLUSION

This chapter has highlighted the relevance of legal rules from international, EU, and national legal systems for constituting a complex web of regulation for agricultural GMOs. While the international and EU legal framework foreground scientific discourses as the main framework within which to debate the advantages and disadvantages of GMO agricultural products, actual authorization practices within EU GMO authorizations have further enhanced the role of risk assessments as the main basis for risk regulatory decision-making. But the chapter has also highlighted how precarious distinctions between the 'scientific' and 'political' elements of risk regulatory decision-making actually are, and how other dichotomies, such as between 'rational' administrative decision-making and 'emotional public reactions' to transgenic agriculture, do not capture the nature of EU GMO authorizations that also rely on appeals to trust in science, experts, and regulatory procedures. It is likely that without the trust into GMO agricultural products that EU GMO authorizations seek to generate there would be no trade in these products. Trust—both as catalyst for and outcome of EU GMO authorizations—constitutes an important social foundation of environmental law in relation to GMOs. These emotional dynamics of the legal regulatory regime for GMOs, however, still leave unresolved the significant legitimacy and accountability challenges that this regulatory regime faces. Significant legal powers to regulate GMOs are allocated to the international and supranational level in this multi-level governance regime. This means that currently the regulatory regime is fairly unresponsive to citizens' concerns. Law's ability as a communicative system to facilitate an open and comprehensive consideration of various points of view in relation to the advantages and disadvantages of agricultural GMOs seems worryingly limited.

INDEX

A

Aarhus Convention 265–9
  access to information 265–9
  access to justice 369, 376–94, 400
  administrative law 166–7, 265–9
  Air Quality Framework
    Directive 626
  courts and tribunals, role of 366,
    368–9, 400
  direct effect 381–2
  England and Wales 376–8,
    383–92
  Environmental Assessment
    Directive 846, 848, 859,
    863, 865
  environmental information,
    definition of 266–8
  Environmental Information
    Regulations 2004 200,
    268–9
  Environmental Liability
    Directive 379
  errors of law 383
  Espoo Convention 267
  EU law 146, 166–7, 200, 266,
    267–8, 376–83, 400
  Habitats Directive 382–3
  high-level governmental
    policy 449
  implementation 200, 266, 268–9,
    378, 383, 400
  institutions 392–5
  interpretation 383
  legitimacy 166–7
  non-governmental
    organizations 383
  procedural autonomy 378–9,
    382–3
  protective costs orders 386
  public, definition of 266
  public interest litigation 385–92
  public law 255, 304
  public participation 265–8, 449,
    846, 848, 859, 863, 865
  specialist court, arguments
    for 400

  standing 377, 383–5
  symbolism 268
abatement notices 347, 351–4
abuse of power 285, 370–1
access to information *see*
    Environmental
    Information Regulations
    2004; information
access to justice 369–94, 400
accountability
  administrative law 164, 168, 258,
    263, 265, 279–82, 521
  certification 524–5
  constitutions 279–80
  definition 519–20
  democracy 520–2
  dynamic accountability 523
  EU law 115, 164, 168, 302–3
  governance 501, 519–26, 533–4
  industrial modernity 533
  institution of UK EL, as 95,
    109–11
  international law 1026–7
  judicial review 255, 283, 520–1
  legitimacy 164, 168, 522–6
  managerialism 521
  market 525–6
  multiple accountabilities 279
  new forms 521–2
  new public management 525
  ombudsmen 279–80
  parliamentary oversight 279
  peer review 522, 525
  political accountability 525–6,
    533
  planning inspectors 281–2
  public law 255, 258
  public participation 265, 278,
    524–5
  regulation 109–10, 279, 488–9
  rule of law 520
  select committees 279–80
  sustainable development 474
  transparency 524
  tribunals 279, 281–2
  Water Framework Directive 574
acid rain 30, 605, 607–8, 610

Acts of Parliament 87–8, 95
administrative
    constitutionalism 76
administrative law 254–8, 259–83
  Aarhus Convention 166–7,
    265–9
  accountability 164, 168, 258, 263,
    265, 279–82, 521
  challenges of environmental
    law 261–9
  common law 262–3
  constitutional law 110, 255–7,
    261
  consultation 264–5
  criminal offences 305–6
  definition 257
  development 164–8
  discretion 86, 89–94, 114, 258,
    263
  Environmental Information
    Regulations 2004 270–7
  EU law 164–8, 259, 302–3
  good administration, principles
    of 258
  governance 164
  information and expertise 263–4
  judicial review 269–70
  knowledge 263
  legal culture 302–3
  legislation 262
  legitimacy 164–8
  local authorities 257
  non-governmental
    organizations 257–8
  policy 452
  prerogative powers 257
  problems, nature of interests
    in 261–3
  public administration,
    empowerment and
    limiting 257
  public law 254–8, 259–63, 302–3
  public participation 264–5,
    277–8
  regulation 269–83
  relationship with environmental
    law 254